Oct. 29–Nov. 1, 2017
Baltimore, MD, USA

Association for Computing Machinery

Advancing Computing as a Science & Profession

ASSETS'17

Proceedings of the 19th International ACM SIGACCESS Conference on

Computers and Accessibility

Sponsored by:

ACM SIGACCESS

Supported by:

National Science Foundation, Microsoft Research, Facebook, IBM Research, and University of Maryland, Baltimote County

Association for
Computing Machinery

Advancing Computing as a Science & Profession

The Association for Computing Machinery
2 Penn Plaza, Suite 701
New York, New York 10121-0701

Notice to Past Authors of ACM-Published Articles
ACM intends to create a complete electronic archive of all articles and/or other material previously published by ACM. If you have written a work that has been previously published by ACM in any journal or conference proceedings prior to 1978, or any SIG Newsletter at any time, and you do NOT want this work to appear in the ACM Digital Library, please inform permissions@acm.org, stating the title of the work, the author(s), and where and when published.

ISBN: 978-1-4503-4926-0 (Digital)

ISBN: 978-1-4503-5681-7 (Print)

Additional copies may be ordered prepaid from:

ACM Order Department
PO Box 30777
New York, NY 10087-0777, USA

Phone: 1-800-342-6626 (USA and Canada)
+1-212-626-0500 (Global)
Fax: +1-212-944-1318
E-mail: acmhelp@acm.org
Hours of Operation: 8:30 am – 4:30 pm ET

ASSETS 2017 Foreword

We are happy to welcome you to the *19th International ACM SIGACCESS Conference on Computers and Accessibility (ASSETS 2017)*. The ASSETS conference is the premier computing research conference exploring the design, evaluation, and use of computing and information technologies to benefit people with disabilities and older adults. In our 19th year, the ASSETS conference will continue its tradition of presenting innovative research on mainstream and specialized assistive technologies, accessible computing, and assistive applications of computer, network, and information technologies.

We are excited about this year's technical papers program, which features 33 papers. The technical papers track was quite competitive; we received 126 submissions, which means our acceptance rate this year was 26.2%. The 33 papers span a variety of topic areas relevant to computers and accessibility. This include technology by and in support of individuals with diverse motor, cognitive, and sensory abilities.

This year, we introduced a new track within technical papers, short papers, which are for more succinct research contributions. 5 of the 33 papers this year are from the short papers category. Additionally, we encouraged authors of papers introducing novel systems or interaction techniques to submit video figures illustrating these systems; these video figures will be hosted with the papers in the ACM Digital Library. We also introduced an optional HTML-based authoring application, which is one of many approaches the SIGACCESS Steering Committee is considering to increase the accessibility of our proceedings; we appreciate the efforts and feedback of those who helped pilot-test this effort.

In addition to the technical papers program, ASSETS 2017 features many other exciting presentation venues. This year papers that appeared in the journal TACCESS as well as Experience Reports will be presented in a novel format that combines a short talk with a poster presentation. There will also be work-in-progress poster sessions, a demo session, a doctoral symposium, and presentations from the ACM student research competition.

The ASSETS 2017 program is organized as follows:
On Monday (Day 1), the program starts with a keynote presentation by Karen Peltz Strauss on Disability Access and the Federal Communications Commission. Karen is the Deputy Chief of the Consumer and Governmental Affairs Bureau at the Federal Communications Committee (FCC). Following the keynote, we will have a series of technical paper sessions organized around Interaction Techniques and Frameworks, Technology for Neurodiverse Users, The Future of Work and the Web for People with Vision Impairments. The poster sessions during the day will feature poster and demo papers, along with Student Research Competition and SIGACCESS Travel Scholarship recipients. The day will end with a Reception at the conference hotel.

On Tuesday (Day 2), the program will continue with sessions on Memory and Motor Impairments, Sign Language and Captioning, Tactile, Haptic and Augmented Reality Interfaces for Vision Loss. We will also hear short talks from the finalists in the ACM Student Research Competition. The poster sessions on this day will include the poster and demo papers, along with posters from our Doctoral Consortium participants. The day will conclude with a reception at the National Federation of the Blind.

On Wednesday (Day 3), the program will conclude with a morning of short talks and a poster session dedicated to technical sessions summarizing recent publications in the TACCESS journal and Experience Reports. This will be followed by a technical session on Supporting Communication, followed by a technical session on Navigation and Safety. We will close the program by introducing next year's chairs to talk about ASSETS 2018.

Organizing ASSETS 2017 was a large collaborative effort. We would like to thank our authors for submitting high quality research to the conference, which has enabled us to assemble this exciting program. We are grateful to the program committee who worked very hard together in reviewing papers and providing feedback for authors. We also thank the members of our organizing committee: our Treasurer and Registration Chair David Flatla, our Posters and Demos Chairs Erin Brady and Luz Rello, our Doctoral Consortium Chairs Jennifer Mankoff, Chieko Asakawa, and Shaun Kane, our Experience Reports Chair Dianne Pawluk, our Student Research Competition Chairs Stacy Branham and Lizbeth Escobedo, our TACCESS Special Issue Chair Anke Brock, our Best Papers Committee Chair Anne Marie Piper, our Mentoring Chair Kyle Rector, our Local Arrangements Chair Robin Brewer, our Web Chair Lourdes Morales-Villaverde, our Accessibility Chair Erin Buehler, our Publicity Chair Aqueasha Martin-Hammond, our Graphic Design Chair Abdullah Ali, our Sponsorship Chair Michele Williams, and our Halloween Chair William Easley for all their contributions to the conference and these proceedings.

Finally, we would like to thank our supporters: Microsoft Research and IBM Research, the National Science Foundation, and our sponsors ACM and SIGACCESS for their support.

We hope that you will enjoy this exciting program of research in computing accessibility and that the conference will provide you with an opportunity to connect with other researchers and practitioners from institutions around the world.

Welcome to ASSETS 2017!

Amy Hurst
ASSETS 2017 General Chair
University of Maryland, Baltimore County, USA

Leah Findlater
ASSETS 2017 Program Co-Chair
University of Washington, USA

Meredith Ringel Morris
ASSETS 2017 Program Co-Chair
Microsoft Research, USA

Table of Contents

Session: Memory Impairments & Motor Impairments

Session Chair: Jacob O. Wobbrock *(University of Washington)*

Session: Sign Language & Captioning

Session Chair: Raja Kushalnagar *(Gallaudet University)*

Session: Tactile, Haptic, and Augmented Reality Interfaces for Vision Loss

Session Chair: Tiago Guerreiro *(University of Lisbon)*

Session: Supporting Communication

Session Chair: Robin Brewer *(University of Michigan)*

Session: Navigation & Safety

Session Chair: David Flatla *(University of Dundee)*

Poster Session 1

Student Research Competition

Experience Reports

ASSETS 2017 Conference Organization

General Chair: Amy Hurst *(University of Maryland, Baltimore County, USA)*

Program Chairs: Leah Findlater *(University of Washington, USA)*
Meredith Ringel Morris *(Microsoft Research, USA)*

TACCESS Special Issue Chair: Anke Brock *(Inria Bordeaux, France)*

Best Papers Committee Chair: Anne Marie Piper (*Northwestern University, USA)*

Treasurer and Registration Chair: David Flatla *(University of Dundee, UK)*

Posters and Demonstrations Chairs: Erin Brady (*Indiana University-Purdue University Indianapolis, USA)*
Luz Rello *(Carnegie Mellon University, USA)*

Doctoral Consortium Chairs: Jen Mankoff *(University of Washington, USA)*
Chieko Asakawa *(Carnegie Mellon University, USA & IBM Research, Tokyo, Japan)*
Shaun Kane *(University of Colorado Boulder, USA)*

Experience Reports Chair: Dianne Pawluk (*Virginia Commonwealth University, USA)*

Student Research Competition Chairs: Stacy Branham *(University of Maryland, Baltimore County, USA)*
Lizbeth Escobedo *(University of California, San Diego, USA)*

Mentoring Chair: Kyle Rector *(University of Iowa, USA)*

Local Arrangements Chair: Robin Brewer *(University of Michigan, USA)*

Accessibility Chair: Erin Buehler *(Facebook, USA)*

Web Chair: Lourdes M. Morales-Villaverde *(UC Santa Cruz, USA)*

Publicity Chair: Aqueasha Martin-Hammond *(Indiana University-Purdue University Indianapolis, USA)*

Sponsorship Chair: Michele Williams *(Pearson, USA)*

Halloween Chair: William Easley *(University of Maryland, Baltimore County, USA)*

Steering Committee Chair: Shari Trewin *(IBM, USA)*

Steering Committee: Matt Huenerfauth *(Rochester Institute of Technology, USA)*
Faustina Hwang *(Reading University, UK)*
Jinjuan Heidi Feng *(Towson University, USA)*

Program Committee: Chieko Asakawa *(Carnegie Mellon University, USA & IBM Research, Tokyo, Japan)*
Shiri Azenkot *(Cornell Tech, USA)*
Armando Barreto *(Florida International University, USA)*
Jeffrey Bigham *(Carnegie Mellon University, USA)*
Davide Bolchini *(Indiana University-Purdue University Indianapolis, USA)*
Erin Brady *(Indiana University-Purdue University Indianapolis, USA)*
Anke Brock *(INRIA Bordeaux, France)*
James Coughlan *(Smith-Kettlewell Eye Research Institute, USA)*
Ed Cutrell *(Microsoft Research, USA)*
Alistair Edwards *(University of York, UK)*
Jon Froehlich *(University of Washington, USA)*
Kathrin Gerling *(University of Lincoln, UK)*
Tiago Guerreiro *(University of Lisbon, Portugal)*
Kotaro Hara *(Carnegie Mellon University, USA)*
Anthony Hornof *(University of Oregon, USA)*
Matt Huenerfauth *(Rochester Institute of Technology, USA)*
Faustina Hwang *(University of Reading, UK)*
Hernisa Kacorri *(Carnegie Mellon University, USA)*
Shaun Kane *(University of Colorado, USA)*
Sri Kurniawan *(UC Santa Cruz, USA)*
Raja Kushalnagar *(Gallaudet University, USA)*
Richard Ladner *(University of Washington, USA)*
Walter Lasecki *(University of Michigan, USA)*
Jonathan Lazar *(Towson University, USA)*
Clayton Lewis *(University of Colorado, USA)*
Sergio Mascetti *(University of Milan, Italy)*
Kathy McCoy *(University of Delaware, USA)*
Scott McCrickard *(Virginia Tech, USA)*
Joanna McGrenere *(University of British Columbia, Canada)*
Karyn Moffatt *(McGill University, Canada)*
Kyle Montague *(Newcastle University, UK)*
Cecily Morrison *(Microsoft Research, United Kingdom)*
Hugo Nicolau *(University of Lisbon, Portugal)*
Anne Marie Piper *(Northwestern University, USA)*
Cynthia Putnam *(DePaul University, USA)*
Kyle Rector *(University of Iowa, USA)*
Luz Rello *(Carnegie Mellon University, USA)*
John T. Richards *(IBM Research, USA)*
Hironobu Takagi *(IBM Research, Tokyo, Japan)*
Shari Trewin *(IBM Research, USA)*
Ha Trinh *(Northeastern University, USA)*
Khai Truong *(University of Toronto, Canada)*
Bruce Walker *(Georgia Tech, USA)*

Program Committee (continued): Annalu Waller *(University of Dundee, UK)*Gerhard Weber *(Technische Universitat Dresden, Germany)*
Maria Wolters *(University of Edinburgh, UK))*
Shaomei Wu *(Facebook, USA)*
Koji Yatani *(University of Tokyo, Japan)*
Tom Yeh *(University of Colorado, USA)*
Yeliz Yesilada *(Middle East Technical University, Northern Cyprus)*

Additional Reviewers:

Dragan Ahmetovic	Masatomo Kobayashi
Miguel Ballesteros	Varsha Koushik
Cristian Bernareggi	Annika Muehlbradt
Sukru Eraslan	Eshed Ohn-Bar
Kentarou Fukuda	Uran Oh
Andrea Gerino	Maria Rauschenberger
João Guerreiro	Toshiroh Takase
Tatsuya Ishihara	Marco Visentini

ASSETS 2017 Sponsors & Supporters

Sponsor:

SIGACCESS

Special Interest Group on Accessible Computing

Doctoral Consortium Supporter:

NSF

Student Research Competition Supporter:

Microsoft Research

Gold Supporter:

facebook

Silver Supporters:

IBM Research

Microsoft Research

information systems UMBC

Disability Access and the Federal Communications Commission

Karen Peltz Strauss
Federal Communications Commission
445 12th Street, SW
Washington, DC 20554
karen.strauss@fcc.gov

Keywords
Accessibility; disability; policy; law.

BIOGRAPHY

Karen Peltz Strauss is the Deputy Chief of the Consumer and Governmental Affairs Bureau at the Federal Communications Commission (FCC), where she helps to oversee implementation of the Commission's disability policies. As one of the country's premier disability rights attorneys for more than three decades, Strauss has led nationwide efforts to adopt federal policies that ensure that persons with disabilities have access to communications and video programming services and equipment. Prior to joining the FCC, Strauss authored various landmark disability laws, including Title IV of the Americans with Disabilities Act (ADA), closed captioning and telecommunications accessibility requirements in the Communications Act, and the Twenty-First Century Communications and Video Accessibility Act (CVAA). As part of efforts to enact the latter statute, Strauss founded the Coalition of Organizations for Accessible Technology (COAT), whose membership reached 300 national and regional organizations, and whose grassroots support was pivotal to the passage of the CVAA in 2010.

Through her regulatory work both prior to and at the FCC, Strauss has been instrumental in drafting policy to secure disability access to telecommunications products and services, closed captioning, video description, hearing aid compatibility, telecommunications relay services, and 911 services. Strauss's goal has been to ensure that people with disabilities are full participants in our nation's communications systems, especially as our country migrates from legacy to ever-changing Internet-based and wireless communications technologies. One of Strauss's proudest achievements has been the establishment of an FCC-based nationwide program that distributes free communications equipment to low income people who are deaf-blind. The program continues to provide thousands of individuals the tools they need to lead independent and productive lives.

Early in her career, Strauss was legal counsel first, for Gallaudet University's National Center for Law and Deafness and later, for the National Association of the Deaf. Strauss next spent several years consulting for non-profit, governmental and private organizations on communications-related matters. Throughout her career, Strauss frequently has been called upon by Congress to testify as an expert witness on accessibility legislation, and has presented at hundreds of conferences across the United States and other countries. Strauss' 2006 book – A New Civil Right: Telecommunications Equality for Deaf and Hard of Hearing Americans – chronicles decades of accessibility advocacy efforts by Americans who are deaf and hard of hearing in their quest for telecommunications access.

In 2011, Strauss received an honorary doctorate degree from Gallaudet University for her work on communications accessibility. She has also been the recipient of awards from the National Consumers League, Telecommunications for the Deaf and Hard of Hearing, Inc., the National Association of the Deaf, the D.C. Mayor's Office, and the Alliance for Public Technology. Strauss holds a J.D. from the University of Pennsylvania Law School and an L.L.M. from the Georgetown University Law Center.

ASSETS '17, October 29-November 1, 2017, Baltimore, MD, USA

ACM ISBN 978-1-4503-4926-0/17/10.
https://doi.org/10.1145/3132525.3132526

Epidemiology as a Framework for Large-Scale Mobile Application Accessibility Assessment

Anne Spencer Ross[1], Xiaoyi Zhang[1], James Fogarty[1], Jacob O. Wobbrock[2]
[1]Computer Science & Engineering, [2]The Information School
DUB Group, University of Washington Seattle, WA 98195 USA
{ansross, xiaoyiz, jfogarty}@cs.washington.edu, wobbrock@uw.edu

ABSTRACT

Mobile accessibility is often a property considered at the level of a single mobile application (app), but rarely on a larger scale of the entire app "ecosystem," such as all apps in an app store, their companies, developers, and user influences. We present a novel conceptual framework for the accessibility of mobile apps inspired by epidemiology. It considers apps within their ecosystems, over time, and at a population level. Under this metaphor, "inaccessibility" is a set of *diseases* that can be viewed through an epidemiological lens. Accordingly, our framework puts forth notions like *risk* and *protective factors*, *prevalence,* and *health indicators* found within a *population* of apps. This new framing offers terminology, motivation, and techniques to reframe how we approach and measure app accessibility. It establishes how app accessibility can benefit from multi-factor, longitudinal, and population-based analyses. Our epidemiology-inspired conceptual framework is the main contribution of this work, intended to provoke thought and inspire new work enhancing app accessibility at a systemic level. In a preliminary exercising of our framework, we perform an analysis of the *prevalence* of common *determinants* or accessibility barriers. We assess the *health* of a stratified sample of 100 popular Android apps using Google's Accessibility Scanner. We find that 100% of apps have at least one of nine accessibility errors and examine which errors are most common. A preliminary analysis of the frequency of co-occurrences of multiple errors in a single app is also presented. We find 72% of apps have five or six errors, suggesting an interaction among different errors or an underlying influence.

CCS Concepts

• **Human-Centered Computing→Accessibility→Accessibility Theory, Concepts and Paradigms**

Keywords

Mobile computing; mobile accessibility; app accessibility; accessibility assessment; conceptual framework; epidemiology.

1. INTRODUCTION

Mobile applications (apps) play increasingly important roles in many aspects of life, including personal finances, communication, community engagement, and transportation. Supporting access to

ASSETS '17, October 29-November 1, 2017, Baltimore, MD, USA © 2017 Copyright is held by the owner/author(s). Publication rights licensed to ACM.
ACM 978-1-4503-4926-0/17/10...$15.00
https://doi.org/10.1145/3132525.3132547

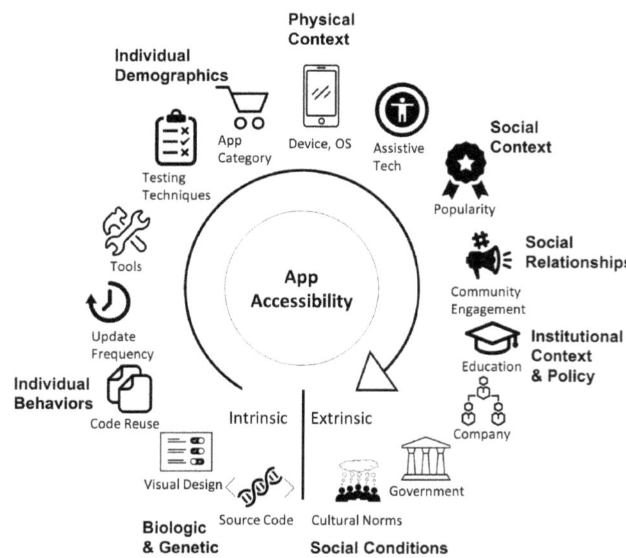

Figure 1. As a systems science, epidemiology can serve as a metaphor that changes the way we think and work with mobile app accessibility. Here, the concept of a multi-factor ecosystem from epidemiology has been applied to mobile app accessibility. An app's accessibility is a product of many factors ranging from individual and intrinsic to population-level and extrinsic. These factors include: source code and design, behaviors, demographics, physical context, social context and relationships, institutional context and policies, and cultural norms. Accessibility is affected by factors at all levels. Figure inspired by [34].

these impactful technologies for all people is important. Yet, for the approximately 15% of the world population with disabilities [35], many of these apps are inaccessible. Understanding the extent and causes of app inaccessibility is imperative for creating successful solutions. To date, most approaches to understanding and improving app accessibility have focused on specific issues within individual apps, such as developer guidelines [1,4], app scanners [5,19], and compiler warnings [2]. But apps do not exist in isolation. They might come from the same developers or studios, utilize the same libraries or code repositories, mimic the same popular design patterns, or simply be subsequent versions of prior releases. These factors can perpetuate accessibility problems, but the factors are rarely, if ever, analyzed at a "multi-factor" or "population level" over myriad apps. Expanding how we approach app accessibility to encompass the rich ecosystem in which apps exist can drive innovations in how we work to enhance accessibility. Fortunately, other areas of study provide a model for multi-factor population-level analyses. One such area is *epidemiology*, which examines health on a population level from a systems perspective. Whereas a physician treats a single patient, an epidemiologist considers the health of a whole population of patients. Analogously, a designer or developer might address the inaccessibility of an individual app, but a population perspective on app accessibility might reveal the causes of systemic problems and suggest potential solutions. An example would be discovering that a widely-used interface toolkit was responsible for inaccessible widgets used in many apps.

We propose an epidemiology-inspired framework for the examination of mobile app accessibility. We emphasize that this metaphor supports the social model of disability [29]. App accessibility is a community responsibility, as captured by our multi-factor framing (see Figure 1) that guides how different parts of the community can contribute to app accessibility. As more companies invest resources into accessibility and more researchers investigate app accessibility, it becomes increasingly beneficial to have a conceptual framework from which to guide thought and action. Conceptual frameworks (e.g., [7]) give a common vocabulary to ground discussion, guide efforts to improve accessibility with known strategies, and illuminate opportunities not previously considered. We acknowledge that the concepts in our framework are numerous, but we believe that this is indicative of the richness of the framework and of its potential to inspire and inform thought and action.

Adapting a model from epidemiology [34], Figure 1 illustrates many factors that act upon an app during its creation, distribution, maintenance, and usage. These factors range from *intrinsic factors* that are tightly encapsulated within each individual app to *extrinsic factors* that indirectly but influentially affect app populations. Example factors, listed from intrinsic to extrinsic, include source code, visual design, development and testing tools, operating systems, assistive technologies used, app popularity, company and government policies, and public opinions. As this framing exemplifies, apps do not exist independently of one another or of their environments. A natural extension is to recognize that neither do their accessibility strengths or weaknesses. Understanding how these factors interact and influence the accessibility of apps over time can help in improving app accessibility through development of preventative measures and post-release repairs [37].

Developing an understanding of how a variety of factors contribute to app accessibility requires recognizing the value of varying levels of analysis, from individual entities to populations at specific moments and over time. Many well-established scientific disciplines have benefitted from longitudinal population-level analyses, such as ecology [33], oceanography [22], and computer security [9]. As stated, we chose epidemiology [20] as our metaphor for our app accessibility framework. We construct our epidemiology-inspired framework and, although no metaphor is perfect or without limitations, we advance the claim that the study of app accessibility can benefit from epidemiology's well-developed language and approach to collecting, analyzing, and acting upon longitudinal multi-factor population-based data. To the best of our knowledge, ours is the first attempt to frame app accessibility as a "population science."

To put our conceptual framework through its paces, we apply it in an analysis of accessibility barriers in popular Android apps available on the Google Play Store. We analyze a sample of 100 apps for nine *determinants*, or causes, of a variety of "inaccessibility diseases" using Google's Accessibility Scanner [19]. We present the *prevalence* of different determinants, motivated by the objective of "Determining the Extent of the Disease" in the population (see Section 4.2). We then reflect on how our framework and preliminary data informs future work.

Our research contributions are twofold:

- A novel conceptual framework for monitoring, analyzing, and acting upon longitudinal multi-factor large-scale data on mobile app accessibility. Our framework highlights wide-ranging intrinsic and extrinsic factors that influence app accessibility, motivates the collection and analysis of large-scale data, and guides opportunities for enhancing treatments for app "diseases" of inaccessibility.
- Empirical results from a framework-guided analysis of a stratified sample of 100 apps from the Google Play Store. Motivated to determine the extent of the disease in the population, we found high *prevalence* with 100% of apps having an "inaccessibility disease" based on the nine *determinants* scanned for.

2. REAL-WORLD EXAMPLES

We present two real-world examples of population-level factors that influence app accessibility and how they fit into the epidemiology-inspired framework. The examples present elements that are *infectious agents* that carry inaccessibility within Android Studio [2] and Android's Floating Action Button design tutorial [17]. These examples both exemplify how factors apart from developer-written source code affect the likelihood of an accessibility barrier.

2.1 Android Studio App Designer

Android Studio is the development environment released by Google for creating Android apps and is one of the most popular tools for Android developers. Due to its widespread use, the accessibility of the Android features it provides has a large impact on the accessibility of the whole population of Android apps.

Android Studio includes a drag-and-drop WYSIWYG Layout Editor. The editor provides basic widgets including Image Buttons for common functionality, such as a star icon for "favoriting." When an icon button is dragged onto an interface, Android Studio generates the layout code in a separate file that defines the button, its layout size, and other basic features. A notable omission within the generated code is the Content Description, the field a screen reader uses to describe an icon button. If that field is not manually added by the developer, the app will have an inaccessible button for people using a screen reader. As an approach to addressing this, when the content description field is non-existent or has no content, Android Studio will issue a warning that provides options to: (1) guide the developer to add the field, or (2) set a flag to ignore all warnings of that type.

This example illustrates the *transmission* of an inaccessible button *disease* from an *infectious agent*, the icon button, to a *host* app. The *determinant*, or cause of the disease, is the missing content description. Our epidemiology-inspired framework then motivates an in-depth analysis to *evaluate the existing preventative treatment* of the warning to determine if it is sufficient at preventing the spread of the disease.

2.2 Android Floating Action Button Design

Floating action buttons are a part of Google's Material Design for Android, a guide for a more unified design in Android apps [24]. Floating action buttons are already being adopted in popular apps such as Skype, Gmail, Facebook Messenger, and Dropbox. Floating action buttons, however, are potential *infectious agents* carrying inaccessibility. These buttons are typically separate from standard menu bars, "floating" in a visually prominent location, such as in the bottom-right corner of the screen, highlighting the most important action. Android provides design guidelines for how to employ these buttons in interfaces, including outlining how the buttons should look, act, animate, and function. Such buttons might become accessibility barriers to people who are blind or have a motor impairment because they are not anchored to traditional menus, making their location in the linear navigation order unexpected or inconvenient. Switches and linear screen reader navigation are examples of assistive technologies that depend on linear navigation orderings. Floating action buttons might also cause other accessibility barriers with explore-by-touch screen readers because the design guidelines recommend that floating action buttons animate, move, or switch functionality with changes in app state, which might be difficult to track non-visually.

This example illustrates *transmission* of a second inaccessible button *disease* from an *infectious agent*, the floating action button design, to a *host* app. One *determinant* of the disease is the lack of intuitive integration of the button into linear navigation order. Another *determinant* is the lack of feedback for floating action button state transitions. This *infectious agent* lives in the *repository* of Google's Material Design.

3. RELATED WORK

We see two major strands of related work, that of mobile app accessibility and that of population-level or large-scale analyses of the web for accessibility or of apps for other purposes. We address both in the subsections that follow.

3.1 Mobile App Accessibility

There is limited work assessing the accessibility of mobile apps. Milne et al. [25] investigated nine mobile health apps on Apple iOS for adherence to seven accessibility features and found that all of the apps had at least one feature missing. Moreover, many of the barriers were not covered in Apple's accessibility guidelines, which focus primarily on individual elements versus interactions between elements. This study fits into our conceptual framework by looking at *prevalence* of inaccessibility, although on a small scale. It also fits the objective of assessing existing treatments (i.e., the guidelines).

Yu et al. [36] assessed the interface and navigation accessibility of six mobile health apps through user tests with six people with spina bifida. They identified many enhancements that would increase the app's accessibility. These studies begin to establish the *lethality,* or severity, and *prevalence* of accessibility barriers. They also fit the objective of inspiring new treatments. Our framework would also motivate the collection of data needed to assess if the new enhancements were effective.

To guide developers in enhancing app accessibility, Google [1] and Apple [4] have mobile accessibility guidelines. W3C also issued a note on how to apply existing web accessibility guidelines to mobile devices [15]. Studies analyzing the success of web guidelines suggest that guidelines are not sufficient for ensuring accessibility, due to a number of factors that include lack of developer knowledge, difficult to implement recommendations, difficulties testing for adherence, or the mismatch between actual user concerns and guideline recommendations [13,23,26]. Google's Accessibility Scanner [19] and Apple's Accessibility Inspector [5] are tools for app accessibility analysis. Both tools run on an app interface, screen by screen, and return an analysis flagging common accessibility barriers such as buttons that are too small, images lacking text descriptions, and elements with problematic color contrast. These tools can only be applied to a single app at a time and must be guided interactively. Our framework motivates the development of advancements in analysis tools to allow for larger-scale analyses with more detail on accessibility problems.

3.2 Large-Scale Analyses

Large-scale app analyses have been conducted to understand the effectiveness of web accessibility guidelines, vulnerabilities in apps, app usage patterns, and popular designs. This prior work demonstrates insights that can be gained from such analyses and provides further motivation for designing and leveraging population-level analyses for app accessibility.

How well the existing guidelines and tools work to address accessibility is largely under-studied. Hanson and Richards [21] performed a longitudinal study of changes in web accessibility on over 100 websites over 14 years. They concluded that government websites tended to be more accessible than non-government sites and that accessibility overall was getting better, but most sites still failed on at least one simple accessibility feature.

Richards, Montague, and Hanson [30] further investigated potential indirect factors influencing accessibility, including changes in coding practices, devices, browser capabilities, and the importance of page rank. They concluded these indirect factors might account for some increase in web accessibility and discussed the potential of considering indirect accessibility when developing new technology.

Bigham et al. [8] studied web accessibility by analyzing differences between sighted and blind people's browsing behaviors. Participants used a web proxy to perform their normal web browsing in their home on their own equipment over the course of a week. The data collected was analyzed for statistical differences between sighted and blind people's browsing experience using metrics such as number of websites visited that had images with alt text, number of interactions with dynamic content, and timing spent on common tasks. They used the differences in these metrics as a measure of the frequency of accessibility barriers on the web and how those impact browsing experiences.

These works exemplify the types of insights that can be gained through large-scale and longitudinal studies. Creating techniques that allow for such studies of mobile apps could allow similar insights into how successful existing interventions are, into potentially impactful unconsidered influences, and into opportunities for improvement. Our epidemiology-inspired framework helps to structure our approach to creating those techniques.

Large-scale analyses of app usage can reveal patterns in terms of duration, app category, and context (e.g., time of day, location) [10,27]. The results of these studies aim to inform app design [27] or to provide a basis for an app recommendation system [10]. These types of analyses have yet to be applied with a focus on mobile accessibility, but could be insightful. For example, analogous to prior analysis of web accessibility [8], the difference in time spent in communication apps between those who use a screen reader and those who do not could suggest an accessibility barrier.

Population-level analyses have also been used to explore interactions between apps and more extrinsic factors through analyzing code reuse [28], design reuse [16], and widget and layout popularity [31]. For example, Mojica et al.'s [28] insights support the interdependence of apps by highlighting the prominence of code reuse. The ERICA project [16] similarly analyzed interface designs and user traces with the aim of informing future designers. App interdependence is a key component of our epidemiology-inspired framework, and motivates extending analyses to include the impact of such code reuse and popular design patterns on accessibility.

Computer security also has a long history of using large-scale studies to understand the prevalence of security vulnerabilities, their sources, and how they spread. In work that is perhaps most similar to ours, Gil et. al. [18] propose a "genetic epidemiology approach to cyber-security" using large-scale automated analyses to create tools to determine the probability of a network being susceptible to a threat. The authors focus on computer networks and genetic mutation detection concepts from genetic epidemiology. By contrast, we create a broader framework utilizing many more concepts from general epidemiology applied to mobile app accessibility.

4. EPIDEMIOLOGY FRAMEWORK

Epidemiology regards human health as holistic physical, emotional, and social well-being, not just the absence of illness. Epidemiology acknowledges that an individual's health cannot be understood in isolation and is instead the product of continuous interaction with environmental and social factors [11]. We utilize key terminology, concepts, and techniques from epidemiology to frame mobile app accessibility in a similarly holistic fashion. A *healthy* app is one whose essential functionality is accessible and usable to all, not just an app that has no rudimentary accessibility errors. Our framework defines a single app as a potential *host* of one or more *diseases* of inaccessibility. A *population* consists of a large group of apps, such as: all apps in existence, all Android apps, all apps that use the Google Map library, or all shopping apps.

Inspired by epidemiological concepts and the five objectives of epidemiology presented by Gordis [20], we offer a conceptual framework to guide the thoughts and actions of researchers and developers concerning app accessibility. We present the terminology for this framework in Tables 1a-d, showing the analogies drawn between epidemiology and app accessibility, with examples.

4.1 Identify Factors and Causation

Addressing a disease requires understanding what causes it and what factors make the entity more *(risk factor)* or less (*protective factor*) likely to contract it. The same is true for various "inaccessibility diseases" that arise in apps. By understanding where diseases come from, how they spread, and what factors affect an app's risk, we can better guide the development of *treatments*.

We define a *factor* as characteristics of an app, or of the ecosystem in which an app is developed, maintained, and used, that impact the likelihood of an app having an inaccessibility *disease*. There are *risk factors* that increase the likelihood of disease and *protective factors* that reduce the likelihood. Figure 1 presents a structure for understanding the many factors within the *ecosystem* that impact accessibility. Much of the language and structure of the framing are inspired from the "model for analysis of population health and health disparities" presented in epidemiology [34].

Epidemiological elements move from *intrinsic* to *extrinsic* factors. Intrinsic factors include the core of an individual app. At the other end of the spectrum are highly extrinsic factors, or those that impact many apps in a manner that is removed from their source code.

Starting at the intrinsic end of the spectrum (see Figure 1), there are the metaphorical *biological* and *genetic factors* (i.e. an app's source code and design). Progressing toward extrinsic factors, the spectrum continues into factors that directly impact the biological characteristics. These factors include *individual behavior* such as code reuse through libraries, copying from repositories or tutorials, frequency of updates, testing techniques, and tools used. Factors such as tools, testing, and code provenance not only reflect what app building strategies are used but also the trust in those strategies. Having high trust in a tool might reduce developer sense of responsibility for investigating accessibility barriers. *Individual demographics* are closely tied to these factors. These include app age and category (e.g., travel, shopping, entertainment). The next section of the spectrum is more extrinsic than intrinsic. Within *physical context*, there is the device upon which the app is running, the OS and OS version, and any accessibility software or hardware being used. These elements have fewer direct interactions with the app's biological and genetic factors. Yet physical context can impact an app's accessibility based on how the source code and physical context interact and support one another. For example, different versions of a screen reader might interact differently with app source code, resulting in different levels of accessibility within the same app, dependent on physical context.

Table 1: Epidemiology-inspired terminology and its mapping to mobile app accessibility with examples. (a) Terms describing a single app

(a) Terms Describing an App

Term	Epidemiology	Accessibility	Example(s)
Health	State of complete physical, social, and mental well-being, not just the absence of disease	State of complete accessibility and usability, not merely the absence of obvious accessibility problems	An app has all its buttons labeled but their labels so poorly describe their functions that the app is almost impossible to use
Disease	A condition that interferes with a vital physiological process	An accessibility barrier	An app with a calendar that cannot be traversed with a screen reader would have an "inaccessible calendar disease"
Host	An organism that can be infected	An app that can have an accessibility barrier	A specific app (e.g., the Yelp app)
Case	An instance of a particular condition	A single instance of an app with an inaccessibility disease	An instance of the Toggl app with an unlabeled button
Infectious Agent	An entity that carries and transmits a disease	A component that carries or transmits disease	The icon button widget from Android Studio (see Section 2.1)
Determinant	A factor (entity, characteristic, behavior, or event) that directly influences disease occurrence	The root cause (element, characteristic, code, or design) of an accessibility barrier	The missing content description within the button's source code
Factor	An aspect of behavior, lifestyle, environment, or inherited characteristic that is associated with increased occurrence of a disease	A characteristic of an app or of the ecosystem in which an app is developed, maintained, and used that impact the likelihood of an app having an inaccessibility disease. Can be *risk* or *protective*	(See Factors and Causation Section 4.1)
Usual Source of Care	The place a patient usually goes when sick or needing advice about health	The way an app is normally tested for accessibility	Automated tests; Blindfolded developer
Diagnosis	The process of determining by examination the nature and circumstances of a disease	The process of determining the existence and cause of an accessibility barrier	By hand exploration; Google Accessibility Scanner
Life Expectancy	Average number of years of life remaining based on individual, population, and environment characteristics	How long before an app is abandoned based on its risk and protective factors, environment, and characteristics. Can be of development or use	How long app is maintained; Time between download and abandonment

Table 1 cont. (b) Terms describing a disease. **(c)** Population-level terms. **(d)** Terms for taking action on epidemiology-inspired data.

(b) Terms Describing a Disease

Term	Epidemiology	Accessibility	Example(s)
Reservoir	The habitat in which an infectious agent normally lives, grows, and multiplies	A harbor for accessibility barriers	Toolkits; Design guides
Contagiousness	How capable a disease is of being transmitted by contact or close proximity	The ease at which an accessibility barrier can be transmitted given its host and environment	Highly contagious: An accessibility barrier within core library source code
Natural History of a Disease	The temporal course of disease from onset to fatal termination, remission, relapse, or recovery	The process of an accessibility barrier being introduced, encountered, fixed or ignored, and perpetuated or permanently remedied. May be of use or development	See Section 4.3
Incidence	Measure of the frequency of a new case of the disease occurring in a population over time	A measure of the frequency of new occurrences of an accessibility barrier in a population over time	Number of new cases of inaccessible buttons in the Top 100 apps released in a month
Prevalence	The number or proportion of cases of a disease in a given population	The number or proportion of apps with a particular disease in a given population	Number of apps in Top 100 with an inaccessible button
Lethality	How likely is a disease to cause death or complications	How likely is an app to be abandoned due to accessibility barriers	Highly lethal: An log-in button that can't be activated with a screen reader
Transmission	Any mode or mechanism by which an agent is spread	How an accessibility barrier enters an app	Copy-paste repository code; Using a drag-and-drop tool

(c) Population-Level Terms

Term	Epidemiology	Accessibility	Example(s)
Population	The total number of persons in a particular group (e.g., all people with a certain occupation)	The apps or a group of apps under consideration	Google Play Store Top 100; All transportation apps
Census	The enumeration of an entire population with details including residence, occupation, age, etc.	An enumeration of all apps including versions, release dates, APK, platform, health status, etc.	The Androzoo [3] collection of apps, versions, and security vulnerabilities
High-Risk Group	A group in the population with an elevated risk of disease	A group of apps at elevated risk of having a particular accessibility barrier	Android apps are more at risk for inaccessibility than iOS apps
Outbreak	The occurrence of more cases of a disease than expected in a given area or group over a particular period of time	Occurrence of more cases of accessibility barriers or a particular determinant than expected in a period of time	Significant increase in number of unlabeled buttons in a week
Mortality Rate	The measure of frequency of death in a population during a specified time interval	A measure of how often apps are abandoned, for any reason, during a specified time interval	70% of apps are abandoned within a week of downloading
Herd Immunity	The resistance to an infection of an entire group because of a substantial proportion being immune. Herd immunity is based on having a substantial number of immune persons, thereby reducing the likelihood that an infected person will encounter a susceptible one.	An app's resistance to an accessibility barrier because its ecosystem is dominated by factors that are accessible	Minimizing the number of widgets in Android Studio that introduce accessibility barriers
Health Indicator	A measure that reflects, or indicates, the state of health of people in a population	A measure that reflects, or indicates, the state of accessibility within a population of apps	The number of apps with unlabeled buttons
Detection Bias	Can occur when people with a risk factor are more likely to have a disease detected because of intense follow-up	Can occur when certain apps are more likely to have accessibility barriers detected because of closer scrutiny	Apps built by developers who themselves have a disability might be more likely to have early diagnosis of accessibility barriers than other apps
Common Source Outbreak	An outbreak that results from a group of persons being exposed to a common disease agent	When there is a common source for an increased incidence of an inaccessibility disease	An OS update that causes widespread inaccessibility

(d) Terms about Taking Action

Term	Epidemiology	Accessibility	Example(s)
Public Health	Systematic collection, analysis, interpretation, and dissemination of ongoing health data to gain knowledge of disease patterns, and to control and prevent disease	Systematic collection, analysis, interpretation, and dissemination of ongoing app accessibility data to gain knowledge of accessibility patterns and to control and prevent barriers to access	Community reporting by and for people with disabilities about the accessibility of certain apps
Treatment	Techniques to combat a disease. Includes prevention and therapy.	An intervention designed to reduce or eliminate an accessibility barrier or its impact. Includes prevention and therapy.	App developer tools that aid in the detection and remedy of accessibility barriers
Prevention	Treatment measures to prevent disease (e.g., immunization, limiting exposure to risk factors)	Treatment measures that prevent an app from having an accessibility barrier	Screening toolkits; Thorough testing
Therapy	Measure to treat a contracted disease, reduce its impact on health, or reduce its spread	A treatment that repairs an existing inaccessibility disease	Adding custom labels to buttons
Universal Precautions	Recommendations issued to minimize the risk of transmission of pathogens by health care and public safety workers	Population-based prevention with best practices that all apps should follow to reduce inaccessibility	Accessibility guidelines; Integration of accessibility testing into general quality assurance

Social context encompasses the popularity of an app and how that popularity can impact the accessibility standards to which the app is held. *Social relationships* cover how vocal people in the community are about accessibility, how active people are in demanding that an app be accessible, and how responsive an app is to adapting to critical feedback.

The final, most extrinsic factors include those on the institutional and societal level. Within *institutional context*, there are education, company, and government influences. *Education* influences include the education of developers for creating accessible apps, of users on existing accessibility support, of the community on the importance of advocating for accessibility, and of institutional leaders on the importance of prioritizing and integrating accessibility considerations.

Company factors consider how companies can impact the accessibility of their apps by dedicating resources to accessibility, choosing tools to help enhance accessibility, and creating policies that enforce accessibility within their organizations. *Government* factors are similar, but on a larger scale. The government's role in funding allocation, public initiatives, policies, lawmaking, enforcement, and advocacy all play into the accessibility of apps. At the extrinsic end of the spectrum is *social condition*. This covers the cultural norms and public expectations of a whole society. For example, whether accessibility is viewed as a bonus or an essential requirement and how much society supports the allocation of resources for achieving better accessibility.

All factors throughout the spectrum interact with one another and shape the ecosystem in which an app is created, maintained, and used. Changes in any one can impact others up and down the spectrum, potentially affecting accessibility. Structuring our understanding of *how* these factors affect an app's risk for acquiring an "inaccessibility disease" can guide accessibility enhancing treatments.

4.2 Determine the Extent of a Disease

In a world of limited resources, it is essential to direct those resources toward the most impactful problems. Epidemiologists determine the extent of a disease in a community, through measures such as *incidence* and *prevalence*, to plan health services, facilities, and health-provider training. App accessibility could benefit from similar metrics. These metrics include disease *prevalence*, or the extent to which "inaccessibility diseases" occur in an app population. For a given disease, metrics also include identifying the prevalence of *determinants,* or causes of diseases. Properties of the *determinant* can also be measured, such as *lethality*, a measure of severity defined as the likelihood an app will be abandoned due to an accessibility barrier. Finally, metrics such as *incidence* that measure how many new *cases* are emerging over time can help identify whether a new risk factor has emerged that impacts many apps. An example would be an accessibility barrier created by a widespread OS update. The objective of determining the extent of a disease gives a data-driven focus to addressing app inaccessibility.

4.3 Study Natural Histories

Our next inspiration from epidemiology is the study of the progression of a disease in a host. Epidemiologists map disease progression from exposure to a *risk factor* or *infectious agent*, to early *disease onset*, to the appearance of *symptoms*, to *diagnosis*, and finally to *outcome*. This progression model, known as the *natural history of the disease*, informs what risk factors and symptoms to be alert for, what impact the disease will have if untreated, and where in the timeline there exist opportunities for preventative or therapeutic treatments [20]. Rather than modeling the natural history of an "inaccessibility disease," we use similar concepts to model the progression of an app through two important phases of its existence: (1) its creation and maintenance, and (2) its usage [12]. Modeling how an app progresses through these phases frames thinking about when a host app might be exposed to a risk factor or infectious agent, at what stages in the progressions the disease might manifest and be diagnosable, and what impact the disease might have. The natural histories also inspire when a treatment, *preventative* or *therapeutic*, might be applied most effectively.

4.3.1 *Natural History of App Development*

The "Natural History of App Development" (Figure 2) outlines the stages of app creation and maintenance. Pre-birth, or before an app is released, the app goes through iterative steps of conception, design, implementation, and testing. Interventions within this period are *preventative treatments*. A successful preventative intervention will treat an "inaccessibility disease" before the app is released for use. As with epidemiology, preventative treatment is preferred to *therapeutic treatment* (i.e., after release), as it prevents placing a burden on the user community.

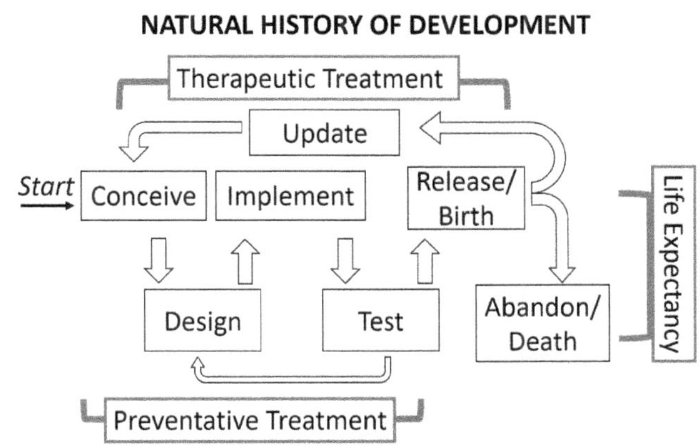

Figure 2. The natural history of app development model represents the design and implementation process an app goes through pre-release and post-release. It serves as a framework for where new treatments might be introduced.

However, it is difficult to prevent all "diseases" in an app before the app is released. We then consider the next stages of the app's post-birth life, which is an iteration on pre-birth stages through a series of updates [12]. These updates might be driven by bug fixes, end-user feedback, the app creator's desire for new or extended features, or any number of other factors. This update stage might occur at varying rates, from daily to yearly. This stage presents an opportunity for *therapeutic treatments* that address accessibility barriers or vulnerabilities in released apps. It is unfortunately possible that updates might introduce or worsen "inaccessibility diseases." It is therefore beneficial to monitor an app's accessibility over time.

The last important milestone in the natural history of development is death. In this stage of natural history, death is defined as when an app is no longer being maintained. A "dead" app will not benefit from treatment aimed at developers or maintainers, such as guidelines or source code testing tools, and requires other forms of remediation.

4.3.2 *Natural History of App Usage*

We also present the "Natural History of App Usage" (Figure 3), which focuses on the environment of usage on a device by an end user. An app's usage is born at the beginning of its active use. Pre-birth stages include finding and downloading an app. Preventative treatment can be introduced at these stages. For example, by adding the ability to filter searches for healthy, accessible apps or by adding an accessibility rating to an app download page. Such preventative treatments would allow a user to understand the health of the app and potentially avoid trying apps that are "diseased."

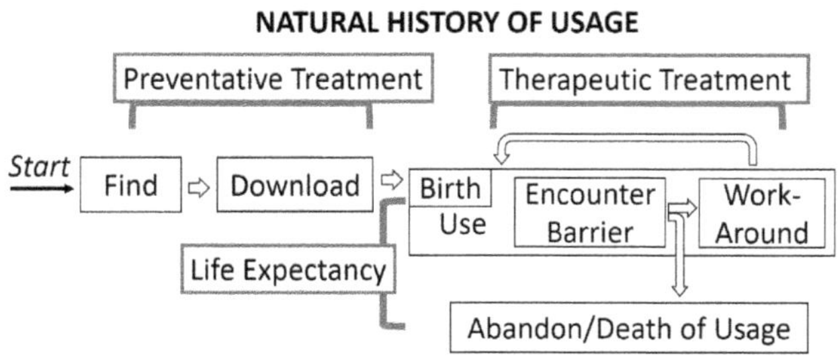

Figure 3. The natural history of app usage model represents the process by which an end user finds, downloads, uses, and abandons an app. The usage stage includes first usage, or *birth* of usage. Within usage, someone might cycle through the stages of encountering a barrier and trying to work around it. The progression could ultimately end when a user abandons an app and usage *dies*.

An app's usage-birth happens when it is first opened on the device. During usage, barriers caused by "diseases" might be encountered and work-arounds might be attempted. Usage-death occurs when the person discontinues use entirely. Therapeutic methods could be introduced within usage or abandonment. An example of an existing treatment is found in Apple's and Google's screen readers, an end-user can create custom button labels for fixing poorly labeled elements. A post-death treatment could prompt a user to submit feedback on why an app's usage has ceased.

4.4 Evaluating Existing and New Treatments

Epidemiology is motivated to collect information to guide the development of intervention methods and modes of health care delivery. A key component to achieving that is being able to evaluate the effectiveness of interventions in order to focus efforts on the most promising strategies.

App accessibility efforts would benefit from expanding evaluation techniques, such as those motivated by our epidemiology-inspired framework. Existing accessibility enhancement techniques include preventative treatments such as developer guidelines [1,4] and automatic interface analysis tools [5,19] as well as therapeutic treatments such as adding custom labels for screen readers and forums where people can search for assistance [6].

Some existing treatments might have been tested on a small scale with user testing or on a small number of apps, but systematic population-based longitudinal multi-factor analyses are lacking. Such analyses could provide more insights into the effectiveness of treatments that address accessibility diseases and highlight opportunities for improvement.

Example metrics from epidemiology include: (1) tracking the *prevalence* or *lethality* of different disease *determinants*, or causes, in the *population* (e.g., how many Android apps have an unlabeled image button, or how many apps in that same population are abandoned because of that "inaccessibility disease"); (2) performing such tracking before and after a treatment is introduced (e.g., adding the empty content description warning in Android Studio), and (3) examining whether a treatment influences factors as expected (e.g., logging whether missing content description warnings are frequently muted in Android Studio). An impactful treatment should be reflected in the metrics of the whole population. By collecting population-level longitudinal multi-factor data, we can better evaluate the strength of different approaches.

4.5 Breaking the Chain of Infection

Although not one of Gordis' five objectives of epidemiology [20], the *Chain of Infection* [14] (Figure 4) is another helpful concept for understanding how different factors interact in the spread of disease. The chain portrays the links between a disease agent, a susceptible host, and how a disease spreads. We similarly conceptually model different *hosts*, *agents*, and *reservoirs* for app accessibility barriers. This model structures an understanding of the interactions between agents, hosts, and transmission.

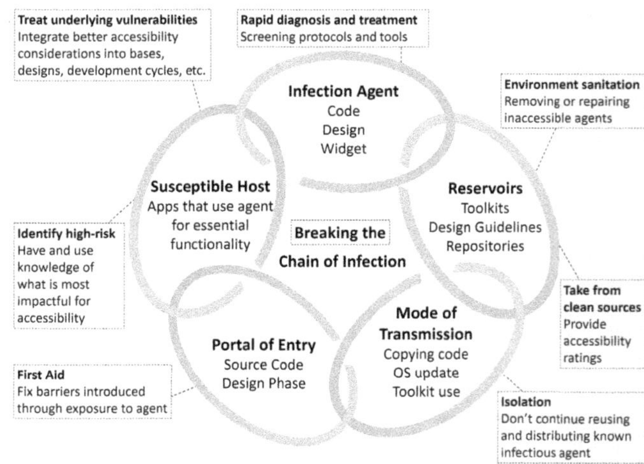

Figure 4. The Chain of Infection helps visualize where an accessibility barrier originates and how it spreads into host apps. Working to break the chain at any one major link—infectious agent, reservoir, transmission, portal of entry, or susceptible host— can guide where treatments are introduced. Inspired by [14].

This model is further useful with its extension into *Breaking the Chain of Infection* [14]. If any link of the chain is broken, then the disease cannot spread. By looking at each component in the chain as an opportunity to disrupt the flow of a disease, we can better consider where interventions could be introduced effectively, what those interventions might look like, and what resources need to be involved for intervention success.

This cycle can be applied to the Android Studio unlabeled icon button case study (see Section 2.1). We start by defining the app as a susceptible *host* for the inaccessible button *disease.* The icon button widget acts as the *infectious agent* with the disease *determinant* being its missing content description. The agent resides in the *reservoir* of the Android Studio design interface. It is *transmitted* through the developer's use of that interface with a *port of entry* at the source code implementation stage.

Establishing the links between the elements helps to structure the consideration of possible interventions. Currently, Android Studio provides a compilation warning for the missing content description, effectively applying *first aid* (i.e., a warning) in the *portal of entry* (i.e., the source code). The existing accessibility guidelines for Android act to *treat underlying vulnerabilities* of the host app in the form of addressing lack of education of developers. A potential *treatment* at the *agent* (i.e., Image Button widget) link could be to create a default content description for default Android icon buttons. Framing accessibility within this chain provokes thinking about causes of inaccessibility in greater granularity and inspires new opportunities for addressing this problem.

4.6 Inform Public Policy and Regulation

Epidemiology's consideration of multi-factor and population-level influences on health within an ecosystem guides data collection and analysis. In turn, that data can be applied to impact public health. Mirroring Gordis' [20] final objective for epidemiology, *Informing Public Policy and Regulation*, we consider how a population-based model of app accessibility can change the app environment to enhance the health of apps. Changes could include legislation (e.g., web accessibility [32]), company-enforced vetting of apps, initiatives to inform developers, or initiatives to educate people on available treatments for their apps. Data-driven direction and structure can propel these changes to happen. For example, as in the introduction of this paper, the percentage of people in the world with disabilities is often used as motivation for accessibility work. Similar data around the *prevalence* and *lethality*, or impact, of app accessibility problems could compel policy changes. An epidemiology-inspired framework helps inform what data collection, analysis, and presentation might look like.

5. EXERCISING THE FRAMEWORK

Our chief contribution in this paper is conceptual, providing a new framework that reshapes how we think about and work to improve app accessibility. To demonstrate how this framework guided our own thinking, we present an initial empirical study of the *prevalence* of various "inaccessibility diseases" in Android apps.

5.1 Method

We took a stratified sample from the *population* of top free Android apps. Apps were selected from the "top downloaded, free" lists in the Google Play Store in each of ten categories (i.e., our strata): Business, Communication, Education, Entertainment, Health and Fitness, Maps and Navigation, Medical, Productivity, Shopping, and Social. We excluded apps that required a specialized log-in (e.g., a bank account or subscription) or blocked automated scanning (e.g., banking apps often block taking screenshots). Ten apps from each category were analyzed, totaling 100 apps. For each app, 4-8 primary tasks were identified. For example, in the "Indeed Job Search" app, the tasks were as follows: recover forgotten password, log-in, search for jobs, apply for jobs, and access settings. Google's Accessibility Scanner [19] was the *diagnostic tool* used to scan each screen required to complete the tasks for *determinants* of various "inaccessibility diseases" (Table 2).

Table 2. The accessibility errors, or *disease determinants*, reported by Google's Accessibility Scanner provide a *health indicator* for apps.

Error	Description
Clickable Items	Overlapping clickable items
Editable Image Label	TextView has a content description. This might interfere with a screen reader's ability to read the content of the text field
Image Contrast	Low contrast in image or icon
Item Descriptions	Items with identical speakable text
Item Label	Missing element label
Item Type Label	Item label ends with type, e.g., "Play Button." TalkBack automatically announces item type, so information is redundant
Link	URL in link may be invalid
Text Contrast	Low text contrast between foreground and background
Touch Target	Item is too small

5.2 Results

The *prevalence* of each disease *determinant* is the number of apps in which each error occurred (Figure 5). The most prevalent determinants are Touch Target (95% of apps), Item Label (94%), and Text Contrast (94%). Slightly less prevalent are Item Descriptions (85%), Image Contrast (85%), and Clickable Items (57%). The least prevalent determinants were Item Type Label (20%), Editable Item Label (10%), and Link (1%).

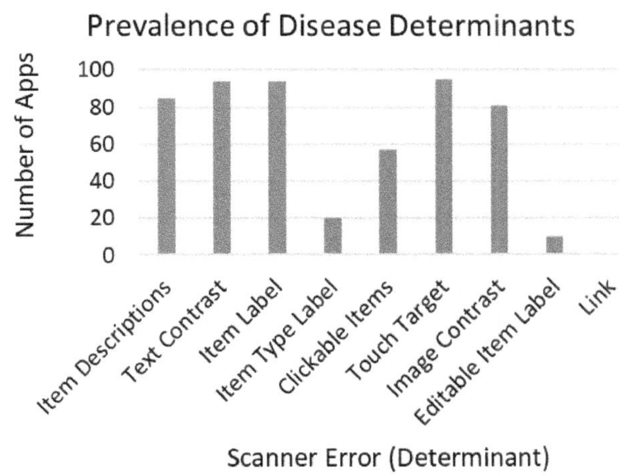

Figure 5. The high prevalence of disease in the tested apps highlights that apps are still largely inaccessible, even for simple determinants like item labels. All of these determinants can result in various "inaccessibility diseases," like the "inaccessible button disease."

To provoke thinking about whether determinants co-occur, Figure 6 presents the distribution of disease determinants per app. Based on the determinants tested, all of the apps had some form of an "inaccessibility disease;" in other words, they all *presented* at least one of the nine determinants as *symptoms*. Seventy-two percent of apps were diagnosed with either five or six determinants (36% each). The remaining distribution is skewed slightly left with 3% of apps diagnosed with one determinant, 2% of apps with two, 2% with three, 9% with four, 10% with seven, 3% with eight, and no apps presenting a case with all determinants. It is important to note the limitations of the Google Accessibility Scanner *diagnostic tool* and the impact those limitations have on the results. For example, the three apps with a single determinant all presented a single Item Label error on all tested screens. In each case, the single error reflected the fact that their entire interface was a canvas that presented itself as a single item to the accessibility API (i.e., the entire screen is inaccessible, but only one error is reported).

5.3 Discussion of Results

To our knowledge, there is no large-scale *census* of how prevalent different accessibility barriers are in mobile apps. The *prevalence* report presented above works toward such a census on the most prominent accessibility barriers in the *population* of top Android apps. Our findings, albeit preliminary, show that significant accessibility barriers, such as missing item labels, are still widely prevalent in apps. Situating these findings within our new conceptual framework, we can see how this type of data can motivate the need for dedicating resources to reducing even basic accessibility barriers and serve as a metric for evaluating the effectiveness of existing interventions.

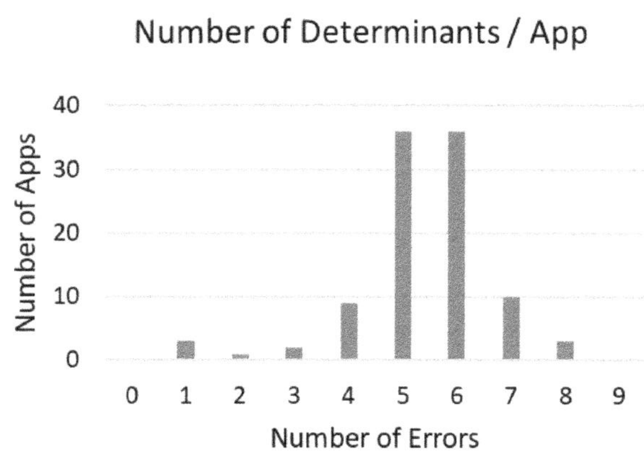

Figure 6. The distribution of the number of errors in each app explores co-occurrences of different disease determinants. Co-occurrence might suggest different underlying influential factors.

Although *prevalence* is one useful metric of app accessibility, it does not alone capture disease causes or impact. The *lethality* of each case of inaccessibility varies due to the determinant and context. For example, the Item Label error is more lethal than the Item Type Label for a screen reader user. A Touch Target error may be more lethal for someone with a motor impairment than an Item Label error. These observations motivate the development of advanced diagnostic tools and techniques that can give deeper insights into the most impactful determinants.

There are many co-occurrences of different determinants of inaccessibility (Figure 6). Cases where different lethalities of similar determinants co-occur are of special interest. For example, Item Description and Item Label are similar errors but Item Label is usually more lethal. An Item Label error will result in a screen reader saying "unlabeled button" versus an Item Description error will cause it to redundantly say "save button button." The co-occurrence of these determinants raises the question of why some elements get poor labels while others get none. The fact that the co-occurrence was not an isolated incident (at least 11% of apps tested had both errors) suggests that there might be underlying common factors involved. A more detailed analysis of what tools, education, or other factors contributed to some elements being labeled while others were not would give insight into: (1) in what stages of an app's natural history of development and usage it might be exposed to different infectious agents and determinants (e.g., what libraries are associated with unlabeled versus poorly labeled elements); (2) the effectiveness of current treatments; and (3) where in the chain of infection new treatments might be most effective.

Our results also highlight the limitations of current accessibility analysis tools. As noted above, the three apps that only have one error are due to the whole interface canvas being represented as a single, unlabeled element. This design makes them among the most inaccessible apps for screen reader users. Yet our current approach of counting types of errors, based on the granularity of the Accessibility Scanner, does not reflect the magnitude of those single error cases. Advancements in diagnostic tools would allow for the collection of better overall *health metrics*.

6. TAKEAWAYS AND FUTURE WORK

Our epidemiology-inspired framework has influenced how we approach app accessibility, driving our initial *prevalence* analysis. Situating our analysis and findings within the framework guided our methods, structured the types of phenomena we investigated, and gave us language to discuss the results and how they impact the larger ecosystem of app accessibility. The framework also provided many opportunities for considering future work in understanding and enhancing app accessibility.

The primary purpose and contribution of this paper is to introduce the epidemiology-inspired framework for app accessibility and to put a small piece of it through its paces in a preliminary analysis of disease *prevalence*. But, as the size of the entire framework makes clear, there are many other aspects of accessibility that can be measured in future work. Creating tools that allow for large-scale population-level analyses, tracing "inaccessibility diseases" in apps to identify potential *agents* (e.g., the Android Studio icon button example), and designing novel interventions beyond guidelines and individual developer tools are priorities for future work. Our new conceptual framework provides the motivation and structure to explore these opportunities. We acknowledge the sheer size and complexity of the epidemiology-inspired framework, but find it proportional to the problems and opportunities associated with improving the accessibility of the entire mobile app ecosystem.

7. CONCLUSION

We have shown how epidemiology's motivation, language, techniques, and models are highly transferrable to the challenge of mobile app accessibility on a population-level, beyond just addressing individual apps. It is our hope that our epidemiology-inspired framework will shape, guide, and inform our current methods and priorities for addressing app accessibility by incorporating multi-factor, longitudinal, and population-level concepts.

8. ACKNOWLEDGMENTS

We thank Anat Caspi of the Taskar Center for Accessible Technology at the University of Washington for her insights and feedback. This work was funded in part by the National Science Foundation under awards IIS-1053868, IIS-1702751, and DGE-1256082; the Wilma Bradley Endowed Fellowship in Computer Science & Engineering; a Google Faculty Award; and The Mani Charitable Foundation.

9. REFERENCES

1. Android Accessibility Developer Guidelines. https://developer.android.com/guide/topics/ui/accessibility
2. Android Studio. https://developer.android.com/studio/index.html
3. Androzoo. https://androzoo.uni.lu/
4. Apple Accessibility Developer Guidelines. https://developer.apple.com/accessibility/ios/
5. Apple Accessibility Scanner. https://developer.apple.com/library/content/documentation/Accsssibility/Conceptual/AccessibilityMacOSX/OSXAXTestingApps.html
6. AppleVis. http://www.applevis.com/
7. Victoria Bellotti, Maribeth Back, W. Keith Edwards, Rebecca E. Grinter, Austin Henderson, and Cristina Lopes. (2002). Making Sense of Sensing Systems: Five Questions for Designers and Researchers. *Proc CHI 2002*, 415–422. http://doi.org/10.1145/503376.503450
8. Jeffrey P. Bigham, Anna C. Cavender, Jeremy T. Brudvik, Jacob O. Wobbrock, and Richard E. Lander. (2007). WebinSitu: a Comparative Analysis of Blind and Sighted Browsing Behavior. *Proc. Assets 2007*, 51–58. http://doi.org/10.1145/1296843.1296854

9. Matt Bishop. (2003). What is Computer Security? *IEEE Security & Privacy Magazine*, *1*(1), 67–69. http://doi.org/10.1109/MSECP.2003.1176998
10. Matthias Böhmer, Brent Hecht, Johannes Schöning, Antonio Krüger, and Gernot Bauer. (2011). Falling Asleep with Angry Birds, Facebook and Kindle – A Large Scale Study on Mobile Application Usage. *Proc. MobileHCI 2011*, 47–56. http://doi.org/10.1145/2037373.2037383
11. Urie Bronfenbrenner. (1979). *The Ecology of Human Development: Experiments by Nature and Design*. Harvard University Press.
12. Parmit K. Chilana, Andrew J. Ko, Jacob O. Wobbrock, Tovi Grossman, and George Fitzmaurice. (2011). Post-Deployment Usability: a Survey of Current Practices. *Proc. CHI 2011*, 2243–2246. http://doi.org/10.1145/1978942.1979270
13. Raphael Clegg-Vinell, Christopher Bailey, and Voula Gkatzidou. (2014). Investigating the Appropriateness and Relevance of Mobile Web Accessibility Guidelines. *Proc. W4A 2014*, 1–4. http://doi.org/10.1145/2596695.2596717
14. Association for Professionals in Infection Control. (2017). Break the Chain of Infection. *Infection Protection and You: Healthcare Professionals*.
15. Michael Cooper, Peter Korn, Andi Snow-Weaver, Gregg Vanderheiden, Loïc Martínez Normand, and Mike Pluke. (2013). *Guidance on Applying WCAG 2.0 to Non-Web Information and Communications Technologies (WCAG2ICT)*. http://www.w3.org/TR/wcag2ict/
16. Biplab Deka, Zifeng Huang, and Ranjitha Kumar. (2016). ERICA: Interaction Mining Mobile Apps. *Proc. UIST 2016*, 767–776. http://doi.org/10.1145/2984511.2984581
17. Floating Action Button Usage Guidelines. https://www.material.io/guidelines/components/buttons-floating-action-button.html
18. Santiago Gil, Alexander Kott, and Albert-László Barabási. (2014). A Genetic Epidemiology Approach to Cyber-Security. *Scientific Reports*, *4*, 5659. http://doi.org/10.1038/srep05659
19. Google Accessibility Scanner. https://play.google.com/store/apps/details?id=com.google.android.apps.accessibility.auditor
20. Leon Gordis. (2004). *Epidemiology*. Saunders, Philadelphia, PA.
21. Vicki L. Hanson and John T. Richards. (2013). Progress on Website Accessibility? *ACM Transactions on the Web*, *7*(1), 1–30. http://doi.org/10.1145/2435215.2435217
22. Dale F. Leipper. (1961). Oceanography—A Definition for Academic Use. *Transactions, American Geophysical Union*, *42*(4), 429. http://doi.org/10.1029/TR042i004p00429
23. Jennifer Mankoff, Holly Fait, and Tu Tran. (2005). Is Your Web Page Accessible?: a Comparative Study of Methods for Assessing Web Page Accessibility for the Blind. *Proc. CHI 2005*, 41–50. http://doi.org/10.1145/1054972.1054979
24. Material Design. https://material.io/guidelines/
25. Lauren R. Milne, Cynthia L. Bennett, and Richard E. Ladner. (2014). The Accessibility of Mobile Health Sensors for Blind Users. http://scholarworks.calstate.edu/handle/10211.3/133384
26. S. Milne, A. Dickinson, A. Carmichael, D. Sloan, R. Eisma, and P. Gregor. (2005). Are Guidelines Enough? An Introduction to Designing Web Sites Accessible to Older People. *IBM Systems Journal*, *44*(3), 557–571. http://doi.org/10.1147/sj.443.0557
27. Trinh Minh, Tri Do, Jan Blom, and Daniel Gatica-perez. (2011). Smartphone Usage in the Wild : a Large-Scale Analysis of Applications and Context. *Proc. ICMI 2011*, 353–360. http://doi.org/10.1145/2070481.2070550
28. Israel J. Mojica, Bram Adams, Meiyappan Nagappan, Steffen Dienst, Thorsten Berger, and Ahmed E. Hassan. (2014). A Large-Scale Empirical Study on Software Reuse in Mobile Apps. *IEEE Software*, *31*(2), 78–86. http://doi.org/10.1109/MS.2013.142
29. Mike Oliver. (1990). The Individual and Social Models of Disability. *Joint Workshop of the Living Options Group and the Research Unit of the Royal College of Physicians*, Vol. 23.
30. John T. Richards, Kyle Montague, and Vicki L. Hanson. (2012). Web Accessibility as a Side Effect. *Proc. ASSETS 2012*, 79-86. http://doi.org/10.1145/2384916.2384931
31. Alireza Sahami Shirazi, Niels Henze, Albrecht Schmidt, Robin Goldberg, Benjamin Schmidt, and Hansjörg Schmauder. (2013). Insights Into Layout Patterns of Mobile User Interfaces by an Automatic Analysis of Android Apps. *Proc. EICS 2013*, 275–284. http://doi.org/10.1145/2494603.2480308
32. Section 508. https://www.section508.gov/
33. Arthur Tansley. (1987). What is Ecology? *Biological Journal of the Linnean Society*, *32*(1), 5–16. http://doi.org/10.1111/j.1095-8312.1987.tb00406.x
34. Richard B Warnecke, April Oh, Nancy Breen, Sarah Gehlert, Electra Paskett, Katherine L Tucker, Nicole Lurie, Timothy Rebbeck, James Goodwin, John Flack, Shobha Srinivasan, Jon Kerner, Suzanne Heurtin-Roberts, Ronald Abeles, Frederick L Tyson, Georgeanne Patmios, and Robert A Hiatt. (2008). Approaching Health Disparities From a Population Perspective: the National Institutes of Health Centers for Population Health and Health Disparities. *American Journal of Public Health*, *98*(9), 1608–15. http://doi.org/10.2105/AJPH.2006.102525
35. World Health Organization. (2011). World Report on Disability. http://www.who.int/disabilities/world_report/2011/report/en/
36. Daihua X Yu, Bambang Parmanto, Brad E Dicianno, and Gede Pramana. (2015). Accessibility of mHealth Self-Care Apps for Individuals with Spina Bifida. *Perspectives in Health Information Managemen, American Health Information Management Association*, *12*(Spring). http://www.ncbi.nlm.nih.gov/pubmed/26755902
37. Xiaoyi Zhang, Anne Spencer Ross, Anat Caspi, James Fogarty, and Jacob O. Wobbrock. (2017). Interaction Proxies for Runtime Repair and Enhancement of Mobile Application Accessibility. *Proc. CHI 2017*, 6024–6037.

BrailleSketch: A Gesture-based Text Input Method for People with Visual Impairments

Mingzhe Li, Mingming Fan, Khai N. Truong
Department of Computer Science
University of Toronto
franklin.li@mail.utoronto.ca, mfan@cs.toronto.edu, khai@cs.toronto.edu

ABSTRACT

In this paper, we present BrailleSketch, a gesture-based text input method on touchscreen smartphones for people with visual impairments. To input a letter with BrailleSketch, a user simply sketches a gesture that passes through all dots in the corresponding Braille code for that letter. BrailleSketch allows users to place their fingers anywhere on the screen to begin a gesture and draw the Braille code in many ways. To encourage users to type faster, BrailleSketch does not provide immediate letter-level audio feedback but instead provides word-level audio feedback. It uses an auto-correction algorithm to correct typing errors. Our evaluation of the method with ten participants with visual impairments who each completed five typing sessions shows that BrailleSketch supports a text entry speed of 14.53 word per min (wpm) with 10.6% error. Moreover, our data suggests that the speed had not begun to plateau yet by the last typing session and can continue to improve. Our evaluation also demonstrates the positive effect of the reduced audio feedback and the auto-correction algorithm.

CCS Concepts

• Social and professional topics→ Professional topics→ Computer profession → Assistive technologies

Keywords

Blind; Braille; text input; mobile devices; sketch; gesture.

1. INTRODUCTION

Text entry is an important communication mechanism. For people with visual impairments this can be accomplished by writing Braille. Traditionally, this is done manually by using a slate, a stylus, and Braille paper. However, it can be difficult for people with visual impairments to learn to hold the stylus up-right and write Braille backward. Six-key Braille typewriters, such as the Perkins Brailler [21], have since enabled people to type by simultaneously pressing keys that correspond to the different Braille dots accordingly.

Over the past decade, mobile devices have become increasingly more powerful and accessible. With commodity mobile devices, people with visual impairments are able to enter text using the onscreen keyboard with screen reader software, such as Apple's VoiceOver. However, this approach results in a very low text entry speed [4]. Alternatively, people can use speech recognition software to input text at a much faster rate [3]. However, speaking in public places may not always be appropriate and can introduce privacy concerns. A growing body of research has been exploring ways to leverage the user's ability to perform touch and multi-touch gesture inputs on mobile devices. For example, BrailleTap [9], TypeInBraille [15], Perkinput [4], and BrailleEasy [23] enable the user to type Braille by performing multiple taps sequentially to specify the dot codes for the desire letter—this can be time consuming. Methods such as Perkinput [4] and BrailleTouch [22] have also explored how touchscreen mobile devices can be used to support 6-finger chorded typing, as done on the Perkins Brailler.

Researchers have also explored gesture-based approaches [10][17] that allow users to draw gestures that are interpreted into letters. These approaches include methods which require the user to learn a new unistroke alphabet (*e.g.*, MoonTouch [10]) as well as those which allow the user to draw a gesture to represent the intended Braille code (*e.g.*, Edge Braille [17]). Approaches, such as EdgeBraille, allow people to leverage their knowledge of the Braille alphabet. There is only a low learning curve in this situation because people do not need to learn a new alphabet.

Inspired by this line of research, we present BrailleSketch (see Figure 1), a gesture-based text entry method for people with visual impairments to type Braille by drawing a path. To use

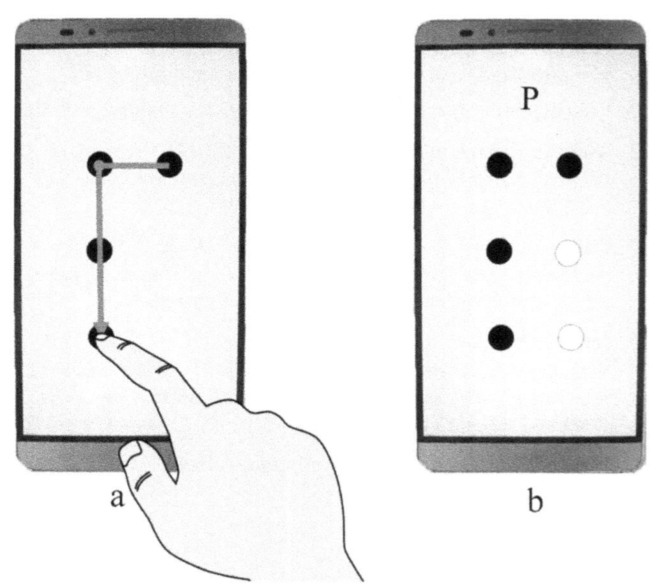

Figure 1. With BrailleSketch, a user simply sketches a path that connects all dots in a Braille code to type the corresponding letter.

ASSETS '17, October 29-November 1, 2017, Baltimore, MD, USA

ACM ISBN 978-1-4503-4926-0/17/10.
https://doi.org/10.1145/3132525.3132528

BrailleSketch, the user simply places her finger anywhere on the touch screen and sketches a path that passes through all the dots in a Braille code in a way that is intuitive to her. Different from existing approaches of typing Braille on the touchscreen, such as BrailleTouch [25], our design leverages the user's knowledge of the Braille alphabet but does not require users to know how to type Braille by performing 6-finger chorded input, as done with a Perkins Brailler. Our method also differs from other gesture-based text entry methods, such as MoonTouch [10], because it does not require people with visual impairments to learn an additional alphabet. We conducted a user study with people with visual impairments to evaluate the performance of BrailleSketch. Our results show that after ~100 minutes of typing, participants on average were able to type 14.53 word per minute (wpm) with 10.6% error rate. The fastest speed achieved overall was 19.32 wpm.

2. RELATED WORK

In this section, we review three general text entry approaches for people with visual impairments. The first approach explores the use of audio feedback to enable the user to input text. The second approach investigates typing-based and tapping-based methods for a variety of mobile devices, such as touchscreens and wearables. The final approach enables the user to perform gestures that are recognized into text.

2.1 Audio-based Methods

People with visual impairments often do not need to use a special keyboard when they use a computer. However, they require special screen reader software that voices the keys that are pressed. On mobile devices, the touchscreen accessibility function, such as Apple's VoiceOver, can help the user identify the keys that she touches in order to enter text. However, previous studies have shown that this method supports very low text entry rate (*e.g.,* 4.5 wpm [4], 4.3 wpm [3], 0.66 wpm [5]). To improve upon this, No-Look-Notes [5] explores dividing the screen into 8 pie segments with each corresponding to a set of characters (*e.g.,* 'ABC') that are easier to select. When the user touches a segment, the system reads the set of characters located in that segment. She can then tap the region with a second finger to select it and all of the characters get arranged vertically on the screen. When the user's finger touches the screen again, the system reads the character located at that position. She then can tap the screen with a second finger to select that letter or slide the finger to find the desired letter. In their evaluation of the system, Bonner *et al.* showed that participants were able to input text using No-Look Notes at a rate of 1.32 wpm with 11% error and VoiceOver at 0.66 wpm with 60% error.

Another audio-based approach to entering text is via speech. Azenkot and Lee's study [3] shows that the average text entry speed via speech is 19.5 wpm. However, speech interaction can potentially be inappropriate in public spaces and may introduce privacy concerns.

2.2 Typing- and Tapping-based Methods

The Perkins Brailler [21] is a typewriting tool that includes six keys which map to the six dots in a Braille code. To type, the user must simultaneously push the keys corresponding to the dots for the intended Braille code.

With the advent of mobile devices, researchers have explored additional ways to allow users to input Braille codes. For example, BrailleTap [9] maps inputs from the phone's physical keypad into dots in a Braille code. Guerreiro *et al.* showed that BrailleTap supports a rate of 3.6 wpm with 6.55% error. BrailleType [19] divides the touchscreen of a phone into a 3×2 grid. The user can sequentially perform a long-press in different grid cells, one cell at a time, to input dots in a Braille code. The user completes the typing of a character by performing a double tap. An evaluation of the system showed that participants were able to input text at a rate of 1.49 wpm with 9.7% error rate. With SingleTapBraille [1][2], users perform a series of sequential taps on the touchscreen to indicate the positions of the dots in a Braille code. Alnfiai and Sampalli evaluated SingleTapBraille and showed that participants achieved 4.71 wpm with 11% total error rate. TypeInBraille [15][16] allows users to input a Braille code by performing three multi-finger tap gestures sequentially. Each tap gesture types a row of dots in the Braille code. A 1-finger tap on the left side of the screen inputs the left dot in a row, while a 1-finger tap on the right side of the screen inputs the right dot in a row, a 2-finger tap input both dots, and a 3-finger tap inputs no dots in a row. This method results in a speed of 6.3 wpm with 3% error.

The Perkins Brailler design and 6-key chording method have also been extended to work on touchscreens and wearables. For example, BrailleEasy [23] and Perkinput [4] allow users to type a column of a Braille code one at a time by simultaneously tapping different fingers of one hand on the touchscreen. With Perkinput, on small touchscreen devices, the two columns of a Braille code can be tapped one after another. The simultaneous chording of 6-keys can also be supported on larger touchscreen devices with both hands touching the screen at the same time. Alternatively, two small devices can be paired to support input from a different hand. In their evaluation of the system, participants were able to achieve 6.05 wpm with 3.52% uncorrected error rate. BrailleTouch [8] allows users to cradle a mobile phone with two hands and type a Braille code with both hands at the same time. Much like how users would type with a Perkins Brailler, three fingers from each hand would be used to type each column of dots in a Braille code. With BrailleTouch, expert users were able to achieve a rate of 23.2 wpm with 14.5% error rate [25] while slower users reached 9.40 wpm with 39.3% error rate. Apple iOS natively includes Braille keyboard that uses a similar method to BrailleTouch. However, one drawback of these methods is that the number of people who know how to type Braille using Perkins-like methods is less than those who can read Braille [6].

Additionally, researchers have also examined glove based wearable text input methods. Lee *et al.* [18] designed a pair of chording gloves that allowed people with visual impairments to type Braille on any surface as if they were typing on a Braille typewriter. An evaluation of the work showed that participants were able to reach a rate of 24.3 wpm and 5.2% error rate [11]. Despite the high text entry speed, glove based methods require users to wear additional hardware on their hands.

2.3 Gesture-based Methods

Researchers have also explored the use of gestures as an intuitive method for people with visual impairments to input text. For example, EdgeBraille [17] users can enter a Braille code by swiping their finger along a mobile device's edges, which contain areas that could be touched to input dots. Participants achieved a speed of 7.17 wpm with 8.43% error with EdgeBraille. Because the dots are input by touching areas along the edge of the screen, users have to move their finger across the entire screen to draw Braille codes, which results in long travel distances. Inspired by EdgeBraille's design, our design removes these two constraints by allowing users to place their finger anywhere on the screen and to

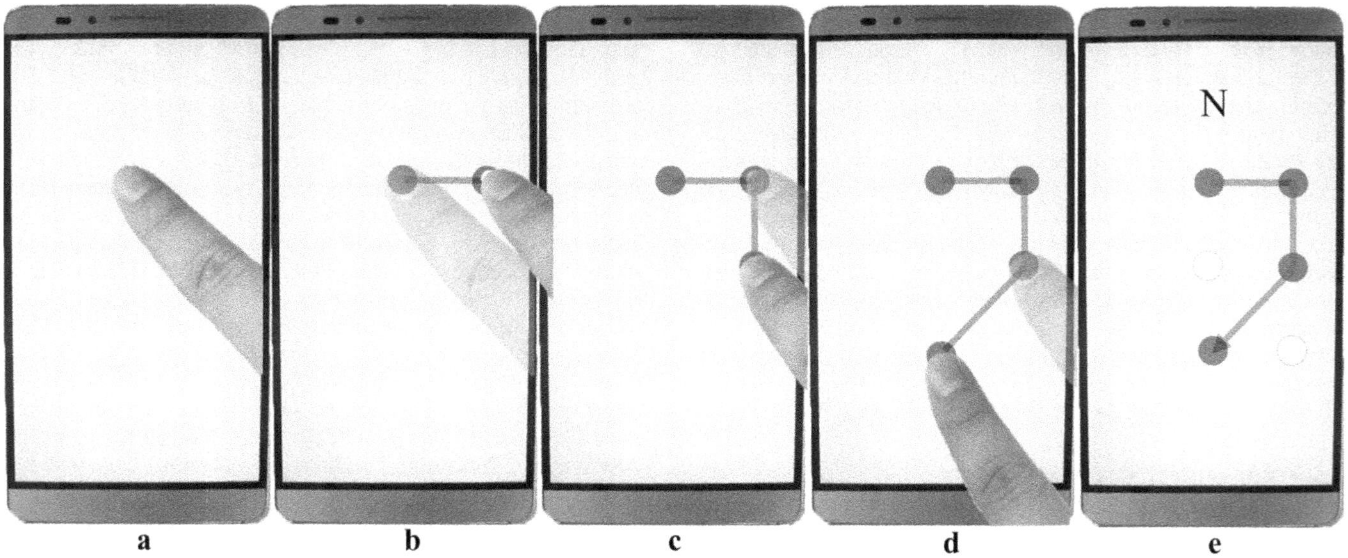

Figure 2. BrailleSketch on a smartphone. A user types the Braille code for 'N' by touching a finger anywhere on the screen first (a), then moving it horizontally to the right (b), then vertically to the bottom (c), then diagonally to the bottom left (d), and finally lifting the finger off the screen (e). The sketched path passes through the 4 dots in the Braille code of 'N' in a single gesture.

sketch the gesture without needing to reach specific positions. Our design also allows users to draw the same Braille code differently.

Another type of gesture-based text entry methods for people with visual impairments is to draw pre-defined gestures for each English letter. For example, Moontouch [10] allows users to draw gestures in Moon Alphabet to input English letters. Heni *et al.*'s evaluation of their approach shows that participants were able to type at 10.14 wpm. In contrast, our work examines the speed at which participants would be able to input text using gestures based on their knowledge of the Braille alphabets instead of learning a different alphabet, such as Moon.

3. SYSTEM DESCRIPTION

In this section, we describe how we implemented BrailleSketch as a gesture based text input method that allows people with visual impairments to sketch Braille codes on a touchscreen.

3.1 High-Level Design

We will first describe how users input a Braille code by performing a gesture. We will then discuss specific audio feedback provided to help the user to sketch the code without sight.

3.1.1 Sketching a Braille Code

To input a letter, the user simply sketches a path that connects all the dots in the desired Braille code. We illustrate how the user would type 'N' using BrailleSketch in Figure 2. The Braille for the letter 'N' contains 4 dots: 2 dots in the top row, one in the right column of the middle row, and one in the left column of the last row. In this example, the user simply places her finger anywhere on the screen to input the top left dot. Then, the user drags her finger to the right to input the top right dot. Next, the user drags her finger downwards to input the dot on the right side of the middle row. Finally, the user drags her finger downwards diagonally to input the fourth dot on the left side of the bottom row. Once the user lifts her finger from the screen, the letter 'N' is recognized.

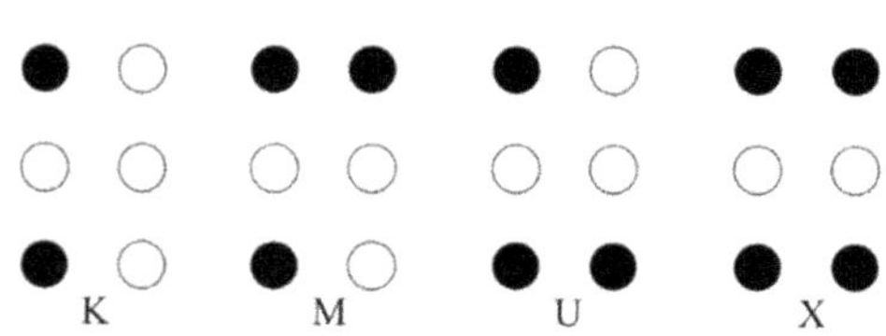

Figure 3. Braille codes for "K", "M", "U", and "X".

Most Braille codes can be drawn in more than one way. To make the system easy to use, BrailleSketch allows users to sketch the Braille code however it seems most natural to them. In Section 3.2.1, we discuss how the system recognizes the dots intended in the path drawn by the user and why this enables the gesture to be drawn flexibly.

Braille codes for the letters 'L', 'M', 'U', and 'X' (see Figure 3), do not have dots in the middle row. However, we designed our method to always input the next adjacent dot after the gesture is continued along a direction for a particular distance. Thus, to enable the user to input Braille codes that do not include dots in the middle row, the user must draw two gestures that are recognized together. A gesture path drawn very shortly (<500 ms) after another gesture path is treated as part of the previous gesture. For example, a 'K' is drawn using a double tap; 'X' is drawn using two lines; 'M' is drawn with a horizontal line first and then a dot; 'U' instead is drawn with a dot first and then a line.

3.1.2 Audio Feedback

To help people with visual impairments better perceive whether they have sketched is correct, the system provides different audio cues. Specifically, a 1000 HZ sine-wave audio sound will be played when a new dot is in a cardinal (*i.e.*, horizontal and vertical) direction adjacent from the previously added dot, and a 200 HZ sine-wave audio sound will be played if it is in an ordinal (*i.e.*, diagonal) direction from the previous dot. For example, when typing the Braille code for the letter 'N', the user will hear the same audio cue in Figure 2*b* and Figure 2*c*, because the new dot is cardinally adjacent to the previous dot. However, she will hear a different audio cue in Figure 2*e* because the new dot is ordinally adjacent to the previous dot. In this way, the user knows when she

Figure 4. A 5x3 grid of dots used to recognize the gesture drawn by the user is computed and centered where the finger touches the screen.

has incorrectly inputted a letter. For example, to draw 'C', the user simply needs to drag her finger horizontally, on the screen; and to draw an 'E', the user would drag her finger downwards diagonally left to right. If the user wants to type 'C', but hears a 200 HZ sine-wave audio sound, then she would know that the gesture was drawn incorrectly.

Previous research suggests that reading each letter during typing can decrease the text entry speed. Specifically, Mackenzie and Castellucci [14] showed that providing feedback after typing a word, rather than after each letter, can increase the typing speed. Inspired by this idea, our system does not provide letter level feedback. Instead, it only reads aloud the entire word after the user types a space to complete a word. The system, however, does provide an immediate audio feedback ("*no*"), if the sketched gesture cannot be recognized as any letter. Additionally, our design does not support correction while drawing the gesture. To correct an error, the user must delete the wrong gesture and type it again.

3.2 Implementation

In this section, we discuss how BrailleSketch recognizes a gesture as a Braille code and how it maps Braille dots. Then we describe how BrailleSketch implements the auto-error correction and supports the input of additional keys (*i.e.*, space, delete, and enter).

3.2.1 Sketch Recognition

We implemented BrailleSketch as an Android application. We used HUAWEI Ascend Mate7 phone running Android version 4.4.2 as the testing device. It has a 6.0-inch screen. The height and width are 157 mm and 81 mm respectively, and the resolution is 1080 × 1920 pixels. BrailleSketch allows the user to touch anywhere on the screen to start a gesture. When the user touches the screen, BrailleSketch computes a 5 rows × 3 columns grid of dots centered at the touch point (see Figure 4). We set the size of the grid to be 5×3 so that the touch point can be any dot of a 3×2 Braille code. For example, in Figure 4, depending on the direction that the user draws the gesture next, the touch point can be the bottom right dot of the 3×2 Braille code or it can also be the top left dot of the Braille code, *etc*. The diameter of each dot in the grid is 2/15 of the screen's height (*i.e.*, the longer edge), which is 2.1 cm on the testing phone. This is slightly larger than the average width of the pad of the index finger for adults (1.6 to 2 cm) [7]. The distance between the centers of two adjacent dots is 1/6 of the screen's height.

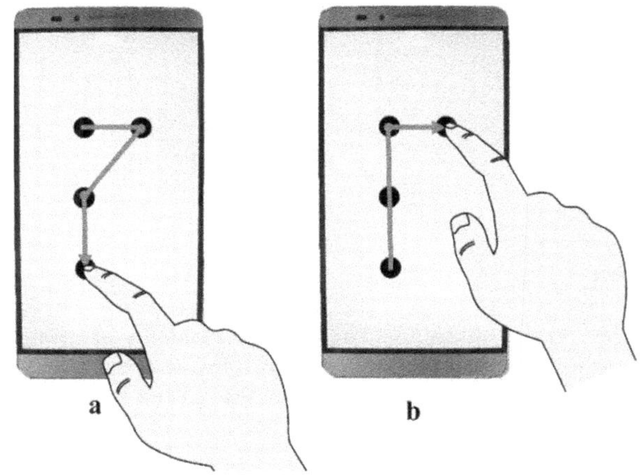

Figure 5. Two different ways of sketching the Braille code for the letter "P" beyond the one shown in the Figure 1.

BrailleSketch supports different ways of typing a letter. For example, Figure 1 shows one way to type the letter 'P' by starting from the top right corner dot, moving up to the top left corner dot, and finally ending at the bottom left corner dot. Alternatively, the user can also start from the top left corner dot, move to the top right corner dot, then move diagonally to the middle left dot, and finally end at the bottom left corner (see Figure 5 a). The user can also start from the bottom left dot, move up to the top left dot, then move horizontally to the right and end at the top right dot (see Figure 5 b). Thus, BrailleSketch allows the user to sketch Braille codes flexibly. The Grade 1 Braille alphabet design enables our method to use the subsequent dots in a gesture to determine the position of the first touchpoint. For example, if the subsequent dots in the pattern are above the dot added at the initial touch point, then the system determines the first touchpoint must be in one of the bottom two rows.

3.2.2 Auto-Correction

BrailleSketch implements an auto-correction algorithm [14] to correct errors in typed words. The algorithm works as follows: if the word typed by the user is in the dictionary, then it is left alone. The algorithm uses a dictionary that contains 10,000 words taken from the British National Corpus [24]. If a word is not in the dictionary, it computes the minimum string distance (MSD) between the inputted word and all words in the dictionary. The system then generates three lists of words with MSD equals 1, 2 and 3. It then sorts each list of words based their frequency. It combines the three lists and moves all the words that have the same length as the inputted word to the front of the combined list. The word at the top of the list is used to replace the inputted word. It is also possible that the algorithm does not find any match to the word. In that case, the auto-correction leaves the typed word as is. Future implementations of the autocorrection algorithm will explore how to include a dictionary with all words from the British National Corpus.

3.2.3 Additional Keys

Aside from the 26 English letters, BrailleSketch also allows the user to type three additional keys: *Space, Delete* and *Enter* (see Figure 6). When the keyboard is active, we override the functionality of the *volume* buttons. The user can type *Space* to finish a word by pressing the *volume down* button (located on the right side of the phone). She can type *Enter* by pressing anywhere on the screen for more than 2000 ms. Finally, she can delete a letter by performing swipe right gesture that leaves the screen.

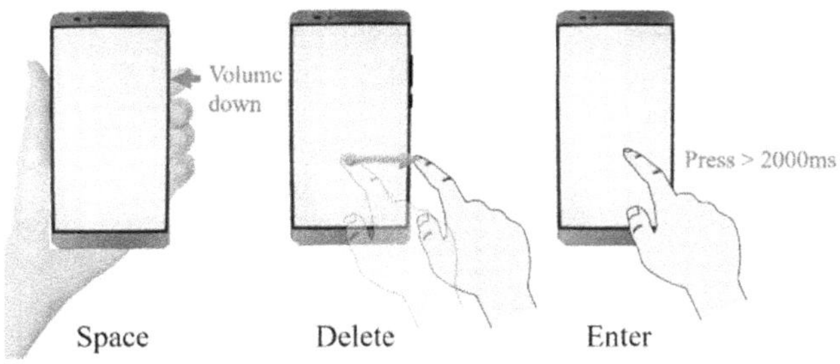

Figure 6. Three additional keys implemented: pressing volume down key to type the Space; swiping to the right to delete a letter; pressing anywhere on the screen for more than 2s to type "Enter".

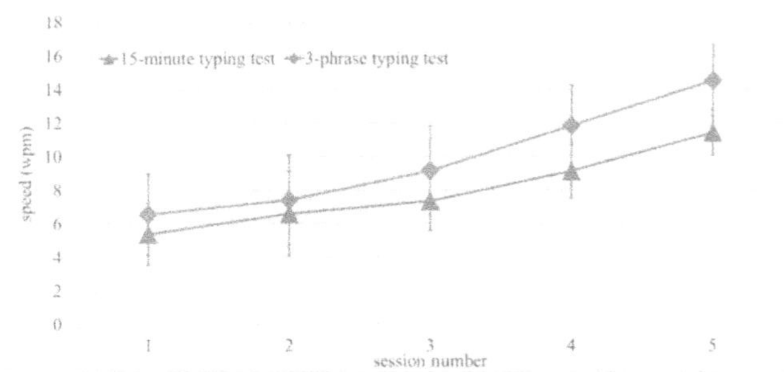

Figure 7. Typing speed for each session of the two typing tests. The horizontal axis is session number and the vertical axis is speed (wpm). Bars show standard deviations.

4. EVALUATION

4.1 Method

We next investigated the typing performance that participants with visual impairments were able to achieve with BrailleSketch. We describe the participants and the procedure involved in our evaluation of the BrailleSketch method.

4.1.1 Participants

We recruited 10 participants with visual impairments (2 males and 8 females) from CNIB (Canadian National Institute for the Blind) via emails and snowball sampling. The average age of the participants was 50.3 (SD=11.4). The average year of experiencing Braille was 32.3 (SD = 8.1). All participants were legally blind. Four of the participants were blind since born. All participants have used Braille-based typing devices before the study.

4.1.2 Procedure

Our study consisted 5 test sessions (1 to 5). Before the first test session, we provided participants with a training session (~10 minutes) to learn and practice typing using BrailleSketch. Then during each test session, BrailleSketch presents the participant with one text phrase at a time by reading it aloud using the Android's text to speech synthesizer. We asked participants to type this phrase as fast and accurately as possible using only lower-case letters and spaces, with no punctuation or numbers. Participants can press the volume up button located on the right side of the phone to request the system to speak the phrase out again. We created five sets of phrases by shuffling the standard set of 500 English phrases which was developed by Mackenzie and Soukoreff [13]. In this standard set, the frequency of each letter is highly correlated with the English language. Each test session used a different shuffling of the phrase set, and all participants were presented with the same shuffling of the phrases in the same order.

Each test session consists of two parts. First, participants were asked to type as many phrases as possible for 15 minutes. After each 15-minute typing session, we also asked the participants to type 3 additional phrases in order to be able to directly compare our results with a Heni *et al.*'s gesture-based text input method for people with visual impairments[10].

We arranged a 5-minute break between each two test sessions to let the participants relax. After the participants completed all test sessions, we interviewed them about problems that they might have encountered, and to collect their feedback about BrailleSketch.

We compensated each participant $65 for completing the study. We also offered a $50 gift card to the participant who had the highest average speed across all five sessions to motivate them to keep typing as quickly and accurately as they could throughout the entire study.

4.2 Results

The ten participants completed a total of 50 15-minute typing test sessions and 50 3-phrase typing test sessions. We analyzed the speed, error rate, gesture per character of the data collected using the StreamAnalyzer [26]. We treated the test session as one independent variable (IV) with 5 levels (*i.e.*, five test sessions) and the type of typing test as the second IV with 2 levels (*i.e.*, the15-minute typing test and the 3-phrase typing test). We performed a 2-way repeated measure ANOVA to examine whether the changes between sessions and the difference between two typing tests were statistically significant or not. When a statistically significance was found, we performed pairwise comparisons with Bonferroni correction to identify the pair(s) that exhibited significant difference. We reported partial eta square as the measure of the effect size in addition to the p-value.

4.2.1 Speed

Figure 7 shows the average typing speeds in wpm for each session of the two typing tests. For the 15-minute typing tests, the speed in the first test session was 5.37 wpm (SD = 1.86). It grew session after session and reached 11.39 wpm (SD = 1.36) in the last session. The best performance in the final session was 13.30 wpm, while the worst performance was 9.748 wpm.

For the 3-phrase typing tests, the speed in the first test session was 6.56 wpm (SD = 2.43). It also grew session after session and reached 14.53 wpm (SD = 2.13) in the last session. The best performance in the final session was 19.32 wpm, while the worst performance was 11.53 wpm.

There was a significant effect of the type of typing test on the text entry speed ($F_{1,9}$= 31.02, $p < .001$, η_p^2= .78). There was a significant effect of the test session on the text entry speed too ($F_{4,36}$= 121.5, $p < .001$, η_p^2= .93). Pairwise comparisons show that the differences between each two sessions were statistically significant ($p < .05$).

4.2.2 Error Rates

We calculated the average uncorrected, corrected, and total error rates for two typing tests. We first computed the average error rates per session per person. We then averaged all participants' error rates for each session to compute the average error rate for

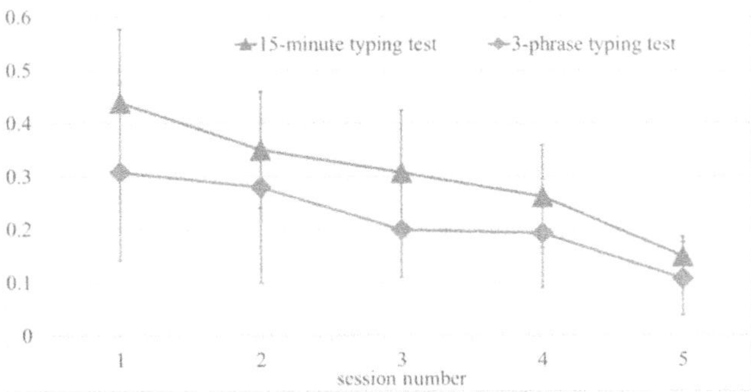

Figure 8. Total error rate for each session of the two typing tests.

each test session. The total, uncorrected, and corrected error rates are shown in Figure 8, Figure 9 and Figure 10 respectively.

4.2.2.1 Total Error Rates

Figure 8 shows the total error rates for the two typing tests over the five test sessions. For the 15-minute typing tests, the total error rate decreases from 0.439 (SD = 0.139) in the first session to 0.308 (SD = 0.166) in the last session. For the 3-phrase typing tests, the total error rate decreases from 0.148 (SD = 0.036) in the first session to 0.106 (SD = 0.069) in the last session.

There was a significant main effect of the typing test on the total error rate ($F_{1,9}$= 13.78, p < .01, η_p^2= .61). There was a significant effect of the test session on the total error rate too ($F_{4,36}$= 22.64, p < .01, η_p^2= .72). Pairwise comparisons show that the differences between the two sessions were significant (p < .05) except between session 1 and session 2 (p = 0.96) and between session 2 and 3 (p = 0.66).

4.2.2.2 Uncorrected Error Rates

Figure 9 shows the uncorrected error rates for the two typing tests over the five test sessions. For the 15-minute typing tests, the uncorrected error rate decreases from 0.105 (SD = 0.0908) in the first session to 0.047 (SD = .036) in the last session. For the 3-phrase typing tests, the uncorrected error rate decreases from 0.0804 (SD = 0.100) in the first session to 0.03 (SD = 0.040) in the last session.

There was a significant main effect of the typing test on the uncorrected error rate ($F_{1,9}$= 5.36, p < .05, η_p^2= .37). There was a statistically significant effect of the test session on the total error rate too ($F_{4,36}$= 3.12, p < .05, η_p^2= .26). Pairwise comparisons show no significant differences between any two sessions.

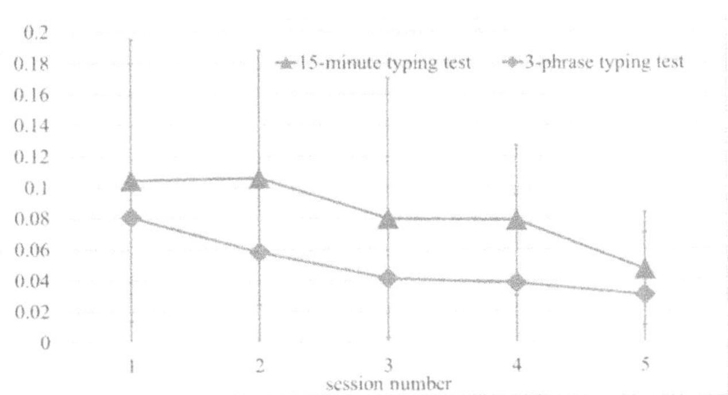

Figure 9. Uncorrected error rate for each session of the two typing tests.

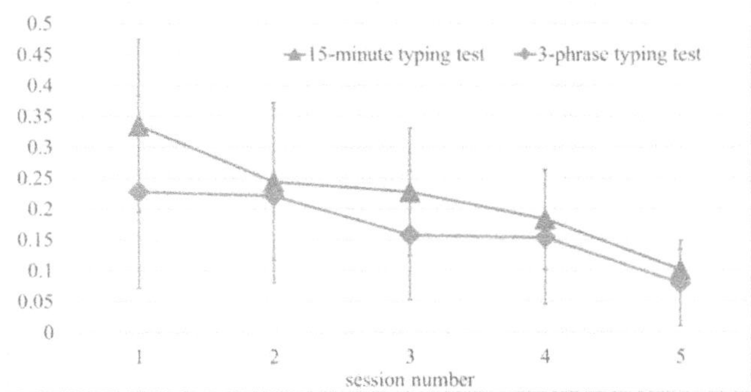

Figure 10. Corrected error rate for each session of the two typing tests.

4.2.2.3 Corrected Error Rates

Figure 10 shows the corrected error rates for the two typing tests over the five test sessions. For the 15-minute typing tests, the corrected error rate decreases from 0.33 (SD = 0.14) in the first session to 0.10 (SD = 0.03) in the last session. For the 3-phrase typing tests, the uncorrected error rate decreases from 0.23 (SD = 0.16) in the first session to 0.079 (SD = 0.07) in the last session.

There was a significant effect of the typing test on the corrected error rate ($F_{1,9}$= 13.85, p < .01, η_p^2= .61). There was a significant effect of the test session on the corrected error rate too ($F_{4,36}$= 16.09, p < .01, η_p^2= .64). Pairwise comparisons show that the differences between the last session and the first three sessions were significant (p <.05). There was a trend towards significance between the last session and the fourth session (p=.053) and between the fourth session and the first session (p=.070). There was no significant difference between any other sessions.

4.2.3 Gesture Per Character (GPC)

GPC denotes the number gestures taken on average to input a letter. GPC provides an indication of the accuracy and efficiency of an input method. A high GPC value indicates low accuracy and low efficiency. The closer the GPC value is to 1, the more accurate and efficient the method is.

Figure 11 shows the GPC for two typing tests over 5 test sessions. For the 15-minute typing tests, GPC decreases from 2.16 (SD = 0.506) in the first session to 1.24 (SD = 0.096) in the last session. The best GPC was 1.05 (SD = 0.055) in the last session. For the 3-phrase typing tests, the uncorrected error rate decreases from 1.81 (SD = 0.79) in the first session to 1.193 (SD = 0.145) in the last session. The best GPC was 1 in the last session.

There was a trend towards significance between the two typing

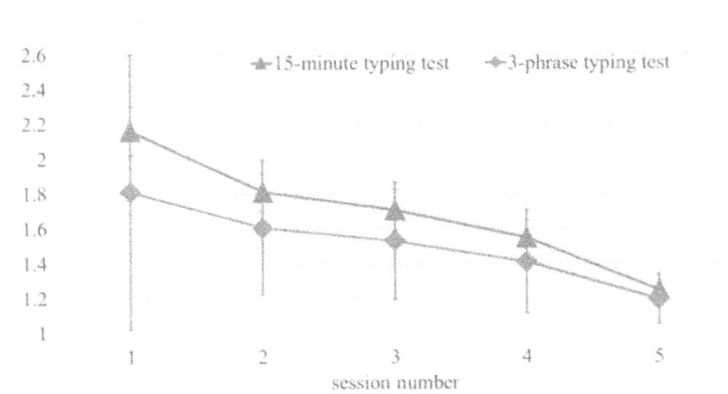

Figure 11. GPC for each session of the two typing tests.

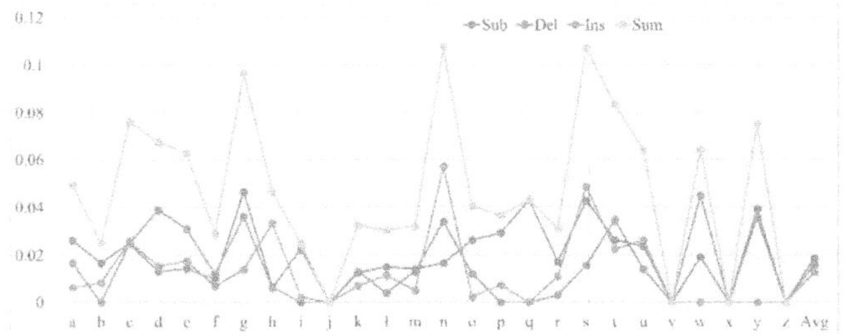

Figure 12. Three types of uncorrected error per letter in the last session of the 15-minute typing tests. "Sum" represents the total uncorrected error rate for each letter. "Avg" represents the average uncorrected error rates of all letters.

tests ($F_{1,9}$= 4.98, p = .053, η_p^2= .36). There was a significant effect of the test session on the GPC too ($F_{4,36}$= 15.61, p < .001, η_p^2= .64). Pairwise comparison results show that the differences between the last session and the first three sessions were significant (p <.05). There was a trend towards significance between the last session and the fourth session (p=.052). There was no significant difference between any other sessions.

4.2.4 Unpacking the Errors

We analyzed the data from the last session of the 15-minute typing test to gain a better understanding of the errors that participants made when using BrailleSketch. We used the data from the 15-minute typing tests, because participants typed more phrases in the 15-minute typing tests than the 3-phrase typing tests and also made significantly more errors. Additionally, statistical analysis shows a significant difference or a trend towards significant difference between the last session and any of the first four sessions.

4.2.4.1 Detailed Uncorrected Errors

Figure 12 shows the different uncorrected errors per letter in the last session of the 15-minute typing tests. From the figure, we can see that *Substitution* error was the most common type of error. It was followed by *Deletion* error and then *Insertion* error. N, S and G were the top-3 letters with the highest total uncorrected errors. G, S, and Y were the top-3 letters with the highest *Substitution* errors. On the other hand, I, V, and X were the top-3 letters with the lowest *Substitution* errors.

	a	b	c	d	e	f	g	h	i	j	k	l	m	n	o	p	q	r	s	t	u	v	w	x	y	z
a	193	0.6	0.11	0.67	0.56	0.54	0	0.06	0	0	0	0.01	0	0	1.9	0	0	0.06	0	0.41	0.22	0	0.01	0	0.11	0
b	1.2	134	0	0	0	0	0	0	0	0	0	0.6	0	0	0	0	0	0	0	0	0	0	0	0	0	0
c	0.27	0	164	0	0	0	0	0	0	0	0	0	0	0.4	0	0	0	0	0	0.23	0	0	0	0	0.07	0
d	0.4	0	0	103	0.25	0	0	0	0	0	0	0	0	0.14	0	0	0	0.33	0	0.5	0	0	0	0	1	0
e	0.68	0	0	0	155	0	0	0.03	0	0	0.5	0	0	0	0	0	0.4	0	0	0	0.08	0	0.1	0	0.33	0
f	0.4	0	0	0.48	0.4	78	0	0	0	0	0	0	0	0	0	0	0	0	0	0.08	0	0	0	0	0	0
g	0	0	0.5	0	0	0	132	0	0	0	0	0	0	6.5	0	0	0	0	0.24	0.31	0.1	0	0	0	0	0
h	0	0	0	0	0	0	0	121	0	0	0	0	0.17	0	0	0	0.2	0	0.33	0	0	0	0	0	0	0
i	0.3	0.2	0	0	0	0	0	0	36	0	0	0	0.12	0	0.53	0	0	0	0	0	0.06	0	0	0	0	0
j	0.5	0	0	0	0	0	0	0	0	14	0	0	0	0	0	0	0.4	0	0	0	0	0	0	0	0	0
k	0	0	0	0	0	0	0	0	0	0	32	0	0	0	0	0	0	0	0	0	0	0	0	0	0	0
l	0.03	0.3	0	0	0	0.1	0.5	0.5	0	0	0	112	0	0	0.29	0.01	0	0.33	0	0.54	0.01	0	0.5	0	0	0
m	0	0	0.1	1	0	0	0	0	0	0	0.6	0.1	38	0	0	0	0.4	0	0	0	0	0	0	0	0	0
n	0	0	0	0.25	0	0	0	0	0	0	0	0	0	234	0	0	0	0.33	0.5	0	0	0	0	0	0	0
o	0	0	0.61	0.19	0.55	0	0	0	0	0	0	0.1	0.17	0	64	0	0	0.14	0.75	0.29	1	0	0	0	0.1	0
p	0	0	0	0	0	0.2	0.5	0	0	0	0	0	0	0	0	182	0	0	0	0	0	0	0	0	0	0
q	0	0	0	0	0	0	0	0	0	0	0	0	0	0	0	2.5	52	0	0	0	0	0	0	0	0	0
r	0.67	0	0	0.13	0.04	0	0	0	0	0	0	0.33	0	0	1	0	0	64.4	0	0.21	0	0	0	0	0.67	0
s	0.2	0	0	0	0	0	0	0	0	0	0	0.1	0	0	0	4.5	0	0	93	0	0	0	0	0	0.25	0
t	0	0	0	0	0	0.5	0	0	0	0	0	0.33	0	0	0	0	0	0	2.5	126	0	0	0	0	0	0
u	0	0	0	0	1.25	0	0	0	0	0	0	0	0	0	0	0	0.4	0	0	0	47	0	0.5	0	0	0
v	0	0	0	0	0	0	0	0	0	0	0	0	0	0	0	0	0.3	0	0	0	0	10	0	0	0	0
w	0	0	0	0	0	0	0	0	0	0	0	0	0	0	0	0	0	0	0	0	0	0	74	0	0	0
x	0	0	0.06	0	0	0	0	0	0	0	0	0	0	0	0.25	0	0	0	0	0	0	0	0	17	0	0
y	0	0	0	0	0	0	3.4	0.3	0	0	0	0	0	0	0	0	0.4	0	0	0	0	0	0	0	63	0
z	0	0	0	0	0	0	0	0	0	0	0	0	0	0	0	0	0	0	0	0	0	0	0	0	0	12

Figure 13. The confusion matrix of the substitution errors of the last session of the 15-minute typing test.

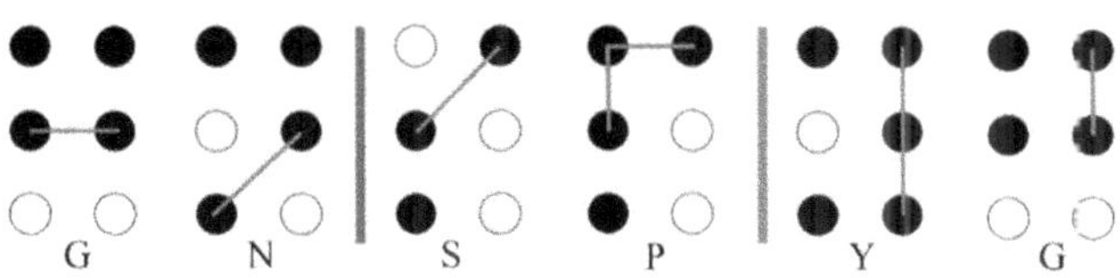

Figure 14. The three letters with the highest substitution errors and what they were mistyped as. Red lines represent the part of the sketched gesture path that contributed to the confusion between these pairs of letters.

We further analyzed the most common type of error, the *Substitution* error, by computing a confusion matrix [26]. Figure 13 shows the confusion matrix of the *Substitution* errors for all letters in the last session of the 15-minute typing tests. Each cell in row x and column y of the matrix contains the number of occurrences of a substitution error where the presented letter x was transcribed as y. The counts were weighted by all possible alignments and thus may not be integers [12]. We found that: 1) all letters, as expected, appeared unevenly in the testing phrases; 2) most letters fell in the diagonal line, which were correctly transcribed; 3) G, S, and Y had the highest *Substitution* errors and were mistyped as N, P and G respectively. Figure 14 shows the Braille codes of these letters. The difference between G and N and the difference between S and P were the direction of the initial (or final) part of the gesture path (see the first two groups in Figure 14). The difference between Y and G was the length of a vertical line in the gesture paths (see the last group in Figure 14).

4.2.4.2 *Detailed Corrected Errors*

Corrected errors happen when participants delete incorrectly typed letters and change them. We computed the corrected error rate of each letter by dividing the number of corrections for a letter by the total number of times that the letter appeared in the testing phrases. Figure 15 shows the corrected error rate of each letter in the last session of the 15-minute typing test. We found that the letters with the highest corrected error rate were: N, V, and Z. The letters with the lowest three corrected error rates were: J, Q, and X.

4.2.5 *Subjective Feedback*

Participants were generally positive about using BrailleSketch. For example, one participant commented that "*Typing with one finger is nice. I found that it is easy to use, even though I am used to typing with the Perkins Brailler. I am getting faster after getting used to drawing on the phone. It is also helpful for people to learn Braille.*" Participants also felt excited about the potential uses of BrailleSketch. For example, one participant suggested the need to integrate a method such as BrailleSketch with home appliances, such as the microwave, because more and more appliances are equipped with a touch screen that are difficult to use without sight. More generally, participants encouraged us to release BrailleSketch for the iOS system so that more people with visual impairments could download and use it.

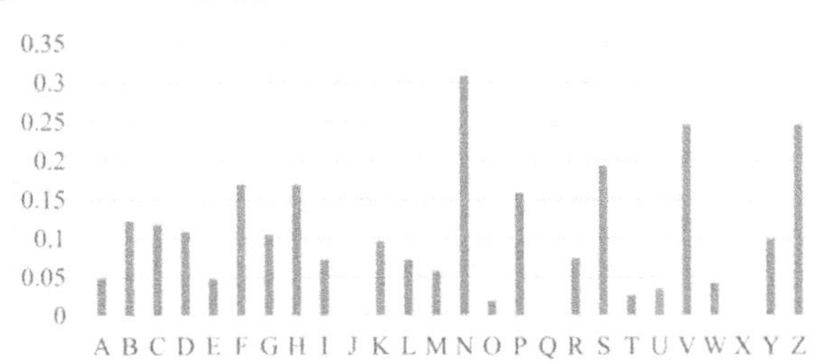

Figure 15. The corrected error rate per letter for the last session of the 3-phrase typing tests.

5. DISCUSSION

In this section, we first discuss our system's performance in comparison to other gesture based text entry methods. We then discuss the speed and error rate achieved with BrailleSketch and compare them with other text entry methods for people with visual impairments. Afterwards, we analyze the performance of the automatic error correction algorithm that we used in BrailleSketch. Finally, we discuss the effect of the delayed audio feedback that BrailleSketch used and the intuitiveness of the method.

5.1 Gesture based Text Input Methods

Like BrailleSketch, EdgeBraille [17] and MoonTouch [10] are two input methods that allow people with visual impairments to draw gestures that are interpreted into text. EdgeBraille, similar to BrailleSketch, leverages the user's familiarity with the Braille alphabet. However, EdgeBraille requires that users draw gestures that touch areas along the edges of the touchscreen to specify the dots in the intended Braille code; this requires long travel distances on the touchscreen. On the other hand, MoonTouch requires that users learn the Moon alphabet. However, MoonTouch allowed the users to draw gestures of any size anywhere on the screen. This enabled MoonTouch users to input text faster than EdgeBraille users (at 10.14 wpm [10] *vs.* 7.17 [17] respectively).

In this work, we examine how to develop a gesture-based method that leverages the users' familiarity with the Braille alphabet without requiring the user to target specific locations on the screen to support accurate input. We designed the evaluation procedure to include the 3-phrase typing test following the 15-minute typing tests in order to formally compare BrailleSketch with MoonTouch [10]. In particular, Hani *et al.*'s evaluation of the MoonTouch system included 5 evaluation sessions in which participants were asked to type three phrases as quickly and accurately as possible after "learning sessions" for "learning the system and interacting with it during a time interval of at least 15 min and at most 20 min" [9]. Participants typed at an average speed of 10.14 wpm in the fifth session with 1.22 GPC when using MoonTouch. In contrast, participants typed at an average speed of 14.53 wpm with 1.19 GPC when using BrailleSketch.

5.2 Other Braille-based Text Input Methods

Table 1 shows the average speed and error rate of other Braille-based text input methods from the literature and our BrailleSketch. We also added training time and study time whenever we could find them from the related papers. The speed achieved with BrailleSketch (14.53 wpm) outperformed the other methods listed except BrailleTouch's rate achieved by expert and moderate performance groups. The typing speed with BrailleTouch in the last three sessions were not significantly different from each other [25], which suggested that the reported speed probably has begun to plateau. However, the typing speed between any two sessions with BrailleSketch system was significantly different ($p < .05$). This shows that typing speed achieved with BrailleSketch has not begun to plateau by the last session yet and still has the potential to increase if participants keep using it. On the other hand, the error rate made by participants using BrailleSketch (0.11) had already dropped lower than that of BrailleTouch.

Table 1. Speed and error rate of Braille-based input method.

Braille-based text entry method	Speed (wpm)	Error rate	Training Time (min)	Study Time (min)
BrailleType [20]	1.49	0.07	10 ~ 15	N/A
SingleTapBraille [1]	4.71	0.11	20	40 ~ 60
Perkinput [4]	6.05	0.04	75	525
TypeInBraille [15]	6.3	0.03	10	N/A
EdgeBraille [17]	7.17	0.08	5	N/A
BrailleEasy [23]	9.82	0.10	40	40
BrailleTouch [25] (poor performance group)	9.4	0.39	N/A	450
BrailleTouch [25] (moderate performance group)	21	0.33	N/A	450
BrailleTouch [25] (expert performance group)	23.2	0.15	N/A	450
BrailleSketch (our system)	14.53	0.11	10	~100

5.3 Audio Feedback

Inspired by previous research that showed removing immediate per letter feedback could increase text entry speed [14], BrailleSketch does not speak out the typed letter immediately after users type it. Instead, it only speaks out the entire word after users finish typing it.

To examine the effect of the reduced audio feedback strategy, we also implemented BrailleSketch with the immediate letter-level audio feedback that reads aloud the letter immediately after it was typed. We tested it with one participant using the same study protocol. The participant was born blind and has used Braille extensively for over 30 years. The typing speed of his last session using the system with immediate letter-level audio feedback was 8.37 wpm, which was lower than the lowest speed of any participants in the last session when using BrailleSketch without immediate letter-level audio feedback (11.53 wpm). The total error rate of his last session in this test (0.113) was roughly equal to the average total error rate of BrailleSketch without immediate letter-level audio feedback (0.106). These results suggest that the reduced audio feedback in the current BrailleSketch implementation (*i.e.,* no immediate letter-level audio feedback) improved its text entry speed without increasing the error rate. However, we only tested the audio feedback with one participant. Further evaluation with more participants are needed to further validate the effect of different audio feedback strategies.

In our current design, BrailleSketch provides an immediate audio feedback ("*no*") to the users, if the sketched gesture cannot be recognized as any letter (erroneous input). Our evaluation shows that participants did not confuse the word "no" with erroneous input because words are only read aloud after being completed with *Space* or *Return*. However, a better audio feedback, such as non-word sounds, should be considered in the future.

While designing the audio feedback to indicate the direction the users are sketching their gesture paths, we tested different sound frequencies internally before choosing 1000 HZ and 200 HZ. However, we did not systematically evaluate how different audio feedback may affect text entry performance, which is an important future topic of discussion regarding input methods for people with visual impairments.

5.4 Automatic Error Correction

To evaluate the effect of the auto-correction algorithm that our system used, our system also recorded the transcribed texts before using the auto-correction algorithm. We compared the transcribed phrases before and after the auto-correction was applied with the presented phrases in the 3-phrase typing tests. We found among the total 770 presented words, 62 words were mistyped before using auto-correction. The auto-correction properly corrected 34 words, which was 55% of the mistyped words. Of the 28 words that auto-correction failed to correct, 15 were changed to incorrect words and 13 were left as-is. Future works will examine how to improve the auto-correction algorithm.

5.5 Intuitiveness of BrailleSketch

BrailleSketch can be used quickly by people who already know the Braille alphabet because it allows users to create their own mappings of the Braille pattern for letters into gestures without any training needed. The system can recognize different gestures for the same letter based on the sketched paths after completed (Figure 5). Whichever is the most natural mapping for the user, they can draw it. For many other Braille typing methods, users need to know how to type Braille in Perkin-like methods.

To correctly type letters, participants either know the gestures that they can use or are able to guess it. Thus, to some extent, our study tested the intuitiveness of BrailleSketch. We also analyzed the errors caused by touching too high/low on the screen through the five test sessions. The average total error rate of all participants in all test sessions due to touching too high/low on the screen was 0.85%. This low error rate suggests that participants were able to land or adjust their finger to avoid the edges of the phone during the typing test.

6. CONCLUSION

In this paper, we presented BrailleSketch, a Braille-based text entry method that allows users to input text by sketching a path that connects all the dots in the intended Braille. The average speed achieved using BrailleSketch by participants in our study was 14.53 wpm with 10.6% error and 1.19 GPC. We showed that the speed has not begun to plateau by the last session yet and still has the potential to increase. Our results show that gesture-based Braille text entry method with reduced audio feedback and auto-correction is potentially better than most tapping and typing methods for people with visual impairments who already know how to read Braille. Our approach does not require people with visual impairments to learn an additional alphabet and is faster than other alphabet based gesture methods.

7. ACKNOWLEDGES

This research was approved by the Social Science, Humanities, and Education Research Ethics Board (REB) at the University of Toronto under the protocol reference #32798. This work was supported by the Natural Sciences and Engineering Research Council of Canada (NSERC).

8. REFERENCES

[1] Alnfiai, M. and Sampalli, S. 2016. An Evaluation of SingleTapBraille Keyboard. *Proceedings of the 18th International ACM SIGACCESS Conference on Computers and Accessibility - ASSETS '16* (New York, New York, USA, 2016), 161–169.

[2] Alnfiai, M. and Sampalli, S. 2016. SingleTapBraille: Developing a Text Entry Method Based on Braille Patterns Using a Single Tap. *Procedia Computer Science*. 94, (2016), 248–255.

[3] Azenkot, S. and Lee, N.B. 2013. Exploring the use of speech input by blind people on mobile devices. *Proceedings of the 15th International ACM SIGACCESS Conference on*

Computers and Accessibility - ASSETS '13 (New York, New York, USA, 2013), 1–8.

[4] Azenkot, S., Wobbrock, J.O., Prasain, S. and Ladner, R.E. 2012. Input finger detection for nonvisual touch screen text entry in Perkinput. *Proceedings of Graphics Interface* (2012), 121–129.

[5] Bonner, M.N., Brudvik, J.T., Abowd, G.D. and Edwards, W.K. 2010. No-Look Notes: Accessible Eyes-Free Multi-touch Text Entry. *Proceedings of International Conference on Pervasive Computing* (2010), 409–426.

[6] Braille profiling project - RNIB: *https://www.rnib.org.uk/sites/default/files/braille_profiling.doc*. Accessed: 2017-05-05.

[7] Dandekar, K., Raju, B.I. and Srinivasan, M.A. 2003. 3-D finite-element models of human and monkey fingertips to investigate the mechanics of tactile sense. *Journal of biomechanical engineering*. 125, 5 (2003), 682–691.

[8] Frey, B., Southern, C. and Romero, M. 2011. BrailleTouch: Mobile Texting for the Visually Impaired. *Universal Access in Human-Computer Interaction. Context Diversity*. Springer Berlin Heidelberg. 19–25.

[9] Guerreiro, T., Lagoá, P. and Santana, P. 2008. NavTap and BrailleTap: Non-visual texting interfaces. *Proceedings of the Rehabilitation Engineering and Assistive Technology Society of North America Conference* (2008).

[10] Heni, S., Abdallah, W., Archambault, D. and Uzan, G. 2016. An Empirical Evaluation of MoonTouch: A Soft Keyboard for Visually Impaired People. *Proceedings of International Conference on Computers Helping People with Special Needs* (2016), 472–478.

[11] Lee, S., Hong, S.H., Jeon, J.W., Choi, H.-G. and Choi, H. 2004. Design of Chording Gloves as a Text Input Device. Springer, Berlin, Heidelberg. 201–210.

[12] MacKenzie, I.S. and Soukoreff, R.W. 2002. A character-level error analysis technique for evaluating text entry methods. *Proceedings of the second Nordic conference on Human-computer interaction - NordiCHI '02* (New York, New York, USA, 2002), 243.

[13] MacKenzie, I.S. and Soukoreff, R.W. 2003. Phrase sets for evaluating text entry techniques. *CHI '03 extended abstracts on Human factors in computing systems - CHI '03* (New York, New York, USA, 2003), 754.

[14] MacKenzie, S. and Castellucci, S. 2012. Reducing visual demand for gestural text input on touchscreen devices. *Proceedings of the 2012 ACM annual conference extended abstracts on Human Factors in Computing Systems Extended Abstracts - CHI EA '12* (New York, New York, USA, 2012), 2585.

[15] Mascetti, S., Bernareggi, C. and Belotti, M. 2011. TypeInBraille: a braille-based typing application for touchscreen devices. *The proceedings of the 13th international ACM SIGACCESS conference on Computers and accessibility - ASSETS '11* (New York, New York, USA, 2011), 295.

[16] Mascetti, S., Bernareggi, C. and Belotti, M. 2012. TypeInBraille: Quick Eyes-Free Typing on Smartphones.*Computers Helping People with Special Needs* (2012), Springer, Berlin, Heidelberg. 615–622.

[17] Mattheiss, E., Regal, G., Schrammel, J., Garschall, M. and Tscheligi, M. 2014. Dots and Letters: Accessible Braille-Based Text Input for Visually Impaired People on Mobile Touchscreen Devices. Proceedings of the *International Conference on Computers for Handicapped Persons (2014)*. Springer, Cham. 650–657.

[18] Myung-Chul Cho, Kwang-Hyun Park, Soon-Hyuk Hong, Jae Wook Jeon, Sung Il Lee, Hyuckyeol Choi and Hoo-Gon Choi A pair of Braille-based chord gloves. *Proceedings. Sixth International Symposium on Wearable Computers,* 154–155.

[19] Oliveira, J., Guerreiro, T., Nicolau, H., Jorge, J. and Gonçalves, D. 2011. Blind people and mobile touch-based text-entry. *The proceedings of the 13th international ACM SIGACCESS conference on Computers and accessibility - ASSETS '11* (New York, New York, USA, 2011), 179.

[20] Oliveira, J., Guerreiro, T., Nicolau, H., Jorge, J. and Gonçalves, D. 2011. BrailleType: unleashing braille over touch screen mobile phones. *In Proceedings of the INTERACT 2011* (2011), 100–107.

[21] Perkins Braillers: *http://www.perkinsproducts.org/about-perkins-braillers*. Accessed: 2017-04-15.

[22] Romero, M., Frey, B., Southern, C. and Abowd, G.D. 2011. BrailleTouch: Designing a Mobile Eyes-Free Soft Keyboard. *Proceedings of the 13th International Conference on Human Computer Interaction with Mobile Devices and Services - MobileHCI '11* (New York, New York, USA, 2011), 707.

[23] Šepić, B., Ghanem, A. and Vogel, S. 2014. BrailleEasy: One-handed Braille Keyboard for Smartphones. *Studies in health technology and.* (2014), 1030–1035.

[24] Silfverberg, M., MacKenzie, I.S. and Korhonen, P. 2000. Predicting text entry speed on mobile phones. *Proceedings of the SIGCHI conference on Human factors in computing systems - CHI '00* (New York, New York, USA, 2000), 9–16.

[25] Southern, C., Clawson, J., Frey, B., Abowd, G. and Romero, M. 2012. An evaluation of BrailleTouch: mobile touchscreen text entry for the visually impaired. *Proceedings of the 14th international conference on Human-computer interaction with mobile devices and services - MobileHCI '12* (New York, New York, USA, 2012), 317.

[26] Wobbrock, J.O. and Myers, B.A. 2006. Analyzing the input stream for character- level errors in unconstrained text entry evaluations. *ACM Transactions on Computer-Human Interaction*. 13, 4 (Dec. 2006), 458–489.

Investigating Microinteractions for People with Visual Impairments and the Potential Role of On-Body Interaction

Uran Oh[1,2], Lee Stearns[1], Alisha Pradhan[3], Jon E. Froehlich[1,4], Leah Findlater[3,5]

[1]Department of Computer Science
[3]College of Information Studies
University of Maryland, College Park

[2]Robotics Institute
School of Computer Science
Carnegie Mellon University

[4]Computer Science and Engineering
[5]Human Centered Design and Engineering
University of Washington

uranoh@cmu.edu, lstearns@umd.edu, alisha93@terpmail.umd.edu, jonf@cs.umd.edu, leahkf@umd.edu

ABSTRACT

For screenreader users who are blind or visually impaired (VI), today's mobile devices, while reasonably *accessible*, are not necessarily *efficient*. This inefficiency may be especially problematic for microinteractions, which are brief but high-frequency interactions that take only a few seconds for sighted users to complete (*e.g.,* checking the weather or for new messages). One potential solution to support efficient non-visual microinteractions is on-body input, which appropriates the user's own body as the interaction medium. In this paper, we address two related research questions: *How well are microinteractions currently supported for VI users? How should on-body interaction be designed to best support microinteractions for this user group?* We conducted two studies: (1) an online survey to compare current microinteraction use between VI and sighted users (*N*=117); and (2) an in-person study where 12 VI screenreader users qualitatively evaluated a real-time on-body interaction system that provided three contrasting input designs. Our findings suggest that efficient microinteractions are not currently well-supported for VI users, at least using manual input, which highlights the need for new interaction approaches. On-body input offers this potential and the qualitative evaluation revealed tradeoffs with different on-body interaction techniques in terms of perceived efficiency, learnability, social acceptability, and ability to use on the go.

CCS Concepts

• **Human-Centered Computing → Accessibility → Empirical Studies in Accessibility**

Keywords

Visual impairments; mobile; microinteraction; wearable technology; on-body interaction.

1. INTRODUCTION

Today's mobile devices are reasonably *accessible* for blind and visually impaired (VI) users but are not necessarily *efficient*. This inefficiency may be especially problematic for microinteractions—that is, brief but high-frequency interactions that typically take sighted users only a few seconds to complete [3]. Manually finding and playing a song, for example, can take 15 seconds for a blind user [20] while entering a four-digit passcode to unlock a smartphone requires on average eight seconds, leading many blind users to forgo this security feature altogether [6].

ASSETS '17, October 29-November 1, 2017, Baltimore, MD, USA
© 2017 Association for Computing Machinery.
ACM ISBN 978-1-4503-4926-0/17/10...$15.00
https://doi.org/10.1145/3132525.3132536

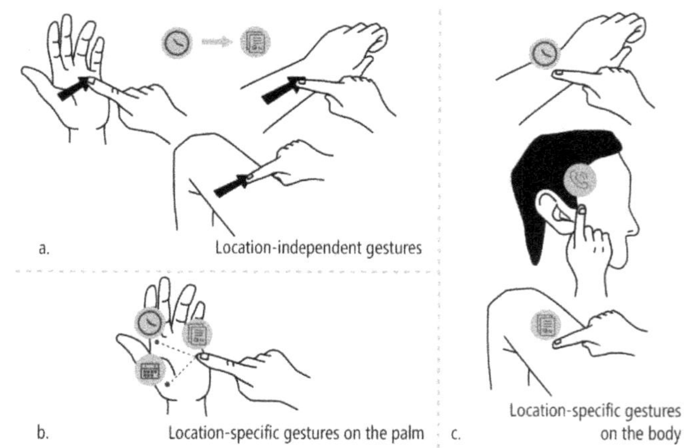

Figure 1. The three on-body interaction techniques explored for microinteractions in Study 2: (a) location-independent taps and swipes that can be performed anywhere on the body, (b) location-specific input that allows users to directly access a specific set of applications by tapping a dedicated location on the palm only or (c) on the body. See also video figure.

While many approaches could be taken to support efficient non-visual microinteractions, one particularly promising direction is *on-body input* [16,17], which appropriates the user's own body as the interaction medium. Prior work has shown that on-body input can be more efficient than touchscreen interaction for non-visual use, even without including the time to first retrieve the smartphone from a pocket or bag [14,26].

In this paper, we address two interrelated research questions: *(1) How well are microinteractions currently supported for blind and visually impaired users? (2) How should on-body interaction be designed to best support microinteractions for this user group?* Prior work in on-body interaction for users who are blind or visually impaired has identified a desire for socially acceptable input locations and the potential to support use on-the-go [25]. However, important issues related to efficient input remain, including understanding VI users' experiences with existing microinteractions (*e.g.,* on smartwatches, smartphones) and reactions to on-body interaction, as well as how to best leverage the body for microinteraction input (*e.g.,* taps and swipes anywhere on the body *vs.* at specific locations; Figure 1).

To investigate current support for accessible microinteractions and the design of on-body microinteractions for VI users, we conducted two studies. The first study was a formative online survey with 117 users (56 sighted and 61 VI) to characterize current microinteraction use and identify barriers therein. For the second study, we recruited 12 screenreader users who participated in an in-person semi-structured interview on the same themes and completed a qualitative evaluation of a real-time on-body interaction prototype that we developed. For the latter, participants compared three complementary on-body interaction techniques: location-independent gestures (*i.e.*, taps and swipes anywhere on the body), location-specific gestures on the hand (*i.e.*, pointing to different hand locations), and location-specific gestures on the body (*i.e.*, pointing to different hand and body locations).

Our findings suggest that efficient microinteractions are not currently well-supported for VI users, at least using manual input. While speech input is a common alternative, it is not always appropriate, thus highlighting the need for new approaches to support frequent and fast non-visual interactions. The qualitative evaluation of the three on-body interaction techniques to support microinteractions revealed tradeoffs in terms of perceived efficiency, learnability, social acceptability, and the ability to use on the go. For example, participants considered input at *specific* locations across the body to be the least efficient whereas location-independent gestures, which can be performed anywhere, were seen as supporting learning and offering flexibility for use on-the-go. In summary, the primary contributions of this paper are: (1) an identification of the needs, barriers, and strategies for enabling microinteractions for users with visual impairments in comparison to sighted users, and (2) design implications for supporting microinteractions for VI users via on-body input.

2. RELATED WORK

Our research is informed by prior work on microinteractions and mobile and wearable technologies for VI users.

2.1 Microinteractions

Microinteractions are defined by Ashbrook [3] as interactions that take less than four seconds to complete, such as changing the volume or dialing a number. These interaction durations are important because they can profoundly influence usage of an application or device [28,34]. Mobile contexts also increase the need for efficient interaction: Oulasvirta *et al.* [28] showed that mobile interaction typically occurs in short bursts of attention that are only four to eight seconds long.

Research on understanding and supporting microinteractions has largely focused on sighted users. Pizza *et al.* [29] found that the most frequent smartwatch interactions under 10 seconds were glancing at the watch face, accessing notifications, and setting and checking timers. As well, in an analysis of over 4,000 Android smartphone users, Bömer *et al.* [7], found that tasks related to communication (*e.g.*, text messaging, phone calls) were among the shortest and most frequently used tasks. Efforts to support more efficient microinteractions have largely focused on wearable devices because wearables enable quicker access times and less disruptive transitions between the device and the physical world compared to mobile phones [4,22,24]. In comparison to sighted users, however, VI users—our focus—typically have longer interaction times [5,6], which is particularly problematic in mobile contexts since device access is already limited [1,33,39]. While some wearable devices for VI users arguably support microinteractions (e.g., *EyeRing*'s barcode scanning and currency identification [24]), to our knowledge, no study has thoroughly examined VI users' microinteraction needs and how well these needs are currently supported.

2.2 Accessible Mobile/Wearable Interaction

Mobile technology plays an important role for VI users, particularly in supporting independence [21]. Yet, touchscreen smartphones are not innately accessible due to a heavy reliance on visual cues and the minimal tactile feedback of the smooth touchscreen [18,23]. One approach for non-visual use is to employ location-insensitive gestures that do not require accurate hand-eye coordination [8,13,20]. For example, *Apple VoiceOver*[1] and *Google TalkBack*[2], two popular mobile screenreaders, provide location-insensitive taps and swipes that can be performed anywhere on the screen. These solutions also support location-specific interaction by allowing users to touch down and move the finger around to hear audio output for each element that is touched. Despite these advances, however, touchscreen interactions can still be time-consuming for VI users [5,6,20,39]—likely impacting microinteraction efficiency.

Accessible wearable interaction has largely focused on supporting tasks in the physical world, such as way-finding [11], object or character recognition [32,35], and currency detection [24]. For instance, *OrCam* includes a wearable camera and provides speech output for reading or identification when the user points to a document, object, or face [27]. A smaller body of work has focused on providing mobile digital information access through wearable technologies for VI users, such as Ye *et al.*'s [39] study of a wristband that pairs with a phone to control audio screenreader output. That study also investigated the advantages and limitations of wearable devices over smartphones for VI users and found that potential advantages included quick interaction, discretion, and use on the go. We build on these prior studies by focusing on microinteractions specifically and the ability of on-body input to support these interactions for VI users.

On-body input [16,17] offers the same advantages as most other wearable input: portable and quick to access. Moreover, with tactile and proprioceptive feedback from the user's own body, on-body input is efficient for eyes-free use [14]—a finding that has been extended to VI users [26]. Studies on the *design* of on-body interaction have focused primarily on sighted users (*e.g.*, [15,38]). For example, Weigel *et al.* [38] investigated characteristics of different skin input modalities and preferred input locations, and found that the most preferred location was the palm. As an exception, Oh and Findlater [25] studied the design of on-body input by asking VI users to create on-body input gestures and to compare location-independent input gestures on the hand to on a touchscreen phone. Findings showed that input on the hands and arms was considered relatively socially acceptable and on-body input in general was seen as valuable compared to the phone during hands-busy use (*e.g.*, one hand holding a cane or dog leash). However, the authors did not investigate *location-specific* on-body input, which has been shown to offer potential performance benefits over touchscreen interaction [26].

3. STUDY 1: MICROINTERACTION SURVEY

We conducted an online survey with 61 VI and 56 sighted smartphone users to compare microinteraction usage patterns between these two groups. We targeted VI users who interact primarily through audio output (*e.g.*, screenreaders) rather than visual output (*e.g.*, screen magnifiers). Thus, our VI group only includes participants who reported using screenreaders most or all of the time when interacting with their mobile device.

[1] http://www.apple.com/accessibility/ios/voiceover/

[2] https://play.google.com/store/apps/details?id=com.google.android.marvin.talkback

Smartwatch: A smartwatch offers many of the same features as a smartphone, but has a smaller screen that is roughly the size of a large watch face. Smartwatches often include a camera, speaker, microphone, and sensors that can track information like the number of steps you've taken.

On-body interaction: Imagine a small wearable device such as a wristband or a ring that can sense when you do taps, swipes or other gestures on the surface of your body. This device can be paired with a small speaker for audio output or with a projected image on your arm or hand and would allow you to do many of the same actions as you can do on a smartphone or smartwatch. For example, you can perform taps and swipes on your bare palm in the same way you usually use the touchscreen on a phone or smartwatch. You can also tap or perform other gestures at specific locations on your body, such as the wrist, a fingertip, or ear to execute specific actions (e.g., check the time, answer a phone call, change a song's volume).

Figure 2. Descriptions of smartwatches and on-body interaction used in the online survey.

The survey focused on microinteractions with smartphones and smartwatches but also solicited open-ended feedback about on-body interaction. We hoped to learn:

1. What are the most common microinteractions currently used by sighted and VI users?
2. What tasks, if any, are not supported as microinteractions for VI users but would be valuable to support in the future?
3. How do users perceive the use of wearable devices (specifically, smartwatches) for microinteractions compared to smartphones?
4. How do people react to the idea of on-body interaction and what potential use cases do they foresee?

3.1 Method

We created an accessible online survey via *SurveyMonkey*, which was designed to take ~25 minutes for screenreader users. Smartphone owners were recruited to participate through email lists, a university bulletin board, community organizations, Facebook, and word of mouth. After completion, participants could opt into a drawing for a $100 Amazon gift certificate.

3.1.1 Survey Design

The survey, included in Appendix A, consisted of 32-36 questions depending on the participant's level of vision. For smartwatch owners, we asked an additional 24 questions. Questions included general background (*e.g.*, age, gender), current mobile and wearable technology use (*e.g.*, device type, frequency of use), and perceived tradeoffs between smartphones and smartwatches. The survey also asked respondents to estimate the time needed for them to complete specific microinteractions that are common for sighted users on mobile and wearable devices [2,37]—see Table 1. At the end of the survey, we also solicited feedback on the idea of on-body interaction. To aid understanding, we provided brief descriptions of smartwatches and on-body interaction (Figure 2).

3.1.2 Data and Analysis

During a one-month period, we received 134 fully completed and 13 partially completed survey responses (dropout rate of 8.8%). Fifty-six participants reported normal or corrected-to-normal vision (*sighted* participants) and 61 participants reported having a visual impairment and using a screenreader most or all of the time (*VI* participants); an additional 17 VI participants who were infrequent screenreader users were excluded from analysis. Of the VI group, one participant had 20/70 to 20/200 vision, 13 were legally blind (at best 20/200), 17 were blind with some light perception, and 30 were totally blind. Participants were asked to specify their age within a range (*e.g.*, 35–44, 45–54); the median age range was 45–54 for VI participants (38 female, 22 male, 1 other) and 25–34 for sighted participants (30 female, 26 male).

Table 1. The ten microinteractions examined in our online survey. This list is based on [7,29].

Task Label	Task Description
Alarm	Set an alarm or timer
App launch	Find and open a specific app
Calendar	Check your calendar for an overview of the day's schedule
Clock	Check the current time
Music	Pause a music player
Navigation	Set a destination to get navigation directions
Phone calls	Dial a phone number
Read message	Read a text message that is two sentences long
Respond to msg.	Respond to a text message with a two-word reply
Weather	Check the weather

Table 2. Mobile tasks reported as being frequent and fast to complete (≤ 10 seconds) by at least five VI or sighted participants, sorted by popularity among VI participants. Bolding and '*' indicate tasks that were significantly different between the two user groups.

Task	VI (*N*=61)	Sighted(*N*=56)
Email interactions, primarily checking for new email	80.3%	73.2%
Text message interactions, primarily checking for new messages	68.9%	76.8%
Checking the weather*	41.0%	21.4%
Voice call interactions (*e.g.*, answering or declining calls, dialing, checking missed calls)*	34.4%	10.7%
Checking the time	31.1%	28.6%
Checking notifications other than calls, emails, text messages, social media	26.2%	19.6%
Social media, primarily checking for updates	19.7%	30.4%
Information search (*e.g.*, trivia, bus schedule)	19.7%	17.9%
Music player control	18.0%	8.9%
Changing device settings (*e.g.*, volume, wifi)	9.8%	5.4%
Calendar interactions	8.2%	8.9%

We used chi-square tests of independence to analyze the impact of user groups (VI *vs.* sighted) on frequency data (*e.g.*, from multiple-choice questions on microinteraction usage). For the seven open-ended questions in the survey, we followed an iterative coding process [19]. Two researchers together developed initial codebooks for each question, then independently coded a randomly selected subset of 20-40 responses. Cohen's kappa was computed to assess interrater reliability for each code and problematic codes were refined; three to four iterations of this process were completed for each question. The average kappa score across all codes after the final iteration was 0.87 ($SD = 0.12$; range 0.53–1.0).

3.2 Findings

We describe participants' experiences with microinteractions, perceived tradeoffs between smartphones and smartwatches, and responses to the idea of on-body interaction. Asterisks in tables and figures indicate statistically significant differences ($p < .05$) between the VI and sighted participant groups.

3.2.1 Device Ownership and Frequency of Use

As required to complete the survey, all participants owned smartphones. Most VI participants had iOS devices (59 iOS, 8 Android, 1 other), while sighted participants were more evenly split (29 iOS, 30 Android, 5 other), confirming previously identified patterns of adoption [5,37,39]; some participants reported multiple devices. Participants used their devices frequently: 56 VI and 55 sighted participants reported using their smartphone at least once every few hours. Thirteen participants (4 VI, 9 sighted) owned a smartwatch and all reported using it at least every few hours.

3.2.2 Frequently Used Microinteractions

To compare what current smartphone tasks can be classified as microinteractions for VI users versus sighted users, we asked

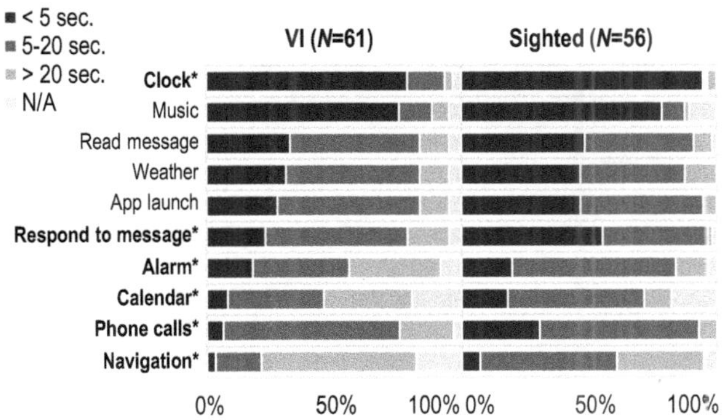

Figure 3. Percentage of survey participants reporting different task completion times across 10 common microinteraction tasks, sorted by the percentage of VI participants who reported '*< 5 seconds*'.

participants to list tasks that were *frequent* and *fast* (≤ 10 seconds to complete). This was an open-ended question and responses are shown in Table 2. While overall trends are similar across the two groups, VI participants were significantly more likely to list *'checking the weather'* (41% *vs.* 21%; $\chi^2_{(1)} = 5.16$, $p = .023$, $\phi = .21$) and *'voice call interactions'* (34% *vs.* 11%; $\chi^2_{(1)} = 9.25$, $p = .002$, $\phi = .28$) than sighted participants. The voice call interactions by VI users consisted primarily of checking for missed calls and voicemails. These differences may reflect the utility of auditory information for VI users, such as hearing a weather forecast versus looking out the window or talking versus composing a text message. As for accessibility-specific tasks such as OCR or identifying colors, only one participant reported such a task as taking 10 seconds or less to complete: *'identifying currency'*.

3.2.3 Task Completion Time for Microinteractions

To quantify how screenreader use impacts microinteraction task completion time, we asked participants to estimate their time to complete each of the 10 microinteractions listed in Table 1 using manual input (*i.e.*, without speech dictation); options were *'< 5 seconds'*, *'5-20 seconds'* and *'> 20 seconds'*. Figure 3 shows the reported durations for each task. Generally, a greater percentage of sighted participants reported being able to complete the tasks in *'< 5 seconds'* compared to VI users. The frequencies of reported completion times were significantly different between the two participant groups for more than half of the tasks (Table 3). While prior work has shown that screenreader users are slower at mobile tasks than sighted users [5,21], these results emphasize how widespread this trend is for tasks that are often deemed to be microinteractions. Focusing on the responses that were *'< 5 seconds'* (a microinteraction duration), the most substantial difference between the two groups was related to text entry (*'Respond to Message'*). Only 23% of VI participants reported *'< 5 seconds'* for this task compared to 55.4% of sighted participants, perhaps due to the inefficiency of manual text entry for users with visual impairments [5,8].

3.2.4 Use of Speech Input

Motivated by studies showing that speech input (*e.g.*, *Apple Siri*) is more popular for blind users than sighted users [5,39], we examined speech input use for microinteractions. Overall, and confirming prior work, a significantly greater number of VI participants (36.1%) reported using speech input at least *'most of the time'* compared to sighted participants (8.9%); chi-square test ($\chi^2_{(1)} = 12.11$, $p = .001$, $\phi = .32$). We also asked participants to indicate whether they *'usually'* use speech input for each microinteraction

Table 3. Chi-square test results comparing reported microinteraction task durations between the sighted and VI groups (does not include responses of "N/A"). Only the six tasks (of 10) that were significantly different are listed.

Task	N_{VI}	$N_{Sighted}$	$\chi^2_{(2)}$	p	ϕ
Clock*	59	56	6.57	.038	.24
Respond to Message*	58	55	15.84	<.001	.38
Phone Calls*	59	56	13.38	.001	.34
Alarm*	56	54	10.59	.005	.31
Calendar*	49	46	10.84	.004	.34
Navigation*	50	53	15.18	.001	.39

Table 4. Percentage of participants who '*usually*' use speech input for each of ten given microinteractions, with chi-square test results comparing the two participant groups. Bolding and '*' indicate tasks that were significantly different between the two user groups.

Task	VI (N=61)	Sighted (N=55)	$\chi^2_{(3)}$	p	ϕ
Phone calls*	73.8%	25.0%	27.78	<.001	.49
Alarm*	72.1%	33.9%	17.15	<.001	.38
Respond to message*	67.2%	17.9%	28.93	<.001	.50
Navigation*	63.9%	30.4%	6.73	.01	.24
Weather*	52.5%	21.4%	11.98	.001	.32
App launch*	50.8%	16.1%	15.67	<.001	.37
Read message*	34.4%	7.1%	12.94	<.001	.33
Clock*	34.4%	7.1%	12.94	<.001	.33
Calendar*	32.8%	7.1%	11.78	.001	.32
Music	16.4%	7.1%	2.37	.124	.14

listed in Table 1 (responses: yes/no). VI participants were significantly more likely to use speech input than sighted participants for all tasks except *'Music'* (Table 4). The biggest effect size was for *'Respond to Message'* where VI users were almost 4x as likely to use speech, again perhaps reflecting the difficulty of manual text entry for this user group [5,8].

3.2.5 Comparison of Smartphones and Smartwatches

While wearable devices like smartwatches have been shown to be particularly useful for supporting microinteractions for sighted users [3], we wanted to understand whether perceptions differ for VI users. Specifically, we asked four open-ended questions comparing smartwatches and smartphones: two about perceived advantages/disadvantages of smartwatches (Table 5) and two about tasks conducive to each technology. Because only a small number of participants owned a smartwatch (9 sighted, 4 VI), our analysis does not just focus on their responses but instead includes all 117 participants.

Table 5 shows smartwatch advantages and disadvantages mentioned by at least five participants in either user group, along with chi-square test results comparing the groups. VI participants were significantly more likely to mention advantages due to the watch's small size (*e.g.*, lightweight, portable) (30.9% *vs.* 12.7%), while sighted participants were significantly more likely to mention disadvantages due to size (*e.g.*, small input/output area) (72.7% *vs.* 53.7%). VI participants were also significantly more concerned about *'sound-related issues'* such as low volume or not being able to pair with/plug in headphones (16.7% *vs.* 0.0%). Overall, these differences may reflect a reliance on visual output by sighted users compared to audio output by VI users.

When participants were asked about tasks they would prefer to do on a smartwatch compared to a smartphone, the top responses were fitness tracking (39.3% of VI *vs.* 33.9% of sighted participants), clock (32.8% *vs.* 37.5%), and text messaging (32.8% *vs.* 33.9%). Interestingly, 29.3% of VI participants said they would prefer the

Table 5. Perceived advantages and disadvantages of smartwatches compared to smartphones mentioned by at least five VI or sighted participants, sorted by popularity among VI participants. Items with significantly different response rates between the two groups are bolded and marked with '*'.

Advantages	VI (*N*=55)	Sighted (*N*=55)	$\chi^2_{(1)}$	*p*	ϕ
Quick/easy access	50.9%	52.7%	0.04	.849	-.02
Small – lightweight*	**30.9%**	**12.7%**	**5.33**	**.021**	**.22**
Portable	21.8%	14.5%	0.98	.323	.09
Not having to hold a device	9.1%	9.1%	0.00	1.00	.00
Less distracting*	**0.0%**	**9.1%**	**5.24**	**.022**	**-.22**

Disadvantages	VI (*N*=54)	Sighted (*N*=55)	$\chi^2_{(1)}$	*p*	ϕ
Small – input/output space*	**53.7%**	**72.7%**	**4.25**	**.039**	**-.20**
Limited functionality	22.2%	16.4%	0.60	.438	.07
Sound-related issues*	**16.7%**	**0.0%**	**9.99**	**.002**	**.30**
Not a stand-alone device	14.8%	10.9%	0.37	.542	.06

phone for all tasks compared to only 13.2% of sighted participants; this difference was significant ($\chi^2_{(1)} = 4.24, p = .040, \phi = .20$).

3.2.6 Attitude Toward On-body Interaction.

Finally, we asked two open-ended questions about on-body interaction: overall reactions to the concept and for what specific tasks, if any, such interaction may be useful. Five VI participants did not answer this question and are excluded from this analysis. Participants were roughly evenly split in mentioning potential benefits or concerns of on-body interaction. 48.2% of VI and 60.7% sighted participants mentioned at least one benefit, such as quick/easy access or larger interaction surface than a smartphone. However, 46.4% of VI and 46.4% of sighted participants also mentioned at least one concern, such as social acceptability, technical challenges (*e.g.*, sensing accuracy), and learning curve. The most frequent concern for VI users was social acceptability, although this was mentioned by only 12.5% of VI participants; 3.6% of sighted participants reported the same. Fifty-five VI users and 51 sighted users provided suggestions for tasks where on-body interaction would be especially useful. The most common were making phone calls (29.1% of VI and 39.2% of sighted responses) and checking the time (27.3% of VI and 31.4% of sighted responses). Other suggestions included changing device settings, reading/checking new messages, and controlling a media player.

3.3 Summary

Our findings emphasize differences between VI and sighted users' experiences with microinteractions. VI users took longer to complete microinteractions for most tasks and were more likely to use speech input. In terms of attitudes towards smartwatches, VI users were more likely to appreciate the small size of the device but to also be concerned about audio quality compared to sighted users. Both groups of participants responded largely similarly to the idea of on-body interaction, expressing potential benefits (*e.g.*, larger interaction space) and some concerns (*e.g.*, social acceptability).

4. Study 2: Interview & Prototype Evaluation

We conducted an in-person study with 12 VI participants to re-examine the survey themes in more depth and to subjectively compare different on-body interaction techniques for microinteractions. Previous work has shown that on-body input is more efficient for VI users than smartphone input when using *location-specific* gestures—such as pointing to different areas of the hand [26]. But, how does such input compare subjectively to more flexible *location-independent* input, such as taps or swipes

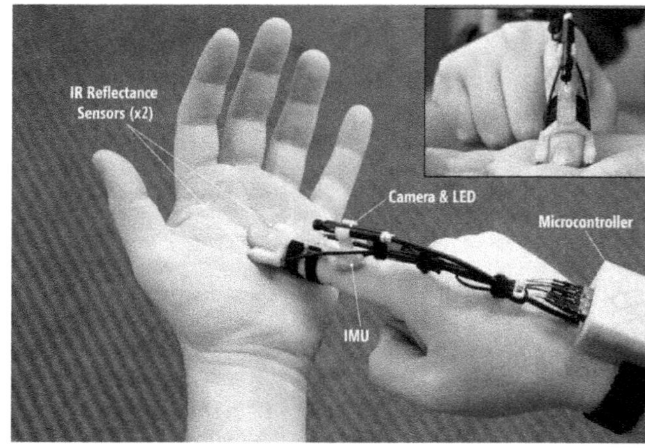

Figure 4. Our wearable, on-body interaction prototype system consists of a finger-worn package including a camera and LED, two IR reflectance sensors, and an IMU. Computer vision and machine learning algorithms are used to support location-specific, on-body gestural interaction.

anywhere on the body? Moreover, for location-specific input, do users value semantic mappings between locations and microinteractions (*e.g.*, tapping the wrist to hear the time) or more discreet but less meaningful locations? To address these questions, we built and asked participants to use a real-time system that supported three on-body interaction techniques: location-independent input, location-specific input at different body locations, and location-specific input on only the hand.

4.1 Participants

We recruited 12 smartphone users with visual impairments (7 female) through email lists, local organizations, and word of mouth; three of them (P1, P6 and P9) also participated in Study 1. Nine were blind and three had low vision. They were on average 46.2 years old (*SD* = 12.0, range 29–65). All participants had owned a smartphone for more than a year and used a screenreader "*all of the time*", except for P11 who used a screenreader "*most of the time.*" P5 used an Android phone, while the remaining participants used iPhones. Only two participants owned a wearable device: P10 had a fitness tracker and P5 had previously owned a smartwatch but rarely used it. As with the survey, the use of speech input was prevalent: ten participants used speech at least some of the time; seven of these reported regular use. Participants were compensated $60 for their time and travel costs.

4.2 Real-time Wearable System

We built a real-time wearable system, shown in Figure 4, to explore microinteractions using three different on-body interaction techniques: location-independent gestures, location-specific gestures on the palm only, and location-specific gestures at a wider variety of body locations.

4.2.1 System and Algorithms

The system includes several finger-worn sensors, as shown in Figure 4: a pair of infrared (IR) reflectance sensors[3] near the tip of the finger to sense *touch-down* and *touch-up* events, a camera[4] that localizes the user's touch using computer vision, an LED to provide consistent lighting for the camera, and an inertial measurement unit (IMU)[5] for sensing movements and recognizing gestures. Placing the sensors on the gesturing finger rather than elsewhere on the

[3] Fairchild Semiconductor QRE113GR
[4] Awaiba NanEye GS Idule Demo Kit
[5] Adafruit Flora LSM9DS0

Table 6. Our system supports 16 microinteractions organized in a two-level hierarchical menu. An * identifies items that we asked participants to select in our user study.

Category	Application	Description
Clock	Time	Check the current time
	Alarm*	Check the next alarm
	Timer*	Check the time remaining
	Stopwatch	Check the time elapsed
Daily Summary	Date	Check today's date
	Calendar*	Check the next event
	Weather*	Check the current temperature and weather conditions
Notifications	Summary	Summarize notifications (*e.g.*, "one missed phone call and two new messages")
	Missed phone call*	Check missed phone calls (*e.g.*, "missed phone call from Alice")
	New message #1	Check first new message (*e.g.*, "message from Bob")
	New message #2*	Check second new message (*e.g.*, "message from Charlie")
Health and Activities	Distance	Check the miles traveled
	Steps*	Check the number of steps taken
	Calories	Check the calories burnt
	Heart rate*	Check the heart rate
Speech Input*	(No sub-menu)	Activate voice input

body mitigates the camera framing issues that VI users often face [2] and enabled flexible input at a variety of locations.

Our system use the camera images that occur between touch-down and touch-up events to localize patches of skin, an approach adapted from [36]. While the algorithms are not the focus of the current paper, in short, the approach is as follows. The visual texture, represented as a histogram of rotation-invariant local binary patterns at multiple scales, is classified using support vector machines (SVMs). To achieve real-time use (~35 fps), we remove the geometric verification stage reported in [36] and compensate for the resulting loss in accuracy by combining location estimates across 20 video frames (~570ms window). Once the location has been classified, an SVM trained on accelerometer, gyroscope, and IR features classifies the gesture itself (*e.g.*, tap, directional swipe). The image-based localization step requires training per participant, as described in the procedure section below.

The hardware components were mounted on the user's index finger via a 3D-printed ring and Velcro strips, and were positioned to avoid interfering with the user's fingertip sensitivity or range of motion. The IMU and IR sensors were connected to a wristband containing an Arduino microcontroller[6], which in turn connected along with the camera to a desktop computer[7]. Speech feedback was provided through a pair of speakers using the *Microsoft .NET* speech synthesis libraries. This prototype was intended to explore possible on-body interaction designs, and we envision a future system to be much smaller and self-contained.

4.2.2 *Interaction Techniques*

The system allowed users to access 16 applications that align with the microinteraction findings in Study 1. As shown in Table 6, the applications were arranged in a two-level menu hierarchy with five top-level categories; only the *Speech Input* category had no sub-menu. We implemented the following three interaction techniques, shown in Figure 1 and in the accompanying video figure, for accessing the top-level categories.

Location-independent gestures (LI). Touching anywhere on the body and swiping left and right allows the user to linearly navigate through the top-level menu categories, while a double-tap activates

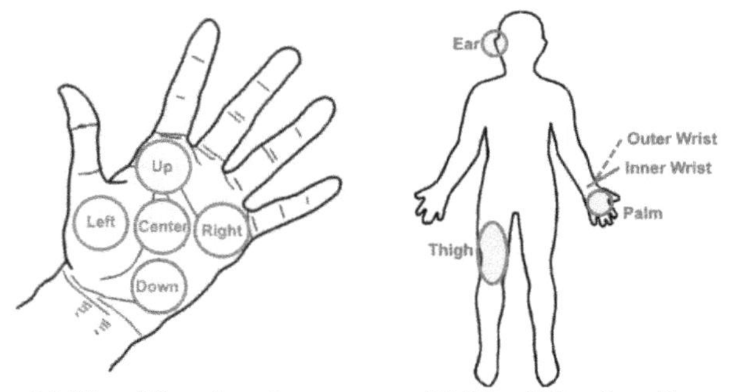

(a) Five LS_{palm} locations (b) Five LS_{body} locations

Figure 5. Locations used for LS_{palm} and LS_{body} interaction techniques: (a) LS_{palm} mapped five microinteraction categories arbitrarily to five locations on palm; (b) LS_{body} mapped the categories when possible to semantically meaningful body locations (e.g., wrist for *Clock*).

the currently selected category. This interface is simple and flexible, but similar location-independent interaction on the touchscreen has been shown to be time-consuming for VI users navigating a long list of items [20].

Location-specific gestures on the palm (LS_{palm}). The top-level categories are arbitrarily mapped to the five palm locations shown in Figure 5a: up (*Notifications*), left (*Clock*), right (*Daily Summary*), down (*Health and Activities*), and center (*Voice Input*). Users can select a category by directly tapping on its location or they can "touch and explore"—touching down anywhere on the palm, sliding the finger around to hear each touched item read aloud, then lifting up when the desired item is found. VoiceOver and TalkBack support a similar touch-and-explore functionality.

Location-specific gestures on the body (LS_{body}). The top-level categories are mapped to five locations on the body, with semantic mappings where possible (Figure 5b). Semantic body mappings, have shown promise for body-centric mobile interactions [10,12]. The five locations included: tapping the outer wrist for *Clock*, the ear for *Speech Input*, and the thigh for *Health and Activities* (*e.g.*, step count). Other mappings were the palm for *Notifications* and the inner wrist for *Daily Summary*.

Once the top-level category is selected and activated using one of these three interaction techniques, users swipe left/right to navigate the submenu items and double-tap to select the current item. This submenu interaction is similar to basic interface navigation with VoiceOver and TalkBack, with which our participants were familiar (all were screenreader users). Of the three interaction techniques, the location-specific options should theoretically be fastest because they allow for direct access to menu categories, while the location-independent option provides more flexibility.

4.3 Procedure

The study session began with a background questionnaire, followed by semi-structured interview questions (~20 minutes) that focused on the same themes as the survey. After the interview, we calibrated and trained the localization component of the wearable on-body interaction prototype (~30 minutes), which included collecting several images of each location shown in Figure 5. The three interaction techniques were then presented in counterbalanced order. For each interaction technique, participants were given a short introduction (~5 minutes) before independently completing a set of 10 microinteractions. Each microinteraction consisted of navigating to, selecting, and briefly using an application (*e.g.*,

[6] Sparkfun Arduino Pro Micro (5V/16MHz)

[7] Dell Precision T7910 (Intel Xeon, 8-core, 2.1Ghz, NVIDIA GeForce GTX 750Ti)

Alarm item within the *Clock* category). The set included two applications from each of the five menu categories (Table 6) except for the *Speech Input* category, which was simply selected twice since it had no submenu items. For each microinteraction, the tester stated which application to select along with its category. The session concluded with open-ended questions about the user experience and comparison of the three interaction techniques in terms of preference, ease of use, efficiency, and use in public.

4.4 Data Analysis

We audio-recorded and transcribed participants' open-ended responses for analysis. For questions that were also in the online survey, we reused the same analytical codebook (*e.g.*, "*What tasks or actions do you do frequently on your phone?*"). Other questions were analyzed by one researcher based on themes of interest [9] (*e.g.*, one-handed use of phone, interaction on-the-go), while allowing for new, emergent themes.

4.5 Findings

We briefly cover findings that confirm and extend the survey responses on general microinteraction use before presenting subjective responses to the on-body interaction techniques.

4.5.1 Current Microinteraction Experience

In general, trends were similar to the survey responses from VI participants, thus we highlight only new findings and examples.

Overall microinteraction use. The most frequently used and fast (≤ 10 seconds) smartphone tasks with manual input were: voice call interactions (*N*=9 participants out of 12), text message interactions (*N*=8), looking up information (*N*=6), and checking the weather (*N*=4). Seven participants specified that some tasks take less than 10 seconds only when using speech input (*e.g.*, voice search, dictation) emphasizing again the importance of speech input for supporting efficient interaction for VI users. In terms of accessibility-related tasks, three participants mentioned frequent use of *TapTapSee*[8], a money/object identification app, although it was not considered fast (≤ 10 seconds).

Microinteractions on-the-go. Previous work on the design of on-body interaction for VI users emphasized the importance of one-handed interaction to support use on-the-go, since users may be holding a cane or service dog leash [25]. Participant responses confirm that finding. When asked about using their phone with one hand, eight participants commented that one-handed use is important when walking. At the same time, nine participants also preferred not to use their phone at all when using a cane due to safety concerns, confirming that the perceived cost of interacting with a mobile device on-the-go is high for VI users [1,33,39]. For example, P8 said, *"See, when I'm walking, I have to use my cane, so I don't even be [sic] on the phone. To me, that's almost like driving and being on the phone. [...] That'll put a blind person in danger."* Although limited to answering/rejecting a call or using speech input, six participants reported that they use a headphone or a headset to remotely control their phone while walking.

Advantages and limitations of smartwatches. We also asked about perceived advantages and limitations of smartwatches compared to smartphones. In general, responses reflected trends seen in the survey, such as advantages of quick/easy access (*N*=6), hands-free (*N*=5), and portability (*N*=4), and limitations related to the small size (*N*=9), functionality (*N*=3), need for a paired phone (*N*=3), and sound-related issues (*N*=2). Of the nine participants who

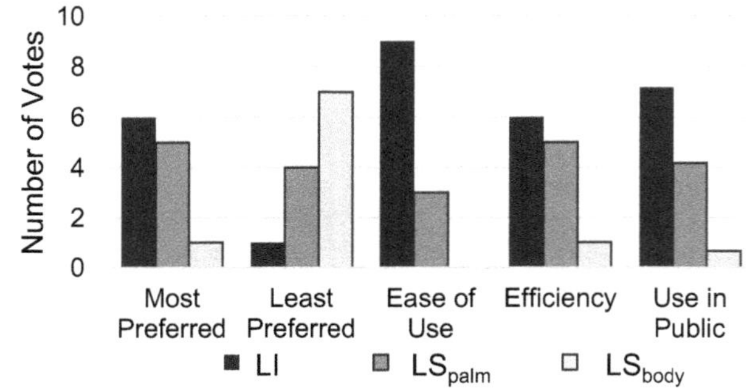

Figure 6. Vote counts for the interaction techniques that are the most and least preferred overall, most efficient, easiest to use, and most comfortable to use in public. Participants were allowed to vote for multiple options for *Use in Public*, but in such cases the votes were adjusted to sum to 1.0 per participant. (*N* = 12)

reported limitations related to size, eight specified that the small screen would make input difficult, for example:

> *"...because [the phone] has [a] wider space so I can find the layout of the keyboard, and I'll have a wider area of navigation between the letters and the keys. But in the case of [a] smartwatch, it's much, much smaller, so it will be compact and difficult to locate each letter."* (P1)

4.5.2 On-body Prototype Evaluation

We summarize overall reactions to on-body interaction then compare subjective responses to our three interaction techniques.

General reactions. We asked participants for their thoughts about on-body interaction *before* using our prototype and again *after* using it in comparison to smartphones and smartwatches (open-ended). Most participants (*N*=9) reacted positively beforehand, citing similar reasons as in the survey: quick and easy access (*N*=7), being able to map different body locations to different interactive tasks (*N*=6), and not having to hold the phone in hand (*N*=4). After use, when compared with a smartwatch or a smartphone, reactions focused on technical/physical aspects of the interaction, such as the number of devices to be carried (*N*=6) or sensor/speaker locations (*N*=6). After using the prototype, three participants still felt that they would prefer to use their phone due to familiarity. For instance, P9 said: *"I would rather use the phone. [...] I have no problem with using the body. It's just that I'm not used to it."*

Preferred interaction techniques. Figure 6 shows the subjective votes along several dimensions: overall most and least preferred, easiest to use, most efficient, and most appropriate for public use. Due to the sample size (*N*=12), we do not report on statistical tests on this data, but instead analyze the subjective rationale provided to support the votes. For overall preference, location-independent gestures (*LI*), where taps and swipes could be performed at any location, and gestures performed at specific locations on the palm only (LS_{palm}) were preferred to gestures performed at specific locations across the body (LS_{body}). The reasons for these preferences are broken down in the sections below.

Ease of use and learnability. As shown in Figure 5, most participants (*N*=9) felt that *LI* was the easiest to use of the three interaction techniques, for reasons such as: the microinteractions were easy to perform (*N*=7), the interaction was similar to that on a phone (*N*=6), and the input location was flexible (*N*=5). At the same time, about half of the participants considered the need to learn and remember specific locations to be a drawback of both LS_{palm} (*N*=7)

[8] http://www.taptapsee.com

and LS_{body} (N=6), although the semantic mappings of LS_{body} (*e.g.*, tap wrist for *Clock*) were seen by some (N=5) as beneficial for learning. Another valued interaction was the touch-and-explore feature of LS_{palm}, which four participants noted as supporting learning, even for novices. For example:

> *"So someone who's new to it, I think they can pick it up fairly simple. [...I like] the browsing part and being able to also open the apps. I can go back the center of my palm and still browse through that." (P5)*

Efficiency. We expected that *LI* would be perceived as less efficient than the two *LS* interfaces, since *LI* required a longer sequence of inputs (several swipes) compared to selecting a category by simply tapping its dedicated location. However, as seen in Figure 5, participants were roughly split between *LI* and LS_{palm} as the most efficient interaction technique, while only one participant selected LS_{body}. Seven participants commented that LS_{body}'s efficiency was impacted by the large motion required to point to different locations, which was especially of concern before learning the mappings. For instance:

> *"[With LS_{palm}] it's easy to search through. Because if it's not here, it's somewhere in this area. But [with LS_{body}] if you have it on your wrist and then your palm and on your ear, you gotta remember which one you need to touch." (P12)*

Social acceptability. Social acceptability is an important concern for wearable interaction [31] and for on-body interaction for VI users specifically, as seen both in prior work [25] and in Study 1. Nine participants felt they would be most comfortable using either *LI* or LS_{palm} in public compared to LS_{body} because the latter was less discreet. The remaining three participants felt that all three interaction techniques would be equally appropriate or inappropriate for public use. For example, P1 stated *"[LS_{body}] looks weird and a bit obnoxious. I mean, not pleasing for the onlooker. [...] So I don't feel comfortable using it publicly."* The specific body locations included in the interface, however, would likely impact this perception (as found in [25]). For example:

> *"The [outer] wrist, I think is okay. I guess the inside of the wrist is okay, too. [...] But ear, nose, thigh, all those things would be more uncomfortable." (P6)*

Interaction on-the-go and input availability. We found that participants appreciated having multiple options for input locations, especially for mobile contexts where one hand is busy. For this reason, six participants liked that *LI* did not restrict the input location, whereas microinteractions in the *LS* conditions could only be accessed from their dedicated input location, which may not always be available. For instance, P10 preferred locations other than the palm for flexibility, commenting, *"If you have something in your hand, it's like for me, if I'm holding my cane, or I'm standing somewhere, I want to check the time, I can just tap on my wrist. So it's easier, because my hand is not always going to be free."*

Customization. At the end of the study, we asked participants if they would want to customize the prototype to support different apps. A variety of preferences emerged, in terms of both interaction location and tasks to support. While seven participants wanted to use the palm for input, others suggested different body locations. P12, for example, wished to use specific locations for different tasks, suggesting some possibilities that had not been evaluated in the study, such as fingertips for making phone calls, ear lobe for answering phone calls, wrist for checking the time, thigh for notifications, and even lips for activating voice input. Furthermore, participants differed in the applications they wanted to support. For instance, P2 wanted to perform only phone call-related tasks, while P8 wanted a wider variety of tasks, such as opening apps like a calendar, a clock, and games, as well as checking notifications and heart rate. This diversity suggests that customization may be beneficial.

4.5.3 Summary

Our interview findings reinforced the survey responses regarding current support for microinteractions, specifically strategic use of voice input. The perceived trade-offs between three interaction techniques from the real-time system evaluation revealed VI users' needs and preferences for on-body interaction in terms of ease of use (*e.g.*, touch-and-explore to support learnability), efficiency (*e.g.*, downside of LS_{body}'s large movements), and use in public (*e.g.*, differences across body locations). The ability to support use on-the-go by supporting flexibility of input was also important.

5. Discussion

We reflect on the implications of our findings, focusing on how to better support microinteractions for people with visual impairments.

5.1 Accessible Microinteractions

Our findings suggest that efficient manual input for microinteractions is not well-supported for users with visual impairments. Only two microinteractions, checking the time and controlling a music player, were reported as taking < 5 seconds for most of our VI survey respondents. As seen in both the survey and interviews, voice input is a valuable tool for addressing the inefficiencies of screenreaders for microinteractions. This finding reflects previous more general studies showing that voice input is more popular for VI users than for sighted users [5,39]. However, because voice input may not always be appropriate due to background noise or privacy concerns [1,5,39], it is also important to develop more efficient manual input approaches to better support non-visual microinteractions.

Tasks that use mobile technology to increase the accessibility of the physical world, such as OCR, currency detection, and object recognition, arose rarely in the survey and interviews. This was, perhaps, because our focus was on tasks that are frequent *and* fast. Responses from three interview participants support this possibility: all three mentioned using their phone frequently for accessibility-specific tasks but not efficiently enough to qualify as a microinteraction; only one of the 61 survey respondents mentioned such a task (currency detection) as taking < 10 seconds. There is thus an opportunity for new wearable devices or even redesigned smartphone apps or operating systems to much more efficiently support accessibility-specific physical world tasks.

As already mentioned, wearable devices are particularly well-suited to support microinteractions [4,22,24]—whether smartwatches, on-body interaction, or other devices. However, differences in how VI and sighted users perceive smartwatches suggest that the ideal wearable form factor for each user group may differ, particularly in terms of the bulk and size needed to support visual versus auditory output modalities. VI users were more likely than sighted users to perceive the small size of a smartwatch to be an advantage, whereas sighted users, who rely on the visual output of the display, were more likely to see this size as a disadvantage. Still, some VI users were concerned about the touchscreen size from a gestural input perspective.

5.2 On-body Input for Microinteractions

While a variety of approaches—such as new wearable devices and redesigned touchscreen interactions—should be considered for future work on non-visual microinteractions, our findings provide specific guidance for implementing an on-body solution. Overall, there were tradeoffs between the three on-body interaction techniques in efficiency, learnability, use on-the-go, and social acceptability. For efficiency, we had expected that the location-specific interaction techniques would fare well because they allowed for direct access to menu items or applications rather than requiring a series of swipes to find a specific item. However, participants felt that the two techniques that supported interaction within a small space were the most efficient: location-specific palm gestures and location-independent gestures, the latter of which participants often did on their hand. This finding suggests that quick access to all information within a constrained, discreet space may overshadow the efficiency advantages of direct selection at more distributed locations on the body, as well as the utility of semantic mappings (*e.g.*, wrist for time, ear for volume).

Learnability of the interface was also a concern. Half the participants mentioned that a strength of the location-independent gestures was not having to memorize the mappings between locations and menu items. Although we had expected that the touch-to-explore feature of location-specific gestures would allow users to discover items and support novice use, this was not seen in our study. However, a larger set of menu items and a longer-term study (rather than a single session) would likely affect perceptions of learnability. As users transition to experts, they may better appreciate the speed with which they can directly access items at specific hand and/or body locations. Thus, enabling both location-independent and location-specific gestures may best support both novice and expert users, similar to how iOS and Android support both gesture-based navigation as well as exploration by touch.

The three interaction techniques vary in their ability to support use on-the-go since not all input locations will always be available (*e.g.*, hand or thigh). Thus, in mobile contexts, input locations that move less when the whole body is in motion (*e.g.*, chest *vs.* leg) or that can be used even when one hand is busy (*e.g.*, holding a cane or bag) may be preferred. Alternatively, location-independent gestures, which are not restricted to a specific location, would allow for the flexibility to adapt the interaction to any given body posture or movement. As with issues of learnability, a combination of location-independent and location-specific input may also be useful to explore for use on-the-go. Regardless, complementing manual input with voice input is critical for efficient, on-the-go interaction.

Finally, social acceptability is a common concern with wearable assistive technology for VI users [30,39]. This concern arose with on-body interaction in Study 1 but was less pronounced in Study 2 where participants had experience using a real-time prototype. The gestures at locations across the body (*e.g.*, ear, thigh, wrist) were seen as less appropriate for use in public than the other two interaction techniques, which supported much smaller input areas. Socially acceptability concerns may be mitigated by supporting location-independent gestures as users can choose any input location that they consider discreet or by mapping all applications to a concentrated area that can support subtle gestures. Allowing users to customize body locations may also be useful, as appropriate locations may differ from one person to another (*e.g.*, due to gender or personal preference).

5.3 Limitations

A limitation of the online survey and first portion of the in-person study is that the data on microinteraction timing and frequency of use is based on subjective estimates. As such, it important for future work to complement these findings with log data of actual use. Another survey limitation is that the VI user group was older than the sighted user group, which may have impacted results. For the in-person study, while our system offered real-time interaction, it was still an early prototype and had drawbacks that could have impacted user perceptions. Most notably, the wearable components were bulkier than we envision a future system would be and the system required a lengthy training process (~30 minutes) to collect training images of the user's hands and body. As well, the system included only five application categories, which were accessed via location-specific taps or location-independent swipes and taps. A larger number of top-level items in the interface may change how users view the efficiency tradeoffs between the different interaction techniques. Finally, a longer-term evaluation of the on-body interaction techniques may yield different tradeoffs by addressing novelty effects and allowing users to develop expertise.

6. CONCLUSION

Our goal is to support not only *accessible* mobile interaction for users with visual impairments but *efficient* interaction. We investigated how well microinteractions are supported on smartphones and smartwatches for people with visual impairments compared to sighted users. Our findings suggest that manual input does not sufficiently support efficient non-visual microinteractions, highlighting the need for new interaction approaches. Speech input was a commonly used workaround for VI users in our online survey, but is not always appropriate due to privacy and noise concerns. As an alternative manual input approach, we evaluated three different on-body interaction techniques, which revealed tradeoffs in terms of perceived efficiency, learnability, social acceptability and ability to use on the go. Future work should examine to what extent it is possible to combine the strengths of these different on-body interaction techniques into a single system to ultimately allow for efficient and socially acceptable input.

7. ACKNOWLEDGEMENTS

We thank our participants, David Ross and the Atlanta VAMC, Liang He, and the National Library Service for the Blind and Physically Handicapped. This work was supported by the Office of the Assistant Secretary of Defense for Health Affairs under Award W81XWH-14-1-0617.

8. REFERENCES

1. Abdolrahmani, A., Kuber, R., and Hurst, A. 2016. An Empirical Investigation of the Situationally-Induced Impairments Experienced by Blind Mobile Device Users. *ACM W4A '16*: 21.
2. Adams, D., Morales, L., and Kurniawan, S. 2013. A qualitative study to support a blind photography mobile application. *ACM PETRA '13*, 1–8.
3. Ashbrook, D. L. 2010. Enabling Mobile Microinteractions. *PhD Thesis*.
4. Ashbrook, D. L., Clawson, J. R., Lyons, K., Starner, T. E., and Patel, N. 2008. Quickdraw: The Impact of Mobility and On-Body Placement on Device Access Time. *ACM CHI '08*, 219–222.
5. Azenkot, S. and Lee, N. B. 2013. Exploring the use of speech input by blind people on mobile devices. *ACM ASSETS '13*: 11.
6. Azenkot, S. Rector, K., Ladner, R., and Wobbrock, J. O. 2012. PassChords: Secure Multi-Touch Authentication for Blind People. *ACM ASSETS '12,* 159–166.
7. Böhmer, M., Hecht, B., Schöning, J., Krüger, A., and Bauer, G. 2011. Falling Asleep with Angry Birds, Facebook and Kindle: A Large Scale Study on Mobile Application Usage. *ACM MobileHCI '11*, 47–56.
8. Bonner, M. N., Brudvik, J. T., Abowd, G. D., and Edwards, W. K. 2010. No-look Notes: Accessible Eyes-free Multi-touch

Text Entry. *Springer-Verlag Pervasive '10*, 409–426.

9. Braun V. and Clarke, V. 2006. Using Thematic Analysis in Psychology. *Qualitative research in psychology* 3, 2: 77–101.
10. Chen, X. A., Marquardt, N., Tang, A., Boring, S., and Greenberg, S. 2012. Extending a mobile device's interaction space through body-centric interaction. *ACM MobieHCI '12*, 151–160.
11. Dakopoulos. D. and Bourbakis, N. G. 2010. Wearable obstacle avoidance electronic travel aids for blind: a survey. *Systems, Man, and Cybernetics, Part C: Applications and Reviews, IEEE Transactions on* 40, 1: 25–35.
12. Guerreiro, T., Gamboa, R., and Jorge, J. 2007. Mnemonical body shortcuts for interacting with mobile devices. *International Gesture Workshop*, 261–271.
13. Guerreiro, T., Lagoá, P., Nicolau, H., Gonçalves, D., and Jorge. J. 2008. From Tapping to Touching: Making Touch Screens Accessible to Blind Users. *IEEE MultiMedia '08.*
14. Gustafson, S., Rabe, B., and Baudisch, P. 2013. Understanding Palm-based Imaginary Interfaces: The Role of Visual and Tactile Cues when Browsing. *ACM CHI '13*, 889–898.
15. Gustafson S., Holz, C., and Baudisch, P. 2011. Imaginary Phone: Learning Imaginary Interfaces by Transferring Spatial Memory from a Familiar Device. *ACM UIST '11*, 283–292.
16. Harrison, C., Ramamurthy, S., and Hudson, S. E. 2012. On-body Interaction: Armed and Dangerous. *ACM TEI '12*, 69–76.
17. Harrison, C., Tan, D., and Morris, D. 2010. Skinput: Appropriating the Body As an Input Surface. *ACM CHI '10*, 453–462.
18. Hoggan, E., Brewster S. A., and Johnston, J. 2008. Investigating the Effectiveness of Tactile Feedback for Mobile Touchscreens. *ACM CHI '08*, 1573–1582.
19. Hruschka, D. J., Schwartz, D., St.John D. C., Picone-Decaro, E., Jenkins, R. A., and Carey, J. W. 2004. Reliability in Coding Open-Ended Data: Lessons Learned from HIV Behavioral Research. *Field Methods* '04: 16(3), 307–331.
20. Kane, S. K., Bigham, J. P., and Wobbrock, J. O. 2008. Slide Rule: Making Mobile Touch Screens Accessible to Blind People Using Multi-touch Interaction Techniques. *ACM ASSETS '08*, 73–80.
21. Kane, S. K., Jayant, C., Wobbrock, J. O., and Ladner, R. E. 2009. Freedom to Roam: A Study of Mobile Device Adoption and Accessibility for People with Visual and Motor Disabilities. *ACM ASSETS '09*, 115–122.
22. Loclair, C., Gustafson, S., and Baudisch, P. 2010. PinchWatch: A Wearable Device for One-Handed Microinteractions. *ACM MobieHCI '10:*10
23. McGookin, D., Brewster, S., and Jiang, W. 2008. Investigating Touchscreen Accessibility for People with Visual Impairments. *ACM NordiCHI '08*, 298–307.
24. Nanayakkara, S., Shilkrot, R., Yeo, K. P., and Maes, P. 2013. EyeRing: A Finger-worn Input Device for Seamless Interactions with Our Surroundings. *ACM AH '13*, 13–20
25. Oh, U. and Findlater, L. 2014. Design of and Subjective Responses to on-Body Input for People With Visual Impairments. *ACM ASSETS '14*: 8.
26. Oh, U. and Findlater, L. 2015. A Performance Comparison of On-hand versus On-phone Non-Visual Input by Blind and Sighted Users. *ACM TACCESS '15:* 7(4), 14.
27. OrCam Technologies Ltd. http://www.orcam.com. .
28. Oulasvirta, A., Tamminen, S., Roto, V., and Kuorelahti, J. 2005. Interaction in 4-Second Bursts: The Fragmented Nature of Attentional Resources in Mobile HCI. *ACM CHI '05*, 919–928.
29. Pizza, S., Brown, B., McMillan, D., and Lampinen, A. 2016. Smartwatch in Vivo. *ACM CHI '16*, 5456–5469.
30. Profita, H., Albaghli, R., Findlater, L., Jaeger, P., and Kane, S. K. 2016. The AT Effect: How Disability Affects the Perceived Social Acceptability of Head-Mounted Display Use. *ACM CHI '16*, 4884–4895.
31. Profita, H. P., Clawson, J., Gilliland, S., Zeagler, C., Startner, T., Budd, J., and Do, E.Y. 2013. Don't Mind Me Touching My Wrist: A Case Study of Interacting with On-body Technology in Public. *ACM ISWC '13*, 89–96.
32. Shilkrot, R., Huber, J., Ee, W. M., Maes, P., and Nanayakkara, S. C. 2015. FingerReader: A Wearable Device to Explore Printed Text on the Go. *ACM CHI '15 Extended Abstracts*, 2363–2372.
33. Shinohara, K. and Wobbrock, J. O. 2011. In the Shadow of Misperception: Assistive Technology Use and Social Interactions. *ACM CHI '11*, 705–714.
34. Starner, T. E., Snoeck, C. M., Wong, B. A., and McGuire, R. M. 2004. Use of Mobile Appointment Scheduling Devices. *ACM CHI '04 Extended Abstracts*, 1501–1504.
35. Stearns, L., Du, R., Oh, U., Jou, C., Findlater, L., Ross, D. A., and Froehilich, J. E. 2016. Evaluating Haptic and Auditory Directional Guidance to Assist Blind Persons in Reading Printed Text Using Finger-Mounted Cameras. *ACM TACCESS '16:*9(1), 1–38.
36. Stearns, L., Oh, U., Cheng, B. J., Findlater, L., Ross, D., Chellappa, R., and Froehlich, J.E. 2016. Localization of Skin Features on the Hand and Wrist from Small Image Patches. *IEEE ICPR '16*, 1003–1010.
37. WebAIM. *Screen Reader User Survey #4. http://webaim.org/projects/screenreadersurvey4/#demographics.*
38. Weigel, M., Mehta, V., and Steimle, J. 2014. More Than Touch: Understanding How People Use Skin As an Input Surface for Mobile Computing. *ACM CHI '14*, 179–188.
39. Ye H., Malu, M., Oh, U., and Findlater, L. 2014. Current and Future Mobile and Wearable Device Use by People with Visual Impairments. *ACM CHI '14*, 3123–3132.

In-context Q&A to Support Blind People Using Smartphones

André Rodrigues[1], Kyle Montague[2], Hugo Nicolau[3], João Guerreiro[4], Tiago Guerreiro[1]
[1]LASIGE, Faculdade de Ciências, Universidade de Lisboa
[2]Open Lab, Newcastle University
[3]INESC-ID, Instituto Superior Técnico da Universidade de Lisboa
[4]Carnegie Mellon University
afrodrigues@fc.ul.pt, kyle.montague@newcastle.ac.uk, hman@inesc-id.pt, jpvguerreiro@cmu.edu, tjvg@di.fc.ul.pt

ABSTRACT
Blind people face many barriers using smartphones. Still, previous research has been mostly restricted to non-visual gestural interaction, paying little attention to the deeper daily challenges of blind users. To bridge this gap, we conducted a series of workshops with 42 blind participants, uncovering application challenges across all levels of expertise, most of which could only be surpassed through a support network. We propose Hint Me!, a human-powered service that allows blind users to get in-app assistance by posing questions or browsing previously answered questions on a shared knowledge-base. We evaluated the perceived usefulness and acceptance of this approach with six blind people. Participants valued the ability to learn independently and anticipated a series of usages: labeling, layout and feature descriptions, bug workarounds, and learning to accomplish tasks. Creating or browsing questions depends on aspects like privacy, knowledge of respondents and response time, revealing the benefits of a hybrid approach.

CCS Concepts
• **Human Centered Computing→ Empirical studies in accessibility; Accessibility systems and tools;**

Keywords
Blind; Smartphone; Human Computation; Assistance.

1. INTRODUCTION
Learning to use a smartphone device or application can be challenging for blind people, particularly when adopting these for the first time. Prior work has predominantly focused on improving physical touchscreen accessibility, particularly in the text-entry domain [7], either by measuring performance [6], understanding gestures [5] or providing alternative interaction methods [9].

ASSETS '17, October 29-November 1, 2017, Baltimore, MD, USA

ACM 978-1-4503-4926-0/17/10…$15.00
https://doi.org/10.1145/3132525.3132555

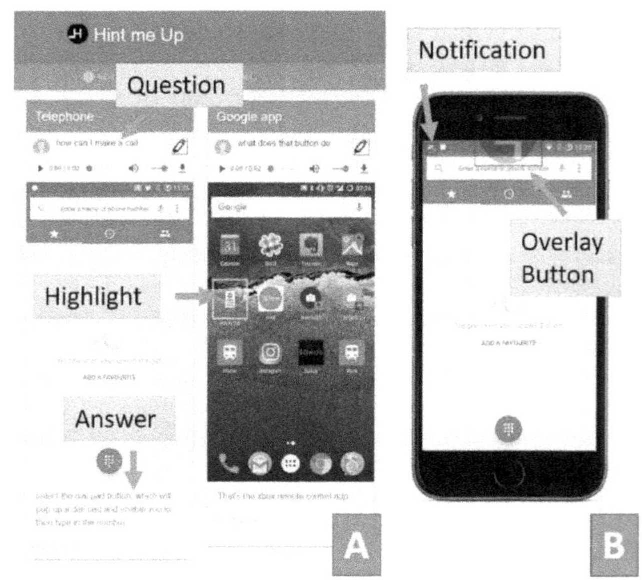

Figure 1 - A) Volunteer web app. It shows two answered questions, one with a specific element of the interface highlighted. B) Hint Me! with the always available button on the top of the screen, and a notification showing the user he received an answer

Rodrigues et al. [8] found that the barriers that blind people must overcome are not only related with the physical performance of touch gestures, but also in understanding the new paradigm that accompanies these devices and apps. For many, these challenges included being able to perform basic operations with the device, such as placing a call or sending a text message. Due to the lack of support for smartphones and apps, users found themselves resorting to friends and family to overcome these hurdles. However, the study results were drawn from assessing the adoption process of five blind people, putting forward the need for broader evaluations.

To better understand the extent of the challenges and current coping mechanisms, we conducted a series of workshops with 42 blind participants, from newcomers to expert smartphone users with different devices and operating systems. We found challenges that originate from the lack of guidance when using new features or layouts that are only surpassed with the support of others.

Prior research in crowdsourcing has allowed users to identify and locate objects in the real-world through visual questions using a smartphone (e.g. [1]). Following a similar approach, the Social Accessibility project [10] provided a collaborative metadata authoring mechanism to enhance webpage accessibility. Chilana et al. [4] have enabled Q&A in-context into web applications. Based on our workshop findings and inspired by these prior work, we developed *Hint Me!*, a human-powered service that allows blind users to get in-app smartphone assistance. Using *Hint Me!* as a design probe, we conducted a user study with six blind participants to elicit their perceptions on the usefulness and acceptance of human-powered networks for smartphone support.

In this paper, we extend the domain knowledge of the challenges blind users experience when interacting with smartphones. We propose *Hint Me!* as a solution to leverage the collective knowledge of others, and we share design considerations for future human-powered assistance technologies aimed at backing smartphone usage by blind people.

2. ISSUES AND COPING STRATEGIES

We recruited 42 blind people through social media, word of mouth, and through the centre for the blind where the workshops took place. Participants were required to be screenreader users. Over a two day period, we conducted five workshop sessions for newcomers and novice users (i.e. three on Android and two on iOS), and two for experts (i.e. one Android and one in iOS). Each session lasted two to three hours and each participant attended only one. Although the workshops were conducted informally, newcomers and novices were guided throughout basic phone tasks, while experts sessions were centered around their questions and doubts. Participants were free to ask questions and collaborate during the sessions.

Participant smartphone expertise ranged from newcomers (17), and novice (18) to expert (7). Newcomers were people who had never used a smartphone; novice users already owned a smartphone but were only able to do simple tasks, such as placing/receiving calls or send/read text messages; and, experts were able to use more advanced features, such as web services (e.g. Dropbox, Facebook). Our goal was to gain a broader understanding of smartphone barriers faced by blind users and their current learning and coping mechanisms. We extend prior work by including participants with different ability levels and devices. We gathered qualitative insights about initial reactions to smartphones; how participants currently use these devices; common and critical challenges; and how they cope with them. We conducted inductive thematic analysis [3] on researchers' notes of the workshops, which resulted in the following three main themes.

2.1 Challenges Beyond Touch Interaction

Participants thoroughly discussed issues they experienced with smartphones. For newcomers, their problems were related with touchscreen interactions and simple gestures. However, the cause of their struggles quickly became the lack of understanding on how the underlying interfaces were behaving. Although advanced gestures (e.g. 'L' gesture or rotor) were challenging for users of all expertise levels, it did not prevent them from accomplishing their goals. Moreover, some of their difficulties came from the lack of knowledge on how to perform the gesture rather than its execution.

All participants reported issues with smartphones, independently of expertise level and device. However, expert users focused more on application-specific issues, such as 1) unawareness of available options (*"In one app I had no way of sharing to Facebook. When I pressed More Actions nothing happened. What I found out afterwards, when I asked a friend, was that the option was there but it was not yet on the screen. I had to scroll on a new window that appeared."*), 2) using advanced features (*"I am not able to listen to music from my Dropbox in offline mode"*), or 3) accessibility problems (e.g. unlabeled buttons). Interestingly, all issues were solved with simple instructions.

2.2 Independent and Community Learners

Participants strongly rely on others to surpass challenges, often asking for help from people they consider to be technology experts. We found that users informally created communities that relied on the same specialist; two of them were present in our workshops. They were tech savvy, autodidact, and highly motivated to learn about technology. They regularly read blogs, forums, and mailing lists about assistive technologies, and even contact developers to report bugs and request features. Several participants in the workshop relied on them to cope with daily problems. They provided assistance through a variety of channels (e.g. calls, SMS, Skype) and often about the same issue but to different people.

During the workshops, experienced users would often help by guiding others step-by-step, while doing the actions on their own devices and waiting for others to finish each step. For gestural interaction, some participants went further and performed the gesture on the back of the other users' hand. Nevertheless, it was clear that people preferred an active learning approach rather than giving their device to others.

2.3 Issues in Surpassing Challenges

For some issues, the only possible solution was asking for help from a sighted friend (e.g. screenreader started speaking in a foreign language). However, participants discussed some situations where help from sighted friends and family was challenging due to their unfamiliarity with screenreaders. All but one participant mentioned how they preferred to be helped by screenreader users *"Often the problem is not them [sighted users] not knowing how to solve the problem, the problem is not knowing how to explain to us how we can solve it"*). Although sighted people are seen as valuable sources of assistance, most of them are oblivious to the challenges of screenreader users. They usually know the steps needed to accomplish a given task, but are unaware on how to perform them using accessibility services.

Availability and over-reliance on others was recurrently mentioned. For specialists, it can become a burden in their daily lives, even though they enjoy helping others, as the wife of one of the specialists described: *"He helps everyone except me! He spends his evenings helping everyone, on the phone or on the computer, but has no time to talk with me."*.

3. HINT ME! IN-APP ASSITANCE

The workshops extended prior work [8], revealing a frequent need for other people's assistance, despite expertise level. It is worth highlighting that people benefit from explanations given to the person next to them; this knowledge was 'contagious', spreading from one person to another, creating a collaborative learning experience. The exposure to similar doubts alongside the celerity at which people were able to learn together revealed both an opportunity and a need to enlarge the support networks beyond their current reach.

Currently, users are limited to relying on others for help, or searching online for answers, which is cumbersome, takes the user out of the context the problem arouse in, relies on the user being able to portrait his issue, and often will not produce any result.

To augment current support networks, we propose *Hint Me!*, a human-powered in-app assistance tool for smartphone usage. It is an integrated Android service that enables users to connect with a support network of people willing to provide assistance. With *Hint Me!*, every question is linked with the context it was created in. Using an overlay button users may quickly browse existing questions and answers associated with the app, current screen, or with a particular element they select. Moreover, since it is an independent service it is available system-wide in any mobile application. *Hint Me!* supports, among others, workflow guidance (e.g., *how to perform an action?*), layout description, labeling, and learning workarounds for inaccessible content.

3.1 Creating a Question

Users are able to ask questions, within any application, through an ever-present quick launch overlay button (e.g. Figure 1 B). Questions are recorded and their text is extracted relying on Google Voice Recognition technology. Additional information is collected to enable us to present the question to volunteers in diverse environments (e.g. web-app, Facebook, in-app context) augmented by, in-app contextual information aimed at providing volunteers with an enriched view over the applications and obstacles faced by the user (e.g. Figure 1 A).

In order to provide context, *Hint Me!* automatically captures a screenshot of the device alongside all element's details (e.g. alternate text, text, position, dimensions), creating the DOM tree structure of the interface and enabling its re-creation; in case the question relates to a specific element of the interface, users can select it in order to be highlighted.

3.2 Getting an Answer

Hint Me! gradually builds a shared knowledge-base with the answers to previously asked questions. Volunteers are able to edit the question for clarity or to correct errors from the speech conversion. Questions only become available when they have been validated and answered. When an answer is submitted, the question author receives a notification.

Users can browse through all Q&A associated with their current context, or through their asked questions. Within their current context, Q&A will be filtered according to their current app or screen. Additionally, users can select a particular interface element to navigate content specifically associated to it. Users can select an answer to pin it to the *Hint Me!* overlay button. Long pressing the button accesses the answer, enabling users to follow long and hard answers without the need to memorize them.

4. PERCEPTIONS OF HINT ME!

We conducted a design probe study in an institution for visually impaired people where we recruited 6 participants, 3 females. Their ages were comprehended between 31 and 62 years old (M=45.7; SD=12.6). All had previous experience with smartphones: P2 a month, P1 and P3 a year, P4 two years, P5 and P6 over three years, all were legally blind and screenreader users. We used a Vodafone Smart Platinum 7 smartphone running Android 6.0 with Talkback. We relied on *Hint Me!* to allow users to explore the possibilities behind a human-powered assistant for smartphone usage in order to elicit comments and opinions for the interview thereafter.

The study was divided in two sessions, each lasting one hour: 1) posing questions; 2) browsing existing content. The content generated in the first session populated *Hint Me!* with Q&A derived from the users' needs. One researcher acted as the volunteer through a web-app (Figure 1 A), the optimal scenario of a volunteer being an expert user. The researcher had previous knowledge of the tasks and was able to listen to the user interacting with the device. Although our focus was to understand the perceptions of the end-users receiving assistance, we also report on the volunteer experience.

Each session started with a description of *Hint Me!*, then participants performed four tasks, two in each of the selected apps (i.e. Facebook, WhatsApp, Du Speed Booster, and Spotify). Applications were counterbalanced between sessions and were selected from the top Play Store applications, discarding apps from the same category. Tasks were created based on the Play Store descriptions such as: check <John's> friend profile; send <John> your location; release memory; and play music.

Participants could resort to *Hint Me!* when they felt they could benefit from it. Each task started with the researcher reading aloud the task description; participants could, at any point during the task, prompt the researcher to repeat. Participants could only ask questions through *Hint Me!*. When a question was submitted, the researcher used the volunteer web-app to provide an answer. After the second session, we conducted a semi-structured interview to investigate the perceived usefulness and acceptance of *Hint Me!* and its underlying approach.

In the first session, a total of 21 questions were created (e.g. "*How is the page organized?*", "*How can I reach the artist since I cannot find him in the list?*", "*Which button is the optimize?*"), and each participant did at least two. In the 24 tasks of the second session, *Hint Me!* was opened 18 times and 16 answers were consulted, with all participants relying on them at least once.

Two researchers inductively created a codebook from a set of three interviews. They coded independently and reached a Cohen's Kappa agreement of k=0.67. Below, we detail our findings, anchored to the four main identified themes followed by the experience report from the researcher that acted as a volunteer.

4.1 From Aid to Self-Organized Learning

All participants reported positively showing interest in installing the app in their devices. P1 and P4 felt that having direct answers to their very specific questions was the most useful feature, allowing them to surpass many of the barriers previously encountered. P2 stated: "*For example, nowadays I don't use the Internet on my phone. But, if I had access to Hint Me I would have started using the Internet already. I am sure*". In this case, *Hint Me!* was seen as a safety net to explore new applications, knowing that he could always ask someone for assistance, if needed.

Hint Me! was seen as a learning tool that would give users autonomy to fully control their devices, as P4 stated "*[with Hint Me!] we have greater autonomy in using the device because we are not dependent on others to tell us how something is done*". Interestingly, P2 and P4 felt that *Hint Me!* allowed them to learn without the dependency on others. Although we explicitly told them that someone would be answering their questions online, these comments suggest that *Hint Me!* has the potential to reduce the social barriers associated with asking for help: "*Sometimes people don't have the time to explain to us [how to do things]. If I had this service I wouldn't need to bother other people, I would just do them [the questions] here*".

P6 explicitly valued the active learning approach; that is, it is the users who perform the actions by learning and following a set of instructions: "*I like this does not work as remote assistance, people have access to an image but can't control the device*".

Participants identified several scenarios where the tool would be helpful. Four participants mentioned *Hint Me!* could be useful when exploring new apps or after an update. P1 stated "*[I see myself using this app] mainly in an app that I am using for the first time, or maybe after an update, when new features are made available. Or there can even be a bug which already has workarounds available*". The system was also seen as a tool to report and deal with malfunctions or interface elements that had unexpected behaviors.

P6 saw *Hint Me!* as an in-app training tool, rather than a questioning app: "*It is useful to describe the app, it's structure and layout. It helps. A lot of blind people do not have a mental model [of the app] and can't do things easily - oh it's on the center of the screen or a little more to the right - they don't have that mental picture*".

On the other hand, P2 focused on using *Hint Me!* to surpass accessibility problems, such as mislabeled or unlabeled buttons: "*I recently installed news apps and some of them are not accessible at all. With this app I could understand which button to press to get to certain sections*".

4.2 Questioning vs Browsing: A Trade-off

Participants identified value in both being able to create a new question and browsing previous stored knowledge. However, when asked about the foreseen usage of the system, they revealed different perceptions and preferences, namely in regards to the way they would retrieve knowledge.

P5 showed a preference for browsing and would only create questions if he couldn't find a response: "*I think I would check the database first. This way, I wouldn't risk making a question that was already asked. If I couldn't find it, I would then add one more question*".

On the other hand, P6 considered the perceived the availability of an answer to be a deciding factor: "*It is always easier to ask a question if the answer comes right away; if it is about the app's layout, I would search for an [existing] question, because that question was probably made, and it would be faster to search rather than ask a new question; if it is something that probably no one asked before, it's easier to ask*".

Other participants reinforced time of response as being relevant in their foreseen operation of the system. P4 stated "*having the list of questions is very relevant as there may not be people available to timely answer our questions*". Time was not the only reason for a browse first approach; other participants felt leaned to it as they had doubts about their ability to accurately formulate a question.

Participants expressed thoughtful concerns, namely to what relates to application versions. P1 told us: "*If the answers provided were for the same version, I would search for an available answer; if not, I would make a question since it is likely that the answer is no longer valid for my version*".

4.3 Anonymity and Answer Quality

We asked participants about whom they would send their questions to, particularly between unknown volunteers, close friends, or their broad social network. Participants preferred directing the questions to the volunteer group, choosing anonymous communication. The main reasons were related to not overburdening their family and friends, and due to the limited knowledge that this closer group may have ("*...in their case it would be harder to get the answer*", P1).

There is a common belief that the group of volunteers would be more qualified, both at the application and accessibility level ("*[closer] people are not aware of accessibility (i.e., Talkback), probably they will not be able to help much*", P1).

However, sharing their in-app information with unknown people was considered a possible issue, where additional contextual information is required, as stated by P5: "*I'm not sure what the screen capture shows. I think it would be important for us to understand how much of is being captured*".

Asking questions to close people was considered useful when sensitive information was involved. P6 stated: "*If it had [personal] information, [...], I would be more comfortable asking someone I know. But if it was - what is this button in this app, where personal information is not shown, in this case I wouldn't mind asking a broader group of people*".

People disliked the possibility of having questions posted in their Facebook. They do not feel it is private nor safe ("*Facebook is public. One thing is to ask an anonymous question to a specific group [...] A different thing is to post it on Facebook*", P6). Similar findings were reported in Brady et. al. [2] where blind people were reluctant to use social networks for visual Q&A (i.e. a question associated with a photo) due to the perceived social cost.

When asked about sighted or blind people volunteers, participants reinforced volunteers should be experienced with accessibility services to ensure useful responses.

4.4 The Role of the Volunteer

The volunteer provided answers that accommodated different navigation methods (explore by touch or swiping) by providing both spatial and positional instructions (e.g. "*The Optimize button is on the center top of the screen; navigating from the start it is the second button without a label*").

There is often a mismatch between the visual information and the output of the screenreader. Without using a screenreader or having additional contextual information, the volunteer would not have been able to answer all questions. One example was a mislabeled option when searching for an artist on Spotify, the first step involved opening a menu incorrectly labeled as "*Go Up*". In some cases, even layouts with correct labels may not be enough to incite a clear answer (e.g. duplicate labels).

Without rich contextual information, sighted people will struggle to provide clear answers. On the other hand, there are questions that are only trivial to sighted volunteers (e.g. "*How is this page organized?*", "*What is this button?*").

5. IMPLICATIONS FOR DESIGN

Participants showed interest in using *Hint Me!* to learn at their own pace, thus removing the need to rely on others' availability. Still, they expressed concerns on how to ensure the quality of the answers and their own privacy. They saw different usages for questioning and browsing, from addressing an issue to finding features or workarounds they were unaware of. The following implications derived from their desires and concerns and the insights on the volunteer role:

Enable Self-Organized Learning. Facilitating smartphone usage is not just about overcoming challenges; it is also about promoting serendipitous discovery of new features. Assistance must allow users to have control on content consumption in order to learn at their own pace.

Support the Workforce. For a successful assistance, the human supporter must be provided with enough information to become domain competent and aware of the communication needs of the end-user. As such, we should compensate the potential mismatch between the user' experience and the volunteer, augmenting his understanding of the user's context and doubts (e.g leveraging DOM trees to portrait the information available to the screenreader).

Gather Knowledge. Technologies that rely on human input should not waste contributions in single use, but instead iteratively build a shared knowledge-base. Moreover, we must look for opportunities to preemptively generate knowledge (e.g. describe layout structure) enabling better coverage and availability.

Nurture Knowledge. The variety of mobile devices, applications versions and frequent updates demands a continuous re-assessment of the gathered knowledge validity.

Respect Privacy. Smartphones are inherently private and hold personal data. Human-powered approaches must provide users with control over what they share and with whom, awareness of what is being shared, and selection of supporter-group based on information sensitivity. Alternatively, we must find novel ways to take advantage of context by removing all private and identifiable information.

6. LIMITATIONS

With the guarantee of the quality of the answers we were able to understand the potential of the approach. However, it limited our understanding of the issues the users face with answers of variable quality. We relied on a screenshot of the user interface to provide context, limiting the solution to sighted volunteers. However, we also collect DOM tree structure enabling the recreation of the contents accessible to the screenreader. With it, the pool of volunteers can be expand to users with a wide range of abilities.

7. Conclusions

Our findings show that support networks are essential to surpass everyday barriers. Although existent human-powered tools help blind users making sense of the real-world, supporting smartphone usage has been an unexplored avenue. We present *Hint Me!*, a human-powered assistance tool that mimics the qualities of in-person support and collaborative learning. Initial perceptions showed positive and promising results related to in-app support and self-organized learning. Future work will need to address privacy issues, leverage created knowledge, guarantee adequate assistance, and target a larger segment of users (e.g. older adults).

8. ACKNOWLEDGEMENTS

We thank the Fundação Raquel e Martin Sain in Lisbon and, particularly, Dr. Carlos Bastardo for his help in the discussion of the work and recruitment of participants. This work was partially supported by Fundação para a Ciência e a Tecnologia (FCT) through funding of the scholarship and ref. SFRH/BD/103935/2014, LASIGE Research Unit, ref. UID/CEC/00408/2013, INESCID Research Unit, ref. UID/CEC/50021/2013, and EPSRC award number DERC EP/M023001/1 (Digital Economy Research Centre).

9. REFERENCES

[1] J. P. Bigham, C. Jayant, H. Ji, G. Little, A. Miller, R. C. Miller, R. Miller, A. Tatarowicz, B. White, S. White, and T. Yeh. Vizwiz: Nearly real-time answers to visual questions. In Proc. of ACM Symposium on User Interface Software and Technology, UIST '10, pages 333-342, 2010.

[2] E. L. Brady, Y. Zhong, M. R. Morris, and J. P. Bigham. Investigating the appropriateness of social network question asking as a resource for blind users. In Proc. of Conference on Computer Supported Cooperative Work, CSCW '13, pages 1225-1236, 2013.

[3] V. Braun and V. Clarke. Using thematic analysis in psychology. Qualitative Research in Psychology, 3(2):77-101, 2006.

[4] P. K. Chilana, A. J. Ko, and J. O. Wobbrock. Lemonaid: Selection-based crowdsourced contextual help for web applications. In Proc. of SIGCHI Conference on Human Factors in Computing Systems, CHI '12, pages 1549-1558, 2012.

[5] S. K. Kane, J. O. Wobbrock, and R. E. Ladner. Usable gestures for blind people: Understanding preference and performance. In Proc. of SIGCHI Conference on Human Factors in Computing Systems, CHI '11, pages 413-422, 2011.

[6] H. Nicolau, K. Montague, T. Guerreiro, A. Rodrigues, and V. L. Hanson. Typing performance of blind users: An analysis of touch behaviors, learning effect, and in-situ usage. In Proc. of ACM SIGACCESS Conference on Computers and Accessibility, ASSETS '15, pages 273-280, 2015.

[7] J. Oliveira, T. Guerreiro, H. Nicolau, J. Jorge, and D. Gonçalves. Blind people and mobile touch-based text-entry: Acknowledging the need for different flavors. In Proc. of ACM SIGACCESS Conference on Computers and Accessibility, ASSETS '11, pages 179-186, 2011.

[8] A. Rodrigues, K. Montague, H. Nicolau, and T. Guerreiro. Getting smartphones to talkback: Understanding the smartphone adoption process of blind users. In Proc. of ACM SIGACCESS Conference on Computers and Accessibility, ASSETS '15, pages 23-32, 2015.

[9] C. Southern, J. Clawson, B. Frey, G. Abowd, and M. Romero. An evaluation of brailletouch: Mobile touchscreen text entry for the visually impaired. In Proc. of the International Conference on Human-computer Interaction with Mobile Devices and Services, MobileHCI '12, pages 317-326, 2012.

[10] H. Takagi, S. Kawanaka, M. Kobayashi, T. Itoh, and C. Asakawa. Social accessibility: Achieving accessibility through collaborative metadata authoring. In Proc. of ACM SIGACCESS Conference on Computers and Accessibility, Assets '08, pages 193-200, 2008.

Improving Smartphone Accessibility with Personalizable Static Overlays

André Rodrigues[1], André Santos[1], Kyle Montague[2], Tiago Guerreiro[1]
[1]LASIGE, Faculdade de Ciências, Universidade de Lisboa
[2]Open Lab, Newcastle University
afrodrigues@fc.ul.pt, abranco@lasige.di.fc.ul.pt, kyle.montague@newcastle.ac.uk, tjvg@di.fc.ul.pt

ABSTRACT

The physical keypads that used to dominate our mobile devices provided additional support for non-visual interaction - the keys could be recognized tactually, the interfaces were simpler and consistent. When combined with a screen reader, these devices could be easily operated by blind people. The advent of smartphones, with their rich, feature-filled applications and interfaces, have brought forward additional challenges for blind users. Apps and features are no longer developed by a single entity leading to an overwhelming variety of interfaces. We present an approach that superimposes a virtual overlay to all other interfaces ensuring interface consistency by re-structuring how content is accessed in every screen. To explore the approach, we split the screen, dedicating half to a configurable set of static options mimicking always available physical buttons regardless of context; while the other enables the standard content navigation gestures with the ability to re-order content and apply filters. In a qualitative study with nine visually impaired participants, the virtual overlays were reported as simpler to use, while still providing full-fledged usage of the system and the third party applications, and were seen as effective and useful, particularly for novice users.

CCS Concepts

• **Human Centered Computing →Accessibility**

Keywords

Blind; Smartphone; Accessibility; Personalizable Interface

1. INTRODUCTION

According to WebAim[1] surveys, 69% of the inquired screenreader users in 2015 also rely on a mobile screenreader. From those who do, 20% are still using feature phones or restrictive accessibility services on smartphones. There is a considerable share of the visually impaired population that are yet to fully transition to smartphones. Moreover, with keypads users were able to use a phone without a screenreader but smartphones cannot be operated without one. Many people, particularly less tech-savvy people wish they could continue using their dated feature phones with physical keypad and consistent interfaces [4]. Unfortunately, due to market pressure such devices are being produced less and less.

The default screen readers for today's top mobile operating systems, *VoiceOver* and *Talkback*, have provided basic access to smartphones for blind and visually impaired people. Although smartphones are powerful, they have been reported as challenging to adopt. Rodrigues et al [4] exposed that the barriers go beyond touchscreen accessibility, spawning from the mismatch between users' application mental models and the actual interfaces. Moreover, independent of user expertise, smartphone navigation and interfaces can be construed as inconsistent due to the freedom each developer has in structuring its apps interfaces and navigation (e.g. a confirm button can be in different places both physically and in the navigation hierarchy). This represent a substantial leap from the feature phones with their always available physical keypads with standard behavior's. In an environment where new apps and updates are made available everyday users have to continuously adapt to new interfaces.

Prior approaches have tried to replicate the consistency found in previous systems by replacing the entire operating system - limiting the user to the set of bespoke apps (e.g. *Mobile Accessibility* and *GeorgioPhone* on Google Play Store). Although it guarantees the consistency and accessibility of the apps provided, it negates the benefits of thousands others. Custom and implicitly restrictive assistive technologies can have also have the adverse effect of stigmatizing people that would rather be able to use mainstream applications and devices [5].

Other work on mobile accessibility has been mostly focus on input, namely text-entry [3] and gestures [1]. In recent work, Zhang et al. [6] address the issues found in the particular sub-context of mobile web browsing by adapting all web pages to be provided using a single personalized hierarchical view of the content, thus allowing users to quickly skim through content. At an application level, other approaches [2] have tried to facilitate the learning process of older adults by exposing users first to an interface with reduced functionalities before allowing full control. Zhang et al. [7] introduces the concept of interaction proxy allowing third party developers to augment mobile application accessibility by adapting how a specific application is rendered and accessed by the user.

Currently mobile screen readers allow users to access all the content available, but unlike custom made applications they cannot guarantee a consistent interface or navigation. Targeted application adaptations [7] can improve learnability and accessibility. However, similarly to custom made applications, these require adaptations for each app individually, hindering their scalability.

In an effort to combine the advantages of both paradigms, that is, providing the consistency and personalization of custom solutions,

[1] http://webaim.org/projects/screenreadersurvey6/

ASSETS '17, October 29-November 1, 2017, Baltimore, MD, USA

ACM 978-1-4503-4926-0/17/10…$15.00
https://doi.org/10.1145/3132525.3132558

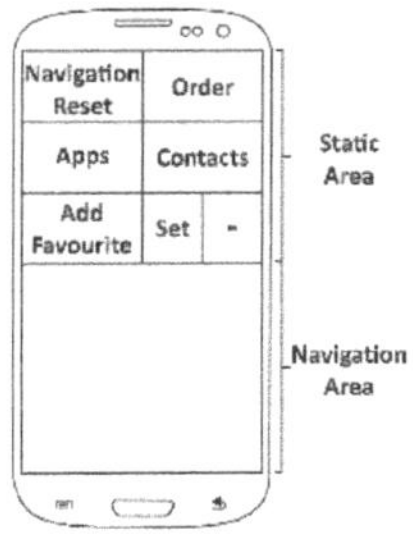

Figure 1 - Default template for PSI.

without sacrificing system wide access to all applications; we propose resorting to virtual layers that adapt and abstract how users access content. In a possible parameterization of such approach, targeted at blind people, we propose a virtual overlay with two main components: 1) a set of static always-available options, mimicking options associated with physical buttons in the old feature phones; and 2) a navigation area, that allows and abstracts access (e.g., ordering elements alphabetically or by usage frequency) to all applications and interface elements underneath. We developed an Android accessibility service that instantiates this approach adapting how it is presented and navigated by its users.

In this paper, we investigate the benefits and shortcomings of a personalizable, static and consistent interface (PSI) on mobile devices for non-visual access, alongside its acceptance by blind people (novice and expert users). In a lab study, we exposed nine smartphone screen reader users to PSI and all its features. Through thematic analysis of the interviews conducted, consistent layers were perceived as simpler to use and held potential benefits when first learning to use a smartphone. Furthermore, for users who struggle with current methods, believed these layers could enable them to take full advantage of their device.

2. PERSONALIZABLE STATIC OVERLAY

Many features were lost with the demise of physical keypads. They provided a consistent interface with multiple shortcuts, from always being a press away from the messaging app or speed dialing a contact. We aimed to provide a consistent and familiar interface to the user regardless of what application was being explored. With PSI, our goal was for users to only need to learn to use one interface in order to interact with all apps. To achieve it, we developed the PSI Android accessibility service, that adapts how content is transverse by the Talkback screen reader. Since PSI only adapts how content is navigated it provides system-wide access while presenting a consistent interface that was only previously available in custom restrictive approaches.

2.1 User Interface

The interface was split in two: the Static Area (SA) and Navigation Area (NA). The static area contains a set of options that are always available on screen and occupies half the screen. The other half contains the navigation area that is used to access all content. PSI adapts every interface as described except for text-entry.

2.1.1 Static Area

In its default state, the SA has seven options, Navigation Reset, Order, Contacts, Applications, Add Favourite, PSI Settings and Minimize. To access these options the user can rely on touch-to-explore (i.e. drag their finger on the screen to focus an element and double tap to select) or swipes when a static element is focused. Whenever a static element is selected it affects the content that is accessible in the navigation area.

2.1.2 Navigation Area

In the NA using the Talkback standard gestures of swiping left/right and double tap to select, users can access the content being displayed on screen. With a dedicated navigation area we intend to reduce focusing errors from swipes that are misinterpreted as touch-to-explore focus actions. Moreover, with the added control over navigation PSI is able to sort and filter elements.

2.1.3 Special Cases

In text-entry, when an edit box is selected the static area is hidden and the NA is displayed on the top half. The keyboard is displayed on the bottom half while allowing users to navigate on the top half, once the keyboard is closed PSI resumes its standard interface.

2.2 Personalizing PSI

When PSI is first launched on a device the default layout template is shown (Figure 1). Through the PSI Settings, users can create and edit the template options (with the exception of the PSI Settings and Minimize buttons which are locked). PSI rows always fill the full width of the screen, and in each row every option occupies the same space with the exception of PSI Settings and Minimize. There are two ways to create a new template: easy or expert mode. In easy mode users select options to be displayed in a layout of rows of three. In expert users are able to add as many options as they see fit in a table structure. When editing a template users are able to add and remove options. When adding, users first select the type of element (i.e. feature or shortcut) and then choose its position. To remove users simply select the unwanted option.

2.3 PSI Featured Options

PSI allow users to personalize their templates with several options. The Navigation Reset focus the navigation area and its first element. Order allows users to sort and filter content in the NA. Applications opens the list of applications installed. Contacts sets a list of contacts in the navigation area that when selected initializes a call. Add to Favorites stores the current focused element as a favorite in that screen. In the PSI Settings menu, the user is able to customize the template including adding shortcuts. Lastly, Minimize pauses PSI, similarly to Talkback, PSI can then be resumed through a sticky notification.

2.3.1 Sorting Elements

Users can sort how content is navigated to quickly reach their intended target. Currently, it can order: default, alphabetically, most used, most recently used, favourites (i.e. favorites displayed first) and interactive (i.e. filters out all non-interactive elements). PSI filters work on a per-screen per-app basis. To do so, PSI counts and locally stores user's interaction with each element in each application screen to provide the filters to order by frequency and recency. The PSI system is designed to ensure easy addition of other filters in future developments.

2.4 PSI Personalized Shortcuts

There are three types of shortcuts that can be added to the static area: app, contact and task. App opens the corresponding app; contact speed dials a contact; and task performs a pre-defined sequence of commands. In the current iteration of PSI we define tasks for a given application and version (e.g. open last email in Inbox, open last text message in Messages).

3. USER EVALUATION

To evaluate our approach we conducted a lab study where nine participants were exposed to PSI. We analyzed the qualitative data collected from the debriefing interview to understand the benefits and shortcomings of our approach.

3.1 Participants

We recruited nine smartphone screen reader users (i.e. four used Android and five had an iPhone). Participants self-reported as being capable of performing basic phone (i.e. making and receiving calls and messaging). Age ranged from 27 to 58

Table 1 - Participants experience in months and list tasks able to perform marked with an Y for yes and N for not.

ID	Months	Tasks						
		Listen music	Receive Email	Send Email	Browse Internet	Social Apps	Install Apps	Assist. Apps
P1	30	Y	N	N	N	N	N	N
P2	72	Y	Y	N	Y	Y	Y	Y
P3	48	Y	Y	N	Y	Y	Y	Y
P4	0,5	Y	N	N	N	Y	N	N
P5	72	Y	Y	Y	Y	Y	Y	Y
P6	36	Y	N	N	Y	N	N	N
P7	48	Y	Y	Y	Y	Y	Y	Y
P8	12	N	Y	Y	Y	Y	N	Y
P9	6	Y	Y	Y	Y	Y	N	Y

(M=43.3, SD=10). Smartphone experience and ability to perform a broad set of tasks varied amongst our participant, as shown in Table 1. The two participants able to perform all tasks in Table 1 are accessibility instructors who provide training for other blind and visually-impaired people on how to use screen readers. Participants were recruited from a local social institution and all were legally blind.

3.2 Apparatus

We used a Samsung Galaxy S3 with Android Nougat 7.0, running our PSI accessibility service. PSI operates as a foreground service acting as a proxy between the content on the screen and the screenreader. Talkback was enabled and used as the default screen reader.

Table 2- Tasks performed by the participants with PSI.

TASK
Explore all the static options on the top half of the screen.
Use the *navigation area* and to find *settings*.
Use the alphabetic filter to find the option *Accessibility* in *Settings*.
Go to Apps and order by *frequency* to find the most used app.
Use the *contacts* shortcut and to call the last most used contact.
Mark *sound* in *settings* as *favourite*. Use the filter *favourites*.
Use PSI *settings* to add a fixed shortcut to the contact john snow.
Use PSI *settings* to add a fixed shortcut to *open last received email*.

3.3 Procedure

Participants were informed the purpose of the study was to explore Personalizable Static Interfaces to identify its benefits and shortcomings. Participants were introduced to PSI and given an overview of all its features. They were then guided through a set of eight tasks. The researcher first gave a short explanation of the feature and the current window content followed by the task to be performed. Participants could ask questions freely and assistance was provided on request. Each participant performed the tasks depicted in Table 2 in the same order, this process took about 30 minutes. Finally, we conducted a debriefing session where we performed a questionnaire and a 10-30 minutes semi-structured interview. Participants were asked for their views regarding PSI consistent and personalizable characteristics.

3.4 Data Analysis

Interviews were recorded and transcribed. Two researchers coded two interviews to inductively create a codebook[2]. The researchers coded the remaining interviews independently with the resulting codebook and reached a Cohen's Kappa agreement of k=0.71.

3.5 Findings

All participants were able to successfully complete the tasks. Five themes emerged from the data analysis, herein we present our findings framed by the themes. In *Challenges to Smartphone Usage* we discuss the participants views on the challenges they faced since first starting to use a device and on its effects. *Personalize, Organize, and Simplify* aggregates the discussion surrounding PSI interface. The main advantages brought forward by PSI are reported in *Learnability & Autonomy*. The remaining two themes are *Concerns & Limitations* and *Improving PSI* where participants expressed the perceived drawbacks of PSI and how PSI could be refined. In this section we will refer to users that reported to be able to do six of the seven tasks in Table 1 as experts.

3.5.1 Challenges to Smartphone Usage

As found in prior work [4] participants reported to have struggled when getting started with their smartphone. When asked to reflect on their own experiences, some participants could not remember the specific origins of the issues (happening up to three years ago), however, vividly described the deep sense of frustration they faced at the time. Accessibility features have improved over the years, however, we haven't reached a point where adopting a device is a streamlined experience. One of the lesser experienced participants explained their initial difficulties and the reliance of peer support to get going when everything was new. "*My first challenges was to not throw it against a wall. I didn't know how to do anything. I tried to explore on my own but my daughter would end up mad at me because I kept modifying stuff without realizing it. With your app I am sure I would be scolded a lot less." (P4)*

Despite P4 having the desire to explore the device alone, they felt it was dangerous to do so, as they were inadvertently editing settings and configurations. From an expert view many of the issues that plague novice and less experienced users spawn from a lack of spatial ability to overcome the challenges presented. Consequently, users often get lost and feel frustrated. *"If we don't have spatial awareness we will navigate left, right, left, right, left, left, right. (...) If we can't visualize the paths in our head it's like trying to find the metro. If I don't know the way I will end up circling a post" (P5)*

Getting started with a screen reader on a smartphone can be overwhelming. Less tech-savvy users struggle to understand what is happening since the interface seems to change completely every time an option is selected. Not only is navigation confusing and seems to change from app to app, but the variety of gestures can be a burden. *"It's Facebook and email and all those troublesome gestures, swipe with two fingers, swipe with one, up and down, blah blah blah it annoys me. I would rather have these. [PSI interface]" (P4)*

Ultimately for novice users this all leads to a lack of autonomy when interacting with their device. Even experienced users are not necessarily experts. In some cases even after years of usage, they can still struggle with navigation to a point where discoverability becomes an issue. For P1 he can still only perform basic tasks and

[2] https://goo.gl/7JzSUi

struggles to find the options he is looking for. *"I often receive messages with bills to pay and I would like to forward them to my wife. Unfortunately I am unable to, I usually end up memorizing the reference codes and write a new message." (P1)*

3.5.2 Personalize, Organize and Simplify

PSI permanent options and dedicated screen areas brought structure to how content can be accessed. *"Everything used to be scattered, but with the options present in the top I will no longer need to search for them, it is easier" (P9)*

By dedicating an area of the screen exclusively to swipe navigation and establishing a clear rule to how content is structure users perceived the interface as simpler. *"For example if I had that navigation area when I was in the Messages application I would probably be able to find the forwarding button" (P1)*

PSI ability to order content on demand was seen by users as a way to facility interaction and promote discoverability. For some users this simply meant they would need to spend less time learning the different gestures for advanced options while for others the adaptability would allow them to have different navigation strategies depending on the app. *"Today I could be using Alphabetic ordering but I could change to Most Use, all depending on the application and on what I intended to do" (P3)*

Participants acknowledged different users have different interaction needs. Moreover, needs can easily change. Thus, the ability to personalize the static area and add the different types of shortcuts was a key feature for some users. *"The ability to add contacts and tasks, it makes it easier because we have an open door to what we want. (...) For example I could be contacting frequently John Snow, but if for whatever reason it stopped happening. Instead of having a lot of fixed buttons I could remove them." (P1)*

3.5.3 Learnability and Autonomy

PSI was seen has a simpler interface to interact with smartphones. Participants believed they would have had less problems if they would have PSI during their adoption period. *"It would have been a lot easier. You see, I had a phone with normal keys, and it suddenly broke down... I bought a smartphone and I couldn't even answer a call. (...) To start with this would have been much better." (P8)*

Furthermore, participants reported that people with additional difficulties either due to being less tech-savvy, or having less spatial abilities could benefit from a consistent interface. *"Some people have a lot difficulties using a smartphone. Why? Because things are never in the same place, buttons move from one place to another. I believe this would help." (P3)*

Two expert participants mentioned how PSI should be incorporated in default screen readers as an "easy mode" that could be a stepping stone before using the de facto screen reader navigation. *"You should sell this to Talkback, we would benefit from it. The user would start with this, when he felt he was familiarized with the system he could start to try the original." (P5)*

However, they also believed people with additional difficulties would never be able to fully adapt to current screen reader navigation thus PSI would be the first and final step. *"They are forced to use a touchscreen screen. A phone without any physical keys. I believe your app is not just for getting started. They would always rely on it." (P5)*

As a side effect PSI consistency users felt an additional sense of security and independence when exploring the system. *"It [Static Area] is something that gives us a bit more confidence when exploring" (P2)*

For some participants PSI was more than a stepping stone. They believed the ability to order and add shortcuts would improve their performance. *"When you get used to that menu (static options) you will do things faster, and the shortcuts facilitate a lot." (P3)*

3.5.4 Concerns and Limitations

For one instructor PSI had the severe limitation of breaking the norms established by the de facto screen readers on smartphones. PSI content navigation does not support touch-to-explore navigation and gestures shortcuts do not affect the content on the navigation area. As such he believed users with good spatial abilities and a high understanding of the interface (i.e. experts) benefit more from the standard screen reader. *"For someone who already know how to use touch-to-explore he will use touch-to-explore. (...) Another issue is when you are dividing the screen in half you are also blocking the standard gestures used in Android" (P7)*

Participants often described scenarios where they had requested sighted assistance to overcome an issue. One participant was concerned if sighted users would be able to provide assistance if PSI was running on the device. *"The applications that make our life easier, make the smartphone difficult to interact for sighted people. People already think Talkback is weird enough. (...) What does a sighted people see when interacting with it?" (P1)*

3.5.5 Improving PSI

When queried about how we could improve PSI all users suggested more customization options. For some that meant having the ability to change the size and position of the dedicated areas. For others that meant a fixed toggle button to order content in a specific way rather than a button with all possible sorting options. Others mentioned the desire to create their own shortcuts to tasks. *"I would like to have more shortcuts to tasks. The type? Well that depends on what people use more often on their phones. Maybe users could be given the chance to create their own tasks." (P6)*

Several participants mentioned PSI should be incorporated natively in screen readers. For one expert user this would mean PSI would not only support standard gestures but it could allow the creation of shortcuts using gestures. *"For example if I want to open Whatsapp I would do a W." (P7)*

The two instructors expressed how physical cues and interfaces can still play a fundamental role both in adoption and navigation. One is still wishing for old physical interfaces to return, suggesting we should provide a physical directional pad on the phone allowing users to navigate as they used to. The other instructor suggested adding a physical tactile line in PSI to reinforce and facilitate learning the distinction between the dedicate areas. *"It could have a physical line to divide it. (...) A line almost imperceptible just so we can tell tactile if we are in one area or the other." (P5)*

4. DISCUSSION

4.1 The Benefits of a Consistent Approach

Smartphones lost the similarities between applications that was once the norm. For screen readers' users this led to having to understand an infinite amount of app structures and navigation approaches to reach the intended elements. With PSI we provide dedicated areas and clear rules to how content is structured and accessed. Having the SA allowed users to have a consistent point of reference which granted a sense of constant awareness. The fixed set of customizable options brought back the quick access, ever present "physical keys" favoured in the feature phone devices. Specifically, the ability to order content established an expectation of which content is going to be transversed. Thus, information was not perceived as scattered or disorganized.

4.2 Same Functionalities, Simpler Interface

Talkback allows full access to the system by modifying how users interact. It provides two navigation methods: swiping for next and previous item; and dragging the finger through the screen until the location of the desired item is found. Both interactions methods have their strengths and weaknesses. We took advantage of each method with a clear divide where to navigate content and where to access permanent static features. Touch-to-explore is particular adequate to deal with quick access and static options. On the other hand swipe navigation allows users to navigate without any previous knowledge. The main disadvantage to sequential navigation is the time required to reach options in cluttered applications. For a system to succeed with it, it must provide opportunities for users to quickly reach content. In Talkback the answer was gesture shortcuts and touch-to-explore. In our approach we provided ordering filters with a single button.

PSI breaks the paradigm of direct manipulation of content in conventional smartphone screenreaders in favor of providing a consistent interface. Currently blind users are required to have strong spatial abilities to quickly interact with their smartphone. PSI was built to adapt all interfaces to a single one by taking advantage of the same DOM tree structure available to Talkback. With PSI users only needed to understand a single screen in order to understand them all, which is particular beneficial for users with less spatial abilities. Therefore, users perceive our consistent interface as simpler, organized and ultimately, easier to learn.

4.3 Personalizing, Customizing and Adapting

When asked what they would improve in PSI most of what was mentioned was further customization options. Users showed interest in continually adapting their interface through the introduction and removal of the different types of shortcuts. In addition to simple contact and application shortcuts the ability to create task oriented ones may prove to be crucial to support more demanding users. Therefore, similar approaches that take advantage of permanent static elements must ensure a straightforward personalization process. Furthermore, every user is different and it expects different things out of his/her device, for a consistent interface to succeed it needs to give users the ability to adjust to their needs.

4.4 Static Overlays from Novice to Expert

Participants unanimously believed a personalizable static overlay provides a simpler interface. One of the referred key benefits was to facilitate the adoption process without having to compromise functionality. For some, consistent interfaces can be just a stepping stone to ease the transition to smartphones. However, for a large segment of users with additional difficulties, it may be the only way to take full control of their smartphone. Static overlays were not seen as a less performant method by some of the more advance users. Users expected the ability to create a wide variety of shortcuts, customizing the interface and adaptive ordering filters could have a positive effect in their current navigation.

However these interfaces provide diminishing returns for users that rely on their spatial abilities and mental capacities to memorize the location of each option in each app. Moreover, advanced users often rely on gestures shortcuts (e.g. first item, next page) that were not supported by PSI. Going forward solutions relying on consistent interfaces should not neglect advance users and support the advanced shortcut gestures.

5. CONCLUSIONS

Today's accessibility services must accommodate the large diversity of mobile apps. They provide access to often conflicting interface paradigms. As such they are not particular designed for any interface; leading to a more complex and less effective interaction. Current screenreaders enable touching to explore, swiping to navigate to next/previous elements, and performing special gestures, all in the same area. The complexity of these interactions together with the complexity of the interfaces disables a large portion of the population to use mobile devices effectively. As such, we are proposing personalized interface layers that allow users to create a consistent presentation experience for themselves, regardless of the application they are interacting with. Recognizing the additional difficulties faced by blind users with dual interaction spaces, we developed a solution that provides clearly separated interaction areas. Providing a simpler navigation area that enables a more flexible, but still complete, access to available interface elements in the applications underneath. This approach is perceived by users as simpler to use and learn, and to enable an easier transition to these devices. Future work should seek to explore the impact PSI could have in the adoption process. There is an opportunity to reconsider mobile accessibility approaches to be more modular and customizable, enabling higher degrees of personalization and thus supporting at all levels of expertise.

6. ACKNOWLEDGEMENTS

We thank the Fundação Raquel e Martin Sain in Lisbon. This work was partially supported by Fundação para a Ciência e a Tecnologia (FCT) through funding of the scholarship and ref. SFRH/BD/103935/2014, LASIGE Research Unit, ref. UID/CEC/00408/2013 and EPSRC award number DERC EP/M023001/1 (Digital Economy Research Centre).

7. REFERENCES

[1] S. K. Kane, J. O. Wobbrock, and R. E. Ladner. 2011. Usable gestures for blind people: understanding preference and performance. In Proc. of the SIGCHI Conference on Human Factors in Computing Systems (CHI '11). ACM, New York, NY, USA, 413-422.

[2] R. Leung, L. Findlater, J. McGrenere, P. Graf, and J. Yang. 2010. Multi-Layered Interfaces to Improve Older Adults' Initial Learnability of Mobile Applications. ACM Trans. Access. Comput. 3, 1.

[3] H. Nicolau, K. Montague, T. Guerreiro, A. Rodrigues, and V. L. Hanson. 2015. Typing Performance of Blind Users: An Analysis of Touch Behaviors, Learning Effect, and In-Situ Usage. In Proc. of the 17th International ACM SIGACCESS Conference on Computers & Accessibility (ASSETS '15).

[4] A. Rodrigues, K. Montague, H. Nicolau, and T. Guerreiro. 2015. Getting Smartphones to Talkback: Understanding the Smartphone Adoption Process of Blind Users. In Proc. of the 17th International ACM SIGACCESS Conference on Computers & Accessibility (ASSETS '15).

[5] K. Shinohara and J. O. Wobbrock. 2011. In the shadow of misperception: assistive technology use and social interactions. In Proc. of the SIGCHI Conference on Human Factors in Computing Systems (CHI '11).

[6] D. Zhang, L. Zhou, J. O. Uchidiuno, and I. Y. Kilic. 2017. Personalized Assistive Web for Improving Mobile Web Browsing and Accessibility for Visually Impaired Users. ACM Trans. Access. Comput. 10, 2.

[7] X. Zhang, A. S. Ross, A. Caspi, J. Fogarty, and J. O. Wobbrock. 2017. Interaction Proxies for Runtime Repair and Enhancement of Mobile Application Accessibility. In Proc. of the 2017 CHI Conference on Human Factors in Computing Systems (CHI '17).

Introducing People with ASD to Crowd Work

Kotaro Hara
HCI and Robotics Institutes
Carnegie Mellon University
kotaroh@cmu.edu

Jeffrey P. Bigham
HCI and LT Institutes
Carnegie Mellon University
jbigham@cs.cmu.edu

ABSTRACT
Adults with Autism Spectrum Disorders (ASD) are unemployed at a high rate, in part because the constraints and expectations of traditional employment can be difficult for them. In this paper, we report on our work in introducing people with ASD to remote work on a crowdsourcing platform and a prototype tool we developed by working with participants. We conducted a six-week long user-centered design study with three participants with ASD. The early stage of the study focused on assessing the abilities of our participants to search and work on micro-tasks available on the crowdsourcing market. Based on our preliminary findings, we designed, developed, and evaluated a prototype tool to facilitate image transcription tasks that are increasingly popular on crowd labor markets. Our findings suggest that people with ASD have varying levels of ability to work on micro-tasks, but are likely to be able to work on tasks like image transcription. The tool we introduce, Assistive Task Queue (ATQ), facilitated our participants' completion of image transcription tasks by removing ambiguity in finding the next task to work on and in simplifying tasks into discrete steps. ATQ may serve as a general platform for finding and delivering appropriate tasks to workers with autism.

CCS Concepts
• **Human-centered computing → Accessibility →Accessibility technologies.**

Keywords
Autism Spectrum Disorder; crowdsourcing

1. INTRODUCTION
Autism Spectrum Disorder (ASD) is a developmental disorder that is characterized by communication deficiencies, social interaction challenges, and restricted, repetitive patterns of behavior (*e.g.,* stimming) with varying levels of severity [36, 39]. In the U.S., more than 3.5 million people are estimated to have ASD [1], of which 50-75% of adults are expected to be unemployed [15]—a rate much higher than people without disabilities [6]. The lack of job opportunities not only negatively impacts the independence and self-esteem of the affected population, but also has a broader economic effect [8, 23].

Prior work in ASD has largely focused on understanding the causes of autism [35], designing intervention methods and technologies to reduce the impact of disorders on people with ASD [24], and creating technologies to support children and their caregivers [13, 21]. However, we know little about the challenges that adults with ASD in traditional workplace face, and we know even less on how technology can mitigate the vocational challenges for individuals with ASD. Recent work has examined how people with ASD work, but this was focused on high-functioning individuals who work in the technology-industry [30]. Zyskowski *et al.* [42] investigated the demographics of people with disabilities who knew about or had experience in crowd work. The research showed that some people with ASD use crowdsourcing already. However, the study did not reveal the challenges that this population face in working on micro-tasks.

In this paper, we investigate the opportunities and challenges in introducing people with ASD to work in a crowdsourcing environment. Some aspects of crowd work, such as bypassing the social norms of a traditional workplace, may be beneficial for people with ASD. Our hope is to improve the independence of those who face vocational challenges. This has become more possible as some states in the U.S. (*e.g.,* Pennsylvania) have changed their laws so that people receiving Social Security Income can earn more supplemental income without losing their eligibility for benefits [1]. Crowd work, however, could also introduce new challenges, such as requiring persons with ASD to navigate an overwhelming variety of job opportunities to successfully secure work. Our research questions include: Does crowd work present a feasible job opportunity for individuals with severe ASD? If so, what types of tasks would be best suited? And, could technology be designed to facilitate this kind of work?

To evaluate the potential of crowd work for providing individuals with ASD with new job opportunities, we conducted an iterative user-centered design study with three individuals with ASD. We assessed how well they were able to negotiate the existing crowd work environment (we focused on Amazon Mechanical Turk or AMT) and whether we could design technologies to facilitate their completion of micro-tasks. The study involved six weekly sessions with three participants with ASD. We dedicated the first four sessions to developing a better understanding of the participants' capacities in using the existing AMT interface to search and perform micro-tasks. We designed the sessions with an expert consultant with ASD. Based on findings from this stage, we designed, developed, and evaluated a prototype tool—Assistive Task Queue (ATQ)—to support our participants while working on image transcription tasks. Although, it is impossible to generalize from three participants, even with only three participants we observed substantial diversity of abilities. Over six weeks, we were nevertheless able to iterate toward approaches that seemed to work well for each participant, suggesting broader applicability of our general approach.

Our findings from the in-lab observations and in-lab studies suggest that our participants' abilities to work on micro-tasks vary significantly. But all could perform some tasks. Our participants performed best on tasks that required a low degree of executive function. For example, they could complete image description and

[1] PA ABLE. http://www.paable.gov

ASSETS '17, October 29-November 1, 2017, Baltimore, MD, USA

ACM 978-1-4503-4926-0/17/10…$15.00
https://doi.org/10.1145/3132525.3132544

image transcription that required limited working memory and relied on visual perception. On the other hand, they struggled with a writing task that taxed working memory. We also found different levels of ability to search and explore the micro-tasks available on AMT. One of our participants could independently search and find tasks to work on, while the other two needed guidance from a researcher. Our findings are complicated by comorbid cognitive impairments in all participants, although such a combination of disabilities is common in this population [2]. In evaluating ATQ, we showed that the tool could facilitate our participants with ASD to find and work on image transcription.

This work qualitatively and quantitatively showed that our participants with ASD can perform crowd work. And, they benefited from simplification and guidance of micro-tasks and help with automated task search. More broadly, we contribute: (i) the first formative evaluation of challenges in introducing people with ASD in a crowd work environment, (ii) the assessment of how different types of micro-tasks are suited for providing individuals with ASD with new job opportunities, and (iii) the design and evaluation of a ATQ to facilitate work on image transcription tasks for our participants with ASD.

2. Background and Related Work

We describe the challenges that traditional workplace settings pose to people with ASD. We also introduce the HCI research that focuses on supporting this population.

2.1 Employment for Adults with ASD

It is estimated that there are approximately 3.5 million people with ASD in the U.S. [1], of which 50-75% of adults are unemployed [15]. Unemployment not only affects independence and self-esteem, but also significantly impacts the economy. For instance, it is estimated that $1.4-2.4m is needed to support an individual with ASD over their lifespan [8, 23]. Even those who are considered higher functioning are less likely to be employed and make less money compared to people without ASD.

While the symptoms manifested by adults with ASD vary across individuals [36], interaction and behavioral difficulties negatively impact employment [15, 19]. Prior work reports that interaction disorders pose the largest difficulties for individual with ASD in the workplace [15]. The challenges include difficulties understanding directions, in face-to-face communications (*e.g.*, reading facial expressions), and communicating in an inappropriate manner. Furthermore, behavioral difficulties such as throwing tantrums, physical aggression, self-injury, and ritualistic behaviors (*e.g.*, stimming) can create employment barriers [10].

Cognitive dysfunction and comorbidity (*i.e.*, the simultaneous presence of two or more chronic conditions) with other psychiatric symptoms could also negatively affect job opportunities. Difficulties in task execution due to problems with attention, motor planning, and working memory likely negatively impact work performance [32]. Acclimating to new job routines and managing changes in the work setting often pose additional challenges (though it can be overcome [20]). The individuals with ASD are sometimes also diagnosed with symptoms like depression and anxiety [22], which requires additional care.

Vocational programs and societal changes have been improving the situation [11, 14–16]. The programs attempt to help individuals prepare for and gain employment through various interventions, including job placement support (*e.g.*, job matching), on-the-job support (*e.g.*, increasing the awareness of employer toward ASD), and workplace modifications (*e.g.*, reducing over stimulating distractions). More recently, major technology companies—such as Microsoft and SAP—has been hiring people with ASD because they may be well-suited for the types of jobs offered in the technology-industry. Survey and interview studies conducted by Morris *et al.* revealed that software engineering tasks that require attention to details (like software testing) seems to be well suited for adults with ASD. While valuable, skill-matching alone does not address challenges with securing/keeping jobs and the volume of jobs offered by the pioneering companies are limited. Clearly, more work in addition to these efforts is needed to improve the situation.

	Age	Spectrum	Comorbidity	Occupation	Living
P1	28	Autism disorder	Intellectual disability	Janitor	with parents
P2	23	Asperger's syndrome	ADHD; Intellectual disability; OCD; Schizophrenia	Janitor	with housemates
P3	22	Autism disorder	Intellectual disability	Packaging	with parents

Table 1. Participant demographics from the survey, interview, and conversation with the participants' caregivers.

The crowdsourcing environment could offer new work opportunities for people with ASD. For example, a work environment where communication is nonverbal and asynchronous in nature may be favored by people with ASD [15, 20]. At the same time, however, aspects of crowdsourcing such as the lack of on-site support and overwhelming diversity of types of work offered could prevent people with ASD from working on crowdsourcing markets. Crowdsourcing has been studied for more than a decade, but limited research has assessed the potential benefits and drawbacks of crowdsourcing for people with ASD.

2.2 HCI Research on ASD

A range of HCI research has investigated the roles that technology could play in supporting people with ASD and their caregivers. Researchers have studied online communication by people with ASD [9, 34], designed methods/technologies for education and intervention [25, 33], and designed technologies to support children and their caregivers [13, 21]. For example, Hayes *et al.* developed CareLog, a tool to support school teachers to better conduct functional behavior assessment [13]. For more comprehensive survey of HCI research on ASD, see the recent survey by Kientz *et al.* [21].

The above research focused on supporting children and caregivers, and limited work looked into vocational support for adults with ASD. Morris *et al.* surveyed a neuro-diverse population (including people with ASD) to understand the challenges and opportunities they find while working at a large technology company [30]. While related, the focus was not understanding how people with ASD use crowdsourcing. Hong *et al.* studied the design of a social network to support the independent living of adults with ASD [17]. However, it was about designing systems to let people with ASD learn life skills through online collaborations. Finally, Swaminathan *et al.* investigated web accessibility of the crowd work environment [38] and Zyskowski *et al.* investigated who works on AMT [42], but their focus was not on people with ASD.

3. Study Method

Our study used the iterative user-centered design inspired by the participatory design method [37], a process that uses continual participation of the target population. The method was uniquely suited for this study; iteratively conducted study sessions not only let us understand how our participants use AMT, but also allowed us to simultaneously envision and shape new tools [37]. Furthermore, the method has been previously applied to accessibility research [29, 40]. We used AMT because it is widely used both in HCI research and in practice, and it offers a variety of micro-tasks. We asked our participants to perform the types of tasks that are common in the crowdsourcing market, such as image tagging, image transcription, and survey tasks [7, 12, 38].

Working with a local research partner, we recruited three participants with ASD through referral (Table 1). Our participants had other disabilities, too (Table 1). Participants had prior experience in using a computer. The participants used the computer in our lab to work on tasks administered in the study. The participants were compensated $20 per session in addition to what they earned by completing Human Intelligence Tasks (HITs) on AMT. All study sessions were audio and video recorded and interviews were transcribed by the researchers. The participants' interactions were recorded using a screen recorder. In each session, one participant and participant's caregiver attended the meeting. The study lasted for five to six sessions per participant.

4. Iterative User-Centered Design

The study lasted for six weeks from March to May in 2017. The first four weeks were spent to explore the participants' abilities to search and work on micro-tasks. In the following week, we designed, developed, and evaluated an assistive tool to support people to perform image transcription tasks—task that is prevalent on AMT and could be performed by all of our participants.

We describe the study and the summary of the findings from each week. We also discuss how the findings affected the subsequent weeks' research directions. In designing the sessions, we got feedback from an expert consultant who also has high-functioning ASD. The in-lab studies necessarily used within-subjects design given the expected variability between our participants. We relied on researcher observations more often than think-aloud because our participants' cognitive and communication disabilities made it hard for them to fully articulate their thoughts.

4.1 Week 1: Introductory Session

4.1.1 Method

We administered a background survey to collect demographic information including name, age, sex, comorbidity with other disabilities, employment status, and experience with using computing devices. When needed, the researcher and/or caregiver explained the intent of the questions. We then introduced the basic mechanism of crowd work, AMT specific concepts (*e.g.,* HITs), how to interact with the AMT interface, and types of tasks available. In the interview, we asked about their experiences on the current/most recent occupation, interpersonal challenges they face, their preferences on work location/time flexibility, their expectations toward crowd work, and experience in remote work.

To see how people with ASD use the crowdsourcing platform, the participants were asked to freely explore and work on AMT tasks. We were interested in their task search behaviors, task selection behaviors (*e.g.,* types of tasks they select), and how they work on the tasks. When the participants struggled to find tasks to work on, we offered the following keywords for searching: *data collection*, (image/audio/video) *transcription,* (image/video) *description*, *survey*, and *writing*. These suggestions were made based on the types of task that are common on AMT [7, 12]. If the participants further struggled, we ask them to work on the micro-tasks of the above categories that we made and posted on AMT.

4.1.2 Result

P1 and P2 participated from Week 1. P3 participated from Week 2 but went through the Week 1 procedure except for working on AMT. The sessions with P1 and P2 took 64 and 72 minutes. All participants were male. The age ranged from 22 to 28. P1 and P3 had autism disorders, and P2 had Asperger's syndrome. All participants had comorbidity (*e.g.,* intellectual disabilities—see Table 1). All participants found their current or most recent occupations through our research partner's referral. P2 earned $77-130 per week; P1 and P3 did not know their weekly earnings.

I would be interested in crowd work because I could	P1	P2	P3*
earn money	4	4	5
do something interesting or fun	4	5	5
do something that's stimulating or challenging	4	4	5
learn new skills	4	5	5
feel like I'm contributing to the society	3	5	5
help other people on their projects	3	5	5
participate with family and friends	4	5	5
work without interpersonal communication	3	5	5
work anonymously	2	3	5
work remotely at anywhere I want	4	4	5
work at anytime.	2	3	5

Table 2. Participants' motivation for working on crowdsourcing. The scale ranged from 1 (strongly disagree) to 5 (strongly agree). *The response from P3 are from Week 2.

When asked about their work preferences, P1 and P2 said they like routine jobs with fixed schedules. None had prior experience in remote work. They had no knowledge about crowdsourcing until they heard about the study. They had no preference whether the work was on-site or remote. We asked to rate why they were interested in crowd work in 5-point scale—see Table 2. When asked if they want to treat crowd work as either main source of income or supplementary source of income, all responded that they want to work on crowd work in addition to other jobs.

P1 and P2 were asked to freely work on AMT tasks. We observed their varying abilities to search and work on micro tasks (*i.e.,* HITs). P1 who has an autism disorder required extensive help and guidance from the researcher. The researcher provided step-by-step instructions on searching for HITs and prompted him to work on them. Completing a HIT was also difficult. For example, when P1 worked on an image description task where he was asked to provide a title and an alt-text for a given image, he had trouble focusing on what to describe. Seeing the struggle, the researcher decided to ask P1 to work on an image classification task that we prepared, where the participant was asked to confirm the presence of a target object in a series of pictures, which he could complete. P2, on the other hand, could independently use the AMT interface and find HITs that he could work with minimal guidance.

4.1.3 Week 1 Summary

In general, our participants were motivated to work on AMT tasks. The factors like *earning money*, *do something interesting or fun* and *stimulating*, *learning new skills*, and being able to work *with caregiver* seemed to be important for all participants. *Anonymity* and *work time flexibility* seemed to matter less for P1 and P2. Although they had no preferences on on-site or remote work, they were still interested in the remoteness of crowd work.

The abilities of P1 and P2 to work on micro-tasks varied. P1 struggled on searching and completing HITs, whereas P2 had no problem navigating the AMT interface. It is important to note that both participants could work on some HITs, suggesting the feasibility of introducing adults with ASD to work on micro-tasks. We further investigated what kinds of micro tasks they could work on in Week 2 and 3. We also studied how we could support them to find HITs in Week 4.

Figure 1. The examples of images used in the Week 2 tasks. (a) *Image classification*: prompted yes/no question like "is this this woman smiling?" (b) *Image description*: prompted to describe what is in the image. (c) *Image transcription*: prompted to transcribe parts of the image. like the first name in the business card.

4.2 Week 2: Task Completion Efficacy 1

To better understand our participants' abilities to work on micro-tasks, we asked them to work on a variety of micro-tasks. P3 joined and he went through the Week 1 procedure, except for the part where we asked to freely explore AMT. Overall, the sessions with P1, P2, and P3 took 68, 67, and 108 minutes.

4.2.1 Method

We prepared the following five categories of tasks: (i) *image classification*, (ii) *image description*, (iii) *image transcription*, (iv) *survey*, and (v) *writing*. The goal was to prepare tasks of varying types and difficulty levels that exist on AMT. For image classification and image description tasks, we downloaded 5 images for each from ImageNet that were previously tagged by AMT workers (Figure 1a). The image classification task prompted the participant to answer five yes/no questions like "is this woman smiling?" The image description task asked the participants to describe and enter what is in each image (Figure 1b).

For the image transcription, survey, and writing tasks, we downloaded the HITs' HTML files and media contents that were available on AMT at the time, and re-posted them as our HITs. We had two images for the image transcription task: a shopping receipt and a business card (Figure 1c). The participants were asked to find and transcribe 12 pieces of information like "total amount of transaction in the receipt" and "email address in the business card." The survey task asked to score the relevancy of 9 search results for a given term "Frozen Yogurt". The query results included items like "Dawns Deli" and "YoGo Factory Frozen Yogurt" and the participant were asked to provide 5-point Likert response that ranged from highly relevant to highly irrelevant.

In the writing task, participants received two lists of information about two imaginary restaurants. Each list included restaurant's name, location and cuisine, as well as the qualities of decor, food, and service (*e.g.*, "Neighborhood is Palo Alto", "Service is mediocre."). The participants were asked to generate a fluent description that compares the two restaurants. All the tasks were posted on AMT. We compensated the participants with $0.05-0.10 per task (in addition to the $20 session pay). In addition to *in-situ* observation, we report the time they took to complete each task as a proxy of how hard the tasks were for the participants.

4.2.2 Result

The participants spent 28 seconds to 21.6 minutes to complete the types of the tasks that we prepared (Table 3).

Image Classification. Image classification tasks took the least amount of time for P1 and P2, but P3 took longer than the others. While P2 had no problem, P1 and P3 required guidance in answering the questions; the researcher needed to prompt for an answer to each question (*e.g.*, asking "is this a picture of soccer game?"). P3 also had challenge in providing accurate classifications. He had tendency to answer "yes" to all the classification questions. Note that he knew the correct answer, but the answer was not correctly registered. For example, for one question with a picture of people playing soccer that asked "is this a picture of people playing baseball?" P2 correctly said it is soccer, but he still selected "yes" for the answer.

	Image Classification	Image Description	Image Transcription	Survey	Writing
P1	1.72	3.68	10.75	7.40	21.62
P2	0.47	0.73	2.63	1.08	7.95
P3	6.17	3.40	19.87	3.72	10.88

Table 3. Task completion time (min) for each task category. The participants finished classification and description tasks relatively quickly. P1 and P3 took long time to complete transcription and writing tasks.

Image Description. The image description task took a moderate amount of time for the participants. All participants provided accurate descriptions for the pictures. Like in the image classification task, the researcher needed to initiate each question for P1 and P3 by asking "what is in the next image?"

Image Transcription. P2 completed the image transcription without guidance, but P1 and P3 struggled to initiate transcription, like in previous tasks. P1 and P3 took a long time to complete the task because searching for the right information in the images was hard. In the name card transcription, for instance, the researcher needed to provide step-by-step guidance like "is the company name on the image?", "where do you see it?", "what is the company name?", and "can you transcribe that?"

Survey. P1 and P3 struggled to complete the task. It seemed that the task was more taxing for P1; he took two times longer than P3 to complete it and four times more than the time he spent on image classification. P2 had no problem completing the task.

Writing. The writing task took the most time for P1 and P2. It took a significant amount of time for P3, too. Constructing natural sentences while using the given lists of information seemed taxing for the participants. The generated text were also not fluent. For example, P3 wrote *"restaurant are lemongrass and benjarong in palo alto. cuisine is thai. decor is excellent. food quality is excellent. service is mediocre and good,"* which is almost an exact copy of the information provided on the lists.

4.2.3 Week 2 Summary

The abilities to complete the tasks varied across the participants; P2 could perform most of the tasks that we prepared, but P1 and P3 struggled. The participants could perform image description and survey tasks although P1 and P3 needed help starting to answer. Image classification could be performed relatively easily by all, but P3 had a unique challenge in registering what he observed in the given picture to the yes/no answer. This could mean that he was fixated on answering "yes" to all the questions, he did not understand the question, or both.

The tasks that required too much information processing seemed to be hard. All participants struggled to perform the writing task. It seemed challenging to keep the given list of information in short-term memory and synthesize it to generate text. This observation could be explained by the current understanding of executive dysfunction in people ASD. That is, writing tasks such as what we administered tax working memory [28].

In the image transcription task, reading and transcribing seemed doable for our participants, but finding the right information on the image seemed hard for P1 and P3. It is not clear, however, whether this is the side-effect of executive dysfunction (*i.e.*, challenge to plan and systematically search for the information to

Figure 2. The task interfaces for Week 3. (a) *Survey control*: 10 questions from AQ were listed on a single page. (b) *Survey mini*: 10 questions from AQ were administered one-by-one to the participant. (c) *Transcription control*: we asked the participant to provide business name, transaction date, and total amount of payment for each receipt in a single page. (d) *Text detection*: the participant used the interface to draw a bounding box around the target information like business name. (e) *Transcription mini*: The participants were asked to transcribe what was on the cropped image of the receipts.

transcribe) or visual attention bias. Since P2 seems to be unaffected, we think it is not common across all people with ASD.

4.3 Week 3: Task Completion Efficacy 2

Given the results from Week 2, we decided to further investigate whether our participants could perform image transcription tasks. We also investigated the performance on the survey task as it was not clear how well our participants performed on these tasks. We also decided to administer these tasks due to their increasing prevalence on AMT [12, 38]. Overall, the sessions with P1, P2, and P3 took 62, 37, and 59 minutes respectively.

4.3.1 Method

In addition to assessing our participants' ability to work on image transcription and survey tasks, we also investigated the potential effect of task simplification. Both survey and transcription tasks had control and simplified interface conditions. We measured accuracy and task completion time.

Survey. We used questions from the Autism-Spectrum Quotient (AQ) [3]. AQ was used primarily because of its tested internal consistency of the survey items and secondarily because we wanted to see how our participants respond to the questions. We had two conditions: *control* interface that has the questions in a single page (Figure 2a) and a simplified *mini* interface where the questions were served one-by-one. Each condition had a set of 10 questions. Each set took a pair of two questions from the five different areas of constructs in the AQ—social skill, attention switching, attention detail, communication, and imagination—and each pair consisted one "agree" response and "disagree" response [3]. This was done to test the repeatability.

Image Transcription. In preparing the image transcription tasks, we downloaded images from receipt transcription HITs that were available on AMT. The task involved transcribing business names, transaction dates, and total transaction amounts from 10 receipts. We tested two methods: (i) a *control transcription* condition in which we showed the image transcription interface that replicated the original HIT (Figure 2c), and (ii) a simplified *mini transcription* condition where the participants were asked to transcribe string in each image where the target area was cropped (Figure 2e). The mini transcription condition therefore reduced the burden of searching for the right information to transcribe. In

	Survey Control	Survey Mini	Transcription Control	Transcription Mini	Text Detection
P1	0.6 (3/5)	0.0 (0/5)	1.0 (30/30)	1.0 (30/30)	1.0 (30/30)
P2	0.2 (1/5)	0.2 (1/5)	0.9 (27/30)	0.97 (29/30)	0.77 (23/30)
P3	0.2 (1/5)	0.0 (0/5)	0.8 (24/30)	1.0 (30/30)	0.8 (24/30)

Table 4. Task accuracy for the Week 3 survey tasks and transcription tasks. For survey control and mini conditions, we used repeatability as a proxy for the accuracy.

addition, we asked them to work on *text detection* in which we asked them to draw bounding box around the target information (Figure 2d). Our goal was to see the time cost and the accuracy of visual search. For each condition, there were two practice tasks.

Measures. For image transcription tasks, we measured task completion time and accuracy. Transcribed strings were compared to researcher-prepared ground truth transcription to measure the accuracy. Special characters (*e.g.*, '$') were omitted from the analysis and the date format was disregarded (*e.g.*, "Mar 29 '17" and "29 03 2017" were treated as same). Accuracy for the bounding boxes in text detection tasks were visually assessed by a researcher. Because transcribing three items (business name, transaction date, and transaction amount) were split in the *mini transcription* and *text detection*, we added the time in each triplet to compare with the *control* condition. Similarly, we measured task completion time and accuracy for the survey tasks. Because there is no "correct" answer for surveys in general, we use the repeatability as a proxy for accuracy. Repeatability was measured by counting agreements of responses to the items in the same construct (*e.g.*, items "I find social situations easy" and "I would rather go to a library than a party" are in the same construct *social skill* that have opposite polarity). For example, if responses in 3 out of 5 constructs agree, then the overall agreement is 60%.

4.3.2 Accuracy

Survey. The repeatability measures were 0.6, 0.2, and 0.2 for the *control* tasks and 0, 0.2, 0 for *mini* tasks for P1, P2, and P3 respectively (Table 4). The responses from P2 and P3 had low repeatability in both conditions. Interestingly, the response from P1 had lower repeatability in the *mini* condition. The researcher who observed the session noted that P1 seemed to be fixated on choosing the same answer on the *mini* condition rather than reading and answering the questions.

Transcription. P1, P2, and P3 transcribed the images with 100%, 90%, and 80% accuracy in the *control* condition and 100%, 97%, and 100% in the *mini* condition (Table 4). P1 transcribed text perfectly in both conditions. P2 made typos when entering total transaction amount, which seemed more prevalent in *control* interface. P3 made 6 errors, of which 5 were mistakes where he entered addresses of the businesses instead of the business names. To compare the transcription accuracies between *control* and *mini*, we used generalized linear mixed model (GLMM) [4]. We used GLMM instead of the oft-used repeated-measures ANOVA to incorporate the random effect (*i.e.*, subject variability). As the responses were binary (correct/incorrect), we used a logit link function. We had interface (*i.e.*, *control vs. mini*) as the main effect, and we had the intercepts for the participants as the random effect. There was a significant main effect of the interface ($\chi^2(1, N{=}180){=}7.9$; $p{<}0.01$), showing that simplifying tasks had a significant positive effect on the accuracy of the task.

Text detection accuracies varied across participants. P1 performed the task perfectly, but P2 and P3 made some mistakes (Table 4). The source of P2's errors were bounding boxes that contained not only the target information like business name, but also other things like business addresses.

4.3.3 Task Completion Time

Survey. On average, P1, P2, and P3 took 21.6, 4.5, and 23.1 seconds to answer items in the survey *control* condition, and 11.7, 5.3, and 15.3 seconds to complete in the survey *mini* condition. Figure 3 shows that P1 and P3 took less time to answer questions on the *mini* condition, but it seems that there was a limited effect for P2. To test the significance, we used a linear mixed model (LMM). Like the accuracy analysis, we had *interface* as the main effect and *participants* as the random effect. We observed the significant main effect of the interface type ($\chi^2(1, N{=}60){=}9.65$; $p{<}0.01$). This shows that simplifying the survey task made task completion significantly faster. Note, however, the speed up may be due to P1 getting fixated on repeating (*i.e.*, not reading and comprehending the questions) rather than task simplification.

Transcription. On average, P1, P2, and P3 took 64.9, 27.4, and 57.6 seconds to transcribe a receipt in the *control* condition, 45.4, 24.6, and 37.0 seconds in the *mini* condition. Text detection took 90.2, 41.4, and 74.6 seconds on average. Looking at Figure 3, participants, especially P1 and P3, seem to have transcribed images faster in the *mini* condition compared to the *control* condition. We used LMM to test the significance of the effect of interfaces. We observed a significant main effect of interface ($\chi^2(1, N{=}60){=}21.2$; $p{<}0.001$). This shows that removing the visual search component of the transcription task significantly reduces the task completion time. Note, however, making mini interface requires text to be detected and cropped (Figure 3). When our participants worked on text detection, it took significantly longer time than the *control* transcription ($\chi^2(1, N{=}60){=}17.6$; $p{<}0.001$) due to the added cost of the image cropping interaction.

4.3.4 Week 3 Summary

The participants finished survey tasks faster due to task simplification. However, breaking the survey into smaller pieces had an unexpected negative impact on the participants' response quality. For instance, P1 selected "slightly agree" repeatedly to all the questions in the *mini* condition. We asked why he chose the same answer for every question, but he could not articulate the reason. The speed-quality tradeoff makes it unclear whether it is

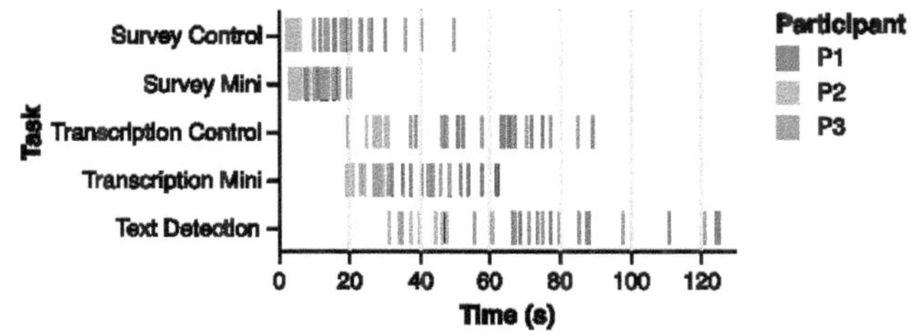

Figure 3. The strip plot of task completion time by each participant. The x-axis is completion time in seconds and y-axis is the category of the task.

beneficial to break down the survey only to make it easier for the participants with ASD. While we believe the low repeatability was because of the participants' limited abilities to comprehend the survey questions, we cannot strongly argue this was not dues to the insufficient internal consistency of the survey questions as we used a subset of the items in AQ (instead of the original AQ).

We observed a significant positive effect of task simplification on both quality and speed for image transcription. The improvement in the task speed is likely due to the reduced burden on searching for relevant information to transcribe. We were somewhat surprised to see the positive effect on the transcription accuracy for P2 and P3. Reduced task complexity that allowed people to focus on what to transcribe may have influenced the accuracy. However, this could also be a learning effect as the *mini* condition was administered after the *control* condition.

Reducing task complexity itself takes time. For example, *text detection* alone took significantly longer than *transcription control*. Note that breaking tasks down into smaller pieces has the added benefit of giving more flexibility on how to split the task between workers. Thus, for example, those who can detect text could work on text detection, and those who are good at transcribing could focus on text transcription. *Subcontracting microwork* [31] could facilitate the process. Future work should further investigate the cost-benefit tradeoff of task simplification.

4.4 Week 4: Task Search Behavior

We observed that searching for HITs introduced added interaction complexity and reduced the productivity of P1. To further investigate how our participants search and explore HITs, we asked them to search for image transcription tasks using the AMT interface and observed their behaviors.

4.4.1 Method

We asked our participants to find image transcription tasks using the AMT's default search interface. We presented the top page of the AMT's worker page, then asked them to use the keyword "transcribe" to find image transcription tasks using the AMT interface. We asked them to complete five transcription tasks.

Measures. In addition to the *in-situ* observation, we counted the number of the tasks they completed during the approximately hour-long session, the number of times that they opened the non-image transcription tasks (*e.g.*, audio/video transcription tasks), how long it took to find the task to work on, and how long it took to complete each task. We did not measure transcription accuracy because the tasks differed across the participants.

4.4.2 Result

Our participants spent, on average, 9.9% of their time on the task search. P1, P2, and P3 completed 2, 5, and 4 tasks respectively.

P1: During the 68.2 minutes session, P1 found and completed two image transcription tasks. He spent 5.9 minutes for task search—8.6% of the session. Finding HITs to work on required support from the researchers as the participant could not figure out how to

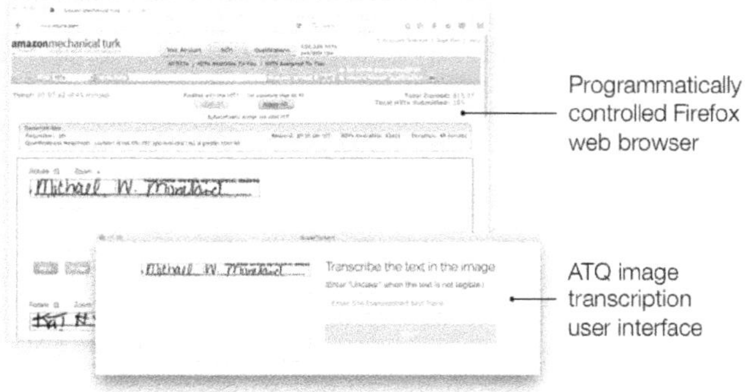

Figure 4. The ATQ prototype. The system has a custom desktop UI for image transcription, a programmatically controlled Firefox web browser, and a Selenium browser automation tool that runs on the background.

navigate AMT's search interface. Completing two tasks took more than an hour. The tasks that he worked on involved transcribing scanned images of hand written text. Decoding unclear handwriting seemed more challenging compared to transcribing printed texts in receipts or business cards (which he did in Week 2 and 3). P1 often got stuck when he could not read unclear text and the researcher intervened. For example, the researcher instructed to enter "unclear" if the text is not legible.

P2: P2 found and completed 5 transcription tasks in 20.1 minutes. He spent 1.3 minutes for searching the tasks (6.4% of the time to complete 5 transcription tasks). For both task search and working on image transcription, he did not require help from the researcher.

P3: P3 completed 4 transcription tasks in 59 minutes. He spent 8.6 minutes searching for the tasks and 50.2 minutes for completing the HITs. Task search took 14.6% of the session. While searching for the image transcription tasks, he opened two audio transcription tasks. Because he did not know how to go back and search for image transcription tasks, the researcher intervened and instructed how to resume the search. While working on HITs, P3 did not get stuck but often made errors.

4.4.3 Week 4 Summary

The observations from Week 4 revealed that our participants spent a non-negligible amount of time looking for HITs. For example, while searching for a task to work on, P3 clicked and opened two audio transcription tasks. Because the goal was to find and work on image transcription tasks, we asked him to search for another task in those cases. Note, while this restriction was artificial (*i.e.*, he may be able to work on audio transcription), it is not unrealistic that he will encounter many tasks that he cannot perform if he were to freely use AMT. It appears crucial to reduce worker task search time, which is unpaid work.

Our findings from Week 1 to 4 pointed to two potential research directions. First, because abilities of people with ASD and skills required to perform certain HITs both vary widely, it seems that technologies that match people and tasks based on both of these features seem helpful. Second, we believe technologies that semi-automatically simplify searching and working on micro-tasks will improve the productivity of people with ASD. In the rest of the paper, we focus on the latter and leave the former as future work.

4.5 Assistive Task Queue

We designed and developed a prototype Assistive Task Queue (ATQ) that simplifies working on image transcription micro-tasks for our participants with ASD. ATQ was developed with three design principles: (i) provide tasks that can be performed by the participants with ASD, (ii) remove the complexity of searching for HITs, and (iii) breaking a large task into smaller pieces that are more digestible for the participants with ASD.

First, given the limited abilities of our participants with ASD to perform AMT tasks, feeding them the tasks that they can perform is likely important for them to successfully complete the HITs. Based on our findings from Week 1 to 4, we believe that tasks that do not tax working memory and executive function in general would be good candidates for our participants. For example, image description, image classification, and image transcription that relies more on perception and less on comprehension and synthesis of ideas seem more feasible. This observation and the popularity of image transcription tasks on AMT [12] made us to focus on designing tools to facilitate image transcription tasks.

Second, we design ATQ to reduce the time for task search. ATQ automatically crawls, finds, and accepts image transcription tasks on behalf of its user. Third, ATQ breaks down the web interface of an image transcription HIT into smaller pieces and feeds them one-by-one to its user.

We use the following components to implement the prototype ATQ: the custom desktop transcription UI developed with HTML, CSS, and JavaScript, Firefox web browser, and Selenium browser automation tool (Figure 4; Video Figure). When the user opens the ATQ, Selenium requests the browser to search for a list of available image transcription HITs on AMT using predefined search queries. Once HITs appear on the browser window, Selenium parses the HIT titles and match them with predefined titles of image transcription tasks. The first task that matches gets programmatically accepted. Once the HTML content of the accepted HIT appears on the browser window, the content gets sent to the transcription interface by Selenium and it gets parsed. We use a predefined pattern for each HIT to parse its HTML.

Based on the parsed information, the image transcription interface shows an image to transcribe as well as the input field. One image is presented at a time. The transcription interface then prompts the user to transcribe the shown image like what the original interface asks the user to do. Once the user types in the information to the input field and click "Next" or hit enter, the transcribed information is sent to the Firefox browser and fills the corresponding input field on the original HIT. Once all the input fields were entered, the HIT was automatically submitted.

4.6 Week 5: ATQ Evaluation

We evaluated the usability with the three participants to investigate the utility of ATQ. Overall, the sessions with P1, P2, and P3 took 48, 31, and 44 minutes.

4.6.1 Method

Procedure. The participants were asked to work on transcribing text from a series of scanned images, each containing a line of hand written text (Figure 4). There were two conditions: the *control* condition that used the original interface that was posted on AMT and the *ATQ* condition. We downloaded the image transcription tasks posted by a requester *p9r* and re-posted them as our tasks. This was necessary to administer the same images across the participants. In both conditions, the participants were asked to transcribe twelve practice images and twenty images. The images included strings like names, email addresses, and medical conditions. The tasks were served in the following order: practice control task, control task, practice ATQ task, and ATQ task. At the beginning of each task, we instructed the participant to start transcribing the image. We measured the time for transcribing each image. Once a participant started a task, we intervened as little as possible, but if he was stuck for more than

	Transcription Accuracy					
	Control (N=20)			ATQ (N=20)		
	Correct	Incorrect	Unclear	Correct	Incorrect	Unclear
P1	9	3	8	17	3	0
P2	17	3	0	16	2	2
P3	12	8	0	14	6	0

Table 5. The numbers of correct/incorrect transcription responses. Unclear indicates how many times the participant noted the text is not legible.

10 seconds, we gave instructions (*e.g.*, we told to type "unclear" and move on when the text on an image was not clear).

Measures. In addition to in-situ observation, we looked into the transcription accuracies and interaction intervals. A member of the research team transcribed all the images and matched them with the participants' transcripts to assess the accuracy. Up to two character typos were forgiven. Interaction intervals (*e.g.*, how long each participant spent typing) and total task completion time were measured from the screen recording.

4.6.2 Accuracy

P1, P2, and P3 transcribed 9, 17, and 12 out of 20 images correctly in the *control* condition, and 17, 16, and 14 out of 20 correctly in the *ATQ* condition. P1 and P3 transcribed text more accurately using ATQ, while P2 performed equally correctly in the both conditions (Table 5). We used GLMM with a logit link function to assess the significance. We had *interface* as the main effect. We had a random intercept for participants. We did not observe a significant main effect of interface, but there was a possible trend ($\chi^2(1, N=120)=3.74$; $p=0.053<0.1$). This suggests that more work is needed to investigate whether the interface condition affected the transcription accuracy.

4.6.3 Task Completion Time.

P1, P2, and P3 took 13.2, 4.9, and 9.5 minutes respectively to complete the task on the *control* condition. All participants finished the task faster in the *ATQ* condition; P1, P2, and P3 took 10.0, 3.4, and 8.8 minutes respectively (Figure 5; Table 6). We used LMM to evaluate the significance of the difference between the conditions. We had *interface* as the main effect and *participant* as the random effect. A significant main effect of *interface* was observed ($\chi^2(1, N=120)=4.02$; $p<0.05$). Faster task completion time in the *ATQ* condition was not due to the faster typing speed, but because of the reduced interaction complexity. For example, ATQ condition did not require the participant to scroll the browser window to move to the next transcription image.

P1: P1 required more interventions than the others during the control task; the researcher suggested to enter "unclear" when he was stuck and paused for more than 10 seconds. We intervened 8 times in the control condition. He also made consistent mistakes on transcribing email addresses, where he usually skipped what was after "@". He consistently substituted special characters like "-" with spaces.

P2: P2 completed the tasks in the both conditions without problems (except for some typos), thus we did not intervene. He told us that ATQ condition "made the task more competitive," probably because it gave more game-like feeling (*e.g.*, task images showed up one after the other quickly).

P3: P3 completed all the task both in AMT interface and ATQ without any interventions. He made some errors in transcription.

4.6.4 Week 5 Summary

We evaluated the utility of ATQ to support our participants with ASD on image transcription. We observed a significant improvement in task completion time due to reduced interaction

	Transcription Task Completion Time (minutes)					
	Control			ATQ		
	Overall	Typing	Other	Overall	Typing	Other
P1	13.2	10.7	2.5	10	8.2	1.8
P2	4.9	3.3	1.6	3.4	2.9	0.5
P3	9.5	8.1	1.4	8.8	7.6	1.2

Table 6. Task completion time. Both conditions (*control* and *ATQ*) involved transcribing 20 images of text.

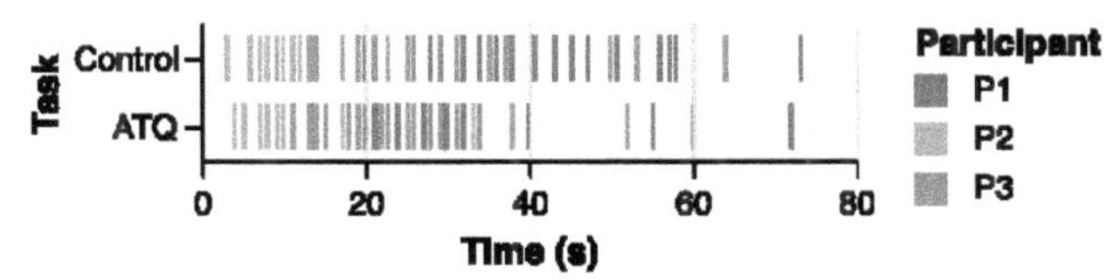

Figure 5. A strip plot of time spent on transcribing each image. P1 and P3 took longer to complete transcription in the *control* condition.

I would be interested in crowd work because I could	P1	P2	P3
earn money	5	5	4
do something interesting or fun	5	4	4
do something that's stimulating or challenging	5	4	4
learn new skills	4	5	4
feel like I'm contributing to the society	4	4	5
help other people on their projects	4	5	4
participate with family and friends	4	4	5
work without interpersonal communication	4	4	4
work anonymously	3	4	5
work remotely at anywhere I want	4	4	4
work at anytime.	4	4	5

Table 7. Participants' motivation for working on crowdsourcing in the future. The responses were measured during the exit interview. The scale ranged from 1 (strongly disagree) to 5 (strongly agree).

complexity. We also note that this speed up is in addition to the benefit of reducing the task search time that ATQ automatically takes care of. There was no significant main effect of interface type to transcription accuracy.

We also identified potential improvements that we could make to ATQ. For example, we could build task dependent instruction to reduce some systematic errors. For example, we may be able to prevent a user from forgetting to transcribe domain names in email addresses by prompting them to transcribe the entire text in the image. Limitations of the prototype are: it focused on searching and parsing predefined tasks on the market. The researcher programmed what tasks to search and how to parse the task, which will not scale in the real-life setting. Future work should investigate potential methods to populate variety of tasks that can be fed into ATQ.

4.7 Week 6: Exit Interview

We conducted exit interviews with our participants. We investigated if their motivation to work on crowdsourcing changed over the period of this study. The sessions took 32, 18, and 27 minutes for P1, P2, and P3 respectively.

Method. We conducted a structured interview. The same set of questions from the interview in Week 1 were used, but were phrased to ask if participants are interested in working on AMT after working on the crowd work during the study. We also asked questions like "are you satisfied with what you made by working on AMT tasks," "how much time do you want to spend on crowd work per week," and "do you use AMT outside of the study?"

Result. Overall, our participants were motivated to work on AMT in the future (Table 7). This did not seem to change significantly from Week 1 (Table 1). P1, P2, and P3 made \$1.17, \$3.00, and

$1.03 by completing HITs over the study sessions. P1 and P2 told us they would like to make more than what they earned. For example, P1 noted that he would like to make minimum wage. None of our participants used AMT outside of the study. P1 and P2 were still going through the process of making their own accounts, which took a long time because Amazon requested personal information to set up the payment accounts, which meant our research partner had to help them make their AMT accounts. P3 created his own AMT account, but he did not use it.

5. Discussion

All of our participants with ASD were able to successfully work on Amazon Mechanical Turk. The tasks that each individual could best perform varied between people, depending in part on the how their ASD and other disabilities manifest. This research was motivated by the premise that the crowdsourcing could provide people with ASD an alternative option for work environment. Crowd work seems to have traits that may benefit this population. For example, interaction difficulties associated with ASD that account for the biggest vocational impact [15] could be mitigated by the non-verbal nature of online crowd work. This aligns with the findings from prior work [5, 27] that reported people with ASD felt more control in social communication over textual media (*e.g.,* chat and forum). Although the types of tasks that can be performed by our participants varied, this study suggests that there are some micro-tasks that people with ASD can perform. Assistive tools like ATQ could improve their productivity, too.

So, *is crowd work good for people with ASD?* We are confident that it is feasible to introduce many people with ASD to crowd work given our experiences with our participants, but a few challenges need to be overcome so that we can confidently suggest them to work on this environment. The challenges include *effective job matching, scalable work guidance,* and *hourly wage*.

Worker-Job Matching. Many job options were overwhelming to our participants. As mentioned in the Week 4 summary, we believe that technologies that match people and tasks based on users' abilities and skills required to perform tasks would be helpful and necessary. Such technologies would need to: efficiently assess the abilities that the user possess; automatically tease out what skills are needed to perform certain HITs; and optimally match the user with the HITs based on the extracted information. This also aligns with prior research in ASD and the ethos of ability-based design [25, 41]. Future work includes the design, implementation, and evaluation of such mechanisms.

Scalable Work Guidance. We showed that ATQ could improve the productivity of image transcription tasks. But the current prototype relied on a predefined search query and an HTML parsing format. Future work should investigate how to scalably search and identify tasks that could be broken down. The types of work that ATQ supports should be expanded, too. This is important; although the volume of image transcription tasks that are available on AMT was high at the time of the study, the number of jobs available on the market could diminish.

Low Hourly Wage. The low hourly wage of crowd work has been discussed extensively in the prior work [18, 26]. It is difficult to earn the U.S. minimum wage currently on AMT. For example, Horton and Chilton reported that median wage is $1.38 per hour [18], only a fraction of the U.S. federal minimum wage ($7.25). The problem would be exacerbated for our participants, who performed tasks more slowly than workers without ASD. That said, experts on AMT claim hourly wages of over $10; tools that make workers for efficient may help workers in general.

6. Limitations

A limitation of our work is that only three people with ASD participated, with the tradeoff that participants were observed over multiple sessions. Opportunities for future work include a larger user study with people with ASD. We solely focused on the capacity of people with ASD to perform crowd work and did not explore the roles that caregivers could play. We plan to explore how they could support people with ASD to perform micro-tasks. Our participants had comorbidity (*e.g.,* intellectual disability, ADHD). This may have affected our observations and make it hard for us to argue all the findings are due to ASD. Nevertheless, studying this population is important as comorbidity is common in people with ASD (*e.g.,* the CDC estimates that 56% of children with ASD have below average intellectual abilities [2]). We did not exhaustively test the types of the micro-tasks available on AMT. The tasks were often selected by the researchers and not by the participants. This was necessary for the in-lab studies. More work is needed to explore what types of tasks they can best perform.

7. Conclusion

We conducted an iterative user-centered design study to investigate the challenges and opportunities in introducing people with ASD to crowdsourcing work environment. The process was central to understanding the abilities of people with ASD to perform crowd work and simultaneously design technology to support the target population. We found that our three participants had varying levels of abilities to work on micro-tasks. We believe that the tasks such as image description and image transcription that do not tax their executive function are easier for them to perform, while highly cognitive tasks like writing pose challenges. This work qualitatively and quantitatively showed that our participants with ASD could perform crowd work and they benefited from simplification and guidance of micro-tasks. Based on the findings, we designed and evaluated an assistive tool to improve the productivity of people with ASD to perform image transcription, a task type prevalent on crowdsourcing market.

8. ACKNOWLEDGMENTS

We thank Sarah Lehman for her feedback. We also thank Liz Carter and Jill Lehman for their advice in structuring our research. This work was developed under grants from the National Institute on Disability, Independent Living, and Rehabilitation Research (NIDILRR grant numbers 90DP00610100 and H133E140039).

9. REFERENCES

[1] Autism Costs More Than $2 Million Over Patient's Life: 2014. *https://www.bloomberg.com/news/articles/2014-06-09/autism-costs-more-than-2-million-over-patient-s-life.*

[2] Autism Spectrum Disorder - Data & Statistics: Prevalence: 2016. *https://www.cdc.gov/ncbddd/autism/data.html.*

[3] Baron-Cohen, S., Wheelwright, S., Skinner, R., Martin, J. and Clubley, E. 2001. The Autism-Spectrum Quotient (AQ): Evidence from Asperger Syndrome/High-Functioning Autism, Malesand Females, Scientists and Mathematicians. *Journal of Autism and Developmental Disorders.*

[4] Bates, D., Maechler, M., Bolker, B., Walker, S. and others 2014. *lme4: Linear mixed-effects models using Eigen and S4.*

[5] Benford, P. and Standen, P. 2009. The internet: a comfortable communication medium for people with Asperger syndrome (AS) and high functioning autism (HFA)? *Journal of Assistive Technologies.*

[6] Brault, M.W. 2012. *Americans With Disabilities: 2010, Household Economics Studies.*

[7] Brewer, R., Morris, M.R. and Piper, A.M. 2016. "Why Would

Anybody Do This?": Understanding Older Adults' Motivations and Challenges in Crowd Work. *Proceedings of the 2016 CHI Conference on Human Factors in Computing Systems*.

[8] Buescher, A.V.S., Cidav, Z., Knapp, M. and Mandell, D.S. 2014. Costs of autism spectrum disorders in the united kingdom and the united states. *JAMA Pediatrics*.

[9] Burke, M., Kraut, R. and Williams, D. 2010. Social Use of Computer-mediated Communication by Adults on the Autism Spectrum. *Proceedings of the 2010 ACM Conference on Computer Supported Cooperative Work*.

[10] Burt, D.B., Fuller, S.P. and Lewis, K.R. 1991. Brief report: Competitive employment of adults with autism. *Journal of Autism and Developmental Disorders*.

[11] Cullum, P.M. and Ennis-Cole, D. 2014. Preparing adults with autism spectrum disorders for employment. *Online Journal for Workforce Education and Development*.

[12] Difallah, D.E., Catasta, M., Demartini, G., Ipeirotis, P.G. and Cudré-Mauroux, P. 2015. The Dynamics of Micro-Task Crowdsourcing: The Case of Amazon MTurk. *Proceedings of the 24th International Conference on World Wide Web*.

[13] Hayes, G.R., Gardere, L.M., Abowd, G.D. and Truong, K.N. 2008. CareLog: A Selective Archiving Tool for Behavior Management in Schools. *Proceedings of the SIGCHI Conference on Human Factors in Computing Systems*.

[14] Hedley, D., Uljarević, M., Cameron, L., Halder, S., Richdale, A. and Dissanayake, C. 2016. Employment programmes and interventions targeting adults with autism spectrum disorder: A systematic review of the literature. *Autism*.

[15] Hendricks, D. 2010. Employment and adults with autism spectrum disorders: Challenges and strategies for success. *Journal of Vocational Rehabilitation*.

[16] Hillier, A., Campbell, H., Mastriani, K., Izzo, M.V., Kool-Tucker, A.K., Cherry, L. and Beversdorf, D.Q. 2007. Two-Year Evaluation of a Vocational Support Program for Adults on the Autism Spectrum. *Career Development for Exceptional Individuals*.

[17] Hong, H., Kim, J.G., Abowd, G.D. and Arriaga, R.I. 2012. Designing a Social Network to Support the Independence of Young Adults with Autism. *Proceedings of the ACM 2012 Conference on Computer Supported Cooperative Work*.

[18] Horton, J.J. and Chilton, L.B. 2010. The Labor Economics of Paid Crowdsourcing. *Proceedings of the 11th ACM Conference on Electronic Commerce*.

[19] Howlin, P., Goode, S., Hutton, J. and Rutter, M. 2004. Adult outcome for children with autism. *Journal of Child Psychology and Psychiatry*.

[20] Keel, J.H., Mesibov, G.B. and Woods, A. V 1997. TEACCH-Supported Employment Program. *Journal of Autism and Developmental Disorders*.

[21] Kientz, J.A., Goodwin, M.S., Hayes, G.R. and Abowd, G.D. 2013. Interactive Technologies for Autism. *Synthesis Lectures on Assistive, Rehabilitative, and Health-Preserving Technologies*.

[22] Kim, J.A., Szatmari, P., Bryson, S.E., Streiner, D.L. and Wilson, F.J. 2000. The Prevalence of Anxiety and Mood Problems among Children with Autism and Asperger Syndrome. *Autism*.

[23] Leigh, J.P. and Du, J. 2015. Brief Report: Forecasting the Economic Burden of Autism in 2015 and 2025 in the United States. *Journal of Autism and Developmental Disorders*.

[24] Lindgren, S. and Doobay, A. 2011. *Evidence-based interventions for autism spectrum disorders*.

[25] Madsen, M., el Kaliouby, R., Goodwin, M. and Picard, R. 2008. Technology for Just-in-time In-situ Learning of Facial Affect for Persons Diagnosed with an Autism Spectrum Disorder. *Proceedings of the 10th International ACM SIGACCESS Conference on Computers and Accessibility*

[26] Martin, D., Hanrahan, B. V, O'Neill, J. and Gupta, N. 2014. Being a Turker. *Proceedings of the 17th ACM Conference on Computer Supported Cooperative Work and Social Computing*.

[27] Mazurek, M.O. 2013. Social media use among adults with autism spectrum disorders. *Computers in Human Behavior*.

[28] McCutchen, D. 2000. Knowledge, Processing, and Working Memory: Implications for a Theory of Writing. *Educational Psychologist*.

[29] Moffatt, K., McGrenere, J., Purves, B. and Klawe, M. 2004. The Participatory Design of a Sound and Image Enhanced Daily Planner for People with Aphasia. *Proceedings of the SIGCHI Conference on Human Factors in Computing Systems*

[30] Morris, M.R., Begel, A. and Wiedermann, B. 2015. Understanding the Challenges Faced by Neurodiverse Software Engineering Employees: Towards a More Inclusive and Productive Technical Workforce. *Proceedings of the 17th International ACM SIGACCESS Conference on Computers and Accessibility*

[31] Morris, M.R., Bigham, J.P., Brewer, R., Bragg, J., Kulkarni, A., Li, J., Savage, S. and Savage, S. 2017. Subcontracting Microwork. *Proceedings of the SIGCHI Conference on Human Factors in Computing Systems*

[32] Patterson, A. and Rafferty, A. 2001. Making It to Work: Towards Employment For the Young Adult with Autism. *International Journal of Language & Communication Disorders*.

[33] Picard, R.W. 2009. Future affective technology for autism and emotion communication. *Philosophical Transactions of the Royal Society B: Biological Sciences*.

[34] Ringland, K.E., Wolf, C.T., Boyd, L.E., Baldwin, M.S. and Hayes, G.R. 2016. Would You Be Mine: Appropriating Minecraft As an Assistive Technology for Youth with Autism. *Proceedings of the 18th International ACM SIGACCESS Conference on Computers and Accessibility*

[35] De Rubeis, S. et al. 2014. Synaptic, transcriptional and chromatin genes disrupted in autism. *Nature*.

[36] Seltzer, M.M., Krauss, M.W., Shattuck, P.T., Orsmond, G., Swe, A. and Lord, C. 2003. The Symptoms of Autism Spectrum Disorders in Adolescence and Adulthood. *Journal of Autism and Developmental Disorders*.

[37] Spinuzzi, C. 2005. The Methodology of Participatory Design. *Technical Communication*.

[38] Swaminathan, S., Hara, K., Bigham, J.P., Swaminathan Saiganesh, H.K. and Bigham, J.P. 2017. The Crowd Work Accessibility Problem. *Proc. of the Web for All Conference*

[39] Wakefield, J.C. 2013. DSM-5: An Overview of Changes and Controversies. *Clinical Social Work Journal*.

[40] Wobbrock, J. and Myers, B. 2006. Trackball Text Entry for People with Motor Impairments. *Proceedings of the SIGCHI Conference on Human Factors in Computing Systems*

[41] Wobbrock, J.O., Kane, S.K., Gajos, K.Z., Harada, S. and Froehlich, J. 2011. Ability-Based Design: Concept, Principles and Examples. *ACM Trans. Access. Comput.*

[42] Zyskowski, K., Morris, M.R., Bigham, J.P., Gray, M.L. and Kane, S.K. 2015. Accessible Crowdwork? Understanding the Value in and Challenge of Microtask Employment for People with Disabilities. *Proc. of CSCW 2015* (2015).

Digital Strategies for Supporting Strengths- and Interests-based Learning with Children with Autism

Cara Wilson, Margot Brereton, Bernd Ploderer, Laurianne Sitbon and Beth Saggers
Queensland University of Technology
Brisbane, Australia
+61 7 3138 8365
{cara.wilson, m.brereton, b.ploderer, laurianne.sitbon, b.saggers}@qut.edu.au

ABSTRACT
Technologies to support children with autism tend to use predefined content to enhance specific skills, such as verbal communication or emotion recognition. Few mobilise the child's own (often very specific) interests, strengths and capabilities. Digital technologies offer opportunities for children to personalise learning with their own content, following their own interests and enabling their self-expression. This project sought to engage children to record and express their own interests within their contexts of support – the home and the classroom. The vehicle for self-expression was an audio-visual calendaring app called MeCalendar. Implementation was kept open-ended to allow teachers to use it in ways that best fit with their existing embedded practices. In this paper we report on how the prototype has been appropriated in two classrooms by teachers in an autism-specific school setting with children aged 6 to 7. Our contribution is an understanding of how technologies for self-expression led to enhanced verbal communication, positive reinforcement through video modelling, engagement in class tasks and enhanced social interaction. Children appropriated the design in unimagined ways, leading them to self-scaffold and to catalyse their confidence in social interaction and self-expression. Teachers played an integral role in appropriating the design in the classroom, specifically through their in-depth knowledge of each child and their individual needs, strengths and interests.

CCS Concepts
•**Human-centered computing → Accessibility technologies**
•**Human-centered computing → User centered design**

Keywords
Child-Computer Interaction; Autism; Appropriation; Classroom

1. INTRODUCTION
Individuals with autism typically have challenges in a number of areas, often described as the presence of both impaired social communication and interaction, as well as restricted, repetitive patterns of behaviours, interests or activities [1]. However, and as highlighted in the recently revised Diagnostic and Statistical Manual of Mental Disorders – Fifth Edition (DSM-5[1]), children on the spectrum are an extremely heterogeneous group and express these criteria in very different, eclectic ways [29]. It is important to note that there is much debate around the terminology used to describe autism. Kenny et al. [27] discuss that there continues to be divided preference on whether person-first language (i.e. "a person with autism") or identity-first language (i.e. "an autistic person") should be used. The term Autism Spectrum Disorder (ASD) has been criticised for being deficit-focussed, i.e. centring on the disabilities, not the abilities, of people on the spectrum and for being so inclusive as to trivialise the issues of some forms of autism [27]. Thus, we see that the debate here is complex. Here we use the person-centred term "child with autism" as it is most commonly used in the community of our study participants, where children are still developing their identities.

While we are witnessing both an increase in technologies to support children with autism, and the inclusion of developmentally diverse children in the design process [8], technology to support children with autism is often limited to predefined content to enhance particular skills. It is common to see scripted scenarios to teach topics such as emotion recognition [26], social skills for specific situations [22, 23], or specific behaviours [39]. While such technologies have demonstrated efficacy, in our research we sought to approach learning from a different perspective, asking how we can begin by building on the children's own interests, competences and motivations, expressed through their daily activities.

In summary, we investigated how to empower children with autism by supporting them to document and communicate their own interests and competencies using technology. We examined how both teachers and children appropriated and used the technology. We also observed other classroom support mechanisms employed by teachers and how they integrated the new technology into their practices. We present several considerations when designing supportive technology for and with children with autism.

The study utilised an open-ended implementation of our prototype, an audio-visual calendaring app named MeCalendar [10], which enabled children and their teachers and caregivers to document activities of interest to them on a daily basis. We aimed to explore how both children and teachers appropriated this technology in the classroom and further, to understand how this supported children's interests and competencies.

Our contribution is an understanding of how children's communication and engagement improves when they are supported to communicate about their own interests through flexible design prototypes. Children appropriated the design in unimagined ways, leading them to self-scaffold and to catalyse

ASSETS '17, October 29-November 1, 2017, Baltimore, MD, USA

ACM 978-1-4503-4926-0/17/10…$15.00
https://doi.org/10.1145/3132525.3132553

their confidence in communicating. Teachers also played an integral role in appropriating the design in the classroom, specifically through their in-depth knowledge of each child and their needs.

2. RELATED WORK

2.1 Autism and Technology

Research at the intersection of autism and HCI has led to increasing development of technologies which aim to support various aspects of autism [4]. Technologies designed to support children with autism have included; interactive environments to support movement and gesture [28], mobile technologies to encourage play and social interaction [24, 5] and learning through touch-based games [6]. These technologies aim to enhance self-expression and some encourage activities children enjoy in order to enhance specific abilities or skills [22, 23].

Assistive Technology has emerged as the dominant design approach when working with developmentally diverse groups, the underlying goal being to create technology that increases, maintains, or improves functional capabilities of individuals with disabilities [30]. However, in line with Frauenberger et al. [19], we believe it may be time to think *beyond assistance and intervention,* in designing with and for those with autism, and towards a more holistic approach which supports individuals towards self-expression and self-empowerment. There is increasing discussion on the importance of ability-based design, noting that interactive technologies which adapt to users' abilities, different user skills, and changing user contexts can support ability-based design [41]. Further, the Autism Co-operative Research Centre's recent Australian Educational Needs Analysis report [33] found that technology was reported to be an effective support for learning in areas such as writing, communication needs, transition needs and socio-emotional needs, with parents and teachers reporting the use of a wide range of technological supports in both school and at home contexts. It was found that iPads were one of the most common technologies used in these contexts (ibid). In terms of classroom-specific technologies, Hourcade et al. [22] highlight, there are many commercial apps available which claim to support children with autism in the classroom, but few are empirically verified. Examples of those which are backed by research include Hirano et al. [21], who developed a digital scheduling tool, vSked, for use by the teacher in classroom settings in supporting visual scheduling. Other studies have looked into the use of visual supports [16] and motion-based activities [6] to engage students with autism in the classroom. Hourcade et al [22, 23] developed a suite of flexible apps which aimed to encourage children with autism to engage in social interactions while undertaking activities that they enjoy. Their goal here was to encourage interaction by associating it with a pleasurable activity, so that the interaction in turn became desirable. The tools were designed open-endedly, to ensure the children felt free to express themselves.

The aforementioned technologies notwithstanding, few technologies explicitly aim to foster the individual child's interests and aspirations, and find ways to help communicate these central human desires to proxies and communities. Winter-Messiers [40] discusses the importance of special interest areas (SIAs) in the enhancement of young people with autism's socia communication, emotional, sensory and fine motor skills, noting the critical need for teachers to understand and value the special interests of these students. By integrating SIAs into academic work, teachers may see the generalisation of these motivations into classwork activities, providing a forum for children to demonstrate their true abilities. This work led to the development of a strengths-based model of SIAs, which proposes that 'deficits' traditionally associated with autism, such as language, body language, social communication, emotions, sensory, and fine motor skills, consistently *diminished* when children with autism engaged with their own special interests in education contexts. As Winter-Messiers [40, p.149] succinctly puts forward: "We must see SIAs for the gold mine they are in helping our students progress toward their academic, social, emotional, communication, and behavioural goals." As Hourcade [23] points out, children's uses of technologies are as diverse as the children themselves, thus, the need for personalisation and individual focus is clear. We would add that design which provides scope for the expression and sharing of these diverse interests acknowledges the concept of children as experts in their own interests. Thus, we see the need for a tool which is flexible, both in its design and in its implementation, and which supports children's interests.

2.2 Appropriation and Open-Ended Design

Dourish [12, p.465] describes appropriation as "the process by which people adopt and adapt technologies, fitting them into their working practices". As Brereton et al. [10] note, successful appropriation depends on the ability for technologies to fit with the users' skills, values and goals. Indeed, some argue that it is part of the design process itself [11]. This leads us to the concept of scaffolding, i.e. the support given to learners to enable them to achieve objectives they would not have achieved without support [2, 4]. This is a common approach in autism education, often used to teach social behaviours [34] by providing tiers of support from core to targeted to intensive. We propose this may be extended to appropriation of digital tools with children with autism. Indeed, Kellogg and Erickson [25, p.31], in their work on appropriation and social scaffolding, suggest that, for users to appropriate technology, they must "both understand its capabilities and have scaffolding mechanisms for collectively discovering, structuring, iterating, and promulgating practices that enable the technology to become a... 'resource'". These perspectives are especially important in autism-specific contexts in which social communication and interaction is often challenging and scaffolding on the part of teachers may be required in order to enable appropriation.

We propose that open-ended technologies which afford customisation and appropriation [3] can help us move beyond assistance and intervention [19] to allow children with autism to record, express and share their interests and competencies, on a personal level. Work on autism and virtual reality by Ringland et al. [31] highlights that accessibility can be fostered through appropriation of "mainstream" or "mundane" technologies, in order to enhance user experience, emphasising the importance of flexible designs which can be customised by the user in accordance with their own interests and preferences. This allows users to more freely express their identities. Their work centres on the importance of these "DIY approaches", that is designing technologies which can be easily adopted and adapted (i.e. appropriated) by the child with autism to foster certain skills or competencies. Here, our work is similar in its intentions, but investigates appropriation in a classroom context as opposed to a virtual reality context. Sengers and Gaver [35] promote the value of staying open to design interpretation through the support of multiple meanings in design and evaluation. Further, Lucy Suchman [36] identifies the often-common incidence of

Figure 1. Screenshots from MeCalendar depicting (a) the Homepage which allows the user to choose between making a new entry, going directly to the calendar, or reviewing their tagged skills, (b) an entry by one child showing his pets with the caption 'My Guinea Pigs Bert and Cooper', and (c) the calendar view depicting all entries in a monthly layout.

discrepancy between designer assumptions and user interpretations of design in real-world situations. Suchman's concept is echoed by Frauenberger and colleagues, who discuss that "deliberately open" design briefs for supportive technologies allow for designs which are "un-imaginable to the neuro-typical adult designers" [17, p. 130]. This is particularly relevant in relation to those with developmental differences as users often appropriate technology "in ways designers do not envision, to support needs that may not have been fully understood or anticipated" [31, p33].

2.3 Relevant theories

Relevant theories from the fields of Psychology and Sociology support the notion that children's interests and social contexts merit attention. Self-Determination Theory [32] is primarily concerned with the potential of social contexts to provide experiences that satisfy people's universal needs for feelings of competence (a need for challenge and feelings of effectiveness), autonomy (a sense of willingness and volition) and relatedness (social connection with others). Satisfaction of these three needs has been shown to yield enhanced self-motivation and wellbeing.

Turning to Speech and Language therapy, we highlight the child-led approaches employed by professionals in this area. Greenspan et al. [20], for example, emphasise the importance of 'floor-time interactions' with a 'child with Sspecial needs', an approach which encourages parents to get down on the floor with their child and interact and play, following the child's interests and motivations. The Floor-Time Approach describes its four goals as the encouragement of; attention and intimacy, two-way communication, logical thought, and the expression and use of feelings and ideas. As Greenspan et al. [20, p123] highlight "through interactions, you can mobilise your child's emotions in the service of his learning" and suggest doing so through following her interests and motivations. The Hanen Centre's 'More Than Words' (MTW) approach [37] is a socio-interactionalist program developed for the parents of children with autism who also have speech and language delays. The key here is that adults can enhance the child's social participation in interaction by interpreting and responding to the child's communicative attempts as if they were intentional. This means following the child's lead to create communicative interactions around the child's interests or focus of attention. We consider these approaches and ask; how can we mobilise and support this learning through digital strategies? How can we extend these approaches to the digital sphere? We know of few studies which investigate how to extend these theories from other disciplines into a digital context. We ask: how do we take approaches beyond therapy settings and intensive one-to-one parent-child activities, to enable the child to bring their personal explorations to a shared place? Theoretically, therefore, we aim to build on child-led approaches and competency-based approaches in the digital sphere, embedding these into daily living through digital means and to answer the question: how do we use digital support for real world interactions?

3. STUDY DESIGN

The aim of this study was to explore how children with autism and their teachers appropriate the open-ended design of supportive technologies for use in classroom settings. To achieve this aim, we employed the use of an existing concrete prototype, previously developed by the research team. MeCalendar is an audio-visual calendar app for the iPad, which supports children to communicate daily personal activities through photos and videos [10]. The prototype is set up in a typical calendar layout (Fig. 1c). Children, teachers and parents are encouraged to click on the date, and select between uploading a photo or video from the device's gallery, or taking a new photo or video (Fig. 1a). These can then be annotated in the notes section and written information or audio clips about the photo or video can be added (Fig. 1b). The entry is then saved to the chosen day and can be shared between home, school, and other settings. MeCalendar was developed prior to the present study and the full details of the design evolution can be found in work by Brereton et al. [10]. The design concept grew from co-design work with teachers and parents at a special needs school. The idea of a calendar structure emerged to help children develop a sense of time as well as planning skills. The researchers' and parents' experiences of using tablet computers such as the iPad also contributed to the design concept and this ultimately led to the development of the present concrete prototype, MeCalendar.

The research draws upon best practices from established methods for engaging participants, such as Participatory Design (PD) [15] and Action Research [13], and engages with these methods in ways appropriate to the participants. We partnered with an autism-specific primary school in Brisbane, Australia, working closely with two classes of six children, aged 6-7 years old, and two class teachers, over 10 weeks. The children had varying levels of ability and verbal skills, however, we do not find it pertinent to expound these here, as this project is about supporting individual strengths, not dwelling on individual "deficits". Children were each provided with an iPad Mini 2, on which we disabled Internet access, at the teachers' request, thus the iPads were used solely for MeCalendar. Teachers were asked to use the app in any way they wished in the classroom and had complete freedom over its implementation. Design implementation was kept open-ended to allow teachers to use it in ways that best fit with their existing embedded practices and close understanding of each child. Insights into the appropriation of MeCalendar were gathered through diary data, participant observation, and interviews. Teachers were asked to reflect on their use of MeCalendar in a diary or Teacher Reflective Log. In total we spent 5 days in the classroom. Observations were recorded as field notes. Additionally, we took photos and video-recorded over 20 hours of classroom interactions involving children and teachers interacting with MeCalendar. Finally, we conducted interviews with each teacher before, during and after the school term to discuss their experiences with MeCalendar and to reflect on our observations of MeCalendar use.

Data analysis followed the process of thematic analysis [9], based on a variety of rich data: diary entries from teachers, field notes from our observations of use in classroom, transcripts from interviews with teachers, and video, audio, photo-visual and text data collected from the children's iPads. We sought to interpret the data and define the themes from the perspectives of both the teachers as well as the perspectives of the children to show whether and how the design might have empowered them to support their ways of teaching, learning, and interest-based engagement. Hence, the findings contain two sections to report on appropriation by teachers and by children. All direct quotes are from teacher interviews, where 'TA' represents Teacher A, and 'TB', Teacher B. The names of the children have been changed in line with ethical consent. While teacher opinions on the technology were explicitly gathered through interviews, understandably, explicit quotes from minimally-verbal children are not often obtained. Thus, we base our findings from the 'child-led appropriation' perspective on participant observations of the children and their use of the tool over several observation sessions. We hope to address this imbalance in future work which focuses on supporting the design contributions of minimally-verbal children with autism.

4. FINDINGS

We found that appropriation in the classroom was two-fold, comprising both teacher-led (explicit) and child-led (observed) appropriation. While teacher-led appropriation was predominantly based on learning and behavioural outcomes, child-led appropriation was based predominantly on their own interests.

Each teacher implemented the prototype in different ways, drawing attention to the nuanced and variable meta-practices at play in each teacher's classroom. This was then either built on by children and appropriated as a learning activity, or children appropriated the technology in independent ways. With child-led appropriation, the importance of the child's own interests became apparent, as they used the prototype to support these, as well as learning activities, as described below. We call this independent appropriation by children "self-scaffolding" (e.g. Bickhard, 2013) and will elaborate in the discussion section.

4.1 Teacher-led Appropriation

Each teacher had different perspectives on how the calendar might be best implemented and used in their classroom, best defined as *structured* vs. *free-use*. For example, TA used it in a very systematised way, specifically appropriating it for use during language and handwriting tasks at set times each day and providing a rotational one-to-one session with each child (structured). TB used it more broadly (free-use), as a motivational tool and as a support for modelling behaviours, noting: "*So yes, mine sounds a lot more chaotic than hers [laughs]. I'd say ours is very warm, causal, informal kind of thing and yeah, I use it a lot for motivation*" [TB].

Despite these differences, however, both teachers had some similar implementation techniques, the most prominent being that each used the tool as a support for a weekly 'Show and Share' session, whereby children would be invited to the front of the class to discuss a photo or video they had taken in MeCalendar, either at home, at school, or elsewhere. This suggests that the tool lends itself to particular forms of common appropriation. The differences in appropriation show that the tool was flexible, as well as the importance of an open-ended approach to implementation. Through this approach, we were able to see the vast array of activities the teachers imagined for the tool as well as how they integrated the tool into existing practices, strategies and expertise.

4.1.1 Verbal Ability

Teachers reported that some non-verbal students had begun to talk in class, using spontaneous language to describe their MeCalendar photos and videos. Differences in verbal ability, such as late development of speech, are common in autism, and many children with autism present limited or no verbal abilities, and may be described as *minimally-verbal* [38]. As previously discussed, the teachers in our study both appropriated MeCalendar as a 'Show and Share' support tool. In this context, children were asked to come to the front of the class and discuss a photo or video they had taken in MeCalendar, either at home, at school, or elsewhere. The social expectation and attention of the full class could be seen as very daunting for the child, and the teacher used the exercise to encourage confidence in speech and communication. Despite the difficulty of the task, teachers reported that using the prototype as a visual prompt provided great support for the children. *"Mikey has no spontaneous, or had no spontaneous, language. He really struggled to make eye contact and even just, you know, to stand in front of the group. Now, he's willing to get up there and he's spontaneously using language"* [TA].

In this case, the teacher reported that there was not a lot of language, perhaps a few key words, such as "brother" or "dog" but that this in itself was a great increase in the verbal skills of the child. In children who were already verbal, the teachers found that the prototype helped encourage more focussed and descriptive language, as well as functional language: *"I go "what's this one" and he's like "oh a swimming pool, oh yes I went there for a swim with my brother in the back yard and..." so you know, huge stories, very different, very different!"* [TB].

Although not specifically intended as a visual prompt, we found that the calendar was appropriated as such, perhaps due to the personal nature of the image (Fig.3): *"My non-verbal kids are talking. They are so motivated having their picture in front of them, on their screen. We've had lots of Halloween pictures and so that's inspired conversations, so they're really motivating."* [TA].

4.1.2 Classwork

We found that teachers naturally used the app to support class tasks, with particular focus on using it towards achievement of the child's IEP (Individualised Education Programme) goals. These goals are individual, curriculum-based goals set for each child, often relating to behavioural skills which enable classwork, such as "I will sit at my desk when I am asked". Enhancing writing skills was of particular interest to TA and thus the prototype was appropriated for use in handwriting tasks. Due to common fine motor difficulties in autism, handwriting is often not a well-liked activity, requiring concentration and precision. Indeed, children with autism can often show resistance to such exercises in the classroom. *"Handwriting is a particular issue in this classroom but I have no resistance from any of them now"* [TA].

Teacher A's approach was to implement a routine for handwriting around MeCalendar. Children would be asked to take a photo at home which they could then discuss with the class during their Show and Share slot. The next day, the teacher initiated a one-to-one activity with the child whereby they would think of vocabulary related to their photo and then create sentences with the selected words. She found that even the children who usually showed resistance to handwriting were "willingly" attempting it: *"His handwriting is one of his IEP goals, and he hated handwriting, um, and would show all sorts of resistant behaviours, drop to the floor, cry, run away, even become aggressive with us. This was last week's [shows an example worksheet]. He's now willingly talking about his photo and then when I ask him to write it down, he's willingly writing it down, which is just great."* [TA]

One child preferred to have his MeCalendar beside him on the desk during handwriting tasks so that he could carefully copy words. TA explained why she thought this strategy works: *"It's because it's his own calendar, and the words he's writing match his calendar and his photos, so they mean more to him"* [TA].

4.1.3 Socialisation

We found that, through teachers' strategies and expertise, the app was implemented in such a way that socialisation was enhanced, both in broad social communication areas such as child-to-child interaction and whole class bonding, as well as in more specific areas such as turn taking, eye contact and body language. We use the broad term "social skills" here, referring to everything from body language, to verbal communication, to listening, to eye contact, to turn-taking. For example, for one child, Cody, standing in front of the class and communicating about their calendar was very daunting, however, through using the calendar as a visual prompt: *"The non-verbal children, even just to get them to stand up, like one of them yesterday for the first time stood facing the group [for Show and Share] which has never happened before... But he's actually turning now to face them [his classmates], he still can't give direct eye-contact, but his body language is indicating that he's open to questions, so that's huge for him."* [TA].

For another child, the teacher tailored her approach in order to address his difficulty with staying on-topic in conversations and providing an "in" in terms of something to pin conversations on that is interesting to him while also providing the teacher with the learning outcomes she wishes to pursue with the child: *"It's given us something to talk about... it has opened up the lines of communication. So, for Daniel, there's more joint communication, on topic, about something, rather than him rabbiting on about a story that he's seen on TV or something. So, there's definitely increased functional communication."* [TB].

Further, in terms of child-to-child interaction, the teachers felt that using the prototype was creating a "warmth" in the classroom, enabling the children to get to know each other better through their Show and Share sessions: *"Yeah, it's knocking down a couple of little boundaries! Actually I think we're getting to know each other better. I feel as though we're, you know, getting a bit closer. I feel as though we're bonding [laughs]... We're sharing a lot "oh you did that on the weekend". So it's definitely bringing a positive feeling, like a warmth. It is, it's creating a little warm feeling."* [TB]

4.1.4 Behaviour and Modelling

Teacher B teacher organically used MeCalendar as a video modelling tool. The teacher took photos and videos of the children while they were exhibiting a positive behaviour, such as sitting at their desk and completing their classwork (Fig. 2). She notes: *"I do little interviews with the kids while they're doing their work. Some kids get particularly motivated if it's a hard task like writing or something or other and I say "Oh shall I get a picture of you and you can show it to mummy and daddy?" when they're sitting down and competing their work."* [TB].

Figure 2. An example of modelling - a child working at his desk

She discusses another child: *"Daniel, I've recorded him for five or six minutes straight. I stood there with the video going while he did a maths sheet. He's one to give up very quickly very easily - so it was six minutes well spent. And there he his, diligently working away and I'm recording comments going "Well done!"* [TB].

4.1.5 Calendar Format

The teachers provided feedback on the calendar format of the app and why this particular structure seems to have been useful. TA noted: *"Using their interests is so crucial and I think that, putting it in that calendar format gives them that sense of time too. Because a lot of our students haven't got that concept of before and after. But through this, Robin was able to say to me "I went camping a long time ago" because he was able to see on his calendar that we were now in November and he'd been camping in October. So he's starting to put his own time frames to things. He's now putting the pieces together himself which is ten times more important than anything I could teach him in class."* [TA].

When asked if any form of photos or videos might provide the same support, teachers responded that they valued the structure afforded by the calendar layout, and this also allowed for the teaching of calendaring and time concepts. TA noted that the calendar format allowed the children to track their progress and, further, to remind themselves that they had successfully shared information with the class previously, thus encouraging confidence in sharing again: *"I don't think it would have as much meaning without the calendar format. For my particular students who are really engaging with it, I think because they're able to personally track themselves. And, just by putting up the calendar on the whiteboard Colby can see that he had success last week on Wednesday by telling us about his bike riding, that then gives him that little bit more confidence and motivation to talk again. And he does, he gets up there and he puts it on the screen and he reflects on it and you can see his little chest puff out! So it's given them a sense of security because they can see, "Well I've already done this, I know what I'm doing."'* [TA].

4.1.6 Using Interests

TA reflected on why encouraging the children's interests through the app was beneficial in her class: *"Instead of me trying to find the stimulus that interests them, and me having to try and direct their learning, they are doing it for me [laughs]. They are giving me the stimulus, they're giving me the feedback, so it's very easy for me just to run with it, which I'm just loving, absolutely loving. Um, because we're not seeing any avoidance, because these are their interests. So they're both sitting at their desks and working away, they can access MeCalendar independently, they can access their photos independently, and because its got the multiple photos for each day they're loving having the flexibility of choosing which one."* TA noted about another child, Ryan: *"He loves presenting to the rest of the class. But only if it's a photo, a personal photo. If I were to give him something else to provide a description of, he wouldn't be as willing to do it, we'd have to do a lot of prompting."*

4.2 Child-led Appropriation

Beyond teachers' strategies for implementation, the children had their own ideas and strategies for appropriation of the prototype. To that end, we have structured the following section with headings which we feel reflect the child's perspective and reflect the interest which is driving their appropriation. This child-centred language arose as part of the analytic method, whereby we attempted to approach the data from the child's perspective.

4.2.1 Breaking Routine / I want to try something new

Children with autism commonly need routine and structure however, flexibility is a crucial part of the curriculum. TA had a daily classroom activity known as "Change of the Day", in which the children had to do something differently from how it was usually done, while she supported them in the change. Our findings suggest that appropriating a technology to communicate about their interests can scaffold children to help them "break" a routine. We see this as a form of self-scaffolding using technology. The willingness of children to break their own routine in order to stand at the front of the class and communicate was still surprising to teachers. This also suggests that this routine rigidity may not be as important to the child if they are confident in discussing something they are interested in or have a deep knowledge of e.g. their pet cat.

One child, Mikey, who the teacher notes is usually extremely rigid in his routine, was adamant that he would have a turn at Show and Share, despite the fact that it wasn't his usual day to do so. The same child is also very limited verbally and so his confidence in standing up and talking to the class (Fig. 3) was extremely "pleasing and emotional" for TA: *"When you were here last time, you remember he actually insisted on having a Show and Share, even though it's not his day, which, for Mikey who is such a routine, regimented, child, he knows, Wednesday is his day to do Show and Share, for him to break his own routine is phenomenal"*

4.2.2 Unprompted handwriting / I want to write

Despite usually showing high levels of resistance to writing tasks e.g. running away or crying, Matthew spontaneously began to write a list by copying words from MeCalendar. In a one-to-one session, the teacher asked the child to think of words related to his photo on MeCalendar, in this case a photo of a pumpkin being carved for Halloween: *"He was completely inspired to copy and trace the words and then he drew his own picture of a pumpkin, completely unprompted and then he wrote his name, all of which he doesn't usually do. So it's all becoming very spontaneous"* [TB]. This uncharacteristic action suggests that perhaps the child did have an inherent want to be able to write, but needed a support in his attempts to do so.

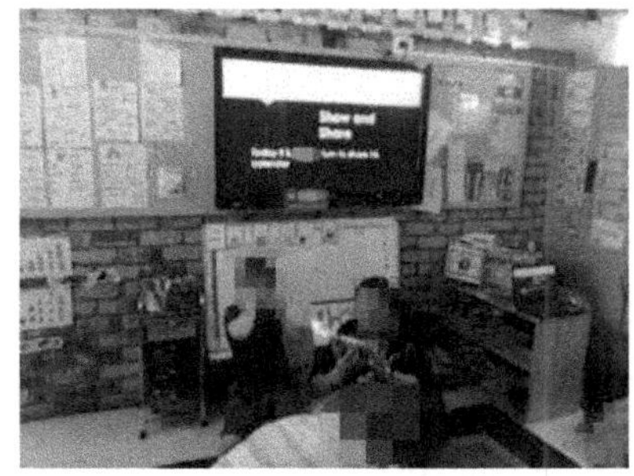

Figure 3. Mikey breaking his routine in order to take part in Show and Share

4.2.3 Modifying Class Tasks / I want to learn this differently

Children used the prototype to approach classroom learning in adapted ways. Children's confidence in using the tool in new ways may suggest that the tool helps them express and explore their own interests with confidence. In this context, the children were gathered on the floor at the front of the classroom, looking at the interactive whiteboard on which the teacher was discussing the day, date, month, year, and weather. After going round each child and asking them to tell her one of the above components of the calendar, she asked the children to then write down the information from the whiteboard on a worksheet. During our observation session, one of the children decided they would prefer to take a photo of the whiteboard using MeCalendar, then typing up the requested information in the comments section below the photo. He wrote down all the requested information – day, date, month, year, and weather – and then continued to write more about the day e.g. "*It is very sunny. I am very happy*". Thus, we see that, while some activities may be difficult for the child e.g. handwriting, there are other forms of support to allow them to pursue their creativity, without having to concentrate on a fine motor task.

4.2.4 Positive Reinforcement / I'm proud of myself

Children were observed by the teachers and the research team replaying videos and audio clips taken by the teacher of them exhibiting good behaviour in class. The teachers identified this as an act of positive reinforcement through watching themselves successfully completing a task: *"I noticed that on all the ones I've videoed of him doing his work, he's pressing the play button so he can listen to it himself and, you know, he's sitting there smiling, he's engaged [laughs]. So, yeah, that's all very good... He was independently checking that out"* [TB].

Teacher A also found that children enjoyed sharing these positive comments with friends: *"And at the end, when they've finished I'll say "Do you want to get a picture of it?" and they'll go and get their iPads and take a picture, because they're very proud of their work too". And if it's been particularly good I'll press the microphone and say "Wow Matthew you've done an awesome job!" Then I press stop and they're so pleased, playing it again and showing it to their friend with my voice over the top, because it's so exciting.*"

4.2.5 Fun / I want to play

Perhaps an obvious way for children to appropriate a new technology is through fun and play. One child, Tyler, showed us a photo of himself in his martial arts uniform. In the classroom, there are rotations of activities, and one such rotation involved time for each child to use MeCalendar in whatever way they would like. This unstructured, free-use approach allowed us to observe one child replaying a video of himself and his dad singing. *"For him, the most motivating ones are of himself singing"* [TB].

Other children used the calendar to store and review their hobbies and interests, which included; gnomes, Aikido, playing the Wii, fire engines, pets, scootering, trains, drawing, swimming and hot water systems. The children took photos and videos in MeCalendar of the things they found fun and annotated these e.g. "My toys I love the best". The teachers liked that the children had appropriated the technology in this way as it allowed for unprompted writing and speaking practice, when annotating or adding audio clips.

4.2.6 Sharing /I want to share what I like and make friends

Children appropriated the technology as a tool to help them communicate and share with each other, fostering child-to-child interaction in the classroom. Interaction between children with autism can be nuanced, as the child's understanding of the social world around them can be limited or overwhelming [34]. In this example, two of the children leveraged the prototype as a social interaction tool, using it to show each other photos of interest to them, as well as to take photos of one another on their MeCalendars. This enhanced and scaffolded their friendship and their understanding of each others' lives outside of school. TB comments: *"I know that Kyle and Bobby like sharing with each other, definitely, like they've got a nice little friendship now and they've definitely shared with each other without me asking them... It's technology, so they love it. Now they are taking photos of each other and go home and show their parents "this is my friend at school'"* [TB].

5. DISCUSSION

The findings indicate that, given an open-ended implementation approach, teachers gravitate towards appropriating technology in classrooms in ways which support children in the pursuit of their verbal, social and behavioural goals, as well as the classwork goals which support these. Teachers were found to scaffold educational and social activities in order to support each child's individual interests or competencies, tailoring them specifically through their in-depth knowledge of each child. We call this *teacher-led appropriation.* Secondly, we found that the way in which children with autism appropriate design in the classroom centred around the enhancement or communication of their own interests. Children were found to engage in *self-scaffolding* activities, whereby they used the MeCalendar prototype to support their personal interests (i.e. to verbally express or to visually represent interests), effectively integrating it into their daily lives. We call this *child-led appropriation.* This work highlights the need for design which supports child interests and competencies, the effectiveness of open-ended design implementation, and the role of self-scaffolding in the appropriation of a technology by children with autism. The findings can be categorised into three main elements; interest-focussed approach, scaffolding structures, and classroom integration.

5.1 Interest-focussed Approach

The interest-focussed approach provided by the app enabled teachers to engage the children in classroom activities and child participants to reflect, share, and strengthen their interests. Teachers commented that the use of interests was crucial in engaging the children on a deeper, more personal and holistic level with their classwork and broader skills work, supported by work in special education research [33, 40]. That teachers found they could step back and let the children direct their own learning through use of their own stimuli suggests appropriation on a meta level. In terms of extending the child-led approaches from Speech and Language disciplines [20, 37], we see a strengthening of child-led approaches to learning through children using their own personally relevant stimuli. The calendar design was perceived to mobilise confidence within the children, perhaps due to an enhanced sense of competence when talking about a topic they know well, or an item or activity they love, such as fire engines or gnomes. We suggest that the children feel competent because they can express their interests, and because they are encouraged and supported by teachers to express these. Perhaps the prototype has acted as a catalyst, tapping into the child's genuine interests and providing a vehicle through which to convey these to others. This, in turn, is supported by teacher expertise, as they appropriate the technology and shape the child interests towards the enhancement of skills and competencies. The idea of mobilising confidence within children with autism certainly fits with the theoretical lens of Self-Determination Theory. We suggest that the calendar satisfies three components; competence (I am able to use this tool / I am an expert on my own interests), autonomy (I can choose what I want to include in my calendar) and relatedness (I can communicate my interests to others through MeCalendar/ People understand me). Ryan and Deci [32] propose these are essential components of self-motivation and mental wellbeing.

5.2 Scaffolding Structures

The prototype provided scaffolding structures for both teachers and children. These arose in the form of four distinct but interrelated types of scaffolding structure; teaching structures, temporal structures, audio-visual structures, and child-led self-scaffolding structures.

Teaching structures influenced both teachers' inherent understanding of each child (social) and the underlying curricula to which their classroom activities are pinned (educational). It would perhaps be difficult to support children's interests and indeed for children to appropriate classroom technology without teachers' expert strategies and knowledge. Thus we see the teachers' expertise is crucial to the way in which the technologies are appropriated, in line with literature from the field of education and Assistive Technology [16]. Teachers use their expertise to provide a broad scaffold: children construct their own self-scaffolding within this.

Teachers appropriated the calendar layout as an opportunity to teach temporal aspects. The prototype was found to provide temporal structure through its calendar format, leading to holistic learning of time and date concepts for children who may be described as 'higher-functioning', as well as broader sequencing concepts, such as "tomorrow" and "yesterday", for children who may be described as 'lower-functioning'. In line with literature which suggests that structure and routine is important in autism support [34], we found that the structured format of the calendar layout provided children and teachers alike with referential boundaries in which to create, organise and retrieve audio-visual content. This was of particular use for children for whom days, dates and time are very abstract concepts.

The audio-visual structure provided by the prototype enabled several instances of prompting for interaction and expression. Often, photos were used as visual prompts through which to engage the children in discussion or to make abstract concepts concrete. Audio clips of teacher's praise were replayed by the children in acts of positive reinforcement, feeding into the larger IEP goals of e.g. completing classwork or sitting at one's own desk. While we recognise such functionalities may already be provided by tablets (through e.g. camera function, video camera function, and voice note function), teachers commented that it was the integration of photos, videos and text into an accessible tool which allowed such activities as self-tracking, independent search and self-reassurance of previously completed tasks. In turn, this allowed for ease of use and access, for teachers and children alike. We found that the integration of the audio-visual element into a calendar structure provided children with an understanding of concepts which teachers were keen to teach. Through leveraging the children's own interests, the calendar became less about explicitly teaching sequencing of time and days, and more about the 'when' of everyday life. Through this approach, children began to learn about sequencing of time and days more holistically.

The ways in which the technology was appropriated as child-led self-scaffolding structures were of particular interest as they were unexpected and yet frequent. Teachers commented on how the children broke routine, adapted learning activities and extended social interaction beyond their usual scope. This was surprising for the teachers and led to new insights into how the prototype can support children's latent needs. For example, when Mikey became upset that it wasn't his day to present his Show and Share, and then insisted on presenting on his topic of interest – videos of himself singing. On one level, this was an example of a child standing up in front of his class and explicitly conveying an interest to the group. On another, deeper level, he could be considered to have self-scaffolded a learning opportunity for himself, whereby the support environment surrounding him had allowed him to be opportunistic, supported by his photos and videos in MeCalendar. If we take scaffolding to mean the support given to learners to enable them to achieve objectives they would not have achieved without support [2, 4], we see that in this example, the child is providing the support to himself, using the technology as a prompt. This could be described as an act of self-scaffolding, whereby children use their own interests, and supporting media, to scaffold their interactions, rather than using pre-defined scaffolds provided by others. As one teacher remarked, the children were able to provide their own stimulus, and thus direct their own learning. The above observations about scaffolding resonate with related work. Frauenberger [18] discusses how a technology can also be a catalyst which scaffolds human interaction which surrounds it. In our case, the technology provided a visual prompt and memory tool, armed with which children could feel confident about the interests they were trying to express. Frauenberger [18] discusses that, despite having some pre-defined notions as to what a technology might achieve, it can also act as a catalyst for the scaffolding of other outcomes. Importantly, he notes that our designs can scaffold interactions. They can "mediate and empower" [18, p.57]. He also suggests that when design is appropriated in this way, the outcome, in this case expression of interests and competencies, can become meaningfully situated and implicit as opposed to instructional. Thus, we suggest that technology which can be appropriated by children for self-scaffolding and supported by teachers' expert knowledge, may lead to growth in confidence in the expression of interests and competencies, which in turn are used by teachers to support learning.

5.3 Classroom Integration

Teachers employ a great number of strategies in order to elicit and enhance social skills in children with autism. Noticeably, both teachers employed a different integration strategy; one structured, one free-use. MeCalendar seemed to provide a broad scope for support, allowing the teacher to use it for particular social aspects for particular children, and each in her own style. By all accounts and purposes, this app is very simple in its conception and design: a calendar layout which allows insertion of photos, videos and comments for each day. The prototype was also physically accessible, meaning the children could easily carry it in their schoolbags between home and school, use it around school and when doing other activities too, encouraging everyday, integrated use.

The observations about appropriation in the classroom extend related work in several ways. Firstly, while previous work explored the interests of children with autism through playful interactivity in virtual worlds [31], our research highlights that these interests can also be successfully integrated with more formal learning activities in classroom settings. Similar to Hourcade et al. [22, 23], we focussed on enhancing skills through interactive tablet applications and deliberately open-ended work. In contrast to their design, however, MeCalendar extended work to the specific context of children with autism and we left it to the teachers and children to adapt and adopt the design according to their needs and interests, without the intention of enhancing one specific ability.

It is important to note the limitations of this research and how it can be improved. One aspect of the design implementation which requires further work is parental participation. Despite indicating interest and engagement at the beginning of the project, parental participation was low throughout the study. In terms of limitations of the tool itself, for example, we found that children at times found the buttons too small to be accurately pressed and some became frustrated at inadvertently pressing the incorrect button (e.g. 'Home' instead of 'Add Photo'). Addressing this is of particular importance as some child participants had fine motor skill challenges which led to challenges in dexterity. Another challenge described by teachers was the number of steps between taking a photo or video and having it successfully added to the calendar. Having to confirm the use of the photo two separate screens was problematic (currently users must click 'Use Photo' on in the entry window, and then again click 'Save' once they have entered a title for the entry). This is supported by observational data which showed that children often became impatient with this process, thus, a more streamlined media entry process will be developed. Teachers also provided design feedback regarding opportunities to extend the app, for example extending the current function to add smiley faces to any entry to include different colours of faces to reflect the four Zones of Regulation, a curriculum-wide ranking strategy in which children use colours to express how they are feeling. Teachers suggested that the incorporation of this into the MeCalendar design could help the children rank and self-regulate their zones throughout the day, also providing the teacher and parents with a record of the child's mood over time.

The work presented here suggests several future directions. Those discussed above - increased parental involvement, improved features for dexterity, integration of teachers' suggestions – will be addressed in a new iteration of the app. We also suggest it is imperative to focus on how best to support design contributions from children themselves in this research context. We aim to apply a Speech and Language therapy approach to this problem, hoping to edge closer to understanding the true design needs of children with autism, especially those who are minimally-verbal.

6. CONCLUSION

In conclusion, this study has investigated the appropriation of a flexible support technology in classrooms by children with autism and their teachers. We highlight the importance of encouraging open-ended implementation and use, suggesting that such an approach can yield surprising results through empowering and leveraging the imagination, expertise and interests of our participants. Simple, audio-visual technologies can act as a catalyst for confidence in the expression of these interests and competencies. The findings here suggest a move towards a focus on child-led appropriation based on personal strengths and interests, as, when attempting to support and enhance child competencies and abilities, these are the true motivators of child experience and learning.

7. ACKNOWLEDGMENTS

We thank all of the participants for their on-going enthusiasm for this project. This research is supported in part by the Cooperative Research Centre for Living with Autism (Autism CRC) under Project No. 2.027. The authors acknowledge the financial support of the Autism CRC, established and supported under the Australian Government's Cooperative Research Centres Program.

8. REFERENCES

1. American Psychiatric Association. 2013. *Diagnostic and Statistical Manual of Mental Disorders, Fifth Edition (DSM-5).* Arlington VA: American Psychiatric Association
2. Adrian Ashman and Robert Conway. 1997. *An Introduction to Cognitive Education: Theory and Applications*. Routledge, London.
3. Saskia Bakker, Elise van den Hoven, and Berry Eggen. 2012. FireFlies: supporting primary school teachers through open-ended interaction design. In *Proceedings of the 24th Australian Computer-Human Interaction Conference* (OzCHI '12), ACM, New York, NY, USA, 26-29. http://doi.org/10.1145/2414536.2414540
4. Mary Barry and Ian Pitt. 2006. Interaction design: a multidimensional approach for learners with autism. In *Proceedings of the 2006 conference on Interaction design and children* (IDC '06). ACM, New York, NY, USA, 33-36. http://doi.org/10.1145/1139073.1139086
5. Laura Bartoli, Franca Garzotto, Mirko Gelsomini, Luigi Oliveto, and Matteo Valoriani. 2014. Designing and evaluating touchless playful interaction for ASD children. In *Proceedings of the 2014 conference on Interaction design and children* (IDC '14). ACM, New York, NY, USA, 17-26. http://doi.org/10.1145/2593968.2593976
6. Arpita Bhattacharya, Mirko Gelsomini, Patricia Pérez-Fuster, Gregory D. Abowd, and Agata Rozga. 2015. Designing motion-based activities to engage students with autism in classroom settings. In *Proceedings of the 14th International Conference on Interaction Design and Children* (IDC '15). ACM, New York, NY, USA, 69-78. http://doi.org/10.1145/2771839.2771847
7. Mark Bickhard. 2013. Scaffolding and self scaffolding: Central aspects of development. LT Winegar, Sc. Valsiner (Eds), Chz'ldreri 610: 33-52
8. Peter Börjesson, Wolmet Barendregt, Eva Eriksson, and Olof Torgersson. 2015. Designing technology for and with developmentally diverse children: a systematic literature review. In *Proceedings of the 14th International Conference on Interaction Design and Children*, 79-88. http://doi.org/10.1145/2771839.2771848
9. Virginia Braun and Victoria Clarke. 2006. Using thematic analysis in psychology. *Qualitative research in psychology* 3, 2: 77-101. http://doi.org/10.1191/1478088706qp063oa
10. Margot Brereton, Laurianne Sitbon, Muhammad Haziq Lim Abdullah, Mark Vanderberg, and Stewart Koplick. 2015. Design after design to bridge between people living with cognitive or sensory impairments, their friends and proxies. *CoDesign* 11,1: 4-20. http://doi.org/10.1080/15710882.2015.1009471
11. Jennie Carroll. 2004. Completing Design in Use: Closing the Appropriation Cycle. ECIS 2004 Proceedings. Paper 44. http://aisel.aisnet.org/ecis2004/44
12. Paul Dourish. 2003. The Appropriation of Interactive Technologies: Some Lessons from Placeless Documents. *Comput. Supported Coop. Work* 12, 4 (September 2003), 465-490. http://doi.org/10.1023/A:1026149119426
13. Bob Dick. 2004. Action research literature: Themes and trends. Action Research 2, no. 4: 425-444.
14. Alan Dix. 2007. Designing for appropriation. *Proceedings of the 21st British HCI Group Annual Conference on People and Computers: HCI... but not as we know it-Volume 2*, British Computer Society, 27–30. Retrieved January 14th 2017 from http://dl.acm.org/citation.cfm?id=1531415
15. Pelle Ehn. 1989. *Work-oriented design of computer artifacts.* Hillsdale, NJ: Lawrence Erlbaum Associates
16. Charles Fage, Léonard Pommereau, Charles Consel, Émilie Balland, and Hélène Sauzéon. 2014. Tablet-based activity schedule for children with autism in mainstream environment. *In Proceedings of the 16th international ACM SIGACCESS conference on Computers & Accessibility* (ASSETS '14). ACM, New York, NY, USA, 145-152. http://doi.org/10.1145/2661334.2661369
17. Christopher Frauenberger, Judith Good, Alyssa Alcorn, and Helen Pain. 2012. Supporting the design contributions of children with autism spectrum conditions. In *Proceedings of the 11th International Conference on Interaction Design and Children* (IDC '12). ACM, New York, NY, USA, 134-143. http://doi.org/10.1145/2307096.2307112
18. Christopher Frauenberger. 2015. Rethinking autism and technology. *Interactions* 22, 2 (February 2015), 5759. http://doi.org/10.1145/2728604
19. Christopher Frauenberger, Judith Good, and Narcis Pares. 2016. Autism and Technology: Beyond Assistance & Intervention. In *Proceedings of the 2016 CHI Conference Extended Abstracts on Human Factors in Computing Systems* (CHI EA '16). ACM, New York, NY, USA, 3373-3378. http://doi.org/10.1145/2851581.2856494
20. Gillian R. Hayes, Sen Hirano, Gabriela Marcu, Mohamad Monibi, David H. Nguyen, and Michael Yeganyan. 2010. Interactive visual supports for children with autism. *Personal Ubiquitous Comput.* 14, 7 (October 2010), 663-680. http://doi.org/10.1007/s00779-010-0294-8

21. Sen H. Hirano, Michael T. Yeganyan, Gabriela Marcu, David H. Nguyen, Lou Anne Boyd, and Gillian R. Hayes. 2010. vSked: evaluation of a system to support classroom activities for children with autism. In *Proceedings of the SIGCHI Conference on Human Factors in Computing Systems* (CHI '10). ACM, New York, NY, USA, 1633-1642. http://doi.org./10.1145/1753326.1753569

22. Juan Pablo Hourcade, Natasha E. Bullock-Rest, and Thomas E. Hansen. 2012. Multitouch tablet applications and activities to enhance the social skills of children with autism spectrum disorders. *Personal Ubiquitous Comput.* 16, 2 (February 2012),157-168. http://doi.org/10.1007/s00779-011-0383-3

23. Juan Pablo Hourcade, Stacy R. Williams, Ellen A. Miller, Kelsey E. Huebner, and Lucas J. Liang. 2013. Evaluation of tablet apps to encourage social interaction in children with autism spectrum disorders. In *Proceedings of the SIGCHI Conference on Human Factors in Computing Systems* (CHI '13). ACM, New York, NY, USA, 3197-3206. http://doi.org/10.1145/2470654.2466438

24. Wendy Keay-Bright. 2009. ReacTickles: playful interaction with information communication technologies. *International Journal of Arts and Technology*, 2, 1: 133-151. http://doi.org/10.1108/17549450200800026

25. Wendy Kellogg and Thomas Erickson. 2005. Supporting appropriation work with social translucence, collective sensemaking, and social scaffolding. *International Reports on Socio-informatics* 2, 2: 30-43.

26. Peter Leijdekkers, Valerie Gay and Frederick Wong. 2013. CaptureMyEmotion: A mobile app to improve emotion learning for autistic children using sensors. *In Proc. IEEE International Symposium on Computer-Based Medical Systems*, CBMS 2013, Porto, 381 – 384. http://doi.org/10.1109/CBMS.2013.6627821

27. Lorcan Kenny, Caroline Hattersley, Bonnie Molins, Carole Buckley, Carol Povey, and Elizabeth Pellicano. 2015. "Which terms should be used to describe autism? Perspectives from the UK autism community." *Autism* 20(4), 442-462. http://doi.org/10.1177/1362361315588200

28. Narcís Parés, Anna Carreras, Jaume Durany, Jaume Ferrer, Pere Freixa, David Gómez, Orit Kruglanski, Roc Parés, J. Ignasi Ribas, Miquel Soler, and Àlex Sanjurjo. 2005. Promotion of creative activity in children with severe autism through visuals in an interactive multisensory environment. In *Proceedings of the 2005 conference on Interaction design and children* (IDC '05). ACM, New York, NY, USA, 110-116. http://doi.org/101145/1109540.1109555

29. Malinda Pennington, Douglas Cullinan and Louise Southern. 2014. Defining autism: Variability in state education agency definitions of and evaluations for autism spectrum disorders. *Autism Research and Treatment* (June 2014), 1-8. http://doi.org/10.1155/2014/327271

30. Marshall Raskind. 1994. Assistive technology for adults with learning disabilities: A rationale for use. In Gerber, P.J. and Reiff, H.B. (Eds.) Learning disabilities in adulthood: Persisting problems and evolving issues. Stoneham, MA: Andover Medical (1994), 152-162.

31. Kathryn E. Ringland, Christine T. Wolf, LouAnne E. Boyd, Mark S. Baldwin, and Gillian R. Hayes. 2016. Would You Be Mine: Appropriating Minecraft as an Assistive Technology for Youth with Autism. In *Proceedings of the 18th International ACM SIGACCESS Conference on Computers and Accessibility* (ASSETS '16). ACM, New York, NY, USA, 33-41. https://doi.org/10.1145/2982142.2982172

32. Richard Ryan and Edward Deci. 2000. Intrinsic and extrinsic motivations: Classic definitions and new directions. *Contemporary Educational Psychology* 25, 1: 54-67. http://doi.org/10.1006/ceps.1999.1020

33. Beth Saggers, David Klug, Keely Harper-Hill, Jill Ashburner, Debra Costley, Trevor Clark, Susan Bruck, David Trembath, Amanda A. Webster, and Suzanne Carrington. 2016. Australian Autism Educational Needs Analysis-What are the needs of schools, parents and students on the autism spectrum?. (2016) Accessed 12th May 2016 from http://www.autismcrc.com.au/download/886/Australian%20Educational%20Needs%20Analysis%20-%20FINAL%20REPORT_20160505_WEB%20LIVE.pdf?redirect=node/440

34. Frank Sansosti. 2004. A research synthesis of social story interventions for children with Autism Spectrum Disorders. Focus on Autism and other Developmental Disabilities, 19(4), 194-204.

35. Phoebe Sengers and Bill Gaver. 2006. Staying open to interpretation: engaging multiple meanings in design and evaluation. In *Proceedings of the 6th conference on Designing Interactive systems* (DIS '06). ACM, New York, NY, USA, 99-108. http://doi.org/10.1145/1142405.1142422

36. Lucy Suchman. 1987. *Plans and Situated Actions* Cambridge: Cambridge UP.

37. Fern Sussman. 1999. More than words: Helping parents promote communication and social skills in children with Autism Spectrum Disorder. Toronto, Ont. The Hanen Centre.

38. Helen Tager-Flusberg and Connie Kasari. 2013. Minimally Verbal School-Aged Children with Autism Spectrum Disorder: The Neglected End of the Spectrum. *Autism research* 6, 6: 468 – 478. http://doi.org/10.1002/aur.1329

39. Tracy Westeyn, Gregory Abowd, Thad Starner, Jeremy Johnson, Peter Presti and Kimberley Weaver. 2012. Monitoring children's developmental progress using augmented toys and activity recognition. *Personal and Ubiquitous Computing,* 16, 2: 169-191. http://doi.org/10.1007/s00779-011-0386-0

40. Winter-Messiers, Mary Ann. 2007. From tarantulas to toilet brushes: Understanding the special interest areas of children and youth with Asperger syndrome. *Remedial and Special Education.* 28, 3: 140-152. http://doi.org/10.1177/07419325070280030301

41. Jacob O. Wobbrock, Shaun K. Kane, Krzysztof Z. Gajos, Susumu Harada, and Jon Froehlich. 2011. Ability-Based Design: Concept, Principles and Examples. *ACM Transactions on Accessible Computing* 3, 3: 1–27. http://doi.org/10.1145/1952383.1952384

CymaSense: A Novel Audio-Visual Therapeutic Tool for People on the Autism Spectrum

John McGowan
Edinburgh Napier University
School of Computing
Edinburgh
+441314552461
J.McGowan@napier.ac.uk

Grégory Leplâtre
Edinburgh Napier University
School of Computing
Edinburgh
+441314552709
G.Leplatre@napier.ac.uk

Iain McGregor
Edinburgh Napier University
School of Computing
Edinburgh
+441314552788
I.McGregor@napier.ac.uk

ABSTRACT

Music Therapy has been shown to be an effective intervention for clients with Autism Spectrum Condition (ASC), a lifelong neurodevelopmental condition that can affect people in a number of ways. This paper presents a study evaluating the use of a multimodal 3D interactive tool, CymaSense, within a series of music therapy sessions. Eight adults with ASC participated in an 8-week period using a single case experimental design approach. The study used qualitative and quantitative methodological tools for analysis within and beyond the therapy sessions. The results indicate an increase in communicative behaviours for both verbal and non-verbal participants.

ACM Classification Keywords

H.5.2. Information interfaces and presentation: Graphical User Interfaces (GUI); Prototyping; Screen Design; User-Centered Design; Visualization Theory, Concepts and Paradigms.

Keywords

Autism Spectrum Condition (ASC); Assistive Technologies; Music Therapy; Interactive Audio-Visual; Multi-Sensory Environments; Cymatics.

1. INTRODUCTION

People with autism typically have difficulties with communication, social interaction and self-esteem. From a historical perspective, recognised interventions for autism are largely behavioural based. Applied behavioural analysis (ABA) being considered the most effective and widely used [16]. Some critics, however, have pointed out that ABA relies heavily on responding to vocal-based instructions with vocalised responses, which can be difficult for many people with ASC. It can also be restrictive to the individual's freedom of expression [3]. Music therapy was established in the 1950s and can provide a non-verbal means of communication with autistic clients. A level of predictability within musical structure offers people with ASC a channel of communication through which to express themselves, which can result in a number of benefits. Lim states that the inherent structure of music stimuli and intact capacity of pattern perception and production in children with ASC has a positive effect on speech production [26]. Not all of the successes of music therapy are easy to quantify, however, as they can integrate medical, educational, sociological, psychological and musicological discourses within their practices [34]. This is largely due to the lack of randomised controlled trials that can be run with groups of people with autism. The nature of the spectrum condition being that no two groups or individuals have the same abilities or requirements. Consequently, this can lead to many funding bodies asking for longer term objective studies to back up existing case histories [33]. Simpson and Keen recognise that there is limited evidence to back up the efficacy of music interventions, but more research needs to be conducted, particularly within more naturalistic settings [44]. Nonetheless, case studies continue to back the validity and success of music therapy techniques, in particular, the improvisational techniques used by Nordoff and Robbins [52].

Music and arts therapists often use technology within their practice to stimulate the senses of autistic clients. Simple and inexpensive iPad apps through to sophisticated music production tools are available, and in use within practices [19]. Computers have been shown to provide a certain amount of predictability and stability for people on the autism spectrum, providing an attractive environment due to the lack of human contact and stress involved in reading emotional cues from faces [15]. However, not all therapists are well informed about or proficient in the use of modern technology, and effective use of assistive technologies can be limited. Previous studies have shown beneficial use of interactive multimodal systems for children with ASC. The Reactable tangible user interface visualises synthesised sound as animated 2D graphical connections between modular blocks [51]. Gestural systems like SensoryPaint use sound to highlight animated movement [38]. Interactive Surfaces, like BendableSound, use tactile, visual and audio feedback to engage children with autism [5]. It is arguable that music therapy could be made more engaging if the musical channel of communication it aims to open between therapist and client were augmented by a visual modality.

This paper presents a study in which CymaSense, an interactive multimodal interface that generates real-time 3D visual stimuli based on Cymatics, was used to augment music therapy sessions involving adults with ASC [27]. The development of CymaSense was based on interviews conducted with music therapists. The study which involved eight adults with ASC intends to assess the hypothesis that use of an audiovisual tool within music therapy, such as CymaSense, could improve communication and self-esteem for people with autism. The following section lays out related work, in terms of autism, interventions, and the potential for constructive use of technology within current music therapy practices.

2. RELATED WORK

2.1 Autism

Autism Spectrum Condition (ASC), also known as Autism Spectrum Disorder, is a lifelong neurodevelopmental condition where people share the following features in their diagnosis [2]:

ASSETS '17, October 29-November 1, 2017, Baltimore, MD, USA

ACM ISBN 978-1-4503-4926-0/17/10...$15.00
DOI: https://doi.org/10.1145/3132525.3132539

difficulties in social communication and interaction; problems in the use of language and verbal communication; limited and stereotypical behavioral patterns [35]; problems in perceptual processing; and inhibited use of their imagination [31]. A 2014 study by the Centres for Disease Control found that the condition affects one child in every 68, and has encouraged health professionals to consider ASC as a critical and urgent public health concern [36]. Research has shown that autism is a strongly genetic condition, however, not all of its genetic or biological signature has yet been identified [50].

People on the autism spectrum are said to be unconscious of the amount of control they can exert over their environment and obtain a coherent response, even when it is they themselves who are responsible for changes in their environment [31]. They can have little sense of the cause-and-effect a neurotypical person takes for granted, thus increasing a sense of lack-of-control and frustration. The isolating nature of this condition has shown higher rates of anxiety and depression, regardless of intellectual and linguistic abilities [32], prompting researchers to find solutions to a condition where relatively little is known concerning its causes [28]. Much of early and current research has focused on behavioural approaches to intervention, which provide success in terms of treating symptoms, but do not address the core emotional deficits of people with ASC [35]. Issues of low self-esteem, anxiety and attitudes towards relationships with peers can create additional negative physical and psychological illnesses [18]. Support for people on the autism spectrum seems to be lacking for both the adolescent and adult communities, partly due to the rising numbers of people being diagnosed with ASC at the beginning of the 21st century [18]. It has even been noted that there exists more support for parents of autistic children than for adults on the autism spectrum [35].

2.2 Interventions

Music therapy is considered an effective approach for addressing language and communication skills for children with ASC and can provide a non-verbal means of communication [27]. Improvisational approaches encourage freedom of expression within individuals, often improving confidence and independence [43]. In addition to traditional acoustic instruments and use of the human voice, music and arts therapists continue to embrace technology within their practice to achieve a greater sense of agency and stimulate the senses of autistic clients. This can include: electronic interfaces like the iPad or Launchpad [30]; existing assistive technologies and tangible user interfaces (TUI) like the Skoog [45] or Reactable [51], which have been shown to improve social interaction and play in people with ASC through a shared space [11]. Research has shown that sensory integration therapy has encouraged development of independence amongst autistic people [40].

2.3 Augmented music therapy

For people with autism, cause-and-effect can be problematic due to issues with sensory impairment. Therapeutic approaches involve teaching children how to combine sensory integration and body awareness therapies, known as Multi-Sensory Environments (MSE), which can aid in the attainment of therapeutic goals. MSEs have demonstrated the efficacy of this approach through previous research [38], but have not been widely adapted for use within music therapy sessions. Cibrian et al. successfully facilitated music therapy sessions using their BendableSound prototype which uses animation and sound in conjunction with a fabric-based interactive surface, designed to encourage attention and motor development, but is somewhat restricted to the playing of the interactive surface itself [5].

Current audio-visual applications that demonstrate simple cause-and-effect take many forms, from: web-based visualisers [4]; stand-alone applications that link to audio and media players [47]; iPad apps [17]; and VJing software for use in art installations and public performances. However, the majority of these use arbitrary visualisation of sound based on the amplitude of the audio and are not designed for people on the autism spectrum. Augmenting the auditory modality with real-time visual feedback may be an effective means of strengthening a sense of causality within a music therapy scenario. In order to achieve this goal, a suitable real-time music visualisation system is required.

2.4 Cymatics

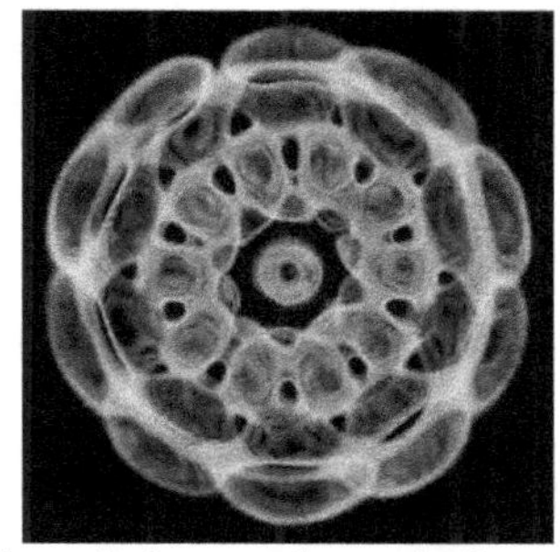

Figure 1: Cymatic image of sound vibrated through water

Cymatics are physical impressions of sound created in media such as water (see Figure 1) or by particulate material on a brass plate (Figure 2)[21]. They are the result of diffraction and refraction of sound waves created within the visualising medium [8].

Figure 2: Chladni plate

Software simulations of these phenomena exist and are employed by artists including: the KIMA collective in performance and installations [14]; Graham Wakefield's 2D and 3D patches for a software Tonoscope, created in the Max visual programming language [48]. Chladni's 18th century principles, which are the basis for these visualisations, are merely a mechanism for visualising a cross section of a sonic bubble created by the resonant tone of a particular size of plate, not the shape of sound. Sound does not travel in longitudinal waves within rectangular blocks but rather propagates spherically in air due to diffraction. Water-based Cymatic visualisations provide greater detail due to their ability to visualise a wider spectrum of frequencies. Small changes in sound timbre can create complexities within the observable patterns, creating dramatic and aesthetically interesting results. These patterns are, however, deterministic and are used by some instrument makers to visualise the tonal qualities of their instruments. The combination of predictability and surprise that Cymatic patterns exhibit, as well as their physically accurate representations of sounds can make them a fascinating sound visualisation paradigm.

3. REQUIREMENTS

A preliminary series of semi-structured interviews were conducted to identify the needs of autistic clients within therapy sessions, and the potential for a visualisation tool. Two with clinical music therapy practitioners; one with a community music therapist; and one with the head music therapist of a charitable organisation. The goals of the interviews were: to outline current practice; highlight the ways in which technology is currently used; indicate where potential lies for augmented working practices using new tools; and to produce a requirements analysis for a prototype tool. The audio recorded interviews were transcribed and coded using NVivo data analysis software. The details of that study will be the topic of a separate paper. The information formed the basis for the development of CymaSense, a real-time music visualisation application based on Cymatics. The interviews identified a need for: clear cause-and-effect; customisability in terms of colour and Cymatic shapes; the use of tangible user interfaces for efficacy and to enable social interaction through sharing. It was decided that a proposed system for processing and mapping appropriate audio data to the visual domain would have to include: MIDI data (Musical Instrument Digital Interface); and the conversion of analogue sound into the digital domain. This would allow visualisation of a wide range of electronic and acoustic instruments.

Research into the use of shared interfaces has indicated improvements in turn-taking and eye contact amongst participants with ASC [51]. To facilitate visual musical interaction between a music therapist and client, implementation of a single and two-user version of the tool was recommended by the therapists. Information about the design and behavior of the tool is provided in the next section. For additional details, please refer to [27].

4. CYMASENSE

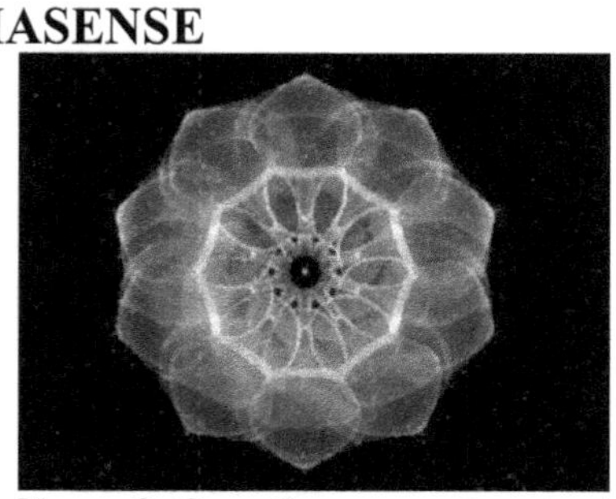

Figure 3: CymaSense sample output

CymaSense is an interactive application that visualises acoustic and electronic audio input. Processed audio is transformed into translucent 3D Cymatic shapes and projected onto a screen or interactive surface (Figure 3). Changes in volume affect the scale of the shapes being presented. Variations in timbre modify the surface qualities of the shapes being visualised. Changes in pitch determine which Cymatic shape (out of twelve) is chosen, as well as lightness of colour. A user interface allows background and Cymatic shape colour choices to be made. A single-user version displays a single set of Cymatic shapes in the centre of the screen, while a 2-user version displays shapes side-by-side on screen.

High definition Cymascope images of individual frequencies were used as templates for the creation of twelve 3D Cymatic shapes (Figure 4), relating to each of the semitones within a musical octave. The MIDI and audio inputs are analysed in real-time using Cycling'74 Max [7]. Relevant data (amplitude, pitch, harmonic content, velocity, pitch bend) is transmitted using the Open Sound Control (OSC) to the Unity games engine in which the visualisation is generated.

The CymaSense prototype comprises of (1) an interface to control audio input and visual output for single or multi-user interaction and (2) a separate output screen (Figure 3).

4.1 Mapping

The mapping between audio and visual attributes is based on audio visual associations validated by previous studies [13]. However, the novelty of the visualisation paradigm implemented in CymaSense also afforded experimentations with the less obvious aspects of the mapping. Amplitude to scale of Cymatic shape and particle size – mapping amplitude to scale is commonly referred to in literature [23].

Pitch to Cymatic shape – This is consistent with Cymatic shape behaviours observed. The 3D shapes created were inspired by Cymascope reference images [8] (see Figure 4).

Figure 4: 3D Cymatics shapes modelled in Autodesk Maya

Pitch to colour lightness - lightness of colour is altered by MIDI note or microphone frequency, implementing a pitch to lightness relationship, referred to in synesthesia and cross-modality literature [53]. The higher the pitch, the lighter the visual component. This aids in differentiating the same Cymatic shape over several octaves.

Timbre to Cymatic shape surface quality – timbre is considered the most difficult characteristic of tone to describe [46]. It is also referred to as a potentially useful tool in audio-visualisation by therapeutic practitioners. Colour is commonly associated with timbre in audiovisual mappings, but colour was used for other purposes in the application. Therefore, it was decided to experiment with surface qualities as a means of representing the spectral qualities of a sound. The Cymatic shapes generated for a given frequency were modified using a 3D morphing technique as follows: the shapes of bright sounds were made to appear sharper, while dark sounds were transformed to appear more rounded.

4.2 Additional Interface Options

Cymatic shape colour and background colour choice - colour was identified in literature [6] and through interviews with therapists, as key to empowering clients in relation to facilitating their own choices. Each CymaSense shape is comprised of an external shell and two sets of animated particles. Colour assignment to both the shell and particles are possible to allow a variety of colour combinations. User selection of: Cymatic shape outer material colour; main particle colour; internal particle colour; and background colour have been made available directly from the interface.

Cymatic shape rotation – through observation of Cymatic shapes created in water, it has been noted that in addition to changes in shape dependent on frequency, subtle rotation occurs. A simple on/off button for no or random rotation values was deemed sufficient for the initial prototype where a change in frequency or MIDI note triggers a random quaternion rotation on all three axes between a value of -1 and 1, providing immediate but subtle audio-visual feedback. (Please refer to the video figures.)

5. EVALUATION

This section presents an evaluation carried out with TouchBase, a centre run by Sense Scotland charity [42] for people with a variety of disabilities, including autism.

5.1 Study Development

The intention of the study was to utilise CymaSense within a music therapy environment to test whether it would be of benefit to the communication and self-esteem of its autistic clients. Observation and analysis of the sessions were facilitated through a combination of video observation and a post-study survey. The creation of a Communicative Responses and Acts Score Sheet (CRASS) allowed detailed analysis of each session, where the time for an occurrence of musical and non-musical behaviours were totalled each week and used for comparative purposes. For example, participating in rhythmic give and take, matching a beat, creating a verbal response or establishing eye contact. The use of CRASS was based on the Edgerton method of determining the effectiveness of improvisational music therapy on communicative behaviours [10]. A post-study behavioural change survey with the participants' parents/guardians, care workers and tutor gathered information concerning observable musical and non-musical behaviours of the participants outside of the sessions.

5.2 Participants

Six adult males and two adult females, who have been clinically diagnosed as being on the autism spectrum, were recruited from Scottish Autism [41] and Sense Scotland [42] for the 8-week study. One of the males and one female worked together as a group (G1), while the other six participants took part in one-to-one sessions with the music tutor (P1-P6). Participants' diagnosis of autistic impairment ranged from severe to mildly impaired. Deficits in communication skills were common to all participants. Four participants were non-verbal, and two participants demonstrated limited functional language skills. None of the participants had visual or aural deficiencies. Parents or guardians provided informed consent for their children to be involved in the study. All participants were between the ages of 18 and 28 years.

5.3 Procedure

A single subject design [1] was used consisting of two phases: (A) a baseline stage was determined over two weeks; (B) the intervention was introduced and tested over a subsequent six-week period. This is the same protocol use by Yang et al. [54] used to examine social behavior in 7-to-9 year old children with ASC, and by Hutchins [20] and Norris [29] researching the effects of Social Stories on autistic children. Each participant was scheduled for a 30-minute session per week for eight weeks, with the exception of the group who were scheduled for a 60-minute session each week. Due to illnesses and unforeseen circumstances not all the participants were able to attend all sessions. During the non-intervention baseline stage (A) the music tutor used a number of improvisational musical techniques. The techniques were aimed at establishing contact with and facilitating responses from the participants, and development of their musical and rhythmical abilities. The music tutor played guitar, percussion, electronic keyboard and/or sang, and provided each participant with the opportunity to do the same. Lazar et al. discuss ways to empower adults with cognitive impairments through art therapy via the Third Hand technique, where the therapist draws on and enables the skills of the client, builds on previous sessions and provides support [24]. Similarly, the tutor was sensitive to the desires, goals, and emotions of the clients, by providing support intent on minimising the imposition of meanings, ideas, or preferences onto their work.

In designing creative spaces for people with ASC, Makhaeva et al. discuss the advantages of participatory design with autistic users [12]. They highlight that the common contradictory misconception between autism and creativity can be overcome through subtle interplay and space that allows meaningful participation. By combining a well-known activity with familiar, but slightly modified elements, participants felt free to appropriate them in original ways. The authors employ a Play Partner and Active Observer which contribute to facilitating a creative process. Adopting this approach prior to the intervention stage (B), discussion between the music tutor (as Play Partner) and the researcher (as Active Observer) took place. Any new changes or tasks for people on the autism spectrum can be stressful, therefore, a phased approach should minimise the effects on each participant. Ringland and Cibrian discuss the importance of natural user interfaces to support body awareness and sensory stimulation within multi-sensory environments, regarding their respective SensoryPaint and BendableSound interventions for children with ASC [38][5]. Similarly, adoption of the participants' natural body interactions with the tutor from a musical perspective were taken into account. Designed to identify and agree upon each participant's communication and musical abilities, a short interview with the music tutor confirmed the most appropriate way to customise and introduce the intervention (see 6.2 for details). The intervention phase (B) was introduced gradually within a session, once the participant was identified as being comfortable. The intervention involved projecting the visualisation of the sound produced by the participants' respective instruments, either on a screen, or using an interactive table (see 5.4 for details) (Figure 5).

The music tutor could alter the lighting levels in the music room over the session allowing the participants to become more aware and engaged with the audio-visual interaction (Video Figure 2). During the intervention phase, the music tutor continued to respond to each participant's individual needs, based on the amount of gestural, verbal, vocal and musical responses and acts within each session.

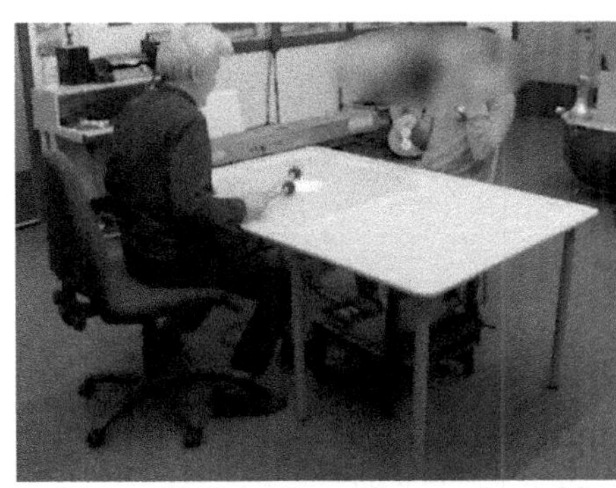

Figure 5: CymaSense Interactive table

5.4 Materials/Settings

The music sessions took place in a large room with adjustable roof blinds and windows to allow control of available light and air entering the space, and had the following musical instruments available: acoustic and electric guitars; microphones; an assortment of acoustic and electronic percussion; a harp; electronic keyboard. All instruments could be height adjusted to suit each participant either sitting or standing. Chairs were available for both participants and tutor. A variety of beater and drum sticks were also available. In addition, two video cameras were installed to record the sessions: one mounted on top of a cymbal stand in the corner of the room; another placed on a small stand near the entrance to the room.

The CymaSense prototype was run on a laptop connected to an audio interface, placed at the side of the room. The prototype was used in three distinct ways. These were tailored to the needs of each autistic participant, which were monitored prior to, and during, the intervention sessions (see 6.2). Firstly, a microphone on a stand was used to capture all of the audio signals within the room. This allowed the tutor to use any instrument within the room and minimise changes to the established routine for the participants. A tripod-based projector on one side of the room projected the visual output from the laptop onto a screen (Figure 6, Video Figure 1). Secondly, two microphones captured audio inputs for the 2-user version of the prototype, allowing the tutor and participant to control their own set of shapes through the use of voice or chosen instrument. The 2-user version was also projected onto the screen with each set of Cymatic shapes positioned side by side (Video Figure 2). Thirdly, an interactive table was used as an alternative means of using the prototype, presented as a tangible user interface within the room. This facilitated the needs of those participants who were less capable of eye-hand coordinated activity – playing an instrument and looking at the screen – as well as those who were driven by rhythm-based activities (Video Figure 3). The table design comprised of: a Perspex transparent surface; a contact microphone to pick up audio vibrations; an interface adapter for iPad; an iPad app to generate synthesised sounds; a small amplifier; and a projector to visualise the CymaSense prototype on the underside of the table surface (see Figure 5, Video Figures 1 and 4). The music tutor was alone in the room with the participants with the exception of a few unanticipated interruptions and on occasion when the researcher's help was required with the prototype.

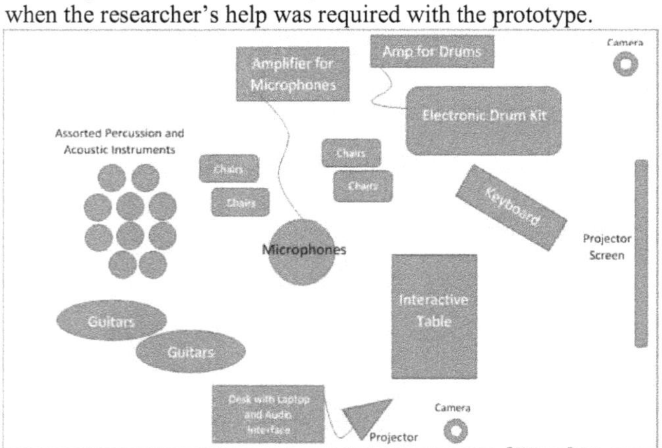

Figure 6: Music room overview

5.5 Sessions

The sessions were customised for each participant, however, a general set of structured activities were as follows: (1) Directed activity – the tutor began sessions with an introductory welcome and interaction with a chime bar. He would continue with personalised interaction with the participants' chosen instruments and/or voice. At the end of the sessions conclusory activities included simple breathing and stretching exercises to finalise the session. (2) Free activity – the music tutor would identify favoured instruments for each participant and encourage them to initiate interaction during the sessions. Independent play was also encouraged with the tutor being on-hand whenever the participant required assistance or encouragement.

5.6 Hypotheses

This research was designed to test the following hypotheses: (1) there is a significant difference between the number of musical and non-musical communicative responses demonstrated by the autistic participants in the first and last sessions of the eight week study (see 6.1); (2) there is a significant difference between the number of musical and non-musical communicative responses demonstrated by the autistic participants in their last non-intervention and first intervention sessions; (3) there will be observable changes in the communicative, social/emotional or musical behaviours of the autistic participants by parents, care workers or tutor at the conclusion of the 8-week period.

5.7 Measurement

Villafuerte et al. [51] used a composite variable based on social interaction when evaluating the Reactable tangible user interface for children with ASC. Their approach was to measure self-initiated contact and responses to social interaction. In this study, the contingent measurement was communicative behaviours. The CRASS scoresheet, described by Edgerton to evaluate improvisational music therapy approaches, was used as a basis for data gathering [10]. Divided into two sections: musical CRASS data deals with communicative responses influenced by the tutor and actions initiated by the participant that demonstrate an element of independence; non-musical CRASS data similarly details responses and actions including eye-contact, verbal, vocal and gestural communication. Non-musical CRASS data could be considered the more significant communicative factor beyond the music sessions and is referred to in more detail in Table 3. The frequency of musical and non-musical CRASS data was totalled for each session and was used to validate hypotheses (1) and (2). A post-study questionnaire provided qualitative data concerning observable changes in the participants' behaviours outside of the sessions. The survey questions were grouped into three categories: communicative behaviours; social/emotional behaviours; and musical behaviours. This data was used to validate hypothesis (3).

5.7.1 Quantitative Data

A total of 57 hours of video were analysed (two cameras recorded six weekly 30-minute sessions plus one 60-minute group session over eight weeks – minus absences). The number of occurrences of musical and non-musical communicative behaviours were observed and totalled for each participant for comparative analysis (see 6.1).

5.7.2 Qualitative Data

In addition to the video material, this research used interview and questionnaire methods for qualitative analysis. The objective was to gather data concerning the participants' behaviours outside of the sessions that could contribute to understanding results concerning communicative behaviours (see 6.2).

6. RESULTS

The recorded video material was analysed in order to elaborate all of the research results. Each participant was due to participate in eight sessions in total: two sessions of baseline non-intervention improvisational music therapy, and six intervention sessions with the CymaSense prototype. Entries in Table 3 indicate which sessions were attended by each participant.

6.1 Quantitative Analysis

Figure 7 shows the means for musical, non-musical and combined communicative acts and responses (CRASS) for all participants over the eight sessions. An overall increase was noted, however, reduction in scores in sessions 2 and 4 are notable and could be explained by absences skewing the data. This will be discussed in Section 7. To evaluate the six individuals and one group of two (G1), we decided to analyse the data in two ways: (i) by including the group in the analysis and (ii) by excluding it (see Table 1). All participants' last session scores were greater than their first session scores indicating a positive level of change over the eight sessions. The combined musical and non-musical scores ranged from 55 to 213 points, with a mean of 75.7 with G1, and a mean of 69.8

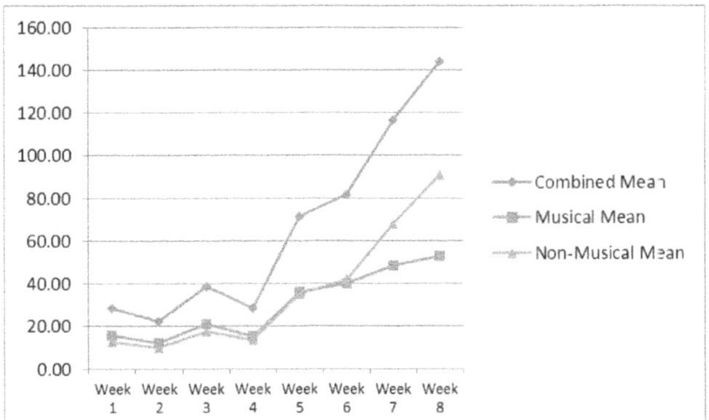

Figure 7: One-to-one and group mean scores over 8 sessions

without G1 included. Musical scores ranged from 23 to 77 including G1 data, 23 to 62 without, with mean scores of 35 including G1 and 32.6 without. Non-musical scores ranged from 38 to 174 points, with a mean of 40.6 with G1 data included and 37.2 without.

The Wilcoxon Matched-Pairs Signed Ranks Test was used to determine whether the differences observed between weekly sessions were significant. The average scores were compared between the following weeks: (a) the first and last sessions of the trial; (b) the first and last sessions of the intervention stage; (c) the third and last sessions of the intervention stage – this was to test the effect of resistance to change autistic people display [9].

Table 1: Wilcoxon Matched-Pairs Signed Ranks Tests Overview (one-tailed)

Test	Combined Musical and Non-Musical p-value	Musical Only p-value	Non-Musical Only p-value
a(i)	.009	.014	.009
a(ii)	.014	.023	.014
b(i)	.022	.034	.022
b(ii)	.034	.055	.034
c(i)	.014	.022	.009
c(ii)	.022	.038	.014
d(i)	.034	.034	.034
d(ii)	.055	.055	.055
e(i)	.014	.014	.014
e(ii)	.023	.023	.023

It is assumed that by the third intervention week, resistance to change is minimal; (d) sessions two and three, designed to be the last non-intervention and first intervention session – however, absences led to missing data; (e) the last non-intervention and first intervention session for all participants – this would vary on a session number basis as five of the participants' initial intervention stage was affected by absence. For all of the above, tests were conducted for the combined musical and non-musical data, musical data only, and non-musical data only (see Table 1).

A significant difference was observed between first and last session scores for all conditions a(i) and a(ii). The difference between the first and last sessions with intervention were significant for all conditions except b(ii) for musical scores only, Z=-1.6; p=0.055 (one-tailed), which showed no significant change. To validate the introduction of the intervention session for all participants, barring absences, sessions test c(i) and c(ii), indicate a more accurate level of significant change for all musical, non-musical and combined conditions. Sessions two and three d(i) showed significant differences for one-to-one sessions only at the .034 level (one-tailed, Z=-1.8). However, the follow-up test, e(i) and e(ii) comparing all last non-intervention sessions with first interventions sessions, indicate significant levels for all conditions.

The post-study Behaviour Change Survey was completed by four parents, four care workers and one music tutor. Twenty surveys were distributed and sixteen were returned (80% return rate). The survey consisted of a series of 7 point Likert-type scale questions, where a value of: 1 represented the negative end of the scale; 4 represented the central position; 7 represented the positive end of the scale. Table 2 shows an overview of the means for each. The means from all three behavioural categories fell between 5 and 6, indicating a change from slightly more to somewhat more. The musical category had a mean of 5.7 whilst both the communications and social/emotional categories had a mean of 5.6.

Table 2: Mean Scores for Behaviour Change Survey

Communicative Behaviours	5.6
Social/Emotional Behaviours	5.6
Musical Behaviours	5.7
Overall	5.6

6.2 Qualitative Analysis - Participant Results

6.2.1 Participant 1

P1 has ASC and was 18 years old. He was a non-verbal communicator, but used facial expressions, body language, gesturing and pictorial methods to communicate. P1 vocalised, although he did make verbal sounds and could say some words such as "Night, night", "Where", "Da Da". He could be loud in his vocalisations. He appeared to respond more positively to short, simple sentences. He usually required time to process information as well as transitions to and from different activities. Initial observations of the non-intervention sessions noted that he had a preference for percussion.

"If we brought in that extra element then he realises that his percussion instruments can be triggering visuals." [Tutor]

Table 3: Non-Musical CRASS Data

	P1	P2	P3	P4	P5	P6	G1
Week 1	19	14	13	10	4	14	16
Week 2	13	-	16	8	6	11	17
Week 3	37	9	-	22	-	20	34
Week 4	-	19	-	23	17	-	35
Week 5	41	39	24	41	20	45	36
Week 6	52	-	-	95	12	46	87
Week 7	66	44	51	117	26	71	101
Week 8	51	85	34	182	68	84	133

For the first intervention sessions, a microphone was used to visualise room sounds and project them onto the screen. The interaction with CymaSense indicated an improvement in his sense of agency through encouragement to vocalise and see the results.

However, the interactive table was chosen by the tutor as a more suitable intervention, for sessions 4 to 8, due to his preponderance toward leaning slightly forward and using his energy in a percussive manner (Video Figure 3). During subsequent interventions, P1 became more communicative through eye contact and gestural interactions (Table 3).

"[P1] developed greater understanding of the Cymatics environment and sharing these activities... He did so with curiosity, energy and enthusiasm...could be extremely valuable and meaningful to explore music and creative expression receiving such rich auditory and visual feedback to his verbal and non-verbal actions." [Tutor]

One of P1's parents expressed interest in the techniques used within the sessions - "We are interested...to learn how you carried out these sessions and if we could replicate them at home".

6.2.2 Participant 2

P2 has ASC, had been diagnosed with "profound learning disability" and was 27 years old. He was hypersensitive to loud noises or boisterous environments, and would seek out quieter areas. He communicated using non-verbal means by using different vocalisations to express happiness, distress or anger. He also used facial expressions, body language, gestural communication and objects of reference to communicate.

Initial observations of the non-intervention sessions revealed that he responded to the music tutor sitting close with turn-taking rhythmic activities on the keyboard or electric guitar. "He likes quite subtle sounds, tones. So that could be interesting finding something that's sensitive enough to have the visual responses to his sounds." [Tutor]

His first two intervention sessions had a microphone set up to visualise any sound on a screen. However, this approach did not seem effective as he has a tendency to look toward the instrument and was not capable of playing and watching the screen simultaneously. Subsequent intervention sessions used the interactive table, which indicated a more effective increase in cause-and-effect and subsequent sense of agency, as well as an increase in non-musical CRASS data (Video Figure 4) (Table 3).

"He gradually came to understand and interact with the Cymatics environment as well as with me. Developing a verbal and non-verbal, dialogue between us...I can see gradual sustained focus, attention levels and a greater sense of sharing and communication with me in these creative, expressive activities. All towards greater independence and initiating activity, away from his typical repetitive behaviours...very significant developments...often a motivating, and joyous experience..." [Tutor]

6.2.3 Participant 3

P3 has ASC, was non-verbal and was 24 years old. Her care workers commented that she often displayed a sense of detachment, withdrawal and non-participation, and had an obsession with spending lengthy periods of time in the bathroom. This led to the absences within the study and issues concerning participation within the sessions in which she was present. The music tutor commented: "I feel that she wasn't ready to explore new unfamiliar activity, for example Cymatics, when fundamentally the trust between us had to be embedded first...In the latter sessions there were some small but significant moments, where she was 'opening up' and feeling more at ease with gradual confidence." Consequently, the intervention did not indicate any significant improvements within her communication levels.

6.2.4 Participant 4

P4 has ASC, was 28 years old and had been diagnosed as non-verbal. He did not have functional language skills but used vocal expressions, body language, gesturing and pictorial methods to communicate. He was known to have an interest in computers, but little was known concerning his interests as he was the only participant not to have worked with the tutor before.

During the sessions, P4 developed a relationship of trust and understanding with the music tutor. He identified a number of plucked and percussive instruments that appealed to him and, similarly to P2, the initial two intervention sessions used a microphone which would visualise any sound on a screen. These sessions indicated a small change in communication levels but also established a set of rules for further exploration. "This was all about creating an environment relating to [P4]'s requirements and levels of communication, social rules, personal space, where he could establish a sense of trust and agency in the sessions". [Tutor]

Subsequent sessions changed the intervention to the interactive table, where greater improvements in communication were notable (Table 3). This allowed him to experiment with a range of percussive instruments that could be placed on top of the table simultaneously visualising the sound. He also developed a greater sense of agency through increased use of the CymaSense interface by choosing his own colour schemes at will. The tutor noted: "There were so many positive developments here over the 8 weeks towards greater confidence choice making, independence and gradual co-improvisation. Would certainly like to explore Cymatics possibilities further with [P4]."

One of his parents also commented: "For 20 to 30 minutes after each session, [P4] is extremely animated and puts more words together than he does in any other circumstances (for example, five words in a row 'music room good go back'). He tries to tell friends and family about the sessions and uses the tutor's and researcher's names (in his own special pronunciation). These sessions have definitely produced a positive effect in his overall communication."

6.2.5 Participant 5

P5 has ASC, was non-verbal and was 25 years old. He did not have functional language skills but expressed himself though vocalisations, using a microphone within previous music therapy sessions. It was evident through his use of the microphone that it would be suitable to introduce the intervention as a projection on screen that could provide meaningful audio-visual feedback. The tutor commented: "The consistency of the setting supported a sense of anticipation and excitement to grow in him, as he looked for the visual responses to his actions independently and also within our vocal and musical interplay."

P5 developed a musical relationship with the tutor that showed significant improvements in non-musical CRASS data toward the end of the sessions with the introduction of the two-user version of CymaSense (Table 3). His care worker noted "I have noticed in [P5]'s diary entries, an increase in singing at home." The tutor commented: "The use of the two-way Cymatics microphone set up really promoted this...I could observe some significant exchanges between us with some very meaningful pauses, and emotional peaks, which [P5] expressed with laughter, and greater close direct eye-to-eye contact than previously before the study...also to motivate him to initiate expressive ideas and encourage choice making within our musical interaction." (Video Figure 2)

6.2.6 Participant 6

P6 has ASC and was 22 years old. His language skills were functional and his communication was spontaneous. Having previously worked with the tutor, he was known for creatively expressing himself through musical improvisation. His tutor commented: "[P6]'s quite set in that he creates improvised songs. So he likes to sing and he likes to play an instrument…and he's playing on his own. And then we can have parts we do where he'll ask me to play drums or accompany him." A combination of using the microphone to visualise sounds and use of the interactive table allowed P6 to fully express himself and enhance his creativity (Video Figure 1). At the end of the first intervention session P6 commented on CymaSense to the tutor: "I love it! It gives you more focus on the song itself…it affects you…better as a singer."

The tutor went on to highlight P6 "…seemed inspired working within the Cymatics creative environment, enjoying control of the visual responses. He enjoyed the dynamic movement and intense colour responses to his energetic musical improvisations. A very immersive and personalised environment…"

6.2.7 Group 1

Finally, the group of two (G1) comprised two 24 year olds with ASC. One non-verbal male (M1) and one female (F1) with functional language skills. They were childhood friends and had subsequently participated within a number of therapeutic sessions together. Due to the diversity of both of their needs (M1 preferred percussion and strumming guitar, F1 preferred singing and percussion), a combination of using the microphone to visualise sound on screen was used, in addition to the interactive table.

They were both quite fluent with the use of computers and became more comfortable and confident in choosing their own colour schemes via the CymaSense interface. As the sessions developed they became more enthused creatively and communicatively and as their care workers noted: "Since Cymatics, [F1] has been more into her music and happier that she has something else music related…" - "Her clarity in singing has improved greatly…instead of humming…She has disclosed that this is her favourite activity, both verbally and using symbols…I can also see [F1]'s skills at drama has improved, maybe due to more [involvement] at Cymatics."

M1 seemed to develop his level of immersion with the intervention over the course of the sessions but not out-with the sessions. His care worker noted: "It appears to increase his social/musical interests during sessions. But he hasn't shown any long-term changes that I have observed." Their combined level of non-musical CRASS data indicate significant improvements over the sessions (Table 3).

7. DISCUSSION

The results of the study indicate that the combination of improvisational music therapy and use of CymaSense can improve communication for people with ASC, thus validating the hypotheses. These results support other studies related to music therapy [25], TUIs [51][5], and with natural user interfaces (NUI)[38], with respect to enhancing communication for people with ASC. This study differs through employing a combination of music therapy techniques, NUIs and TUIs. It provides the participants with an additional sense of agency and independence through the ability to experience tactile, auditory and visual feedback, within an improvisational music setting. The study suggests they can create a greater sense of predictability and control through use of the interface to control visual elements.

A surprising dip in P1's score for the final session can be noticed. It was noted that he was suffering from a heavy cold that day and his subsequent energy levels could have affected his poorer than expected performance. Similarly, P5 had dental treatment prior to sessions 4 and 5, making him physically tired and less energetic than normal. Participants' absences have already been stated with regard to their emotional health, additionally the physical health of some participants is likely to have affected their scores and consequently the results of this study.

One recognised trait of people with ASC is the fear of novelty or change within a situation [49]. In this study, there was no negative novelty effect observed. The results show there was no decrease in CRASS scores when the tool was introduced, and that scores typically increased with use. Multimodal NUIs have also been identified as a means of alleviating potential stress for people with ASC [38]. In addition, the tutor had experience working with all but one participant, P4, prior to the start of the study, further reducing potential change-related stress for the majority of participants.

One limitation to interpretation of the data relates to the single subject AB design used in the study. The experimental design used may not be as strong as one where the intervention is withdrawn and then reintroduced [37]. A withdrawal phase was considered but was advised against by a music therapy expert as it would run the risk of distressing participants if a successful intervention was withdrawn. The practicalities of carrying out this type of study were an important factor that affected its design. It is challenging to secure the participation of a therapist and participants for a long duration, which limits the duration of the different stages of the study. The baseline (A) phase was thus decided to be a two-week period, a compromise that enabled us to run the intervention over a longer stretch of time, which we judged preferable. However, consideration for a repeat or continuation of the study is on-going for further validation. An additional BAB reversal design would provide comparative data to highlight the effect of the music therapy itself compared to the intervention.

It could be argued that CymaSense, when used as an interactive table, not only visualises interaction with the table surface itself, but also creates a novel percussive instrument. This creates new opportunities for social interaction through a shared space and turn-taking, while independent use could also encourage cause-and-effect and a subsequent sense of agency.

Interpretation of the data, from an audio-visual perspective, relied on a number of variables relating to the study environment and the nature of each participant's level of ASC. For example, the amount of light within the room may affect the comfort levels of the participants in differing ways. Hypersensitivity and hyposensitivity is well known within autism and may be a factor [39]. However, the lighting conditions were altered and continually assessed during each session by the tutor for the participants' comfort levels.

The size and location of the projected image may have affected the participant's ability to appreciate the cause-and-effect nature of the system. This was noted by the researcher and the tutor through constant review of sessions and video, and subsequent decisions were made as noted in the results section (6.2).

Colour may have affected how participants experienced the sessions. The tutor initially used the default colours (black background and spectrum colours for the Cymatic shapes) for a number of sessions to allow familiarity with the tool. Alternative colours were chosen at random by the tutor in future sessions while some participants chose their own colour schemes. None of the participants were diagnosed with visual or auditory impairments. However, further studies would be required to determine the effectiveness of the colours chosen and the effect of environmental factors like temperature or noise - for example, the hum of the projector. Similarly, little is known concerning how the animation of the shapes themselves affected each participant. Again, however, participants with functional language provided positive feedback concerning the dynamic movement and colour responses.

8. CONCLUSION AND FUTURE WORK

The majority of participants used CymaSense successfully. Although it is difficult, or even impossible, to gather a homogenous group of people with ASC, the design, implementation and results based on the sample population in our study support the initial hypothesis that the use of an interactive audio-visual tool can improve communication for people on the autism spectrum. Further research is planned to include interviews with parents in an attempt to identify the elements of CymaSense that make it successful. In addition, the effectiveness of the audio-visual mapping implemented in CymaSense is currently being evaluated in a study in which the response of neurotypical respondents is compared to that of autistic users.

This evaluation of CymaSense opens up new possibilities for other sensory impaired groups. The CymaSense system architecture can support visualisation of any sound through 3D graphics, making customisation for alternative groups simple. Future studies concerning its use by children and by alternative disability groups, including the hearing impaired, may promote social interaction and self-esteem by encouraging group play and turn-taking.

TUI interventions [51] or NUI interventions [38], used in other studies, promote communication and social interaction within autistic children. In this study, which involved eight autistic adults, four of which were non-verbal and two only exhibited limited language skills, we have demonstrated that significant improvements in communication can be observed by augmenting music therapy with real-time visual feedback. The single case qualitative analysis has provided specific insight into the usefulness of the intervention and of the system developed.

9. ACKNOWLEDGMENTS

The Authors would like to acknowledge the IIDI (Institute for Informatics and Digital Innovation) for their financial support, and TouchBase for their assistance in the organisation of the study.

10. REFERENCES

1. David Aldridge. 2003. *Case Study Designs in Music Therapy*. Jessica Kingsley Publishers.
2. American Psychiatric Association. 2013. *Diagnostic and statistical manual of mental disorders (5th ed.)*. .
3. Carolynn Bredek, Doreen Granpeesheh, Kathy Thompson, and Renat Matalon. 2014. Visual and Other Sensory Modifications. In *Evidence-Based Treatment for Children with Autism*. Elsevier, 115–132.
4. Butter Churn. 2017. Butterchurn visualizer. Retrieved March 14, 2017 from https://butterchurnviz.com/.
5. Franceli L. Cibrian, Oscar Peña, Deysi Ortega, and Monica Tentori. 2017. BendableSound: An elastic multisensory surface using touch-based interactions to assist children with severe autism during music therapy. *International Journal of Human-Computer Studies* 0: 1–16.
6. Peter Ciuha, Bojan Klemenc, and Franc Solina. 2010. Visualization of concurrent tones in music with colours. *Proceedings of the international conference on Multimedia - MM '10*, ACM Press, 1677.
7. Cycling '74. 2017. Max. Retrieved February 14, 2016 from https://cycling74.com/products/max/.
8. Cymascope.com. 2015. Physics :: Cymascope Research. Retrieved December 30, 2015 from http://cymascope.com/cyma_research/physics.html.
9. Theo Dimitriadis and Henk Smeijsters. 2011. Autistic spectrum disorder and music therapy: theory underpinning practice. *Nordic Journal of Music Therapy* 20, 2: 108–122.
10. C. L. Edgerton. 1994. The Effect of Improvisational Music Therapy on the Communicative Behaviors of Autistic Children. *Journal of Music Therapy* 31, 1: 31–62.
11. William Farr, Nicola Yuill, and Hayes Raffle. 2010. Social benefits of a tangible user interface for children with Autistic Spectrum Conditions. *Autism* 14, 3: 237–252.
12. Christopher Frauenberger, Julia Makhaeva, and Katharina Spiel. 2017. Blending Methods : Developing Participatory Design Sessions for Autistic Children. .
13. Kostas Giannakis. 2006. A comparative evaluation of auditory-visual mappings for sound visualisation. *Organised Sound* 11, 3: 297.
14. Oliver Gingrich, Alain Renaud, and Eugenia Emets. 2013. KIMA - A Holographic Telepresence Environment Based on Cymatic Principles. *Leonardo* 46, 4: 332–343.
15. Ofer Golan and Simon Baron-Cohen. 2006. Systemizing empathy: Teaching adults with Asperger syndrome or high-functioning autism to recognize complex emotions using interactive multimedia. *Development and Psychopathology* 18: 591–617.
16. Gina Green and J Ricciardi. 2015. *Findings and conclusions: National standards project, phase 2*. .
17. Haruki Hasegawa. 2015. Music Visualizer. Retrieved July 19, 2017 from https://music-visualizer.h6ah4i.com/.
18. A. Hillier, G. Greher, N. Poto, and M. Dougherty. 2012. Positive outcomes following participation in a music intervention for adolescents and young adults on the autism spectrum. *Psychology of Music* 40, 2: 201–215.
19. Juan Pablo Hourcade, Stacy R. Williams, Ellen A. Miller, Kelsey E. Huebner, and Lucas J. Liang. 2013. Evaluation of tablet apps to encourage social interaction in children with autism spectrum disorders. *Proceedings of the SIGCHI Conference on Human Factors in Computing Systems - CHI '13*: 3197–3206.
20. Tiffany L Hutchins and Patricia a Prelock. 2006. Using Social Stories and Comic Strip Conversations To Promote Socially Valid Outcomes for Children with Autism. *Seminars in Speech and Language* 27, 1: 047–059.
21. Hans Jenny. 1968. CYMATICS. *The Sciences* 8, 7: 12–18.
22. Ronna S Kaplan and Anita Louise Steele. 2005. An analysis of music therapy program goals and outcomes for clients with diagnoses on the autism spectrum. *Journal of music therapy* 42, 1: 2–19.
23. Mats B. Küssner. 2014. Shape, Drawing and Gesture: Cross-Modal Mappings of Sound and Music. .
24. Amanda Lazar, Raymundo Cornejo, Caroline Edasis, and Anne Marie Piper. 2016. Designing for the Third Hand : Empowering Older Adults with Cognitive Impairments through Creating and Sharing. *Proceedings of the Designing Interactive Systems Conference (DIS '16)*: 1047–1058.

25. H a Lim. 2007. The Effect of" Developmental Speech-Language Training through Music" on Speech Production in Children with Autism Spectrum Disorders. *Journal of Music Therapy* XLVII, 1: 2–26.

26. H a Lim and E Draper. 2011. The Effects of Music Therapy Incorporated with Applied Behavior Analysis Verbal Behavior Approach for Children with Autism Spectrum Disorders. *Journal of Music Therapy* 48, 4: 532–550.

27. John McGowan, Grégory Leplâtre, and Iain McGregor. 2017. CymaSense. *Proceedings of the 2016 ACM Conference Companion Publication on Designing Interactive Systems - DIS '17 Companion*, ACM Press, 270–274.

28. Francois Michaud and Catherine Theberge-Turmel. 2002. Mobile Robotic Toys and Autism. In K. Dautenhahn, A. Bond, L. Cañamero, and B. Edmonds, eds., *Socially Intelligent Agents: Creating relationships with Computers and Robots*. Kluwer Publishers, 125–132.

29. Christine Norris and John Dattilo. 1999. Evaluating Effects of a Social Story Intervention on a Young Girl with Autism. *Focus on Autism and Other Developmental Disabilities* 14, 3: 180–186.

30. Novation. Launchpad | NovationMusic.com. Retrieved from https://global.novationmusic.com/launch/launchpad#.

31. Narcís Parés, Anna Carreras, Jaume Durany, et al. 2005. Promotion of Creative Activity in Children With Severe Autism Through Visuals in an Interactive Multisensory Environment. .

32. S Parsons and P Mitchell. 2002. The potential of virtual reality in social skills training for people with autistic spectrum disorders. *Journal of Intellectual Disability Research* 46, 430–443.

33. M. Pavlicevic. 2014. Afterword: Knock knock... *Psychology of Music* 42, 6: 2014–2016.

34. Mercédès Pavlicevic, Nicky O'Neil, Harriet Powell, Oonagh Jones, and Ergina Sampathianaki. 2013. Making music, making friends: Long-term music therapy with young adults with severe learning disabilities. *Journal of intellectual disabilities : JOID*: 5–19.

35. Katherine Paxton and Irene A Estay. 2007. Counselling people on the autism spectrum: A practical manual. *Counselling people on the autism spectrum: A practical manual*.

36. J. Preis, R. Arnon, D. Silbert, and A. Rozegar. 2015. Does Music Matter? The Effects of Background Music on Verbal Expression and Engagement in Children with Autism Spectrum Disorders. *Music Therapy Perspectives*: 1–10.

37. Brian Reichow, Peter Doehring, Domenic V. Cicchetti, and Fred R. Volkmar. 2011. *Evidence-based practices and treatments for children with autism*. .

38. Kathryn E. Ringland, Rodrigo Zalapa, Megan Neal, Lizbeth Escobedo, Monica Tentori, and Gillian R. Hayes. 2014. SensoryPaint: A Multimodal Sensory Intervention for Children with Neurodevelopmental Disorders. *Proceedings of the 2014 ACM International Joint Conference on Pervasive and Ubiquitous Computing - UbiComp '14 Adjunct* September: 873–884.

39. Jodi Robledo, Anne M Donnellan, and Karen Strandt-Conroy. 2012. An exploration of sensory and movement differences from the perspective of individuals with autism. *Frontiers in integrative neuroscience* 6, November: 107.

40. Roseann C. Schaaf and Lucy Jane Miller. 2005. Occupational therapy using a sensory integrative approach for children with developmental disabilities. *Mental Retardation and Developmental Disabilities Research Reviews* 11, 2: 143–148.

41. Scottish Autism. 2017. Scottish Autism - Autism Awareness Charity & Services for Children & Adults in Scotland. Retrieved April 4, 2017 from http://www.scottishautism.org/.

42. Sense Scotland. 2017. Sense Scotland. Retrieved April 4, 2017 from http://www.sensescotland.org.uk/.

43. Stephen M Shore. 2003. The Language of Music: Working with Children on the Autism Spectrum. *Journal of Education* 183, 2.

44. Kate Simpson and Deb Keen. 2011. Music interventions for children with autism: Narrative review of the literature. *Journal of Autism and Developmental Disorders* 41, 11: 1507–1514.

45. SkoogMusic. Skoogmusic | We create music technology that lets anyone make music. Retrieved July 3, 2015 from http://www.skoogmusic.com/.

46. S.M. Smith and G.N. Williams. 1997. A visualization of music. *Proceedings. Visualization '97 (Cat. No. 97CB36155)*, IEEE, 499–503.

47. Soundspectrum. 2017. SoundSpectrum. Retrieved March 14, 2017 from https://www.soundspectrum.com/.

48. Lewis Sykes. 2011. The augmented tonoscope. ... *conference on Electronic Visualisation and the Arts*: 1–6.

49. Colwyn Trevarthen. 2002. Autism, sympathy of motives and music therapy. *Enfance* 54, 1: 86.

50. Erez Tsur, Michael Friger, and Idan Menashe. 2016. The Unique Evolutionary Signature of Genes Associated with Autism Spectrum Disorder. *Behavior Genetics* 46, 6: 754–762.

51. Lilia Villafuerte, Milena Markova, and Sergi Jorda. 2012. Acquisition of social abilities through musical tangible user interface. *Proceedings of the 2012 ACM annual conference extended abstracts on Human Factors in Computing Systems Extended Abstracts - CHI EA '12*, 745.

52. Barbara L. Wheeler. 2015. *Music Therapy Handbook*. Guilford Publications.

53. Mitchell Whitelaw. 2008. Synesthesia and Cross-Modality in Contemporary Audiovisuals. *The Senses & Society* 3, 3: 259–276.

54. Tsung-Ren Yang, Pamela J Wolfberg, Shu-Chin Wu, and Pey-Yun Hwu. 2003. Supporting children on the autism spectrum in peer play at home and school: piloting the integrated play groups model in Taiwan. *Autism : the international journal of research and practice*.

Good Background Colors for Readers: A Study of People with and without Dyslexia

Luz Rello
Human-Computer Interaction Institute
Carnegie Mellon University
luzrello@cs.cmu.edu

Jeffrey P. Bigham
Human-Computer Interaction Institute &
Language Technologies Institute
Carnegie Mellon University
jbigham@cs.cmu.edu

ABSTRACT

The use of colors to enhance the reading of people with dyslexia have been broadly discussed and is often recommended, but evidence of the effectiveness of this approach is lacking. This paper presents a user study with 341 participants (89 with dyslexia) that measures the effect of using background colors on screen readability. Readability was measured via reading time and distance travelled by the mouse. Comprehension was used as a control variable. The results show that using certain background colors have a significant impact on people with and without dyslexia. Warm background colors, *Peach*, *Orange* and *Yellow*, significantly improved reading performance over cool background colors, *Blue*, *Blue Grey* and *Green*. These results provide evidence to the practice of using colored backgrounds to improve readability; people with and without dyslexia benefit, but people with dyslexia may especially benefit from the practice given the difficulty they have in reading in general.

Keywords

Background colors, Dyslexia, Readability, Reading Speed

Categories and Subject Descriptors

K.4.2 [**Computers and Society**]: Social Issues—*Assistive technologies for persons with disabilities*; K.3 [**Computers in Education**]: Computer Uses in Education—*Computer-assisted instruction*

1. INTRODUCTION

More than 10% of the population has dyslexia, a specific learning disability with a neurobiological origin [15, 17, 32]. The *World Federation of Neurology* defines dyslexia as a disorder in children who, despite conventional classroom experience, fail to attain the language skills of reading, writing, and spelling commensurate with their intellectual abilities [33].

ASSETS '17, October 29-November 1, 2017, Baltimore, MD, USA

DOI: https://doi.org/10.1145/3132525.3132546

The use of different background colors to enhance reading performance of those with dyslexia has been broadly discussed in previous literature and has been recommended by institutions such as the *British Dyslexia Association* [4]. To the extent of our knowledge the existing recommendations are not based on objectives measures collected with large user studies. In this paper, we present the first study that measures the impact of ten background colors on the reading performance. The user study was carried out with a large number of participants (341) with and without dyslexia, allowing for a statistical comparison between groups.
The main contributions of this study are:

- Background colors have an impact on the readability of text for people with and without dyslexia, and the impact is comparable for both groups.

- Warm background colors such as *Peach*, *Orange*, or *Yellow* are beneficial for readability taking into consideration both reading performance and mouse distance. Also, cool background colors, in particular *Blue Grey*, *Blue*, and *Green*, decreased the text readability for both groups; however, this do not necessarily mean that such colors need to be avoided.

- When reading on screen, people with dyslexia present a significantly higher use of the mouse in terms of distance travelled by the mouse.

The next section focuses on dyslexia, reviews related work, and explains the relationship of dyslexia to visual stress syndrome (Meares-Irlen syndrome). Section 3 explains the experimental methodology and Section 4 presents the results, which are discussed in Section 5. In Section 6 we derive recommendations for dyslexic-friendly background colors and mention future lines of research.

2. DYSLEXIA AND COLORS

According to the *International Association of Dyslexia*, dyslexia is characterized by difficulties with accurate and/or fluent word recognition and poor spelling and decoding abilities. These difficulties typically result from a deficit in the phonological component of language that is often unexpected in relation to other cognitive abilities and the provision of effective classroom instruction [20]. Therefore, in theory, dyslexia is not related to the color in which the text or the background is presented. However, there are a number of studies and recommendations regarding colors and dyslexia. One possible explanation for this is that visual stress syndrome (Meares-Irlen syndrome) is associated with dyslexia. In this section we explain both, (i) the previous work regarding color recommendations and dyslexia, and (ii) the relationship of dyslexia to Meares-Irlen syndrome.

2.1 Related Work

McCarthy and Swierenga stated that poor color selections are one of the key problems encountered by people with dyslexia when reading on a screen [21]. There are a number of studies that have recommended the use of certain fonts or background colors. According to Perron, high contrast creates so much vibration that it diminishes readability [23]. Likewise, Bradford recommends avoiding high contrast and suggests pairing off-black/off-white for font and background respectively to enhance Web accessibility for people with dyslexia [3]. In a user study carried out by Gregor and Newell [12, 13] mucky green/brown and blue/yellow pairs were chosen by people with dyslexia.

An eye-tracking study of 22 participants with dyslexia [28] showed that a black font over a cream background presented shorter fixation durations among the participants, being the most readable pair. The same experimental setting was later performed with a larger group of participants (92 people, 46 with dyslexia and 46 as a control group) giving comparable results [26]. Similarly, a cream background color is recommended by the *British Dyslexia Association* [4].

Our study advances previous work in two ways (i) we are using 10 background colors with black font similar to the color overlays used to treat Meares-Irlen syndrome, even if it is not a language based disorder, given their previous success in that target population (see Section 2.2); (ii) it is the first time that a mouse tracking measure is used to address text readability for participants with dyslexia; and (iii) the user study was carried out with a large number of participants with and without dyslexia allowing a statistical comparison between the groups.

2.2 Dyslexia and Meares-Irlen syndrome

Dyslexia rarely occurs alone. Dyslexia has a wide range of comorbities, that is, conditions that exist simultaneously but are independent to dyslexia. The most common ones are: dysgraphia, attention deficit disorder and attention deficit hyperactivity disorder, and visual stress syndrome (Meares-Irlen syndrome). Among the visual difficulties associated with dyslexia that could be alleviated by modifications of the visual display [10], the most studied is Meares-Irlen syndrome [18].

Meares-Irlen Syndrome is a perceptual processing disorder, meaning that it relates specifically to how the brain processes the visual information it receives. Unlike dyslexia, it is not a language-based disorder but it is comorbid with dyslexia.

Of individuals with dyslexia, 25.84% in Spanish-speakers [1] to 46% in Portuguese-speakers [14] have Meares-Irlen Syndrome. These estimations are of native speakers of Spanish and Portuguese, respectively. Meares-Irlen syndrome is characterized by symptoms of visual stress and visual perceptual distortions that are alleviated by using individually prescribed colored filters. Patients susceptible to pattern glare, perceptual distortions and discomfort from patterns, may have Meares-Irlen syndrome and are likely to find colored filters useful [11].

Kriss and Evans [18] compared colored overlays on a group of 32 children with dyslexia with a control group of same size. The differences between the two groups did not reach statistical significance. The authors conclude that Meares-Irlen syndrome is prevalent in the general population and possibly somewhat more common for people with dyslexia. Children with dyslexia seemed to benefit more from colored overlays than non-dyslexic children. The authors stress that Meares-Irlen syndrome and dyslexia are separate entities and are detected and treated in different ways [18].

Moreover, Jeanes *et al.* [16] showed how color overlays improved the reading performance of children in school without taking into consideration dyslexia or other visual difficulties. Gregor and Newell [13], and later Dickinson *et al.* [7] have shown that visual changes in the presentation of text may alleviate some of the problems generated by dyslexia and visual comorbidities.

3. METHODOLOGY

To study the effect of background colors on screen readability, we conducted a user study where 341 participants (89 with dyslexia) read 10 comparable texts with varying background colors. Readability was measured via reading speed and a mouse-tracking measure, while comprehension was used as a controlled variable measured by comprehension tests.

3.1 Experimental Design

3.1.1 Independent variables

In our experimental design, *Background Color* served as an **independent variable** with 10 levels. The text color used in all samples was black (f00000). Following we present each of the levels of *Background Color* followed by the RGB color values, the hex color value; and the luminosity contrast ratio[1]). Since all the color contrasts are greater than 7:1 they all meet the WCAG[5] color contrast requirements for AAA.

- *Blue:* RGB(150, 173, 252); #96ADFC; 9.68:1.
- *Blue Grey:* RGB(219, 225, 241) #DBE1F1; 16.05:1.
- *Green:* RGB(219, 225, 241) #A8F29A; 15.83:1.
- *Grey:* RGB(168, 242, 154) #D8D3D6; 14.21:1.
- *Orange:* RGB(216, 211, 214) #EDDD6E; 15.17:1.
- *Peach:* RGB(237, 221, 110) #EDD1B0; 14.35:1.
- *Purple:* RGB(237, 209, 176) #B987DC; 7.56:1.
- *Red:* RGB(185, 135, 220) #E0A6AA; 10.2:1.
- *Turquoise:* RGB(224, 166, 170) #A5F7E1; 16.99:1.
- *Yellow:* RGB(248, 253, 137) #F8FD89; 19.4:1.

We chose to study these colors because they have been recommended and studied in previous literature about dyslexia [4, 12, 26] and Meares-Irlen syndrome, which is comorbid with dyslexia [1, 14]. See Section 5 for a comparison of our results with previous studies.

[1]Color Contrast Tester available at: https://www.joedolson.com/tools/color-contrast.php

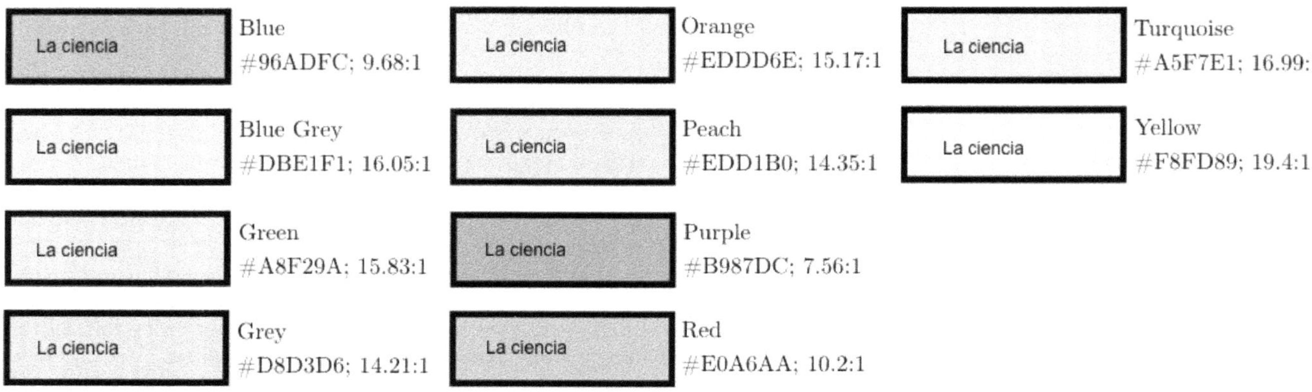

Figure 1: The 10 background colors used in the experiment as independent variables using black font including their Hex color values and the luminosity contrast ratio between the black font and the background color: *Blue*, *Blue Grey*, *Green*, *Grey*, *Orange*, *Peach*, *Purple*, *Red*, *Turquoise*, **and** *Yellow*.

3.1.2 Dependent Variables

For quantifying readability, we use three **dependent measures**: *Reading Time* and *Mouse Distance.* The latter one was extracted using mouse-tracking. To control **Comprehension** of the text we use two comprehension questions as *control variables.*

To track mouse movements we used an an open source, client-server architecture mouse tracking tool called smt2 [19].[2]. This software allowed us to log mouse movements at fixed-time intervals. This process does not interfere with the user's browsing experience or introduce delays associated with data capture.

- *Reading Time:* Shorter reading durations are preferred to longer ones as faster reading is related to more readable text. Therefore, we use *Reading Time*, *i.e.* the time it takes a participant to completely read one text sample, as a measure of readability.

- *Mouse Distance:* The total number of pixels that the mouse travelled over the text. Having a computer with a mouse was a requirement for the study so no finger movements were recorded as mouse movements. Mouse movements were possible but not required during the reading of the text (except for pushing the "ok" button when the participant finished reading the text). The main measure to address readability is *Reading Time* and *Mouse Distance* can be treated as a secondary readability indicator. A user study with 90 participants [22] found that the more complex the text was, the more mouse tracking movements the participants made. Hence, we can conclude that shorter mouse distances could be related to higher text readability.

3.1.3 Control variable

To check that the text was not only read, but also understood, we used two literal questions, that is, questions that can be answered straight from the text. We used multiple-choice questions with three possible choices: one correct choice, and two wrong choices. We use these comprehension questions as a *control variables* to guarantee that the data analyzed in this study were valid. If the reader did not choose the correct answer, the corresponding text was discarded from the analysis.

[2]Available at: https://smt.speedzinemedia.com/downloads.php

3.1.4 Design

We used a *within-subject* design, that is, all the participants contributed to all the conditions reading 10 different texts with all 10 different background colors. We counterbalanced the colors to avoid sequence effects, hence there were 10 different variants of the experiment where the order in which a certain background color appeared was not repeated. Therefore, the data were evenly distributed with respect to text order and color combinations .

We also controlled having a balanced participant representation of all the experimental variants. Each of the 10 variants was undertaken by no less than 33 participants and no more than 35 participants (34.1 participants x 10 variants equals our 341 participants). The distribution of the groups -with and without dyslexia- contributing to each of the variants was also controlled. Participants with dyslexia contributed to all the variants, and their distribution ranged from 16.13% to 25.71%.

3.2 Participants

Overall, 341 participants undertook the experiment, including 89 people (69 female, 20 male) with dyslexia or at risk of having dyslexia (Group Dyslexia). Their ages ranged from 18 to 60 ($\bar{x}$ = 38.38, s = 11.02). The control group (Group Control) had 252 people (195 female, 57 male). Their ages ranged from 18 to 60 ($\bar{x}$ = 37.79, s = 10.31). They were all Spanish native speakers, although 160 were bilingual (50% in group Control and 38.20% in Group Dyslexia) in Catalan, Galician, Basque, and English.

Participants were recruited through a public call that dyslexia associations distributed to their members; 66 participants had a confirmed diagnosis of dyslexia including the date the place where they were diagnosed; 23 subjects were at risk of having dyslexia (under observation by profession-

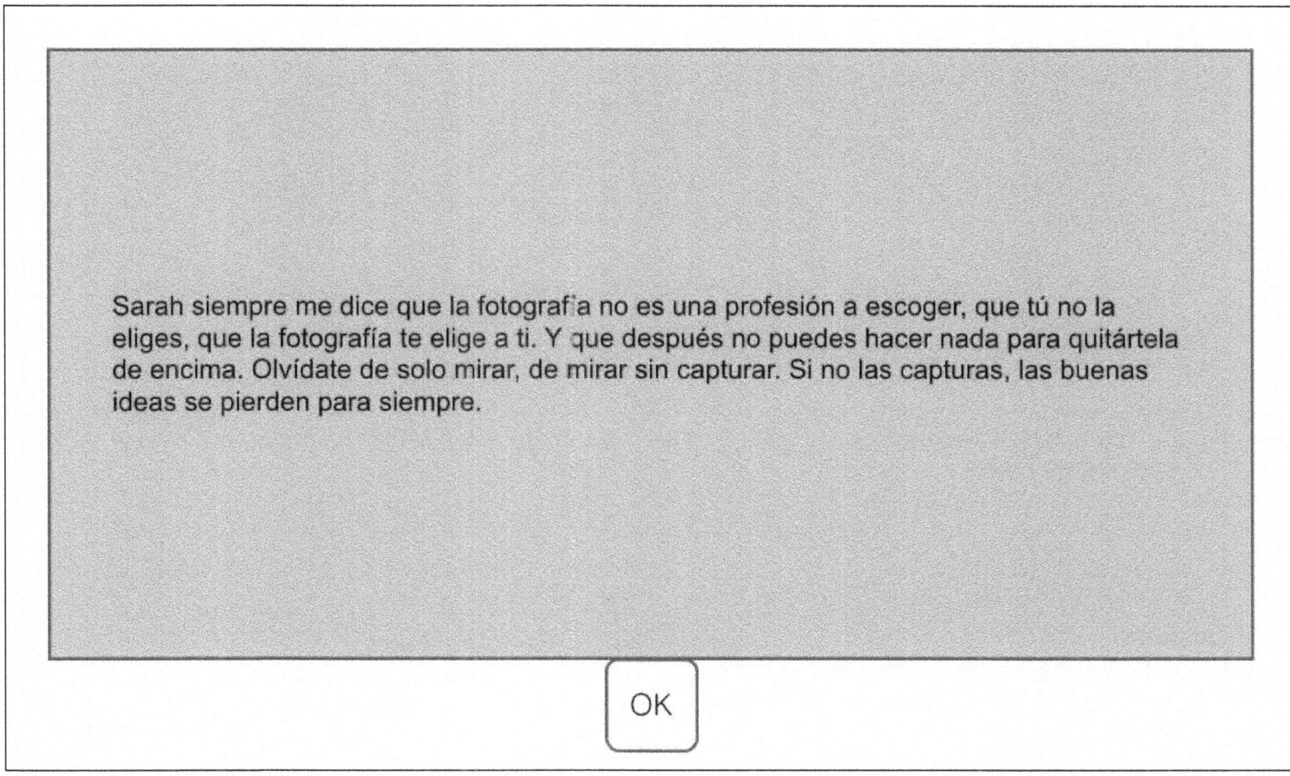

Figure 2: Sample slide used in the study with background color *Blue*.

als) or suspected to have dyslexia. Note that all the participants were adults and finding adults with confirmed diagnosis of dyslexia is more challenging than finding children with a confirmed diagnosis. Participants from the control group were also volunteers responding to the call for volunteers made through dyslexia associations as well as family and friends from the group with dyslexia. Participants took the experiment from different Spanish speaking countries; there were participants from Spain (212), Argentina (76), Mexico (16),Chile (9), Venezuela (5), USA (5), Peru (4), Colombia (2), and Panama (2).

Overall, the participants presented a high education profile as 83.28% had a college degree or higher: primary education (6 participants), secondary education (23), professional education (28), college (66), university (131), masters (62), and Ph.D. (25).

It is worth noting that Meares-Irlen syndrome remains undiagnosed in Spanish speaking countries. We specifically asked our participants if they were diagnosed with any visual stress syndromes. Only one of them, who had previously lived in the United Kingdom, was diagnosed with Meares-Irlen syndrome in addition to dyslexia.

3.3 Materials

To isolate the effects of the background color presentation, the texts need to be comparable in complexity. In this section, we describe how we designed the study material.

3.3.1 Texts

All the texts used in the experiment meet the comparability requirement because they all share parameters commonly used to compute readability [9]. All the texts were extracted from a chapter of the same book, *Impostores ('The Impostors')* , by Lucas Sánchez [30]. Each paragraph shared the following characteristics: (i) same genre; (ii) same style; (iii) same number of words (55 words)[3]; and (iv) absence of numerical expressions and acronyms because people with dyslexia encounter problems with such words [6, 27]. See Figure 2 for an example of one of the texts used.

3.3.2 Text Presentation

Text presentation has an effect on the reading speed of people with dyslexia [13], hence we used the same layout for all the texts (except for the *Background Color* condition): The texts were left-justified [4], using an 18-point sized [29] *Arial* font type [25]. The font color was black, the most frequently used on the Web.

3.3.3 Comprehension Control Questions

After the participants read the texts, there were two literal comprehension control questions. The order of the correct answer was counterbalanced. An example of one of these questions is given below.

- *The neighbors of the story...*
  Los vecinos de la historia...
    - *were happy when the tree was cut down.*
      se alegraron cuando cortaron el árbol.
    - *liked the tree very much.*
      les gustaba mucho el árbol.

[3]If the paragraph did not have that number of words we slightly modified it to match the number of words.

Group Dyslexia		*Reading Time*		*Group Control*		*Reading Time*	
Color	$\tilde{x}$	$\bar{x} \pm s$	%	Color	$\tilde{x}$	$\bar{x} \pm s$	%
Peach	13.72	14.85 ± 6.29	100	Peach	11.32	12.28 ± 5.09	100
Orange	20.19	15.33 ± 6.02	103	Orange	11.78	12.32 ± 4.07	100
Yellow	15.07	16.30 ± 6.06	109	Yellow	12.81	13.43 ± 4.52	109
Purple	16.58	17.21 ± 6.28	115	Purple	14.03	14.68 ± 5.38	119
Red	17.18	17.47 ± 5.96	117	Red	13.90	14.97 ± 6.05	121
Turquoise	17.47	17.59 ± 5.99	118	Turquoise	13.64	14.54 ± 4.76	118
Grey	17.48	18.05 ± 5.95	121	Grey	14.88	16.03 ± 5.97	130
Blue	17.84	19.42 ± 7.61	130	Blue	15.12	16.24 ± 5.71	132
Green	18.78	19.42 ± 7.18	130	Green	14.81	16.45 ± 6.77	133
Blue Grey	20.19	21.57 ± 6.93	145	Blue Grey	18.15	18.82 ± 6.00	153

Table 1: Median, mean and standard deviation of *Reading Time* in seconds. Colors are sorted by the mean $\bar{x}$. We include the relative percentage for *Reading Time*, our main readability measure, with respect to the smallest average value, *Peach*.

- *talked and babbled with the tree.*
  hablaban y balbuceaban con el árbol.

3.4 Procedure

We sent an announcement of the study to the main associations of dyslexia in countries with large Spanish-speaking populations, including the United States. Interested potential participants contacted us, and after we checked their participation requirements (age, native language, and technical requirements, *i.e.* having a laptop or desktop computer with the Chrome browser installed as well as the use of mouse), we set up a date to supervise the study. We met the participants on-line. After they signed the on-line consent form, we gave them specific instructions and they completed the study. They were asked to read the 10 texts in silence and complete the comprehension control questions. While answering the questions they could not look back on the text. Each session lasted from 10 to 15 minutes long.

4. RESULTS

In the first step we cleaned up the data considering the answers of the comprehension questions. We discarded the data of 4.9% of the participants (17) due to failing the comprehension test.

We use the Shapiro-Wilk test for checking if the data fits a normal distribution. The test showed that none of the data sets (10 for each group) were normally distributed for *Reading Time* and *Mouse Distance*. As our data set was not normal, we include the median and box plots for all our measures in addition to the mean and the standard deviation. For the same reason, to study the effects of the dependent variables (repeated measures) we used the two-way Friedman's non-parametric test for repeated measures plus a complete pairwise Wilcoxon rank sum post-hoc comparison test with a Bonferroni correction that includes the adjustment of the significance level. In the post-hoc tests we used the Bonferroni adjustment [2] because it is the most conservative approach in comparison with other adjustment methods. Finally, we used the Spearman's rank-order correlation for nonparametric data to understand the strength of the association between groups and the main indicator of dyslexia in Spanish, *Reading Time* [31] and *Mouse Distance*.

We used the R Statistical Software 2.14.1 [24] for our analysis, with the standard condition of $p < 0.05$ for significant results. We only report post-hoc test results when significant effects were found.

4.1 Reading Time

Table 1 shows the main statistical measures[4] of the main readability indicator *Reading Time* for participants with and without dyslexia in each of the *Background Color* conditions.

There was a significant effect of *Background Color* on *Reading Time* ($\chi^2(9) = 1154.81$, $p < 0.001$).

- **Between Groups:** Participants with dyslexia had significantly longer reading times ($\bar{x} = 17.73$, $s = 20.28$ seconds) than the participants without dyslexia ($\bar{x} = 14.98$, $s = 20.17$ seconds, $p < 0.001$).

  For *Reading Time* the Spearman's correlation coefficient between groups is $\rho = 0.964$, and it is statistically significant ($p < 0.001$).

- For **Group Dyslexia** there was a significant effect of *Background Color* on *Reading Time* ($\chi^2(9) = 299.16$, $p < 0.001$) (Table 1, Figure 3). The results of the post-hoc tests show that:

  - *Peach* had the shortest mean reading time. Participants had significantly shorter reading times using *Peach* than *Blue Grey* ($p < 0.001$), *Green* ($p < 0.001$), *Blue* ($p < 0.001$), *Grey* ($p = 0.002$), *Turquoise* ($p = 0.026$), and *Red* ($p = 0.035$).
  - *Orange* had the second shortest mean reading time. Participants had significantly shorter reading times using *Orange* than *Blue Grey* ($p < 0.001$), *Green* ($p = 0.001$), *Blue* ($p = 0.002$), and *Grey* ($p = 0.002$).
  - Similarly, *Yellow* had the third shortest reading time, significantly shorter than using *Blue Grey* ($p < 0.001$), *Green* ($p = 0.029$), and *Blue* ($p = 0.040$).
  - *Blue Grey* had the longest reading time. This background color lead to significantly longer reading times than using *Peach* ($p < 0.001$), *Orange* ($p < 0.001$), *Yellow* ($p < 0.001$), *Purple*

[4]We use $\bar{x}$ for the mean, $\tilde{x}$ for the median, and s for the standard deviation.

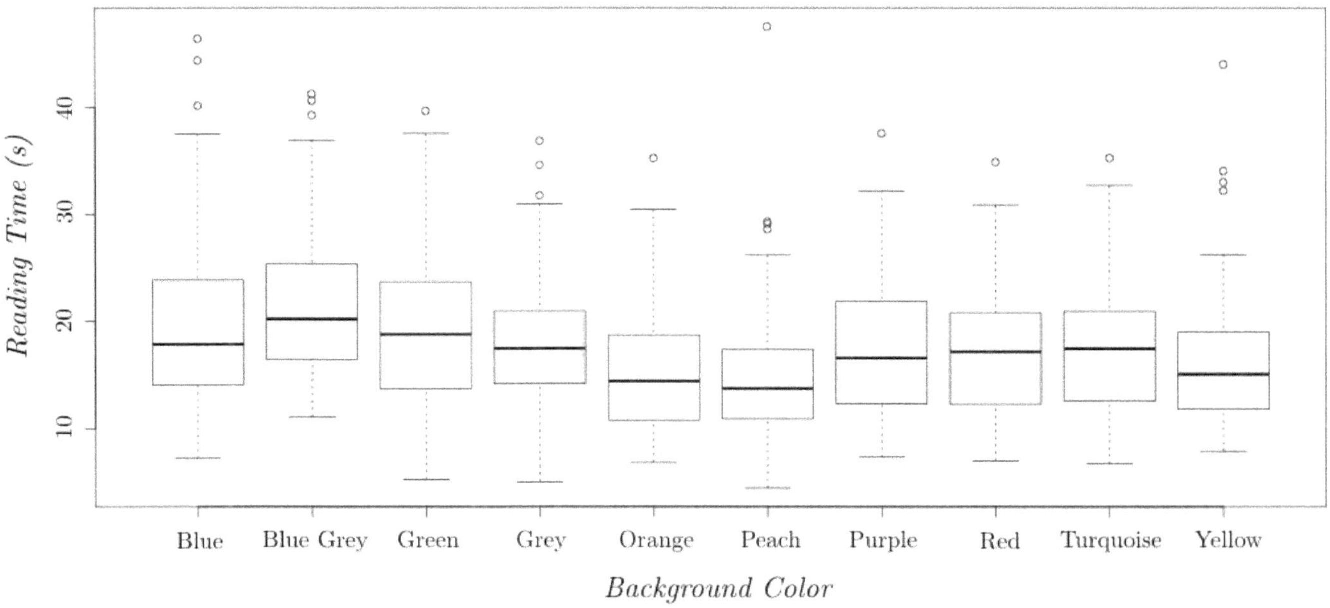

Figure 3: ***Reading Time*** **box plots by** ***Background Color*** **for Group Dyslexia.**

($p = 0.001$), *Red* ($p = 0.004$), and *Turquoise* ($p = 0.005$).

- Likewise, in **Group Control** there was a significant effect of *Background Color* on *Reading Time* ($\chi^2(9) = 859.37$, $p < 0.001$) (Table 1, Figure 4). The results of the post-hoc tests show that:
  - *Peach* had the shortest reading time, significantly shorter than the rest (all with $p < 0.005$) except *Orange*, which had the second shortest duration.
  - *Orange* had the second shortest reading time, significantly shorter than the rest of the background colors ($p < 0.001$) except for *Peach* and *Yellow*, having *Yellow* the third shortest reading time.
  - *Yellow* had the third shortest reading time, significantly shorter than *Purple* ($p = 0.046$), *Red* ($p = 0.032$), *Grey* ($p < 0.001$), *Blue* ($p < 0.001$), *Green* ($p < 0.001$), and *Blue Grey* ($p < 0.001$).
  - *Turquoise* had the fourth shortest reading time, significantly shorter than *Grey* ($p = 0.030$), *Blue* ($p = 0.009$), *Green* ($p = 0.033$), and *Blue Grey* ($p < 0.001$).
  - *Blue Grey* had the longest reading time, significantly longer than the rest: *Peach* ($p < 0.001$), *Orange* ($p < 0.001$), *Yellow* ($p < 0.001$), *Purple* ($p < 0.001$), *Red* ($p < 0.001$), *Turquoise* ($p < 0.001$), *Grey* ($p < 0.001$), *Blue* ($p < 0.001$), and *Green* ($p < 0.001$).
  - *Blue* had the second longest reading time, significantly longer than *Peach* ($p < 0.001$), *Orange* ($p < 0.001$), *Yellow* ($p < 0.001$), *Purple* ($p = 0.022$), *Red* ($p = 0.046$), and *Turquoise* ($p = 0.010$).

4.2 Mouse Distance

There was a significant effect of *Background Color* on *Mouse Distance* ($\chi^2(9) = 215.47$, $p < 0.001$).

- **Between Groups:** Participants with dyslexia had significantly longer *Mouse Distance* ($\bar{x} = 1954.64$, $s = 262.62$ pixels) than the participants without dyslexia ($\bar{x} = 1546.90$, $s = 285.54$ pixels), $p = 0.015$).

  For *Mouse Distance* between groups, the Spearman's correlation coefficient is $\rho = 0.794$, and it is statistically significant ($p = 0.010$).

- For **Group Dyslexia** there was a significant effect of *Background Color* on *Mouse Distance* ($\chi^2(9) = 24.66$, $p = 0.003$). The results of the post-hoc tests show that:
  - *Blue Grey* had the longest mean *Mouse Distance* time and lead to significantly longer distances than: *Grey* ($p = 0.026$), *Orange* ($p = 0.039$), and *Red* ($p = 0.010$).

- For **Group Control** there was a significant effect of *Background Color Mouse Distance* ($\chi^2(9) = 196.01$, $p < 0.001$).

  The results of the post-hoc tests show that:
  - *Blue Grey* also had the longest *Mouse Distance* mean and lead to significantly longer distances than the rest of the background colors (all with a $p - value < 0.001$). *Blue* had the second longest *Mouse Distance* and participants reading over *Blue* had significantly longer mouses distances than *Grey* ($p = 0.033$) and *Red* ($p = 0.008$).

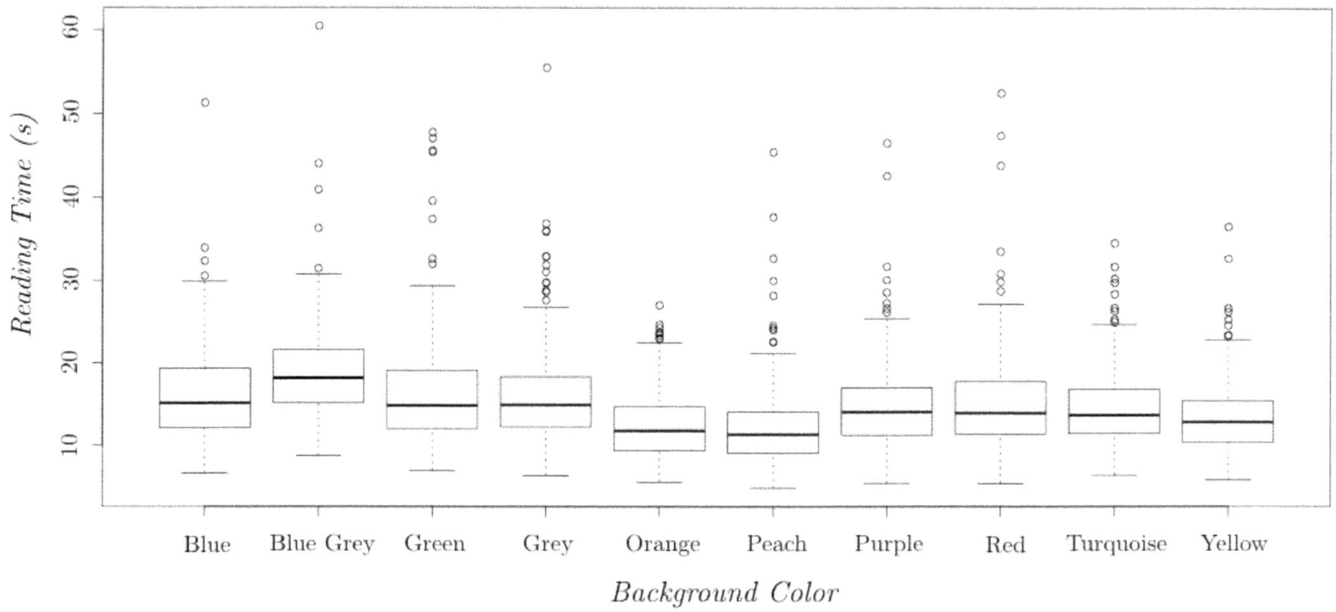

Figure 4: ***Reading Time*** **box plots by** ***Background Color*** **for Group Control.**

5. DISCUSSION

First, our results on reading performance provide evidence that background colors have an impact on readability. Second, these results are consistent with previous studies and most of the current text design recommendations for people with dyslexia. *Peach*, *Orange*, and *Yellow* background colors with black fonts lead to shorter reading times. These are similar to the "cream" color recommended by the *British Dyslexia Association* [4] which is used on their website. [5] It is also consistent with previous research using eye-tracking data with 92 people (46 with dyslexia) where the shortest fixation duration mean was collected when participants read black text over a cream background color [26].

Overall, if we group the colors as *warm colors* and *cool colors* we can observe a consistent behavior of the participants for all measures. *Warm colors*, *i.e.* *Peach*, *Orange*, and *Yellow* lead to significantly faster readings and less mouse movements, while *cool colors*, *Blue Grey*, *Blue*, and *Green*, lead to significantly longer reading times and more concentration of mouse movements. These results do not necessarily mean that *warm colors* are recommended for people with and without dyslexia. Normally, warm colors are used to stimulate observers. For instance, the human retina has a higher response to yellow hues than to any other colors.[6] To the contrary, cool colors are generally used to calm and relax the viewer. Some readers might prefer a cool color rather than a warm color if that color relaxes the reader. Further studies would need to explore the interaction between reading performance and reading preferences to make a sound background color recommendation.

Another conclusion that could be derived from this experiment is that both participants with and without dyslexia behave consistently against similar background color stimuli. For both groups, *warm colors* (*Peach*, *Orange*, and *Yellow*) lead to faster reading. Likewise, *cool colors*, especially *Blue Grey* and *Blue*, lead to significantly shorter readings for both groups. In fact, the correlations between groups for *Reading Time* and *Mouse Distance* measures are strong and significant, $\rho = 0.964$ ($p < 0.001$) and $\rho = 0.794$ ($p = 0.010$) respectively. This is consistent with previous literature, as there is a common agreement in specific studies about dyslexia and accessibility that the application of dyslexic-accessible practices, *i.e.* *Sans Serif* fonts or the use of larger font sizes, benefits readability for users without dyslexia [8, 21, 26].

People with dyslexia also present significantly more mouse movements (*Mouse Distance*) when reading text than people without dyslexia. Even if this was not the focus of this study, to the extent of our knowledge, this is the first result reported on this.

6. CONCLUSIONS AND FUTURE WORK

The main conclusions are:

- Background colors have an impact on text readability for people with and without dyslexia, and the impact is comparable for both groups.
- Warm background colors such as *Peach*, *Orange* or *Yellow* are beneficial for readability, taking into consideration both reading performance and mouse tracking measures. Also, cool background colors, in particular *Blue Grey*, *Blue*, and *Green*, decreased the text readability for both group.
- When reading on screen, people with dyslexia present a significantly higher use of the mouse in terms of the distance travelled by the mouse.

In future work we plan to address the current limitations of this study, taking into account other measures such as

[5] http://www.bdadyslexia.org.uk/

[6] http://www.scribblelive.com/blog/2011/12/07/the-use-of-yellow-in-data-design/

the user's preference. We plan to compare the most beneficial background colors (*Peach*, *Orange* and *Yellow*) with the most common background colors used on the Web such as white or off-white. Since the current study only used back font, we will also explore other font and background combinations used in previous literature.

7. ACKNOWLEDGMENTS

We thank all the participants who volunteered for this study and Sergi Subirats for his help implementing the test. Our special thanks to all the dyslexia and teacher's and therapist's associations who contributed to distribute the call of the study *ADA Dislexia Aragón*, *Adixmur (Asociación de Dislexia y otras dificultades de aprendizaje de la Región de Murcia)*, *Asociación ACNIDA*, *Asociación Catalana de la Dislexia*, *Associació de DislÃĺxia Lleida*, *Asociación Orientación y Educación Madrid*, *COPOE Confederación de Organizaciones de Psicopedagogía y Orientación de España*, *COPOE. Orientación y Educación Madrid*, *Fundació Mirades Educatives*, *Disfam*, *Asociación Dislexia y Familia*, *Disfam Argentina*, *Dislexia & Dispraxia Argentina*, and *Madrid con la Dislexia*.

This paper was developed under a grant from the US Department of Education, NIDRR grant number H133A130057; and a grant from the National Science Foundation (#IIS-1618784)

8. REFERENCES

[1] M. Bernal et al. Prevalencia del síndrome meares-irlen/estrés visual que afecta la lectura en niños de tercer grado. 2015.

[2] C. E. Bonferroni. Teoria statistica delle classi e calcolo delle probabilità. *Pubblicazioni del Regio Istituto Superiore di Scienze Economiche e Commerciali di Firenze*, 8:3–62, 1936.

[3] J. Bradford. Designing web pages for dyslexic readers, 2011. http://www.dyslexia-parent.com/mag35.html.

[4] British Dyslexia Association. Dyslexia style guide, January 2012. http://www.bdadyslexia.org.uk/.

[5] B. Caldwell, M. Cooper, L. G. Reid, and G. Vanderheiden. Web content accessibility guidelines (WCAG) 2.0. *WWW Consortium (W3C)*, 2008.

[6] F. Cuetos and F. Valle. Modelos de lectura y dislexias (Reading models and dyslexias). *Infancia y Aprendizaje (Infancy and Learning)*, 44:3–19, 1988.

[7] A. Dickinson, P. Gregor, and A. F. Newell. Ongoing investigation of the ways in which some of the problems encountered by some dyslexics can be alleviated using computer techniques. In *Proc. ASSETS'02*, pages 97–103, Edinburgh, Scotland, 2002.

[8] M. Dixon. Comparative study of disabled vs. non-disabled evaluators in user-testing: dyslexia and first year students learning computer programming. *Universal Access in Human Computer Interaction. Coping with Diversity*, pages 647–656, 2007.

[9] B. Drndarevic and H. Saggion. Towards automatic lexical simplification in Spanish: an empirical study. In *Proc. NAACL HLT '12 Workshop PITR '12*, Montreal, Canada, 2012.

[10] B. Evans. *Dyslexia and vision*, volume 5. Wiley, 2001.

[11] B. J. Evans, A. Cook, I. L. Richards, and N. Drasdo. Effect of pattern glare and colored overlays on a simulated-reading task in dyslexics and normal readers. *Optometry & Vision Science*, 71(10):619–628, 1994.

[12] P. Gregor, A. Dickinson, A. Macaffer, and P. Andreasen. Seeword: a personal word processing environment for dyslexic computer users. *British Journal of Educational Technology*, 34(3):341–355, 2003.

[13] P. Gregor and A. F. Newell. An empirical investigation of ways in which some of the problems encountered by some dyslexics may be alleviated using computer techniques. In *Proc. ASSETS'00*, ASSETS 2000, pages 85–91, New York, NY, USA, 2000. ACM Press.

[14] R. Guimarães, M. Guimarães, L. Faria, M. Pinotti, L. Guerra, and F. Soares. Prevalência da síndrome de mears-irlen em portadores de dislexia, 2017. http://fundacaoholhos.com.br/artigos/prevalencia-da-sindrome\\-de-mears-irlen-em-portadores-de-dislexia/.

[15] Interagency Commission on Learning Disabilities. *Learning Disabilities: A Report to the U.S. Congress.* Government Printing Office, Washington DC, 1987.

[16] R. Jeanes, A. Busby, J. Martin, E. Lewis, N. Stevenson, D. Pointon, and A. Wilkins. Prolonged use of coloured overlays for classroom reading. *British Journal of Psychology*, 88(4):541–548, 1997.

[17] S. Katusic, R. Colligan, W. Barbaresi, D. Schaid, and S. J. Jacobsen. Incidence of reading disability in a population-based birth cohort, 1976-1982, rochester. *Mayo Clinic Proceedings*, 76(11):1081, 2001.

[18] I. Kriss and B. J. W. Evans. The relationship between dyslexia and Meares-Irlen Syndrome. *Journal of Research in Reading*, 28(3):350–364, 2005.

[19] L. A. Leiva and R. Vivó. Web browsing behavior analysis and interactive hypervideo. *ACM Transactions on the Web*, 7(4), 2013.

[20] G. R. Lyon, S. E. Shaywitz, and B. A. Shaywitz. A definition of dyslexia. *Annals of Dyslexia*, 53(1):1–14, 2003.

[21] J. E. McCarthy and S. J. Swierenga. What we know about dyslexia and web accessibility: a research review. *Universal Access in the Information Society*, 9:147–152, June 2010.

[22] V. Navalpakkam and E. Churchill. Mouse tracking: measuring and predicting users' experience of web-based content. In *Proceedings of the SIGCHI Conference on Human Factors in Computing Systems*, pages 2963–2972. ACM, 2012.

[23] C. Perron. Colour choices on web pages: Contrast vs readability, 2012. http://www.writer2001.com/index.htm.

[24] R Development Core Team. A language and environment for statistical computing (computer software)., 2011. http://www.R-project.org.

[25] L. Rello and R. Baeza-Yates. Good fonts for dyslexia. In *Proc. ASSETS'13*, Bellevue, Washington, USA, 2013. ACM Press.

[26] L. Rello and R. Baeza-Yates. How to present more readable text for people with dyslexia. *Universal Access in the Information Society*, pages 1–21, 2015.

[27] L. Rello, S. Bautista, R. Baeza-Yates, P. Gervás,

R. Hervás, and H. Saggion. One half or 50%? An eye-tracking study of number representation readability. In *Proc. INTERACT '13*, Cape Town, South Africa, 2013.

[28] L. Rello, G. Kanvinde, and R. Baeza-Yates. Layout guidelines for web text and a web service to improve accessibility for dyslexics. In *Proc. W4A '12*, Lyon, France, 2012. ACM Press.

[29] L. Rello, M. Pielot, M. C. Marcos, and R. Carlini. Size matters (spacing not): 18 points for a dyslexic-friendly Wikipedia. In *Proc. W4A '13*, Rio de Janeiro, Brazil, 2013.

[30] L. Sánchez Sampedro. *Impostores (Impostors)*. Crowdfunding, Madrid, Spain, 2012. http://www.impostores.es.

[31] F. Serrano and S. Defior. Dyslexia speed problems in a transparent orthography. *Annals of Dyslexia*, 58(1):81–95, 2008.

[32] S. Shaywitz, M. Escobar, B. Shaywitz, J. Fletcher, and R. Makuch. Evidence that dyslexia may represent the lower tail of a normal distribution of reading ability. *New England Journal of Medicine*, 326(3):145–150, 1992.

[33] World Federation of Neurology (WFN). Report of research group on dyslexia and world illiteracy. Dallas: WFN, 1968.

Imagining Artificial Intelligence Applications with People with Visual Disabilities using Tactile Ideation

Cecily Morrison
Microsoft
Cambridge, UK

Edward Cutrell
Microsoft
Redmond, WA, USA

Anupama Dhareshwar
Microsoft
Bangalore, India

Kevin Doherty
Microsoft
Cambridge, UK

Anja Thieme
Microsoft
Cambridge, UK

Alex Taylor
Microsoft
Cambridge, UK

ABSTRACT

There has been a surge in artificial intelligence (AI) technologies co-opted by or designed for people with visual disabilities. Researchers and engineers have pushed technical boundaries in areas such as computer vision, natural language processing, location inference, and wearable computing. But what do people with visual disabilities imagine as their *own* technological future? To explore this question, we developed and carried out tactile ideation workshops with participants in the UK and India. Our participants generated a large and diverse set of ideas, most focusing on ways to meet needs related to social interaction. In some cases, this was a matter of recognizing people. In other cases, they wanted to be able to participate in social situations without foregrounding their disability. It was striking that this finding was consistent across UK and India despite substantial cultural and infrastructural differences. In this paper, we describe a new technique for working with people with visual disabilities to imagine new technologies that are tuned to their needs and aspirations. Based on our experience with these workshops, we provide a set of social dimensions to consider in the design of new AI technologies: social participation, social navigation, social maintenance, and social independence. We offer these social dimensions as a starting point to forefront users' social needs and desires as a more deliberate consideration for assistive technology design.

Keywords

Visually impaired, blind, accessibility, design, ideation, multicultural, AI, artificial intelligence

1. INTRODUCTION

There is a strong industrial push to create (artificial) intelligent agents that utilize speech and computational vision to enable new experiences. While intended for the mainstream, it is people with visual disabilities who have become especially proficient power users of conversational agents [30]. More recently, there have been more explicit explorations of how computational vision might enable the agent experience for people with visual disabilities. We see products that: find and read text [35], identify objects and people [39], [25], as well as describe images on social media [58].

As artificial intelligence matures, it becomes increasingly important to understand the kinds of things that people with visual disabilities would like to have as part of their tech toolkit. While there is a growing literature on what people find challenging *now* (e.g., [37],[55]), we wanted to prompt those with visual disabilities to imagine what artificial intelligence might offer *in the future*. Such a future may address practical problems that users currently face, or include a set of new abilities that we have not yet considered.

Helping people imagine novel ideas is often done through structured ideation methods [22]. However, typically, these methods rely on overt visual activities such as using ideation cards to prompt ideas as well as subtler visual activities such as recording the outcome of an exercise with post-it notes. Moreover, in group work - even in sharing physical models - collaboration can be highly visual. To work with people with visual disabilities, it is clear new ideation tasks are needed that do not rely on vision. In this paper, we describe a set of novel ideation tasks that we adapted to use with a diverse group of people with visual disabilities.

As people with visual disabilities are a very diverse group, we wanted to reflect that diversity in our participants. In particular, while much research and development in assistive technology has focused on resource-rich environments with advanced infrastructure, about 90% of the world's 285 million people with visual disabilities live in low-income settings [57]. As we explore how intelligent agents can enable people with visual disabilities, we wanted to consider how differences in context, culture, and resource availability would affect the ideas generated. To this end, we used our ideation methods in two contrasting contexts, UK and India.

The central focus of this paper is a synthesis of the ideas generated using adapted, tactile ideation techniques with visually disabled participants in workshops held in the UK and India. We found that participants, despite different cultural contexts, focused on intelligent technologies that enabled them to interact more easily with others. Even mundane challenges were couched very directly in the social context in which they were raised. These findings suggest that we need to take careful consideration of the social dimensions of the lived experiences of people with visual disabilities.

ASSETS '17, October 29-November 1, 2017, Baltimore, MD, USA

ACM 978-1-4503-4926-0/17/10…$15.00
https://doi.org/10.1145/3132525.3132530

In doing so, we might extend the common emphasis on wholly practical or functional challenges this user group faces, such as identifying money or navigating a floorplan. A design space might thus be opened up that focuses on the subtler, but equally important set of challenges introduced by participating in rich and varied social settings, that have yet to receive substantial attention.

This paper makes three specific contributions:

1. The concept and realization of tactile ideation workshops specifically developed for people with visual disabilities;
2. A cross-cultural comparison of ideas generated by people with visual disabilities in the UK and India, illustrating a consistent desire for social experience;
3. An articulation of a set of social dimensions to further a more deliberate design consideration for users' social needs and desires in assistive technology design.

2. RELATED WORK

We begin this section with a brief overview of the types of systems being developed for people with visual disabilities in recent years. We then draw upon a large, diverse literature on ideation, capturing relevant key ideas that can be utilized for tactile ideation, and summarize related literature on designing with people who have a visual disability. As these literatures are diverse and spread across academic fields and industry, we do not attempt to cover them exhaustively, but highlight elements that are particularly relevant to the findings within this paper.

2.1 Systems Research in Visual Disability

There is a considerable literature on developing systems to make life easier for those who with visual disabilities. Recent papers have focused on: the creation [11] and use [20] of tactile graphics; improvements to screen readers, such as concurrent audio [24] or access to charts [62]; reading out visual information with finger-mounted cameras [47]; 3D printed tactile maps [50]; supporting code navigation [8]; and not least, blind photography [1]. The majority of these systems, while diverse, are motivated by access issues, providing support for actions and activities available to people with sight.

The most heavily researched area has been that of navigation and orientation. These range from spotting zebra crossings [3] to the use of guide drones [6]. Other examples include: finding bus stops [17]; traversing open spaces [18]; navigating in buildings [26], and indoor navigation more generally [2]. In addition to this work, there are many technical contributions supporting system development for navigation such as the use of computer vision [10]. We are also beginning to see navigation technologies reach a large number of users through industrial efforts, such as *Microsoft Soundscape*, [36] a 3D spatialized audio navigation system, and American Printing House for the Blind's *Nearby Explorer* app [4].

A newer area of concentration is object and image identification. Early explorations allowed users to crowd-source picture and object recognition [9]. More recently, research has identified the challenges of recognizing images on social networking sights [33], and addressed them by designing an automatic captioning service [58]. Others have looked at object identification more directly through a proposal for a personalized object detector [27]; studies understanding image capture for object identification [32]; as well as design experiments to understand object identification for people with low vision [59]. With these studies, we see design proposals or initial uses of artificial intelligence for practical tasks.

There is now a growing literature that focuses on the lived experience of people with visual disabilities rather than the technology *per se*. Research has pointed out that assistive technology can impede social interaction [46], the authors introducing the term *social accessibility* to prompt designers to think beyond the assistance a device provides to its practicality in social settings [44]. Zolyomi et al. take this one step further to consider the social dimensions of adopting a sight assistive technology [61]. These authors pull out several examples in which people chose to access visual cues from the system to support social participation through understanding the surroundings or a conversational reference.

The social dimensions of the lived experience, however, have only received limited attention by system builders. One group of researchers have explored a social assistant [40]. Made from a camera and vibrating belt, the system indicates the location and distance of an interaction partner and their facial expression. This work illustrates how system and person co-adapt. Other research explores the capture of emotional valence and head nodding, and delivers the determined responses verbally. They illustrate the challenge of generating categorical responses that may be context dependent [38]. There is also work (building on affect recognition) that focuses on communicating gaze direction through tactile feedback. However, so far, the system is only beginning to be tested with visually disabled users [41].

2.2 Ideation Methods

Ideation is the creative process of generating new ideas. While there are many methods, Graham and Bachmann delineate nine approaches [22]. Some of these approaches are to solve specific problems, such as a known accessibility issues. Others are intended to create entities or experiences not yet known. There are two types of methods in this latter category that we would particularly like to highlight as relevant here: 1) *derivative ideas* that involve changing an existing entity; and 2) *symbiotic ideas* which come from combining multiple ideas into a singular entity. These two approaches, particularly suited to engendering new ideas, have been embodied in a range of different techniques.

Ideation cards offer a common technique used in designing interactive experiences with technology. Such cards help participants reflect on specific aspects of a design or combine unexpected ideas. Golembewski, for example, has shown how designers might create their own cards, helping them mix people, place, and objects in serendipitous ways [21]. There are a number of card sets available around specific topics, such as humanistic aspects of design [19] or legal and ethical aspects in technology design [31]. Woelfel provides an overview of existing tools [56].

Another ideation technique, and one that is more tactile, is Lego Serious Play (LSP). LSP is a facilitated workshop in which participants respond to tasks by building symbolic and metaphorical models using LEGO and produce accompanying narratives. There is an emphasis on concrete expression of experiences and ideas that are otherwise abstract. The practical challenges of implementing this method have been nicely documented for imagining health futures [48]. This work describes how to build the confidence of participants in the ideation process, gradually scaling up the exercises. It also talks about the importance of mixing individual and group tasks to enable the sharing and building on others' ideas. While tactile, LSP relies heavily on sight to build and narrate the concept.

There are many other ideation activities and games that enable idea generation through derivation, symbiosis, and spontaneity [23]. Other methods that we have drawn upon include: *show-and-tell*, *object brainstorming*, and *critique*. *Show-and-tell* is an activity in which everyone brings an object and describes how it represents an activity, enabling any of the three idea generation types. Similarly, *object brainstorming* utilizes objects chosen at random as a source for inspiration. *Critique* of current systems is a mechanism to provide insights into design issues by populations who do not currently use a technology, e.g. older people and banking [52]. These methods provide the starting points for creating tactile ideation methods.

2.3 Design with People with Visual Disabilities

A range of methods have been used to give voice to visually disabled users in the design process. A common method is *in situ interviewing or observation*. For example, Branham and Kane [13]interviewed blind individuals and their partners in their homes, exploring how they collaborate in creating accessible home spaces. Describing how "can't do" activities can move to "can do" activities with preparation help from a partner, this method enabled the authors to highlight the range of existing strategies that people already have to achieve an accessible home, and how the social dimensions must be accounted for in technology design.

User-centered design approaches shift the focus from understanding the user to encouraging the user to articulate their needs through a design process. Ye et al. [59], for example, use a wearable probe to provide a sense of the material and the practical experience of interacting with a wearable device through a speech-interface. The authors used the probe to help participants articulate their views on both form and function, giving users a voice in design problems scoped by the designer.

Participatory design attempts to integrate users into the design process itself, to capture tacit knowledge in the production of all aspects of the design from concept to features. We find examples of participatory design with people with visual disabilities in a range of contexts. Azenkot et al. [7] for example used interviews and a method inspired by contextual inquiry to explore with blind participants how they would prefer interacting with a building service robot. A designer controlled and spoke for a robot guiding the participant down a hallway. Throughout, probing and clarifying questions were asked to gain insight into indoor navigation challenges and strategies as well as actionable design recommendations.

Brock [15] describes the use of a multi-touch screen, a tactile paper map and audio output in the design of accessible interactive map prototypes for investigating haptic exploration strategies on spatial cognition with people with VI. Their approach involved brainstorming sessions, Wizard-of-OZ prototyping using raised-line maps and simulated speech output of proposed interaction concepts, and finally a comparative study to evaluate first system, assessing effectiveness and efficiency of their proposed solution and informing further improvements.

Designng a wearable navigation aid, Williams et al. [54] employed low-fidelity prototyping with craft materials as an alternative to sketching. However, participants preferred talking in a question-answer style rather than utilizing the craft materials, leaving the facilitator to construct prototypes based on the discussions. The authors reflect that more structure would have helped people engage in this unfamiliar task. In a later activity, participants were asked to assemble a set of electronic components to design a device in response to a particular scenario. While this enabled detailed conversations about the device's physical design, it did not help them generate new ideas.

Metatla et al. [34] employed a range of methods in their PD process. Amongst others they found that hands-on experiences with technology demonstrations helped build understanding of the state of the art in accessible systems and a shared vocabulary for expressing non-visual design ideas. Similar to Williams et al [REF], in the creation of audio-haptic mock-ups, participants drifted away from the material and were found to only focus on verbal descriptions. Malleable digital prototypes in comparison were generative as they provided alternative ways to support a task. Finally, audio diaries provided a useful resource of extra feedback outside of design sessions.

Sahib et al. [45] describe the use of scenarios as a basis for inviting dialogue with blind users to simulate how they would interact with a search interface. This enabled participants to provide formative feedback and critique proposed designs as well as to provide new ideas based on their experiences with assistive technologies.

Andrews [5] also presents a host of methods used over a number of years to engage blind and partially sighted people in participatory design processes. These included: moodboards, foam models, cards, existing product feedback and storytelling. One of the key adaptations needed to make these activities work was the use of the designer as transcriber to questions posed; an approach that heavily relies on how the sighted person summarises and prioritises what is said, and that potentially risks taking the direct voice away from people with VI. Other issues identified included the use of low-fidelity prototyping to inspire open-ended conversation. The reliance on touch instead often encouraged detailed feedback, before moving to the general concept. While this emphasis is understandable, it ran counter to the purpose of the low-fidelity forms. This suggests the tactile and auditory experience of materials, rather than their visual form, might be considered in design activities.

Lastly, Ratto et al. [43] detail their engagement in PD to design a better blind tennis ball. Blind tennis athletes and several hackers/engineers started with a discussion of the sport and problems faced. Following, they focused on prototyping with the labor divided between sighted people (building) and blind people (testing and commenting). To address this, the authors built tools for blind prototyping, including tactile overlays for circuit boards and a digital multimeter, highlighting the complex relationship between the materials being used and participation.

3. METHOD

Our primary methodological contribution is the design of tactile ideation tasks. Our proposal draws on two types of idea generation introduced above: derivative ideas and symbiotic ideas. Moreover, we have sought to adapt some of the existing approaches above to be orientated much more to non-visual interaction. In this section, we first present the concept of these tactile ideation tasks. We then discuss the two settings in which the workshops were carried out in UK and India. Finally, we describe how we synthesized the results of the ideation process for presentation in this paper.

3.1 Tactile Ideation Tasks

The workshop concept is built around the notion of a sixth sense, or a superpower, that the participants would like to have. A focus on a sixth sense was chosen to help people articulate a desire for a world augmented in some way while being technologically agnostic. More specifically, it was intended to question information need irrespective of technology, while respecting highly developed individual strategies and preferences to sense and form an understanding of the world. The workshop consists of two activity sessions.

3.1.1 Activity Set 1

The first session starts by asking people in small groups to describe, with the support of an object they are asked to bring, a sixth sense or super power that they would like to have. Objects (e.g. a pair of glasses) are passed around from participant to participant during description. The use of an object draws inspiration from the combination of two approaches: show and tell and object brainstorming [23] (see above for explanations of these). The use of objects was a deliberate one to provide a tactile way to share and reference ideas.

This initial activity is then developed through asking each participant to choose a sixth sense that is not their own (referenced through the objects) and a talking button that speaks pre-recorded text. Talking buttons have place names on them, such as: at home, at the mall, at work, at the temple, etc. Participants are then asked to imagine how they would use their new sixth sense in that particular location. To keep their hands busy and create something that can be shared with the group, each participant is asked to create an accessory for their chosen sixth sense from a lump of clay given to them. Participants are then asked to discuss and hand their accessories to each other, before choosing one to give to the participants in another group.

The aim of this task, similar to ideation cards, is to juxtapose the unexpected and to stimulate creative thinking beyond a person's own initial ideas. The use of clay draws upon the research from Lego Serious Play that proposes that making with the hands inspires different kinds of the ideas [42]. The choice of making an accessory is intended to take the focus off having to find a form for the sixth sense. The need to choose a single concept from all of those made by the participants is intended to stimulate the discussion and prioritization of the benefits or disadvantages of a particular sixth sense. This approach was also envisioned as a means to examine the commonality of participants' suggestions.

Finally, each group integrates the sixth sense and scenario received from the other group with an existing technology that they currently use to make a new technology. This can be either an entirely digital technology, such as an app, or a physical technology, such as a liquid level meter. The session finishes with both groups sharing their final concepts. This final activity provides an opportunity for the facilitator to explore current technology use. It also brings the sub-groups together to discuss all the generated ideas.

3.1.2 Activity Set 2

While the first set of activities is bottom up, with no constraints around the technology; the second set of activities is top down, ideating around a specific set of technologies, explicitly exploring opportunities for artificial intelligence, with a particular focus on computational vision. This set of activities starts with a discussion of what artificial intelligence technologies are capable of now and what is predicted they might be capable of in 10 years' time.

Participants are then asked to design a technology that they would like to use from a set of widgets given to them. In the first round, they are asked to choose one artificial intelligence (AI) widget and one output widget. The AI widgets were previously decided upon during a workshop with computational vision researchers, and include: a person recognizer, an object recognizer, an object aligner, and a room mapper. The output widgets include: speech, vibration, 3D audio, and tactile display. For example, participants may create a system that recognizes the alignment of two objects and provides feedback via vibration. These widgets are recorded on a talking button and given to participants in a shared 'craft box'.

Participants are further encouraged to use their own personal box of craft materials to illustrate a scenario in which their invented technology would be used. Included in the craft materials are: pipe cleaners, paper clips, clay, balloons, lego figures, a safety blanket, foam, and double-sided sticky pads. The making approach is in line with the theories from Lego Serious Play, with individual boxes aimed at reducing the problem of materials being too far away to reach or undiscoverable, a problem raised in the literature review.

After 15 minutes, people can add a second widget. The final designs, are then passed around on trays, described, and discussed across both groups.

3.2 UK Cohort

Six participants (2 women) were recruited through personal contacts of the lead researcher who is an active member of the local blind community. They were chosen to represent the diversity of the blind community. Participant ages ranged from 8 (represented by his mother) to 60 years old; vision levels ranged from none to ability to read adapted text; and both early and late blind were included. All participants were heavy technology users and could be seen as early adopters.

The ideation workshop took place at a research lab in Cambridge, UK. Participants worked in groups of three at small round tables for the first activity set. For the second, they sat in the same groups at larger rectangular tables, as more space was needed. The session was intended to last three hours, but intense discussions made it last more than four. Each group had a facilitator.

3.3 India Cohort

Eight blind and partially sighted individuals (4 women) were recruited from Enable India, a charity that teaches computer skills (e.g. keyboarding, and screen reader use) along with workplace skills (e.g. interacting in a sighted workforce). Participants ranged in age from late teens to thirties; sight levels ranged from adapted text to no sight; and included early and late blind users. All were learning to use technology to gain better jobs. Three were smartphone owners.

The workshops took place in a research lab in Bangalore, India. Participants were split into two rooms by gender, to enable a freer discussion in a culture where gender plays a strong mediating role. Each group sat around a small round table with a facilitator. While all participants spoke English, some were more confident than others. Local languages such as Kanada and Tamil were also spoken during the workshop, particularly in the women's group. Several helpers sat around the outside of the table, helping with translation.

The ideation tasks were adapted based on the experience of the UK session as well as practical need. This workshop focused entirely on activity set 1 due to the resistance we saw in the UK workshop to using clay and craft materials (as discussed below). As we did not have direct contact with participants beforehand, we supplied various objects for Activity Set 1. These included: pipe cleaners,

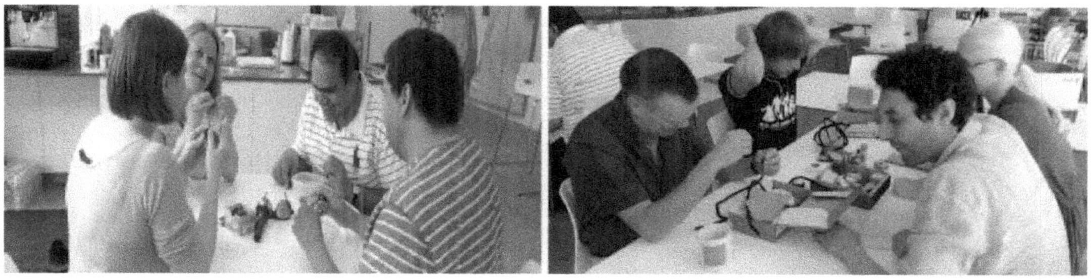

Figure 1. Tactile ideation workshop in the UK. (Left) Object-based show and tell; (Right) Craft-based scenario generation.

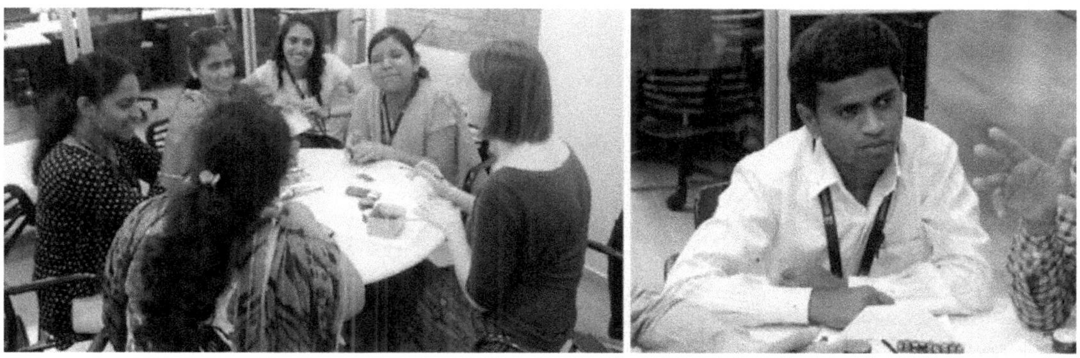

Figure 2. Tactile ideation workshop in India. (Left) Women's breakout with facilitators; (Right) Men's breakout with a participant.

pebble magnets, survival blanket, stress ball, blue-tac, and paper-clips. Participants used these to help think of a sixth sense. The places used in the place activity were adapted to be culturally relevant: Market, Temple, Relative's house, and Work or School.

3.4 Data Synthesis

All of the workshops were video and audio recorded. The facilitators of each group also took notes during and after the session. Each workshop group had two people draw out the ideas which were then placed in a spreadsheet. Related context, such as use examples of proposed ideas or details about the participants' background that helped interpretation, were also included. The authors worked together to cluster the data in meaningful ways. This was an iterative process informed by immersion in the literature as well as other related studies with people with visual disabilities. Permission was given for the use of photos in publications.

4. FINDINGS

The two ideation sessions were both highly generative, spawning a large and varied number of ideas. Some of those ideas were direct descriptions of what a technology would do: "identify an official at an office or summon a guide" (Ip7). Others described how a technology might do something: "The accessory would transfer the patterns in the environment to me in a silent way, not involving vibration or audio. I want it to go directly to my brain." (UKp5). Many of the ideas came as part of stories. Those stories communicated how a particular need would impact the participants; or, the participants integrated a variety of ideas generated through the iterative activities into a single proposed scenario. Below are two such examples, respectively.

> A sixth-sense to tell me when I've offended someone as I can't read people's reactions anymore. You wouldn't know if you queue jumped and someone was offended. People are likely to tell you when you are pleased, but may try to hide their frustration or anger. (UKp3)

> The system already knows who your relatives are (because you interact all the time). Detect changes in furniture from last time visited. Who is present today? Is cousin there? Facial expression may indicate that family folks aren't that interested in having you around. (Ip6).

Most notable about the ideas generated is that the majority mention people either as objects of identification or as part of the story. If we break down our data into singular ideas and remove duplicates from the same group, we count 66 ideas of which 28 are from the UK. Four of the imagined sixth senses were not specific to people with a visual disability, focusing on "knowing the future" or "diagnosing illness through feeling the hand." Forty of the remaining 62 ideas mentioned people in some way. While these are rough estimates given the difficulty of quantifying "an idea," they do give a sense of how pervasive and important people are in the ideas that surfaced. We focus the remaining analysis on articulating the different ways people feature in our data set.

4.1 Identifying People

Many of the examples focused on identifying and locating known people. Some participants wanted to identify friends in a temple (Ip4), or know when their manager was passing by at work (UKp4). These two examples are illustrative of a range in which other strategies, such as voice or handshake recognition, could not be used because of social protocol. Two other situations were singled out as challenging for identifying people: networking events and chance meetings on the street. The noise and crowd of a networking event made navigation to sought-for people difficult. On the street, there was little in the way of context to help with sense-making and surmising who might be around.

> When networking, it can be hard because you know people are in the room, but you don't know where (UKp1).

As illustrated through these examples, identifying people had a number of purposes beyond engagement with a person: First, some of our participants pointed out with a wry sense of humor that identifying people also enables their avoidance. Avoiding people is something a person with a visual disability cannot easily do. Second, in an extended example from the India workshop, identifying which relatives were in the house when looking for "cousin" was desired (Ip8). This provided a social context to ascertain the socially appropriate manner for engaging with a cousin, even if the other people were not the intended focus of the visit.

Identifying people was not limited to a known person. It was also important to identify people routinely in the same environment. Participants spoke about how they often felt disconnected from the communities in which they lived and worked.

> I live in a village. People know what I look like and they will often say hello to me, but I have no clue who they are. If they come and speak to me, they say, I've known you for 20 years. But I haven't known you for 20 years, you've never spoken to me before. (UKp5)

There was almost a fascination with how sighted people could meet each other without directly interacting just by being in the same space. These examples stretch the idea of people we know by name to those we know by sight, or the familiar stranger.

Not least, there were several examples in which the person's role was more important than identity. In the most direct sense, there was a need to identify assistance when entering a building (Ip7). This could also extend to temporary roles, such as finding people who may be going to lunch (UKp4). The most general form of this was understanding who is around. For example, understanding where people are walking and praying in a temple enables navigating around them (Ip4). Equally, people ubiquitously wanted to know where people were absent, in order to find an empty seat.

4.2 Managing Social Interactions

Beyond the identification of people, many examples focused on the identification of social cues to enable the management of social interaction. Some participants emphasized the desire for the low-bandwidth communication provided by eye-contact (UKp5). Another participant pointed out that it provides a back channel for communicating with someone when others are present (UKp3). This is captured in the example below:

> I want to be able to look at [blind son] across the room to let him know that he should stop what he is doing without drawing everyone's attention by speaking aloud. (UKp6)

Others wanted a more sophisticated way to read reactions to modulate their own behavior, whether it be in a doctor-patient relationship or just with family.

> A way to know how someone is responding when I'm breaking bad news [as a doctor] in a hospital context. (UKp2)

> Relatives aren't always that interested in having you around. It would be useful to gauge attention and interest from them in a conversation. (Ip6)

Interestingly, people were more concerned with getting negative cues rather than positive, pointing out that people are more forthcoming when they are pleased, but attempt to be neutral when displeased. This attempt at understatement made reading intent from audio cues alone far more challenging. Finally, people wanted to access non-verbal cues critical for interaction, such as an extended hand or a head nod. Non-verbal cues also extended to understanding attention.

> I want to understand that the priest has extended his hand with an offering of Prasad. (Ip1)

> Suppose we have gone to a vendor to buy some stuff and we are keeping on telling him something, but he is talking to the customer beside us. So we are not able to understand whether he is talking to *me* or the person beside me. (Ip5)

While one group in the UK mused over why people continued to use such non-verbal interactions with people they knew could not see, the groups in India did not question the phenomenon, assuming it was their responsibility to fit in socially.

4.3 Social Stories

There were also a large number of examples in which people featured prominently in stories, but were not necessarily the object of recognition. While the quotation below has seemingly little to do with people, unpacking it with the participants led to a discussion around conversational participation. When out-and-about, it was common to fall into a relationship in which the world was described by the sighted person and the description absorbed by the visually disabled person.

> Here are a pair of glasses and they are magical, or technical, same thing. They can do pattern detection. I am very competitive and no matter what the situation my wife or colleagues can do better when it comes to matching patterns. (UKp4)

Conversations, when out-and-about, are often about visual similarity – "that is similar to the houses we saw in Sweden last year" – or visual difference – "that shop is now closed." Our participants felt that the more visual cues they had, the more opportunity they had to initiate conversation.

On the surface, the next example may describe the mechanistic challenge of recognizing and distinguishing coins, yet the social story underling this instance rather highlights the desire to take part in activities without disrupting social norms.

> At the temple, we find it hard to recognize the coins (1 Rupee or 2 Rupees) to offer during the prayers to the priest. It is also hard to distinguish notes to offer. With shops, we can always ask what note it is and exchange

> it with the right one if wrong. But at a temple, we are embarrassed to ask and exchange notes or coins. We want to be able to tell accurately. (Ip2, Ip3)

This example illustrates that the motivation for a simple recognition technology is influenced by the social setting in which it is required. While such technologies may be useful in a range of places, our examples highlighted how social spaces often reduce the availability of other strategies to gain information, making social participation more difficult. Social participation also took on a new shape with examples in which the imagined technology arose from wanting to avoid being taken advantage of.

> I want a talking ATM. My friends or relatives help me now, but sometimes they take a tip. (Ip3)

> The seller gives me something other than what I ask for. I tell him that this is not right, but he doesn't believe me. I need something to prove that I'm right. (Ip1)

These examples show that social participation is not only a matter of desire, but also of necessity. The ability to demonstrate competence and "normality" is a key driver of informational need in some circumstances. While we only saw such examples in India, we know that there is related research that suggests a similar need in Western contexts, such as the demonstration of professionalism among blind people at work [12].

Socially motivated technology use also came from the need for social independence. Some of our examples highlight that a lack of information keeps young people from gaining the social independence they desire as illustrated in the quotation below.

> My parents do this now, but I'd like my phone to be able to tell me about obstacles or steps (Ip8).

Most of the examples, like this one, asking for practical solutions did not reference people, but could be seen as socially motivated. While gaining social independence is perhaps the opposite of social participation, they are linked in that independence for mundane tasks enables effort to be put towards inherently social interactions unencumbered by need, creating an equity in interaction.

4.4 People across Cultures

The most striking aspect of our data is the similarity of ideas generated across the two workshops. The UK and India have substantial cultural and infrastructural differences. We had expected that this might lead to different ideation results, but this was largely not the case. The only differences were: the UK had ideas unrelated to visual disability; and India started the conversation with very direct day-to-day needs people wanted met, such as better walking directions. However, once settled into the activities, the ideas across the two localities became much more similar. The most compelling examples are found in those quotations which mirror human desires across cultures and locations.

> If I'm talking to someone and they're not that interested in speaking to me, their facial expression will show: So you can finish the conversation quickly. She's just not that into you. (Ip5)

> A way to read emotions during the [name] therapy groups; when girls are eyeing me. I can guess a lot less about what people think now that I cannot see their faces. (UKp1)

5. DISCUSSION

We have presented the method and synthesis of findings from ideation workshops with visually disabled people in the UK and India in order to understand how this user group might imagine their own future with (artificial) intelligent agents. We were surprised to find that when taking an ideation approach agnostic to technology and current everyday needs, our participants focused on technologies that could help them in their social encounters. In some cases that was a matter of recognizing people. In others, it meant being able to participate in social situations without their disability being obtrusive. It was striking that this was consistent across the UK and India, despite substantial cultural and infrastructural differences.

In the discussion, we tease out what the social dimensions of the lived experience of this user group might look like in a design process. We also comment on the particularities of the tactile ideation workshop method and its role in forefronting social interaction in our findings. It must be said that the findings apply more broadly than the original topic of intelligent agents and can be addressed potentially by a wide range of technologies.

5.5 Enabling Social Experiences

The most striking aspect of our workshops was the strong, cross-cultural focus on the sociality of the lived experience. This stands in contrast to the political motivation of access and accessibility often referenced in the technology community. While access to education, work, or culture mediated through technology is critical, we should not forget that peoples' lives are situated socially. In our workshops, the desire for nuanced communication and interaction with other people rose above the more practical challenges that our participants undoubtedly faced, such as getting to work.

This strong focus on social situations in the workshops was underpinned by a set of stories that suggested examples in which existing strategies were not sufficient. All our participants in the UK and most in India had strategies for getting to work and other daily activities. They were also skilled in using broader resources of context to infer social behavior [16]. However, participants developed strategies that often broke down when there was a need to respect formal social structure. Indeed, participants felt that eliciting social information in many social settings foregrounded their disabilities in an undesired way.

Identifying people and their associated attributes was a prominent theme in our findings: knowing who is around, who is a familiar stranger, or who is in an official role. Our findings also highlight that sociality for our participants extended beyond recognizing people and their attributes. Participating socially often meant doing what others are doing, simulating a range of visual capabilities, such as object or text recognition. While this may be seen as simply an access issue, it is the social context which shapes why and how some of these needs might be met with technology. It may not be appropriate to use an expensive mobile phone in an Indian temple.

It is possible that social experiences featured strongly in our ideation workshops because of the inherently human implications of positive and negative social interaction for one's sense of self [28]. People are strongly motivated by loss aversion, and social awareness can provide a safety net for our behavior. Previous research has shown that avoiding deviations from social norms features strongly among uses of technology envisaged by some people with visual disabilities [29]. Our findings suggest the same, prompting us to consider the design space of enabling social experiences in assistive intelligent technologies.

To support designers and technologists in thinking about what it might mean to enable social experiences, we identified social dimensions that were prevalent across our data.

Three of these dimensions span activities which enable meaningful social interaction: Social Participation, the process of participation in social interaction through shared grounding within (knowledge of) the general social context; Social Navigation, the process of identifying and entering into opportunities for social interaction; and Social Maintenance, the process of managing engaged interaction through knowledge of other participants' social cues.

A fourth category, Social Independence, emerged as an important factor in enabling and motivating these activities (see Table 1). These dimensions are highlighted with the intention of broadening future thinking in ideation and design practice. By focusing on these actions and their meanings, we attempt to ensure that we design technologies that go beyond meeting people's functional needs, to include those social needs that make us inherently human.

This design space, with compelling initial explorations (e.g. social interaction assistant [40]), must be approached with nuance. Literature, for example, has already alluded to the challenges of expressing continuous aspects of non-verbal interactions (e.g. facial expression) with the labelled classes machine learning systems can produce [38]. Indeed, mapping the visual recognition of identified people in space to an audible representation raises a host of questions about how location, space and identify are co-constituted (see, for example, [33]). For those with little to no sight, there may be significantly different notions of people in space that are not easily aligned with visual modes of recognition. These insights remind us of the importance of social accessibility [44], both in the use of technology and priority in designing it.

Table 1. Categories of social activities and motivations

Axis	Definition	Example
Social Participation	The ability to participate in a given social interaction.	At the temple, we find it hard to recognize the coins to offer during the prayers to the priest. … But at a temple, we are embarrassed to ask and exchange notes or coins. We want to be able to tell accurately. Visual cues of the environment provided the opportunity to initiate conversation.
Social Navigation	The process of identifying and entering into opportunities for social interaction.	When networking it can be hard because you know people are in the room, but you don't know where. Finding people who look like they are going to lunch.
Social Maintenance	The process of managing interaction through knowledge of other participants' social cues.	I want to understand that the priest has extended his hand with an offering of Prasad. A way to know how someone is responding when I'm breaking bad news [as a doctor] in a hospital context.
Social Independence	The ability to be free from the constraints of social interaction through independent abilities.	I want a talking ATM. My friends or relatives help me now, but sometimes they take a tip. My parents do this now, but I'd like my phone to be able to tell me about obstacles or steps.

5.6 A Reflection on Method

The ideas generated in the workshops undertaken are without doubt shaped by the methods that we used. A key element of the method was to focus on encouraging participants to imagine a sixth sense rather than a technology per se. Interestingly, participants in the UK did not contain their ideas to visual disability; many wanted to predict the future. In India, the participants started out focused on daily challenges they experienced ignoring the idea of a sixth sense. Gradually, through the layering of exercises that built on and changed previous ideas, our participants started to reach beyond what they thought was possible, to what they would really like.

It was striking that in the UK, in which the sixth sense activities were followed by activities imagining a new technology, this lead to dramatically different ideas. In the first set of activities, all the participants focused on ways of connecting with others. In the second , all participants built navigational and mapping tools. We can surmise that this dramatic change may illustrate the difficulty people have in imagining the form of new technologies or how they'd work. It may have been also an issue of the difficulties of prototyping without vision. One participant said: "I'm only doing maps because they are more fun to make." Regardless, it is clear that methods that draw people away from solving daily problems open up the space for imagining future technologies.

A substantial part of the workshop relied on physical objects as a means to support ideation and communication between participants. Objects worked well in both the UK and India as "fiddle" things: ways to keep the hands busy and not feel compelled to talk as ideas formed. In the UK, they also worked well for sharing concepts and helping people keep track of ideas. In India, some of the participants treated the objects quite literally: the safety blanket was like a parachute to get off a plane; blue-tac could be used to make art work with one's children for school. The use of objects as prompts for lateral thinking seemed to be an unfamiliar idea to some. This likely has less to do with the use of objects, but rather familiarity with design-led methods for those with particular educational backgrounds [49].

Prototyping, the creation of new objects as a means to explore or present ideas, did not work well. It was enjoyed by those with partial-sight, but those with less vision found it difficult. While people enjoyed playing with the materials, wrapping a fluffy pipe cleaner around the neck or playing with clay as putty, it was difficult to put things together in a coherent scene. The spatial understanding needed taxed people in a way that did not encourage ideation. Making the materials easily available in personal boxes and providing bounded trays for the work was not enough. The clay also made people's hands sticky, a problem if you use your hands to make sense of the world. It could be interesting to explore the adaptation of methods, such as invisible design, that elicit discussion through ambiguous film without ever showing the design [14].

We present in this paper the ideas generated through the ideation process; however, there was also a lot of insightful side talk. The sessions naturally encouraged people to volunteer information about their current technology use. We got, for example, several excellent comparisons between available technologies. Participants talked at length about the appropriate form-factor of devices. Not least, participants, both in India and UK, were very forthcoming about their thoughts and choices related to living with a visual disability. This openness built as the session went on, with some of the most poignant discussions at the end. We felt that tactile engagement worked well as a means for empathetic engagement to conduct enquiry into people's lives without intruding [53].

6. CONCLUSIONS

As artificial intelligence matures, it becomes increasingly important to understand the kinds of things that people with visual disabilities would like to have as part of their tech toolkit. In this paper, through findings of tactile ideation workshops in both the UK and India, we highlight an underexplored space for imagining technologies for people with visual disabilities that forefronts the inherent sociality in which they live. As designers, technologists, and researchers work to imagine how intelligent technologies can partner with people to increase *capabilities* [51], we encourage a more deliberate focus on users' social needs and desires.

7. REFERENCES

[1] D Adams, S Kurniawan, C Herrera, V Kang, and N Friedman. 2016. Blind Photographers and VizSnap: A Long-Term Study. In Proc ASSETS '16.

[2] D Ahmetovic, C Gleason, C Ruan, K Kitani, H Takagi, and C Asakawa. 2016. NavCog: a navigational cognitive assistant for the blind. In Proc MobileHCI '16.

[3] D Ahmetovic, R Manduchi, J M Coughlan, and S Mascetti. 2015. Zebra Crossing Spotter: Automatic Population of Spatial Databases for Increased Safety of Blind Travelers. In Proc ASSETS '15.

[4] American Printing House for the Blind. Nearby Explorer. http://louis.aph.org/product/Nearby-Explorer,142793.aspx?FormatFilter=8

[5] C Andrews. 2014. Accessible Participatory Design: Engaging and Including Visually Impaired Participants. In Inclusive Designing. Springer.

[6] M Avila, M Funk, and N Henze. 2015. DroneNavigator: Using Drones for Navigating Visually Impaired Persons. In Proc ASSETS '15.

[7] S Azenkot, C Feng, and M Cakmak. 2016. Enabling building service robots to guide blind people: A participatory design approach. In Proc Human Robot Interaction HRI '16.

[8] C M Baker, L R Milne, and R E Ladner. 2015. StructJumper. In Proc CHI '15.

[9] J P Bigham, C Jayant, H Ji, G Little, A Miller, R C Miller, R Miller, A Tatarowicz, B White, S White, and T Yeh. 2010. VizWiz: nearly real-time answers to visual questions. In Proc UIST '10.

[10] S Blessenohl, C Morrison, A Criminisi, and J Shotton. 2015. Improving Indoor Mobility of the Visually Impaired with Depth-Based Spatial Sound. In ICCVW '15 IEEE Int Conf on Computer Vision Workshops.

[11] J Bornschein, D Prescher, and G Weber. 2015. Collaborative Creation of Digital Tactile Graphics. 117–126. In Proc ASSETS '15.

[12] S M Branham and S K Kane. 2015. The Invisible Work of Accessibility: How Blind Employees Manage Accessibility in Mixed-Ability Workplaces. In Proc ASSETS '15.

[13] S M Branham and S K Kane. 2015. Collaborative Accessibility: How Blind and Sighted Companions Co-Create Accessible Home Spaces. In Proc CHI '15.

[14] P Briggs, M Blythe, J Vines, S Lindsay, P Dunphy, J Nicholson, D Green, J Kitson, A Monk and P Olivier. 2012. Invisible design: exploring insights and ideas through ambiguous film scenarios. In DIS '12.

[15] A M Brock. 2013. Touch the map!: designing interactive maps for visually impaired people. SIGACCESS Access. Comput. 105: 9-14.

[16] J S Brown and P Duguid. 1994. Borderline issues: Social and material aspects of design. Human–Computer Interaction 9, 1: 3–36.

[17] M Campbell, C Bennett, C Bonnar, and A Borning. 2014. Where's my bus stop?: supporting independence of blind transit riders with StopInfo. In Proc ASSETS '14.

[18] A Fiannaca, I Apostolopoulous, and E Folmer. 2014. Headlock: a wearable navigation aid that helps blind cane users traverse large open spaces. In Proc ASSETS '14.

[19] B Friedman and D Hendry. 2012. The envisioning cards: a toolkit for catalyzing humanistic and technical imaginations. In Proc CHI '12.

[20] G Fusco and V S Morash. 2015. The Tactile Graphics Helper: Providing Audio Clarification for Tactile Graphics Using Machine Vision. In Proc ASSETS '15.

[21] M Golembewski and M Selby. 2010. Ideation decks: a card-based design ideation tool. In DIS '10.

[22] D Graham and T Bachmann. 2004. Ideation: The Birth and Death of Ideas. Wiley.

[23] D Gray. 2010. Gamestorming: A Playbook for Innovators, Rulebreakers, and Changemakers.

[24] J Guerreiro and D Gonçalves. 2015. Faster Text-to-Speeches: Enhancing Blind People's Information Scanning with Faster Concurrent Speech. In Proc ASSETS '15.

[25] Horus. https://horus.tech/horus/?l=en_us

[26] D Jain. 2014. Path-guided indoor navigation for the visually impaired using minimal building retrofitting. In Proc ASSETS '14.

[27] H Kacorri, K M Kitani, J P Bigham and C Asakawa. 2017. People with Visual Impairment Training Personal Object Recognizers: Feasibility and Challenges. In Proc CHI'17.

[28] N J Kemp. 1981. Social psychological aspects of blindness: A review. Current Psyc Rev 1, 1: 69.

[29] S Krishna, D Colbry, J Black, V Balasubramanian and S Panchanathan. 2008. A systematic requirements analysis and development of an assistive device to enhance the social interaction of people who are blind or visually impaired. In Wkshp on Comp Vis Apps for the Vis Impaired.

[30] E Luger and A Sellen. 2016. Like Having a Really Bad PA: The Gulf between User Expectation and Experience of Conversational Agents. In Proc CHI '14.

[31] E Luger, L Urquhart, T Rodden, and M Golembewski. 2015. Playing the Legal Card: Using Ideation Cards to Raise Data Protection Issues within the Design Process. In Proc CHI '15.

[32] R Manduchi and J M Coughlan. 2014. The last meter: blind visual guidance to a target. In Proc CHI '14.

[33] D Massey. 2013. Space, place and gender. John Wiley.

[34] O Metatla, N Bryan-Kinns, T Stockman, and F Martin. 2015. Designing with and for people living with visual impairments: Audio-tactile mock-ups, audio diaries and participatory prototyping. In CoDesign 11(1), 35-48.

[35] Microsoft. 2016. https://blogs.msdn.microsoft.com/accessibility/2016/04/07/seeing-ai/

[36] Microsoft. 2014. https://blogs.windows.com/devices/2014/11/14/microsoft-research-3d-soundscape-technology-helps-visually-impaired/#ODbbB3H3y22YqHsD.97

[37] M R Morris, A Perkins, C Yao, S Bahram, J P Bigham, and S K Kane. 2016. "With most of it being pictures now, I rarely use it": Understanding Twitter's Evolving Accessibility to Blind Users. In Proc CHI '16.

[38] L Murray, P Hands, R Goucher, and J Ye. 2016. Capturing social cues with imaging glasses. In Proc Ubicomp '16.

[39] Orcam. http://www.orcam.com/

[40] S Panchanathan, S Chakraborty and T McDaniel. 2016. Social Interaction Assistant: A Person-Centered Approach to Enrich Social Interactions for Individuals With Visual Impairments. IEEE J Sel Top in Signal Processing, 10, 5.

[41] S Qiu, M Rauterberg, and J Hu. 2016. Tactile Band: Accessing Gaze Signals from the Sighted in Face-to-Face Communication. In Proc TEI '16.

[42] Rasmussen Consulting. 2012. The Science Behind the LEGO SERIOUS PLAY method. Retrieved from http://seriousplayground.squarespace.com/storage/The Science Behind the LEGO SERIOUS PLAY Method.pdf

[43] M Ratto, I Record, G Coons, and M Julien. 2014. Blind tennis: extreme users and participatory design. In Proc PDC '14, 2, 41–44

[44] K Shinohara and J O Wobbrock. 2016. Self-Conscious or Self-Confident? A Diary Study Conceptualizing the Social Accessibility of Assistive Technology. ACM Transactions on Accessible Computing (TACCESS) 8, 2: 5.

[45] N G Sahib, T Stockman, A Tombros, and O Metatla. 2013. Participatory design with blind users: a scenario-based approach. In Proc INTERACT '13.

[46] K Shinohara and J O Wobbrock. 2011. In the shadow of misperception. In Proc CHI '11.

[47] L Stearns, R Du, U Oh, Y Wang, L Findlater, R Chellappa, and J E Froehlich. 2014. The design and preliminary evaluation of a finger-mounted camera and feedback system to enable reading of printed text for the blind. In Euro Conf on Computer Vision.

[48] D Swann. 2011. NHS at Home: Using Lego Serious Play to Capture Service Narratives andEnvision Future Healthcare Products. INCLUDE 2011 Proceedings. http://eprints.hud.ac.uk/13355/1/SwannpdfF358_1689.pdf

[49] R Talhouk, S Mesmar, A Thieme, M Balaam, P Olivier, C Akik, H Ghattas. 2016. Syrian refugees and digital health in Lebanon: Opportunities for improving antenatal health. In Proc ASSETS '16.

[50] B Taylor, A Dey, D Siewiorek and A Smailagic. 2016. Customizable 3D Printed Tactile Maps as Interactive Overlays. In Proc ASSETS '16.

[51] A Taylor. 2017. Becoming more capable. In Platypus, the CASTAC Blog. Ret April 27, 2017 from http://blog.castac.org/2017/04/becoming-more-capable

[52] J Vines, M Blythe, S Lindsay, P Dunphy, A Monk, and P Olivier. 2012. Questionable concepts: critique as resource for designing with eighty somethings. In Proc ASSETS '12.

[53] J Wallace, PC Wright, J McCarthy, DP Green, J Thomas, and P Olivier. 2013. A design-led inquiry into personhood in dementia. In Proc CHI '13.

[54] M A Williams, E Buehler, A Hurst, and S K Kane. 2015. What not to wearable: using participatory workshops to explore wearable device form factors for blind users. In W4A '15, Web for All Conference.

[55] M A Williams, C Galbraith, S K Kane, and A Hurst. 2014. "just let the cane hit it." In Proc ASSETS '16.

[56] C Wölfel and T Merritt. 2013. Method card design dimensions: a survey of card-based design tools. In Proc INTERACT '13.

[57] World Health Organization. 2013. Factsheet on Visual impairment and blindness. Retrieved from http://www.who.int/mediacentre/factsheets/fs282/en/

[58] S Wu, J Wieland, O Farivar, and J Schiller. 2017. Automatic Alt-text: Computer-generated Image Descriptions for Blind Users on a Social Networking Service. In Proc CSCW '17.

[59] H Ye, M Malu, U Oh, and L Findlater. 2014. Current and future mobile and wearable device use by people with visual impairments. In Proc CHI '14.

[60] Y Zhao, S Szpiro, J Knighten, and S Azenkot. 2016. CueSee: exploring visual cues for people with low vision to facilitate a visual search task. In Proc Ubicomp '16.

[61] A Zolyomi, A Shukla, and J Snyder. 2016. Social Dimensions of Technology-Mediated Sight. In Proc ASSETS '16.

[62] H Zou and J Treviranus. 2015. ChartMaster: A Tool for Interacting with Stock Market Charts using a Screen Reader. In Proc ASSETS '15.

Interviews and Observation of Blind Software Developers at Work to Understand Code Navigation Challenges

Khaled Albusays
Computing and Information Sciences Ph.D. Program
Rochester Institute of Technology
Rochester, NY 14623
khaled@mail.rit.edu

Stephanie Ludi
Department of Computer Science & Engineering
University of North Texas
Denton, TX 76207
stephanie.ludi@unt.edu

Matt Huenerfauth
Golisano College of Computing and Information Sciences
Rochester Institute of Technology
Rochester, NY 14623
matt.huenerfauth@rit.edu

ABSTRACT
Integrated Development Environments (IDEs) play an important role in the workflow of many software developers, e.g. providing syntactic highlighting or other navigation aids to support the creation of lengthy codebases. Unfortunately, such complex visual information is difficult to convey with current screen-reader technologies, thereby creating barriers for programmers who are blind, who are nevertheless using IDEs. To better understand their usage strategies and challenges, we conducted an exploratory study to investigate the issue of code navigation by developers who are blind. We observed 28 blind programmers using their preferred coding tool while they performed various programming activities, in particular while they navigated through complex codebases. Participants encountered many navigation difficulties when using their preferred coding software with assistive technologies (e.g., screen readers). During interviews, participants reported dissatisfaction with the accessibility of most IDEs due to the heavy use of visual abstractions. To compensate, participants used multiple input methods and workarounds to navigate through code comfortably and reduce complexity, but these approaches often reduced their speed and introduced mistakes, thereby reducing their efficiency as programmers. Our findings suggest an opportunity for researchers and the software industry to improve the accessibility and usability of code navigation for blind developers in IDEs.

CCS Concepts
•Human-centered computing→ User studies; •Social and professional topics→ Assistive technologies; •Software and its engineering→ Requirements analysis; •Human-centered computing→ Empirical studies in accessibility

Keywords
Accessibility; Blind Programmers; Programming Challenges; Code Navigation Difficulties; User Studies.

1. INTRODUCTION
Integrated Development Environments (IDEs) is software which integrates a text editor, file management, compiler, and other tools to promote an efficient workflow for modern computer programmers. IDEs play an important role in the modern software development process, especially when creating lengthy codebases. The text editors in these systems often include visual aids that use indentation to indicate scope level, different colors for syntax highlighting, and various other features to help programmers understand their code structure and navigate through it more easily.

ASSETS'17, October 29-November 1, 2017, Baltimore, MD, USA

ACM ISBN 978-1-4503-4926-0/17/10…$15.00
https://doi.org/10.1145/3132525.3132550

Figure 1. A participant using JAWS with an 80-cell Brilliant Braille Display, while programming in Java using the Eclipse Integrated Development Environment (IDE).

Prior research on blind programmers has found that the information conveyed through visual metaphors in IDEs are often not conveyed by screen readers [2], which creates challenges for blind programmers [9, 18], putting them at a disadvantage when compared to their sighted peers [7, 11]. IDEs provide a particular benefit when programmers are working on large pieces of software, to help (sighted) programmers understand the structure and relationships between lines of code. Blind programmers who are using screen readers or braille displays (which convey information linearly, one line at a time) have difficulty understanding structural relationships quickly [11, 19, 23]. Screen reader users also have access to fewer advanced IDE features for quickly moving through a large codebase, often forcing them to navigate code line-by-line or jump to different locations using "find/search" features [2].

Section 2 discusses how most prior studies on blind programmers have based their findings on case study observations or feedback from a relatively small number of users, e.g. 8 or 12 participants [11, 19]. To build a foundation for future research addressing users' challenges, there is a need for larger empirical studies. Our recent survey of 69 blind programmers explored a broad set of issues [1], and participants listed navigating through code and understanding its structure as key concerns. However, we had not conducted follow-up interviews to analyze these issues more deeply. To address this, we conducted this current observation and interview-based study to specifically investigate how 28 blind programmers navigate through code, using their own preferred development tools while performing common programming activities.

To preview for the reader, our study had three key findings:

1. Programming software (e.g., IDEs) did not meet participants' needs for code navigation; they regularly struggled when performing typical programming activities with these tools. Nevertheless, participants still preferred to use IDEs, even though they encountered these navigation difficulties.
2. Assistive technologies and specific accessibility features of some IDEs did not provide adequate support to enable users to navigate through code comfortably. Although some users were able to customize their assistive technology to better convey the information displayed by the IDE and trigger specific commands, the inefficiency of code navigation made participants feel a loss of control, and they often reported disorientation in the code.
3. Participants felt uncomfortable disclosing their programming needs (e.g., navigation difficulties) and their disability status to colleagues or researchers, which may prevent them from understanding the need to improve the accessibility of IDEs.

In summary, our findings provide greater empirical evidence about the need to improve code navigation features in IDEs for blind programmers, and it identifies opportunities for researchers and industry for addressing these needs. This study contributes to the literature by providing more detailed, firsthand feedback from a relatively large number of participants.

This paper is structured as follows: Section 2 surveys prior work in various tools and techniques to help blind individuals overcome programming barriers. Section 3 outlines our specific research questions to investigate how blind programmers navigate through a lengthy codebase, using their own preferred development tools and while performing common programming activities. Section 4 provides an overview of the methodology used in this paper to investigate the outlined research questions in Section 3. Section 5 explains our interview and observation results, and Section 6 summarizes our conclusions and future research directions.

2. LITERATURE REVIEW

Globally, the number of students entering the Computer Science discipline has increased over the past 10 years [7], however, people with disabilities remain underrepresented in computing [12]. Students who are blind must overcome significant educational and technological barriers, including the heavy use of images and visual abstractions in classrooms; prior researchers have examined how the traditional curriculum in Computer Science has not been designed with assistive technologies in mind [18, 23]. While there has been significant prior research on investigating particular design interventions to benefit blind programmers, e.g. audio cues (Section 2.1) or navigation aids (Section 2.2), there have been relatively few studies that have explored the challenges faced by blind programmers more broadly (Section 2.3).

2.1 Design Interventions: Audio Cues

Significant prior research has examined how to create audio-based accessibility tools for computing students with visual disabilities or other professional software developers [16, 21]. For instance, Sanchez and Aguayo 2005 developed a custom programming tool called Auditory Programming Language (APL) aimed to help blind students write software code comfortably [17]. They demonstrated that audio could convey important information to non-visual users. However, their tool provided a limited set of commands (e.g., input, output, cycle, condition, and variable) making it difficult to scale.

Similarly, Stefik et al. [23] created a tool called Sodbeans based on NetBeans IDE for Java programming, to help convey certain information to students who are blind. The tool used audible cues [6] so that blind students can learn programming concepts. These cues were designed to be browsed in a hierarchical tree manner, to support navigation. In addition, blind students have a rich set of programming environments and tools that they can use beyond the use of Java (e.g., Java, PHP, Ruby). The tool was evaluated based on the students' ability to master the programming concepts.

Various researchers, e.g. [20], have examined the potential of auditory cues to benefit programmers, including the potential benefits of non-speech audio for blind programmers: For instance, Vickers and Alty [25] found that such audio helped programmers locate bugs in their code. Specifically, musical cues proved useful for conveying information to programmers during a debugging process. Boardman et al. [4] created a tool called LISTEN to investigate the use of sounds when analyzing various program behaviors; their goal was to instrument computer programs so that different audible sounds were mapped to different behaviors during the program execution. Stefik et al. [22] investigated the use of audio cues to convey lexical scoping relationships in software code; different cues were played when a change in scope was detected.

Some researchers have examined the limits of understandability of audio cues: In [13], researchers conducted an experiment to investigate the usefulness of auditory cues for navigating menus on mobile phones. These authors also compared two techniques, *Earcons* (a hierarchical progression of variable tones) and *Spearcons* (spoken directions, compressed and sped up) as navigation methods [26]; they found that *Spearcons* helped blind users navigate through cell phones quickly and comfortably. They also found that short cues were more effective than more complicated cues, for conveying certain types of information.

In summary, audible cues have been found to be helpful for a variety of programming activities. Further investigation might help indicate whether audio cues can benefit non-visual users (programmers) to locate errors and debug code faster, mainly to reduce the amount of time blind programmers take to navigate through lengthy codebases.

2.2 Design Interventions: Code Navigation

Several prior researchers, e.g. [8], have proposed interventions to help enhance code navigation. By "code navigation," we refer to the ability of blind programmers to understand lengthy codebases better and how each code statement is nested within the code, which results in enabling blind programmers to navigate code quicker.

Smith et al. [19] developed an Eclipse plug-in to help non-sighted users understand code structure, to speed navigation through a codebase. The authors used keyboard inputs and speech/sound outputs of the hierarchical structure of the codebase to convey certain information to non-visual users. In their work, authors performed a usability test using hyperbolic browser method that employs a fisheye technique [10]. The fisheye technique refers to zooming-in on a single node in a hierarchy tree structure, with the details of the ancestors and descendants presented in reduced detail. Such an approach helped researchers identify strategies that sighted developers tend to use while moving through familiar and unfamiliar trees. Based on this, the authors defined a set of user requirements for an accessible tree navigation system.

Similarly, Baker et al. [2] created an Eclipse plug-in called StructJumper that aimed to help screen reader users navigate through a large amount of codebase quickly. The tool was designed to create a hierarchical tree representation based on the codebase, which presents hierarchical tree-based information about the nesting structure of a Java class. In their tool, blind programmers used a *TreeView* feature to get an overview of the code structure. In addition, they could use a *Text Editor* feature to get an idea of where they are within the nested structure of the code. Thus, blind programmers could look up contextual information about their code without having to lose their position. For example, with the use of shortcut keys, blind developers could press a defined key to find which statement of the code he or she is working on. Such a technique allows a blind developer to quickly jump to the node corresponding to the current location. This approach was similar to that used by other researchers to recognize code in order to present a tree-like structure in a hierarchical tree representation [19].

Other researchers have examined technology interventions to improve code understanding for sighted developers: For example, researchers in [5] created a system where code is presented in "bubbles", which are editable views of, e.g., specific methods or collections of variables; each bubble is in a different color. Of course, the heavy use of visual abstractions is not suitable for blind programmers; further study would be needed to determine whether this bubble metaphor could benefit non-visual users.

2.3 Programming Challenges

While a variety of studies have been published focused on the design and evaluation of specific technology interventions to benefit blind programmers, there have been relatively fewer empirical studies to explore and identify programming challenges. For example, Mealin and Murphy-Hill (discussed below) interviewed 8 participants [11], and Smith et al. [19] conducted an experiment with 12 participants to evaluate a code navigation plug-in. We discuss two prior studies, most closely related to our work:

Mealin and Murphy-Hill conducted an interview study with eight experienced blind developers to highlight their programming difficulties [11], and they identified a number of challenges: First, they noticed that developers were not using the tools available within the IDEs. It was unclear from their study whether users were unaware of the tools offered within these IDEs, found the tools to be too complex, or if the tools were not easily accessible. Second, they found that many blind developers were using a temporary text buffer to store programming notes and to work in it. During the interviews, participants also mentioned challenges with debugging, inaccessible UML diagrams, code navigation, complexity of IDEs, and working in teams with sighted programmers. The authors discussed how blind developers use workarounds or other strategies to overcome the above-mentioned challenges.

We recently conducted an online survey of 69 blind programmers to identify challenges [1]. Similar to the findings of [11] regarding the use of temporary text buffers, we found that blind developers felt overwhelmed when using existing IDEs (e.g., Eclipse, NetBeans, etc.), and therefore they preferred to use simpler editors to write software code comfortably (e.g., Notepad, Notepad++, etc.). In addition, participants indicated that navigating through code and understanding its structure were key concerns. However, the focus of our survey had been on programming challenges broadly, and the survey methodology did not permit us to conduct follow-up discussions with our participants to probe for additional details about code navigation or conduct an in-depth analysis.

3. RESEARCH QUESTIONS

To better understand blind programmers' challenges and build a foundation for future research addressing these problems, we have therefore conducted an observation and interview-based study to specifically investigate how blind programmers navigate through code, using their own preferred development tools and while performing common programming activities. This new study also allowed us to more specifically investigate this issue of code navigation that had been raised in our prior survey [1]. Specifically, we wanted to investigate the following questions:

- **RQ1:** What difficulties do blind developers encounter when navigating through a codebase?
- **RQ2:** What tools do they use in their development work?
- **RQ3:** What workarounds or strategies do they use to overcome any code navigation barriers?

4. METHODOLOGY

As methodological inspiration, we have drawn upon the recent work of Szpiro et al., who conducted a study using contextual inquiry and qualitative data analysis to understand the challenges faced by people with low vision when accessing computing devices [24]. Their goal was to uncover challenges and identify opportunities for researchers and industry to improve low vision accessibility tools, and we have similar aims in regard to code navigation for blind programmers. In this work, we used observations and semi-structured interviews with blind programmers to identify code navigation difficulties, the tools they used, and any workarounds they employ. This methodology will help us gain deeper insight, relative to our prior survey-based study in [1]. In addition to identifying future research opportunities, another goal was to involve blind programmers in the research and to gather firsthand comments and suggestions from these users.

4.1 Interview Design

Prior to the main study, we conducted pilot tests (mock interviews with five sighted programmers) to ensure that our semi-structured question plan, interview technique, and procedure were well-formed. As a result of these pilot tests, the interview questions and procedure were modified, e.g. the wording of some of the questions were changed to use terminology more familiar to this user group.

The planned questions included five multiple-choice and 16 open-ended questions, which were grouped into several topics:

- **Demographics:** user characteristics such as age, gender, country, visual acuity, and level of expertise in software development.
- **Languages and Tools:** to identify a list of programming languages and programming tools (e.g., Eclipse, etc.).
- **Assistive Technologies:** to identify participants' preferences of assistive technologies such as screen readers or braille displays.
- **Development Style:** to capture and observe blind programmers' strategies when developing software, mainly to navigate code.
- **Navigation Difficulties:** to uncover navigation difficulties and how it impacted blind developers' performance.
- **Navigation Tools:** to investigate existing code navigation tools and how it helped overcome navigation difficulties.

- **Working in Teams:** to understand how blind programmers work in teams, mainly with sighted programmers.

4.2 Participants

We recruited participants using a private mailing list from previous studies (individuals had agreed to join this mailing list and had previously indicated an interest in participating in studies) and by posting advertisements on private groups (Google, LinkedIn, and AppleVis) for people who are blind. A total of 36 people responded. We conducted an initial screening interview over *Skype* and *Google Hangouts* to first determine the eligibility of the participants. To participate, individuals had to be an experienced developer (5+ years in programming), 18 years or older, self-identified as fully blind, actively engaged in programming either as a job or a hobby, and a user of assistive technologies (e.g., screen reader or braille display). Eight respondents were excluded from the study due to the use of magnifiers and corrective lenses. (The focus of this study was on users of screen readers or braille displays.)

Afterward, we conducted the interview sessions with the remaining 28 blind programmers. Participants (all male) varied in age from 22 to 52 (mean =29.68, SD=6.59). Our sample showed variation in programming experience (lowest = 5 years, highest = 24 years) and employment status (e.g., retired, employed, unemployed, freelancer). Few unemployed participants are searching for job opportunities. All participants use screen readers, and 8 participants used braille displays (see **Table 2**). Participants were from five different countries: United States (n = 22), United Kingdom (n = 3), Australia (n = 1), India (n = 1), and the Netherlands (n = 1).

4.3 Procedure

The interview took place online via *Skype* and *Google Hangouts* per the participants' preference. Prior to the interview, participants were provided with informed consent documents and the interview questions (so they could familiarize themselves with the interview topic in advance). Each interview lasted approximately one hour and occurred during January to December 2016. Enrollment had not been fixed; rather, recruitment was discontinued (at 28) after the researcher observed that no new issues were raised during the sessions conducted with participants 27 and 28. All participants were compensated for their time with $50 Amazon gift cards.

The session began with the brief semi-structured interview (questions in section 4.1). This was followed by an observation period when we asked participants to engage in common programming activities. The participant transmitted their voice and their computer's audio output, and in addition, they transmitted the video image of what was displayed on their computer screen. The interviews and observations were recorded with the participants' prior approval, using *Screencast-omatic* software.

Since our goal was to understand code navigation difficulties and observe how participants deal with these navigation problems, we identified in advance a set of programming activities, which we requested the participant to perform during the observation:

- Conducting a programming walk through using any language or tool: We asked the participant to open some code that they had been editing recently as part of their professional work and to explain the code, giving a demonstration of its structure.
- Demonstrating for the researcher some code navigation difficulties they encounter frequently.
- Navigation walk through of some other programmers' codebase with which the participant had no prior knowledge.
- Demonstrating any strategies or workarounds that the participant uses to overcome navigation difficulties.
- Demonstrating any solutions or tools and how they helped.

We observed participants perform the above-mentioned programming tasks, and we occasionally interrupted them with questions. For each question, we encouraged participants to speak freely and openly (explaining that their feedback was very valuable and this research might benefit other programmers in the future) so that we can elicit more detailed answers. We did not insist that participants use specific programming languages or development tools, mainly because participants owned various platforms and had their own preferences. In a few cases, some participants did not wish to perform one of the asks or were unable to do so, and we did not insist in those cases. Our priority during the session was to elicit comments and impressions from the participants about code navigation difficulties that they encountered when performing these tasks, to capture information about: what assistive technologies that they use and why, how they used them, how they completed these activities, and how they felt when performing it.

4.4 Data Analysis

During the session, we captured the following data:

- Responses to closed-ended questions were recorded.
- Additional written notes were taken for open-ended responses, with particular focus on capturing direct quotations.
- Timestamps were noted when an important issue was raised, to facilitate the researcher reviewing key portions of recordings.
- All notes were stored and duplicated for further analysis.

We followed a qualitative methodology for our data analysis. The data was managed and annotated using NVivo qualitative data analysis software. Following an open-coding method [15], we analyzed open-ended questions based on their content using a set of codes that we developed to represent recurring ideas or problems raised by participants. We assigned codes to segments of text transcription or experimenter notes in our dataset.

Two researchers performed coding independently, reading and organizing the participants' transcripts. Afterwards, they met periodically to discuss code categories (e.g., navigation challenges, assistive technologies, programming tools, workarounds, and user needs). In rare cases when coders disagreed (inter-rater reliability = 67%), they held a meeting to reach an agreement and form a consensus coding. We generated a set of themes based on the number of times each issue was raised. For example, high occurrences indicate higher demand or importance. Themes were developed using affinity diagramming [3], which is a useful technique for organizing and analyzing large-scale qualitative data.

5. RESULTS

In this section, we describe key findings, illustrated with examples of our participants' behavior or comments from the interview sessions. Quotations are labeled with code numbers preceded by the letter P that represent individual participants (e.g., P1, P2, etc.). This section is organized based on the major themes that arose during our data analysis: code navigation challenges (Section 5.1), tools (e.g., assistive technologies, programming languages and tools) (Section 5.2), and strategies to overcome navigation difficulties (Section 5.3).

5.1 RQ1: Code Navigation Challenges

In software development, programmers regularly use their sight to obtain information about their software codebase, which allows them to formulate an understanding of their code structure and navigate throughout the code. Blind programmers rely on other senses (e.g., hearing and touch) to acquire contextual and structural information about their software codebase. We observed our participants encountering several code navigation difficulties when performing various programming activities, and participants discussed this issue in their interview responses. We summarize a taxonomy of sub-types of navigation difficulties in **Table 1**; next to each description, we provide the number of participants who mentioned each issue. Due to length constraints, the remainder of this section will summarize some key points, along with illustrative examples and quotations from participants.

Navigation Difficulties	# Participants
Debugging: difficulty navigating through the code in the process of understanding a wrong output.	24
Line by Line: difficulty navigating through code to locate specific information without having to go through the entire codebase linearly, line-by-line.	23
Indentation: unable to distinguish the level of whitespace using a screen reader in indentation-based languages, e.g. Python.	22
Nesting: difficulty navigating through nested methods, loops, functions, or classes.	20
Back Track: difficulty returning quickly to a specific line (in a lengthy codebase) when reviewing other code statements in various files.	18
Errors: difficulty quickly locating code errors while navigating through lengthy codebases.	14
Scope: difficulty understanding the scope level, e.g. while navigating deeply nested methods or loops.	14
Characters: difficulty perceiving certain characters, operators, and parentheses, e.g. missing some characters while coding.	10
Autocomplete: difficulty accessing the autocomplete feature due to incompatibility with the screen reader.	9
Relationship: unable to distinguish the relationship between code entities within a codebase, e.g. the relationship between a class and its subclasses.	9
Line Numbers: difficulty accessing line numbers in the code editor as they were not designed to be readable by a screen reader, e.g. using PyCharm with VoiceOver.	7
Elements: unable to quickly locate a specific element within a given array, class, function or loop, e.g. locating values or variables.	5

Table 1. List of navigation difficulties and number of participants who mentioned each during interviews; the difficulties are sorted based on this number.

Debugging: When a failure occurs in software, programmers must perform three main activities to correct the failure. First, they need to perform fault localization to identify the code statement responsible for the software failure. Second, they need to complete a fault understanding activity that involves understanding the origin of the software failure. Third, they must perform a fault correction activity, to determine the best way to remove the cause of the software failure. All three of these activities are commonly referred to as "debugging," which is an essential skill in software development [14]. Our participants indicated that they understood the importance of debugging and how it helps to correct unwanted software behaviors. However, participants indicated that they tend to rely on simple debugging techniques, mostly because of the accessibility issues in current debugging tools (e.g., *FindBugs*, *Firebug*, etc.). For example, P4 examined several available debugging tools to find one that is compatible with their screen reader. He found that most debugging tools were not accessible as they were designed with vision in mind. Therefore, P4 and many other participants (n = 19) decided to rely on simple debugging techniques such as inserting print commands in the code or tracing:

"I rely on printf *to fix code defects. I also tried to test different tools like* FindBugs *or* Firebug*, but they were not fully accessible to [my] screen reader." (P4)*

P26, on the other hand, discussed the difficulty of navigating through a lengthy codebase to find logic errors. He explained that debugging techniques, such as *printf*, may take longer as there is no clear indication where to find the problem that caused the software to behave incorrectly. While most participants relied on simple debugging techniques, some (n = 9) used advanced debugging tools:

"I was trained to use advanced debugging tools by my sighted colleagues even with the accessibility issues. I think the training helped me use them better." (P8)

Although participants vary in their own debugging experiences, most participants mentioned that debugging is a significant barrier to blind programmers, mostly because it is difficult to interpret software control flow while debugging.

Line by Line: We have discussed previously how vision helps software developers get an overview of the entire codebase. To get an overview of code, most of our participants (n = 18) indicated that they tend to go through a codebase line by line, mainly because screen readers encourage users to move through text in a linear fashion. P5, for example, explained a difficulty that they encountered when working with complex codebase:

"How to accomplish things in my complex code [is] frustrating. I need more time to understand each line and more time to remember what each code block is doing." (P5)

While several participants discussed the difficulty of navigating linearly with a screen reader, some (n = 8) used other techniques, e.g. searching through the codebase using keywords, to avoid scrolling through the entire codebase line by line. While P13 and others enjoy using keywords, another participant (P20) indicated that keyword searching is time-consuming and often frustrating, because the same keyword might appear in several locations within the same codebase. P6 and a few others, on the other hand, agreed that keywords are very popular among blind developers to find a specific code statement. But considering that some cases where the same keyword is used twice or even more, blind programmers often need to review a few code statements before and after the keyword location to ensure that they have found the right line:

"Keywords [are] useful when you deal with the small code, but not a large one, especially when you try to find a variable that [has] been used several times in different locations. Which code block I am reviewing is hard to distinguish with keywords." (P6)

Indentation: Indentation-based languages (e.g., Python, Occam, etc.) use whitespace indentation to delimit code blocks, instead of using keywords or curly braces. In these languages, an increase in indentation may indicate a new, deeper code block, and a decrease in indentation indicates the end of the code block. Python was the most commonly used programming language among our participants (n = 18), mainly because of their job requirements. To navigate through an indentation-based language, most participants indicated that they tend to go through it block by block instead of line by line, mainly to avoid the verbalization of whitespaces (indents) using a screen reader. By "block by block," we refer to instances when blind programmers wish to skip-over code blocks (e.g., in a loop, a function definition) to avoid reading one code statement at a time while browsing the entire codebase. For example, P10 explained that a screen reader will verbalize an indentation as a sequence of individual "space" characters, rather than a single indent of a particular length. When a screen reader user navigates through indentation based languages, the blind programmer will hear his or her screen reader verbalizing whitespaces as a single space (e.g., "space, space, space") rather than a count ("three spaces").

P21 explained how to overcome the whitespace problem using a screen reader. The solution involves writing a custom script (a modification of the typical functionality of a screen reader for a particular application) that forces the screen reader to calculate whitespaces and verbalize it as a complete list of whitespaces:

"I found it useful to write script that forces my screen reader to calculate the whitespaces and then present it [to me]. I designed the script to say, for example, 'four spaces' instead of saying 'space' four different times." (P21)

P3 explained a similar approach:

"Instead of listening to my own screen reader telling me all the spaces separately. I wrote [a] script to give me the level of indentation in my code." (P3)

Although calculating whitespaces and verbalizing it helped several participants (n = 5), others (n = 4) found a braille display much more helpful in determining the level of whitespaces. For instance, P16 reported that a braille display provides valuable assistance in determining the level of whitespaces, through touch. Section 5.2 discusses how users mitigate this whitespace issue by using a braille display in conjunction with their screen reader:

"I use a screen reader and [also] braille display with Python, it helps [me] feel the indentation in my code." (P16)

5.2 RQ2: Tools in Software Development

In this section, we discuss the participants' behavior or experiences towards assistive technologies, programming languages, as well as development tools. We also describe each method and technique used by participants to perform various development activities. We presented each category with the actual number of users based on the participants' use of each language or tool.

5.2.1 *Assistive Technologies*

Assistive technologies refer to any specialty hardware or software add-ons that were designed to increase the functional capabilities of people with disabilities. These assistive tools, whether developed by the industry or privately customized by the end users, provide freedom and independence to people with special needs to accomplish tasks that are difficult without getting help from those who are sighted. In this paper, participants used two different forms of assistive technologies; screen readers and braille displays. A screen reader enables blind users to access the computer display by linearizing the presentation of information from the graphical user interface and verbalizing this information using a speech synthesizer (or transmitting this information to a braille display).

Participants described a variety of experiences performing common programming activities using their screen reader. For example, P2 prefers to use the Non-Visual Desktop Access (NVDA) screen reader when working with a Python codebase:

"I use NVDA because its free, made by a blind user, and helps me convert text into [a] Braille Display." (P2)

P10 uses NVDA for programming activities, mainly because it allows for personal customization. He uses *PyCharm* to write Python applications, despite challenges in using this tool with his screen reader. P10 indicated that *PyCharm* is very complex platform, and it poses many programming problems:

"I like to use PyCharm to write python application, I modified NVDA script to ignore unwanted features and to help [me] reduce its complexity." (P10)

Although many participants (n = 12) decided to use NVDA for personal reasons or financial constraints, others (n = 16) preferred to use a different type of screen reader (see **Table 2**). For instance, P13 uses JAWS with development software, mainly because it allows users to load specific scripts (customized modifications of its behavior) for each platform:

"JAWS provide me with great functionality. You can assign specific script to each application, it helps reduce the time I take to navigate through the entire application." (P13)

A refreshable braille display is an electro-mechanical device to translate information from the computer display into braille characters. It uses round-tipped pins in a flat surface that are raised through holes to convey information to blind users. These devices are available in different sizes (different number of characters that can be displayed in a line simultaneously, e.g., 18, 40, 80) based on the user's needs. In this paper, several participants (n = 8) indicated that they use a refreshable braille display with a screen reader to perform various programming activities (see **Figure 1**). For example, P24 preferred to use a braille display when working with Python codebases, mainly to understand the level of indentation as its difficult to understand when using a screen reader alone:

"Braille display is much better than screen reader when it comes to detecting indentation level. [The] screen reader will say 'space', 'space', 'space', etc. Which is too much to handle with complex code." (P24)

Some participants (n = 6) explained that they preferred to use a refreshable braille display to navigate through a codebase because it was quicker than a screen reader. Others (n = 2) tend to use braille displays because it reduced their "hearing load," i.e. the stress they experience from attending too much information conveyed on the audio channel in an interface. For example, P28 discussed how a screen reader creates significant hearing load when performing programming activities at work:

"I read texts and software code using braille display, [it] helps reduce [the] hearing load and makes me aware of the surrounding, especially in work settings." (P28)

Other participants (n = 2) explained that they used a multi-line braille display. (Most braille displays present a single line of characters, but some are capable of presenting multiple rows of characters simultaneously.) Participants indicated that this device helped them to read several lines of code to get a better overview of the code structure, rather than using a screen reader or a single-line braille display, which presents information linearly:

"Navigating code [is] difficult with screen reader, you feel isolated to one line at a time, I use multi-line braille display which helps me read more than one line at a time." (P16)

5.2.2 Development Languages & Tools

Our participants' knowledge and experience in programming languages and development tools varied. Some (n = 15) were proficient in more than one programming language, and others (n = 13) were experienced in a single language only. This variation was mainly due to their specific job requirements or constraints that are presented by the structure of the programming language.

Participants were asked to the list the programming languages and tools that they use to develop software (see **Table 2**). Our results showed that Python was the most used language among all participants. In fact, 18 participants (n = 64%) indicated that they use Python to write software code for several reasons, including: its simplicity, its rising popularity, and the fact that can be used as an interpreted language – thereby providing users with the ability to dynamically inspect and change their programming code. Although Python was the most used language among all participants, other participants (n = 10) preferred to use Java, again, mostly for job requirements. For example, P27 developed several applications that run on computers, smart cards, and cell phones for the company:

"I developed the company clients support application with other colleagues that was written in Java. [We] choose Java because [of] its well-written libraries. [We] use other languages as well, but mostly Java." (P27)

Operating Systems	#
Windows	23
Linux	8
Mac OS	4

Assistive Technology	#
NVDA	12
JAWS	10
ORCA	5
VoiceOver	4
LSR	3
Windows-Eyes	1
Braille Display	8

Programming Languages	#
Python	18
Java	10
C++	10
SQL	7
C	6
Swift	4
Ruby	3
C#	2
Objective-C	2
PHP	2
Perl	1

Programming Editors	#
Notepad++	18
PyCharm	16
Visual Studio	12
NetBeans	8
Notepad	6
Notepadqq	5
Eclipse	4
Xcode	4
CODA	4
Atom	2
IDLE	1
TextMate	1
Padre	1

Table 2. Number of participants in our study using various operating systems, assistive technologies, programming languages, and programming editors.

In regard to development tools, all participants preferred to use simpler editors rather than current IDEs. Participants explained that simpler editors (e.g., *Notepad*, *Notepad++*, *Notepadqq*, etc.) were popular due to their simplicity and flexibility with assistive technologies and programming languages. *Notepad++*, for example, was especially popular among users of the Windows operating system as it available for free. P4 explained that his reason for using *Notepad++* was due to its wide range of plug-ins, that helped facilitate writing software code. While some participants (n = 7) favored plug-in features to install tools that had previously been developed by the blind programming community, others (n = 8) find it useful to write their own plug-ins. For example, P15 worked with several blind programmers to develop a plug-in that allows screen reader users to navigate through autocomplete functionality, mainly to make it more accessible. Autocomplete is a common feature in most IDEs in which the system displays a pop-up menu of predictions of what the programmer is about to type next, based on the first few characters of the word they have typed. But this feature is not fully accessible to screen reader users, mainly because it appears on the screen as a pop-up which the screen reader does not recognize. Although most participants preferred to use simpler editors when performing various programming activities, all participants agreed that IDEs are necessary at times, despite accessibility problems.

5.3 RQ3: Programming Strategies

In the midst of a discussion about navigation difficulties with our participants, it would have been easy for participants to forget to mention positive information, such as navigation workarounds or strategies. For this reason, we specifically asked participants to demonstrate or explain some examples of these. Our participants discussed a myriad of strategies to overcome various programming challenges, mainly code navigation difficulties. Due to length constraints, this section will summarize some key points, along with illustrative examples and quotations from participants.

Simple Editors: As discussed above most participants (n = 26) indicated that they rely on simple editors to write software code; we highlight here how several of our participants reported using simple editors in concert with IDEs – to overcome inaccessible features in existing IDEs. For example, several participants (n = 8) explained how they use simple editors to record code errors, bugs status, and where variables located to enhance navigation. Other participants (n = 7) use them to avoid losing their current spot while reviewing other code statements. For example, P18 demonstrated how to use *Notepad* to navigate through a complex codebase that was written by other programmers:

"The code I am showing is large and long. I work with other programmers to maintain it and mostly to modify it. I use Notepad to record code errors while reviewing other statements for reference." (P18)

Custom Scripts: Our participants expressed mixed feeling about the use of assistive technologies, mostly screen readers. In this work, most participants (n = 19) modified screen reader settings to match their own personal needs. Others (n = 9) wrote custom scripts to overcome many issues including programming difficulties. Participants explained that creating a custom script is not a perfect solution, yet it still provides an alternative method to solve some of the problems they experience when interacting with current IDEs. For example, P11 showed a script that was designed to force the screen reader to locate elements on the *PyCharm* (IDE) which was not fully accessible. P9, on the other hand, reported that his screen reader will not read line numbers on some of the IDEs, mainly because line numbers was not designed to be readable by a screen reader. Therefore, he wrote a custom script to force the screen reader to read line numbers:

"I wrote many custom scripts to help do my job faster. My screen reader will not catch line numbers on some of the IDEs, so I coded [a] script to force my screen reader catch line numbers. (P9)

Shortcut Keys: as researchers, we were interested to know how blind programmers get a high-level overview of the entire codebase for navigation purposes. Screen readers navigate through codebase linearly, forcing the user to read the entire codebase one line at a time. To overcome this problem, several participants (n = 9) indicated that they use shortcut keys as a navigation strategy. For example, P4 relies on shortcut keys to locate specific code statements without scrolling through the entire codebase. Other participants (n = 12) use them to get structural information about their codebase. However, P1 argues that shortcut tools like *find* comment (to search for text strings) can help programmers find content in the codebase using keywords, but often a single keyword is not enough to jump through all the associated content (for e.g. in programming languages like Java and C++, jumping through all the functions in a code using a single search keyword can be ineffective as all related functions might not use those specific keywords).

However, P12 said that the use of shortcut keys was inefficient since it forces users to jump between code blocks, which is difficult for someone who is blind, especially for unfamiliar codebases:

"Depending on the language, the start of the block may not be easy to follow without reading through all lines. In cases like that, shortcut keys may not be [a] helpful strategy at all." (P12)

P19, on the other hand, was annoyed that various IDEs make use of specific shortcut key combinations that are also used by his screen reader, leading to conflicting functions:

"I rely on shortcut keys to navigate through code, but there are overlapped keys between several applications. I had to write a custom script to control overlapped shortcut keys for me." (P19)

Code Comments: In software development, commenting involves placing different readable descriptions inside code blocks to detail the purpose of each block. Most blind developers rely on them to make code maintainable and debugging easier. Commenting is an important technique, especially when a project involves other programmers. In this work, most participants (n = 16) used commenting, not in the traditional manner (to make source code readable or document how a certain function works), but rather to overcome navigation barriers. For example, P3 used commenting to locate software bugs that need to be addressed immediately with other software programmers. Although some participants (n = 6) used commenting to locate code errors or bugs, others (n = 9) use it to highlight code statements that require further review:

"When modifying some of my code function, I use comments to locate them fast, especially while checking other statements so I can get back to them fast." (P22)

Sighted Help: Our participants indicated that seeking help from others, especially from those who are sighted, is avoided by many blind individuals in workplace settings, often due to embarrassment about the amount of time they take to accomplish certain tasks. Additionally, many participants indicated that they wanted to demonstrate that their visual loss had no impact on their ability to fulfill their job requirements. Although most participants (n = 16) tended to avoid seeking help from sighted co-workers, others (n = 10) found it necessary. For example, P25 seeks sighted help to get an overview of the entire codebase when a new implementation takes place. This helps reduce the amount of time a blind programmer takes to get an overview of the entire implementation. P7 agreed that requesting sighted help is understandable since blind programmers are unable to simply glance at codebase due to the linear nature of the screen reader:

"Reviewing another programmer's code with a screen reader takes longer than someone who is not blind, I seek help sometimes to get [a] quick overview of the new implementation." (P7)

P13 shares a similar opinion about the importance of requesting sighted help whenever needed:

"I enjoy working with sighted programmers, you always learn many tips." (P13)

5.4 The Need for Better Navigation

As part of our interview, we also discussed with participants some possible future features that could be added to IDEs to improve their accessibility. In some cases, the participants requested features prior to being prompted. For all participants, we included a section in the interview in which we briefly described several possible future enhancements to IDEs – to gauge the interest our participants had in each option. Overall, 82% of our participants (n = 23) showed interest in using these various features (listed below), while 18% said that they might be willing to try them. The set of possible future enhancements to IDEs discussed during our interviews included the following:

Tree View: Most participants expressed the need to have an alternative feature to navigate through codebase, mostly to avoid going through it line by line. For example, several participants suggested a hierarchical navigation feature in which codebase could be presented as a tree, mainly to hide code complexity. (This is in agreement with prior findings of Baker et al. [2].) In fact, 18 participants (64%) showed interest in using such a feature. Tree view (or tree list) is already available feature in some of the IDEs but is not fully accessible to screen readers:

"Going through code line by line is very difficult with [a] screen reader, especially when you deal with complex software code. As blind programmers, we discuss many ideas about accessibility in programming. In fact, we thought to program [a] tool that presents the software code as tree instead of navigating through line code, which takes forever." (P14)

"I would love to see a tool that shows code in a different way, not line by line." (P27)

Auditory Feedback: Several participants (n = 7) suggested that sounds should become a core integration component when interacting with programming activities, especially for blind programmers. For example, some participants (n = 3) indicated that sounds would help them monitor background processes in development tools while attending other tasks. One advantage is that auditory cues can help blind programmers split their attention between an immediate task and waiting for the result of some background process. Participants also suggested that sounds could be used to help provide additional information regarding syntax errors, invalid statements, and current location in code in order to reduce programming difficulties. (This is in agreement with findings of Vickers and Alty [25].) In fact, 19 participants were interested in using auditory feedback (68%), while 9 (32%) participants said that they would be willing to try it:

"It would be nice to have audio feedback when we make code mistakes. It will help locate errors while navigating through code or maybe highlight any syntax error." (P8)

"The way how programming relies on visual representation is the major impact in almost all difficulties that we face as blind individuals. We need another way of programming, maybe with audio or something else as I can't think of different way that could help us." (P24)

Bookmarks or Tags: Our participants described how they used comments to leave keywords at particular locations in their code, which they could then jump to more easily by using a search feature. Participants also reported that they tend to remove all of these comments before sharing their code with others, especially sighted people, mainly because they feel embarrassed. Several participants expressed the need to have a bookmark feature in which they could tag specific line of code and return to it later for further modification (without making use of comments and searching to accomplish this task). Participants cautioned that the bookmark feature should be designed to jump to a specific code statement, rather than to a specific line number (which may shift when additional code is inserted or deleted). Bookmark or Tag features are already available in Visual Studio and other IDEs, further investigation may indicate whether such tools are fully accessible and beneficial for non-visual users. In fact, 24 participants (86%) showed interest in using bookmark feature, while 4 (14%) participants said that they might try it:

"I always wanted to build [a] tool that tags code for personal use. You could build it in [a] way that any line can be tagged either for private or public comments. You could also use shortcut keys to locate each tag to quickly find them. I guess I did not find the right time to develop it." (P22)

Nesting & Scope Level: Nested code is commonly used in software development where various programming logic structures are combined to one another (e.g., embedded within one another). Deeply nested code can pose challenges for blind users because it is harder to read. When nested code goes beyond three levels of indention, it can be difficult to understand and navigate. To handle nested code, sighted programmers tend to use *code folding* in software editors. This feature allows them to collapse an entire code block (visually hide the full text of the code and replace it with a small visual placeholder instead), which allows programmers to have a better view of the surrounding code statements. Several of our participants also suggested that it would be valuable to have a scope and nesting level indicator feature. This would read aloud the current cursor location when a special shortcut key combination is pressed. We are not aware of any similar study or tool in this regard. In fact, 19 (68%) of our participants were interested in having nesting and scope level indicators, while 9 (32%) participants said that they might try it:

"I find it difficult to know my location when working with nested code block. You can't tell with a screen reader unless you read the entire block. I think a good solution is to have a tool that gives [me] the location and how deep I am within the nested code." (P5)

Class Relationships: In object-oriented programming, a class is used to describe one or more objects, mainly to serve as a template for creating various objects within a program. Each object is created from a single class – this one class could be used many times, mostly to instantiate multiple objects. It can be also used by software developers to isolate specific objects so that their internal variables or methods are not accessible from all parts of the program. This prevents the programmer from changing internal implementation details of some code, which might break other parts of the codebase. Programmers tend to use classes to help create more structured programs that can be easily modified. The inheritance relationships for classes can become complex, especially when there are multiple subclasses that inherit all or some of the characteristics of the main class. To understand class relationships, sighted programmers often rely on diagrams (e.g., how components are interrelated). Diagrams can be difficult to understand by blind programmers. Our participants expressed the need to have some method of conveying class relationship features, e.g. audio cues as they navigate through classes or subclasses in order to provide an overview of classes in a codebase. We are not aware of any similar study or tool in this regard. In fact, 17 (61%) of our participants expressed interest in using a class relationship feature, while 11 (39%) participants said that they might use it:

"It would be interesting to have class relationship tools where you get instant feedback through audio. Maybe [by] pressing shortcut keys to get audio feedback whenever I need to know all the subclasses of a class." (P18)

6. CONCLUSION AND FUTURE WORK

In this paper, we presented our exploratory study aimed at understanding code navigation challenges encountered by blind programmers when using various development tools. We illustrated and discussed our methodology for learning about code navigation difficulties from our participants: blind software developers. Our study offers a new perspective into the use of common development tools (e.g., Eclipse, NetBeans, etc.) alongside assistive technologies by developers who are blind. Most previous studies have based their findings on a small number of participants [2, 11, 19]. Our results arose from observing and interviewing a much larger sample, and our findings highlight various code navigation difficulties based on different programming languages and tools.

Our findings indicated that participants struggled to navigate through codebases using existing development software alongside assistive technologies (e.g., screen reader). Although accessibility tools provided benefits, they failed to give enough support for blind programmers to navigate through codebases quickly and comfortably. Since navigation options in IDEs are restricted to sighted users, blind programmers prefer simpler editors (e.g., *Notepad*, *Notepad++*). Participants explained and demonstrated how diverse programming environments, in combination with assistive technologies, lead to various challenges, often because these IDEs were designed without accessibility in mind.

Most of our participants preferred to use a screen reader (despite its limitations) to write software code. Others found this difficult, and therefore, favored using a braille display instead. However, several of our participants indicated that they could not afford to purchase a braille display. While most IDEs were not fully accessible, blind programmers still rely on them to accomplish their work. Moreover, some blind programmers may seek sighted help for various reasons, mostly to access content that is not accessible with assistive technologies. Although some blind programmers seek sighted help, others prefer writing custom scripts to overcome many programming challenges. For example, several blind programmers wrote custom scripts to enhance navigation in indentation-based languages. Others wrote scripts for each IDEs, mainly to access features difficult to use with a screen reader.

There were some limitations of our study: First, we only explored navigation difficulties encountered by experienced developers, who were totally blind, actively engaged in programming either as a job or hobby, and used assistive technologies to access the computer display (e.g., screen reader, braille display, or both). It was beyond our scope to study novice programmers or individuals with greater diversity in their visual acuity. A further investigation into such an important user group may reveal different findings. Secondly, while the qualitative design of this study allowed us to gather firsthand comments and experiences from our user group, and to discover new issues that arose, in future work, it may be important to follow up this study with a survey administered to a larger group of participants, to verify some of our findings.

The navigation challenges identified in this study illustrate the need for further research on improving the usability and accessibility of current IDEs. For example, participants showed interest in using a new forms of code navigation, e.g. using hierarchical navigation approaches. Participants also indicated a desire for bookmarks (or tags) features that would allow blind programmers to tag specific line of code and return to it later for further modification. They also expressed interest in scope and nesting level indicator, auditory additional feedback, and methods for conveying class relationships, which could make programming more accessible for these users.

Finally, while the participants in our study expressed interest in various technology interventions to address their needs, it would be necessary in future work to conduct formal evaluations of the efficacy of such technology in studies with blind developers. In fact, we are specifically planning, in our future work, to explore some form of auditory feedback which could help convey important information while users are navigating through lengthy codebases. Several participants expressed interest in this technology. Participants also suggested that audio cues could be used in various other programming activities. We plan to conduct participatory design research to understand how to best use auditory cues in a code navigation system.

In summary, the results of this study provide future accessibility researchers a foundation for understanding the needs of blind programmers, which may support their work in creating and evaluating new technologies to address those needs.

7. ACKNOWLEDGMENTS

We acknowledge scholarship support from the King Salman Scholarship Program. We would like to thank our participants and our anonymous reviewers for their valuable feedback and insights.

8. REFERENCES

[1] K. Albusays and S. Ludi. Eliciting programming challenges faced by developers with visual impairments: exploratory study. In *Proceedings of the 9th International Workshop on Cooperative and Human Aspects of Software Engineering*, pages 82–85. ACM, 2016.

[2] C. M. Baker, L. R. Milne, and R. E. Ladner. Structjumper: A tool to help blind programmers navigate and understand the structure of code. In *Proceedings of the 33rd Annual ACM Conference on Human Factors in Computing Systems*, pages 3043–3052. ACM, 2015.

[3] H. Beyer and K. Holtzblatt. *Contextual design: defining customer-centered systems*. Elsevier, 1997.

[4] D. B. Boardman, G. Greene, V. Khandelwal, and A. P. Mathur. Listen: A tool to investigate the use of sound for the analysis of program behavior. In *Computer Software and Applications Conference, 1995. COMPSAC 95. Proceedings., Nineteenth Annual International*, pages 184–189. IEEE, 1995.

[5] A. Bragdon, R. Zeleznik, S. P. Reiss, S. Karumuri, W. Cheung, J. Kaplan, C. Coleman, F. Adeputra, and J. J. LaViola Jr. Code bubbles: a working set-based interface for code understanding and maintenance. In *Proceedings of the SIGCHI Conference on Human Factors in Computing Systems*, pages 2503–2512. ACM, 2010.

[6] S. A. Brewster. Using nonspeech sounds to provide navigation cues. *ACM Transactions on Computer-Human Interaction (TOCHI)*, 5(3):224–259, 1998.

[7] J. M. Francioni and A. C. Smith. Computer science accessibility for students with visual disabilities. In *ACM SIGCSE Bulletin*, volume 34, pages 91–95. ACM, 2002.

[8] A. Z. Henley and S. D. Fleming. The patchworks code editor: toward faster navigation with less code arranging and fewer navigation mistakes. In *Proceedings of the 32nd annual ACM conference on Human factors in computing systems*, pages 2511–2520. ACM, 2014.

[9] M. Konecki, A. Lovrenčić, and R. Kudelić. Making programming accessible to the blinds. In *MIPRO, 2011 Proceedings of the 34th International Convention*, pages 820–824. IEEE, 2011.

[10] J. Lamping, R. Rao, and P. Pirolli. A focus+ context technique based on hyperbolic geometry for visualizing large hierarchies. In *Proceedings of the SIGCHI conference on Human factors in computing systems*, pages 401–408. ACM Press/Addison-Wesley Publishing Co., 1995.

[11] S. Mealin and E. Murphy-Hill. An exploratory study of blind software developers. In *Visual Languages and Human-Centric Computing (VL/HCC), 2012 IEEE Symposium on*, pages 71–74. IEEE, 2012.

[12] National Science Foundation, National Center for Science and Engineering Statistics. 2017. *Women, Minorities, and Persons with Disabilities in Science and Engineering: 2017*. Special Report NSF 17-310. Arlington, VA. Available at www.nsf.gov/statistics/wmpd/.

[13] D. K. Palladino and B. N. Walker. Learning rates for auditory menus enhanced with spearcons versus earcons. Georgia Institute of Technology, 2007.

[14] C. Parnin and A. Orso. Are automated debugging techniques actually helping programmers? In *Proceedings of the 2011 international symposium on software testing and analysis*, pages 199–209. ACM, 2011.

[15] J. Saldaña. *The coding manual for qualitative researchers*. Sage, 2015.

[16] J. Sánchez and F. Aguayo. Blind learners programming through audio. In *CHI'05 extended abstracts on Human factors in computing systems*, pages 1769–1772. ACM, 2005.

[17] J. Sánchez and F. Aguayo. Apl: audio programming language for blind learners. *Computers Helping People with Special Needs*, pages 1334–1341, 2006.

[18] R. M. Siegfried. Visual programming and the blind: the challenge and the opportunity. *ACM SIGCSE Bulletin*, 38(1):275–278, 2006.

[19] A. C. Smith, J. S. Cook, J. M. Francioni, A. Hossain, M. Anwar, and M. F. Rahman. Nonvisual tool for navigating hierarchical structures. In *ACM SIGACCESS Accessibility and Computing*, number 77-78, pages 133–139. ACM, 2004.

[20] A. C. Smith, J. M. Francioni, and S. D. Matzek. A java programming tool for students with visual disabilities. In *Proceedings of the fourth international ACM conference on Assistive technologies*, pages 142–148. ACM, 2000.

[21] A. Stefik, R. Alexander, R. Patterson, and J. Brown. Wad: A feasibility study using the wicked audio debugger. In *Program Comprehension, 2007. ICPC'07. 15th IEEE International Conference on*, pages 69–80. IEEE, 2007.

[22] A. Stefik, C. Hundhausen, and R. Patterson. An empirical investigation into the design of auditory cues to enhance computer program comprehension. *International Journal of Human-Computer Studies*, 69(12):820–838, 2011.

[23] A. M. Stefik, C. Hundhausen, and D. Smith. On the design of an educational infrastructure for the blind and visually impaired in computer science. In *Proceedings of the 42nd ACM technical symposium on Computer science education*, pages 571–576. ACM, 2011.

[24] S. F. A. Szpiro, S. Hashash, Y. Zhao, and S. Azenkot. How people with low vision access computing devices: Understanding challenges and opportunities. In *Proceedings of the 18th International ACM SIGACCESS Conference on Computers and Accessibility*, pages 171–180. ACM, 2016.

[25] P. Vickers and J. L. Alty. When bugs sing. *Interacting with Computers*, 14(6):793–819, 2002.

[26] B. N. Walker, A. Nance, and J. Lindsay. Spearcons: Speech-based earcons improve navigation performance in auditory menus. Georgia Institute of Technology, 2006

9. ONLINE APPENDIX

Supplemental materials have been uploaded to the ACM Digital Library to accompany this paper, including two comma-separated value (CSV) files: (1) a table of additional quotations from participants and (2) a table listing the operating system, assistive technologies, programming languages, and programming editor uses by each participant (complementing the summarized information found in Table 2 in this paper). In addition, these materials are also available online at our laboratory website at the following URL: http://latlab.ist.rit.edu/assets2017code

The Effects of "Not Knowing What You Don't Know" on Web Accessibility for Blind Web Users

Jeffrey P. Bigham
HCI Institute
Carnegie Mellon University
jbigham@cs.cmu.edu

Irene Lin
HCI Institute
Carnegie Mellon University
iwl@andrew.cmu.edu

Saiph Savage
HCI Lab
West Virginia University
saiph.savage@mail.wvu.edu

ABSTRACT

Web accessibility and usability have been extensively studied for blind web users. The focus has generally been on making it technically possible for blind users to access content, or on helping to make the web more usable. This paper explores a challenge at the intersection of these two lenses, which is the effects of blind web users not knowing what they don't know. On the web, this often means that the user is having a problem completing a task, but does not know whether the problem is because the information is there and not accessible, whether the information is simply difficult to access, or whether the information is not present at all. We first discuss how this issue has manifested itself in other work in this space. We then present the results of a study with 30 sighted web users and 30 blind web users exploring the phenomenon, demonstrating that not knowing the source of a problem causes frustration and wastes time. We conclude with recommendations for future research to help understand and address this problem, as well as design implications for future technology that may assist non-visual web navigation.

CCS Concepts

•Human-centered computing → *Accessibility theory, concepts and paradigms; Empirical studies in accessibility;*

Keywords

accessibility; web; usability; blind; screen reader

1. INTRODUCTION

Accessing the web is a vital part of modern life, and remains more difficult for blind web users [18]. The focus on this problem has been on making the web more accessible, with guidelines [15, 24], assessment tools and processes [29, 26, 19], and automatic and crowd-powered fixing [27, 8]. These efforts have had mixed success [17]. Yet, we know that many of the barriers that blind web users experience are not due to accessibility problems, *per se*, but rather usability problems that have the effect of making content much more difficult to access (effectively inaccessible) [22].

ASSETS '17, October 29-November 1, 2017, Baltimore, MD, USA

ISBN 978-1-4503-4926-0/17/10...$15.00

DOI: https://doi.org/10.1145/3132525.3132533

One such problem that blind web users encounter while using the web is that it is often unclear to them what information is available, and what is available but inaccessible [24]. An example is a phone number on a restaurant's web site that is in an image without an alternative text description. The information is on the web site, but as a blind user without access to the image, you wouldn't be able to know for sure (let alone get the phone number). Information that you would expect to find on a web page is often not there[1]. Some restaurants really don't have their phone number on their web page.

Knowing whether the information you want is on the page is important because it determines the best action for you to take: if the information is not there, you should look for it elsewhere; whereas, if the information is there but inaccessible, it might make sense to employ more costly strategies for accessing it [9], request a fix [27, 8], or find a sighted person to help [4, 7]. Given the pervasiveness of technically inaccessible content, many blind web users develop such strategies for accessing this content.

We call the generalization of this problem "not knowing what you don't know" (NKWYDK). We have hypothesized that blind web users have greater difficulty in recognizing when expected information is not present, in part because sometimes that information is present but inaccessible. A consequence could be that while a sighted user can quickly move on once encountering inaccessible information, a blind user takes longer or becomes more frustrated.

In this paper, we explore NKWYDK with 60 participants, 30 sighted and 30 blind, in a controlled study. We created tasks that were designed to be easy, hard, technically inaccessible, and impossible for blind users (described in more detail later). We note that sighted users are faster and more successful across easy and hard tasks, as would be expected from prior work [6]. We also find that sighted users are (not surprisingly) more successful in solving the inaccessible tasks. Some blind participants were particularly resourceful in solving them as well, confirming that "inaccessible" does not always mean impossible. Underscoring the point about NKWYDK, we find that blind participants spent similar amounts of time on inaccessible and impossible tasks, and often incorrectly assigned blame in both cases, i.e., thought inaccessible tasks were impossible, and impossible tasks were inaccessible.

2. RELATED WORK

The traditional way to think about accessibility for the web has been in terms of compliance with accessibility standards. The most popular standard is the World Wide Web Consortium (W3C)'s Web Content Accessibility Guidelines (WCAG). The first version, WCAG 1.0, was defined in 1999 [15], and was updated to WCAG 2.0 in 2008 [13]. While there are substantial differences between the

[1] XKCD humorously illustrated this in the case of university web pages: https://xkcd.com/773/

two [24], both are comprised of a number of guidelines and checkpoints within those guidelines that is each assigned a priority level. WCAG has formed the basis for much of the web accessibility legislation that has been passed in various countries, and, thus, achieving compliance is a significant part of what tools test for and what accessibility professionals help to do [12].

Standards such as WCAG fail to adequately capture many impactful usability problems [22, 24]. This is problematic because severe usability problems have similar effects as inaccessible content on a blind web user: the task intended to be completed cannot be successfully completed. Blind people use various strategies to overcome accessibility and usability problems on web pages [9]. Strategies for making the web more efficient to navigate include using CTRL+F to find relevant content, and browsing through a list of links on a page instead of its full content. Strategies for overcoming accessibility problems include using the screen reader's built-in virtual cursor to explore visual elements on the web page, or even using an image's filename to guess at its contents.

Effectively employing these strategies is difficult because *(i)* they do not always work, and *(ii)* using them effectively generally requires some technical knowledge about how web pages are built and how the screen reader interprets them. If NKWYDK causes greater uncertainty about what is on a web page, it may make it more difficult to employ such strategies effectively. Viewed through the theoretical lens of information foraging [23, 14], blind web users likely miss out on useful information because of NKWYDK as compared to sighted users.

Power *et al.* studied the problems that blind web users encountered on the web that were not captured by standards like WCAG [24]. Major categories of problems not covered by WCAG included: *(i)* content found in pages where not expected by users, *(ii)* content not found in pages where expected by users, *(iii)* pages too slow to load, *(iv)* no alternative to document format (*e.g.*, PDF), *(v)* information architecture too complex (*e.g.*, too many steps to find pages), and *(vi)* broken links. At least *(i)* and *(ii)* could be interpreted through the lens of NKWYDK, and these two categories collectively accounted for 13.5% of all problems that users encountered in their study. In particular, the *content not found in pages where expected by users* category was described as follows:

> *"...describes problems where users confidently followed a link to a page, but a piece of information that they expected to find there was missing. For example, on a museum website, users followed a link to an object in the museum collection, but did not find any information about the room in which that object is displayed, which they expected."*

Given that this is already a known problem, we might expect the problem to be even worse if it turned out blind users could not reliably tell if they had encountered it or not. Blind web users seem to behave in ways that one might expect if they were unsure as to whether desired information was on a page they visited. For instance, a behavior noticed in the WebinSitu study was what the authors called "probing," which was when participants visited a web page and then quickly left [6]. Blind participants exhibited this behavior much more than sighted participants did, potentially because they were using the behavior to resolve uncertainty about what the web page contained. Given that redundant information exists on the web, a useful strategy may be to visit web pages, quickly determine if they satisfy your information need, and move along to the next web page if they do not. It may make sense to employ even imperfect heuristics if the cost of trying to find non-existent information is high enough (as seems likely).

NKWYDK also has implications for technology designed to fix accessibility problems based on user requests. For instance, the crowdsourced Social Accessibility project could fix web accessibility problems for blind web users, but the crowd would only be asked to fix problems when requested by users. They note that many of their users had difficulty knowing when and what to ask due to uncertainy about whether problems encountered were because of accessibility or not [28]:

> *"One of the most important findings of the service was the high ratio of users who are not aware of the nature of the problems they are facing. Skilled and experienced users are aware of their problems, and they can easily report them. However, we were surprised by how many users were unaware of the real causes of their difficulties."*

Similar observations were made by Petrie *et al.* in noting that remote participants don't always know why they are experiencing problems while running remote users studies with blind participants [21]. We might reasonably expect that blind users therefore under-report accessibility problems to the owners of web sites, even when companies have methods for reporting problems [4, 10].

The phenomenon of NKWYDK is not restricted to blind web users. NKWYDK naturally comes up in the context of accessibility, especially for those with perceptual disabilities. For instance, one of the use cases described in Scribe4Me was for deaf people to use the system to retroactively understand what hearing people were reacting to [20]. In effect, it was a tool for helping deaf people query into the past for what they didn't know. However, they would only know to make such a query when something in their environment signaled that they should ask. One of the primary challenges that the visual question answering service VizWiz ran across was blind users not knowing whether they had captured the necessary information to answer their question in the photos that they took [11]. NKWYDK also causes problems for people without disabilities, often when making decisions for which some information is unknown (because of time or other costs in retrieving it) [25].

3. METHODOLOGY

To explore the effects of not knowing what you don't know on web usability, we designed a study, which was conducted remotely. Prior research has shown that remote studies can be effective for people with disabilities [21]. Some problems will go under-reported, and so our study was designed to explicitly consider this problem – we wanted users to deal with the uncertainty about the problems they faced independently. Remote studies may be more ecologically valid for blind web users because each participant uses their own screen reader and settings [6].

The study asked participants to complete 8 information finding tasks. It included 4 difficulty conditions (Easy, Hard, Inaccessible, and Impossible). Participants completed 2 tasks in each condition across a total of 8 trials. Task difficulty was counterbalanced and presented in a random order. Each participant completed only one task on each of 8 different web pages to avoid learning effects, with the assignment of condition to web page also randomized. Participants were informed of what the study entailed and signed a consent form prior to participating in the study.

3.1 Web Pages and Tasks

Eight web pages were selected for the study (Figure 1). These web pages were chosen so that participants were unlikely to have visited them before (and thus were unlikely to have been familiar

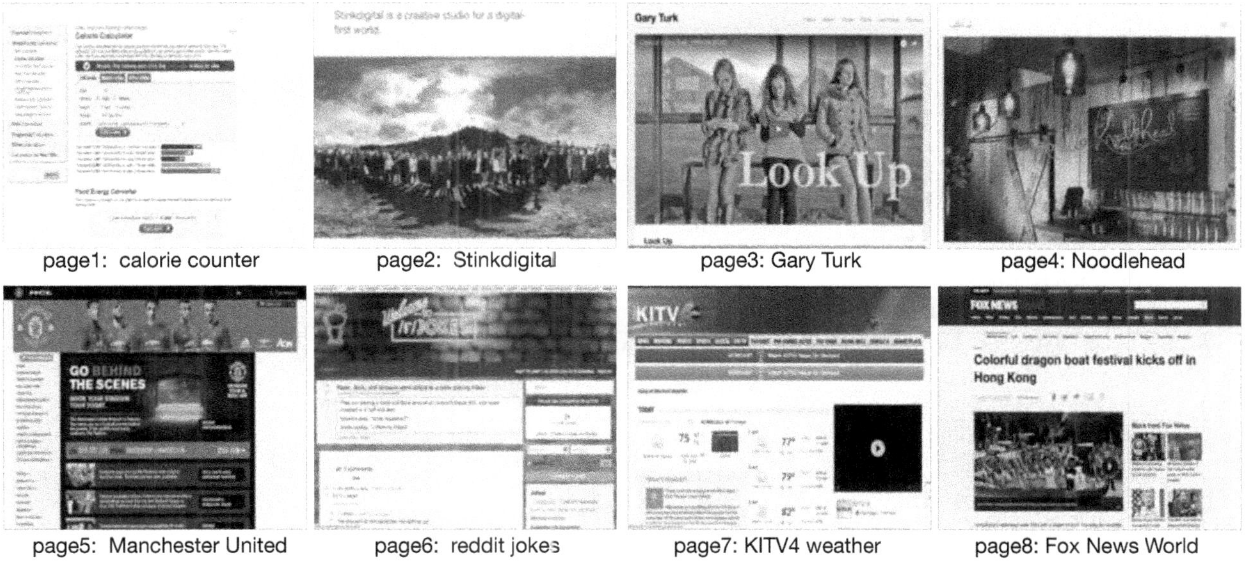

Figure 1: The tasks that participants were asked to complete were created using saved versions of the eight web pages above. All were real web pages, chosen so that participants were unlikely to have experience using them. They were slightly modified as necessary to create tasks of the four types (Easy, Hard, Inaccessible, and Imposible). The full task pages are included with this paper as supplementary material and are described in detail in Table 1.

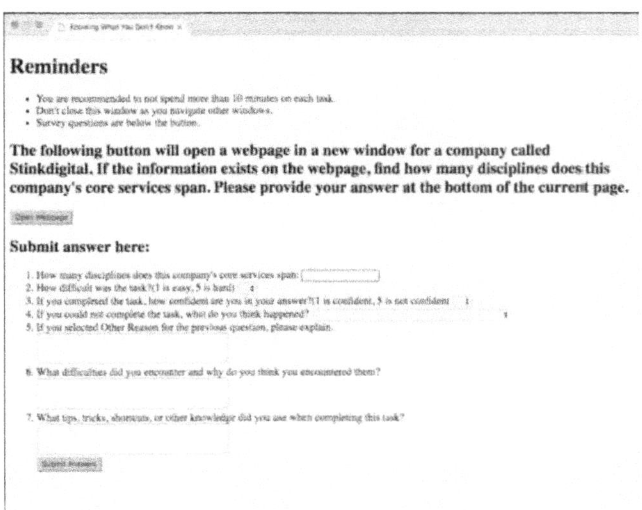

Figure 2: An example task page from our study, which asks participants to answer a question on the given page, times how long they take to answer, and asks them questions about the task.

with their structure)[2]. The web pages chosen varied in accessibility according to WCAG 2.0, with the most common problems relating to lack of alternative text for each image, lack of proper use of headings, and lack of form labels. For each page, we created four tasks with each of the following difficulties, sometimes modifying the page slightly, but often using the page as it was:

- **Easy:** information can be found without major obstacles; nearly all participants should be successful.
- **Hard:** not easily searchable, hidden, or requires an aggregate view (or skim) of the page; many participants should be successful, but it may require longer.
- **Inaccessible:** requires access to content that is inaccessible to screen reader users according to WCAG; some blind participants may still get these correct, but not many.
- **Impossible:** the requested information doesn't exist on the page; no one should get this correct.

[2]The task pages have been included as supplementary material.

In order to reduce bias when users approached a task, instructions were designed to avoid blind participants from assuming "the information will be there." This might have caused participants to spend more time than they might otherwise. The following points were made on the instructions page in addition to other clarifying instructions:

- Some tasks are difficult or impossible. Please spend no more than ten minutes trying to find the answer.
- It is acceptable to answer "I don't know" if you do not have an answer.

Participants were aware that they would receive no penalty for not being able to find an answer, although all participants typed something into the answer box, whether it was a guess or simply "I don't know," and submitted it. The directions also gave a recommended time allotted for each question of no more than 10 minutes. After this time, an alert would pop up asking the participant to move on to the next task. This was to encourage the participant to move on if they got stuck on a particular task, especially given that some tasks were not possible to complete. Participants were able to terminate their session whenever they chose and were encouraged to take breaks between tasks, as needed. They were, however, asked to complete each individual task without interruption.

3.2 Data Collection

We collected three types of data from participants in our study while they completed the 8 tasks. The first was the answer to the questions that we asked, the second was automatic timing data, and the third was a set of questions designed to elicit what participants thought of each task they completed (Figure 2). Task completion time was measured as the time between when the participant initially opened the webpage to begin searching for an answer (when

Task	Description	Explanation
Easy - information can be found without major obstacles		
page1-ez	How many calories are needed to lose 1 pound per week?	Located at the top of the page.
page2-ez	How many disciplines does this company's core services span?	Can be located with CTRL+F.
page3-ez	Name the person who filmed and edited the video?	Located at the top of the page.
page4-ez	How many days a year is this restaurant open?	Located at the top of the page.
page5-ez	This web page provides a link to what social media?	Located at the top of the page.
page6-ez	How many comments are there?	Mentioned twice.
page7-ez	What is the UV index?	Can be located with CTRL+F.
page8-ez	When was this article published?	Logically located after the article title.
Hard - not easily searchable, hidden, or requires an aggregate view (or skim) of the page		
page1-hrd	How many kilojoules per ounce are there in ethanol?	Located in unmarked table.
page2-hrd	Name one award Stinkdigital earned?	HTML (DOM) is not in a logical order.
page3-hrd	What is the length of the video?	Requires pressing play and knowledge of where information would be located.
page4-hrd	What is the price of beef soup?	No heading tags, only CSS styling.
page5-hrd	Name one prize this business boasts on its webpage?	No obvious label.
page6-hrd	What does the sub-comment say?	No obvious distinction between comment and subcomment.
page7-hrd	What is the low in Honolulu for today?	Styling error causes most screenreaders to overlook.
page8-hrd	What is the image caption for the first image?	No <img> tag; the caption is not obvious and blends into the main article.
Inaccessible - technically inaccessible with a screen reader user because of something that is inaccessible on the page		
page1-in	How many calories are needed to lose 1 pound?	Uses inaccessible HTML <canvas>.
page2-in	Name a client of Stinkdigital?	Client logos are displayed as background images.
page3-in	Name the person who did sound engineering for the video?	Requires mouse click because of mousedown event.
page4-in	Name one $8 noodle dish that is indicated as spicy?	Spiciness is indicated by color styling only.
page5-in	What is the email address to contact regarding stadium tours?	Information is contained in an unlabeled image.
page6-in	How many upvotes does the original post have?	Uses aria-hidden tag.
page7-in	When is the sunrise in Honolulu for today?	Requires mouse click because of mousedown event.
page8-in	Find what the image caption about the duck in the river says?	Located in the last slide of carousel of images.
Impossible - information doesn't exist on the page		
page1-imp	How many calories are needed to lose 1 pound?	Does not exist.
page2-imp	Name a client of Stinkdigital?	Does not exist.
page3-imp	Who did sound engineering for the video?	Does not exist.
page4-imp	Name one $8 noodle dish that is indicated as spicy?	Does not exist.
page5-imp	What is the contact email address for stadium tours?	Does not exist.
page6-imp	How many upvotes does the original post have?	Does not exist.
page7-imp	When is the sunrise in Honolulu for today?	Does not exist.
page8-imp	What does the image caption about the flag say?	Does not exist.

Table 1: The 32 tasks of varying difficulty across 8 web pages along with brief descriptions explaining how each met the requirements of its condition. Tasks and problems were based on those found naturally on the selected pages, although in some cases pages were altered to make content accessible or inaccessible as appropriate for the given difficulty.

the user clicked the "Open Webpage" button in Figure 2) to when the participant began inputting a response in any of the required form fields. Data was stored per user in a text file using PHP. Participants were also asked to complete a pre-survey and a post-survey asking about their experience using the web and their experience completing the study, respectively.

4. STUDY WITH SIGHTED PARTICIPANTS

To validate our apparatus and provide a comparison point to our later study with blind participants, we first ran our study with 30 sighted participants recruited from Amazon Mechanical Turk (Table 2). Participants were required to have completed at least 1000 HITs and have a 95% approval rate on the platform. Workers were paid $5.00 for their participation, which for sighted participants averaged less than 15 minutes, resulting in an average hourly wage of more than $20.00/hour.

One goal of running the study first with sighted participants was to validate our study apparatus. We expected that sighted participants would answer most questions correctly across the first three conditions (Easy, Hard, and Inaccessible) but would not be able to answer the Impossible question. The results from sighted participants agreed with these expectations (Figure 3). Overall, sighted participants answered 88.6% of the Easy, Hard, and Inaccessible questions correctly, and failed to answer any of the the Impossible questions correctly (suggesting the answers could not be easily guessed, and were not accidentally on the page). Sighted participants also took longer to complete the Impossible tasks. It required sighted participants an average of 110.57 seconds (SD = 66.55 s) to

Years of Web Experience	# of Participants
5 years or less	0
Between 6 - 10 years	5
Between 11-15 years	5
Between 16-20 years	17
21+ years	3

Table 2: Sighted User Web Experience Levels

complete Impossible tasks, compared to 84.2 seconds (SD = 105.04 s) to complete Inaccessible tasks, presumably because they spent time trying to find the answer before giving up at some point.

When sighted participants were asked in the pre survey about when they felt confused on the web, most sighted participants said that they do not often get confused. One sighted participant responded, *"Not particularly [confused often]. I believe by enough searching that you can find the answer to anything and everything."* When sighted users could not find information, they tended to try modifying their search terms or believed they were looking in wrong place. One sighted participant wrote, *"If the information is not in the place I would expect it to be I get a bit confused. Or if the information is in a format I do not understand."* It was rare for sighted participants to believe that it was the website's fault too. Most sighted participants indicated a solution similar to this user's approach: *"I try harder to find it."*

5. STUDY WITH BLIND PARTICIPANTS

For this study, we recruited 30 blind participants by advertising our study on Twitter. Participants were paid $35.00 for their participation, which required approximately one hour of work. We regularly pay more for blind participants who have proficient skill in using a screen reader, just as we would pay more for other rare individuals with specialized skills.

In the presurvey,many blind participants mentioned that they had trouble identifying the root of problems which they experienced on the web, for instance, *"Yes I do feel this way because sometimes I am not sure if certain links are hidden or if certain content on the page is difficult to find."* Some commented on specific aspects of a website layout, such as an overabundance of links, misuse of ARIA labels or information not presented in an accurately logical and orderly manner. One participant's response ties these comments about the layout together: *"I have found a growing trend toward information being buried in graphics or only available when clicking, tapping or otherwise moving some other part of the interface. The model of a static web 'page' with everything it has to say being said in a straightforward fashion seems to be changing into a far more dynamic and, often, less usable experience for me."* A few users said that since they consider themselves accessibility experts, they don't get confused because they believe the presence of information is binary: *"it's either there or not."* An overwhelming majority indicated that when choosing a website to navigate, content matters more than accessibility. As one user said, *"If a website has better content and is accessible enough, then I will put up with minor accessibility issues to get access to that superior content."*

5.1 Task Completion Times and Accuracy

Overall, it required blind participants 107.1 seconds (SD = 65.07s) on average to complete Easy tasks, 189.9 seconds (SD = 140.32s) to complete Hard tasks, 172.5 seconds (SD = 105.62s) to complete Inaccessible tasks, and 223.7 seconds (SD = 146.35s) to complete Impossible tasks. We conducted a two-way ANOVA to study the effects that the type of task *i.e.*, Easy, Hard, Inaccessible, or Impossible, and being either a sighted or blind individual, had on the time it took people to complete the task (*i.e.*, the type of task and being blind/sighted were the independent variables). There was no significant difference between the amount of time that a blind/sighted participant took to do the task given the task category (F=1.05, p<.38). In other words, the time differences observed between sighted/blind people on a particular task category appear to be explained by being sighted/blind, rather than by the task category itself.

Years of Screen Reader Experience	# of Participants
<= 5 years	9
6 - 10 years	6
11-15 years	4
16-20 years	8
21+ years	2

Screen Reader Used	# of Participants
JAWS	14
NVDA	12
VoiceOver	5

(Note: Some participants use more than one screen reader)

Table 3: Experience and screen reader preferences of blind participants. In this study, we define "blind web users" as those who primarily use a screen reader to browse the web.

In order to study in greater detail how the task difficulty affected the task completion time for blind participants, we conducted an ANOVA test. This test considered for blind people the effect of time to complete the task given the difficulty, *i.e.*, Easy, Hard, Inaccessible, or Impossible. The Bonferonni correction accounted for repeated tests [1]. A significant difference emerged between the amount of time that a blind participant took to complete the task given the difficulty (F=9.87, p<0.0001). Most of the pair-wise task completion times were also significantly different at the $p < 0.01$ level: Easy vs. Hard, Hard vs. Impossible, Inaccessible vs. Hard, and Inaccessible vs. Impossible.

Nearly all blind participants (95.1%) were able to successfully complete the Easy tasks, whereas only 37.7% of blind participants successfully completed the Hard tasks, and 24.6% of blind participants completed the Inaccessible tasks. The distributions of the Easy and Hard conditions differed significantly (Wilcoxon signed-ranks, $Z = -5.0162, p < 0.01$). The distributions of the Hard and Inaccessible conditions were not detectably significant (Wilcoxon signed-ranks, $Z = -1.3207, p = .18$).

Some users were able to use various strategies to correctly complete 4 of the 8 Inaccessible tasks even though it was technically inaccessible according to the guidelines. 5 answered *page3-in* by managing to click the button to display the dynamic content, and then finding the desired information; 1 answered *page4-in* by using built-in screen reader functions to determine the color of the font; 1 answered *page5-in* by using an OCR plug-in; and 8 answered *page7-in* by using the built-in screen reader search function to find hidden content that happened to list the correct answer, although for a day other than the one asked about. We explore these clever solutions in greater detail in Section 5.2.

Given that some of the technically inaccessible tasks were nevertheless answered correctly by some users, primary analysis was repeated using only the tasks that were not solved by any users (tasks 1,2,6, and 8). The average time for correct answers was 130.20 seconds (SD = 103.76), while the average time for incorrect answers was 188.38 seconds (SD = 102.12). Thus, the inaccessible tasks that users could not solve were closer to the average time required to solve those tasks that were impossible.

Participants generally found the desired information when completing the Easy and Hard tasks. Blind users took an average of

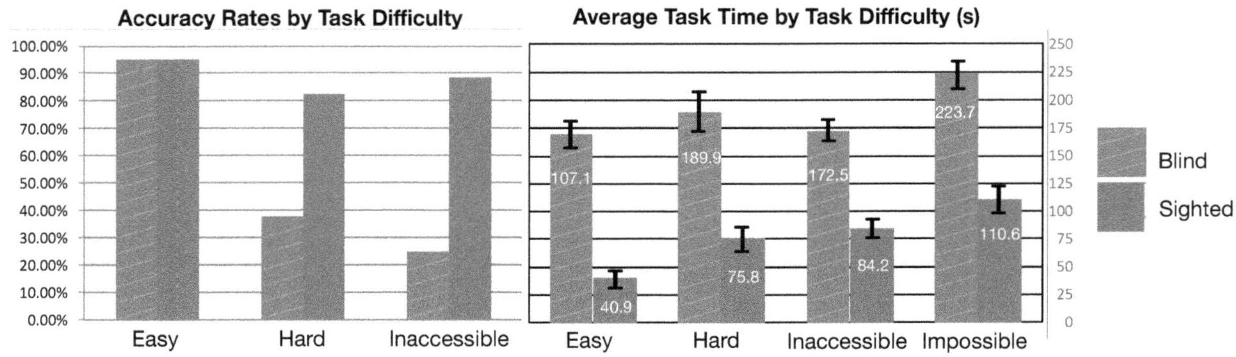

Figure 3: Accuracy and time for blind and sighted participants across the four difficulty conditions. Sighted participants were fairly accurate in all possible conditions, whereas blind participants did well in the Easy tasks, but much worse while adapting the Hard (37.7%) and Inaccessible (24.6%) conditions. Blind participants answered some fraction of the Inaccessible tasks correctly for four of the eight tasks, which we explain in the text. Overall, blind participants required approximately twice as long to complete tasks in each condition in comparison with other participants. Tasks in the Hard condition took slightly longer than tasks in the Inaccessible condition.

107.14 seconds (SD = 65.07s) to complete Easy tasks and average 189.91 seconds (SD = 140.32s) to complete Hard tasks. Blind users had more difficulty isolating the cause of problems in the Inaccessible and Impossible conditions (average of 172.45 seconds (SD = 105.62 s) to complete Inaccessible tasks, compared to 223.7 seconds (SD = 146.35s) to complete Impossible tasks.)

After completing each task, participants were asked to answer the following question: *"If you could not complete the task, what do you think happened?"* Five options were provided: 1) "Not Applicable"; 2) "The information was hidden or not easily searchable"; 3) "I cannot access the information with my screen reader"; 4) "The information does not exist on the page"; and 5) "Other Reason." This question was asked in order to gauge the participant's perceived difficulty level of the task. The first four options respectively represent Easy, Hard, Inaccessible, and Impossible. "Other Reason" provides an alternative to the other options if the participant felt that their response did not fall into any of the first four categories. Sighted participants were able to figure out the cause of problems they were experiencing, but blind participants had much more trouble, often confusing the Hard, Inaccessible, and Impossible categories. Results are summarized in Figure 4.

5.2 Who Receives the Blame

After each task, blind users were asked to explain what they believed was the cause of any experienced difficulties in navigating the web. Researchers used open coding to analyze every blind participant's survey response. Themes emerged from the iterative coding and refinement of the responses.

5.2.1 Bad HTML Design

This category is about blaming the design of the website for the problems experienced. Blind participants thought that faulty HTML was to blame for the problems they experienced 31% of the time. In this instance, the user did not consider that the problem they were experiencing was because they were blind, but rather it was a problem experienced by all users of that site (including sighted individuals.) For example, one participant was not able to find a price on a website, and blamed the page layout:

"There were too many things to click on, and I must admit I didn't have the patience to check every single thing the prices could have been hidden under."

Another participant was unable to find an email on a website and thought it was because most people design websites to not include an email address:

"...I just didn't find an Email address. The contact link didn't reveal it either. I rarely do find E-mail addresses, so I thought they weren't often provided..."

5.2.2 Web Accessibility Problems

25% of the time, blind users believed that the obstacles they experienced came from websites that had accessibility issues. In this case, users thought that the designers of the page had not made certain elements available to them, considering only that sighted users might be able to access the information. For instance, this user mentions how he believes the information he is looking for is in an inaccessible image: *"I think the required information was written in a not labelled graphic."*

A few blind users were able to access the unaccesible information from website through several different hacks, and then stated that it was actually an easy task to do. For instance, the following person was asked to find how spicy was a certain dish, but spiciness of a dish was embedded in a chili icon that has no alternative text. The person hacked a solution that studied the page's html to figure out what was the level of spiciness.

> *"Spicy dishes are indicated using an alternative font size/colour. To figure this out, I had to locate the "Indicates Spicy" text, and check how the formatting of it differed from the surrounding text on the page. I then had to check the formatting for every $8 dish to determine which ones were spicy."*

5.2.3 Self Blame

This category is about blind users blaming themselves for not being able to access or obtain certain information. 13% of the time, people did not blame the website's design or the accessibility of the site, but rather their own abilities. *"I'm sure this information is there but I couldn't find it."* 31% of the time, blind users did not blame anyone or anything else for issues they experienced.

5.3 Power Users

In the individual task feedback, we received a number of interesting responses from users, who offered clues about how they either did solve some of the tasks in the study, or how they would generally approach these problems. Some responses and behaviors indicated a level of technical expertise necessary to effectively overcome challenges in what seem like routine challenges. Given that these users were among those who seemed to adapt to the prob-

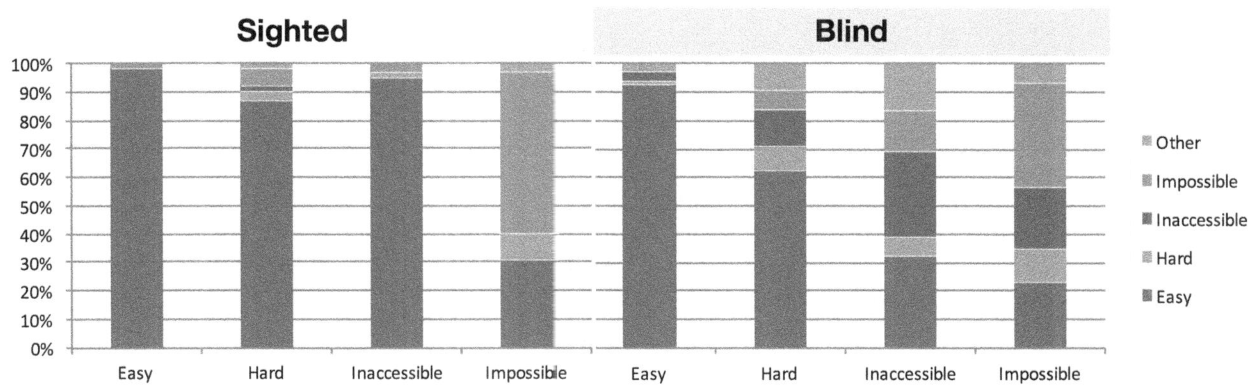

Figure 4: Distribution of blind and sighted participant ratings by difficulty. Sighted participants did not experience a change in task difficulty, and therefore tended to label all of the Easy, Hard, and Inaccessible tasks as being easy. In contrast, as the tasks got more difficult, blind participants indicated they had more difficulty, and frequently confused Hard, Inaccessible, and Impossible tasks.

lems in our tasks most easily, they may provide clues into how to make such tasks easier in the future.

Power users revealed themselves on tasks of each difficulty. On Easy tasks, they described their process of finding the requested information. For example:

> *"If you use the screenreaders ability to bring up links, move to sign up, and below that is the twitter information."*
> *– Task5 (EASY)*

Despite employing various clever strategies, power users sometimes had difficulty with the Hard tasks, such as in this example:

> *"I first looked through the tabbed items (links, buttons, form controls etc) that the site offered and came across mostly buttons. Links seemed to only exist for the contact information. Second, I searched for the word "award" using my screenreader's find facility. It mentioned several times "most awarded" and then a single word on its own line: "Awards". I thought I had hit my jackpot until I saw the list below and saw text quoted from magazines and the like. As a last resort, I even tried looking through the HTML source and could see only a jumble of div, span and path tags with the text seemingly buried way beneath this complete haystack."*
> *– Task2 (Hard)*

The following two example give hints as to how the power users among our participants were able to complete "inaccessible" tasks:

> *"Read the menu. I was interested in all they might have. At the bottom, I found "indicates spicy" I read character at a time to see if there was a symbol my screen reader did not announce. There wasn't, so I checked the font and found spicy was in red. Read the $8 noodles again checking the font of each line. Found the first red one."*
> *– Task4 (Inaccessible)*

> *"I used my favorite method, which was the JAWS find command. I then checked how many times rise was found on the page. Then I checked to see if the placement and time I found for sun rise on the page made sense."*
> *– Task7 (Inaccessible)*

Power users also seemed to choose when to give up based on how much they cared about receiving the information:

> *"Screen reader find function (search for 'clients'). Screen reader mouse cursor function (to try and activate the unlabelled buttons). It's worth noting that, if some of the untagged images on the web page contain client names, I could possibly have obtained them using OCR. I did not do this in this case, because in every day life I wouldn't be aware beforehand that I was looking for client information, so I would simply assume that the information was not there."*
> *– Task2 (Impossible)*

Another power user revealed insight about a realistic mindset when searching for information. They revealed strategies they could have employed, but probably would not use in practice:

> *"I was going to open the page source to find out what <img> or class was used to indicate 'spicy.' I would do this if information was critical to me but on a page like this I would typically live with the mystery."*
> *– Task4 (Impossible)*

6. DISCUSSION

We have explored the effects of NKWYDK on blind web users performing information finding tasks. Overall, our results demonstrated that this does indeed cause confusion, although participants illustrated that the effects of task difficulty are not necessarily straightforward. It was somewhat difficult, for instance, to tease apart the effects of NKWYDK from routine web accessibility and usability problems. Some blind participants also exhibited sophisticated strategies for finding out the information they did not know, and seemed to use heuristics developed through experience to give them insight into what was available on the page (or not). Overall, we believe our study confirmed the impact that subtle usability problems like NKWYDK can have on the experienced accessibility of the web and highlights the richness of this area for future inquiry.

6.1 Sighted vs. Blind Web Browsing

Our study validated differences in sighted and blind web browsing, which were noted at least 10 years ago [6]. For instance, blind people still seem to require about twice as long as sighted people do to accomplish the same task. Interestingly, this same ratio held even when blind people were looking for information that was not contained on the task page, suggesting that the potential added confusion did not slow them down additionally. This inefficiency penalty paid by blind web users certainly has effects on what they are able to accomplish and how effectively they are able to compete. Power users among our blind participants seemed to be especially aware of how the accessibility of web pages could impact their experienced usability of them, reflecting prior results on the relationship between accessibility and usability [22]. These participants occasionally indicated that they did not expect to find the information they were looking for given features of the page and so chose not to try especially hard.

6.2 Difficult, Inaccessible, or Impossible

Participants had nearly as much trouble completing the tasks that we designed to be Hard as they did completing the Inaccessible tasks. This result fits with prior arguments about poor usability being an under-appreciated cause of inaccessibility in some cases [5, 22, 24]. The fact that only about a third of blind participants were able to find information that more than 80% of sighted participants were able to find highlights this continuing problem. Especially novice users may confuse not only inaccessible and impossible tasks, but also difficult, inaccessible, and impossible tasks. This broadened our idea of what kinds of problems fit into the NKWYDK framework to include Hard tasks.

6.3 Confusing Inaccessible with Impossible

Inaccessible information was confused with impossible information in those cases in which the blind participants were unable to get past the accessibility problem. In the individual task feedback, some blind participants reported inaccessible tasks as being impossible, and impossible tasks as being inaccessible. Impossible tasks required nearly an additional minute of time for blind participants to complete. This observed difference suggests that blind web users may be wasting significant time looking for information that is not even there. One of the biggest practical challenges for equalizing access between blind and sighted people is figuring out how to lower the time penalty blind users pay. Future work may consider interfaces that could inform blind web users of the likelihood of finding a particular piece of information given the patterns of what data is usually shared in other websites and also the accessibility that was detected on the page.

6.4 Limitations

Like most studies, ours had limitations. The blind population that we recruited was likely more technically savvy than the average blind computer user, and certainly more technically savvy than the average blind person (using a screen reader is not easy, and so those who master it can generally be considered technically adept). They used a variety of different screen readers, had varying levels of experience with those screen readers, and various levels of experience with the Web. Some were able to solve the tasks that were technically inaccessible, although we were able to separate out these tasks in our analysis. Given that participants likely had no intrinsic motivation to answer the questions, they might have given up more easily than they would have if they truly needed the information they were looking for. Despite these limitations, which mostly leaned toward users we would expect to be best prepared to handle confusing situations, we still observed effects of usability causing substantial inefficiency for our blind participants and NKWYDK appearing to cause substantial confusion.

7. FUTURE WORK

In this paper, we have shown that not knowing what you don't know about information availability and accessibility can affect how successful blind users are in browsing the web. Our findings suggest a number of opportunities for future work in better understanding the effect of NKWYDK on web users and in creating tools to help mitigate its effects.

The first is in expanding our findings in web accessibility. Our study was with blind web users on a specific set of designed web pages; it would be interesting to validate these results in a larger-scale study *in-the-wild*. It is likely that other users may also experience problems from not knowing what they don't know. For instance, deaf web users miss out on auditory information, and web users who do not use the mouse miss out on content that is only accessible that way. In some cases, not being able to access this content may cause similar confusion about what is available and how to best access it. We suspect that the kind of information missing and how it affects different user groups is not the same as how it affects blind web users.

We believe our results may generalize to other challenges faced by people with disabilities off of the web. While we highlighted some examples in our related work section, there are likely others. For instance, blind travelers likely face similar problems when navigating unknown physical spaces (especially indoors where navigation assistance is much more limited), or realizing when their environment changes [2]. There may be an opportunity to develop a uniting theory of NKWYDK that would connect these challenges, and potentially even predict when they are likely to occur.

Finally, we believe there are opportunities to develop tools to help users overcome the problems that we have described here, and that this represents a rich area for future research. We noticed that our more technically savvy blind participants used their knowledge of HTML and CSS in order to access inaccessible information. One idea is to make it easier for less technically savvy users to employ some of the same tactics. Tools might also somehow expose accessibility information to web users so that they can make better decisions about how much time to invest looking for information given global information about a particular site, that either may not contain that information or where the information they are looking for is actually inaccessible. Prior approaches for automatic assessment [30], machine learning prediction of accessibility [3], and end user approaches for fixing inaccessible content [8] may be relevant.

8. CONCLUSION

In this paper, we have explored the concept of not knowing what you don't know, and how it affects blind web users as they complete tasks on the web. A specific and actionable finding from this paper for future research is that confusion between not knowing if information exists on a web page or is simply inaccessible leads to confusion and wasted time, especially for blind web users. Information finding is still less efficient for blind users than it is for sighted users. Power users have developed strategies requiring significant skill to overcome some of these effects, but these strategies are not easily available to less technical users. Our results demonstrate opportunities for future research in further understanding this phenomenon and creating tools to help address it.

9. ACKNOWLEDGEMENTS

This work was developed under grants from the National Institute on Disability, Independent Living, and Rehabilitation Research (NIDILRR grant numbers 90DP0061 and H133E140039), as well as research grants from the J. Wayne and Kathy Richards Faculty Fellowship in Engineering. We thank Sina Bahram for comments on our study design, and thank the participants in our studies for their time and feedback.

10. REFERENCES

[1] Hervé Abdi. 2007. The Bonferonni and Šidák corrections for multiple comparisons. *Encyclopedia of measurement and statistics* 3 (2007), 103–107.

[2] Nikola Banovic, Rachel L. Franz, Khai N. Truong, Jennifer Mankoff, and Anind K. Dey. 2013. Uncovering Information Needs for Independent Spatial Learning for Users Who Are Visually Impaired. In *Proceedings of the 15th International ACM SIGACCESS Conference on Computers and Accessibility (ASSETS '13)*. Article 24, 8 pages.

[3] Jeffrey P. Bigham 2007. Increasing web accessibility by automatically judging alternative text quality. In *Proceedings of the 12th international conference on Intelligent user interfaces IUI '07*. 349–352.

[4] Jeffrey P. Bigham, Jeremy T. Brudvik, and Bernie Zhang. 2010. Accessibility by Demonstration: Enabling End Users to Guide Developers to Web Accessibility Solutions. In *Proceedings of the 12th International ACM SIGACCESS Conference on Computers and Accessibility (ASSETS '10)*. 35–42.

[5] Jeffrey P. Bigham and Anna C. Cavender. 2009. Evaluating Existing Audio CAPTCHAs and an Interface Optimized for Non-visual Use. In *Proceedings of the SIGCHI Conference on Human Factors in Computing Systems (CHI '09)*. 1829–1838.

[6] Jeffrey P. Bigham, Anna C. Cavender, Jeremy T. Brudvik, Jacob O. Wobbrock, and Richard E. Ladner. 2007. WebinSitu: A Comparative Analysis of Blind and Sighted Browsing Behavior. In *Proceedings of the 9th International ACM SIGACCESS Conference on Computers and Accessibility (Assets '07)*. 51–58.

[7] Jeffrey P. Bigham, Chandrika Jayant, Hanjie Ji, Greg Little, Andrew Miller, Robert C. Miller, Robin Miller, Aubrey Tatarowicz, Brandyn White, Samual White, and Tom Yeh. 2010. VizWiz: Nearly Real-time Answers to Visual Questions. In *Proceedings of the 23Nd Annual ACM Symposium on User Interface Software and Technology (UIST '10)*. 333–342.

[8] Jeffrey P. Bigham and Richard E. Ladner. 2007. Accessmonkey: A Collaborative Scripting Framework for Web Users and Developers. In *Proceedings of the 2007 International Cross-disciplinary Conference on Web Accessibility (W4A) (W4A '07)*. 25–34.

[9] Yevgen Borodin, Jeffrey P. Bigham, Glenn Dausch, and I. V. Ramakrishnan. 2010. More Than Meets the Eye: A Survey of Screen-reader Browsing Strategies. In *Proceedings of the 2010 International Cross Disciplinary Conference on Web Accessibility (W4A) (W4A '10)*. 10 pages.

[10] Erin Brady and Jeffrey P. Bigham. 2014. How Companies Engage Customers Around Accessibility on Social Media. In *Proceedings of the 16th International ACM SIGACCESS Conference on Computers & Accessibility (ASSETS '14)*. 51–58.

[11] Erin Brady, Meredith Ringel Morris, Yu Zhong, Samuel White, and Jeffrey P. Bigham. 2013. Visual Challenges in the Everyday Lives of Blind People. In *Proceedings of the SIGCHI Conference on Human Factors in Computing Systems (CHI '13)*. 2117–2126.

[12] Giorgio Brajnik, Yeliz Yesilada, and Simon Harper. 2010. Testability and Validity of WCAG 2.0: The Expertise Effect. In *Proceedings of the 12th International ACM SIGACCESS Conference on Computers and Accessibility (ASSETS '10)*. 43–50.

[13] Ben Caldwell, Michael Cooper, L Guarino Reid, and Gregg Vanderheiden. 2008. Web content accessibility guidelines (WCAG) 2.0. *WWW Consortium (W3C)* (2008).

[14] Ed H Chi, Peter Pirolli, Kim Chen, and James Pitkow. 2001. Using information scent to model user information needs and actions and the Web. In *Proceedings of the SIGCHI conference on Human factors in computing systems*. 490–497.

[15] W Vanderheiden Chisholm and G Jacobs. 1999. I.(editors)(1999) Web Content Accessibility Guidelines (WCAG). *W3C* (1999).

[16] Juliet M Corbin and Anselm Strauss. 1990. Grounded theory research: Procedures, canons, and evaluative criteria. *Qualitative sociology* 13, 1 (1990), 3–21.

[17] Vicki L. Hanson and John T. Richards. 2013. Progress on Website Accessibility? *ACM Trans. Web* 7, 1, Article 2 (March 2013), 30 pages.

[18] Jonathan Lazar, Aaron Allen, Jason Kleinman, and Chris Malarkey. 2007. What Frustrates Screen Reader Users on the Web: A Study of 100 Blind Users. *International Journal of Human-Computer Interaction* 22, 3 (2007), 247–269.

[19] Jennifer Mankoff, Holly Fait, and Tu Tran. 2005. Is your web page accessible?: a comparative study of methods for assessing web page accessibility for the blind. In *Proceedings of the SIGCHI conference on Human factors in computing systems*. 41–50.

[20] Tara Matthews, Scott Carter, Carol Pai, Janette Fong, and Jennifer Mankoff. 2006. *Scribe4Me: Evaluating a Mobile Sound Transcription Tool for the Deaf.* Springer Berlin Heidelberg, Berlin, Heidelberg, 159–176.

[21] Helen Petrie, Fraser Hamilton, Neil King, and Pete Pavan. 2006. Remote Usability Evaluations With Disabled People. In *Proceedings of the SIGCHI Conference on Human Factors in Computing Systems (CHI '06)*. 1133–1141.

[22] Helen Petrie and Omar Kheir. 2007. The Relationship Between Accessibility and Usability of Websites. In *Proceedings of the SIGCHI Conference on Human Factors in Computing Systems (CHI '07)*. 397–406.

[23] Peter Pirolli and Stuart Card. 1999. Information foraging. *Psychological review* 106, 4 (1999), 643.

[24] Christopher Power, André Freire, Helen Petrie, and David Swallow. 2012. Guidelines Are Only Half of the Story: Accessibility Problems Encountered by Blind Users on the Web. In *Proceedings of the SIGCHI Conference on Human Factors in Computing Systems (CHI '12)*. 433–442.

[25] Ulrike Schultze and Charles Stabell. 2004. Knowing What You Don't Know? Discourses and Contradictions in Knowledge Management Research. *Journal of Management Studies* 41, 4 (2004), 549–573.

[26] Hironobu Takagi, Chieko Asakawa, Kentarou Fukuda, and Junji Maeda. 2004. Accessibility designer: visualizing usability for the blind. In *ACM SIGACCESS Accessibility and Computing*. 177–184.

[27] Hironobu Takagi, Shinya Kawanaka, Masatomo Kobayashi, Takashi Itoh, and Chieko Asakawa. 2008. Social Accessibility: Achieving Accessibility Through Collaborative Metadata Authoring. In *Proceedings of the 10th International ACM SIGACCESS Conference on Computers and Accessibility (Assets '08)*.

[28] Hironobu Takagi, Shinya Kawanaka, Masatomo Kobayashi, Daisuke Sato, and Chieko Asakawa. 2009. Collaborative Web Accessibility Improvement: Challenges and Possibilities. In *Proceedings of the 11th International ACM SIGACCESS Conference on Computers and Accessibility (Assets '09)*.

[29] Jim Thatcher, Cynthia Waddell, and Michael Burks. 2002. *Constructing accessible web sites*. Vol. 34. Glasshaus Birmingham.

[30] Markel Vigo and Giorgio Brajnik. 2011. *Automatic web accessibility metrics: Where we are and where we can go.* Interacting with Computers, Vol. 23:2: 137–155. Oxford University Press Oxford, UK.

Speed-Dial: A Surrogate Mouse for Non-Visual Web Browsing

Syed Masum Billah[1] Vikas Ashok[1] Donald E. Porter[2] IV Ramakrishnan[1]
[1]Department of Computer Science, Stony Brook University, NY, USA
{sbillah, vganjiguntea, ram}@cs.stonybrook.edu
[2]Department of Computer Science, University of North Carolina at Chapel Hill, NC, USA
porter@cs.unc.edu

ABSTRACT

Sighted people can browse the Web almost exclusively using a mouse. This is because web browsing mostly entails pointing and clicking on some element in the web page, and these two operations can be done almost instantaneously with a computer mouse. Unfortunately, people with vision impairments cannot use a mouse as it only provides visual feedback through a cursor. Instead, they are forced to go through a slow and tedious process of building a mental map of the web page, relying primarily on a screen reader's keyboard shortcuts and its serial audio readout of the textual content of the page, including metadata. This can often cause content and cognitive overload.

This paper describes our Speed-Dial system which uses an off-the-shelf physical Dial as a surrogate for the mouse for non-visual web browsing. Speed-Dial interfaces the physical Dial with the semantic model of a web page, and provides an intuitive and rapid access to the entities and their content in the model, thereby bringing blind people's browsing experience closer to how sighted people perceive and interact with the Web. A user study with blind participants suggests that with Speed-Dial they can quickly move around the web page to select content of interest, akin to pointing and clicking with a mouse.

CCS Concepts

- **Human-centered computing ~ Haptic devices**
- **Human-centered computing ~ Accessibility technologies.**

Keywords

Semantic web browsing; tactile interaction; Microsoft Surface Dial; visual impairment; screen reader; tactile exploration.

1. INTRODUCTION

For web browsing, people with vision impairments employ screen readers (e.g., JAWS, VoiceOver, NVDA, and many more listed in [2]), which reads aloud the textual content of the Web in serial order, generally ignoring layout and graphics.

Blind users predominantly rely on keyboard shortcuts to accelerate content navigation. Without shortcuts, blind users cannot skip past or skim content; skimming is essential functionality, as websites often have complex visual layouts, inline advertising, and aggregate content from multiple sources. Forcing a listener to hear all content would significantly and disproportionately harm users with vision impairments. Thus, modern screen readers feature numerous shortcuts to accelerate web navigation.

Even with these shortcuts, however, screen readers have significant usability problems for web browsing [11, 27]. First, blind users have to train on these shortcuts and learn a number of browsing strategies before they can efficiently browse the Web [11]. Second, because one cannot judge the importance of content before listening to it, blind users must listen to reams of irrelevant content before they find what they need. Third, screen readers alone are of little help in understanding the semantics of a page's contents, as screen readers are not aware of the fact that web content is organized into several logical blocks or semantic entities. For example, consider a list of products with their prices, features, and short descriptions in a tabulated HTML list. Most screen readers do not capture the relationships between these elements, and therefore treat these list elements as separate items. Consequently, the user cannot easily know that elements are related to each other, or when she has navigated past the end of the list. In short, there is no overview, and the user must assemble the semantic structure in her mind as the content is being read. The end result of this is that the current state of web browsing places significant and needless cognitive load on people with vision impairments.

These problems are particularly acute for common tasks in content-rich web sites with several semantic entities. For example, sighted users can purchase something online or make a reservation in just a few minutes with a few mouse clicks, whereas screen-reader users often need 10 minutes or more to complete the same tasks [34].

The reason for this difference is that sighted users can perceive the semantic structure of a page at a glance, via visual cues such as white space, fonts, and colors. For example, a sighted user can easily differentiate search results from advertisements on a side panel. Further, with the mouse, the user can quickly place the cursor on any element of interest in the page, select it, and operate on it. In contrast, blind users must explore the screen by brute force, read aloud by a screen reader, in order to construct their own semantic model of the page. The visual feedback of a mouse is not useful for blind users.

To address the aforementioned problems in non-visual web browsing, speech and haptic interfaces have been explored as alternatives to keyboards (e.g. [7, 39]). Although these interfaces can alleviate the extensive use of keyboard shortcuts to a certain extent, they still fall short of adequately addressing the cognitive and content overload problem in non-visual web browsing (details in sections 2 and 5).

This paper describes our research contribution towards reducing the gap in the web-browsing experience between sighted people and those with vision impairments. Specifically, this paper presents the Speed-Dial Non-Visual Browsing System for desktop platforms—a novel interaction paradigm that provides an intuitive and quick

ACM 978-1-4503-4926-0/17/10…$15.00
https://doi.org/10.1145/3132525.3132531

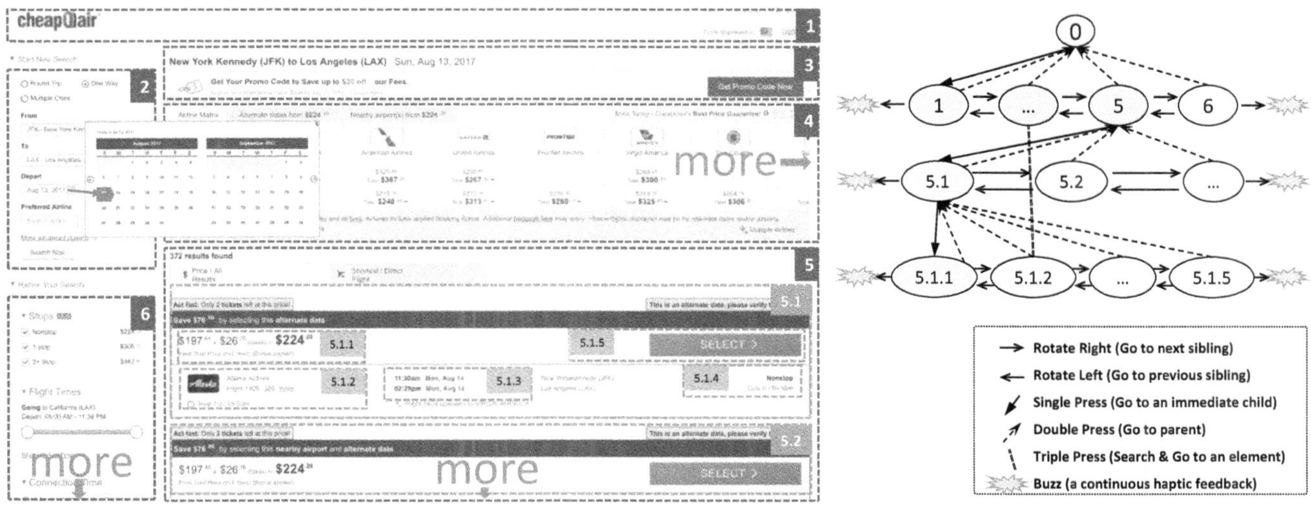

Figure 1: An illustration of Speed-Dial. On the left is a flight-reservation web site, which is divided into six logical blocks or semantic entities. Entity 5 is further divided into (sub)-entities. On the right is the corresponding semantic tree, and a list of valid gestures offered by the Dial to navigate on the tree.

access to the various entities and their content on the web page. Speed-Dial automatically generates a model, based on [7], explicitly capturing the semantics of the page that sighted users implicitly construct visually. This semantic model is interfaced with the interaction mechanics of an off-the-shelf physical Dial for web navigation.

The Speed-Dial prototype uses the recently announced Microsoft Surface Dial[1]; in principle, Speed-Dial should work with other Dial devices as well. The Surface Dial is a small, cylindrical puck, 1 ½" tall and 2 ½" in diameter. The Dial accepts three very simple gestures as input—press it like a button and rotate it left and right. The Dial can provide haptic feedback through vibration as output. Pressing and holding the Dial can activate a radial menu, which the user can navigate by rotating the Dial left or right. The Dial's behavior can be customized per-application.

The semantic model on which Speed-Dial operates is tree-structured, to provide blind users with an understanding of the hierarchical relationship of the elements in the page. Individual elements, such as buttons or text, are represented as nodes, whereas aggregate objects with clear visual boundaries, such as frames or lists, are represented as sub-trees. The semantic model used in Speed-Dial is created using techniques published in the extensive research literature on understanding the semantics of web pages (detailed in Section 2). The challenge is presenting the semantic model in a format amenable to quick access by a user.

Figure 1 illustrates how Speed-Dial can be used to navigate the search results page corresponding to a flight search, and the corresponding semantic tree. The page has six semantic entities, numbered 1 through 6, reflected by the six nodes at the 1st level in the tree. Each node at this level can be expanded further to reveal its (sub)-entities. The tree is traversed breadth-first. The press gesture at a node navigates down the subtree rooted at that node. The rotate right/left gestures traverse the nodes in a level bi-directionally. A special haptic feedback, denoted by the "buzz" indicates no more nodes remain to be traversed. When a node is visited, the screen reader reads out all the information associated with the entity, such as the price in node 5.1.1.

This illustration shows the distinctive features of Speed-Dial. Unlike shortcuts, there are a few, simple gestures. Gestural motions such as rotations and presses are almost instantaneous. The top-level semantic entities give a quick, high-level overview of the page, helping the user find an entity of interest quickly (i.e., with few gestures). The haptic feedback helps orient to the user within the page, such as indicating they have reached the end of a list. Speed-Dial can work with any screen reader, and provides uniform experience across different screen readers—an attribute that is highly desired by blind screen reader users [10]. Lastly, Speed-Dial exemplifies the well-known "information visualization mantra", namely, *overview, zoom, details on demand* [38] but in the context of non-visual web browsing.

A user study with 12 blind participants indicates that Speed-Dial is a promising approach to solve the content and cognitive overload problem with non-visual web browsing—the participants took 77% less time with Speed-Dial compared to that with a screen reader, and 49% less time compared to that with a screen reader augmented with speech interface to complete their tasks. In summary, Speed-Dial enables users to rapidly access any web content, thereby serving as a surrogate for the mouse.

2. RELATED WORK

Augmenting screen readers with different kinds of interaction modalities for web browsing continues to attract serious research attention, with audio-haptic and speech being the most popular.

Audio-haptic Interfaces for Web Browsing

In addition to the standard Braille displays [1], several research works [23, 24, 31, 39, 42, 43] have demonstrated the usability and applicability of audio-haptic interfaces for web browsing. These interfaces not only provide vibrations and audio cues, but also communicate the presence of HTML elements and various shapes on a page by using force-feedback [24, 28, 43], and tactile pin representations [33, 36, 39]. Prior work proposed guidelines for

[1] https://www.microsoft.com/en-us/surface/accessories/surface-dial

designing appropriate haptic sensations (e.g. tactons) for people with vision impairments [23].

Although audio-haptic devices are very helpful in obtaining an overview of a webpage, the unrestrained freedom of movement within the page is a hindrance for precise navigation and information finding; users may navigate past visual delimiters, such as white space. The user may have a sense of direction from the overview, but may still spend a lot of time searching for specific content of interest, such as the fare of a flight.

Extant audio-tactile interfaces incorporate a very limited notion of content semantics; in particular, they only represent the boundaries of various web entities on the page. The Dial-based system described in this paper utilizes the semantic meaning of the entities to organize navigation.

Closely related to haptic interfaces are tactons that provide vibrotactile feedback through the cutaneous senses to convey non-visual information [9, 13, 26, 32, 37, 40]. Sensory pulses of different durations that encode different kinds of taps such as single, double, etc. and amplitude of sensory stimulation that encode different values are some examples of tactons [12]. Speed-Dial system incorporates the idea of tactons for navigating the semantic model.

Speech Interfaces for Web Browsing

Natural-language interfaces for web browsing have been explored since inception of the Web, and have the potential to alleviate the extensive use of keyboard shortcuts by using spoken commands. House et al. [20] proposed a modified version of the NCSA Mosaic system [5] that was capable of translating user utterances to simple browsing actions. However, their system supported only a few basic actions on browser controls such as opening URLs or new windows. Dragon NaturallySpeaking [30] supports a slightly larger set of user commands to control websites by speech—besides browser controls, it has commands to operate on a few syntactic elements like links, buttons, forms, and form fields—all of which are readily identifiable by their HTML tags [21]. However, Dragon [30] relies on visual cues and a graphical user interface, thereby reducing accessibility. JSay [19] improves the accessibility of Dragon by interoperating with the popular JAWS screen reader. But JSay is also limited to a handful of basic functions, such as accessing application controls, scrolling, and refresh. A far richer set of more flexible commands is supported by Capti-Speak [6] that, like JSay, integrates a speech-interface with a screen-reader. All of the previously-mentioned, speech-driven interfaces, including Capti-Speak, operate only at the syntactical level, and do not incorporate the semantics of page content.

We also mention that generic voice-based Assistants such as Siri, Cortana, and Echo are being used to manage one's daily activities, but their focus is not web browsing.

Perhaps the closest related research to Speed-Dial is the spoken-dialog Assistant system proposed by Ashok et al. [7]. With their Assistant, users can not only navigate the page using spoken dialog, but also query the page content for certain information, such as the price of a product or duration of a flight. Further, the Assistant supports interaction at a semantic level, i.e., the users can communicate directly with the web entities present in the page without having to understand HTML markup. However, the Assistant, like all other speech interfaces, is heavily reliant on the availability and accuracy of automatic speech recognition (ASR).

Speech interfaces have several open challenges to widespread use for non-visual browsing. ASRs require high-fidelity microphones to accurately capture speech and eliminate spurious background noise; the built-in microphones in most desktops or laptops often corrupt the speech and cause substantial recognition errors. Moreover, the latency of ASR-based browsers is significant. Speech cannot be used in all scenarios, such as in public places where privacy and security may be compromised [3]. Speech alone is also unsuitable and tiring for ad-hoc navigation. For instance, skimming through a list of several products on a shopping website requires speaking "go to next product" repeatedly. We believe that rotating a dial is faster and less cumbersome for users. Under the best of circumstances, speech only addresses the element selection problem, not the content navigation problem.

Web Page Semantics

A principal component driving the Dial interface is the semantic model or semantic representation of the web page content. Semantic understanding of web pages is a classic research topic dating back to the inception of the Web (e.g., [16-18]). The use of web page semantics in accessibility is a long-standing research topic (e.g., [22, 35]). The starting point for semantic understanding of web pages is a web ontology. Broadly speaking, an ontology explicitly encodes a shared and common understanding of a particular domain, in this case the Web. The encoding captures commonly-used concepts in the domain, namely descriptions of web entities in the Web domain such as forms, text-boxes, menus, buttons, and widgets; attributes associate these concepts and relationships among them. With a web ontology in hand, one can create a semantic model of a web page. Web entity data extraction for constructing this semantic model is based on well-established web segmentation techniques [4, 8, 15, 44, 45]. Broadly speaking, these techniques partition a web page into semantically-related units, based on the observation that related items in a Web page often exhibit consistency in presentation style and spatial locality. We note that Apple's VoiceOver screen-reader also employs a basic notion of semantics using Web spots—landmarks that separate different segments on the webpage, some of which may be semantic entities. However, the caveat is that the user must manually associate segments with semantic entities.

A semantic model, in essence, is a tree that is similar in structure to the HTML DOM of the web page. Conceptually, the semantic layer is an abstract layer over the DOM tree. The semantic model in this paper is similar to the one developed by Ashok et al. [7], in that a collection of hand-coded web entity descriptions in the web ontology provides the necessary blueprints for identifying and representing various web entities, their characteristics, and their relationships as a hierarchy in the semantic model.

3. SPEED-DIAL INTERFACE DESIGN

We now explain the various components of Speed-Dial in detail.

Figure 2 depicts the workflow and the architectural schematic of the Speed-Dial system. A user can interact with a webpage using either the standard screen reader shortcuts or the Dial gestures. A special gesture (press & hold) brings up a radial menu (Figure 3) listing out several choices, such as navigate by heading or web-entity overview; each option determines the meaning of the other dial gestures, such as *rotating* or *tapping*.

We note that the radial-menu choices, as well as the interpretation of the gestures, also depend on the semantics of the page content. For example, if the screen-reader focus is presently on a text-box, the Dial radial menu contains characters (Figure 4); if the focus is on a date form field, the radial menu contains options to change the day, month, and year (Figure 7); if the focus is on a flight-result item (Figure 8), a single tap with subsequent *rotate* gestures will

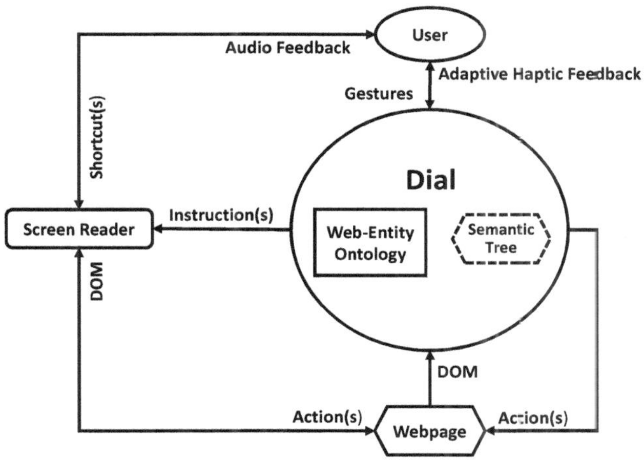

Figure 2. Architectural schematic and workflow of Speed-Dial system.

enable the user to quickly navigate through the important details, such as price or duration.

To obtain the semantic structure and composition of the webpage from the DOM, the Dial leverages a custom-defined Web-Entity Ontology [7] that provides the necessary blueprints or "class definitions" to identify and represent various web entities, such as forms, filters, menu, search-results, and calendars, as well as their characteristics and relationships. The Dial models this abstracted information as a Semantic Tree – a "cleaned-up" semantics-based non-visual presentation of the HTML DOM. The Semantic Tree then forms the basis for gestural navigation as illustrated in Figure 1. Additionally, a blueprint in the Web-Entity Ontology may also specify custom radial menu choices and gesture interpretations, which will be applied to the Dial interface whenever the corresponding entity is in focus.

Note that it is also possible to navigate the raw HTML DOM with Dial. But this reduces to navigating the HTML DOM element-by-element at the syntactic level, and hence inherits all the "content and cognitive" overload problems associated with navigating using keyboard shortcuts.

Finally, depending on the radial-menu option selected and gesture performed by the user, the Dial either performs the intended action (e.g., fill a form text field) directly on the webpage content, or instructs the screen reader to perform certain actions (e.g., navigate to the next heading). For users' convenience, the Dial also provides audio-haptic feedback, such as a tick with a small vibration when navigating to the next element.

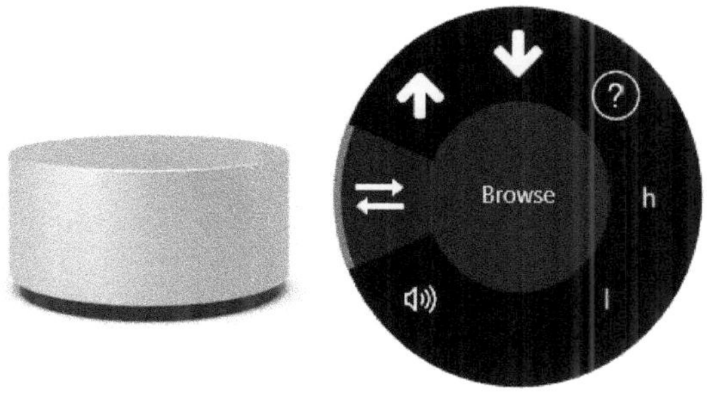

Figure 3: Surface Dial (left) and custom Dial menu (right)

It is instructive to mention that it is certainly possible to navigate the semantic model with keyboard alone without using the Dial device, although this will require either new shortcuts that do not overlap with standard shortcuts or overriding existing shortcuts. Consequently, the new shortcuts will likely be non-uniform across screen-readers. In contrast, Speed-Dial interface is uniform across all screen-readers, and requires users to remember less to efficiently navigate webpages.

3.1 The Speed-Dial

This subsection describes the important components of the Speed-Dial interface.

3.1.1 Hardware and Gestures

We did not build our own hardware; instead we used an *off-the-shelf* input device—the Surface Dial (see Figure 3) from Microsoft. It is a wireless rotational peripheral device (dimensions: 59 mm x 30 mm, weight: 145 g) with adaptive haptic feedback and 3,600 points of precision. The Surface Dial is designed to be placed on the screen of the Microsoft Surface tablet, but the Surface Dial also works off-screen with any PC, laptop or tablet running the Windows 10 Anniversary Update platform version.

Gestures. By default, the Surface Dial supports four basic types of gestures; a user can (i) rotate left, (ii) rotate right, (iii) quick press or just *press*, and (iv) press and hold. The press and hold or *long press* gesture brings up a radial Dial menu (Figure 3). Additionally, adaptive haptic feedback lets the user feel every action. Using the Surface Dial SDK, we customized the interface and the controls to suit our specific needs, including the addition of two custom gestures: double presses and triple presses (Figure 1, bottom-right).

Haptic Feedback. Speed-Dial also uses two tactons (haptic feedback) [32] to inform users about either the movements of the virtual navigational cursor, or the boundaries of the entities on the page. For navigational movements, we used a short, tick-like feedback on every rotation; and for entity-boundary notifications, we used a continuous buzz-like vibratory feedback (Figure 1).

3.1.2 Web-Entity Ontology

Web ontology has been extensively studied in the context of information extraction from web-pages. It has also been applied to improve accessibility [25]. The Web-Entity Ontology is based on our prior work on Web-Entity-Description Library described in [7], which followed well-studied methodologies and algorithms [4, 7, 29, 44, 45]. The Ontology contains hand-crafted descriptions or blueprints of various entities, such as forms, tables, filters, menu, search results, and calendars. The descriptions of web entities can be thought of as Java classes (from a programmer's perspective), whereas the entities in the Semantic Tree generated from the webpage can be thought of as corresponding instances or objects. Each description contains the following information:

(i) The characteristics and properties (i.e., data and methods) of the corresponding entity type. For example, a search-results entity contains fields to store the list of result items, a pointer to the root node (in the DOM), and a list of strings containing keywords such as "flight" or "tickets;
(ii) Algorithms to identify or extract the entities belonging to that entity type on the page; and
(iii) Custom Dial-interface specifications (more details in the next subsection).

To create the Web-Entity Ontology, we built and analyzed a training dataset of 200 popular websites from various domains including shopping, social networking, music, sports, banking, flight/hotel reservations, government, video-streaming, and news. We identified the common aspects of the entities belonging to the same type but on different websites (e.g., list of products on different shopping websites), and designed generic descriptions for these types. Overall, our Web Entity Ontology consists of over 100 descriptions. Note that new descriptions for new web-entity types can be easily added to the Ontology manually without modifying the other components of Speed-Dial, thereby making it scalable across multiple websites.

Accuracy. Depending on the type of semantic entity, our extraction accuracy varied from 75% to over 90%. For example, the accuracy was over 90% for identifying calendars, menus, sort-options, and filter-options; over 85% for forms and search-results; and 75% for individual news-articles. Almost all errors were false negatives (i.e., not able to identify the entity on the page) as opposed to false positives (i.e., identifying one entity incorrectly as some other entity). In case of false negatives, the users can still find the corresponding entities using keyboard shortcuts.

3.1.3 Custom Interface Specifications

In this subsection, we describe how we encode custom navigational behavior for different semantic entities onto the Dial interface. Because the Dial gestures, such as rotation, are strictly one dimensional, we convert any two-dimensional (2-D) information on the web page into multiple one-dimensional (1-D) lists.

Not all web entities require a custom Dial interface. For example, the Dial can directly operate (press) on buttons, radio-buttons, and check-boxes. However, some semantic elements require special adaptation, including the autocomplete text-box; date-picker or calendar; drop-down or combo-box; and generic search-results list. As shown in prior studies [29], screen-reader users have a hard time interacting with these complex UI entities due to their inconsistent behavior, appearance, and the inaccessibility of underlying JavaScript libraries. Therefore, whenever such elements are in focus, the Dial offers customized interfaces to improve their usability. Next, we present the details of custom interfaces for a few key entity types.

Basic/Leaf. We consider an entity that does not have any children or sub-entities to be a leaf entity. Examples of this type include buttons, radio-buttons, check-boxes, and links. For these entities, the Dial does not offer any custom interface; it simply brings focus to the HTML element underlying the entity. User action (or the press operation) is directly performed on the HTML element by calling the HTML element's corresponding in-built function.

Text-Box. In text-box entity, user can enter text using either the default keyboard, or an onscreen radial keyboard provided by the Dial. To bring up the radial keyboard (Figure 4), user needs to perform the press & hold gesture (*long press*). Once the radial

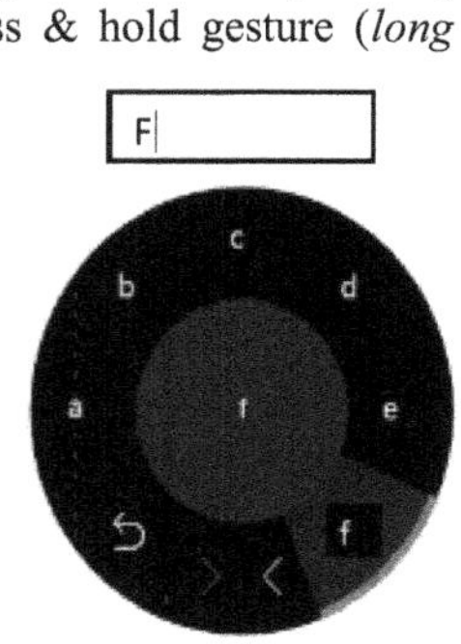

Figure 4: On-screen radial keyboard in Dial for entering text

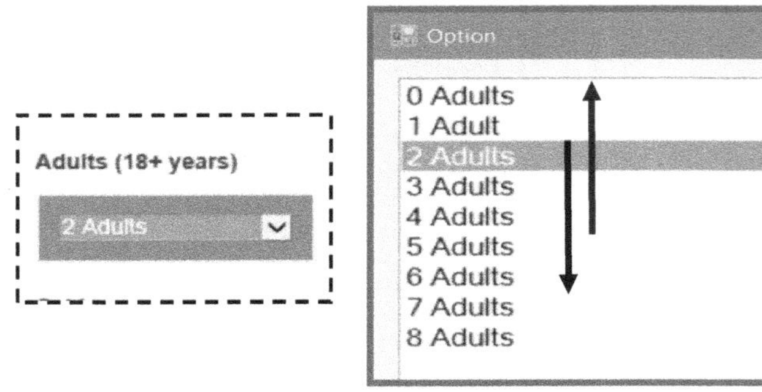

Figure 5: A sample HTML drop-down (left), and its equivalent custom drop-down widget for Dial (right).

keyboard is on, the user rotates the Dial left/right to select a character and then *press* once to add the character to the text-box. Although this radial keyboard is not suitable for lengthy textual input, it is handy for entering a few characters.

Drop-Down/Combo-Box. The custom interface for a drop-down is a popup containing a list-box that populates data dynamically from the available options in the underlying HTML element (i.e. <li> elements under a <ul> HTML markup tag). The user rotates the Dial left/right to move down/up the list. A *press* gesture finalizes the selection and dismisses the custom-interface popup (Figure 5).

Autocomplete. Similarly, the custom interface for the autocomplete text-boxes includes a popup that contains a text-box for input, and a list-box for storing dynamically-generated auto-complete suggestions (Figure 6). The user can type the first few characters using either the keyboard, or the radial keyboard (Figure 4). Then the user rotates the Dial left/right to go through the suggested list items, and performs *press* to select a list item. The selected value is entered into the HTML autocomplete text-box and the custom-interface popup is dismissed automatically.

Calendar. Calendar is one of the most difficult widgets to interact with a screen reader [29]. Different websites may have different presentations of the calendar widget (e.g., showing only days of a month, or days of two months; or having small arrows and dropdowns to change the month and year). A few websites do not even permit users to manually enter the date, thereby forcing them to use a cumbersome and often inaccessible calendar widget. Even if the date-field is editable, sometimes there is no mention of the expected date format (e.g., 01/05/2017, or 01-05-2017, or 01/05/17, or May 1), and thus the users are unable to proceed due to form-validation errors, which screen readers often times fail to report.

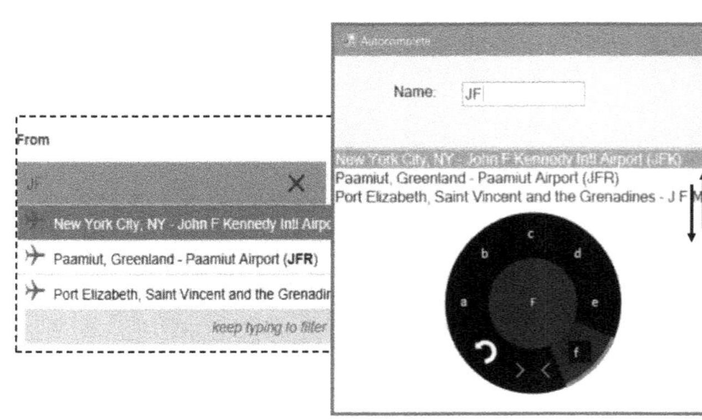

Figure 6: A sample HTML autocomplete box (left), and its equivalent custom autocomplete widget for Dial (right).

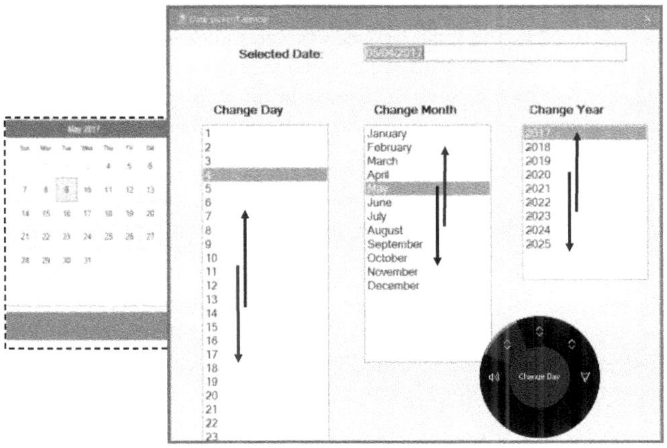

Figure 7: A sample HTML calendar (left), and the custom (generic) calendar widget for Dial (right)

To address these usability concerns, our custom calendar interface (popup) has three separate 1-D lists containing (i) days of a month, (ii) months of a year, and (iii) recent years (Figure 7). The access to these 3 lists is provided via 3 separate options on the radial menu, and the contents of each list can be easily accessed by simply rotating the dial after selecting that list with a press gesture. Once the user has settled on a date, a double press gesture populates the underlying HTML date-field with the chosen date while dismissing the custom popup.

Search Result/Data-grid. A lot of content on the web is tabular in nature. However, different websites may format tabular content differently, e.g., as lists, tables, or nested `div` elements. To represent tabular content, we use a custom data-grid view (Figure 8, in the foreground), where each column contains semantically-identical elements. For example, consider the search results in Figure 8 (in the background), and its equivalent custom interface (in the foreground). Each search-result item is represented as a row, and columns represent different properties of an item such as fare, duration, itinerary, and airline. The user can navigate either along the direction of a row or along a column using rotational gestures, with the press gesture for toggling between these two directions. Thus, the users not only can get a quick overview of the important details of any single flight, but also rapidly navigate over the properties (e.g. prices) of all the flights in the results list.

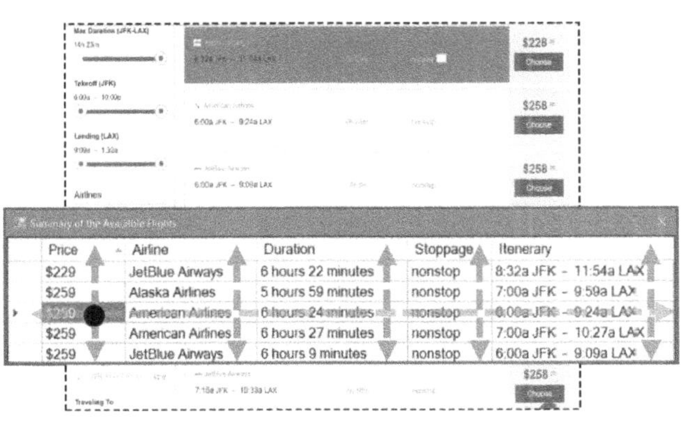

Figure 8: An HTML data-grid view (background), and its equivalent custom data-grid view for Dial (foreground). The green lines show the direction of Dial cursor.

3.2 Screen Reader Integration

We encoded a few essential screen-reader shortcuts (e.g., *h*: go to next heading, *l*: go to next link) in the default Dial radial menu (see Figure 3). Selecting such a menu option (e.g., *h*) enables users to navigate by headings using rotational gestures. This is particularly helpful for less-experienced screen-reader users with limited shortcut vocabulary. Additionally, it reduces cognitive overload by promoting uniformity, since different screen readers may have different key-bindings for the same function (e.g., `R` in JAWS vs. `D` in NVDA to go to the next landmark). In other words, given an action and a screen reader, the onus of determining the right shortcut for this purpose is shifted from the user to the Dial; the Dial examines what screen reader the user is currently using, and then simulates the appropriate, low-level keystroke. Thus, by playing the role of an intermediary between the user and a screen reader, the Dial ensures uniformity of user experience, and minimizes the disruption when a user switches from one screen reader to another—a feature highly desired by blind users [10].

3.3 System Implementation Notes

Speed-Dial was developed with the C# visual studio .NET framework version 4.6.2. It was a Windows Form application with an embedded browser (*WebBrowser* form control) object. Internally, this embedded browser shares the same rendering engine with Microsoft's Internet Explorer (IE) web browser. Therefore, from the perspective of screen readers, our application was equivalent to IE, and therefore the same screen-reader shortcuts can be used to browse the web.

In future work, we can integrate the Speed-Dial with any other browser through a custom plug-in or browser-extension. Our initial study selected IE because studies have shown that IE still remains the most popular browser among blind users [41].

For generating adaptive haptic feedback, we manipulated the value of the *RotationResolutionInDegrees* property exposed by the Dial API. For instance, setting this property value to 1.0 generates a continuous buzz-like feedback, whereas values greater than 10.0 generate a simple tick.

4. USER STUDY

To assess the effectiveness and usability of Speed-Dial, we conducted an IRB-approved user study aimed at validating the following primary and secondary hypotheses:

H: Speed-Dial significantly improves web usability compared to: (i) popular screen readers and (ii) screen readers augmented with speech interfaces. We test the following secondary hypotheses:

- **H1**: Higher efficiency in web tasks involving continuous navigation within the page.
- **H2**: Lesser effort to locate, understand and interact with desired web element.
- **H3**: Higher usability rating.
- **H4**: More intuitive interaction with webpage contents.

4.1 Participants

We conducted a user study with 12 visually-impaired participants who had no hearing or speech impairments. All participants were familiar with the IE web browser and the JAWS screen reader. They varied in age from 25 to 65 (mean=40, median=36, SD=12.5), and gender (7 males, 5 females). Regarding screen-reader expertise, 5 participants considered themselves to be "experts", whereas the remaining 7 participants were "beginners". On average, the participants browse internet for 1.5 hours per day.

4.2 Study Setup

We assigned tasks to the participants that were transactional in nature, requiring a sequence of steps spanning multiple web pages. Users with vision impairments typically find these tasks challenging. We assigned the following 3 types of tasks:

- **T1**: On a travel booking site, find the form for reserving a flight, booking a hotel, renting a car, or purchasing a vacation package. Fill-out the form with experimenter-provided data (such as *From city*, *To city*, *Departure date*, *Number of travelers*), and hit the *search* button.
- **T2:** On the search-results page of the same travel booking site, find the search-results list, and identify the top 3 search results satisfying predefined criteria (i.e., flight-related criteria were cheapest airfare, shortest travel time, or number of layovers).
- **T3:** On the search-result page, use different filters to narrow down the search-results list, and consider any special deals. This task was purely exploratory, and, as such, we did not record any objective measurements.

We choose the following 3 travel booking websites: priceline.com, expedia.com, and cheapoair.com, based on the observation that these websites differ considerably in appearance, accessibility support, richness of contents, and content placement. Additionally, all the participants indicated that they were not that familiar with these websites. For each website, a participant was supposed to perform the 3 aforementioned tasks under each of the following 3 conditions, thereby totaling 9 tasks per participant:

- **Screen-Reader Only (SR).** Participants could only use the standard keyboard shortcuts supported by JAWS. This was also considered as the baseline condition.
- **Screen-Reader with Speech Command (SR+Speech).** Participants could use the standard keyboard shortcuts of JAWS, and high-level speech commands described in [7], e.g., "select this item", "pick the next item", "go to search-result", or "choose 5th for departure date".
- **Screen-Reader with Speed-Dial (SR+Dial).** Participants could use the standard shortcuts of JAWS, as well as the gestures offered by the Speed-Dial interface.

To avoid confounds, we used the same underlying semantic model in both SR+Speech and SR+Dial conditions. To minimize the learning effect, we counterbalanced the ordering of the websites, the conditions, and the tasks T1 & T2.

Prior to the study, participants were given sufficient instructions and time (~30 minutes) to familiarize themselves with all three conditions. We chose the following 3 websites for practice runs: Craigslist (classifieds), Twitter (social), and CNN (news).

Each participant was allotted 30 minutes to complete tasks T1 & T2. If a participant completed both tasks within the allotted time window, only then he or she was requested to perform T3 for the remaining time. All conversations during the study were in English.

4.3 Data Collection and Analysis

We used the publicly-available software *globalmousekeyhook*[2] to record participants' keystrokes and time spent on each page. We also audio-recorded all sessions and transcribed them later for post-analysis. For tasks T1 and T2, we recorded the following measures: (i) completion time; (ii) number of shortcuts used under each condition; (iii) number of speech commands used; (iv) number of times each Dial gesture was used; (v) number of times a participant navigated back and forth between the boundaries of an entity; (vi) number of times the participant sought moderator's help; and (vii) reasons for failure, such as automatic speech recognition (ASR) errors, content inaccessibility, semantic error, or Speed-Dial error.

We also recorded any unusual browsing behavior that delayed the completion of assigned tasks, such as repeatedly navigating over the same content, confusion due to form-validation errors, or failure to recognize the entities.

At the end of the experiment, the participants were asked to complete the standard System Usability Scale (SUS) questionnaire [14], and a set of open-ended questions eliciting comments and suggestions for all 3 study conditions.

5. RESULTS

In this section, we analyze the collected measurements and subjective feedback, as well as compare the participants' performance and web browsing experiences under the 3 different study conditions (i.e., SR, SR+Speech, and SR+Dial). We conducted one-way ANOVA test with Tukey's honestly significant difference (HSD) post hoc test to determine if any differences in measures between these 3 conditions were statistically significant.

Completion time. We found significant effect of study conditions on completion time for both tasks T1 ($F_{2,33} = 47.6$, $p < .0001$) and T2 ($F_{2,33} = 18.4$, $p < .0001$). The mean completion times for tasks T1 and T2 under each condition are shown in Figure 9. For task T1, when using SR+Dial, the mean completion time (60.4s) was reduced by 73.0% compared to that of the baseline SR (224.2s), and 5.7% compared to the SR+Speech condition (66.2s). For task T2, these reductions were 80.2% and 62.8% respectively (SR+Dial: *mean*=76.9s, SR: *mean*=389.6s, SR+Speech: *mean*=207.0s).

Number of shortcuts. We also found a significant effect of study conditions on number of shortcuts issued in tasks T1 ($F_{2,33} = 32.5$, $p < .0001$) and T2 ($F_{2,33} = 28.4$, $p < .0001$). Figure 10 shows the mean number of shortcuts. When using SR+Dial (*mean*=2.6), participants typed 97.1% and 90.6% fewer shortcuts than when using SR (*mean*=92.4) and SR+Speech (*mean*=27.91) in task T1. In task T2, these reductions were 95.5% and 89.5% respectively (SR+Dial: *mean*=8.1, SR: *mean*=181.1, SR+Speech: *mean*=77.6).

The post-hoc pairwise comparison with Tukey HSD test indicated that the differences in means in completion time and shortcut usage for tasks T1 and T2 were statistically significant ($p < .01$) between the pairs of SR & SR+Speech and SR & SR+Dial. However, between SR+Speech & SR+Dial the differences were not significant for task T1, but significant ($p < .05$) for task T2.

A closer inspection of the collected data reveals the reason behind this significant difference for task T2. For each spoken utterance, the Speech interface in SR+Speech condition incurred an (unavoidable) overhead of about 1.0 to 1.5 seconds for converting speech to text, interpreting this text, and translating the interpretation to actions. Additionally, the Speech interface occasionally encountered speech-recognition failures, errors, and natural-language ambiguities, such as vague commands matching two or more elements with identical names and tags. The situation was further exacerbated on the search-results page for task T2 that contained many semantic entities and related content. For navigation, participants had to speak the same commands (e.g., "go

[2] https://github.com/gmamaladze/globalmousekeyhook

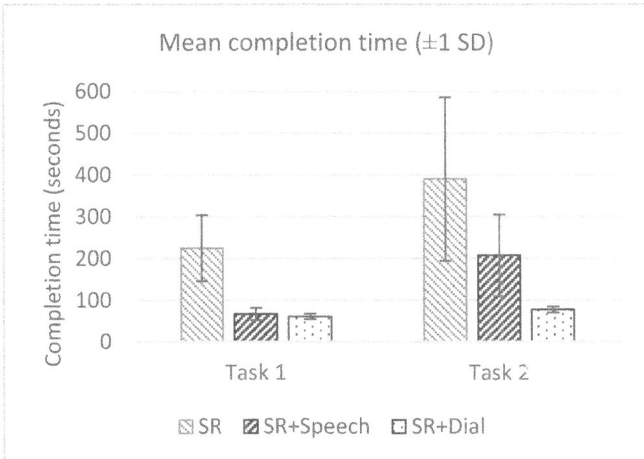

Figure 9: The mean time to complete task T1 (left) and task T2 (right) in 3 conditions. Error bars show ±1 SD.

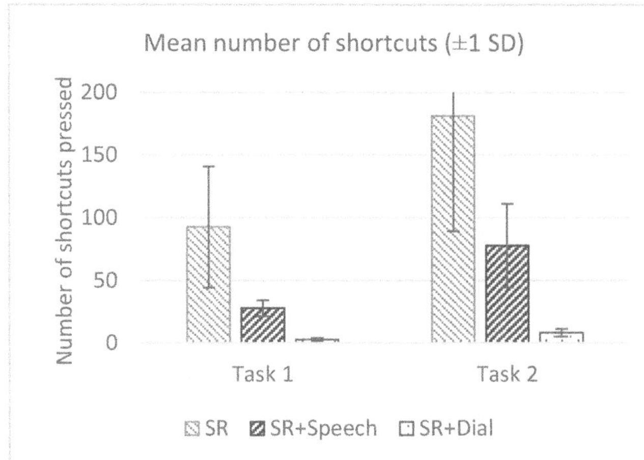

Figure 10: The mean number of shortcuts issued in task T1 (left) and task T2 in 3 conditions. Error bars show ±1 SD.

next", "how much is the price?", "what is the duration?") over-and-over again for each search-result item. The overhead accumulated to the point that participants reduced the usage of speech commands and reverted to using keyboard shortcuts.

In contrast, in SR+Dial condition, the participants did not encounter these issues because: (1) the Dial interface gave them feedback almost immediately—within 0.3 seconds on every rotation, while also providing haptic feedback whenever the focus reached the boundaries of entities. All participants liked this feature, and stated that it gave them confidence and a better understanding of their orientation in a webpage; and (2) the semantics-driven content-presentation style of Speed-Dial was straightforward to navigate, requiring only a few simple gestures. Therefore, even though the search-results webpage contained many entities, almost all participants systematically and *semantically* explored the page with Dial gestures rather than falling back to keyboard shortcuts that operated on the *syntactic* HTML content. The participants also explicitly stated that they pressed a few keyboard shortcuts in SR+Dial condition due to their habitual reflex or by accident, and not because they needed those shortcuts.

Note however that, for the form-filling task T1, there were no statistically significant differences in average measure values between SR+Speech vs SR+Dial. Because in SR+Speech condition, participants simply gave speech commands to choose the dates, thereby avoiding the painful screen-reader interaction with the calendar widget. Regardless, the above results and observations validate our hypotheses H1, H2, and H4.

5.1 Interaction Behavior and Subjective Feedback for Speed-Dial

We observed an interesting behavioral pattern with Speed-Dial—the participants kept rotating the Dial even after finding their content of interest until they reached the boundary. Then, they rotated the Dial to navigate back to the desired content, and perform the desired action. When asked, the participants explained that they were always afraid of missing important information as well as losing focus and orientation—something that they claimed as a frequent occurrence while browsing web with screen readers. For example, when they press a 'TAB' shortcut, the screen readers might sometimes inexplicably take them to a different, undesired section of the webpage. As a result, they subconsciously became cautious and less exploratory while navigating a webpage (with screen reader). But with Dial, the participants were more confident exploring the content given that they would never unknowingly navigate past the boundaries of entities—Speed-Dial always confines the navigation within these boundaries unless the user explicitly instructs it to move to other entities.

Regarding the usage of custom gestures, we noticed that the participants frequently used the double press gesture to move "one level" up in the Semantic Tree so that they could reorient themselves. 9 out of 12 participants stated that traversing up in the Semantic Tree until reaching the top level with Dial was much better than pressing 'ESC' multiple times with JAWS to get to the beginning of a page. If they wanted to return to their previously-focused location, with JAWS, they had to use multiple shortcuts once again; whereas with the Dial, they could find the previous location with fewer steps (at most, the height of the Semantic Tree). Surprisingly, they did not use the triple press gesture often; only 2 out of 12 used that gesture, and said that it slowed them down.

While participants were using only the screen reader, we observed that the expert users spent quite a bit of time guessing the features supported by the entities. For example, they checked if a text-box, had the "autocomplete" feature by entering a few characters, and pressing the down-arrow key. With Speed-Dial, they said that they did not have to guess anymore due to the custom-Dial interface that is consistent across all websites.

5.1.1 Usability Rating

At the end of each session, each participant was asked the standard System Usability Scale (SUS) questionnaire where participants rated positive and negative statements about each study condition on a Likert scale from 1-strongly disagree to 5-strongly agree, and 3-being neutral. We found significant effect of study conditions on SUS score ($F_{2,33} = 15.5$, $p < .0001$). The mean SUS score of SR+Dial (85.0) was 18.3% higher than that of SR (69.3) and 4.6% higher than that of SR+Speech (81.04). Post hoc comparisons using the Tukey HSD test indicated that the pairwise differences in means in SR vs. SR+Speech and in SR vs. SR+Dial were statistically significant ($p < .01$). However, it was not significant in case of SR+Speech vs. SR+Dial ($p = .36$). Still, participants stated that they preferred Speed-Dial to others, as SR was the most cumbersome to use, and the Speech interface was becoming cumbersome to use for task involving continuous navigation. Furthermore, with the Speech interface, speech commands often interfered with listening to the page content—a problem avoided by using Speed Dial.

5.2 Post-Evaluation

Finally, we administered a brief, Likert-type questionnaire (1-strongly unfavorable, 5-strongly favorable response) to solicit participants' opinions and suggestions regarding Speed-Dial. As shown in Table 1, all participants liked the "buzz" feedback indicating entity boundaries (Question 3). They also liked the uniformity of interaction experience (Question 10), and the ease of learning (Question 2). The participants were undecided about the potential of using Dial for text entry (Question 9) as well as the triple press gesture for the "search & go" feature. Finally, there was a strong consensus that Speed-Dial can indeed serve as a mouse surrogate (Question 6).

5.3 Feature Requests

The participants expressed a desire for more custom gestures, such as *press & turn* to immediately select a menu option. They also wanted a relatively stronger haptic feedback, and incorporation of rotational momentum to skip multiple entities in one go. Integration of Speed-Dial with smartphones was also highly coveted.

Table 1. Post-experiment questionnaire and responses.

Question: On a scale of 1 to 5	Avg	SD
1. How easy is it to rotate the Dial compared to pressing keyboard shortcuts?	4.50	0.65
2. How easy is it to learn Speed-Dial?	4.75	0.43
3. How important is it to know the entity boundaries?	5.00	0.00
4. How useful is vibration feedback?	4.17	0.90
5. How useful is the combination of audio and vibratory feedback?	3.17	1.40
6. Can Speed-Dial serve as a mouse?	4.50	0.65
7. Is "search & go" feature useful?	3.83	0.99
8. How easy is it to fill forms with Speed-Dial?	4.42	0.76
9. How useful is the radial keyboard?	3.33	1.11
10. Does Speed-Dial provide uniform interaction experience?	4.75	0.43

6. CONCLUSION

This paper explores the applicability of an off-the-shelf, physical Dial as a surrogate for a computer mouse in the context of non-visual web browsing. Our experimental results demonstrate that the combination of Dial & semantic model has a bestter constructive synergy over extant non-visual web browsing systems that combine speech interface and semantic model. A unique aspect of Speed-Dial is that it provides uniformity of interaction experience regardless of the underlying screen reader. Uniformity can eliminate the need to learn new screen readers, thereby reducing training effort and associated cost. In fact, this was affirmed by a participant who said: "If I have this, I shouldn't spend my time in computer class". Speed-Dial enables blind users to quickly move around the web page to select content of interest, akin to pointing and clicking with a mouse, i.e., it serves as a surrogate for the computer mouse.

7. ACKNOWLEDGMENTS

We thank Glenn Dausch, Yevgen Borodin, and the anonymous reviewers for their insightful feedback that helped shape this paper. Asmita Negi, Leela Bharath Kumar, and Rakesh Agarwal contributed to the implementation of Speed-Dial. This research was supported in part by NSF: IIS-1447549, CNS-1405641; National Eye Institute of NIH: R01EY026621; and NIDILRR: 90IF0117-01-00. The content is solely the responsibility of the authors and does not necessarily represent the official views of NIH nor represent the policy of NIDILRR.

8. REFERENCES

[1] AFB, Refreshable Braille Displays. Retrieved from http://www.afb.org/ProdBrowseCatResults.aspx?CatID=43.

[2] AFB, Screen Readers. Retrieved from http://www.afb.org/ProdBrowseCatResults.aspx?CatID=49.

[3] Ahmed, T., Hoyle, R., Connelly, K., Crandall, D., and Kapadia, A., 2015. Privacy Concerns and Behaviors of People with Visual Impairments. In *Proceedings of the Proceedings of the 33rd Annual ACM Conference on Human Factors in Computing Systems*. ACM, 3523-3532.

[4] Álvarez, M., Pan, A., Raposo, J., Bellas, F., and Cacheda, F., 2010. Finding and extracting data records from web pages. *Journal of Signal Processing Systems 59*, 1, 123-137.

[5] Andreessen, M., 1993. NCSA Mosaic technical summary. *National Center for Supercomputing Applications 605*.

[6] Ashok, V., Borodin, Y., Puzis, Y., and Ramakrishnan, I. V., 2015. Capti-Speak: A Speech-Enabled Web Screen Reader. In *Proceedings of the Proceedings of the 12th Web for All Conference*. ACM, 327-328.

[7] Ashok, V., Puzis, Y., Borodin, Y., and Ramakrishnan, I., 2017. Web Screen Reading Automation Assistance Using Semantic Abstraction. In *Proceedings of the Proceedings of the 22nd International Conference on Intelligent User Interfaces*. ACM, 407-418.

[8] Baluja, S., 2006. Browsing on small screens: recasting web-page segmentation into an efficient machine learning framework. In *Proceedings of the Proceedings of the 15th international conference on World Wide Web*. ACM, 33-42.

[9] Bardot, S., Brock, A., Serrano, M., and Jouffrais, C., 2014. Quick-glance and in-depth exploration of a tabletop map for visually impaired people. In *Proceedings of the Proceedings of the 26th Conference on l'Interaction Homme-Machine*. ACM, 165-170.

[10] Billah, S. M., Ashok, V., Porter, D. E., and Ramakrishnan, I. V., 2017. Ubiquitous Accessibility for People with Visual Impairments: Are We There Yet? In *Proceedings of the Proceedings of the 2017 CHI Conference on Human Factors in Computing Systems*. ACM, 5862-5868.

[11] Borodin, Y., Bigham, J. P., Dausch, G., and Ramakrishnan, I. V., 2010. More than meets the eye: a survey of screen-reader browsing strategies. In *Proceedings of the Proceedings of the 2010 International Cross Disciplinary Conference on Web Accessibility (W4A)*. ACM, 1-10.

[12] Brewster, S. and Brown, L. M., 2004. Tactons: Structured Tactile Messages for Non-Visual Information Display. In *Proceedings of the Fifth Australasian User Interface Conference (AUIC2004)*. ACS, 15-23.

[13] Brock, A., Kammoun, S., Macé, M., and Jouffrais, C., 2014. Using wrist vibrations to guide hand movement and whole body navigation. *i-com 13*, 3 (2014-12-10), pp. 19-28.

[14] Brooke, J., 1996. SUS-A quick and dirty usability scale. *Usability evaluation in industry 189*, 194.

[15] Cai, D., Yu, S., Wen, J.-R., and Ma, W.-Y., 2004. *VIPS: A vision based page segmentation algorithm.* Microsoft technical report.

[16] Chung, C. Y., Gertz, M., and Sundaresan, N., 2002. Reverse engineering for web data: From visual to semantic structures. In *Proceedings of the Proceedings 18th International Conference on Data Engineering*. IEEE, 53-63.

[17] Dill, S., Eiron, N., Gibson, D., Gruhl, D., Guha, R., Jhingran, A., Kanungo, T., Rajagopalan, S., Tomkins, A., and Tomlin, J. A., 2003. SemTag and Seeker: Bootstrapping the semantic web via automated semantic annotation. In *Proceedings of the Proceedings of the 12th international conference on World Wide Web*. ACM, 178-186.

[18] Fensel, D., Decker, S., Erdmann, M., and Studer, R., 1998. Ontobroker: Or how to enable intelligent access to the WWW. In *Proceedings of the Proceedings of the 11th Banff Knowledge Acquisition for Knowledge-Based Systems Workshop*. CiteSeer.

[19] Hartgen Consultancy, 2017. J-Say. Talk to Your Computer, It Talks Back! Retrieved from http://www.ngtvoice.com/products/software/astec/j-say/.

[20] House, D., Novick, D., Fanty, M., and Walpole, J., 1995. Spoken-Language Access to Multimedia (SLAM).

[21] HTML5.2, 2017. Hyper-Text Markup Language v.5.2. Retrieved from http://w3c.github.io/html/.

[22] Huang, A. W. and Sundaresan, N., 2000. A semantic transcoding system to adapt Web services for users with disabilities. In *Proceedings of the Proceedings of the 4th International ACM Conference on Assistive Technologies*. ACM.

[23] Kuber, R., Yu, W., and McAllister, G., 2007. Towards Developing Assistive Haptic Feedback for Visually Impaired Internet Users. In *Proceedings of the Proceedings of the SIGCHI conference on Human Factors in Computing Systems*. ACM, 1525-1534.

[24] Kuber, R., Zhu, S., Arber, Y., Norman, K., and Magnusson, C., 2014. Augmenting the non-visual web browsing process using the geomagic touch haptic device. *SIGACCESS Access. Comput.*, 109, 4-10.

[25] Labský, M., Svátek, V., and Nekvasil, M., 2008. Information Extraction Based on Extraction Ontologies: Design, Deployment and Evaluation. *Ontology-based Information Extraction Systems (OBIES)*, 9.

[26] Lawrence, M. M., Martinelli, N., and Nehmer, R., 2009. A Haptic Soundscape Map of the University of Oregon. *Journal of Maps 5*, 1, 19-29.

[27] Lazar, J., Allen, A., Kleinman, J., and Malarkey, C., 2007. What Frustrates Screen Reader Users on the Web: A Study of 100 Blind Users. *International Journal of human-computer interaction 22*, 3, 247-269.

[28] Magnusson, C., Tan, C. C. S., and Yu, W., 2006. Haptic access to 3D objects on the web. In *Proceedings of the Eurohaptics*.

[29] Melnyk, V., Ashok, V., Puzis, Y., Soviak, A., and Borodin, Y., 2014. Widget Classification with Applications to Web Accessibility. In *Proceedings of the International Conference on Web Engineering (ICWE)*.

[30] Nuance, 2017. Dragon Naturally Speaking Rich Internet Application. Retrieved from http://www.nuancesoftwarestore.com/dragon-naturallyspeaking-premium/.

[31] O'Modhrain, M. S. and Gillespie, B., 1997. The moose: A haptic user interface for blind persons. In *Proceedings of the Proc. Third WWW6 Conference*.

[32] Pielot, M., Poppinga, B., Heuten, W., and Boll, S., 2011. A tactile compass for eyes-free pedestrian navigation. In *Proceedings of the Proceedings of the 13th IFIP TC 13 international conference on Human-computer interaction - Volume Part II*. Springer-Verlag, 640-656.

[33] Pietrzak, T., Crossan, A., Brewster, S. A., Martin, B., and Pecci, I., 2009. Creating Usable Pin Array Tactons for Nonvisual Information. *IEEE Transactions on Haptics 2*, 2, 61-72.

[34] Puzis, Y., Borodin, Y., Puzis, R., and Ramakrishnan, I. V., 2013. Predictive Web Automation Assistant for People with Vision Impairments. In *Proceedings of the proceedings of the 22th international conference on world wide web*. ACM, 1031-1040.

[35] Ramakrishnan, I. V., Stent, A., and Yang, G. L., 2004. HearSay: enabling audio browsing on hypertext content. In *Proceedings of the International World Wide Web Conference (WWW)*.

[36] Rotard, M., Knödler, S., and Ertl, T., 2005. A tactile web browser for the visually disabled. In *Proceedings of the Proceedings of the sixteenth ACM conference on Hypertext and hypermedia*. ACM, 15-22.

[37] Rümelin, S., Rukzio, E., and Hardy, R., 2011. NaviRadar: a novel tactile information display for pedestrian navigation. In *Proceedings of the Proceedings of the 24th annual ACM symposium on User interface software and technology*. ACM, 293-302.

[38] Shneiderman, B., 1996. The eyes have it: A task by data type taxonomy for information visualizations. In *Proceedings of the Visual Languages, 1996. Proceedings., IEEE Symposium on*. IEEE, 336-343.

[39] Soviak, A., Borodin, A., Ashok, V., Borodin, Y., Puzis, Y., and Ramakrishnan, I., 2016. Tactile Accessibility: Does Anyone Need a Haptic Glove? In *Proceedings of the Proceedings of the 18th International ACM SIGACCESS Conference on Computers and Accessibility*. ACM, 101-109.

[40] Tsukada, K. and Yasumura, M., 2004. ActiveBelt: Belt-Type Wearable Tactile Display for Directional Navigation. In *UbiComp 2004: Ubiquitous Computing: 6th International Conference, Nottingham, UK, September 7-10, 2004. Proceedings*, N. DAVIES, E.D. MYNATT and I. SIIO Eds. Springer Berlin Heidelberg, Berlin, Heidelberg, 384-399.

[41] WebAIM, 2015. Survey of Preferences of Screen Readers Users. Retrieved from http://webaim.org/projects/screenreadersurvey6/.

[42] Wong, E. J., Yap, K. M., Alexander, J., and Karnik, A., 2015. HABOS: Towards a platform of haptic-audio based online shopping for the visually impaired. In *Proceedings of the Open Systems (ICOS), 2015 IEEE Confernece on*. IEEE, 62-67.

[43] Yu, W., Kuber, R., Murphy, E., Strain, P., and McAllister, G., 2006. A novel multimodal interface for improving visually impaired people's web accessibility. *Virtual Reality 9*, 2-3, 133-148.

[44] Zhai, Y. and Liu, B., 2005. Web data extraction based on partial tree alignment. In *Proceedings of the Proceedings of the 14th international conference on World Wide Web*. ACM, 76-85.

[45] Zhu, J., Nie, Z., Wen, J.-R., Zhang, B., and Ma, W.-Y., 2006. Simultaneous record detection and attribute labeling in web data extraction. In *Proceedings of the Proceedings of the 12th ACM SIGKDD international conference on Knowledge discovery and data mining*. ACM, 494-503.

"But, I Don't Want/Need a Power Wheelchair": Toward Accessible Power Assistance for Manual Wheelchairs

Dafne Zuleima Morgado Ramirez
University College London,
UCLIC66-72 Gower Street, London,
WC1E 6BT, UK
+44 02031087070
d.morgado-ramirez@ucl.ac.uk

Catherine Holloway
University College London,
UCLIC66-72 Gower Street, London,
WC1E 6BT, UK
+44 02031087990
c.holloway@ucl.ac.uk

ABSTRACT
Power assist devices help manual wheelchair users to propel their wheelchair thus increasing their independence and reducing the risk of upper limb injuries due to excessive use. These benefits can be invaluable for people that already have upper limb joint pain and reduced muscular strength. However, it is not clear if the way that assistance is provided by such devices is what manual wheelchair users need and expect. 12 manual wheelchair users were interviewed to understand: the situations in which they find it difficult to propel their wheelchairs; situations they considered paramount to have power assistance; their experience or knowledge of power assist devices; and likes and dislikes of commercially available power assist devices. Finally, they were asked to comment on their ideal form factor of a power assist device. Users have suggested improvements of the devices' accessibility and visualized new ways in which they could interact with the technology. These interactions involve "chairable" devices independent from, but not excluding, wearable devices and mobile applications. We have identified the need of monitoring emotions and the need for designing an open source do-it-yourself wheelchair propelling assistance device which we believe is required equally in developed and in developing countries.

CCS Concepts
• H.5.2 (Information Interfaces and Presentation) User interfaces: User-centered design, Prototyping
• J.3 (Life and Medical Sciences) Health
• K.4.2 (Computers and Society) Social Issues: Assistive technologies for persons with disabilities

ASSETS '17, October 29-November 1, 2017, Baltimore, MD, USA

ACM ISBN 978-1-4503-4926-0/17/10…$15.00
https://doi.org/10.1145/3132525.3132529

Keywords
Manual Wheelchair; Power Assist Device; Participatory Design; Interviews; Assistive Technology; Human-Centered; Accessibility; Interaction Design

1. INTRODUCTION
The World Health Organization estimates that there are 70 million people that need a wheelchair worldwide and only 5% to 15% have access to one [57]. There are around 1.2 million wheelchair users in the United Kingdom [56]. A wheelchair user is a person that uses a wheelchair for personal mobility due to difficulty in walking or moving around as a result of different neuromusculoskeletal impairments [58]. Manual wheelchair users often injure their upper limbs due to continuous and excessive use. The incidence of shoulder pain is reported to range from 42% [13] to 66% [17], with the most commonly reported injury occurring to the rotator cuff muscles [1]. Bilateral carpal tunnel syndrome is also a common side effect of handrim manual wheelchair propulsion [6]. Those injuries can be prevented by reducing the frequency of wheelchair use, reducing the weight of both the wheelchair and the wheelchair user and adding a power assist system [31]. Injuries are thought to arise in part to the cyclical nature of the wheelchair push cycle [39, 47]. They are exasperated by the low gross mechanical efficiency of wheelchair pushing - only 10% of effort goes directly into making a person and the wheelchair move forwards [14] and this is when pushing along flat, smooth surfaces such as a hospital floor. On more challenging surfaces, such as ramps, side slopes and rough or loose surfaces (e.g. gravel) the push forces required are much higher [24], which increases the risk of injury.

There is broad agreement in the literature that using an electric motor to augment a manual wheelchair user's power, has multiple benefits. It reduces metabolic demand [2, 12, 22, 43], increases mechanical efficiency of manual wheelchair propulsion [5, 44], helps decrease repetitive strain injuries [11, 30-33, 36] and enables users to propel their wheelchairs for longer, farther [35]. In addition, people travel through places they never travelled with a conventional manual wheelchair [3, 34]. A power assist device attaches to a manual wheelchair to help the user propel the wheelchair. Power assist devices are typically installed in front, behind or replace the wheels hub. It is not a device that converts the manual wheelchair into a joystick controlled electric or power wheelchair.

We present the findings from the exploratory stage of a new project. The aim is to set the requirements of future manual wheelchair propelling assistive technology. In later work these shall be designed. The contributions of this paper include: (1) a review of previous work on power assist devices for self-propelled manual wheelchairs, (2) an examination of the current market of power-assist devices from a user and human computer interaction (HCI) perspective; (3) similarities between form factors of ideal power assist devices and (4) the identification of opportunities to improve the usability, interaction and user experience with power assist devices for manual wheelchair users.

2. RELATED WORK

Only three studies have explored the perceptions of pushrim activated power assistance by manual wheelchair users [18, 20, 26]. They each assess a different power-assist device: e-motion by Alber [54], Servomatic by Meyra GmbH [41] and one undisclosed device [26]. They found that 5 out of 12 users had a positive experience with power assist. In other study [18], users indicated that although the addition of power assist enabled them to have access to new activities, greater social life and less fatigue, the devices were still cumbersome, prohibitive in public transport and had battery problems. Guillon, Van-Hecke [20] found lower user satisfaction for e-motion in contrast with using a manual wheelchair and Servomatic. User satisfaction was also low for power assist devices during indoor use and while performing car transfers.

Only one study assessed three power-assist devices in terms of their performance against the standards of the American National Standards Institute and the Rehabilitation Engineering and Assistive Technology Society of North America available in the year 2008 [29]. These standards assess the safety, durability and efficacy of wheelchairs by testing: static and dynamic stability, braking effectiveness, maximum speed, maximum acceleration, maximum retardation, energy consumption, statics strength, impact strength and fatigue strength. The study was completed as power-assist wheels are an addition to the wheelchair frame and as such they must not adversely affect the safety, durability and effectiveness of the manual wheelchair. Through fatigue tests they found that the e-motion had the least estimated life years (1.3-2.3) in comparison with the Xtender (3-5). The e-motion was found to have "extraordinary" rates of failure, most of them related to the design of the device (weight, size, location within the wheelchair) [29]. Despite these failures the e-motion wheels are still a popular choice for manual wheelchair users in the UK.

Although a geared fully mechanical wheelchair wheel exists, it only has two gears which require undesirable sustained user's effort and greater time when ascending ramps [25]. The concept of a fully mechanical assistance device is desirable but it requires improvements in order to be able to compare against powered assist devices.

In conclusion, there has been limited work conducted in the area of power assist devices for self-propelled manual wheelchairs. In terms of interaction and overall user experience the handful of studies which have been conducted have all found failings in the current product range.

3. POWER ASSIST DEVICES OFFERED

We focused on the power assist devices that are available in the UK market. There are six popular power assist devices commercially available in the UK, all with price tags over £4k ($4.9k). Images of these devices can be seen in the supplementary information. These vary in the method they attach to a manual wheelchair. There are three attachment methods: (1) anchor to the frame of the wheelchair behind and below the seat, (2) replaces rear wheels and (3) anchors to the wheelchair frame below and in front of the seat converting the wheelchair into a tricycle. The SmartDrive [38] is the only one that attaches to the frame using method (1). The Twion [54], e-motion [54], WheelDrive [52] and Xtender [53] attach to the wheelchair using method (2). Batec handbike [7] is an example of attachment method (3). The devices also differ regarding their weight, their color, their modes of operation and accessibility features (Table 1). The SmartDrive and Pushtracker were recently released (December 2016), which promise to enable a better user experience through an updated wristband and a mobile application.

The expected user ability also varies among devices. All devices require good upper body stability and coordination of arm strength (apart from e-motion wheels). Any user with little residual or reduced upper limb strength can use all devices excluding the Twion wheels. Users with unequal arm strength can use all devices with exception of the Twion wheels and the WheelDrive. Regarding appearance, greys and blacks predominate. SmartDrive is black including its wristband. Twion wheels is offered in light grey with dark grey details. The Batec hybrid handbikes have hardware in black as standard with colorful frame options: red, orange, blue, green, light grey or pink.

Although power assist devices have been available in the market for some time, it is unknown how the users perceive these devices and if the current interaction with the user is what users expect and need.

4. PROCEDURE

Twelve manual wheelchair users, with different ranges of experience in using power assist devices, were interviewed individually for an average of 1.5 hours each using an in-depth, semi-structured method [8]. Users were recruited through a website, posters and the UK National Health Service wheelchair services. Eight were interviewed in person and four by telephone. A synthesis of the interview questions is:

a) When propelling your wheelchair, what issues do you have and what is your greatest need?
b) What type of journeys do you find difficult and why?
c) Which power assist devices do you know and which have you used before or use currently?
d) What do you think of power assist devices?
e) Under what conditions do you need power assistance?
f) How would you like power assist devices to work and what do you think they should look like?
g) Would you like the power assist device to give you information and if so, in which form and what?
h) Can you please describe your dream power assist device?

Questions were adapted depending on the experience of participants with power-assist devices. Interviews were transcribed and analyzed by the first author. An inductive approach was used, where the data was used to form codes and themes. Data was analyzed using thematic analysis akin to the approach by Braun and Clarke [8]. Themes and concepts were developed in order to interpret data; and to identify key concepts and relationships between them. Transcripts were analyzed iteratively until no new concepts emerged (saturation) [55]. A discussion and review of the themes was done with the second author. Thematic analysis was used as it enabled the creation of rich descriptions of the needs, expectations and form factors and to identify implicit and explicit ideas within the data, such as social and functional accessibility.

Table 1. Characteristics of power assist devices available in the market.

Device	Weight (Kg)	Accessibility features
SmartDrive MX2+ with PushTracker	6.1	Wrist band: senses movement, digital display of number of pushes and controls the device through inertial gestures. Mobile application to track push count, distance and time during assistance and no assistance modes. LEDs for battery status. Double tap on handrim and single tap activate specific responses from the motor. Double tap: start up or ramp up speed if already moving or slow down if already moving. Single tap: coast at current speed. Rollback prevention. Modifiable tap sensitivity, top speed and acceleration.
Twion wheels	6.3 each wheel	Handrim activated. Mobile application: track distance, battery status, speed, altitude, use GPS of mobile for visualizing journeys and remote control of unoccupied wheelchair. LEDs for battery status. Reverse assistance.
e-motion wheels	10 each wheel	Handrim activated. Wireless hand held control with a digital screen and buttons for adjusting device settings. LEDs for battery status. Rollback delay. Left/right power adjustment to different arm strengths.
WheelDrive	11.5 each wheel	Double hand rims. Outer rim assists while the inner rim provides continues drive. LEDs for battery status. Three levels of power assistance: low, medium and high. Reverse assistance. Battery can be detached for travel.
Xtender	17	Handrim activated. LEDs for battery status. Rollback prevention, downhill speed control and one arm drive possible.
Batec hybrid handbikes	29	Digital display panel and button controls. LEDs for battery status. Manual, hybrid or fully powered propelling assistance.

Table 2 Participant's characteristics.

User	Age (years)	Time using a manual wheelchair (years)	Power assist device use experience	Disability
U1	24	8.5	e-motion user for 2.5 years	Spinal cord injury (SCI), tetraplegia
U2	29	3.75	Batec hybrid handbike for 2.5 years, e-motion for 0.5 years	SCI, level C6
U3	37	1.16	Tested e-motion wheels and SmartDrive MX2 in a mobility shop	Spina bifida meningocele and hydrocephalus with SCI level C4/C5 and syringomyelia with SCI between T1 and T10.
U4	43	23	Tested SmartDrive M1 and emotion for a few hours	SCI, level L1
U5	69	0.75	Tested similar to Batec handbike for a few hours in a hospital	Spinal stroke, T11
U6	48	32	None	Spina bifida with carpal tunnel syndrome on both wrists for last 3 years
U7	44	11	e-motion for 11 years and M1 SmartDrive for a few hours	SCI, level C5/C6 complete
U8	21	16	e-motion for 3 years	Cerebral palsy
U9	59	2.5	e-motion for 3.5 years	Multiple sclerosis
U10	55	53	None	Post poliomyelitis syndrome
U11	36	32	None	Spina bifida, paralysis from waist down
U12	53	1.16	Tested e-motion wheels for a few hours in a hospital	SCI, level C3/C4 motor incomplete

5. FINDINGS

Although participants were of different ages, had different levels of experience using power assist devices and had different disabilities, there was a strong agreement in their responses regarding daily struggles using a wheelchair. We present these barriers as physical and non-physical. The individual form factors of an ideal power assist device showed similarities and offered an insight into individual preferences that could become ubiquitous forms of interaction with power assist devices. Differences in opinions were more evident regarding the way in which they wanted to interact or not interact with the assistance device.

5.1 Physical barriers

Physical barriers were identified in relation to the built environment, wheelchair propelling skills, non wheelchair users, weather, and the length of a journey in distance. Users had different strengths in their arms, thus the difficult situations they faced were at different levels and in different priorities. Challenging situations related to the UK built environment are: up and down level changes (curbs), negotiating rough surfaces (with gravel, cracks, gaps, broken pavement, cobble stones, thick carpets, park grass that hasn't been cut), potholes, door thresholds, side slopes, ascending steep inclines like ramps including those used in buses and trains (due to the need of power) and descending inclines. For example, U6 said *"on thick carpets you feel that you are sinking down and you have to do a special effort to move the chair"*.

Wheelchair skills that users found difficult are stopping suddenly and reversing. Regarding the length of their journey, wheeling long distances is difficult for every manual wheelchair user, regardless of the smoothness of the surfaces and the strength of their arms. Other people become a barrier when travelling through a crowd and having people crashing into their wheelchair accidentally. For instance, U4 pointed out *"it is not about the device, it is about how the world works and how unpredictable situations can be"*.

Weather poses challenges in autumn when surfaces become slippery with wet tree leaves or when surfaces are difficult due to dry tree leaves accumulation. Winter snow and frost were least mentioned. U3 said *"if it is wet it is horrible, I try not to go out if it is raining as it is difficult to get traction"*.

5.2 Non-physical barriers

Non physical barriers were identified as lack of awareness, incorrect understanding, lack of interest and the experience of emotion and it consequences.

The majority of users showed a lack of awareness of current technology available in the market and this added to the sometimes incorrect understanding of what the devices did. Similarly, lack of interest in understanding power assist devices was observed, signaling: a lack of interest in preventing repetitive strain injury as getting older, a lack of awareness of repetitive strain injury and a lack of awareness that handrim wheelchair propulsion is inefficient. Users that are interested in power assist devices appear to rely strongly on the experience and knowledge of other manual wheelchair users regarding wheelchair technology. For instance, U8 confessed to having thought that the assistance device would allow him to get fitter and then progressively he would have been able to return to use a manual wheelchair without assistance.

The experience of emotion is an additional barrier that manifests itself as physical pain. Stress and anxiety commonly cause shoulder pain which affects the user's ability to propel their wheelchair.U6 said *"at the moment my shoulders are quite sore but that is because of stress with the current season (Christmas), starting a new job, and setting up at a new desk"*.

All users agree that the cost of the technology is too high.

5.3 In which situations do users need power assist?

Most of the situations identified were to compensate for the barriers of the built environment. Adding power assistance is needed not only to wheel for longer distances and for a longer time; but also to be able to hold the weight of the user and the wheelchair down a slope for safety. Particular situations are: ascending (add power) and descending (rollback prevention) inclines, travel across side slopes, to complete an emergency stop (especially when the user has reduced arm strength and coordination), and rough terrain as mentioned in the previous section. Power assistance is also needed at the end of the day when tiredness is experienced. U4 said: *"I struggle with having to propel my wheelchair for long distances. After 2 hours you can notice aches and pains"*.

5.4 Social accessibility

Assistive technology that has a socially accessible design is a tool that conveys both ability and social identity. Social discourse is facilitated when the user's identity is not only functionally but also socially supported; acting as complementary dimensions [48]. This concept is supported by the users since they like power assist devices that conceal their function by integrating themselves within the wheel hub; as in not modifying significantly the general accepted appearance of a manual wheelchair. Assist devices which are easy to install and charge are also seen as likable. Upon the discovery of mobile applications able to synchronize with power assist devices, users expressed interest and inquisitiveness but caution. U2 and U12 expressed the importance of stability of the wheelchair with the power assist installed and gave greater importance to it over appearance. U1 said: *"I would have made them look nicer, closer to (what) a manual wheelchair looks like"*.

Other than the hybrid handbike, the color range of power assist devices are not an issue for users although one considered it either medical (grey) or "futuristic but old" like a "90's PC" (U2). U3 said *"the appearance of the e-motion is not best looking, it looks medical. I think they should be black. Being grey and white they look like a hospital. I think they should be able to come in any color"*.

5.5 Functional Accessibility

The main objective of assistive technology is to maintain or improve functioning thereby facilitating well-being through independence, dignity and participation in society [57]. In this paper functional accessibility refers to the capacity of assistive technology to maintain or improve functioning of its user.

Physical spaces are being modified or created in order to be accessible to wheelchairs, therefore users rightly point out that it is expected that chairable devices would not increase the width of their wheelchair to the extent that they can no longer travel through door thresholds or increase the weight of their wheelchair to the extent that they cannot propel the wheelchair with the device turned off. Power assist devices that have sensors installed on the handrims make these the weak and delicate feature of the wheelchair creating problems when someone handles the wheels from the handrim when boarding cars and airplanes. In general users are comfortable with the current battery duration and charging time required. Reported problems of batteries not lasting enough during the day are due users forgetting to charge the devices rather than a problem with the batteries themselves. However, some sealed batteries that cannot be separated from the hub of the wheels during air travel are not seen as practical. U4 said *"the downside of e-motion is that when you are flying the fact that the batteries are in built (you cannot separate the battery from the wheels), some airlines have problems with the battery being inside the wheels"*.

Power assist devices designs that are installed at the hub require the owner not to lift the wheels from the handrim in order to avoid damaging the sensors. Users fear that even family members fail to remember not to handle the wheels through the handrim, let alone strangers that want to be helpful but end damaging the sensors.

This highlights a major design problem, where the user was not taken into account. Regardless of how careful the users themselves are with handling their wheelchairs and power assist devices, the power-assist devices are often broken by other people moving and lifting their wheelchair e.g. in taxis, airports and restaurants. As U2 said *"no one wants to have to grip the wheels by the tire where it is dirty and rough"*.

The hybrid handbike user expressed disappointment due to the lack of assistance when moving the wheelchair in reverse and that sometimes the motor provides too much power (even at the lowest power setting) creating a loss of control. Although vibration is expected when traveling at higher speeds, the hybrid handbike user finds such vibration disorienting causing occasional crashes. U2 said: *"I think I can manoeuver the obstacle but then I can't. The power is instant and is always there, even on the lowest setting, you can control the speed but it is not as fine as using your own hands."*

Regarding the PushTracker's option to track the number of pushes, U8 highlighted that the technology may affect self-esteem of manual wheelchair users if they start comparing their daily number of pushes while forgetting that everyone has different abilities. Comparing pushes among wheelchair users with different abilities is not only clinically invalid, but has potential for creating negative emotional responses when there is a significant difference in the number of pushes between wheelchair users.

In general users are comfortable with receiving assistance to hold the wheelchair while going downhill (such as with the SmartDrive).

5.6 Ideal form factors

We gathered the personal ideal form factors of each user and found similarities and differences. Similarities focused on the form of the hardware used. Functional requirements, including interaction methods, where differences arose, have been adapted into a range of modular options for the ultimate power-assist device. In offering a range of functional options we aim to make the power assist device accessible to users with different abilities. What we are not attempting is to suggest an ideal form factor that fits every wheelchair and suits every user.

5.6.1 Hardware

The ideal power assist device would attach to the user's most comfortable and favorite manual wheelchair regardless of the weight, size and type of rear wheels of the wheelchair. The power assist should be concealed by attaching it below the chair where it "clicks" into the axle powering the rear wheels through a mechanical transmission (Figure 1) just as electric bike motors. The feasibility of this design needs to be tested. Ideally, the battery also clicks below the seat where a concealed connection feeds the motor, a system similar to the battery of the WheelDrive. The battery can be a set of two installed below the seat on each side, but not on the back wheels, and these can be separated from the device for air travel. In this way, backup batteries can fit into a backpack, just like books. User U4 believes the ideal attachment weight would be 0.5 Kg without batteries and 2 Kg with batteries, which may only be achieved if the battery is separated into various components of maximum 2Kg each. Reducing the weight of the device will ensure that wheelchair users who drive a car will be able to lift their wheelchair into their car without having to detach the ideal power assist device and without additional struggle since the added weight of the power assist device would not be significant.

"At home, I could reverse the chair and click and it starts charging, then in the morning I just move forward unclick and go" - U3

5.6.2 Functions

All users expressed their desire to be able to control the amount of power the device provides, and this control should be through a concealed and easy to use interface "while on the go". Most users suggested having as a minimum three different power settings; one user suggested having an unlimited choice of power through a sliding or rotating control (comparable to a volume control). User (U1) suggested a control system that could predict the risk of tipping in order to be able to use the wheelchair without anti-tippers. Two other users also expressed a dislike for the appearance of the anti-tippers and their choice of not using them regardless of the risk of tipping over. User U2 suggested adding a downhill break feeding and charging the battery, to make it last longer. One user (U2) suggested an automatic change of power to the minimum level of assistance as soon as the battery reaches a certain low level, in order to enable the user to reach a charging point. This should be accompanied by a timely notification to the user. The way notifications are desired is covered in the next section. Users indicated that it is better to have an optional reverse downhill and forward downhill slow down settings (activated by the user rather than an automated feature), especially when using public transport ramps.

Users also agree that the use of a power assist devices should be intuitive rather than requiring the users to learn to use a wheelchair like they have never used one before. U1 said *"I would like them to work closer to what a manual wheelchair is like" and U4 said "a power assist device needs to feel part of the wheelchair rather than being something unpredictable".*

U6 was interested in the device being able to remember the easy and the difficult journeys, a feature which is possible with current technology [21].

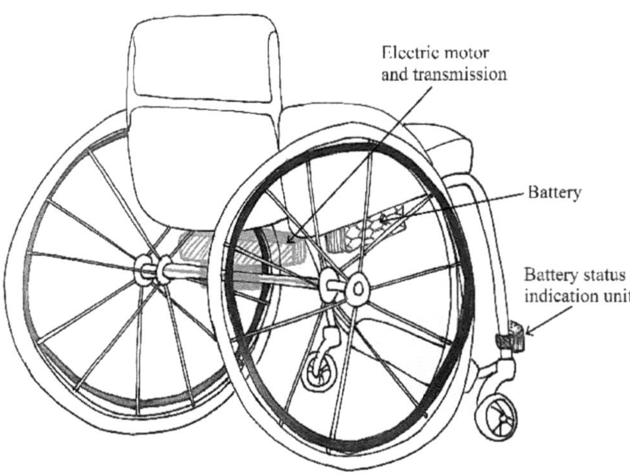

Figure 1 Sketch of power assist electric motor and transmission feeding the rear wheels through the axel. One battery on each side to distribute weight, only right battery visible on sketch. Also an alternative battery status indication unit, when the user cannot turn around to read LEDs on the back wheels hub or behind the chair, the unit is attachable to any part of the wheelchair frame. © Dafne Zuleima Morgado Ramirez

5.6.3 *Interactions*

Eleven users were comfortable with the idea of interacting with the device through a mobile application. However, they stressed the importance of having the flexibility of not having to access a mobile device to setup and use the device, but having the opportunity to do so. Thus the use of smartphones was perceived as inaccessible for some manual wheelchair users. U5 said *"I am not sure I want anything that operates with my mobile phone, unless I have a third hand"* in contrast with U8 that said *"Like my phone recognizes my voice, I would like to be able to speak to my mobile phone or directly to my power assist in order to change settings on the go"*.

One user suggested using a portable Raspberry Pi computer [45] with a small interface that could be attached to any part of the wheelchair frame to control the device without the need of a smartphone (U4). This additional interface could look like and be installed just as the battery status indication unit in Figure 1. U6 suggested tactile buttons below the seat, accessible in between the knees for quick and easy power and speed settings control and on/off choice. Thus, users appear to prefer both a primary and secondary ways of controlling and setting up their ideal power assist devices, where one of those ways does not require them to have and use a smartphone with an application.

"I would like some sort of touch identification, or recognize the person sitting on the wheelchair. Identifying me and then automatically activating my preferred settings" - *U8*

Most users are interested in being able to track wheelchair pushes and have a mild interest in being able to set a fitness program (desired pushes per day). U3 said *"I would also like the device to help me remain fit, be able to tell the device how many pushes I want to do, to not get lazy. Being able to set up a program"*. U4 suggested being able to monitor the correlation between the number of pushes and shoulder pain, in order to receive a notification before becoming too tired and getting pain. This could be possible with a learning algorithm. U4 said *"maybe I can have an app on my mobile and after I have used the device at the end of the day I can indicate to the app how much pain I had that day"*. Similarly, we identified an interest in knowing the amount of effort they put in versus the work done by the power assist device.

Regarding data, users would like to be able to fully customize notifications, warnings and reports in order to suit their interests, including having the option to turn off all notifications. Data they indicated an interest in are: time and distance travelled, number of pushes, power provided by the device, battery status in percentage or LEDs or a coating or thin film installed on one handrim that changes color according to battery level (Figure 1), distance and time that can be travelled with the current battery, heart rate, calories consumption and global positioning system tracking not relying on a smartphone. U8 indicated that the power assist device could include GPS and keep track of the location of the user in order to provide suitable weather forecast and transport information, not only during the morning when starting the day but also throughout the day. U10 and U12 were interested in being able to record a journey and then indicate to a mobile app synchronized with the power assist the destination (user input), they then expected confirmation or rejection of the proposed journey depending on the battery status (sufficient or not to complete a single or return journey; and recommended charging time required if rejected).

Optional detailed reports on effort, journeys and comparisons would also be interesting. Most users indicated that they would like to have more information regarding the battery status, such as a percentage in addition to the LEDs. One user (U7) would like the device to be able to identify the propulsion pattern [50] and notify if the incorrect one is being used. Current technology can identify propulsion patterns [23].

The handrim tapping gesture sensed by the wristband (Table 1) available with the PushTracker of the SmartDrive MX2 is a HCI feature that was thought provoking. Suggested improvements to the PushTracker were the addition of gestures (up and down movement with palm facing down and frozen wrist) and voice notifications from the device to the user.

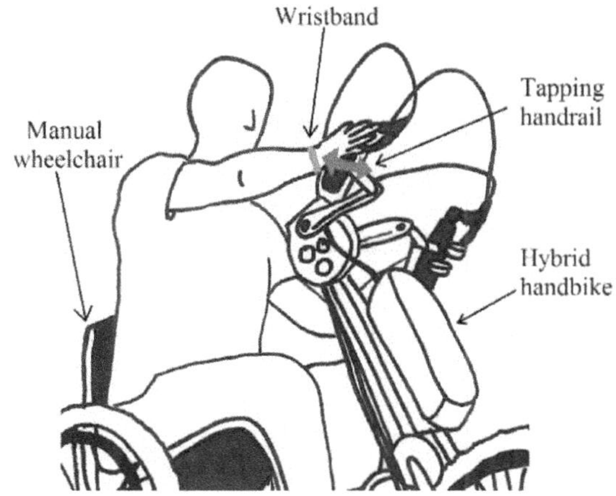

Figure 2 Sketch of tapping gesture on the handrail of a hybrid handbike being detected through a wrist worn device. © Dafne Zuleima Morgado Ramirez

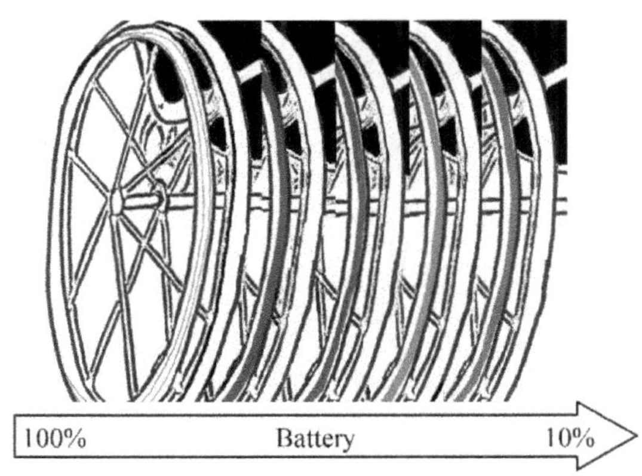

Figure 3 Sketch of battery indication option when user cannot turn around to read LEDs on the back wheels hub or behind the chair, thin LED film covering the handrim changes color according to battery status. Suggested by U8. © Dafne Zuleima Morgado Ramirez

U10 and U12 suggested being able to interact with a handbike through a wrist band, just as the SmartDrive does with the PushTracker. U10 suggested the gesture of tapping on the handrail of the handbike to increase/decrease the power when negotiating inclines – wearing a wristband for detection (Figure 2). The suggestion of providing a smartphone docking area between the handles of the handbike was appealing to most users, given the ease of access to on-screen interaction possibilities such as: battery status, changing power assistance, switching between manual and hybrid modes and also keeping track of their other applications such as social media.

U8 also pointed out that there is generally the assumption that manual wheelchair users cannot move their legs, but with certain disabilities this is possible and in his case he considers possible and desirable to have the option to propel the wheelchair or control the power assist device through his legs and feet.

5.7 Summary of findings

Table 3. Summary of findings.

Physical barriers	built environment, wheelchair propelling skills, non wheelchair users, weather, and the length of a journey in distance
Non physical barriers	lack of awareness, incorrect understanding, lack of interest and the experience of emotion and it consequences
Needs	compensate for the barriers of the built environment, power assist devices that preserve socially and functionally accessible
Expected Hardware	concealed below the wheelchair, lightweight, attach to the user's chosen manual wheelchair regardless of its weight, size and type of wheels, optional backup batteries
Expected Functions	control power like volume, tipping risk prediction, downhill break feeding battery, automatic low power set at low battery with notification to user, user selectable downhill and forward downhill resistance, intuitive, location and journey tracking with intelligent journey memory
Expected Interactions	mobile and no-mobile app control options, portable Pi computer attached to wheelchair frame, tactile buttons below the seat for speed, power and on/off control, track wheelchair pushes, distance travelled, set fitness program, pain tracking, statistics of user work versus power assist, customizable notifications, warnings and reports, battery status in percentage apart from LEDs or visually interactive on one handrim, smart weather forecast and transport information based on location, journey feasibility prediction based on battery status, propulsion patterns identification with notification to user, handrim tapping gestures

6. DISCUSSION

We interviewed manual wheelchair users with various levels of experience using power assist devices. To our knowledge, this is the first study exploring the user's perceptions and expectations on power assist devices for UK users and the most recent after a previous study published in 2010 in which manual wheelchair users were interviewed after they used only the e-motion for 6 weeks [18]. The results of this study offers suggestions regarding different devices and interactions that could be prototyped and tested through participatory design workshops with manual wheelchair users. This study has shown that there is a general lack of awareness among users of the existing devices in the market and the literature that has tested and evaluated their designs and performance.

Manual wheelchair users work very hard and for long periods of time in order to develop and acquire wheelchair skills that help them negotiate inaccessible built environments, which prevail [40, 46]. During this process they also become so familiar with their wheelchair that it becomes part of them, as indicated by the users interviewed in this study. Users have stressed that an ideal power assist device would attach to their current and favorite manual wheelchair, preserving its current width, appearance and blend in with their wheelchair skills. Rather than forcing them to get a new wheelchair and learn to use it again. User's experience with power assist devices have meant that they have had to learn to use the wheelchair in an entirely different way, like if they have never used it before, especially with the e-motion wheels. Most power assist devices claim to offer assistance during everyday tasks; but in reality they offer assistance under their own conditions, which are frequently not representative of daily situations faced by manual wheelchair users.

The presentation of the outputs given to the users need to be improved, in particular outputs that do not require the user to take out a mobile and access an application. Alternatives to prevent the need of a "third hand" to handle a smartphone while propelling a wheelchair are needed. A possible chairable output and input device [10] we suggest is a thin flexible film LEDs or organic LED which combine touch sensitivity with luminosity [37], which could be attached to the wheelchair frame. Even greater interaction possibilities are possible as the assist devices are already detecting force which could be displayed to users to indicate effort or be used to activate/deactivate features. Another chairable device that power assist devices require is miniaturized network of sensors that should be able to sense the environment, for instance to identify the roughness of the surface travelled and be aware of people and other wheelchairs (to prevent unplanned collisions).

The results show that most users wish to maintain the social accessibility [48] of the wheelchair by preferring power assist devices that have minimal impact on the generally accepted appearance of the manual wheelchair. Evidently, there are users that give priority to functional accessibility over social accessibility, as seen in this study. Existing technology in power assisted bicycles could serve as a reference in order to create a power assist device capable of rotating the wheels through the axle and adding regenerative braking [19]. The alternative of propelling the wheelchair through the residual strength of the lower limbs is also possible [51]. Although some people and demographics (e.g. young adults) have suggested chairables, such as the LEDs on the handrim and clearly find these socially acceptable, these suggestions may not be the case for everyone [49]. Generally, personalization is an important factor in acceptability and one which requires further investigation.

The lack of will or motivation is a non physical barrier for wheelchair users that has been identified before [40]. Affective disorders (anxiety, depression, etc.) can cause muscular and joint pain and lack of attention to their immediate environment, which consequently can reduce the manual wheelchair propelling ability. Affective disorders can also cause apathy and carelessness which can put at risk the maintenance of the assistive technology. For instance, although there is no technical problem with the battery of power assistive devices, some users forget to charge the device overnight or not take care of delicate parts as they would when feeling positive and motivated. The technology to monitor the sympathetic nervous system and identify stress, arousal, engagement and excitement already exists [15]. We believe that power assist devices could be more responsive to the mental and physical status of the user and provide assistance not only based on requested power, surface roughness travelled, heart rate and fitness level but also based on the current affective disorders

Seven interviews were performed before the announcement of the MX2+ and PushTracker on December 2016. It incorporates some of the most interactive features ever seen in power assist devices such as a wrist worn device that works as a Fitbit [16] but modified in order to measure wheelchair pushes and other mobility actions. These are similar to the latest Apple Watch Series 2 [4] but with the advantage of being less power hungry. The MX2+ can also synchronize with a mobile application in order to track mobility activity over time. However, since the release of the PushTracker, users have had problems regarding the battery consumption of the PushTracker wristband (battery lasts 3 hours only) and with the Bluetooth connectivity from the PushTracker with the SmartDrive (extending the arm wearing the wristband, 10 to 15 cm away from the wheelchair cuts connectivity and the SmartDrive turns off) [42]. Therefore, the promised user interaction features are not living up to the expectation due to battery and Bluetooth connectivity issues caused under the normal shoulder range of motion. These could potentially have been mitigated by more of a participatory design approach to the technology, including user behavioral analysis. The SmartDrive MX2 and PushTracker has been released in the UK since March 2017, where possible, we recommend a detailed user study of this device.

Generally, user behavior analysis with biomechanics and participatory design would enable the identification of current or new ways in which the users interact with the technology. These should take account of cultural factors. For example, European wheelchair users use public transport (buses, trains, metro) more frequently than cars, whereas areas of the USA would have high car usage. Therefore assuming wheelchair users in Europe frequently ascend multiple ramps and make longer journeys to get to and from the public transport options, they may have a greater need for power-assist and are at greater risk of shoulder. Thus, the results of this study should be interpreted in the context of a public-transport centric city.

There are still HCI features that could be improved upon and other major design features which require a rather urgent redesigns (delicate handrims, hub-installed power assist devices, and heavy hardware). Recent technology could enable the distribution of the battery "body" by dividing it into smaller cells and allocating it along unobvious surfaces of the wheelchair, for instance, below the seat [28]. Some wheelchair users, when pushing the handrim, may push off the wheel rather than parallel and forward to the wheelchair due to reduced muscular force control. In these cases, gestures read by a wristband will need to offer alternative calibration for those gestures that the user is capable of performing. Similarly, people with a SCI very often have a combination of muscular weakness, spasms and lack of feeling, which may interfere with articulating inputs through a wristband. Learnings from this study are transferable to other assistive technology. For instance, reducing the weight of any chairable device but also accounting for the need of robustness and personalization.

Beyond the individual form factors presented in this study, we believe that an ideal power assist device would affordable and consist in a mechanism that can be installed below the wheelchair seat or behind it or in front of the wheelchair mounted on a handbike. With traditional tools and 3D printers, manual wheelchair users should have access to well explained, open source DIY alternative attachments that they could produce as they are or modify them to their needs. This information could be readily available through DIY online communities such as Instructables, Thingverse and other online blogs [27]. Low cost solutions have been developed for interacting with wheelchairs [9] but we could not find anyone designing a propelling assistance device that can be either fully mechanical or powered, that can keep its production costs low, be reparable by the owner, adaptable to individual needs and preserve the socially accepted appearance of the wheelchair. A high quality, low cost propelling assistance device would not only enable a greater number of wheelchair users in developed countries to increase their independence, but also those users in in-development countries.

7. CONCLUSION AND FUTURE WORK

In this study we have explored the physical and non-physical barriers that manual wheelchair users face when propelling their wheelchair. We have also identified specific situations in which users consider power assistance paramount and the social and functional accessibility of the power assist devices currently available in the UK market. We discussed similarities found among form factors of 12 individual ideal power assist devices. We have described a system that is installed below the seat of the wheelchair and that enables the detachment of batteries. We have also gathered previous literature and users experiences regarding the methods of attachment of power assist devices and found evidence that strongly points out that power assist devices installed at the hub of the wheels suffer from fatigue failure, are too heavy and fragile for daily use. We encourage power assist designers and manual wheelchair users to give preference to devices that are either installed behind, below or in front of the wheelchair.

We present opportunities to design outputs for users of power assist devices and improvements to be made to the current user interfaces such as implementing hand gestures with existing wristbands. Most users are comfortable with wearing a wrist band to control the device and interact with mobile applications. But chairable input and output devices that allow users to control the wheelchair power assist device without the need of a mobile phone or a wearable device are required. Power assist devices that enable interactions through mobile phones and wrist worn devices are starting to appear in the market however they require improvements in terms of battery capacity and Bluetooth connectivity.

Our suggestions included the identification of a great opportunity in improving the interaction with the user by monitoring emotions and by providing interactive visual outputs while propelling the wheelchair. We also suggest the need for the design of two open source wheelchair propelling assistance devices that could empower manual wheelchair users by being do-it-yourself: a fully mechanical version and a powered version.

Future work should consider the role of caregivers/support workers which push and pull wheelchairs and that could benefit from using power assist devices to make their caring work easier. In addition, a field test of the latest monitoring devices and HCI inputs should be investigated. A core design challenge in the future will be in reducing device weight, which we believe can be achieved using novel power methods and these should be investigated; in particular those which offer modular power options.

8. ACKNOWLEDGMENTS
We thank all the volunteers and our mentor for helping through the submission to ASSETS. The research is funded by the Engineering and Physical Sciences Research Council (EPSRC, EP/N022971/1) in partnership with the Queen Elizabeth Olympic Park, and forms part of the founding projects in the Global Disability Innovation Hub (GDIHub).

9. REFERENCES
1. Akbar, M., et al., *Prevalence of Rotator Cuff Tear in Paraplegic Patients Compared with Controls.* The Journal of Bone & Joint Surgery, 2010. **92**(1): p. 23-30.
2. Algood, S.D., et al., *Impact of a pushrim-activated power-assisted wheelchair on the metabolic demands, stroke frequency, and range of motion among subjects with tetraplegia.* Archives of Physical Medicine and Rehabilitation, 2004. **85**(11): p. 1865-1871.
3. Algood, S.D., et al., *Effect of a pushrim-activated power-assist wheelchair on the functional capabilities of persons with tetraplegia.* Archives of Physical Medicine and Rehabilitation, 2005. **86**(3): p. 380-386.
4. Apple Inc. *Physical and Motor Skill Accessibility - Apple Watch.* 2017 [cited 2017 8th January]; Available from: http://www.apple.com/uk/accessibility/watch/physical-and-motor-skills/.
5. Arva, J., et al., *Mechanical efficiency and user power requirement with a pushrim activated power assisted wheelchair.* Medical Engineering & Physics, 2001. **23**(10): p. 699-705.
6. Asheghan, M., et al., *The prevalence of carpal tunnel syndrome among long-term manual wheelchair users with spinal cord injury: A cross-sectional study.* The Journal of Spinal Cord Medicine, 2016. **39**(3): p. 265-271.
7. Batec Mobility S.L. *Batec Mobility - Add-on handbikes for wheelchairs: manual and power handbikes easy to attach to the wheelchair. Revolutionary anchoring system.* [cited 2017 8th January]; Available from: http://batec-mobility.com/en.
8. Braun, V. and V. Clarke, *Using thematic analysis in psychology.* Qualitative Research in Psychology, 2006. **3**(2): p. 77-101.
9. Buehler, E., et al., *Sharing is Caring: Assistive Technology Designs on Thingiverse,* in *Proceedings of the 33rd Annual ACM Conference on Human Factors in Computing Systems.* 2015, ACM: Seoul, Republic of Korea. p. 525-534.
10. Carrington, P., A. Hurst, and S.K. Kane, *Wearables and chairables: inclusive design of mobile input and output techniques for power wheelchair users,* in *Proceedings of the 32nd annual ACM conference on Human factors in computing systems.* 2014, ACM: Toronto, Ontario, Canada. p. 3103-3112.
11. Chow, J.W., et al., *Longitudinal stroke cycle characteristics of pushrim-activated power-assisted wheelchair propulsion.* Journal of Biomechanics, 2007. **40**(Suplement 2): p. S468.
12. Cooper, R.A., et al., *Evaluation of a pushrim-activated, power-assisted wheelchair.* Archives of Physical Medicine and Rehabilitation, 2001. **82**(5): p. 702-708.
13. Dalyan, M., D. Cardenas, and B. Gerard, *Upper extremity pain after spinal cord injury.* Spinal Cord, 1999. **37**(3): p. 191-195.
14. de Groot, S., et al., *Consequence of feedback-based learning of an effective hand rim wheelchair force production on mechanical efficiency.* Clinical Biomechanics, 2002. **17**(3): p. 219-226.
15. Empatica Inc. *Real time physiological signals - E4 EDA/GSR sensor wirstband.* 2017 [cited 2017 8th January]; Available from: https://www.empatica.com/e4-wristband.
16. Fitbit Inc. *Fitbit Official Site for Activity Trackers and More.* 2017 [cited 2017 8th January]; Available from: https://www.fitbit.com/uk.
17. Fullerton, H.D., J.J. Borckardt, and A.P. Alfano, *Shoulder Pain: A Comparison of Wheelchair Athletes and Nonathletic Wheelchair Users.* Medicine & Science in Sports & Exercise, 2003. **35**(12): p. 1958-1961.
18. Giacobbi, P.R.J., et al., *Wheelchair Users' Perceptions of and Experiences with Power Assist Wheels.* American Journal of Physical Medicine & Rehabilitation, 2010. **89**(3): p. 225-234.
19. Guarisco, M., F. Gao, and d. Paire, *Autonomy and User Experience Enhancement Control of an Electrically Assisted Bicycle With Dual-Wheel Drive.* IEEE Transactions on Industry Applications, 2017. **53**(2): p. 1476-1484.
20. Guillon, B., et al., *Evaluation of 3 Pushrim-Activated Power-Assisted Wheelchairs in Patients With Spinal Cord Injury.* Archives of Physical Medicine and Rehabilitation, 2015. **96**(5): p. 894-904.
21. Gupta, M., et al. *A comparison between smartphone sensors and bespoke sensor devices for wheelchair accessibility studies.* in *2015 IEEE Tenth International Conference on Intelligent Sensors, Sensor Networks and Information Processing (ISSNIP).* 2015.
22. Haubert, L.L., et al., *Comparison of Energy Expenditure and Propulsion Characteristics in a Standard and Three Pushrim-Activated Power-Assisted Wheelchairs.* Topics in Spinal Cord Injury Rehabilitation Fall, 2005. **11**(2): p. 64-73.
23. Holloway, C., et al. *Street rehab: Linking accessibility and rehabilitation.* in *2016 38th Annual International Conference of the IEEE Engineering in Medicine and Biology Society (EMBC).* 2016.
24. Holloway, C.S., et al. *Linking wheelchair kinetics to glenohumeral joint demand during everyday accessibility activities.* in *37th Annual International Conference of the IEEE Engineering in Medicine and Biology Society (EMBC).* 2015.
25. Howarth, S.J.a., et al., *Use of a geared wheelchair wheel to reduce propulsive muscular demand during ramp ascent: Analysis of muscle activation and kinematics.* Clinical Biomechanics, 2010. **25**(1): p. 21-28.
26. Hubbard, S., et al., *Poster 27: Characterizing Successful Pushrim-Activated Power-Assist Wheelchair Users.* Archives of Physical Medicine and Rehabilitation, 2007. **88**(10): p. e13.
27. Hurst, A. and S. Kane, *Making "making" accessible,* in *Proceedings of the 12th International Conference on Interaction Design and Children.* 2013, ACM: New York, New York, USA. p. 635-638.
28. Jervis, R., et al., *Design of a miniature flow cell for in situ x-ray imaging of redox flow batteries.* Journal of Physics D: Applied Physics, 2016. **49**(43): p. 434002.
29. Karmarkar, A., et al., *Evaluation of Pushrim-Activated Power-Assisted Wheelchairs Using ANSI/RESNA Standards.* Archives of Physical Medicine and Rehabilitation, 2008. **89**(6): p. 1191-1198.
30. Kloosterman, M.G.M., et al., *Exploration of shoulder load during hand-rim wheelchair start-up with and without power-assisted propulsion in experienced wheelchair users.* Clinical Biomechanics, 2016. **34 Supplement**(C): p. 1-6.
31. Kloosterman, M.G.M., et al., *A systematic review on the pros and cons of using a pushrim-activated power-assisted wheelchair.* Clinical Rehabilitation, 2013. **27**(4): p. 299-313.
32. Kloosterman, M.G.M., et al., *Effect of power-assisted hand-rim wheelchair propulsion on shoulder load in experienced wheelchair users: A pilot study with an instrumented wheelchair.* Medical Engineering & Physics, 2015. **37**(10): p. 961-968.
33. Kloosterman, M.G.M.a., et al., *Comparison of shoulder load during power-assisted and purely hand-rim wheelchair propulsion.* Clinical Biomechanics, 2012. **27**(5): p. 428-435.
34. Levy, C.E., et al., *Variable-ratio pushrim-activated power-assist wheelchair eases wheeling over a variety of terrains for elders.*

Archives of Physical Medicine and Rehabilitation, 2004. **85**(1): p. 104-112.

35. Levy, C.E.M.D., et al., *Use of Power Assist Wheels Results in Increased Distance Traveled Compared with Conventional Manual Wheeling.* American Journal of Physical Medicine & Rehabilitation, 2010. **89**(8): p. 625-634.

36. Lighthall-Haubert, L., et al., *Comparison of Shoulder Muscle Electromyographic Activity During Standard Manual Wheelchair and Push-Rim Activated Power Assisted Wheelchair Propulsion in Persons With Complete Tetraplegia.* Archives of Physical Medicine and Rehabilitation, 2009. **90**(11): p. 1904-1915.

37. LTM Consortium. *Light.Touch.Matters | The product is the interface.* [cited 2017 11th January]; Available from: http://www.light-touch-matters-project.eu/index.php?tag=home.

38. MAX Mobility. *PushTracker - MAX Mobility.* 2016 [cited 2017 8th January]; Available from: http://www.max-mobility.com/pushtracker.

39. Mercer, J.L., et al., *Shoulder joint kinetics and pathology in manual wheelchair users.* Clinical Biomechanics, 2006. **21**(8): p. 781-789.

40. Meyers, A.R., et al., *Barriers, facilitators, and access for wheelchair users: sbstantive and methodologic lessons from a pilot study of environmental effects.* Social Science & Medicine, 2002. **55**(8): p. 1435-1446.

41. MEYRA GmbH. *Servomatic, MEYRA.* 2017 [cited 2017 24th March]; Available from: https://www.meyra.de/hmv-suche/hmv-details/product-446/.

42. Milgate, N., *Current issues of the SmartDrive MX2 and Pushtracker,* M.R. Dafne Zuleima, Editor. 2017, Equipment for the Physically Challenged (EPC) Wheelchairs Ltd.: London, United Kingdom.

43. Nash, M.S., et al., *Power-Assisted Wheels Ease Energy Costs and Perceptual Responses to Wheelchair Propulsion in Persons With Shoulder Pain and Spinal Cord Injury.* Archives of Physical Medicine and Rehabilitation, 2008. **89**(11): p. 2080-2085.

44. Pavlidou, E., et al., *Rolling resistance and propulsion efficiency of manual and power-assisted wheelchairs.* Medical Engineering & Physics, 2015. **37**(11): p. 1105-1110.

45. Raspberri Pi Foundation. *Raspberry Pi - Teach, Learn and Make with Raspberry Pi.* 2017 [cited 2017 8th January]; Available from: https://www.raspberrypi.org/.

46. Rimmer, J.H., et al., *Physical activity participation among persons with disabilities.* American Journal of Preventive Medicine, 2004. **26**(5): p. 419-425.

47. Sabick, M.B., B.R. Kotajarvi, and K.-N. An, *A new method to quantify demand on the upper extremity during manual wheelchair propulsion1.* Archives of Physical Medicine and Rehabilitation, 2004. **85**(7): p. 1151-1159.

48. Shinohara, K. and J.O. Wobbrock, *Self-Conscious or Self-Confident? A Diary Study Conceptualizing the Social Accessibility of Assistive Technology.* ACM Trans. Access. Comput., 2016. **8**(2): p. 1-31.

49. Shinohara, K. and J.O. Wobbrock, *In the shadow of misperception: assistive technology use and social interactions,* in *Proceedings of the SIGCHI Conference on Human Factors in Computing Systems.* 2011, ACM: Vancouver, BC, Canada. p. 705-714.

50. Slowik, J.S., et al., *The influence of wheelchair propulsion hand pattern on upper extremity muscle power and stress.* Journal of Biomechanics, 2016. **49**(9): p. 1554-1561.

51. Stein, R.B., et al., *Improved efficiency with a wheelchair propelled by the legs using voluntary activity or electric stimulation.* Archives of Physical Medicine and Rehabilitation, 2001. **82**(9): p. 1198-1203.

52. Sunrise Medical LLC. *WheelDrive wheelchair power assist.* 2016 [cited 2017 8th January]; Available from: http://www.sunrisemedical.eu/wheelchairs/quickie/wheelchair-power-assist-wheeldrive.

53. Sunrise Medical LLC. *Quickie Xtender Power Assist Wheelchair Accessory.* 2016 [cited 2017 8th January]; Available from: http://www.sunrisemedical.com/manual-wheelchairs/quickie/manual-power-assist/xtender.

54. Ulrich Alber GmbH. *Wheelchair Drives.* 2017 [cited 2017 8th January]; Available from: https://www.alber.de/en/products/wheelchair-drive.html.

55. Weed, M., *Capturing the essence of grounded theory: the importance of understanding commonalities and variants.* Qualitative Research in Sport, Exercise and Health, 2017. **9**(1): p. 149-156.

56. Wheelchair Leadership Alliance. *NHS England - Improving wheelchair services.* 2017 [cited 2017 26th April]; Available from: https://www.england.nhs.uk/ourwork/pe/wheelchair-services/.

57. World Health Organization. *Assistive Technology, Fact Sheet.* 2016 [cited 2017 11th April]; Available from: http://www.who.int/mediacentre/factsheets/assistive-technology/en/.

58. World Health Organization, International Society for Prosthetics and Orthotics, and United States Agency International Development, *Guidelines on the provision of manual wheelchairs in less-resourced settings.* 2008, Geneva, Switzerland. 131.

Understanding Fatigue and Stamina Management Opportunities and Challenges in Wheelchair Basketball

Patrick Carrington, Denzel Ketter, Amy Hurst
Department of Information Systems
University of Maryland, Baltimore County
Baltimore, Marlyand 21250 USA
{carpat1,dketter1,amyhurst}@umbc.edu

ABSTRACT
Wearable fitness devices have demonstrated the capacity to improve overall fitness and athletic performance. Previous research has identified a need for these technologies to take into consideration a broader range of abilities to create more inclusive fitness communities. The adaptive sports community offers opportunities to explore technology use within a specialized community wherein physical activity is central to its identity. In this paper, we explore the current use and future potential of fitness technologies for stamina and fatigue management in wheelchair basketball, a team-based sport originally created for paraplegic athletes. We present findings from observations, seven interviews, and a survey (76 responses) with wheelchair basketball players and coaches. We present findings relating to their experience with and interest in automatic tracking of fatigue and stamina related metrics for themselves and their players.

CCS Concepts
• **Social and professional topics~People with disabilities**

Keywords
Wheelchair Basketball; Wearable; Fitness; Stamina and Fatigue Management; Adaptive Sports;

1. INTRODUCTION
Wearable technology continues to thrive and be a popular and controversial topic today. Recently, there has been a growing interest in the development of wearable fitness technologies which are suitable for people with a broader range of attributes and abilities. While many fitness devices still function primarily for able-bodied individuals, some consumer devices, such as the Apple Watch 2, have taken deliberate action to develop features specifically for users with disabilities. In addition, research projects have targeted the design and development of mobile and wearable fitness technologies for use by people with disabilities [3],[11],[17]. However, more research is needed to understand the role that wearable devices can serve for wheelchair sports to build more inclusive fitness communities.

ASSETS '17, October 29-November 1, 2017, Baltimore, MD, USA

ACM 978-1-4503-4926-0/17/10...$15.00
https://doi.org/10.1145/3132525.3132543

Figure 1. Wheelchair Basketball is one of the world's most popular adaptive sports. It is a team sport that incorporates multiple roles and is designed to be inclusive of people with differing abilities.

Adaptive sports provide an opportunity to explore physical activity within a context where there is a baseline of physical activity relating to participation in a sport. For team sports, like wheelchair basketball, there are formally defined roles, a structure of activities (e.g. training, practice, competition, etc.), and multiple people who have both individual and shared goals. Wheelchair basketball incorporates different competition levels, and people with a range of functional abilities. The sport is also structured to support inclusion of these different functional and competitive levels, in part, through their use of a functional classification system. This makes wheelchair basketball an ideal sport to study.

Quantification has been shown to contribute positively to performance and training for sports [21]. Stamina and Fatigue are an important aspect of team and player/athlete management in all competitive sports. The US Women's soccer team uses Polar heart rate monitors during their training to provide insight to coaches and develop athlete-specific training routines. Also, the World Champion German Men's Soccer team described their use of the Adidas miCoach platform and its contributions to their success in the 2014 World Cup. We use fatigue and stamina management to focus our investigation and contextualize the results among other technologies used in competitive athletics.

In this paper, we investigate the current use and potential of wearable fitness technologies for stamina and fatigue management in the sport of wheelchair basketball. We conducted an interview study with five wheelchair basketball players and two wheelchair basketball coaches to understand habits, practices, and opportunities for fitness tracking technologies. Following the interviews, we conducted a survey with 76 wheelchair basketball players and coaches to learn about their interest in automatically tracking fatigue and stamina related metrics for themselves and their players.

Research Question. We aim to answer the following research question:

1) How can we design mobile and/or wearable technologies for wheelchair basketball players to support stamina and fatigue management?

To answer our primary research question, we must also consider the context in which this technology would be used. Thus, we also address the following questions:

a) What is wheelchair basketball and how does it differ from "stand up" basketball?
b) Who are the stakeholders involved in stamina and fatigue management in wheelchair basketball?

2. RELATED WORK

2.1 Automatic Tracking and Fitness Technologies

Pedometers have been used to record step counts and have been used to improve participation in physical activities[5],1]. Today's wearable fitness devices often build on this and can capture this information and more. Many of the commercially available wearable fitness devices, such as the Fitbit[1], can track information such as step count, calorie expenditure, and overall physical activity by tracking motion. Morris et al.'s [12] Recofit system used an armband to capture repetitive motions for strength training which makes it possible to count repetitions when lifting weights or stretching. The commercially available Microsoft Band[2] can measure many details such as distance, calories burned, motion activity, sleep activity, heart rate, steps taken, and skin temperature from a single device. In contrast, people also may use multiple devices to track these features.

Quantified Self (QS) describes the social and technical movement surrounding tracking data about one's habits and using that objective data to learn and understand one's habits [14]. MacLeod et al. [10] explored the motivations and opportunities for personal informatics to be used by people with chronic illnesses. They described the disparity between presumed and actual motivations for self-tracking and behavior change. In this case, having an understanding and control over their data motivated participants to self-track.

Whooley et al. [23] described the integration of multiple data sources to identify correlations between actions such as sleep and cognitive performance. Through the process of reflection and reintegration, the data can be used in many more ways than simply direct measurement. In addition, Rooksby et al. [18] discussed how people use tracking data from different sources. A single tracker may not give a full representation of a person's activity. They also point out that reviewing and sharing data with others can create new connections and provide a platform for sharing experiences. For this research, we explore and build on these ideas and capabilities to identify opportunities for wearable fitness devices to support wheelchair basketball players.

2.2 Stamina and Fatigue Management in Competitive Sports

In professional and collegiate sports, managing the health of the athletes is essential to the success of the team. Athletes are expected to perform at the peak of their ability whenever they compete and to improve they are routinely asked to perform at or beyond the edge of their abilities. Over time, performance will inevitably decrease, but strategies can be implemented to understand and reduce the performance impact. This constant boundary pushing puts a strain on the body and if not properly managed can lead to fatigue and/or injury.

Several strategies have been employed for stamina and fatigue management in competitive sports. The most effective methods involve detailed analytics, constant assessment, and are multi-faceted interventions including detailed exercise programs, nutrition regimens, mental training, and rest [1],[1][1]. Often these programs involve a significant mental training and awareness component where athletes must learn about their own bodies and abilities. Technology has been used as an effective tool to support physiological awareness and learning about one's body.

2.3 Fitness Devices for People with Disabilities

Specifically, this work focuses on fitness devices for people with motor impairments. Researchers have begun to identify a research agenda and illuminate important implications for the design of mobile fitness technologies for people with disabilities. However, more research is needed to understand the potential for wearable fitness devices among people with disabilities.

Currently, the Apple Watch with watchOS 2.0 update is the only consumer-available wearable fitness device with features to specifically address wheelchair use. It offers a wheelchair mode, which enables the ability track pushes instead of steps, and converts some exercises to be more appropriate for someone using a wheelchair.

Few research projects have explored fitness tracking for people with motor impairments. Carrington et al. [3] and Malu and Findlater [11] introduced several accessibility challenges relating to the design of fitness devices for people with motor impairments. Both Carrington et al. and Malu et al. took a general perspective on the accessibility of wearable fitness devices for people with motor impairments to identify accessibility challenges associated with using wearable fitness devices, in general. This paper identifies opportunities for the use of automatic tracking particularly for wheelchair basketball players.

3. OBSERVATIONS OF WHEELCHAIR BASKETBALL AT THE NWBT

The National Wheelchair Basketball Tournament (NWBT) attracts hundreds of athletes, annually. It is managed by the National Wheelchair Basketball Association (NWBA) We attended the tournament for the past two years (2016 and 2017) to observe the community and learn more about wheelchair basketball, the NWBA, and the rules and practices of the sport.

In 2016, we observed interactions within the community and had informal conversations with community members, players, coaches, and tournament staff. These observations informed the design of our future interviews observations at the tournament in 2017.

[1] http://www.Fitbit.com/

[2] http://www.microsoft.com/microsoft-band/

Participants in the fitness technology interviews mentioned that different factors of the games including game speed, scheduling, and availability of substitute players impacted their management of fatigue. During the 2017 tournament, we looked for examples of these factors and recruited for the survey and other future studies.

Competition Levels. At the NWBT, there are three levels of competition for adults: Division I, Division II, and Division III. All three of these divisions are co-ed. The NWBA also governs a collegiate division, with Men's and Women's teams, and manages the US National Wheelchair Basketball Team. Division I through III are based on the level of competition with I being the highest and III being the lowest. Players in the collegiate division may also play on a division I, II, or III team, or the national team. Elite players from any division may be selected for the National team.

Game Speed and Competition Level. We observed that Division I level games moved at a faster pace because players tended to move at higher speeds. We also observed that Division I games tended to also have a lot of time when the clock is stopped for different in game events, timeouts, fouls, and short pauses. These in-game events allow the athletes to pause for a moment before resuming the high-intensity activities of the game. This also occurred in Division II and III games, but with longer pauses and overall the pace of the games was slower.

Functional Classification and Inclusive Competition. The functional classification system is used to group players into categories based on their physical ability to execute fundamental basketball movements (Table 2). Each player is assigned a class from 1.0 to 4.5 based on their abilities. This classification is used to ensure every player has an equal right and opportunity to be an integral member of a team. According to NWBA rules, each team is allowed a maximum of 15 points total for the five active players on the court at any given time. This ensures a balance of the total functional abilities for each team.

The functional abilities of players can vary significantly and not all wheelchair basketball players used a wheelchair when they were not playing. At the end of a game, some people will roll to the sideline unstrap from their chairs and walk away. It is difficult to tell what a player's functional classification might be unless you are trained to do so. For instance, one may confuse a physical limitation for fatigue or a fatigue-related response. The classification process involves watching and interviewing individual players by a panel of classification reviewers to receive an official classification. This is one of the other roles that the NWBT serves for this community. All classifications are verified during the registration process for the tournament to ensure that no team has an unfair advantage.

Fatigue Related Incidents. At the tournament, there is a medical staff onsite in case of injuries or other emergencies. Most of these incidents involved cuts or other physical injuries. However, there were also a few instances where people received medical treatment due to fatigue, overheating, or fainting. While we observed very few of these events, it is one extreme situation relating to fatigue that could be prevented with the right prior information. These observations informed this work and the idea for automatic tracking of this information.

4. FITNESS TECHNOLOGY INTERVIEWS

We conducted semi-structured interviews with five wheelchair basketball players and two wheelchair basketball coaches. The interviews focused on understanding the opportunities for using fitness tracking technologies for wheelchair basketball.

4.1 Participants

Participant details are in Table 1. Participants were volunteers and were recruited through the National Wheelchair Basketball Association, via email, and by word of mouth. All participants in the interviews were compensated for their time.

4.2 Interview Structure

The semi-structured interviews were approximately 30 minutes and consisted of the following sections.

4.2.1 Background (~5 minutes)

This section covered demographic information about the participants, their amount of experience with wheelchair basketball, and roles they have on their wheelchair basketball teams. For players, we also covered information about their basketball wheelchair and official classification.

4.2.2 Experience with Mobile Tracking (~5 minutes)

We asked participants to describe any previous experiences they have had with mobile or wearable fitness tracking technology. We asked about their overall impressions of the devices and the experience of using them.

4.2.3 Current and Desired Tracking and Training Activities (~15 minutes)

We asked participants about the activities that they are currently tracking with respect to their individual training, team practices, and competition. These activities included sport specific statistics, drills, metrics, performance assessments, as well as fitness related activities. We also asked about desired or potential activities that participants would like to automatically track using mobile or wearable technologies.

4.2.4 Ideal Mobile Tracking Solution (~5 minutes)

In this section, we asked participants to describe their ideal mobile tracking solution or device and its capabilities. We asked participants to describe the potential benefits of this proposed technology. We also asked questions about any existing restrictions that might limit the use of such a technology in training, practice, or during competition.

4.3 Analysis

Each interview was transcribed and coded. We used a thematic analysis approach to code the interview data and identify relevant themes based on the interview transcripts and field notes from observations. Resulting themes included device requirements, fatigue management, past experiences, wheelchair basketball routines, tracking behaviors, and desired information.

4.4 INTERVIEW FINDINGS

The findings from the preliminary interviews will be presented in the following subsections based on the structure of the interview provided above.

Table 2. Description of the functional classification system. Adapted from NWBA functional classification descriptions http://www.nwba.org/page/show/2023335-functional-classification.

Class	Description
1.0	No active movement of the trunk in the vertical, forward or sideways plane.
1.5	Has characteristics of a class 1.0, but more trunk stability
2.0	Has active use of upper trunk in the vertical and forward planes, able to rotate the upper trunk while upright in both directions, able to hold the ball forward with both arms extended, able to lean the trunk into the forward plane about 45 degrees with control and return to the upright sitting position, able to actively bring upper trunk off the backrest of the chair, and uses hands to return to upright of trunk if no thighs-unless knees are significantly higher than the hips.
2.5	Has characteristics of class 2.0, but able to lean forward and return to upright sitting position possibly with difficulty
3.0	Displays active use of the upper and lower trunk in the forward and vertical planes: Can lean forward 90 degrees, placing chest on thighs and return to upright with ease without knees significantly higher than hips, can hold the ball with both hands outstretched in front of face without loss of stability, can rotate upper and lower trunk as a unit not supported by wheelchair backrest, rotation of the trunk occurs at the level of the pelvis not the waist, unable to maintain stability leaning sideways, and works within a 'Cylinder'
3.5	Has characteristics of a class 3.0, but able to move partially out into the sideways plane and return to upright sitting, able to remain upright in hard contact situations forward, able to sit with hips higher than knees, often raises and lowers trunk with each push, able to generate some power in legs with pushing, able to retrieve a ball with two hands on the floor slightly to the side and return to upright position, can lean to the side but remains within his base of support, plays within a WIDER cylinder than a Class 3.0 player, does not have full volume of action to either side.
4.0	Displays the ability to move the trunk maximally in all planes of movement with weakness to one side, has one strong side and one weaker side, can hold the ball with outstretched hands in front or overhead without loss of stability even in contact situations, no need to counterbalance even in contact situations unless contact is forceful and directed into the weaker side.
4.5	Displays the ability to move the trunk maximally in all planes of movement with no significant weakness in any direction, full volume of action in all planes, displays ability to lean to either side during shooting, passing, contesting a shot or trying to intercept a pass.

Table 1. Demographics and Background of Participants

ID	Age	Gender	Years Exp.	Class	Occupation
P1*	ND	Male	25	N/A	Coach
P2	26	Male	15	1.0	Academic Advisor
P3*	31	Female	3	N/A	Adaptive Sports Coordinator
P4	26	Male	14	1.0	Engineer
P5	34	Male	20+	2.5	Receptionist
P6	38	Male	7	1.0	Recreational Director
P7	23	Male	<1	3.0	Accountant

*This participant was a coach

4.4.1 Previous Experience with Tracking

Participating in organized competitive wheelchair basketball exposed each of our participants to some aspect of tracking or quantifying their performance. However, for the purposes of this research we focused on automatic tracking using some type of mobile or wearable device. Three of the five players had experience using a mobile or wearable fitness tracker.

P2 used a Fitbit but did not have a great experience with it:

"I have tried a Fitbit for a little bit, for a little while...but I had troubles with it actually tracking how much activity I had. I mean like I don't take steps of course but I got to the end of the day and it had 500 steps for example. or umm the actual miles. all the calculations seemed roughly quite off. umm I don't know it just doesn't recognize movements the same way... but it definitely wasn't correct..."

"I tried it for 2...2 weeks I think. [I got it because] I liked the idea behind the accountability you could have with other people. umm to kind of push each other. for me it didn't do a whole lot for me." -P2, Player

P4 also used a Fitbit but had a better impression and still uses the device:

"I have a Fitbit... um it tracks it does track my steps and heart rate and calories burned and all that sorta stuff. um I just have the simple version of the Fitbit I don't have the fancy one with the touch screen and all that...Yeah, I find it useful I like it. It does keep track of things pretty well I feel like. so I do like it...I've had it for a little over a year now..." –P4, Player

P5 owns an Apple Watch and likes what it currently does for him, but would like it to do more:

"I do have an Apple Watch. That I use... I think it works pretty well you know there's a few things that I don't that I don't necessarily care for like it doesn't. It keeps track of your pushes but it doesn't keep track of the miles you know so it will tell you you've done 2000 pushes but I'm like ' well how far is that?' but I guess it's kind of push is different for everyone"

– P5, Player

The remaining two players did not have direct experience with automatic tracking but had either seen or heard of others using fitness devices.

4.4.1.1 Summary of Previous Experience

Participants had mixed experiences with fitness tracking devices. Three players had direct experience with a device either a Fitbit or Apple Watch. Two participants were not satisfied with the information provided by their devices. One participant stopped using the device because of this. The other participants had not used a device themselves.

4.4.2 Current and Desired Tracking and Training Activities

Current Activities. Participants mentioned several activities that they currently track as part of their training and preparation:

P4 described how he wears his Fitbit, measures the time it takes for him to perform different exercises, and his shooting percentages:

"When I have been training, I like to like time certain exercises in terms of agility and speed and that sort of thing. And then in terms of shooting just kind of count uh percentage wise say I shoot 50 shots form a spot um just kind of keep track of how many makes and a percentage." – P4, Player

P5 mentioned using his Apple Watch to track his activities in practice:

"I use it when I work out. just uh when I'm playing basketball I'll war it at practice and stuff just to know how far I've gone or whatever, you know, as far as pushes and you know burning calories it keeps track of that and you know your heart rate and all that fun stuff too." – P5, Player

Coaches Perspective

P1 described how as a coach measuring and assessing performance is part of the regular routine for training:

"We do preseason testing...testing for med ball throws, chin ups, bench press, baseline to free throw sprint and then 20meter sprint, with and without the ball...[We measure] time and power output...We have laser timers for all of our sprint work.

We'll do 30-minute drill every day and they have to complete it and give us their time. So for beginners they'll come in and it'll take them the whole 30 minutes. Our guys that have been here 3-4-5 years they can now complete it in 18-21 minutes. So, we use that kind of as a bench mark for fitness." – P1, Coach

Desired Activities. In addition, participants expressed an interest in tracking the following metrics and activities:

P2 was interested in tracking the distance travelled as well as speed and acceleration:

"I don't know if you ever see an NFL game I think it would be interesting to see the distance travelled. Some people might go straight down the court and back. other people are picking, and they're um hand on the ball and going around all sorts of people., you know they might travel twice as far in the same vertical distance." –P2, Player

"I think uhh different speeds like a top speed or acceleration track could be measured. or like stopping distance. Like somebody is flying down the court and they they power stop how quickly do they stop. a deceleration over a long range?"

–P2, Player

P4 described his desire for having something to give warning signs for fatigue before it becomes a problem:

"Instead of waiting to actually feel tired and waiting for that fatigue to actually set in if this technology can like give you a sign beforehand. like hey you're running low or you're slowing down type of thing. um that could kind of be proactive and prevent that. that fatigue from setting in." – P4, Player and Coach

He also mentioned that heart rate could be beneficial for measuring fatigue:

"I think heart rate would be beneficial. I don't know what else I don't have a great medical background in terms of signs and stuff for fatigue that would be useful for that."

– P4, Player and Coach

Coaches Perspective

In addition to individual metrics described by and for individual players, coaches were also interested in determining the position of players on the court at different times:

"Their movement their position um where they are and let's say a certain player you can pull that up and say look on this play you were over here whereas maybe you should have been in this position type of thing." – P4, Player and Coach

4.4.2.1 Summary of Current and Desired Tracking

Players and coaches engaged in tracking different activities currently. Two players described using their existing devices to track their physical activity during practices. Coaches also described their measurement and tracking routines. They also described desired tracking activities, providing individual metrics of interest such as distance travelled, heart rate, player movements, and positions.

4.4.3 Ideal Mobile Tracking Solution

Participants suggested locations on the wheelchair to attach devices and sensors. P2 suggested a location under the seat of the chair would be a safe place:

"There's like a cross bar under there um that doesn't have direct contact with other wheelchairs so if you fall down you're not going to crunch it. If there was a way to secure it to that I think that would be the probably safest point." – P2, Player

He also suggested that wearing something on the body might also be permitted:

"I mean yeah you could wear a head band or a sleeve, an arm band...I don't know if you could integrate it into one of those...I don't see any reason why a ref would tell you to take it off." – P2, Player

P4 also suggested that wearing a chest strap for respiration might be desirable. P5 described his desire for something that could attach to his chair but also something that might contact the body:

"You could possibly use it if it was attached to the chair someway for sure. and it wasn't so big and bulky you don't want it to be heavy. but like a wrist band would work. and then also we have like a click strap which are basically like ski straps that clench down into your chair. If you could figure out most people have wrist bands that they put over the clicky part to keep you from, you know getting jabbed by it if you fall on them, so something in there could work. If you could figure that out, it'd be a good place for something." – P5, Player

The descriptions of an ideal mobile tracking solution seemed to be as much about what to track as how and when it is tracked. Participants identified important considerations for both personal preference and adherence to the rules, regulations, and practices of people who play the sport.

"Everybody pushes harder in games. everybody goes harder in games. um you may not get the same effect in practice when maybe you're not going at 100% or you're not in that high speed environment of a game. so, I think it would be more beneficial in game." – P4, Player

P7's discussed how a device that detected movement and speed information might useful at the national level of competition:

"I think probably to have like a national level it would probably apply the most. I don't see why you wouldn't want to do that if you're at the national level and if I were them I would already be doing that. I just think at that point its one way to measure yeah measure any type of show or perform with it. and I just think from a health perspective there some way to kind of motivate." – P7, Player

He also described that such a device might also be useful for people at every level but would likely be too expensive for newer players, like him, to make that kind of investment. Three other participants also mentioned that tracking information like this might be most useful at elite or national levels, since they are more likely to use that type of "analytical information".

Coaches Perspective

Coaches confirmed possible form factors by were generally interested in having more information about their players. One coach described the lack of options out there and the opportunity for improvement:

"It is a wide-open space. There's nothing out there but we definitely need information if were gonna maximize our training with our athletes just like with the able-bodied athletes." – P1, Coach

4.4.3.1 Summary of Ideal Mobile Tracking Solution

Participants described that a solution for mobile tracking might involve attaching sensors or devices to the wheelchair. These devices would need to be attached in such a way that they would be shielded or out of reach from collisions or contact with other players. On-body sensing devices would need to take on the form factors of existing, approved, athletic equipment. This includes headbands, hats, a chest strap or fabric. Both coaches and players were interested in new information regarding their performance. However, given that few people use devices every day, participants especially one coach felt that there is an unmet need for more information.

4.5 Summary of Fitness Tech Interviews

Participants in the interviews had some experience with automatic tracking for fitness but, as expected, all were concerned with their performance and assessment of their goals or team's goals. Specific metrics such as heart rate, number of pushes, and speed were mentioned as well as several different basketball related activities or situations for when this information might be useful. These interviews were used to focus our observations and survey questions. The results from the interviews informed the design of the survey questions including desired metrics and activities.

5. NWBT SURVEY

We conducted a survey to learn more about wheelchair basketball players' and coaches' interest in automatic tracking for stamina and fatigue management. Specifically, we were interested in the following questions:

1) How interested are players and coaches in automatic tracking for fatigue and stamina management?
2) What are players' and coaches' motivation for automatically tracking stamina and fatigue related data?
3) What are the potential benefits of collecting this information?
4) What concerns do players and coaches have with automatically tracking this kind of data?
5) What form factor preferences do players and coaches have for devices to automatically track this data?

5.1 Survey Design

The survey consisted of 19 questions and took approximately 10-15 minutes to complete. We designed the survey to be short so it could be completed during breaks at the tournament, while allowing an opportunity for participants to take part in future interviews. The survey was divided into 2 main sections, one for players and the other for coaches. If a person was a player, but had no experience with coaching, they were not presented with the section for coaches, and vice versa. Each of the two sections consisted of ~9 questions asking about the following:

- Levels of competition (National, Division I,II,III)
- Functional classification (Table 2)
- Overall Interest in Automatic Tracking of S&F
- Interest in- Stamina and Fatigue related metrics (derived from interviews)
- Open-ended questions about motivations, potential benefits, and concerns related to automatic tracking

The survey was administered online through Google Forms and available for two weeks following the start of the tournament.

5.2 NWBT Survey Results

The survey link was shared with all players and coaches who registered with an adult team at the 2017 NWBT (48 teams). There was a total of 94 responses. We checked the responses for erroneous data (entering short answers to numerical questions etc.) and incomplete responses (blank sections, multiple skipped questions, etc.) and removed those entries. We ended with a total of 76 responses representing 59 players, 7 coaches, and 10 who were both players and coaches. Each of the five adult competitive divisions and eight functional classes are represented in the sample (Table 3 and Table 4). The results of the survey are summarized in the following subsections.

5.2.1 Interest in Automatic Tracking

Participants were asked to indicate their level of interest in automatic tracking both overall and their interest in specific metrics on a 5-point scale from "Not Interested" to "Extremely Interested". Overall, the results of the survey confirm that there is interest from both players and coaches in automatically tracking this kind of information. More than 85% of players and more than 97% of coaches indicating that they were at least "Somewhat Interested" in tracking. The distributions of overall interest levels are shown in Table 5. Coaches were extremely interested in automatic tracking because of the benefits it could provide their team in the form of information.

Table 3. Highest Competition levels for Players and Coaches.

Players		Coaches	
(Inter-) National	6	(Inter-) National	2
Division I	15	D1	2
Division II	20	D2	3
Division III	20	D3	5
College	8	College	2
		Varsity	3
Total	69	Total	17

Table 4. Functional Classification of Survey Participants

Classification	Number of Players
1.0	10
1.5	4
2.0	8
2.5	11
3.0	9
3.5	4
4.0	9
4.5	10
Not Provided	4
Total	69

Table 5. Overall Interest in automatic tracking of stamina and fatigue for Players and Coaches.

	Players (n=69)*	Coaches (n=17)*
Extremely Interested	18.8%	43.8%
Very Interested	24.6%	18.8%
Somewhat Interested	42.0%	31.3%
Slightly Interested	13.0%	6.3%
Not Interested	1.4%	0.0%

***These sample includes 10 responses from players who were also coaches. These responses were counted for both groups.**

We also asked participants to rate their interest in specific metrics that were identified through the interviews. Those metrics included "Number of pushes", "Movement/Speed", "Heart Rate", "Distance Travelled", and "Respiration". Only coaches were given the option for "Position of players" due to an interest expressed during an interview. Coaches wanted to know whether players are in correct the positions, or locations, at different times. The results are summarized in Table 6 and Table 7.

Table 6. Distribution of level of interest in individual metrics of players about themselves.

	Extremely Interested	Very Interested	Somewhat Interested	Slightly Interested	Not Interested
Number of Pushes	20.3%	31.9%	34.8%	7.2%	5.8%
Movement/ Speed	34.8%	37.7%	17.4%	7.2%	2.9%
Heart Rate	26.1%	36.2%	26.1%	8.7%	2.9%
Distance Travelled	29.0%	24.6%	34.8%	8.7%	2.9%
Respiration	30.4%	36.2%	24.6%	8.7%	0.0%

Table 7. Distribution of level of interest for individual metrics of coaches for about their players.

	Extremely Interested	Very Interested	Somewhat Interested	Slightly Interested	Not Interested
Number of Pushes	52.9%	29.4%	5.9%	11.8%	0.0%
Movement/ Speed	82.4%	11.8%	5.9%	0.0%	0.0%
Heart Rate	52.9%	35.3%	11.8%	0.0%	0.0%
Distance Travelled	47.1%	23.5%	11.8%	5.9%	11.8%
Respiration	64.7%	23.5%	11.8%	0.0%	0.0%
Position of Players	52.9%	17.6%	29.4%	0.0%	0.0%

5.2.2 Device Form Factor Preferences

Survey participants were asked to indicate their preferred form factors for a device by choosing from four options shown in Table 8. Each participant could cast multiple votes for multiple options. For players (91 total votes), "something that could attach to either" receiving the most votes, followed by "part something you wear and part something attached to the chair", then "something that attaches to your chair", and finally "something you wear on your body". The results for coaches (23 total votes) were similar. However, there were equal number of votes for "something that attaches to your chair" and "part something you wear and part something attached to the chair". Form factor results are summarized below in Table 8.

Table 8. Summary of form factor preferences indicated by survey participants.

Form Factors [Something worn on]	Players (For Self)	Coaches (For Players)
Body	12	3
Chair	19	5
Either, Body OR Chair	34	10
Both, Body AND Chair	26	5
Total	91	23

6. DISCUSSION

6.1 Fatigue Management – Self vs Team

Overall, fatigue and stamina management are important to playing the game of wheelchair basketball and being competitive. However, there is an interesting transition from different levels of competition. One of the most important distinctions to make is that of the player and the coach. First, players are interested in automatic tracking primarily for self-management of their own performance. In contrast, coaches are interested in their players' information primarily to manage the team, and secondary to manage individual players.

There were several central ideas relevant to the discussion of fatigue management that we noticed through the observations, interviews, and survey.

Awareness. One such idea is this concept of awareness. Four players were interested in learning more about themselves and having a better sense of their bodies. All three coaches expressed interest in improving their awareness of their players. As stated by one player and two coaches, managing fatigue is often a shared responsibility between player and coach.

There is a difference between what a player may want for their own self-management and what that same person may want when assuming the role of a coach. This appears to be related to the idea of awareness. As a coach, your job is to manage the team and thus rely on information to make informed decisions and plan strategy.

Management of Individual Training. Two coaches and three players described the benefits of knowing more about individual players, to better tailor training programs to individual needs and set better individual goals. As demonstrated by the Olympic soccer teams' example[3,4], this can make a huge difference when preparing for intense competition and keeping players healthy. This idea has been explored briefly through a pilot study which provided a data set relating to player activities in rugby and basketball [21]. The researchers suggested that the dataset might be useful in replicating game conditions during practice sessions. Our findings also support this use case for automatically tracked information. In addition to game information, players may take advantage of recorded metrics to compare their performance across practices or for assessment purposes.

Management of Team Strategy. Two coaches and one player described the coach's responsibility of managing team strategy and substitutions. Given the functional classification requirements for active players, it is important to make smart decisions when substituting players. Coaches in the survey mentioned one of the potential benefits would be if the automatic tracking would be able to assist with managing their line-ups. A participant in the interviews also mentioned this idea of making smarter substitutions based on automatically tracked real time information.

6.2 Movement and Biomechanics

Athletes and coaches were excited about the idea of automatically tracking motion and muscle activity as they related to the biomechanics of the different motions they make. For instance, one participant was intrigued by the idea of being able to better understand his muscle activity as he performed pushes in different situations to ensure he was getting the most power that he could out of every push. One survey participant also mentioned their motivation would be to learn to "push smarter, not harder". This is important to the management of fatigue because it allows players to make efficient movements. Improving the efficiency of movements improves a player's ability to maintain their performance for longer periods of time.

As P1 pointed out, it is important to understand how each person is moving to make sure you are doing what is right for them. Given the varying degrees of motor impairment and function it is important to understand each individuals' potential and challenges.

"I would like to know how each athlete is generating power so that we can see actually what functionally they have access to, and how we can help them maximize their functional capacity." – P1, Coach

This information would allow coaches to intervene more effectively:

"You could uh identify it early enough to not get into some of the bad habits. Are they using the hip flexors or are they using the triceps or lats? What are they using to generate power in their push or their stops? Umm...I think to be able to see that in their training and can use that to teach stroke mechanics and maximizing their stroke technique. That would be mean more to me..." – P1, Coach

6.2.1 Injury and Fatigue Prevention

Shoulder pain is a common condition among wheelchair users especially for wheelchair basketball players. A study conducted by Curtis and Black [8] described the prevalence of shoulder pain among female wheelchair basketball players. They also describe movements in wheelchair basketball involving the upper body that lead to upper body soft tissue injuries. Shoulder injury is very prominent among wheelchair basketball players and has been studied in relation to other factors [24][20].

6.3 Form Factor and Device Preferences

The interview and survey results confirm the opportunity for a device to be used to support wheelchair basketball players and teams. Interview participants described characteristics of existing devices that they liked including common form-factors like wrist-worn devices, chest straps, or ankle-worn devices. There were also some other devices that people were interested in using such as a smart basketball:

"You know they have like the basketball that like knows your form or whatever and knows the rotation of the ball and something to incorporate that into your training would be nice. To have some kind of wearable technology that knows the angle of your shot or where you release it or something like that." – P5

Participants also mentioned how feedback might need to be interpreted by coaches. P4 said:

"The coach would have to be trained in terms of what those that information that you're receiving back really means. So, I don't know if any coach would be able to be like oh this person's level of oxygen or whatever is low. take them out or whatever so I mean there would necessarily need to be some training involved." – P5, Player

[3] https://www.sporttechie.com/u-s-womens-national-team-training-polar-wearables/

[4] http://www.geekwire.com/2015/german-national-soccer-team-used-wearable-technology-win-world-cup/

6.3.1 Wheelchair-Attached Sensing

From the survey, we confirmed that having an option or combination of locations (on-body and/or wheelchair-attached) for devices would be preferable. This is consistent with findings from related work suggesting the use of the wheelchair to deliver solutions [3]. Players suggest utilizing the space around and under the seat to attach devices. The reason for this suggestion is to avoid direct contact between the device and other players. Due to the nature of the sport, it is important that devices are out of the way for the safety of the wearer as well as other players they encounter during a game. Sporner et al. [21] utilized a miniature data logger (MDL) to collect quantified measurements of activity for wheelchair users. This approach has been used in other settings to learn about everyday characteristics of manual wheelchair use among veterans[22] and children[7]. The MDL requires processing of the data after the activity is completed. Given the advancement of current and emerging fitness tracking technologies and sensing, more real-time or near-real-time feedback is expected from participants.

6.4 Community Characteristics

The wheelchair basketball community is structured to allow competition at multiple levels and to incorporate people with different abilities at all levels. The functional classification system allows someone who might have low functional motor abilities to compete at all levels based on their basketball skill. Also, there is a strong commingling of people who play professionally, internationally, and recreationally across different teams and levels of competition. While a minimum documented disability is required to play the sport officially, this is not a requirement for coaches or people who want to play recreationally. Thus, the sport itself while adaptive is not closed to people who would be considered "able-bodied". Informally, an able-bodied person would receive a classification of 4.5 to keep the teams balanced.

7. Limitations and Future Work

Some limitations of the survey were that the data discussed here is ordinal data and may not provide a consistent scale between options on the 5-point scale. In addition, given the small samples and uneven groupings of participants by class or competition level, we would be unable to perform proper between-group comparisons for their preferences.

For future work, we intend to collect additional data to explore comparisons by competition level and functional classification. We also intend to more deeply explore the interface requirements for the proposed class of devices to support the unique and shared needs of players and coaches at all levels.

8. Conclusions

This research explores the development of mobile and wearable devices for automatic tracking of stamina- and fatigue-related information for the sport of Wheelchair Basketball. In this paper, we described an exploration into how automatic tracking might be used by wheelchair basketball players and coaches to support stamina and fatigue management. We conducted an interview study to identify potential metrics and uses for automatic tracking. We presented the results of a survey with 76 people, including 69 wheelchair basketball players and 17 coaches, to validate our interview findings and capture a more general sense of the interest in stamina and fatigue management.

This research provides new insight for mobile and wearable technology designers to improve existing solutions and to create new systems that provide relevant feedback for this population of athletes. We intend to expand this research to include other adaptive sports. Our goal is to create more versatile mobile and wearable technology solutions that are useful in different active situations.

9. ACKNOWLEDGMENTS

We would like to acknowledge our participants, the National Wheelchair Basketball Association, Claudia Lepore, Brandon McBeain, and the UMBC ISRC and Prototyping and Design Lab. This work was partially funded by Microsoft and Nokia.

10. REFERENCES

[1] Bravata, D. M., Smith-Spangler, C., Sundaram, V., Gienger, A. L., Lin, N., Lewis, R., ... & Sirard, J. R. (2007). Using pedometers to increase physical activity and improve health: a systematic review. Jama, 298(19), 2296-2304

[2] Calvo, R.A. and Peters, D. (2013). The irony and re-interpretation of our quantified self. (New York, New York, USA, Nov. 2013), 367–370.

[3] Carrington, P., Chang, K., Mentis, H., & Hurst, A. (2015). But, I don't take steps: Examining the Inaccessibility of Fitness Trackers for Wheelchair Athletes. In Proceedings of the 17th International ACM SIGACCESS Conference on Computers & Accessibility (pp. 193-201). ACM.

[4] Cervantes, C. M., & Porretta, D. L. (2010). Physical activity measurement among individuals with disabilities: A literature review. *Adapted Physical Activity Quarterly*, *27*(3), 173-190.

[5] Chan, C. B., Ryan, D. A., & Tudor-Locke, C. (2004). Health benefits of a pedometer-based physical activity intervention in sedentary workers. Preventive medicine, 39(6), 1215-1222.

[6] Cheshire, W. P., & Freeman, R. (2003). Disorders of sweating. In *Seminars in neurology* (Vol. 23, No. 4, p. 399).

[7] Cooper, R. A., Tolerico, M., Kaminski, B. A., Spaeth, D., Ding, D., & Cooper, R. (2008). Quantifying wheelchair activity of children: a pilot study. *American journal of physical medicine & rehabilitation*, *87*(12), 977-983.

[8] Curtis, K. A., & Black, K. (1999). Shoulder pain in female wheelchair basketball players. *Journal of Orthopaedic & Sports Physical Therapy*, *29*(4), 225-231.

[9] Lupton, D. (2014). Self-tracking cultures: towards a sociology of personal informatics. In *Proceedings of the 26th Australian Computer-Human Interaction Conference on Designing Futures: the Future of Design* (pp. 77-86). ACM.

[10] MacLeod, H., Tang, A., & Carpendale, S. (2013). Personal informatics in chronic illness management. In *Proceedings of Graphics Interface 2013* (pp. 149-156). Canadian Information Processing Society.

[11] Malu and Findlater (2016) Toward accessible health and fitness tracking for people with mobility impairments. In *Proceedings of the 10th EAI International Conference on Pervasive Computing Technologies for Healthcare (PervasiveHealth '16)*, 170-177.

[12] Montgomery, P., Pyne, D., Hopkins, W., Dorman, J., Cook, K., Minahan, C. (2008) The effect of recovery strategies on physical performance and cumulative fatigue in competitive basketball. *Journal of Sports Sciences,* 26(11), pp. 1135-1145.

[13] Morris, D., Saponas, T. S., Guillory, A., & Kelner, I. (2014). RecoFit: using a wearable sensor to find, recognize, and

count repetitive exercises. In *Proceedings of the 32nd annual ACM conference on Human factors in computing systems* (pp. 3225-3234). ACM

[14] Patel, M. S., Asch, D. A., & Volpp, K. G. (2015). Wearable devices as facilitators, not drivers, of health behavior change. *Jama*, *313*(5), 459-460.

[15] Postma, K., Berg-Emons van den, H.J.G., Bussmann, J.B.J., Sluis, T.A.R., Bergen, M.P. and Stam, H.J. (2005). Validity of the detection of wheelchair propulsion as measured with an Activity Monitor in patients with spinal cord injury. Spinal Cord. 43, 9 (Apr. 2005), 550–557.

[16] Rampinini, E., Impellizzer, F., Castagna, C., Coutts, A., Wisloff, U. (2009). Technical performance during soccer matches of the Italian Serie A league: Effect of fatigue and competitive level. Journal of Science and Medicine in Sport. 12(1), pp. 227-233.

[17] Rector, K., Milne, L., Ladner, R. E., Friedman, B., & Kientz, J. A. (2015, October). Exploring the Opportunities and Challenges with Exercise Technologies for People who are Blind or Low-Vision. In *Proceedings of the 17th International ACM SIGACCESS Conference on Computers & Accessibility* (pp. 203-214). ACM.

[18] Robson-Ansley, P., Gleeson, M., Ansley, L. (2009) Fatigue Management in the preparation of Olympic athletes. *Journal of Sports Sciences*, 27(13), 1409-1420

[19] Rooksby, J., Rost, M., Morrison, A., & Chalmers, M. C. (2014). Personal tracking as lived informatics. In *Proceedings of the 32nd annual ACM conference on Human factors in computing systems* (pp. 1163-1172). ACM.

[20] Souza, A. L., Boninger, M. L., Fitzgerald, S., Shimada, S. D., Cooper, R. A., & Ambrosio, F. (2005). Upper limb strength in individuals with spinal cord injury who use manual wheelchairs. *The journal of spinal cord medicine*, *28*(1), 26-32.

[21] Sporner, M. L., Grindle, G. G., Kelleher, A., Teodorski, E. E., Cooper, R., & Cooper, R. A. (2009). Quantification of activity during wheelchair basketball and rugby at the National Veterans Wheelchair Games: A pilot study. *Prosthetics and orthotics international*, *33*(3), 210-217.

[22] Tolerico, M. L., Ding, D., Cooper, R. A., & Spaeth, D. M. (2007). Assessing mobility characteristics and activity levels of manual wheelchair users. *Journal of rehabilitation research and development*, *44*(4), 561.

[23] Whooley, M., Ploderer, B., & Gray, K. (2014). On the integration of self-tracking data amongst quantified self members. In *Proceedings of the 28th International BCS Human Computer Interaction Conference on HCI 2014-Sand, Sea and Sky-Holiday HCI* (pp. 151-160). BCS.

[24] Yildirim, N. U., Comert, E., & Ozengin, N. (2010). Shoulder pain: a comparison of wheelchair basketball players with trunk control and without trunk control. *Journal of back and musculoskeletal rehabilitation*, *23*(2), 55-61.

Narratives of Older Adults with Mild Cognitive Impairment and Their Caregivers

Galina Madjaroff & Helena M. Mentis
Department of Information Systems
University of Maryland Baltimore County
{galina1, mentis}@umbc.edu

ABSTRACT
The design of assistive technology is dictated by the narratives surrounding a particular impairment and its impact on one's life. This in turn affects the perceptions of the users – both the role of technology as well as their own sense of identity. In the case of those with a mild cognitive impairment, a precursor to dementia, home-based technologies that are disability and change focused shape the identity of the very people they are to help – reifying their dependency and their loss of self. With this study, we set out to better understand the narratives of people living with a mild cognitive impairment as well as their partners that live with them and provide care. Within this investigation, we uncovered the predominance of a disease-focused narrative – one that laments loss of identity and the struggles of daily care. However, we also uncovered a different narrative centered on the role of technology to provide support within the dyads' life. These technology narratives were evidence of a need to support the biopsychosocial aspects of autonomy for both parties and improved relationships. We use our findings to further discuss the driving force behind design goals for home-based technologies for those with a mild cognitive impairment.

CCS Concepts
• **Human-centered computing→Empirical studies in HCI** • **Human-centered computing→Accessibility** • **Social and professional topics→Seniors**

Keywords
Cognitive impairment; Dementia; Home-based technology.

1. INTRODUCTION
For those with a cognitive impairment, technology has typically aimed to improve a care recipient's memory and cognition [3] prevent their falls [7], or generally protect the vulnerable care recipient [7, 44] through close monitoring via sensors [8], [11] and assistive technologies [20, 22, 24]. Likewise, caregiver-based technology solutions have focused on the burdens of caring for someone with cognitive impairment [1, 21, 43, 48], including characterizing the caregiver as the second invisible patient and attempting to improve their quality of life through mobile applications that aid in connecting to peer support [4, 33, 45, 48]. In this regard, the problematization and solution for technology interventions has been focused on the medical, declinist, and disease model driven view of cognitive impairment [46]. In other words, the care receiver is often seen as deficient and in need of help while the caregiver is shouldering a burden and needing relief.

ASSETS'17, Oct. 29–Nov. 1, 2017, Baltimore, MD, USA.

ACM ISBN 978-1-4503-4926-0/17/10…$15.00.
DOI: http://dx.doi.org/10.1145/3132525.3132554

This framing in the development of new technologies ultimately is apparent to the users of that technology [19, 35, 50]. A declinist perspective is not lost on both the care receivers and caregivers and so this technological framing, in turn, affects how the person with cognitive impairment and the caregiver sees themselves, their role, and their relationship to one another. In essence, technology based on the medical model reifies an illness narrative held by the impaired and their caregivers and even may elevate it to a prominent place in their daily lives [35]. Over the long term, such a framing can have consequences on one's quality of life through a loss of one's autonomy, which does not promote a very person-centered perspective [46]. Technology that is framed by the medical model is a pervasive concern in the ASSETS community and has spurred the exploration of other models for technology design. For instance, a social model focuses its efforts on obtaining access, reducing oppression, and supporting activism [35]. These alternative frames can in turn produce technology that shapes the personal and social narratives one may have of the impact of their impairment and their place in society and relationships.

Our study was motivated to identify the potential of a model for framing the design of home-based technology for those with a progressive cognitive impairment and their spouses that serve as a caregiver. This is ultimately in hopes of creating technology that elevates one's personhood and provides a realm where technology improves the narratives of care in the home leading to a better quality of life. We set out to do this by first investigating the narratives that the population holds – both in their daily lives, but also in technology's place in those narratives.

In the following paper, we present evidence from our interviews with older adults with mild cognitive impairment (MCI) and their caregivers. These interviews revealed how the disease narrative view was prevalent in how caregivers and care recipients defined their experiences, expectations, and relationships. However, when the pair discussed the benefit of technology in the home to be used by both actors, the discussion moved to one of opportunity for *autonomy* and *safety* for both actors. This change in perspective reframes the role of the caregiver and care recipient from one of managing burden to that of recognizing opportunity – from an Illness Narrative [39] to a Biopsychosocial Narrative [23]. From these findings, we discuss how this can manifest in different forms of technology support in the home. One that can complement the current illness narrative-led design motivation – thus, not eschewing it completely – but, rather one that can inspire new technology directions for the home to offset the predominance of the illness narrative.

2. RELATED WORK

2.1 Models for Design

Within the ASSETS community, there has been a shift in how to think about and design for disability or impairment. Mankoff et. al [35] began this discussion with literature from Disability Studies as a lens to critically reflect on the work in assistive technology. In particular, they argued that the model that a researcher or designer holds had a determining effect on the technology that was designed as well as the way it was evaluated. Consequently, they highlighted the technology may have negative consequences on a user's life experiences. For instance, the *medical model* of disability can be oppressive and lead to ostracization and segregation. And, importantly, any technology resulting from this mindset, no matter how much the designers think they are coming from a helpful place, is ultimately complicit in feeding these negative outcomes.

The medical model of aging is a fairly prominent viewpoint in the HCI and ASSETS literature, specifically. There is a tendency to view aging and any age-related disease as experiencing some form of deficit and that the role of technology is to alleviate the effects of that deficit. Carroll et. al [10] highlighted this problem in the assumption that older people are living in isolation and technologies are needed to connect them to family and friends. However, Carroll points out that this is often not the case and older adults currently play key roles in communities.

But this medical model dominates much of the studies of older adults and, in turn also dominates the body of knowledge that HCI researchers draw upon in their framing of technology support. Vines et al's [50] discourse analysis of 644 SIGCHI-venue papers also highlighted the framing of technology as solving the "problem" of aging. It is difficult to blame technology designers as there is much to be desired by this framing. Focusing on one's physical and functional limitations provide actionable challenges and a mechanism to show measurable results [35]. However, Vines et al [50] highlighted how a turn away from a medical model allows for the individual to define for themselves what successful aging is and how that may provide the needed sense of worth in the face of any illness or challenges.

As an antidote of sorts to the medical model, Mankoff et al. [35] highlighted the benefits of a *social model* that may allow for a designer to turn their attention away from "fixing" the individual and instead address the problems of access, oppression, and activism. This in turn highlights the need to care for the individual as a person and putting the power of leading that care in the hands of the individual with the impairment. Mankoff et al.'s social model was further termed the *social creationist* model by Frauenberger [19] to better distinguish it from the post-modern *social constructivist* model. The latter model's focus is instead on how language is used to define what is a disability and how that does or does not open up a space for one's disability to be viewed as a form of "normal".

Frauenberger [19] expertly pointed out, though, that all of these models are reductionist in nature. They see disability as being defined and best addressed by one factor and, so, the technological solutions guided by these models are too one-sided. Frauenberger [19] attempted to put forth a philosophical position to address the dichotomy between the medical model and social models of disability. The *critical realist* model that he puts forth argues that it is not fruitful to be fixated on conceptualizing disability as either determined in the biological condition or as a purely social construct. This dichotomy simply leads to technologies that either focus on individual support or attempt to change the environment. He instead argues for a multi-layered and interactional conceptualization of disability, which addresses multiple aspects of the disabled experience: the biological, the psychological, the psychosocial and emotional, the cultural, and so on, all at the same time. This creates a need for a problem-solving approach that has aspects of both the medical and social models, particularly because the experience of those with a disability and those who care for them is multidimensional and diverse [19].

Finally, Lazar et. al [31] recently built on this epistemological turn and argued for the *critical dementia* perspective in design for those specifically with dementia-related impairments. This framework recognized people with cognitive impairment as making meaning in a contextualized and social manner, engaging in similar physical and embodied interactions that display meaning, responding to and participating in the world through sensory experiences, and continuing to engage in emotion and affective experience. Thus, very much a perspective that engages in technology design for both intrinsic and extrinsic values as Frauenberger argued for.

All of these models can inform how HCI researchers engage with the experience of those with cognitive impairment and ultimately how technology design can be focused in its fulfillment of user needs [31]. What is not clear is how these models relate to the lived experiences of those with dementia. To better understand this lived experience, we turned our attention to the literature on Life Narratives that are both a product of experiences as well as a shaping force on one's lived experience.

2.2 Life Narratives

Although the Models for Design outlined above are useful for conceptualizing and designing for the disability experience, how one views themselves and how others view and treat them is encompassed in one's Life Narrative. Multiple components of identity including, personal, social, illness, and their story lines make up an individual's experience. In the gerontology literature, these components are referred to as "narratives" – the way one frames one's experiences as well as how their world is being framed by others [9]. As individuals, we all have narratives in which we conceptualize our lives and our relationships, however with the introduction of an illness or in this case a cognitive impairment diagnosis, one's narrative can significantly change. There is a dominant issue of identity, and how that may change and transforms for those with the impairment as well as those around them or who care for them – for example labeling from "normally functioning" to "cognitively impaired" and from "spouse" to "caregiver". A new diagnosis alters the relationship between the person, how they view themselves, and how they view their surrounding world. This leads to the attempt of "reconstructing" one's life story [52]. In order to make sense of what is happening, to give meaning to this disruption, the newly diagnosed individual is forced to direct their attention and efforts to rebuilding their identity after diagnosis, in the framework of this new life [26] – this is facilitated and evidenced by the narratives they hold and share. The person has to work to reconstruct their narrative in order to understand their illness in terms of past social experience and to reaffirm the impression that their life still has meaning and purpose [52]. This narrative view is less about the factual account and more about understanding how an individual makes meaning that they live by after a diagnosis. Similar to the models in disability discourse and assistive technology, there are two narratives that are prominent in the gerontology literature that can be applied to those with a physical or cognitive impairment: the illness narrative and the biopsychosocial narrative.

The *illness narrative* is a story a person tells and significant others retell to give coherence to the disruptive events that have had an effect on the family system and all actors in it. This typically results in a narrative of loss and change that can be overwhelming for all people involved. The individuals with cognitive impairment see themselves as well as are seen through the lens of their illness, which identifies them based on condition, disease and diagnosis [47]. Such views position those with cognitive impairment as "objects" of their illness rather than "participants" in it [13]. If this narrative persists, it becomes difficult for the person to maintain their sense of identity and self-esteem, which should continue to be maintained for as long as possible. Fostering 'personhood' and psychosocial factors of dementia is essential to care [15].

The *biopsychosocial (BPS) narrative* can provide a more accurate and complete picture of the experience of the individual with cognitive impairment. The BPS narrative is a holistic approach to care that brings empathy and compassion into medical practice [5]. Its main pillars include self- awareness when caring for someone with an illness, active cultivation of trust, empathy, forming a therapeutic relationship and communicating in order to foster dialogue not just medical application of protocol. This model fosters a more productive emotional climate between patient and clinician [5]. We extend this narrative framework to our work with caregivers and care recipients, specifically couples. By shifting the illness narrative to one that is more positive, supportive and constructive, a biopsychosocial narrative can provide opportunity for the dyadic interactions to not only be viewed as influenced by the stressors of change, but also as an opportunity for a positive outcome. Seeing dementia as a social process full of opportunity helps one understand the role of experience of memory loss rather than giving prominence to the disease [23]. If technologies used early on in the disease cycle – i.e. while the care recipient is still able to remain in their home – can be designed to shift the narrative from that of illness to that of biopsychosocial success, then we can support and enhance the lives of all actors in the family system going through this disruptive process.

3. METHODS

As it is often the goal in HCI studies to generalize, a typical user study does not consider the "universe of one" of those dealing with a progressive cognitive impairment [36]. The deficits experienced by those with cognitive impairment are often highly variable and prohibit attaining generalizability, and so those of us who are interested in working with this population should consider the best methods to approach such studies. Because of this, building relationships with the dyads was critically important for our study and we employed empathy as a defining characteristic of our research [53]. "Knowing the user" and understanding the shared experience of the dyads starts with a conversation, particularly building "empathy through dialogue" [53]. Methodologically, HCI has adopted several qualitative approaches for eliciting experiences in order to understand the user in the design process, including interviews, narratives, scenarios, simulations, and role playing [3].

Mulvenna et.al [40], discuss that it is imperative that voice is given to both the caregiver and care-recipient with dementia in order to gather the most appropriate, user centric data from technology studies. This approach to technology studies and dementia have led to a more person-centered or "emotion oriented" method that focuses on the individuals suffering from the disease and uncovering their experiences *as well as* those caring for them. Thus, an integral part of these interviews was to consider the caregiver-care recipient as a unit as opposed to separate entities. The sense of identity of the person with cognitive impairment is a product of the dyadic caregiver- care recipient relationship, which is both dynamic and multidimensional [51].

3.1 Participants

For this study, we focused on individuals with mild cognitive impairment (MCI). MCI is defined by a noticeable decrement in cognitive functioning that goes beyond normal changes seen in aging [42], but is not clinically defined as dementia as of yet. Studies from the Mayo Clinic have demonstrated that close to 15% of individuals over the age of 70 have cognitive impairment [41] and there is a significant rate at which individuals progress from MCI to dementia – 10% per year [41]. We began with this population due to their interest in staying in their home for as long as possible and the increased likelihood of sustaining an extended length interview.

The first phase of our study included participants from the Integrace Institute, which serves the local community and helps families and patients deal with a dementia diagnosis. The participants were part of the Institute's outpatient clinic and do not live on the premises as residents, but rather at home with a family member. Participants were recruited with the help of the Institute's Director of Research. The inclusion criteria was a diagnosis of mild cognitive impairment by an on-staff neurologist at the clinic. In total, five couples were interviewed. The sample size was constrained due to (1) the narrow inclusion criteria of a diagnosis of MCI and limited availability of clinical sites and (2) saturation was quickly reached by five dyads. Applicable demographics are presented in Table 1.

Table 1. Care Receiver and Caregiver Demographics

Participant Dyad ID	Care Receiver	Caregiver Relationship
D1	P1 Male	C1 Wife (did not attend)
D2	P2 Female	C2 Husband
D3	P3 Female	C3 Husband
D4	P4 Male	C4 Wife
D5	P5 Female	C5 Husband

3.2 Procedure

Patients were recruited from the Institute with the help of the Director of Research. A flier was distributed to all of the applicable clinic patients indicating for them to call the Dementia Research and Education Associate at the Integrace Institute if they were interested in participating in the study. Those who indicated an interest in being involved would then schedule a visit with the first author of this paper through telephone or email. The interviews with the first author occurred on the Institute's premises (D1, D2) in a private conference room or in the participant's homes (D3, D4, D5) if they preferred. Participants had to have the ability to provide informed written or verbal consent to being involved in the research.

A strong ethical framework was essential in guiding our research [34], particularly because we were working with a vulnerable population. This framework focuses on several aspects: respect of the individual with impairment and their caregiver (not looking at our participants through the medical model lens, or as disabled or sick); making sure the opportunities for research participation are available in the least intrusive and restrictive way [34] and assuring that all confidentiality protocols have been followed closely, including gathering and storing our data. We have firmly complied with our IRB's requirements to "do no harm" to those who are considered vulnerable, particularly cognitively impaired older adults [34]. There is a general consensus that a diagnosis of a dementing illness does not presume incompetence [37]. In order to participate in this study, we asked that the person's caregiver or "surrogate" [25] provide consent for them; in our case surrogate consent was provided by the partner. We also asked the individual with cognitive impairment to provide written and if unable, verbal consent. Upon completion of the IRB requirements we proceeded with our interview.

Semi-structured interviews were employed including questions focusing on home technology use adapted from Davis [14]. The interviews began by getting to know the family unit with a background on events prior and following the diagnosis of cognitive impairment. We asked them to share any family history they felt comfortable with, and on more than one occasion we would hear about love stories, children, and be shown Bat Mitzvah home videos. All of the participants in this study were kind enough to share details about their daily life, daily care and how they were coping with everyday life. Specifically, we asked them how using technology in their home enhanced their experience as a caregiver in providing daily care and how using technology in their home enhanced their experience as a care-recipient in their daily care.

3.3 Data Collection

Interviews were video and audio recorded and later transcribed for detailed content analysis. Since we were asking participants about technologies they enjoy using, they sometimes showed us their smart phone or other device so video recording was essential to capture these demonstrations. The video recordings allowed us to revisit important elements of the conversations and pick up on cues, particularly from the person with MCI. The recordings also serve as evidence on which interpretations can be made by others in order to establish validity [17]. By using a semi-structured interview method, we were able to elicit deep and meaningful narratives about the family's lives. The primary advantage of conducting interviews in a health related problem space is to allow the researcher to focus on the participants' perceptions and ultimately inform about their experiences and those of their caregivers [17]. Marital relationships and coping with dementia have been discussed as an important aspect of analysis [2, 12, 16, 32]. This perspective is also important in how we chose to conduct our interviews – involving both partners in the caregiver/care-recipient marital relationship.

3.4 Analysis

Thematic analysis was chosen to systematically analyze the data while also allowing us to tap into latent themes that manifested in the data collected [6]. This provided us with the ability to move beyond surface level similarities to more tacit themes [38]. Subsequent integration of these latent themes with our interpretation of the literature on technology design for the home helped us form the basis for the introduction of technology that should support alternative narratives [18]. The analysis focused on how the dyads spoke of their life experiences as well as their perspective on the place for technology in the home. Coding was organized first around the broad theme of 'narratives'. The evidence that narratives were different depending on if they were speaking of current experiences or future technology needs led to further classifying the data into the type of narratives that were prominent in each of these reflection points. The two main themes that emerged were the predominance of an illness narrative when discussing the couple's everyday lives and the predominance of a biopsychosocial narrative when discussing their current use of technology or needs for technology in the future. All quotes are evidence of the existence of those two main themes. There is no interrater reliability as the researchers brought varied but valid perspectives to identify themes in the data.

4. RESULTS

4.1 The Prominent Illness Narrative in Everyday Life

A large portion of every interview allowed the participants to speak of their lives and reflect on their experience living with MCI and caring for someone with MCI. The dynamics of the relationship change after the diagnosis [2] as can be seen by the narratives that will follow – there was sometimes tension, anger and uncertainty about what life would be like. Each dyad had their own set of coping mechanisms and ways to continue to preserve their way of life, but the illness narrative dominated when discussing their daily lives. It became apparent that each of the participants had established their roles in the family as either caregiver or care-recipient, which was evident in their narratives. The pressures and responsibilities that the caregivers felt were often overwhelming at the initial stages of the diagnosis. This was also the case for the individual receiving the diagnosis. When asked to share some of their initial experiences with the diagnosis, our participants centered their discussion around coping, managing and understanding the illness. The illness narrative was evident particularly in how the disease was managed by the medical staff which often lacked compassion.

> *P5: "Yea, and he said [the physician] you have dementia and walked out!"*
>
> *C5: "Not as quickly as that but basically that's- he has a certain amount of time he spends with patients and regardless of what's going on it's like when that time is up, he goes out of the room and I remember one time we were sitting and I actually stopped him. I said, "Hold on, doctor" and he froze and I said "I have some questions". I got him to come back in but he looked at [P5], got some background and he gave her some tests and he just said- just said nonchalantly "You have dementia"."*

On several occasions the partners shared their disappointment with how their treatment was handled by medical staff and how little information was given to them about the diagnosis and how to find resources. The lack of psychosocial support for both caregiver and care recipient was evident with our couples.

> *C5: And then when I asked what to do, they gave me a list of internet sites and books and I'm thinking where do I start? And then one of the things they said was that they usually have the book "The 36 Hour Day" and they didn't have any copies of that in the library but I found it online. I had to read it 'cause I needed to get the information- it scared the daylights out of me. And it still is a frightening book to read. Because it's worse case scenario. It just simply gives you all the facts but there's no good ending to it. And I said no no…this is not going to be [P5]. I said no way in my mind- I either blocked it or I said we're gonna find something but this is not the case…*

P5: We got to do everything we can do.

Once the family navigated through this new phase in their life, they shared that it was often difficult to go back to the way things were. For example, some partners took their new role as caregiver very seriously – they felt they had to helicopter over their loved one, making sure they are safe, secure and all the details of their care is anticipated. For example, C3 discussed an incident with his wife where he was out of town for a day and she had forgotten to feed herself, felt faint, and had to be taken to the hospital by neighbors.

Figure 1. Dyad 3, P3 on right. Interview occurred in their home.

C3: "If I go somewhere she goes with me, it's just that's what we do... if only occasionally, last year I had a strike which put me on an emergency assignment which left her in a really rough spot there about 53 days as I drove to Eastern Shore and back every day. I would've been staying there but I couldn't because I had to be home at least at night and my son works. She was here 3 days so we had coverage, even her daughter would get on the phone and walk with her every day... so I had a period of time where I had to be away during summer but that was the last time I think and she only ended up in the emergency room once during that time."

P3: "What was that for?"

C3: [to his wife] "Because you didn't eat!"

C3: [to the interviewer] "So she didn't eat and got shaky so she described that to her daughter in Florida who can't see her, so she didn't know but I knew it was cause of low sugar cause my grandfather used to get it. She doesn't have diabetes or anything like that..."

P3: "Peanut butter jelly works for me."

C3: "So they [the neighbors] took her to the hospital. I would have taken her to the urgent care if I was there."

This event evidently caused him great distress, which really shifted the nature of their partnership to managing the illness. This has manifested in several activities he has now taken control over, including handling her medications:

C3: "I sort the medications now...she used to always do them by herself and put them in the pill boxes herself, but I noticed she was getting confused so I took that over. I have a tendency, if something really makes her miserable...and to me crying is miserable and if she's crying because she's confused over something I will help her or take over, she doesn't have to do it... that may not be the perfect solution but I don't want her suffering more than necessary..."

This caregiver was very much focused on supporting his wife's needs and wanted to make sure she is safe and taken care of. He approached her care from a positive standpoint, however it seemed that he may have hindered some of her autonomy in order for her to be safe, or rather for him to feel that she is safe.

Dyad 4 had a similar relationship where the caregiver felt that having everything very organized and regimented would benefit her partner and his well-being. She mentioned that her background as a teacher has helped her with this:

C4: "I like organization, everything has its place and it does! And has something been done with dementia and that? With organization... because I'm just, I mean both of us have backgrounds in Special-Ed... you know he has been very very very good! The glasses, the wallet, and the keys, he has done very well. Another reason why I say that is that medication is a very important aspect and believe me we are going through all that. I found out unless you have a routine I mean he has two pillboxes and so I do the 7 days..."

As we can see from this quote, C4's narrative was dominated by handling her partner's daily tasks and ensuring that he was prepared to take on the daily schedule. She shared that it made life easier for both if she was very well organized. Her partner would then expect for her to plan his day and follow the schedule, which did not allow much room for him to make autonomous decisions. It was also interesting to note her decision to take her husband off his medication, so he would enjoy himself on their vacation:

C4: "You know in Florida we took an 11-day cruise and we had a grand time, there were some mix ups but we had a grand time and I took him off his medication and I had a reason for that because we were having wine and eating so I didn't want them to interact and so we enjoyed it..."

Interviewer: So it was the right thing for you?

C4: "For him too, I would like to go back and I think photographs are important and have many of those... and I think the most important thing is the acceptance and realistic. If things get overwhelming then for two people to be down then that can't be. I even looked into programs like that but we are not there yet..."

The autonomy of the care-recipient would often be compromised due to the need for safety that was expected by the caregiver. Like most caregiver-care recipient relationships, this was not associated with any negative intentions. The caregiver felt this was the best decision for their care partner at that time and coping with the illness narrative was often difficult:

C4: "So as a caregiver you have to get over your anger because he was the one doing everything and he was mad and I was mad also because I had to change my schedule...and then I realized it's a process and you kind of feel alone. And you have to think about the whole process and see what you can do. I think I have gotten over it..."

The illness narrative becoming the predominant daily narrative was most striking in our experience with Dyad 1. The caregiver for P1 chose not to participate in this study after a phone conversation with the first author of this paper. From that conversation and comments from the staff at the clinic, it was observed that C1 was not interested in being that involved in P1's care at the Institute or to be involved in any studies with him.

Clinic Director via email: "[C1] is really not as informed as [P1], they are very different than the [D2]. She hasn't been as involved in his care. I'm happy to reach out, but I can imagine you won't be able to get as much from her..."

From our conversation with P1, it became clear that his wife was burdened by his diagnosis and felt overwhelmed with all that she was now having to take on where at one time he took care of everything.

P1: "Sure I can do online banking, I can set up most of these things. Once in a while the password doesn't work. But more than not it's my wife...she was never interested in doing this and she still has difficulty but she's taken on a lot of that from me too... ...Yeah the responsibility to check it."

[A little while later, he continued on this thread]

"I am not saying that I have Alzheimer's because they don't know exactly, but I am on that track, I lose things all the time, you know, when am I going to find them, but I still have good driving skills. My wife prides me on the fact but I am very cognizant that I need to kind of schedule myself and without the help of my wife to help me do that schedule, that would be very difficult for me."

Although P1 did not directly comment on why his wife did not wish to participate in this study, it became evident that as the primary breadwinner he had been responsible for a lot of the household and financial responsibilities and those obligations had to be taken on by his wife following his diagnosis and progressive cognitive decline.

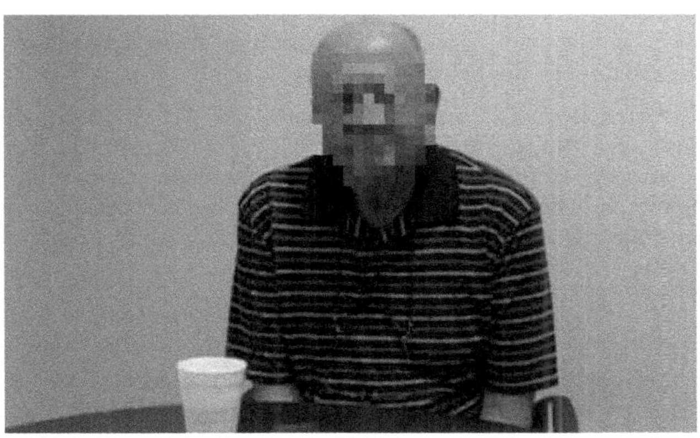

Figure 2. P1 during his interview. His wife did not join him.

The illness narrative, specifically the loss of self and search for identity of the person with MCI was particularly evident when the discussion reached a point of tension. This was evident when the care recipient would say something "odd" or not in the same grain as the conversation. C4, for example, felt extremely uncomfortable when her husband took over the discussion and reflected on a negative memory from his childhood:

P4: "The book is about two things it starts off first part about where I lived and born and was brought up and I was like...because I was left handed my mother did not want me my mother would call me "my black baby" so... and it was because I was left handed they thought I was retarded but I knew everything other kids knew too..."

C4 immediately refocused the conversation indicating that this was not something she felt comfortable sharing and really determined to show the research team that her husband was successful and accomplished prior to his diagnosis. The caregiver would then sometimes act as a gatekeeper who may be well meaning but perpetuates the idea that their partner is no longer themselves and must be supervised.

C4: "He was writing his book, and I think my husband has been a very successful person I mean he was very successful in high school he got full scholarship going to college, he was on the dean's list, but his interest has always been in sports and when he graduated from college I didn't know but found out he was a terrific basketball player, he was third round draft for the Detroit Pistols... you know when he graduated from college he was fantastic but something happened, someone ran into him and that was his end of career..."

Despite the predominance of an illness narrative in all of our discussions, some couples still attempted to balance autonomy and safety. This is a struggle within an illness narrative that required a lot of concerted effort and work. It can manifest in attempts to do more activities together, such as planning travel, participating in research projects, and even retiring at the same time in order to adjust to the changes as a couple. For example, C2 noted that having a better understanding of the genetic components of his wife's condition was now his role as a caregiver.

C2: "See it's up to me to read up about my wife, I know what's going on with the latest research now that she's in these studies, then I'll participate in that because it's meaningful to me. I'm doing a lot of what I'm doing with my wife is because she has a possible gene that could affect the brain, as the years go on I want to make sure I understand and can be there for her as best as I can."

Likewise, D5's relationship demonstrated that it was led by the illness narrative and coping with the loss. Thus, C5 felt protective of his wife's needs and safety; however, over time he realized he also needed to encourage her to continue to remain as independent as possible.

C5: At the beginning, I realized I was finishing P5's sentences she would hesitate and then I stopped and I said lemme see where she's going with this. She's able to...

P5: Talk.

C5: And whatever you're thinking of. And sometimes we have a signal, she will hit a word and I think you just did it before, she'll be looking for it and so I'll fill it in. Like yesterday we were talking to this group they asked her the address and I know sometimes P5 has problems with numbers but I said alright because the last time someone asked for an address and you turned to me. But this time you ended up answering it and I just sat back."

P5: "I answered it the whole way. I did it."

C5: "You knew the address, you knew the phone number and so I don't jump in. I know I can be, my first thought was that-I have to be protective. I have to be able to let her do what she can do."

As the diagnosis became a permanent part of the couples' daily life, the majority of our participants felt the most important aspect in coping with this life event was to simply control the effects of the illness to the best of their ability. This often overrode other aspects of a healthy relationship such as simply supporting one another, continuing to do the things they enjoyed, and finding a balance. This is not the life experience that we want to support. It is one that, with the introduction of technology with a medical model bent, would persist. However, in the following section, when the couples began discussing the place for technology in their lives, we see a noticeable shift. One that does not play into the illness narrative that was so prevalent in the prior discussion, but rather how technology was actively supporting a biopsychosocial perspective.

4.2 Technology Shaping a Place for the Biopsychosocial Narrative

When our interviews shifted to technologies each partner enjoyed using or was familiar with, the narratives used to frame their experiences seldom centered on the illness. The focus was often on being able to connect with family and friends, personal entertainment, or managing finances or schedules online – in other words, continuing to live their life to the fullest. All of the care recipients had an example of some technology that was continuing to engage them in their lives: P3's children lived in Florida and she used Facebook to look at their photos and videos, P4 was adamant about pulling his iPhone from his pocket to show us his calendar and tell us about the book he's writing about his life, P2 and P3 discussed their favorite games, and P5 talked about doing puzzles on the Kindle and watching shows with his wife on their Roku. This in turn led to the caregivers to also discuss the place of new technologies in their lives that were not focused on an illness narrative.

C5: "My kids got me a Roku for my birthday a couple of years ago I had no idea what it was. I figured it out and discovered all the channels- because I had Amazon we had some movies there. We had Netflix so I switched it over to streaming. But [P5] would be sitting here watching television and say there's nothing on. Like Saturday night there's nothing on television. I said well there's Roku, it's set up I can show it to you. It's got all the shows you like, and you can go to it and select a show you like."

In fact, all of our dyads felt technology was valuable when used to benefit them and their partner's well-being. C2, 3, 4 and 5 utilized technology in their "down time" to relax and consume media that was enjoyable for them. P2 was interested in playing games and engaging her cognitive abilities.

P2: "I play a word game on there [iPad] a lot. I have Jackpot Party which ... I don't know what you call it... I can't think of the word for it! ...Slot machine! Slot machine!" And I just got two new things that are for elderly people it's supposed to be helping with their memory. One's called Brain IQ and one's called Lumocity"

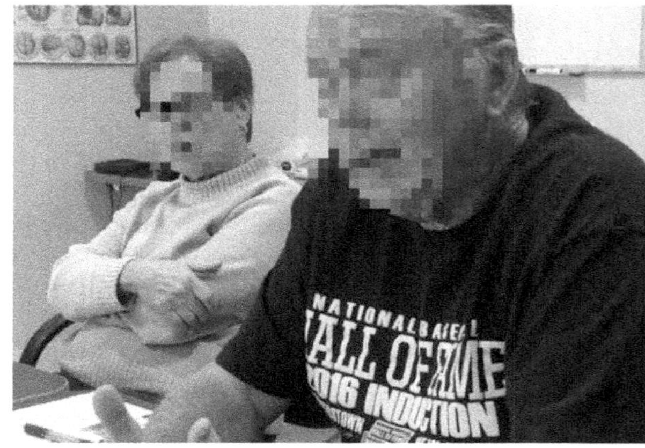

Figure 3. Dyad 2. C2 (right) discussing the computer games P2 (left) likes to play.

C3 was particularly interested in his partner being more engaged with technology in their home that could support their family unit.

C3: Well her favorite thing, I will tell you more about me but her favorite thing right now is solitaire so she plays it right over there, she still beats it, she can figure it out and so for me well I don't know... I keep trying to figure out how I could use the technology to make it better for her or to make it better for me or both of us, because I think the technology for her would be different than for me so if you look at it at a caregiver perspective its different."

Technology also provided a sense of independence for both actors in the family system which was important in order to achieve some balance in the caregiving relationship. C3 talked about being on his phone late at night after his wife had gone to sleep, as "me time", when he could watch a show or browse the net and do activities he enjoyed.

Likewise, P1 and P2 were proud of the fact that they were the ones who booked the family trips online, even though the final supervisory step (i.e. checking that all information was correct before pressing the final button) was done by their caregiver, it gave them a sense of autonomy and their care partner a sense of safety.

P1: "So after I get her [caregiver wife] more involved in this technology [booking vacations, paying bills online] over time... and given she's done fairly well in doing that. And so I'm relying on the fact that if my problems were to increase that she would be there to do that for me."

Providing the space for the care recipient to be independent and engage in things they enjoy doing or even new activities was realized and encouraged by the caregivers. Our caregivers used technology as a form of engagement and relationship building that we didn't see when they were discussing their everyday lives. For instance, C5 was always looking for new games that P5 might enjoy and both of them were very proud of her ability to complete them.

C5: "We discovered Jigsaw puzzle on the kindle and..."

P5: I love it!

C5: At the beginning, she couldn't finish them I would see where she would have one piece at the wrong place and the she would show it to me and I started to pull those out and I would say ok try it again and then she would finish it...she hasn't asked me to do it in weeks...

P5: "Yea I can do that"

P5: "Of course I did read something that said you need to vary the kind of things you're doing if all you did were jigsaw puzzles then it just means you'd be very good at jigsaw puzzles..."

Figure 4. Dyad 5 showing the technology both C5 (right) and P5 (left) use in their home.

It is evident from these discussions that everyday technology that was not built from the frame of a medical model, was better at engaging the participants and enriching their relationships and daily life. This in turn led to a biopsychosocial narrative surrounding the use and need for technology in their daily lives. Most technology that was used in the home was able to support the individual and collective needs of the partners without much fear of safety or loss of autonomy for both actors. This ultimately indicates that the narratives of daily life of older adults with cognitive impairment is critical in inspiring new directions for designing technologies to support the family system. This perspective on design could potentially elevate the lived experience and shift the narrative to one of biopsychosocial opportunity over that of illness.

5. DISCUSSION

In this study, we have uncovered the predominance of an illness narrative of daily life of caregivers and care recipients with MCI. This narrative was one that gave prominence to the impact of how their lives have changed since the diagnosis. It gave prominence to a concern over the continued safety and management of the person with the cognitive impairment. However, when the discussions shifted to that of current commercially available technology the couples were using, a biopsychosocial narrative was much more prevalent. In our conversations around technology, we were told stories that aligned with the psychosocial aspects of the couples' lives. The illness was still present, yet the idea that the dyad could continue to be successful and supported through technology was evident. It is clear that a focus on the illness and disease can hinder the lived experience, self-esteem, and identity of the individual with cognitive impairment and restrict the potential for a BPS narrative to have a positive shaping effect on the relationship between the care partners. However, technology designed and used in the context of cognitive impairment care does not need to reify this illness narrative; instead it can be a central figure in a BPS narrative.

Our findings also challenge the perspective that the caregiver or care recipient need support separately. We argue that the family system is deeply affected by the onset of the illness and must cope with it together in order to reach a more opportunistic narrative. Technology that supports the family system has the potential to further foster the BPS narrative and provide a space for the rebuilding of each partner's identity in the relationship.

Finally, we show that being immersed in the narratives of daily life of those with MCI and their caregivers provides researchers with an opportunity to "successfully engage" [29]. It is important for those of us working with disabled or impaired individuals to apply the critical realist model in order to better understand the multidimensional aspects of the lived experience of those with dementia and related disorders. This could also provide us with the ability to better understand this unique population's experience – specifically how the family system is affected by the onset of the illness and examine the dynamic of the relationship. Because of our findings and experiences learning from our participants, we have formulated both a framework to understand how there is a relationship between the concepts of autonomy, safety, and narratives as well as a goal for the design of technologies to support the biopsychosocial lives of those with cognitive impairment and their caregivers.

5.1 The Relationship between Autonomy and Safety in Narratives

Two distinct aspects emerged from the analysis of the narratives—the sense of autonomy and feelings of safety for *both* partners in the family system. Autonomy, in the context of the dyadic relationship, is defined by how a person's sense of autonomy is affected by those around them. This means that both actors depend on the other for support in gaining more autonomy [27]. Safety concerns for both partners includes managing and preventing physical injuries, including falls, wandering, and misuse of medications [28].

When discussing their daily lives, our findings demonstrate that *both* of the carepartners' autonomy was caught up in the illness narrative, which in our participants' cases focused on coping with the burdens of the diagnosis and care of cognitive impairment. The caregiver had to cope with, determine the boundaries of, and understand their new role after the diagnosis (D4, D5) and the illness narrative made it clear that their autonomy was impeded by this new set of responsibilities. This meant that in the balance of the relationship, some of their autonomy was forfeited, which, in turn, affected their new life narrative. Similarly, the care recipient's sense of autonomy was disrupted after the diagnosis, which led to the realization that they are now dependent on their partner in some capacity, which in turn shifted the focus of their narrative to one of illness. The shift in autonomy was manifested when the caregiver would have to make the best decision possible in a difficult or challenging situation (D4), for example to withhold medication for their partner, or give up some of their independence in order to support the needs of their partner (D3, D4), for instance lack of focus on their own emotional and physical well-being. We observed the caregiver choosing to "rescue" their spouse from what was perceived as an uncomfortable situation (P4 discussing racial issues), thus taking away some of their partner's choice to share aspects of their experience [51]. Thus, a loss of autonomy for both partners was evident in the illness narratives told by all of our participants.

Similarly, when safety concerns for the care recipient arose during discussions, the caregiver would often tell a story of taking a well-meaning, yet paternalistic approach to supporting the care recipient's needs. The caregivers were tempted to substitute their own judgement, particularly when they felt they had better insight into what constituted a safe environment for their partner. This in turn would be agreed upon by the care recipient and thus intensify the illness narrative. For instance, following an incident where P5 forgot to turn off the stove, C5's reaction was to take over the cooking responsibilities and P5 quickly relented. Thus, there was a hyper concern for safety that was evident in the illness narrative that led to potentially more drastic than necessary measures to be put into place in order to secure the safety of the care recipient. These measures were decided upon by the caregiver, but were readily agreed to be the care recipient – again indicative of the shaping effect of the illness narrative on both actors perception of their roles and needs.

Thus, there is clearly a relationship between autonomy and safety that manifest in an imbalance for both actors leading to as well as exacerbated by the illness narrative in their daily lives. The illness narrative they began with soon after diagnosis led to a predominant concern for safety. This led to the caregiver instilling and monitoring the safety of the care recipient, which in turn diminished the autonomy of both carepartners. Thus, continuing to reify the illness narrative in their lives.

However, we saw a slightly different dynamic between autonomy and safety when discussing the use of technology in their lives. In the BPS-centered narratives of technology use, there was a focus on how to engage technology in a way that balanced both of their needs for autonomy and safety. For instance, P1's initiative to continue to book vacations for the family with C1 signing off prior to completing the final step. Thus, both maintained a semblance of their own autonomy and yet, safety for the care recipient was still achieved. This balance in autonomy in turn continued to reify a BPS narrative. This shows us that couples could cope with new challenges surrounding the diagnosis and find a solution that balanced the relationship between autonomy and safety. This balance is what the design of technology for those with a cognitive impairment should strive for.

5.2 Designing Technology for a Biopsychosocial Narrative

The narratives that shape the experiences of our care receivers and caregivers is a different concept than the disability frameworks spoken of in prior work. What we attempt to clarify through the accounts here is that the models we focus on as designers and researchers shape how we approach designing technologies to support those with cognitive impairment and their caregivers at home. In turn, those technologies have a shaping effect on the narratives that are predominant in one's use of the technology. Prior work has focused on moving away from designing through the lens of the medical model and taking a more holistic, person-centered approach to designing for impairment and disability [30, 49]. In particular, the work by Frauenberger [19] highlighted how the complex relationship between the many factors those individuals with disabilities experience, including biological, cultural and psychosocial, are important to consider in order to support diverse experiences. We particularly agree with this model for design as the illness narrative led to a constraining of options for our participants while a biopsychosocial narrative was cognizant of how the impairment could be addressed in a multidimensional manner that allowed for relational opportunities to be realized.

A deeper analysis of the dominant narratives in the family system can provide for a better understanding of how the context of dementia can influence design. Our findings open up the potential for technology in the lives of older people with cognitive impairment and their caregivers. Specifically, we show how there is an opportunity for greater relationship support in the dyad. One way to achieve this is to support the autonomy of both individuals while maintaining the safety of the impaired person. For instance, technology can afford those affected with MCI with the self-reliance they thought they loss, afford the caregiver with a feeling of safety for the person they care for, and afford both actors with a sense of maintaining their own autonomy as the disease progresses.

A mutually supportive technology – a technology that could potentially maintain both actor's biopsychosocial needs – will allow for an adequate negotiation of autonomy and safety between the care recipient with MCI and their familial caregivers. This, in turn, may shift the actors' predominant narrative from the impact of the decline on both actors to the state of the biopsychosocial well-being of both actors. Specifically, in order to design technology that is supportive of the family system, we must consider several aspects. First, technologies that support the autonomy of both actors. For the care recipient, this means avoiding a catch all paternalistic approach and focusing on one that respects the individual's wishes and choices. For the caregiver, honoring their new role while supporting their ability to live a fulfilling life. Second, understanding that designing for safety and risk, whilst important, must not sacrifice the care recipient's sense of autonomy or take away from their BPS narrative.

6. CONCLUSION

The consideration of the life narratives of those living with cognitive impairment can provide a clearer lens in designing technologies for the home to support the family system. Building on prior work on models for assistive technology design, [19, 29, 30, 35] we have presented an approach to better understand the life narratives of older adults living with cognitive impairment and their caregivers in the home. Our work provided an insight into the daily life of couples where a partner has been diagnosed with a life-changing illness and how narratives play a role in shaping autonomy and the sense of safety of both the older adult with cognitive impairment and their caregiver. Our approach revealed that although an illness narrative was dominant in the discussions around their daily lives, the role of technology could shift that narrative to a more opportunistic model – one of biopsychosocial success. Further, this perspective can be the driving force behind design goals for home-based care technologies for those with progressive cognitive impairment.

7. ACKNOWLEDGMENTS

We would like to thank the team at the Integrace Institute for their continued support. We would also like to thank the undergraduate students at UMBC who contributed to the paper by collecting and analyzing data, Ms. Feizian and Ms. Paul.

8. REFERENCES

[1] B., S. et al. 2010. Factors determining the impact of care-giving on caregivers of elderly patients with dementia. A systematic literature review. *Maturitas*.

[2] Baikie, E. 2002. The impact of dementia on marital relationships. *Sexual and Relationship Therapy*. 17, 3 (2002), 289–299.

[3] Bharucha, A.J. et al. 2009. Intelligent Assistive Technology Applications to Dementia Care : Current Capabilities, Limitations and Future Challenges. *American Journal of Geriatric Psychiatry*. 17, 2 (2009), 88–104.

[4] Boots, L.M.M. et al. 2014. A systematic review of Internet-based supportive interventions for caregivers of patients with dementia. *International Journal of Geriatric Psychiatry*.

[5] Borrell-Carrio, F. et al. 2004. The biopsychosocial model 25 years later: Principles, practice, and scientific inquiry. *Annals of Family Medicine*. 2, 6 (2004), 576–582.

[6] Braun, V. and Clarke, V. 2006. Using thematic analysis in psychology. *Qualitative Research in Psychology*. 3, 2 (2006), 77–101.

[7] Brodaty, H. and Donkin, M. 2009. Family caregivers of people with

dementia. *Dialogues in Clinical Neuroscience*.
[8] De Bruin, E.D. 2008. Wearable systems for monitoring mobility-related activities in older people: a systematic review. *Clinical Rehabilitation*. 22, (2008), 878–895.
[9] Bruner, J. 1991. The narrative construction of reality. *Critical Studies*.
[10] Carroll, C. et al. 2017. Robin: Enabling Independence For Individuals With Cognitive Disabilities Using Voice Assistive Technology. *Proceedings of the 2017 CHI Conference Extended Abstracts on Human Factors in Computing Systems* (2017), 46–53.
[11] Carswell, W. et al. 2009. A review of the role of assistive technology for people with dementia in the hours of darkness. *Technology and Health Care*. 17, 4 (2009), 281–304.
[12] Clare, L. 2002. We'll fight it as long as we can: coping with the onset of Alzheimer's disease. *Aging & mental health*. 6, 2 (2002), 139–148.
[13] Cotrell, V. and Schulz, R. 1993. The perspective of the patient with Alzheimer's disease: a neglected dimension of dementia research. *The Gerontologist*.
[14] Davis, F.D. et al. 1989. User acceptance of computer technology: a comparison of two theoretical models. *Management Science*. 35, (1989), 181–192.
[15] Downs, M. 1997. The Emergence of the Person in Dementia Research. *Ageing & Society*. 17, (1997), 597–607.
[16] Fitting, M. et al. 1986. Caregivers for Dementia Patients: A Comparison of Husbands and Wives. *The Gerontologist*. 26, 3 (1986), 248–252.
[17] Fitzpatrick, R. and Boulton, M. 1994. Qualitative methods for assessing health care. *Quality in Health Care*. 3, 2 (1994), 107–113.
[18] Forsythe, D.E. 1999. "It's Just a Matter of Common Sense": Ethnography as Invisible Work. *Computer Supported Cooperative Work*. 8, 1–2 (1999), 127–145.
[19] Frauenberger, C. 2015. Disability and Technology A Critical Realist Perspective. *Assets'15*. (2015), 89–96.
[20] Frazer, A. 2007. Universal Usability. *Communications of the ACM*. (2007).
[21] Gitlin, L.N. et al. 2001. A randomized, controlled trial of a home environmental intervention: effect on efficacy and upset in caregivers and on daily function of persons with dementia. *The Gerontologist*. 41, 1 (2001), 4.
[22] Gregor Peter , Newell, A.F.Z.M. 2002. Designing for Dynamic Diversity - interfaces for older people. *Proceedings of the fifth international ACM conference on Assistive technologies*. (2002), 151–156.
[23] Harris, P. 2002. *The Person with Alzheimer's Disease: Pathways to Understanding the Experience*.
[24] Hirsch, T. et al. 2000. The ELDer project: social, emotional, and environmental factors in the design of eldercare technologies. *Design*. (2000), 72–79.
[25] Hougham, G. et al. 2003. Empirical research on informed consent with the cognitively impaired. *Irb*. (2003), 1–7.
[26] Hyden, L.-C. 1997. Illness and narrative. *Sociology of Health and Illness*. 19, 1 (1997), 48–69.
[27] Izal, M. et al. 2005. Caregivers' expectations and care receivers' competence: Lawton's ecological model of adaptation and aging revisited. *Archives of Gerontology and*. (2005).
[28] Lach, H.W. and Chang, Y.-P. 2007. Caregiver perspectives on safety in home dementia care. *Western journal of nursing research*. 29, 3 (2007), 993–1014.
[29] Lazar, A. et al. 2017. A Critical Lens on Dementia and Design in HCI. *Proceedings of the 2017 CHI Conference on Human Factors in Computing Systems - CHI '17*. (2017), 2175–2188.
[30] Lazar, A. et al. 2016. Designing for the Third Hand : Empowering Older Adults with Cognitive Impairments through Creating and Sharing. *Proceedings of the Designing Interactive Systems Conference (DIS '16)*. (2016), 1047–1058.
[31] Lazar, A. et al. 2017. Supporting People with Dementia in Digital Social Sharing. *Proceedings of the 2017 CHI Conference on Human Factors in Computing Systems - CHI '17* (2017), 2149–2162.
[32] Lewis, R.D.H. 1998. The Impact of the Marital Relationship on the Experience of Caring for an Eldelry Spouse with Dementia. *Ageing & Society*. 18, 2 (1998), 209.
[33] Lyons, K.S. et al. 2002. Caregiving as a dyadic process: Perspectives from caregiver and receiver. *Journals of Gerontology Series B-Psychological Sciences and Social Sciences*. 57, 3 (2002), P195–P204.
[34] Mahoney, D. et al. 2007. In-home monitoring of persons with dementia: Ethical guidelines for technology research and development. *Alzheimer's &*. (2007).
[35] Mankoff, J. et al. 2010. Disability studies as a source of critical inquiry for the field of assistive technology. *Proceedings of the 12th international ACM SIGACCESS conference on Computers and accessibility - ASSETS '10*. (2010), 3.
[36] Mcgrenere, J. 2006. Designing Technology for People with Cognitive Impairments. *CHI*. (2006), 1635–1638.
[37] Melnick, V.L. and Dubler, N.N. 1985. Alzheimer's Dementia: Dilemmas in Clinical Research. *Clifton., N.J.: Humana.Press.;*. (1985).
[38] Merton, R.K. 1976. Structural Analysis in Sociology. *Approaches to the Study of Social Structure*. 21–52.
[39] Miyashiro, G.M. 1991. The illness narratives: suffering, healing and the human condition. *Cadernos de Saúde Pública*. 7, 3 (1991), 430–435.
[40] Mulvenna, M. and Martin, S. Designing & Evaluating a Cognitive Prosthetic for People with Mild Dementia.
[41] Petersen, R.C. et al. 2001. Current concepts in mild cognitive impairment. *Archives of neurology*. 58, (2001), 1985–1992.
[42] Petersen, R.C. 2006. Mild cognitive impairment. *American Academy Of Neurology*. 367, 9527 (2006), 1979.
[43] Piper, A.M. et al. 2016. Technological Caregiving. *Proceedings of the 2016 CHI Conference on Human Factors in Computing Systems - CHI '16* (2016), 5311–5323.
[44] Piper, A.M. et al. Technological Caregiving: Supporting Online Activity for Adults with Cognitive Impairments.
[45] Powell, J. et al. 2008. A systematic review of networked technologies supporting carers of people with dementia. *Journal of telemedicine and telecare*. 14, 3 (2008), 154–6.
[46] Ronch, J., Bowman, C., & Madjaroff, G. 2013. *Culture Change in Elder Care*.
[47] Ronch, J. 2004. Changing institutional culture: Can we re-value the nursing home? *Journal of Gerontological Social Work*. (2004).
[48] Schulz, R. et al. 2002. Dementia caregiver intervention research: In search of clinical significance. *Gerontologist*.
[49] Shinohara, K. et al. 2014. In the shadow of misperception: Assistive technology use and social interactions. *Proceedings of the 17th ACM conference on Computer supported cooperative work & social computing* (2014), 705–714.
[50] Vines, J. et al. 2015. An Age-Old Problem : Examining the Discourses of Ageing in HCI and Strategies for Future Research. *Tochi*. 22, 1 (2015), 1–27.
[51] Whitlatch, C.J. et al. 2006. Dyadic intervention for family caregivers and care receivers in early-stage dementia. *The Gerontologist*. 46, 5 (2006), 688–694.
[52] Williams, G. 1984. The genesis of chronic illness: narrative re-construction. *Sociology of Health & Illness*. 6, 2 (1984), 175–200.
[53] Wright, P. and McCarthy, J. 2008. Empathy and experience in HCI. *Proceeding of the 26th annual CHI conference on Human factors in computing systems* (2008), 637–647.

AMI: An Adaptable Music Interface to Support the Varying Needs of People with Dementia

P. Frazer Seymour[1,2], Justin Matejka[1], Geoff Foulds[3], Ihor Petelycky[3], Fraser Anderson[1]

[1] Autodesk Research
Toronto, ON
{first.last}@autodesk.com

[2] University of Guelph
Guelph, ON
research@frazerseymour.com

[3] LifeMusic System
Toronto, ON
{first.last}@lifemusicsystem.com

ABSTRACT
Dementia is a progressive, degenerative syndrome that erodes cognition, long term memory, and the ability to maintain social relationships. Anxiety is common among those with dementia, and ranges from momentary and mild, to chronic and severe. Listening to familiar music from childhood or early adulthood has been shown to provide therapeutic and positive quality of life effects for individuals with dementia, but most modern interfaces are unfamiliar and difficult to use which may add frustration and stress that music is intended to relieve. To enable individuals with dementia to control playback of music, we present AMI, a tangible music player that can be reconfigured and adapted to meet the changing needs and preferences of individuals. AMI provides a set of input components (e.g., buttons, switches, knobs) with varying physical properties which can be easily interchanged by a non-technical user (such as a caregiver). This work contributes the system design, results of user tests with the target population, as well as a set of design principles that can be used in the development of future interfaces.

CCS Concepts
H.5.2 [Information Interfaces and Presentation]: User Interfaces

Keywords
Tangible input; dementia; music and audio; accessibility; personalization.

1. INTRODUCTION
Over 46 million people are currently living with dementia, and this total is expected to double every 20 years [29]. Characteristic symptoms include disturbances of memory, thinking, and learning, as well as deteriorating emotional control [5], though the development and severity of symptoms is highly variable between individuals. Specific memories and abilities can be lost or altered as the syndrome progresses [4], which have adverse effects on quality of life, including depression [9, 18]. As dementia tends to occur later in life, people with dementia often cope with additional physical impairments. The combination of these factors can limit the individual's ability to perform certain actions or operate certain interfaces.

ASSETS '17, October 29-November 1, 2017, Baltimore, MD, USA

ACM 978-1-4503-4926-0/17/10…$15.00
https://doi.org/10.1145/3132525.

Figure 1: AMI, a reconfigurable tangible music player. By reconfiguring modules in the base, the player can be customized to a user's specific needs.

Listening to music has been shown to improve the mental state of people with dementia [14]. Touch based tablets and music players are commonly available to seniors [3], but are difficult for people with dementia to access independently [20, 22, 28], which adds to their stress and that of their caregivers. Traditional interaction design assumes that users will become more competent with practice, however, diminishing short-term memory makes this a challenge for people with dementia. To properly accommodate this population, new, adaptable hardware and software is needed.

To address these issues, we present AMI: an Adaptable Music Interface which provides a configurable, modular system that caters to the unique needs of users with dementia. This paper contributes a description of the AMI system and its implementation; observations from sessions where AMI was used by people with varying cognitive and physical impairments; and design guidelines for tangible and adaptable interfaces for people with dementia. While the current work is motivated by people with dementia, many of the concepts and principles are more broadly applicable to older adults, or those with various motor or visual impairments.

2. RELATED WORK
This work builds upon prior work developing technology and music interfaces targeted at people with dementia [2, 13, 15, 22] and is inspired by recent work in HCI which explores reconfigurable tangible interfaces. The development of AMI was guided by research into interaction difficulties of people with dementia [7, 11].

2.1 Music Interfaces for People with Dementia

With the increased interest in music as a therapeutic tool for people with dementia [1, 12, 19, 20] and for creating assistive devices for people with dementia [8, 14, 18], there have been a number of projects that aim to make music playback more accessible for this population.

One approach to accessibility is to use existing touch-screen interactions but cater the graphical elements to the target population [5, 10]. CIRCA, for instance [5] provides a touch screen interface that enables users to browse music and other media content with the goal of facilitating reminiscence therapy and providing access to content relevant to the user's history. Similarly, the ENABLE project [24] provides a touch screen interface for users to select music from a list interface and displays related lyrics and images to provide context for a song. While these approaches allow for some degree of customization in terms of the media that is played and presented, many applications on touch-screens are unfamiliar for users with dementia, and the physical actions (e.g., tap, swipe) themselves cannot be adapted to accommodate target users and their decreasing cognitive and physical abilities.

Other researchers have addressed the difficulty of touchscreen interfaces for older individuals and people with dementia by developing simplified tangible interfaces. For instance, INDEPENDENT [19] created a physical music playing device similar in size to a CD player. The device consisted only of a lid and a single button; this enabled the selection of music to a very limited extent, and could be used unaided by users even in advanced stages of dementia. However, this device and the various similar commercial products [24, 25] are not adaptable to a user or their changing needs, and provide only very limited control.

2.2 Configurable Interfaces

Within the domain of HCI, several research projects have developed systems which allow designers to quickly interchange and reconfigure input components to support rapid prototyping of interfaces. For example, Switcharoo and VoodooIO allow users to select components for each function of a system and position them anywhere they would like in order to control software [6,25]. Several commercial projects explore hardware-based approaches to prototyping, such as Phidgets [11] and Gadgeteer [26]. These approaches simplify hardware prototyping by standardizing an interface, allowing for plug-and-play abilities with a diverse set of components. Additionally, there are approaches that allow graphical user interfaces to adapt to the particular hardware they are being displayed on [10].

AMI builds on this work by adapting their use to the domain of media playback for people with dementia and simplifies the process of configuring inputs. By providing a set of standard components, and eliminating software configuration steps, AMI ensures that non-technical end users can readily exchange the input devices. The software allows AMI to map that functionality to the correct controls to enable a dynamic, adaptable test bed.

3. AMI

To address issues found in commercial media playback devices and research prototypes, we developed the Adaptable Music Interface (AMI). AMI is comprised of three parts (Figure 2): an iPad tablet, containing the music and acting as the display; input components, which are used to control the system; and a microcontroller, to translate the analog input into digital signals recognized by the software. Once configured with the help of a caregiver, AMI is intended to be usable by people with dementia and other impairments without assistance.

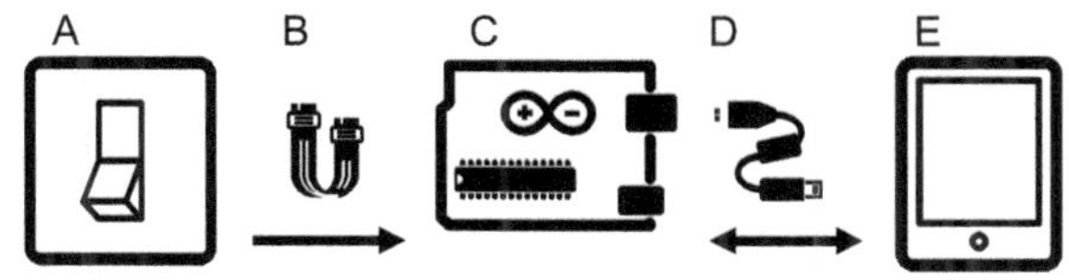

Figure 2: System overview: Input components (A) connect using ribbon cables (B) to an Arduino (C) in the chassis, which communicates via a serial cable (D) to an iPad (E).

It should be noted that the touch-screen functions of the iPad are used only by the caregiver during configuration. The tangible controls are used to operate the playback functions.

3.1 Input Components and Chassis

Thirteen modular input components have been fabricated to connect to a base unit. Each input component is comprised of an electronic device (such as a button, switch, or rotary encoder) mounted on a panel along with a 10-pin ribbon cable connector. Each panel contains alignment pins that provide stability and guide panel placement, allowing the components to be attached and removed easily. Panels can be 'single width' (5cm wide) or 'double width' (10cm) to facilitate a greater range of components. Panels can be attached to the chassis in any position and combination.

Each electronic device is directly wired to the connector. AMI utilizes six of the ten available pins, providing power, ground, an analog connection, two digital connections, and a "heartbeat" connection. Components can make use of these pins as needed, allowing users to connect analog and digital components without needing to understand the underlying electronic complexity.

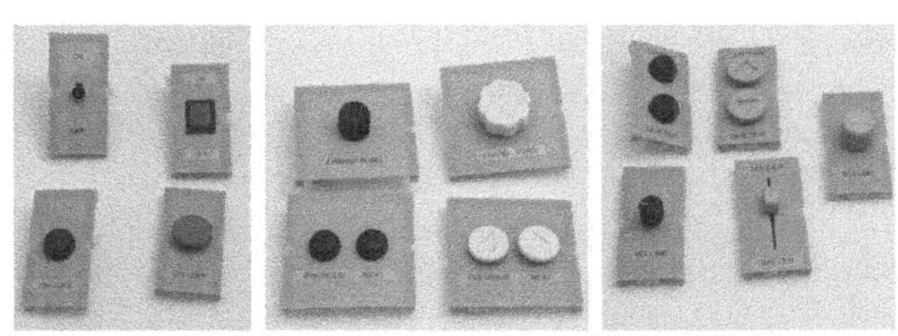

Figure 3: Modular components used with AMI. Left) power components; Centre) tuning components; Right) Volume

A wide range of input components are supported to increase the chance that users find a familiar control (Figure 3), or that a component will satisfy combinations of impairments. These components included professional, off-the-shelf devices such as knurled metal knobs, as well as several custom fabricated input devices that varied in color, shape, activation force, haptic feedback, etc. Currently, the system supports two types of toggle switches, several buttons, linear and rotary potentiometers, and rotary encoders.

The chassis (Figure 4, Left) provides power to the system and houses circuitry which manages the communication between the input components and the tablet application. Four 10-pin connectors are mounted within the chassis, and are wired to the analog and digital pins on an Arduino Uno. The Arduino polls these pins at 20Hz to monitor for changes in input values, and communicates with the iPad via using a Redpark serial cable [32].

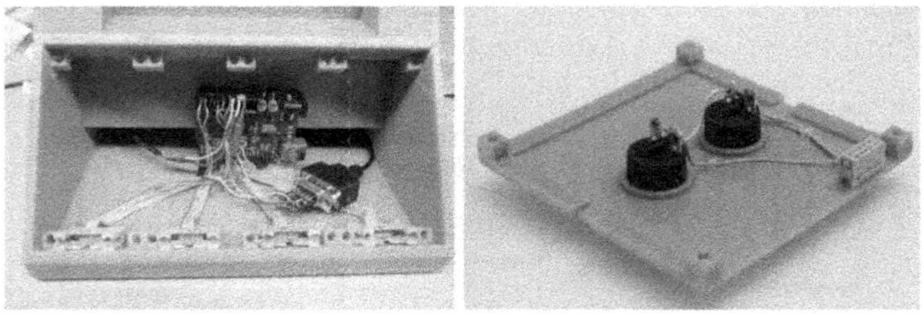

Figure 4: Left) Internal view of chassis, showing connectors and circuitry; Right) Wiring for sample input component.

3.2 Display and Audio Software

A custom iOS application runs on the iPad to provide functionality for media playback, display, and input handling. The application uses the existing iOS library for access to music the individual likes, and communicates with the attached Arduino using a serial connection.

When the system is in its *off* state, the tablet's screen dims and displays a treble clef, musical staff, and notes to provide a familiar visual indication of the device's functionality. When the system is in its *on* state, music immediately begins to play. Album art for the selected song is displayed in the centre of the screen, with *next* and *previous* tracks displayed to the left and right. When the selected track is changed (e.g. by navigating with next or previous buttons) the newly selected track rotates into place.

3.3 Configuration

To support the dynamic and changing needs of individuals, AMI supports simple reconfiguration of input components. When the tablet application opens in an unconfigured state, all functions are set to "safe" default behaviours (i.e., a random track will start playing at a pre-set volume, turning off after a pre-set time). Input components can be added or removed at any time into any position on the base unit while the application is running. An icon at the top of the display indicates what functionality a component will be mapped to.

To illustrate the utility of the configurable nature of AMI, we present a selection of sample configurations that could be designed for users living with dementia. (Figure 5) These configurations represent users presenting a variety of combinations of cognitive, motor, and visual impairments and show the spectrum of users supported with AMI.

4. FEEDBACK SESSIONS

To build an understanding of the utility of interchangeable controls, we conducted two informal feedback sessions with members of the target population (Figure 6). Sessions took place in two settings: an organized event for testing accessible products, and a daycare for people with dementia. In the former, the person with dementia was accompanied by a family caregiver, some of whom live with visual impairment; in the latter, a professional caregiver accompanied the person with dementia. Informed consent was obtained from all participants or their caregiver. In total, ten individuals participated in the study, with eight completing a personalized device. Two individuals stopped the session before completing a device.

We began by explaining the functionality of the system, and that it was a music player. Then, we presented AMI (or an auxiliary bank (Figure 6, left)) assembled with various input components. We asked the participant to use one of the components to achieve a desired functionality (e.g., turn on the device). Alternative components for that functionality were then presented to the participant, and they were asked to use them. If participants could understand and operate multiple components, they were asked for a preference, presenting them side-by-side for comparison. Once the participant selected one, the same process occurred for the next function (e.g., change song). When components for all functions had been selected, we presented the participant with a fully configured device to ensure they were able to use it.

4.1 Results

There were six unique configurations among the eight completed designs, and there were important individual differences between the devices constructed for each participant. For instance, one user did not understand the affordance of the large, yellow knob and tried to press it. Several others mistook some of the coloured buttons for knobs and attempted to turn them unsuccessfully. For these individuals, the availability of other components enabled them to configure a device that they would otherwise not have been able to use.

Figure 5: Sample configurations illustrating the adaptability to a variety of needs and use cases of fictitious, simplified personas. These examples serve to highlight how different components may support varied function, and are not meant to be a 'definitive' radio for any particular segment of people. The leftmost device may be used by someone without impairments (A), followed by an individual with cognitive impairment (B), visual impairment (C), physical impairment (D), and a combination of multiple impairments (E).

The utility of modular components was also apparent as participants' varied backgrounds impacted their preference and ability to operate the components. For instance, one participant, when asked how he would increase the volume with a knob, replied that he would "crank it up!". Further discussions with the caregiver revealed that the particular individual came from a musical background and was familiar with using knobs to control volume.

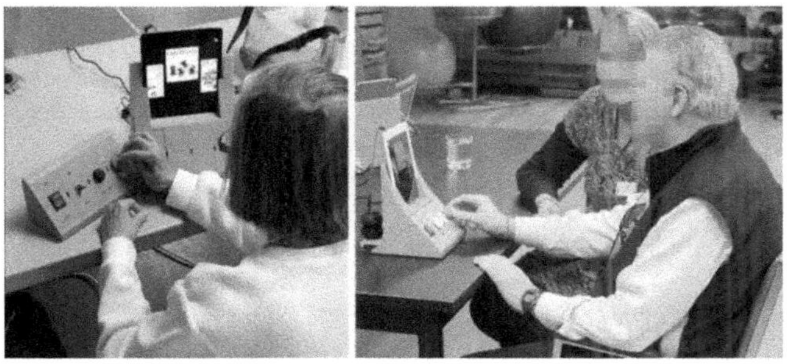

Figure 6: Individuals from each of the two sessions configuring AMI by testing components.

Overall, there was a broad coverage of input components used in the final devices. For power, four individuals selected rocker switches, three selected a toggle switch, and one chose a button. Knobs and buttons were almost equally preferred for song selection with five participants using buttons and three selecting knobs. Finally, the slider was the most popular volume component, used in four of the completed configurations, the others choosing a knob or buttons. This variation indicates that users could benefit from the ability to select and customize the input components.

Some users were unable to produce a configured radio by growing uncomfortable and ending the session early. This is not uncommon in dementia research, as individuals can become confused or anxious. In these cases, it may be worthwhile to provide indicators on the components that signal their functionality very clearly so the user may still be able to operate the device at a later time.

5. DISCUSSION

The results of the user study demonstrated the utility of the approach, and usability of the prototype. From the experiences we observed during the study, we present a set of recommendations to help guide future work targeting tangible interfaces for people with dementia. These recommendations build on existing work [7, 13, 18] as well as consultation with domain experts from four research groups and three care facilities. Many of the aspects described here are more broadly applicable to users who do not have dementia, but may have some form of physical or visual impairment.

5.1 Adaptation

Due to the variation between individuals with dementia, as well as the dynamic and progressive nature of the syndrome, it is important that interfaces which target this population are able to adapt to the specific person and their abilities over time [4]. Adaptation need not necessarily be automatic or accessible by the person themselves, but should be simple and intuitive as we found caregivers often have limited time to become familiar with a new interface and may be nontechnical. Adaptation should be possible not only at deployment-time, but also throughout the use of the device. If a user is no longer able to operate a specific functionality, that functionality should be removable or replaceable.

5.2 Familiar Metaphors

People with dementia often have varying experiences with devices (such as music players), and that experience may not be accurately remembered, so it is important to provide each person with interaction metaphors that are familiar [7]. To that end, familiar input metaphors should be used, such as flipping a switch, turning a knob, pressing a button, etc. Depending on the person's exposure to prior interfaces, they may better understand different metaphors (e.g., jukebox, 8-track, radio) and the associated controls. As the effects of dementia are widely variable [18], as much diversity should be supported as possible, e.g., differentiating form, action, and feel of each component.

5.3 Support Multiple Impairments

There are common impairments (loss of vision, motor impairments, etc.) which often concurrently impact people with dementia, as dementia tends to take affect at later ages. These impairments can prevent users from being able to touch or grasp small targets, operate high-force interfaces, or perform fine motor tasks. Additionally, visual impairments may hinder the user's ability to visually discriminate between the size, shape, or color of input components. To support a wide range of impairments, a system should attempt to provide a variety of input options and modes of feedback.

5.4 Limitations and Future Work

Improvements can be made in the software to allow for more complex mapping of functionality; e.g., a *configuration by example* approach where a component is connected and activated, then mapped to the next action made on the tablet such as decreasing the volume or pausing playback. Alternately, a touch-based interface that could be quickly used to map inputs to functionality could be useful to a caregiver or another user without dementia.

Additionally, the in-situ efficacy of AMI needs to be evaluated with a longitudinal study. This type of study would give insight into the utility of being able to reconfigure the device as the symptoms progress, and has the potential to provide new information to guide the design of future interfaces and technology.

6. CONCLUSIONS

Many individuals are impacted by dementia and its related effects, which cause a lack of independence and often with it depression and many associated afflictions. AMI aims to enable these individuals to control the playback of music using intuitive, tangible controls. With this type of interface, AMI intends to provide more independence and better access to music to people with dementia. The lessons learned while developing and testing the device can serve to inform the design of future devices targeted at individuals with dementia.

7. REFERENCES

[1] David Aldridge. 2000. *Music therapy in dementia care: More new voices.* Jessica Kingsley.

[2] Norman Alm, Richard Dye, Gary Gowans, Jim Campbell, Arlene Jean Astell, and Maggie Ellis. 2007. A communication support system for older people with

dementia. *IEEE Comput.* (2007). Retrieved from research-repository.st- andrews.ac.uk/handle/10023/ 1589

[3] M. Anderson. 2016. *Technology Device Ownership: 2015. Pew Research Center; 2015.*

[4] J. Wesson Ashford and Frederick A. Schmitt. 2001. Modeling the time-course of Alzheimer dementia. *Curr. Psychiatry Rep.* 3, 1 (2001), 20–28.

[5] Arlene J. Astell, Maggie P. Ellis, Lauren Bernardi, Norman Alm, Richard Dye, Gary Gowans, and Jim Campbell. 2010. Using a touch screen computer to support relationships between people with dementia and caregivers. *Interact. Comput.* 22, 4 (July 2010), 267–275.

[6] Daniel Avrahami and Scott E. Hudson. 2002. Forming interactivity: a tool for rapid prototyping of physical interactive products. In *Proceedings of the 4th conference on Designing interactive systems: processes, practices, methods, and techniques*, 141–146.

[7] Suzanne Cahill, Jurate Macijauskiene, Aase-Marit Nyg\a ard, Jon-Paul Faulkner, and Inger Hagen. 2007. Technology in dementia care. *Technol. Disabil.* 19, 2, 3 (2007), 55–60.

[8] Marilyn Cash. 2003. Assistive technology and people with dementia. *Rev. Clin. Gerontol.* 13, 04 (2003), 313–319.

[9] Peijun Chen, Mary Ganguli, Benoit H. Mulsant, and Steven T. DeKosky. 1999. The temporal relationship between depressive symptoms and dementia: a community-based prospective study. *Arch. Gen. Psychiatry* 56, 3 (1999), 261–266.

[10] Krzysztof Gajos and Daniel S. Weld. 2004. SUPPLE: Automatically Generating User Interfaces. In *Proceedings of the 9th International Conference on Intelligent User Interfaces* (IUI '04), 93–100.

[11] S. Greenberg and C. Fitchett. 2001. Phidgets: easy development of physical interfaces through physical widgets. 209–218.

[12] I. Hagen. 2004. Development of a Protocol for the Assessment of Assistive Aids for People with Dementia. *Dementia* 3, 3 (October 2004), 281–296.

[13] Tizneem Jiancaro, Susan B. Jaglal, and Alex Mihailidis. 2017. Technology, design and dementia: an exploratory survey of developers. *Disabil. Rehabil. Assist. Technol.* 12, 6 (2017), 573–584.

[14] Susan M. Koger, Kathryn Chapin, and Melissa Brotons. 1999. Is music therapy an effective intervention for dementia? A meta-analytic review of literature. *J. Music Ther.* 36, 1 (1999), 2–15.

[15] Amanda Lazar, Raymundo Cornejo, Caroline Edasis, and Anne Marie Piper. 2016. Designing for the Third Hand: Empowering Older Adults with Cognitive Impairment through Creating and Sharing. In *Proceedings of the 2016 ACM Conference on Designing Interactive Systems*, 1047–1058.

[16] Alex Mihailidis and Geoffrey R. Fernie. 2002. Context-aware assistive devices for older adults with dementia. *Gerontechnology* 2, 2 (2002), 173–188.

[17] Kellie Morrissey, Gavin Wood, David Green, Nadia Pantidi, and John McCarthy. 2016. "I"m a rambler, I'm a gambler, I'm a long way from home': The Place of Props, Music, and Design in Dementia Care. In *Proceedings of the 2016 ACM Conference on Designing Interactive Systems*, 1008–1020.

[18] R. Orpwood. 2004. User Involvement in Dementia Product Development. *Dementia* 3, 3 (October 2004), 263–279.

[19] R. Orpwood, J. Chadd, D. Howcroft, A. Sixsmith, J. Torrington, G. Gibson, and G. Chalfont. 2010. Designing technology to improve quality of life for people with dementia: user-led approaches. *Univers. Access Inf. Soc.* 9, 3 (August 2010), 249–259. DOI:https://doi.org/10.1007/s10209-009-0172-1

[20] Linnéa Persson. 2015. *Experienced issues with tablet computer interfaces among older adults: An exploratory study using a human centred interaction design approach.* Retrieved from http://www.diva-portal.org/smash/record.jsf?pid=diva2:872166

[21] Louise Robinson, Katie Brittain, Stephen Lindsay, Dan Jackson, and Patrick Olivier. 2009. Keeping In Touch Everyday (KITE) project: developing assistive technologies with people with dementia and their carers to promote independence. *Int. Psychogeriatr.* 21, 03 (2009), 494–502.

[22] Élvio Rodrigues, Micael Carreira, and Daniel Gonçalves. 2016. Enhancing typing performance of older adults on tablets. *Univers. Access Inf. Soc.* 15, 3 (2016), 393–418.

[23] H. B. Svansdottir and J. Snaedal. 2006. Music therapy in moderate and severe dementia of Alzheimer's type: a case–control study. *Int. Psychogeriatr.* 18, 04 (2006), 613–621.

[24] P. Topo. 2004. Assessment of a Music-Based Multimedia Program for People with Dementia. *Dementia* 3, 3 (October 2004), 331–350.

[25] Nicolas Villar, Kiel Gilleade, Devina Ramdunyellis, and Hans Gellersen. 2007. The VoodooIO gaming kit: a real-time adaptable gaming controller. *Comput. Entertain. CIE* 5, 3 (2007), 7.

[26] Nicolas Villar, James Scott, Steve Hodges, Kerry Hammil, and Colin Miller. 2012. . NET gadgeteer: a platform for custom devices. In *International Conference on Pervasive Computing*, 216–233.

[27] Jayne Wallace, Anja Thieme, Gavin Wood, Guy Schofield, and Patrick Olivier. 2012. Enabling self, intimacy and a sense of home in dementia: an enquiry into design in a hospital setting. In *Proceedings of the SIGCHI Conference on Human Factors in Computing Systems*, 2629–2638.

[28] Jenny Waycott, Sonja Pedell, Frank Vetere, Elizabeth Ozanne, Lars Kulik, Alan Gruner, and John Downs. 2012. Actively engaging older adults in the development and evaluation of tablet technology. In *Proceedings of the 24th Australian Computer-Human Interaction Conference*, 643–652.

[29] Dementia statistics | Alzheimer's Disease International. Retrieved September 20, 2016 from http://www.alz.co.uk/research/statistics

[30] CD Boom Box. Retrieved January 10, 2017 from http://enablingdevices.com/catalog/AdaptedElectronics/CD_Players_Boom_Boxes/cd-boom-box

[31] Music Player For Alzheimer's and Dementia I Simple Music Player I Alzstore. *www.alzstore.com.* Retrieved from http://www.alzstore.com//ProductDetails.asp?ProductCode=2115

[32] Lightning Serial Cable for iOS – Redpark Product Development. Retrieved September 20, 2016 from http://redpark.com/lightning-serial-cable-l2-db9v/

Deaf and Hard-of-Hearing Perspectives on Imperfect Automatic Speech Recognition for Captioning One-on-One Meetings

Larwan Berke
Rochester Institute of Technology
152 Lomb Memorial Drive
Rochester, NY 14618 USA
larwan.berke@mail.rit.edu

Christopher Caulfield
Rochester Institute of Technology
152 Lomb Memorial Drive
Rochester, NY 14618 USA
cxc4115@rit.edu

Matt Huenerfauth
Rochester Institute of Technology
152 Lomb Memorial Drive
Rochester, NY 14618 USA
matt.huenerfauth@rit.edu

ABSTRACT

Recent advances in Automatic Speech Recognition (ASR) have made this technology a potential solution for transcribing audio input in real-time for people who are Deaf or Hard of Hearing (DHH). However, ASR is imperfect; users must cope with errors in the output. While some prior research has studied ASR-generated transcriptions to provide captions for DHH people, there has not been a systematic study of how to best present captions that may include errors from ASR software nor how to make use of the ASR system's word-level confidence. We conducted two studies, with 21 and 107 DHH participants, to compare various methods of visually presenting the ASR output with certainty values. Participants answered subjective preference questions and provided feedback on how ASR captioning could be used with confidence display markup. Users preferred captioning styles with which they were already most familiar (that did not display confidence information), and they were concerned about the accuracy of ASR systems. While they expressed interest in systems that display word confidence during captions, they were concerned that text appearance changes may be distracting. The findings of this study should be useful for researchers and companies developing automated captioning systems for DHH users.

CCS Concepts

• **Human-centered computing~Empirical studies in accessibility** • **Human-centered computing~Accessibility design and evaluation methods** • *Social and professional topics~Assistive technologies*

Keywords

Deaf and Hard of Hearing; Automatic Speech Recognition; Real-Time Captions; Communication; User Study; Feedback.

1. INTRODUCTION

Advances in speech and language technology can benefit people who are Deaf or Hard of Hearing (DHH) by providing access to spoken information. Many of these users currently benefit from a wide range of services such as e-mail/instant messaging [3], American Sign Language (ASL) in-person interpretation, real-time transcription or captioning services, and Video Relay Service [6].

ASSETS'17, October 29-November 1, 2017, Baltimore, MD, USA
© 2017 Association for Computing Machinery.
ACM ISBN 978-1-4503-4926-0/17/10…$15.00
https://doi.org/10.1145/3132525.3132541

However, in many work or education settings, DHH individuals may lack access to sign language interpreting services due to their high cost or the need to arrange such services in advance. Further, DHH individuals who do not identify as culturally Deaf or older adults who have lost hearing later in life may prefer text-based accessibility tools, rather than sign language interpretation.

With recent advances in Automatic Speech Recognition (ASR), researchers have considered whether fully automatic solutions for providing text transcriptions of spoken language could be useful for DHH users [35]. An exploratory survey of DHH participants by Elliot *et al.* [10] revealed that users were agreeable to the idea of having ASR support their workplace conversations, but the study did not provide users with an opportunity to try a prototype of this technology. Kawas *et al.* [23] found that participants felt more autonomous when using a current ASR platform for real-time captioning, but their study focused on a classroom setting, and with a small number of participants.

While these prior studies suggest the promise of ASR for workplace meeting captioning, an empirical study with a large number (100+) of DHH participants is needed to identify factors important to users. Similar to [23], we expect that DHH users may be better able to provide feedback after they have an opportunity to try a prototype ASR captioning system, in our case, with a simulated workplace meeting, and with word-confidence information displayed. This paper describes a pair of studies we have conducted with 128 total DHH users trying such a prototype and providing feedback.

1.1 ASR Tools for DHH Individuals

Several researchers have investigated how to produce captioning tools to benefit DHH users via ASR technologies. Some focused on non-real-time applications, e.g., ASR producing a transcript of classroom lectures, after the lecture is concluded, to enable students to review material after class [44]. Others examined whether ASR can automatically caption the content of online videos [38]. In these above settings, the user must wait for offline ASR processing.

Other researchers have investigated semi-automated real-time applications of ASR for DHH users: In [24], students viewed lectures with real-time captioning, to achieve good accuracy, their ASR used a human-prepared dictionary for each course. As another example, in some Communication Access Realtime Translation (CART) services, a professional clearly re-speaks the words of the lecturer into a high-end microphone, to achieve high ASR accuracy [29]. While ASR technology has improved, there are still errors in the output, especially in noisy and complex environments. To boost the accuracy of imperfect ASR, some researchers have created systems in which human overseers fix mistakes in ASR output [15] or have crowdsourced the task of transcribing audio (thereby bypassing the use of ASR) [17]. The business model for these services requires some regular payment for the human labor.

Some researchers have experimented with fully automated real-time systems for DHH users: Some examined whether augmented reality glasses can overlay ASR-produced captions on the field of view of DHH users [31], but they found that the quality of several ASR engines was insufficient for DHH users, due to noisy environments in daily life that led to low accuracy, e.g. 60%. Kawas *et al.* [23] performed a qualitative study of ASR in classrooms and had similar findings; their participants struggled with low quality captioning from a real-time ASR application.

In contrast to prior work, our research focuses on a context in which ASR may work better: during live one-on-one meetings between a DHH individual and a hearing person. By removing a major source of noise from the environment (e.g. classroom with crowds and background sounds) and focusing on one speaker, ASR engines are capable of producing output with higher accuracy. Furthermore, contrast this setting to a public lecture: A lecturer may not change how they speak based on ASR output since they are busy attending to their entire diverse audience; in contrast, during a live one-on-one meeting, a speaker might adjust their voice or speaking style to lead to better ASR results if they notice errors in the ASR output.

We focus on a scenario in which ASR results are displayed on a mobile tablet device viewable by the DHH participant in a one-on-one meeting with hearing individuals. To prototype how captions may appear, we produced simulation videos of a business meeting (Figure 1) with a camera focused on an actor who is sitting at a table (across from the camera). The layout for this mock conversation is shown in Figure 1 with the text captions appearing in a black area at the bottom of the video window, containing the output from the ASR engine, representing where the DHH user might view a tablet device below the line of-sight with their conversational partner. Additional details about these videos appear in Section 1.3.

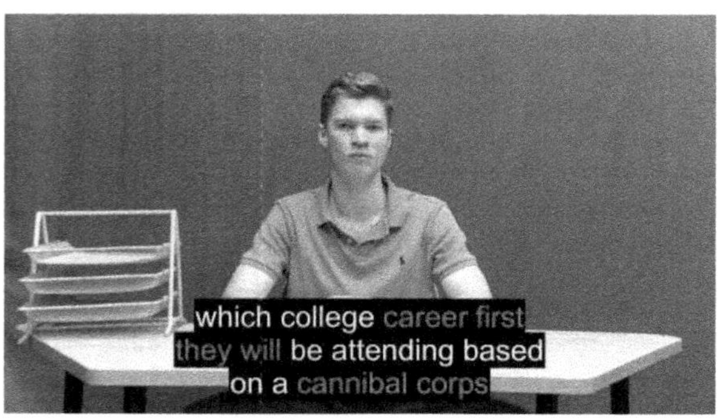

Figure 1. The prototype tool examined in this work

1.2 Displaying Confidence

Prior research has found that users may benefit from captions, even if only a portion of the speech audio was successfully captioned. For example, a participant in one study using ASR captioning said: "knowing the context and searching for keywords are essential steps to build their capacity of understanding." [34] This finding is valuable since ASR systems are currently not perfectly accurate in identifying the words spoken, especially in noisy environments.

There is additional information we can provide to DHH users: ASR engines assign confidence metrics to the words they hypothesize are being spoken in an audio input; this information could be utilized by the viewer to know which portions of the text they should trust. Most ASR applications do not convey this information to the user. We investigate whether knowing the difference between high-confidence (confident) and low-confidence (uncertain) words, given some threshold, may benefit DHH users of automatically produced captions (which will naturally contain errors).

In addition to investigating *whether* providing ASR confidence information benefits DHH users, we also examine *how* we should display this information visually. We must consider how to reduce the complexity of the information that is presented to users. In a live one-on-one meeting, the DHH participant must read the caption and attend to the face and body language of their conversational partner. We seek a method of displaying uncertain words/phrases in a way that does not create additional communication barriers for DHH users by making the visual presentation too complex.

Several researchers have studied how to present ASR captions on screen, including whether to indicate if the ASR was not confident about some of the words. Figure 2 lists how prior researchers have modified the appearance of captions, including a few researchers who have specifically examined how to possibly convey the ASR confidence level to viewers (which is the focus of our research).

Changing the appearance to convey ASR confidence:

Appearance Changed	Prior Published Research
Font Change	Piquard-Kipffer *et al.* [34]
Font Color	Shiver and Wolfe [39]
Underlining	Vertanen and Kristensson [42]

Changing the caption appearance for other reasons:

Appearance Changed	Prior Published Research
Colored Borders	Vy [43]
Dynamic Positioning	Hong *et al.* [18]
Dynamic Size	Wang *et al.* [45]
Emoji	Lee *et al.* [28]
Removal of Text	Ferdiansyah and Nakagawa [12]
Syllables	Secară [38]
Text Spacing	Nambo *et al.* [32]
Tracked Display	Kushalnagar *et al.* [25]
Transparency	Miller *et al.* [30]

Figure 2. Captioning Display Styles

Piquard-Kipffer's team [34] indicated words for which the ASR was confident using **bold** text, and uncertain words, in regular text. They experimented with conveying ASR-uncertain words with phonetic spelling (like a dictionary pronunciation listing), but DHH users did not like that approach. Noting that only those participants who knew phonology of the spoken language could benefit from the extra information, the authors explained that their method may not benefit members of the DHH community who utilize sign language as their primary language.

Shiver and Wolfe [39] used white text (on a black background) to indicate words for which the ASR was confident, and darker gray text for the word for which ASR was uncertain. Some participants in their study liked this approach. However, when the authors tried to measure the impact of this addition through comprehension-question testing, they did not measure an effect. The authors used caution in drawing conclusions from their comprehension-question results: "even when there were no captions available, participants answered more than 50% of the content questions correctly... Also, the performance on the perfectly-captioned video was lower than that on the two videos captioned through ASR." [39]

DHH users were not the focus of [42], but those researchers studied the use of red underlines to indicate ASR-uncertain words in the text output of a dictation application. They studied how visualizing ASR errors could help hearing individuals correct the output, but the authors noted that confidence visualization did not improve participants' ability to find errors [42]. However, the authors noted that when their system accurately added "uncertain" underlines to erroneous words, participants were more successful at fixing the ASR dictation output, as compared to a baseline condition with no underlining. Their work revealed that the potential benefits of uncertainty marking may depend on the ASR accuracy level.

While prior work has examined methods of marking words in captions, e.g. [34, 39], the literature lacks an empirical comparison of various approaches for conveying confidence, based on reactions from DHH users – especially in the context of one-on-one meetings between a DHH individual and a hearing person. Such a study can identify promising design directions, which could be further explored and refined through additional design work and evaluation.

1.3 Prototype and Stimuli for Our Studies

To support our study, we built a prototype that uses ASR to process speech from videos to automatically add captions, with appearance dependent on the confidence numbers in the ASR output. Figure 1 showed an example of the output of our current prototype.

As discussed in Section 1.1, while we envision a future application in which users may hold a tablet device that displays captions during a one-on-one meeting with a hearing individual, we have created videos of a mock business meeting scenario with captions displayed onscreen. Crabb *et al.* [7] recommended the captioning be positioned below and outside of a video frame when captioning online videos. In our case, we are simulating where a person may hold a tablet device displaying live captions, below the line of sight of their conversational partner; in the prototype videos, the user can see the real-world environment to the left and the right of the captions, as they would to the left and right of a tablet they may hold at that location in real life. The ASR output appears onscreen one word at a time, similar to C-Print [11], rather than appearing as entire phrases or sentences at once. Further, onscreen text is limited to 3 lines so that it does not take up too much visual space, following recommendations in Kushalnagar *et al.* [26].

In Figure 1, red indicated words for which the ASR engine had a low confidence value. The speaker actually said "which college *career fairs they will* be attending based on *the candidate requirements*." The prototype can be configured to format text in a variety of ways, and the automatically generated caption text can be modified manually to insert or remove errors, for testing purposes. Determining the optimal threshold of ASR confidence for determining when to apply text formatting is an open question because it greatly depends on the specific ASR engine. Another open design question is the span of the text to use as the granularity for the uncertainty marking. For the research in this paper, we shall assume a per-word confidence based on ASR engine confidence rather than calculating confidence over multi-word chunks of text.

In this paper, we use this prototype to compare various methods of displaying word confidence to DHH users and elicit their feedback. With Figure 2 as a starting point, we wanted to select a set of visual parameters to convey word-confidence to a DHH user reading captions. To reduce our design space, we considered captioning standards, e.g. digital television captioning includes basic ASCII plus a few special characters [2], and some standards recommend the look and speed of video captions [9]. Other researchers recommend avoiding animated text [36], avoiding small/large font sizes [5], avoiding text/background color combinations that clash or are too similar [8], and encouraged the use of sans serif fonts for legibility [21]. Figure 3 displays the caption appearance options we decided to investigate in a preliminary study (Section 2.1). We included some "opposites" such as *Bold on Confident* (bold_c) and *Bold on Uncertain* (bold_u), but some caption markup styles lacked a logical opposite, e.g. *Empty Underline on Uncertain* (del_u).

To produce stimuli that could be repeated across participants with variations in the captioning display, we simulated a one-on-one meeting by creating a short film of a business meeting. We wrote a script with someone discussing upcoming plans for a project with the person viewing the video: A human resources office was recruiting job candidates at an upcoming event. An actor performed the meeting script in a sound-proof video studio, with an office desk and plain background (Figure 1). The actor's voice was captured by a professional microphone on an overhead boom. The script was composed of 12 stimulus paragraphs, with an average of 88.3 words in each paragraph (ranging in duration from 19 to 46 seconds).

Example of Markup on Captioning	**Description (label)**
	Baseline condition: no markup (no_change)
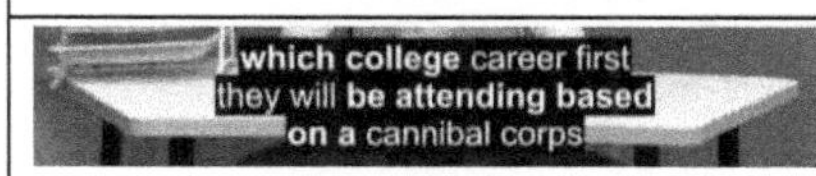	Bold on Confident (bold_c)
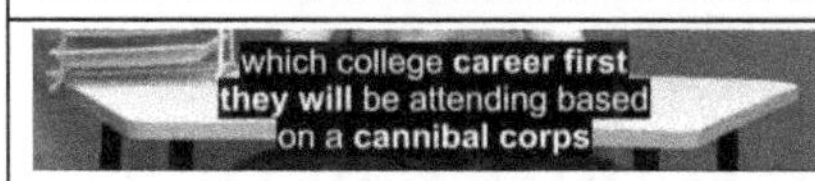	Bold on Uncertain (bold_u)
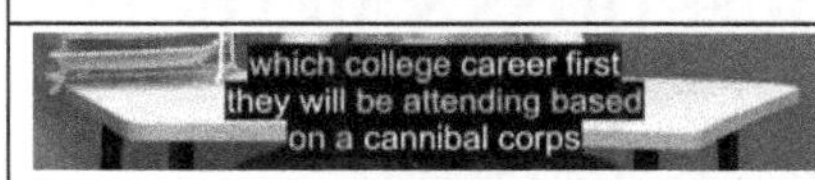	Green on Confident (color_c)
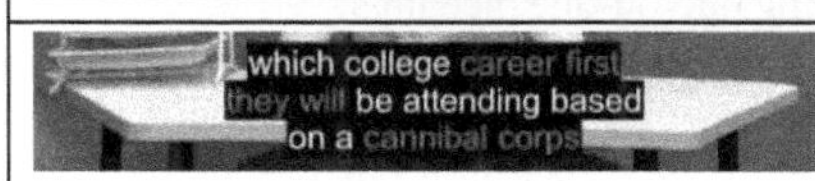	Red on Uncertain (color_u)
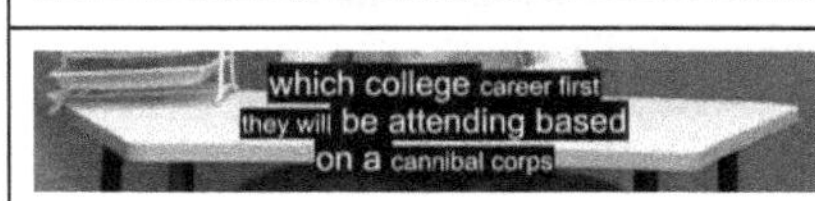	Small font size on Uncertain (size_u)
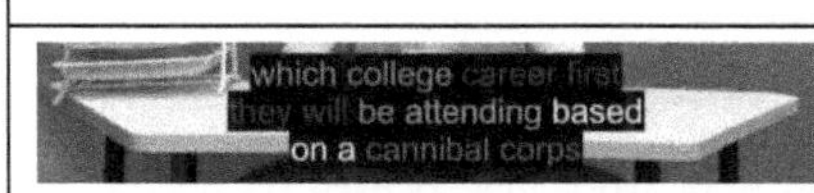	Levels of gray color based on confidence (r_gray)
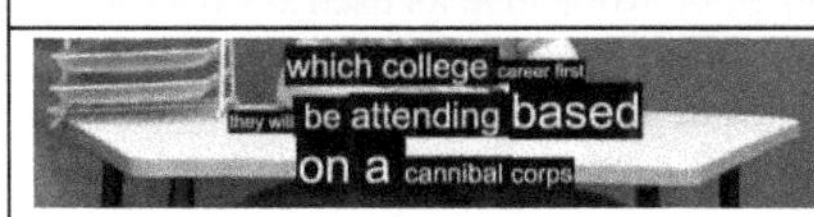	Levels of font size based on confidence (r_size)
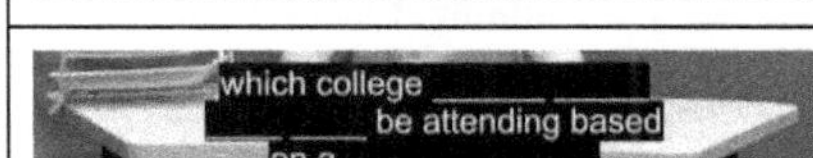	Empty underline on Uncertain (del_u)
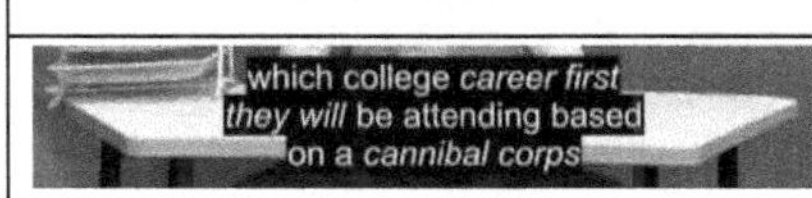	Italics on Uncertain (it_u)
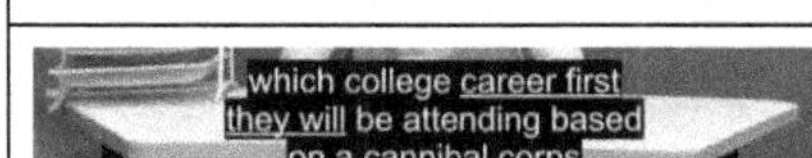	Underline on Uncertain (ul_u)
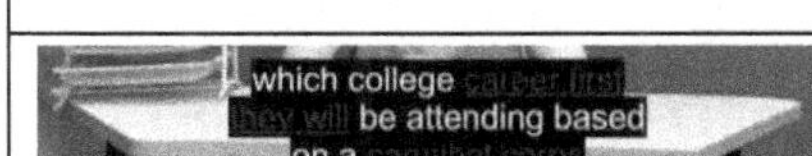	Underline and gray color on Uncertain (ul_gray_u)

Figure 3. Markup conditions in the pilot study (Section 2.1)

To generate realistic ASR output (containing errors), the audio from the videos was processed using the Sphinx open-source ASR engine [27]. Accuracy is reported using Word Error Rate (WER), based on the number of substitutions, insertions, and deletions in the output when compared to the actual script. The average WER of our stimuli was 23.2%. We selected this rate because we needed sufficient errors to appear in our caption texts so that participants would see at least a few words with markup in each stimulus. If the WER were any worse, we were concerned that participants would find the captions so unhelpful that they would not remain engaged during the study.

To decide which words should receive markup, a confidence threshold must be defined so that words can be categorized as either *Confident* (above the threshold) or *Uncertain* (below it). Based on our observations and feedback from a small number of DHH users who viewed initial prototype videos, we selected a probability threshold of 0.995. (It was not the intent of this study to determine an optimum threshold value; we leave this for future work.) It is important to note that the confidence value is not a perfect indication of the ASR accuracy for individual words. That is, some words correctly recognized by the ASR may be labeled as "uncertain," and conversely, some words that were incorrectly recognized by the ASR may be labeled as "confident." For the 1060 words in our stimuli, 789 were correct and confident, 197 were correct yet uncertain, 39 were incorrect yet confident, and 69 were incorrect and uncertain.

Finally, all 12 stimulus-paragraph videos were generated using all 12 markup conditions in Figure 3, to yield 144 videos.

2. RESEARCH QUESTIONS & METHODS

This paper investigates several research questions:

RQ1: Are DHH users receptive to the idea of using ASR to caption spoken content during one-on-one meetings?

RQ2: What issues/factors do DHH users consider important when they are using ASR captioning as an assistive technology?

RQ3: When viewing captions of speech in a one-on-one meeting, what confidence markup do DHH users subjectively prefer?

RQ4: What applications do DHH users believe are most suitable for the use of ASR-based automatic captioning tools?

As we mentioned in Section 1, prior researchers have found that displaying caption markup for ASR applications has promise: in particular, as measured through subjective preferences of users. However, we did not find prior work that focused on one-on-one meetings nor determined which method of visual markup is preferred by DHH users. One study that closely resembled our research questions was done by Kawas *et al.*, however they did not exclusively focus on ASR as a captioning tool for one-on-one meetings nor did they discuss displaying confidence [23]. While prior guidelines for caption display helped to narrow our design space, we still had quite a long list of word-markup parameters to consider (Figure 2). It was infeasible to expect our participants to give reasonable answers when presented with this many choices. Therefore, we split our research into two parts: a "pilot" study to narrow down the markup choices, and a larger follow-up study. The design of the first (pilot) study is a single-question quantitative survey, while the second, larger "comparison" study used both quantitative and qualitative methods to analyze responses to subjective scalar questions and open-ended feedback questions.

2.1 Pilot Study to Narrow the Markup Set

The goal of this pilot study was to identify a subset of the most promising visual markup styles. DHH participants viewed videos of a mock one-on-one meeting situation, with captions displayed. This within-subjects study had 12 conditions: the 11 visual display styles listed in Figure 3 and a baseline condition (white text on black background, with no indication of word confidence). Each participant viewed and subjectively evaluated a total of 12 videos, with one video of each of the different markup methods. The 12 conditions were assigned to the 12 paragraph-length stimuli videos (Section 1.3) using a Latin-squares schedule, to rotate conditions among the individual videos. The 12 video stimuli of the business meeting were presented to participants in chronological order.

We designed videos on a MacBook Pro 15-inch laptop with a web browser displayed stimuli and questions; the laptop was pre-installed with a PHP server and hosted the stimuli locally. A native ASL signer research assistant was with the participant at all times in order to provide guidance on using the application and technical troubleshooting when necessary. The application presented a typical HTML form that the participant completed and pressed "Next" to proceed through the study.

We reached out to participants by e-mail and flyers on the university campus. Participants were eligible if they answered "yes" to both screening questions: Are you Deaf or hard-of-hearing? Do you use captions when viewing television? They made an appointment with the researchers and participated in the study in a private office as to ensure a distraction-free environment. Participants were paid $40 for the 50-minute study. A total of 21 DHH individuals participated, with self-identified gender of 13 males and 8 females and self-identified hearing-status of 14 people who are Deaf and 7 people who are Hard of Hearing.

After completing consent forms and a demographic questionnaire, participants were shown an introductory video to introduce the scenario and explain the purpose of the visual markup. Participants were informed that the words they would see were produced by a computer that was trying to identify what was spoken automatically; further, they were informed that the computer wasn't always confident in what it heard, and the changes in appearance of the text indicated this. After each video stimulus, participants answered a Yes/No question: "Did you like the style of captioning in this video clip?" The question was modeled after the Quality of Perception (*QoP*) scale shown to be effective for DHH individuals in [16]. Figure 4 displays mean scores (No=0/Yes=1) for each markup style. The differences shown in Figure 4 are not statistically significant; it was not the intent of this pilot study to conclusively select a best markup method: Our goal was to identify the most promising candidates from this large set of visual mark-up styles, which would be further examined in a large follow-up study. Section 2.2.1 discuss how this selection was made.

At the end of the study, participants were asked to write open-ended feedback comments about any aspect of the study.

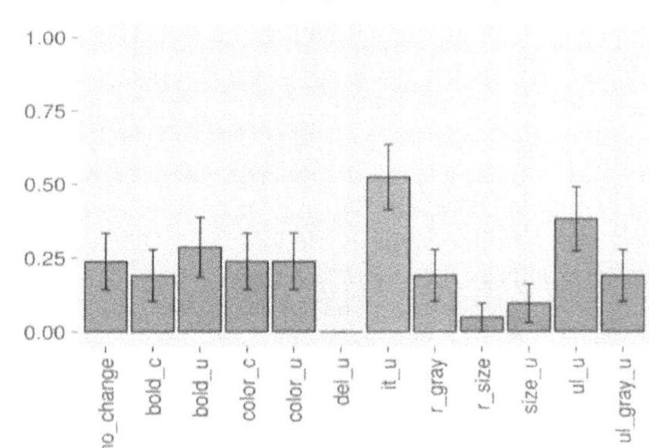

Figure 4. Pilot Study Preference Results

2.2 Larger Study

A subset of the most preferred visual markup styles in the preliminary study were compared in a subsequent study containing a larger number of participants. While the design of this larger study was mostly identical to the first study, a few modifications and refinements were made, summarized in the following subsections.

2.2.1 New List of Markup Styles

The first step was to reduce our set of markup styles by analyzing the results from the preliminary study. Given practical limits on the number of DHH participants who could be recruited for this study, we wanted to reduce our study design to only four conditions: a baseline and three visual markup styles. We used the following criteria to select the four conditions in this follow-up study:

1. *Retain the baseline:* The captions without any visual markup (no_change) were retained for the larger, comparison study so that we could compare this ubiquitous form of captioning to the new captioning methods that included visual markup.
2. *Retain the markup styles that received the highest subjective preference scores in the preliminary study:* Videos that used *italics* to indicate uncertain words (it_u) had the highest scores, and videos that used underlining to indicate uncertain words (ul_u) had the second highest scores in Figure 4.
3. *Eliminate styles that markup confident words:* The subjective preference results were less clear-cut for the remaining videos, but videos that utilized color or **boldness** seemed to have the highest scores among those that remain. In feedback comments, several participants indicated that applying markup to confident words was visually distracting. Since this issue will only be exacerbated as the accuracy of ASR systems improves over time, we decided to eliminate any markup styles that apply visual markup to text that was confidently identified by the ASR system (bold_c, color_c). Therefore, we were left to consider whether to retain the Bold on Uncertain (bold_u) or Color on Uncertain (color_u) markup style for inclusion in our larger, comparison study
4. *Considering colorblindness accessibility:* The set of visual markup styles in the preliminary study included both Color on Uncertain (red) and Color on Confident (green); with the red/green meant to convey a negative/positive distinction. However, one participant in our preliminary study indicated that he had difficulty distinguishing the red/green colors from the "unmarked" white text. For this reason, we decided to merge the Bold on Uncertain and Color on Uncertain styles to create a new style, "Bold and Color on Uncertain," that redundantly conveyed the information through both color and boldness. While the specific way in which an individual may experience color vision deficiency may be unique [22, 13], there are trends: We selected a yellow color (red 100%, green 100%, blue 0%) which retained contrast with both the black background and also with the unmarked white text, across a variety of common forms of colorblindness.

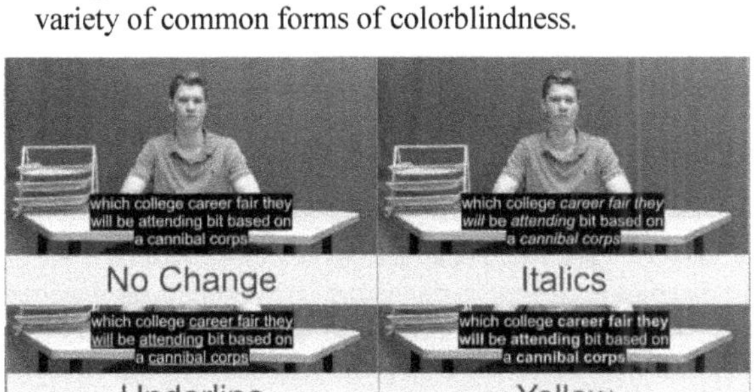

Figure 5. Markup conditions in larger study (Section 2.2)

Therefore, we settled on a list of 4 markup styles for the expanded study: *Baseline ("No Change"), Italics on Uncertain, Underline on Uncertain,* and *Yellow+Bold on Uncertain* – as shown in Figure 5.

2.2.2 Comprehension Questions

After each video clip, we asked participants four multiple-choice comprehension questions about information conveyed in the speech audio of the stimuli videos. We used "text-explicit" (TE) style comprehension questions [20] wherein the participant is not required to infer from information in memory. None of our research questions specifically focus on whether different caption markup may lead to different comprehension score results: Therefore, our rationale for including these questions was simply to introduce pressure on the participants to understand what was said, to more realistically simulate using captioning in live meetings, so that our participants would have a higher fidelity prototype experience, prior to answering preference questions at the end of the study.

2.2.3 Preference Questions

Since we reduced the number of markup styles in this larger study, there was time to add questions. Yannakakis and Hallam [47] found that participants may provide different subjective evaluations when they are asked to provide a subjective rating for an item in isolation or when they are asked to rank a set of items; their work suggested the merit of utilizing both methods, especially when there may be serial-presentation contrast effects in a study design, despite the use of randomized Latin squares ordering for the markup styles. In addition to asking subjective preference questions after each markup type (including 5-point Likert-type items and binary Yes/No questions), after all 12 videos were shown, participants in this larger study were asked to rank the 4 captioning styles. The participants were presented a page with pictures of all 4 styles to remind them of each style, and they used four drop-down lists with the markup styles to provide a ranking.

Finally, at the end of the study we asked participants a battery of open-ended questions to elicit their opinion on the confidence markup and their opinions on the use of ASR for captioning. Our questionnaire and videos can be downloaded from our website: http://latlab.ist.rit.edu/assets2017dhh

2.2.4 Number of Participants and Demographics

We recruited a total of 107 DHH participants (those that participated in our pilot study were excluded) from our university campus and they self-identified their hearing status as (69 Deaf, 36 Hard-of-Hearing, 2 other), and gender as (59 males and 48 females). Participants' ages ranged from 18-30 years old.

3. QUANTITATIVE RESULTS

This section presents the results of our quantitative analysis of the closed-ended question items during our larger study.

After each video, we asked participants the same question in the pilot study, "Did you like this style of captioning?" Figure 6 displays the mean scores (No=0/Yes=1) for each markup style. A Kruskal-Wallis test indicated significance for the factor of markup style [$\chi 2=17.587$, DF=3, $p=0.000535$]. To compare the markups in a pairwise manner, a Wilcoxon rank-sum test with Bonferroni correction was used for post-hoc analysis; the following pairs differed significantly in their medians: *No Change / Underline*: $p= 0.00085$, *No Change / Yellow*: $p=0.00211$, *No Change / Italics:* $p=0.02307$. Notably, our participants had significantly higher preference scores for the markup condition with *No Change*, in which no confidence information was displayed.

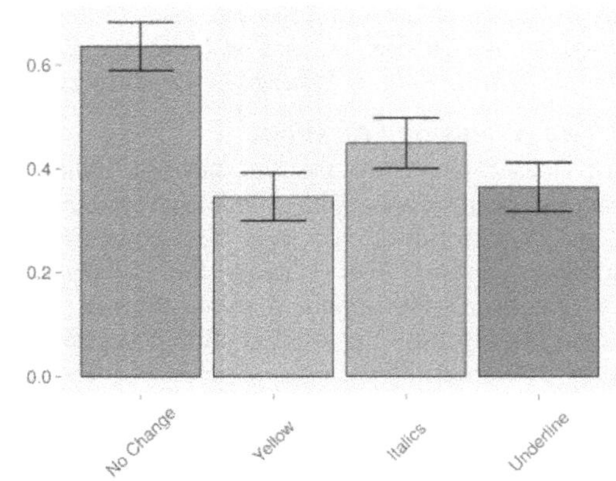

Figure 6. Larger Study: Preference Responses (binary)

We followed up on this question with another binary question: "Was this style of captioning distracting?" Figure 7 displays the mean scores (No=0/Yes=1) for each markup style. The Kruskal-Wallis test indicated significance [$\chi2$=22.692, DF=3, p=4.682e-05]. Post-hoc pairwise Wilcoxon signed-rank tests revealed significant differences for the following pairs: *No Change / Yellow*: p=3.7e-05, *No Change / Underline*: p=0.00035, *Italics / Yellow*: p=0.00187. Participants seemed to prefer captions without confidence markup or which used italics to convey confidence, from the perspective of reducing distraction.

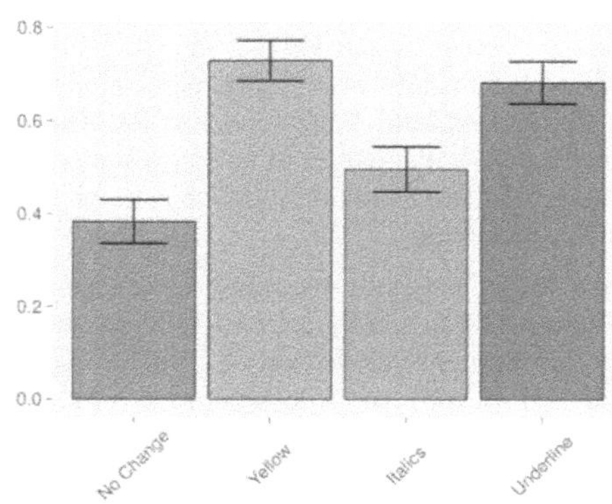

Figure 7. Larger Study: Distracting Responses (binary)

The participants were asked a 5-point Likert question, "I think this captioning style would be helpful during face-to-face meetings with hearing people." Figure 8 displays responses for each markup style. The Kruskal-Wallis test did not indicate significance for this question [$\chi2$=3.771, DF=3, p=0.2873].

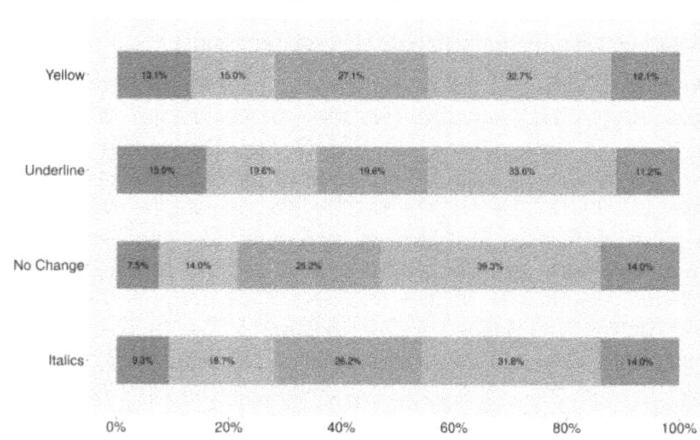

Figure 8. Larger Study: Helpful Responses (Likert)

Lastly, we asked participants to rank the markup styles at the end of the experiment with the question "Please select and rank the captioning display styles." Figure 9 displays the percentages of the ranks for each markup style. The Friedman rank sum test indicated significance [$\chi2$=26.559, DF=3, p=7.284e-06]. Post-hoc pairwise Wilcoxon signed-ranks test with Bonferroni corrections revealed significant differences for the following pairs: *No Change / Underline*: p=0.00014, *No Change / Yellow*: p=0.00025, *No Change / Italics*: p=0.01576. Similar to the results on the binary preference questions (Figure 6), participants indicated a subjective preference for captions without any confidence information.

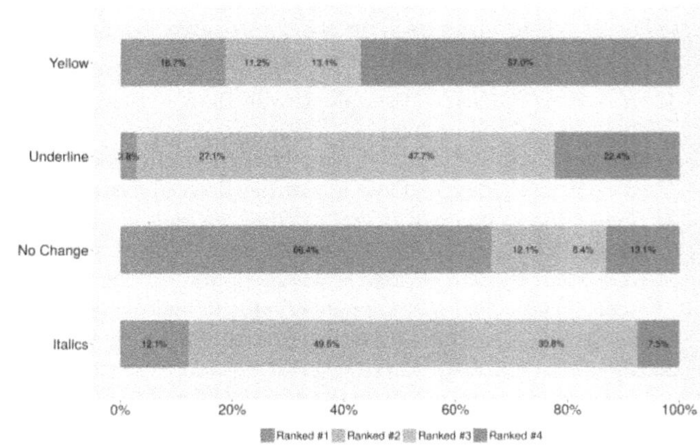

Figure 9. Larger Study: Ranking of Markup Types

The findings in this section primary address research question RQ3 from Section 2: "When viewing captions of speech in a one-on-one meeting, which confidence markup do DHH users subjectively prefer?" In addition, the results presented for the question about distraction partially address research question RQ2. Overall, participants expressed a preference for captions without any such markup. In Section 5, we speculate why this might be the case.

4. QUALITATIVE RESULTS

This section describes how we analyzed the open-ended responses collected during the larger study using a qualitative methodology. After collecting text comments from 107 participants during the larger study, we obtained a total of 364 individual comments (a total of 6,112 words) from those whom responded – after we had excluded responses such as "no comment" or equivalent. Following the methodology of [40], we began with a round of open-coding in which two annotators independently coded the texts. After meeting to discuss their independent codes, a revised code list was produced, and the annotators formed a consensus coding. One annotator was a Deaf native ASL signer, and the other was a hearing individual: this was done intentionally to reflect the multiple perspectives that are relevant during a meeting between a DHH user and a hearing user. Next, we performed affinity diagramming and thematic analysis of the data to identify common themes for our research questions. The annotators separately considered what themes were relevant to our research questions before meeting again to form the final list. Below, major findings from this analysis are presented, grouped in subsections that correspond to our four research questions from Section 2.

4.1 RQ1: Initial view of ASR captioning

At the beginning of the study, before the participants watched the videos, we asked them if they had prior experience with ASR, as we wanted to know if they were already using ASR in their daily lives. Approximately 20% of our participants had prior experience with ASR tools, which may indicate some interest (but significant opportunity for growth) among DHH users. For those that answered affirmatively, we then followed up with a question, "If you selected 'Yes' please explain your experience with ASR." Our coding of this data indicated that participants had both **positive experiences** and **negative experiences** with ASR. Several who reported a positive experience indicated that they appreciated the fact that they could communicate with hearing people or understand spoken content:

> "I did use my iphone app to pick up news like CNN since sometime CNN do not provide closed caption on live tv" (P97)

> "AVA app and it was great! most of the time accurate and it becomes funny when it has errors." (P27)

Among those that shared negative experiences, a common theme that arose was that they were **dissatisfied with ASR accuracy** and they felt that it was too **frustrating** to follow the captioning. Participants believed that they **noticed when there were errors**:

> "I believe they have this on youtube and such it becomes really annoying when the captions are all messed up because i really want to understand what is being said" (P88)

> "The hearing participate communicated through ASR app on the phone with me. It was quite interesting even there were several errors and possibly barriers in the communication between us." (P79)

4.2 RQ2: Key Issues in Assistive ASR Tools

Our second research question centered on what issues or factors DHH users believed to be important when using ASR captioning as an assistive tool. Our survey included the question: "Could you explain your perspective on computer captioning as an assistive technology?" As mentioned in the previous research question and discussed further in Section 4.3.2, the most frequent issue (N=43) that participants discussed was **ASR accuracy** and how it directly impacted their ability to understand spoken content. Other than accuracy, participants mentioned that they were resistant to using ASR for a variety of reasons, including: concern about **replacing ASL interpreting**, the **lack of bidirectional communication**, and lacking **reliable access** to technology for impromptu ASR interactions. For example:

> "It can be beneficial. I fear that people would abuse the use of assistive technology as it will not be fully reliable. Using a live interpreter will always have my vote." (P14)

> "I do support the idea of ASR but there is one issue.. it help us to understand what hearing people are saying but how can we input our message to them through ASR. I cant even speak at all and how can they receive information from me?" (P96)

> "I think it is a wonderful technology but the situation is that sometimes people doesn't carry their computers if something comes up." (P81)

4.3 RQ3: Preference of Confidence Display

For each of the four markup styles presented in the larger study, we asked participants to discuss their opinion via an open-ended question: "Do you have any comments about this captioning style?" In the following subsections, we will discuss major themes that emerged from the participants' responses to this question (ordered by frequency, beginning with the most frequent issue below).

4.3.1 Distraction from Markup

By far, the most common issue (N=32) raised by participants was that they felt like they could not focus on the information content of the "business meeting" scenario video because the markup style was **too distracting**. It is important for the reader to note that the numerical information in the output of ASR that indicates its confidence on individual words can be wrong: incorrect words for which the ASR was "confident, yet wrong" or correct words for which the ASR was "uncertain, but actually correct." When reading captions with markup, the participants had to cognitively process the markup, the word, and the overall sentence context before they could figure out whether they should trust the captioning (or if they needed to guess what was actually spoken). Many participants indicated that this activity was mentally taxing and unpleasant:

> "In this case this change in fonts is distracting because sometimes styled words are correct sometimes they are not. So I do not know which is correct or not. I also notice some mistakes in non-styled words. In this case the change in styles does not serve its purpose." (P11, *Italics*)

> "It is actually distracting if it highlights so many words that are pointless to be acknowledged about what speaker was talking about." (P43, *Underline*)

> "Honestly I don't like the highlighted words because it's very distracting and it can be misleading to read. So I wouldn't recommend this kind of captioning style." (P68, *Yellow*)

4.3.2 Perception of Accuracy when Errors Visible

The responses indicated that the majority of participants realized that when markup was added to the captioning, they could readily spot errors. However, it appeared that increasing the visibility of the errors led participants, in some cases, to believe that the captions with markup were less accurate (relative to captions without markup). Although there was no actual difference in the ASR accuracy rate across the different markup conditions, the use of visible markup seemed to increase the ***perceived inaccuracy***, which could reduce acceptance of this technology among users (N=21).

> "The caption was good but some mistake words and no period or comma" (P100, *Italics*)

> "however the video in this research did not underlined incorrect words. Not sure if it is a system error or what" (P45, *Underline*)

> "It does point out when something is typed wrong and its not what the person said" (P72, *Yellow*)

4.3.3 Resistance to Unfamiliar Captioning Markup

Some (N=13) participants mentioned that they were accustomed to watching movies or television with closed captioning (or subtitles) and wanted consistency of experience. They did not see sufficient benefits of confidence markup to offset this **unfamiliarity**:

> "today we have close caption on the television or movie and their closed caption perfectly smooth" (P6, *Italics*)

> "The underline don't need it and I suggest to you used from Netflix it is way to better used CC" (P87, *Underline*)

> "White/black only. It is very common closed captions." (P97, *Yellow*)

4.3.4 Confusion Regarding the Intent of Markup

A few (N=7) participants expressed confusion regarding what the markup was supposed to convey. The study had begun with a brief video, in ASL (and a handout containing the script in English), explaining the purpose of the study and what the markup was meant to indicate. Despite this, several participants were **confused about their purpose**, revealing that training may be necessary for use of confidence markup captions:

> "It makes no sense for some words in the captions to be italicized." (P60, *Italics*)

> "I actually got confused with the captions because I was not sure if the underline makes words look important or not." (P64, *Underline*)

> "I think Yellow means it fixes the errors if that is true then I 100% strongly agree!" (P94, *Yellow*)

4.3.5 Overall experience of confidence markup

At the end of the larger study, we asked two questions to elicit opposing perspectives on captioning with confidence markup. The first question was, "Could you list what you liked about the confidence display that you saw today?" The responses had an overall positive tone, even though 37% of participants mentioned that this has been their first time seeing captions with confidence information. The most frequently mentioned themes were: markup leading to more **awareness about errors** in captions, markup helping users understand **how ASR works**, and markups leading to **increased user confidence in ASR as a tool**. For example:

> "It was interesting to see what the captioning wasn't confident about. I didn't know that's what was happening." (P71)

> "bad captions are better than no captions" (P76)

> "I like knowing which one is wrong and which one is right" (P81)

> "It will display accurate word to word. I was amazed about that." (P59)

We then asked a question to elicit more critical feedback, "Could you list some things that should be improved?" As previously discussed in Section 4.3.2, most participants mentioned that if ASR accuracy was improved, they would be more enthusiastic to use the technology. Other than **accuracy**, participants brought up a wide range of issues such as: **styling / appearance** of the captioning, **emphasis on certain words**, and the **learning curve**. Our participants were not able to control the appearance of the captions in this study (e.g. number of lines, font size), yet it is feasible for those issues to be addressed in an actual application. Some participants had unique ideas which could be explored further:

> "I wish the caption could be filled with highlighter so that we cannot miss any important information." (P106)

> "Example of sounds. Showing who is voices. Showing specific of sounds."(P73)

One challenge for the participants was to become acquainted with the concept of reading **imperfect captioning generated by ASR**, as opposed to generated by human (which typically has no errors). This learning curve might not be easy for some DHH users to acquire, but one participant summed it up nicely:

> "Beginning was crazy and awkward but slowly understanding more better." (P94)

4.4 RQ4: Other applications of ASR tools

To capture how our DHH participants may imagine themselves using ASR tools they experienced during our study in other contexts, we asked, "Could you list other ways that Automatic Speech Recognition could be used?" Many participants saw potential utility from ASR technology and proposed locations or situations where they thought ASR would be useful: **public places**, **appointments**, **family events**, **travelling**, and **cultural events** (e.g. concerts). Participants indicated a desire to have more access to spoken information, e.g. public announcements. This comment was typical of what we observed from many responses:

> "At an airport when announcing arrived or departed flights automatic speech recognition could come in handy for the deaf and hard of hearing. The same goes for the train bus cruise or any type of station." (P58)

Furthermore, some participants wanted to use ASR as an archiving tool so they could peruse content at their own time and pace:

> "Save the video and can read replay captioning." (P103)

5. CONCLUSION

This study has investigated whether it is possible to utilize the confidence values from an ASR engine, to provide DHH users with additional information in an automatic captioning system, for supporting meetings between DHH and hearing users. Through a pair of studies with 128 total DHH participants, we have compared multiple forms of visual display to present this confidence information, and we collected subjective preferences from DHH users on each. In addition, after asking DHH participants to engage in a simulation of a one-on-one meeting with a hearing person, with automatically generated captions that included confidence markup, we surveyed participants about their opinions on this technology. Quantitative and qualitative analysis of these responses suggested several major findings, as discussed in Sections 3 and 4 above:

- Participants **expressed interest** in adding markup to captioning to indicate the words for which ASR was uncertain.
- However, after experiencing such captions during a simulated meeting, participants expressed subjective preferences for captions that **did not include** any confidence markup.

We speculate various potential explanations for this contrast:

- Participants may have disliked the specific set of visual markup display approaches used in the larger study.
- Participants did not consciously notice any benefit from the additional confidence information, e.g. perceiving that any benefits were outweighed by the potential for distraction.
- Participants' prior experience with captions without confidence markup led to their subjective preference for a familiar technology, and the exposure to other conditions during this simulation was too brief for them to learn how to utilize this information. It is conceivable that if standard methods of confidence display were widely adopted, then users may gain familiarity in interpreting and utilizing this information in ASR captions.
- The simulated nature of the one-on-one meeting activity in the larger study did not adequately capture real-word aspects of an interactive meeting with a hearing conversational partner, thereby obfuscating potential benefits of this technology.
- Potential benefits of this technology may only occur under specific conditions, e.g. particular ASR accuracy rates, text reading complexity, or participant literacy levels – as discussed in Section 6 below, a wide variety of settings for these parameters would need to be examined in future work.

Our qualitative analysis of the feedback from participants also led to several findings about factors that DHH consider important in automatic captioning and useful applications that users foresee:

- **Accuracy** was salient for DHH users considering the potential of ASR captioning; additional concerns included the potential **loss of ASL interpreting services**, supporting **bidirectional** communication, and the **reliability** of the technology.
- In regard to the confidence markup they experienced in the study, participants were concerned about **distraction** caused from changes in text appearance. Some commented on how markup made **errors more apparent** and how changes in text appearance during captions were **unfamiliar**. A few

participants **did not understand the purpose** of markup, which may indicate a need for more introduction or training.

- Participants suggested potential **applications** for ASR-generated captions, e.g. for announcements in public places, appointments, family gatherings, or cultural events.

The overall aim of this study has been to explore the potential of ASR captioning technology for use in meetings, especially whether conveying confidence may benefit DHH users. The goal of our analysis has been to distill our findings into a form that may be useful for future researchers interested in this application. In particular, by identifying key concerns of DHH participants, it may be possible to explore alternative designs for this technology to mitigate perceived deficiencies or address key concerns.

6. LIMITATIONS AND FUTURE WORK

Section 1.3 described the Word Error Rate (WER) of the ASR-generated captions in our study, but ASR accuracy has been improving in recent years, e.g. [19, 46]. This study did not examine how variation in WER might have influenced participants' preference scores of confidence markup or influenced their views on the use of ASR for captioning. The findings of this study may be specific to particular error rates in caption text, and a future study would be needed to examine this issue.

In future work, it may be useful to consider the intersection of literacy and text complexity. Most of our participants were students on a university campus, and it is known that most deaf college students have reading levels below that of sixth grade (11-12 years old) [1, 33]. To analyze the reading complexity of our stimuli, we analyzed them using the Flesch-Kincaid [14] formula: the Flesch Reading-Ease Score was (FRES: mean=69.76, median=69.21 with SD=9.69) and the Flesch-Kincaid Grade Level was (FKGL: mean=8.6, median=8.73 with SD=2.28). Based on those scores, the text appearing in the captions of our video stimuli was at the 8th grade reading level (13-14 years old) approximately. In future work, we may examine stimuli with a range of text reading complexity (and measure the literacy rate of our participants on a standardized test) to investigate if these factors may influence participants' preferences in an ASR based captioning system.

While this study employed subjective preference questions and open-ended feedback to probe DHH participants' views of ASR captioning technology, additional measurements are possible:

- Prior work has utilized eye-tracking technology to study how DHH participants utilize captions [41] and how modifications to text appearance influences their eye movements [37]; we may employ eye-tracking on ASR captioning for meetings and the use of confidence markup in future work.
- Our larger study included comprehension questions to encourage participants to engage in the simulated meeting task. While none of our research questions in this study focused on potential changes in users' comprehension scores based on different markup types, out of curiosity, we conducted an ANOVA to compare comprehension scores for different markup types, but we found no statistically significant differences, similar to [39]. This may illustrate the difficulty in measuring comprehension differences from displaying captions with different forms of confidence markup. Interestingly, while participants indicated that some markup styles were distracting (Section 3), there were no differences in comprehension scores in this study. We plan to investigate comprehension scores in a future study, considering the methodology of [4], who measured DHH students' comprehension of an educational lecture.

7. ACKNOWLEDGEMENTS

This work has been supported by a Google Faculty Research Award and by the National Technical Institute for the Deaf (NTID). Kasmira Patel and Anmolvir Kaur assisted with data collection.

8. REFERENCES

[1] J. Albertini, C. Mayer. 2011. Using miscue analysis to assess comprehension in deaf college readers. *The Journal of Deaf Studies and Deaf Education*, 16(1):35.

[2] Consumer Electronics Association. 2013. Cea-708-e (ansi): Digital television (dtv) closed captioning.

[3] F. G. Bowe. 2002. Deaf and hard of hearing Americans' instant messaging and e-mail use: A national survey. *American Annals of the Deaf*, 147(4):6–10.

[4] A. Brandão, H. Nicolau, S. Tadas, V.L. Hanson. 2016. Slidepacer: A presentation delivery tool for instructors of deaf and hard of hearing students. In *Proceedings of the 18th International ACM SIGACCESS Conference on Computers and Accessibility* (ASSETS '16), ACM, New York, NY, USA, 25–32. DOI: http://dx.doi.org/10.1145/2982142.2982177

[5] CaptionMax. 1993. *Suggested Styles and Conventions for Closed Captioning*. WGBH Educational Foundation, Boston.

[6] Federal Communications Commission. 2015. *Video relay services*. http://www.fcc.gov/guides/video-relay-services

[7] M. Crabb, R. Jones, M. Armstrong, C.J. Hughes. 2015. Online news videos: The UX of subtitle position. In *Proceedings of the 17th International ACM SIGACCESS Conference on Computers & Accessibility* (ASSETS '15), ACM, New York, NY, USA, 215-222. DOI: http://dx.doi.org/10.1145/2700648.2809866

[8] M. Davoudi, M. B. Menhaj, N. S. Naraghi, A. Aref, M. Davoodi, M. Davoudi. 2012. A fuzzy logic-based video subtitle and caption coloring system. *Advances in Fuzzy Systems*. DOI: http://dx.doi.org/10.1155/2012/671851

[9] DCMP. 2016. DCMP Captioning Key - Quality Captioning. http://www.captioningkey.org/quality_captioning.html

[10] L. Elliot, M. Stinson, J. Mallory, D. Easton, M. Huenerfauth. 2016. Deaf and hard of hearing individuals' perceptions of communication with hearing colleagues in small groups. In *Proceedings of the 18th International ACM SIGACCESS Conference on Computers and Accessibility* (ASSETS '16), ACM, New York, NY, USA, 271-272. DOI: http://dx.doi.org/10.1145/2982142.2982198

[11] L.B. Elliot, M.S. Stinson, B.G. McKee, V. S. Everhart, P.J. Francis. 2001. College students' perceptions of the c-print speech-to-text transcription system. *Journal of deaf studies and deaf education*, 6(4):285–298.

[12] V. Ferdiansyah, S. Nakagawa. 2013. Effect of captioning lecture videos for learning in foreign language. In *Proc. SLP Meeting of Info. Processing Society of Japan*. SLP-97, No. 3.

[13] D.R. Flatla, C. Gutwin. 2012. Situation-specific models of color differentiation. *ACM Trans. Access. Comput.* 4, 3, Article 13, 44 pages. DOI: http://dx.doi.org/10.1145/2399193.2399197

[14] R. Flesch. 1948. A new readability yardstick. *Journal of applied psychology*, 32(3):221-223.

[15] Y. Gaur, W.S. Lasecki, F. Metze, J.P. Bigham. 2016. The effects of automatic speech recognition quality on human transcription latency. In *Proceedings of the 13th Web for All Conference* (W4A '16). ACM, New York, NY, USA, Article 23, 8 pages. DOI: https://doi.org/10.1145/2899475.2899478

[16] S.R. Gulliver, G. Ghinea. 2003. How level and type of deafness affect user perception of multimedia video clips. *Universal Access in the Information Society*, 2(4):374–386.

[17] R.P. Harrington, G.C. Vanderheiden. 2013. Crowd caption correction (ccc). In *Proceedings of the 15th International ACM SIGACCESS Conference on Computers and Accessibility* (ASSETS '13). ACM, New York, NY, USA, Article 45, 2 pages. DOI: http://dx.doi.org/10.1145/2513383.2513413

[18] R. Hong, M. Wang, M. Xu, S. Yan, T.-S. Chua. 2010. Dynamic captioning: video accessibility enhancement for hearing impairment. In *Proceedings of the 18th ACM international conference on Multimedia* (MM '10), ACM, New York, NY, USA, 421–430. DOI: http://dx.doi.org/10.1145/1873951.1874013

[19] X. Huang, J. Baker, R. Reddy. 2014. A historical perspective of speech recognition. *Comm. ACM*, 57(1):94–103.

[20] D.W. Jackson, P.V. Paul, J.C. Smith. 1997. Prior knowledge and reading comprehension ability of deaf adolescents. *Journal of Deaf Studies and Deaf Education*, 2(3):172–184.

[21] J. Jankowski, K. Samp, I. Irzynska, M. Jozwowicz, S. Decker. 2010. Integrating text with video and 3d graphics: The effects of text drawing styles on text readability. In *Proceedings of the SIGCHI Conference on Human Factors in Computing Systems* (CHI '10). ACM, New York, NY, USA, 1321-1330. DOI: http://dx.doi.org/10.1145/1753326.1753524

[22] L. Jefferson, R. Harvey. 2006. Accommodating color blind computer users. In *Proceedings of the 8th international ACM SIGACCESS conference on Computers and accessibility* (Assets '06). ACM, New York, NY, USA, 40-47, DOI: http://dx.doi.org/10.1145/1168987.1168996

[23] S. Kawas, G. Karalis, T. Wen, R.E. Ladner. 2016. Improving real-time captioning experiences for deaf and hard of hearing students. In *Proceedings of the 18th International ACM SIGACCESS Conference on Computers and Accessibility* (ASSETS '16). ACM, New York, NY, USA, 15-23, DOI: http://dx.doi.org/10.1145/2982142.2982164

[24] R. Kheir, T. Way. 2007. Inclusion of deaf students in computer science classes using real-time speech transcription. In *ITiCSE'07*, ACM, NY, NY, USA, 261-265, DOI: http://dx.doi.org/10.1145/1268784.1268860

[25] R.S. Kushalnagar, G.W. Behm, A.W. Kelstone, S. Ali. 2015. Tracked speech-to-text display: Enhancing accessibility and readability of real-time speech-to-text. In *Proc ASSETS'15*, ACM, NY, NY, USA, 223-230, DOI: http://dx.doi.org/10.1145/2700648.2809843

[26] R.S. Kushalnagar, W.S. Lasecki, J.P. Bigham. 2014. Accessibility evaluation of classroom captions. *ACM Trans. Access. Comput.* 5, 3, Article 7, 24 pages. DOI: http://dx.doi.org/10.1145/2543578

[27] P. Lamere, P. Kwok, E. Gouvea, B. Raj, R. Singh, W. Walker, M. Warmuth, P. Wolf. 2003. The CMU sphinx-4 speech recognition system. In *Proc ICASSP'03*, 2–5.

[28] D.G. Lee, D.I. Fels, J.P. Udo. 2007. Emotive captioning. *Computers in Entertainment (CIE)*, 5(2):11.

[29] M. Marschark, G. Leigh, P. Sapere, D. Burnham, C. Convertino, M. Stinson, H. Knoors, M. P. Vervloed, W. Noble. 2006. Benefits of sign language interpreting and text alternatives for deaf students' classroom learning. *Journal of deaf studies and deaf education*, 11(4):421–437.

[30] D. Miller, K. Gyllstrom, D. Stotts, J. Culp. 2007. Semi-transparent video interfaces to assist deaf persons in meetings. In *Proc ACM-SE 45*, ACM, NY, NY, USA, 501-506. DOI: http://dx.doi.org/10.1145/1233341.1233431

[31] M. R. Mirzaei, S. Ghorshi, M. Mortazavi. 2012. Using augmented reality and automatic speech recognition techniques to help deaf and hard of hearing people. In *Proc VRIC'12*, ACM, NY, NY, USA, Article 5, 4 pages. DOI: http://dx.doi.org/10.1145/2331714.2331720

[32] H. Nambo, S. Seto, H. Arai, K. Sugimori, Y. Shimomura, H. Kawabe. 2012. Visualization of non-verbal expressions in voice for hearing impaired: Ambient font and onomatopoeic subsystem. In *Proc ICCHP'12 volume 1*, 492–499.

[33] S.J. Parault, H.M. Williams. 2010. Reading motivation, reading amount, and text comprehension in deaf and hearing adults. *J. of Deaf Studies and Deaf Educ.*, 15(2):120-135.

[34] A. Piquard-Kipffer, O. Mella, J. Miranda, D. Jouvet, L. Orosanu. 2015. Qualitative investigation of the display of speech recognition results for communication with deaf people. In *SLPAT'15*, 36-41. Assoc. of Comp. Linguistics.

[35] S.S. Prietch, N.S. de Souza, L.V.L. Filgueiras. 2014. A speech-to-text system's acceptance evaluation: would deaf individuals adopt this technology in their lives? In *UAHCI'14*, 440–449.

[36] R. Rashid, Q. Vy, R.G. Hunt, D.I. Fels. 2007. Dancing with words. In *Proc C&C'07*, ACM, NY, NY, USA, 269–270. DOI: http://dx.doi.org/10.1145/1254960.1255007

[37] K. Rathbun, L. Berke, C. Caulfield, M. Stinson, M. Huenerfauth. 2017. Eye movements of deaf and hard of hearing viewers of automatic captions. Journal on Technology & Persons with Disabilities, 5, 130-140, http://hdl.handle.net/10211.3/190208

[38] A. Secară. 2011. RU ready 4 new subtitles? Investigating the potential of social translation practices and creative spellings. In M. O'Hagan (ed.), *Translation as social activity: Community translation 2.0 [Special issue]. Linguistica Antverpiensia New Series*, 10, 153–172.

[39] B. Shiver, R. Wolfe. 2015. Evaluating alternatives for better deaf accessibility to selected web-based multimedia. In *Proc ASSETS'15*, ACM, New York, NY, USA, 223–230. DOI: http://dx.doi.org/10.1145/2700648.2809843

[40] Strauss, A., & Corbin, J. (1998). Basics of qualitative research: Techniques and procedures for developing grounded theory (2nd ed.). Thousand Oaks, CA: Sage.

[41] A. Szarkowska, I. Krejtz, Z. Klyszejko, A. Wieczorek. 2011. Verbatim, standard, or edited?: Reading patterns of different captioning styles among deaf, hard of hearing, and hearing viewers. *American annals of the deaf*, 156(4):363–378.

[42] K. Vertanen, P.O. Kristensson. 2008. On the benefits of confidence visualization in speech recognition. In *Proc CHI'08*, ACM, New York, NY, USA, 1497–1500. DOI: http://dx.doi.org/10.1145/1357054.1357288

[43] Q.V. Vy. 2012. Enhanced captioning: speaker identification using graphical and text-based identifiers. *Theses and dissertations.* Paper 1702.

[44] M. Wald. 2005. Using automatic speech recognition to enhance education for all students: Turning a vision into reality. In *Proc IEEE FIE'05*, S3G-S3G. IEEE.

[45] F. Wang, H. Nagano, K. Kashino, T. Igarashi. 2015. Visualizing video sounds with sound word animation. In *Proc ICME'15*, 1–6. IEEE.

[46] W. Xiong, J. Droppo, X. Huang, F. Seide, . Seltzer, A. Stolcke, D. Yu, G. Zweig. 2016. Achieving human parity in conversational speech recognition. *Computing Research Repository (CoRR)*, http://arxiv.org/abs/1610.05256

[47] G.N. Yannakakis, J. Hallam. 2011. *Ranking vs. Preference: A Comparative Study of Self-reporting*, In: S. D'Mello, A. Graesser, B. Schuller, J.C. Martin JC (eds) *Affective Computing and Intelligent Interaction. ACII 2011. Lecture Notes in Computer Science*, 6974. Springer, Berlin.

Evaluating the Usability of Automatically Generated Captions for People who are Deaf or Hard of Hearing

Sushant Kafle
Rochester Institute of Technology
152 Lomb Memorial Drive
Rochester, NY, 14623
+1-585-475-2700
sushant@mail.rit.edu

Matt Huenerfauth
Rochester Institute of Technology
152 Lomb Memorial Drive
Rochester, NY, 14623
+1-585-475-2700
matt.huenerfauth@rit.edu

ABSTRACT
The accuracy of Automated Speech Recognition (ASR) technology has improved, but it is still imperfect in many settings. Researchers who evaluate ASR performance often focus on improving the Word Error Rate (WER) metric, but WER has been found to have little correlation with human-subject performance on many applications. We propose a new captioning-focused evaluation metric that better predicts the impact of ASR recognition errors on the usability of automatically generated captions for people who are Deaf or Hard of Hearing (DHH). Through a user study with 30 DHH users, we compared our new metric with the traditional WER metric on a caption usability evaluation task. In a side-by-side comparison of pairs of ASR text output (with identical WER), the texts preferred by our new metric were preferred by DHH participants. Further, our metric had significantly higher correlation with DHH participants' subjective scores on the usability of a caption, as compared to the correlation between WER metric and participant subjective scores. This new metric could be used to select ASR systems for captioning applications, and it may be a better metric for ASR researchers to consider when optimizing ASR systems.

CCS Concepts
• **Human-centered computing~Empirical studies in accessibility** • **Human-centered computing~Accessibility design and evaluation methods**

Keywords
Accessibility for People who are Deaf or Hard-of-Hearing; Automatic Speech Recognition; Real-time Captioning System; Caption Usability Evaluation

1. INTRODUCTION
Over 37 million people in the U.S are Deaf and Hard-of-Hearing (DHH) [4], and many benefit from offline captioning (e.g., for pre-recorded television programming) or real-time captioning services (e.g., in classrooms, meetings, and live events). Over the past few decades, automated speech recognition (ASR) technologies have seen major progress in their accuracy and speed. With its increasing maturity, ASR technologies are now being used commercially for many consumer applications. Due to its low cost and scalability, ASR has potential for the task of captioning [2][11][13]. Broadly, our research investigates the use of automatic speech recognition (ASR) to provide captioning services for DHH users, especially in real-time contexts such as meetings with hearing colleagues. The focus of this paper is on designing and evaluating a metric for evaluating the quality of an ASR system, to determine whether its output would produce understandable captions for DHH users.

Section 1 describes the use of ASR for captioning and motivates why the most common evaluation metric for ASR systems (Word Error Rate, WER) is insufficient for evaluating ASR for generating captions for DHH users. Section 1.3 introduces our new metric and outlines our major research questions. Section 2 describes prior work on the limitations of WER and on identifying new evaluation metrics. Section 3 provides details about the design and development of our new metric. Section 4 outlines the hypotheses examined in this paper. Section 5 describes the stimuli preparation strategy and the methodology of our study with DHH participants. Finally, sections 6 and 7 present our results and conclusions.

1.1 Automated Captioning Technologies
Real-time captioning services are usually provided by a human transcriptionist who transcribes the audio information to text using a keyboard, with the captions being displayed on a screen. Although well-trained transcriptionists can produce accurate real-time captions with a speed of over 200 words per minute, systems that rely on trained transcriptionists, e.g. Computer-Aided Access Real-Time (CART) or similar services [39], are not suitable for impromptu meetings or extremely brief conversational interactions, given the overhead cost of arranging a transcriptionist. Recently, a crowd-sourced technique to generate real-time captions [26] has been shown to produce accuracy comparable to that of a trained transcriptionist, with lower cost. However, the proposed system relies on the Amazon Mechanical Turk platform, and the business model for providing captioning services is not yet clear.

Researchers have also investigated architectures for providing real-time captioning using ASR, including: use of an ASR system to generate automated captions directly [2][11][13] or the use of non-experts to inspect the output of an ASR system [20][40][41]. While asking humans to correct errors in captions generated by ASR sounds promising, it has been found that manually identifying and correcting errors in ASR generated captions can take more time than producing the transcript without the support of ASR [16]. With recent improvements in ASR, recent work has investigated the potential of ASR technologies (without any human intervention) for captioning live meetings [9] or for classroom lectures [23].

ASSETS'17, October 29-November 1, 2017, Baltimore, MD, USA

ACM ISBN 978-1-4503-4926-0/17/10…$15.00
https://doi.org/10.1145/3132525.3132542

1.2 Word Error Rate as an ASR Metric

Accurate, large-vocabulary, continuous speech recognition is still considered an unsolved problem. Although there have been recent leaps in the performance of these systems [43], ASR performance is generally not on par with humans, who currently provide most caption text for DHH users. Noise in the input audio, the ambiguity of human speech, or unforeseen speaker characteristics (e.g. a strong accent) can lead to ASR errors. As researchers continue to improve ASR accuracy, they generally report the performance of their systems using a metric called Word Error Rate (WER). Given the ubiquity of this metric, it is reasonable that reducing WER may be a goal of many ASR research efforts (implicitly, if not overtly).

$$WER = \frac{S + D + I}{N}$$

Figure 1: Formula for Word Error Rate (WER), based on *S* (number of erroneous substitutions of one word for another), *D* (number of deletions, i.e. erroneous omissions of words that were spoken), *I* (number of insertions of spurious words in the ASR output), and *N* (number of words actually spoken).

As shown in Figure 1, WER is calculated by comparing the "hypothesis text" (the output of the ASR system) to the "reference text" (what the human actually said in the audio recording). The metric considers the number of misrecognitions in the hypothesis text, normalized by the word-length of the reference text. Notably, WER does not consider whether some words may be more important to the meaning of the message or whether some words might be more predictable than others in a text. In fact, researchers have previously found that humans perceive different ASR errors as having different degrees of impact on a text – some errors might distort the meaning of the text more harshly than others [31]. Others have found that the impact of errors may be dependent upon the specific application in which ASR is used [10][33].

1.3 Metric of ASR Quality for DHH Readers

The premise of this paper is that rather than simply counting the number of errors, it would be better to consider which words are incorrect or where they occur in the sentence, when evaluating ASR text output for captioning applications for DHH users. As discussed in section 2, some researchers have previously examined the limits of the WER metric and have considered some alternatives. A novel aspect of our research is that we are specifically interested in measuring the quality of ASR output for a captioning application for DHH individuals, and we evaluate our proposed metric in a user-study with DHH participants.

There are reasons to believe that it is important to create and evaluate metrics of ASR output quality specifically targeted for DHH users. Anecdotally, some accessibility researchers have argued that ASR-generated errors on captions are more comprehension-demanding than human produced errors [2][25]. Further, there are known differences in literacy rates and reading mechanisms among DHH readers, which differ from their hearing peers: In standardized testing in the U.S., English literacy rates have been measured to be lower for deaf adults [21][29]. Furthermore, literacy researchers have hypothesized that the basic mechanism employed by many deaf adults to understand written sentences differs from hearing readers: That is, deaf readers may identify the most frequent content words and derive a complete representation of the meaning of the sentence, ignoring other words [3][6]. This reading strategy is often referred to as a "keyword" strategy, and it suggests that a subset of the words in a caption text might be of very high importance to DHH users (for text understandability).

Following this same reasoning, it might be disadvantageous to penalize each error in a caption text equally. Some errors may be very consequential to the understandability of the text (with the potential to mislead or confuse the readers), while other errors may have little impact (perhaps easily ignored by readers). Our goal is to develop a metric that can predict the quality of an ASR text output based on the usability of the text as a caption for DHH users. Unlike WER, we want our metric to distinguish between harmful errors in the caption (likely to degrade the quality of caption for DHH users) and less harmful errors; the metric should use this distinction when penalizing a text for each type of error.

With this aim, we developed the Automated-Caption Evaluation (ACE) metric, which measures the impact of errors on the understandability of a caption for DHH users. ACE makes use of a word predictability score (entropy of a word given its context) as a measure to identify keywords in a text and, it uses semantic distance (between the error words and actual words in the reference text) as an approximation of the deviation in meaning due to errors. Using these two measures, ACE computes an impact score for the errors in the text, which is used to predict the degree of usability of the ASR output as a caption text for DHH users.

The focus of this paper is on comparing the performance of our ACE metric on this task and to explore two research questions:

Q1. Do DHH users subjectively rate ASR-generated captions preferred by the ACE metric as having greater usability than ASR-generated captions that are not preferred by ACE?

Q2. Does the ACE metric correlate better with the subjective quality judgments of DHH users on ASR-generated captions, as compared to their correlation with WER scores?

2. PRIOR ASR EVALUATION RESEARCH

This section surveys prior research on the limitations of WER as an evaluation metric for ASR research, efforts to design alternative metrics, and methods to identify important words in a text for DHH readers – which is an aspect of our new alternate evaluation metric.

2.1 Limitations of WER

While WER has been the most commonly used evaluation measure for speech recognition performance, spoken language technology researchers have argued for alternative evaluation measures that would better predict human performance on tasks that depend on ASR text output usability [30][32]. While WER has a lower bound of zero (indicating that a hypothesis text is a perfect match for a reference text), researchers have criticized WER since it lacks an upper bound [30], making it difficult to evaluate WER scores in an absolute manner. Further, some researchers have argued that WER is ideally suited to evaluation of ASR quality only for those applications in which the human can correct errors by typing, since the WER metric is based upon counting errors – which directly relates to the cost of restoring the output word sequence to the original input sequence [30].

In other applications, researchers have observed a weak relationship between WER and human task performance. For example, in the task of spoken document retrieval (in which a user searches for a speech audio file, that has been transcribed by ASR, by typing search terms for desired information), researchers have found that the WER of the ASR system has little correlation with the retrieval system performance [15][18]. Moreover, in [42] researchers saw improvements in a spoken language understanding task, even during a significant increase in WER.

2.2 ASR Evaluation Methods

Several researchers have proposed alternative metrics to WER for evaluating the performance of ASR for specific applications:

Some researchers have weighted errors based on their Term Frequency-Inverse Document Frequency (TF-IDF) measure [33]. TF-IDF is commonly used by researchers studying information retrieval; it assigns high scores to words that are generally "rare" but which appear in great frequency in a particular document, e.g., if a rare word like "penguin" appears very frequently on a particular webpage, then it is reasonable to think that the word "penguin" is an important "keyword" for that webpage. Researchers have used TF-IDF as a "loss function" during the decoding step of their ASR system [33]. (During decoding, the ASR system aims to determine the most likely sequence of words that corresponds to speech information.) The loss function penalized errors on keywords more heavily than errors on other words, when choosing from a list of output candidates. The authors explored using this metric as a weighting factor in a Boolean fashion (keyword or non-keyword) or by using the actual numerical TF-IDF scores as weights.

Researchers in [15] attempted to modify WER to weight "content words" more heavily than other words. Generally speaking, content words include nouns, verbs, adjectives, and adverbs that convey semantic meaning, rather than "function words," e.g. determiners, that convey grammatical information. The authors used ASR in an information retrieval application; users searched for content in spoken audio recordings. The authors found a nearly linear relationship between the proposed metric and retrieval performance across different systems: i.e., ASR systems that recognized content words more accurately provided the best input for their retrieval task. Thus, both [15] and [33] found that keyword identification (to differentially weight specific kinds of errors) led to useful ASR metrics for applications related to information search.

Some researchers have considered applications of ASR that are even closer to our focus on automatic captioning: For instance, some have proposed a metric for evaluating ASR output on a speech transcription task [31]; their metric was based on opinion scores collected from humans who judged the quality of ASR-generated voicemail-to-text transcripts. Scores from their metric correlated with the human judgments better than WER did. Their metric learned the cost of different error types (namely, insertion, deletion, and substitution) and learned a weight factor called the "saliency index" to predict the text understandability. While not focused on creating a fully automatic metric, researchers in [1] investigated different categories of captioning errors (e.g., substitution of a word with an incorrect tense) and weighted each category to design a "weighted WER" metric. This metric was proposed for evaluating the accuracy of captions for television.

The "match error rate" (MER) and "word information loss" (WIL) metrics were introduced in [32], as replacements for WER in settings where high error rates are common. The MER metric is similar to WER except that it is properly normalized and thus computes the "probability" of a given match (between the reference text and the hypothesis text) being incorrect. Similar to MER, WIL is a probabilistic approach that approximates the proportion of the word information lost due to the presence of errors.

Our work is also heavily inspired by the work of [30], which discusses the problems of application-oriented evaluation of ASR systems. In their work, the researchers proposed a generic framework to evaluate the ASR output based on information retrieval concepts like "precision" and "recall." Their proposed framework assumes that the speech recognition task is analogous to an information retrieval task, i.e. the goal for transcription is to retrieve all the relevant information (i.e. the spoken word) from in the original speech signal. Their framework also provided room to incorporate application-dependent importance weights for words and for different ASR error types. However, for our application of real-time captioning for DHH users, the assumptions made in their framework are less appropriate: they treated words as independent units of information, without considering their position in a sentence, i.e. under this assumption identical words located at different positions in a sentence will have identical weights.

In contrast, section 3 describes how our new metric considers the predictability a word at its position in a sentence. Motivation for considering word-predictability in context is discussed in section 2.3. In addition, our new metric considers the semantic deviation between the error word and the actual reference word (section 3).

2.3 Word Predictability

We previously discussed how some researchers [6][7] have hypothesized that deaf readers use a sentence-understanding strategy in which they seek content words in order to derive a representation of sentence meaning, potentially ignoring other information, e.g. morphosyntactic relationships between words. Research on the eye movements of deaf readers has also revealed that deaf readers visually fixate on approximately 30% of the words in a text. The skipped words were largely determined by lexical factors such as how frequent a word is, the length of the word, and the predictability of the word in that sentence [3]. Similarly, in [37], researchers found that both the length of the word and predictability of the word in context were related to whether readers skip over a word and also on the amount of time readers spent on non-skipped words. In general, highly predictable words have been shown to be read faster and skipped more often than unpredictable words by most readers [34], even more so with less skilled readers [3].

Furthermore, word predictability has been a common theme in prior research on assessing the readability of a text or the reading comprehension skills of a participant [8][24][35][36] . For instance, the "Cloze procedure" is an assessment methodology that has been around for years and is one of the most common ways of evaluating both the readability of a text and the reading skills of participants. In this task, the participant is given a text with one word omitted, and they must guess the missing word. Most standardized English-language tests (e.g., TOEFL, GRE, WRAT) utilize some variation of the Cloze technique to evaluate participants' reading skills.

The predictability of a word refers to the degree to which a reader can use the context to guess the word. For example:

The _____ was barking at the mail-man.

The predictability of the word *dog* is high given the context. The context of the word is powerful enough to provide a hint as to what the word is. Conversely, in the sentence:

The meeting is scheduled on _____.

The predictability is very low – suggesting that the readers might not be able to rely on the context to predict the word.

Given the use of word predictability in reading assessment (Cloze tests) and given the aforementioned eye-tracking research (indicating that DHH readers are more likely to skip over highly predictable words), we decided to include word predictability in our new measure of ASR output quality for captioning for DHH users. Specifically, section 3 presents how we estimate word predictability and use it to identify important keywords in the sentence – ultimately allowing us to invent a new metric for evaluating the impact of ASR errors on caption usability.

	Caption Text	WER	ACE
Reference Text	based on the information we gather we will send it off to the lead recruiter for each of those teams	--	--
ASR Hypothesis 1	on the information we gather we will send it off to *relief worker* for each of those *chains*	0.25	0.65
ASR Hypothesis 2	based the information gather will send it off the lead recruiter for each those teams	0.25	0.28

Table 1: This example demonstrates how ACE penalizes captions containing different errors, as compared to how the WER metric evaluates each. Higher ACE or WER values indicate "worse" output for each metric.

3. AUTOMATED-CAPTION EVALUATION

As discussed in section 1, we are interested in the potential for ASR systems to be used as a real-time captioning tool for impromptu meetings. There are many commercial and research ASR systems available, each with different capabilities, e.g., adapting to the voice of specific speakers, operating in contexts with different types of background noise, or recognizing different vocabulary or genres [19][27][28]. A natural question is how to compare ASR systems to determine their suitability for use in this context, and given the limitations of WER discussed in section 2, we therefore present a new Automated-Caption Evaluation (ACE) metric.

ACE considers two primary factors: (a) the predictability of a word given its context and (b) the semantic deviation between the error word and the reference word. These two factors are used to predict the impact of an error in the caption text as follows:

$$I(e_i) = \alpha * E(w_i) + (1 - \alpha) * D(w_i, e_i) \quad (1)$$

where $E(w)$ represents the predictability score of the reference word w, $D(w, e)$ represents the semantic distance between the reference word w and the error word e and $I(e)$ represents the impact score of the error e. Alpha (α) represents the interpolation weight, which determines how much each factor contributes to the overall impact score. In other words, the overall impact of an error is determined by the weighted combination of the predictability of the word and the semantic distance of the error and the reference word. The weighting factor is determined by the value of alpha (α). Section 3.4 describes how this per-word impact score $I(e)$ is used to calculate an overall ACE metric for an entire sentence.

To preview for the reader the benefits of this new metric (before beginning our detailed discussion of the technical details behind its calculation), we provide Table 1, which demonstrates how ACE evaluates caption quality, as compared to WER. Two ASR output texts are shown that have identical WER scores; however, our ACE metric assigns different scores to the texts. ASR Hypothesis 1 has errors on words that are less predictable and the semantic difference between the substituted words and their original reference is great (e.g. "chains" vs. "teams"); for this reason, the ACE metric assigns a higher score (indicating worse output) to that text.

The following sections explain how we calculate key components of this metric and how we use them to create our final metric. An evaluation of the efficacy of this metric (in a study with DHH participants evaluating captions) is presented in section 3.3.

3.1 Word Predictability Sub-Score

To compute the predictability score of a word, we utilized several n-gram language models; these models are based on how frequently certain sequences of words, of various length, have appeared in large collections of text. Similar models are commonly employed in word-prediction systems for text-entry applications, e.g. [14]. Based on the probability score assigned to the predictions by the language model, we compute the predictability score for the word.

3.1.1 Language Model

We trained our n-gram models (n = 1 to 5) on Switchboard [17], English CALLHOME and TED-LIUM [38] corpora, which contain a total of 1.9 million unique words. These corpora were selected because they closely represent text from conversational speech dialogs (similar to the one-on-one meeting context in which we are considering the use of ASR for real-time captioning).

The n-gram models were used bidirectionally, to make predictions using both left and right word-sequence contexts, independently. To rank the possible word candidates using each context, a Stupid Back-off [5] mechanism was utilized. For ranking predictions from left context, the following scoring function was used:

$$S\left(w_i \middle| w_{i-k+1}^{i-1}\right) = \begin{cases} \dfrac{\text{count}(w_{i-k+1}^{i})}{\text{count}(w_{i-k+1}^{i-1})} & \text{if count}\left(w_{i-k+1}^{i}\right) > 0 \\ \lambda\, S\left(w_i \middle| w_{i-k+2}^{i-1}\right) & \text{otherwise} \end{cases}$$

where a recommended value of 0.4 was used for lambda (λ) [5]. A similar scoring function was used to rank the candidates from the right context. The predictions from both the right and left contexts were combined and then ranked for later use.

3.1.2 Word Entropy

To obtain a predictability score from these predictions, we first selected the top (N_c=20) ranked unique candidates and transformed their count probabilities to normalized probabilities (that sum to 1). For instance, in the "the meeting is scheduled on ___" example, the language model might predict various possible words, e.g. "Monday, Friday, Tuesday, etc." The model will predict that each of these words has some probability of appearing in that context.

Based on the distribution of probability among the candidates, an entropy score was calculated as follows:

$$E(w) = \sum_{i=0}^{N_c} - P\big(w_c(i)\big) * \log\big(P(w_c(i)\big) \quad (2)$$

where $E(w)$ represents the entropy of a word w (at a unique position in the text). $w_c(i)$ is a candidate of the word w predicted by the language model and $P(w_c)$ is the probability of the candidate w_c as determined by the language model.

The entropy score calculated in Equation 2 is a measure often used in information theory to calculate the unpredictability of a state. In our application, it is the measure of the degree of unpredictability

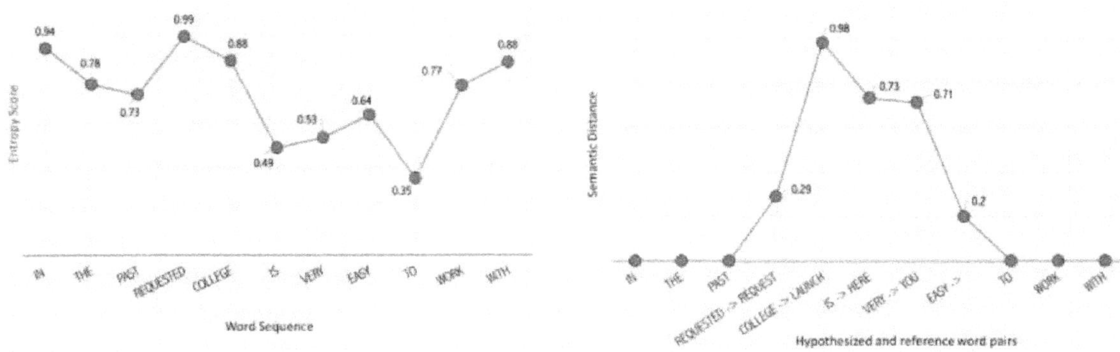

(a) Word Predictability Score (b) Semantic Distance

Figure 2: Word predictability and semantic distance values are demonstrated here for an example sentence. (a) Each word is assigned an entropy score where the greater score indicates the unpredictability of the word. (b) Each hypothesized word is aligned with the reference word (reference word -> hypothesized word), and for each error, semantic distance is approximated. Greater distance score indicates larger deviation in the spoken message due to the error word.

of a word given the context. A higher value indicates that the chances of picking the right word from the list of candidates is low – meaning it is difficult to predict the word. Whereas, a lower value would indicate that some words in the list of candidates clearly have higher probability than others – meaning it is easier to predict the word. The entropy is normalized to get a predictability score within a (0, 1) range. Figure 2(a) provides a visual example of how this metric assigns scores to a text. As shown in the figure, some words in the example text are highly unpredictable (with higher entropy score) – like *requested, college,* etc., while some are fairly predictable – like *is, to,* etc. in the text.

In conclusion, for each error word, the entropy score of the corresponding reference word (w) is calculated to estimate the word predictability score ($E(w)$). For insertion errors, where there could be two adjacent reference words that could be responsible for the error, an average entropy score is computed based on the adjacent reference words.

3.2 Semantic Distance Sub-Score

The second factor that is considered in our ACE metric is the degree to which the meaning of a word in the output text differs from the meaning of the actual word that was spoken. In order to compute this semantic disagreement between the error word and the actual reference word, we utilized a pre-trained word2vec tool from Google[1]. The Word2vec tool provides a vector representation of words which can be subsequently used in many natural language processing applications and research. In this paper, the word2vec tool is used to compute semantic distance between the two words.

The semantic distance measure is used to represent the cost of an error. As shown in Figure 2(b), semantic distance score for minor errors (for e.g., *'requested' -> 'request'*) would receive a small score, while an extreme misrecognition (for e.g., '*college*' -> '*launch*') would receive a high semantic distance score. However, for insertion and deletion errors, the length of the word is used to approximate the distance. For insertion and deletion errors, a constant value of 0.05 was chosen to scale the word length to get the semantic distance which was decided empirically from the analysis of errors from ASR system on a separate dataset[2].

[1] https://code.google.com/archive/p/word2vec

3.3 Selecting a Weight between Sub-Scores

The word predictability sub-score (section 3.1) and the semantic distance sub-score (section 3.2) are combined using a weighted sum to produce an error impact score (as shown in Equation 1), but that equation requires us to select a tuning parameter alpha (α) to specify how much each sub-score contributed to the overall error impact score. To learn the appropriate value of alpha (α), we "fit" the value of this parameter, using response data provided to us by researchers who had conducted a prior study with DHH participants regarding the impact of various ASR errors in captioning [22], with the following demographic characteristics: ages 20 to 32 (mean = 22.63 and deviation= 2.63), 12 men and 18 women, 26 participants self-identified as Deaf and 4 as Hard-of-Hearing.

In that prior study, DHH users were presented with imperfect English text passages (containing errors that had been produced by an ASR system when the text had been spoken aloud and then automatically recognized), and they were asked to answer questions that required understanding the information content of those passages. Each question was based on information from a single sentence in the passage, and each sentence contained 0 or 1 ASR errors. Participants received a score of 1 if they answered a question correctly, and 0, if answered incorrectly.

From all the data collected during that prior study, we examined the subset of question-responses that corresponded to English sentences that had contained ASR errors. This data was used to calculate a "comprehension score" for each sentence, by averaging the scores from the 30 participants for questions about that sentence. For each sentence, we examined the ASR error within and calculated word-predictability and semantic-distance sub-scores. Given this new dataset, the value of the alpha parameter was tuned using a grid search to maximize the prediction accuracy of our impact score metric in Equation (1). We obtained an alpha (α) value of 0.65, suggesting that in our task the impact score depended slightly more on the word predictability score, rather than on semantic distance.

3.4 Metric Formulation

The ACE metric makes use of the impact scores of the errors in the text to compute the final evaluation score. One way to formulate

[2] https://catalog.ldc.upenn.edu/ldc93s1

our metric would have been to compute this score is by summing over the impact scores of each error and normalizing it by the length of the reference text, as had been done for WER in Figure 1, e.g.

$$\text{Version1\_ACE} = \frac{\sum I(e_i)}{N}$$

where $I(e)$ is the impact of error (e) on the usability of the captions and, N is the length of the reference text. This style of formulation for a metric is quite common [1][31][32], and its value would be equal to WER if all the error impact scores were to equate to 1. However, this above formulation of the metric has some limitations:

- For each error (e) in the hypothesized text, we compute an impact score by considering a single error (e) at a time in the reference text – consequently ignoring any non-linear impact due to a cascade of errors (effect of an error in presence of others). Thus, a sum of impact scores of individual errors is insufficient for capturing the true impact of such situations.
- Since the impact score of each error lies between the 0 and 1, the metric will always be less than or equal to WER, i.e.

$$0 \leq \text{Version1\_ACE} \leq WER$$

This is because, N (the length of the reference text) is not the true normalizing constant for our metric.

Due to these limitations above, we invented a new (and final version) of the ACE metric as follows:

$$\text{ACE} = \frac{\max_{e \in \text{E}} I(e)}{\log(N) - \log(n)}$$

where E is the set of all the errors (substitution, insertion and deletion) in the hypothesized text. $I(e)$ represents the impact of each error, defined in Equation (1). N is the length of the reference text, and n is the total number of errors in the hypothesized text.

In this new version, the impact due to errors the *maximum* score among all the individual impact scores $I(e)$ for all errors in the text. When calculating alternative versions of this metric on example texts, we found that taking the *maximum* value represented our subjective impression of error impact across a single sentence better than other common alternatives, e.g. mean or median. Intuitively, if a sentence contains a major error, the overall effect on the sentence understandability can also be major; furthermore, the number of additional words in the text does not subjectively "improve" the sentence in a linear manner, which would be suggested by our Version1_ACE metric shown previously. There are limitations of this approach, e.g. extending this approach to longer, multi-sentential texts; section 7 discusses some limitations.

Similarly, the final version of our metric discounts the effect of N on the impact score, as compared to the previous version. As the length of the reference text increases, it slowly mitigates the impact of individual errors – the rationale being that as readers have more context (more surrounding words), it is easier to decipher the true meaning of the text. The rate of this change is regulated in a non-linear fashion using log. But, if the number of error increases with the reference text, the impact of errors is counterbalanced (note the subtraction of a log(n) term in the denominator).

Like WER, ACE is also an error measure, meaning that a *lower* ACE score indicates a *better* caption text. Similar to WER, ACE does not have an upper bound; however, we note that it is trivially possible to modify the metric to prevent it from exceeding some limit, e.g. $\max(1, \text{ACE(W)})$ would prevent it from exceeding 1.

In summary, our intention when designing this new ACE metric was to penalize ASR output texts that contain errors that are likely to lead to misunderstanding; specifically, the ACE metric considers errors at locations in a text that are less predictable and errors that deviate semantically from the actual word.

4. EVALUTING THE EFFICACY OF ACE

While the goal of our overall project is to develop a metric that could automatically evaluate the usability of a caption for DHH users, we must select a more specific scope in order to design a study to evaluate the efficacy of this new metric. We have selected to focus on measuring the efficacy of ASR for providing captions during a business meeting between a hearing person (speaking English) and a DHH participant. The rationale for this focus is that impromptu one-on-one meetings in a workplace may be a situation in which it is unlikely for professional captioning services to be available. Therefore, there is an opportunity for using automatic methods like ASR technology as a captioning tool. With this focus, we predict that DHH users will subjectively prefer ASR text output that is predicted as less erroneous by our ACE metric (as compared to ASR text output predicted as being less erroneous by the traditional WER metric).

Specifically, if we ask DHH users to evaluate the quality of ASR text output, we hypothesize the following:

H1: If we compare ASR output texts predicted as better by WER (i.e. with low WER-to-ACE ratio) to ASR output predicted as better by ACE (i.e. with high WER-to-ACE ratio), DHH participants will subjectively prefer texts preferred by ACE.

H2a: The subjective preference judgments of DHH participants on ASR output texts will correlate significantly with ACE.

H2b: There will be a significantly higher correlation between DHH human judgments and ACE, as compared to the correlation between DHH human judgments and WER.

5. OVERVIEW OF STUDY DESIGN

To investigate these hypotheses, a comparative evaluation study was designed where the performance of the evaluation metrics (ACE and WER) was assessed based on their agreement with DHH participant's judgment scores on the usability of captions generated by an ASR system.

5.1 Preparation of Stimuli

To create caption texts to display to our DHH participants during the study, we made use of some staged and prerecorded videos (provided to us by Christopher Caulfield and Larwan Berke, details in Acknowledgements). These videos display one side of a two-person business meeting communication – the speaker leading the conversation in the video is made to look like he is interacting to the participant who is watching the video, as shown in Figure 3.

Figure 3: Preparation of a fake meeting transcript.

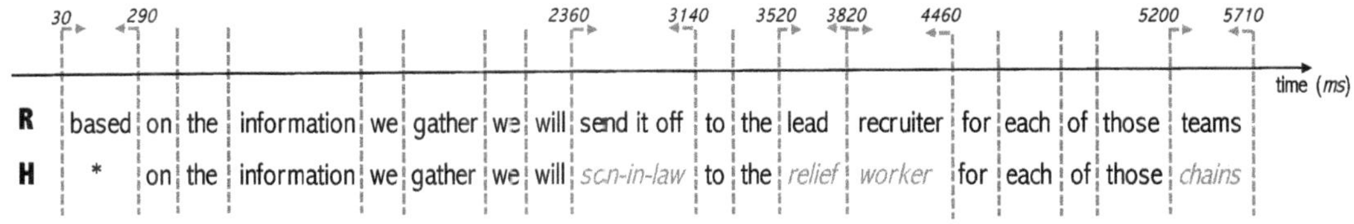

Figure 4: Time based alignment of reference (R) and hypothesized (H) text. The grouping with red dotted arrowhead lines indicates individualized errors aligned with corresponding reference text based on word level timestamps.

We extracted the verbatim script of what the human actor said during the videos, and we used the entire text of this video as a potential source of stimuli sentences for inclusion in this study (details in 5.1.1 and 5.1.2 below). Next, we processed the original audio recording from these videos using an ASR system that we expected to make a large number of errors (it is important for our stimuli selection process described in 5.1.2 for us to have many possible errors to choose from). For this processing, we used the CMU Sphinx 4 system with its off-the-shelf US English acoustic and language models which have been previously disseminated to the research community[3].

While a simplistic approach for creating stimuli for the study would have been to simply display the raw output of the ASR system to users, we were interested in obtaining judgments from participants on texts that had a variety of ACE metric scores. Furthermore, to investigate hypothesis H1, we were interested in presenting users with some pairs of ASR text output that displayed multiple hypotheses (i.e. two different guesses from the ASR system about what it heard), with one of the texts having a low WER-to-ACE score ratio (indicating that WER believed the text to be good, but ACE did not) and the other with a high WER-to-ACE ratio. Since ASR systems actually consider a wide variety of hypotheses when they analyze a speech audio file (with one hypothesis correct, and the remainder containing some variety of errors), we wanted to search the space of ASR output candidate hypotheses to select texts to display in our study with various WER-to-ACE ratios. Sections 5.1.1 and 5.1.2 describe our procedure for identifying ASR output hypotheses to display in our study with diverse WER-to-ACE ratios. Rather than inventing artificial errors to insert into the texts, our procedure obtains a large number of real ASR errors on a text and selects a subset of these errors to include in the texts displayed.

5.1.1 Time-based Alignment

After we prepared the meeting script and ran it against our low-accuracy ASR system, the next step was to align the reference text (the verbatim script of what the human actually said) and the hypothesis text (the output of the ASR system) to obtain a list of all the errors in the ASR output. While the ASR output hypothesis text already included timestamps of when the ASR believed each word had been spoken, we needed to identify timestamps for each word in the reference text. We manually compared the reference text to the original audio to obtain timestamp values for each word.

Next, we needed to time-align the hypothesis text to the reference text, to correctly identify all the errors in the hypothesis text. Standard alignment tools like [12] were ill-suited to this task because they are designed to compute the edit distance of the reference text from the hypothesis text. Our task required alignment of the text to capture the exact regions of errors – the goal of which is different slightly from the edit distance computation. For the purpose we wrote code to identify different error regions in the ASR output. Often, there is no one-to-one correspondence between an error word and a reference word. Multiple reference words can be misrecognized as a single word (substitution followed by deletions) and a single reference word can be misrecognized as multiple words (substitution followed by insertions) [22][32]. Our time-based error alignment software uses word-level timestamps to group the errors appropriately, as shown in Figure 4. The output of our processing is a list of confusion pairs for each sentence. For the example in Figure 4, the confusion pairs would be: (based, *); (send it off, son-in-law); (lead, relief); (recruiter, worker); (teams, chains).

5.1.2 Stimuli Selection

The alignment of the bad hypothesis output from the ASR system with the reference transcripts (in section 5.1.1 above) provided us with the list of confusion pairs, with each pair corresponding to an independent error (no overlap in the time frames) the ASR system made. We note that the reference text and the list of confusion pairs can be thought of as specifying an entire "space" of possible ASR outputs: Considering the reference text as a starting point, and considering each confusion pair as an "insert an error" operator, one can imagine an entire network of possible ASR text outputs that are possible. Each ASR output contains some subset of the errors from the list of confusion pairs.

Given this space of possible ASR outputs, our goal is to identify two output texts for each reference text, with these properties:

- The output texts should reflect reasonable performance of a commercial ASR system in noise typical of a workplace setting when the speaker is not wearing a special headset microphone; so, we wanted to identify text candidates with WER of approximately 0.25 (ranging between 20% and 30%).
- We wanted to identify one text candidate that has a low WER-to-ACE ratio and another candidate with a high WER-to-ACE ratio. We selected two candidates with identical WER: one with a high ACE score, and the other with a low ACE score.

Thus, the two text candidates identified represent two possible outputs from an ASR system. The errors that appear in the texts are realistic: They were actual errors made by an ASR system, and the overall WER error rate for the sentences is approximately 0.25. We can think of one of these text candidates as being "preferred by WER" (the one with the low WER-to-ACE ratio), and the other as being "preferred by ACE" (with the high WER-to-ACE ratio).

We wrote code to execute a search procedure through the space of possibilities to identify a pair of text candidates that fit the above criteria. We executed this code on 45 text sentences that had been extracted from the verbatim script of what the human spoke in our business meeting videos, and we thereby obtained 45 pairs of ASR text output candidates (two per sentence). Example stimuli from are available here: http://latlab.ist.rit.edu/assets2017ace

[3]https://sourceforge.net/projects/cmusphinx/files/Acoustic%20and %20Language%20Models/

5.2 Study Setup and Procedure

During the study, each participant was presented with 45 pairs of text output; each pair was displayed simultaneously, as shown in Figure 5. The reference text (what the human actually said) was provided at the top of the screen, and the two text candidates were presented on the left and right side of the screen (positioned as captioning text in a black box below the video image).

The participant was asked to provide an individual subjective quality rating for each of the two videos, using a ten-level scale (frown face to smiley face) with endpoints labeled as "Useless" and "Useful." At the beginning of the study, participants were provided with instructions on the study procedure and a practice item, prior to being presented with the 45 sentence pairs.

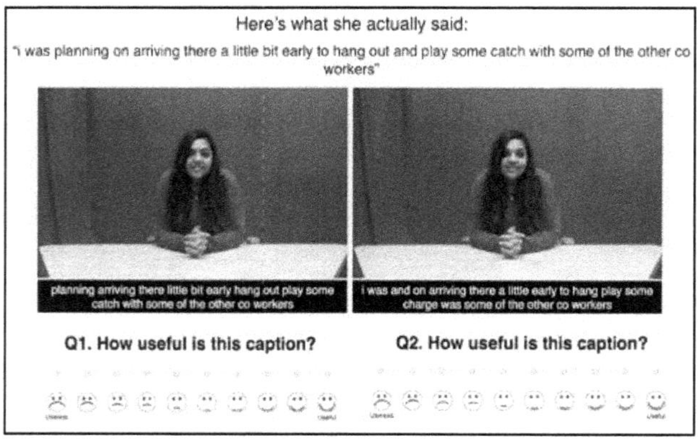

Figure 5: Screenshot from the study, with side-by-side comparison of caption-text automatically generated by ASR. Each pair of texts (left and right) have identical WER scores, but one text in each pair was preferred by our ACE metric.

The WER score was identical for the two text candidates that were shown in each pair; across all 45 pairs, the WER was in the range of 0.25 to 0.3. The two versions of text differed in their ACE score; one had a higher ACE score while other had a lower score. The presentation of text candidates on the left or right side was randomized throughout the study.

5.3 Participants

We recruited participants from the Rochester Institute of Technology and surrounding campus community. We collected data from 30 DHH participants (age distribution with mean = 23.53 and standard deviation= 4.92), which included 17 men and 13 women. Among our participants, 14 people self-identified as deaf, 8 people identified themselves as Deaf, and 8 people of the participants as hard-of-hearing. All of the participants reported that they were familiar with the use of captioning technology, and they regularly used captioning when watching television programming.

6. RESULTS AND DISCUSSION

We collected 2700 responses in total from our 30 participants (subjective scores for each sentence, for 45 stimuli pair per participant). Figure 6 presents the average subjective judgment rating for each participant in the study, displaying their average score across all text candidates that they evaluated: the text output preferred by the ACE score (with high WER-to-ACE ratio) and the text output not preferred by ACE. Figure 7(a) presents the summarized response data across all participants, and Figure 7(b) visualizes a linear correlation best-fit line for the relationship

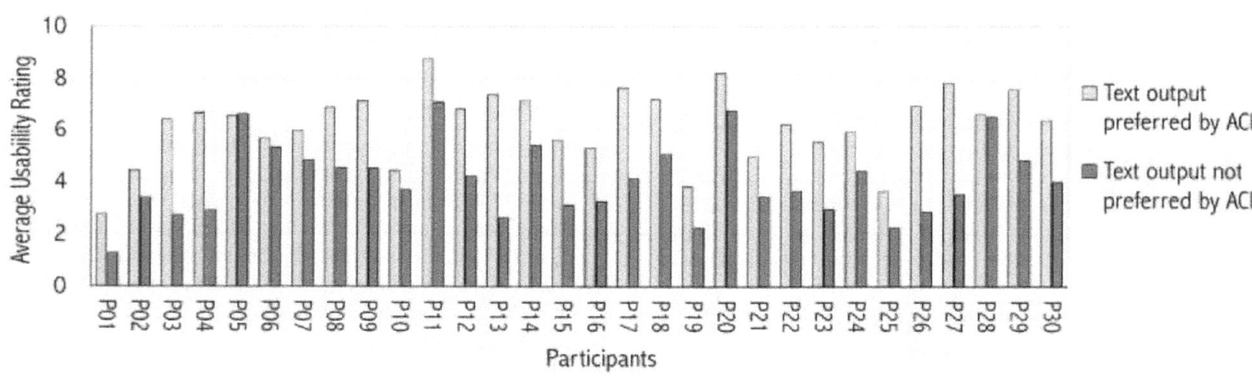

Figure 6: Average usability rating variation among participants.

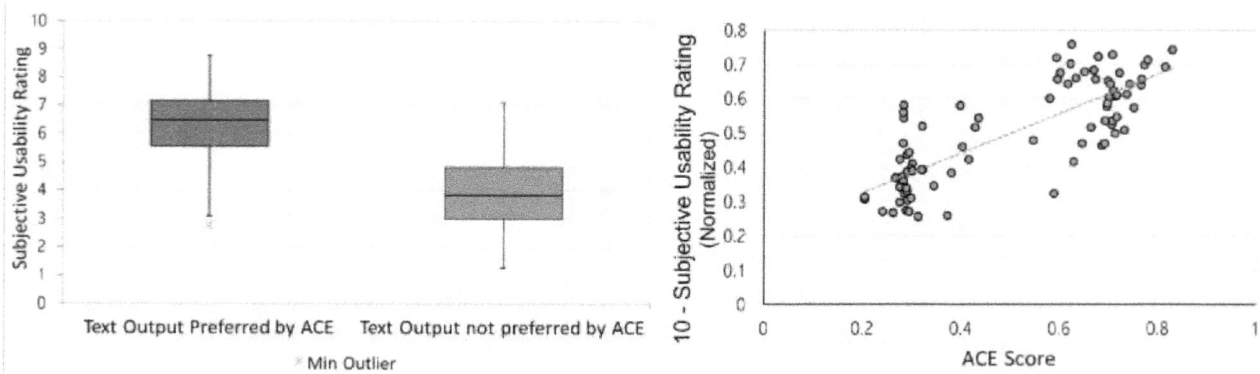

(a) Usability rating across stimuli (b) Correlation Analysis

Figure 7: Analysis of the ACE metric with participant's usability rating.

between the ACE scores of each sentence and the participants' subjective judgment rating.

Hypothesis H1 considered whether DHH users reported a subjective preference for captions that were predicted as "better" by our ACE metric, as compared to the captions that were predicted as "worse" by our ACE metric (high WER-to-ACE ratio vs. low WER-to-ACE ratio). The median difference (subjective score on "better" texts – subjective score on "worst" texts) was 2.5; the DHH users had higher subjective ratings for texts that had been preferred by the ACE metric. A boxplot summarizing the subjective rating scores from the participants for each stimulus (text predicted as "better" by ACE vs text predicted as "worse" by ACE) is shown in Figure 7(a). The distribution of the two groups differed significantly (Wilcoxon signed-rank W= 643394.00, N = 1350, N_test = 1226, P-Value < 0.0001). Thus, hypothesis H1 was supported: DHH users preferred predictions from the ACE metric.

For Hypothesis H2a, we considered if the usability scores from DHH users correlated with the ACE score significantly. We computed Spearman Rho Correlation score for the two scores. The correlation coefficient was found to be rho = 0.742791 with a p-value <0.0001. Figure 7(b) shows the corresponding correlation graph. This supports H2a: DHH user's judgments on the usability of the caption text correlated with scores from ACE metric.

For Hypothesis H2b, we performed significant difference testing on the correlations between 1) the human subjective preferences and the ACE score (r_{ha}) and, 2) the human subjective preferences and the WER score (r_{hw}). We performed a Fisher r-to-z transformation in order to perform an asymptotic z-test. For $r_{ha} = 0.742791$ and $r_{hw} = 0.108852$, we found a significant difference between the two coefficients (z-score = 5.771, 1-tail P-value < 0.0001). Thus, hypothesis H2b was supported: The subjective judgment of DHH participants about the quality of ASR captions was more highly correlated with ACE, as compared to their correlation with WER.

7. CONCLUSIONS AND FUTURE WORK

We have designed a new evaluation metric that analyzes the output of ASR systems to predict the impact of various ASR recognition errors on the usability of automatically generated captions for DHH users, and we have compared this new ACE metric to the traditional WER metric in a study with DHH participants. In a side-by-side comparison of pairs of ASR text output with identical WER score, the texts favored by our new metric were also preferred by DHH participants. Our metric also had significantly higher correlation with DHH participants' subjective scores on caption usability, as compared to the correlation between WER and their scores. Our new ACE metric can be used to select ASR systems for captioning applications, and researchers may utilize ACE as a loss function when training ASR systems for DHH captioning applications. The error impact module used in the metric could also find its use in error marking systems alongside word uncertainty measures to indicate readers of harmful errors in the caption.

While we have identified word predictability and semantic distance as useful predictors of the usability of an automatically generated caption text, there are still limitations in our metric, which we will address in future work, e.g., empirically evaluating alternatives to the use of *maximum* for combining error impact sub-scores (as discussed in section 3.4), e.g. to accommodate longer texts with multiple sentences. Rather than using word2vec similarity scores alone to compute semantic distance, we may also explore additional semantic features (such as sentiment). We also plan to conduct a user-study with a larger number of users to explore the relationship between additional linguistic features for identifying important words, to enable us to build and compare metrics that predict the understandability of a text; in particular, we may train a statistical model of feature weights on the usability scores collected from a larger number of DHH participants on diverse stimuli. More broadly, we will also continue our research on improving ASR based captioning for DHH users, as described in section 1.

8. ACKNOWLEDGMENTS

This material was based on work supported by the National Technical Institute for the Deaf (NTID). We are grateful to Christopher Caulfield, who assisted with data collection for this study, and to our collaborators Larwan Berke, Michael Stinson, Lisa Elliot, Donna Easton, and James Mallory. Larwan Berke and Christopher Caulfield, our colleagues at RIT, provided us with the stimuli videos described in section 5.1.

9. REFERENCES

[1] T. Apone, B. Botkin, M. Brooks and L. Goldberg. 2011. Caption Accuracy Metrics Project. *Research into Automated Error Ranking of Real-time Captions in Live Television News Programs, WGBH.* Retrieved from http://ncam.wgbh.org/file_download/136

[2] K. Bain, S. H. Basson, M. Wald. 2002. Speech recognition in university classrooms: liberated learning project. In *Proc. ASSETS '02*, ACM, New York, NY, USA, 192–196. DOI: http://dx.doi.org/10.1145/638249.638284

[3] N. N. Belanger and K. Rayner. 2013. Frequency and predictability effects in eye fixations for skilled and less-skilled deaf readers. *Visual cognition,* 21(4):477–497

[4] D. L. Blackwell, J. W. Lucas, T. C. Clarke. 2014. Summary health statistics for us adults: national health interview survey, 2012. *Vital and health statistics. Series 10, Data from the National Health Survey*, (260):1–161

[5] T. Brants, A. C. Popat, P. Xu, F. J. Och, J. Dean. 2007. Large language models in machine translation. In *Proc. EMNLP-CoNLL '07,* Prague, Czech Republic, 858–867, Association for Computational Linguistics.

[6] A.-B. Dominguez, J. Alegria. 2010. Reading mechanisms in orally educated deaf adults. *Journal of deaf studies and deaf education,* 15(2): 136–148. DOI: https://doi.org/10.1093/deafed/enp033

[7] A.-B. Dominguez, M.-S. Carrillo, M. del Mar Perez, J. Alegría. 2014. Analysis of reading strategies in deaf adults as a function of their language and meta-phonological skills. *Research in developmental disabilities*, 35(7):1439–1456. DOI: https://doi.org/10.1016/j.ridd.2014.03.039

[8] J. Duffy, T. Giolas. 1971. *The effect of word predictability on sentence intelligibility*. Technical report, Submarine Medical Research Laboratory.

[9] L. Elliot, M. Stinson, J. Mallory, D. Easton, M. Huenerfauth. 2016. Deaf and hard of hearing individuals' perceptions of communication with hearing colleagues in small groups. In *Proc. ASSETS '16*, ACM, New York, NY, USA, 271–272. DOI: http://dx.doi.org/10.1145/2982142.2982198

[10] B. Favre, K. Cheung, S. Kazemian, A. Lee, Y. Liu, C. Munteanu, A. Nenkova, D. Ochei, G. Penn, S. Tratz, et al. 2013. Automatic human utility evaluation of ASR systems: does WER really predict performance? In *Proc. Interspeech '13*, 3463–3467.

[11] M. Federico, M. Furini. 2012. Enhancing learning accessibility through fully automatic captioning. In *Proc. W4A '12*, ACM, New York, NY, USA, Article 40, 4 pages. DOI: http://dx.doi.org/10.1145/2207016.2207053

[12] J. Fiscus. 1998. *Sclite scoring package version 1.5.* US National Institute of Standard Technology, Retrieved on May 1, 2017 from http://www. itl. nist. gov/iaui/894.01/tools.

[13] I.R. Forman, B. Fletcher, J. Hartley, B. Rippon, A. Wilson. 2012. Blue herd: automated captioning for videoconferences. In *Proc. ASSETS '12,* ACM, New York, NY, USA, 227–228. DOI: http://dx.doi.org/10.1145/2384916.2384966

[14] N. Garay-Vitoria, J. Abascal. 2006. Text prediction systems: a survey. *Univers. Access Inf. Soc.* 4, 3 (February 2006), 188-203. DOI: http://dx.doi.org/10.1007/s10209-005-0005-9

[15] J.S. Garofolo, C.G.P. Auzanne, E.M. Voorhees. 2000. The TREC spoken document retrieval track: A success story. In *Content-Based Multimedia Information Access - Volume 1, RIAO '00,* Paris, France, 1-20.

[16] Y. Gaur, W. S. Lasecki, F. Metze, J. P. Bigham. 2016. In *Proc. W4A'16.* ACM, New York, NY, USA, Article 23, 8 pages. DOI: https://doi.org/10.1145/2899475.2899478

[17] J.J. Godfrey, E.C. Holliman, J. McDaniel. 1992. Switchboard: Telephone speech corpus for research and development. In *IEEE International Conference on Acoustics, Speech, and Signal Processing, volume 1,* 517–520. IEEE.

[18] D. Grangier, A. Vinciarelli, H. Bourlard. 2003. *Information retrieval on noisy text.* Technical report, IDIAP.

[19] S.S. Gray, D. Willett, J. Lu, J. Pinto, P. Maergner, N. Bodenstab. 2014. Child automatic speech recognition for US English: child interaction with living-room-electronic-devices. In *Proc. WOCCI,* 21–26.

[20] R.P. Harrington, G.C. Vanderheiden. 2013. Crowd caption correction (CCC). In *Proc. of ASSETS '13. ACM, New York, NY, USA, Article 45, 2 pages. DOI: http://dx.doi.org/10.1145/ 2513383.2513413*

[21] D. W. Jackson, P. V. Paul, J. C. Smith. 1997. Prior knowledge and reading comprehension ability of deaf adolescents. *Journal of Deaf Studies and Deaf Education,* 2(3), 172–184.

[22] S. Kafle, M. Huenerfauth. 2016. Effect of speech recognition errors in text understandability for people who are deaf or hard-of-hearing. In *Proceedings of the 7th Workshop on Speech and Language Processing for Assistive Technologies (SLPAT), Interspeech'16,* San Francisco, CA, USA. 20–25.

[23] S. Kawas, G. Karalis, T. Wen, R.E. Ladner. 2016. Improving real-time captioning experiences for deaf and hard of hearing students. In *Proc. ASSETS'16,* ACM, New York, NY, USA, 15-23. DOI: https://doi.org/10.1145/2982142.2982164

[24] R. Kliegl, E. Grabner, M. Rolfs, R. Engbert. 2004. Length, frequency, and predictability effects of words on eye movements in reading. *European Journal of Cognitive Psychology,* 16(1-2):262–284. DOI: http://dx.doi.org/10.1080/09541440340000213

[25] R.S. Kushalnagar, W.S. Lasecki, J.P. Bigham. 2014. Accessibility evaluation of classroom captions. *ACM Trans. Access. Comput. 5,* 3, Article 7, 24 pages. DOI: http://dx.doi.org/10.1145/2543578

[26] W.S. Lasecki, J.P. Bigham. 2014. Real-time captioning with the crowd. *interactions,* 21, 3 (May 2014), 50–55. DOI: https://doi.org/10.1145/2594459

[27] X. Lei, A.W. Senior, A. Gruenstein, J. Sorensen. 2013. Accurate and compact large vocabulary speech recognition on mobile devices. In *Proc. Interspeech'13, vol. 1,* 662–665.

[28] J. Li, L. Deng, Y. Gong, R. Haeb-Umbach. 2014. An overview of noise-robust automatic speech recognition. *IEEE/ACM Trans. Audio, Speech and Lang. Proc.* 22, 4 (April 2014), 745-777. DOI: http://dx.doi.org /10.1109/TASLP.2014.2304637

[29] J.L. Luckner, C.M. Handley. 2008. A summary of the reading comprehension research undertaken with students who are deaf or hard of hearing. *American Annals of the Deaf,* 153(1):6–36. DOI: http://dx.doi.org/10.1353/aad.0.0006

[30] I.A. McCowan, D. Moore, J. Dines, D. Gatica-Perez, M. Flynn, P. Wellner, H. Bourlard. 2004. *On the use of information retrieval measures for speech recognition evaluation.* Technical report, IDIAP.

[31] T. Mishra, A. Ljolje, M. Gilbert. 2011. Predicting human perceived accuracy of ASR systems. In *Proc. Interspeech'11,* 1945–1948

[32] A.C. Morris, V. Maier, P.D. Green. 2004. From WER and RIL to MER and WIL: improved evaluation measures for connected speech recognition. In *Interspeech'04,* 2765-2768.

[33] H. Nanjo, T. Kawahara. 2005. A new ASR evaluation measure and minimum Bayes-risk decoding for open-domain speech understanding. In *Proc. IEEE International Conference on Acoustics, Speech, and Signal Processing, vol. 1,* 1053–1056.

[34] K. Rayner. 1998. Eye movements in reading and information processing: 20 years of research. *Psychological Bulletin,* 124(3):372-422 DOI: http://dx.doi.org/10.1037/0033-2909.124.3.372.

[35] K. Rayner, X. Li, B.J. Juhasz, G. Yan. 2005. The effect of word predictability on the eye movements of Chinese readers. *Psychonomic Bulletin & Review,* 12(6):1089–1093. DOI: http://dx.doi.org/10.3758/BF03206448

[36] K. Rayner, E.D. Reichle, M.J. Stroud, C.C. Williams, A. Pollatsek. 2006. The effect of word frequency, word predictability, and font difficulty on the eye movements of young and older readers. *Psychology and Aging,* 21(3):448. DOI: http://dx.doi.org/10.1037/0882-7974.21.3.448

[37] K. Rayner, T.J. Slattery, D. Drieghe, S.P. Liversedge. 2011. Eye movements and word skipping during reading: effects of word length and predictability. *Journal of Experimental Psychology: Human Perception and Performance,* 37(2):514-528. DOI: http://dx.doi.org/10.1037/a0020990

[38] A. Rousseau, P. Deleglise, Y. Esteve. 2012. Ted-lium: an automatic speech recognition dedicated corpus. In Proc. of *LREC,'12* 125–129. ELRA, Paris, France.

[39] M.S. Stinson, P. Francis, L.B. Elliot, D.Easton. 2014. Real-time caption challenge: C-print. In *Proc. of ASSETS '14,* ACM, New York, NY, USA, 317-318. DOI: http://dx.doi.org/10.1145/2661334.2661337

[40] H. Takagi, T. Itoh, K. Shinkawa. 2015. Evaluation of real-time captioning by machine recognition with human support. *In Proc. W4A'15,* ACM, New York, NY, USA, Article 5, 4 pages. DOI: http://dx.doi.org/10.1145/2745555.2746648

[41] M. Wald. 2011. Crowdsourcing correction of speech recognition captioning errors. In *Proc. W4A'11,* ACM, New York, NY, USA, Article 22, 2 pages. DOI: https://doi.org/10.1145/1969289.1969318

[42] Y.-Y. Wang, A. Acero, C. Chelba. 2003. Is word error rate a good indicator for spoken language understanding accuracy. In *Proc. IEEE Workshop on Automatic Speech Recognition and Understanding,* 577–582. IEEE.

[43] W. Xiong, J. Droppo, X. Huang, F. Seide, . Seltzer, A. Stolcke, D. Yu, G. Zweig. 2016. Achieving human parity in conversational speech recognition. *Computing Research Repository (CoRR),* http://arxiv.org/abs/1610.05256

Design and Psychometric Evaluation of an American Sign Language Translation of the System Usability Scale

Matt Huenerfauth
Rochester Institute of Technology
152 Lomb Memorial Drive
Rochester, NY 14618 USA
matt.huenerfauth@rit.edu

Kasmira Patel
Rochester Institute of Technology
152 Lomb Memorial Drive
Rochester, NY 14618 USA
kxp3157@rit.edu

Larwan Berke
Rochester Institute of Technology
152 Lomb Memorial Drive
Rochester, NY 14618 USA
larwan.berke@mail.rit.edu

ABSTRACT
In usability studies, designers and researchers frequently use subjective questions to evaluate participants' impression of the usability of some product. The System Usability Scale (SUS) is a popular standardized questionnaire consisting of ten English statements about the usability of a product, to which participants indicate their agreement on a five-point scale. Many deaf adults in the U.S. have lower levels of English reading literacy, but there are currently no standardized questionnaires similar to SUS for Deaf and Hard-of-Hearing (DHH) users who are fluent in American Sign Language (ASL). To facilitate the inclusion of such users in studies, we created an ASL translation of SUS following accepted methods of survey translation: using a bilingual team including native ASL signers who are members of the Deaf community, along with back-translation evaluation to determine whether the meaning of the original was preserved. To validate whether key psychometric properties were preserved during translation, we deployed the ASL instrument in a study with 30 DHH participants. By comparing the results to users' responses to another measurement instrument, along with scores from 10 additional DHH participants responding to the original English SUS, we verified the criterion validity and internal reliability of the new "ASL-SUS." We are disseminating the translated instrument to promote the inclusion of DHH users in HCI research studies or in usability testing of consumer products.

CCS Concepts
• Human-centered computing~Empirical studies in accessibility • Human-centered computing~Accessibility design and evaluation methods

Keywords
System Usability Scale, SUS, American Sign Language, Translation, ASL-SUS, Criterion Validity, Internal Reliability

1. INTRODUCTION
To ensure that technology is accessible to diverse users, researchers and designers should ideally include people with disabilities during evaluation studies: The focus of our research is on finding ways to make it easier for researchers to include people who are Deaf or Hard-of-Hearing (DHH) in such studies. Often, designers will gather feedback from study participants by asking them to respond to questions about their impression of a system, and many studies will use pre-existing questionnaires for this purpose.

One popular instrument is the System Usability Scale (SUS), which consists of a ten-item Likert scale with English statements about the usability of some product [5]. For each item, participants indicate their agreement on a five-point scale from Strongly Disagree to Strongly Agree. From these responses, researchers use a rubric to calculate a final score on a range from 0 to 100, with higher scores indicating that the participant believed the product to be very usable. SUS has been used to evaluate a wide range of products, including hardware, computer software, websites, and mobile applications. Given the ease with which it is administered and scored, it has become a ubiquitous measurement instrument in HCI research and in commercial HCI usability testing.

One logistical challenge that designers face when including DHH users in empirical studies is that many people who are DHH prefer to communicate using American Sign Language (ASL). In fact, studies indicate that there are a half-million people who consider ASL as a primary means of communication [23]. Previous research on English literacy among U.S. deaf adults has found that many have lower literacy than their hearing peers [29]. In a usability study, DHH participants with lower English literacy may not fully understand questions presented in the form of English text, which may lead to discomfort or responses which are less reliable [13].

We therefore investigate how to translate SUS, one of the most commonly used usability questionnaires, into ASL. By making this translated instrument (in the form of ASL videos with translated instructions and question items) available to the HCI research community, our goal is to enable researchers to more easily include DHH participants in their studies, alongside hearing participants. In addition to creating this ASL translation, we have also conducted an evaluation to determine whether it preserves the meaning and other characteristics of the original English version, to enable researchers to compare scores across both versions.

This paper is organized as follows: Section 2 surveys prior work on HCI research with DHH users, standardized questionnaires, and prior efforts to translate them into other languages. Sections 3 and 4 outline our research questions and methodology for creating and evaluating the ASL version. Section 5 presents our evaluation results, and Section 6 summarizes our conclusions and future work.

2. LITERATURE SURVEY

2.1 Technology Research with DHH Users
It is difficult to quantify how often people with disabilities are *excluded* from usability studies or research due to the perception among some researchers that logistical barriers to inclusion are too

ASSETS'17, October 29-November 1, 2017, Baltimore, MD, USA

ACM ISBN 978-1-4503-4926-0/17/10…$15.00
https://doi.org/10.1145/3132525.3132540

great, especially when the study's focus is on the general population rather than on people with disabilities specifically. As discussed in [27], while HCI researchers generally agree that the participants in a study should be representative of the population of users, there can be a variety of challenges in recruiting participants with disabilities. People with disabilities are often not included in user testing, which can lead to inaccurate results [27]. In fact, a popular research-methods textbook for training future HCI professionals devotes an entire chapter to motivating students that people with disabilities should be included in studies and explaining how to overcome logistical barriers to doing so [19]. Some researchers include proxy users, e.g. sighted users wearing blindfolds or hearing users with the computer muted, rather than recruit users with disabilities [19, 27]. Others have examined the use of remote testing for people with disabilities, which addresses some barriers to recruitment due to population sparsity or difficulty traveling, but remote testing but does not address the English literacy issues of many DHH users (discussed above), unless steps are taken to provide question items using ASL videos, e.g. as in [26, 28].

Computing accessibility researchers publishing their work at competitive research conferences or journals will generally include people with disabilities in their empirical studies [27]. For example, researchers studying technologies related to sign language animation or recognition often conduct evaluation studies with participants who are DHH [10, 16]. Technology researchers who are studying current challenges or barriers faced by people who are DHH will also include DHH participants in studies: For instance, researchers have examined the communication challenges of DHH users in business or educational contexts [8, 11, 17].

Research on DHH users has tended to employ non-standardized survey questions, created specifically for each particular project; often, these question items are provided in the form of ASL videos, sometimes alongside English text versions of the items. For instance, one online survey of DHH students included both English and ASL versions of each question, to study the communication approaches used during meetings with hearing peers [11]. Another online survey used ASL videos to present question items, in order to collect judgments from ASL signers about the intelligibility of ASL videos of various levels of quality [28].

Some prior accessibility researchers have created and disseminated standardized survey instruments in the form of ASL videos. In [16], researchers sought to identify relationships between DHH participants' opinions about ASL animation technology and their responses to standardized surveys about technology use (originally designed for older users). In support of this research, the authors created ASL translations of pre-existing English survey questions about technology use and displayed these items to their participants in the form of ASL videos. However, the authors did not conduct a formal assessment of the quality of their ASL translations. In [15, 16], researchers disseminated sets of question items (in the form of both English text and ASL video) that could be used to evaluate the quality of ASL animation generation systems, to promote a standardized set of evaluation instruments among that community to enable comparisons of results across studies. However, none of this prior research produced translations of commonly used HCI usability survey instruments, nor did these prior studies include a formal assessment of translation quality.

A key premise of our work is that if there were greater availability of question items (available as both English text and ASL videos) suitable for evaluating usability of software or websites, more HCI researchers may include of DHH participants in their studies, even when the study is not specifically focused on DHH users.

2.2 Standardized Usability Questionnaires

When conducting a study to measure participants' subjective opinion about the usability of some technology, HCI researchers often use *standardized* questionnaires, i.e. official, accepted versions of questionnaires with a commonly agreed-upon set of questions, presented in a particular order, and with rubrics for how to calculate a final score based on a participant's responses. When the same questionnaire is used, it is easier to compare results across studies. Further, it is possible to archive participant scores across a large number of studies, perhaps subcategorized as to the type of technology evaluated. This set of published response values (or tables containing mean and standard deviations) is referred to as "norms," and the existence of this large quantity of historical data makes it easier to evaluate the results of a new study. That is, after a researcher has used a standardized instrument to produce a score representing the usability of some technology, they can compare their participants' responses to these norms to understand how their new results compare, in general, to prior studies. Often, the items included in a standardized questionnaire were chosen from an initially larger pool of questions, through a process of psychometric validation, to create a measurement instrument with a set of desirable psychometric properties [20, 25]. Since we discuss some properties in this paper, we provide brief definitions below for how we use some terms; detailed definitions appear in [1, 20, 25].

- **Construct Validity** refers to whether the instrument actually measures the real-world phenomena it is meant to, e.g. usability; this property is often assessed by examining the internal factor structure, i.e. whether subsets of questions on the questionnaire are correlated and whether these clusters relates to specific sub-scores or factors to be measured.
- **Criterion Validity** refers to whether the instrument relates to some other external property that can be measured; this property is often assessed based on whether the resulting score is correlated with some other trusted measure that respondents complete concurrently (i.e. another instrument they complete at the same time) or to its ability to predict some outcome.
- **Content Validity** refers to whether the questionnaire covers all of the essential aspects of the real-world phenomena it is supposed to measure; this property is often assessed by asking a panel of expert judges to evaluate the individual items.
- **Internal Reliability** refers to its internal consistency, i.e. whether all of the items in the instrument contribute equally to its score; this property is often assessed by calculating the Cronbach's alpha coefficient for the group of items [7].

2.3 Translating Surveys to Other Languages

It is known that asking participants to respond to a questionnaire in their non-native language affects their response scores [13]. So, researchers have established customary methods for translating a standardized survey into another language and evaluating whether the meaning of the original was preserved [13]. Further, researchers who translate a standardized questionnaire often evaluate the new version to determine whether certain desirable psychometric properties of the original (section 2.2) were preserved during the translation process. This section describes prior work in translating standardized usability questionnaires to other languages and the methods used to evaluate the success of those efforts. The four projects summarized below are the primary focus of this section:

- **English-to-Persian SUS:** Researchers in Iran translated the SUS into Persian, with a goal of creating an Iranian version that retained the psychometric properties of the original [9]. To ensure that the content of the new instrument was valid, a panel of 10 experts first analyzed the Persian version of the questions. Next, the authors conducted a study with 202 university students to evaluate the resulting survey scores.

- **English-to-Slovene SUS:** Researchers translated SUS into the Slovene language [4]. To evaluate the translation, the authors assembled a committee of reviewers with multidisciplinary backgrounds. The authors also evaluated their new instrument in a user study with 182 participants.
- **English-to-Turkish CSUQ:** Researchers translated the Computer System Usability Questionnaire (CSUQ) from English into Turkish [12]. While the focus of our project is SUS, CSUQ is a similar standardized usability questionnaire; so, the process by which researchers translated and evaluated it is relevant for us to consider. After conducting their translation, the authors evaluated the validity of the Turkish version by using the instrument in a user study with 97 participants to evaluate its psychometric properties.
- **English-to-German SUS:** Researchers authored a German translation of SUS based, in part, on an online crowdsourcing effort by a large group of volunteers [22]. However, no formal evaluation was conducted of the quality of the resulting translation nor of its psychometric properties.

We analyze these prior efforts to translate standardized usability surveys into other languages along several dimensions, which correspond to the three sub-sections below. Throughout this survey, key methodological elements of these prior studies are highlighted in **bold** font, and the research methodology for our translation of SUS from English to ASL (section 4) incorporates many key elements of the methodology of these prior translation projects.

2.3.1 Who translated the questionnaire, and how?

The methodology used in prior work for translating the survey instrument has varied. In some studies, a **team of experts** have performed the translation, sometimes as part of a multi-disciplinary team: For example, in the English-to-Turkish CSUQ project, a multidisciplinary research group of language professionals and reviewers were responsible for the translation. The group consisted of five native Turkish reviewers, two were bilingual reviewers, a native Turkish language expert and also usability expert who was responsible for coordinating the translation effort [12]. In the English-to-Persian SUS project [9], an ergonomics specialist conducted the initial translation. In [22], a **group of volunteers** suggested through online crowdsourcing how to translate the questions into German. An advantage of this approach is that it reduces the cost for researchers in conducting the translation, and it also provides a method by which questions could be translated into a wide variety of languages. However, the quality must be assessed, e.g., researchers in [22] had to edit the final version to improve the translation quality, subsequent to the crowdsourcing.

Section 4 will discuss how, in our project, we have asked a small **team of experts** to translate SUS into ASL.

2.3.2 How was the translation evaluated to determine if the original meaning was preserved?

There are several ways that the quality of the translation can be evaluated to determine whether it is fluent and whether it has preserved the meaning of the original English version.

In some projects, the team responsible for producing the translation conducts **multiple rounds of revision**, sometimes interleaved with rounds of user testing: For instance, in the English-to-Turkish CSUQ project [12], the quality of the translation was evaluated through a committee review process. After a draft of the translation to Turkish was developed from the original, the draft underwent a three-stage review process. This was aimed at modifying the Turkish version to preserve the meaning of the original English questions. Different participants were involved in each of the three stages. The nine members of the translation team independently evaluated the results after each round of testing and adjusted their translation to ensure that the meaning of the original questions were preserved. Each member of the research group reviewed the original and the revised versions of the Turkish SUS independently [12]. In the English-to-Persian SUS project [9], researchers conducted a study with 30 participants to identify linguistic problems in the translation; this pilot study led to the identification and integration of amendments into the final Persian SUS. In the English-to-Slovene SUS project [4], the translation process involved ten reviewers from the computer and natural sciences fields and three independent translators who were native Slovene speakers also fluent in English. The translation process was carried out in multiple stages, with members of the translation team considering comments from evaluators after each round. In the German-to-English SUS project [22], researchers edited the output of the crowdsourced translations written by volunteers online.

In some projects, a **back-translation procedure** is used to identify problems in the translated text: In this approach, after the team has produced their initial forward translation of a questionnaire from language "A" to language "B," then the researchers set up an evaluation study in which some new group of people translate each question back into the original language A. By comparing the original version of the survey (A) to this back-translated version (A-to-B-to-A), the researchers can determine if some meaning or concepts were lost during the original A-to-B translation phase. For example, in the English-to-Persian SUS project [9], two professional translators, who had lived in English-speaking countries, performed a back-translation after the original forward translation (English to Persian) had been carried out by the ergonomic specialist on the translation team. In the English-to-Slovene SUS project [4], the final round of revision included a back-translation procedure to look for any missing concepts.

Section 4 will discuss how, in our project, we have decided to use a translation process that incorporates both: **multiple rounds of revision** along with a **back-translation procedure** to identify any translated items that fail to preserve the meaning of the original.

2.3.3 How was the new version of the questionnaire evaluated to determine whether it preserved the useful psychometric properties of the original?

In addition to evaluating the text itself, researchers have evaluated whether key statistical characteristics of the questionnaire were preserved after the translation process. For example, in the English-to-Turkish CSUQ project [12], the researchers evaluated their translated version by using it in a usability study. Since CSUQ has a factor structure (i.e. it consists of several sub-scales, each based on a subset of questions), the researchers evaluated its **construct validity** by examining whether scores for clusters of items in the newly translated version were appropriately correlated.

In the English-to-Persian SUS project [9], a qualitative evaluation was also conducted involving a panel of ten experts to assess the **content validity** of the new instrument. Feedback from the expert group led to a revision of the translation of some items. Researchers also assessed their instrument through a study with 201 university students who evaluated a university food reservation system. The psychometric measures that were assessed based on these results included **construct validity** and **internal reliability** [9].

In the English-to-Slovene SUS project [4], a study involving 182 respondents (114 males, 86 females) was carried out using the new Slovene SUS to evaluate the usability of the Google Gmail website. The researchers evaluated their newly translated instrument's **internal reliability**, **criterion validity**, and **construct validity**.

Section 4 describes how we conducted a usability test with DHH participants responding to our new ASL version of SUS; we assessed **internal reliability** of our items using Cronbach's alpha [7]. We also asked participants to complete an additional usability questionnaire, which had previously been used in [2], to assess the **criterion validity** of our ASL translation of SUS.

2.4 Translating Surveys to ASL

Prior researchers have translated English surveys into ASL for health-related studies; although they had a focus on medical issues, these researchers' methodologies are also relevant to our work.

Health researchers have translated the Behavioral Risk Factor Surveillance System survey (a standardized survey conducted across the U.S.) into ASL using a **team of experts** consisting of bilingual individuals, with a mix of Deaf community members and health researchers [14]. The team strove for ASL with **meaning equivalence rather than word-for-word translation** and for ASL that would be understandable to a wide set of deaf individuals [14]. After the team produced an **ASL script** (a text file containing sequences of English words representing sequences of ASL signs, in appropriate ASL word order), a researcher not on the translation team **back-translated** the material to English. These were compared to the original English questions; in some cases, the translation team edited their ASL translations based on the results of this back-translation evaluation [14]. Finally, **native ASL signers** (people who grew up using ASL since early childhood) performed the ASL versions while being video recorded; an additional native ASL signer **"coach"** sat behind the camera, watching the script, to ensure that the performer followed the script that had been produced by the translation team.

Other researchers have translated the Multidimensional Health Locus of Control survey from English into ASL [24]. They convened a focus group of both bilingual members of the Deaf community who were **native ASL signers** and **ASL interpreters**. This first focus group produced an ASL translation for each English question item. Next, the researchers convened a second focus group (with similar membership composition) to produce an English **back-translation** for each ASL item; this second focus group also evaluated how close their English back-translation was to the original English version of the question items. In cases of divergence, the second focus group was asked to recommend a modification to the ASL version to better preserve the meaning of the original. During the back-translation evaluation, there were many cases (15 of 24) in which back-translation **lacked word-for-word equivalence** with the original English item, yet the focus group determined that the meaning was sufficiently preserved [24].

Section 4 will discuss how, in our project, the **team of experts** conducting the translation included **native ASL signers**. During translation, we created an **ASL script**, and during recording, a **coach** sat behind the camera while a **native signer** was recorded. During our evaluation, a group of **ASL interpreters** produced the **back-translations**, and when evaluating them, we considered **meaning equivalence rather than word-for-word translation**.

3. RESEARCH QUESTIONS

The goal of this study was to translate SUS, one of the most commonly used standardized questionnaires, from English into ASL to make it suitable for use with DHH users who prefer to communicate using ASL. Our challenge was to preserve the meaning of the questions and other desirable characteristics (section 2.2) so that results from our ASL instrument are comparable to results on the original English version. For convenience, we refer to our translated version as "ASL-SUS." In the remainder of this paper, we examine the following questions:

RQ1: Do the items in the ASL-SUS preserve the meaning of the original English SUS items, as measured through a back-translation study, in which ASL interpreters produce English back-translations and the meaning equivalence is compared to the original items?

RQ2: Deployed as the evaluation metric in a user study with DHH participants evaluating a university website, does ASL-SUS possess several key psychometric properties listed below?

a) **Internal Reliability**, as measured by Cronbach's alpha [7], indicating correlation among the set of ASL-SUS items
b) **Criterion Validity**, as measured by comparing the correlation between ASL-SUS and another measurement instrument collected concurrently from users: the adjective scale of [2]

4. RESEARCH METHODS

Our study included five phases: The first was the translation of SUS items into ASL. In phase two, a native ASL signer produced video recordings of the items, and the third phase consisted of back-translation and revision of the ASL videos. The fourth phase consisted of user studies with DHH users responding to the ASL-SUS items, to evaluate the quality of the translation and to assess the psychometric properties mentioned in RQ2 above. Finally, in phase five, we disseminate ASL-SUS to the research community. Details of each phase are discussed below.

4.1 Translation into ASL, Initial Revisions

During the first phase, a translation team was assembled, consisting of experts with skills in HCI and fluency in ASL and English:

- The first member was a doctoral student in computing, with several years of experience in the computing industry, who had completed two semester-long courses in HCI and was conducting research in HCI. This student was a fluent, native signer of ASL, born Deaf into a Deaf family of ASL-signers, and a graduate of a primary/middle/secondary school for the Deaf and from a university with instruction in ASL.
- The second member was a master's degree student in an HCI graduate program who had completed four semester-long courses in HCI, with experience conducting hundreds of hours of user testing, especially in-person studies with people who are DHH. This student was a fluent, native ASL signer who was born Deaf and used ASL since birth, and a graduate of a primary/middle/secondary school for the Deaf and from a university with instruction in ASL and English.
- The third member was a faculty member with a PhD in computing who publishes research in HCI and accessibility, and who had experience in corpus-based ASL computational linguistics research. This faculty member was a fluent signer who learned ASL as an adult, having completed 10 university courses in ASL, including 2 summer ASL immersion programs, and regularly uses ASL with DHH lab members.

The members of the team fell into specific roles: The faculty member suggested translation options and particular ASL linguistic structures (e.g. rhetorical questions, use of reference points in the signing space, etc.) to convey the original SUS question meaning. The doctoral student had final authority on the fluency of the ASL translations, given this student's "Deaf-of-Deaf" background and native signing skills. The masters student identified terminology about technology likely understood by DHH participants in usability studies and when particular ASL options proposed by the doctoral student were so idiomatic as to be difficult to understand for a DHH participant who may possess non-native ASL fluency.

To begin the process, the translation team held several meetings to create draft concepts for how the SUS instructions[1] (presented at the beginning of the questionnaire) and the ten question items could be conveyed in ASL. During this time, the team found it useful to use a mobile phone video camera to record themselves producing alternatives and saving brief video clips representing alternatives. Multiple revisions were made for each SUS item, through this process, until a consensus set of ASL items were produced. The team avoided using an overly word-for-word transliteration of the original English items, to avoid producing non-fluent English-like signing videos. Instead, the team strove to preserve the overall meaning of each item, while using ASL structure. These casually-recorded videos were transcribed to produce an ASL script representing each item (see appendix A for more details).

4.2 Recording of High Quality ASL Videos

In phase two, high-definition videos were recorded of a native ASL signer performing each of the ASL-SUS items, in a video recording studio with professional-quality overhead lighting. The ASL signer wore solid-color black shirt (which contrasted with the signer's skin color, as shown in Figure 1), and a plain blue background (contrasting with both the skin and shirt color) was behind the signer. The master's degree student on the translation team acted as a coach, behind the camera, with a copy of the script, observing the ASL produced by the native signer being recorded to ensure that the performance matched the intended ASL translations.

4.3 Back-Translation, Final Revisions

In this third phase, we conducted a back-translation experiment to determine whether the translation preserved the meaning of the original. We recruited nine participants (5 female, 4 male) for this study, who were advanced students (3rd- or 4th-year) in a bachelor's degree program in ASL interpreting at Rochester Institute of Technology. Our rationale for recruiting interpreting students is that they regularly complete assignments in which they view and critique videos of ASL signing, and they have skills in discussing translation alternatives. The age of participants ranged from 20 to 26 (median 22). Three reported having deaf family members, including one participant who self-described as a Child of Deaf Adults (CODA). Aside from the CODA, who had used ASL since birth, the remaining participants had been using ASL for 3 to 8 years (mean 5.25). Participants were paid $40 for participating in this one-hour study, which was approved by the university IRB.

The participants were presented with each ASL-SUS video, and they were asked to write an English translation for each. Afterward, participants were shown the original English SUS, and they were asked to compare their translation to the original and to provide written feedback about any cases in which the meaning diverged. Participants were asked to offer suggestions about how the ASL video translation could be revised so that it would have been more successful at conveying the meaning of the original English item.

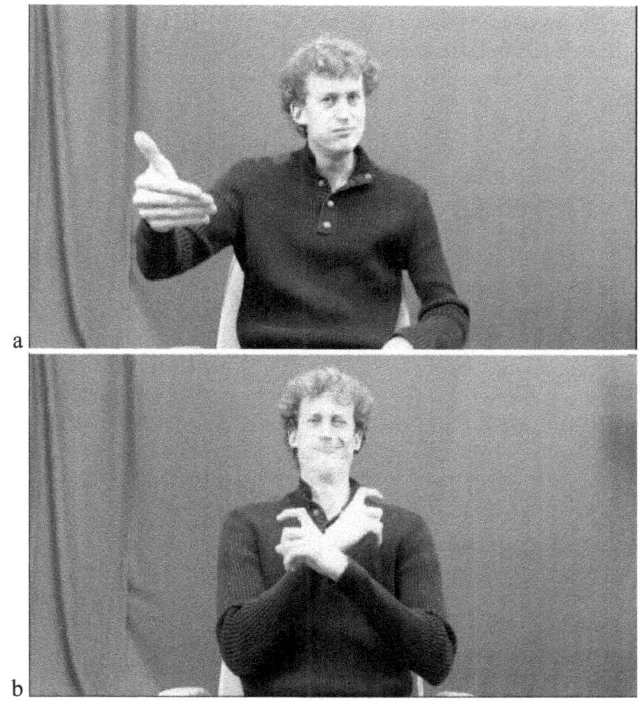

Figure 1. Example screenshots from videos of a native ASL signer performing some of the ASL-SUS items: (a) Excerpt from ASL-SUS for "I think that I would like to use this frequently," showing ASL sign FREQUENT, with cheeks-puffed-air-released-on-side facial expression to increase the degree of magnitude of the concept "frequently"; (b) Excerpt from ASL-SUS for "I found the system unnecessarily complex," showing ASL sign COMPLEX, with a negative-grimace facial expression to indicate bemused irritation.

The translation team (section 4.1) analyzed the back-translations and feedback comments from this study in order to identify any ASL videos for which the back-translations diverged from the meaning of the original English item or for which the participants had indicated suggestions of how the ASL video could have been improved. The translation team identified 2 items that needed to undergo major revisions based on the feedback, and 4 items that needed some small changes. Some examples of revisions made to our original ASL videos based on this feedback include:

- The initial translation (section 4.1) of SUS question 8 "I found the product very awkward to use" into ASL was as follows: I LOOK $\text{THIS}_{\text{down}}$, topic-eyebrow-raise{USE} AWKWARD. OVERWHELM (shrug). (Appendix A describes our notation used for ASL transcription.) Some participants indicated that the signer's performance of AWKWARD in the video was somewhat fast and difficult to perceive. Furthermore, several indicated that the use of OVERWHELM suggested that the fault lay with human user (who was not able to understand the technology), rather than the technology having some flaw. For instance, one back-translation was "This is over my head." Therefore, in the revised version of this item, the translation

[1] In translating the instructions to ASL, additional explanatory content had to be added. For instance, the instructions had to explain that participants would need to watch *videos* of ASL and then circle items on paper, and the disagree/agree scale had to be explained in ASL (since the English questions would not appear on the paper). Further, the original SUS instructions mentioned the user's "reactions to the website today." Researchers generally change the word "website" to "device" or "software" as needed. To avoid producing multiple versions of our ASL videos, we needed the instructions to explain that the questions referred to the website, software, or device that the person had just used.

team decided to omit the sign OVERWHELM, and the sign AWKWARD was slowed down (with a "disgust-tense" facial expression added) to improve intelligibility.

- Our original translation of SUS question 5 "I found the various functions in the product were well integrated" into ASL was as follows: I LOOK THIS$_{\text{down}}$, DO-DO$_{\text{repetitive-circular-sweeping}}$ cheek-puff{ MAINSTREAM-INTEGRATE } check-puff-side-release{ SMOOTH }. In the feedback comments, most participants indicated that they had not understood the signer's use of a repeated DO-DO sign performed in a circular sweeping arc motion to convey that the product does lots of things. For instance, one of the back-translations was "I can see all the pieces coming together." We decided to make use of the ASL sign ACTIVITY to more overtly refer to the many functions of the system[2]. The revised ASL version of this item was: I LOOK THIS$_{\text{down}}$, MANY ACTIVITY (signer sets up a list buoy[3], with rhythmic nodding when pointing to each item) I CAN USE TOGETHER FINE, WAVE-WOW.

We confirmed that our revisions had addressed the concerns raised in the back-translation study by evaluating the revised videos in a second back-translation study with 10 new participants (8 female, 2 male; ages 20 to 23; mean 9.4 years of ASL usage; all in the 3rd and 4th year in the ASL interpreting degree program).

4.4 Summative User Study Evaluation

To evaluate our revised ASL-SUS items, we conducted two studies in which DHH participants evaluate the usability of a university website. The only difference between the studies was the number of participants (30 in study #1, 10 in study #2) and whether they responded to the ASL-SUS (study #1) or the original English version (study #2), after they interacted with the website. Participants were paid $40 for participating in either one-hour study; both were approved by our university IRB.

4.4.1 Summative User Study #1 with ASL-SUS

In determining whether ASL signing participants could easily understand and respond to a SUS survey presented via ASL videos, we conducted a usability study with 30 participants (15 female, 15 male) from the Rochester Institute of Technology and surrounding community. Participant ages ranged from 19 to 27 (mean 22.5). Of the 30, 25 self-identified as Deaf, and 5, as Hard-of-Hearing. Twenty participants had used ASL since infancy, 6 since age 3, and the remainder by age 5. Eleven participants indicated that they had grown up in households with ASL signing parents.

Using a methodology similar to a prior study that had used SUS [6], we asked participants to access our university website and perform information-seeking tasks, without using a search engine:

- What events are happening on campus on March 9th, 2017?
- Find the textbook that you must buy for a given course.
- Find the phone number for the student employment office.
- Where is a particular building on the campus map?
- Find the latest issue of some university publication.
- Where in the library is "the Notebook" by Nicholas Sparks?
- What is on the menu today at the cafeteria?
- What are the opening hours for the academic support office?
- What's the phone number and office hours for the registrar?
- When does the freshman orientation event begin?

A fluent ASL signer conducted each experimental session in ASL, and the participant was handed a sheet of paper with the list of items above (written in English). Participants were asked to complete each task in sequence, and some tasks required up to five minutes. Most participants struggled with a few of the items on the list, with many commenting that they usually use the search engine to find information, rather than using the navigation bars on the website. Participants' computer screens were recorded during the session.

After completing the tasks, the participants were asked to view the ASL-SUS videos (consisting of an introductory video with instructions, followed by the ten Likert-type items). (Appendix A contains transcripts of the ASL-SUS items and a URL where the videos can be downloaded or viewed.) Participants indicated their answer choice for each Likert item on a piece of paper that contained a list of numbers from 1 to 10 arranged vertically, with a set of five checkboxes next to each. The leftmost checkbox was labeled "strongly disagree," and the rightmost, "strongly agree." No other English questions or instructions appeared on the paper.

In order to evaluate the criterion validity of ASL-SUS, it is useful to collect responses from participants on a second pre-existing usability instrument. In [2], researchers wanted to identify English adjectives that corresponded to various SUS scores [2]; so, they asked 964 English-speaking participants (mean age 40.4; 474 female, 490 male) to evaluate a variety of websites and software, across several studies. The participants responded to the original English version of the SUS questionnaire, and in addition, they responded to a novel seven-point "adjective scale" designed by the researchers. Participants were asked to select a word that indicated how user-friendly they believed the website or software to be. The scale consisted of adjectives, scored as ordinal values: Worst Imaginable (1), Awful (2), Poor (3), OK (4), Good (5), Excellent (6), Best Imaginable (7). We decided to ask our participants to respond to this adjective scale in our study: since this instrument had previously been compared to the original English SUS, we could perform a similar analysis of our new ASL-SUS. Since our participants were fluent ASL signers, we provided an ASL video translation of the Adjective Scale user-friendliness question and the answer choice levels (see Appendix A), but the paper answer-sheet presented the seven options using the original English adjectives.

4.4.2 Comparison Study #2 with English SUS

While there are many published results and norms available for English-speaking users responding to original English SUS items, we wanted to gather a small set of response data from additional DHH participants evaluating the university website. Section 5 discusses how this comparative data is used to evaluate the ASL-SUS. In this study #2, 10 DHH participants (4 female, 6 male) were recruited from the university campus and surrounding community. Participant ages ranged from 20 to 27 (mean 22.4). Of the 10, 5 self-identified as Deaf, and 5, as Hard-of-Hearing. Three had used ASL since infancy, 2 since age 4, 2 since age 7, and the remainder by age 16. Five participants indicated that they had grown up in households with ASL signing parents. The procedure and tasks in this study were identical to those in study #1, with one difference: Instead of responding to the ASL-SUS, these participants

[2] While some ASL signers use a specific sign for "function," the native ASL signers on the translation team felt that this was an English-influenced sign, using an "F" handshape initialization, and it may not be widely understood by signers less familiar with computer jargon.

[3] In ASL, a "list buoy" refers to a linguistic construction in which the signer raises the non-dominant hand into the signing space with some number of fingers extended, to represent a list of items that is being communicated. The signer generally points to each finger when referring to or introducing each item in the list. Here, the list buoy is used in a non-specific sense, to indicate that there are a multitude of functions.

responded to the original English SUS items on a paper questionnaire.

4.5 Dissemination of ASL-SUS

In the final phase of our study, we have disseminated our new ASL-SUS, to share this resource with the research community. Appendix A provides a transcript of each item, and the final version of the ASL videos and PDFs of the paper answer sheets are available at http://latlab.ist.rit.edu/assets2017sus

To provide the research community with additional information about participant responses on these new instruments, we share the raw numerical response data from study #1 and #2 (on ASL-SUS, English SUS, and Adjective Scale) in Appendix B.

5. Results

This section analyzes the results from our evaluation of ASL-SUS, with a focus on addressing the research questions in section 3.

Our first research question (**RQ1**) was whether we had preserved the meaning of the original English SUS during the translation process used to produce ASL-SUS. This issue was primarily examined in a formative manner, during the translation and back-translation evaluation process. To ensure that meaning was preserved during translation, we used several commonly accepted methodologies: a team of experts produced the translation, multiple rounds of revision occurred, a back-translation evaluation was conducted prior to the final revision, and native ASL signers participated in the translation process. Informally, we note that the mean scores for ASL-SUS in study #1 (52.25) and the original English SUS in study #2 (50.5) were quite similar; this is a reasonable result since DHH participants evaluated an identical website and performed identical search tasks in both studies.

Although not a formal research question identified in this study, we were also interested in the overall usability of the ASL-SUS, i.e., whether DHH participants found any of the videos confusing or difficult to understand. During summative study #1 (section 4.4.1), we invited participants to indicate if they were unsure of the meaning of any ASL-SUS videos or had difficulty in responding to any questions. At the end of the study, participants wrote feedback comments about their experience participating in the study. None of the 30 participants indicated that they experienced difficulty in understanding or responding to the ASL-SUS questions.

In regard to **RQ2**, sections 5.1 and 5.2 analyze the results from studies #1 and #2 to examine two key psychometric properties: **internal reliability** and **criterion validity**.

5.1 Internal Reliability

To evaluate the internal reliability of ASL-SUS, i.e. whether all items contribute to the overall score, we calculated Cronbach's alpha [7]. Since even-numbered items on SUS are reverse-scored (they have negative polarity), we inverted those items. For responses from the study #1 participants, the alpha for ASL-SUS was 0.69. Generally, alpha scores of 0.7 and above are considered acceptable [18]; so, our ASL-SUS is on the borderline.

To assess the internal reliability of our new ASL-SUS, we compare this alpha value above with two other alpha values:

- In a **prior study** examining the internal reliability of the original English SUS, researchers reported alpha scores of 0.91, based on responses from 2,324 hearing participants [3].
- In our **study #2**, 10 DHH participants responded to the original English SUS, while evaluating an identical university website as in study #1; we calculated an alpha value of 0.79.

Given the alpha value of 0.69 for ASL-SUS in study #1 (and the relatively similar alpha values for English SUS in study #2, also with DHH participants), we conclude there is evidence for the internal reliability of the ASL-SUS. However, the alpha for ASL-SUS was lower than published values for the original English SUS on response data from a large number of hearing participants.

5.2 Criterion Validity

One method of evaluating criterion validity is to determine how convergent an instrument is with other instruments that measure the same abstract concept. Section 4.4 described how our DHH participants, in addition to responding to ASL-SUS, also responded to the Adjective Scale from [2]. To assess whether the scores from each participant on the ASL-SUS were correlated to the scores from that participant on the Adjective Scale, we calculated the Pearson's coefficient $r=0.684$, $p<0.001$. This result indicated a significant correlation between participants' responses to these instruments.

To assess the criterion validity of ASL-SUS, we compare this correlation above with two other correlations:

- **Previously Published Correlation between English SUS and Adjective Scale:** In [2], the authors calculated the correlation between their participants' English SUS scores and their Adjective Scale scores: Pearson's $r=0.822$, $p<0.01$. We performed a Fisher's r-to-z transformation to determine whether this ASL-SUS-to-Adjective-Scale correlation from study #1 was significantly different than the English-SUS-to-Adjective-Scale correlation reported in [2]; no significant difference was observed ($p=0.09$, $z=1.67$).
- **Study #2 Correlation between English SUS and Adjective Scale:** The participants who provided the response data in [2] consisted almost entirely of hearing participants. To compare our study #1 correlation above with data from a more similar group of users, we can examine the data from study #2, in which 10 DHH participants responded to the original English SUS and to the Adjective Scale. We calculated the correlation between SUS and Adjective Scale for these users: Pearson's $r=0.633$, $p<0.5$. To compare our study #1 results and study #2 results, a Fisher's r-to-z transformation was performed to determine whether our study #1 ASL-SUS-to-Adjective-Scale correlation was significantly different than the study #2 English-SUS-to-Adjective-Scale correlation; no significant difference was observed ($p=0.42$, $z=0.21$).

Thus, we conclude that there is strong evidence that the ASL-SUS has comparable criterion validity to the original English SUS, using the adjective scale of [2] as our criterion.

6. CONCLUSIONS AND FUTURE WORK

The specific goal of this project was to create and evaluate an ASL translation of the popular SUS questionnaire, commonly used by HCI researchers and practitioners to quickly evaluate the usability of websites or software. We investigated (sections 2.3.1 and 2.4) and utilized (sections 4.1, 4.2, and 4.3) accepted methodologies for formally translating a pre-existing English instrument into ASL.

We also investigated (sections 2.3.2 and 2.3.3) and utilized (sections 4.4 and 5) accepted methodologies for evaluating whether a translated instrument has preserved the meaning of the original version and whether it possesses various psychometric properties. Our results provide strong evidence of the criterion validity of ASL-SUS (as related to the adjective scale of [2]) and moderate evidence of its internal reliability (based on a Cronbach's alpha calculation). In summary, the results of our summative evaluation of ASL-SUS indicate that this instrument is suitable for use by researchers who wish to evaluate software or websites through studies with DHH participants.

The broader goal of this study has been to facilitate the participation of people who are DHH in HCI research studies or in commercial usability testing by HCI practitioners, including during studies that primarily include hearing participants. By making it easier for HCI researchers to provide DHH users with an understandable version of this common usability questionnaire (SUS), we hope to reduce a barrier for including DHH participants.

6.1 Limitations

While providing ASL versions of standard surveys may address the issue of lower English literacy rates among many deaf individuals that would make English instruments difficult to use, this study has not addressed other potential barriers, including: providing access to low-literacy DHH individuals with weaker ASL skills, helping researchers find and recruit DHH individuals for studies, or supporting communication of task instructions or other information for DHH users that is necessary for participation in the study.

While we evaluated several psychometric properties, there are additional properties that should be evaluated in subsequent studies, e.g. external reliability (i.e. whether someone re-taking ASL-SUS on another occasion obtains a similar score). Furthermore, our analysis was based on data collected from DHH participants who evaluated a single website; it would be valuable to obtain ASL-SUS scores for a wider variety of products to serve as a broader basis for subsequent psychometric evaluations – to determine if ASL-SUS behaves similarly to original SUS in a variety of evaluation circumstances. Additionally, the DHH participants in our study were mostly university students between ages 20 and 27; for future psychometric evaluation, we should record responses from a wider age range of DHH participants.

6.2 Future Work

While an in-person evaluation study with 30 DHH users is reasonable in size, given comparable prior published accessibility studies with DHH users [15, 16], some recommend [12] recruiting a total number of participants equal to five times the number of items on an instrument that is being psychometrically validated, i.e. 50 in the case of SUS. Our lab regularly conducts usability studies with ASL users, and we intend to continue to make use of ASL-SUS, to enlarge our collection of response data – and to replicate our psychometric evaluation of ASL-SUS. As we collect this additional data, we will address several of the limitations outlined above (e.g. evaluating different technology artifacts, and including a wider age range of participants), and we intend to evaluate additional psychometric properties of ASL-SUS in future work. For instance, a prior study [2] concluded that SUS had a single factor structure (based on an examination of the results of a single-factor analysis), yet researchers in [21] discuss how specifically investigating multi-factor solutions led them to conclude that SUS actually consists of two factors: Learnability (based on the responses to items 4 and 10) and Usability (based on the responses to the remaining items). We would like to evaluate the construct validity of ASL-SUS, by determining whether this factor structure had been preserved during the process of translating the items to ASL. However, our study #1 only included 30 participants. In future work, we plan on collecting additional response data and then conducting a common factor analysis with varimax rotation, as in [21], to compare the factor structure of ASL-SUS to the factor structure of the original SUS.

7. ACKNOWLEDGMENTS

This material is based upon work supported by the National Science Foundation under award number 1400802 and 1462280, and it has been supported by a Google Faculty Research Award and by the National Technical Institute for the Deaf (NTID).

8. REFERENCES

[1] American Educational Research Association, Psychological Association, and National Council on Measurement in Education. 1999. *Standards for Educational and Psychological Testing*. AERA, Washington, DC.

[2] Bangor, A., Miller., J., Kortum, P. 2009. Determining what individual SUS scores mean: adding an adjective rating scale. *Journal of Usability Studies* 4(3), 114-123.

[3] Bangor, A., Kortum, P., Miller, J.T. 2008. An empirical evaluation of the system usability scale. *International Journal of Human-Computer Interaction*. 24, 574-594

[4] Blažica, B., Lewis, J.R. 2015. A Slovene translation of the system usability scale: the sus-si. *Int J of Hum-Comput Interact* 31(2), 112-117. DOI: http://dx.doi.org/10.1080/10447318.2014.986634

[5] Brooke, J. (1996). SUS-A quick and dirty usability scale. Usability evaluation in industry, 189(194), 4-7.

[6] Chaparro, B.S. 2008. Usability evaluation of a university portal website. *Usability News*. (October 2008) Retrieved May 1, 2017 from http://usabilitynews.org/usability-evaluation-of-a-university-portal-website/

[7] Cronbach, L.J. 1951. Coefficient alpha and the internal structure of tests. *Psychometrika,* 16, 297–334. DOI: http://dx.doi.org/1010.1007/BF02310555

[8] Da Silva Alves, A., Ferreira, S. B., De Oliveira, V.S., Da Silva, D.S. 2012. Evaluation of potential communication breakdowns in the interaction of the deaf in corporate information systems on the web. *Procedia Comput Sci* 14, 234-244. DOI: http://dx.doi.org/10.1016/j.procs.2012.10.027

[9] Dianat, I., Ghanbari, Z., Asghari Jafarabadi, M. 2014. Psychometric properties of the Persian language version of the system usability scale. *Health Promotion Perspectives* 4(1), 82-89. DOI: http://dx.doi.org/10.5681/hpp.2014.011

[10] Dilsizian, M., Tang, Z., Metaxas, D., Huenerfauth, M., Neidle, C. 2016. The importance of 3D motion trajectories for computer-based sign recognition. In *Proceedings of the 7th Workshop on the Representation and Processing of Sign Languages: Corpus Mining, The 10th International Conference on Language Resources and Evaluation (LREC 2016)*, Portoroz, Slovenia. ELRA, Paris.

[11] Elliot, L., Stinson, M., Mallory, J., Easton, D., Huenerfauth M. 2016. Deaf and hard of hearing individuals' perceptions of communication with hearing colleagues in small groups. In *Proceedings of the 18th International ACM SIGACCESS Conference on Computers and Accessibility (ASSETS '16)*. ACM, Reno, NV, USA, 271-272. DOI: http://dx.doi.org/10.1145/2982142.2982198

[12] Erdinç, O., Lewis, J.R. 2013. Psychometric evaluation of the T-CSUQ: the Turkish version of the computer system usability questionnaire. *Int J of Hum-Comput Interact* 29(5), 319-326. http://dx.doi.org/10.1080/10447318.2012.711702

[13] Geisinger, K.F. 1994. Cross-cultural normative assessment: Translation and adaptation issues influencing the normative interpretation of assessment instruments. *Psychological Assessment* 6(4), 304–312.

[14] Graybill, P., Aggas, J., Dean, R. K., Demers, S., Finigan, E., Pollard, R.Q. 2010. A community-participatory approach to adapting survey items for deaf individuals and American Sign Language. *Field Methods* 22(4), 1-20.

[15] Huenerfauth, M., Kacorri, H. 2014. Release of experimental stimuli and questions for evaluating facial expressions in animations of American Sign Language. In *Proceedings of the 6th Workshop on the Representation and Processing of Sign Languages: Beyond the Manual Channel, The 9th International Conference on Language Resources and Evaluation (LREC 2014),* Reykjavik, Iceland. ELRA, Paris.

[16] Kacorri, H., Huenerfauth, M., Ebling, S., Patel, K., Menzies, K., Willard, M. 2017. Regression analysis of demographic and technology-experience factors influencing acceptance of sign language animation. *ACM Trans. Access. Comput.* 10, 1, Article 3 (April 2017), 33 pages. DOI: http://dx.doi.org/10.1145/3046787

[17] Kawas, S., Karalis, G., Wen, T., Ladner, R.E. 2016. Improving real-time captioning experiences for deaf and hard of hearing students. In *Proc. 18th International ACM SIGACCESS Conf. on Computers and Accessibility.* ACM, New York, NY, USA, 15-23. DOI: http://dx.doi.org/10.1145/2982142.2982164

[18] Landauer, T.K. 1997. Behavioral research methods in human-computer interaction. In M. Helander, T. K. Landauer, and P. Prabhu (eds.) *Handbook of human–computer interaction, 2nd ed.*, 203–227. Elsevier, Amsterdam

[19] Lazar, J., Feng, J.H., and Hochheiser, H. 2017. *Research Methods in Human-Computer Interaction, Second Edition.* Morgan Kaufmann, San Francisco, CA, USA.

[20] Lewis, J.R. 1995. IBM computer usability satisfaction questionnaires: Psychometric evaluation and instructions for use. *Int'l Journal of Human–Computer Interaction,* 7, 57–78.

[21] Lewis, J.R., Sauro, J. 2009. The factor structure of the system usability scale. In *Proc. of Human Computer Interaction International conference (HCII 2009)*, San Diego CA.

[22] Lohmann, K., Schäffer, J. 2013. System usability scale (SUS)-An improved German translation of the questionnaire. (September 2013) Retrieved May 1, 2017 from http://minds.coremedia.com/2013/09/18/sus-scale-an-improved-german-translation-questionnaire/

[23] Mitchell, R., Young, T., Bachleda, B., and Karchmer, M. 2006. How many people use ASL in the United States? Why estimates need updating. *Sign Lang Studies* 6(3):306-335.

[24] Samady, W., Sadler, G.R., Nakaji, M., Malcarne, V.L. 2008. Translation of the multidimensional health locus of control scales for users of American Sign Language. *Public Health Nursing* 25(5), 480-489. DOI: http://dx.doi.org/10.1111/j.1525-1446.2008.00732.x

[25] Sauro, J., Lewis, J.R. 2012. *Quantifying the user experience: Practical statistics for user research.* Elsevier, Amsterdam

[26] Schnepp, J., Shiver, B. 2011. Improving deaf accessibility in remote usability testing. In *Proceedings of the 13th international ACM SIGACCESS conference on Computers and accessibility (ASSETS '11).* ACM, New York, NY, USA, 255-256. DOI: http://dx.doi.org/10.1145/2049536.2049594

[27] Sears, A., Hanson, V. 2011. Representing users in accessibility research. In *Proceedings of the SIGCHI Conference on Human Factors in Computing Systems (CHI '11).* ACM, New York, NY, USA, 2235-2238. DOI: http://dx.doi.org/10.1145/1978942.1979268

[28] Tran, J.J., Johnson, T.W., Kim, J., Rodriguez, R., Yin, S., Riskin, E.A., Ladner, R.E., Wobbrock, J.O. 2010. A web-based user survey for evaluating power saving strategies for deaf users of mobileASL. In *Proceedings of the 12th international ACM SIGACCESS conference on Computers and accessibility.* ACM, New York, NY, USA, 115-122. DOI: http://dx.doi.org/10.1145/1878803.1878825

[29] Traxler, C. 2000. The Stanford achievement test, 9th ed: national norming and performance standards for deaf & hard-of-hearing students. *J Deaf Stud & Deaf Educ* 5(4): 337-348.

9. APPENDIX A: ASL TRANSLATIONS

Videos of the ASL version of the SUS question items appear online at this URL: http://latlab.ist.rit.edu/assets2017sus

A gloss transcription of each ASL video, using English words to informally represent ASL signs, appears below for the reader's convenience. We include below some notes on notational conventions used in this appendix and in section 4.3: There are a wide variety of notational conventions used by ASL linguists and interpreters to informally represent ASL signing in a written form; for this paper, we have used the following conventions:

- Capital letters will be used to represent individual signs. When multiple English words are being used to represent a single ASL sign, then hyphens will be used, e.g., DON'T-MIND is a single sign in ASL (i.e. right index finger sliding off the nose and then pointing forward away from the body).
- Lowercase letters and braces (i.e. "{ }") indicate non-manual aspects of the performance and the span of words during which they occur, e.g. disgust-face-without-head-shake{ DIFFERENT} indicates that the signer performs the sign DIFFERENT while simultaneously producing a negative disgust facial expression (without any side-to-side head shaking, which often co-occurs with this facial expression).
- Additional gestural aspects of the performance that are difficult to convey using the above notations are simply indicated with lowercase words in parentheses, e.g., (shrug).

9.1 ASL Translation of SUS

Prior to the 10 question items, the SUS customarily begins with brief instructions. The ASL translation below differs in content from the English text since the participant must be instructed to watch videos in the ASL version. In addition, the signer explains the Likert-style response scale for the question items, with options: strongly disagree, disagree, neutral, agree, and strongly agree.

Introduction: *English:* "Instructions: For each of the following statements, mark one box that best describes your reactions to the website today." *ASL Transcript:* HELLO, rhetorical{ THIS QUESTION WHAT}, SEE THIS PAPER, HAVE SENTENCE. I WILL SIGN EACH SENTENCE. rhetorical{ YOU DO-DO } WATCH POINT SENTENCE, WATCH, WONDER YOU AGREE OR DISAGREE, wh-question{ WHICH }. yes-no-question{ REMEMBER BEFORE }, YOU PLAY $\text{THIS}_{\text{down}}$ THING, VARIOUS, MAYBE PROGRAM, MAYBE WEBSITE, MAYBE ELECTRIC, DIFFERENT. PLAYING $\text{THIS}_{\text{down}}$ TEST. NOW, YOU DREAM-BUBBLE-IMAGINE QUESTION ASL. rhetorical{ AGREE OR DISAGREE, HOW ANSWER}. SEE POINT BOX 1 2 3 4 5, (nodding). rhetorical{ 1 WHAT } STRONGLY DISAGREE. rhetorical{ 2 WHAT } OKAY DISAGREE. rhetorical{ 3 WHAT } NEUTRAL. rhetorical{ 4 WHAT } OKAY AGREE. rhetorical{ 5 WHAT } STRONGLY AGREE. YOU OBSERVE, PICK ONE, CIRCLE ANSWER.

Note: The ASL signer in the video introduction above pointed to a location in the lower region of the signing space to represent the concept of the product, website, or software that the participant had just used. In the transcriptions below, whenever the signer refers to the "product," he points to this region in the signing space again. This avoids the redundancy of the signer repeating the phrase "software, website, or product" for every question item below. This pointing sign is glossed using $\text{THIS}_{\text{down}}$ in the transcriptions below.

Question 1: *English:* "I think that I would like to use this product frequently." *ASL Transcript:* I LOOK $\text{THIS}_{\text{down}}$, head-nod-with-mouth-morpheme-cheek-puff{ DON'T-MIND USE OFTEN }

Question 2: *English:* "I found the product unnecessarily complex." *ASL Transcript:* I LOOK $\text{THIS}_{\text{down}}$, negative-grimace{ WAVE-WOW COMPLEX }

Question 3: *English:* "I thought the product was easy to use." ASL Transcript: I LOOK $\text{THIS}_{\text{down}}$, head-nod-with-mouth-morpheme-cheek-puff{ EASY USE UNDERSTAND }

Question 4: *English:* "I think that I would need the support of a technical person to be able to use this product. " ASL Transcript: I DREAM-BUBBLE-IMAGINE $\text{THIS}_{\text{down}}$ USE, I NEED TECHNOLOGY HELP_{me} (emphatic-nod)

Question 5: *English:* "I found the various functions in the product were well integrated." *ASL Transcript:* I LOOK $\text{THIS}_{\text{down}}$, MANY ACTIVITY (list buoy using the left hand with four fingers extended to indicate list items, using right index finger to point to each item one-by-one, with rhythmic nodding when pointing to each item) I CAN USE TOGETHER FINE, WAVE-WOW.

Question 6: *English:* "I thought there was too much inconsistency in this product." *ASL Transcript:* I LOOK $\text{THIS}_{\text{down}}$, MANY ACTIVITY (list buoy using the left hand with four fingers extended to indicate list items, using right index finger to point to each item one-by-one, with rhythmic nodding when pointing to each item) disgust-face-without-headshake{ DIFFERENT } disgust-face-with-negative-headshake{ NOT SAME }

Question 7: *English:* "I imagine that most people would learn to use this product very quickly." *ASL Transcript:* I DREAM-BUBBLE-IMAGINE LOOK $\text{THIS}_{\text{down}}$, LEARN USE FAST (shrug)

Question 8: *English:* "I found the product very awkward to use." *ASL Transcript:* I LOOK $\text{THIS}_{\text{down}}$, I USE disgust-face-without-head-shake-with-tense-grimace{ AWKWARD }

Question 9: *English:* "I felt very confident using the product." *ASL Transcript:* I LOOK $\text{THIS}_{\text{down}}$, I USE happy-positive-face{ CONFIDENT }

Question 10: *English:* "I needed to learn a lot of things before I could get going with this product." *ASL Transcript:* I LOOK $\text{THIS}_{\text{down}}$, WAVE-WOW I MUST LEARN MANY MANY, I FINALLY USE

9.2 ASL Translation of Adjective Scale

The adjective scale was designed in [2]. The translation team decided that the terms "user-friendliness" and "product" needed some expansion in ASL to convey the meaning, e.g. to suggest that the person might have seen a website, a computer program, etc.

English: "Overall, I would rate the user-friendliness of this product as: worst imaginable, awful, poor, OK, good, excellent, best imaginable." *ASL Transcript:* yes-no-question{ REMEMBER BEFORE YOU PLAY THIS THING } VARIOUS, MAYBE PROGRAM, MAYBE WEBSITE, MAYBE ELECTRIC. PLAY, TEST, (nodding). NOW, I CURIOUS, WHAT YOUR OPINION $\text{THIS}_{\text{down}}$. rhetorical-question{ HOW EXPLAIN THIS } yes-no-question{ SEE BOX (points to first checkbox on paper sheet) } YOU OBSERVE, I EXPLAIN. FIRST, RIGHT SIDE BOX, NO GOOD disgust-face{ WORST } NEXT, disgust-face{ AWFUL } NEXT, disgust-face{ POOR } NEXT, grimace{ OK } NEXT, shrug{ GOOD } NEXT, positive-face{ EXCELLENT } NEXT, positive-face{ CHAMP-BEST } NOW, OBSERVE $\text{THIS}_{\text{down}}$, YOU PICK ONE, CIRCLE.

10. APPENDIX B: USER STUDY DATA

This appendix contains the raw data collected in study #1 and study #2, described in section 4.4. The Tables 1 and 2 contain the following columns: "Partic. ID #" (a code number used to refer to each participant), "Q1" to "Q10" (the raw scores from participant responses to individual Likert-type items, with 1 indicating Strongly Disagree and 5 indicating Strongly Agree), the ASL-SUS score based on these ten responses, and the "Adj. Scale" indicating the numerical values corresponding to the adjective choice of the participant on this item (scoring details appear in section 4.4.1). Because half of the individual items on SUS have negative polarity, overall scores are calculated according to this formula, from [5]:

$$\mathbf{SUS} = 2.5 \cdot (\,(\mathbf{Q1}\text{-}1) + (5\text{-}\mathbf{Q2}) + (\mathbf{Q3}\text{-}1) + (5\text{-}\mathbf{Q4}) + (\mathbf{Q5}\text{-}1) + (5\text{-}\mathbf{Q6}) + (\mathbf{Q7}\text{-}1) + (5\text{-}\mathbf{Q8}) + (\mathbf{Q9}\text{-}1) + (5\text{-}\mathbf{Q10})\,)$$

Table 1: Raw data from user study #1 with ASL-SUS.

Partic. ID #	Q1	Q2	Q3	Q4	Q5	Q6	Q7	Q8	Q9	Q10	ASL-SUS	Adj. Scale
1	3	2	3	2	5	4	4	1	4	2	70	5
2	3	1	5	4	3	4	5	2	5	3	67.5	6
3	4	4	2	3	4	4	2	4	2	4	37.5	4
4	3	2	3	1	3	3	5	4	3	3	60	5
5	3	4	4	5	4	5	5	3	4	4	47.5	5
6	3	4	2	4	4	4	4	2	3	2	50	5
7	5	4	4	4	4	4	3	3	4	4	52.5	5
8	3	2	3	4	4	2	3	2	5	5	57.5	5
9	4	3	2	3	4	2	3	3	4	3	57.5	5
10	3	2	4	1	3	5	4	2	4	3	62.5	5
11	5	2	4	2	4	3	2	2	4	3	67.5	6
12	3	2	3	4	4	4	4	3	3	5	47.5	7
13	2	4	2	3	4	4	2	3	2	4	35	4
14	1	4	2	2	2	4	1	2	2	4	30	1
15	2	4	2	3	3	4	2	4	1	5	25	2
16	4	2	4	2	2	4	4	2	4	4	60	5
17	3	4	2	3	3	4	2	3	4	3	42.5	5
18	4	3	4	3	2	4	4	3	3	3	52.5	5
19	5	3	4	4	5	4	3	3	5	4	60	5
20	1	4	4	5	5	5	5	5	5	5	40	6
21	1	3	3	3	3	3	2	5	3	3	37.5	4
22	2	4	3	4	2	2	1	3	3	5	32.5	4
23	3	2	4	3	5	5	4	4	4	4	55	5
24	4	3	2	4	4	4	3	5	3	5	37.5	4
25	5	3	3	5	4	2	2	1	3	3	57.5	5
26	4	2	3	2	4	1	5	1	4	4	75	6
27	4	4	3	4	4	3	4	4	3	4	47.5	5
28	5	2	4	2	4	1	3	2	4	2	77.5	6
29	3	2	4	2	4	2	3	3	3	2	65	5
30	5	4	5	4	5	5	5	4	5	4	60	6

Table 2: Raw data from user study #2 with English SUS.

Partic. ID #	Q1	Q2	Q3	Q4	Q5	Q6	Q7	Q8	Q9	Q10	English SUS	Adj. Scale
31	4	5	5	1	5	2	3	2	4	1	75	6
32	3	3	4	2	5	3	4	2	4	2	70	5
33	4	3	4	4	3	4	3	3	3	3	50	4
34	2	1	3	1	4	1	5	3	4	5	67.5	4
35	2	3	3	5	4	3	4	5	2	4	37.5	4
36	4	3	4	2	4	3	3	3	4	2	65	6
37	2	5	3	2	3	4	1	5	4	1	40	4
38	1	5	4	1	1	5	3	4	4	4	35	3
39	3	4	2	5	3	3	2	5	3	3	32.5	5
40	2	4	2	4	3	4	3	3	3	5	32.5	4

Speed-Accuracy Tradeoffs for Detecting Sign Language Content in Video Sharing Sites

Frank M. Shipman, Satyakiran Duggina, Caio D.D. Monteiro, Ricardo Gutierrez-Osuna
Department of Computer Science and Engineering
Texas A&M University
College Station, TX 77843-3112
1-979-862-3216
shipman@cse.tamu.edu

ABSTRACT
Sign language is the primary medium of communication for many people who are deaf or hard of hearing. Members of this community access online sign language (SL) content posted on video sharing sites to stay informed. Unfortunately, locating SL videos can be difficult since the text-based search on video sharing sites is based on metadata rather than on the video content. Low cost or real-time video classification techniques would be invaluable for improving access to this content. Our prior work developed a technique to identify SL content based on video features alone but is computationally expensive. Here we describe and evaluate three optimization strategies that have the potential to reduce the computation time without overly impacting precision and recall. Two optimizations reduce the cost of face-detection, whereas the third focuses on analyzing shorter segments of the video. Our results identify a combination of these techniques that yields a 96% reduction in computation time while losing only 1% in F1 score. To further reduce computation, we additionally explore a keyframe-based approach that achieves comparable recall but lower precision than the above techniques, making it appropriate as an early filter in a staged classifier.

CCS Concepts
• **Information systems** → Multimedia and multimodal retrieval
• **Social and professional topics** → Assistive technologies

Keywords
Sign language detection; signal processing; computer vision.

1. INTRODUCTION
Many applications rely on identifying moments where communication takes place in a recording. For spoken languages, this involves voice detection in an audio signal. For sign languages (SLs), this involves detecting sign language in a video signal. This paper describes and evaluates optimizations for SL detection algorithms aimed at reducing computation without severely impacting accuracy.

Sign language is the medium of communication for many people who are deaf or hard of hearing. With the rising popularity of video sharing sites like YouTube and Vimeo, the volume of SL content available is steadily growing. The SL community often shares these videos through email or posts in social media, passing direct links to the content. However, when an information consumer, rather than an information provider, wants to locate SL content on a particular topic, they must rely on the existence of metadata that identifies both the topic and language used in the video. Unfortunately, studies have shown that metadata is frequently applied inconsistently [5]. Studies of metadata-based access to SL videos on particular topics have found precision rates of 43% [8]. As a result, many in the SL community do not search for SL content. Automatic SL detection would help this situation.

We have been exploring how to identify SL video in video sharing sites. Our earliest work explored the relative value of a set of video features [6] on detecting SL content, but was limited to videos containing a single person facing the camera. In later work [4], we relaxed the constraints to enable detection in videos including multiple visible people and improved the recall but with considerable computational cost. In this later approach, likely signing activity in each frame of a video is modeled using polar coordinates (angle and distance) in a polar motion profile (PMP) which relies on background modeling and subtraction [10] and face detection using Haar features [9]. These combine to create a computationally intensive process. Reduction in computation time is needed to scale the solution to the quantity of videos uploaded to video sharing sites. Once a fast approach to detecting sign language in videos is available, more computationally expensive techniques can be applied to detect which sign language it is.

In this work, we propose techniques to reduce the amount of computation needed to generate PMPs for a video. We evaluated the impact of using alternate face detectors, varying the length of the video segments analyzed, and detecting faces for sampled video frames on the precision and recall of the classifier. These results lead to a recommended combination of these optimizations, which is analyzed in terms of both computation and accuracy. Finally, we explore the potential for computing PMPs from sampled frames without generating a background model – an approach that further reduces computation but comes with a greater reduction in accuracy.

2. RELATED WORK
Sign language involves hand gestures, facial expressions and postures of the body to communicate. A significant amount of research has aimed at transcribing American Sign Language into written words. Such a capability would be useful for those not in the SL community to understand the videos in SL and would also

ASSETS'17, Oct. 29–Nov. 1, 2017, Baltimore, MD, USA.
© 2017 ACM. ISBN 978-1-4503-4926-0/17/10…$15.00.
DOI: http://dx.doi.org/10.1145/3132525.3132559

enable search over the content of SL. However, this is a hard problem and not currently applicable to the inconsistent quality of shared videos. Most current research on SL transcription recognizes signs or parts of signs in constrained contexts such as with limited vocabularies, limited signing speed, and/or limitations on the signer's position and the background.

Instead of transcribing SL, our focus is more modest: detecting SL. Related to this problem, Cherniavsky et al. [1] developed an activity detection technique to reduce the bandwidth of mobile video communication when the user is making gestures. But this approach was not meant to differentiate between sign language and other forms of human gesturing and hand/arm motion.

To address this problem, our early work used off-the-shelf video analysis techniques to develop five features that were expected to discriminate between SL videos and other types of videos [6]. The results showed that a measure of the symmetry of movement relative to face was the best feature for classifying SL videos. Expanding on this result, we developed polar motion profiles (PMPs) to model quantity of motion relative to the faces of potential signers [4], enabling videos with multiple people visible simultaneously. This later approach relies on accurate face detection and uses multiple face detectors based on Haar-like features in parallel. Here we explore techniques to speed up the generation of PMPs without negatively affecting the outcome.

Once a video is believed to include sign language, techniques are needed to identify which sign language it is. Gebre et al. [2, 3] tackled the problem of distinguishing between specific sign languages based on video features with a corpus of professionally produced SL videos. We have shown that PMPs can be used to similarly distinguish between certain pairs of sign languages although the accuracy of results are considerably lower for the type of videos found on video sharing sites than they are for the professionally produced SL videos [7].

3. POLAR MOTION PROFILES

Polar motion profiles (PMPs) are a translation and scale invariant measure of the amount of activity, computed on a polar coordinate system centered on each face. In this technique, PMP needs prior information extracted by both face detection and background subtraction modules. Figure 1 shows the steps involved on the computation of a PMP for a given video.

Face detection information is obtained using an ensemble of the individual face detectors provided by the openCV library (*Default, Alt, Alt2, Alt Tree, Profile.*) In this approach, a majority vote is used to determine the face locations. Based on the location of the detected faces, regions of interest (ROI) are defined in every frame of the video. Each ROI is computed to be large enough to capture the arm and hand movements for the person detected. Activity inside each ROI is identified using foreground-background separation based on the adaptive Gaussian mixture model described in [10].

Given the ROI and the foreground pixels, PMPs are computed to represent the activity in a video. The resulting PMP is a feature vector with 460 elements, 360 representing each angular coordinate and 100 elements for radial coordinates. Equation 1 details the computation for the angular coordinate (θ) features; a similar equation is used to obtain the radial coordinate features.

$$PMP(\theta) = \frac{1}{T}\sum_{t=1}^{T}\frac{1}{R(t)}\sum_{r=1}^{R(t)} PMP_r(\theta, t) \quad (1)$$

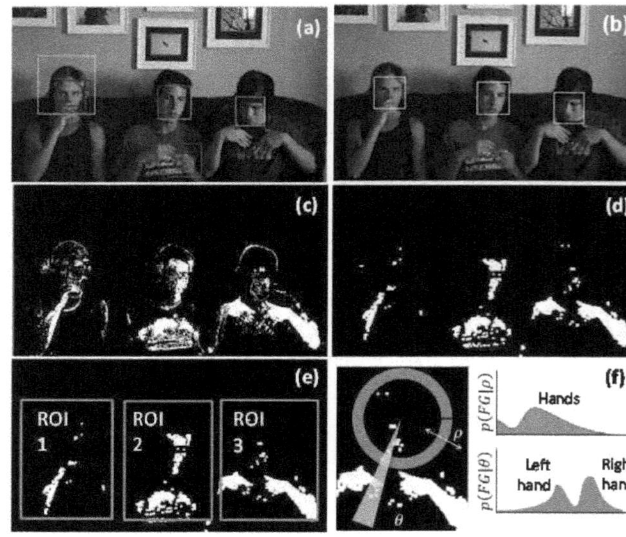

Figure 1. (a) Faces identified by each face detector. (b) Faces from the ensemble of the detectors. (c) Foreground (FG) pixels returned by the background subtraction. (d) Refined FG after morphological de-noising. (e) Regions of interest (ROI) defined for each face detected in the frame. (f) Computation of PMPs for a video frame.

where $R(t)$ is the number of ROIs at frame t, T is the total number of frames in the video, and $PMP_r(\theta, t)$ is the ratio of foreground pixels (FG) to the sum of foreground pixels and background pixels (BG) at polar coordinate θ for region r and frame t.

$$PMP_r(\theta, t) = \frac{FG_r(\theta, t)}{FG_r(\theta, t) + BG_r(\theta, t)} \quad (2)$$

The end result is the probability of finding a foreground pixel in the portion of the ROI represented by the element of the PMP feature vector. Principal Components Analysis (PCA) is applied to map the 460 feature elements into six features, which are then passed to a support vector machine (SVM) classifier.

4. OPTIMIZATIONS

There are a variety of approaches available to reduce the computation time. Each of these techniques may detrimentally affect classification accuracy. We initially explored (1) reducing face detection computation time by using a single face detector instead of the ensemble approach, (2) applying face detection to a reduced number of frames, and (3) reducing the length of the video segments used for classification. The initial goal was to match the performance of background subtraction, which happens at real-time, i.e., a second of a video is processed in a second. If the face detection time can match the background subtraction, then the lag to generate PMPs can be minimized since the two efforts can be executed in parallel.

4.1 Face Detection Computation Time

Face detection is computationally expensive. The ensemble of five face detectors proved to be effective in reducing false positives but at the expense of computational cost. False positives in face detection can introduce PMPs with no signer in the region. When there is no signer, the activity in the region of interest might become trivial due to morphological opening (erosion and dilation) after background subtraction. Hence, the PMP for false positive faces may not significantly affect the performance of the classifier, allowing the use of a single face detector to reduce computation time. To support this hypothesis, we replaced the ensemble of face detectors with each of the individual face detectors, and measured precision, recall, and computation time.

A second approach to reducing computation for face detection examines how performing face detection on every Nth frame affects SL detection. We had reason to believe that sub-sampling would have limited effects since signers' faces and bodies tend to be relatively stationary in many of the SL videos on video sharing sites. The ROIs for the frames between sampled frames were the last computed ROI – that is the ROIs are in static positions for the frames in between frames where face detection is computed.

4.2 Shorter Video Segments

A one minute segment of the original video was used to perform classification in our earlier studies. This means that face detection and background subtraction was performed on each frame in that segment. Reducing the length of the chosen segments reduces computation but the resulting PMPs may be less representative of the overall video. How short is too short? Answering how varying the length of the segment affects SL detection not only informs the design of optimized SL detectors but helps answer to what degree fine-grained diarization (i.e., discriminating segments of a video that include SL from those that do not) can be achieved.

4.3 Recommended Approach

Using the results from the above assessments, we identify a recommended configuration that substantially lowers computation time while not sacrificing precision and recall. We report the computation time and accuracy of this configuration.

5. EVALUATION

The dataset used for assessing the current work is the same as in [4]. It was collected from online video sharing sites and each video was manually labeled as SL or Non-SL video. This corpus contains 111 SL videos and 116 non-SL videos considered related to the SL videos in the corpus by the video sharing site – that is the non-SL videos were returned as results for queries including terms like "sign language" or were recommended as related to known SL videos. The videos in this corpus are not limited to videos with a single potential signer facing the camera as in our earliest evaluations [6, 8] As such, this dataset closely resembles the set of videos that need to be classified in real-world scenarios.

For all experiments, we compare the recall (a measure of false negatives) and precision (a measure of false positives) achieved by our new approaches with the earlier ensemble approach. The F1 score is the harmonic mean of precision and recall. Each value reported is the average of 50 iterations, with each iteration dividing the dataset into training and testing samples randomly.

5.1 Time to Process a Minute of Video

We ran the five individual face detectors in openCV and the ensemble technique on the videos from the dataset to determine their computational time requirements. The length of each video segment was chosen to be one minute and the resolution 240p. The results are shown in Table 1. The focus here is on the relative time requirements as the computation was performed on a quad-core 3.5 GHz Windows PC with 8 GB of memory so may not be indicative of performance on a modern server.

Table 1. Average time for face detectors for 1 minute video.

Ensemble	Default	Alt	Alt 2	Alt Tree	Profile
896 s	94 s	161 s	130 s	107 s	174 s

Using a single face detector instead of the 5-detector ensemble can reduce face-detection time by a factor of 5-10, depending on the particular selection. The time required for the ensemble also indicates that running all five face detectors in parallel takes more time than the sum of time when running them individually.

5.2 Using Single Face Detector

While using a single face detector is much faster, such a choice may negatively affect the accuracy of results. To answer this question, we evaluated classifiers based on each of the five individual face detectors and a classifier that used the 5-detector ensemble. Figure 2 presents the F1 score as a function of the dataset size. As shown, the ensemble is the best face detection technique to be used when training with a limited number of samples and performs well overall. As the number of training samples increase, classifiers with frontal face detectors employing a cascade of stage classifiers and adaptive boosting i.e., alt and alt2, performed best. Overall, the range of F1 scores shows that using a single face detector instead of the ensemble detector does not substantially impede SL detection.

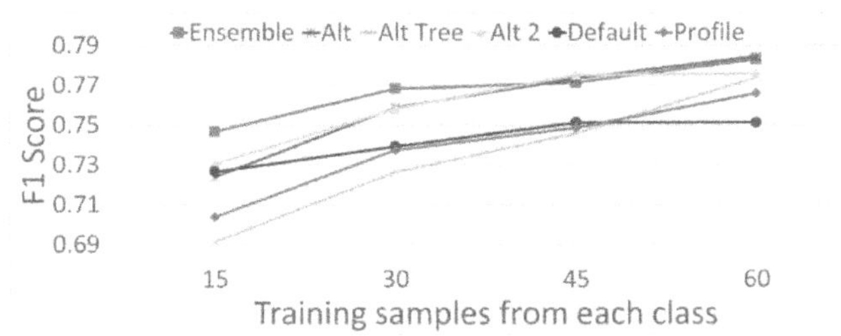

Figure 2. F1 scores for face detectors and training set sizes

Taking both accuracy and computation time into consideration, we chose the alt2 frontal face detector over the alternatives for our recommended configuration.

5.3 Sampling Frames for Face Detection

As already mentioned, the body and head of signers in SL videos tend to be relatively stationary. Hence, instead of detecting faces at each frame, we tested sub-sampling frames at regular intervals and detecting faces at only those frames. The frame rate of the videos in the dataset is 30 frames per second. We tested the effect of sampling intervals ranging from 1 (each frame) to 120 (one frame every 4 seconds) for each of the face detectors. The alt and alt2 face detectors consistently performed better than the other individual face detectors. Figure 3 shows that the ensemble and alt2 face detectors performance was relatively stable up to sampling every 20th frame, at which point the performance gradually decreased and became inconsistent.

This indicates that a sub-sampling rate of 1/20 significantly reduces computation time without losing much accuracy. Additionally, the slow degradation in F1 score as the number of frames sampled is reduced indicates the potential for frame sampling at much longer intervals, as is explored in Section 6.

5.4 Processing Shorter Video Segments

Shortening the length of video segments for feature extraction and classification provides two advantages: first, the computation time for feature extraction can be substantially reduced; second, it enables the identification of shorter segments of SL content in videos (i.e. diarization). We evaluated classifiers with the individual face detectors to find how they performed relative to the ensemble classifier with shorter segments of videos. To select the shorter segment, we took the segment at the center of the first-

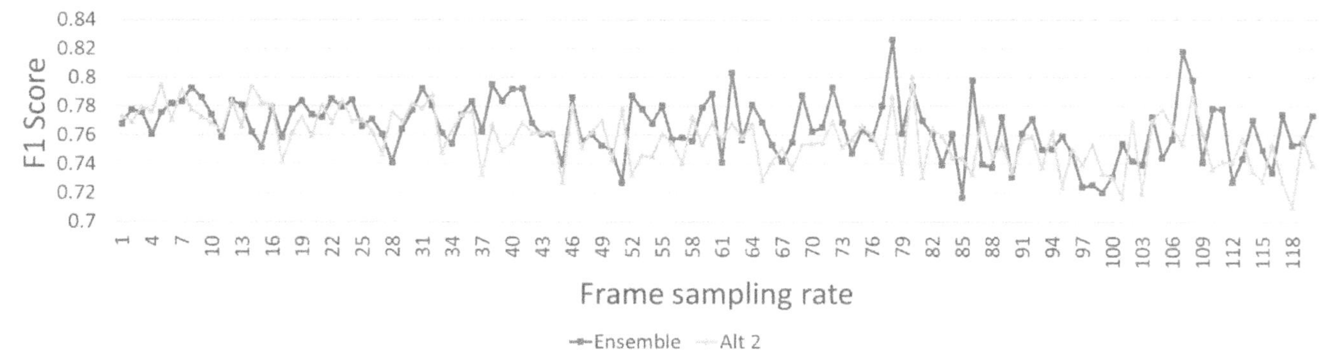

Figure 3. F1 scores for applying face detection to sampled frames. The erratic nature of the results are likely due to the deterministically sampled frames being more or less representative of the video as the starting frame was fixed for each iteration.

minute segment of the full video. For training the classifier, we used 50 samples from each of the SL and non-SL corpus.

Figure 4 shows the F1 scores for the face detectors as the segment lengths vary. The performance degrades as the segment length is decreased. The results reaffirm the selection of alt2 as an appropriate choice for our recommended configuration, but do not identify a shorter segment length for the recommended model discussed next.

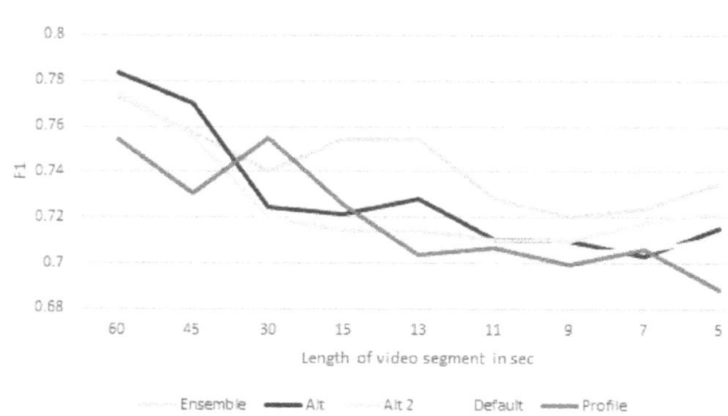

Figure 4. F1 scores for different segment lengths.

5.5 A Recommended SL Detection Approach

Based on the above findings, we chose alt2 frontal face detector as the face detector to compare against the original voting scheme. The other design choices considered are detecting faces at a sub-sample rate of 1/20 with 60 training samples from each of the SL and non-SL corpus. Table 2 presents the results. Results were about 2% lower on precision, had the same recall, and a 1% lower F1 score when compared with the original approach. Yet these optimizations reduced computation time by 96% (from 896 seconds to 31 seconds) for the one minute segments of video.

Table 2. Evaluation of recommended approach

	Karappa et al. Approach	Recommended approach
Average face detection time	896 sec	31 sec
Precision	85 %	83 %
Recall	71 %	71 %
F1 Score	78 %	77 %

Our recommended approach did not explore how segment length would affect computation time and accuracy when combined with sampling. Shortening the segment lengths tended to have a more significant impact on performance but is clearly crucial for diarization, a topic for future work.

6. KEYFRAME-BASED SL DETECTION

Given the huge volume of videos that are uploaded to video sharing sites every day, the optimizations above improve the applicability of SL detection to this context but do not solve the problem. What is needed is a pre-processing stage that identifies videos that warrant such analysis. Towards this end, and based on the results from frame sampling for face detection, we developed a keyframe-based SL detector that uses the same PMP features as before but computes these features for a small set of frames within the video rather than computing them for each frame in the video. Because this approach does not examine every frame, foreground pixels must be identified by alternative means.

As with the above approaches, the keyframe-based approach relies on face detection to identify a region of interest. Within each region of interest, the foreground model is generated via frame subtraction with the prior frame – i.e. the prior frame is used as the background model. More specifically, foreground pixels in a keyframe are the result of applying a median filter to the two greyscaled frames, subtracting the frames, then thresholding the results. Finally, image opening is applied to remove noise among the identified foreground pixels. The resulting foreground image is then used to generate PMPs which are passed to the SVM for classification.

The advantage of a keyframe-only approach when compared to the above techniques is that only a small number of frames have to be considered. The limitation of using such an approach is that, without a dynamic background model and without information about the intermediate position of the potential signers' arms, the foreground identified is likely to include change within the field of view not associated with hand/arm motions. Changes in body position, lighting, etc. could overwhelm the foreground data associated with human gestures, creating too much noise for accurate SL detection.

To characterize the performance of keyframe-based SL detection, performance of the resulting classifier was examined as the number of keyframes selected from the video varied. These results were examined for both 30 second and 60 second video segments. The keyframes included in the analysis were evenly distributed in the video segment. Thus, if 5 frames are chosen from a 60 second video segment, the frames are chosen at the 0, 15, 30, 45 and 60 second points for generating the PMPs.

The results in terms of F1 scores using the same corpus of SL and non-SL videos as before is shown in Figure 5. The F1 scores of the classifier are clearly better with the longer (60 second) source videos. Since the longer video for the same number of frames doubles the time between examined frames, this indicates that changes in background are not the main cause of incorrect classifications for this approach. Overall performance in terms of the F1 score leveled off when at least 10 keyframes were selected for analysis at about 71% for the longer videos.

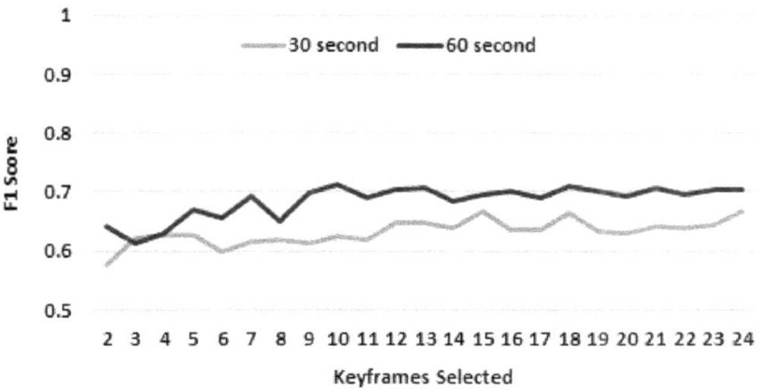

Figure 5. SL vs. Non-SL F1 score for 30 and 60 second videos.

When the results for this approach are compared to the ensemble approach described in [4], the keyframe-based approach achieves similar or slightly better recall but at a considerable loss in precision. This is shown in Table 3.

Table 3. Comparison of keyframe and Karappa approach.

	Karappa et al. Approach	Keyframe Approach
Precision	85 %	69 %
Recall	71 %	74 %
F1 Score	78 %	71 %

While the performance of the keyframe-based SL detector is lower in terms of precision and F1 score, it reduces the number of frames extracted and analyzed from 1800 to 10. This makes the classifier much faster. Indeed, in our studies with this approach, feature generation is reduced to such a point that frame extraction can become a bottleneck depending on how the video is encoded.

In terms of performance within a staged classifier, given the relatively strong recall, there is the potential to include a frame-based classifier as an initial filter. Videos identified as likely including SL content by this filter could then be more carefully analyzed by a second, more powerful SL detector.

7. DISCUSSION AND FUTURE WORK

We report on the possibility of reducing the computational time involved in feature extraction when detecting sign language video. Polar Motion Profiles depend on face detection and background subtraction, and the generation of PMPs has to wait until data from both are computed. Although background subtraction is real time, face detection could take more than 10 minutes to compute for a video of one-minute length, using the ensemble approach. We were able to bring down the computation time for face detection to at or below the time requirement for background subtraction without greatly impacting precision and recall.

We focused on three approaches to reduce the time in the face detection module. First we assessed the impact on system performance when the ensemble of face detectors is replaced with individual face detectors. Then we focused on detecting faces on sampled frames of the videos rather than for each frame. Finally, we focused on shortening the length of video segments analyzed.

The recommended configuration obtained was close to the performance of the original model and reduced the computation time in the face detection module by 96%.

Further exploration of a frame-based classifier removed the need for background modeling. While this resulted in a considerable loss in precision, the frame-based classifier had a relatively high recall with computation costs at the level required for frame extraction. This combination makes it a good candidate as an early filter in a staged classifier. We are investigating whether a such a staged classifier can both improve accuracy and reduce the average computation time for our current single stage classifier.

The above results show that PMP-based classifiers perform well on the types of videos uploaded to video sharing sites, but rely on background subtraction to identify signing activity. The current approach will not work on videos that are edited to include short segments with different backgrounds. For such videos, alternative techniques for identifying hand motion are needed. Another class of video where the current approach may fail are videos that have both SL and non-SL segments. For such videos, the classification of the video as containing sign language is needed. At the same time, the system must also identify the SL segments of the video for signers looking for accessible content (i.e. diarization.)

8. REFERENCES

[1] Cherniavsky, N., Ladner, R., Riskin, E. 2008. Activity detection in conversational sign language video for mobile telecommunication. *IEEE Int. Conf. on Automatic Face and Gesture Recognition*, 1–6.

[2] Gebre, B., Wittenburg, P. and Heskes, T. 2013. Automatic sign language identification. *2013 IEEE Int. Conf. on Image Processing*, 2626–2630.

[3] Gebre, G., Crasborn, O., Wittenburg, P., Drude, S. and Heskes, T. 2014. Unsupervised feature learning for visual sign language identification. *Proc. of Annual Meeting of the Association for Computational Linguistics*, 370–376.

[4] Karappa, V., Monteiro, C., Shipman, F. and Gutierrez-Osuna, R. 2014. Detection of sign-language content in video through polar motion profiles. *IEEE Int. Conf. on Acoustics, Speech and Signal Processing (ICASSP)*, 1290–1294.

[5] Marshall, C. 2009. No Bull , No Spin : A comparison of tags with other forms of user metadata. *Proc. of the ACM/IEEE-CS Joint Conf. on Digital Libraries (JCDL '09)*, 241–250.

[6] Monteiro, C., Gutierrez-Osuna, R. and Shipman, F. 2012. Design and evaluation of classifier for identifying sign language videos in video sharing sites. *Proc. of the ACM Conf. on Computers and Accessibility*. (2012), 191–198.

[7] Monteiro, C., Mathew , C., Gutierrez-Osuna, R. and Shipman, F. 2016. Detecting and Identifying Sign Languages through Visual Features, *Proceedings of IEEE International Symposium on Multimedia 2016*, 2016, pp. 287-290.

[8] Shipman, F., Gutierrez-Osuna, R. and Monteiro, C. 2014. Identifying Sign Language Videos in Video Sharing Sites. *ACM Transactions on Accessible Computing*. 5, 4 (Mar. 2014), 1–14.

[9] Viola, P. and Jones, M. 2001. Rapid object detection using a boosted cascade of simple features. *Computer Vision and Pattern Recognition, CVPR 2001*, I--511.

[10] Zivkovic, Z. 2004. Improved adaptive Gaussian mixture model for background subtraction. *Proc. of the 17th Int. Conf. on Pattern Recognition*, 28–31.

FluxMarker: Enhancing Tactile Graphics with Dynamic Tactile Markers

Ryo Suzuki[1], Abigale Stangl[2], Mark D. Gross[2], Tom Yeh[1]
[1]Department of Computer Science, [2]ATLAS Institute
University of Colorado Boulder
Boulder, CO, USA
{ryo.suzuki, abigale.stangl, mdgross, tom.yeh}@colorado.edu

ABSTRACT

For people with visual impairments, tactile graphics are an important means to learn and explore information. However, raised line tactile graphics created with traditional materials such as embossing are static. While available refreshable displays can dynamically change the content, they are still too expensive for many users, and are limited in size. These factors limit wide-spread adoption and the representation of large graphics or data sets. In this paper, we present FluxMaker, an inexpensive scalable system that renders dynamic information on top of static tactile graphics with movable tactile markers. These dynamic tactile markers can be easily reconfigured and used to annotate static raised line tactile graphics, including maps, graphs, and diagrams. We developed a hardware prototype that actuates magnetic tactile markers driven by low-cost and scalable electromagnetic coil arrays, which can be fabricated with standard printed circuit board manufacturing. We evaluate our prototype with six participants with visual impairments and found positive results across four application areas: location finding or navigating on tactile maps, data analysis, and physicalization, feature identification for tactile graphics, and drawing support. The user study confirms advantages in application domains such as education and data exploration.

CCS Concepts

•**Human-centered computing → Accessibility technologies;**

Keywords

visual impairment; interactive tactile graphics; tangible interfaces; dynamic tactile markers

1. INTRODUCTION

For people who are blind or visually impaired, tactile graphics are essential resources to learn and explore non-textual information such as maps, graphs, and pictorial diagrams. Students with visual impairments often use tactile graphics to understand an abstract concept in physics, the structure of molecules in chemistry, or a human brain model in biology classes. Although such tactile

ASSETS '17, October 29-November 1, 2017, Baltimore, MD, USA

ISBN 978-1-4503-4926-0/17/10... $15.00

DOI: https://doi.org/10.1145/3132525.3132548

Figure 1: FluxMarker User Interaction with Dynamic Markers

representations are useful in presenting spatial and visual information, the form to associate the visual and textual information has been limited; tactile graphics can only present a fixed and limited amount of information to tactile readers [6]. Braille labels and keys are often used to annotate the content [1], but this annotation is not accessible for many blind users, as approximately 90 percent of blind people in the United States cannot read braille [3, 4].

To overcome these limitations, recent work has focused on enhancing traditional tactile graphics with interactive tactile graphics, which leverage multimodal interaction to provide more accessible and adaptable information associated with the visual information. These interactive graphics can detect touch input and annotate content with an audio description [5, 26] or haptic feedback [45], which allows readers to explore the tactile content more efficiently than classical tactile maps or diagrams [6, 20]. However, the tactile representations of these systems are still static and they cannot render dynamic content in tactile form [16]. Through our formative study, we found that the current way to present dynamic tactile representations is largely limited with small-size and expensive refreshable braille displays, which can significantly limit both potential applications and wide-spread adoption.

This paper proposes *dynamic tactile markers*, a new approach to enhancing tactile graphics with reconfigurable multiple tactile elements. Dynamic tactile markers are movable, self-adjusting physical elements that can render the dynamic information on top of a traditional tactile graphic such as swell paper or thermoformed plastic. In contrast to prior approaches, which utilize audio or haptic feedback, our approach aims to enhance *tactile* feedback which can provide the real-time affordances and the physical guides for blind or low visions users to explore the spatial information.

We explore four application scenarios where the dynamic tactile markers assist blind users accomplish the following tasks: (1) find locations on a map, (2) read and analyze dynamic data, (3) locate and identify specific features on tactile graphics, and (4) draw through dynamic assistance. In these scenarios, the dynamic tactile markers can be used as a tangible data point for data visualization, a location or navigating path on a map (Figure 1), or spatial reference points for guided drawings.

This approach is motivated by a formative study in which we asked four blind participants the needs and challenges of the current tactile representations. From the study we learned that high cost and small working space size are the major limitations for accessing the technology, which suggests an opportunity for a new type of interaction with tactile graphics. Based on these findings and the consideration of different actuation techniques, we explore an electromagnetic actuation as a low-cost and scalable design for enhancing existing tactile graphics with dynamic tactile markers.

To demonstrate this concept, we present FluxMarker, a software and hardware prototype that actuates magnetic elements on top of a static tactile graphic. FluxMarker can move multiple small magnets to a grid of possible locations by using an array of electromagnetic coils. The coils are fabricated with standard printed circuit board (PCB) manufacturing techniques, which can enable the low-cost fabrication (40 USD for a 16x16 grid and 15cm x 15cm dimension, and 500 USD for a 160x160 grid and 150cm x 150cm dimension). With modular design, the size of the display easily scales up without significant increase of cost and fabrication complexity, while allowing independent multiple magnets control.

We evaluated our prototype with six people with visual impairments to investigate the plausibility of the application scenarios identified during our formative work. We found that all participants were able to use the FluxMarker to identify specific features on the tactile graphics faster than when they did not have a reference point, albeit they wanted to have the markers move along paths to guide them between landmarks. They were also interested in using the markers to create raised lines around specific tactile elements so that they could feel the boundaries and the contained tactile information. Our participants also noted the possibility for the system to annotate graphics in real-time, which would help understand their data sets, interpret tactile graphics at the same time as teachers present the same information visually during lectures, and with building in situ ways to navigate. Finally, our participants confirmed that the FluxMarker would help people learn to draw, in particular, young students.

In summary, our contributions are as follows:

- An approach to enhancing the tactile graphics with dynamic tactile markers
- A design of low-cost, scalable actuated tangible markers, informed by a formative study with four blind people.
- A hardware prototype of the PCB manufactured electromagnetic coils and its technical evaluation.
- A user evaluation study with four blind participants and two low vision participants, which illustrates the potential benefits of dynamic tactile markers in four application scenarios.

2. RELATED WORK

2.1 Interactive Tactile Graphics

Although the benefits of tactile graphics are well documented, there are several limitations. The first limitation of a tactile graphic is its finite capacity to hold information [6]. It is difficult to add information, such as captions or annotations, without making a tactile graphic overly complicated [40]. Take for example a tactile map with roads, intersections, and several landmarks. It would not be feasible to add a tactile label to every map feature. Researchers have been exploring the use of other modalities to augment a tactile graphic with additional information. Two of the most promising modalities are sound [5, 26] and haptics [45]. Sound has been applied to annotate the content of a tactile graphic to give a text-to-speech description based on QR code [5], object recognition [12], or touch input [26]. Haptic-tactile maps [32, 46] can generate force feedback based on the user interaction. Compared with traditional tactile graphics these interactive tactile graphics can improve the efficiency in exploring content and facilitate learning [6, 20]. However, sound and haptics have their own limitations: they limit users' ability to obtain quick overviews of spatial information with two handed interaction [25] and using the hands as a marking or reference points to compare different parts of the graphic spatially [32]. In contrast, our proposed dynamic markers are designed to improve *tactile* feedback by providing physical guides and affordances directly on a tactile graphic for blind users to explore and comprehend spatial information.

2.2 Dynamic Tactile Graphics

Another limitation of a tactile graphic is its static content and the high cost of production [16]. Although recent work has demonstrated tools to automate the design of tactile graphics [7, 18, 37], once it is created a static tactile graphic cannot be easily modified. A dynamic tactile graphic can enable updating of its content in response to users' inputs. HyperBraille [31] is a commercially available refreshable braille display that has one of the largest touch-sensitive pin-matrix display (7200 pins arranged in 60 rows). Researchers have demonstrated interactive systems that leverage such commercially available refreshable displays to produce a dynamic tactile map with geographic annotation [35, 47]. However, the cost of a dynamic tactile display like HyperBraille is prohibitive, ranging from 2,000 USD for an 18-character display to 50,000 USD for a half page of braille.

Recently, a wide variety of novel actuator technologies has been proposed, including electromagnetic actuators [44], piezo-electric actuators [9, 43], electroactive polymers [8], hydraulic and pneumatic actuation [22, 34], and shape memory alloy [41]. However, piezo-electric actuators are still the only technology found in commercially available devices [34], and the cost of a single piezo-powered braille cell is approximately 100 USD, bringing the cost of even a single line refreshable braille display to over 1,000 USD [33]. To enable dynamic updating of tactile content, we explore an alternative approach where instead of developing an alternative refreshable braille display we augment a tactile graphic. Our hybrid approach allows a blind user to interact with the tactile content dynamically, while allowing size and resolution to scale without a significant increase in cost and fabrication complexity.

2.3 Tangible Interaction

One emerging form of dynamic tactile graphics are those enabled by a tabletop tangible user interface. Tabletop tangible user interfaces were first created to allow users to interact with digital information by moving or actuating physical objects [15, 27, 28], and these systems have been applied to many domains, including urban planning [42], remote collaboration [11], education [14], and data visualization [21]. Recently, researchers have investigated ways to use tangible interfaces for assistive applications [25, 36]. For example, Tangible Graph Builder [25] is specifically designed for visually impaired users to allow them to access graph and chart-based data through tangible interface. Tangible Reels [10] helps visually impaired users to construct a tangible map by their own with sucker pads and retractable reels. These devices allow visually impaired people to dynamically create tactile maps and retrieve specific information related to points and links. Inspired from these work, we explore how *actuated* tangible objects can enhance the exploration and interaction with tactile graphics for visually impaired users.

3. FORMATIVE STUDY

We conducted a formative study with four blind individuals (male: 2, female: 2) to understand their current uses of tactile graphics, challenges they encounter, and opportunities where dynamic tactile markers may be helpful for them. The age of the participants ranged from 22 to 28 (Mean=25.75, SD=2.6). All participants were students (one undergraduate and three graduate students) in various fields (biology and neuroscience, astrophysics, and computer science) at a local university. We chose students as main target users because tactile graphics are heavily used in education, particularly in STEM fields. Throughout a 30-minute semi-structured interview, we focused on three aspects: (1) current use of tactile graphics, (2) challenges and limitations in the current use of tactile graphics, and (3) opportunities for an alternative approach to enhancing tactile representations. Next we present our findings.

3.1 Current Uses

We first asked the participants when and why they use tactile graphics. All participants have used tactile graphics for their coursework or research. For example, P2 said that she uses tactile graphics to access visual material in the textbooks of her biology and neuroscience classes. She uses a tactile representation of the brain model to spatially understand the functionality of each anatomical region. A particularly important use scenario is data exploration and analysis. P4 was involved in a space grant project that sends a balloon with instruments to high attitude to collect data. P4 mentioned that a tactile graphic would be a good medium to represent the data in an accessible way for analysis.

3.2 Challenges

Participants reported several challenges in using a *static* tactile graphic for data analysis and learning resources. First, they found it difficult to understand changes in data. P4 pointed out that this difficulty is due to the lack of dynamicness in tactile representation. In addition, when there is too much information, a graphic can be too complex to interpret [6, 40]. P2 commented that *"P2: When you try to add all the information on a single tactile graphic, this can be too complex."*

Participants also reported several limitations in the current form of a *dynamic* tactile representation. First, the current devices for displaying dynamic tactile graphics are very costly. All participants commented on this cost issue as a hindrance for wider adoption. P2 said that *"P2: I don't have any of these [refreshable braille displays]. I want, but the cost of thousands of dollar is just too expensive for me."* Second, the size is too small [39]. P1 mentioned that the small size of these displays makes it difficult to use for data analysis applications: *"P1: braille display can show the 40 characters or maybe 80. That's about it. [...] I know there is an effort to make 4 lines or 5 lines of the braille display, but I'm not sure how successful they are. These can be very expensive."* P3 mentioned that these [refreshable braille displays] are only designed for reading text, not showing data. *"P3: It's too small and can't express, for example, weather map, or complicated graph of 5000 data point."*

In summary, a static tactile graphic lacks the ability to represent changes and can be overly complex, whereas a dynamic tactile graphic is costly and too small. Neither is ideal for supporting data analysis and interactive information retrieval.

3.3 Opportunities

The key opportunity we identified from the formative study is to consider a hybrid method that combines both static and dynamic tactile graphics. P2, who did not own a refreshable display, mentioned that *"It would be cool if it can dynamically label the part or change the texture, so that it can keep the tactile graphic simple but as accurate as possible."* In other words, only a part or a few parts of a graphic need to be dynamic, while the rest of the content remains static.

Another opportunity worth noting is a common desire to understand changes in data analysis. P1 mentioned that *"I'm actually more talking about the dynamics over time, say, ... how much snow falls over time, earthquake data, or global warming data, anything that are changing over time. I don't know what any of these look like in the real world."*

3.4 Design Requirements

Our formative study inspired us to develop FluxMarker, a technique for controlling a set of dynamic tactile makers to move around a static tactile graphic to support data exploration and analysis. Informed by our findings, we identified the following design requirements for FluxMarker:

1. **Support:** It needs to support a range of traditional static tactile graphics.
2. **Dynamic Update:** It needs to dynamically update its location in response to user inputs.
3. **Multiple Markers:** It needs to be capable of controlling multiple markers independently.
4. **Perceptibility:** Its location as well as changes in location need to be perceivable by users via hands.
5. **Scalability:** Its cost needs scale well as the display area increases, preferably linearly.

4. DYNAMIC TACTILE MARKERS

To address the limitations of the current tactile graphics, we propose *dynamic tactile markers*, a new approach that uses movable self-adjusting physical elements to dynamically render points of information on top of a traditional tactile graphic. The markers are magnets that are manipulated above a bed of electromagnetic coils, whose movements are controlled by software. The magnetic, dynamic tactile markers create real-time and adjustable tactile reference points, which can easily reconfigure the tactile content and enrich the spatial information. While dynamic tactile markers can be applied more generally in any tangible user interface, we specifically explore the design space of augmented tactile graphics for people with visual impairments. This section describes the interaction design and use scenarios that led us to investigate the design of a system to render dynamic markers.

4.1 Interaction and Application Scenarios

The main goal of dynamic tactile markers is to provide real-time tactile affordances on an otherwise static tactile graphic in order to direct a user's attention to specific features of the graphic. This type of interaction is especially important when users explore spatial content. In contrast to the refreshable braille display, the hybrid approach using the combination of a static tactile diagram and dynamic markers makes the display content persistent without losing the user's spatial memory [39]. This enables users to easily recognize the position of the marker by referring the static outline as a constant reference, while allowing update context-dependent contents based on the user's needs, such as a location in a map or data points of a graph. Here we describe four application scenarios where dynamic tactile markers can be useful for people with visual impairments.

4.1.1 Location Finding and Feature Identification

Tactile maps provide blind people a means to explore geographical information. For example, a tactile map of a campus will display a layout of buildings and braille labels associated with each building. However, finding a particular location is often a tedious task; unlike a sighted person's ability to scan a map and quickly identify a specific location, blind users usually explore the map sequentially and must orient themselves to the whole graphic before finding a specific location. Moreover, although the information is often labeled with braille, reading braille takes time and is inaccessible for those who cannot read braille. Audio feedback can help to orient users to the name or feature of the current location, however, this technique makes it difficult to orient oneself to specific locations on the page.

Dynamic tactile markers can help to identify a spatial location quickly. For example, responding to "Where is the nearest coffee shops?" in a local area map or "Where is the Black Sea?" in a geographical world map, the dynamic tactile markers can move around on the tactile map, and the blind user can use their hands to quickly skim the map to identify the location of the marker (Figure 2). They can quickly find the marker position relative to their current location or an outline of surrounding areas on an existing tactile map. In this way, they do not lose contact with spatial reference points or the spatial memory they have developed. In addition, responding to the query, "How can I get to this place?", other markers can instantly draw the tactile path by aligning dots on the map. Once the user is satisfied by finding the location or route, the dynamic tactile markers can be reset, and cleared from the tactile graphic.

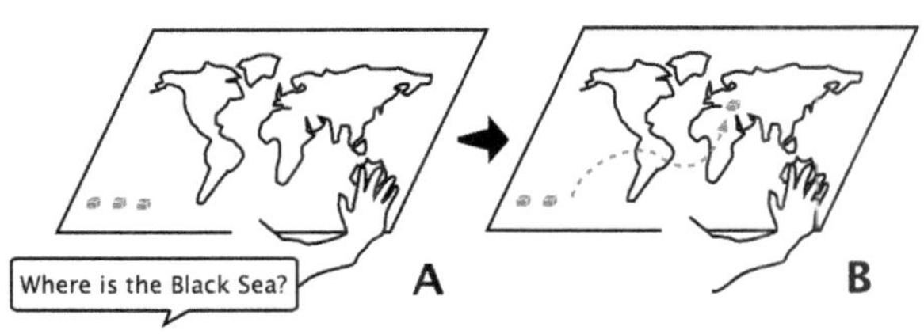

Figure 2: FluxMarker's Location Finding and Feature Identification Application

Similar to location finding, the dynamic tactile marker can be used to locate a specific feature on a tactile map based on a user's question. For example, a student with visual impairments is given a brain model to use in her biology class. She can ask "which region of the brain has a memory function?", the dynamic tactile marker can point out the domain of a hippocampus by positioning the marker within that region of the organ. This is a similar, but different interaction from existing interactive tactile graphics, which explains the feature of each region triggered by the user's pointing, while the dynamic tactile marker can point out the location triggered by the user's question. In another scenario, a student is in a lecture, and the professor is presenting a graphical representation of a cell via PowerPoint, and uses a laser pointer to identify the cell nucleus for the sighted students. The student with visual impairment, who has a tactile version of the graphic, can ask the dynamic tactile marker to move to the corresponding location.

4.1.2 Data Analysis and Physicalization

Data analysis is one of the most challenging tasks for people with visual impairments. As the visualized data is not accessible for blind users, they often find it difficult to interact with the data. Dynamic tactile markers can help blind users make sense of data through data physicalization [17].

One advantage of using dynamic tactile markers is the ability to update the data for a different context. For example, a blind user who wants to analyze the temperature of a city over time might want to know the pattern throughout the year, maximum temperature, and minimum temperature of the city. Twelve dynamic tactile markers can position themselves to display a plot graph to represent the temperature data of each month. By touching the data point and referring to the scale, which can be given by a static embossed paper, the user can find the maximum and minimum temperature of the city. While understanding the pattern of the data can be challenging with audio representation alone, with dynamic tactile markers, she can also comprehend the pattern of the graph by recognizing spatial positions. If she wants to analyze the temperature data a different city, she can just ask "render the data point" with the city name. Then, the dynamic tactile markers can be repositioned to render the requested data point.

4.1.3 Guided Drawing Assistant

In addition to supporting an interpretation of a content or analyzing the data, the dynamic tactile marker can also support students to create their own tactile graphic representations. Many students with visual impairment have limited exposure to drawing or making their own representations of information due in part to the lack of educational practices and materials [13]. The dynamic tactile marker can help blind users to make their own tactile representations by guiding them with reference points of the drawing. For example, when a blind user is trying to draw a hexagon, six dynamic tactile markers would appear, marking the reference points of each corner of the shape. The user can touch the markers to position themselves with the nondominate hand, and guide them to draw the line to the next point (Figure 3). Or, the tactile markers can form a nearly solid edge that the user could mark alongside. This guided drawing can be particularly useful when creating their own tactile graphics when used in conjunction with inexpensive physical tactile drawing boards such as the Sensational Art Board [1], the inTact Sketchboard [2] and 3D printing Doodle Pens [3].

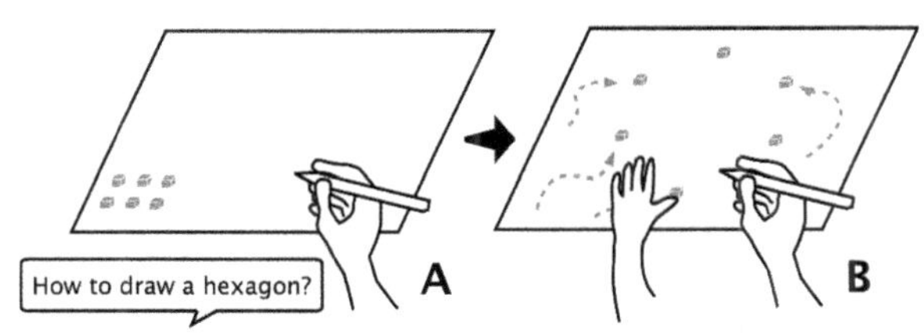

Figure 3: FluxMarker's "Guided Drawing Assistant" Application.

5. DESIGN CONSIDERATIONS

Many different actuation techniques can enable dynamic tactile markers, but an appropriate design should meet the design requirements that we identified through our formative study. In order to ensure that our design meets these requirements, we evaluated a variety of actuation approaches that have been proposed in different areas such as tangible user interface, robotics, and accessibility. These actuation methods include mechanical actuators (e.g., DC motors, servo motors, stepper motors), piezoelectric actuators (e.g., piezo-elastomer, piezo-electric linear motor, ultrasonic motor), electrostatic actuation, magnetic actuation, electromagnetic actuation, pneumatic and hydraulic actuation, and material-based

[1] http://www.sensationalbooks.com/products.htmlblackboard
[2] http://www.easytactilegraphics.com/
[3] http://the3doodler.com/

actuation (e.g. shape memory alloy). Given the technical considerations, we decided to explore electromagnetic coils to actuate a passive magnet as a marker. Three primary considerations rose to the surface while conducting this evaluation: cost, scalability, fabrication complexity, and compliance. This section describes the design rationale behind our decision.

5.1 Cost

One of the most important considerations is the cost of fabrication. Although mechanical actuation such as motors and linear actuators is the straightforward design choice, these parts are expensive. For example, coordinated self-positioning robots like Zooids system [21] can be used as dynamic tactile markers, but parts and assembly costs 50 USD for each robot so it is costly to increase the number of markers. In contrast, components that can be fabricated with existing PCB manufacturing technique are inexpensive [38], for example, electromagnetic [29, 38] or electrostatic actuation [19]. Piezo-electric actuation such as ultrasonic motors and piezo-electric linear actuators can be also integrated with PCB board [4], but the fabrication process requires piezoceramic materials and specialized manufacturing process, which increases the cost of fabrication. Another low-cost actuation method is pneumatic or hydraulic actuation as the parts are relatively inexpensive.

5.2 Size and Scalability

As we found through the formative interviews, display size is another important consideration. Existing approaches that use one actuator for each pixel of a dynamic tactile display, including refreshable braille [2] or raised-pin displays [11, 23, 30], do not scale well. For example, a 10x10 pin size raised-pin display that uses either mechanical or piezo-electric linear actuation requires only 100 actuators. However, a 100x100 display size requires 10,000 individually actuated pins. Even with relatively low-cost actuators, cost increases exponentially with display size (e.g., using a 5 USD servo motor, a 100x100 pixel display will cost at least 50,000 USD).

In contrast, PCB manufactured electromagnetic actuation scales relatively well because many coils can be aligned on a PCB. For example, in our design an 8x8 array of coils can be aligned on a 10cm x 10cm PCB, costing only 0.50 USD. While the cost of printed circuit board increasees with the size of the board, the cost increase is trivial, and the cost of transistors to drive a high current for electromagnetic actuation is also inexpensive compared to mechanical or piezo-electric components.

5.3 Fabrication Complexity

In addition to cost and scalability, we value the simplicity of fabrication and control mechanism which allows the larger accessibility community to quickly adapt, replicate, and test. As mentioned above, pneumatic and hydraulic actuation methods are also promising approaches. Researchers have proposed using a fluidic logic circuit to switch the pressure of pneumatic actuators and control the state of each pixel in a refreshable braille display [34]. The complexity of design and fabrication of hydraulic actuation can be alleviated with advanced 3D printing technology [24], but it is still difficult to design complex fluidic circuits that can control the multiple pixels individually. In short, the fabrication and control mechanisms of such pnuematic actuated devices are a challenge.

In contrast, using electromagnetic coils leverages commercially available PCB manufacturing for fabrication, and a standard circuit design for the control mechanism. Thus, we chose to develop an electromagnetic actuation technique that meets all the considerations we identified previously, while allowing the simple control and fabrication process.

[4]http://pcbmotor.com/

6. SYSTEM DESIGN & IMPLEMENTATION

To instantiate the concept of the dynamic tactile marker, we present FluxMarker, a software and hardware system that actuates magnetic markers with low-cost, scalable electromagnetic coil arrays (Figure 4). The hardware system is comprised of markers, coils, circuits, a controller, and a corresponding GUI. In the following section, we describe the specifications of the elements we used to construct the system.

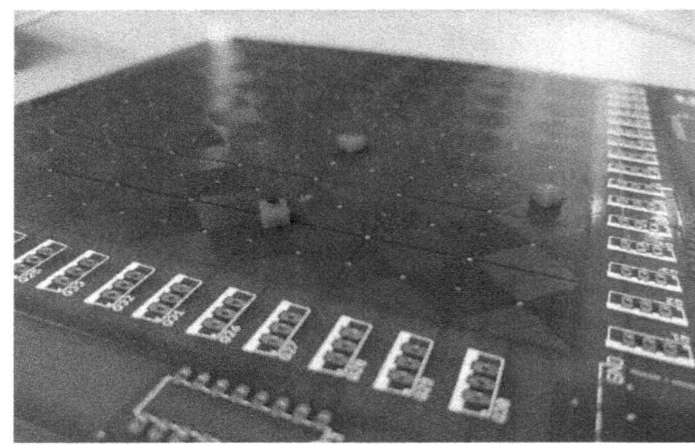

Figure 4: Overview of PCB Coil Board

6.1 Hardware

6.1.1 System Design

Coil Design: FluxMarker consists of magnetic passive markers and arrays of electromagnetic coils. The electromagnetic coil arrays can be fabricated with standard PCB manufacturing technique. We use a two-layer printed circuit board and each layer contains a set of micro-coils with horizontal and vertical offsets. Each coil has an identical rectangular shape and is arranged in the shape of a tile (see Figure 4).

Running current through the circuit coils generates a local magnetic field within the area of the coil such that each coil can only attract a single magnet located within its area. If the PCB had only one layer, there would be no way to move the magnet from the center of one coil to the next because the magnet is located beyond the range of the second coil. Thus, the pattern of coils on the top and bottom layers are offset so that their effective areas overlap. Figure 6 illustrates the movement of the magnet. The microcontroller switches a sequence of coils on and off to move the magnet across the coils. As the top layer and bottom layer are offset both horizontally and vertically, the magnet travels in a zig-zag path from one coil (on the top layer) to the next (on the bottom layer) rather than in a straight line.

The coil arrays are fabricated with standard PCB manufacturing so the size of each array is limited by the capability of the PCB factory. To address this, we designed our electromagnetic coil arrays as a scalable module. Each 16 x 16 magnetic coil array board is a module of a certain size (e.g., 15cm x 15cm). Modular boards can be soldered together side to side as tiles, allowing the overall size of the coil array to be as large as desired (Figure 5).

Circuit Design: Switching current to each coil turns on and off its magnetic field. The standard approach to switching the current is to use a single MOSFET transistor for each coil, but this increases the complexity of the circuit design as it requires several of I/O lines

Figure 5: Modular and Scalable Design

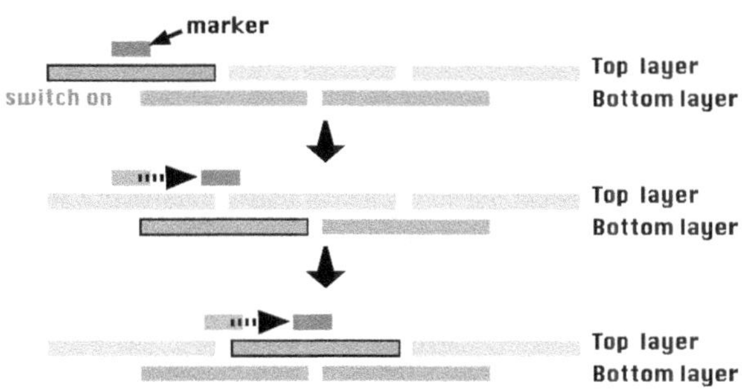

Figure 6: Diagram of the Dynamic Marker's Movement Across the Coil Board

to drive each MOSFET transistor. Instead, we use a multiplexing technique with a diode array to more efficiently control and drive many coils in an array. Consider a 4x4 array of coils where each coil is connected to a diode (Figure 7). Similar to a LED matrix display, only one row of coils can be on at any time. By switching through each row quickly (e.g., 10-100ms), a coil at any position can be activated. For example, setting only row A as HIGH and the other rows (B, C, and D) as LOW, while setting column 1 and 3 as LOW and the other columns (2 and 4) as HIGH will turn on only coils (A, 1) and (A, 3). Next, if we set row B as HIGH and the other rows (A, C, and D) as LOW, and set column 1 and 4 as LOW and the other columns (2 and 3) as HIGH, we can turn on (B, 1) and (B, 4). In this way we can control 16 coils using only 8 (4 + 4) I/O pins on the microcontroller. This design decreases the complexity of the circuit and reduces the required number of microcontroller I/O pins as well as MOSFETs, which cost more than diodes.

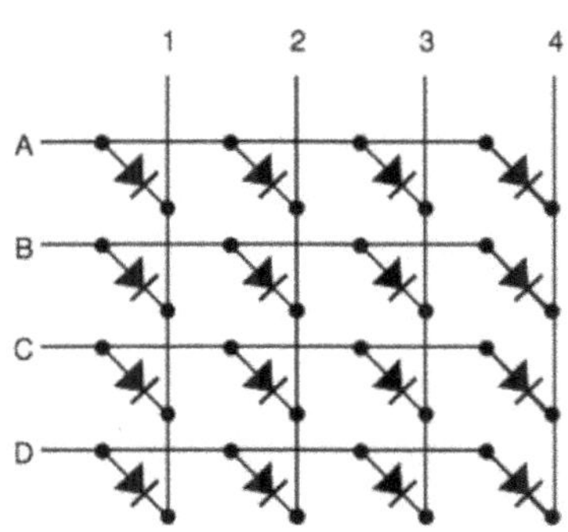

Figure 7: Multiplex Coil Matrix

While LEDs can be switched with relatively low current (e.g., 20mA) directly supplied by the microcontroller, the electromagnetic coil requires higher current (e.g., 0.5-1A). Thus, we use half-bridge MOSFET transistor switches to amplify and control the current to each coil. The half-bridges are made from a push-pull pair of P-channel and N-channel power MOSFET transistors. One terminal from each coil is tied to a P-channel MOSFET transistor, and another terminal is tied to an N-channel MOSFET transistor. The gate of both MOSFET transistors are controlled by an I/O line from the microcontroller, and the source voltage comes from an external 9V power supply.

Controller Design: In this scheme, each half-bridge transistor uses two I/O pins of the microcontroller, so the number of I/O pins on the microcontroller limits the number of available transistor switches (e.g., the Arduino microcontroller has only 14 digital I/O pins). To further reduce the required number of I/O pins, we use daisy-chained shift registers. Each shift register switches multiple MOSFET transistors with serial-in/parallel-out data transmission. By using a chain of shift registers any number of transistors are controlled using only a few microcontroller pins.

By generating a local magnetic field, each coil attracts a magnetic marker located in its range. To move the marker from one point to another, the program analyzes the shortest path, and then switches coils on and off sequentially along this path to move the magnet. As a blind or low vision user interacts with a marker, the system keeps the coil charged so that the marker cannot accidentally be pushed aside.

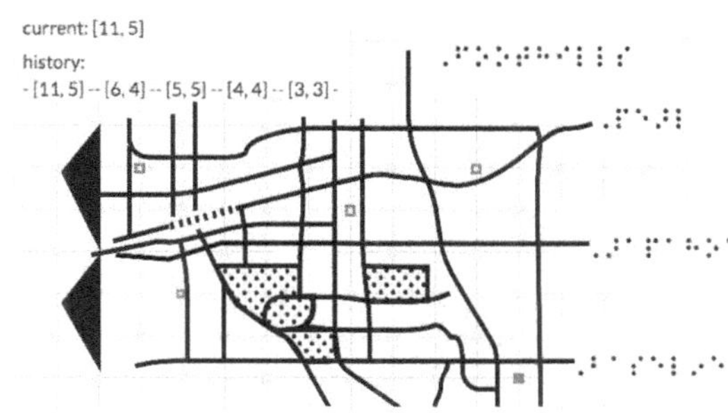

Figure 8: GUI Software

6.1.2 *Implementation*

Markers: We use N50 neodymium disc magnets (2mm diameter and 3mm thickness) to act as tactile markers that are dynamically actuated by electromagnetic forces. We added a laser-cut square cap to stabilize the orientation so that the magnets do not flip over. In our prototype, each magnetic marker costs approximately 0.20 USD.

Coils: Our current prototype comprises 16x16 grid coils and is 15cm x 15cm in size. Each coil has 22 turns and the size is 15.85mm width and height. The width and spacing of each line in the coils is 0.1524mm (0.006 inches), the minimum trace width and separation of our PCB manufacturer, to maximize the number of turns in each coil.

Circuits and Microcontrollers: We use an ESP8266 microcontroller, which switches the current to the coils using 8-bit HC595N shift registers. Each shift register can drive 8 coils which are switched using a half-bridge MOSFET transistor. An N4001 diode attached to each coil prevents reverse current flow in the diode array. We use FQP27P06 and IRF740 for P-channel and N-channel MOSFETs, respectively. A 9V AC-DC line voltage adapter powers the MOSFETs.

Fabrication Cost: Our prototype costs approximately 40 USD, including the cost of 32 MOSFETs, 128 diodes, 4 shift registers, a printed circuit board, and a microcontroller. We estimate the cost of

160x160 grid coils will be 500 USD for the total parts cost (MOSFETs: 128 USD, diodes: 147 USD, shift registers: 20 USD, PCB: 200 USD, and microcontroller: 15 USD). In the production of our prototype hardware system, we manually assemble these parts, but this process can automate with PCB assembly machines.

6.2 Software

We developed software to support the task of specifying the locations of dynamic tactile markers and controlling their movements. This software consists of a web-based graphical user interface (GUI) and a web server that communicates with the display hardware. Using our GUI, the task of creating a hybrid tactile graphic is as follows. First, a sighted tactile graphic designer will specify the static elements of the graphic by drawing lines and polygons or by importing an existing graphical file. Second, the designer will specify a spatial configuration of markers (e.g., the locations of coffee shops on a local tactile map, or the position of hippocampus in the human brain model). Third, the designer will specify the input commands associated with this particular configuration (e.g., voice command of "show me the nearest coffee shops" or "which region of the brain is the hippocampus?"). Finally, if the designer wants to specify a sequence of such spatial configurations, the system supports the creation of a step-by-step guide or a drawing aid (Figure 8).

The main functions of the web server component of our software are to compute the display logic given a particular marker configuration and to communicate this logic to the display hardware. The communication is through a wireless HTTP (HyperText Transfer Protocol) connection. On the hardware side, an ESP8266 microcontroller enables wireless communication with a built-in Wifi chip module. Each coil in the display matrix has a unique ID. The web server can send messages to individual coils to turn them on or off. The display logic specifies the sequence and timing of these messages in order to move markers to desired locations and the software tracks the history of each marker position. Once the task is finished, the system moves the markers to the corner of the display away from the tactile graphic. The microcontroller program is written in C++ and the control GUI is written in JavaScript.

7. USER STUDY

The goal of the user study was to use the prototype to assess the use case scenarios we identified during our formative research and background research, and to probe users about other possible applications of the FluxMarker. In particular we observed how the tool supported participants' ability to find specific locations within a tactile graphic, supported participants ability to relate content knowledge to elements on a tactile graphic; engaged participants in drawing tasks; and affected participants perceptions of how information can be communicated with tactile graphics and their interactions with assistive technologies.

7.1 Participants

Six people with visual impairments participated in the user study (3 male, 3 female); three participants were also part of the earlier formative study. P1 (male) P2 (male) P3 (female) identified as being totally blind. One female participant identified as being legally blind with a little bit of light perception (P4). One male (P5) and one female (P6) participant identified as having a visual impairment, but had functional vision through the use of assistive technologies. Figure 1 summarizes the characteristics of participants in terms of frequency of use of tactile graphics, familiarity with science graphics, familiarity with tactile maps, and braille fluency.

7.2 Method

We conducted a 45-minute session with each participant. During each session we presented an overview of the research, introduced the prototype and described how it worked in conjunction with the graphics, and then showed the participant two embossed tactile graphics from the local university's accessible media lab so that they would have basic familiarity with the graphics. The graphics included (A) an embossed tactile map of Eastern Europe and Russia and (B) an embossed tactile graphic representing a sectional view of a human brain. At the beginning of the session we provided the participants with the context in which these graphics might be used and provided time for them to explore the graphics. We then asked the participants to (C) draw a hexagon on a piece of trace paper, in order to observe their familiarity with drawing without any aids. Figure 9 shows examples of user study sessions.

To observe how the participants used the FluxMarker we laid the embossed tactile graphics on top of the display and asked the participants to read graphics A and B, and perform a series of tasks with the aid of the dynamic markers. When evaluating FluxMarker with Graphic A, we asked participants to first find a region on the map without the aid of the marker, and then find a specific point on the graphic as marked with the FluxMarker. Subsequent to finding the marker, we asked participants to identify other geographic features. This allowed us to observe how each participant used the marker as a reference point throughout their search. We performed the same order of operations with Graphic B, albeit the graphic was more detailed and the representation of the brain had less "regions" and more features represented. We asked participants to identify these features in relation to each other.We also asked participants to follow a moving marker to draw a hexagon on a piece of trace paper. While the participants were performing the task, we answered any questions that arose. We observed their actions, recorded their commentary. After these activities we conducted 10-minute semi-structured interview where we asked about their experience with the FluxMarker in relation to their first and third experience with the graphics. We also asked for feedback about the prototype and their view of its current and future application. To analyze the data we reviewed the video of the sessions and captured questions and comments that arose during the testing, and identified themes that arose from the interview questions.

7.3 Findings & Discussion

7.3.1 Applications

In order to assess the application of FluxMarker we asked participants to use the tactile map, tactile graphic, and drawing paper to preform a task with the tool. Each participant performed those tasks in slightly different ways, and provided unique feedback and new ideas about the effectiveness of the tool.

Spatial Navigation: When viewing the tactile map, P1 rapidly scanned the display area with two hands and found the boundaries of the countries represented on the map without guidance; he said that he loves geography and is good at geometry. He immediately started looking for the Black Sea, at which point we used the FluxMarker to help him locate the sea. He found the marker within seconds and noticed that it was positioned in the middle of the sea. P1 compared his experience with this tool as being similar to working with a teacher of the visually impaired (TVI), who might manually place a simple magnet or sticker on the map to mark a location. He suggests that we use the FluxMarker to guide someone to follow a path in order to discover a landmark, in this case *"the Yangtze River"* if this map also included China. At the end of the user study he said *"The best application I could see this being used for is to*

Participant	P1	P2	P3	P4	P5	P6
Gender	Male	Male	Female	Female	Male	Female
Age	22	28	26	36	23	26
Visual Impairment Status	Blind	Blind	Blind	Blind	Low Vision	Low Vision
Frequency of Tactile Graphic	Medium	Medium	High	Medium	None	None
Familiarity with Science Graphics	None	Medium	Medium	Medium	None	None
Familiarity with Tactile Maps	High	High	Low	High	Low	Low
Braille Fluency	High	High	High	Medium	Low	Low

Table 1: Characteristics and Experience of Participants in Our User Study

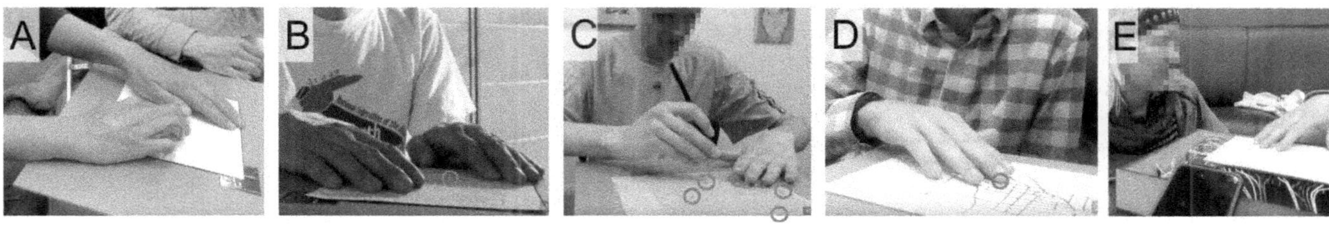

Figure 9: User study. Participants used our system to (A) identify a point of interest, (B) explore a sectional view of a human brain, (C) draw a shape, and (D) navigate a street map, where red circles indicate the positions of one or more FluxMarkers. (E) A participant was shown the inner working of our system.

have the marker move with the user following along, so that the teacher could trace a path out for me in real-time."

P3 also identified real-time mapping as an important application of the tool. She suggested *"If you could have a tactile map, where then you could locate two buildings [using the markers], and then figure out pathways between those markers [which represent the buildings], you could then start populating the map with landmarks using these markers."* P5 and P6, both low vision, explored the tactile graphic visually and did not have any ideas for how this tool would support them with navigation.

Feature Identification and Locating: In addition to using the markers to identify specific landmarks or geolocations, P3 wanted the markers to form into a raised line around specific regions of the tactile graphic to make the boundaries more amplified. When viewing the tactile map with the marker, it was located in the middle of an empty space. She asked, *"I was wondering, is the marker in the middle [of the country]?"* She then suggested that the dynamic markers would be more beneficial if they could outline the boundary of the country or entity one was trying to find.

When using the dynamic markers to explore the map, P2 started brainstorming other possible applications. He provided the scenario of using Google to find restaurants with four stars, and the then using the FluxMarker to automatically populating the location of the restaurants to narrow his decisions about where to go.

When using the markers to find Kazakhstan on the tactile map, P4 indicated that the markers provide a sense of independence. *"It works better than having another person poking at the spot. Even if you know where their finger is, and you start taking time to explore around, they might think you are lost–which you are not–and try to show you around."* She also mentioned that if an instructor was talking about a specific location on a graphic or map, it would be easier to keep up if the marker was in the corresponding position on the display. *"This would be useful if it was synced up with a lecture and graphics, or even if it was synced with an instructors laser pointer; if it was tracking what was up on the board, and I could follow along, that would be amazing."*

P6 elaborated on this concept, indicating that as somebody with low vision, she has a hard time following lectures that have slides. *"I usually ask the presenter to give audio cues when they are changing slides so I can follow along with the slides in front of me, but they usually forget to do that. Or if they have annotated graphics and they forget to describe that...then this tool would be very helpful. If this could be used to help track those animations on a print out of their slides. I think this would be great for low vision."*

Data Analysis and Visualization: P3 mentioned wanting to be able to rapidly zoom into a specific area of a graphic, and see the details in higher resolution. She envisioned that the user could specify a region of a graphic, and FluxMarker could dynamically represent the zoomed in region in higher resolution next to the original view. P2 suggested that FluxMarker could be used to display incoming financial data from wall street to show how the market fluctuates.

P4, an astrophysicist, remarked that while FluxMarker is not yet useful for her work, she enthusiastically recommended connecting FluxMarker to Excel so that she could create diagrams of her data in real-time using multiple markers. *"If they [the markers] were more stable and you had an ordinary piece of tactile graphic paper, you could add the markers on top of that and make a line graph. That would be very useful. That would absolutely be helpful to me in my professional career. On of the things that happens when I am writing a paper is preparing my data in Excel, I can't get any feedback from that graph. If I had something like this plugged into my computer, I could see if it graph matches my numbers. I could actually check my own work before publishing. That is a big deal!"*

Drawing or Tracing Guide: All participants found the task of following the dynamic marker to draw a hexagon to be slow and troublesome as they already had strategies for how to draw the shape. For example, when drawing a hexagon freehand, P4 first drew a square and then used her spatial understanding to add additional sides. She remarked that it was not different from following a real person and it did not provide the tactile feedback that a drawing board would. P2 remarked that the FluxMarker would be difficult to use to draw organic shapes due to the orthogonal layout of the coil grid. He also remarked that it would be more useful if the markers could be closer together. However, P1 pointed out that it could provide a sense of independence for people who want to practice drawing on their own; P3 thought that the FluxMarker would be a good resource for young children learning to draw.

7.3.2 Technical Evaluation

The user study provided us an opportunity to evaluate the technical characteristics of the FluxMarker. Here we discuss users' comments with respect to support, perceptibility, and scalability:

Support: The design of the physical prototype enabled the user to directly place embossed tactile graphics on the PCB display. During the user study, we found that the markers moved well along embossed paper graphics, but Swell paper was too thick for the current level of magnetization to maintain contact with the display. Throughout the user study the participants remarked that the markers felt loose and that they moved too easily when touched; they wanted them to have a stronger magnetic connection to the PCB display. P4 remarked *" If I was taking a test and was in a hurry looking around, and moved the marker, it would slow me down." We noted that in some cases this made participants hesitant to freely explore the graphics."*

Perceptibility: P4 and P5 explicitly said something about the markers. P4 noted that the marker stands out in comparison to the rest of the page. P5 wanted to make sure that they would not cover any important graphic content. P1, P3, and P4 each remarked on the heat of the magnets and underlying PCB display. When looking for the marker P4 said, *"In some ways I think the heat is a good indicator of where the marker is going to be...because the marker is a very specific spot, but the heat is a region."* The heat she was referring to is the result of current flowing through the coil, which turns out to be a useful side-effect for P4. In contrast, P2 found the heat less favorable and noted that if we increase resolution of the markers, the heating problem would need to be addressed.

Scalability: All participants were impressed by the low cost of the prototype and the prospect of a larger display size. P1 mentioned that if the resolution were lower (the markers more spread out), a mechanism would be needed to help users find their starting reference point. Without this it would be laborious to find the marker. P3 was satisfied with the current size of the display since she could explore the whole display in a short amount of time.

8. LIMITATIONS & FUTURE WORK

Our system, while promising, has several limitations that require future research. First, our user study is largely based on qualitative findings, rather than quantitative measures from controlled experiments. Although the focus of our study was to explore the application space with a proof-of-concept prototype, we acknowledge the importance of more in-depth and rigorous user study about the various aspects of the system. For example, our system has a GUI component to enable designers to specify dynamic marker configurations, but we have not tested this formally. For the future work, we will recruit other stakeholders including family members, teachers of visual impairments, and professional tactile transcribers to gain insight into content creation involving dynamic markers.

Second, our system currently does not detect the positions of the markers. Instead, it assumes the initial positions of the markers are known and tracks their movements based on users' commands. We are interested in developing a closed-loop system which can detect markers' locations by using camera-based tracking or reed switch arrays, and then feed location information back to the system in real-time. Such system can improve the accuracy and robustness of marker movement.

Finally, the current system uses dynamic markers as *output* of information, but the markers can be also used by users to provide *input*. For example, one participant was excited about the potential use scenarios where he can use tactile markers to find nearby restaurants, and then he can ask context-aware questions such as open hours, ratings, or a menu of the restaurant by touching the marker, just like Google Maps. In these scenarios, tactile markers should be enhanced to respond to real-time information requests. For the future work, we are interested in integrating touch sensing or gesture tracking mechanisms into the system to open up a new interaction model for visually impaired users and explore the possible design space of dynamic tactile markers.

9. ACKNOWLEDGMENTS

We would like to thank the participants for their time and helpful feedback. We also would like to thank Shohei Aoki and Ron Pelrine for their technical advice and feedback. This research was supported by the NSF CAREER award IIS 1453771 and the Nakajima Foundation.

10. REFERENCES

[1] Braille authority of north america, http://www.brailleauthority.org/tg/.

[2] Hyperbraille, http://www.hyperbraille.de.

[3] The braille literacy crisis in america, 2009.

[4] Blindness statistics, 2015.

[5] C. M. Baker, L. R. Milne, J. Scofield, C. L. Bennett, and R. E. Ladner. Tactile graphics with a voice: using qr codes to access text in tactile graphics. In *Proceedings of ASSETS*, pages 75–82. ACM, 2014.

[6] A. M. Brock, P. Truillet, B. Oriola, D. Picard, and C. Jouffrais. Interactivity improves usability of geographic maps for visually impaired people. *Human–Computer Interaction*, 30(2):156–194, 2015.

[7] C. Brown and A. Hurst. Viztouch: automatically generated tactile visualizations of coordinate spaces. In *Proceedings of TEI*, pages 131–138. ACM, 2012.

[8] P. Chakraborti, H. K. Toprakci, P. Yang, N. Di Spigna, P. Franzon, and T. Ghosh. A compact dielectric elastomer tubular actuator for refreshable braille displays. *Sensors and Actuators A: Physical*, 179:151–157, 2012.

[9] H.-C. Cho, B.-S. Kim, J.-J. Park, and J.-B. Song. Development of a braille display using piezoelectric linear motors. In *SICE-ICASE, 2006. International Joint Conference*, pages 1917–1921. IEEE, 2006.

[10] J. Ducasse, M. J. Macé, M. Serrano, and C. Jouffrais. Tangible reels: construction and exploration of tangible maps by visually impaired users. In *Proceedings of CHI*, pages 2186–2197. ACM, 2016.

[11] S. Follmer, D. Leithinger, A. Olwal, A. Hogge, and H. Ishii. inform: dynamic physical affordances and constraints through shape and object actuation. In *Proceedings of UIST*, volume 13, pages 417–426, 2013.

[12] G. Fusco and V. S. Morash. The tactile graphics helper: providing audio clarification for tactile graphics using machine vision. In *Proceedings of ASSETS*, pages 97–106. ACM, 2015.

[13] S. Hayhoe. Reducing passive cultural exclusion of people with disabilities, an epistemological approach. 2014.

[14] M. S. Horn, E. T. Solovey, R. J. Crouser, and R. J. Jacob. Comparing the use of tangible and graphical programming languages for informal science education. In *Proceedings of CHI*, pages 975–984. ACM, 2009.

[15] H. Ishii and B. Ullmer. Tangible bits: towards seamless interfaces between people, bits and atoms. In *Proceedings of CHI*, pages 234–241. ACM, 1997.

[16] R. D. Jacobson. Navigating maps with little or no sight: An audio-tactile approach. *Proceedings of Content Visualization and Intermedia Representations*, pages 95–102, 1998.

[17] Y. Jansen, P. Dragicevic, P. Isenberg, J. Alexander, A. Karnik, J. Kildal, S. Subramanian, and K. Hornbæk. Opportunities and challenges for data physicalization. In *Proceedings of CHI*, pages 3227–3236. ACM, 2015.

[18] C. Jayant, M. Renzelmann, D. Wen, S. Krisnandi, R. Ladner, and D. Comden. Automated tactile graphics translation: in the field. In *Proceedings of CHI*, pages 75–82. ACM, 2007.

[19] M. E. Karagozler, S. C. Goldstein, and J. R. Reid. Stress-driven mems assembly+ electrostatic forces= 1mm diameter robot. In *Proceedings of IROS*, pages 2763–2769. IEEE, 2009.

[20] S. Landau and L. Wells. Merging tactile sensory input and audio data by means of the talking tactile tablet. In *Proceedings Eurohaptics*, volume 3, 2003.

[21] M. Le Goc, L. H. Kim, A. Parsaei, J.-D. Fekete, P. Dragicevic, and S. Follmer. Zooids: Building blocks for swarm user interfaces. In *Proceedings of UIST*, pages 97–109. ACM, 2016.

[22] J. S. Lee and S. Lucyszyn. A micromachined refreshable braille cell. *journal of microelectromechanical systems*, 14(4):673–682, 2005.

[23] D. Leithinger and H. Ishii. Relief: a scalable actuated shape display. In *Proceedings of TEI*, pages 221–222. ACM, 2010.

[24] R. MacCurdy, R. Katzschmann, Y. Kim, and D. Rus. Printable hydraulics: a method for fabricating robots by 3d co-printing solids and liquids. In *Proceedings of ICRA*, pages 3878–3885. IEEE, 2016.

[25] D. McGookin, E. Robertson, and S. Brewster. Clutching at straws: using tangible interaction to provide non-visual access to graphs. In *Proceedings of CHI*, pages 1715–1724. ACM, 2010.

[26] J. A. Miele, S. Landau, and D. Gilden. Talking tmap: Automated generation of audio-tactile maps using smith-kettlewell's tmap software. *British Journal of Visual Impairment*, 24(2):93–100, 2006.

[27] G. Pangaro, D. Maynes-Aminzade, and H. Ishii. The actuated workbench: computer-controlled actuation in tabletop tangible interfaces. In *Proceedings of UIST*, pages 181–190. ACM, 2002.

[28] J. Patten and H. Ishii. Mechanical constraints as computational constraints in tabletop tangible interfaces. In *Proceedings of CHI*, pages 809–818. ACM, 2007.

[29] R. Pelrine, A. Wong-Foy, B. McCoy, D. Holeman, R. Mahoney, G. Myers, J. Herson, and T. Low. Diamagnetically levitated robots: An approach to massively parallel robotic systems with unusual motion properties. In *Proceedings of ICRA*, pages 739–744. IEEE, 2012.

[30] I. Poupyrev, T. Nashida, S. Maruyama, J. Rekimoto, and Y. Yamaji. Lumen: interactive visual and shape display for calm computing. In *ACM SIGGRAPH 2004 Emerging technologies*, page 17. ACM, 2004.

[31] D. Prescher, G. Weber, and M. Spindler. A tactile windowing system for blind users. In *Proceedings of ASSETS*, pages 91–98. ACM, 2010.

[32] M. Rice, R. D. Jacobson, R. G. Golledge, and D. Jones. Design considerations for haptic and auditory map interfaces. *Cartography and Geographic Information Science*, 32(4):381–391, 2005.

[33] N. Runyan and D. Blazie. Eap actuators aid the quest for the'holy braille'of tactile displays. In *SPIE Smart Structures and Materials+ Nondestructive Evaluation and Health Monitoring*, pages 764207–764207. International Society for Optics and Photonics, 2010.

[34] A. Russomanno, R. B. Gillespie, S. O'Modhrain, and M. Burns. The design of pressure-controlled valves for a refreshable tactile display. In *World Haptics Conference (WHC), 2015 IEEE*, pages 177–182. IEEE, 2015.

[35] B. Schmitz and T. Ertl. Interactively displaying maps on a tactile graphics display. In *Proceedings 2012 Workshop on Spatial Knowledge Acquisition with Limited Information Displays*, pages 13–18, 2012.

[36] J. Schneider and T. Strothotte. Constructive exploration of spatial information by blind users. In *Proceedings of ASSETS*, pages 188–192. ACM, 2000.

[37] R. Štampach and E. Mulíčková. Automated generation of tactile maps. *Journal of Maps*, 12(sup1):532–540, 2016.

[38] E. Strasnick, J. Yang, K. Tanner, A. Olwal, and S. Follmer. shiftio: Reconfigurable tactile elements for dynamic affordances and mobile interaction. In *Proceedings of CHI*. ACM, 2017.

[39] S. Swaminathan, T. Roumen, R. Kovacs, D. Stangl, S. Mueller, and P. Baudisch. Linespace: A sensemaking platform for the blind. In *Proceedings of CHI*, pages 2175–2185. ACM, 2016.

[40] A. Tatham. The design of tactile maps: theoretical and practical considerations. *Proceedings of international cartographic association: mapping the nations*, pages 157–166, 1991.

[41] P. Taylor, A. Moser, and A. Creed. A sixty-four element tactile display using shape memory alloy wires. *Displays*, 18(3):163–168, 1998.

[42] J. Underkoffler and H. Ishii. Urp: a luminous-tangible workbench for urban planning and design. In *Proceedings of CHI*, pages 386–393. ACM, 1999.

[43] T. Völkel, G. Weber, and U. Baumann. Tactile graphics revised: the novel brailledis 9000 pin-matrix device with multitouch input. *Computers Helping People with Special Needs*, pages 835–842, 2008.

[44] F.-H. Yeh and S.-H. Liang. Mechanism design of the flapper actuator in chinese braille display. *Sensors and Actuators A: Physical*, 135(2):680–689, 2007.

[45] W. Yu, R. Ramloll, and S. Brewster. Haptic graphs for blind computer users. In *Haptic human-computer interaction*, pages 41–51. Springer, 2001.

[46] L. Zeng and G. Weber. Audio-haptic browser for a geographical information system. *Computers Helping People with Special Needs*, pages 466–473, 2010.

[47] L. Zeng and G. Weber. Atmap: annotated tactile maps for the visually impaired. In *Cognitive Behavioural Systems*, pages 290–298. Springer, 2012.

Designing Interactions for 3D Printed Models with Blind People

Lei Shi
ls776@cornell.edu

Yuhang Zhao
yz769@cornell.edu

Shiri Azenkot
shiri.azenkot@cornell.edu

Jacobs Technion-Cornell Institute, Cornell Tech, Cornell University
New York, NY, USA

ABSTRACT
Three-dimensional printed models have the potential to serve as powerful accessibility tools for blind people. Recently, researchers have developed methods to further enhance 3D prints by making them interactive: when a user touches a certain area in the model, the model speaks a description of the area. However, these interactive models were limited in terms of their functionalities and interaction techniques. We conducted a two-section study with 12 legally blind participants to fill in the gap between existing interactive model technologies and end users' needs, and explore design opportunities. In the first section of the study, we observed participants' behavior as they explored and identified models and their components. In the second section, we elicited user-defined input techniques that would trigger various functions from an interactive model. We identified five exploration activities (e.g., comparing tactile elements), four hand postures (e.g., using one hand to hold a model in the air), and eight gestures (e.g., using index finger to strike on a model) from the participants' exploration processes and aggregate their elicited input techniques. We derived key insights from our findings including: (1) design implications for I3M technologies, and (2) specific designs for interactions and functionalities for I3Ms.

CCS Concepts
• **Human-centered computing~Participatory design**

Keywords
Interactive 3D printed models; visually impairments; exploration behaviors; elicitation

1. INTRODUCTION
Recent developments in 3D printing technologies have made 3D models much more available to blind people. With relatively affordable, consumer grade 3D printers, teachers and blind students can print tactile models at schools and their homes [6]. In addition, "makers" around the world [10], DIY hobbyists who use 3D printing and other rapid prototyping technologies, have shared millions of 3D printable models online. Such models include architectural structures, cartoon figures, human organs, and many others. These models can help blind people learn complex concepts (e.g., the structure of a molecule) that cannot be conveyed from text alone.

ASSETS '17, October 29-November 1, 2017, Baltimore, MD, USA

ACM 978-1-4503-4926-0/17/10…$15.00
https://doi.org/10.1145/3132525.3132549

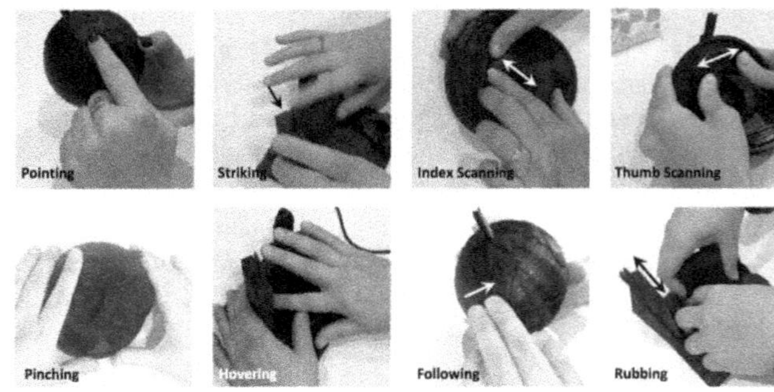

Figure 1. The eight gestures identified in the Elicitation section of the study. The movements of dynamic gestures are marked with arrows.

Seeing the potential of 3D models, researchers have developed methods of enhancing them by augmenting them with audio descriptions. They created interactive 3D printed models (I3Ms) with sensors like cameras [25, 31], capacitive sensors [9, 17, 38], and microphones [30, 32]. These interactive models can sense a blind user's gestures and speak corresponding audio information to the user. However, prior work focused on the technical aspects of sensing input on the models and producing output; no work has investigated the methods and behaviors of blind people as they explore tactile 3D models and determined their needs for interactivity. To date, most I3Ms supported straightforward interactions designed by researchers (e.g., pointing to a continent on a globe model to get its label). These designs didn't fully explore the design space and power of I3Ms.

In this paper, we aim to understand blind people's needs and preferences for the design of interactivity in 3D printed models. Specifically, we investigate two research questions:

RQ1: How do blind people explore tactile models (that are not interactive)?
RQ2: What interaction techniques are effective in I3Ms?

Answering both questions is critical to our aim. I3Ms are a new medium that present undiscovered design opportunities. Unlike designing interactions for traditional web browsers [23] or desktop systems [42] that have established functionalities, interaction design for 3D printed models is not established and we do not yet know what functions are needed or useful. The goal of interactive systems is to support and adapt to users' behaviors [8], rather than the opposite. Thus, RQ1 contributes to the fundamentals of I3Ms, while RQ2 takes a direct action to seek interaction techniques for I3Ms.

To answer the questions, we conducted a two-section study with 12 legally blind participants. In the first section of the study, we observed participants as they performed several tasks to explore and identify 3D printed models and their components (RQ1). In the second section of the study, we elicited interactions from participants [42], asking them to define input techniques for five interactive functions for an I3M (RQ2). We used three models throughout the study: a globe, a cell, and a map.

Our findings reveal that 3D model exploration involves five major types of exploration activities (e.g., counting similar tactile elements), four hand postures (e.g., using one hand to hold a model on the table), and eight gestures (as seen in Figure 1) In the second section of the study, participants suggested touch gestures on the model, speech commands, and buttons to trigger interactive events. We conclude with a design for I3Ms along with implications for future I3M technologies.

In summary, our contributions include:

(1) An in-depth analysis of blind people's exploration behaviors of 3D printed models.
(2) A set of user-defined input techniques for various I3M functionalities.
(3) Design implications for I3Ms and a specification for an I3M system.

2. BACKGROUND AND RELATED WORK

2.1 3D Printing

3D printing technology is becoming more and more available. 3D printers have evolved from pieces of industrial equipment to personal tools, and are widely used in fabrication activities like prototyping and repairing [20]. People can already print tools and models with printers found in community maker spaces, schools, and libraries. Some printers cost as little as $100 [41].

Researchers have created printable content to help people with disabilities solve their own accessibility problems. People have designed specialized devices for prosthetics users [13] and people with motor and mobility impairments [5]. For blind people, personal printers can create tactile learning materials that benefit blind people in education. Prior work designed 3D printed graphics to help blind people learn programming [14], design [21], mathematics [3, 6], and basic literacy skills [15, 34].

As 3D printing technology continues to evolve, blind people will be able to print models at home, at school, or at their local library. Our work aims to make these printed models more powerful, by understanding how researchers and designers can add interactive elements to best address blind people's needs and preferences.

2.2 Interactive 3D Printed Models

Accessibility researchers have explored different methods to create I3Ms. Equipped with sensors, these I3Ms can sense a blind user's gestures and provide audio feedback to the user.

Shi *et al.* [32] used acoustic sensing to add audio labels to 3D printed models. To add a label, a designer added a printable percussive component called a "Ticker" to the model that could be strummed with a flick of the finger. Each ticker generated a unique sound that was then detected by a mobile application. The application would then speak the label associated with the strummed Ticker. In a user study with nine blind participants, the application classified Ticker sounds with a mean accuracy of 93 percent, and participants enjoyed using the application.

Another approach to adding interactivity to a 3D printed model is to embed conductive filament into the model. When a model is placed on a touchscreen, users can touch the conductive parts of the model to trigger inputs on the touchscreen. In this way, audio information can be associated with touches on the model that are sense by the capacitive sensor. Kolitsky [17] and Taylor *et al.* [38] used this technique to add audio labels to printed tactile graphics and maps. Similarly, LucentMaps [9] combined this technique with speech input to make printed maps more accessible to visually impaired people. LucentMaps provided both audio and visual feedback to explain and highlight elements in printed transparent maps.

Computer vision has been applied to I3Ms as well. Reichinger *et al.* [25] used a depth sensor to allow blind people to explore tactile reliefs with audio guidance. They designed three gestures to retrieve audio labels, get detailed audio descriptions, and turn on or turn off audio feedback on tactile reliefs. CamIO [29] and our previous work [31] also used similar approaches to add audio labels for 3D models.

This growing number of accessibility research indicates the importance of I3Ms to blind people. However, prior work mostly focused on the technical challenges of creating I3Ms, and these systems only had straightforward interactions designed by researchers. Our study contributes to I3M design by understanding users' behaviors and needs, and eliciting interactions f them.

2.3 Tactile Perception

Tactile perception consists of cutaneous perception and haptic perception. According to Hatwell *et al.* [1] [12], cutaneous perception perceives information using the skin in a stationary process. Haptic perception, on the other hand, involves moving one's muscles and the whole shoulder-arm-hand system. People use tactile perception to sense temperature, shape, texture, pressure, vibration, and pain.

Prior work has studied the exploration process and object properties that people use to identify an object. Lederman *et al.* [19] defined Exploratory Procedures (EPs) as stereotyped movement patterns that do not correspond to any configuration of the hand or gesture. They found participants performed different EPs to examine a specific property of a 3D object (e.g., performing static contact EP to examine temperature, while performing pressure EP to examine hardness). Klatzky *et al.* [16] further confirmed three properties contributed to tactile object identification: the material, the size, and the shape of an object. Both studies were conducted with sighted participants.

Compared with sighted people, blind people used different strategies in tactile perception tasks. Previous studies suggested that blind participants preferred to use two hands and multiple fingers, while sighted participants usually chose to use one hand with only one or two fingers in tactile perception tasks [7, 26, 35]. Also, researchers found that blind participants completed tactile perception tasks with higher accuracy and at a faster speed than sighted participants [7, 22, 26].

Unlike traditional tactile objects, 3D printed models are unique learning tools. Perceiving information from printed 3D models is a more complex task than the tactile perception tasks performed in the work mentioned above. Although prior work yielded us insights about tactile perception, no prior research has examined blind people's experiences when interacting with 3D printed models. We aim to fill this gap by understanding blind people's exploration behaviors on 3D printed models. Our study highlights the major activities, hand postures, and gestures blind people used, which sheds light on the design opportunities for I3Ms.

[1] There are different definitions for haptic and cutaneous perception. We used the one introduced by Hatwell *et al.* [12].

3. STUDY DESIGN

3.1 Study Objectives

We aim to draw design implications from (1) blind people's exploration behaviors of 3D printed models and (2) user-defined input techniques. Thus, we conducted a two-section study to answer the two research questions posed in the introduction.

3.2 Participants

We recruited 12 legally blind participants (4 males, 8 females) whose ages ranged from 23 to 60 years (mean = 40.75, SD = 13.15). Eleven participants identified as blind, while the remaining one identified as low vision. Eight participants had a college or graduate degree, and four participants had only graduated from high school. Eleven participants were familiar with Braille, but four of them didn't read it regularly. Eleven participants had iPhones, while the remaining one did not use a smartphone. We compensated each participant 15 USD per hour and reimbursed transportation expenses up to 60 USD.

3.3 Procedure

The study consisted of one session that was about 60 minutes long. The session included two sections, which we refer to as *Exploration* and *Elicitation*[2]. After introducing the project to a participant, we began the Exploration section, in which we asked them to explore three models by performing three tasks. Then, we began the Elicitation section. In a typical elicitation study, researchers prompt a user with the effects of an action, known as *referents*, and the user is expected to provide the causes of the action, known as *signs* [8]. In our study, we asked users to define signs (input techniques) for six Referents (functions) with the three models.

We designed tasks for the Exploration section that would prompt participants to both explore the models as a whole and examine smaller model components. Hatwell [11] and Lederman *et al.* [18] found that exploration using tactile perception involves two stages: an overview and detailed exploration; participants would stop exploring at the first stage if no further instruction was given. Thus, our three tasks were:

Task 1. *Identify the Model.* We asked participants to tell us what the model represented. If a participant didn't know what the model was, the researchers told her.

Task 2. *Describe the Shape of an Element.* We asked participants to describe a designated element on each model: Nucleus in the Cell model, North America in the Globe model, and the round building in the Map model. If a participant couldn't find the specific element, the researchers showed her the location of the element.

Task 3. *Describe the Shapes of Nearby Elements.* After Task 2, we asked the participant to explore and describe the elements near the designated element from Task 2.

When performing the tasks, we asked participants to think aloud and explain what they were feeling and doing. If they asked questions about the content on the models, we would answer them after they finished the tasks. We gave the participant one model at a time, and counterbalanced the order in which the models were presented with a Latin triangle. The Exploration lasted around 20 minutes, and participants were encouraged to take a break after finishing each model.

[2] We used "elicitation" instead of "gesture elicitation" to include other modalities in addition to gestures.

During the Elicitation section, we invited participants to design input techniques they wanted to use to get audio output from I3Ms. We used the same models we used during Exploration, and asked each participant to define input techniques for six functions, henceforth referred to as referents. The first four referents were demonstrated in interactive printed maps [9, 38]. The last two referents were discussed by Shi *et al.* [32]. All referents used audio as feedback. These referents included the following, with examples from a globe model:

Referent 1. *Get General Model Information.* The system provides a high-level description of a model: "this is a globe with seven continents."

Referent 2. *Select an Element and Get its Name.* the user selects a continent and the system speaks its name: "North America."

Referent 3. *Select a Sub-Area of an Element and Get its Name.* The user selects an area on North America and the system says: "This is where the Rocky Mountains are."

Referent 4. *Get More Information.* The system provides information about the Rocky Mountains from Wikipedia.

Referent 5. *Record Notes.* The user performs a technique to record notes about the Rocky Mountains.

Referent 6. *Retrieve Notes.* The system speaks the previously recorded notes about the Rocky Mountains.

As is standard with elicitation studies [42], we went through each referent with a participant and asked her to elicit input with the help of Wizard-of-Oz audio feedback. We prompted her by saying "If the models can sense your behaviors and understand your speech, how would you like to interact with the models?" Then, a researcher demonstrated the audio output for each referent. For example, when demonstrating Referent 1 for the Globe model, the researchers used a script to produce synthesized speech for the sentence: "This is a globe model. You can find Asia, North America, South America, and Africa in this model." After demonstrating all referents, the participant was asked to design input techniques to trigger these referents. When the user performed a possible input technique, the researcher played the audio output to simulate the complete interaction.

For each referent and each model, participants were asked to define one input technique. They could use the same inputs for the three models. If they felt that one of the referents was unnecessary for a given model, we allowed them to skip this referent. As with the Exploration section, we gave each participant one model at a time, and counterbalanced the order in which the models were presented with a Latin triangle.

3.4 Apparatus and Materials

We printed three models for the study. We downloaded these models from Thingiverse and OpenStreetMap Buildings [24], online 3D maps containing the models of building geometries. Since most interactive models require auxiliary components (e.g., visual trackers [29]) to sense users' touches, we added a stick to the top of each model to represent an auxiliary component, as shown in Figure 2. The models were printed on a Makerbot 5th generation printer. The three models included:

1. *Cell*: A cell model modified from thing: 689381 [1]. The model has a Nucleus, two Golgi Apparatuses, three Mitochondrion, and four semi-spheres representing Peroxisomes.
2. *Globe*: A globe model modified from thing: 17336 [40]. The model has seven continents.
3. *Map:* A map model downloaded from OpenStreetMap Buildings. The model includes several buildings.

We developed a Python script that used the text-to-speech engine in a Macbook to speak texts, which provided Wizard-of-Oz audio feedback.

3.5 Analysis

We used two cameras to record the study: a fixed camera mounted on the table and a hand-held camera operated by a researcher. Two researchers analyzed the videos recorded by two cameras.

We analyzed the video data from the Exploration section in three stages, following Lederman *et al.*'s video coding method [19]. This method allowed us to combine data from our observations of participants' behavior and their reported thought process. In the first stage, we carefully reviewed the videos from the hand-held camera, and coded them using digital note cards. A note card contained a static frame from the video, an identification code, and text explaining this frame and related dialog from the video. A researcher initiated the transcription process by creating a series of note cards for a video clip. Then the other researcher validated the note cards to make sure the cards represented the video clip.

In the second and third stages, two researchers categorized the note cards into themes in an iterative process. In the second stage, the researchers printed the note cards, and clustered them into several groups based on the performed hand postures and gestures described in the note cards, as shown in Figure 3. Then, they identified themes, like common exploration activities and questions participants asked about the models. In the third stage, the researchers independently reviewed each note card with the identified themes, and validated the themes. We collected and coded a total of 300 note cards.

For data from the Elicitation section, we sorted suggested input techniques, and transcribed only the audio data of the videotapes. We calculated the Max-Consensus and Consensus-Distinct Ratio for each Referent, following Morris *et al.*'s approach [23]. We developed themes from the transcription using axial coding [27].

4. FINDINGS: EXPLORATION

We describe the findings from the Exploration section of our study. We found that participants performed five distinct exploration activities, frequently used four hand postures, and performed eight gestures during the exploration tasks.

4.1 Exploration Activities

When a participant explored a model, she sensed the texture and shape of the model, measured the size of the elements, counted the number of elements, compared similar elements, and communicated with the researcher. In the study, these activities appeared in all three tasks, including Task 2 and 3 where participants could complete the tasks by only sensing the texture of a model and describing the shapes of its elements. Thus, all these five activities are important in tactile exploration.

Figure 2. Three printed models used in the study. From left to right: the Cell model, the Globe model, and the Map model.

Figure 3. A researcher was clustering the note cards. Another participating researcher took the photo.

Sensing

Sensing the shape and texture of a model was the most common activity participants performed when exploring the models. Most of the time participants moved their fingertips back and forth against the model to sense its texture; they occasionally used their palms and fingernails as well. To feel the shape of a model, they performed static gestures like holding the model firmly in their hands.

Measuring

Five participants used their hands to approximately measure the sizes of components on the models. Participants measured components on the Map model most, feeling the heights and widths of the rectangular buildings and the radius of the round building using proprioception. Participants performed these "measuring" activities during all tasks and for all models.

Comparing

Four participants mentioned they compared the shapes of two elements to confirm whether they represented the same concept. For example, P8 and P11 touched two semi-spheres on the Cell model to check whether they both represented Peroxisomes.

Counting

When a specific shape appeared more than twice, many participants counted the instances of the shape. We noted a counting activity whenever a participant verbally counted similar shapes, and found seven participants performed counting activities when exploring the Cell and Map models across three tasks. On the Cell model, participants counted the holes in the Nucleus. On the Map model, they counted the buildings and components of the buildings (e.g., the entrances of the round building).

Communicating

Eight participants communicated with the researchers during the three tasks. Their communication generally served three purposes:

- *Indication*: They used different gestures to tell the researchers that they found the specified element in Task 2.
- *Explanation*: They described their behavior and pointed out certain elements to the researchers.
- *Inquiry*: They asked questions about the identities of elements during the three tasks.

4.2 Hand Postures

Identified Postures

Participants held and manipulated the models using four distinct postures. Sometimes they only used one hand to explore the model, leaving the other hand to hold or stabilize the model. In other cases, they used both hands to explore the model. As shown in Figure 4, we identified four postures: *Grabbing, Stabilizing, Diverging, and Converging*. We described the four postures and their advantages in Table 1. All participants used the four postures throughout the exploration tasks except for P12, who only used the Grabbing posture.

Patterns of Hand Postures

We found participants actively and unconsciously switched among postures to explore the models. The posture a participant adopted depended on (1) the shape of the model being explored, (2) the size of the area the participant was perceiving, and (3) the exploration activity performed.

The shape of a model afforded the postures participants used to explore it. For example, ten participants only used the Grabbing posture when exploring the Globe model. P5 reflected on his posture and said, "I think it's easier with my hands [to hold the Globe model in the air]." While P6 thought she didn't use the Grabbing posture on the Map model because "I don't feel comfortable holding it." On the other hand, participants were more likely to put stable models (e.g., the Cell and the Map models) on the table and adopt the Stabilizing, the Diverging, and the Converging postures. P1 said he put the Map model on the table because "it has a solid base." P7 said she would have put the Globe model on the table if it had "the shape of a teardrop."

The size of the area participants explored also influenced their hand postures. For example, participants tended to use the Diverging posture when exploring large elements (e.g., the Golgi Apparatuses on the Cell model).

Postures also varied depending on what exploration activity the participant was performing. For example, all comparison activities were associated with the Diverging posture, with which participants could examine two elements at a same time.

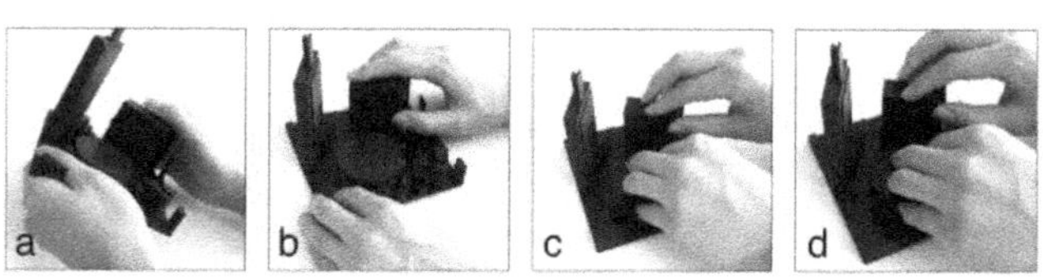

Figure 4. The four identified hand postures. From left to right: Grabbing, Stabilizing, Diverging, and Converging.

Meanwhile, in all communication activities participants used the Grabbing and the Stabilizing postures. Participants used one hand to grab or stabilize the models while using the other hand to point out elements to the researchers.

4.3 Gestures

Identified Gestures

We found eight gestures in the study. We classified a gesture by which parts of the hands were involved and whether it was static or dynamic. We define a *static gesture* as a gesture in which a participant pauses in the middle of performing an action with her hand. By contrast, we define a *dynamic gesture* as a gesture in which a participant performs an action that involves continuous movement. Static gestures were associated with cutaneous perception, while dynamic gestures involved haptic perception as well. In the study, participants performed four single-finger gestures (*i.e.*, *Pointing*, *Striking*, *Index Scanning*, and *Thumb Scanning*, as shown in Figure 5) and four multi-finger gestures (*i.e.*, *Pinching*, *Hovering*, *Following*, and *Rubbing*, as shown in Figure 6). The Pointing, Pinching, and Hovering gestures were static gestures, while the others were dynamic. We described the gestures in Table 2.

Patterns of Gestures

Participants unconsciously chose gestures based on (1) the ongoing activities and (2) properties of the areas they were exploring.

Participants used different gestures for different exploration activities. Table 3 shows the Gesture-Activity matrix, where we marked all combinations that appeared in the study. While the Rub gesture was more capable and could support all five activities, the other gestures served fewer activities. Three gestures only served a single type of activity.

The Pointing and the Striking gestures were only used when participants communicated with the researchers. Participants only used the Thumb Scanning gesture to sense the texture and shapes of elements of a model.

In addition to the influence of the activities, participants also chose gestures based on the complexity and the sizes of the areas they were exploring. When a model was simpler, they tended to use fewer fingers with gestures like Index Scanning, Thumb Scanning, and Hovering. P2 said, "If it's a larger, general model, I would use even the palms of my hands… I want to get everything at once, when I want to be specific, I will revert to my pointers." Other participants also shared similar thoughts. This is because fingers, especially fingertips, have a greater density of receptors, and are more sensitive to detailed tactile information [12]. On the other hand, the palms have larger contact surfaces and can sense larger elements or an entire model at the same time.

	Posture	Description	Advantages
Exploring Using One Hand	Grabbing	Use one hand to hold the model in the air, and perceive tactile information from the other hand.	Allowing a participant to use one hand to navigate and rotate the model freely.
	Stabilizing	Use one hand to fix a model on the table, and the other hand to learn the model.	Not only enabling a participant to explore the model stably, but also providing a reference point from his fixed hand.
Exploring Using Two Hands	Diverging	Put two hands on two elements separately, and each hand could perform different gestures.	Enabling a participant to explore two elements at the same time.
	Converging	Use both hands to explore a single element.	Allowing a participant to explore large elements (e.g., the Golgi Apparatuses in the Cell model) using both hands.

Table 1. The four identified hand postures.

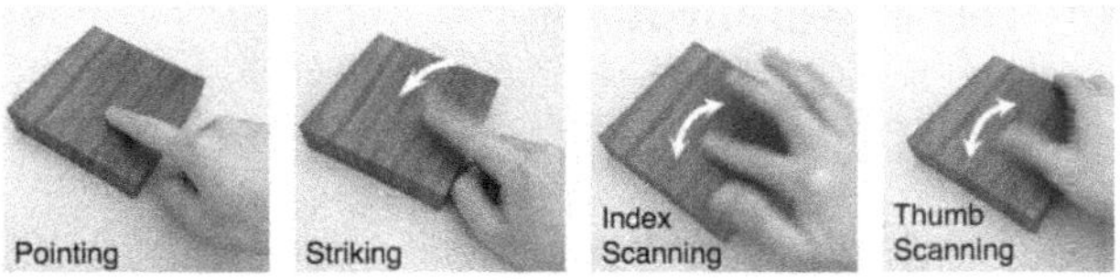

Figure 5. The four identified single-finger gestures. The movements of dynamic gestures are marked with arrows.

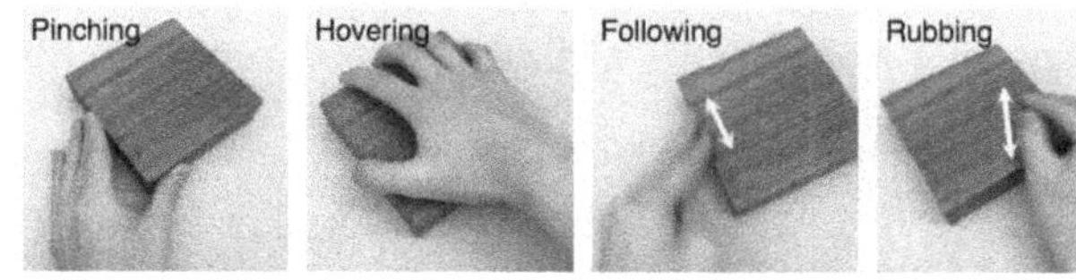

Figure 6. The four identified multi-finger gestures. The movements of dynamic gestures are marked with arrows.

	Posture	Description	Movement	Parts of Hands
Single-finger Gestures	Pointing	Hold an index finger on a model. Five participants used this Pointing gesture.	Static	Index fingers
	Striking	Strike a point on a model with quick light blows. Six participants performed this gesture.	Dynamic	Index fingers
	Index Scanning	Use index fingers to scan an area. Nine participants did this gesture.	Dynamic	Index fingers
	Thumb Scanning	Use thumbs to scan an area. Four participants did this gesture.	Dynamic	Thumbs
Multi-finger Gestures	Pinching	Grip a model using thumb, index, and middle fingers, and hold this gesture for a while to perceive tactile information. Five participants did this gesture.	Static	Thumbs, index, and middle fingers mainly
	Hovering	Put an entire hand on a model without observable movement. Eight participants used this gesture.	Static	Fingertips, palms, and finger pads
	Following	Use more than two fingers together to follow the edge of an element. Ten participants used this gesture.	Dynamic	Fingertips and finger pads
	Rubbing	Use nails, fingertips and finger pads to move around an area. All participants used this gesture.	Dynamic	Nails, fingertips and finger pads

Table 2. The eight gestures identified in the Exploration section.

	Sensing	Measuring	Comparing	Counting	Communicating
Pointing					X
Striking					X
Index Scanning	X	X	X	X	
Thumb Scanning	X				
Pinching	X	X			
Hovering	X	X		X	
Following	X				X
Rubbing	X	X	X	X	X

Table 3. The Gesture-Activity matrix. We marked all the combinations of exploration activities and gestures that appeared in the Exploration section of the study.

5. FINDINGS: ELICITATION

Ten of the 12 participants designed input techniques for all referents. Most used the same input techniques for referents across the three models. P5 thought recording notes and retrieving notes were unnecessary, and P12 thought selecting an area was not a reasonable referent. We report the input techniques participants proposed and summarized patterns from their designs.

5.1 User-Defined Input Modalities

In total, participants proposed 82 interactions for six referents, 58 of which were distinct on a per-referent basis. The suggested interactions covered three input modalities: gestures, speech input, and buttons. In Table 4, we divided the interactions into three modalities. Among all user-defined interactions, gestures were the most common modality and had the biggest variations.

	Total Techniques	Distinct Techniques
Gestures	56 (68.3%)	40 (70.0%)
Speech Input	13 (15.9%)	9 (15.5%)
Buttons	13 (15.9%))	9 (15.5%)
Total	82	58

Table 4. The total and distinct Techniques broken down by different interaction modalities.

Gestures

All participants except for P12 wanted to perform gestures on the models to trigger some referents. Some gestures they mentioned are commonly available on touchscreens or supported by screen reader software, such as tapping, touching, pressing with force, holding for a while and swiping. Some gestures had variations. For example, participants brought up different tapping gestures like a single-finger single tap, a two-finger single tap, and a two-finger triple tap. Participants sometimes combined two gestures to create a new gesture (e.g., a tapping gesture followed by a press gesture).

Several participants designed gestures that were not based on current eyes-free touchscreen interaction. P2 wanted to shake a model to get general information about it, and squeeze an element to get its name. P10 used her fingers to follow the edge of an area, which we defined as the Following gesture (see above), to select it. P9 scratched an area to select it.

Two participants described principles that guided their proposed gestures. P6 used speed as a parameter to trigger different referents. For example, a user could perform a swiping gesture quickly on an element to get general information about it, and then slow down to retrieve more detailed information. P8 introduced the Rochester Method [28], also known as Visible English. He drew a symbol representing a question mark (as defined by the Rochester Method) to retrieve general information about a model.

Speech Input

Five participants mentioned speech input. They used simple commands such as "what is it?" "more information," and "save information." P11 said these commands were inspired by Siri on the iPhone.

Buttons

Participants designed buttons to fulfill different functions, and arranged them in different locations. For example, P5, P7, P12 wanted to have a button that could turn on the audio feedback of an I3M, and speak general information about the model. P3 designed buttons to get detailed information and take notes. However, three participants emphasized that the buttons should not be incorporated into the models. P7 commented on the effect of buttons on the tactile information represented on a model, saying that "adding buttons to the structure almost takes away from actually teaching someone what is the thing you are touching." They suggested placing the buttons at the bottom of a model or on an auxiliary component like the long stick we added.

5.2 Elicited Interactions for Referents

On average, each referent got 13.7 input techniques, and 9.7 distinct input techniques. When broken down into the three input modalities (gestures, speech, and buttons), there were 6.7 distinct gestures, 1.5 distinct speech input commands, and 1.5 distinct button arrangements per referent.

To further understand user agreement of proposed interactions for each referent, we calculated the max-consensus (MC) and consensus-distinct ratio (CDR). MC is the percent of participants who suggested the most popular input technique for a referent or referent/input modality combination. A higher MC value indicates more user agreement on the most popular user-defined input technique. For a referent or referent/interaction technique combination, CDR is the percent of the distinct techniques that achieved a given consensus threshold among participants. This metric indicates the diversity of techniques that fulfill a certain user agreement. We used a threshold of two in the analysis.

In Table 5, we list MC, CDR, and the distinct input techniques that were above the consensus threshold for each referent. Across all referents, gestures received more user agreement with a mean MC of 20.8%, compared to speech input (mean MC = 11.1%) and buttons (mean MC = 12.5%). However, speech input and buttons were more favored for referents that do not involve specific model elements. For example, the referent "Get General Model Information" had a MC of 25% for buttons, but a MC of 17% for gestures. The referent "Get More Information" had a MC of 25% for speech input, compared to a MC of 17% for gestures. P3, who designed a button for "Get General Model Information," said that "it doesn't matter if you are feeling it (the model)."

For each referent, we can choose the technique with the highest number of the supporting participants (i.e., the first action in each row) as its elicited interaction. In this study, our elicited interaction set is conflict-free. Prior work [42] introduced a method to eliminate conflicts in elicited interactions.

6. DESIGNING I3MS

We conclude design implications for I3Ms from the study, and propose a set of recommended interactions and functions.

6.1 Design Implications

We draw design implications from both sections of the study. These implications can be used as design guidelines for future I3Ms.

Improving Tactile Information

I3Ms are augmented 3D printed objects. Thus, we need to consider the printed model itself when design an I3M. The findings from the study imply that designers should make tactile information clearer, and consider potential technology failures in 3D prints.

We could design different versions of a model to meet the needs of users with varied tactile perception abilities and avoid overwhelming information. Participants said that some models contained an overwhelming amount of details. For example, when exploring the Globe model, P6 said, "In North America, there are so many details, and I can't distinguish what they are and what they mean." Another participant, P12, thought the raised edges on the Globe model were unnecessary and confusing, and suggested that we produce different models to meet the needs of people with varied educational backgrounds. For example, when designing a model for a continent, we could have a detailed version where

Referent	MC/CDR Type	MC	CDR	Above Threshold Distinct input actions	#
Get General Model Information	Overall	25%	23%	• Push a button on the long stick to turn on the model	3
	Gestures	17%	22%	• Use index finger to press the model at beginning	2
	Speech	8%	0%	• Use index finger to touch the model at beginning	2
	Buttons	25%	50%		
Select an Element and Get its Name	Overall	25%	40%	• Use index finger to tap once on the element	3
	Gestures	25%	44%	• Use index finger to press the element	3
	Speech	-	-	• Use index finger to touch the element	2
	Buttons	8%	0%	• Use index finger to tap twice on the element	2
Select a Sub-Area of an Element and Get its Name	Overall	33%	29%	• Use index finger to swipe on the area	4
	Gestures	33%	17%	• Push a button on the long stick to switch the level of information	2
	Speech	-	-		
	Buttons	17%	100%		
Get More Information	Overall	25%	40%	• "more information"	3
				• Use index finger to swipe on the element/area	2
	Gestures	17%	38%		
	Speech	25%	100%	• Use index finger to tap twice on the element/area	2
	Buttons	8%	0%	• Use index finger to tap on the element/area and hold	2
Record Notes	Overall	17%	22%	• "record notes"	2
	Gestures	17%	20%		
	Speech	17%	50%	• Use index finger to tap on the element/area twice	2
	Buttons	8%	0%		
Retrieve notes	Overall	17%	22%	• "retrieve notes"	2
	Gestures	17%	20%		
	Speech	17%	50%	• Use index finger to tap on the element/area twice	2
	Buttons	8%	0%		

Table 5. Six referents and their max-consensus (MC) values, consensus-distinct ratios (CDRs), and distinct input actions that were above a consensus threshold of two. The MC and CDRs were also broken down into three input modalities. Two referents didn't get any speech interaction. For each distinct input action, we list the number of the participants reporting in the "#" column.

major cities are marked. In addition, we could create a simplified version that only has general geographic information. Since 3D printers produce low-cost models in a relatively short time, blind users can print and experience different versions of a model to meet their needs. Moreover, recent research on 3D printers allows us to modify an existing model [39]. Using similar tools, a blind user can learn from a simplified version and ask a printer to add more details when she gets a better understanding of the model.

To overcome potential technology failures, we propose using specific tactile patterns to avoid imperfections, and using software solutions to optimize 3D prints. For example, designers could mark each element on a globe model with different tactile patterns. In this way, users will understand which part belongs to an element and they could learn to ignore printing imperfections. In addition, designers can use software applications like MeshMixer [2] that increase the durability and printing quality of models.

Controllable and Changeable Digital Content

In the Elicitation section, four participants specifically point out the potential issue of overwhelming audio feedback. They worried that the models would keep providing unnecessary audio output when they were exploring the models. P5 said, "It's annoying, if you are feeling, it keeps saying nucleus, nucleus, nucleus, every time you touch it, that would be irritating." P7 further explained the reason behind this, "People don't take a ton of information well, instead, it overwhelms them. So, they need to be very much in control of the information they are accessing."

We propose to use modes to change content and avoid overwhelming the user with information. In the study, four participants said they would like to be able to switch among different modes using a switch or a button. The most basic modes they mentioned were turning on and turning off the audio output. In addition, the embedded audio content of an I3M could be customized to meet varied needs from different users. P3 and P5 also thought the models could have modes with different levels of information. For example, P3 mentioned "national mode," "state mode," and "city mode" for the Globe model. In addition, P4 thought these models could also serve different purposes. He designed two settings as an example, "One setting is to give general information, or element information. Another setting is to allow people to guess [the name of an element]."

Supporting Exploration Behaviors

I3Ms should contain adequate information to support the exploration activities blind people perform when perceiving a model. Prior work [9, 17, 25, 30–32, 38] only provided simple label information for each element on a 3D model. However, in the Exploration section, blind people also showed their interest in the dimensions of elements, similarities among elements, and the number of repeated elements.

We also need to consider blind people's exploration behaviors when designing auxiliary components for I3Ms. I3Ms rely on additional sensors to sense users' behaviors. Some auxiliary components require a fixed model, and might not be suitable for models without a stable base. For example, prior work [9, 17, 38] used conductive filament and touchscreens to create I3Ms, which required users to attach the model onto a tablet when use it. This method could fail in the case of a model that does not have a stable base (e.g., the Globe model), because blind people tended to hold that model in the air and use the Grabbing posture to explore it. When designed in a suitable form, an auxiliary component could help tactile exploration. For example, P3 used the long stick as a handle so she could hold models steadily, as shown in Figure 7.

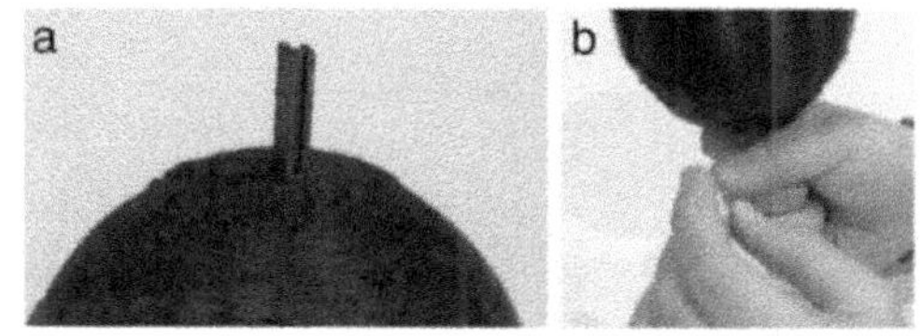

Figure 7. Participants took advantage of (a) the long stick we added on each model. For example, (b) P3 used it as a handle to stabilize and manipulate the model.

Learnable and Distinguishable Gestures

When using gestures as the main input modality for I3Ms, we should consider the learnability of the gestures, as well as how to distinguish the gestures from regular exploration behaviors.

On the one hand, we should use common gestures to lower the learning curve of interactive models. In the Elicitation section of our study, the participants designed common touchscreen gestures. P7 attributed her reasons for doing this to the learnability of gestures, and said "every time you do something, there is a learning curve," a thought shared by other participants as well. In addition to the gestures from the Elicitation section, we also identified some learnable gestures in the Exploration section. For example, the Pointing, Striking, and Following gestures are used in communication activities to inquire information. These gestures are intuitive ways to communicate with I3Ms.

On the other hand, I3Ms should also be able to distinguish deliberate gestures from exploration behaviors. Some participants also expressed their concerns about gesture recognition. When designing gestures, a designer should consider the exploration behaviors we highlighted and avoid potential confusion.

Interaction Techniques for Small Models

Three participants felt that the small size of the models limited the design space for gestures. When designing input techniques for the Globe model, P3 said, "If you want multiple state information, it would be hard to do in an item that's small."

Since current mainstream printers could only produce models with a limited size, we should combine different interaction techniques to overcome this constraint. For example, while selecting a state in the Globe model was difficult, the participants chose other methods like speech input to retrieve information.

6.2 Proposed Design

Our proposed design uses an RGB camera, a microphone, and a touchscreen from a tablet as sensors, and is an extension of our ongoing work [31, 33]. With these sensors, a user can use gestures, speech input, and physical and virtual buttons to interface with an I3M, as shown in Figure 8. We describe the functions and interactions of the proposed design in Table 6.

The findings from both sections of the study contributed to our proposed design. The exploration behaviors we identified implied the potential functions blind people need. For example, the proposed design enables them to compare elements or areas and inquiry the dimension information of an element. The elicited input techniques yielded insights about blind participants' preferences for different interaction techniques, as well as their opinions about I3Ms. For instance, we design virtual and physical buttons that enable users to control information flow. The I3Ms we design have two modes: "Element" and "Area." For example, on a globe model, users can perform inquiries about continents in the "Element" mode, and the "Area" mode provides information about countries.

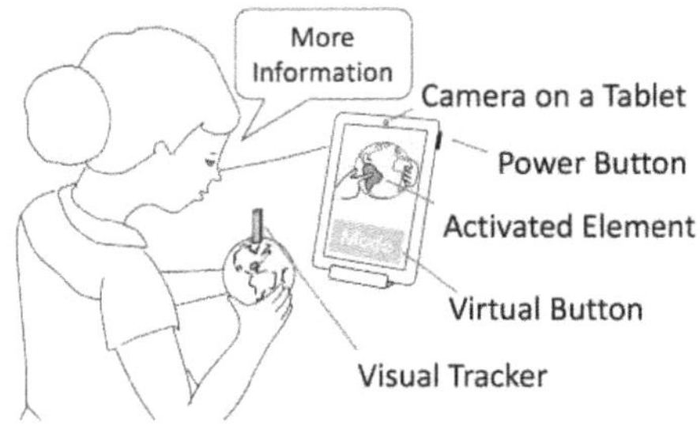

Figure 8. A use case for the proposed design. A user selects an element with her index finger, and says "more information" to retrieve further information about the element.

Functions	Interactions
Turn on/off	Power button
Switch modes	Virtual button
Select a Sub-Area of an Element and Get its Name	Use index finger to tap once on the element/area
Compare two elements/areas	"Comparison" + Use index finger to tap once on two elements/areas
Get dimension	"Dimension" after selecting
Get more information	"More information" after selecting

Table 6. The functions and interactions for the proposed design.

7. DISCUSSION

We conducted a study with blind participants and discussed design implications for I3Ms. In addition to I3Ms, the findings from our study can also contribute to the design of passive printed models. Passive printed models also faced challenges in terms of design and technology, as we described in Section 6.1. Thus, model designers should consider our guidelines to improve tactile information for passive printed models. Moreover, designers should provide accessible information (e.g., tactile Braille prints, audio books) to explain the information included in the models to avoid confusion, if that information isn't accessible interactively.

In the Exploration section of our study, we developed a new taxonomy to analyze exploration behaviors. We classified each note card in three dimensions: exploration activities, hand postures, and gestures. We defined hand postures based on the functionalities of hands, and specified each gesture by its movement and which parts of the hands it involved. With this taxonomy, we coded all note cards. While prior work on tactile perception [19] and elicitation [23, 42] introduced several taxonomies that might yield other perspectives, we believe our inductive approach captured a range of salient behaviors in the relatively unexplored space of the perception of 3D models.

In the Elicitation section of our study, we asked participants to design input techniques to retrieve audio information about models and their components. We used audio as the default output since all prior work on I3Ms provided audio feedback. However, other output modalities, such as smells and vibrations, can also be applied to I3Ms [4]. Visual feedback can also be important for people with low vision, who comprise the majority of the population of people with visual impairments [36, 37]. We plan to conduct further studies to explore potential output techniques.

We proposed a design of I3Ms using the sensors in a tablet. The sensors a designer chooses will affect the design of I3Ms. For example, RGB cameras are ubiquitous, but they are less capable of differentiating touching and pressing gestures. Moreover, sensors can also affect the design of auxiliary components. In the study, we added a long stick on each model to represent an auxiliary component. We found that such components wouldn't bother users if they were designed to support users' exploration behaviors. Model designers should choose sensors based on use cases, and adopt the findings from this study.

The proposed design enables a blind user to retrieve information from I3Ms, but we think I3Ms themselves could take more initiative and guide users through the exploration process of a model. Prior work [22] suggested that by following some exploration patterns, blind users could learn tactile information more efficiently. I3Ms should be able to help users find the best strategy to explore models. However, we need further research to design accessible and efficient instructions to guide this process.

The findings of our study could be more substantial with future research. The identified exploration behaviors should be confirmed with more participants, and the design implications we concluded should be further examined. Moreover, the proposed design should be validated in an iterative design process.

8. CONCLUSIONS

In this paper, we conducted a study with 12 legally blind participants to understand blind people's exploration behavior with 3D printed models and elicit interactions for future I3Ms. With the design implications concluded from the study, we proposed a design of I3Ms. The findings in the study lay an important foundation for future research and design of I3Ms which could serve as powerful accessibility tools.

9. ACKNOWLEDGEMENTS

This work has been supported by AOL and the Connected Experiences Lab. We thank Niti Parikh for helping us print models. We also thank all participants for their time and valuable suggestions.

10. REFERENCES

[1] Animal Cell - Thingiverse: *http://www.thingiverse.com/thing:689381*. Accessed: 2017-04-04.

[2] Autodesk Meshmixer: *http://www.meshmixer.com/*. Accessed: 2017-05-04.

[3] Brown, C. and Hurst, A. 2012. VizTouch: automatically generated tactile visualizations of coordinate spaces. *TEI '12*, 131–138.

[4] Brule, E., Bailly, G., Brock, A., Valentin, F., Denis, G. and Jouffrais, C. 2016. MapSense: Multi-Sensory Interactive Maps for Children Living with Visual Impairments. *CHI '16*, 445–457.

[5] Buehler, E., Hurst, A. and Hofmann, M. 2014. Coming to grips: 3D printing for accessibility. *ASSETS '14*, 291–292.

[6] Buehler, E., Kane, S.K. and Hurst, A. 2014. ABC and 3D: opportunities and obstacles to 3D printing in special education environments. *ASSETS '14*, 107–114.

[7] Davidson, P.W. 1972. Haptic judgments of curvature by blind and sighted humans. *Journal of Experimental Psychology*. 93, 1 (1972), 43–55.

[8] Good, M.D., Whiteside, J.A., Wixon, D.R. and Jones, S.J. 1984. Building a user-derived interface. *Communications of the ACM*. 27, 10 (Oct. 1984), 1032–1043.

[9] Götzelmann, T. 2016. LucentMaps: 3D Printed Audiovisual Tactile Maps for Blind and Visually Impaired People. *ASSETS '16*, 81–90.

[10] Hatch, M. 2013. *The Maker Movement Manifesto: Rules for Innovation in the New World of Crafters, Hackers, and Tinkerers.* McGraw Hill Professional.

[11] Hatwell, Y. 1987. Motor and cognitive functions of the hand in infancy and childhood. *International Journal of Behavioral Development*. 10, 4 (Dec. 1987), 509–526.

[12] Hatwell, Y., Arlette, S. and Edouard, G. 2003. *Touching for knowing: cognitive psychology of haptic manual perception*. John Benjamins Publishing.

[13] Hofmann, M., Harris, J., Hudson, S.E. and Mankoff, J. 2016. Helping Hands: Requirements for a Prototyping Methodology for Upper-limb Prosthetics Users. *CHI '16*, 1769–1780.

[14] Kane, S.K. and Bigham, J.P. 2014. Tracking@ stemxcomet: teaching programming to blind students via 3D printing, crisis management, and twitter. *SIGCSE '14*, 247–252.

[15] Kim, J. and Yeh, T. 2015. Toward 3D-Printed Movable Tactile Pictures for Children al Impairments with Visual Impairments. *CHI '15*, 2815–2824.

[16] Klatzky, R.L., Loomis, J.M. and Lederman, S.J. 1993. Haptic identification of objects and their depictions. *Perception & Psychophysics*. 54, 2 (1993), 170–178.

[17] Kolitsky, M.A. 2016. 3D printing makes virtual world more real for blind learners. *e-mentor*. 1 (63) (2016), 65–70.

[18] Lederman, S.J. and Klatzky, R.L. 1993. Extracting object properties through haptic exploration. *Acta Psychologica*. 84, 1 (1993), 29–40.

[19] Lederman, S.J. and Klatzky, R.L. 1987. Hand movements: A window into haptic object recognition. *Cognitive Psychology*. 19, 3 (1987), 342–368.

[20] Lipson, H. and Kurman, M. 2013. *Fabricated: The new world of 3D printing*. John Wiley & Sons.

[21] McDonald, S., Dutterer, J., Abdolrahmani, A., Kane, S.K. and Hurst, A. 2014. Tactile aids for visually impaired graphical design education. *ASSETS '14*, 275–276.

[22] Morash, V.S., Pensky, A.E.C., Tseng, S.T.W. and Miele, J.A. 2014. Effects of using multiple hands and fingers on haptic performance in individuals who are blind. *Perception*. 43, 6 (2014), 569–588.

[23] Morris, M.R. 2012. Web on the Wall: Insights from a Multimodal Interaction Elicitation Study. *ITS '12*, 95–104.

[24] OpenStreetMap Buildings: *https://osmbuildings.org/*. Accessed: 2017-04-04.

[25] Reichinger, A., Fuhrmann, A., Maierhofer, S. and Purgathofer, W. 2016. Gesture-Based Interactive Audio Guide on Tactile Reliefs. *ASSETS '16*, 91–100.

[26] Rovira, K., Deschamps, L. and Baena-Gomez, D. 2011. Mental rotation in blind and sighted adolescents: The effects of haptic strategies. *Revue Europeene de Psychologie Appliquee*. 61, 3 (2011), 153–160.

[27] Saldana, J. 2015. *The Coding Manual for Qualitative Researchers*. Sage.

[28] Scouten, E.L. 1967. The Rochester method, an oral multisensory approach for instructing prelingual deaf children. *American annals of the deaf*. 112, 2 (Mar. 1967), 50–5.

[29] Shen, H., Edwards, O., Miele, J. and Coughlan, J.M. 2013. CamIO: A 3D computer vision system enabling audio/haptic interaction with physical objects by blind users. *ASSETS '13*, 1–2.

[30] Shi, L. 2015. Talkabel: A Labeling Method for 3D Printed Models. *ASSETS '15*, 361–362.

[31] Shi, L., McLachlan, R., Zhao, Y. and Azenkot, S. 2016. Magic Touch: Interacting with 3D Printed Graphics. *ASSETS '16*, 329–330.

[32] Shi, L., Zelzer, I., Feng, C. and Azenkot, S. 2016. Tickers and Talker: An Accessible Labeling Toolkit for 3D Printed Models. *CHI '16*, 4896–4907.

[33] Shi, L., Zhao, Y. and Azenkot, S. 2017. Markit and Talkit: A Low-Barrier Toolkit to Augment 3D Printed Models with Audio Annotations. *UIST '17*.

[34] Stangl, A., Kim, J. and Yeh, T. 2014. 3D printed tactile picture books for children with visual impairments. *IDC '14*, 321–324.

[35] Symmons, M. and Richardson, B. 2000. Raised Line Drawings are Spontaneously Explored with a Single Finger. *Perception*. 29, 5 (May 2000), 621–626.

[36] Szpiro, S., Zhao, Y. and Azenkot, S. 2016. Finding a store, searching for a product: a study of daily challenges of low vision people. *UbiComp '16*, 61–72.

[37] Szpiro, S.F.A., Hashash, S., Zhao, Y. and Azenkot, S. 2016. How People with Low Vision Access Computing Devices. *ASSETS '16*, 171–180.

[38] Taylor, B., Dey, A., Siewiorek, D. and Smailagic, A. 2016. Customizable 3D Printed Tactile Maps as Interactive Overlays. *ASSETS '16*, 71–79.

[39] Teibrich, A., Mueller, S., Guimbretière, F., Kovacs, R., Neubert, S. and Baudisch, P. 2015. Patching Physical Objects. *UIST '15*, 83–91.

[40] Textured Earth - Thingiverse: *http://www.thingiverse.com/thing:17336*. Accessed: 2017-04-04.

[41] The Peachy Printer - The First $100 3D Printer: *https://www.kickstarter.com/projects/117421627/the-peachy-printer-the-first-100-3d-printer-and-sc*. Accessed: 2017-05-05.

[42] Wobbrock, J.O., Morris, M.R. and Wilson, A.D. 2009. User-defined gestures for surface computing. *CHI '09*, 1083.

Evaluating Wrist-Based Haptic Feedback for Non-Visual Target Finding and Path Tracing on a 2D Surface

Jonggi Hong[1], Alisha Pradhan[2], Jon E. Froehlich[1,3], Leah Findlater[2,4]

[1]Department of Computer Science
[2]College of Information Studies
University of Maryland, College Park

[3]Computer Science and Engineering
[4]Human Centered Design and Engineering
University of Washington

{jhong12, alisha93, jonf, leahkf}@umd.edu

ABSTRACT

Precisely guiding a blind person's hand can be useful for a range of applications from tracing printed text to learning and understanding shapes and gestures. In this paper, we evaluate wrist-worn haptics as a directional hand guide. We implemented and evaluated the following haptic wristband variations: (1) *four* versus *eight* vibromotor designs; (2) vibration from only a *single* motor at a time versus from two adjacent motors using *interpolation*. To evaluate our designs, we conducted two studies: Study 1 (N=13, 2 blind) showed that participants could non-visually find targets and trace paths more quickly and accurately with single-motor feedback than with interpolated feedback, particularly when only four motors were used. Study 2 (N=14 blind or visually impaired participants) found that single-motor feedback with four motors was faster, more accurate, and most preferred compared to similar feedback with eight motors. We derive implications for the design of wrist-worn directional haptic feedback and discuss future work.

CCS Concepts

Human-centered computing→Accessibility→Empirical Studies in Accessibility

Keywords

Haptic feedback; haptic wristband; blind user; wearable computing; accessibility.

1. INTRODUCTION

Directional hand guidance can be useful for a range of everyday activities for people who are blind and visually impaired (VI), such as physically tracing printed text to hear text-to-speech output [36, 37], learning handwriting [4] and touchscreen gestures [26], and understanding shapes [13]. To provide this guidance, researchers have explored both audio feedback, such as sonification and verbal guidance [26], as well as haptics, such as finger-mounted vibromotors [36, 37] or force feedback [13].

Smartwatches present new opportunities for directional hand guidance that is proximal to the hand yet embedded unobtrusively into an existing general-purpose device. For example, haptic motors around the wrist, as shown in Figure 1, may be useful for guiding a blind user's hand on a 2D surface. However, how to design this guidance is an open question. While placing a larger

ASSETS '17, October 29-November 1, 2017, Baltimore, MD, USA

ACM ISBN 978-1-4503-4926-0/17/10…$15.00
https://doi.org/10.1145/3132525.3132538

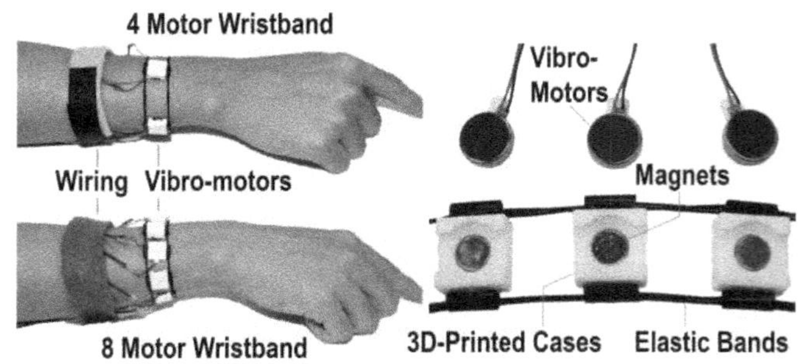

Figure 1. Wristbands with four and eight motors. Image adapted from our prior work [18], which used the same hardware and wristband configuration.

number of haptic actuators around the wrist may offer more precise feedback, it also increases the physical weight and complexity of the device. At the same time, fewer motors may still be useful, particularly if it is possible to create *phantom sensations*, where two closely-placed motors vibrating at once create the perception of a single vibration located between the two [2].

Wrist-worn haptic feedback has been primarily studied with sighted users and, even then, in the context of notifications such as the user's ability to recognize different pulse patterns (*e.g.*, [29]). For blind users, one [7, 8, 20] or four vibromotors [27] have been used on the wrist to support navigation (*i.e.*, directing the user's whole body) but not for precise hand guidance, which is our focus. A small number of studies with sighted users have focused on wrist-worn haptics for directional hand guidance [1, 35, 40]; however, [1, 35] did not compare multiple haptic designs so conclusions about efficacy cannot be drawn. Two exceptions come from Weber *et al.* [40] and Hong *et al.* [18]. Weber *et al.* [40] compared wristbands with four or six haptic motors to verbal instructions (up/left/right/down) to guide sighted users in moving and rotating their arm. However, they did not find statistically significant differences between the haptic designs, and their focus was on guiding hand movement in free space rather than on a 2D surface. Hong *et al.* [18] showed that an 8-motor wristband resulted in small accuracy benefits over a 4-motor design but their experimental task was relatively simple (making a directional swipe) and their study did not include blind users, who may perform differently due to differences in tactile perception (*e.g.*, [16]).

To study directional wrist-worn haptic feedback for blind users and to compare the effectiveness of different feedback designs, we implemented and evaluated the following haptic wristband variations: (1) *four* versus *eight* vibromotor designs; (2) vibration from only a *single* motor at a time versus from two adjacent motors, with the intention of creating an *interpolated*, more precise phantom sensation (vibration) between the two. In theory, eight vibromotors and the use of phantom sensations should provide more precise feedback than the other options but requires more hardware and could also be more cognitively or physically taxing. We conducted two controlled lab experiments: the first study included 11 sighted and 2 blind participants and was aimed at paring down the number of experimental conditions before conducting a second study with 14 blind and VI participants.

Study 1 showed that participants could non-visually find targets and trace paths more quickly and accurately with single-motor feedback than with interpolated feedback, particularly when only four motors were used. Study 2 (with blind participants) eliminated the interpolated feedback conditions and found that single-motor feedback with four motors was faster, more accurate, and most preferred compared to similar feedback with eight motors. In summary, this paper contributes empirical evidence that wrist-worn haptic feedback with a single motor vibrating at once performs better than interpolated feedback, and that embedding four motors in the wristband performs better than eight motors. We also provide design implications for non-visual wrist-worn haptic guidance. Our results have implications for future smartwatch haptic wristband designs.

2. RELATED WORK

We highlight assistive uses of haptic feedback as well as wrist and hand-worn haptic feedback devices.

2.1 Haptic Feedback for Assistive Applications

Haptic feedback has been used for a range of assistive applications for users with visual impairments. Most effort has focused on sensory substitution of visual information (*e.g.*, [31]) and on navigation (*e.g.*, [15]) but other areas have also been investigated, such as hand-worn dynamic braille for deaf-blind users [3, 17]. Sensory substitution maps visual information to alternative channels such as audio or haptics. A well-known example is *BrainPort*, which translates images from a glasses-worn camera into electrical stimulations on the tongue [31]. Another example is *Optacon*, which translates black and white areas on a printed page to dynamic tactile output for the user to touch [33]. Haptic wristbands and gloves have also been used to convey the color of objects under the finger [9, 34].

In this paper, we explore the use of haptics for directional guidance. Here, most work has focused on whole-body navigational support. An early example comes from Ertan *et al.* [15], who employed a 4x4 grid of vibrotactile actuators on the back of a vest to indicate turn information. Similarly, Scheggi *et al.* [32] used wrist-worn devices with two haptic actuators that were controlled by a remote observer to help blind users avoid obstacles while walking. Mann *et al.* [24] employed a haptic helmet combined with a depth camera to help blind users avoid collisions, although no user evaluation was reported. Cosgun *et al.* [12] evaluated a haptic belt with eight motors to provide directional guidance in discrete, 45° increments. They showed that users could recognize which of the eight motors was vibrating with 55-97% accuracy, depending on the motor. Though these studies showed that haptic feedback devices in different form factors are feasible to use for whole-body navigation, the design of wrist-worn haptic feedback for precise hand guidance has not been investigated with blind users.

2.2 Non-visual Directional Hand Guidance

For non-visual directional hand guidance specifically, prior work has explored both audio and haptic channels. For example, Oh *et al.* [26] used verbal feedback and sonification to teach blind users how to make touchscreen gestures. Audio feedback has also been used to help users reach targets in their peripersonal space [28, 41]. Directional audio guidance, however, has the drawback of interfering with other uses of the audio channel, such as screenreader or text-to-speech output [37]. Haptic feedback addresses this issue. Kim *et al.* [21] used four vibromotors mounted on a handheld smartphone to guide users with visual impairments to find targets on a large display. A user study showed that speech plus haptic feedback was faster than speech alone in helping users find targets. Shilkrot *et al.* [36] and Stearns *et al.* [37] both employed haptic actuators mounted on the finger and audio feedback to provide up/down (1D) finger guidance for a blind user tracing along a line of printed text. The latter conducted a controlled experiment with 19 blind participants to compare haptic and audio feedback for this reading task, finding that there were tradeoffs in accuracy and user preference between the two [37]. In contrast to these studies, our paper focuses on using haptic feedback around the wrist for precise 2D directional guidance for blind users.

Wrist-worn directional haptic guidance has been investigated to a greater extent with sighted users. In addition to the Weber *et al.* [40] example mentioned in the introduction, another study that is closely related to ours evaluated the accuracy with which users can perceive four or eight vibromotors placed around the wrist and move their hand in response [18]. In a user study, they vibrated one or two motors at a time to create a phantom sensation that conveyed direction more precisely than the 90° or 45° angular intervals between the four or eight motors. Users were asked users to move their finger in the direction they perceived. The wristband with eight motors was more accurate than the wristband with four motors, though the angular error in movement ranged from ~23–25° for both wristbands. In comparison to that study, our paper focuses on more complex and realistic tasks (target finding and path tracing), includes blind and visually impaired users, and explores a wider range of haptic feedback designs.

Other haptic studies with sighted users have investigated using a grid of motors on one side of the wrist to convey direction instead of placing motors around a band. For example, Lee *et al.* showed that the accuracy of perceiving direction with the grid of motors on the back of a smartwatch is more accurate with sensory saltation (an illusion of stimulus movement) than without it [22]. Another study empirically showed that the accuracy of localizing a vibration within a 3x3 grid layout was ~22–76% depending on the motor [10]. Finally, Matscheko *et al.* [25] compared a grid layout to a wristband layout for directional guidance while users are engaged in tasks that occupy the visual and audio sensory channels. They found the band layout to be more accurate, which supports our decision to use a design with motors around the band rather than in a grid.

3. DESIGN OF HAPTIC GUIDANCE

To evaluate the performance of different haptic feedback designs on 2D hand movement, we implemented two haptic wristbands: one with four motors and the other with eight motors. They employ the same hardware design as in [18] but with different software.

3.1 Hardware

The wristbands, shown in Figures 1 and 2, are identical except for the number of motors. We use eccentric rotating mass (ERM) disc vibromotors 10mm in diameter. [1] ERMs are inexpensive and ubiquitous, their flat design can be easily integrated into a wristband, and they have been used to create phantom sensations

[1] https://www.adafruit.com/product/1201

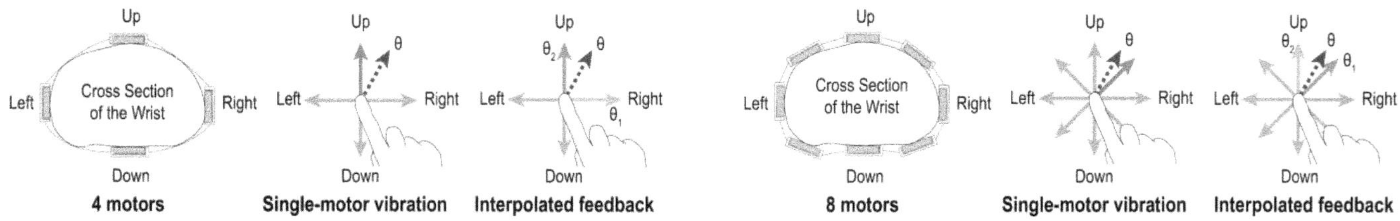

Figure 2. The position of motors around the wrist and an example of haptic feedback of 4 or 8 motors with single motor vibration or interpolation. In this figure, θ is the prompted direction (blue dotted arrow) and red and light red arrows are directions of vibration.

[30]. Additionally, ERMs performed better for our user tasks when compared to a similar wristband design with linear resonant actuators (LRAs) when tested with three internal pilot participants. When mounted on the wristband and worn by a user, we measured the amplitude of the ERMs at 0-1.2g and the frequency at 0-162Hz; Figure 3 shows the measured frequency and amplitude in response to applied voltage. The response time to drive the motor to full vibration from the complete idle state was 100ms.

As shown in Figure 1, our custom wristband design addresses three issues: vibration transfer along the band, variation in wrist size, and the non-uniform shape of a wrist. To isolate the motors and limit vibration transfer, we mounted the motors on a band separate from the wiring and housed them magnetically in 3D-printed cases connected only by thin elastic thread. The band with the wiring connected to an Arduino Mega for communication and power. Because the wrist is not a uniform oval, placing the motors equidistantly around the band (as in [40]) means that the motors are not necessarily at the position the user expects—for example, the right-most location on the wrist may not be midway between the up and down positions. To address variation in wrist sizes and shapes, our prototype is adjustable. The band with the motors is threaded through the motor cases rather than affixed, which allows the cases to slide (with effort) along the band, and allows the band to be tightened or loosened (based on [19]). The experimenter could thus adjust the band per user. The Arduino Mega was in turn connected to a Samsung Galaxy Tab 4 tablet via an on-the-go (OTG) cable. The tablet communicated serially with the Arduino Mega, sending a signal at a frequency of 92 Hz to update the vibration.

3.2 Feedback

We implemented two different vibration types: *single-motor* vibration, which is simpler and thus may be easier to perceive, and *interpolated* vibration, which should offer more precise directional information. To mitigate desensitization that can occur when haptic feedback is continuously applied at a single location [5], our feedback designs provide only *corrective* guidance. That is, when the user's finger moves off course, vibration guides them back to the intended direction (corrects the finger movement). When the finger movement is on course, no vibration occurs. This design was selected among several options based on extensive piloting within our research lab, including options that provided continuous vibration such as dropping to low intensity rather than no vibration.

3.2.1 Single Motor Vibration

For this feedback type, only one motor vibrates at a time, and the location of that motor maps to a direction on a 2D plane (Figure 2). Directions are in 90° increments for the 4-motor wristband and 45° increments for the 8-motor wristband. For example, vibrating the leftmost motor on the wrist indicates that the finger should move to the left on the 2D surface. To convey directions *between* two motors, the single closest motor vibrates (*e.g.*, for a prompted direction of 15°, the rightmost motor, at 0°, vibrates).

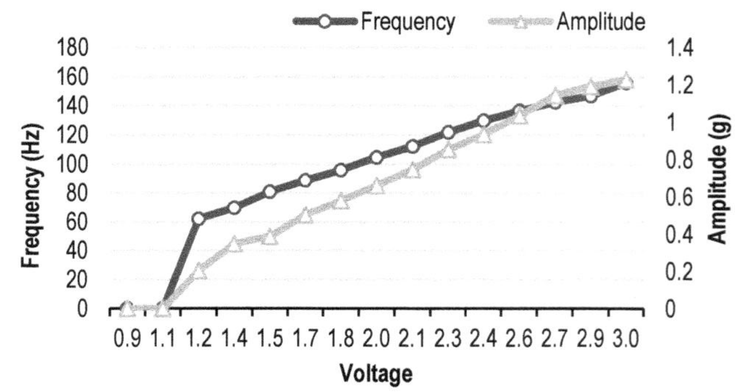

Figure 3. Measured frequency and amplitude of an ERM vibro-motor mounted on a user's wrist as applied voltage changes. Graph adapted from our prior work [18].

To provide corrective guidance, no vibration occurs if the difference between the finger's trajectory and the intended direction is less than 22.5°; 22.5° was selected based on prior work showing the minimum angular accuracy in moving the hand based on vibration around the wrist is at least 23° [18]. As the finger's trajectory diverges from the intended direction, vibration intensity increases: the applied voltage increases linearly from 1V when the user's hand movement trajectory is 22.5° away from the intended direction to 3V (maximum intensity) when the user's trajectory is 90° or farther from the intended direction.

3.2.2 Interpolated Vibration

With the second feedback design, one or two motors vibrate at a time to allow the user to interpolate a more precise direction. Vibrating two adjacent motors should theoretically create an illusory single 'phantom sensation' between the two [2]; varying the amplitude and frequency of each motor impacts the specific location of the phantom sensation. Following [2], we logarithmically adjust the amplitude and frequency based on the precise angle we wish to indicate between the motors. To indicate an angle θ between two motors, we calculate:

$$V_1 = V_{max} \times \frac{log(\theta_2 - \theta + 1)}{log(\theta_2 - \theta_1 + 1)}$$

$$V_2 = V_{max} \times \frac{log(\theta - \theta_1 + 1)}{log(\theta_2 - \theta_1 + 1)}$$

where V_1 and V_2 are the voltages on the two adjacent motors and θ_1 and θ_2 are the angles of directions mapped to the two motors as shown in the Figure 2. As with the single motor vibration design, V_{max} was controlled to avoid continuous vibration on the wrist. V_{max} was set to 3V if the difference between the intended direction and the finger movement was greater than 90°. If the difference was less than 22.5°, V_{max} was 0V. If the difference was in the 22.5–90° range, V_{max} linearly ranged from 1V–3V.

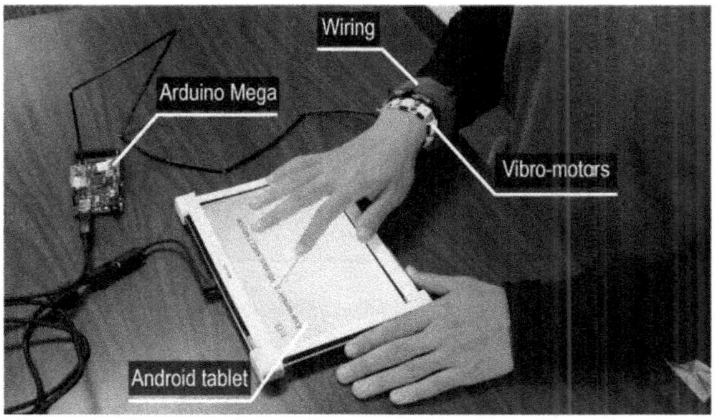

Figure 4. The experimental setup for both studies. Visuals on the screen were for the experimenter and were not visible to sighted participants nor perceptible to blind participants.

4. STUDY 1: INTERPOLATION AND NUMBER OF MOTORS

To gather preliminary data before running a full study with blind and visually impaired participants, we first conducted an initial study with 11 sighted and 2 blind participants. This study included both the 4-motor and 8-motor wristbands as well as the single-motor and interpolated feedback. It was not meant to substitute for evaluation with blind and visually impaired participants but instead allowed us to identify the most promising feedback designs to evaluate later with our VI participants—thus allowing for a simplified and more statistically powerful experimental design.

4.1 Method

4.1.1 Participants

We recruited 11 sighted participants (6 female, 5 male) and two blind participants.[2] The sighted participants were recruited through campus email lists and ranged in age from 19 to 34 (M = 25.3, SD = 4.5); all were right-handed. The blind participants were recruited through a list of potential participants maintained by our research lab. One was 53 years old, male, and right-handed, while the second was 63 years old, female, and left-handed.

4.1.2 Procedure

The study session took up to two hours. We first collected demographic information and touchscreen device experience. The tablet device, which had non-slip feet attached, was placed flat on a table in front the participant, as shown in the Figure 4. The four conditions were presented in counterbalanced order with a five-minute break offered between each one. Sighted participants were blindfolded during the tasks to isolate the effects of the haptic feedback and to provide a better indication of which conditions we should evaluate in the follow-up study with VI participants. The procedure for each condition consisted of the following four steps.

Step 1: Wristband placement and introduction. The experimenter placed the wristband on the participant's wrist and adjusted the position of the motors while the participant held their hand on the tablet screen. To confirm that the motors were perceptually at the correct positions (Figure 2), the experimenter vibrated each one in turn and adjusted its position if the participant reported that it felt off. Participants were then given a brief introduction to the wristband (~5 minutes) that consisted of 16 trials: a motor vibrated, the participant attempted to move their finger in

[2] An additional five sighted participants completed the study but their data was not usable due to a technical problem with Bluetooth where the Arduino and tablet disconnected repeatedly. In Study 2, we resolved this problem by using a wired connection.

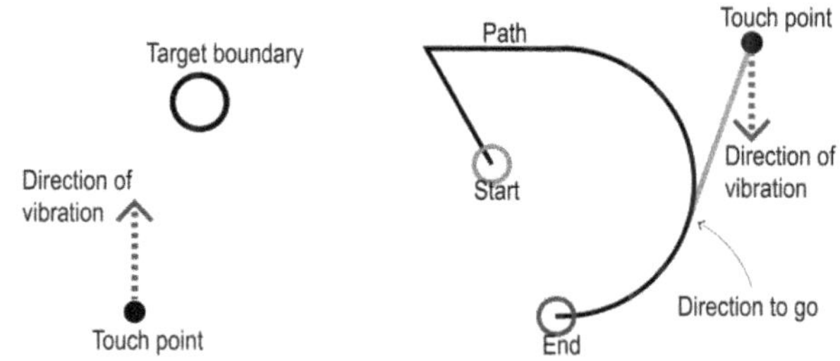

(a) Target-finding task **(b) Path-tracing task**

Figure 5. Single-motor haptic feedback for example target-finding and path-tracing trials. The motor closest to the ideal angle of movement is vibrating. For the path-tracing task, the ideal angle of movement is computed using a tangent line drawn from the touch point to the curve.

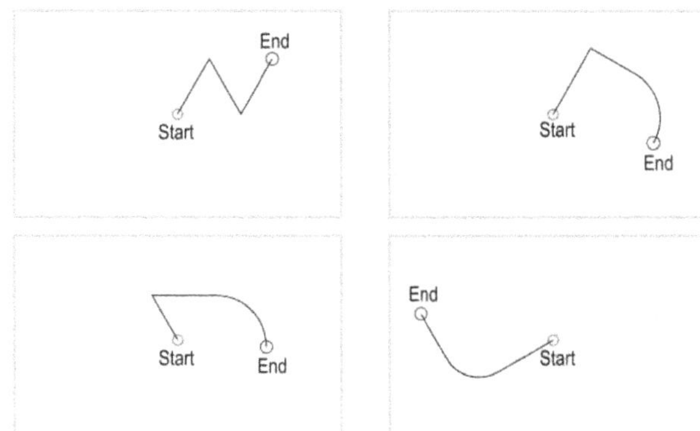

Figure 6. Sample paths used in the path-tracing task. All paths started at the center of the screen.

the direction of the vibration, and the system provided feedback about how close the movement was to the presented angle of movement (perfect: ≤ 5.625° from presented angle, close: > 5.625° and ≤ 22.5°, and incorrect: > 22.5°). If the movement was incorrect, the direction was repeated until the participant moved correctly, with the experimenter giving verbal instructions after two incorrect attempts. For the single-motor feedback conditions, the 16 trials consisted of 4 or 2 trials per motor for the 4-motor and 8-motor wristbands, respectively. For the interpolated feedback conditions, 16 target directions were evenly distributed at 22.5° intervals for both wristbands, with one trial in each direction.

Step 2: Target-finding task (Figure 5a). For the target-finding task, each trial consisted of moving from the center of the touchscreen to a randomly placed circular target (15mm in diameter) with at least 7.5mm buffer (a target radius distance) between the edge of the target and the edge of the screen. A sticker at the center of the tablet provided a tactile indicator of the start location. To begin a trial, the participant placed their finger on the sticker for one second, after which a sound played and wristband vibration indicated the trial had begun. Upon entering the target bounds, an end sound also played. Participants completed 5 training trials and 30 test trials for this task, where the training trials included decreasing levels of experimenter guidance, from physically guiding the participant's finger to having the participant do the trial fully independently. Participants were asked to complete the test trials as quickly and accurately as possible.

Step 3: Path-tracing task (Figures 5b and 6). Following the target-finding task, participants were asked to trace paths (as if they were following a route on a map). We programmatically generated a set of 18 paths based on route features from a real university campus map, including the relative length of segments, the angles between segments, and the ratio of straight to curved segments. Each path consisted of three straight or curved segments, with the constraint that not all three could be curved. The distance between the start and end points of each path was at least 30 mm. The average path length was 140 mm (*SD*=26.4).

During this portion of the study, each participant completed 5 path-tracing training trials presented in the same order followed by 10 test trial paths presented in random order. As with target finding, the experimenter provided decreasing levels of guidance during the training trials. Again, a trial started by placing the finger on the start sticker until a sound played and vibration started. The system then guided the user to trace each segment in turn. For straight segments, the system guided the user to the segment end point in the same manner as guiding to a target in the target-finding task. For curved segments, the system guided the user to the tangent point of a line drawn from the curve to the finger, the location of which was continuously updated as the finger moved (Figure 6). For both straight and curved segments, reaching the "end of the segment" was defined as being within 7.5 mm of the exact end point (*i.e.*, within the radius of a target in the target-finding task). A beep indicated the end of each segment and a chime sound indicated the end of the trial. Again, participants were asked to complete the test trials as quickly and accurately as possible.

Step 4: Subjective feedback. After each condition (*e.g.*, single *vs.* interpolated with 4 *vs.* 8 motors), we asked participants to rate overall experience, ease, accuracy, and speed on 7-point Likert scales, and solicited open-ended feedback. When all conditions were done, we asked participants to select the easiest, fastest, most accurate, most preferred, and least preferred conditions and to provide overall feedback about their experience.

4.1.3 Study Design

The study used a within-subjects design with two factors: *Number of Motors* (4-motor *vs.* 8-motor) and *Vibration Type* (single motor *vs.* interpolation). The order of presentation for the four conditions was counterbalanced using a balanced Latin square and participants were randomly assigned to orders.

4.1.4 Measures and Data Analysis

The main measures were trial completion time and movement error. Trial completion time was computed from the time the vibration started until their finger entered the target bounds for target-finding trials or reached the end of the last segment for path-tracing trials. For target-finding trials, movement error was computed as the ratio of: the actual distance the finger moved during the trial to the Euclidian distance between the start location and the closest point on the target (lower values are better):

$$movement\ error = \frac{finger\ movement\ distance}{shortest\ possible\ distance}$$

For path-tracing trials, movement error was computed by first uniformly resampling the user's actual trace to have one point every 1 mm, then matching the points from the resampled path to the presented path using dynamic time warping (DTW) [6], which measures the distance between two temporal sequences of points. The average of the distances between matched points was then computed as the movement error; lower numbers are better.

For each participant, outlier trials were defined based on trial completion time as being more than 3*IQR (interquartile range) above the upper quartile or less than 3*IQR below the lower quartile within a given experimental condition [39]. In total, 1.6% of trials were excluded from analysis. The trial completion times and movement errors for both tasks violated the normality assumption (Shapiro-Wilk tests, $p < .05$). Therefore, we ran nonparametric analyses using 2-way ANOVA with aligned rank transform (ART) [42]. Bonferroni corrections were used for all posthoc pairwise comparisons.

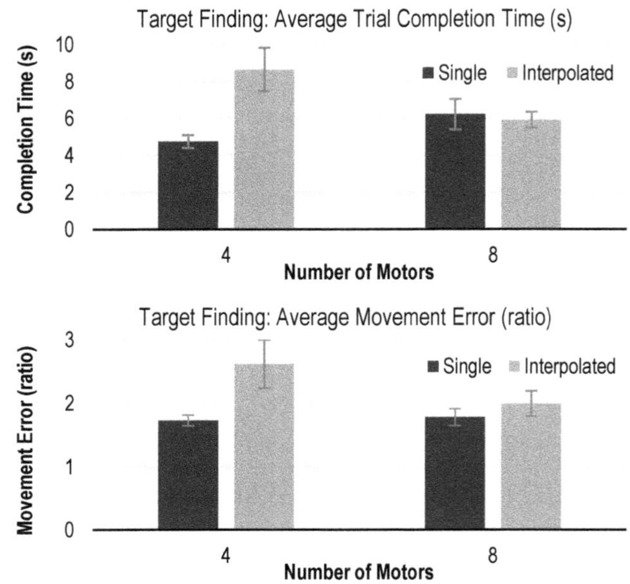

Figure 7. Average trial completion time and movement error for the target-finding task in Study 1, showing interpolated feedback is less accurate than single-motor feedback. Error bars show standard standard error. (*N* = 13)

4.2 Results

We present speed and accuracy for both the target finding and path-tracing tasks, followed by subjective feedback.

4.2.1 Target Finding

Figure 7 (top) shows the average trial completion times for the target-finding task. Overall, the interpolated feedback was slower than the single-motor feedback, at 7.3s per trial on average (*SD* = 3.4) compared to 5.4s (*SD* = 2.3). This difference was significant, as shown by a main effect of *Vibration Type* ($F_{1,36} = 8.83$, $p = .005$, $\eta^2 = 0.21$). While there was no significant effect of *Number of Motors* ($F_{1,36} = 0.53$, $p = .470$, $\eta^2 = 0.04$), there was a significant interaction effect between *Number of Motors* and *Vibration Type*, showing that efficacy of the vibration type depended on how many motors there were ($F_{1,36} = 8.91$, $p = .005$, $\eta^2 = 0.13$). Pairwise comparisons showed that interpolated feedback was slower than single-motor feedback with the 4-motor wristband, at 8.6s per trial on average (*SD* = 4.2) compared to only 4.7s per trial (*SD* = 1.3); this difference was significant with a Wilcoxon signed rank test ($W = 3$, $Z = -2.97$, $p = .001$, $r = 0.58$). In contrast, no difference was found between the two vibration types for the 8-motor wristband with 6.2s per trial (*SD*=3.1) for single motor and 5.9s (*SD*=1.5) for interpolated ($W = 42$, $Z = -0.24$, $p = .839$, $r = 0.05$).

In terms of accuracy (Figure 7, bottom), interpolated feedback also resulted in higher error than single-motor feedback, with a movement error of 2.3 on average (*SD* = 1.1) compared to 1.8 (*SD* = 0.4); this difference was significant, as shown by a main effect of *Vibration Type* ($F_{1,36} = 5.67$, $p = .023$, $\eta^2 = 0.14$). The main effect of *Number of Motors* ($F_{1,36} = 1.71$, $p = .200$, $\eta^2 < 0.01$) and the

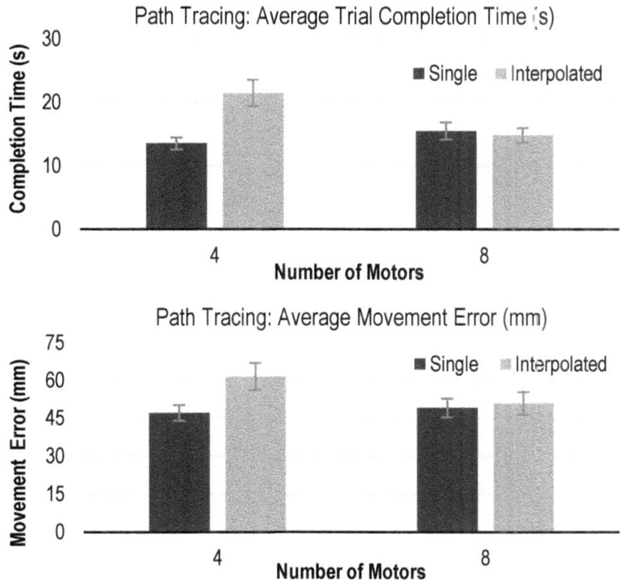

Figure 8. Average trial completion time and movement error for the path-tracing task in Study 1, showing interpolated feedback is slower and less accurate than single-motor feedback. The error bars are standard error. ($N = 13$)

interaction between *Number of Motors* and *Vibration Type* ($F_{1,36}$ = 1.62, p = .212, η^2 = 0.04) were not significant.

4.2.2 Path Tracing

This pattern of findings was similar for the path-tracing task, with interpolated feedback not faring well, particularly with the 4-motor wristband design. Figure 8 (top) shows the average trial completion times. Interpolated feedback was significantly slower than single-motor feedback with average trial times of 18.1s (*SD* = 6.9) compared to 14.5s (*SD* = 4.2); main effect of *Vibration Type* ($F_{1,36}$ = 8.27, p = .007, η^2 = 0.24). The number of motors did not have a significant effect on the trial completion time ($F_{1,36}$ = 4.93, p = .057, η^2 = 0.14); however, there was a significant interaction effect between the *Number of Motors* and the *Vibration Type* ($F_{1,36}$ = 12.5, p = .001, η^2 = 0.15). As with the target-finding task, pairwise comparisons showed that this latter result was due to interpolated feedback slowing participants down only with the 4-motor wristband. Here, trials took on average 21.5s (*SD* = 7.6) with interpolated feedback and 13.5s (*SD* = 3.4) with single-motor feedback, which was a significant difference (W = 90, Z = 3.11, p < .001, r = 0.61). There was no such difference for the 8-motor wristband.

Movement error (Figure 8, bottom) was also significantly higher with interpolated feedback than with single-motor feedback, at 9.5mm on average (*SD* = 3.1) compared to 8.2mm (*SD* = 2.1); main effect of *Vibration Type* ($F_{1,36}$ = 4.66, p = .038, η^2 = 0.11). While the main effect of *Number of Motors* was not significant ($F_{1,36}$ = 2.2, p = .147, η^2 = 0.11), the interaction effect between *Number of Motors* and *Vibration Type* was significant ($F_{1,36}$ = 4.17, p = .048, η^2 = 0.04). As with earlier results, interpolated feedback resulted in higher movement error than single-motor feedback for the 4-motor wristband, at 10.6mm (*SD* = 3.3) versus 8mm (*SD* = 1.9); the difference was significant (W=80, Z = 2.41, p = .013, r = 0.47).

4.2.3 Subjective Responses

Subjective responses reflected the performance results, as shown in Figure 9. Participants consistently rated the 4-motor wristband with interpolation worse than the other three conditions in terms of ease,

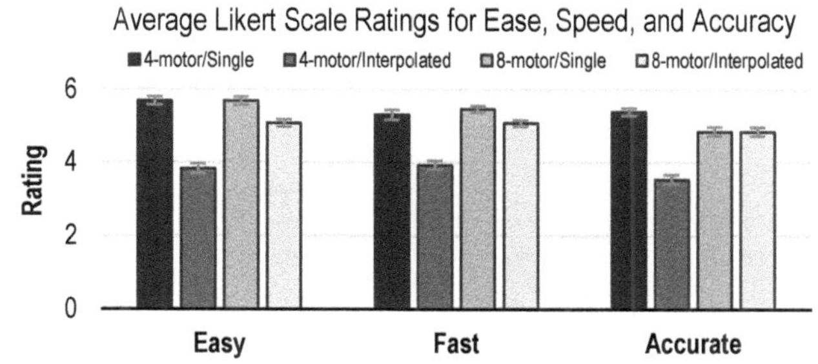

Figure 9. Study 1 subjective ratings on 7-point Likert scales for ease, speed, and accuracy, where 1=*strongly disagree* and 7=*strongly agree.* The single motor condition received higher ratings than interpolated feedback. Error bars are standard error. ($N = 13$)

	4-motors		8-motors	
	Single	Interpolated	Single	Interpolated
Easiest	7	1	4	1
Fastest	6	1	4	2
Most accurate	9	1	3	0
Most preferred	6	2	4	1
Least preferred	0	9	1	3

Table 1. Subjective vote tallies in Study 1, showing 4-motors with interpolation was the least preferred condition. ($N = 13$)

speed, and accuracy. Table 1 shows vote tallies for easiest, fastest, most accurate, and most/least preferred of the four conditions. The single-motor feedback options received more positive votes compared to interpolated feedback options.

4.3 Summary and Discussion

Interpolated feedback was slower and less accurate in both tasks, but was particularly problematic with the 4-motor wristband. Subjective feedback matched this performance data. One limitation of this study is that the sighted participants' performance may not be representative of blind users. However, performance from the two blind participants matched the overall trends comparing single-motor *vs.* interpolated feedback: both blind participants were faster with single-motor feedback for both tasks, while single-motor feedback was more accurate for path tracing for both participants and resulted in mixed accuracy for target finding (one participant was more accurate, one was less accurate). Based on these results, we focused only on single-motor feedback in Study 2 with blind and VI participants.

5. STUDY 2: EVALUATION WITH BLIND AND VISUALLY IMPAIRED USERS

Based on the findings from Study 1, we eliminated the interpolated feedback conditions and conducted a follow-up study with 14 blind and visually impaired participants to compare single-motor feedback with the 4-motor and 8-motor wristbands.

5.1 Method

The study method is largely the same as for the pilot study with a few key changes highlighted below.

5.1.1 Participants

We recruited 14 (8 female, 6 male) visually impaired participants through an existing participant pool and local organizations working with people with visual impairments. Participants were on average 44.8 years old (*SD*=13.9; range 22–64). Seven participants were totally blind, two were blind with light perception, and five were legally blind. All 14 used a screen reader on their computer and/or smartphone. Twelve participants were right handed, one was left handed, and one reported using her left hand for writing tasks and right hand for touchscreen devices (she used her right hand for study tasks). All but one participant owned a touchscreen device. Of the 13 touchscreen device owners, 11 participants reported daily use and 2 participants reported use every few days.

5.1.2 Procedure

The study procedure lasted up to 90 minutes. As we removed the interpolated feedback conditions, we had only two experimental conditions: single-motor feedback with four or eight motors. The conditions were fully counterbalanced and participants completed the same set of tasks with each condition as in Study 1. Due to a steep learning curve that we saw persist into the test trials during Study 1, we also provided more training and increased the number of test trials as follows: (1) After first putting on the wristband, participants completed the same 16 *familiarization* trials as in Study 1; however, an additional trial was appended every time a participant made two consecutive incorrect attempts in a specific direction, up to a maximum of four or eight additional trials depending on the number of motors on the wristband. (2) For the *target-finding* task, participants completed at least 12 training trials including an initial two guided by the experimenter. Additional training trials were added up to a maximum of 20 if the movement error (ratio) was greater than 3.0 in two or more of the most recent five training trials. The number of test trials for target finding also increased from 30 in Study 1 to 36 here. (3) For the *path-tracing* task, participants completed 7 training trials and 12 test trials (up from 5 and 10, respectively in Study 1). (4) Finally, because of comments from some Study 1 participants about desensitization to the haptic vibration, we imposed an eight-minute break between conditions.

5.1.3 Study Design, Measures and Data Analysis

Study 2 included a single experimental factor of *Number of Motors* (4 or 8). This was a within-subjects factor and was fully counterbalanced, with participants randomly assigned to orders. However, to capture possible learning effects, we split the 36 trials in the target-finding task into two blocks of 18 trials each and included *Block* as an additional factor in the analysis of that task. We did not do so for the path-tracing task because of the smaller number of trials and the increased likelihood of any individual trial unduly affecting the average within a block of only nine trials.

As with Study 1, the main measures were *trial completion time* and *movement error*. Outlier trials were detected within each condition per participant using the IQR method as in Study 1. Out of 1,344 test trials in total across the 14 participants, 31 outlier trials (2%) were excluded from data analysis.

Shapiro-Wilk tests showed that trial completion times and movement error violated the normality assumption of parametric tests for both tasks ($p < .05$). Thus, for the target-finding task, a 2-way repeated measures ANOVA (*Number of Motors* x *Block*) with ART was used to anlayze the trial completion time and movement error. We used Wilcoxon signed rank tests to analyze the trial completion time and movement error for the path-tracing task, as well as for subjective ratings.

5.2 Results

We present performance analyses followed by subjective ratings and an analysis of open-ended comments from participants.

5.2.1 Target Finding

As shown in Figure 10 (top), similar to Study 1, participants were again faster with the 4-motor wristband than the 8-motor one, at 7.3s per trial on average ($SD = 4.8$) compared to 9.8ms ($SD = 4.9$). This difference was significant (main effect of *Number of Motors*: $F_{1,39} = 14.51$, $p < .001$, $\eta^2 = 0.05$). The main effect of *Block* was

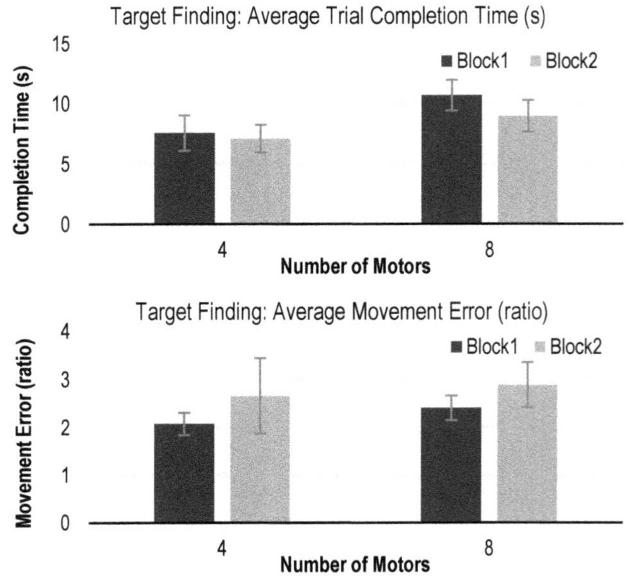

Figure 10. Trial completion time and movement error for the target-finding task in Study 2. The 4-motor wristband was faster and more accurate than the 8-motor wristband. Error bars are standard error. ($N = 14$)

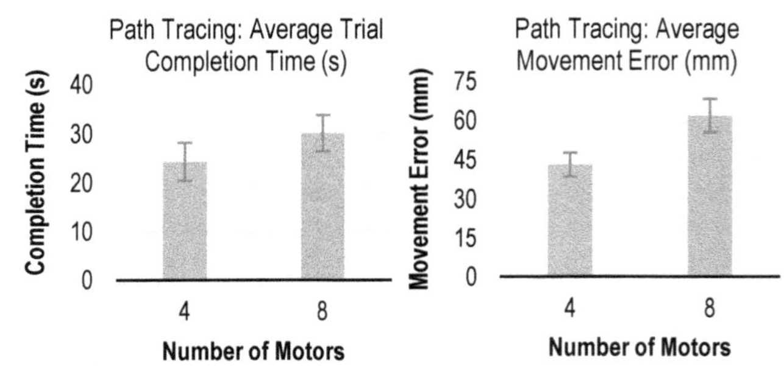

Figure 11. Trial completion time and movement error for the path-tracing task in Study 2. The 4-motor wristband was more accurate than the 8-motor wristband. Error bars are standard error. ($N = 14$)

not statistically significant ($F_{1,39} = 2.54$, $p = .119$, $\eta^2 < 0.01$) nor was the interaction between the two factors ($F_{1,39} = 1.45$, $p = .235$, $\eta^2 < 0.01$).

Participants were also more accurate with the 4-motor wristband than the 8-motor one (Figure 10, bottom). The movement error ratio was on average 2.4 with four motors ($SD = 2.1$) compared to 2.6 with eight motors ($SD = 1.4$), a significant difference (main effect of *Number of Motors*: $F_{1,39} = 5.14$, $p = .029$, $\eta^2 < 0.01$). As with completion time, the main effect of *Block* was not statistically significant ($F_{1,39} = 0.34$, $p = .560$, $\eta^2 = 0.01$) nor was the interaction between the two factors ($F_{1,39} < 0.01$, $p = .947$, $\eta^2 < 0.01$).

5.2.2 Path Tracing

Performance for the path-tracing task is shown in Figure 11. The results partially mirror the target-finding results: participants were not faster with either wristband ($W = 25$, $Z = 1.73$, $p = .091$, $r = 0.33$) but were significantly more accurate with the 4-motor wristband ($W = 12$, $Z = -2.54$, $p = .009$, $r = 0.48$). Trials took on average 24.3s with four motors ($SD = 14.6$) and 30.1s with eight motors ($SD = 13.7$). The movement error was 7.4 mm ($SD = 2.9$) with four motors and 10.6 mm ($SD = 4.1$) with eight motors on average.

	4-motor *M(SD)*	8-motor *M(SD)*	Wilcoxon signed rank test result
Ease of understanding*	6.4 (0.7)	5.2 (1.6)	W=36, z = -2.54, p = .008, r=0.48
Speed	6.1 (0.8)	5.1 (1.2)	W = 61, z = -1.75, p = .085, r = 0.33
Accuracy*	5.9 (1.0)	4.8 (1.1)	W = 59, z = -2.36, p = .021, r = 0.45

Table 2. Subjective ratings on 7-point Likert scales, were 7 indicated strong positive agreement. Measures with statistically significant differences are shown with '*'.

5.2.3 Subjective Feedback

Table 2 shows subjective Likert scale ratings collected at the end of each condition, which largely reflect the performance results. Participants perceived the 4-motor wristband to be significantly easier to understand and more accurate than the 8-motor wristband. No differences were found in perceptions of speed.

When asked about overall preference at the end of the study, participants were split: eight participants preferred the 4-motor feedback while six participants preferred the 8-motor feedback. The most common reason cited for preferring 4-motor feedback was that it was easier to understand (6 participants). For example, P9 said: "*[4-motors] was easier to use and I felt less frustrated. I felt like I did better. I was more sure of [...] which one was vibrating.*" For the 4-motor wristband, some participants mentioned the ease of mapping the vibrations to the four cardinal directions on the tablet screen (one person mentioned this for 8-motor feedback too). One participant also mentioned that with four motors it felt like there was less vibration, whereas with eight motors it felt like the entire hand was vibrating. Finally, one participant appreciated the spacing between motors with the 4-motor option because she had a small wrist.

Reasons for preferring 8-motor feedback included higher perceived accuracy and increased precision. For example, P8 said, "*The feedback is more fine-grained and I like that [...] Instead of a general direction I like precision.*" P3 also mentioned:

> *"...this would be good for [...] not just maps but statistics, because [...] when you put the numbers on a graph, you know, you have more, more to figure out where everything is for charting the graph."* (P3)

At the same time P11 noted the additional information with the 8-motor feedback had some drawbacks, saying: "*I could adjust better [with 8-motor], but I did think that it slowed me down more.*"

Some participants mentioned applications for which they thought the wrist-worn haptic feedback could be useful, including: drawing, navigating maps, plotting graphs, and operating touchscreen devices. At the same time, issues of learning and fatigue arose, suggesting that the haptic designs could be further refined to limit vibration. Eight participants commented that they would have performed better with more practice. For example. P15 mentioned for 8-motor feedback: *"I feel it, I understand. [The] more I was practicing, [the] more I was getting it."* Four participants mentioned that after a while their wrist got tired, and as a result, they had more trouble identifying which motor was vibrating. For example, P07 mentioned for 8-motor feedback: *"After a while [...] the way it jumps [from one direction to another], if there is no constant stopping of vibrations, it kind of starts blending into each other."* We return to this issue in the Discussion section.

5.3 Summary

Study 2 largely reaffirms our Study 1 findings. Participants completed the target-finding task faster and more accurately with the 4-motor wristband than the 8-motor wristband. In the path-tracing task, participants were significantly more accurate when they used 4-motor wristband than 8-motor wristband. The subjective evaluation supported the performance results with positive feedback about the 4-motor wristband.

6. DISCUSSION

Across the two experiments, our findings showed that the fastest, most accurate, and most preferred design was the four-motor wristband with a single-motor vibration. This conclusion is counter to our expectations: we had expected that having more vibromotors (8 *vs.* 4) and attempting to induce precise phantom sensations between adjacent motors would lead to more accurate performance. We discuss this and other issues relevant to future wrist-worn haptic feedback designs below.

6.1 Why Does 4-motor Outperform 8-motor?

We were surprised that doubling the number of haptic actuators around the wrist did not result in performance benefits: the 8-motor design was slower and less accurate than the 4-motor design in both studies. While further work is necessary to uncover why this might be, some possible reasons include vibration transfer, higher cognitive load, and perceptual limitations. Vibration transfer occurs when the actuation of one motor causes one or more adjacent motors to also vibrate. The transfer is a function of the intensity of the actuated motor, the distance and physical connection between the motors, and the wrist itself (*e.g.*, the skin, bone structure). While our elastic band was designed to mitigate vibration transfer, it was not completely suppressed. In particular, because the inter-motor distance was lower with the 8-motor design, transfer would theoretically be higher. The interpolated conditions also used higher combined intensity vibrations than the single-motor conditions, which may have exacerbated transfer problems and created inadvertent phantom sensations or other perceptual issues. In practice, embedding the motors in a solid smartwatch strap or wristband robust enough for daily use will likely result in greater vibration transfer than our elastic design, magnifying the benefits of the 4-motor design over the 8-motor design.

6.2 Designing Wristband Haptics

Creating wrist-worn directional hand guidance systems requires exploring a large design space. In this paper, we built and investigated only a few possible designs. Important design considerations, include: cognitive factors (*e.g.*, understandability, learnability), perceptual factors (*e.g.*, desensitization, phantom sensations), as well as the design of the wristband, haptic hardware, and underlying software algorithms to actuate those haptics.

Early in our design process, we examined a range of haptic hardware, including muscle wire (shape memory Nitinol), tactors, piezoelectrics, and vibromotors. We settled vibromotors based on our internal experiments and results from prior work (*e.g.*, [18]). In the haptics literature, two vibromotor designs are common: ERM and LRA. We initially built and examined prototypes for both. While LRAs are attractive because they offer faster response times than ERMs and allow for independent control of amplitude and frequency, our internal tests showed that our ERM design performed better. For example, in a small pilot test with three participants, all participants performed faster and more accurately with the ERM prototype than the LRA prototype. Consequently, we refined and used the ERM prototype in this paper.

As with the haptic hardware, designing an appropriate haptic feedback signal is a difficult design problem. One needs to consider the hardware response time, the intensity and frequency of the vibration, and the vibro-modulation pattern. To help inform the approach used in this paper, we designed four guidance methods. Three of the four methods used *corrective guidance*—that is, the vibromotors were actuated only when the user's finger trajectory and the intended direction differed by at least 22.5°. Of these corrective guidance approaches, one vibrated at maximum intensity regardless of the magnitude of the difference, one increased linearly as the angular difference increased, and the third increased in a small number of discrete steps as the angular difference increased. A fourth option was to use a pulse vibration (100ms on / 100ms off) to indicate intended direction, regardless of the difference between the actual and intended direction. Among the four methods, the corrective guidance with linear change in vibration was fastest and most accurate in our pilot tests, so it was selected for our studies. However, further work may yield improved haptic feedback designs (*e.g.*, more perceptible feedback patterns).

6.3 Effect of Age and Technology Experience

Before refining our prototypes and approach for Study 2, we attempted to replicate Study 1 with 22 blind participants (M=54.3 years old; SD=10). In contrast to our Study 1 and Study 2 experiences, only 10 of the 22 participants in this interim study could complete the experiment within the allotted time; the other 12 dropped out early or were unable to complete all tasks. This experience partly motivated us to increase the number of training and test trials in Study 2. At the same time, participant age and overall familiarity with technology may have played a role in the low success rates in this interim study. The interim study participants were older than in Studies 1 and 2: on average 54.3 years old (compared to 28.3 in Study 1 and 44.8 in Study 2). Age is an important variable given that older persons have lower sensitivity for perceiving vibration stimulus on the skin [11]. The interim participants also had less experience with touchscreen technology, with only 14 of the 22 owning a touchscreen device, compared to almost all participants in Studies 1 and 2.

6.4 Limitations and Future Work

The results and limitations of our studies reveal several directions for future work. First, some participants mentioned fatigue from using the haptic feedback, which may be partly due to desensitization. While we attempted to mitigate desensitization by providing corrective guidance rather than continuous vibration (Section 3.2), it could have impacted some feedback designs more than others (*e.g.*, interpolated *vs.* simple); for example, desensitization occurs more quickly at higher intensity levels [5] and with more sustained activation [23]. We also included 5-8 minute breaks between conditions, but recovery time between vibration stimuli is still an active area of research (most work suggests 30 secs to 3 mins, *e.g.*, [5, 14, 23]). Ultimately, to limit fatigue, wrist-based haptic feedback may be most applicable to short tasks (*e.g.*, learning a new route, exploring a drawing, reading a flyer) rather than in-depth tasks (*e.g.*, reading a book line-by-line). It is also possible that fatigue lessens as participants gain experience. Future work should explore these concerns further.

Second, some participants indicated needing more time to learn and effectively use our wristband prototypes. While we examined learnability by splitting Study 2 into blocks, we found no clear learning effect during the duration of the target-finding task. Future work should examine how performance changes with time by using a more longitudinal study design.

Third, while our study tasks were developed to model two common real-world tasks, finding a target and tracing a route, more work is necessary to understand whether the observed performance numbers are accurate enough to provide value in practice (*e.g.*, did participants have a strong conceptual understanding of the paths that they tried?). It will also be important to explore other applications, such as drawing, plotting graphs, and operating touchscreen devices in general, as suggested by participants.

Fourth, our focus was on isolating the effects of specific wrist-based haptic designs but non-haptic and hybrid approaches should also be considered (*e.g.*, sonification or vocal directions like "move up"). Note, however, that the audio channel is often overloaded in assistive applications and audio directional guidance can interfere with speech output (*e.g.*, screenreaders) [38].

7. CONCLUSION

In this paper, we report on the design and evaluation of two haptic wristbands, 4-motor *vs.* 8-motor, and two actuation approaches, simple (single motor) *vs.* interpolated (two motor). Our Study 1 findings showed that participants could non-visually find targets and trace paths more quickly and accurately with single-motor feedback than with interpolated feedback, particularly with the 4-motor design. In Study 2, we eliminated the interpolated feedback conditions and found that single-motor feedback with four motors was faster, more accurate, and most preferred by blind participants compared to similar feedback with eight motors. Our results help establish important benchmarks for future work and contribute to the growing body of hand guidance research.

8. ACKNOWLEDGMENTS

We thank Hong Tan, David Ross, and the Atlanta VAMC. This work was funded by the Office of the Assistant Secretary of Defense for Health Affairs under Award W81XWH-14-1-0617.

9. REFERENCES

[1] Aggravi, M., Salvietti, G. and Prattichizzo, D. 2016. Haptic wrist guidance using vibrations for Human-Robot teams. *IEEE 25th Intl Symposium on Robot and Human Interactive Communication (RO-MAN)*, 113–118.

[2] Alles, D.S. 1970. Information Transmission by Phantom Sensations. *IEEE Transactions on Man-Machine Systems*. 11, 1 (1970), 85–91.

[3] Amemiya, T., Yamashita, J., Hirota, K. and Hirose, M. 2004. Virtual leading blocks for the deaf-blind: A real-time way-finder by verbal-nonverbal hybrid interface and high-density RFID tag space. *Virtual Reality Annual International Symposium*. (2004), 165–172.

[4] Arter, C., McCall, S. and Bowyer, T. 1996. Handwriting and children with visual impairments. *British Journal of Special Education*. 23, 1 (1996), 25–28.

[5] Berglund, U. and Berglund, B. 1970. Adaptation and recovery in vibrotactile perception. *Perceptual and motor skills*. 30, 3 (1970), 843–853.

[6] Berndt, D. & Clifford, J. 1994. Using dynamic time warping to find patterns in time series. *KDD workshop'94*, 359–370.

[7] Bosman, S., Groenendaal, B., Findlater, J., Visser, T., de Graaf, M. and Markopoulos, P. 2003. GentleGuide: An exploration of haptic output for indoors pedestrian guidance. *HCI with Mobile Devices and Services'03*, 358–362.

[8] Brock, A., Kammoun, S., Macé, M. and Jouffrais, C. 2014. Using wrist vibrations to guide hand movement and whole body navigation. *i-com*. 13, 3 (Jan. 2014), 19–28.

[9] Carcedo, M.G., Chua, S.H., Perrault, S., Wozniak, P., Joshi, R., Obaid, M., Fjeld, M. and Zhao, S. 2016. Hapticolor:

Interpolating color information as haptic feedback to assist the colorblind. *Proc. of CHI'16*, 3572–3583.

[10] Chen, H.Y., Santos, J., Graves, M., Kim, K. and Tan, H.Z. 2008. Tactor localization at the wrist. *Lecture Notes in Computer Science*. 5024 LNCS, (2008), 209–218.

[11] Cholewiak, R.W. and Collins, A. a 2003. Vibrotactile localization on the arm: effects of place, space, and age. *Perception {&} psychophysics*. 65, 7 (2003), 1058–1077.

[12] Cosgun, A., Sisbot, E.A. and Christensen, H.I. 2014. Evaluation of rotational and directional vibration patterns on a tactile belt for guiding visually impaired people. *IEEE Haptics Symposium, HAPTICS*. (2014), 367–370.

[13] Crossan, A. and Brewster, S. 2008. Multimodal trajectory playback for teaching shape information and trajectories to visually impaired computer users. *ACM Trans. Access. Comput.* 1, 2 (Oct. 2008), 12:1--12:34.

[14] van Erp, J.B.F. 2002. Guidelines for the Use of Vibro-Tactile Displays in Human Computer Interaction. *Proceedings of Eurohaptics*. (2002), 18–22.

[15] Ertan, S., Lee, C., Willets, A., Tan, H. and Pentland, A. 1998. A wearable haptic navigation guidance system. *Proc. of ISWC'98*. 164–165.

[16] Goldreich, D. & Kanics, I. 2003. Tactile Acuity is Enhanced in Blindness. *J. Neurosci.* 23, 8 (Apr. 2003), 3439–3445.

[17] Hirose, M. and Amemiya, T. 2003. Wearable Finger-Braille interface for navigation of Deaf-Blind in ubiquitous barrier-free space. *Proc. HCI International'03*, 1417–1421.

[18] Hong, J., Stearns, L., Froehlich, J., Ross, D. and Findlater, L. 2016. Evaluating Angular Accuracy of Wrist-based Haptic Directional Guidance for Hand Movement. *Proceedings of the 42nd Graphics Interface Conference* (2016), 195–200.

[19] How to Make a Sliding Knot (single knot) - jewelry making tutorial: 2012. *https://youtu.be/t6Qy5WdSq74*.

[20] Kammoun, S., Jouffrais, C., Guerreiro, T., Nicolau, H. and Jorge, J. 2012. Guiding Blind People with Haptic Feedback. *Pervasive 2012 Workshop on Frontiers in Accessibility for Pervasive Computing* (Jan. 2012).

[21] Kim, K., Ren, X., Choi, S. and Tan, H.Z. 2016. Assisting people with visual impairments in aiming at a target on a large wall-mounted display. *International Journal of Human-Computer Studies*. 86, (2016), 109–120.

[22] Lee, J., Han, J. and Lee, G. 2015. Investigating the Information Transfer Efficiency of a 3x3 Watch-back Tactile Display. *Proc of CHI'15*, 1229–1232.

[23] Leung, Y.Y., Bensmaia, S.J., Hsiao, S.S. and Johnson, K.O. 2005. Time-course of vibratory adaptation and recovery in cutaneous mechanoreceptive afferents. *Journal of neurophysiology*. 94, 5 (2005), 3037–3045.

[24] Mann, S., Huang, J., Janzen, R., Lo, R., Rampersad, V., Chen, A. and Doha, T. 2011. Blind navigation with a wearable range camera and vibrotactile helmet. *Proc. of MM'11*, 1325-1328.

[25] Matscheko, M., Ferscha, A., *et al.* 2010. Tactor placement in wrist worn wearables. *Proc. of ISWC'10*, 1–8.

[26] Oh, U., Kane, S.K. and Findlater, L. 2013. Follow That Sound: Using Sonification and Corrective Verbal Feedback to Teach Touchscreen Gestures. *Proc. of ASSETS'13*, 13:1--13:8.

[27] Panëels, S., Brunet, L. and Strachan, S. 2013. Strike a Pose: Directional Cueing on the Wrist and the Effect of Orientation. *Haptic and Audio Interaction Design*. I. Oakley and S. Brewster, eds. Springer Berlin Heidelberg. 117–126.

[28] Parseihian, G., Gondre, C., Aramaki, M., Ystad, S. and Kronland-Martinet, R. 2016. Comparison and evaluation of sonification strategies for guidance tasks. *IEEE Transactions on Multimedia*. 18, 4 (2016), 674–686.

[29] Pasquero, J., Stobbe, S. & Stonehouse, N. 2011. A haptic wristwatch for eyes-free interactions. *CHI'11*, 3257–3266.

[30] Richter, H., Blaha, B. and Wiethoff, A. 2011. Tactile feedback without a big fuss: simple actuators for high-resolution phantom sensations. *Proc. of UbiComp '11*. (2011), 85–88.

[31] Sampaio, E., Maris, S. and Bach-y-Rita, P. 2001. Brain plasticity: "visual" acuity of blind persons via the tongue. *Brain research*. 908, 2 (Jul. 2001), 204–7.

[32] Scheggi, S., Talarico, A. and Prattichizzo, D. 2014. A remote guidance system for blind and visually impaired people via vibrotactile haptic feedback. *22nd Mediterranean Conference on Control and Automation* (Jun. 2014), 20–23.

[33] Schoof, Loren T., I. 1974. An analysis of Optacon usage. (Nov. 1974).

[34] Schwerdt, H.N., Tapson, J. and Etienne-Cummings, R. 2009. A color detection glove with haptic feedback for the visually disabled. *Information Sciences and Systems, 2009. CISS 2009. 43rd Annual Conference on* (2009), 681–686.

[35] Sergi, F., Accoto, D., Campolo, D. and Guglielmelli, E. 2008. Forearm orientation guidance with a vibrotactile feedback bracelet: On the directionality of tactile motor communication. *IEEE/RAS-EMBS Biomedical Robotics and Biomechatronics, BioRob 2008*, 433–438.

[36] Shilkrot, R., Huber, J., Wong, M.E., Maes, P. and Nanayakkara, S. 2015. FingerReader: a wearable device to explore printed text on the go. *Proc. of CHI '15*, 2363–2372.

[37] Stearns, L., Du, R., Oh, U., Jou, C., Findlater, L., Ross, D.A. and Froehlich, J.E. 2016. Evaluating Haptic and Auditory Directional Guidance to Assist Blind People in Reading Printed Text Using Finger-Mounted Cameras. *ACM Trans. on Accessible Computing*. 9, 1 (Oct. 2016), 1–38.

[38] Stearns, L., Du, R., Oh, U., Jou, C., Findlater, L., Ross, D.A. and Froehlich, J.E. 2016. Evaluating Haptic and Auditory Directional Guidance to Assist Blind People in Reading Printed Text Using Finger-Mounted Cameras. *ACM Transactions on Accessible Computing*. (2016).

[39] Upton, G. and Cook, I. 1996. *Understanding statistics*. Oxford University Press.

[40] Weber, B., Schätzle, S., Hulin, T., Preusche, C., Deml, B., Schatzle, S., Hulin, T., Preusche, C. and Deml, B. 2011. Evaluation of a vibrotactile feedback device for spatial guidance. *IEEE World Haptics Conference'11*, 349–354.

[41] Wilson, G. and Brewster, S.A. 2016. Using Dynamic Audio Feedback to Support Peripersonal Reaching in Young Visually Impaired People. *Proc. of ASSETS'16*, 209–218.

[42] Wobbrock, J.O., Findlater, L., Gergle, D. and Higgins, J.J. 2011. The Aligned Rank Transform for Nonparametric Factorial Analyses Using Only Anova Procedures. *Proc. of CHI'11*, 143–146.

Technology-Mediated Sight: A Case Study of Early Adopters of a Low Vision Assistive Technology

Annuska Zolyomi, Anushree Shukla, and Jaime Snyder
Information School
University of Washington
Seattle, WA 98195 USA
{annuska, ashukla3, jas1208}@uw.edu

ABSTRACT
A case study of early adopters of a head-mounted assistive device for low vision provides the basis for a sociotechnical analysis of technology-mediated sight. Our research complements recent work in HCI focused on designing, building, and evaluating the performance of assistive devices for low vision by highlighting psychosocial and adaptive aspects of digitally enhanced vision. Through a series of semi-structured interviews with users of the eSight 2.0 device and customer-facing employees of the eSight company, we sought to better understand the social and emotional impacts associated with adoption of this type of low-vision assistive technology. Four analytic themes emerged from our interviews: 1) assessing the value of assistive technology in real life, 2) negotiating social engagement, 3) boundaries of sight, and 4) attitudes toward and expectations of technology. We introduce the concept of *multiplicities of vision* to describe technology-mediated sight as being a form of skilled vision and neither fully-human nor fully-digital, but rather, assembled through a combination of social and technical affordances. We propose that instead of seeing low-vision users through a deficit model of sight, HCI designers have more to gain by viewing people with low vision as individuals with a distinct type of skilled vision that is both socially and technologically mediated.

CCS Concepts
H.5.1. Information Interfaces and Presentations:
Multimedia Information Systems; K.4.2. Computers and Society: Social Issues.

Keywords
Low vision; assistive technology; head-mounted systems; qualitative research.

1. INTRODUCTION
Globally, 246 million people have "low vision," an umbrella term for moderate to severe visual impairments [39]. While much of this population is completely blind, a larger portion has partial vision. These individuals can experience acuity loss, high sensitivity to light, blind spots, and other disruptions of the visual field.

A growing set of assistive technologies (AT) for people with low vision are emerging that take advantage of recent developments in computer vision, wearable technologies, and battery life. In contrast to permanent and invasive treatment like surgery, these devices provide a temporary, relatively low risk option for those with vision loss. However, users of low vision head-mounted displays (HMDs) are still in the minority among the population of people with low vision. In adopting this technology, tradeoffs are often made between social, emotional, and biological factors. Our study contributes empirical evidence in the form of rich, qualitative descriptions of users' psychosocial experiences when integrating technology-mediated sight into their daily lives.

We conducted a case study of early adopters of the second release of the eSight eyewear (Figure 1), a hands-free assistive device marketed to people with low vision throughout the U.S. and Canada. Through this case study, we ask:

- What is the emergent, social, and emotional nature of visual experience made available to low vision users through AT, specifically the eSight HMD?
- How is this experience of vision assembled via a combination of social and technical affordances?
- What are the implications of these experiences for the design of assistive and augmentative technologies in the future?

Figure 1. Users of the eSight 2.0 device. Credit: eSight Corporation.

To explore these questions, we conducted semi-structured interviews with thirteen users of eSight 2.0 and three eSight employees who direct and conduct customer screening interviews, initial fittings, and training sessions. User narratives about integrating AT into their daily lives surfaced themes regarding 1) assessing the value of AT in real life, 2) negotiating social engagement, 3) boundaries of sight, and 4) attitudes toward and expectations of technology. We introduce the concept of *multiplicities of vision* to describe technology-mediated sight as being 1) a form of skilled vision and 2) neither fully human nor fully digital, but rather, continuously assembled through a combination of social and technical affordances.

ASSETS '17, October 29-November 1, 2017, Baltimore, MD, USA

ACM 978-1-4503-4926-0/17/10$15.00
https://doi.org/10.1145/3132525.3132552

2. BACKGROUND

We describe the experience of low vision, provide a brief overview of current AT for people with low vision, and then describe the eSight 2.0 device used by the participants in our study.

2.1 The experience of low vision

Vision is typically described in terms of three characteristics: visual acuity, contrast sensitivity, and visual field perception [3,16]. There are four levels of visual acuity: normal vision, moderate visual impairment, severe visual impairment, and blindness. "Normal" or typical vision is described as 20/20. If you have reduced visual acuity, for example 20/60 vision, you can see detail at 20 feet that a typically sighted person can see at 60 feet. You are considered legally blind if either: 1) your vision is 20/200 vision or worse, even with corrective lenses, or 2) your visual field is 20 degrees or less [2].

Refractive errors cause conditions such as myopia (nearsightedness), hyperopia (farsightedness), astigmatism (irregular curvature of the lens), or presbyopia (inelasticity of the lens) that can typically be treated with corrective lenses or surgery [38]. However, if these refractive conditions cannot be corrected, the person is considered to have low vision. Other low vision conditions include macular degeneration (degeneration of the retina), diabetic retinopathy (diabetes related disease of the retina), amblyopia (dim vision), glaucoma (distress on the optic nerve caused by pressure within the eyeball), and Stargardt disease (juvenile macular degeneration) [1]. In these cases, people often have some functioning sight but can experience significant blind spots, limited field of view or have other disruptions to their visual field; significant acuity loss; trouble seeing at a distance; and particular sensitivity to light levels. Many also suffer from headaches and eye tremors. Visual impairments such as these "cause a number of disabilities including difficulty with reading, writing, recognizing faces, watching television, orientation and mobility, and completing activities of daily living" [16, p. 495].

2.2 Assistive technologies (AT) for people with low vision

There are currently multiple technologies available to help people with low vision accomplish daily tasks [18,35]. Many of these tools provide access to digital devices such as desktop computers, laptops, mobile phones, and public kiosks [6,34] through screen magnification, text-to-speech, and speech-to-text (dictation and command-and-control) software and hardware. Applications built into operating systems also enable users to enlarge the size of text and elements on the screen using font and zoom settings. Many of these technologies require the text to be in a readable format through Optical Character Recognition [12]. Audio books and video-camera-based magnifiers, including closed circuit televisions (CCTVs), are common tools for people with low vision to access print media. People with low vision use mainstream mobile phone cameras to zoom in on faraway objects and use applications for specific functionality such as scanning a barcode on a product while shopping [35]. However, these strategies are unreliable due to screen glare, poor photo resolution, and concerns about having the phone lost or stolen while in outdoor, public spaces.

As mainstream technology has moved toward mobile and wearable devices, so has the low vision field. A recent trend has been portable HMD, like the eSight device, that provide magnification and contrast enhancements using optoelectronics and video technology. Two notable early examples of HMD for individuals with low vision are the Low Vision Enhancement System (LVES) [23,36] and Jordy [13]. LVES, released in 1994 by Johns Hopkins University and NASA, is a battery-powered, portable system providing real-time video image processing and eye-tracking capabilities [22]. Jordy, launched in 1998 by Enhanced Vision Systems, provides 16 levels of magnification and can be head mounted or used with a docking station [13]. Recently, HCI researchers have turned to augmented reality devices, including Google Glass and custom prototypes [e.g., 10,42,43]. For example, Zhao et al. created ForeSee [42], a general purpose real time video system with five enhancement methods: magnification, contrast enhancement, edge enhancement, black/white reversal, and text extraction. Other HMD for people with low vision have been designed and optimized for specific scenarios, such as exercise [29], theaters [21], and video games [41].

2.3 eSight eyewear

For our study, we focused on early adopters of eSight 2.0 eyewear. Marketed since 2013 by Ottawa-based eSight Corporation, the device is currently used by over one thousand individuals with low vision in the US and Canada and has received attention in popular media [8]. The eSight device is classified as a Class 1 Medical Device and is appropriately registered with the US Federal Drug Administration (USFDA) and Health Canada. It has been the subject of a study conducted by the Canadian National Institute for the Blind (CNIB) which established that it "offers a statistically significant improvement in visual acuity and contrast sensitivity for users" [9].

The head-mounted camera system captures live video sent through a small portable computer (about the size of a paperback book) that is worn or carried by the user. Proprietary software is used to process the video one pixel at a time, optimizing for the user's visual impairment. A full-color digital image is displayed in real-time on high-resolution near-to-eyes organic-LED (OLED) screens that are held in place by an eyeglass frame with adjustable headband. The screens provide 35-degree field of view and 4x3 aspect ratio, with adjustable pupil spacing and integrated prescription lenses. The 2.0 version of the eyewear weighs less than 200 grams, has a battery life of about four hours, and costs approximately US$15,000. (The recently released eSight 3.0 is smaller with improved performance and costs US$10,000 [9] but was not yet available at the time of data collection.)

The device uses a combination of automated settings and physical user controls located on a portable CPU/battery pack. The system permits immersive and bioptic use, including magnification (up to 14x) and color, contrast, and brightness enhancements. Users can instantly switch from near vision (reading a document) to midrange vision (looking up to see who just entered the room) to long range vision (looking out the window to see if it is raining). It is also possible to connect the device directly to a monitor or TV (bypassing the camera) and to take and store still images from video output.

2.4 Challenges to Assistive Technology Acceptance

While HMDs offer promise for the future, there are challenges to getting AT for low vision to the people who stand to benefit most. Potential users can have limited awareness of emerging or established technologies that could meet their needs [25]. Often, acquiring an AT is a decision made not only by the end user, but is a negotiation with family, educators, therapists, and employers. Power dynamics among these stakeholders can influence the priorities assigned to the user's needs, the allocation of resources, and the social acceptance of AT use. [27]. Related concerns have been raised about the expense of devices like eSight and the lack of financial support provided through federal programs or private health insurance [6].

Having a vision impairment and using AT can influence a person's identity and their social interactions in profound ways [17,24], depending on factors such as age of onset or having families members with similar conditions [26]. Users of AT report that mastering their AT gave them an increased sense of independence and productivity [31]. However, social stigma is a key deterrent to use [26,27,31]. Some individuals felt that using non-mainstream technology brought attention to their disability and increased the perceived "otherness" of having a disability. They felt that they were subject to misperceptions that people with disabilities have a continual need for assistance and would be "helpless without their device" [27, p.705]. While social acceptability is a primary concern [18,42], some believe that social stress will lessen as awareness of technology-mediated accommodations grows and social norms change [28].

Further challenges to AT use over time are related to changing user needs depending on task, context, and stage of visual condition [37]. The value that people with progressive or chronic diseases place on AT can change over time, as their condition evolves, degrades, or improves [26]. People with low vision can have complex relationships with technology as a result of personal experiences devising adaptive strategies to work around accessibility issues [18,19]. In spite of the potential for peers and colleagues to express limiting views about their technology-mediated abilities [25], in Lazar's study, blind individuals exhibited a higher tolerance for frustrating web experiences than sighted users.

In summary, the changing landscape of AT for low vision spurred by mainstream advances in mobile, wearable and virtual technologies has highlighted the need to better understand how the use of these technologies unfolds in the real world. Researchers in low vision AT and augmented reality have called for deeper exploration of the lived experiences and friction points of using low vision AT [12,32] and, specifically, wearables [20,42]. Our research contributes to this growing area of research by examining the psychosocial dynamics of vision and AT through the experiences of early adopters of the eSight eyewear.

3. Methods

3.1 Participants

For the user interviews, we worked with eSight to identify 13 users (6 female, 7 male) over the age of 25 (average age of 52) who had a minimum of 5-10 years with vision loss and experienced profound shifts in vision when using the eSight device, as measured by Best Corrected Visual Acuity (BCVA). We conducted interviews over Skype or telephone, which allowed us to reach a broad geographic range across the U.S. and Canada. The participants were trained or employed in, or retired from, occupations such as information technology support, nursing, marine engineering, teaching, electrician, office administration, kitchen design, and visual art.

Many but not all of our participants participated in social services established by government and community organizations such as the CNIB. These services included education services for disabled students in elementary and post-secondary education, vision rehabilitation, occupational therapy, and adaptive sports groups. Our interview participants described having a range of visual conditions, acuity, and physiological experiences with vision loss (Table 1).

Most of our participants described changes in their experience of visual impairment over time, such as lessening eyesight due to chronic degenerative eye disease; unexpected loss of sight due to medical complications; and progressive worsening of congenital eye conditions over time, especially as a result of aging. One participant reported improvement in sight over time.

Participants reported using a variety of low vision aids (LVAs) and AT over time, typically spurred by changes in their visual condition and evolving needs. LVAs included hand held magnifiers, binoculars, CCTVs, large print books, audio books, canes, and guide dogs. For digital access, many reported using the screen magnifier and text-to-speech functions of software such as ZoomText and Kurzweil. Hardware adaptations included large print keyboards and hand-held magnifiers. One participant had previously owned two early HMDs, LVES and Jordy. All participants had been using the eSight eyewear for at least one year.

Table 1. Visual and sensory conditions of participants who use eSight.

#	Visual Condition	Onset
P01	Stargardt disease (Central blind spot; sees colors as tones)	Child
P02	One eye totally blind; other eye low acuity	Adult
P03	Folia of eye unusable; low acuity	Birth
P04	Low acuity; color blind	Birth
P05	Optic Nerve Hypoplasia; low resolution; eyes rotate. Also: Congenital hearing loss; Hand and head tremors	Birth
P06	Macular degeneration	Adult
P07	Macular degeneration; Peripheral vision is green	Adult
P08	Stargardt disease (Central vision is disappearing)	Adult
P09	One eye Glaucoma and Uveitis resulting in loss of eye; other eye Global rupture resulting in no central vision	Child
P10	Myopia; lazy eye; stigmatism; Macular degeneration	Birth
P11	Usher's Syndrome (No colors; no night vision; cannot see faces anymore). Also: Hearing loss	Adult
P12	Visual Ocular Albinism; Nystagmus	Birth
P13	Legally blind. Also: Multiple Sclerosis	Adult

We supplemented the eSight user interviews with semi-structured interviews with three eSight employees who are involved in demonstrating eSight to potential users as well as fitting and training new users. These activities have given these individuals insight into non-use, barriers to adoption, and typical challenges faced by new users.

3.2 Data collection

Our one hour interviews followed a semi-structured format based on the critical incident technique of eliciting and documenting participant narratives [11]. This technique asks participants to recall a specific, significant activity and recount what they "saw, heard or felt" [11, p. 329] during the unfolding of that event. Early transitional experiences with the eSight eyewear were positioned as critical incidents in the long-term adaptation to technology-mediated sight.

Semi-structured interviews with eSight employees focused on initial customer screening, fitting, training, and post-purchase support. The participants were asked to describe the necessary visual qualifications for using eSight, and customers' concerns about adoption and daily use.

3.3 Analysis

Our analytic process followed a grounded and inductive approach [4,5]. Three members of the research team reviewed interview notes and transcripts, collectively identifying a set of emergent *initial codes*, reflecting the concerns, discourse and perspectives of the individuals in our study. Further discussion and review of interviews resulted in these initial codes being refined to a set of 14 *focused codes* across 4 main analytic themes (Table 2).

Table 2. Main themes and focused codes. Frequency of each code is in parentheses ( ).

Assessing the value of AT in real life
• *Rationale*- Why AT was used or not used in a given situation (265) • *Sharing AT*- Accounts of sharing AT with others (both with and without visual impairment), often for the purpose of showing the benefits (48) • *Impairment positives*- Instances where a lack of fully functioning eyesight was described in positive terms (14)
Negotiating social engagement
• *Inclusion*- Having (or lacking) ability to fully participate or perform in social life with a sense of equity or parity (87) • *Independence*- Having (or lacking) ability to accomplish day-to-day tasks without assistance (60) • *Contributing*- Having (or lacking) ability to provide, give, or share through work, wages, labor, etc. (52) • *Discernibility*- Instances where a visual impairment went unnoticed or unnoted (or should/could have) (28) • *Nonverbal communication*- Social interactions that relied on body language, facial expressions, physical proximity, or other nonverbal expressions (19)
Boundaries of sight
• *Depth, distance and transitions*- Instances where the experience of vision was described in terms of space (87) • *Seeing yourself see*- Reflections on what it is like to see, both with and without AT (75) • *Superpowers*- AT giving users the ability to do things that people with typical eyesight could not do (19)
Attitudes and expectations of technology
• *Responses to visual impairment*- Actions taken as a direct response to visual impairment (e.g., help sought, changes to living environment, lifestyle changes) (140) • *Expectations*- Assumptions, anticipations, or suppositions about what the future will hold (125) • *Attitudes and experiences with technology*- References to involvement with or feelings towards technology in general (not just AT) (79)

These codes were applied to the 13 eSight user interviews through a multistep process using nVivo qualitative analysis software. At least two researchers coded each interview; and at least two researchers reviewed each coded segment. Differences were deliberated until consensus was reached. Codes were applied parsimoniously by focusing on the primary concept being discussed by participants in each passage. However, because some emergent themes were complex and inter-related, a small portion of the coded passages were assigned more than one code (approximately 13%). Throughout this process, *analytic search* was used to identify key corroborating and potentially conflicting examples, resulting in a refined annotated codebook (available upon request) [4]. Thematic analysis was also performed on the research memos from the eSight employee interviews.

4. Findings

Here we provide brief summaries of each of the four main themes that emerged from our interviews with eSight users, highlighting focused codes most relevant to our research questions.

4.1 Theme 1: Assessing the value of AT in real life

We observed that the decision to purchase and use a given AT is a fluid, dynamic choice, influenced by growing awareness of different AT and access to financial resources. This finding expanded related research on the challenges of AT use by highlighting the perceived value of AT over the course of a lifetime. As people's visual conditions fluctuated and life circumstances shifted, they experienced changes in their emotional readiness to adopt AT. The majority of our participants had experimented with two or more visual aids. As children, choice of AT was typically initiated by parents or school staff. As the participants became adults, the scope of influence on AT use widened to include key family members, workplace policies, available resources, and advocacy by community organizations like CNIB.

Experimentation with AT use was primarily driven by a need for mobility and to be able to see things at different focal planes. For example, P05 explained: *"Using binoculars were not flexible enough. Constantly having to adjust them for different distances. I'm better off to stand next to [the] presentation screen."* Participants described using more traditional AT, such as walking canes or guide dogs, with mixed feelings about inclusion and stigma. For instance, P02 relied on his cane, saying, "*I don't go anywhere without it*," whereas P09 said "*I'm embarrassed to use my white cane*."

Participants described situations where AT was sufficient in providing fundamental visual access but contextual factors impacted use:

"Using a magnifier...was great for looking at something on paper, but if I was looking at something through a window obviously...I wouldn't be able to do anything with it. If I was in a store, if I could hold it, if it was in my hand...I could see the price on it but if it was something up on a shelf, a magnifier was no good to me." (P06)

"You're trying to scan over a tablet with a magnifier that's only like an inch and a half off the screen. You're always touching something...With the Jordy, I hold it at a reasonable distance from my face. And I use my hands to read the screen while on my own I have all the accessibility [features] turned up." (P04)

With regards to the decision to start using the eSight eyewear, our participants expressed a strong, hopeful reaction when they first learned about the device on TV, online, or at a vision trade show. Our participants learned about the device either first-hand or were passed along information by family, co-workers, and friends. For all but one of our participants this led to contacting eSight for screening and then scheduling a demonstration. (The exception to this process was P04, who purchased eSight after the screening but without a demonstration, relying on his past experiences with HMD (LVES and Jordy) and discussions with eSight.)

In contrast to our participants who ultimately purchased eSight, some individuals who contact the company decide not to pursue this AT. According to the eSight employees we interviewed, the initial screening process can include a recommendation that someone who is experiencing drastic changes in their vision or overall health might not be ready to start using a new AT. Some potential users want to delay their purchasing decision until they can try eSight in specific scenarios that are important to them, such as using their iPad. Others are simply not receptive to eSight after hearing more about the product, citing that they are content with their current AT and workarounds. An eSight employee equated this reported satisfaction with the status quo with generalized resistance to change, citing this as a significant barrier to the adoption of products such as eSight.

The demonstration that follows initial screening is often an emotional experience since the success of eSight, or lack of success, is usually evident upon initial use. Our participants vividly described their first experiences using eSight, many tearing up as they talked about the *"night and day difference"* (P03) in their vision, and feeling *"blown away"* (P06) and overwhelmed:

"Now my first, I still get a little emotional…I put the glasses on and [my wife] is sitting in the conference room and I look at her… I've never seen her face. She cried, I cried. That was a big thing, that was the reason for trying them out." (P11)

P12 got her wish that *"it wouldn't be something that would help just a little bit, … but it was going to be a significant improvement, [if] it's really going to help me then I would know right away. Thankfully it was a big difference."*

The financial commitment required to purchase the eSight device (approximately US $10,000 to $15,000) played an important role in assessing the technology's value. P09 experienced a series of severely degenerative medical events that led at one point to her having complete vision loss. She summarized her decision to spend the money:

"It was super emotional but kind of ridiculously funny at the time. I was like are you kidding me, if someone had told me when I was in the complete dark that for $10,000 you could have some eyesight back I think that would have gotten me through…I can't even explain the emotional component of that. Like how insignificant $10,000 seemed at that time." (P09)

P08 described the mental process of weighing financial costs versus benefits:

"When I saw the cost of it … I thought oh my God you know, how would I, I mean that just seemed like a lot of money for this, but on the other hand it depends on how much you feel the difference it's going to make in your life…if you could make it work somehow." (P08)

Both of these statements reflect the emotional, aspirational, and practical dimensions of embracing AT devices like eSight. The relatively high cost of this technology is not without controversy due to socioeconomic challenges faced by many people living with visual impairment. Most of our participants had concerns about the cost, balancing personal value with available resources. None of the participants in our study expressed regret about purchasing the eSight eyewear, an outcome that we saw as directly related to eSight's deliberate screening and demonstration process. While some individuals paid for the device out of pocket using savings or by selling a car that was no longer needed because of deteriorating vision, the relatively high price tag for eSight meant that many participants engaged closely with a social support network to raise the needed funds. This ranged from families pooling resources to collections at church to social media campaigns like gofund.me. At least two participants received their eSight eyewear as the result of a donor who covered the entire cost of the device.

4.2 Theme 2: Negotiating social engagement

The discernibility of a visual condition influenced social interactions for our participants, contributing to their sense of social acceptance or stigma of disability and AT use. Our participants talked about "passing" as a person without visual impairment. For example, one person described being surprised to learn that people could identify his visual limitations at first sight, for many years not realizing that his eyes were noticeably small and sunken:

"I walk into a room [and]…they'll say would you like some help? Well, I'm okay but I'm kind of wondering why the person, like I ask them did I stumble when I came through the door? Like did I knock something? Like how did they know I had a vision impairment?" (P04)

Others talked with pride about realizing that a co-worker or acquaintance were not aware that they were visually impaired: *"He actually has no idea I can't see…I'd kind of like to keep it that way, like I'm just a person." (P01)*

In talking about the impacts of bringing eSight into their lives, participants directly associated technology-mediated sight with social engagement. While sharing a range of stories about how they were active, social, and adventurous, many participants described situations in which their visual impairments constrained the ways they contributed to their families, communities and work environments. When asked to describe instances when they particularly felt the impacts of adopting the technology, many gave the device credit for greatly supporting their abilities to work, help their children with sports or school work, or more effectively complete household chores like shopping. In contrast to research focused on barriers to social acceptance, technology-mediated sight in these instances was described as explicitly connected to a sense of self-worth and societal value. For example, one participant described what it was like to try to do the family grocery shopping before eSight:

"He won't let me do the grocery shopping because I don't buy any of the right stuff that everybody likes…I would never come home with anything that anybody liked. I thought I was picking the, you know, this jar of peanut butter looks like this jar of peanut butter." (P01)

This person went on to explain that with eSight, she is now able to see small differences in labels, making her better able to respond to her family's preferences. This increased acuity also made her keenly aware of all the things she missed without the device, contributing to feelings of inadequacy and, at times, depression. Here we see evidence of technology-mediated sight being used to negotiate ongoing attempts to balance inconveniences, even stigmas, associated with head-mounted AT with desires for more robust social practices in spite of differences in visual abilities.

Related aspects of social engagement included experiencing degrees of inclusion and independence through use of the eSight eyewear. Having the ability to observe and use non-verbal communication through eye contact, facial expressions and proximity were considered a strong benefit of the device. However, many of the stories shared by participants highlighted challenges to achieving true parity and equity to those without visual impairment. More often they described what could be called satisficing. Their visual experience was a not a replacement for unmediated sight, but offered enough of the same social affordances to be considered valuable:

"It wasn't normal vision but it was vivid enough for me to feel like I was there experiencing it with him again, like I was part of the world that he was living in, I wasn't in a different excluded weird cold place." (P09)

Many people told us that they decided *not* to use the device in some social situations because the opacity and bulkiness of the headgear interfered with their ability to interact in a naturalistic manner:

"...when I first met a client I would not wear my eSight because part of my job with sales was selling the kitchen design and if a person can't see your eyes they have a hard time trusting you.... I'm used to not seeing anyone's eyes, I'm used to using other points, but most people are not, so when they're talking to you they want to see your eyes." (P10)

The eSight device (and similar technology) is not a cure-all for challenges of inclusion, independence, and social integration faced by individuals with low vision. The social reality created using these devices for interpersonal communication and engagement is distinct, valued, and not entirely similar to unmediated interactions. Some users expressed initial disappointment about this gap, yet adjusted to this alternate social reality.

4.3 Theme 3: Boundaries of sight

Measures of visual acuity are typically presented in terms of distance: if my eyesight is 20/80, I can see at 20 feet what normally sighted people can see at 80 feet. In our interviews, we learned that the relationship between sight and space or distance is more complex than that pair of numbers might imply. In addition to the obvious challenges of navigating physical space with a visual impairment, participants also described building skills related to calibrating their own non-visual mental models of the world with versions of the world encountered through social interactions with sighted individuals. For example, where a sighted companion might think of the path to a favorite coffee shop as a series of left and right turns, for someone with low vision, this path might be described in terms of a sound and temperature scape. Many adaptations described by our participants involved developing the skills and insights to reconcile these disparate representations.

In talking about how navigating their physical surroundings changed through use of the eSight eyewear, most people placed a particularly high value on the ability to see at a distance. For many, especially those with degenerative conditions, visual experience of the world became increasingly shallow in depth as their eyesight deteriorated.

One participant described the challenge of having such shallow depth of field: *"To be able to see my wife's face what I would call clearly without the eSight, she has to be within a few inches of my face" (P06)*. Another participant told us that while she could see her son's nose and eyelashes if she held him close, she longed to be able to watch him play: *"I don't see far away, I see stuff but it's super blurry and ... I'd love to be able to sit on my deck and watch my son play in the sandbox." (P09)*

In contrast, another participant described discovering what it meant to "people watch" while using eSight:

"I was sitting in the choir at our church and someone was singing in the front of the auditorium and I could zoom in and I could see the people's faces for the first time...there were people there that weren't there very often and I was asking [my mom] who is this, who's this, and so I was watching them and I told my mom, 'I feel like I'm spying on people because I can see them and they don't know I'm looking at them,' and she said, 'Well, dummy, that's how everybody is!" (P12)

These examples illustrate important ways that seeing over distance impacts social inclusion.

Another way that the boundaries of sight were described by participants had to do with reflective self-awareness of the activity of seeing. We began interviews by asking people to describe to the best of their ability what the world looks like for them. Many people described blind spots, tunnel vision, blurriness, problems with light, and needing to hold things very close to their eyes. Five of the 13 participants also explicitly spoke about the connection between their eyes and brain when describing their experience of sight, for example:

"My eyes tend to move. In my case they rotate in a counterclockwise football shape which makes it hard to try and stabilize the image that I'm looking at. It's very, very hard on the brain because the brain is very good at rectifying that and sort of stabilizing it, integrating it into a stable image, but it still is tiring after a while." (P05)

Some described needing breaks from seeing the world, finding the visual world over-stimulating. None of our participants used the eyewear every moment of the day. Most people reserved hours of use for work or specific tasks. Such intermittent use of the device led P01 to track changes she perceived in her mental model of the world:

"...I took it off and ... then I looked at the TV and then all of a sudden it was like I couldn't process anything. Like everything that I knew in the room when the unit came off was different." (P01)

Participants also spoke about the ways in which using the eSight device increased their awareness of differences between their own experience of sight and those of fully sighted friends and loved ones. Over half of the participants referred at one point or another to being aware that the device gave them "*super powers*," or the ability to see in more detail, at greater distance or under dimmer lighting conditions than fully sighted individuals could. One participant described herself as appearing to look like *"a super hero"* or a *"cyborg mom"* (P01) when she wore the device to pick up her son at school. Another participant described working in a warehouse using eSight to magnify product information:

"I'll be like Robocop and just read everything... They would say, 'What was that part number?' and I'd be like, '1234567 and the serial number ABCD,' and I'd just read it off and it was like they were talking to a walking computer." (P11)

In perhaps one of the best examples from our interviews of the sociotechnical implications of this aspect of AT, a grandfather described what it was like for him to return to watching his grandson's hockey matches after he started using the eSight eyewear:

"[My grandson] was all excited because I was his super fan and he came running up and he still had his skates on and he called to me and said, 'Grandpa, could you see me?" And I said, 'I could see the puck! I could follow the puck all around the rink!'...My grandson got a penalty and he was opposite of me in the arena and he was sitting in the penalty box and my son said, 'I'd like to know what he's doing right now,' and I just beamed up and I told him what he's doing right now. So we had to go find him and [tell him to] be careful when he was in the penalty box because we could see what he was doing." (P06)

4.4 Theme 4: Attitudes and expectations toward technology

Our interviews revealed tensions between an individual's desire to enhance their visual experiences, their confidence in their skills using technology, and their expectations of what technology can deliver. Although our participants exhibited a baseline trait of being comfortable with technology, that is not the case of all potential users. During the screening process, eSight assesses the potential customer's familiarity with technology by asking about their use with everyday technology such as TV remote controls and cell phones.

Our participants exhibited an openness to technology, which appeared to play an important role in their initial willingness to try eSight:

"My first reaction was just yes I'll try anything." (P01)

"I'm a geek to begin with so it was technology based, so sure, I mean I do a lot of reading and I'm willing to try things and that sort of thing." (P05)

Beyond being comfortable with technology, many of our participants had an aspirational attitude toward innovation. This attitude influenced how participants imagined the future, whether speculating about the ways in which devices like eSight could be improved or prospects for even better AT in their lifetime:

"... I figure eventually it will have various overlays. I could see it having sort of two layers, the assistive technology layer and a layer on top of it that will let you say add Android apps or something like that." (P05)

As mentioned previously, participants described sensing a gap between their own mediated encounters with the visual world and what those with more fully functioning sight experience. Few participants expected technology alone to bridge that gap, at least in their lifetime, but many expressed hope for future generations, with at least six of the thirteen referencing their own children or grandchildren in their hopes for the future. Twelve explicitly stated that they actively and enthusiastically shared information about eSight with others, with P06 referring to himself as a kind of "Johnny Appleseed." Many simply wanted others to share in the experience of sight offered by eSight. Others had a more global vision of the possible impact of the technology: "*...My thought was if this works, this is like, this is a historical moment." (P01)*

Overall, the people we spoke with were highly cognizant that their visual status would likely be fluctuating over time. P09 was particularly eloquent in talking about a recent, though possibly temporary, improvement in her sight:

"I don't know what my future will entail sight-wise. The doctors...have no idea how long it will last, what it will look like, eventually they think it will even out but it still fluctuates. It does scare me, I do live in a little bit of a fear ... that I will go back to what I had at that one time of [complete vision loss] and I do not want to do anything to cause that or inhibit my vision from staying where it's at right now, but I do recognize that I can't live in fear for the rest of my life, it's not healthy for me, it's not healthy for anybody around me." (P09)

These anticipated changes and the need to remain adaptive balance positive attitudes towards the HMD.

5. Discussion

We argue that the narratives of eSight users are not just about the adoption of ATs but also provide important insights into the ways in which ATs and HMDs become entwined with personal and social understandings of sight, creating new "ecologies of the visual" [30, p. 4]. Our participants support this sociotechnical argument through their descriptions of the many ways in which, as users of AT for low vision, their experiences of sight have been assembled through a combination of hardware, software, physiology and social engagement.

5.1 Multiplicities of vision

The participants in our study explicitly stated that the eSight device did not "cure" them of their visual impairment, was not a replacement for more fully functional sight, and was not appropriate for all situations. Not only do physical and material variations in the surrounding environment affect what can be seen with the eSight device, individual variations in sight occur on a yearly, monthly, daily and even hourly basis. Rather than describing a stable, static, or standardized experience, many instead referred to visual experiences they had with eSight as something different, a new type of sight that provided them with *an* experience of the visual, if not *the* singular notion of "vision" that they might have held when they first heard about the device.

Caren Yglesias, a visual culture scholar, points out that, "Seeing is more than an optical operation; understanding what is seen is a thoughtful experience" [40, p. 86]. We learned that not just seeing, but *understanding the personal value* of what is being seen was an important aspect of how and why AT is integrated into someone's life. The value that eSight users placed on what was being seen (e.g., the face of a loved one, paperwork involved in a desk job that enabled someone to support a family, the panorama of the Grand Canyon), was entangled with their assessment of the technology, the concessions they were willing to make to use the device (including cost), and ultimately what they came to describe as "adequate" or "enough" sight. In this way, the eSight device (and similar technologies) plays an important role in creating an awareness of the multiplicities of vision, highlighting that sight is not just one thing for all people in all situations.

This observation has implications for more holistic, situated, and longitudinal evaluation of HMD like the eSight eyewear. While measures of visual acuity can describe the ability for AT to replicate more typically functioning eyesight, they do little to help us understand so many of the other types of visual experiences described by the individuals in our study. Replication of normative vision is just one possible outcome; some devices might be far better positioned to introduce entirely new types of visual experiences for low vision users and others. Another outcome may be technologies that focus on creating a rich social or task supports using modalities other than vision to enhance a person's holistic experience. Given the different roles of AT, different desired combinations of modalities, both the design and evaluation of technologies would need to be more nuanced and situated to the person and their abilities, social environment, and task goals.

5.2 Low vision as skilled vision

Technology-mediated vision has been a staple of scientific observation for centuries, initially through microscopes and telescopes and more recently through technologies such as x-rays, MRI and spectroscopy [7]. With new these imaging techniques, novel forms of visual literacy have evolved resulting in new forms of *professional* [14] or *skilled vision* [15]: the process of learning to see the most important or informative details of a visual display through the eyes of a specific community of practice. This type of visual expertise is often tied to professional discourse and norms, and tends to be situated, contextual, and material, involving an apprentice-like experience to acquire.

However, this case study on eSight provides evidence of "vernacular" skilled vision [33], in which daily practices of non-professionals entail adaptive and specialized visual skills. eSight users have learned, often through trial and error, how to make the best use of the visual input they receive. They are developing expertise in learning how to make sense of the visual information provided by the eSight device. For example, one of the distinct differences between a device like eSight and other ATs like magnifiers or smartphone apps is its ability to simultaneously pan, zoom, and focus. This functionality enables users to see *through* space; the visual experience afforded by the eSight device is not just a series of interactions with flat planes, but aspires to provide users with a more fluid ability to make seamless transitions through foreground, middle ground, and background. A majority of our participants have a radically shortened depth of view (e.g., only being able to see things that are inches away from their eyes). Therefore, for many this was the first time (or the first time since the onset of a visual condition) that they had the ability to navigate depth of field using sight.

Recognizing people with low vision – as they navigate their worlds through un-mediated and technology-mediated sight – as people with expertise in skilled vision can open new avenues of investigation and innovation in other visual and multi-modality domains. Designers can gain a deeper understanding of the choices these skilled users make in adopting and operating vision technologies, and therefore, design technologies that are more compatible and usable based on people's specialized sensory abilities.

5.3 Limitations and future work

Case studies enable researchers to dive deeply into a bounded set of experiences in order to surface themes, observations, and opportunities that can then be applied and tested more broadly. For this study, we closely examined one form of AT available to people with low vision. Future work comparing the experiences of eSight users with users of other AT for low vision will enable us to better understand the range of social affordances associated with these emergent technologies. Related, and also previously noted, is that the users in our study were all relatively enthusiastic, no doubt as a result of our recruiting methods. Although our study does focus on the integration of HMD AT in the lives of individuals with low vision, necessarily focusing on those who have gone through this process, interviews with eSight employees helped us to contextualize the choices faced by potential users and to learn more about those who were not enthusiastic adopters. Future work looking more closely at non-use will help us build a more holistic picture of sociotechnical factors in technology-mediated sight. Methodological limitations include relying on self-report rather than benefiting from the richness of direct observation.

6. Conclusion

Interviews with early adopters of eSight eyewear for low users provided the basis for a sociotechnical analysis of technology-mediated sight. Our findings describe 1) sociotechnical experiences of vision offered through this device, and 2) the ways in which these experiences are assembled through a combination of social and technical affordances. In doing so, we argue that the narratives of eSight users are not just about the adoption of ATs but also help us to better understand the way in which technology-mediated sight represents new and emerging sociotechnical ecologies of the visual. This concept of multiplicities of vision can be instrumental to designing nuanced and situated assistive and augmentative technologies.

7. ACKNOWLEDGMENTS

We thank Rob Hilkes and the eSight users and employees who participated in our research. We also thank Jacob O. Wobbrock for his valuable feedback on an early version of this paper.

8. REFERENCES

[1] American Optometric Association. What Causes Low Vision? Retrieved September 14, 2016 from http://www.aoa.org/patients-and-public/caring-for-your-vision/low-vision/what-causes-low-vision?sso=y

[2] Canadian Ophthalmological Society. What is Low Vision? *Canadian National Institute for the Blind*. Retrieved September 14, 2016 from http://cnib.ca/en/your-eyes/eye-conditions/low-vision/Pages/default.aspx

[3] Bill Chapman. 2001. *Coping with Vision Loss: Maximizing What You Can See and Do*. Turner Publishing Company.

[4] Kathy Charmaz. 1983. The grounded theory method: An explication and interpretation. In *Contemporary Field Research*, Robert M. Emerson (ed.). University of California, Waveland Press, Prospect Heights, IL, 109–126.

[5] Kathy Charmaz. 2014. *Constructing Grounded Theory*. SAGE.

[6] Albert M. Cook and Janice Miller Polgar. 2014. *Assistive Technologies: Principles and Practice*. Elsevier Health Sciences.

[7] Johanna Drucker. 2014. *Graphesis: Visual Forms of Knowledge Production*. Harvard University Press, Cambridge, MA.

[8] eSight Corporation. eSight Home Page. Retrieved September 14, 2016 from https://www.esighteyewear.com

[9] eSight Corporation. eSight FAQ. Retrieved July 20, 2017 from https://www.esighteyewear.com/faq

[10] Alexander Fiannaca, Ilias Apostolopoulous, and Eelke Folmer. 2014. Headlock: A Wearable Navigation Aid That Helps Blind Cane Users Traverse Large Open Spaces. In *Proceedings of the 16th International ACM SIGACCESS Conference on Computers & Accessibility* (ASSETS '14), 19–26. DOI:https://doi.org/10.1145/2661334.2661453

[11] John C. Flanagan. 1954. The Critical Incident Technique. *Psychological Bulletin* 51, 4 (1954), 327–358.

[12] Daniel Fok, Janice Miller Polgar, Lynn Shaw, and Jeffrey W. Jutai. 2011. Low vision assistive technology device usage and importance in daily occupations. *Work* 39, 1 (2011), 37–48.

[13] Barry Francis. 2005. The Jordy Electronic Magnification Device: Opinions, Observations, and Commentary. *Journal of Visual Impairment & Blindness* (September 2005), 553–563.

[14] Charles Goodwin. 1994. Professional Vision. *American Anthropologist* 96, 3 (1994), 606–633.

[15] Cristina Grasseni. 2004. Skilled vision. An apprenticeship in breeding aesthetics. *Social Anthropology* 12, 1 (February 2004), 41–55. DOI:https://doi.org/10.1111/j.1469-8676.2004.tb00089.x

[16] Robert Harper, Louise Culham, and Christine Dickinson. 1999. Head mounted video magnification devices for low vision rehabilitation: a comparison with existing technology. *British Journal of Ophthalmology* 83, 4 (1999), 495–500.

[17] Terri Hedgpeth, John A. Black Jr., and Sethuraman Panchanathan. 2006. A Demonstration of the iCARE Portable Reader. In *Proceedings of the 8th International ACM SIGACCESS Conference on Computers and Accessibility* (ASSETS '06), 279–280. DOI:https://doi.org/10.1145/1168987.1169054

[18] Shaun K. Kane, Chandrika Jayant, Jacob O. Wobbrock, and Richard E. Ladner. 2009. Freedom to Roam: A Study of Mobile Device Adoption and Accessibility for People with Visual and Motor Disabilities. In *Proceedings of the 11th International ACM SIGACCESS Conference on Computers and Accessibility* (ASSETS '09), 115–122. DOI:https://doi.org/10.1145/1639642.1639663

[19] Jonathan Lazar, Jinjuan Feng, and Aaron Allen. 2006. Determining the Impact of Computer Frustration on the Mood of Blind Users Browsing the Web. In *Proceedings of the 8th International ACM SIGACCESS Conference on Computers and Accessibility* (Assets '06), 149–156. DOI:https://doi.org/10.1145/1168987.1169013

[20] Tony Liao. 2012. A framework for debating augmented futures: Classifying the visions, promises and ideographs advanced about augmented reality. In *2012 IEEE International Symposium on Mixed and Augmented Reality (ISMAR-AMH)*, 3–12. DOI:https://doi.org/10.1109/ISMAR-AMH.2012.6483982

[21] Janet van der Linden, Terry Braun, Yvonne Rogers, Maria Oshodi, Adam Spiers, David McGoran, Rafael Cronin, and Paul O'Dowd. 2012. Haptic Lotus: A Theatre Experience for Blind and Sighted Audiences. In *CHI '12 Extended Abstracts on Human Factors in Computing Systems* (CHI EA '12), 1471–1472. DOI:https://doi.org/10.1145/2212776.2212491

[22] Robert W. Massof and Douglas L. Rickman. 1992. Obstacles Encountered in the Development of the Low Vision Enhancement System. *Optometry and Vision Science* 69, 32 (1992), 32–41.

[23] Robert W. Massof, Douglas L. Rickman, and Peter A. Lalle. 1994. Low vision enhancement system. *Johns Hopkins APL Technical Digest* 15, 2 (1994), 120–125.

[24] Troy L. McDaniel, Daniel Villanueva, Sreekar Krishna, Dirk Colbry, and Sethuraman Panchanathan. 2010. Heartbeats: A Methodology to Convey Interpersonal Distance Through Touch. In *CHI '10 Extended Abstracts on Human Factors in Computing Systems* (CHI EA '10), 3985–3990. DOI:https://doi.org/10.1145/1753846.1754090

[25] Joyojeet Pal, Tawfiq Ammari, Ramaswami Mahalingam, Ana Maria Huaita Alfaro, and Meera Lakshmanan. 2013. Marginality, aspiration and accessibility in ICTD. 68–78. DOI:https://doi.org/10.1145/2516604.2516623

[26] T. Louise-Bender Pape, J. Kim, and B. Weiner. 2002. The shaping of individual meanings assigned to assistive technology: a review of personal factors. *Disability and Rehabilitation* 24, 1–3 (2002), 5–20.

[27] Phil Parette and Marcia Scherer. 2004. Assistive technology use and stigma. *Education and Training in Developmental Disabilities* 39, 3 (2004), 217–226.

[28] Halley Profita, Reem Albaghli, Leah Findlater, Paul Jaeger, and Shaun K. Kane. 2016. The AT Effect: How Disability Affects the Perceived Social Acceptability of Head-Mounted Display Use. In *Proceedings of the 2016 CHI Conference on Human Factors in Computing Systems*, 4884–4895. DOI:https://doi.org/10.1145/2858036.2858130

[29] Kyle Rector, Lauren Milne, Richard E. Ladner, Batya Friedman, and Julie A. Kientz. 2015. Exploring the Opportunities and Challenges with Exercise Technologies for People Who Are Blind or Low-Vision. In *Proceedings of the 17th International ACM SIGACCESS Conference on Computers & Accessibility* (ASSETS '15), 203–214. DOI:https://doi.org/10.1145/2700648.2809846

[30] Gillian Rose and D. Tolia-Kelly (Eds.). 2012. *Visuality/Materiality: Images, Objects and Practices*. Ashgate Publishing, Surrey, England.

[31] Kristen Shinohara and Jacob O. Wobbrock. 2011. In the Shadow of Misperception: Assistive Technology Use and Social Interactions. In *Proceedings of the SIGCHI Conference on Human Factors in Computing Systems* (CHI '11), 705–714. DOI:https://doi.org/10.1145/1978942.1979044

[32] Kristen Shinohara and Jacob O. Wobbrock. 2016. Self-Conscious or Self-Confident? A Diary Study Conceptualizing the Social Accessibility of Assistive Technology. *ACM Transactions on Accessible Computing* 8, 2 (January 2016), 5:1–5:31. DOI:https://doi.org/10.1145/2827857

[33] Jaime Snyder. 2017. Vernacular Visualization Practices in a Citizen Science Project. In *Proceedings of the 2017 ACM Conference on Computer Supported Cooperative Work and Social Computing*, 2097–2111. DOI:https://doi.org/10.1145/2998181.2998239

[34] Sarit Felicia Anais Szpiro, Shafeka Hashash, Yuhang Zhao, and Shiri Azenkot. 2016. How People with Low Vision Access Computing Devices: Understanding Challenges and Opportunities. In *Proceedings of the 18th International ACM SIGACCESS Conference on Computers and Accessibility*, 171–180. DOI:https://doi.org/10.1145/2982142.2982168

[35] Sarit Szpiro, Yuhang Zhao, and Shiri Azenkot. 2016. Finding a store, searching for a product: a study of daily challenges of low vision people. 61–72. DOI:https://doi.org/10.1145/2971648.2971723

[36] S. Thierfelder, B. Lege, and F. Ulrich. 1998. Low Vision Enhancement System (LVES). Initial clinical experiences with a new kind of optoelectronic rehabilitation system. *Ophthalmologe* 95, 11 (November 1998), 781–783.

[37] Michele A. Williams, Amy Hurst, and Shaun K. Kane. 2013. "Pray Before You Step out": Describing Personal and Situational Blind Navigation Behaviors. In *Proceedings of the 15th International ACM SIGACCESS Conference on Computers and Accessibility* (ASSETS '13), 28:1–28:8. DOI:https://doi.org/10.1145/2513383.2513449

[38] World Health Organization. 2013. What is a refractive error? Retrieved September 14, 2016 from http://www.who.int/features/qa/45/en/

[39] World Health Organization. 2014. Visual impairment and blindness - Fact Sheet N°282. Retrieved June 21, 2016 from http://www.who.int/mediacentre/factsheets/fs282/en/

[40] Caren Yglesia. 2012. Seeing air. In *Visuality/Materiality: Images, Objects and Practices*. Ashgate Publishing, Surrey, England, 85–108.

[41] Bei Yuan and Eelke Folmer. 2008. Blind Hero: Enabling Guitar Hero for the Visually Impaired. In *Proceedings of the 10th International ACM SIGACCESS Conference on Computers and Accessibility* (ASSETS '08), 169–176. DOI:https://doi.org/10.1145/1414471.1414503

[42] Yuhang Zhao, Sarit Szpiro, and Shiri Azenkot. 2015. ForeSee: A Customizable Head-Mounted Vision Enhancement System for People with Low Vision. In *Proceedings of the 17th International ACM SIGACCESS Conference on Computers & Accessibility* (ASSETS '15), 239–249. DOI:https://doi.org/10.1145/2700648.2809865

[43] Yuhang Zhao, Sarit Szpiro, Jonathan Knighten, and Shiri Azenkot. 2016. CueSee: Exploring Visual Cues for People with Low Vision to Facilitate a Visual Search Task. In *UbiComp '16*. DOI:https://doi.org/ttp://dx.doi.org/10.1145/2971648.2971730

Development and Theoretical Evaluation of Optimized Phonemic Interfaces

Gabriel J. Cler
Boston University
635 Commonwealth Ave
Boston, MA 02215
617-358-1395
gcler@bu.edu

Cara E. Stepp
Boston University
635 Commonwealth Ave
Boston, MA 02215
617-353-7487
cstepp@bu.edu

ABSTRACT
In this paper, optimized communication interfaces in which users select phonemes (sounds) instead of letters or whole words are presented and evaluated. Optimization is based on phoneme transition likelihoods (i.e., the probability of transitioning from one phoneme to another in a particular communication corpus), similar to letter-to-letter transition likelihoods used to optimize orthographic interfaces. However, it is unknown to what extent phoneme transition likelihoods vary by corpus, nor how optimizing based on different corpora affects the final interface efficiency. Here we used computational evaluations to compare phoneme transition likelihoods between various phonemic corpora and optimize phonemic interfaces with each corpus. Each interface's efficiency was evaluated against all the corpora. Phoneme-to-phoneme transitions were highly correlated across corpora (r = 0.7-0.86). Optimization based on phoneme-to-phoneme transition likelihoods improved efficiency by around 20-30% compared to random phonemic layouts, regardless of the corpus used to optimize the interface. Optimizations using different corpora were similar, varying only by 3-5%. We conclude that, if possible, future phonemic interfaces should be optimized via a corpus from the intended user's communication. If this is not possible, however, optimization still improved efficiency using all testing corpora, suggesting that optimizing via any relevant corpus is indicated over other layouts.

CCS Concepts
• **Human-centered computing → Human computer interaction (HCI) → Interaction devices → Keyboards • Human-centered computing → Accessibility → Accessibility design and evaluation methods • Human-centered computing → Interaction design → Interaction design process and methods → User interface design**

Keywords
Phonemic interface; augmentative and alternative communication; metropolis algorithm

ASSETS '17, October 29-November 1, 2017, Baltimore, MD, USA

ACM 978-1-4503-4926-0/17/10…$15.00
https://doi.org/10.1145/3132525.3132537

1. INTRODUCTION
Some individuals use augmentative and alternative communication (AAC) methods to communicate, including those who have concomitant motor impairments. For these individuals, AAC use requires both an interface from which to select targets and a method by which to select those targets. Alternative access methods for people with motor impairments range from devices that track head movements [e.g., 30, 31], eye movements [e.g., 11, 12, 16], tongue movements [e.g., 13], sip and puff actions [e.g., 12], or brain signals [e.g., 4, 32]. However, all of these access methods remain noisy and effortful for the user. Despite the technological advances achieved in these areas, target selection can remain slow and effortful, particularly in people with minimal movement capabilities [2, 12]. To improve communication speed and flexibility, further efforts are necessary to improve both AAC access methods and AAC communication interfaces.

1.1 Phonemic Interfaces
AAC interfaces typically provide targets consisting of letters, whole words, or symbols. Each presents benefits and drawbacks, typically compromising between speed and flexibility. Some AAC interfaces have been developed that use phonemes (which represent a particular sound in a spoken language) as targets instead. Phoneme selection allows individuals to create any set of sounds in their language, rather than relying on text-to-speech methods. Of particular interest to speakers with motor impairments, common AAC messages have 14-20% fewer phonemes than letters, depending on the set of vocabulary or messages evaluated (e.g., [5]). This may reduce the time needed to produce messages while retaining full flexibility. The drawback to using phonemes as interface targets is that one must learn to translate intended thoughts into a phoneme set rather than into letters. Typically we spend many years as children learning to translate thoughts into letters (i.e., writing). Sequencing phonemes (or syllables), although more similar to typical oral communication, is also likely to require training in order to produce intended messages. However, the speed and flexibility advantages to phonemic input suggest that it may be appropriate for some users, and thus effort should be expended to develop the most efficient phonemic interface possible.

Phonemic interfaces have previously been proposed for use by a variety of user populations, including children and adults with learning disabilities and/or motor impairments [3, 20, 24, 27]. Some systems contain only a small set of phonemes [3], or display a reduced set of phonemes on the screen at one time [24], such that users must make several motor actions to select one phoneme (e.g., selecting one target to indicate that you wish to select a fricative, and then selecting a target on a second screen that appears to select /f/). Other systems use a reduced set of phonemes and then must disambiguate the intended selections based on prior selections [27], somewhat similar to the T9 texting system [e.g., 14]. Finally, some phonemic interfaces display all possible phonemes, but disable phonemes that are unlikely to be selected next [20]. Unfortunately, these final two methods for increasing efficiency restrict users to selecting only those words contained in the system's dictionary, without allowing for non-words, proper names, or novel utterances.

It has previously been shown that participants without motor impairments could use a noisy AAC access method [8] to produce speech using a phonemic interface in which all phonemes are available to select at all times [5]. This interface had phonemic targets arranged *a priori* based on articulatory features. However, other ways to improve efficiency of phonemic interfaces in which all phonemes are available to select at all times have not yet been explored.

1.2 Efficiency of Orthographic Interfaces

A variety of methods for optimizing orthographic arrangements have been employed, for both physical keyboards (e.g., the Dvorak typewriter keyboard [10]) and onscreen keyboards (e.g., OPTI [17], FITALY [22] or ATOMIK [33]). Many of these were optimized using some combination of trial-and-error and manual incorporation of letter frequency-of-use and letter-to-letter transition likelihoods. Due to the ubiquity of QWERTY keyboards, most users (with and without motor impairments) do not choose a more efficient orthographic keyboard layout. AAC users do sometimes use an alphabetic arrangement or a frequency-based arrangement, particularly if using a very slow scanning method of communication access. However, if users choose to utilize a phoneme-based interface due to its flexibility and the reduced number of selections required, they will not have a previously-learned arrangement of targets (such as QWERTY in an orthographic interface) to produce interference, so learning an optimal target arrangement is likely not appreciably different from learning any other target arrangement.

1.3 Optimizing Interface Efficiency

Direct selection access methods (e.g., finger pointing, head-tracking, eye-tracking) are generally considered to be less cognitively taxing than scanning methods [21], and thus are typically chosen if AAC users have the physical capability to directly select. Optimizing the layout of an interface used in switch scanning typically involves reordering the targets by frequency of use, such that those targets that are likeliest appear in the beginning of the scanning process [15]. There are also methods of optimizing the arrangements of targets on an interface to be used with direct selection; while this efficiency optimization has been implemented for orthographic keyboards (e.g. [33]), it has not been applied to phonemic interfaces.

One way to calculate and then maximize the efficiency of an interface is based on Fitts' law, a fundamental model of directed movements that suggests that the time it takes to select a target is based on the target's distance and size – a nearer target is faster to select because it requires less movement, and a larger target is faster to select because it requires less precise movements. To optimize the efficiency of an interface, one can arrange the targets such that the distance between targets that are often selected sequentially is minimized.

Importantly, methods of calculating efficiency for direct selection rely on the frequency of letter-to-letter transitions, or *digraph statistics*, in which "digraph" means letter pairs. For example, if the word "the" appears in a corpus many times, the digraphs T→H and H→E (and space→T and E→space) will have high probabilities. For orthographic text entry, many researchers use digraph statistics from Mayzner and Tresselt [18]. However, some have noted that these traditional digraph likelihoods do not represent AAC usage [29]. Various text and conversational corpora have been used to calculate digraph likelihoods and to train language models for prediction. Results show that while testing and training models on the same corpus leads to the best keystroke savings, some savings can still be found even when training and testing on different text corpora [29]. It is not clear whether this holds true with *diphone* likelihoods (phoneme-to-phoneme transition likelihoods) and resulting phonemic interfaces.

In this paper we present the results of optimizing and then testing the efficiency of phonemic interfaces using a variety of corpora to determine if phonemic interfaces optimized for AAC must be tailored to each user or if one generic keyboard (e.g., QWERTY, ATOMIK orthographic keyboards) is sufficiently efficient for all users.

1.4 Research Questions and Motivation

It is currently unknown to what extent phoneme transition likelihoods vary by corpus, nor how optimizing based on different corpora affects the final interface efficiency. In this study, we evaluate phoneme transition likelihoods between various phonemic corpora and optimize phonemic interfaces with each corpus. Then we evaluate each interface's efficiency by testing against all the corpora. If interface efficiency is highly impacted by the testing corpus, communication interfaces should be optimized per user. If efficiency is stable across testing corpora, we would expect AAC users to show similar performance using arrangements of phonemes based on any number of corpora. For reference, we additionally evaluated the efficiencies of two potential phonemic interfaces that were not explicitly optimized for efficiency, but potentially offer more immediate ease of use: a phonemic interface in which the phonemes are arranged alphabetically by their label ("Alphabetic"; developed for this study) and a phonemic interface in which phonemes are arranged by articulatory features such as manner and place ("Articulatory"; developed previously and described in [5]).

Here we present a theoretical evaluation of seven different phonemic interfaces against five different AAC/speech corpora. Thoroughly testing this many interface and testing set combinations in AAC users is infeasible, particularly as performance typically improves over time (thus necessitating many testing sessions per interface per user) [6], and because access to these individuals is limited. This paper thus focuses on thoroughly detailing the quantitative processes involved in evaluating various corpora, optimizing interfaces, and performing theoretical evaluations as a means to reduce the set of interfaces upon which to perform the necessary empirical evaluations by AAC users.

2. METHODS

2.1 Phoneme Set

The full set of phonemes used in American English is subject to some debate. For simplicity, the set of phonemes used in this study was the reduced set of phonemes used in the Carnegie Mellon Pronouncing Dictionary [23]; this machine-readable dictionary was used to convert text corpora to phonemes, and its set of phonemes is similar to those used in the Buckeye Corpus ([19]; see *2.2 Corpora*). See Table 1 for the set of phonemes used for most of the interfaces. Note that the articulatory interface (see *3.2.3 Articulatory Interface*) collapsed the phonemes /AA/ and /AO/ into one target.

2.2 Corpora

The usage statistics used to optimize an interface impact its arrangement and thus its efficiency for the end-user. However, there is no one ideal corpus of AAC messages. Therefore, we have compared five corpora (see Table 2 for more details): an unabridged vocabulary list of one young adult AAC user [26], a list of conversational phrases suggested by AAC specialists [9], a bank of simulated AAC messages [28], and the Buckeye corpus of conversational speech [19]. Text corpora were converted to phoneme transition likelihoods by converting text to phonemes via the CMU Pronouncing Dictionary [23] with hand-corrections for words not contained in the dictionary (e.g., "aneurysm"). The Buckeye Corpus has two types of phonemic transcriptions: one that matches the dictionary entry for a given orthographic transcription ('phonemic' by their terminology, or 'dictionary' here for clarity) and one with actual phonemes produced by speaker ('phonetic' by their terminology, but 'direct' here). For example, one speaker said the phrase "tomorrow's my dinner"; the dictionary transcription of "tomorrow's" is /T AH M AA R OW Z/, whereas the direct transcription is /T M AA R AH Z/. Two separate sets of transition likelihoods were calculated using the dictionary and direct transcriptions. For both, any transcriptions that included phonemes that were not in our set (e.g., 'AHN' for a nasalized 'AH'; syllabic 'EL') were converted to in-set phonemes (e.g., 'AH'; 'AH – L').

Table 1. Reduced set of phonemes

Arpabet label	IPA label	Example word
AA*	ɑ	father
AE	æ	at
AH	ʌ, ə	hut
AO*	ɔ	ought
AW	aʊ	cow
AY	aɪ	hide
B	b	be
CH	tʃ	cheese
D	d	dee
DH	ð	that
EH	ɛ	red
ER	ɝ	hurt
EY	eɪ	ate
F	f	fee
G	g	green
HH	h	he
IH	ɪ	it
IY	i	eat
JH	dʒ	just
K	k	key
L	l	lay
M	m	man
N	n	no
NG	ŋ	sing
OW	oʊ	oat
OY	ɔɪ	toy
P	p	pay
R	r	read
S	s	sea
SH	ʃ	she
T	t	tier
TH	θ	think
UH	ʊ	hood
UW	u	two
V	v	veer
W	w	we
Y	j	yield
Z	z	zoo
ZH	ʒ	measure

*These two phonemes are combined into one phoneme in the Articulatory interface

2.3 Calculating Interface Efficiency

Fitts' law (Equation 1) suggests that the movement time (MT) necessary to travel between targets i and j is related to the distance between the centers of target i and target j (D_{ij}), and the width of the second target (W_j). Exact movement times are determined experimentally based on the pointing device employed; these are then used to derive the constants a and b.

$$MT = a + b\left[\log_2\left(\frac{D_{ij}}{W_j}+1\right)\right] \quad \text{Eq. (1)}$$

Table 2. Corpora

Corpus	Description	Number of words	Conversion process
AAC user [26] ("Actual AAC")	Unabridged vocabulary list with use statistics from one young adult AAC user	49,718	Converted each **word** to phonemes via CMUDict (thus missing word-to-word transitions)
AAC conversation al phrases [9] ("Suggested AAC")	Context-specific message list compiled by AAC specialists	3,941	Converted each **message** to phonemes via CMUDict
Simulated AAC messages [28] ("Simulated AAC")	Mechanical Turk simulated AAC messages	25,182	Converted each **message** to phonemes via CMUDict
Buckeye Corpus - dictionary transcription [19] ("Conversati on-dictionary")	40 typical speakers conversing orally with interviewer	284,832	Converted to reduced phoneme set. Calculated transitions by **message** from dictionary phonemic entry of orthographic transcription
Buckeye Corpus - direct transcription [19] ("Conversati on - direct")	40 typical speakers conversing orally with interviewer	284,832	Converted to reduced phoneme set. Calculated transitions by **message** from direct phonetic transcription

The efficiency of a particular target layout is quantified via Equation 2 [33], which is derived from Fitts' law, and suggests

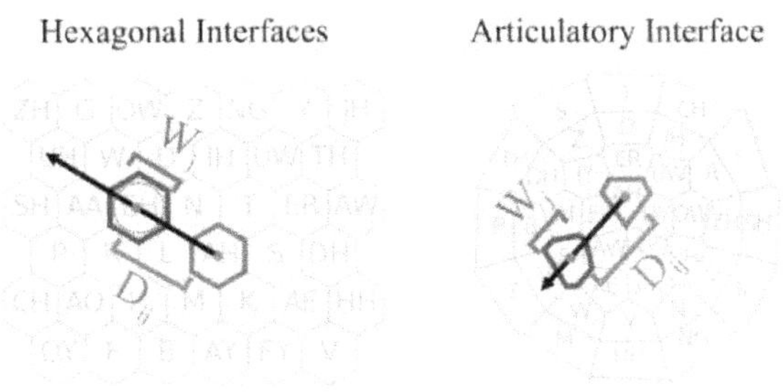

Figure 1. Width (W_j) and distance (D_{ij}) calculations for the interfaces developed and evaluated in this study. Starting phoneme *i* outlined in green, with target phoneme *j* outlined in red. Width is calculated as the distance between the two intersection points of the ideal path from the center of the starting phoneme through the center of the target phoneme (blue dots).

that the average movement time ($\overline{MT}$) of an interface is characterized by the sum of the probability of transitioning between each pair of phonemes (i and j) multiplied by the time it would take to get from phoneme i to phoneme j. Average movement time is converted to words per minute (WPM) as shown in Equation 3 for human readability and comparison with other quantitative orthographic keyboards.

$$\overline{MT} = a + \sum_{i=1}^{39} \sum_{j=1}^{39} \Pr_{ij} * b\left[\log_2\left(\frac{D_{ij}}{W_j}+1\right)\right] \quad \text{Eq. (2)}$$

$$\text{Efficiency (words/min)} = \frac{1\text{ word}}{5\text{ phonemes}} \times \frac{1\text{ phoneme}}{\overline{MT}\text{ (sec)}} \times \frac{60\text{ sec}}{\text{minute}} \quad \text{Eq. (3)}$$

2.3.1 *Fitts' constants*

The constants *a* and *b* in Equations 1 and 2 are Fitts' constants, which are experimentally derived aspects of the pointing device itself. Any change in these arising from choosing a different access method will affect the estimate of efficiency (i.e., some access methods are slower than others), but will not affect the *comparison* of two efficiencies using the optimizing algorithm. Therefore, we have used constants that apply to a stylus type pointing device, in which a is assumed to be 0, b = 1 / 4.9, and a = .127s when $i = j$ in order to compare to other literature [17, 33]. Thus, efficiencies calculated will be considerably higher than those generated by AAC users with noisy access methods, across all interfaces.

2.3.2 *Distance and widths*

Distances between each pair of targets are calculated as the Euclidean distance between the centers of the targets *i* and *j*. Widths are calculated as the width of the second target *j* along the ideal path from the center of the starting phoneme through the center of the target phoneme. For all of the interfaces developed in this study, the target width is consistent, whereas for the articulatory interface (previously developed and discussed in [5]), the target width varies (see Figure 1).

2.3.3 *Transition likelihoods*

Transition likelihoods were calculated from each corpus in Table 2 separately. Any text content was translated to phonemes via the CMU Pronouncing Dictionary [23] and hand-corrected. For the AAC user's vocabulary list, each word's transitions were counted and multiplied by the number of times it was used. For the remaining corpora utilizing messages, all phonemes from the message were concatenated, and each transition was counted.

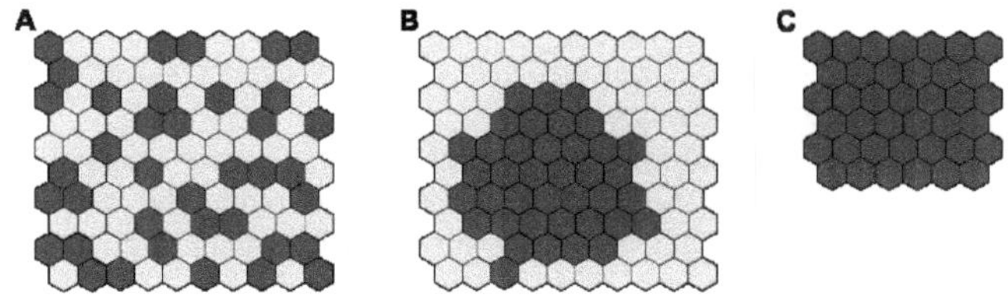

Figure 2. Different configurations of 39 targets; (A) shows a 10x10 interface before the Metropolis algorithm has run, in which 39 hexes have been randomly assigned a phoneme (blue) and the rest are unassigned (grey) (B) shows an interface with high efficiency after running the Metropolis algorithm, which has tightly clustered the targets (max efficiency noted: 39.655 WPM via Suggested AAC corpus). (C) has the 39 targets arranged in a consistent layout both before and after the optimization (max efficiency noted: 39.608 WPM via Suggested AAC corpus).

Then each set of counts was divided by the total number of transitions in the corpus, such that the sum of the probabilities was 1.

Note that the phoneme set in the articulatory interface was slightly different than all others (see section 3.2.3 *Articulatory Interface*). Therefore, to test this interface, separate transition likelihoods for each corpus were recalculated to collapse all X→/AA/, /AA/→X, X→/AO/, /AO/→X, /AA/→/AO/, and /AO/→/AA/ likelihoods as appropriate.

2.3.4 *Words per minute*

Equation 3 includes a standard assumption used for orthographic keyboards, in which the average word is said to require five selections per word (four characters plus the space key). Theoretically, the average number of selections per word for a phonemic interface should be nearer 3, as no space key is necessary or provided, and as there are 14-20% fewer phonemes than letters per word depending on the corpus tested. Regardless, this is left at the orthographic standard of 5 selections/word; values in WPM are presented here only for human readability and could be recalculated at need to represent a "truer" estimate of the phonemic WPM (see section *4.2 Other Efficiency Calculations*).

2.4 Metropolis Optimization Algorithm

Once an interface's efficiency can be quantified, any number of optimization algorithms can be used. One such optimization algorithm is the Metropolis algorithm (see [1] for a review), which is a Markov chain Monte Carlo algorithm with a variety of applications; of particular interest here, it has previously been used to optimize orthographic keyboards.

In this case, the Metropolis algorithm is used as such: one interface of 39 phonemes is randomly generated, and its efficiency is calculated. The interface layout is then optimized via a random walk: two phonemes are randomly swapped and the keyboard efficiency is recalculated. If the new arrangement is more efficient than the current layout, then it is kept and the random walk continues. If the new arrangement is less efficient than the current layout, it may still be kept, according to Equation 4, in which the probability of keeping a less efficient arrangement is quantified by the difference in efficiency (ΔE) and the system temperature (T) multiplied by a scalar (k). The system temperature cycles over time in a process called annealing; this enables the system to break out of local $\overline{MT}$ minima [33].

$$\Pr(\text{keep}_{new}) = 1, \quad \text{if } \overline{MT}_{new} < \overline{MT}_{old} \quad \text{Eq. (4)}$$

$$= e^{-\Delta E/(kT)}, \text{ if } \overline{MT}_{new} \geq \overline{MT}_{old}$$

2.4.1 Interface Shape

The most efficient interface is one in which the targets are tightly clustered, reducing the distances required to move the cursor. Thus target arrangements with hexagonal targets are more efficient than those with rectangular targets arranged in a grid.

The Metropolis algorithm can optimize any interface shape. Initial simulations were done with a large target space (e.g., 10 rows x 10 columns of target locations for the 39 phonemes; Figure 2A) to seek the most efficient layout. After running the algorithm, the most efficient arrangements had targets clustered together (Figure 2B). The tightly clustered targets were in a roughly circular arrangement, which maximizes efficiency (i.e., with phonemes assigned in a particular order, Figure 2B had an efficiency of 39.655 WPM, the maximum output of the algorithm through many iterations), but is less efficient in terms of screen space for end-users, who will need to have other programs on the screen. Therefore, the pre-set target arrangement in Figure 2C was chosen to maximize end-user usability and aesthetics while only slightly reducing efficiency (i.e., highest efficiency with this shape was 39.608 WPM).

2.4.2 Determining Constants

The width of each target was set at 10 to represent the circle circumscribed by the hexagon of the target. The distance between each button was calculated via the Euclidean distance between the centers of each target. As Equations 1 and 2 show, distance is divided by width, making the units arbitrary as long as they are consistent.

The probability of selecting an arrangement that is less efficient (Equation 4) is dependent on the difference in efficiency and two

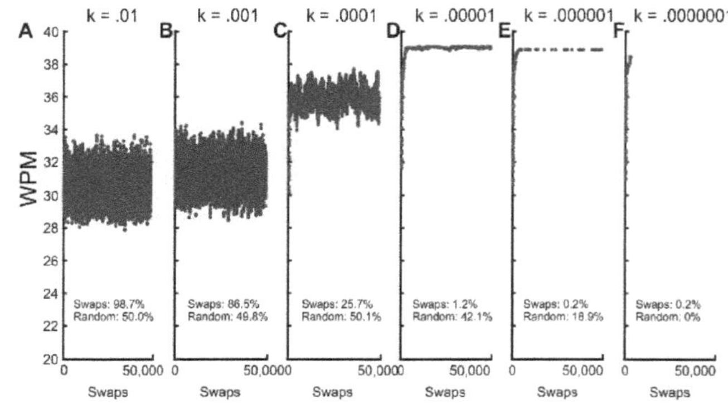

Figure 3. Each panel shows the random walk through the interface space via the Metropolis algorithm with a different value for scalar k with T (arbitrarily) at 10. Each data point represents the WPM for an interface arrangement with a higher efficiency than the "current" arrangement.

scaling variables, k (scalar) and T (system temperature, systematically varied over time). Zhai, Hunter, and Smith [33] present this equation but do not suggest ranges for either k or T.

Figure 3 shows the results of example iterations of the Metropolis algorithm for different values of k, with a static T set at 10. Note that panels A and B stay near the mean random arrangement efficiency ~30 WPM); with this high of a k, many sub-optimal arrangements are kept, and thus the system never approaches an optimal value. Alternately, panels E and F have very few "kept" arrangements; these then are highly dependent on the starting arrangement and do not have the opportunity to get out of local minima. Panels C and D, however, show behavior closer to the goal. Panel C shows a WPM that hovers above the mean. Panel D shows similar behavior to E and F, but with some minor dips in efficiency that eventually lead to higher WPM. Optimal behavior

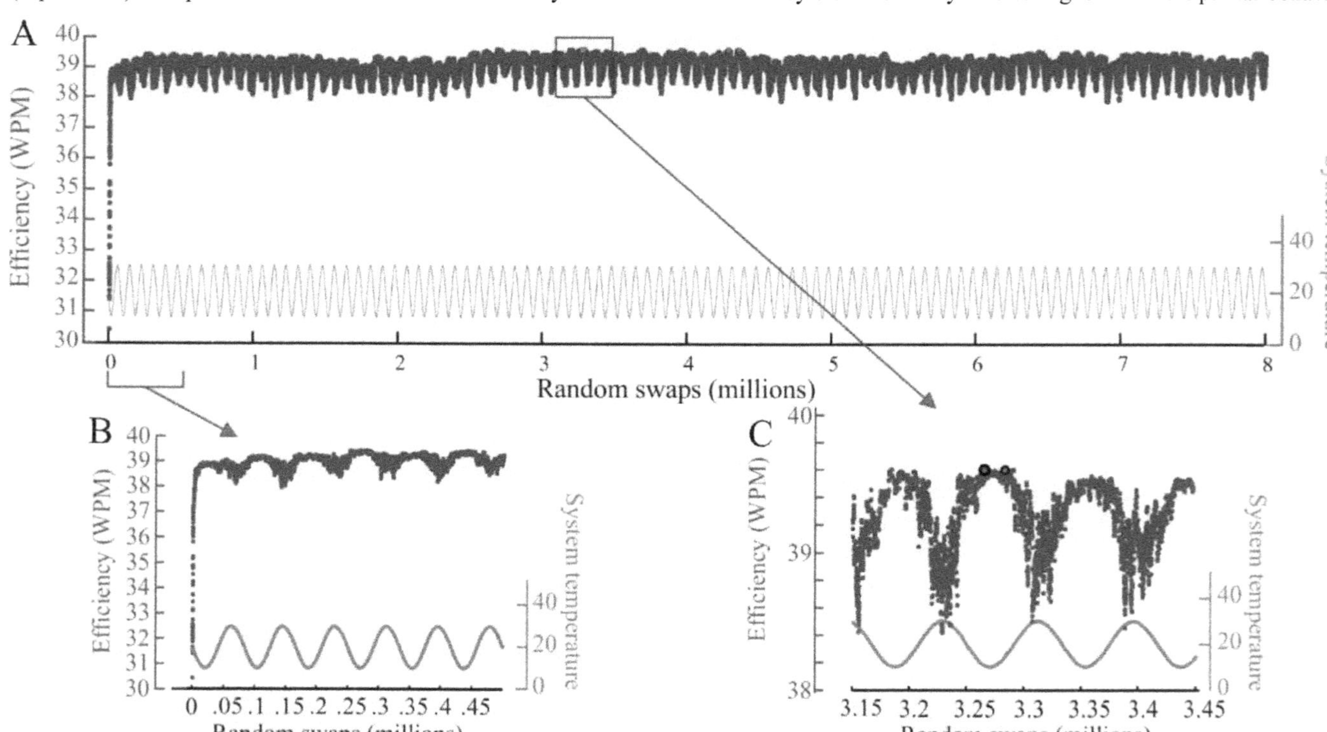

Figure 4. Metropolis algorithm. Top panel shows one iteration of the algorithm, consisting of 8 million random swaps and annealing system temperature. Panel B shows the typical process at the beginning of the algorithm, in which the efficiency quickly rises to the neighborhood of the final "optimized" version. Panel C shows how the annealing process (system temperature in green raising and lowering over time) allows the system to come out of local maxima in order to then approach the optimal solution (red dots).

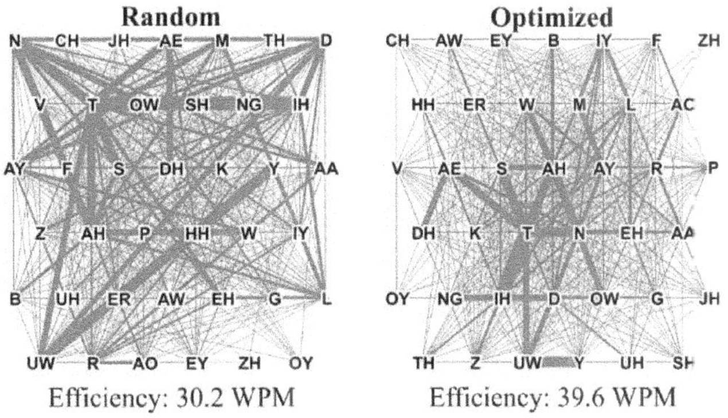

Figure 5. Visual comparison of results of Metropolis algorithm. Left shows a random organization of phonemes; right shows an optimized interface. Width of lines between two targets represents the likelihood of transitioning between them in the AAC conversational phrases corpus.

is likely in between these two numbers, as the algorithm optimizes by periodically choosing a less-optimal solution. Therefore, k was set at .00001 (Panel D), and system temperature was set to vary between 10 and 35, such that the final behavior of the algorithm was between Panels C and D of Figure 3.

For all interfaces, system temperature was varied sinusoidally between 10 and 35 at twelve cycles per million random swaps. The optimization ran for 8 million random swaps for each interface. An example optimization is shown in Figure 4.

2.4.3 Verification of Optimization Outcome

Figure 4 shows the results of one iteration of the optimization algorithm, which consisted of 8 million random swaps. The efficiency first increases rapidly from an average random efficiency (~30 WPM for the suggested AAC messages corpus) to near the final optimum efficiency (~39 WPM; Figure 4B). Next the annealing process (in green; Figure 4C especially) systematically increases and decreases the system temperature, thus increasing and decreasing the likelihood that the algorithm will accept an arrangement with a worse efficiency, as in Equation 4. This allows the system to come out of local maxima in order to then approach the "optimal" solution.

In addition to the efficiency calculations performed at each step by the Metropolis algorithm, representations of the results of the optimization process were evaluated visually to verify the function of the algorithm. Figure 5 shows two different arrangements of 39 phonemes. The left is a random organization, whereas the right shows an optimized arrangement based on the Suggested AAC corpus. The width of the lines represent the transition likelihood between each pair of phonemes. Note that while thick lines occur throughout the random interface (left), the length of thick lines are minimized in the optimized interface; this suggests that when users try to produce the words and phrases common in the corpus (e.g., "you" or /Y-UW/, and "don't" or /D-OW-N-T/), they will not need to move as far to select the required targets. The efficiency of the random interface shown here (30.2) is also the mean efficiency of 100,000 random phoneme layouts using the Suggested AAC corpus to evaluate efficiency.

2.5 Evaluation

Seven interfaces (Figure 6) were evaluated against five corpora (see Table 2). Interfaces A-E were optimized as stated in section *2.4 Metropolis Optimization Algorithm* using diphone probability statistics from each of the five respective corpora. Interface F (Alphabetic) was generated to be the same shape as Interfaces A-

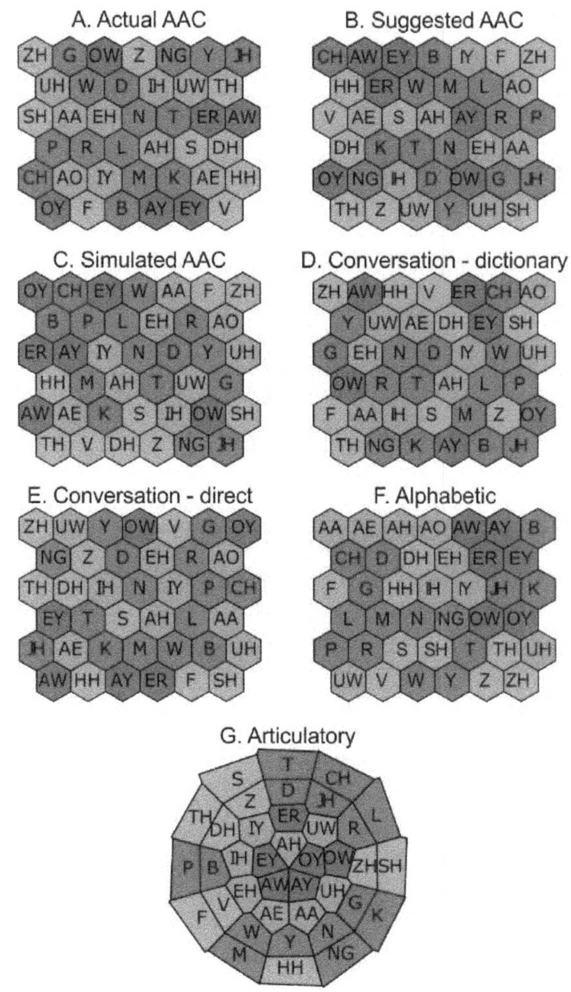

Figure 6. Interfaces developed and evaluated in this study. Target colors show rough groupings of phonemes: simple vowels in green, complex vowels (diphthongs, r-colored vowels) in purple, fricatives and affricates in orange, stops in red, and liquids, nasals, and semivowels in blue.

E, but with the phonemes arranged alphabetically according to their labels. The final interface (Figure 6G; Articulatory) was included to compare to previous studies [6, 7]. Interfaces F and G are included primarily as non-optimized controls in order to evaluate the efficacy of the optimization. Further, while we hypothesized that the Alphabetic and Articulatory interfaces would not provide optimal efficiencies, these interfaces are organized by rules that people can learn, and thus may help users quickly learn where different targets are on the interface. Although the interfaces were not evaluated empirically in this study, future studies may wish to do so. Additionally, if the differences in efficiency are small, users may choose to use the Articulatory or Alphabetic interfaces; whereas if the differences in efficiency are large, they may choose to use an optimized interface instead.

3. RESULTS

3.1 Corpora similarity

Figure 7 shows the correlation of diphone likelihoods between the different corpora tested here. Correlations were high, ranging from .70 to .86. Correlations between text resources (Actual AAC, suggested AAC, and simulated AAC) and conversational

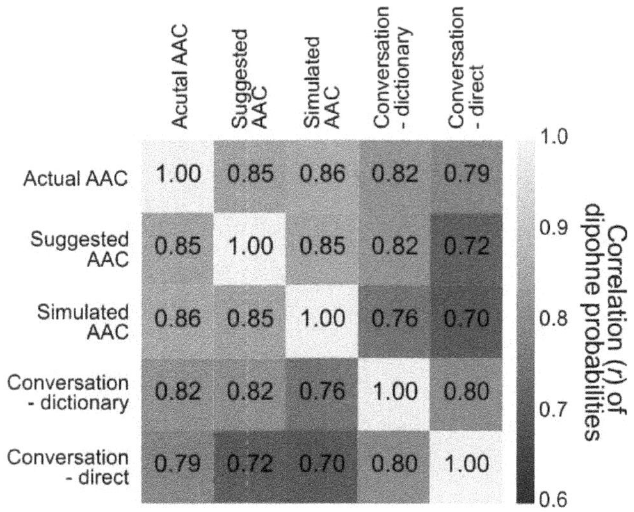

Figure 7. Similarity between phoneme-to-phoneme transition probabilities from different corpora (color represents r-value of Pearson's correlation between all diphone probabilities)

resources (Conversation-dictionary and Conversation-direct) were on the low-to-mid end of the range of correlations, ranging from .70 to .82, while those within text resources were the highest, from .85 to .86. Interestingly, the correlation between the Conversation-dictionary and Conversation-direct probabilities was only .80, despite both being derived from the same conversational source.

3.2 Interfaces

Figure 6 shows the different interfaces developed for this project (A-F) as well as the articulatory interface previously developed (G).

3.2.1 Optimized Interfaces

The first five interfaces (Figure 6A-E) were generated with the Metropolis algorithm as in *Section 2.4 Metropolis Optimization* Algorithm using the diphone probabilities from each respective corpus.

3.2.2 Alphabetic Interface

The alphabetic interface (Figure 6F) used the same layout and phonemes as the optimized interfaces, but arranged the phonemes in alphabetical order based on their label (see Figure 6).

3.2.3 Articulatory Interface

The articulatory interface (Figure 6G) has previously been described in [5]. Briefly, the targets on the interface were arranged manually in a circular layout, such that phonemes were organized based roughly on articulatory features (manner and place of articulation). Phonemes that are differentiated only by voicing (e.g., /TH/ and /DH/) are located at the same angle but different radii. Only 38 phonemes were used for this interface instead of the set of 39 used in the other interfaces in this study; as noted in Table 1, the phonemes /AA/ (*father*) and /AO/ (*ought*) were collapsed into one phoneme. Interface targets were allowed to be directly adjacent (Figure 6G) rather than leaving gaps in between targets as in [5]; this was so that widths were as large as possible in relation to distance between targets, as those in the other hexagonal interfaces are tightly packed.

3.3 Interface efficiency

Efficiency was calculated for each of the seven interfaces against each of the five testing corpora. Results are shown in Figure 8 in terms of WPM. The optimized interfaces had relatively high efficiencies across all testing sets, from 36.5 to 39.6 WPM. Generally efficiencies were highest when the testing corpus was the same as the corpus used to generate the diphone probabilities (shown in Figure 8 on the diagonal, highlighted in black). Variability in WPM for each interface across the different corpora was low, with ideal efficiency to lowest efficiency differing by only 1-3WPM. Efficiencies were lower with both interfaces not optimized by the Metropolis algorithm (30.0-31.4); these were even more consistent across testing corpora, with the Alphabetic only varying by 1.3 WPM across testing corpora, and the Articulatory only varying by 0.7 WPM depending on which corpus was used to evaluate its efficiency.

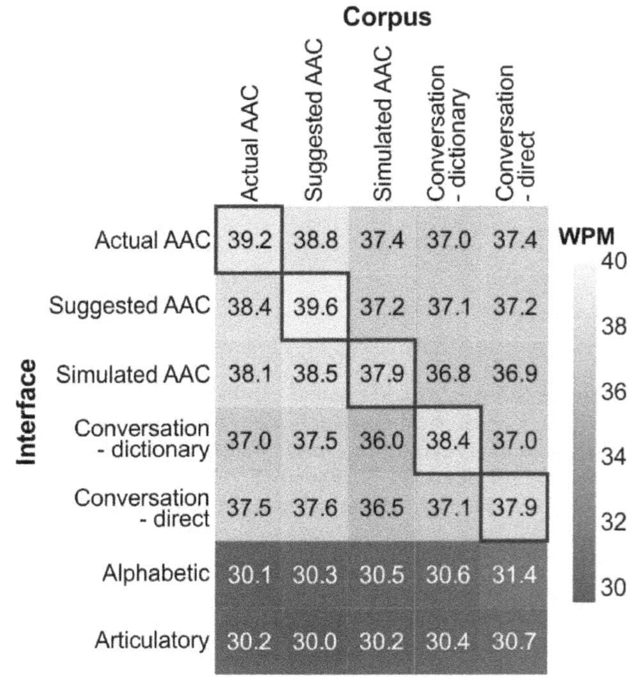

Figure 8. Efficiency in words per minute (WPM) for each interface tested with each corpus. Highlights on the diagonal show when the interface is being tested against the same corpus used to optimize its layout.

4. DISCUSSION

Interfaces not optimized for efficiency (Alphabetic; Articulatory) show efficiencies around 30WPM, which is near the mean random interface efficiency (30.2 WPM). Optimizing an interface using the Metropolis algorithm yields an improvement of around 9 WPM over a random arrangement and the Alphabetic and Articulatory interfaces. However, optimizing by one corpus and testing against another yields differences around 1-3 WPM.

4.1 Benefits of Alp habetic and Articulatory Interfaces

The Alphabetic and Articulatory interfaces may show advantages that are not captured in the efficiency calculation. The organization of the Alphabetic interface gives users some *a priori* information about where targets are located on the interface, as they are arranged via phonemic label. Figure 6F shows that targets arranged by label are also thus somewhat arranged by type of phoneme (note that all nasals are together; vowels are largely grouped). This would likely improve early communication rates via reducing visual search time when users are first learning to use the interface. The Articulatory interface similarly shows

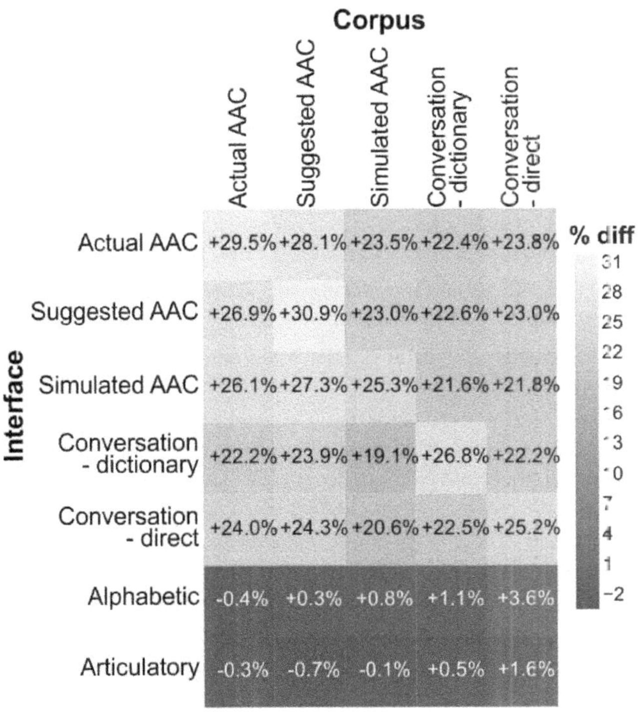

Figure 9. Percent difference in efficiency compared to a random arrangement of phonemes.

organization (Figure 6G), such that all vowels are in the center of the interface, with consonants surrounding them. In addition, the Articulatory interface pairs phonemes that are similar by manner and place of articulation (e.g., /f/ and /v/ are neighbors), which may have initial and ongoing benefits. First, this organization may allow faster learning of the target locations, similar to the Alphabetic interface. In addition, however, this leads to some error tolerance that is not seen in orthographic interfaces or the other phonemic interfaces. If a user overshoots the target and accidentally selects the neighboring pair, the output of may still retain intelligibility that it would not with other interfaces. For example, if a user intends to select /V-OI-S/ ("voice") and instead selects /F-OI-S/ or /V-OI-Z/, a listener would still likely understand that production in context.

4.2 Other Efficiency Calculations

Calculating efficiency in words per minute here relied on two main assumptions that may not hold for phonemic interfaces used by individuals employing alternate access methods.

First, the WPM calculation assumes five letter selections per word, which includes four characters and a space; phonemic interfaces do not require a space, and have fewer characters per word; taking these both into account improves the efficiency calculation for phonemic interfaces.

In addition, alternate access methods are noisier than typical access methods, such as a stylus or physical keyboard. The calculations here used Fitts' constants from a typical stylus to compare to previous work (see section *2.3.1 Fitts' constants*). If we used Fitts' constants derived from an individual with a spinal cord injury using electromyography (EMG) to control a cursor [30], the absolute difference between the interfaces changes. When recalculating Figure 6 using Fitts' constant b=1/2.6, (derived from line of best fit from [30], Figure 5b), the number of estimated words per minute reduces from 30-39 to 8-9 WPM. However, these scale linearly (when using the common assumption that Fitts' a=0). Figure 9 thus shows the improvement in efficiency in percent difference rather than in WPM, as WPM varies by input method, number of characters per word, and by individual skill.

A final way to consider the improvement of the optimization is not in words per minute, but rather as the time it would take to accomplish a task. Table 3 shows time estimates for producing a list of the 1004 suggested AAC messages (the Suggested AAC corpus) with different phonemic and orthographic on-screen interfaces, and using either a typical stylus movement time estimate (in which b=1/4.9) or the EMG cursor movement time estimate (in which b=1/2.6). For the phonemic interfaces, no spaces or punctuation were included. For the orthographic interfaces, no punctuation was included. Fitts' constant remained a=0 for all calculations, as did the special case of movement time when tapping the same target twice (.127s). In these calculations, then, no assumptions were made as to the number of phonemes or letters per word.

The times in Table 3 represent long-term interface usage (i.e., combined time to produce 1004 utterances) using different phonemic (Suggested AAC and Alphabetic, from this study) and orthographic interfaces (orthographic Metropolis interface from [33]; QWERTY keyboard in common use). The optimized phonemic interface shows substantial improvements over orthographic input methods. These improvements increase when the input method is noisy, such as the EMG cursor [30]. Thus, while users with access to typical stylus use may not choose to switch to a phonemic interface, those for whom access is more time-consuming and difficult may find the initial costs of learning a phonemic interface worthwhile (e.g., decreasing time to produce messages from 210 hrs to 102 hrs – roughly 50%). Note, however, that these do not include any prediction, which improves both phonemic and orthographic input rates substantially [25, 27].

Table 3. Time Estimates to Produce Suggested AAC Corpus

Interface	Access Method	
	Stylus (b = 1/4.9)	**EMG cursor by person with spinal cord injury** (b = 1/2.6)
Suggested AAC (phonemic)	54 hrs	102 hrs
Alphabetic (phonemic)	70 hrs	133 hrs
METROPOLIS (orthographic) [33]	78 hrs	147 hrs
QWERTY (orthographic; square targets)	111 hrs	210 hrs

4.3 Clinically Meaningful Speed Improvements

It is not yet clear what degree of improvement in efficiency is clinically meaningful, particularly as AAC users have many different access methods and preferences. Therefore it is also unclear whether the 5-8% improvements due to optimizing per corpus are worthwhile. While producing a new optimized interface once a corpus is obtained is not particularly difficult, it can be somewhat time consuming (converting a given corpus to phonemes often involves some level of hand-correcting for out-of-dictionary terms; running the actual optimization process as described in *2.4 Metropolis Optimization Algorithm* takes approximately twelve hours of computing on a shared computing cluster). Further, it can be difficult to obtain an appropriate corpus. If a user already has an AAC device, they may be willing to allow their AAC specialist to record their usage for some length of time. Although this would be an ideal situation for optimizing an individual AAC interface, only some AAC devices have this recording capability, and recording a person's communication output has privacy concerns.

4.4 Future Directions

4.4.1 Empirical evaluations

An empirical evaluation of these phonemic interfaces is a necessary next step. Although it was not possible to thoroughly evaluate all of the interfaces presented here in AAC users, an empirical evaluation of a small number of interfaces using only one testing set can now be completed to validate the theoretical results. This evaluation should be carried out by users with a variety of motor impairments and access methods. Empirical evaluations should be done to compare the interfaces developed in this study to other existing phonemic interfaces [3, 20, 24, 27].

4.4.2 Individualized optimizations

This paper includes the technical details of the varied quantitative processes that were involved in generating and evaluating the interfaces. These are included specifically so that others can recreate them and produce interfaces optimized based on any given corpus or with weighting factors other than just Fitts'-based efficiency. For example, if a particular user finds left-and-right movements less fatiguing than up-and-down movements, an additional weighting factor could be added for reduced efficiency when the next target is above or below the current target rather than on the same row. Alternate efficiency formulae and weighting could also allow these same algorithms to optimize interfaces intended for use with scanning rather than direct selection methods. In that case, efficiency would be calculated based on time from the onset of scanning to the target's selection, rather than the Euclidean distance between two targets.

4.4.3 Prediction

Finally, another vital way to optimize communication rates is to incorporate online prediction. Studies of existing phonemic interfaces have focused on prediction as the primary way of increasing communication rates [20, 24, 27], without the offline optimizations shown here, and predictive language models can increase phonemic interface communication rates by as much as 100% [24]. Adding prediction to the interfaces presented here is needed in order to compare to other phonemic or orthographic interfaces and to maximize communication rates.

5. CONCLUSIONS

Phoneme-to-phoneme transition likelihoods are highly correlated across corpora, particularly corpora generated from text or AAC use instead of from oral conversation. Optimization based on any corpus increased efficiency from random layouts or from the Alphabetic and Articulatory interfaces by 19-31%. Optimizing and testing on the same corpus led to efficiency improvements of 5-8%, compared to testing on other corpora. Therefore, if possible, future phonemic interfaces should be optimized via a corpus from the intended user's speech. If this is not possible, however, optimization still improved efficiency using all testing corpora, suggesting that choosing an optimized corpus is indicated over other layouts. Future directions include empirical testing and adding prediction to further increase communication rates.

6. ACKNOWLEDGMENTS

This research is supported by NIH grant F31 DC014872 and NSF grant 1452169. Our thanks to Alfonso Nieto Castañón and Frank Guenther for access to their phonemic interface, which was developed under NIH grant R01DC002852.

7. REFERENCES

[1] Beichl, I. and Sullivan, F. 2000. The Metropolis algorithm. *Computing in Science & Engineering*. 2, 1 (2000), 65–69.

[2] Beukelman, D.R. et al. 2007. AAC for adults with acquired neurological conditions: a review. *Augmentative and Alternative Communication*. 23, 3 (2007), 230–242.

[3] Black, R. et al. Introducing the PhonicStick: Preliminary evaluation with seven children.

[4] Brumberg, J.S. et al. 2010. Brain-computer interfaces for speech communication. *Speech Communication*. 52, 4 (2010), 367–379.

[5] Cler, M.J. et al. 2016. Surface electromyographic control of a novel phonemic interface for speech synthesis. *Augmentative and Alternative Communication*. 32, 2 (2016), 120–130.

[6] Cler, M.J. et al. 2016. Surface electromyographic control of a novel phonemic interface for speech synthesis. *AAC: Augmentative and Alternative Communication*. 32, 2 (2016).

[7] Cler, M.J. et al. 2014. Surface electromyographic control of speech synthesis. *Conference proceedings : ... Annual International Conference of the IEEE Engineering in Medicine and Biology Society. IEEE Engineering in Medicine and Biology Society. Annual Conference*. 2014, (2014).

[8] Cler, M.J. and Stepp, C.E. 2015. Discrete vs. continuous mapping of facial electromyography for human-machine-interface control: Performance and training effects. *IEEE Transactions on Neural Systems and Rehabilitation Engineering*. 23, 4 (2015), 572–580.

[9] Context Specific Messages (Suggested by AAC Specialists): *http://cehs.unl.edu/aac/aac-messaging-and-vocabulary/*. Accessed: 2017-01-01.

[10] Dvorak, A. and Dealey, W.L. 1932. US2040248. US2040248 A. 1932.

[11] Frey, L.A. et al. 1990. Eye-Gaze Word Processing. *IEEE Transactions on Systems, Man and Cybernetics*. 20, 4 (1990), 944–950.

[12] Higginbotham, D.J. et al. 2007. Access to AAC: present, past, and future. *Augmentative and alternative communication (Baltimore, Md. : 1985)*. 23, 3 (2007), 243–257.

[13] Huo, X. et al. 2008. Introduction and preliminary evaluation of the Tongue Drive System: Wireless tongue-operated assistive technology for people with little or no upper-limb function. *Journal of Rehabilitation Research & Development*. 45, 6 (2008), 921–930.

[14] Kushler, C. 1998. AAC: Using a Reduced Keyboard. *CSUN Conference on Technology for persons with disabilities* (California State University, Nortridge CA, 1998).

[15] Lesher, G. et al. 1998. Techniques for augmenting scanning communication. *Augmentative and Alternative Communication*. 14, June (1998), 81–101.

[16] Lesher, G.W. et al. 1998. Optimal character arrangements for ambiguous keyboards. *IEEE Transactions on Rehabilitation Engineering*. 6, 4 (1998), 415–423.

[17] MacKenzie, I.S. and Zhang, S.X. 1999. The design and

evaluation of a high-performance soft keyboard. *CHI 99 Conference on Human Factors in Computing Systems*.

[18] Mayzner, M.S. and Tresselt, M.E. 1965. Tables of single-letter and digram frequency counts for various word-length and letter-position combinations. *Psychonomic Monograph Supplements*. Vol 1(2), (1965), 13–32.

[19] Pitt, M.A. et al. 2005. The Buckeye corpus of conversational speech: labeling conventions and a test of transcriber reliability. *Speech Communication*. 45, (2005), 89–95.

[20] Schroeder, J.E. 2005. Improved spelling for persons with learning disabilities. *20th Annual International Conference on Technology and Persons with Disabilities* (Northridge, CA, 2005).

[21] Sevcik, R.A. and Romski, M.B.T.-A.L. 2000. AAC: More Than Three Decades of Growth and Development. 5, 19 (Jul. 2000), 5.

[22] Textware Solutions 1998. The Fitaly one-finger keyboard.

[23] The Carnegie Mellon Pronouncing Dictionary [cmudict. 0.6]: 2005. *http://www.speech.cs.cmu.edu/cgi-bin/cmudict*.

[24] Trinh, H. et al. 2012. iSCAN: A Phoneme-based Predictive Communication Aid for Nonspeaking Individuals. *ASSETS'12*.

[25] Trnka, K. and McCoy, K.F. 2007. Corpus studies in word prediction. *Proceedings of the 9th international ACM SIGACCESS conference on Computers and accessibility - Assets '07*. (2007), 195.

[26] Unabridged Vocabulary Lists with Use Statistics - AAC User: *http://cehs.unl.edu/aac/aac-messaging-and-vocabulary/*.

[27] Vertanen, K. et al. 2012. Applying prediction techniques to phoneme-based AAC systems. *NAACL-HLT 2012 Workshop on Speech and Language Processing for Assistive Technologies (SLPAT)*.

[28] Vertanen, K. and Kristensson, P.O. 2011. The imagination of crowds: conversational AAC language modeling using crowdsourcing and large data sources. *Proceedings of the Conference on Empirical Methods in Natural Language Processing* (2011), 700–711.

[29] Wandmacher, T. and Antoine, J.-Y. 2006. Training language models without appropriate language resources: Experiments with an AAC system for disabled people. *Proceedings of LREC* (2006).

[30] Williams, M.R. and Kirsch, R.F. 2016. Case study: Head orientation and neck electromyography for cursor control in persons with high cervical tetraplegia. *Journal of Rehabilitation Research and Development*. 53, 4 (2016), 519–530.

[31] Williams, M.R. and Kirsch, R.F. 2008. Evaluation of head orientation and neck muscle EMG signals as command inputs to a human-computer interface for individuals with high tetraplegia. *IEEE Transactions on Neural Systems and Rehabilitation Engineering*. 16, 5 (2008), 485–496.

[32] Wolpaw, J.R. et al. 2002. Brain-computer interfaces for communication and control. *Clinical Neurophysiology*. 113, 6 (2002), 767–791.

[33] Zhai, S.M. et al. 2002. Performance optimization of virtual keyboards. *Human-Computer Interaction*. 17, 2–3 (2002), 229–269.

Evaluating an iPad Game to Address Overselectivity in Preliterate AAC Users with Minimal Verbal Behavior

LouAnne E. Boyd[1], Kathryn E. Ringland[1], Heather Faucett[1], Alexis Hiniker[2], Kimberley Klein[1], Kanika Patel[1], Gillian R. Hayes[1]

Department of Informatics
University of California, Irvine
{boydl, kringlan, hfaucett, knklein, kanikap, gillianrh}@uci.edu

Information School
University of Washington
alexisr@uw.edu

ABSTRACT

Overselectivity is a learning challenge that is largely unaddressed in the assistive technology community. Screening and intervention, done by specialists, is time-intensive and requires substantial training. Little to no treatments are available to the broader population of preliterate, minimally verbal individuals. In this work, we examine the impact of an iPad game based on the tenets of behavioral therapy to mitigate overselectivity. We developed software-based techniques and evaluated the system using established methods from the field of Special Education. We present the results of a deployment in a special education school that demonstrates that an assistive tablet game is a feasible means of addressing overselectivity, and we present generalizable technological features drawn from evidenced-based therapies to consider in future assistive technologies. We suggest that designers of assistive technology systems, particularly those who address physical, cognitive, and behavioral difficulties for preliterate AAC users, should consider overselectivity as a potential co-occurring condition.

CCS Concepts

• **Human-centered computing → Accessibility → Accessibility technologies**

Keywords

Autism; AAC; assistive technology; children; tablet games; language development; multiple cue responding; overselectivity.

1. INTRODUCTION

Despite rapid advances in technology, the ability for those who depend on Augmentative and Alternative Communication (AAC) devices to express their wants and needs through such technologies is still highly limited due to a variety of challenges. These devices require intensive setup and often support only the most basic needs [1], such as requesting items or activities. Additionally, commercially available devices, although somewhat customizable, still fail to meet the highly-individualized needs of many AAC users, creating an opportunity for creative solutions.

Improving interactions with these systems has been a continual area of interest for both researchers and practitioners, and assistive technology specialists have identified several potential challenges for AAC users. For example, those with cognitive difficulties may not form sentences as expected [30]. Similarly, those with memory problems (such as aphasia) may not remember how to use the system [1]. AAC devices are restricted to the corpus and categorization provided by the designer, and designs may be limited for those with certain physical disabilities [31]. Finally, because symbols mean different things to different people, these systems do not necessarily work across cultures and contexts. Several studies have focused on making prediction faster because speed of communicating through the device may be prohibitive and lastly, literacy can be an issue for systems that require it [29]. Furthermore, such challenges are often disability specific, leading to more specialized designs. While such specialization is important, this focus does not address challenges that are more general yet still pervasive.

Individuals with pervasive developmental delay often struggle to see the proverbial forest for the trees, meaning that they miss the gestalt overview in exchange for a focus on details, known as "overselectivity" [20,24]. This common learning challenge for students in special education, often called simply "overselectivity," results in overly narrow attention to salient stimuli in the environment and impacts one's ability to learn from observing the environment. Until recently, this phenomenon had been primarily described in children with autism; now, there is growing evidence overselectivity impacts a broad range of people such as people with developmental disabilities, learning disabilities, and hearing impairments [4], many of whom may be AAC users. Overselectivity has also been observed in preliterate AAC users who may not be identified for treatment [5].

Currently, there are very few methods for identifying and treating overselectivity, and the methods that do exist are expensive, time-intensive, highly specialized, and only available for specific populations [11,12]. The pervasive and highly impactful nature of overselectivity provides a compelling reason to develop feasible and accessible treatments to reduce overselectivity in AAC use. The possibility that a larger percent of preliterate AAC users could display overselectivity provides a compelling reason to design systems to reduce overselectivity. Improving issues with overselectivity should improve long-term accessibility as AAC systems are upgraded, often resulting in changes to appearance and to the function of interfaces [5]. We present results from a deployment study of a suite of games, *Go Go Games*, designed by the fourth author to reduce overselectivity in children through behavioral therapy [7]. The results of our evaluation of *Go Go Games* at a special education school demonstrate the potential of reproducible techniques to reduce overselectivity for preliterate, minimally verbal children who display poor uptake of AAC systems.

ASSETS'17, October 29–November 1, 2017, Baltimore, MD, USA.
© 2017 ACM. ISBN 978-1-4503-4926-0/17/10…$15.00.
DOI: http://dx.doi.org/

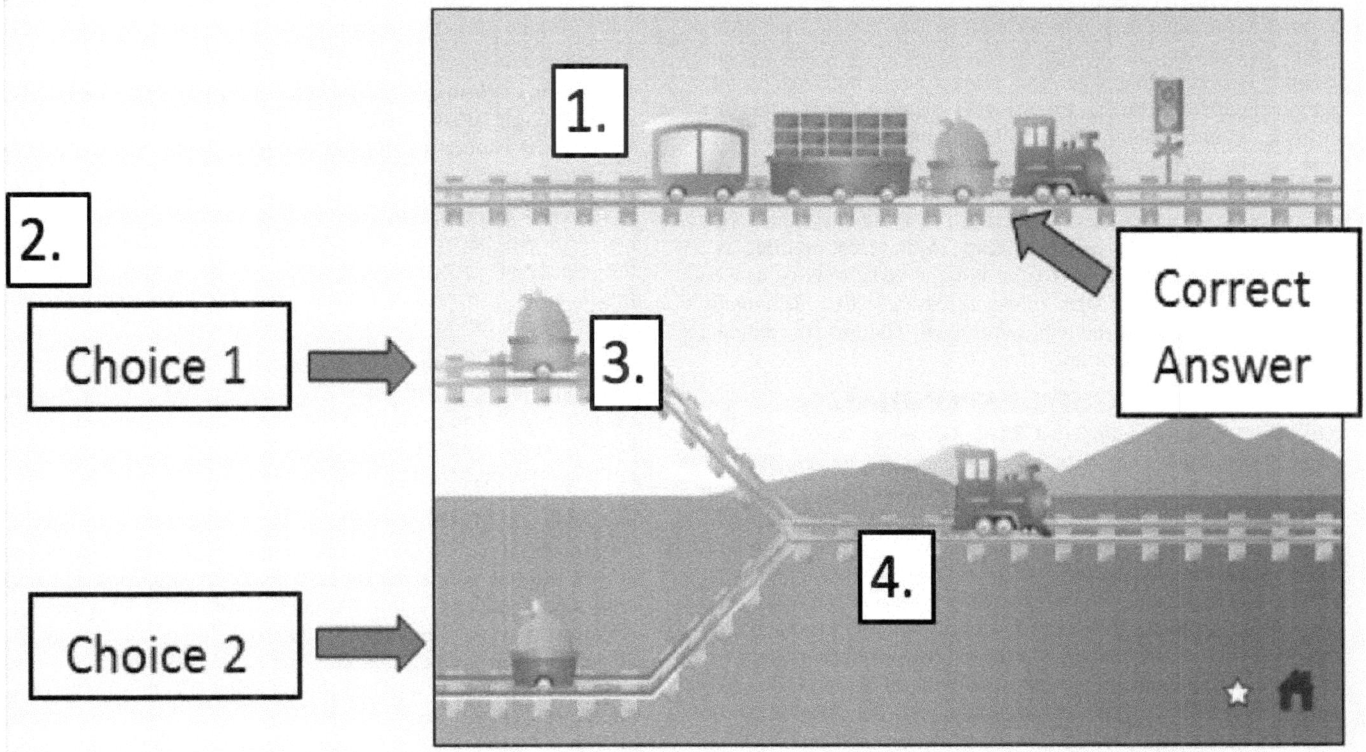

Figure 1. Steps 1-4 show the user interaction in the train minigame: 1. Observe graphic prompt,2. Scan multiple options, 3. Select matching option, and 4. Drag and drop selected choice. © Go Go Games Studios, LLC

2. RELATED WORK

The opportunities to improve the usability and accessibility of AAC devices revolve around a wide variety of innovative ways to adapt the interaction or information (i.e., language set) to support a user's expressive communication. Yet there is an underserved need for assistive technologists to implement replicable techniques to address overselectivity. These techniques, if shown to be feasible and effective, could then be implemented across assistive technology devices to support a range of conditions. To understand the innovative work that has been conducted regarding AAC systems for preliterate, minimally verbal communicators in the ASSETS community, we have found the focus to be predominantly on simplifying the interaction.

Many of these systems incorporate the use of icons as an alternative to verbal, gestural, or written communication. Paper-based systems have relied on icons to support expressive communication for decades [22], and with the affordability and portability of mobile devices, icon-based systems have expanded [15]. Several researchers have extended the utility of icon-based systems such as adding multimedia to the system (e.g., photos, video). For example, Prior et al. [23] developed the *CHAMPION* software project that supported minimally verbal communicators to expressive themselves using–multimedia in the contexts of hospitalization so where unfamiliar staff could understand the user [25]. Similarly, *Vid2Speech* supported early communicators who are preliterate and preverbal by adding video of action words to represent their "dynamic and ephemeral" nature [18]. These systems extend the type of interactions users can have with systems.

Another approach to supporting users with communication is to provide an intervention rather than an alternative form of communication. For example, Black focused on preliteracy skills by developing *PhonicStick*, a joystick that blends and outputs letter sounds to allow for minimally verbal children to explore phonics in an effort to advance emerging literacy skills [2]. Our work also addresses a learning challenge frequently found in preliterate, minimally verbal people--overselectivity.

2.1 OVERSELCTIVITY

Overselectivity to non-relevant or isolated aspects of the environment interferes with children's ability to learn to use language flexibly. Specifically, overselectivity interferes with one's ability to attend to discriminations in language, a skill children typically acquire around the age of three or four. For example, by this age, children can typically respond correctly to the request, "show me the green ball," which requires attention to the object (ball) and color (green). Dube and Wilkinson define stimulus overselectivity as

> *"an atypical limitation in the number of stimuli or stimulus features within an image that are attended to and subsequently learned... For example, the Mayer Johnson PCS symbol for TENNIS shows a gray racquet with a yellow ball... if overselective stimulus control were restricted to the ball only, and the student had learned to identify the symbol on the basis of that one isolated feature alone, then the student may make errors during subsequent symbol use when the symbol BALLOONS is present because that symbol includes a yellow balloon about the same size and color as the tennis ball" [5:4].*

Overselectivity impacts learning in social, speech, and observational learning, as well as intellectual development [26]. Overcoming this barrier is believed to create a path to children accessing more inclusive learning environments [27]. Therefore, determining the therapeutic potential of this technology is critical to understanding a new role technology can play in supporting access to everyday life through improved use of AAC devices and comprehension of language. This project offers both insight into the potential for technical assistance to bridge a gap in accessing existing communication devices, highlighting technical features that can be parlayed into a variety of devices. Support is then sustained over the inevitable changes users experience in devices as interfaces get upgraded or users move on to other systems. This work aims to identify technical features to teach multiple cue responding and mitigate overselectivity. Overselectivity can be problematic for users who move across assistive technology devices, therefore reproducible technical features to mitigate overselectivity, are important.

3. MULTIPLE CUE RESPONDING

Multiple Cue Responding (MCR) is the ability to observe and attend to multiple cues (e.g., color and shape) and recall those cues to make decisions (e.g., find the red triangle in a field of a red square, a blue triangle, and a red triangle). Teaching MCR helps children learn to communicate verbally and may help children use their AAC devices [5]. Pivotal Response Treatment (PRT), one of the only current treatments that teaches MCR, is a therapeutic approach focusing on a child-initiated perspective to target "pivotal" skills that are known to bring about improvements in social, communication, and academic domains [12]. This approach blends the goals of caregivers with the interests of the child to create opportunities for the child to express his or her wants and needs. PRT harnesses the child's motivation to communicate and systematically introduces more complex environments that require the child to then use multiple cues to respond effectively [11].

To examine how the key principles of PRT translate into an iPad game, harnessing children's motivation and systematically exposure children to multiple cues, we developed *Go Go Games* [7]. In this work, we deploy *Go Go Games* to determine the effectiveness of these techniques in assistive technologies which is critical to understanding the role technology can play in MCR intervention. Teaching MCR helps people learn to communicate verbally and also may help children use their AAC devices [5].

3.1 *Go Go Games*

Go Go Games is a publicly available suite of therapeutic video games designed around the principles of Pivotal Response Training (PRT) [12,16]. Players use the system to work through PRT-grounded exercises at their own pace. Players engage with child-preferred digital objects to build trains, direct cars, and assemble robots on screen. To find the correct pieces, they must pay attention to multiple features of the items they see, such as the length, color, and cargo of the train cars they choose. The user interacts with the tablet game by first observing the stimuli presented (i.e., the graphic prompt); 2. scanning options, 3. selecting a match, and 4. dragging selection along path to complete the trial (see Figure 1). Generalizable techniques translated into digital form include:

Repetition of brief user interaction: In *Go Go Games*, users observe, scan, select, drag and drop an item to the correct location along a visual pathway (e.g., train track).

Feedback & Progress Monitoring: In face-to-face therapy, physical token boards represent how much work is expected; this token analogy is visually replicated in the *Go Go Games* interface (see star icon in bottom right corner of Figure 1). Corrective feedback was given by blinking the perimeter of the correct image after the input of an incorrect answers, a progress tracker on the initial screen and in the corner of each game screen, and a congratulatory screen when each level was completed.

Activity is Child-led: *Go Go Games* incorporates child-preferred stimuli (e.g., iPads, trucks, cars, spaceships). Users have flexibility to choose which game and level to play and can turn on or off background music.

Systematic Intervention: The software systematically scaffolds task difficulty based on user performance. Each trial randomizes the placement of correct options on the screen. Immediate feedback is provided for each trial (i.e., visual and audio statements are differentiated based on response).

An additional aspect of a therapeutic iPad game is, unlike traditional therapies, no other person is required to be part of the interactions. We hypothesized that the unique features of *Go Go Games* would support learning MCR as well as increase child motivation to participate in teaching MCR.

4. METHODS

To evaluate if *Go Go Games* can support MCR, we conducted an experiment in a special education school. We conducted this work with school staff providing 6 students with up to 10 minutes of play per day, across nine days (group avg.= 66 minutes, range 30-90 minutes). To ensure that only the game was available during testing sessions, staff reported they enabled a technical feature of the iPad, "guided access." Staff logs were used to calculate minutes of game play, and comments were reviewed for themes about the participants' engagement with the game. Concurrently, we conducted assessments of MCR in the physical world. After the study, we collected usage logs recorded by the teachers and conducted interviews of the teaching staff (n=6).

4.1 Study Design

We employed a single-case experiment design in a special education classroom, as is widely used by special education researchers and clinicians [17]. This evaluation technique is important to the special education community as a body of evidence about the effectiveness of assistive technology in context of use is critical to the inclusion of therapeutic tools in the classroom. Single-case research uses a single participant as one's own control and aims to replicate desired effects across 3-8 participants per study [9]. Additionally, the common practice is to present data on "responders" as well as "non-responders" to add to the knowledge about a specific population [9].

Two of three classroom teachers volunteered to participate in the study, and all students in those two classrooms were invited to participate. After a parent orientation meeting provided by the first author, eleven students' parents gave consent for their children to be in the study. Next, we randomly assigned one class to play the game first (5 students), while the other class played second (6 students). Assessors were blind to which group the participants were in and the amount of game play they received during the study. We employed visual analysis to interpret the assessment data on a case-by-case basis [6,25].

Each participant began the study with a three-day baseline assessment of their MCR skills in the physical world. Group A then began nine days of *Go Go Games* play, while Group B maintained regular classroom activities. After this phase, both groups were measured again, resulting in a post-intervention assessment for Group A, and a repeated baseline measure for Group B. Then Group B began 9 days of *Go Go Games* play while Group A resumed regular school activities. Both groups were measured at the end for a post measure for Group B and a follow up measure for Group A. The strength of this design in an applied setting is that the change that would result from maturation alone is controlled for by staggering the conditions over time [3]. Therefore, if changes are observed between phases, and across multiple baselines, the likelihood the change is due to the intervention is increased. Additionally, if improvements are maintained after the intervention has been removed during the follow up assessment, these changes can be attributed to the intervention.

The staff designated a ten-minute period per day to play *Go Go Games* and logged the start and end time for each student as well as any comments about the interaction. Participants were assessed during the regular school day at the beginning of the study, at the mid-point (between two groups), and at the end (see Table 1).

We assessed the participants' MCR with physical world objects during three phases of the study (beginning, middle, and end) replicating procedures described in behavioral research literature [24]. Assessments occurred one participant at a time in a separate room. Assessment sessions lasted from 3-30 minutes depending on the behavior of the child. We met with the school's behavior therapist for the first 3 days to align our reinforcement schedules to those being used in the classrooms to ensure student comfort. We also aligned our protocol for responding to undesired behavior (e.g., screaming, spitting, throwing objects, hitting, falling to the floor) to that of the school to minimize disruption to their intensive behavioral programming in place for each student.

This resulted in continuing the assessment while engaging in the planned ignoring of disruptive behaviors (i.e., screaming, spitting), and terminating the session for aggressive behaviors (i.e., hitting or non-responsiveness to instructor for 3 minutes).

Table 1: Study design

Days/ Group	1-3	4-12	13-16	17-25	26-28
A	Baseline	Gameplay	Post test	Wait	Follow up
B	Baseline	Wait	Repeated Baseline	Game Play	Post test

4.2 Participants

The school field site provides highly individualized education and therapy during the school day to support academics, functional life skills, social-emotional, and physical development.

One behavior therapist, two lead special education teachers, and six teaching assistants participated in the study as instructional staff. The parents of eleven out of fifteen students with multiple learning challenges, age 6–14, consented to participate. Eleven participants began the study by participating in the baseline screening assessment of MCR (see Table 2). Not all participants were eligible as three demonstrated perfect scores on the screener (P4, P9, P10) and the school administrators had to remove research activities from the schedule under a variety of contexts (i.e., P6 exhibiting aggressive behavior or was not available due to a therapy session). Additionally, measures were missed on multiple days when specific children were absent from school (P7, P8). We present the assessment results of 6, all AAC users, some of whom missed some assessment sessions or game play.

4.3 MCR Probes

To understand the impact of playing *Go Go Games*, we compared performance on a physical MCR assessment before and after the children played the game. The physical assessment and training for these skills incorporate common classroom objects to test the ability to discriminate among objects based on features in their environment [24]. The assessment tasks consisted of fourteen levels of matching 3D objects that grew in complexity from matching dissimilar wooden objects such as a red square and yellow triangle to recalling textures of a red rectangular block, and finally to distinguishing which image was presented between similar 2D images. The final level used physical flashcards we made from digital images in *Go Go Games* as an additional prerequisite level of testing.

The researchers, board certified behavior analysts, and trained assistants, conducted the assessments based on MCR assessment procedure. A researcher holds up a block in front of the child and states, "this one is the correct one" then removes the object from view. A moment later, the researcher places the correct item and its pair in front of the child, holds out her hand for the participant to place the correct block there and then states, "give me the correct one." Before the test starts, the researcher teaches this response by prompting (e.g., pointing at the correct answer) and then moves on to the test phase. In the subsequent trials, the child is expected to independently makes the distinction of the correct block based on differences in features (i.e., shape, color, size, texture, shade, and finally multiple features in 2D images). The school staff requested an additional level of testing be introduced that permitted the items to remain present during the trial. These two phases resulted in 14 levels.

We worked with the school staff to collaboratively determine if the child needed an additional reinforcement system and to receive advice about engaging the child. For example, P1 required an extended interval for her response time given her motor challenges and P5 had a known fixation with items that are red, thus alternative colored blocks were used. During the assessments, two researchers collected data on correct or incorrect responding, and they tallied the scores daily. The complete administration of the test ranged from 5-15 minutes each time and took place in a separate designated room in the school.

4.4 Data Analysis

To measure effectiveness of the game as an intervention for teaching MCR, we compared the distance for each trial between baseline and treatment, a procedure known as "Nonoverlap of All Pairs" (NAP) [14]. "NAP is a 'complete' nonoverlap index as it individually calculated as the number of improving or positive (Pos) pairs plus half of ties (.5 × Ties), divided by all pairs: NAP = ([Pos + .5 × Ties] / Pairs)" [26]. This nonparametric measure of treatment effectiveness is a common method in behavioral research using single-case experiments for autism interventions. This approach is necessary given the small sample sizes typically present in autism intervention research. Using the guidelines for interpretation recommended by Parker and Vannest, NAP scores between 0 and .65 can be classified as "weak effects" (i.e., no effect), 66 to .92 as "medium effects," and .92 to 1.0 as "strong effects" [19].

Table 1 : Participant demographics and MCR assessment results

Group	ID	Age	Mode of Comm.	Edu. Label	Gender	Baseline	#of play sessions	Avg. Mins of usage	Total Mins of usage	%NAP	Effect Size
A	P1	12.8	AAC	ID	F	4/14	9	10	90	22	Weak
A	P2	11.1	AAC	ID	M	6/14	9	10	90	83	Medium
A	P3	6.2	Verbal	AUT	M	14/14	screened out				
A	P4	6.9	Verbal	AUT	M	14/14	screened out				
A	P5	7.3	AAC	AUT	M	0/14	8	8	65	100	Strong
B	P6	13	Verbal	AUT	M	2/14	study terminated for aggression				
B	P7	11.1	AAC	AUT	M	9/14	6	10	60	33	Weak
B	P8	10.7	AAC	ID	F	0/14	3	10	30	54	Weak
B	P9	8.11	Verbal	AUT	M	14/14	screened out				
B	P10	11.5	Verbal	AUT	M	14/14	screened out				
B	P11	11.6	AAC	ID	M	3/14	8	8	66	88	Medium

To understand the experience of using the game, we analyzed data from the six staff interviews alongside our observational notes. The research team individually reviewed the interview notes for initial impressions and then met collectively to discuss trends in the data. Collectively the team then sorted comments into topics. After identifying dominant topics, we re-sorted the comments into themes. We compared these themes with the effectiveness results and presented these findings to the school's behavior analyst for her interpretation of the collective data. With her input, we then analyzed our observational data for evidence for or against these themes in an iterative manner, then we aligned themes with interactions with the software features.

5. RESULTS

We present results in Section 5.1 that indicate that *Go Go Games* was at least moderately effective in improving some students' ability to consider more stimuli in a task. We analyzed interview and observational data from all participants, resulting in findings related to the re-usable interactive features of *Go Go Games,* presented in Section 5.2.

5.1 MCR Assessment Results

Of the eleven participants who were screened, nine qualified and began the study, and six completed enough trials for analysis: three from group A (P1, P2, P5), and three from the extended baseline condition, group B (P7, P8, P11). we present a description of each of the six participants who participated in each phase of the study (excluded from the study were: P3, P4, P9 and P10 who demonstrated mastery of MCR in the screener and P6 who was dismissed from assessment for aggression toward the staff). For these six cases, we conducted a visual analysis [6,25] of the time series data and treatment effect with the non-overlapping procedure described above (see Table 1). A vignette of each participant case assessment is described below.

P1, a 12-year-old girl, has a combination of autistic-like characteristics and a genetic condition called Phelan-McDermid syndrome which often results in delays or impairment with cognition and motor skills [19]. She is minimally verbal and carried an iPad for expressive communication. Her AAC device contained a few choices of words and phrases that she could press on when she wanted to express a feeling or speak about a certain object, such as requesting a snack. Staff described her *Go Go Games* play as prompted due to her delayed motoric responses, and so we permitted extra time during the MCR assessment. P1 played *Go Go Games* over 9 days for 10 minutes. Her MCR assessment results revealed a low level, yet slightly increasing trend in baseline. After nine days (90 minutes of intervention), she exhibited a lower level and slightly more variable trend that persisted during her follow up assessment (see Figure 2). P1's case shows a weak treatment effect as the data only displays a 22% nonoverlap (see Table 2). Because there is no difference between baseline and post-intervention assessments, we conclude the game did not impact her ability to respond to multiple cues in her physical word.

P2 is dually diagnosed with autism and Down syndrome. Staff explained that when he played, they had to prompt him to continue. Visual inspection of P2's baseline assessment shows a low level of MCR with an increasing trend, resulting in a moderate level of performance. P2 played *Go Go Games* over 9 days for 10 minutes. In contrast, P2's post-intervention assessment showed more variability with higher level of performance. During his follow-up (after a nine-day break from his game play), he maintained a moderate level of performance with some variability that is similar to his baseline but at a slightly higher level. Given his two high scores post intervention, his NAP score was 82%, indicating a medium treatment effect as some of the post treatment scores exceed baseline scores.

P5 is a minimally verbal boy with autism and intellectual disability with a reported history of aggressive behavior. Upon entering the assessment room, he laid on the floor. He grabbed a red block and said "R" for the color red. We were told he perseverates over objects that are red so we switched to yellow blocks. On occasion, he signed "all done" and we ended the trial. At times, he would hold the blocks over his head in a gesture that looked like he would throw the blocks. He matched correctly until the second half of the assessment where the task shifts from matching with the cue present to matching from recalling the color of the block. Staff reported that he played the game independently with frequent requests to continue playing at the 10-minute timer. He fluidly moved between mini-games at times taking a break to engage in self-stimulation. Through visual inspection of P5's performance, he scored zero correct in his three baseline sessions. After the intervention phase, his scores varied at moderate levels and were replicated in follow up probes (see Figure 2). P5 exhibited strong positive treatment effects. In baseline, he did not complete even the first level designed to introduce the task. In the post intervention phase, he scored in the mid-range but with less stability and in the follow up sessions, he maintained these mid-level performances. This outcome results in 100% of NAP, a strong effect as all the post treatment points exceed the baseline points (see Table 2).

P7 is a minimally verbal, eleven-year-old boy with autism who demonstrated mastery of the first half of the MCR assessment on the baseline screening. Staff commented on his brief periods of game play "(he) played for 2 minutes then tried to exit the game, teacher redirected.-A staff member from Group A said in the post study interview that, "*he liked it, he had trouble when he hit a harder level go back to an easier level, something he was comfortable with. He would perseverate on the button choice. He would hit me he doesn't like being wrong. When it highlighted another choice, I would hand-over-hand to the correct choice and he didn't like that.*" According to the staff log, he played for 10 minutes per day for the first 6 days. He was absent form school for 1-2 days per week during the duration of the study. His post intervention assessment scores are like his baseline scores except for a dip on the last day of assessment from level 7 to 2, resulting in a weak treatment effect, and a 33% NAP. Our fieldnotes reveal he performed the first two levels without error, then he began screaming, grabbed himself, and ran to the bathroom.

P8 is minimally verbal girl with intellectual disabilities. At the onset of the study she had only attended this school for two weeks and was displaying aggressive behavior. The two baseline sessions she was present for were terminated within 3 minutes for noncompliance. In the extended baseline, she participated until she began to err at level 2. Our fieldnotes indicate she continually chose the block on the left side. In the post sessions, she refused to let go of the block or threw it resulting in 2 of 3 sessions being terminated in first minute resulting in a weak treatment effect, and NAP of 54%. Her log entries for gameplay reveal she played a total of 30 minutes (10 minutes a day) on days 2,5,7 of the nine-day stage. Staff commented in the log that she was distracted, tried to exit out of game, was a bit frustrated and had some difficulty attending. A staff member from Group A reports "*she would not sit for a long, 30 seconds. She concluded stating she "isn't too reinforced by the iPad.*"

P11 is also a minimally verbal boy with autism and cerebral palsy. He is very interested in socializing with staff as he moves throughout the school and stops to visit and chat with others through his iPad. In assessment sessions, he pushed buttons that output "sing happy birthday" & "Where is [staff name]." He was preoccupied with trying to turn on the TV. Staff reported he was usually distracted by the presence others in the room and opportunities to socialize through approaching and greeting. Upon visual inspection on P11's performance, we see his baseline phase was repeated, as he was part of Group B. In the first baseline series, his scores were of a low level and the trend was flat, suggesting the trend was stable. In the second baseline, there was some variability as the middle session shows a mid-level score with no clear trend. These mid-level scores are replicated in the post-intervention assessment and are more stable. His NAP is 88%, a medium treatment effect (see Table 2).

Taken together, the analysis across these six participants indicates that a small dose of intervention, through this tablet-based game, is associated with measurable improvements in MCR performance for minimally verbal children in our sample who use AAC devices. Specifically, three of the six children who received the therapy for the full experimental dosage achieved medium or strong treatment effects (P2, P5, P11).

5.2 Implementation Results

For the participants who did respond positively to playing *Go Go Games,* we explored the generalizable techniques: preferred stimuli (the form factor of an iPad and game content); the simple interaction, and the systematic feedback. Regarding the form factor, our findings reveal variation in the children's inherent responses to the iPad game and the extent to which it could serve as a fun, reinforcing activity. Staff members that worked directly with the respective participants reported that while some "*really enjoyed it and always wanted to keep going after their time was up,*" (P5, P9, P10), other participants were "*not reinforced by the iPad*" (P6, P7, P8). Only one participant verbally responded to the interview question, what did you think of *Go Go Games?* and he, (P10), said "I like trains." These features appeared generally preferred.

Regarding the simple, repetitive user interaction, responses varied between responders and non-responders. The interaction permitted immediate independence for some of the participants. Staff reported that P5 learned interaction easily – "after three prompts P5 understood the game and followed the instructions exactly". Classroom staff reported that participants (P3, P4, P11) "really engaged with the game. The game is exciting to play, [they] engaged with moving the car." Another staff member from group B reported "it's really good because of the repetition." As the iPad game had appeal to the responders, the game mechanics ultimately impacted the success of a student.

One of the biggest indicators of success for this group of participants was the child's tolerance for feedback – both in game and from staff. Staff reported some participants, such as P7, "didn't like being wrong." Therefore, the corrective feedback became a critical feature. Frequently, the staff logs indicated that students were prompted by the staff to continue to play for the suggested 10 minutes, and, in the case of P1, physically assisted to drag the icon to the correct spot once she touched an object. P11 also received assistance to play the game with a staff person sitting with him at times to encourage him to stay seated and playing the game. Children who were willing to receive help from the staff were more likely to complete the requested amount of playtime and repeated assessments.

As with receiving feedback, difficulty stopping play can be a problem for many children. Difficulty transitioning between activities can be very challenging for children with autism [10], sometimes resulting in aggressive or destructive behaviors (i.e., hitting others, throwing a device). Staff reported aggression from P5 when he was asked to hand over the iPad. There is a burgeoning interest among designers to reduce tantrums from turning off tablets by leveraging natural endings [8]. Research states that some caregivers report that they withhold access to technology to avoid battling when it is time to put it away providing natural stopping points and a definitive conclusion has the potential to make the experience more accessible to more families [15]. Addressing this challenge with transitioning away from using the iPad would be a next step to help students like P5 to continue to learn MCR.

Ways we suggest that therapeutic games for this population could be programmed to come to an end smoothly (e.g., the screen could begin fading until it is blank) to make the transition to disengage

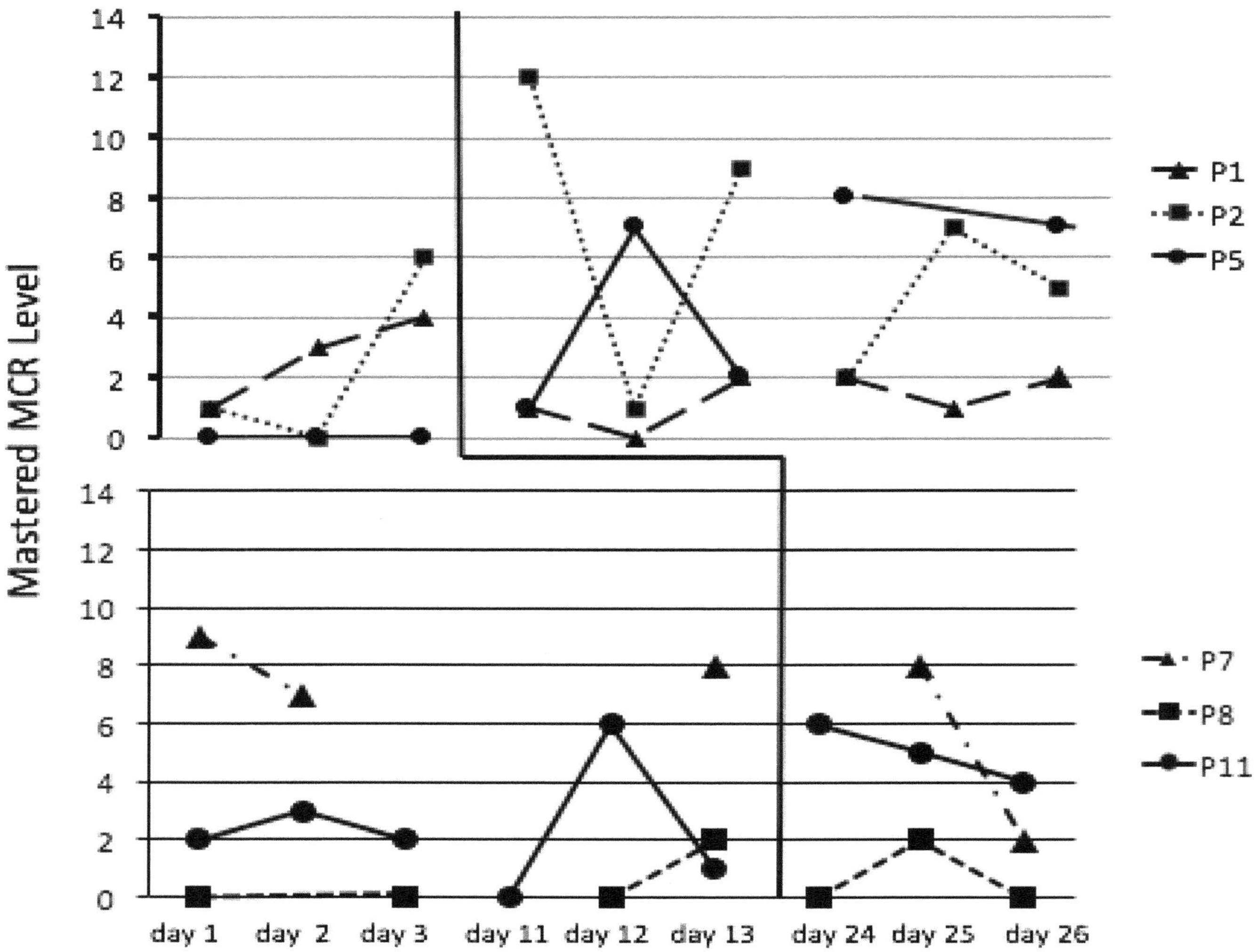

Figure 2: Participant's level of MCR before and after intervention.

more natural. The guided access application used at this school removed the option to exit the game and enter another application but did not address the transition to ending gameplay. An automated way to end play could alleviate some of the discomfort in transitioning (i.e., created a natural ending [8]). Applications can be designed to specifically support terminated iPad game play, methods to do so that do not lead to aggression would require future work.

5.3 Managing Co-Occurring Conditions

Given the complex and varied needs of the AAC users in our study that required or avoided human prompting or sensory input, we present three design considerations to support varied presentations for children who engage in overselectivity, specifically as they related to physical, cognitive, and behavioral challenges. Our analysis highlighted the complexity of the context of classroom settings, in which we deployed *Go Go Games* and which are likely targets for therapeutic game use more generally.

5.3.1 Physical Disabilities

Physical disabilities that co-occur with overselectivity can cause additional challenges, both related to overselectivity and related to the intervention used to improve it. Several staff mentioned visual concerns, for example, saying that the games presented too many details or that the digital objects were too small or too subtle. or making specific suggestions:

"Making the flags or pictures bigger may be helpful for students to see." - Group B staff member

Similarly, our observations and staff reporting indicated that motor issues were a concern for P1 who has a motor disability, who could not easily use the game despite it being designed to tolerate imprecise touch input, allow breaks in smooth drags, and support players who struggle to perform motions that require crossing the midline of their bodies.

These results indicate that all games, and *Go Go Games* should be further modified to allow for additional types of interactions. For example, a touch or tap, instead of a drag would simplify access for children with motor issues. Similarly, personalization of the visual output, as suggested above, could improve access for those with visual challenges. Although wide ranges of input have been explored previously in the literature [28], what is key to our findings here is the challenge of intersectionality within the assistive technology and disabilities communities. It is not enough to design systems with one or even multiple common combinations of disabilities in mind. Children are often evolving in their disabilities experiencing dynamically changing multiple conditions and contexts, requiring intense personalization while still, ideally, making the system accessible for use without professional configuration. This requirement speaks to the need for future therapeutic games to employ intelligence to learn a user's skillset and capabilities as well as to employ personalization at a level that a child, parent, or teacher could engage [32].

5.3.2 Cognitive and Attention Related Disabilities

Just as co-occurring physical disabilities can greatly increase the complexity of a child's struggle with overselectivity, many children in our study also experienced additional *cognitive* and *attention* issues that may have played a role in their engagement with the game. These issues are challenging to differentiate from overselectivity but worth exploring.

As just one example of these challenges, for people to use *Go Go Games* successfully, they must be able to complete a swipe motion. Which can be a challenging concept to learn while playing the game. For P1, staff expressed concerns that this interaction was too cognitively demanding for her but suggested a simpler interaction might help as she does tap her AAC device. Staff also explained that several participants struggled with attention challenges when playing. A staff member from Group A explained that some children "*engage for the whole time, while it was hard for others to maintain engagement.*" Given this variability, it is not clear that all children would be able to attend to the game long enough to see therapeutic benefits.

The context of the environment of assistive technology use can also greatly impact the ability of children to engage. The work in this study was all completed in the classroom environment, in which multiple children of mixed abilities were often present. Staff reported that distractions in the classroom contributed to poor attention and that small visual details in the game were too subtle to hold children's attention. They also explained that some participants struggled to direct their attention to the focal point within the game, and for example, got stuck on one action or spot, or had difficulty understanding where the action was to occur. Others would choose to replay a successful level rather than move on to the increased challenge of the next level. A staff member from Group B suggested that, "*maybe a simpler beginning stage in the game then fade up to full screen of images,*" would provide better scaffolding for learning MCR and support children with attention challenges.

Separately, staff reported that for some participants the background images embedded in the game were distracting. Some staff suggested using minimal visuals on-screen, so that the game would be more accessible to students who are overwhelmed easily. Relatedly, some children engaged with the screen in unintended ways. Since P5 could use the iPad independently, he was observed to engage in self-stimulation with the game where his focus did not appear to be on practicing his matching skills. Despite these unintended interactions, his MCR performance improved dramatically in the post assessment. Perhaps having the opportunity to engage with the game independently, as he chose, afforded him the time to self-regulate. Debates about the appropriate role of educational technology continue in special education settings [13]. Finding a balance between engagement and distraction remains an ongoing challenge and the most productive balance may differ from one child to the next.

These results indicate that there are multiple ways children engage with technology and each way should be considered carefully to determine what, if any, modifications to a system need to occur to support accessibility.

6. DISCUSSION

The results of this research demonstrate that *Go Go Games* can be both usable and effective for learning multiple cue responding for some children with minimal verbal abilities and intellectual disabilities. Our empirical study in an applied setting provides understanding of user experiences across a small yet diverse set of users, leading us to broader questions about the nature of designing assistive technology. In this work, we demonstrated that *Go Go Games* was usable for some in this context. Our small group of diverse participants engaged in scheduled, dose-regulated game play, a necessary precursor to successful therapy. School staff could administer the game doses successfully, another essential component of creating an effective experience. Our interviews with staff members and observations of participants suggest that the app can be deployed as a therapeutic tool in a school setting. However, the fact that several of our participants dropped out before receiving the full treatment also suggests that *Go Go Games* may not be a feasible treatment option in all contexts or for all children given their individual physical, cognitive, and behavioral needs. However, given the fact that the systematic teaching of MCR currently only reaches a very limited user-base (i.e., MCR is therapy target for children with autism [11]), *Go Go Games* has the potential to expand the reach of how many children receive treatment for overselectivity, despite its limitations.

Additionally, we demonstrated effectiveness of *Go Go Games* in teaching MCR to a subset of the population that needs support. The participants who struggled with MCR in their baseline assessment and received the full treatment dose showed improvements in their final assessment. This study has important implications for training this specific skill using this specific game and for training language skills using digital therapies more generally. Given that teaching MCR to reduce overselectivity could potential support the high proportion of preliterate AAC users in more effectively accessing their AAC systems, ongoing research is warranted to understand the role of overselectivity and how to build smart systems to reduce its impact.

People with severe disabilities often exhibit secondary disabilities [21], thus, supporting these circumstances may be essential to the effectiveness of the tool. One way to merge the specialized supports required of these complex conditions would be to train designers of assistive technology for preliterate users in methods to reduce overselectivity, as overselectivity may be a potential co-occurring condition. Alternatively, we could address these complex needs through collaboration across several domains of disability to develop a shared vision of the multitude of needs to address in an assistive technology aimed at a pivotal cognitive skill. This collaborative effort could result in a decision tree for assistive technology designers to concurrently support the unique cognitive, physical, and behavioral as well as social needs of AAC users.

For those relying on AAC devices but struggling with MCR, game mechanisms to reduce overselectivity is paramount. For example, designers of therapeutic games could support a more diverse user base through scaffolding and additional supports and/or build a screener via an experiential tutorial to confirm the user has the prerequisite skills to benefit from the system. A screener could address the wide range of abilities and diverse sets of disabilities (e.g., test various configuration of audio, visual, and motor interactions or even configure itself intelligently based caregiver feedback and user interaction). In this way, input could be varied depending on a user's motor skills, interactions could be varied depending on cognitive skills, and so on as is suggested in ability-based design [32]. For example, P1 who struggles to swipe an image on the iPad may be screened for overselectivity using a variety of interactions (e.g., variations ranging from soft quick tap to sustained drag).

Likewise, system interfaces should be adjustable. For example, the background of a computer game, which can be aesthetically pleasing or a key element to provide enjoyment for some children, can be distracting for children who struggle with overselectivity. A variety of options should be made available during both implementation and game play for customizing these types of non-essential game elements. For example, simply making the game play window smaller limits the visual field the child must interpret. Similarly, being able to toggle on and off various background elements or object size could provide some customizability for children with special needs. Lastly, the mechanics of the reward schedule could be customizable to increase tolerance to in-game feedback. These kinds of solutions are essential for therapeutic games to meet the specific needs of the children who are engaged in them and could be configured by a trained specialist or a parent. However, this kind of customization may also be necessary and useful for a wider variety of games to make them accessible to more children for entertainment or educational purposes.

7. CONCLUSION

In this paper, we presented initial findings toward a body of evidence of the effectiveness of a mobile behavioral intervention in the form of an iPad game for minimally verbal children who struggle with overselectivity. Specifically, single-case design results suggest the mean scores shifted positively for three of six participants after nine days of intervention. Additionally, we describe the conditions under which the system worked well and those areas that require additional design work. We presented generalizable technological design features drawn from evidenced-based therapies to consider in the design of future assistive technologies for people who are preliterate and minimally verbal.

These results leave open research questions regarding the potential for customizing the settings related to vision, motor movements, attention spans, and feedback tolerance for a diversity of issues that challenged users with overselectivity. These design challenges are not trivial, and they represent an important scope of challenge for making technology and games accessible. These systems have the potential to provide both therapeutic benefit and entertainment value. However, this value increasingly relies on the ability to adapt to a variety of users and contexts.

Finally, to truly understand the potential power of these technologies and the barriers to their use, a large evidence-base must be assembled. This work should be followed up with collaborative efforts across a variety of researchers who support preliterate AAC users, as well as evaluation studies that are longer, and therefore provide higher dosages of the game to the children, and include additional participants with other co-occurring challenges to understand the full scope of potential impact and engagement.

ACKNO WLEDGMENTS

We thank the school, staff, children and parents who consented to have their children participated in this work. We thank the behavior therapist, Melissa Kramer, for the translational work that provided a smooth study. We also thank the research assistants, Andrea Conejo-Toledo, and Koramya Arriaga who assisted in the training materials for data collection. We thank STAR lab for early input on this manuscript. We thank Robert and Barbara Kleist for funds to support this work. This research was approved by human subjects protocol #2015-1871.

REFERENCES

[1] Meghan Allen, Joanna McGrenere, and Barbara Purves. 2007. The design and field evaluation of PhotoTalk: a digital image communication application for people. *Proceedings of the 9th international ACM SIGACCESS conference on Computers and accessibility*, ACM, 187–194.

[2] Rolf Black. 2011. The Phonicstick: a joystick to generate novel words using phonics. *The proceedings of the 13th international ACM SIGACCESS conference on Computers and accessibility*, ACM, 325–326.

[3] John O. Cooper, Timothy E. Heron, William L. Heward, and others. 2007. Applied behavior analysis.

[4] Chata A. Dickson, Sharon S. Wang, Kristin M. Lombard, and William V. Dube. 2006. Overselective stimulus control in residential school students with intellectual disabilities. *Research in Developmental Disabilities* 27, 6, 618–631. http://doi.org/10.1016/j.ridd.2005.07.004

[5] William V. Dube and Krista M. Wilkinson. 2014. The Potential Influence of "Stimulus Overselectivity" in AAC: Information from Eye-tracking and Behavioral Studies of Attention. *Augmentative and alternative communication (Baltimore, Md.: 1985)* 30, 2, 172–185. http://doi.org/10.3109/07434618.2014.904924

[6] Gene S Fisch. 2001. Evaluating data from behavioral analysis: visual inspection or statistical models? *Behavioural Processes* 54, 1–3, 137–154. http://doi.org/10.1016/S0376-6357(01)00155-3

[7] Alexis Hiniker, Joy Wong Daniels, and Heidi Williamson. 2013. Go go games: therapeutic video games for children with autism spectrum disorders. *Proceedings of the 12th International Conference on Interaction Design and Children*, ACM, 463–466. Retrieved September 24, 2014 from http://dl.acm.org/citation.cfm?id=2485808

[8] Alexis Hiniker, Hyewon Suh, Sabina Cao, and Julie A. Kientz. 2016. Screen Time Tantrums: How Families Manage Screen Media Experiences for Toddlers and Preschoolers. *Proceedings of the 2016 CHI Conference on Human Factors in Computing Systems*, ACM, 648–660. http://doi.org/10.1145/2858036.2858278

[9] Robert H. Horner, Edward G. Carr, James Halle, Gail McGee, Samuel Odom, and Mark Wolery. 2005. The Use of Single-Subject Research to Identify Evidence-Based Practice in Special Education. *Exceptional Children* 71, 2, 165–179. http://doi.org/10.1177/001440290507100203

[10] Amie M King, Kathryn W Brady, and Grayce Voreis. 2017. "It's a blessing and a curse": Perspectives on tablet use in children with autism spectrum disorder. *Autism & Developmental Language Impairments* 2, 2396941516683183. http://doi.org/10.1177/2396941516683183

[11] Lynn Kern Koegel, Robert L. Koegel, Joshua K. Harrower, and Cynthia Marie Carter. 1999. Pivotal Response Intervention I: Overview of Approach. *Journal of the Association for Persons with Severe Handicaps* 24, 3, 174–185. http://doi.org/10.2511/rpsd.24.3.174

[12] Robert L. |Kern Koegel Koegel. 2006. *Pivotal Response Treatments for Autism: Communication, Social, and Academic Development*. Brookes Publishing Company.

[13] David McNaughton and Janice Light. 2013. The iPad and Mobile Technology Revolution: Benefits and Challenges for Individuals who require Augmentative and Alternative Communication. *Augmentative and Alternative Communication* 29, 2, 107–116. http://doi.org/10.3109/07434618.2013.784930

[14] Bart Michiels, Mieke Heyvaert, Ann Meulders, and Patrick Onghena. 2016. Confidence intervals for single-case effect size measures based on randomization test inversion. *Behavior Research Methods*. http://doi.org/10.3758/s13428-016-0714-4

[15] Pat Mirenda. 2009. Promising Innovations in AAC for Individuals With Autism Spectrum Disorders. *SIG 12 Perspectives on Augmentative and Alternative Communication* 18, 4, 112–113. http://doi.org/10.1044/aac18.4.112

[16] Fereshteh Mohammadzaheri, Lynn Kern Koegel, Mohammad Rezaei, and Enayatolah Bakhshi. 2015. A randomized clinical trial comparison between pivotal response treatment (PRT) and adult-driven applied behavior analysis (ABA) intervention on disruptive behaviors in public school children with autism. *Journal of autism and developmental disorders* 45, 9, 2899–2907.

[17] Samuel L. Odom, Ellen Brantlinger, Russell Gersten, Robert H. Horner, Bruce Thompson, and Karen R. Harris. 2005. Research in Special Education: Scientific Methods and Evidence-Based Practices. *Exceptional Children* 71, 2, 137–148. http://doi.org/10.1177/001440290507100201

[18] Katie O'Leary, Charles Delahunt, Patricia Dowden, et al. 2012. Design goals for a system for enhancing AAC with personalized video. *Proceedings of the 14th international ACM SIGACCESS conference on Computers and accessibility*, ACM, 223–224.

[19] K. Phelan and H. E. McDermid. 2011. The 22q13.3 Deletion Syndrome (Phelan-McDermid Syndrome). *Molecular Syndromology* 2, 3–5, 186–201. http://doi.org/10.1159/000334260

[20] Bertram O. Ploog. 2010. Stimulus Overselectivity Four Decades Later: A Review of the Literature and Its Implications for Current Research in Autism Spectrum Disorder. *Journal of Autism and Developmental Disorders* 40, 11, 1332–1349. http://doi.org/10.1007/s10803-010-0990-2

[21] Jenny Preece, Helen Sharp, and Yvonne Rogers. 2015. Interaction Design: Beyond Human-Computer Interaction. Second Edition. *MyScienceWork*.

[22] Deborah Preston and Mark Carter. 2009. A Review of the Efficacy of the Picture Exchange Communication System Intervention. *Journal of Autism and Developmental Disorders* 39, 10, 1471–1486. http://doi.org/10.1007/s10803-009-0763-y

[23] Suzanne Prior, Annalu Waller, and Thilo Kroll. The CHAMPION software project. *Proceedings of the 13th international ACM SIGACCESS conference on Computers and accessibility*, ACM, 287–288.

[24] Sarah R. Rieth, Aubyn C. Stahmer, Jessica Suhrheinrich, and Laura Schreibman. 2015. Examination of the prevalence of stimulus overselectivity in children with ASD. *Journal of Applied Behavior Analysis* 48, 1, 71–84. http://doi.org/10.1002/jaba.165

[25] Henry S. Roane, Wayne W. Fisher, Michael E. Kelley, Joanna L. Mevers, and Kelly J. Bouxsein. 2013. USING MODIFIED VISUAL-INSPECTION CRITERIA TO INTERPRET FUNCTIONAL ANALYSIS OUTCOMES: FUNCTIONAL ANALYSIS INTERPRETATION. *Journal of Applied Behavior Analysis* 46, 1, 130–146. http://doi.org/10.1002/jaba.13

[26] Laura Schreibman. 1997. The study of stimulus control in autism. *Environment and Behavior*, 203–209.

[27] Laura Schreibman and Robert L. Koegel. 1982. Multiple-cue responding in autistic children. *Advances in Child Behavioral Analysis & Therapy* 2, 81–99.

[28] Shari Trewin, Cal Swart, and Donna Pettick. 2013. Physical Accessibility of Touchscreen Smartphones. *Proceedings of the 15th International ACM SIGACCESS Conference on Computers and Accessibility*, ACM, 19:1–19:8. http://doi.org/10.1145/2513383.2513446

[29] Keith Vertanen. 2013. A collection of conversational AAC-like communications. *Proceedings of the 15th International ACM SIGACCESS Conference on Computers and Accessibility*, ACM, 31.

[30] Tonio Wandmacher, Jean-Yves Antoine, and Franck Poirier. 2007. SIBYLLE: a system for alternative communication adapting to the context and its user. *Proceedings of the 9th international ACM SIGACCESS conference on Computers and accessibility*, ACM, 203–210.

[31] Karl Wiegand and Rupal Patel. 2012. SymbolPath: a continuous motion overlay module for icon-based assistive communication. *Proceedings of the 14th international ACM SIGACCESS conference on Computers and accessibility*, ACM, 209–210.

[32] Jacob O. Wobbrock, Shaun K. Kane, Krzysztof Z. Gajos, Susumu Harada, and Jon Froehlich. 2011. Ability-Based Design: Concept, Principles and Examples. *ACM Trans. Access. Comput.* 3, 3, 9:1–9:27. http://doi.org/10.1145/1952383.1952384

Using Participatory Design with Proxies with Children with Limited Communication

Foad Hamidi
University of Maryland, Baltimore County
Baltimore, MD, USA
foadhamidi@umbc.edu

Melanie Baljko
York University
Toronto, Canada
mb@cse.yorku.ca

Isabel Gómez
University of Seville
Seville, Spain
igomez@us.es

ABSTRACT
Including children with communication disorders in the participatory design and evaluation of digital technologies is challenging, as communication between designers and users — an important part of this approach — can be impacted. Using *Participatory Design with Proxies* (PDwP) supports the inclusion of input from different stakeholders, such as parents, teachers and *Speech-Language Pathologists* (SLPs), who can provide valuable insight and feedback to augment direct input from users, which may be severely limited. We describe how we used PDwP to design a digital living media system that motivates children with disabilities to use digital therapeutic and learning applications and supports communication and collaboration between users. We employed an iterative design process to fabricate three functional prototypes and used them as design probes in participants' home and school settings. We present lessons learned in the form of the strengths and shortcomings of using PDwP for designing systems for children with limited communication abilities.

Author Keywords
Participatory Design with Proxies; Children with Disabilities; Digital Living Media Systems

ACM Classification Keywords
H.5.2. User Interfaces: User-centered Design

INTRODUCTION
A challenge for conducting *Participatory Design* (PD) with users with disabilities is that some disorders severely limit users' communication abilities, making it difficult to gather, interpret and incorporate feedback directly from them [47]. Given the importance of including users with disabilities in the design process of assistive technologies, it is important to explore and refine methodologies that support inclusion despite difficulties [34, 38]. Many such tools and methods are being developed to address these difficulties, including alternative communication tools and techniques for design that are not solely focused on verbal or written mediums [47], and methods for the "designerly" re-interpretation of data gathered from participants [13]. One such approach, *Participatory Design with Proxies* (PDwP), is a variation of PD in which proxies are also included in the early stages of design to gather domain knowledge about a particular design [8, 23]. Proxies are individuals who are very familiar with the target users or who resemble them closely. This approach has been used successfully in the past to design systems with both adults with disabilities [8] and children with disabilities [23].

In this paper, we explore the strengths and weaknesses of PDwP, in the design of an ambient digital living media display that motivates children with disabilities that limit communication abilities to use *target applications* (i.e., digital applications with therapeutic and/or learning outcomes) and communicate more with others. *Digital living media systems* are systems that combine living organisms and electronic components [18, 19]. In this paper, we focus on describing how, when designing one such system, we applied PDwP to gather and interpret useful insights that might otherwise have been impossible to access. We describe the formal evaluation of the system elsewhere [19].

In the next section, we present a review of the research literature on the use of PD with children with and without disabilities. Next, we describe our design process in which we designed and used 3 functional prototypes to gather input from various stakeholders, including *Speech-Language Pathologists* (SLPs), teachers, parents and children. We describe how we used the PDwP method to combine our observations of the children's behavior and feedback from their adult communication partners to interpret the data and address research questions. We conclude with a series of lessons learned.

BACKGROUND
Participatory Design (PD) [40, 42] is a design methodology that emphasizes the incorporation of user domain knowledge and recognizes the importance of collaborating and co-creating technology with users and their community. An essential technique of PD is to actively engage users of technology in its design. Originally, PD was used to develop technologies for the workplace; however, it became apparent that it also offers great value to many other areas

ASSETS '17, October 29-November 1, 2017, Baltimore, MD, USA

ACM ISBN 978-1-4503-4926-0/17/10…$15.00
https://doi.org/10.1145/3132525.3132527

of design and development including designing for users with disabilities [29] and specifically designing with children with disabilities [1, 14, 26]. *Participatory Design with Proxies* (PDwP) is a variation of PD in which proxies, people who are familiar with the target users or who resemble them, are included in the early stages of design to gather domain knowledge about use scenarios [8, 23].

Several PD methodologies have been developed specifically for including children in the design process. *Cooperative Inquiry* is specifically developed to allow children to be design partners and collaborate with adults to come up with novel design ideas [11]. The method views children as potential designers and aims to facilitate their abilities to be design partners through accessible and intuitive methods. It is typically used with small groups of children over long periods of time. Guha et al. are developing an inclusive version of Cooperative Inquiry that provides provisions for involving children with disabilities [17]. Other related approaches view children as co-designers, and include Bonded Design [31] and Informant Design [41]. Moraveji et al. used comics and storyboards as tools to engage children in PD [35].

Participatory Design with Children with Disabilities

Frauenberger et al. have argued strongly for engaging children with disabilities and their community in the participatory design and evaluation of computational interfaces, arguing that the three identified benefits of using PD, namely 1) better understanding of requirements, 2) building realistic expectations in target groups and 3) empowerment of marginalized groups, are amplified in this context [14].

Several projects have used PD to work with children with disabilities to develop new technologies. In the ECHOES project, Frauenberger et al. worked with two high-functioning children on the Autism spectrum and one child with an undiagnosed language disorder, and 30 typically developing 6-years-old children, on the design of a technologically-enhanced learning environment to scaffold the social skill development of both typically-developing children and children on the high functioning end of the Autism spectrum disorder [13, 15]. The researchers found that working with children provided information that otherwise would have been difficult to obtain. Additionally, they found the importance of finding a balance between the benefits of participation and the risks of causing stress or pressure. Finally, they found it essential to interpret and translate children's feedback and ideas into realistic and practical design choices using a "designerly" approach in such a way that the interpretations stay true to the core messages of the children's ideas [13].

The ECHOES project was inspired by the *Reactive Colours* project, which included children on the Autism spectrum as key informants in the design of an interactive software system, *ReacTikles* that provides users with engaging and relaxing activities [28]. The researchers used surveys and interviews with the children's parents to gather feedback about prototypes that they then incorporated into the next iterations of their system. Similarly, Piper et al. included children on the Autism spectrum, in the development of SIDES, a cooperative tabletop computer game for social skills development [36]. They found that interviewing children one-on-one put a lot of pressure on the child and decided instead to conduct interviews in groups.

Brederode et al. involved children with different physical and learning disabilities as design informants in the development and evaluation of *pOwerball*, an augmented reality tabletop tangible game to encourage collaboration and social interaction for children with mixed abilities [9]. This entailed a combination of interviews and observation sessions with children to gather insights that they incorporated into the system. They further evaluated the system with children with and without disabilities. The researchers argued that the child design informants' involvement provided useful insider information about their likes and dislikes about the game and created empathy and understanding between the researchers and the children without creating much stress or pressure.

Several research projects have developed new methods and tools to involve children with different disabilities in the participatory design of new digital systems. These tools and methods include the use of templates and personas [33], low-tech mockups [5], group interaction with prototypes [2], and peer interviews [40].

Including individuals with significant communication and language disabilities in PD can be challenging because of their limited expression when expressing their needs and desires [10, 23, 30]. In the case of children, this is compounded because it can be harder for them than for adults to participate in abstract or hypothetical discussions and scenarios. For these reasons, some researchers have also employed caregivers as "proxy users" to explore the needs of individuals with disabilities [8]. In the case of children, proxy users can include the children's parents, teachers and other individuals who are familiar with them. However, it is clear that working with proxies is not the same as working directly with the users of technology [42] and it should only be used when working directly is impossible because of barriers such as very limited communication or access [42].

Several recent projects have explored using PDwP to design various systems, including serious games and intervention systems. Hirano et al. used a PDwP method to design and evaluate, *vSked*, a visual scheduling tool to support classroom activities for children on the Autism spectrum [23]. To inform their design, they identified and included adult stakeholders (10 teachers and 3 SLPs) as design partners and conducted interviews with them and observed their classrooms and sessions over nine months. They incorporated the results into a working prototype that they co-examined with their design partners. Using stakeholder feedback, they refined the working prototype which they then evaluated with student users in the classroom. The researchers found that incorporating adult stakeholders in the design process was helpful in building a relevant product. In another similar project, Kientz et al. described the major social and behavioral difficulties of working directly with children with disabilities as design partners, and mitigated this using the help of adult proxies (caregivers, parents and teachers of children on the Autism spectrum) to inform the design of a wearable interface to detect self-stimulatory behavior in the children [30].

In another project, Dawe used a "technology probe" (i.e., an early prototype) to develop a communication application for individuals with cognitive disabilities [10]. The probe was developed based on qualitative data (interviews with 20 families of children with cognitive disabilities). It was used to elicit suggestions and ideas from two individuals with cognitive disabilities and their families. Dawe argued that using a technology probe could be an effective tool for the inclusion of individuals with significant cognitive disabilities in the design process as it facilitates dialogue. The concrete instantiation helped overcome difficulties in engaging in abstract or hypothetical discussions. Additionally, Dawe observed that having a concrete object (even in early versions) that can be modified in response to users' suggestion and requests can create ownership and empowerment in users [10].

Thus, previous research show that 1) by including a variety of users and stakeholders in the design process, valuable domain expertise can be uncovered [45], and 2) an important aspect of including users with limited communication in the design process is identifying appropriate communication tools and protocols (i.e., alternatives to spoken or written language) that allow for the expression and integration of their input [38]. We take these results into account by including a diverse group of stakeholders, and by using functional prototypes or probes [26] to elicit feedback. While PDwP has been employed as a methodology in the past, none of the previous projects, to our knowledge, have explored the impact of using it for facilitating access to context-dependent data, such as results that emerge from observing the spontaneous use of a system in the home setting, and in interpreting the impact of interactions beyond the immediate context of use.

DESIGNING A DIGITAL LIVING MEDIA SYSTEM FOR MOTIVATING CHILDREN

Rafigh is a digital system that uses the growth of a living media interface, a living mushroom colony, as a component of its interface. Its purpose is motivate children with disabilities, in a home or school setting, to (1) use digital target applications with positive outcomes, and (2) encourage collaboration and communication between children and their adult communication partners (i.e., teachers, caregivers). It consists of a physical enclosure that houses the mushroom colony and an irrigation system controlled by an embedded computer. Rafigh is designed for use in the home or school setting.

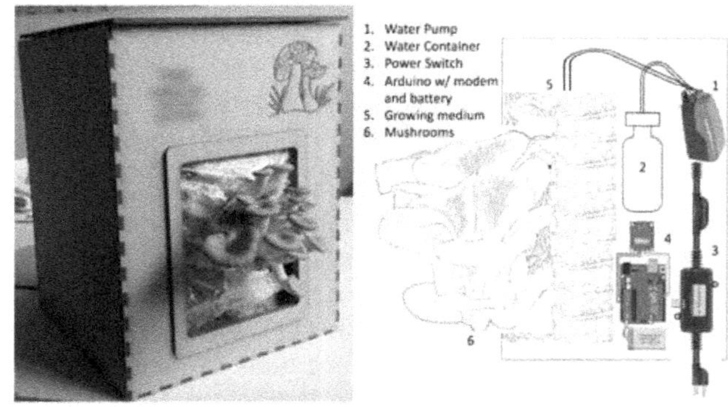

Figure 1. Rafigh (Prototype 3): the physical prototype (left), schematic with component names (right)

Rafigh (Figure 1, left) consists of a physical enclosure that houses a mushroom colony and an irrigation system controlled by an embedded computer. It is designed to be used in conjunction with a customizable suite of 3rd-party digital applications, which we term "target" applications due to their desired therapeutic and/or learning-based anticipated benefits. The choice of target digital applications is a parameter of the system; it is delegated to the child's parents, teachers, SLPs, or other stakeholders who determine the desired therapeutic and/or learning outcomes. Rafigh monitors the use of target digital applications; the more the children use them, the better the adherence to an optimal watering schedule resulting in faster growth. Figure 1 (right) shows the system schematic.

The mushrooms take between 10-16 days to completely grow. For the first few days, there is little change in the visual appearance of Rafigh but in the last 4-5 days of growth the appearance of the mushrooms is more dynamic and visibly changes every few hours. Figure 2 shows the growth of Rafigh over time.

Figure 2. Rafigh's growth over time

Designing Rafigh using PDwP

The current project aimed to study how digital living media systems can (1) better motivate children to use therapeutic and/or learning applications, and (2) support more collaboration and communication between them and their adult communication partners. Work on this initial question lead to another research question: What is an appropriate participatory methodology to design engaging technologies for children with limited communication capabilities? In this paper, we focus on this methodological question.

We decided to frame the research project using the *Research through Design* (RtD) methodology. RtD is used in HCI research to conduct experiential inquiry into a design space through the iterative design and evaluation of artifacts [48, 50]. In this approach, the design and deployment of prototypes, as well as, critical analysis of their affordances and implications, are the primary modes of inquiry [4, 48]. RtD supports the inclusion of multiple stakeholders and multiple points of views and encourages participatory methods [48].

The first phases of RtD, prior to iterative design and reflection phases, involve defining the focus of a project and collecting and synthesizing data to inform it. We conducted a literature review and a series of interviews and focus groups sessions with SLPs. We have reported the results of the review and SLP interviews elsewhere [21] and here briefly summarize their results.

The literature review identified the potential of *Tangible and Embedded Interfaces* (TEIs) for engaging children in the context of communication and behavior intervention, with diverse projects supporting artistic expression [6], collaboration [12] and speech language therapy [18], emerging in recent years. TEIs, also known as *physical* or *digital manipulatives* [50], are characterized by electronic microcontrollers, sensors and actuators that are embedded in either existing or newly designed physical objects [27]. They go beyond the traditional computer screen to engage movement and make the user experience more engaging and accessible. TEIs can be physically more expressive and flexible than traditional desktop interfaces, allowing for the development of novel interfaces that incorporate emotional and ludic cues to the child [50]. *Automatic Speech Recognition* (ASR) has also been previously used to engage children's speech but is found to present challenges in the automatic creation and presentation of meaningful and accurate feedback [3, 21, 44].

SLP interviews consisted of one-on-one, open-ended interviews with 5 SLPs who work with children. Each interview lasted between 45 minutes and an hour. Additionally, we conducted two focus group sessions with SLPs. Three SLPs attended the first meeting and four SLPs attended the second. These sessions lasted between one and a half to two hours. During the interviews and focus group discussions, we asked the SLPs about a possible computational software or hardware solution that could support their practice. We categorized the data into the following 5 design themes:

Intervention-focused Activities: The SLPs believed that a digital system to complement therapy and support communication and collaboration in settings outside of the clinic (e.g., home or school) would be useful. They identified technology's potential to capture children's attention, stating that an interactive toy can be useful if it motivates children to complete complementary speech language exercises at home. Additionally, they stated that it is important that automatic feedback, if provided, be accurate and consistent.

Engagement: The SLPs stated their desire for a digital toy that can sustain the children's speech exercises in the absence of SLPs. They stated that a challenge they often faced was the children's lack of engagement with therapeutic and learning exercises.

Customization: The SLPs identified the need for making the system customizable for each user. They stated that in their practice they customize exercises and intervention activities for each client.

Context of Use: The data indicated a strong need for increased practice of speech and language skills in the home, as well as, school settings. The SLPs emphasized the key role of close family members (e.g., caregivers, parents, siblings), as well as, peers and teachers as communication partners with whom the children can practice language and speech skills. This result points to the importance of considering both *how* and *where* the system is used.

Technological Instantiation: Three of the SLPs already use props such as dolls and physical toys, as well as, images and flash cards to engage children. These toys allow for the development of narrative and the engagement of the children's attention. They stressed that it is useful to have physical toys that children can touch and grasp and are also durable. Two of the SLPs used therapeutic iPad applications regularly to engage their clients.

Based on these results, we developed a general design concept that we used in subsequent PDwP sessions as a communication and discussions tool and consisted of the following description:

Rafigh is an interactive digital system in the form of a digital physical system to support communication and collaboration for children with language and communication disorders in the home setting.

The following series of PDwP sessions were conducted *in situ*. These contexts included the children's school and home settings (as opposed to the lab or clinic settings). In previous research, the importance of using *in situ* evaluations for assistive technology [25] and ubiquitous systems [37] is emphasized. This approach provides higher internal validity and can uncover factors that might go undetected otherwise.

Design Iteration 1

The first series of collaborative design sessions consisted of four one-hour sessions over 4 weeks, with a participating special education teacher (A1) and a 4-year-old boy with speech delay (P1) at a local special education school. At the time of the sessions, A1 had administered speech and language exercises to P1 for close to three months.

During the first 2 sessions, we used the design concept developed above to brainstorm with A1 and also observed the intervention activities and exercises she was using with P1. The exercises consisted of speech drills with animal names and numbers that P1 responded to with vocalizations that sometimes resembled the words but were not clear. A1 used low-tech toys and pictures to emphasize target words and phrases. She suggested that we develop a system to prompt P1 with similar words and provide rewards when they are repeated.

Figure 3. Prototype 1 with LED lights and enclosure (left) and with internal electronics exposed (right)

We incorporated observations from these sessions, input from A1 and results from the literature review and SLP interviews (presented above) into a first prototype, Prototype 1 (shown in Figure 3). Prototype 1 was a tangible cardboard box that housed a microcontroller, LED lights and a bubble blower. The user could activate the lights and bubble blower by repeating after audio and image prompts from a laptop computer that the prototype was placed next to. The software for Prototype 1 consisted of a graphical user interface that prompted the user with a series of animal names. When the child user repeated the words correctly (as determined by an ASR module), the LED lights and bubble blower were activated.

In the next two sessions, we brought Prototype 1 to the school and showed it to A1 and P1. P1 initially showed signs of interest in the water and bubble blower and was happy when bubbles were produced. However, the system did not motivate him to use his speech more: he did not respond to the speech prompts and did not show interest in the software interface. He kept touching different parts of the system and eventually pulled out several of the LED lights. He showed particular interest in the physical box and the electronics inside. He lost interest in the system after about 10-15 minutes.

A1 made several comments and suggestions about the prototype. First, she identified making the system more engaging for P1 as a key requirement. She suggested that an engaging mechanism should be employed that can keep P1's attention over longer periods of time. Additionally, she suggested that the limited software component of the system could not adequately keep P1 interested.

"Both the application and toy have to use brighter colors, more exaggerated sounds, maybe it should be a game they can play. Children this age get distracted easily, you need to make the playing more fun!"

Second, she suggested that if two or more children could use the toy, its appeal might increase. She emphasized that the system should support intervention in the home with complementary exercises. She suggested the family of the child user should be engaged in the intervention. Finally, she observed that P1 liked to touch the system and pull and push on its components. She stated it is important that the system be more robust and have a stronger structure that makes it possible to leave it with the child user over time.

Design Iteration 2

Based on results from sessions with Prototype 1, we decided to design a more engaging and robust prototype. A key outcome of our sessions with prototype 1 was the need to implement an effective means of engagement. We reviewed both the research literature on developing engaging applications for children and the space of existing commercial toys and applications for children. We were inspired by popular toys that simulate living pets, such as *Tamagotchi*, *AIBO* and *Furby*, to explore the idea of using changes in the appearance of living media to engage children. User studies with the *Paro* system, which consists of a responsive physical seal robot, has shown that it can successfully engage and relax both children on the Autism spectrum and elderly users [41, 48]. While simulated toys are easy to control algorithmically, there has also been concern about the possibility of them confusing or disappointing child users when they realize that the system is not alive [43]. We decided to experiment with real living media, to avoid causing these negative emotions in our users and also to study the possibility of combining living media and digital technology in this domain. In this paper, we focus on the design methodology of the system and provide a detailed discussion of previous work on digital living media systems elsewhere [19].

Prototype 2 consisted of a physical housing made from repurposed iPad covers that contained the living media, a living mushroom colony with an initial spore-based state, connected to a micro-controlled irrigation system. The growth rate of the mushrooms was controlled via the watering strategy, which is mostly linearly correlated to growth (but should not involve overwatering, which is detrimental). We also developed an iPad software application for use in conjunction with the system. The application consisted of a story reading activity for the children. The amount of time that the software application was used correlated positively with the amount of water that was administered to the mushrooms. Figure 4 shows Prototype 2 with grown mushrooms.

Our motivation for incorporating the living media was the conjecture that the children would be curious to use the application to see the mushrooms grow faster. The children would have a chance to care for the mushrooms during interaction, possibly being engaged through dynamics of empathy and responsibility. Additionally, we had designed the system to be used collaboratively by the children and be left at their home, a feature that could potentially support increased collaboration and communication between them.

Figure 4. Prototype 2 with mushrooms and iPad

When selecting the specific living medium, we considered potential risks and made provisions to address them. First, we considered the possibility that interacting with living media might pose a physical health risk for the children. Living media, and organic materials in general, if not treated properly can become toxic. Given this possibility, we decided against using plants, such as pea shoots or lentils that need to be planted in soil and compost. We instead chose to use mushroom kits specifically designed and tested for use by children. The kits consist of a growing medium, typically composed from used coffee grounds and inoculated by oyster mushroom spores (the *P. ostreatus* species). Both the mushrooms and the organic material in which they are housed are non-toxic.

Second, we considered the possibility of emotional risks. During interaction with living media, the life forms might die. This situation can pose emotional stress, especially to children, who might hold themselves responsible for the death. Given this possibility, we decided against using sentient animals such as gold fish or sea monkeys as living media because their deaths might have caused emotional distress to the children. Using non-animal life forms, such as mushrooms, in applications that benefit human users is in accord with ethical recommendations by Harvey et al. [18]. Additionally, in the design we provisioned for a scenario when the children do not use the applications, in which case, we would still provide a small amount of water to the mushrooms. Conversely, we would avoid overwatering the mushrooms by limiting the maximum amount of water that can be administered. These provisions mean that the mushrooms cannot be killed through the interaction and only their growth rate can be influenced.

We tested Prototype 2 in the lab for several weeks to verify that we can use it to grow mushroom colonies successfully. We identified several structural problems with the prototype, including a need to separate the electronic and organic components, and to place a lock to avoid tempering by child users. Additionally, our initial experiments with the iPad software application showed that having one application severely limits the usefulness of the system. Thus, we decided to restructure the microcontroller software such that it can be remotely controlled and input with the usage information of a suite of target applications. We incorporated the above insights into Prototype 3.

Design Iteration 3

Prototype 3 (Figure 1, left) consists of a custom-made laser-cut box with separate partitions for a living mushroom colony and a remotely controlled irrigation system that dispenses water based on the child users' usage of target digital applications.

We used Prototype 3 in two separate series of design sessions conducted over 2 weeks in home and school contexts. In each series of design sessions, two children with limited communication and one adult proxy participated. We describe the sessions next.

Prototype 3 in the Home

In the first series of design sessions with Prototype 3, two siblings, a 13-year old boy (P2) and a 10-year old boy (P3), and the children's mother (A2) participated. The siblings, both P2 and P3, both were on the Autism spectrum (P2 on the severe end and P3 on the mild end). A2 is a full-time caregiver and takes care of the children at home.

After contacting A2 and learning about her interest in the project, we started the design sessions with two 1-hour conversations with her. During these sessions, we introduced the project to A2 and asked her to tell us more about P2 and P3. She stated that P2 and P3 rarely communicate with people they are not familiar with (including us). She wanted them to try using learning and therapeutic digital applications expand their vocabulary, improve their communication skills, and to collaborate and communicate more with each other and with her. When we showed her a series of target applications we had identified, she wanted to try to see which ones P2 and P3 would be interested to use. She stated that it is often hard to predict which applications P2 and P3 would like or not. In the past, P2 and P3 had occasionally used some applications (mainly on the family computer before) but they were not using any application on a regular basis.

After the initial sessions, we left Prototype 3 at the participants' house for two weeks. We visited the participants' home approximately every 4 days during this time to collect observations and input from A2. Each visit would last between half an hour to an hour. During this time, we did not talk directly with P2 and twice talked briefly with P3 in A2's presence. We asked A2 to describe how the system worked to the child participants. When we first brought Prototype 3 to the participants' home, A2 placed it on an easy-to-see counter in the kitchen and said that this would make it easy for P2 and P3 to see the mushrooms grow.

In our subsequent visits, A2 stated that P3 had become very interested in the mushrooms' growth and checked them regularly. P2, however, was not interested in them and was more interested in the digital applications. A2 also stated that, together with P2 and P3, she had found several learning applications that the children liked and she had decided that they could use those as target applications. She observed that including the children in the application selection was important.

During the second week, when the mushrooms' growth was more visible, A2 reported that P3 had asked several times about how large the mushrooms would get and had told P2 to use more digital application so the mushrooms would grow more. During this week, P2 and P3 had spent more time together using digital applications. P2 had mentioned the prototype at school and had also shown it to some relatives who were visiting. At the end of the two weeks, once the mushrooms were harvested by A2, she said that P2 had expressed interest in using the prototype to grow mushrooms again.

Prototype 3 in the School

In the next and final series of design sessions, we used Prototype 3 in a school context with two children with Cerebral Palsy and an adult school psychologist (A3). The child participants (P5 and P6) were both 13-year girls who were non-verbal and experienced severe motor impairment arising from Cerebral Palsy; P5 and P6 use alternative communication protocols, including picture books and idiosyncratic systems of head gestures, but not sign-based communication systems/languages. They did not use assistive technologies or alternative means for computer access. A2, P5, and P6 had been working together for about 2 years. However, their communication was limited and they did not use sign language.

During 3 collaborative sessions, each lasting between 20-40 minutes, together with A3, we discussed how Prototype 3 should be adapted for use by the child participants. A3 described that a key task for both P5 and P6 would be to try to learn to use new computer-based *augmentative and alternative communication* (AAC) systems. Prior, both children had tried unsuccessfully to use computers for communication. A3 stated that the most promising options had been single-switch scanning software. *Scanning* refers to a widely-used computer access method in which choices (e.g., letters, words, phrases) are periodically highlighted on a computer screen and the user can select them using a variety of alternative input techniques, including single physical switches or puff switches [7]. According to A3, the children's attempt to use scanning software and a variety of input devices (i.e., puff switches and single switches) had been unsuccessful because (i) using them was difficult and required a lot of practice and effort and, (ii) it was hard for the children to stay interested in performing repetitive tasks such as selecting letters to type their names.

Figure 5. Prototype 3 in the school setting, with custom made switch and projected computer display.

Given this background, A3 suggested that we use Prototype 3 to motivate the children to use the scanning software. With her help, we prepared a setup with a single switch used to control a desktop scanning application, *JClic Fressa* (http://jclic.softonic.com) that helps children practice scanning selection and supports vocabulary development by requiring users to select words that correspond to colors and articles of clothing. Figure 5 shows the set up at the school.

Following the setup, we conducted a series of 6 observation sessions (each between 30-60 minutes) over 20 days with P5 and P6. During the first 2 sessions, each child participant used the target application on its own, and for the next 4 sessions they used Prototype 3 in conjunction with the target. A3 described how the prototype worked to P5 and P6 when it was introduced in the third session. During the sessions, the children could decide how long they wanted to use the prototype, with continuous monitoring by the school psychologist (checking with them every 3-5 minutes to see if they wanted to continue).

We recorded application use times for each child during the sessions. Additionally, A3 took note of any comments the children made about using the application or Prototype 3. Since the child participants were non-verbal, A3 used a small number of questions that the children could reply to using gestures, non-speech vocalization and low-tech communication protocols.

The use-time data showed that, on average, both child participants used the target application longer when used in conjunction with Prototype 3 than on its own (by almost twice as much for P5 and three times as much for P6). A3 stated that, in the presence of Prototype 3, she observed signs of curiosity and interest in both children, especially when they saw the mushrooms growing:

"She (P5) was interested from the beginning but P6 became interested only when she could see the mushrooms growing. They both mentioned the system in between the sessions."

A3 observed that having the physical prototype in the space helped stimulate conversation among other teachers, staff and students who were not directly involved in the project. She stated that given that P5 and P6 are non-verbal, including them in conversations with other students has been challenging. She indicated that several students and teachers commented about Rafigh upon seeing the mushrooms growing and talked to her and P5 and P6 about the project. She believed that placing the prototype in a public visible location was important for this result.

A3 believed working with living media, especially over a long period of time, has the potential to create positive feelings of empathy and responsibility in the children. She suggested that maybe several instances of the system could be set up in a garden that children could grow together by completing therapeutic activities over an extended period. She stated that the children did not clearly know how their collaborating with each other helped grow the mushrooms.

Summary of Design Iteration 3

The feedback from the final series of design sessions was promising and provided evidence that Rafigh motivated children to use the target applications more often and to create more communication and collaboration in home and school contexts. It also revealed several considerations including 1) the importance of involving users in choosing target applications, and 2) the impact of the location where the system is placed. We will include these insights in Rafigh's usage instructions. The design process also revealed several important features of the PDwP approach that we will discuss in the next section.

LESSONS LEARNED

Overcoming logistic and privacy barriers: Given that Rafigh is an ambient system for use in the home or school settings, gathering ecologically valid data about its reception in its context of use poses challenges which were mitigated by the PDwP approach. For instance, we needed the ongoing observations of the adult participants to understand the impact of having Prototype 3 in the children's home and school settings. Using other data-collection schemes, such as video recording or frequent researcher visits, can be disruptive to the family and school staff and can affect the way the children interacted with the system. Thus, using PDwP helped us overcome logistical and privacy barriers. This feature is especially useful for the evaluation of ambient systems in their context of use.

Understanding system impact beyond the individual: Similar to results from previous research [10, 23, 30], we found that working with proxies can provide insight into the impact of the interaction beyond an individual user and outside of the immediate context of use. One of the goals of Rafigh is to increase its users' communication with others. When conducting design sessions with Prototype 3, the proxies provided data about how the prototype had increased child participants' communication with others in both home and school settings. It would have been difficult to find this result without input from the proxies who were observing the children's interaction with others at times other than when the prototype was present.

Overcoming communication barriers: In accordance with previous research [8, 10], we found that using the PDwP approach can successfully overcame communication barriers. In our experience, when conducting the design and evaluation sessions with children, we relied on the adult participants who were familiar with the children to interpret and to communicate insights about the interaction to us. Developing alternative communication protocols and learning to interpret them successfully takes a long time and sometimes requires special expertise (e.g., when using communication protocols). Without the help of proxies, we could not gather input about the prototypes easily.

Indirect representation: When using PDwP, it is important to be aware that the input from the proxies might not necessarily be representative of actual users [42]. Researchers and designers must be aware that while helpful, input from proxy users is not the same as that from actual users. Data reported and interpreted by stakeholders might be impacted by their biases. PDwP should only be used when researchers cannot work directly with the user population and input from proxy users should be verified whenever possible and frequently with members of the target user population. Another related challenge with using PDwP is that data reported and interpreted by stakeholders might be impacted by their biases. When evaluating Prototype 3, we used both qualitative and quantitative data to investigate the interaction.

CONCLUSION

Including participants with limited communication in the participatory design of technology is challenging. We used an iterative *Participatory Design with Proxies* (PDwP) process to better identify the potential of this approach for designing new systems with children with limited communication. We found that using PDwP can provide flexible ways to include and interpret input from users, with whom researchers cannot directly communicate. Additionally, it supports the development of context-dependent systems that need to be designed and evaluated *in situ* and with input from multiple stakeholders. We also found that with this approach it is important to verify data from multiple sources.

In this study, we focused on input from adult participants to interpret children's behaviour or communications. In the future, it would be interesting to explore dynamics that arise when children with and without disabilities interact with each other when using a system. What are some techniques to help combine input from both populations effectively to inform design? How would such a study be different from our current approach?

Another longitudinal study can examine whether the type of suggestions and insights provided by adult and child participants change over time: Would they be more about the form factor and functionality of systems or their underlying design concepts? Finally, a user study can evaluate Rafigh with different user populations and examine the impact of the current design decisions on the interaction.

REFERENCES

1. Alper, M., Hourcade, J. P., and Gilutz, S. Interactive technologies for children with special needs. In *Proc. of IDC'12,* ACM Press (2012), 363-366.
2. Anthony, L., Prasad, S., Hurst, A., and Kuber, R. A participatory design workshop on accessible apps and games with students with learning differences. In *Proc. of ASSETS'12,* ACM Press (2012), 253-254.
3. Bälter, O., Engwall, O., Öster, A., and Kjellström, H. Wizard-of-Oz test of ARTUR: A computer-based speech training system with articulation correction. In *Proc. of ASSETS'05*, ACM Press (2005), 36-43.
4. Bardzell, S., Bardzell, J., Forlizzi, J., Zimmerman, J. and Antanitis, J. Critical design and critical theory: the challenge of designing for provocation. *Proc. of DIS'12*, ACM Press (2012), 288-297.
5. Benton, L., Johnson, H., Brosnan, M., Ashwin, E., and Grawemeyer, B. IDEAS: an interface design experience for the autistic spectrum. In *Proc. of CHI EA'11,* ACM Press (2011), 1759-1764.
6. Bhat, S. TouchTone: An electronic musical instrument for children with hemiplegic cerebral palsy. In *Proc. of TEI'10*, ACM Press (2010), 305-306.
7. Bhattacharya, S., Samanta, D., and Basu, A. Performance models for automatic evaluation of virtual scanning keyboards. *IEEE Trans. on Neural Systems and Rehabilitation Engineering 16*, 5 (2008), 510-519.
8. Boyd-Graber, J. L., Nikolova, S. S., Moffatt, K. A., Kin, K. C., Lee, J. Y., Mackey, L. W., Tremaine, M. M., and Klawe, M. M. Participatory design with proxies: developing a desktop-PDA system to support people with aphasia. In *Proc. of CHI'06,* ACM Press (2006), 151-160.
9. Brederode, B., Markopoulos, P., Gielen, M., Vermeeren, A. and de Ridder, H. pOwerball: the design of a novel mixed-reality game for children with mixed abilities. In *Proc. of IDC'05,* ACM Press (2005), 32–39.
10. Dawe, M. Let me show you what I want: engaging individuals with cognitive disabilities and their families in design. In *Proc. of CHI'07*, ACM Press (2007), 2177-2182.
11. Druin, A. Cooperative inquiry: developing new technologies for children with children. In *Proc. of CHI'99*, ACM Press (1999), 592-599.
12. Fernaeus, Y. and Tholander, J. Looking at the computer but doing it on land: Children's interactions in a tangible programming space. In *Proc. of* HCI'05, (2005), 3-18.
13. Frauenberger, C., Good, J., Keay-Bright, W., and Pain, H. Interpreting input from children: a designerly approach. In *Proc. of CHI'12,* (2012), 2377-2386.
14. Frauenberger, C., Good, J., and Alcorn, A. Challenges, opportunities and future perspectives in including children with disabilities in the design of interactive technology. In *Proc. of IDC'12,* ACM Press (2012), 367-370.
15. Frauenberger, C., Good, J. and Keay-Bright, W. Designing technology for children with special needs: bridging perspectives through participatory design. *CoDesign 7,* 1 (2011), 1-28.
16. Frayling, C. Research in Art and Design. *Royal College of Art Research Papers 1*, 1 (1993), 1-5.
17. Guha, M. L., Druin, A. and Fails, J. A. Designing with and for children with special needs: an inclusionary model. In *Proc. of IDC'08,* ACM Press (2008), 61-64.
18. Harvey, H., Havard, M., Magnus, D., Cho, M. K., and Riedel-Kruse, I. H. *Innocent Fun or 'Microslavery'? An Ethical Analysis of Biotic Games. Hastings Center Report 44*, 6 (2014), 38-46.
19. Hamidi, F., Baljko, M. Engaging Children Using a Digital Living Media System. In *Proc. of DIS '17*, (2017), 711-723.
20. Hamidi, F., Baljko, M. Rafigh: A Living Media Interface for Speech Intervention. In *Proc. of CHI '14*, (2014), 1817-1820.
21. Hamidi, F., Baljko, M. Automatic Speech Recognition: A Shifted Role in Early Speech Intervention. In *Proc. of SPLAT'13*, (2013), 55-61.
22. Hengeveld, B., Hummels, C., Overbeeke, K., Voort, R., van Balkom, H., and de Moor, J. 2009. Tangibles for toddlers learning language. In *Proc. of TEI '09*, ACM Press (2009), 161-168.
23. Hirano, S. H., Yeganyan, M. T., Marcu, G., Nguyen, D. H., Boyd, L. A. and Hayes, G. R. 2010. vSked: evaluation of a system to support classroom activities for children with autism. In *Proc. of* CHI'10, ACM Press (2010), 1633-1642.
24. Hourcade, J. P., Garzotto, F., Rozga, A., Tentori, M. E., Markopoulos, P., Pares, N., Good, J., Pain, H., and Alper, M. Supporting children with complex communication needs. In *Proc. of EA CHI'14*, ACM Press (2014), 119-122.

25. Hurst, A., Hudson, S. E., Mankoff, J., and Trewin, S. Distinguishing users by pointing performance in laboratory and real-world tasks. *ACM Transactions on Accessible Computing 5,* 2 (2013), 5.
26. Hutchinson, H., Mackay, W., Westerlund, B., Bederson, B.B., Druin, A., Plaisant, C., Beaudouin-Lafon, M., Conversy, S., Evans, H., Hansen, H., Roussel, N., and Eiderbäck, B. Technology probes: inspiring design for and with families. In *Proc. of CHI'03*, ACM Press (2003), 17-24.
27. Ishii, H. 2008. Tangible bits: beyond pixels. In *Proc. of TEI'08,* ACM Press (2008), xv-xxv.
28. Keay-Bright, W. E. The Reactive Colours Project: Demonstrating Participatory and Collaborative Design Methods for the Creation of Software for Autistic Children. *Design Principles and Practices: An International Journal 1*, 2 (2007), 7–16.
29. Kensing, F., and Blomberg, J. Participatory design: Issues and concerns. In *Proc. of CSCW'98*, ACM Press (1998), 167-185.
30. Kientz, J.A., Hayes, G.R., Westeyn, T.L., Starner, T. and Abowd, G.D. Pervasive Computing and Autism: Assisting Caregivers of Children with Special Needs. *IEEE Pervasive Computing 6*, 1 (2007), 8-35.
31. Large, A., Nesset, V., Beheshti, J., and Bowler, L. "Bonded design": A novel approach to intergenerational information technology design. *Library and Information Science Research* 28, 1 (2006), 64–82.
32. Menzies, R., Waller, A., and Pain, H. Peer interviews: an adapted methodology for contextual understanding in user-centred design. In *Proc. of Assets'11,* ACM Press (2011), 273-274.
33. Millen, L., Cobb, S. and Patel, H. A method for involving children with autism in design. In *Proc. of IDC'11,* ACM Press (2011), 185-188.
34. Moffatt, K., McGrenere, J., Purves, B., & Klawe, M The participatory design of a sound and image enhanced daily planner for people with aphasia. In *Proc. of the Conference on Human Factors in Computing Systems,* ACM Press (2004), 407-414.
35. Moraveji, N., Li, J., Ding, J., O'Kelley, P., and Woolf, S. Comicboarding: using comics as proxies for participatory design with children. In *Proc. of CHI'07,* ACM Press (2007), 1371-1374.
36. Piper, A. M., O'Brien, E., Morris, M. R., and Winograd, T. SIDES: a cooperative tabletop computer game for social skills development. In *Proc. of CSCW'06*, ACM Press (2006), 1-10.
37. Rogers, Y. Interaction design gone wild: striving for wild theory. *Interactions 18*, 4 (2011), 58-62.
38. Sanders, E. B. N. and Stappers, P. J. Co-creation and the new landscapes of design. *CoDesign: International Journal of CoCreation in Design and the Arts 4*, 1 (2008), 5-18.
39. Scaife, M., Rogers, Y., Aldrich, F., and Davies, M. Designing for or designing with? Informant design for interactive learning environments. In *Proc. of CHI'97,* ACM Press (1997), 343–350.
40. Schuler, D. and Namioka, A. (eds.). *Participatory Design: Principles and Practices.* Lawrence Erlbaum Associates (1993).
41. Shibata, T., Mitsui, T., Wada, K., Touda, A., Kumasaka, T., Tagami, K., and Tanie, K. Mental commit robot and its application to therapy of children. In *Proc. of Advanced Intelligent Mechatronics* (2001), 1053-1058.
42. Simonsen, J., & Robertson, T. (Eds.). *Routledge international handbook of participatory design.* London: Routledge (2012).
43. Turkle, S., Breazeal, C., Dasté, O., and Scassellati, B. Encounters with kismet and cog: Children respond to relational artifacts. *Digital Media: Transformations in Human Communication*, (2006), 1-20.
44. Vicsi, K., Roach, P., Öster, A. M., Kacic, Z., Barczikay, and Tantoa, A., Csatári F., Bakcsi Zs. and Sfakianaki, A. A multimedia, multilingual teaching and training system for children with speech disorders. *Int. Journal of Speech technology 3*, 3 (2000), 289-300.
45. Visser, F. S., Stappers, P. J., Van der Lugt, R., and Sanders, E. B. Contextmapping: Experiences from practice. *CoDesign 1*, 2 (2005), 119-149.
46. Wada, K. and Shibata, T. Living with seal robots—its sociopsychological and physiological influences on the elderly at a care house. *IEEE Transactions on Robotics* 23, 5, (2007), 972-980.
47. Wilson, S., Roper, A., Marshall, J., Galliers, J., Devane, N., Booth, T., and Woolf, C. Codesign for people with aphasia through tangible design languages. *CoDesign 11,* 1 (2015), 1-14.
48. Zimmerman, J., Forlizzi, J. and Evenson, S. Research through design as a method for interaction design research in HCI. In *Proc. of CHI'07,* ACM Press (2007), 493-502.
49. Zimmerman, J., Evenson, S., and Forlizzi, J. Discovering knowledge in the design case. In *Proc. of FutureGround.* Design Research Society (2004).
50. Zuckerman, O., Arida, S., and Resnick, M. Extending tangible interfaces for education: Digital Montessori-inspired manipulatives. In *Proc. of CHI'05*, ACM Press (2005), 859-868.

"Is Someone There? Do They Have a Gun?" How Visual Information about Others Can Improve Personal Safety Management for Blind Individuals

Stacy M. Branham, Ali Abdolrahmani, William Easley,
Morgan Scheuerman, Erick Ronquillo, Amy Hurst
University of Maryland, Baltimore County (UMBC)
Baltimore, MD, USA
{sbranham, aliab1, easley1, morgan.klaus, erick4, amyhurst} @umbc.edu

ABSTRACT
For decades, researchers have investigated and developed technologies that support independent navigation for people who are blind. This has led to systems that primarily aid in detecting routes, landmarks, and building features. However, there has been relatively little inquiry regarding how technologies might support navigation around and in the presence of other *people*. What visual information, if any, do blind navigators wish they had about people on their path? To address this question, we surveyed 58 blind and low vision individuals and interviewed 10 blind individuals. We discovered our participants were interested in using visual information about others to increase their physical safety. For example, they wanted to know if a passerby was holding a weapon, if a presumed official had a proper uniform or badge, and how to describe visual aspects of a criminal to law enforcement. This paper presents one of the only reports documenting accessibility challenges related to physical safety posed by others, including how future assistive tools can empower individuals with disabilities to more actively increase their sense of safety. We call this emerging area *Personal Safety Management* and contribute a set of four broad subareas that deserve further exploration by researchers and designers working within the blind and broader disabilities communities.

CCS Concepts
• **Human-centered computing → accessibility → accessibility technologies → accessibility systems and tools**

Keywords
Visual impairment; blind; disability; assistive technology; facial recognition; violence; crime; police; personal safety management.

1. INTRODUCTION
People with disabilities are disproportionately targeted as victims of crime. People who are blind, in particular, are nearly twice as likely to be victims of violent crime than people without disabilities, according to the Bureau of Justice Statistics [19]. Yet, to our knowledge, there are no commercially-available assistive technologies (AT) that provide visual awareness cues to enable people who are blind to recognize when a person has a gun or knife, locate a police officer in uniform, or describe a criminal suspect or the scene of a crime. Further, a survey of the ASSETS proceedings reveals that relatively few papers have explored threats to physical safety[1]. Those that have broached the topic have tended to focus on environmental safety and obstacle avoidance [6,7,30–32], access to emergency services and alarms [11–13,33], health-risk mediation [14,25–27], and device-oriented safety [2]. But, there is an apparent paucity of literature about the concerns people with disabilities have regarding physical safety in relation to *other people*—here referred to as *interpersonal safety*—and what role AT does or might play.

The current research began as an investigation of navigation aids for people who are blind, and later took a turn to focus on interpersonal safety. Navigation aid research has been concerned with detecting routes, landmarks, and building features [6,7,32]. These concerns are also dominant in commercial navigation technologies such as Guide Dots[2] and BlindSquare[3]. Recent research has established that passersby are also important in navigation [1,31]. For example, a passerby can be a helpful source of on-the-fly directions or be disruptive by grabbing one's white cane [1,31]. This insight seeded our initial research question: what types of information do blind navigators wish they had about *people*—as distinct from landmarks or objects—on their path?

To address this question, we distributed an exploratory survey to 58 people with visual impairments. The survey included both closed and open questions to identify what types of information—particularly visual information about other nearby people—might be useful during independent navigation. The survey revealed that visual information about people was sometimes desired and that interpersonal safety was a critical use case. To further explore these issues, we conducted semi-structured interviews with 10 blind individuals. All 10 interview participants shared stories of times when their personal safety was threatened by others. They expressed a need for access to visual cues that could empower them to more effectively manage their physical safety. In this paper we document and unpack the significance of this finding. Specifically, we call for further investigation into an area we call *Personal Safety Management—informed, agential, and proactive participation in maintaining one's own physical safety*

[1] We use the terms "interpersonal safety," "personal safety" and "physical safety" throughout. Interpersonal safety is used narrowly to refer to (threat of) bodily harm caused by other people via, e.g., assault. Personal safety and physical safety are used generally and interchangeably to refer to bodily harm caused by, e.g., environmental obstacles, lack of access to emergency services, as well as actions of other people.

[2] http://www.guidedots.org/

[3] https://www.blindsquare.com/

ASSETS'17, October 29–November 1, 2017, Baltimore, MD, USA.
© 2017 ACM. ISBN 978-1-4503-4926-0/17/10…$15.00.
DOI: https://doi.org/10.1145/3132525.3132534

2. RELATED WORK

Our work contributes to the existing body of literature relating to how assistive technology (AT) can provide blind individuals with visual information about others through facial detection and recognition. Work in this space has largely examined recognition technologies as a tool to support prosocial interactions (e.g., by reading facial expressions [22,23]) or improve device accessibility (e.g., by taking better photographs of people [3,20]). We extend this work by exploring how recognition technologies can be used to provide visual information about other people that is relevant to assessing and identifying threats to personal safety.

While a great deal of research within the ASSETS community has addressed the unique safety needs of individuals with disabilities, few papers consider the threats to physical safety posed by others. We found that previous research has focused heavily on environmental safety (e.g., obstacle avoidance) or device-oriented safety (e.g., reducing risks associated with device use). In fact, the only paper we found that directly addresses interpersonal safety threats to people who are blind is a recent contribution within the Usable Security community [5].

Our findings complement and extend this corpus by expanding the variety of safety threat scenarios encountered by people who are blind and by offering a map to researchers and designers who plan to further explore this emerging area.

2.1 ATs for Identifying Visual Attributes of People

Prior research has investigated technologies that assist blind individuals with identifying, recognizing, and detecting visual information about other people. Approaches involving computer vision have been very common in this space.

2.1.1 Detecting Faces using Facial Recognition

Prior work has shown that blind individuals, like their sighted counterparts, have a desire to take and organize photographs [3]. Researchers have developed several camera applications that integrate features, such as facial detection, to assist users with capturing better photographs of people and objects [3,20].

2.1.2 Describing People using Facial Recognition

Most work regarding person recognition has been through the development of facial recognition technologies. However, research in this area has largely framed facial recognition as a tool to support effective communication, rather than one that can support personal safety.

In 2005, Krishna et al. [23] developed the iCare Interaction Assistant, a wearable device designed to help blind individuals identify non-verbal cues during social interactions with sighted peers. This initial work sought to identify the most accurate algorithm for this task [23]. Based on the premise that blind users often encounter socially awkward situations in the workplace, Kramer et al. [22] developed a wearable system to identify colleagues and discreetly announce their names to the wearer.

Krishna et al. [24] later contributed a list of eight non-verbal cues that are important but not always accessible to blind individuals. Beyond identifying faces, they note facial expression, eye gaze, and appearance as important cues.

2.1.3 Describing People using Crowd Workers

Brady et al. [10] studied the types of visual questions that users of VizWiz Social asked to crowd workers. VizWiz [9] is a mobile application that allows blind users to photograph something; audio record a question; and then ask either crowd workers, people in social networks, or an image recognition engine to identify what is in the photograph. Brady et al. [10] found that a small portion of users were using VizWiz to ask crowd workers questions about physical appearance of themselves or others.

2.2 ATs for Increasing the Physical Safety of Individuals with Disabilities

Some researchers have discussed and attempted to solve issues around environmental safety and access to health-related services for people with disabilities. Few have examined these through the lens of physical safety, and even fewer have considered the problem of interpersonal safety. In the following sections, we provide an overview of the types of research in the ASSETS community that most directly address physical safety of people with disabilities.

2.2.1 Environmental Safety and Obstacle Avoidance

Many AT researchers have looked at safety in terms of environmental factors that pose obstacles to independent wayfinding. This research focused on different scenarios and populations, ranging from collision avoidance of power wheelchairs for older adults with cognitive impairments [30] to the environmental dangers construction and cars present to people with visual impairments when navigating [6,7,32]. The impact of surrounding people during wayfinding (e.g., by interrupting one's route, offering unwanted directions, or grabbing arms or white canes without consent [31,32]) are referenced primarily as threats to independent navigation.

2.2.2 Access to Emergency Services and Alarms

Past research has investigated the disparate access certain populations have to emergency alerts, alarms, and protocols, as well as to emergency services, such as those provided by emergency call centers or police officers. Bragg, Huynh, and Ladner [11] designed a mobile alert application for hard-of-hearing and deaf users, informed by a survey analyzing the auditory needs of deaf individuals. They noted that emergency alarms, shouting, and gunshots are cues that contain auditory information which can be perceived without sight, but may be missed by deaf or hard-of-hearing individuals. Zafrulla, Etherton, and Starner [33] designed smartphone software to provide more equitable access to emergency call centers for deaf individuals using teletypewriter (TTY) technology. Burton et. al [13] briefly noted ways in which the visual "language" of law enforcement uniforms is unavailable to individuals who are blind, making it impossible to distinguish uniformed police officers from other citizens. Branham and Kane [12] found that blind individuals in the workplace did not have the same access to emergency evacuation routes, emergency tools, and emergency signage as their sighted colleagues. These studies have largely focused on accessibility of general emergency response tools rather than anticipation and navigation of interpersonal safety threats.

2.2.3 Health-Risk Mediation

Addressing health risks and using technology to mitigate them spans a wide range of research, from relieving sore pressure for wheelchair users [27] to combatting barriers to fitness for blind and visually impaired individuals [25,26]. One salient aim of past research has been assisting individuals with disabilities in safely identifying medications [16,17]. Consel, Dupuy, and Sauzéon [14] developed an assistive notification system for older adults that delivered critical and non-critical alerts to users. For example, the system supported reminders to take medication and get out of bed.

2.2.4 *Device-Oriented Safety*
We use the term device-oriented safety to refer to work seeking to limit the harm that devices themselves can cause users. Devices have the ability to induce situationally-induced impairments and disabilities (SIIDs) when they increase the cognitive load of the user in noisy or crowded environments [2]. Distracting audio interfaces can make it more dangerous to navigate traffic, for example [6,32].

2.2.5 *Interpersonal Safety*
Interpersonal safety, or physical safety threats posed by others, is currently not well documented for people with disabilities. Most reports that focus on interactions with strangers do not address physical safety concerns; for example, researchers have identified the threat of others eavesdropping [4], giving unreliable directions [29], or stealing assistive devices worn by the user [26].

One notable exception is a 2016 study by Ahmed et al. [5] which investigated privacy, security, and physical safety concerns of individuals with visual impairments. The portion of their findings related to interpersonal safety identified streets, public transit, ATM booths, and private spaces like the home as four critical safety settings. They offer implications for the design of future wearable devices that might indicate, for example, how many people are in the vicinity and what they are attending to.

Our paper extends Ahmed et al.'s [5] work by documenting new classes of physical safety concerns and scenarios, including how existing ATs impact security and the need for more effective communication with police officers. We additionally provide reflections on how this type of research might be approached and its implications for the ASSETS community.

3. Study Design: What Visual Questions Do Blind Individuals Have About Other People?
This study consisted of an online survey of 58 blind and low vision individuals followed by 10 in-depth phone interviews with blind individuals.

3.1 Survey Methods
We deployed an exploratory survey to investigate the types of visual information people who are blind have about others in their vicinity. Because facial recognition (FR) is becoming pervasive and is already in some degree of use within the blind community, we framed the survey as an exploration of the current use and prospects of FR technologies. Open-ended questions in the survey enabled participants to identify other, sometimes non-visual, types of information they wanted to know about people (e.g., a person's size or their criminal history).

3.1.1 *Survey Design*
The online survey opened with a brief introduction to FR technology along with two applications: identifying any face in the user's surroundings (e.g., strangers and passersby) or recognizing familiar faces (e.g., specific friends, family members, coworkers). Through closed questions, we assessed whether participants had any previous experience using FR and if they would find either of these applications of FR beneficial for their independent navigation or social interactions. Following each closed question, participants were able to elaborate on their answers through free response. We ran the survey as a pilot with five blind participants and then revised the prompts for clarity.

3.1.2 *Survey Participants*
Participants were recruited using a database of contact points of blind individuals who had consented to take part in future studies. There were 58 respondents (39 female, 17 male, 2 preferred not to disclose), ranging in age from 10-57 years (average of 26). To improve the representativeness of the sample, our survey was inclusive of 10 minors (people younger than 18 years old), for which we had IRB approval and parental consent. We refer to survey participants as "SP1" to "SP58."

3.1.3 *Survey Analysis*
The third author reviewed and thematically coded participant responses to each open-ended survey question, generating over 40 unique codes. These codes were organized into high-level categories including physical attributes, demographic information, and nonverbal cues. Codes were iteratively refined in multiple weekly group meetings over a period of months. High-level survey findings are summarized in Section 4.

3.2 Interview Methods
To add context and depth to the findings in our exploratory survey, we conducted semi-structured interviews. We particularly sought examples of times when blind individuals desired visual information about people, including their faces, to improve their independence, social interactions, and safety.

3.2.1 *Interview Design*
Interviews were organized into two sections. The first section asked questions about skills, techniques, and strategies blind individuals use to identify people in different contexts (e.g., navigating, social gatherings, work environments). It also asked participants to describe situations in which they failed to obtain the desired visual information about other people. Finally, it asked how the provision of visual information could (or could not) help them in those situations.

The second section asked questions about participants' familiarity and experiences with FR technology, the potential advantages or disadvantages of assistive aids that use this technology, and how this technology could help them in challenging scenarios mentioned in the first section of the interview. The protocol did not explicitly mention physical safety threats until the end, after most participants had already identified this as an important application without prompt. We ran a pilot interview prior to participant recruitment and made minor revisions to the protocol.

3.2.2 *Interview Participants*
We recruited 10 blind individuals through our participant database and snowball sampling. Participants (six female, four male) ranged in age from 24 to 65 and had varying ages of onset of blindness (Table 1). We refer to interview participants as "IP1" to "IP10."

3.2.3 *Interview Data Collection and Analysis*
Because participants were distributed, all interviews were conducted over the phone. The second author was the primary interviewer in all interview sessions. Most interviews were also attended by a secondary interviewer from the research team who asked follow-up questions and assisted the primary interviewer in taking notes. Interviews lasted approximately 60 to 90 minutes each. After interviews, the primary and secondary interviewers discussed key themes in the interview. Interview insights were presented in multiple weekly group meetings, during which the significance of physical safety threats was identified. The second author listened again to interview recordings and gathered the set

ID	Age	Gender	Visual Impairment Description	Mobility Aid
IP1	28	Female	Legally blind since birth	White cane
IP2	35	Female	Blind since age 18	White cane
IP3	65	Male	Blind since age 18	White cane
IP4	29	Female	Blind since birth	White cane
IP5	38	Male	Blind since age 13	Guide dog before, now white cane
IP6	24	Female	Blind since birth	Both guide dog and white cane
IP7	36	Male	Blind in one eye, some light perception in the other	White cane before, now guide dog
IP8	51	Female	Legally blind since age 13, totally blind since age 45	Guide dog before, now white cane
IP9	52	Male	Blind since age 4	White cane
IP10	30	Female	Legally blind since age 16, totally blind since age 24	White cane

Table 1: Demographic descriptions of interview participants.

of all scenarios in which participants described issues relating to interpersonal safety; these portions of the interviews were transcribed in full by the team. The second author then conducted an iterative card sorting activity with the first author to organize transcribed examples into the thematic categories and subcategories presented in Sections 5.1, 5.2, and 5.3.

4. Survey Findings: Interpersonal Safety is a Concern

Our survey sought to explore potential applications of facial recognition (FR) in the context of blind navigation. We found that 28 of 58 participants had already used FR technology through photography apps that could identify the presence of a face in-frame. Two participants had previously used FR technology that could identify a face and associate it with a name.

The survey asked participants to share *who* they would use FR to identify and *what* information besides names would be valuable to know. Of people to identify, friends and family were mentioned most frequently (28 and 29 statements, respectively), followed by people with whom the user has a professional relationship (25 statements). Twenty-nine statements mentioned wanting to know physical attributes of a person that can be perceived visually (e.g., size of person, hair style, eye color, distinguishing features). Twelve statements mentioned background information about the user's relationship with another person (e.g., how you know the person). Eight statements mentioned non-verbal communication cues that can be perceived visually (e.g., facial expression, eye gaze). Seven statements mentioned demographic information (e.g., age, gender, disability status) which cannot always be perceived visually. Only four responses noted an interest in nearby strangers—as opposed to friends, family, or professional acquaintances. These mentions included seeking strangers on the street in emergency situations, meeting someone for the first time, and finding attractive strangers.

When we asked participants to identify *situations* in which they felt FR could be useful, stranger interactions were much more commonly referenced. Across both types of recognition (recognizing any face or recognizing a particular face), 36 statements explicitly mentioned that FR technology would be useful in helping the user become aware of, or remain aware of, the presence of other individuals (e.g., silent people in elevators and store employees behind service desks). Thirty-five statements indicated that FR would be useful when looking for someone, oftentimes for the purpose of receiving assistance (12 of 35 statements). Another 19 statements mentioned using FR technology to interact with media (e.g., when looking at photos or videos). Ten statements mentioned using FR to assist with identifying non-verbal communication cues (e.g., to identify if a stranger is staring).

While we set out to identify what visual information blind individuals would want about other people in a broad sense, we found numerous responses related to personal safety. Nine statements explicitly mentioned that FR would be useful in promoting safety:

> *"Environments where random people move about. I would like to know immediately when a person enters or exits a room, or my bubble. This is imperative as a blind individual, in case of safety." –SP41*

Four statements mentioned being able to identify emergency personnel and another three mentioned wanting to know the criminal record of others:

> *"If they had a criminal record and what that criminal record would be, then I would make my judgment from there." –SP43*

Our survey findings suggest there may be an implicit connection between the visual information that participants were interested in knowing and decisions about safety. Moreover, personal safety is a distinct concern for people who are blind when they are in the presence of strangers.

5. Interview Findings: Interpersonal Safety Manifests in Multiple Contexts

To gain a deeper understanding of the contexts in which visual information about others might be valuable, we followed our survey with a set of 10 semi-structured interviews. Although our interview protocol did not allude to physical safety until the end, participants' responses raised the topic early and repeatedly. Due to being so rarely and disjointedly presented in prior work, we chose to focus our analysis and reporting on participants' stories of managing physical safety in the presence of others. Findings from our interviews follow.

5.1 ATs Impact Sense of Safety

Perhaps one of our more unexpected findings is that assistive tools can impact user perception of interpersonal safety, even though this is not their primary function. Some participants explained that using an assistive tool or service animal could help them feel safer. Others felt using an assistive tool could pose a safety threat.

5.1.1 ATs Can Increase Sense of Safety

Three participants (IP3, IP6, IP7) described examples where using assistive tools, including their white cane, guide dog or apps on their cellphones could help them feel safer in certain circumstances or in the presence of strangers. IP6 used an app (Aipoly Vision[4]) that leverages computer vision to identify objects and read text on signs, because it made her feel "more confident" and "less vulnerable." She shared an experience where she got off the bus at the wrong station in an unsafe area of the city. She used the app to read the bus numbers, which helped her get out of that area as soon as possible.

IP3 described a situation where he was walking alone late at night in an area of the city that was known to be unsafe gang territory. Suddenly, he could hear several young male voices ahead on the sidewalk. As he approached, he heard footsteps as the presumed gang members surrounded him. He stopped. When there was no greeting, he initiated conversation to examine the situation, but he did not receive any verbal response. Then one of the gang members, who had presumably noticed his white cane, called the others off by saying "not cool man." IP3 believed he was in danger, yet he was ultimately saved by his AT (white cane) signaling his disability to the young men. *"Blindness tends to temper that [threatening] situation,"* IP3 remarked.

IP7 similarly mentioned that his guide dog helped him feel safer while walking in unfamiliar and crowded areas with homeless people around. He believed his dog dissuaded others from approaching or harassing him:

> *"[As] a person with a guide dog, I would say that I ... feel definitely a lot more safer knowing I have my guide dog, than being alone without one and having a cane ... The majority of people whom I interact with ... will not necessarily come toward me, thinking that my dog would be aggressive." –IP7*

Interestingly, IP7 believed that one form of assistive tool (a guide dog) could make him safer than another (a white cane). For both IP3 and IP7, navigation aids served a dual purpose by imparting a sense of protection from potentially threatening people while also helping them navigate.

5.1.2 ATs Can Increase Threats to Safety

While ATs can support feelings of safety, they can also pose threats to safety. Our interviews turned up one example from IP1, who described an incident in which she felt threatened by a person who she connected to through an app for remote visual assistance (Be My Eyes[5]). Using this app, blind users can connect to a network of sighted helpers through live video/audio communication. The agent on the other side of the line indicated that the image was blurry, making it difficult to answer IP1's question accurately. The agent then asked where she was located and suggested he come over to help her in person. Concerned for her safety, she immediately closed the connection and decided to never use this app or similar apps again.

5.2 Communicating with Police or Officials

Half of our participants shared experiences in which they wanted to have better tools to identify and communicate with police and similar security officers. This included being able to locate an officer, being able to communicate effectively with police, and being able to describe criminals to authorities.

[4] Aipoly Vision: http://aipoly.com/

[5] Be My Eyes: http://bemyeyes.com/

5.2.1 Identifying Police Officers and Officials

Five participants (IP1, IP4, IP5, IP8, and IP9) gave examples of times when they felt a need to locate a police officer or security guard for protection in threatening situations, or to verify that they were communicating with a real official. IP4 described being on the train with "all manner of people" and walking on the street alone at night with "people shouting or yelling." When these situations arose, she stated that she would take a longer path to avoid them. She believed that if she were better able to find and identify a police officer, it would put her mind at ease.

Another concern (mentioned by IP1, IP4 and IP8) related to situations in which participants would like to verify if the person communicating with them in a public area was a real authority. IP8 shared a story about a time when she was in a train station, and someone who sounded to her like an official was helping her to find the train:

> *"I thought he was someone who worked at the train station and he said he was gonna walk me to the train ... so we started walking off and another guy ran out from behind the counter, and said "Whoa, whoa where are you taking her?" and it turns out he's just a guy that hangs out." –IP8*

IP8's example shows how inaccessible visual signals—like official uniforms and badges that sighted people rely on to discern who they can trust—may put blind individuals in awkward or even dangerous situations.

5.2.2 Communicating Effectively with Police

Two participants pointed to situations in which they had difficulties communicating effectively with police officers. IP7 described an incident when his apartment was broken into and he needed to communicate with the investigating officers. He explained that the robbery left him feeling "violated", but then he had to deal with critical logistics of talking with an authority:

> *"It would have been nice to also determine what kind of facial expression they were doing too ... You are talking to a cop. Facial expressions are really important. I don't know if he is writing something down, or if he is waiting for more information." –IP7*

Similarly, IP5 explained a case when an Uber driver avoided giving a ride to him because of his wife's guide dog. The situation escalated and the police were called. He indicated that awareness about the facial expressions of the police and the driver could have helped them better understand the dynamics of the situation:

> *"Facial expressions would have been really, really helpful, just to know how the driver was reacting ... if she's just annoyed or ... ready to get physical. ... Are [the cops] sympathetic to our needs or are they more leaning toward what the driver wants?" –IP5*

Like IP7, IP5 was interested in knowing more about the facial expressions of others when communicating with police. Proper communication was considered to be critical to aiding police in documenting a crime (and therefore potentially catching a criminal and recovering damaged or stolen items), as well as protecting their rights and physical safety through persuasive, defensive dialogue.

5.2.3 Describing a Suspicious Scene or Person

IP7 and IP8 pointed to situations where they needed to describe a suspicious person or scene in a potentially dangerous incident. IP8 shared two deeply troubling stories of public indecent exposure and sexual harassment in which she was the target and subsequently needed to communicate the crime to police. She had been on the train with a friend when they discovered that a man sitting in front of them was masturbating while ogling her. The other incident was nearly identical and took place in a public park. IP8 noted that she would not have realized what was going on if she had been alone. Furthermore, she lamented: *"Even if I get threatened or harassed in such situations, I cannot describe the person to authorities."* For IP8, lack of appropriate visual information led her to feel unsafe and unable to help authorities identify the criminal.

5.3 Assessing and Navigating Threats

Participants recounted numerous times they wished they could construct a safer space while navigating. They had concerns about assessing the degree of a threat, dealing with silent or suspicious strangers, navigating public areas safely, getting out of threatening situations, and avoiding them altogether by projecting confidence.

5.3.1 Assessing the Degree of Threatening Situations

Participants shared incidents in which they wanted to know if there was a real threat to their safety and, if so, how to proceed. For example, IP5 described a time he was in a supermarket and heard someone yelling, "He's got a gun!" Without visual information, he could not quickly assess the threat:

> *"I suddenly heard, "He's got a gun!" And so when I heard that, I was like ... we gotta get out of here, let's go. But you know, if I had seen facial expressions, I might have seen people [who] had a kind of fearful, anxious expression, and might have been able to take a cue from that."–IP5*

One technique for assessing threat identified by participants is to listen to the tone of voice of strangers. When seeking assistance from a stranger, IP8 would only ask people who sounded "happy" for directions while intentionally avoiding people who sounded "suspicious." However, she also felt that these auditory cues could be misleading or not provide sufficient information to make accurate judgements about a person' trustworthiness:

> *"Some people could be acting friendly but doing things that are suspicious, I mean they could be talking to you friendly while they're really looking at your wallet." –IP8*

In this case, lack of awareness of eye gaze evoked anxieties about strangers' true intent. IP5 had similar concerns about seemingly friendly people "pulling one over" on him. In one incident, he was walking home from the store with grocery bags in hand when a woman on the street approached and asked him for food. Despite wanting to help, he felt threatened because he could not assess her body language or whether her jacket pocket bulged with a gun:

> *"And I just really felt conflicted because I like to help people if I can, but I'm blind so I don't have that kind of information. So, I just kept on walking ... because I don't wanna be taken advantage of. I got a family to think of, too." –IP5*

In absence of visual information about the degree of threat, IP5 had to choose between honoring his identity as person who helps others and his identity as a person who refuses to be a victim.

IP8 described a situation in an elevator where someone's abnormal behavior contributed to her to desire to have more visual information. Like IP5, she considered body language an important indicator. She also wanted to know about others' clothing:

> *"The way people dress, or if they are covered in tattoos maybe, or if they are skulking in the corner with a hoodie pulled over their head, because they know the consequences of certain ways of dressing and acting. So I'm gonna assume that because they chose to dress or make those motions, that's the message they want to send out." –IP8*

Across these experiences, we see that feedback about fearful or anxious facial expressions, eye gaze fixated on one's valuable possessions, and other non-verbal aspects of self-presentation was desired for assessing the degree of threatening situations. Moreover, lack of visual information was a source of anxiety and manifested as a lack of agency for blind individuals.

5.3.2 Judging if a Silent Person Poses a Threat

People who are blind are often aware of the presence of others nearby. However, in crowded environments, it may be difficult to detect other people and assess whether they pose a threat. Six participants (IP1, IP2, IP3, IP7, IP8, IP10) expressed concern about silent people around them. Specifically, they stated that they were unable to know the direction silent people were looking, their distance, and their facial expression.

> *"It isn't really normal for people to just be quiet." –IP8*

> *"Quiet people may be mysterious and spooky. You don't know if they are looking at you or they are not even in the room. You cannot track people when they are quiet and know if they are a threat." –IP3*

Participants felt that silent people could pose a potential threat due to their unclear intentions, making it difficult to know if their safety was in jeopardy. Participants indicated that not knowing about silent others was a source of discomfort and vulnerability.

5.3.3 Detecting Threats in Crowded Public Spaces

Participants believed that navigating crowded public areas lent itself to threatening situations. IP3 noted that in big public areas and busy streets, any prompt from a stranger could be threatening. He shared an experience about a time he was nearly attacked by a man while walking with his sighted friend. On a crowded street, he unknowingly walked into the personal space of the stranger. His sighted friend interpreted the stranger's "evil" expression and suddenly pulled him out of harm's way:

> *"It looked like he was about to whip out a gun and shoot me or stab me or punch me or whatever, and I had no clue that was going on. This was the kind of dude that people who can see, they stay clear of ... He was looking threatened and ... defensive." –IP3*

As an independent traveler who regularly uses public transit, IP10 revealed that having more information about nearby people would help her feel more safe. She gave the example of a stranger walking on the grass next to her, who she could not recognize due to the sound of busy streets, as being a potential safety concern:

> *"If I am walking around by myself at night ... everyone wants to be more aware of things at that point. And, sometimes the bus transit centers, there are people that hang out, they can be creepy or scary." –IP10*

These examples demonstrate that crowded or noisy areas pose a particular threat because they put pedestrians in close quarters with numerous, unpredictable strangers and make it more difficult to disambiguate aural cues.

5.3.4 Escaping Threatening Situations

Four participants described being in threatening situations that they felt they had to escape. IP1 explained a situation where she was offered help by a stranger via a shortcut to her destination. When he told her they arrived, she realized this was not a short cut and that she was lost and alone with the man. She wanted to find a police officer or citizen to help her, while concurrently trying to conceal her fear from the person who led her there. She was able to convince him to turn around and take her back.

IP9 shared a similar experience where he felt he was being followed by two people and he could not discern their intentions:

> *"A couple of people were following me ... But I was fortunate because somebody fell into step next to me ... and she called over a friend and that person called over a cousin and somebody else called over somebody else and by the time they got done, there was like half dozen people between me and the people who were following me. And I felt a lot safer, because these were the people who tended to police their neighborhood." –IP9*

The lack of information about strangers in the vicinity made IP9 feel unsafe. Like IP1, he sought help from others nearby and was thankful that locals patrolling the neighborhood came to his aid.

IP2 described numerous situations where she was targeted by predatory men interested in using her blindness to their advantage. Below, she described having to use physical force to escape one:

> *"He tried to put on force against me and so he took my cane away, because he knew that I would need that. And so when I told him to leave me alone and give me back my cane ... he told me that it was my fault because I was beautiful. And so that to me is someone who is an attacker ... I am gonna deem that situation as someone who's trying to ... make me the victim and I'm not gonna stand for that. So I kicked him in his knees and he fell and I grabbed my cane and I left. I got myself out of the situation, but it was a little scary." –IP2*

IP2 noted that it would not always be possible to seek help, so she made efforts to prepare to resist attackers by carrying pepper spray and checking her surroundings regularly to ensure no one was following her. She believed that nefarious others might explicitly target blind individuals, presuming it would be easier to conceal their identity and evade repercussions.

IP6 explained a time when she got off the bus in an unsafe area of the city by mistake. While she was focusing on tracking the next bus to a safer location, she would have found it useful to receive notifications of visual information about surrounding people, including whether they were carrying a weapon-like object. All participants mentioned that if more information were provided to them in the moment, they might have been able to manage the situation more effectively. In the absence of critical visual information, participants had to take the risk of escalating the situation themselves or hope that others were nearby to intervene.

5.3.5 Distractions in Critical Situations

Two participants (IP9, IP10) discussed being distracted from their navigational task or startled by people in their vicinity. For example, IP9 was halfway across the street, fully focused on listening to traffic, when a stranger approached him and grabbed his arm—presumably to help. The situation caused IP9 to "flinch", both causing him to worry about the unknown intention of the stranger—perhaps to "steal"—and to lose his concentration on crossing the street safely. He noted that having more forewarning about when other people reach out for him can help prevent unwanted contact and may enable him to stay focused on safe navigation.

5.3.6 Projecting Confidence to Increase Safety

Appearing confident and maintaining awareness of surroundings were two objectives cited by IP1, IP6, IP7, and IP9. They believed this could help them stay safe in unsafe areas. For example, when taken to the wrong location by a stranger, IP1 indicated that projecting calm could facilitate safety: *"I don't want to alert the person I am with that I am scared."* Having access to currently inaccessible visual information through technology may play a role in increasing confidence. Using the Aipoly Vision app on her phone to recognize objects and text, IP6 said:

> *"...knowing more makes you feel more confident. I feel if I am confident, no one will push or grab me. I really like this app because it makes me confident, independent, and less vulnerable, because I am a step forward and have more information about my environment." –IP6*

This suggests that having more information about the situation not simply about reactive defense (e.g., getting on the first bus to a safer place). Feeling or at least appearing confident is an important preventative strategy for avoiding threats.

6. ATs for Increasing Physical Safety is a Nascent Research Area Worth Exploring

After years of investigating accessibility needs of people who are blind within our own research team, we were surprised this study was the first to reveal the significance of interpersonal threats to physical safety. A literature review of the ASSETS contributions over the last 18 years suggests this is an underexplored research topic. As one indication, searching the Proceedings of ASSETS on the ACM portal turned up zero results for search terms "violence," "police," and "law enforcement"—central themes reported here. Instead, papers broaching safety fell into four different categories: environmental safety and obstacle avoidance [6,7,27–29], access to emergency services and alarms [11–13,33] health-risk mediation [14,25–27], and device-oriented safety [2]. In the few cases where interpersonal safety concerns were reported, it was mentioned briefly, as in Williams et al. [31]. This indicates an opportunity to explore how ATs can support *Personal Safety Management—informed, agential, and proactive participation in maintaining one's own physical safety*—not only for people who are blind, but also for people with other or multiple disabilities.

Surprisingly, the only report we found that directly addresses physical safety issues for people who are blind was published in 2016 within the Usable Privacy and Security community. Ahmed et al. [5] present a set of testimonials from blind individuals about how lack of access to visual information can compromise both their physical safety and information security. Notably, our results confirm the threat introduced by others entering one's personal "bubble"; the desire to provide visual details to police to help identify criminals; and the need to support better sense-making in potentially dangerous situations so one can navigate to safety [5]. Our results expand and build on Ahmed et al.'s [5] foundational study by describing how existing ATs already affect real and perceived safety; the need for better ways to interpret and negotiate communication with other citizens and police in contentious situations; the need to support increased confidence as a means of staying safe; and the dual concerns of maintaining safety in crowded areas, as well as areas where it is unclear whether anyone else is around.

HCI has recently begun exploring its role in righting deep social inequalities and power imbalances through incorporating feminist [8] and intersectional [28] theory and contributing to activist technologies that address violence [15] in this vein. People with disabilities are significantly more likely to be targets of violent crime and are often more likely to underreport these crimes to authorities [19]. Our participants tended to raise the topic of interpersonal safety threats after being asked the broad question

"What types of visual information would you like to know about other people?" This suggests that interpersonal safety is a leading concern for people with vision impairments. We therefore see a tremendous opportunity for the ASSETS community to contribute to this space, bringing its values and sensitivities to shaping a research agenda that empowers people with disabilities and demonstrates inclusive excellence. Below, we outline a set of opportunities going forward.

6.1 Opportunity: Answer Visual Questions to Increase Interpersonal Safety

The most basic finding of our study is that many people with vision impairments desire access to visual information about others nearby to increase their personal safety. Like Ahmed et al. [5], we gathered examples that spanned various settings, including crowded public spaces, presumed vacant public spaces, the street, public transit, and one's home. Also like Ahmed et al. [5], we found that participants might benefit from knowing information about how others are moving and behaving around them. This includes how many people are nearby, how far away they are, if they are walking towards them or following them from behind, if they are reaching out toward them, if they are on a collision course, and where they are looking.

Our study adds additional categories to those identified in prior work. Some are visual, others not, and they primarily seek to answer the question "Does this person pose a threat to my physical safety?" These categories include facial expression and emotion, other nonverbal conversational cues, gender, body posture and body size, clothing (e.g., hoodies or official uniforms/badges), indecent exposure, objects-in-hand (particularly weapons like knives and guns), and criminal records.

For designers of AT for the blind, these findings can inspire new tools that leverage computer vision and facial recognition (FR) [5], albeit in less traditional ways (i.e. as more than a conversational aid). We caution, however, that one risk of these technologies is their susceptibility to discriminatory exclusions and characterizations based on personal identities like race and gender. For example, our participants wanted to know if people are in the vicinity. But, in 2015, FR algorithms used by Flickr and Google made headlines by misidentifying black people as "apes" and "gorillas" [18]. The benefits of using FR to increase safety of people who are blind should therefore be weighed carefully with drawbacks related to lack of inclusivity. This may mean taking extra measures to develop inclusive datasets for FR training or seeking alternative technical solutions, like infrared distance and motion sensors.

For the broader disabilities community, there are no doubt different classes of information that will be deemed useful to increasing safety. For example, we can imagine that people who are deaf or hard-of-hearing may benefit from a system that identifies the sound, direction, and distance of gunshots [11]. Existing technologies for Personal Safety Management may be universally valuable. For example, we can imagine the Hollaback! app [15]—which empowers victims to use photographs and storytelling to counter street harassment directed at women—being appropriated or adapted by people with disabilities. Further investigation into the varying safety scenarios and needs of these populations is necessary to design effective tools.

Open research questions in this area include:

- What types of inaccessible information do users want in order to increase interpersonal safety?
- How can assistive devices deliver this information in ways that are appropriately disruptive yet private?
- What technologies are pragmatic in terms of cost, data privacy, and social stigma?

6.2 Opportunity: Continue to Explore the Relationship Between ATs and Safety

We found that assistive tools—including white canes, guide dogs, and apps like Be My Eyes and Aipoly Vision—contributed to an increased or decreased sense of safety. This reaffirms prior findings about how AT can make people feel more safe and confident [7] on the one hand, and put them at higher risk of being grabbed [31] or even mugged [29,32] on the other. Notably, these devices are not explicitly designed for Personal Safety Management. Yet, they impacted how others perceived the blind user or even how the blind user saw themselves, projecting physical vulnerability in some situations and confidence in others. In cases where the device increased a sense of safety, it reinforced the participant's desire to use the technology; the opposite was true for devices that decreased a sense of safety. This suggests that device adoption and abandonment, well-established research topics [1,21,29], may be significantly impacted by concerns about interpersonal safety.

Open research questions in this area include:

- How do we design assistive devices to bolster a sense of confidence and interpersonal safety?
- How can effectiveness be measured?
- How do existing and pervasive ATs already impact users' feelings about safety?

6.3 Opportunity: Explore How ATs Might Facilitate Communication with Police

Several of our participants described situations in which identifying police officers and communicating effectively with them required inaccessible visual information. These findings confirm and build on Ahmed et al.'s [5] documentation of blind individuals' desire to visually describe perpetrators and crime scenes to officials by adding additional scenarios: finding officers in the vicinity, verifying that an individual is a police officer, and communicating effectively and persuasively with police.

Due to various communication challenges outlined by the US Department of Justice [34,35], particularly for people with disabilities, interactions with police are high stakes and can literally be life or death situations. The recent national conversation about deteriorating police-community relations has brought attention to improving the treatment of people with disabilities by law enforcement with programs like COPS[6]. The 2015 Final Report of the President's Task Force on 21st Century Policing[7] notably calls for law enforcement policies prohibiting discrimination based on disability, officer trainings that confront implicit bias and systemic deficiencies in the way police interact with people with disabilities, and adoption of new technologies that will help police better serve people with disabilities.

Open research questions in this area include:

- What visual information can be reliably discerned by AT and how should it be presented for seamless communication?

---

[6] https://cops.usdoj.gov/PolicingTaskForce

[7] https://cops.usdoj.gov/pdf/taskforce/taskforce_finalreport.pdf

- How can technology improve training for police to reduce miscommunication and unnecessary violence?

6.4 Opportunity: Design AT to Empower People to Be Proactive in Safety Management

Our study confirms Ahmed et al.'s [5] finding that additional awareness cues may enable blind individuals to independently and more accurately assess the level of threat in various situations. Our participants wanted to know: *Are silent others present? Are they looking at me? Do they have aggressive or predatory expressions and body language? Are they carrying a gun, knife, or other potential weapon? Are they committing a crime? Are other people noticing the crime, and can they assist me? What's the best route of escape?* They believed that answers to these questions would open new opportunities for them to be *proactive* in their own safety management.

Open research questions in this area include:

- What are the accuracy requirements of ATs that mediate sense-making in potentially critical, dangerous situations?
- Can AT help people with disabilities mount more successful physical self-defense?
- What other sources of information, like live social media posts, might serve this need?

7. LIMITATIONS

While our participants provided many rich stories of their own successes and struggles with safety management, our interview sample size of 10 participants is limited. Since research participants in our sample tended to skew towards relatively higher socio-economic status, there are many scenarios that are unaccounted for and beyond the scope of this investigation. Due to the unexpected focus of semi-structured interviews on physical safety, we missed opportunities to collect demographic information (e.g., race and location) that we believe could have lent additional nuance to our analysis regarding police interactions or general risk of encountering criminals. We look forward to incorporating these insights into future work.

8. CONCLUSION

Despite years of investigating accessibility challenges for people who are blind, our research team was surprised to identify significant concerns surrounding physical safety that are relatively undocumented and unexplored within the ASSETS community. We call this area Personal Safety Management. In this paper, we have laid out a set of examples and resonant themes regarding safety tools, behaviors, and needs as communicated by our participants. We have provided a preliminary map to four promising research opportunities we believe can be explored with other disability populations: 1) understanding interpersonal threats to safety, 2) understanding how pervasive assistive devices already affect safety, 3) understanding accessibility challenges when interacting with law enforcement, and 4) developing AT that empowers people in the safety management process. We hope this map will be a useful guide to researchers and designers working within the blind and broader disabilities communities.

9. ACKNOWLEDGMENTS

We thank our participants for their time and valuable insights. Thanks also to Foad Hamidi for supporting data collection and analysis; Erin Buehler for comments on an early draft; and our reviewers for constructive feedback. This work is supported by Toyota Motor Engineering & Manufacturing North America.

10. REFERENCES

[1] Abdolrahmani, A., Easley, W.B., Williams, M., Branham, S.M., and Hurst, A. 2017. Embracing Errors: Examining How Context of Use Impacts Blind Individuals' Acceptance of Navigation Aid Errors. In *Proceedings of the 2017 CHI Conference on Human Factors in Computing Systems* (CHI '17), 4158-4169.

[2] Abdolrahmani, A., Kuber, R., and Hurst, A.. 2016. An Empirical Investigation of the Situationally-induced Impairments Experienced by Blind Mobile Device Users. In *Proceedings of the 13th Web for All Conference* (W4A '16), Article 21, 8 pages.

[3] Adams, D., Morales, L., and Kurniawan, S. 2013. A Qualitative Study to Support a Blind Photography Mobile Application. In *Proceedings of the 6th International Conference on PErvasive Technologies Related to Assistive Environments* (PETRA '13), Article 25, 8 pages.

[4] Ahmed, T., Hoyle. R., Connelly. K., Crandall, D., and Kapadia, A. 2015. Privacy Concerns and Behaviors of People with Visual Impairments. In *Proceedings of the 33rd Annual ACM Conference on Human Factors in Computing Systems* (CHI '15), 3523-3532.

[5] Ahmed, T., Shaffer, P., Connelly, K., Crandall. D., and Kapadia, A. 2016. Addressing Physical Safety, Security, and Privacy for People with Visual Impairments. In *Proceedings of the 12th Symposium on Usable Privacy and Security (SOUPS '16)*, 341–354.

[6] Amemiya, T. and Sugiyama, H. 2009. Haptic handheld wayfinder with pseudo-attraction force for pedestrians with visual impairments. In *Proceeding of the 11th International ACM SIGACCESS Conference on Computers and Accessibility* (ASSETS '09), 107-114..

[7] Azenkot, S., Prasain, S., Borning, A., Fortuna, E., Ladner, R.E., and Wobbrock, J.O. 2011. Enhancing independence and safety for blind and deaf-blind public transit riders. In *Proceedings of the 2011 Annual Conference on Human Factors in Computing Systems* (CHI '11), 3247-3256.

[8] Bardzell, S. 2010. Feminist HCI: Taking Stock and Outlining an Agenda for Design. In *Proceedings of the SIGCHI Conference on Human Factors in Computing Systems* (CHI '10), 1301-1310.

[9] Bigham, J.P., Jayant, C., Ji, H., Little, G., Miller, A., Miller, R.C., Miller, R., Tatarowicz, A., White, B., White, S., and Yeh, T. 2010. VizWiz: Nearly Real-time Answers to Visual Questions. In *Proceedings of the 23rd Annual ACM Symposium on User Interface Software and Technology* (UIST '10), USA, 333-342.

[10] Brady, E., Morris, M.R., Zhong, Y., White, S., and Bigham, J.P. 2013. Visual Challenges in the Everyday Lives of Blind People. In *Proceedings of the SIGCHI Conference on Human Factors in Computing Systems* (CHI '13), 2117-2126.

[11] Bragg, D., Huynh, N., and Ladner, R.E. 2016. A Personalizable Mobile Sound Detector App Design for Deaf and Hard-of-Hearing Users. In *Proceedings of the 18th International ACM SIGACCESS Conference on Computers and Accessibility* (ASSETS '16), 3-13.

[12] Branham, S.M. and Kane, S.K. 2015. The Invisible Work of Accessibility: How Blind Employees Manage Accessibility in Mixed-Ability Workplaces. In *Proceedings of the 17th International ACM SIGACCESS Conference on Computers and Accessibility* (ASSETS '15), 163-171.

[13] Burton, M.A., Brady, E., Brewer, R., Neylan, C., Bigham, J.P., and Hurst, A. 2012. Crowdsourcing subjective fashion advice using VizWiz. In *Proceedings of the 14th International ACM SIGACCESS Conference on Computers and Accessibility* (ASSETS '15), 163-171.

[14] Consel, C., Dupuy, L., and Sauzéon, H. 2015. A Unifying Notification System To Scale Up Assistive Services. In *Proceedings of the 17th International ACM SIGACCESS Conference on Computers and Accessibility* (ASSETS '15), 77-87.

[15] Dimond, J.P., Dye, M., Larose, D., and Bruckman, A.S. 2013. Hollaback!: The Role of Storytelling Online in a Social Movement Organization. In *Proceedings of the 2013 Conference on Computer Supported Cooperative Work* (CSCW '13), 477-490.

[16] Easley, W., Kuber, R., and Ozok, A. 2016. An empirical study examining medication management among individuals with visual impairments. *Universal Access in the Information Society*. 16, 2 (June 2017), 483-495.

[17] Ervasti, M., Isomursu, M., and Leibar, I.I. 2011. Touch- and audio-based medication management service concept for vision impaired older people. In *2011 IEEE International Conference on RFID-Technologies and Applications* (RFID-TA '11), 244–251.

[18] Hankerson, D., Marshall, A.R., Booker, J., Mimouni, H.E., Walker, I., and Rode, J.A. 2016. Does Technology Have Race? In *Proceedings of the 2016 CHI Conference Extended Abstracts on Human Factors in Computing Systems* (CHI EA '16), 473–486.

[19] Harrell, E. 2016. *Crime Against Persons With Disabilities, 2009-2014 - Statistical Tables*. U.S. Department of Justice, Office of Justice Programs, Bureau of Justice Statistics.

[20] Jayant, C., Ji, H., White, S., and Bigham, J.P. 2011. Supporting Blind Photography. In *Proceedings of the 13th International ACM SIGACCESS Conference on Computers and Accessibility* (ASSETS '11), 203–210.

[21] Kane, S.K., Jayant, C., Wobbrock, J.O., and Ladner, R.E. 2009. Freedom to roam: a study of mobile device adoption and accessibility for people with visual and motor disabilities. In *Proceedings of the 11th International ACM SIGACCESS Conference on Computers and Accessibility* (ASSETS '09), 115-122.

[22] Kramer, K.M., Hedin, D.S., and Rolkosky, D.J. 2010. Smartphone based face recognition tool for the blind. In *2010 Annual International Conference of the IEEE Engineering in Medicine and Biology*, 4538–4541.

[23] Krishna, S., Little, G., Black, J., and Panchanathan, S. 2005. A wearable face recognition system for individuals with visual impairments. In *Proceedings of the 7th International ACM SIGACCESS Conference on Computers and Accessibility* (ASSETS '05), 106-113.

[24] Krishna, S. and Panchanathan, S. 2010. Assistive Technologies as Effective Mediators in Interpersonal Social Interactions for Persons with Visual Disability. In *Proceedings of the 12th International Conference on Computers for Handicapped Persons* (ICCHP '10), 316–323.

[25] Morelli, T., Foley, J., and Folmer, E. 2010. Vi-bowling: a tactile spatial exergame for individuals with visual impairments. In *Proceedings of the 12th International ACM SIGACCESS Conference on Computers and Accessibility* (ASSETS '10), 179-186.

[26] Rector, K., Milne, L., Ladner, R.E., Friedman, B., and Kientz, J.A. 2015. Exploring the Opportunities and Challenges with Exercise Technologies for People who are Blind or Low-Vision. In *Proceedings of the 17th International ACM SIGACCESS Conference on Computers and Accessibility* (ASSETS '15), 203–214.

[27] Rush, R.P. 2009. Sensation augmentation to relieve pressure sore formation in wheelchair users. In *Proceeding of the 11th International ACM SIGACCESS conference on Computers and Accessibility*, (ASSETS '09), 275-276.

[28] Schlesinger, A., Edwards, W.K., and Grinter, R.E. 2017. Intersectional HCI: Engaging Identity Through Gender, Race, and Class. In *Proceedings of the 2017 CHI Conference on Human Factors in Computing Systems* (CHI '17), 5412–5427.

[29] Shinohara, K. and Wobbrock, J.O. 2011. In the shadow of misperception: assistive technology use and social interactions. In *Proceedings of the 2011 Annual Conference on Human Factors in Computing Systems* (CHI '11), 705-714.

[30] Viswanathan, P., Little, J.J., Mackworth, A.K., and Mihailidis, A. 2011. Navigation and obstacle avoidance help (NOAH) for older adults with cognitive impairment: a pilot study. In *Proceedings of the 13th International ACM SIGACCESS Conference on Computers and Accessibility* (ASSETS '11), 43–50.

[31] Williams, M.A., Galbraith, C., Kane, S.K., and Hurst, A. 2014. "Just Let the Cane Hit It": How the Blind and Sighted See Navigation Differently. In *Proceedings of the 16th International ACM SIGACCESS Conference on Computers and Accessibility* (ASSETS '14), 217–224.

[32] Williams, M.A., Hurst, A., and Kane, S.K. 2013. "Pray before you step out": describing personal and situational blind navigation behaviors. In *Proceedings of the 15th International ACM SIGACCESS Conference on Computers and Accessibility* (ASSETS '13), 1–8.

[33] Zafrulla, Z., Etherton, J., and Starner, T. 2008. TTY phone: direct, equal emergency access for the deaf. In *Proceedings of the 10th International ACM SIGACCESS Conference on Computers and Accessibility* (ASSETS '08), 277-278.

[34] "ADA Requirements: Effective Communication." Retrieved July 19, 2017 from https://www.ada.gov/effective-comm.htm

[35] "Commonly Asked Questions About the Americans with Disabilities Act and Law Enforcement." Retrieved July 19, 2017 from https://www.ada.gov/q&a_law.htm

NavCog3: An Evaluation of a Smartphone-Based Blind Indoor Navigation Assistant with Semantic Features in a Large-Scale Environment

Daisuke Sato
IBM Research - Tokyo
dsato@jp.ibm.com

Uran Oh
Carnegie Mellon University
uranoh@cmu.edu

Kakuya Naito
Shimizu Corporation
k.naito@shimz.co.jp

Hironobu Takagi
IBM Research - Tokyo
takagih@jp.ibm.com

Kris Kitani
Carnegie Mellon University
kkitani@cs.cmu.edu

Chieko Asakawa
IBM Research,
Carnegie Mellon University
chiekoa@us.ibm.com

ABSTRACT

Navigating in unfamiliar environments is challenging for most people, especially for individuals with visual impairments. While many personal navigation tools have been proposed to enable independent indoor navigation, they have insufficient accuracy (e.g., 5–10 *m*), do not provide semantic features about surroundings (e.g., doorways, shops, etc.), and may require specialized devices to function. Moreover, the deployment of many systems is often only evaluated in constrained scenarios, which may not precisely reflect the performance in the real world. Therefore, we have designed and implemented NavCog3, a smartphone-based indoor navigation assistant that has been evaluated in a 21,000 m^2 shopping mall. In addition to turn-by-turn instructions, it provides information on landmarks (e.g., tactile paving) and points of interests nearby. We first conducted a controlled study with 10 visually impaired users to assess localization accuracy and the perceived usefulness of semantic features. To understand the usability of the app in a real-world setting, we then conducted another study with 43 participants with visual impairments where they could freely navigate in the shopping mall using NavCog3. Our findings suggest that NavCog3 can open a new opportunity for users with visual impairments to independently find and visit large and complex places with confidence.

CCS Concepts

• **Human-centered computing~Accessibility technologies;** • **Social and professional topics~People with disabilities;** • Information systems~Location based services

Keywords

Indoor navigation; visual impairments; points of interest; voice-based interaction; user evaluation

ASSETS'17, Oct. 29–Nov. 1, 2017, Baltimore, MD, USA.

ACM ISBN 978-1-4503-4926-0/17/10…$15.00
DOI: https://doi.org/10.1145/3132525.3132535

Figure 1. A participant (P5) using NavCog3 heading to a movie theater from a station during Route 1 in Study 1. The smartphone was worn to free the participant's hands while walking.

1. INTRODUCTION

Navigating large, unfamiliar environments in the real-world is a challenging task for people with visual impairments. While sighted individuals can visually obtain semantic information such as doorways, stairs, and shop information to aid navigation, people with visual impairments must rely on non-visual senses [13] or request assistance from another person, who might not be readily available [35]. To facilitate independent mobility for people with visual impairments, many assistive navigation systems have been proposed (see survey by Fallah *et al.* [18]). While much progress has been made towards building prototype systems, many systems have not been deployed at scale in realistic scenarios.

Towards real-world adoption in large environments such as shopping malls, hospitals and airports, we hypothesize that current technologies need to be improved by: (1) achieving more accurate localization to enable more precise instructions, (2) providing non-visual semantic features of the surroundings to help with navigation, and (3) utilizing common devices that are already available to the general public. Many existing indoor navigation systems do not have sufficient accuracy where errors in localization can range from 5 to 10 *m* [4], and do not provide semantic features, which can be extremely useful for orientation and mobility [26, 35]. Moreover, existing systems often require specialized devices for users to carry (e.g., [23, 36]), which may not be practical. Due in part to these key issues, indoor navigation systems have not been successfully deployed nor evaluated in a large-scale environment to meet the needs of people with visual impairments.

On the basis of the hypotheses mentioned above, we will address the following research questions: (1) What level of accuracy can we achieve for indoor navigation, and is it sufficient for turn-by-turn navigation? (2) What are the needs, preferences and expected use cases for accessing semantic features during navigation? (3) To what extent can a navigation system be used to enhance orientation and mobility of individuals with visual impairments?

With the ultimate goal of large-scale adoption in real-world environments, we have designed a smartphone-based navigational assistant for people who are blind or have visual impairments, called **NavCog3**. NavCog3 is based on the initial work of Ahmetovic *et al.* [9, 10], which was only validated in a controlled setting at a university building. Our system uses a similar indoor localization approach using a Bluetooth Low Energy (BLE) beacons network. However, the interface and underlying system architecture is entirely different. It is designed to support people with visual impairment in large-scale indoor environments with semantic features including nearby points of interest (POIs) such as shops and restaurants as well as non-visual landmarks (e.g., doorways).

To address our research questions, we first deployed the system at a large shopping mall (approximately 21,000 m^2), for the evaluation. Finally, we conducted a controlled study with 10 participants with visual impairments consisting three fixed route navigation tasks using NavCog3 (see Figure 1). Lastly, we conducted another user study with a more realistic scenario where we asked 43 participants with visual impairments to use NavCog3 for any destination inside the mall to reflect on natural usages in a large-scale environment.

We measured the localization accuracy while participants were performing navigation tasks for the first study, and the average accuracy was 1.65 *m*, which is comparable to one of the best accuracies achieved by a smartphone-based indoor localization system [3]. With this accuracy, 93.8% of the 260 turns made by participants were successful. We further assessed the turn performance and found that 45° turns were more difficult to make than 90° ones. Findings from the first study confirmed that participants found semantic features to be useful for boosting their spatial awareness (e.g., obstacles), orientation, and mobility (e.g., using elevators). Findings from the second study showed that NavCog3 could enable our participants to reach the shops of their choice, which has not been well supported in other localization systems. These findings suggest that NavCog3 can increase users' confidence in walking independently as well as the opportunities to find and visit new places.

2. RELATED WORK

Our research largely builds on previous work in indoor navigation for people with visual impairments. We were also informed about landmarks and POIs, as well as studies on mobile interactions on-the-go.

2.1 Indoor Navigation and Localization

For safe and independent navigation, many people with visual impairments receive orientation and mobility (O&M) training. However, navigating in an environment can still be challenging as they have to rely on non-visual cues [13]. While commercial navigation tools are often used (e.g., Google Maps[1], Ariadne[2]), these GPS-based navigation systems are limited to outdoor environments only. Thus, many researchers have studied various approaches to support indoor localization for a general purpose [40] as well as for blind navigation [18, 20, 31]. Various localization approaches were explored such as infrared, ultrasound, RFID, lasers and ultra-wideband (UWB) sensors [3, 19, 23, 36]. While these techniques are promising and have sub-meter accuracy, they usually require users to carry a dedicated device (i.e., a receiver).

Approaches that do not require additional devices, other than a smartphone or a sensor installation in a physical environment, include Wi-Fi [15], Bluetooth [29], inertial measurement unit (IMU) sensors [17], a camera [32], or a combination of multiple sensors [24]. While camera-based approaches have the potential for supporting the so called "last meter" problem [30] as they can collect rich visual information about a scene [24, 32], these are not robust enough for a limited field of view and various lighting conditions, which is particularly more problematic for blind users [8]. Although NavCog3 requires the installation of sensors, it does not require additional devices other than a smartphone, is free from line of sight, and can estimate users' location with high accuracy (1.65*m* on average). NavCog3 can provide indoor localization with high accuracy to support reliable navigation assistance for people with visual impairments using built-in IMU sensors in smartphones and Bluetooth Low Energy (BLE) beacons, which are also used in large-scale field studies [5, 6, 28].

2.2 Landmarks and Points of Interest

Both landmarks and POIs can be useful for confirming a person's current location/orientation and understanding the environment while travelling [26, 34]. However, it is difficult for people with visual impairments to be aware of what is around them compared to those without visual impairments who can examine their surrounding at a glance. In this regard, some researchers studied types of semantic features that can be helpful during navigation, particularly for pedestrians with visual impairments [16, 26, 34]. For example, Dias *et al.* [16] interviewed 20 people with visual impairments, and the majority of the participants reported using environmental clues (e.g., smells, sounds) or landmarks (e.g., doorways, elevators) for indoor navigation and orientation. Similarly, Kammoun *et al.* [26] classified semantic features into POIs (e.g., buildings, shops) and landmarks (e.g., ground texture, traffic light) for outdoor environments. In terms of POI information, there are commercial mobile applications that provide POI such as iMove[3] and BlindSquare[4]. BlindSquare, for instance, informs a user of nearby POIs with categories such as education, shopping, and transportation on the basis of the nearest Bluetooth beacon from the user. However, it does not provide turn-by-turn navigation for indoor environment. To the best of our knowledge, NavCog3 is unique as it not only determines if these semantic features are nearby, but also provides their positions and orientations, which is difficult to achieve without accurate localization.

2.3 Interaction On-The-Go

Although the possession of mobile devices is found to increase the independence of mobile contexts for users with visual impairments [27], interacting with mobile devices while walking on a street is difficult as they need to stay alert to ensure their safety [2, 41]. Moreover, since their hands are often occupied by holding a cane or a leash for a guide dog, using a mobile phone is even more challenging unless one-handed or hands-free interaction is supported. [33]. To support hands-free navigation for people with visual impairments, many researchers have focused on wearable technologies [37, 38]. However, these approaches require a custom device, which may not be feasible to support a large population without mass production. In this regard, NavCog3 has been designed as

1 https://maps.google.com
2 https://www.ariadnegps.eu
3 http://www.everywaretechnologies.com/apps/imove
4 http://www.blindsquare.com

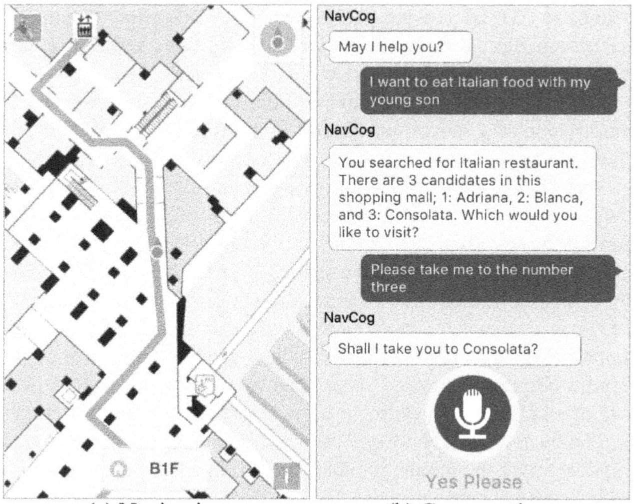

(a) Navigation (b) Conversation

Figure 2. Example screen-shots of NavCog3's interfaces.

a smartphone application to be more readily accessible for users in need. In addition, to minimize the cognitive load, we have added a conversation-based cognitive assistant to NavCog3, which is widely used in many applications such as those for elderly care [22] and knowledge workers [12]. Although evaluating this cognitive assistant is not within the scope of this paper as it is in its early development phase, we expect that speech-based input will relieve cognitive and physical loads, as speech input is known to be faster than manual input [11].

3. THE DESIGN OF NAVCOG3

NavCog3 is a smartphone-based indoor navigation system for people with visual impairments. As a smartphone app, it is readily available to any smartphone user who wishes to get navigational assistance without the need for an additional device. In this section, we describe the navigation instructions and modes of interactions. The details of our implementation can be found in Section 4.

3.1 Navigation

NavCog3 provides turn-by-turn instructions and immediate feedback when incorrect orientation is detected. While speech is used as the our primary feedback for the instructions accessible to people with visual impairments and to enable eyes-free interaction, the system also displays navigation information on the screen (e.g., planned route, current location) to support users who wish to receive visual feedback (see Figure 2a).

3.1.1 Turn-By-Turn Instructions

With the advantage of higher accuracy, NavCog3 can provide turn instructions in a timely manner so that a user with visual impairments can easily make correct turns without visual aid. In addition, it provides "Approaching" notifications prior to the turning point to allow prepare users get prepared. After a turn (or at the start point), the system informs the user of the distance from the current position to the next point and the action that they have to take, either when turning or transitioning between floors (elevator, escalator, or stairs). For sufficiently long distances ($\leq 15\ m$), the system gives a verbal update on the remaining distance every 15 *m*.

At each turning point, the system provides verbal instructions to convey the angle of the turn: a *slight turn* ($22.5° < \theta \leq 60°$), a *regular turn* ($60° < \theta \leq 120°$) and a *big turn* ($120° < \theta$). When a user reaches a turning point, both a short vibration and a short sound effect are provided simultaneously to instruct the user to start turning. Once the user reaches the correct heading, the feedback is provided again to instruct him/her to stop turning and continue walking.

To help users get back on track when they veer from a planned route (by 6 meters), or head in a wrong direction (by 120 degrees), our system provides failure-safe verbal guidance. For example, when a user is walking in the opposite direction, the system would say, "Turn around. You might be going in the wrong direction." If a faster route exists from the user's current location after deviating from the original route, corrective guidance would lead them to the new route accordingly.

Table 1. Categories of semantic features for NavCog3.

	Main	Sub	Information Provided
Landmark	Pathways	Floor	Tactile paving, ramp, step, slope
		Door	Types of doorway (e.g., automatic)
		Obstacles	Existence of object (e.g., trash cans)
	Floor Transition	Elevator	Call button locations, control panel location inside the elevator, Braille button availability, audible announcement availability, wheelchair accessibility
		Escalator	The correct standing side (left or right), directions to adjacent escalator(s)
		Stairs	Shape (e.g., straight, u-shape), number of steps and landings
POI	Shopping and Food	Shop	Type of shops, name
		Restaurant	Cuisine, name
	Facility/ Utility	Restroom	Gender, wheelchair accessibility
		Other	ATM, information center

3.1.2 Nearby Landmarks and POIs

The system provides information about nearby landmarks and POIs so that a user can walk comfortably and confidently. The types of semantic features supported by our system are described in Table 1, which have been recategorized by summarizing previously examined features in [16, 26, 34]. We define landmarks as features that can provide physical or tactile cues to help users to confirm their location such as tactile paving, doorways, and other building infrastructures (e.g. elevator, escalator, and stairs). POIs, such as shops and facilities (e.g., restroom), are defined as places that might interest users during navigation.

In general, information about POIs and landmarks is provided when a user is within proximity to them. However, information about accessibility-related landmarks is already included in the navigation instructions, for example, "Proceed 14 meters on *tactile paving* and turn right at *the end of the corridor*."

3.2 Interactions

3.2.1 Search POI via Conversation

For unfamiliar environments, users may not know what places are available for them to navigate. To help users decide their target destination, NavCog3 enables users to explore nearby POIs by asking the cognitive assistant via speech input. The assistant provides recommendations on the basis of user's request with descriptions. As shown in Figure 2b, a user can initiate a conversation with a request such as "I want to eat Italian food with my young son". The system then provides a set of recommendations on the basis

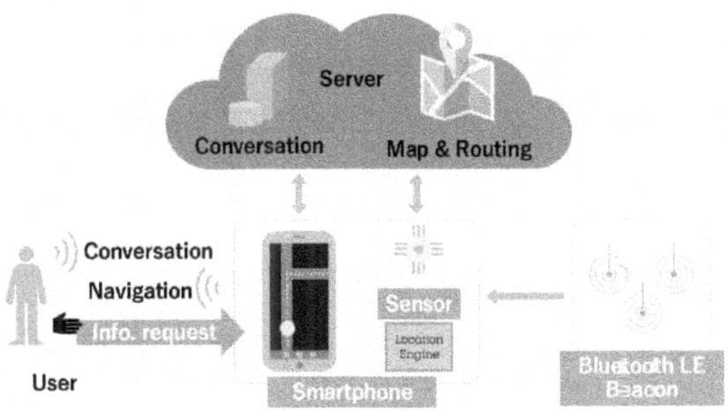

Figure 3. An overview of the system: A user requests navigation or surrounding information via speech-based interaction using a smartphone.

of the search conditions extracted from the users' input; "Italian" and "kids are accepted", in this case. The system also enables users to either manually search for the destination from a POI list or set the destination using speech input if she/he has a specific place in mind.

3.2.2 On-demand Instructions

NavCog3 supports on-demand instructions, which enables users to listen to the current instruction again upon request by simply tapping the screen or pressing a control button on a headset as needed. Example instances include confirming the next action, confirming the surrounding information (e.g., the position of elevator buttons), or checking the remaining distance to the next turning point. The system generates an appropriate instruction on the basis of the current navigation status, user's location, and user's heading.

4. IMPLEMENTATION

In this section, we present the main components implemented for the NavCog3 system (see Figure 3) as well as the deployment process in a large-scale environment with our own evaluation field as an example.

4.1 System Components

4.1.1 Location Engine

We use a hybrid localization technique with a particle filter that combines BLE beacon fingerprinting and pedestrian dead reckoning (PDR), which has been developed as a library component of an open source project[5]. The PDR component uses a filter to recover the delay caused by the smoothing of BLE beacon's RSSI. As a result, using the component to track a user's heading and movement makes the localization responsive and stable. To achieve higher accuracy with the component, proper beacon placement and fine-grained fingerprinting of beacon signals are essential.

Beacon Placement. We first need to place beacons in the environment where we wish to support navigation assistance since the localization is estimated on the basis of detectable beacon signals and their received strength from a user's phone. To achieve high accuracy, the beacon placement interval should be about 7–10 m based on our experience. In addition, the ideal height of the beacon is between 2 and 3.5 m for better radio wave signal reachability; the interference from people passing by is weaker at higher positions, thus, signals with less noise can be received. However, if the position is too high, the accuracy decreases because the variance of the signal power increases as the distance between a device and the beacons increases. Beacons can be hidden if the covering material has little impact on the signal power.

5 https://github.com/hulop/

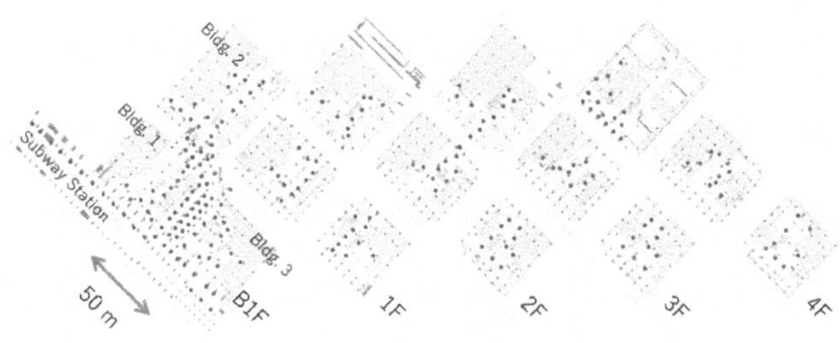

Figure 4. Beacon deployment locations in the environment. Blue dots indicate beacon locations.

Fingerprint Collection. Once all the beacons are placed, fingerprint samples, which are vectors of RSSIs from all beacons within a range of a known location, are collected. Fine-grained fingerprinting is required for accurate location estimation. However, it is time-consuming to manually collect fingerprints point-by-point, and existing alternatives do not guarantee high accuracy [25]. So, we have developed a fingerprinting machine with a LIDAR sensor that can scan the environment with lasers and obtain its coordinates in the environment with an error of centimeter-level. This approach can reduce the radio map creation time by 1/20 compared to that of the point-by-point manual fingerprinting method.

4.1.2 Map & Routing Server

The map data model is an extension a spatial network specification for people with disabilities [1]. It converts a list of physical pedestrian maps and semantic features described in Section 3.1.2 into a spatial graph with semantic features. Each graph edge has attributes detailing path width, gradient, steps, stairs, elevator, escalator, and tactile paving. The routing service computes the optimum route from the available routes given the current location and the destination as well as users' mobility preferences. By default, it avoids escalators and includes routes with tactile paving for users with visual impairments. NavCog3 generates navigation instructions on the basis of these routes and semantic features along them.

4.1.3 Conversation Server

A conversation system has been developed as a Web service that combines two different types of components: (1) a basic conversation script utilizing Watson Conversation API[6] for fixed common facilities and (2) a shop recommendation engine for the shops that can be replaced after a certain period of time. Users' speech input is transcribed using the speech framework of iOS[7] and then submitted to the server. The server runs both components simultaneously and returns the recommendation result if the confidence level of the result is greater than a certain value, otherwise, it returns the result of the conversation script. For shop recommendations, the system requires shop information in text format with annotations such as shop name, shop introduction, opening hours, food menu, and so on. The recommendation engine tries to extract the search conditions from the query text to filter shops that meet the conditions, and then match text in the query with the text in the shop information.

6 https://www.ibm.com/watson/developercloud/conversation.html

7 https://developer.apple.com/reference/speech

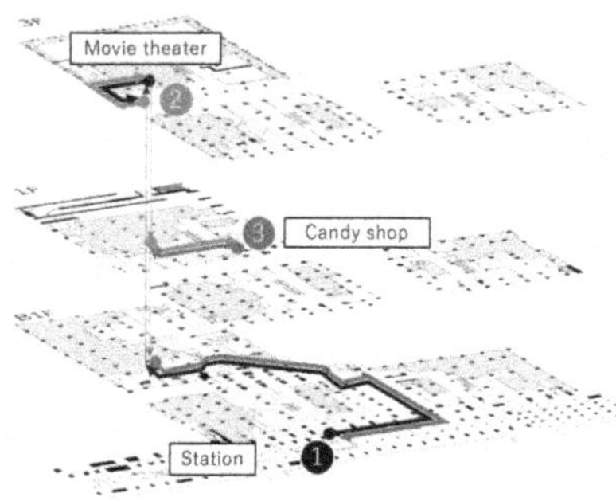

Figure 5. The visualization of three routes for Study 1 in the order of presentation: 1) a station to a movie theater (177*m*), 2) the theater to a candy shop (54 *m*), and 3) the shop to a subway station (176 *m*). Each route included a transition between floors via an elevator.

4.2 Large-Scale Deployment

The deployment area was a shopping mall with three buildings spanning about 21,000 m^2, which is connected to an entrance of a subway station on the first basement level as shown in the Figure 4. The mobile app was built as an iOS app distributed from Apple's App Store[8], which provides indoor localization to the entire deployment area and enables users to navigate to about 100 shops in the shopping mall.

To support indoor navigation for this environment, we first created indoor floor plans for the area from CAD drawings of the building. We then compiled the pedestrian network and POIs for the entire shopping mall from scratch using a map editor. We also collected and annotated text information of the shops from the Webpages of the shopping mall to train the recommendation engine of the cognitive assistant.

In addition, we deployed approximately 220 battery-powered BLE beacons[9] inside the shopping mall, with each costing about $20 and lasting for about one year. Most of the beacons were hidden; placed upon a ceiling while the rest were placed close to the floor if the ceiling was too high in places. The beacon locations are shown as blue dots in Figure 4. All beacons were deployed over two nights during closing hours. Due to ownership issues, we did not deploy beacons inside shop areas, although this would be helpful to navigate users right to the front of the entrance of each shop when it is selected as a destination.

As we used a LIDAR sensor, we were able to collect fingerprints for the map creation of the entire area in 12 hours (three hours for three buildings and corridors on the first basement level). This fingerprint collection was conducted during shop opening hours because the signal strength from beacons can change depending on the environmental changes over time, such as closed shutters. We have also collected approximately 8,000 data points while moving to evaluate the localization error prior to the user study, and the result was 1.47 *m* on average.

5. STUDY 1: FIXED ROUTE

To evaluate the localization accuracy of NavCog3 and to collect subjective feedback on the usefulness of semantic features during navigation, we conducted a 90-minute single-session study with 10 participants with visual impairments. During the study, participants were asked to navigate three fixed routes in a large-shopping mall.

8 https://itunes.apple.com/app/navcog/id1042163426?mt=8

9 http://business.aplix.co.jp/product/mybeacon/mb004ac/

Table 2. Participants' demographic information for Study 1.

PID	Gender	Age	Visual Impairments	Mobility Aid
P1	Female	42	20/2000 for both eyes	White cane
P2	Female	46	20/500 with right eye only	White cane
P3	Male	54	Totally blind	White cane
P4	Female	44	Totally blind	Guide dog
P5	Male	33	Totally blind	White cane
P6	Female	53	20/500 with left eye only	White cane
P7	Male	38	Totally blind	White cane
P8	Female	40	Totally blind	White cane
P9	Male	42	20/500 with left eye only	White cane
P10	Female	48	Totally blind	White cane

5.1 Method

5.1.1 Participants

We recruited 10 participants with visual impairments via a local Braille library (Table 2). Six were totally blind (P2 and P10 were visually impaired since birth), and the rest had low vision (at best 20/500). In terms of smartphone ownership, all but three participants (P7-P9) have used smartphones for at least over a year except for one (P4) had used a smartphone for a week. Four of the participants (P3, P5, P8, P10) reported that they have used a navigation system such as Google Maps before. All have participated in a study with the previous version of NavCog except three participants (P5, P6, P10). Participants were compensated ¥10,000 (approximately $90) for their time.

5.1.2 Apparatus

All participants used a revised version of the NavCog app during the study session. The app was running on an iPhone 6 smartphone, and bone conduction headphones were used to provide audio instructions while not impeding any environmental sounds, which is found to be important for safe navigation [2, 41]. All participants were asked to wear a waist bag with the phone attached to free their hands from holding the phone during navigation, which again is important when walking on a street, especially for users with visual impairments whose hand is often occupied for holding a cane [2, 41]. All participants were provided with a remote control to interact with NavCog3 while the phone was secured in the bag. The app logged every event with a time stamp while the app was running (e.g., instructions), and an experimenter followed and videotaped all participants with a 360-degree camera right behind them.

5.1.3 Procedure

The session began with a background questionnaire. A short training session (5–10 minutes) was then given to the participants who were trying NavCog3 for the first time until they were familiar with the system, such as the navigation voice and the types of information and instructions the system provides during navigation. Prior to the tasks, participants were asked to walk for 5–10 *m* to calibrate their location and heading. They were then asked to navigate three different routes in a shopping mall as shown in Figure 5. The order of the routes was the same for all participants. We instructed the participants to walk normally at their own pace, and the volume and speech rate were adjusted for each participant prior to the tasks. After the task was completed, we collected subjective responses on the usefulness of the semantic features we provided during navigation.

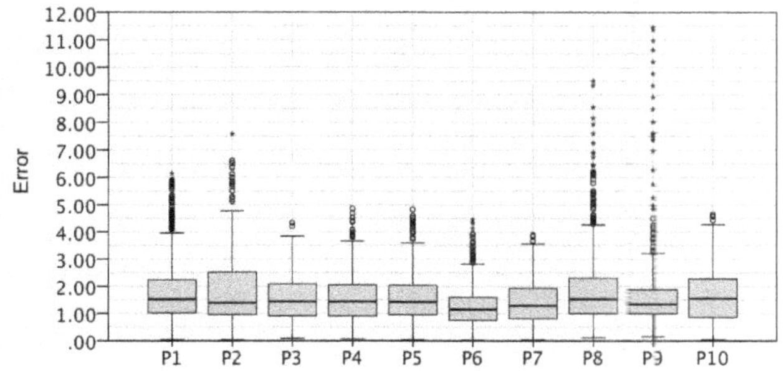

Figure 6. The localization error in meters per participant across three routes (lower value indicates higher accuracy). The boxes indicate 25%, 50% and 75% percentiles. The outliers that do not fall in either 1.5 or 3 times the interquartile range (IQ) from the upper box are shown as circles and asterisks, respectively.

5.1.4 Data Analysis

We visually annotated participants' actual location every second, except for when they were inside an elevator, from the video data for 26 turns per participant. We also annotated their turn performance (i.e., whether they successfully made a turn without the experimenter's help), which varied in terms of turning angle (16 regular, 10 slight turns), and width of a corridor after making a correct turn (M=3.21 *m*; SD = 1.37 *m*; range 1.0–7.3 *m*). We used paired t-test and Chi-square tests for independence throughout the analysis. We also collected audio recordings of participants' comments. The comments were transcribed, translated from Japanese to English, and analyzed on the basis of themes of interest following [14] (e.g., landmark, cognitive load).

5.2 Findings

All ten participants were able to complete the navigation tasks for all three routes. On average, the total task completion time was 990.5 *s* (SD = 129.1), and the total travel distance was 450.0 *m* (SD = 32.4) for all three routes per participant.

5.2.1 Overall Localization Accuracy

The overall localization accuracy of NavCog3 was evaluated in terms of the Euclidian distance between a user's actual location and estimated location. We extracted 7641 actual location points across the three routes from the participants' results. The average error rate was 1.65 *m* (SD = 1.13), which is comparable to the 1.47 *m* accuracy, measured offline prior to Study 1. It is also a better result than that of a former study (1.70 *m*) in a relatively small space (670 m^2) [29]. The localization accuracy per participant is shown in Figure 6. Some participants had higher errors than others (P2, P8, and P9) due to issues with the localization engine. One issue was that the engine stopped working, due to a problem, during navigation while the user kept walking (P9). Another issue was that the heading estimation failed inside an elevator (P2 route 2 and P8 route 1).

5.2.2 Navigation Performance

As our system provides turn-by-turn navigation instructions, we further examined the video data to analyze navigation errors, focusing on participants' turn performance: *success* if they were able to make the turns without requiring help from the experimenter, *fail* if otherwise. Of the 260 turns in total, 221 turns were successful on the first attempt. Of the 39 missed turns, 22 were successful on the second attempt. An experimenter had to interrupt participants for the remaining 17 turns to prevent participants from entering shops (N=8), bumping into people (N=2), because the participant seemed lost (N=2), or due to system-related issues (N=5). In terms of the turn success rate, the average rate per participant across all routes was 85.0% (SD = 10.6%) without any correction, and 93.5% (SD = 5.8%) either with the help of the system's failure-safe guidance (N=18) or by participants themselves (N=4); the average success rate with or without correction was significantly different with the paired t-test (t_9 = -2.43, p = .038). The distribution of localization accuracy with turn performance (*success* vs. *fail*) is shown in Figure 7, where each turn is grouped on the basis of its localization accuracy with an interval of 0.5 *m* (e.g., [0.0, 0.5), [0.5, 1)). We further examined a number of variables that might have affected the turn success rate, focusing on turn angle (regular turn at 90° *vs.* slight turn at 45°) and width of the passage.

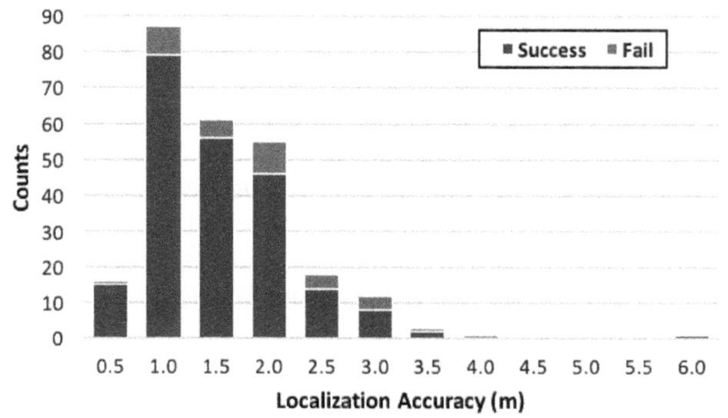

Figure 7. The distribution of localization accuracy in meters (N = 254). Note that x-axis indicates the start of each interval. For example, 0.5 refers to the interval of [0, 0.5).

Turn Angle. Although the average passage width and localization accuracy were not significantly different between the types of turns (*regular* vs. *slight*), a Chi-square test for independence revealed that the turn types significantly impact the turn success rates; $\chi^2_{(1)}$ = 6.245; p = .012; φ = .155. While 89.4% of regular turns were successful, only 78.0% were successful for slight turns, suggesting that regular turns are easier than slight turns. For example, P4 stated that there was no problems when turning 90 degrees, but it was difficult to ask her dog to make slight left turns.

Width of passage. We hypothesized that the turn success rate would be lower as the width of the turn gets narrower. While we were not able to find a correlation between the success rate and the width, some participants commented that making a correct turn is more difficult for narrow widths. For example, P3 mentioned that he would miss the timing of the turn when the corner was narrow due to the width of the corridor being narrow. However, even if he turned into a wide passage too much, he could correct himself later.

5.2.3 Feedback on Semantic Features

Confirming prior findings that surrounding landmarks and POIs are useful for people with visual impairments [26], all participants reacted positively to the semantic features we provided during the navigation, especially for non-visual and silent landmarks such as elevators.

Tactile Paving and Obstacles. All participants considered tactile paving on the floor to be useful except for P4, a guide dog user. She commented that since she walked with a dog, she did not care about tactile paving. The trend was similar for obstacles; eight participants reported that this information was useful for safety. Again, P4, who relies on her guide dog for avoiding obstacles, did not consider this information to be useful.

Elevators. We also provided information on the location of elevators as well as their button locations both inside and outside of them. While one participant (P9), who reported that he tends to rely on his sight whenever he can, did not considered this information to be useful, elevator-related information was appreciated by the rest of the participants. P8, for example, commented that, because elevators these days are mostly silent, she wishes to be notified when the door is open since she does not know whether the elevator is open or closed unless she notices that people are getting on and off.

Points of Interest. All participants considered POIs information to be useful. We noticed that some participants considered POIs would increase the enjoyment of walking places (*N*=4). P10, for example, stated that without NavCog3 she would have never walked into an interesting shop to buy something unless somehow encouraged to do so, and that it was a pleasure to enjoy shopping from the information received. P7 also wished to use POIs information to enhance his spatial awareness. To be specific, he said that the information on nearby shops and vending machine locations were informative as a clue for large crowds (e.g., people coming out from shops, standing in line, etc.) so he can be more cautious.

While POIs may increase the joy of walking around and improve spatial awareness, two participants specified that they would like to receive POI information only upon request or have two modes of navigation such as *exploration mode* where a user can receive detailed information about nearby POIs and *direction-only mode*, which does not provide POI information at all.

Suggested Semantic Features. Besides the information about the existence and location of obstacles, four participants also wished to know the types of obstacles and the distance from them so that they can decide whether they should be alert or not. For example, P10 wished to get more descriptive information, followed by an action suggestion, stating that when told by NavCog3 that there was an obstacle on the right side, because she could not feel it, she was not sure if she had to walk carefully or differently from how she had been. On the other hand, P4, who travels with a guide dog, did not consider the distance information to be useful. Instead, she was more interested in learning about specific directions to the available target so that she can instruct her dog to walk towards it, such as a door or stairs.

Above all, the most commonly suggested landmarks were stairs and escalators, which participants considered to be more accessible than elevators when transitioning between floors (*N*=7). P8 stated that she did not like the elevator because of other people. It would be difficult to determine when to ride the elevator, when the door was open, and whether the floor buttons could be touched or not. She preferred not to use an elevator when alone, even if there was voice guidance, choosing to take the escalator when possible.

5.2.4 Overall Experience

The overall feedback was very positive for all participants. Most or all of the participants considered the timing of the guidance was appropriate (*N*=9), the instructions were easy to understand (*N*=10). In addition, nine participants reported that they would be able to walk alone in any unfamiliar place with NavCog3. Furthermore, all participants expressed their desire to use our system for navigating other places. Here, we summarize the factors that might have influenced the overall experience with NavCog3.

Spatial Mapping. As found in [26], seven participants reported that semantic features helped them to understand the spatial layout of the environment as well as their orientation. For example, P3 mentioned that if he can recall the location from the name of a shop, it would be useful as a reference to other locations (e.g., "next to OO store"). P5 also commented, *"While walking on tactile paving, [NavCog3] taught me the location of a stop, and the name of a shop on the street. So, whether you are going out or returning, you can figure out where you are going by drawing a map inside your head."*

Cognitive Load and Safety. While semantic features may help with spatial understanding of the environment, seven participants reported that this information required extra cognitive load during navigation, which also introduced safety concerns. P6 mentioned that *"If I become distracted by the system announcements, I cannot be aware of the surroundings. Therefore, I cannot avoid obstacles as I can usually do."* P8 also reported that she only needs to listen to the guidance announcements with about 70–80% focus, so that she can concentrate on surrounding sounds and other people. On the other hand, P2 commented that she feels safer using NavCog3 as she felt like she can see the environment as she passes by semantic features using NavCog3. She said that the verbal description of the surroundings makes her feel like she can see the scenery, which reduces her fear while walking.

Hands-Free Interaction. As the needs for hands-free interaction in mobile contexts was found to be important in prior studies for pedestrians with visual impairments [2, 41], half of the participants expressed that they appreciate NavCog3 for enabling hands-free use. P2 said that it was easier to move because she did not have to hold the phone in her hand and could concentrate on using her white cane. P9 specified that he preferred to put the phone in a pocket, especially when in elevators, as it is difficult to find and press the button while holding a phone. Interestingly, while they appreciated the hands-free feature, two participants mentioned that they would rather not use this feature because it requires additional devices, a remote control and a headset in this case, other than the phone (P1), or to feel the haptic feedback better (P8).

6. STUDY 2: FREE ROUTE

To investigate the usability of NavCog3 for supporting large-scale environments and to identify and confirm users' needs for indoor navigation reflecting on their natural usages, we conducted a second study where participants were asked to use NavCog3 for any destination of their choice in a large shopping mall.

6.1 Method

6.1.1 Participants

Forty-three participants (22 males, 21 females) with visual impairments via a local Braille library volunteered for the study. The participants were almost equally split between people who were totally blind (*N*=21) and people with low vision (*N*=22). For the blind user group (**B**), 18 participants used a white cane and three had a guide dog. For the low vision group(**LV**), 17 were cane walkers, two had a guide dog, and three did not use any mobility aid. We did not collect their age or smartphone ownership for this study.

6.1.2 Apparatus

Apparatus was almost the same as the user study. All participants used the same version of NavCog3 as in the user study on an iPhone 6 smartphone. Again, bone conduction headphones were used to convey audio feedback. Unlike the participants in Study 1 who were asked to wear the phone in a waist bag, participants were allowed to carry the phone however they like. For participants who wished to keep their phone in their pocket or a bag, we provided a remote control as an option. The app logged every event with a time stamp while the app was running. No video was recorded for any sessions in Study 2.

6.1.3 Procedure

We had three sessions in parallel, and an experimenter accompanied each participant to ensure their safety. The duration of a session was up to 60 minutes. After a brief explanation on how to use the app at the beginning, participants could freely select the destinations of their choice using the conversational interface. Unlike Study 1, no training was given to any participant. All participants were asked to navigate to at least three different destinations using NavCog3. At the end, we gave short questionnaires and had wrap-up interviews with the participants.

6.1.4 Data Analysis

We audio-recorded participants' comments, which were later transcribed and translated for further analysis. Comments were analyzed on the basis of themes of interest in Study 1 as well as new emergent themes, again following [14]. We also collected usage logs for 188 itineraries from the participants during the study, which includes the distance, duration, and selected destinations. The selected destinations were diverse; of over 100 POIs inside the shopping mall, 52 POIs (47 shops, 5 facilities) were selected at least once. The average travel distance was 152 *m* (*SD*=90.4) and the average travel duration per trip was approximately five minutes (*M*=305 *s*; *SD*=177 *s*).

6.2 Findings

Although no instructions were given to participants to demonstrate the full potential of our system, participants' overall reaction was very positive. Because most of the questions asked in the questionnaire were open-ended, the responses were counted in terms of the number of participants who mentioned it during the wrap-up interview.

6.2.1 Feedback on Semantic Features

Landmarks of Interest. When asked about the perceived usefulness of landmark information (scaled from 1 to 5, where 5 is the best), the majority of the participants showed a positive attitude by giving ratings higher than 3 (*N*=31 out of 43), as confirmed in Study 11wq1. Reflecting Study 1's findings, some participants found some landmarks to be more or less useful than other landmarks. For example, a participant (B13) with a guide dog commented that the information on button location was helpful since dogs cannot recognize buttons. On the other hand, LV5 did not considered Braille availability of the buttons in the elevator to be useful because the participant could not read Braille. The suggestions for other landmarks were more diverse. Some wished to know their current location, chairs, stairs, moving objects and crowds (*N*=2 each). The most frequent requests were related to elevators (*N*=7), which was found to be less preferred than stairs and escalators in Study 1. Again, participants wished to be informed of the current floor location (*N*=3), the arrival time (*N*=2), the heading direction (up/down), as well as which elevator has arrived if there are multiple ones (*N*=1 each).

Points of Interest. In addition to seven participants commenting that they liked the nearby POI information as is, a greater number of participants (*N*=10) expressed a different preference (e.g., level of details). Some wanted more concise announcements especially when shops are on both sides (*N*=2), while five participants wished to get more detailed information on shops. For example, LV21 wished to have a "window shopping mode" with more frequent updates on shops nearby. Other participants wished to turn POI information on and off (*N*=2) or did not want this information at all (*N*=1).

6.2.2 Overall Experience

Cognitive Load and Spatial Awareness. We asked participants if the amount of guidance the system provided was appropriate to not cognitively overwhelm them during navigation. While most of them said the amount was appropriate, some participants showed concerns of losing spatial awareness of surroundings (*N*=5), which could lead to safety issues, as found in Study 1. For example, B11 commented that it was impossible to concentrate on the guidance and create a mental map at the same time, and that it may be safer to cut down the amount of guidance so that one can also be aware of themselves. One solution suggested by five participants was to provide a preview so that they could listen to the guidance prior to their itinerary, and focus on the surroundings while walking.

Independent Navigation. As our primary goal is to support people with visual impairments to navigate independently in any unfamiliar environment, we asked participants if they think our app would allow them to walk alone in other places (i.e., *Navigation Confidence*), and 25 participants reported "yes", not just for unfamiliar environments but also for familiar places at different times of the day (in daytime vs. at night). For example, B12 specified that *"I would be able to navigate places without feeling anxious."* Two participants also liked that NavCog3 would allow them to go out immediately without preparation (e.g., scheduling assistance). The places that participants wished to use NavCog3 for independent navigation included large facilities such as stations (*N*=6), shopping malls, universities (*N*=3 each), offices (*N*=2), hospitals, airports, restroom, and even at home (*N*=1 each).

6.2.3 Other Suggestions for Improvement

In terms of distance, three participants mentioned that they would prefer the distance information to be described in number of steps instead of in meters. As for the turns, four participants from Study 2 also commented that making slight turns was difficult, where two of them suggested using clock position. Interestingly, two participants suggested connecting NavCog3 with other services. B12, for example, wished that our app to link with other services such as Google Maps or shop websites.

7. DISCUSSION

On the basis of our findings, we reflected on the implications for supporting large-scale indoor navigation for people with visual impairments.

7.1 Accuracy Requirements

Overall, most participants could successfully complete tasks without any support at our achieved accuracy. The localization error during the user study sessions was 1.65 *m* on average, which is comparable to one of the best accuracies for an indoor navigation system running on an off-the-shelf smartphone [3, 29]. We observed that most of the errors can be corrected by our fail-safe guidance system without improving the accuracy (Section 5.2.2.). This suggests that our localization accuracy may be sufficient for supporting turn-by-turn navigation as a well-designed fail-safe guidance system can complement the current accuracy limitations. However, it is still important to provide high accuracy for finding small targets such as an elevator button, door knob, or water tap (referred to as a last meter problem [30]).

7.2 Landmarks and Points of Interests

The majority of the participants from both studies considered landmarks that our system provided to be useful (Section 5.2.3 and 6.2.1), confirming the importance of surrounding information for pedestrians with visual impairments to aid their orientation and mobility [17, 26]. Information about elevator locations, for example, was appreciated because they are silent, making them difficult to find. Although our information was largely limited to constructed landmarks such as tactile paving on the floor and doorways, some participants commented that non-physical clues such as sounds from an escalator or changes in light was also useful, confirming that individuals with visual impairments use multiple sensory channels to understand the spatial layout of a physical environment [16]. In this regards, it would be useful to encode information on ambient sounds (e.g., escalator operating sounds) and other types of landmarks into the navigation instructions to inform users what clues to look for on the way.

We found that the landmarks and points that participants found *interesting* or *useful* varied in terms of mobility aid and their objective (i.e., exploration *vs.* way-finding), as found in [39]. For example, the information about obstacles or tactile paving may be less appealing for a guide-dog user compared to white-cane users. Thus, the types of semantic features that a user wishes to be informed about should be personalized or customizable like in BlindSquare [7]. This would also be helpful to reduce the amount of information that may result in cognitive overload while walking, which we will discuss further in the next section.

7.3 Augmenting Navigation Aids

Regardless of which primary mobility aid they use, all participants from the user studies wished to use our system as a complementary means of navigation assistance. In contrast, many participants of our study complained about decreased attention to their surroundings due to the attention to the navigation instructions (Section 5.2.4 and 6.2.2.) For wide adoption, however, seamless augmentation of users' existing navigation skills would be important. To avoid impeding users' mobility, cognitive load should be considered when designing a navigation assistant, so that users can keep their routine during their way-finding. For example, the system can provide instructions when a user is standing still then offer as little guidance as possible when walking so as to not impede users' awareness of surroundings. If they can have a spatial layout of the environment in advance, they can focus on their safety, which is one of the major concerns for people with visual impairments [2, 41].

7.4 Support for Large-Scale Environments

We were able to deploy an indoor navigation system in a large-scale environment (Section 4.2). We demonstrated that our localization accuracy is reliable even in a large shopping mall (Section 5.2.1) that has diverse attributes of an indoor environment (e.g., open space, corridors with various width, crowds, etc.). Findings from Study 2 suggested that users were able to select diverse destinations and navigate to their desired POIs successfully (Section 6.1.4). Moreover, they felt confident walking independently in unfamiliar environments (Section 6.2.2). While important, supporting indoor navigation for a large-scale environment is challenging. As well as deployment costs, collecting landmark information for indoor areas is also time-consuming. We plan to investigate various approaches to help reduce costs such as physical crowdsourcing [21] or computer-based automation. We believe that our system is a great example that shows the feasibility of supporting large-scale environments and how our system can enable independent navigation.

7.5 Limitations

Although attempting to capture the natural usage of our system by allowing participants to navigate to any destination of their choice, a longitudinal field study may reveal additional implications for designing navigation system for people with visual impairments. In addition, we did not control participants' exposure to previous versions of our system, which might have affected navigation errors or subjective responses, although we did not any find noticeable differences. Moreover, different results may have been found had we recruited a different population, especially for the findings related to guide-dog users as the sample size was small. For future work, additional studies with a larger number of guide-dog users or other users with various needs (e.g., wheelchair users, foreigners) would be useful.

8. CONCLUSION

We designed and implemented NavCog3, a smartphone-based indoor navigation assistant for pedestrians with visual impairments. Our system is characterized by turn-by-turn navigation with high localization accuracy and semantic features for spatial understanding. We deployed our system in a large shopping mall and evaluated it with over 50 participants to assess the feasibility of supporting indoor navigation for large-scale environments in the real world. Our study findings show that NavCog3 can achieve high accuracy (1.65 *m* error on average). Subjective responses confirmed that semantic features were perceived to be useful for building spatial map of the environment as they navigate. We also showed that with NavCog3, participants were able to find and navigate to any destination of their choice. All these suggest that our system can be adopted to be used in other large indoor environments, and can open the opportunity for users with visual impairments to freely navigate with confidence.

9. REFERENCES

[1] -Draft development specification for spatial network model for - pedestrians. Ministry of Land, Infrastructure, Transport and - Tourism, Japan, 2017. http://www.mlit.go.jp/common/ - 001177505.pdf visited at 2017-05-01. -

[2] -A. Abdolrahmani, R. Kuber, and A. Hurst. An empirical investigation of the situationally-induced impairments experienced by blind mobile device users. In *Proceedings of the 13th Web for All Conference*, page 21. ACM, 2016.

[3] -Microsoft indoor localization competition - IPSN 2016. https://www.microsoft.com/en-us/research/event/microsoft-indoor-localization-competition-ipsn-2016/ visited at 2017-05-01.

[4] -New version of Google Maps brings indoor floor plans to your - phone. http://edition.cnn.com/2011/11/30/tech/mobile/new-version-google-maps-indoors-wired/ visited at 2017-05-01. -

[5] -SFO app for visually impaired navigation by indoo.rs, 2014. - https://indoo.rs/sfo/ visited at 2017-05-01. -

[6] -Wayfinder app helps the blind navigate the tube, 2014. - http://www.wired.co.uk/article/wayfindr-app visited at - 2017-05-01. -

[7] BlindSquare indoor navigation, May 2015. http://blindsquare.com/

indoor/ visited at 2017-05-01.

[8] -D. Adams, L. Morales, and S. Kurniawan. A qualitative study to support a blind photography mobile application. In *Proceedings of the 6th International Conference on PErvasive Technologies Related to Assistive Environments*, page 25. ACM, 2013.

[9] -D. Ahmetovic, C. Gleason, K. M. Kitani, H. Takagi, and C. Asakawa. Navcog: turn-by-turn smartphonenavigation assistant for people with visualimpairments or blindness. In *Proceedings of the Web for All Conference*, page 9. ACM, 2016.

[10] -D. Ahmetovic, M. Masayuki, C. Gleason, E. Brady H. Takagi, K. Kitani and C. Asakawa. Achieving Practical and Accurate Indoor Navigation for People with Visual Impairments. In *Proceedings of the Web for All Conference*, page 9. ACM, 2017.

[11] -S. Azenkot and N. B. Lee. Exploring the use of speech input by blind people on mobile devices. In *Proceedings of the 15th International ACM SIGACCESS Conference on Computers and Accessibility*, page 11. ACM, 2013.

[12] -P. M. Berry, K. Myers, T. E. Uribe, and N. Yorke-Smith. Task management under change and uncertainty. In *Proceedings of the Workshop on Constraint Solving under Change*, 2005

[13] -A. Black, J. E. Lovie-Kitchin, R. L. Woods, N. Arnold, J. Byrnes, and J. Murrish. Mobility performance with retinitis pigmentosa. *Clinical and Experimental Optometry*, 80(1):1–12, 1997.

[14] -V. Braun and V. Clarke. Using thematic analysis in psychology. *Qualitative research in psychology*, 3(2):77–101, 2006.

[15] -Y.-C. Cheng, Y. Chawathe, A. LaMarca, and J. Krumm. Accuracy characterization for metropolitan-scale wi-fi localization. In *Proceedings of the 3rd international conference on Mobile systems, applications, and services*, pages 233–245. ACM, 2005.

[16] -M. B. Dias, E. A. Teves, G. J. Zimmerman, H. K. Gedawy, S. M. Belousov, and M. B. Dias. Indoor navigation challenges for visually impaired people. In *Indoor Wayfinding and Navigation*, pages 141–164. CRC Press, 2015.

[17] -N. Fallah, I. Apostolopoulos, K. Bekris, and E. Folmer. The user as a sensor: Navigating users with visual impairments in indoor spaces using tactile landmarks. In *Proceedings of the SIGCHI Conference on Human Factors in Computing Systems*, CHI '12, pages 425–432, 2012. ACM.

[18] -N. Fallah, I. Apostolopoulos, K. Bekris, and E. Folmer. Indoor human navigation systems: A survey. *Interacting with Computers*, page iws010, 2013.

[19] -J. Faria, S. Lopes, H. Fernandes, P. Martins, and J. Barroso. Electronic white cane for blind people navigation assistance. In *World Automation Congress (WAC), 2010*, pages 1–7. IEEE, 2010.

[20] -N. A. Giudice and G. E. Legge. Blind navigation and the role of technology. *The Engineering Handbook of Smart Technology for Aging, Disability, and Independence*, pages 479–500, 2008.

[21] -C. Gleason, D. Ahmetovic. (2017) LuzDeploy: A Collective Action System for Installing Navigation Infrastructure for Blind People. In *Proceedings of International Web for All Conference*

[22] -S. Helal, C. Giraldo, Y. Kaddoura, C. Lee, H. El Zabadani, and W. Mann. Smart phone based cognitive assistant. In *UbiHealth 2003: The 2nd International Workshop on Ubiquitous Computing for Pervasive Healthcare Applications*, 2003.

[23] -A. Hub, J. Diepstraten, and T. Ertl. Design and development of an indoor navigation and object identification system for the blind. In *ACM Sigaccess Accessibility and Computing*, number 77-78, pages 147–152. ACM, 2004.

[24] -T. Ishihara, J. Vongkulbhisal, K. M. Kitani, and C. Asakawa. Beacon-guided structure from motion for smartphone-based navigation. In *Winter Conference on the Applications of Computer Vision*. IEEE, 2017.

[25] -S. H. Jung, B.-C. Moon, and D. Han. Performance evaluation of radio map construction methods for wi-fi positioning systems. *IEEE Transactions on Intelligent Transportation Systems*, 2016.

[26] -S. Kammoun, F. Dramas, B. Oriolaand, and C. Jouffrais. Route selection algorithm for blind pedestrian. In *Control Automation and Systems (ICCAS), 2010 International Conference on*, pages 2223–2228. IEEE, 2010.

[27] -S. K. Kane, C. Jayant, J. O. Wobbrock, and R. E. Ladner. Freedom to roam: a study of mobile device adoption and accessibility for people with visual and motor disabilities. In *Proceedings of the 11th international ACM SIGACCESS conference on Computers and accessibility*, pages 115–122. ACM, 2009.

[28] -J.-E. Kim, M. Bessho, S. Kobayashi, N. Koshizuka, and K. Sakamura. Navigating visually impaired travelers in a large train station using smartphone and bluetooth low energy. In Proceedings of the 31st Annual ACM Symposium on Applied Computing, pages 604–611. ACM, 2016.

[29] -D. G. Luca and M. Alberto. Towards accurate indoor localization using ibeacons, fingerprinting and particle filtering. In *2016 International Conference on IndoorPositioning and Indoor Navigation (IPIN)*, 2016.

[30] -R. Manduchi and J. M. Coughlan. The last meter: blind visual guidance to a target. In *Proceedings of the SIGCHI Conference on Human Factors in Computing Systems*, pages 3113–3122. ACM, 2014.

[31] -R. Manduchi and J. Coughlan. (computer) vision without sight. *Communications of the ACM*, 55(1):96–104, 2012.

[32] -R. Manduchi, S. Kurniawan, and H. Bagherinia. Blind guidance using mobile computer vision: A usability study. In *Proceedings of the 12th International ACM SIGACCESS Conference on Computers and Accessibility*, ASSETS '10, pages 241–242, 2010. ACM.

[33] -U. Oh and L. Findlater. Design of and subjective response to on-body input for people with visual impairments. In *Proceedings of the 16th international ACM SIGACCESS conference on Computers & accessibility*, pages 115–122. ACM, 2014.

[34] -J. E. Pérez, M. Arrue, M. Kobayashi, H. Takagi, and C. Asakawa. Assessment of semantic taxonomies for blindindoor navigation based on a shopping center use case. In *The 14th International Cross-Disciplinary Conference on Web Accessibility*, W4A 2017. ACM, 2017.

[35] -P.-A. Quinones, T. Greene, R. Yang, and M. Newman. Supporting visually impaired navigation: a needs-finding study. In *CHI'11 Extended Abstracts on Human Factors in Computing Systems*, pages 1645–1650. ACM, 2011.

[36] -L. Ran, S. Helal, and S. Moore. Drishti: an integrated indoor/outdoor blind navigation system and service. In *Pervasive Computing and Communications, 2004. PerCom 2004. Proceedings of the Second IEEE Annual Conference on*, pages 23–30. IEEE, 2004.

[37] -D. A. Ross. Implementing assistive technology on wearable computers. *IEEE Intelligent systems*, 16(3):47–53, 2001.

[38] -R. Velázquez. Wearable assistive devices for the blind. In *Wearable and autonomous biomedical devices and systems for smart environment*, pages 331–349. Springer, 2010.

[39] -M. A. Williams, A. Hurst, and S. K. Kane. Pray before you step out: describing personal and situational blind navigation behaviors. In *Proceedings of the 15th International ACM SIGACCESS Conference on Computers and Accessibility*, page 28. ACM, 2013

[40] -J. Xiao, Z. Zhou, Y. Yi, and L. M. Ni. A survey on wireless indoor localization from the device perspective. *ACM Computing Surveys (CSUR)*, 49(2):25, 2016.

[41] -H. Ye, M. Malu, U. Oh, and L. Findlater. Current and future mobile and wearable device use by people with visual impairments. In *Proceedings of the SIGCHI Conference on Human Factors in Computing Systems*, pages 3123–3132. ACM, 2014.

Virtual Navigation for Blind People: Building Sequential Representations of the Real-World

João Guerreiro[1], Dragan Ahmetovic[1], Kris M. Kitani[1], Chieko Asakawa[1,2]
[1]Carnegie Mellon University, [2]IBM Research - Tokyo
{jpvguerreiro, dragan1}@cmu.edu, {kkitani, chiekoa}@cs.cmu.edu

ABSTRACT

When preparing to visit new locations, sighted people often look at maps to build an *a priori* mental representation of the environment as a sequence of step-by-step actions and points of interest (POIs), e.g., turn right after the coffee shop. Based on this observation, we would like to understand if building the same type of sequential representation, prior to navigating in a new location, is helpful for people with visual impairments (VI). In particular, our goal is to understand how the simultaneous interplay between turn-by-turn navigation instructions and the relevant POIs in the route can aid the creation of a memorable sequential representation of the world. To this end, we present two smartphone-based virtual navigation interfaces: VirtualLeap, which allows the user to jump through a sequence of street intersection labels, turn-by-turn instructions and POIs along the route; and VirtualWalk, which simulates variable speed step-by-step walking using audio effects, whilst conveying similar route information. In a user study with 14 VI participants, most were able to create and maintain an accurate mental representation of both the sequential structure of the route and the approximate locations of the POIs. While both virtual navigation modalities resulted in similar spatial understanding, results suggests that each method is useful in different interaction contexts.

CCS Concepts

•**Human-centered computing → Accessibility;** *Interaction techniques;*

Keywords

Assistive Technology; Blind Navigation; Cognitive Mapping; Virtual Navigation; Orientation and Mobility.

1. INTRODUCTION

Before visiting a new location, sighted people often explore maps to understand the sequence of actions they need to follow to reach a destination. Both printed and digital maps visually convey information about POIs, which are used to support the construction of a person's mental representation of a route (e.g., turn left **after the post office**). This sequential representation of information is also very common when people provide verbal descriptions to guide someone to a destination. The reduction of a complex physical 3D space into a compact sequential representation is useful because it helps us to store navigational information efficiently. Previous research shows that the same sequential route-based instructions are also used by visually impaired (VI) people when building a mental model of the environment [21, 32]. However, extrapolating a sequential model of the environment requires a way to simultaneously access both the information about the route and POIs along it.

Our goal is to understand how we can provide simultaneous access to turn-by-turn navigation instructions and the POIs in the route to aid the creation of a memorable sequential representation of the world. Moreover we investigate how to use currently available technologies to provide the same kind of integrated knowledge non-visually.

We present a smartphone-based virtual navigation system that supports turn-by-turn navigation and announces POIs at their exact location and orientation along the route (e.g. "Starbucks is on your right"). We describe the design process of the virtual navigation app, including two navigation modalities to simulate route navigation. 1) VirtualLeap allows the user to jump through a sequence of intersections, turn-by-turn instructions and POIs of the route. 2) VirtualWalk simulates step-by-step walking at variable speeds using audio effects and also conveys a sequence of turn-by-turn instructions and POI information.

We performed a user study with 14 participants, using route reconstruction and real-world exposure to both assess users' ability to build sequential representations of the environment and understand the relative benefits and disadvantages of VirtualLeap and VirtualWalk. We gathered user feedback using a think-aloud protocol while using the full system and a semi-structured interview afterwards to inquire about the perceived usefulness, acceptance, and requirements of smartphone-based virtual navigation.

Our results show that the majority of the participants were able to build an accurate sequential representation of the route structure, while a subset was able to locate (all or most of) the POIs in the respective street block. Conversely, participants had difficulty estimating the length of the street blocks. The performance of the two interaction modalities was very similar and participants foresee benefits

ASSETS '17, October 29-November 1, 2017, Baltimore, MD, USA

ISBN 978-1-4503-4926-0/17/10...$15.00

DOI: https://doi.org/10.1145/3132525.3132545

in combining them depending on their goal. *VirtualLeap* was perceived as a faster way to get an overview of the route and relevant POIs (and explore their attributes). In contrast, they preferred *VirtualWalk* for building an accurate sequential representation of the environment.

2. RELATED WORK

VI people's Orientation and Mobility (O&M) depends on non-visual sensing for cognitive mapping of the environment [33]. A cognitive map is a comprehensive spatial representation, which contains information about routes, connections, directions, distances and landmarks [22]. Assistive technologies aim to improve O&M of VI people by supplementing their sensing capabilities or by providing accessible sources of spatial information.

2.1 In-Situ Navigation and Exploration

Assistive navigation caters to the users' need to move independently and to acquire knowledge about the surroundings [3]. In order to support navigation, several solutions convey non-visual turn-by-turn instructions similarly to mainstream apps such as *Google Maps*. These solutions provide a functional understanding of the spatial structure of the environment as a sequence of distances and turns (e.g. [2, 18]). For instance, NavCog [2] is an indoor navigation assistant that relies on Bluetooth beacons installed in the environment to provide accurate localization and turn-by-turn instructions. NAVIG [13] uses GNSS satellite data for localization and camera for near visual sensing, enabling landmark exploration using sonified audio cues.

Other systems and research projects focus on exploring the environment, either by augmenting the users' sensory range through visual detection of features of interest (e.g. crosswalks [20]), or by providing information about nearby landmarks and POIs (e.g. shops), encouraging serendipitous discovery of relevant locations (e.g. [1, 11, 34]). Blum et al. [4] augment this approach by rendering nearby POI through spatialized audio. These approaches provide radial orientation and euclidean distance to surrounding POIs, which conveys the relative disposition of the elements, but no knowledge about the structure of the environment (e.g., buildings and streets between the user and the POI).

These systems are very useful to support VI people's O&M. However, increasing the amount of information conveyed while navigating can be overwhelming to users [26]. For this reason, we combine both turn-by-turn and POI information beforehand, in a controlled environment, in order to increase users' confidence and knowledge about the environment.

2.2 Map Exploration and Virtual Simulation

Apart from real-world exposure, spatial knowledge can also be acquired indirectly [22], for instance through language, maps or virtual simulation. Tactile maps and 3-D models provide spatial information through haptic exploration [33]. However, they require special printers, time and effort to design and print, and they have a fixed resolution which makes it difficult to present detailed and multiscale information [30]. Approaches relying on touchscreen interactive maps try to overcome these limitations, enabling the user to explore the screen while receiving auditory (and sometimes tactile) feedback. Interesting solutions include the use of sonification to convey geometric information [31]; two-handed map exploration on tabletops with simultaneous audio feedback [10]; touchscreens with raised-line overlays [5]; and software overlays that ease the access to spatially structured elements in the map [12]. However, in order to provide detailed spatial information, these approaches often require large touchscreens, which are less widespread and mobile, and therefore more difficult to use on a daily basis.

Other approaches rely on virtual navigation through egocentric exploration, usually relying on 3D audio to increase VI people's spatial knowledge [7, 28]. However, these approaches require quality audio equipment, silence, and are often restricted to specific scenarios that require building comprehensive, specialized virtual environments.

In addition to exploration during mobility, the smartphone app Blindsquare [1] allows users to simulate a static real-world location and examine nearby POIs. SpaceSense [35] extends this approach by enabling virtual route navigation from the simulated location to a selected POI, through sequential turn-by-turn instructions. After each instruction, a vibrotactile matrix addon on the back of the phone provides feedback indicating the direction of and distance to the destination, and to bookmarked POIs near the route. Both BlindSquare and SpaceSense convey the POIs location relative to the user's current location regardless of the user's route (e.g. the POI could be in an adjacent/parallel street). In contrast, we integrate the POIs as elements in the sequential representation of the route with the goal to create a memorable representation of the real-world. This difference, together with SpaceSense need for special hardware and BlindSquare not supporting route navigation makes it difficult to compare them with our two modalities.

3. ENABLING VIRTUAL NAVIGATION

Our virtual navigation system is built on top of NavCog, an open-source turn-by-turn smartphone navigation assistant for VI people [2]. We extend both NavCog's map server, which stores information about the environment, and its iPhone app in order to simulate the user's movement and convey guidance information.

3.1 Populate the Map

The NavCog system relies on a web-based editor to manually insert environment maps and POI. A map consists of a graph-based structure where the edges are walkable areas (corridors or streets), and the nodes are decision points such as intersections or orientation changes. A major concern for the simulation of real-world routes was the ability to automate the process of adding such information for large scale areas without human intervention. The map structure is extracted from the OpenStreetMap (OSM) street layout to automatically generate route edges and nodes. To populate the map with POIs, we combine information from Yelp and FourSquare POI retrieval geo-location services.

We extract POIs from a desired area along with several attributes: name, location, category, description, address, average rating, opening hours, price range, FourSquare tips and a Yelp review. We consider the functional position of each POI in the route, instead of relying on their euclidean distance and radial orientation, often used by existing assistive navigation apps [1, 11]. To link a POI with its respective street, we project the POI coordinates (from OSM, Google Maps, Yelp or FourSquare) on the closest edge having the same street name. When virtually navigating that street, the user is informed of the POI when passing by it.

3.2 Virtual Navigation Interface

The virtual navigation interface was adapted from the most recent version of NavCog [2] through an iterative design process. A preliminary study with three blind subjects aimed at understanding the perceived usability of our initial implementation and how could we improve its functionality in order to better support virtual navigation. We describe the resulting application, which implements two navigation simulation modalities that integrate turn-by-turn instructions and the exploration of POIs and their attributes.

3.2.1 Turn-by-Turn Instructions

NavCog turn-by-turn instructions are grounded on previous research on how to guide VI people (e.g. [24]) and can be divided in three types of messages: distance announcements, action instructions and POI descriptions [2]. Virtual navigation does not use explicit distance announcements as presented in NavCog, since (implicit or explicit) distance information is conveyed by the simulation modalities. It does however provide action instructions in the proximity of decision points (e.g., intersections). When reaching an intersection, the system announces its name, for instance "*Fifth Avenue with Sixth Street*", the action required (e.g. "turn right"), and (after the turn) the distance to the next intersection/turn. When approaching a POI, the system announces its name and its relative position depending on the user's virtual orientation (e.g. "*an obstacle is in front of you*" or "*Starbucks is on your right*"). All interaction with the system in Virtual NavCog relies on gestures.

3.2.2 Virtual Navigation Modalities

We implemented two different modalities for navigation simulation: **VirtualWalk** and **VirtualLeap**. VirtualWalk is based on literature that suggests that virtual exploration may be used to build a mental representation [16] of an environment. In this method, we try to mimic real world navigation by enabling the user to walk and turn in the environment, while being alerted by the surrounding POIs and required actions. The VirtualLeap approach resembles a sequence of instructions similar to what is found in *Google Maps*, but also containing information about the POIs. Herein, the user is able to jump through the relevant points of the route (POIs and intersections) while being informed about the distance the user would need to travel.

VirtualWalk. This approach uses gyroscope data[1] to detect walking and turning gestures (See Figure 1). Tilting the phone down enables walking (Figure 1 a)), with a speed ranging between 0.3 and 0.7 seconds per step. The speed is based on the amount of tilt (using the gyroscope pitch value, with a window of approximately 25 degrees). These walking speeds were obtained empirically based on the feedback from the preliminary study, and answer to the users' need to navigate faster, but not too fast to make sure they can process all information. The tilt range is limited to avoid angles uncomfortable to users, and the system allows users to calibrate their resting pitch inclination.

When reaching a location that requires a turn, the user needs to rotate the phone (detected by the yaw value from the gyroscope) to the announced direction (Figure 1 b)), receiving a confirmation sound when the rotation reaches the required angle. This intends to mimic actual turning

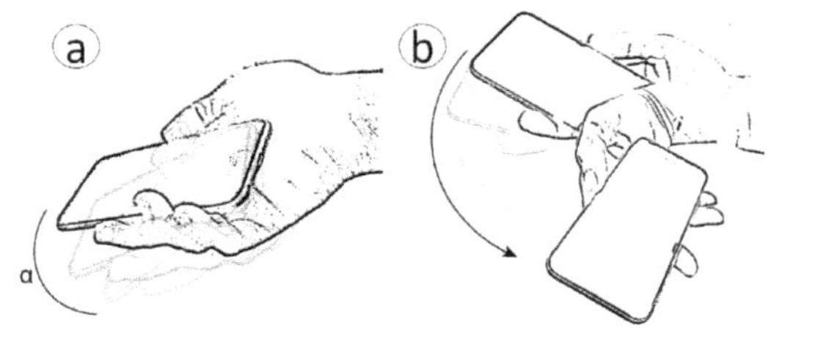

Figure 1: VirtualWalk gestures. a) Walking speed is modified by tilting the phone. b) The user turns by rotating the phone in the required direction.

that occurs in physical locomotion, frequently used in immersive Virtual Environments, which requires less cognitive processing to update the mental representation of the space, when comparing to imagined rotation/turning [29, 15]. After turning, users may rotate the phone back to its previous orientation or maintain its orientation.

Each virtual step is 0.7m long, corresponding to an average human step [23]. To increase the feeling of presence in the virtual environment [25] and to provide feedback on how much the user is walking, we provide auditory feedback of steps. The step length is fixed, but the speed depends on the tilting angle. When the user passes by a POI, it is announced together with its relative location. The user can tilt the phone up instead of down in order to walk backwards while keeping the same orientation. This is useful, for instance, to re-explore a previous POI.

The pilot study supported the addition of a command where users can go through a route at a faster speed, focusing only on the route segments and turns. A two-finger double tap starts an automatic walking mode (at the speed of 0.2 seconds per step), where the user gets auditory feedback about the steps and is required to turn when reaching an intersection but is not alerted about the POIs. The participants' comments are in line with the fact that knowing the environment is a dynamic process that is iteratively updated with supplemental information [8], as they claimed that they would like to learn the route first, and then learn information about the surrounding POIs.

VirtualLeap. This approach relies on swipe gestures (up and down) to move to the next or previous relevant points (intersection or POI) along the route. A *swipe up* gesture announces the distance to the next relevant point (e.g. "walked 50 meters/feet") followed by the respective instruction. For instance, if the user moves to a POI, the system announces its name and relative direction. If the user moves to an intersection, the system reads its name, the required turn, and the distance to the next turn/intersection. In case of a swipe down, the user moves back (e.g. "went back 50 meters/feet"), but the remaining instructions are the same. A two-finger swipe up/down moves the user to the next/previous intersection independently of the presence of POIs.

3.2.3 Explore POIs Information

When next to a POI, users are able to get more information about it, by performing a *swipe right* gesture. The system starts by reading the POI category, and subsequent swipe right (or left) gestures go to the next (or previous) attribute, which can include a short description, average rating, opening hours, address, among others. This gestures

[1]pitch and yaw values from the *iOS Core Motion* framework

intended to ease and quicken the access to POI information, reducing the need to change screens and resume the navigation afterwards. In case there are no near POIs, the system alerts that the user is not next to a POI.

3.2.4 Additional Commands

Additional commands intend to help users orienting themselves in the route. A *double tap* repeats the current instruction. In case the user is not at an intersection nor next to a POI, it reads the name of the street and the distance to the next turn. The *shake gesture* is adapted from current navigation apps [1] and provides the name of and distance to the previous and next intersections. Finally, the user may go back to the starting point by performing a *triple tap*.

4. USER STUDY

The high level goal of our approach and system is to ease autonomous navigation by people with visual impairments. To accomplish that, we rely on the ability to simulate navigating a route using a smartphone to increase the knowledge of a particular location before physically visiting it.

The objective of this user study is to understand the following: 1) blind people's ability to build a mental representation of the sequential instructions and POIs of a route, after using virtual navigation; 2) the relative benefits and disadvantages of VirtualLeap and VirtualWalk modalities; 3) the perceived usefulness, acceptance and requirements of smartphone-based virtual navigation to learn a route while discovering relevant POIs. The study consisted of one session that took two to three hours (average around 2.5 hours), and can be divided in three parts: first, we use route reconstruction as the means to evaluate users' spatial representations of a simulated route; second, users are exposed to a real-world route after using the system; third, users interact with the full system using a think aloud protocol, followed by a semi-structured interview to gather feedback about the system design, usage scenarios and user preferences.

4.1 Participants

We recruited 14 participants (6 female). Their ages ranged from 41 to 75 (M=59.15, SD=11.92) years. Thirteen were legally blind and one had low-vision. Thirteen participants had a congenital or an early-onset visual impairment. Eleven participants own a smartphone (10 iPhone), and all but one walk alone in the street regularly. Besides the white cane or guide dog, nine participants use GPS-based navigation tools, such as *Google/Apple Maps* (5), BlindSquare (4), Nearby Explorer (2), Trekker Breeze (2) or Transit (2). Participants were compensated for their time ($25 per hour).

4.2 Apparatus

We used an iPhone 6 with iOS 10.1.1 and the virtual navigation application that was previously described. We had a set of LEGO blocks and respective base plates, which were used for route reconstruction (Figure 2). We video and audio recorded the whole experiment for further analysis.

4.3 Route Reconstruction Task

Map reconstruction is commonly used to assess route knowledge and the cognitive map of VI people [19, 14, 27, 28, 35]. In this phase, users were able to simulate a route with virtual navigation and build the same route afterwards using LEGO blocks (as in [19, 28]). Users performed two tasks, one with each method (*VirtualWalk* and *VirtualLeap*), and with similar routes. The order of the two methods and the two routes was counterbalanced among participants.

Figure 2: The LEGO blocks and baseplate with a correct representation of the two routes used in the route reconstruction task.

4.3.1 Method

Conditions. The *VirtualWalk* and *VirtualLeap* conditions work as described in the previous section. When using one condition, the commands in the other condition are disabled. Moreover, the function to get more information about the POIs (swipe right and left) is disabled.

Routes. Both routes (Figure 2) have the same length of 130 meters and the same number of intersections (4) and POIs (5). Three of those intersections require a turn. Route complexity is similar to the routes used in *SpaceSense* [35]. Our larger number of POIs reflect our main goal to use virtual navigation to learn the sequential steps of a route, which includes the POIs themselves. The POIs names are based on the most well-known food chains (via lists available in *forbes.com* and *businessinsider.com*), in order to reduce the cognitive load required to memorize the POIs.

LEGO blocks. Participants were required to assemble the LEGO blocks on top of a base plate (Figure 2). We provided four different LEGO lengths to represent the relative differences among the street blocks in the route (as in [35]). Their lengths can be measured in terms of the number of *studs* (the "bumps") on top of the LEGO block: 20, 15, 10 and 5 (each *stud* corresponding to two meters). Participants were informed that they could compose the route by using a single LEGO block for each street block [35]. The relative orientation of the LEGOs indicate the turns. Additional LEGO types include intersections that do not require a turn and the POIs (taller LEGOs with a single stud).

4.3.2 Procedure

After assigning the method for the current condition, the researcher explained all commands to the participants. Participants were able to practice for approximately 10 minutes, while the researcher provided assistance and clarifications if needed. Afterwards, the researcher explained the task, including the need to navigate a route and then build the same route using LEGO blocks. The participant was asked to explore the route until she feels comfortable and ready to reconstruct it. When the participant did not name all POIs, the researcher asks for their names. If at least one name is missing, the researcher informs the name of the remaining POIs and asks if the participant knows to what LEGO element in their route they correspond.

4.3.3 Design and Analysis

We used a within-subjects design where participants performed both conditions (VirtualWalk and VirtualLeap) (in a counter-balanced order), one with each route. We excluded from this analysis one participant with low vision, since she could see, with some effort, the route on the screen. In order to evaluate participants' mental representation of the route, we adapted metrics used in two previous studies [27, 35]:

NumberElementsError: The number of missing or unnecessary street blocks and intersections used to recreate the route. Both routes have five street blocks and four intersections, resulting in nine elements.

FormElementsError: The Levenshtein distance [17] between the correct route and the participant's route composition. This corresponds to the minimum number of operations (deletions, insertions and substitutions) to correct the participant's route and targets the form of the route and not the size (of each block).

PlacementErrors: The number of street blocks used with an incorrect length.

In addition, we extended the analysis to include metrics about the POIs and their locations, and also to assess if participants were able to understand the relative lengths of adjacent streets.

RelativeLengthAccuracy: The accuracy of the perceived relation (longer, shorter or same) between the lengths of adjacent street blocks.

POIsOrderingError: The Damerau-Levenshtein distance [9] between the correct POI order and the users' ordering. It corresponds to the minimum number of operations (deletions, insertions, substitutions, transpositions between adjacent POIs) required to correct the participant's ordering.

POIsInBlockError: The number of POIs that are not in the correct street block or are missing.

POIsOnSideError: The number of POIs that are not in the correct side of the street.

POIsDistanceError: The average distance from the POIs correct location to where the user placed them. The position of the placed POI is re-calculated so it is represented in proportion to the correct length of the block. The distance is then normalized (0 to 1) depending on the block size.

Additionally, we measured participants' **completion times** to explore the route with the application. Shapiro-Wilkinson tests were applied to all dependent variables to check for normality. We ran Paired Samples T-Test to compare both approaches when the variables have a normal distribution, and the Wilcoxon Signed-Rank test otherwise.

4.4 Real-World Exposure Task

Measuring the accuracy of participants' route reconstruction is important to understand the spatial knowledge provided by virtual navigation, but its utility is better assessed in the real world [14]. However, it is very difficult to guarantee a fair quantitative comparison between different methods or alternatives, because external factors such as auditory cues or number of people may impact (positively or negatively) the users' ability to navigate in the real-world [14].

Nevertheless, we wanted to observe how virtual navigation in general, and both navigation methods in particular, could help to build a sequential representation of the environment that can be leveraged when physically navigating the previously simulated route. On one hand, we wanted to focus on the mental representation and not on navigation challenges caused by external factors. In order to accomplish that, instead of freely navigating the route, participants were asked to guide the researcher to the destination using the required turns and POIs as reference. On the other hand, we still wanted to take advantage of the real world sensory cues that help blind people localizing themselves. With this task (guiding the researcher), participants can still make use of such cues to provide more accurate instructions. For instance, if the user perceives she is next to a landmark, such as the elevator due to its particular sound, she can better position herself in her cognitive map.

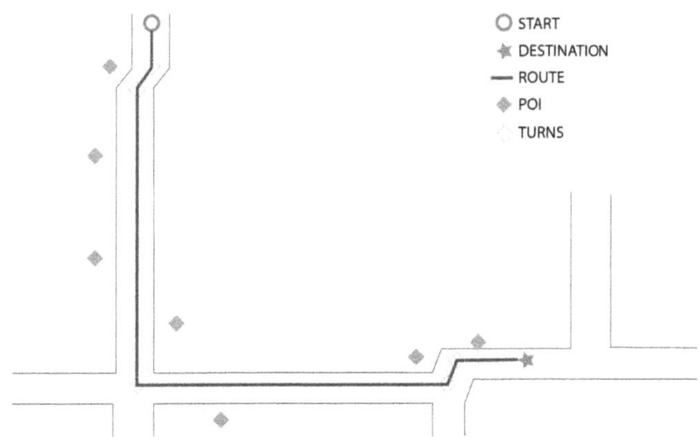

Figure 3: The route used in the real-world exposure task, located at Carnegie Mellon University.

4.4.1 Method

Condition. Participants used the last method they tried in the previous phase. There was no additional practice period, nor additional commands were added.

Route. The route is in the University Center at Carnegie Mellon University and had FedEx as the destination. It has six segments, five turns and seven POIs besides the destination (Figure 3). The POIs include (in the following order): a book store, an exit, an art store, a post office, the career and professional development center, a package pick-up and a lounge with seats and tables.

4.4.2 Procedure

Participants were instructed to explore the route for a maximum of seven minutes (based on the pilot study). They were able to finish their current trial until reaching the destination. They were also informed that afterwards they would need to guide the researcher to the destination using the turns and landmarks as reference. After simulating the route, the participant and the researcher walked to the respective building. It took seven to twelve minutes to get to the starting point.

When reaching the starting point, the researcher asked the participant to hold his elbow and guide him through the same route explored before. The researcher would not provide any new information about the environment, and would only comment about landmarks referred by the participant. For instance, if the participant comments that they *"should be passing by the Art Store"*, possible answers are: *"I do not see the Art Store"*, *"We already passed the Art Store"*, *"I can see it, but we're not next to it"* or provide confirmation (*"yes, we are"*. Moreover, before starting, the researcher in-

Table 1: The description on how we assign accuracy values based on participants' instructions.

Accuracy	Value	Description
High	1	Distance lower than 5 steps
Medium	0.75	Distance between 5 and 10 steps
Low	0.5	Distance higher than 10 steps or vague description (e.g. "don't know the distance, but we should take the next left")
Unnamed	0.25	Acknowledge a POI, but does not recall the name
None	0	Turn error; POI not mentioned; POI in different segment

formed that: 1) he would warn the user when they are about to reach a wall (or obstacles such as chairs and tables) and ask what to do; 2) participants could ask to come back to a known landmark/POI, in case they get lost; 3) the researcher could ask for an estimate on when they are about to reach a landmark or turn mentioned by the participant; this intends to understand participants' distance perception when they refer to elements that are far from their current position (e.g. "we should turn left after the *post office*", when the user is at the beginning of that segment).

4.4.3 Design and Analysis

We used a between-subjects design where participants used one of the navigation methods (VirtualWalk or VirtualLeap) to simulate the route. We collected the users' completion time and interaction behaviours while using the application. Moreover, in order to assess participants' performance guiding the researcher, we observed and coded the videos to account the following:

Reached Destination. It refers to participants ability to reach FedEx.

Route Errors. It refers to the number of wrong turns made by the user.

Missing or Erroneous POIs. POIs not referred by the participant or referred as belonging to a different street segment.

Instruction Accuracy. Accuracy of participants' POI / turn estimation from 0 (error/missing information) to 1 (high accuracy). We defined the maximum value for medium accuracy based on the GPS 4.9 meters accuracy (according to the United States government [2]). Since participants guided the researcher at a slow pace, with shorter steps than a regular step, we estimate this value to correspond approximately to 10 steps. We coded high accuracy as half of this value, meaning less than 5 steps distance. Table 1 describes the different accuracy levels.

Route accuracy. The average of the path instructions (five required turns) accuracy.

POI accuracy. The average of the POI instructions (eight, including the destination) accuracy. We also calculated the accuracy including only POIs that were referred by the participants.

We ran Independent Samples T-Test to compare both groups when the variables have a normal distribution, and the Mann-Whitney U test otherwise.

[2]https://www.gps.gov/systems/gps/performance/accuracy/

4.5 Overall System Exposure and Feedback

After completing the previous tasks, participants were able to explore a popular area in Pittsburgh (the Strip District). They were able to use the full system to navigate in the route while exploring the several POIs existent therein, as well as their attributes with the *swipe-right/left* gestures. First, participants were instructed to explore the route using a think-aloud protocol, where they would verbalize their thoughts about their experience with the system and this particular route. Afterwards, we performed a questionnaire and a semi-structured interview. Besides targeting feedback about the system itself, we intended to understand what the users were learning about the route and the perceived usefulness and acceptance of a system that enables both to simulate a route and to explore and discover relevant POIs along such route. Moreover, we wanted to collect information about additional requirements for such a system.

5. RESULTS

5.1 Route Reconstruction Task

Figure 4 presents the results concerning task completion time and all route and POI accuracy metrics.

5.1.1 Simulation Completion Time

Since in *VirtualLeap* users are able to move faster through the relevant elements of the route, we were expecting users to spend less time exploring the route. However, users took an average of 539.85 (SD=233.92) seconds exploring the route with *VirtualLeap* and 412.54 (SD=188.05) seconds with *VirtualWalk*. A *paired t-test* has shown significant differences between the two conditions ($t(12) = 2.932$, $p<0.05$), which have a mean difference superior to two minutes.

5.1.2 Route Accuracy

Although Figure 4 shows a slight advantage for the VirtualWalk method, differences were not statistically significant. Metrics that concern the route structure independently of the length of the street blocks show that most participants were able to accurately learn the route sequence with both methods. For instance, 10 out 13 participants reconstructed the route structure correctly (*FormElementsError* equals zero) with the VirtualWalk method, while 8 accomplished the same with VirtualLeap. Errors in route reconstruction were mostly caused by adding or omitting a street block.

Although able to grasp the sequential steps of the route, participants had more difficulty estimating the lengths of street blocks, as shown by participants' *PlacementErrors*. *RelativeLengthAccuracy* shows a better understanding of the relative lengths of adjacent street blocks, but still revealing a poor accuracy consistent with prior research (e.g. [35, 16]).

5.1.3 POI Accuracy

Participants placed in their LEGO route an average of 4.54 and 4.69 POIs with VirtualLeap and VirtualWalk, respectively (from a total of 5). Most reconstructed routes included all 5 (17 out of 26) or 4 (8) POIs. Again, the differences between VirtualLeap and VirtualWalk were not statistically significant for any of the POI accuracy metrics. The *POIsInBlockError* metric shows that users were able to add information about the POIs location to their mental representation of the route. In particular, five participants placed all five POIs in the respective street block

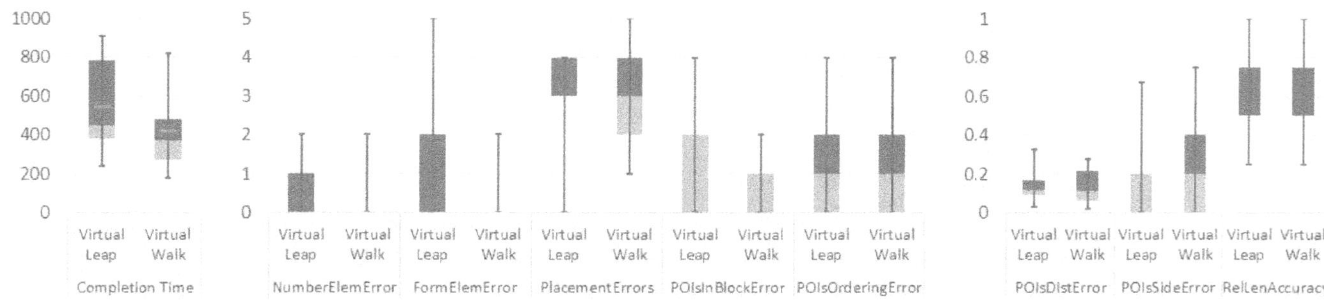

Figure 4: Performance in route reconstruction. BoxPlots show median, IQR, min and max. Green marker indicates the mean for normally distributed variables. Plots without boxes represent measures equal to zero.

in each of the conditions. Moreover, all participants placed at least three POIs in their correct block with the VirtualWalk condition, and eleven participants with VirtualLeap. While participants made a few errors concerning the side of the POIs in the street, they were able to have an approximate idea of the POI location in the respective block (most participants had an average POIsDistanceError below 0.20). *POIsOrderingError* adds up to the *POIsInBlockError* the POIs that are located in the same block but had their order swapped, as well as the POIs that were placed in the correct block but the participants did not recall their names.

5.1.4 Interaction Patterns

The higher completion times for the VirtualLeap method can be explained by participants exploring the route more times (M=9.15, SD=5.16) with that method than with VirtualWalk (M=5.46, SD=3.15). Moreover, participants in both VirtualLeap (7) and VirtualWalk (5) tried, at some point, to explore the route independently of the POIs. Several VirtualWalk users tried to build a better mental map of the route by rotating their body when making a turn (3 users) or by keeping the phone oriented in that direction (6). However, none of the interaction patterns identified caused significant differences in the users' performance.

5.2 Real-World Exposure Task

5.2.1 Virtual Navigation

In both methods, the interaction patterns were very similar to the ones described in the previous task. For instance, VirtualLeap users took an average of 540.6 seconds and explored the route 9.2 times, while VirtualWalk users took an average of 411.6 seconds and explored the route 5.5 times. However, there were no significant differences in user performance depending on the interaction patterns they used.

5.2.2 Real World Navigation

All participants were able to guide the researcher to the destination. Figure 5 depicts the results for all metrics concerning the real world navigation task. The comparison between VirtualLeap and VirtualWalk showed no significant differences between methods, for all metrics.

Overall, participants took an average of 254.23 seconds to reach the destination and made an average of 0.77 errors. Seven participants went through the route without making any error. From the other six participants, four made one (or more) errors at a single point in the route. They often chose to return to a known POI (always right before a turn), being then able to reach the destination. The mean route accuracy (0.82) reflects participants' ability to estimate the distance to the next turn. In general, participants were able to distinguish short and long distances, even when providing less accurate information. The POIs, mainly the ones right before a turn, were key to provide accurate instructions. For instance, seven participants gave the instruction to *"turn left right after passing by the package pickup"*, while eight were aware of the approximate distance to turn left after passing by the post office. When providing less accurate information, participants were also able to benefit from the environment itself (e.g. by reaching a wall or a table and chairs) to understand their next steps. For instance, three participants were aware that they should have the lounge on their left, so when they reached the tables and chairs, they immediately inferred they should turn right.

POI accuracy was much lower (0.48) than route accuracy. However, it is important to mention that participants were not instructed to mention all POIs, but to guide the researcher by providing important information about the environment. For that reason, participants focused more on the POIs that preceded a turn (bookstore, post office and package pickup), resulting in an average of 3.38 of missing or erroneous POIs. If we consider the *referred POI accuracy*, which disregards the POIs that were not mentioned by the user, the mean accuracy increases to 0.82.

Our main goal was to assess the ability of virtual navigation to convey an understanding of the sequential steps of the route, and all participants were able to reach the destination. While seven were able to guide the researcher without making any error, three of them had a combined route and referred POI accuracy above 90%, where two of them referred all POIs.

5.3 Overall System Exposure and Feedback

The participants' comments under the Think-Aloud protocol and during the semi structured interviews were recorded and transcribed for further analysis. The researcher that conducted the study compiled a pre-set of codes based on the questions and notes taken during the interviews. Then, two researchers coded, independently, one interview and discussed their differences until reaching an agreement on the codes and their interpretation. They coded an additional interview and due to the high inter-coder agreement (Cohen's kappa = 0.94) one researcher coded the other interviews [6].

The main themes arising from the interviews were: the comments related to the exploration of a known area, po-

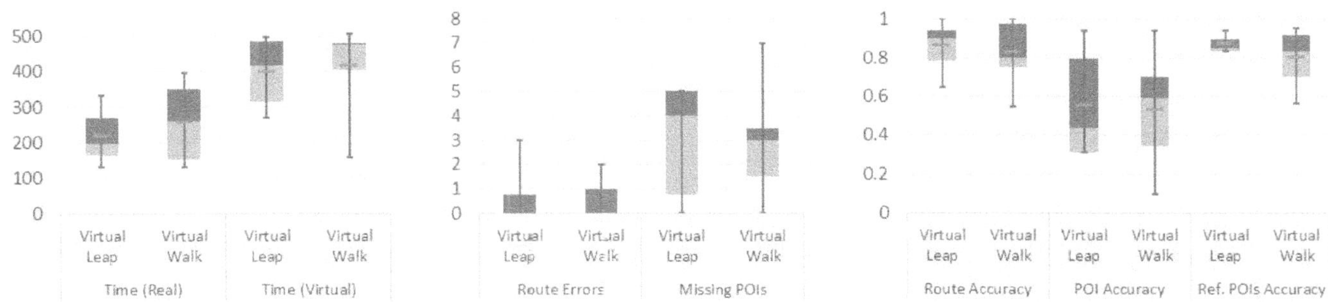

Figure 5: Performance in the real-world exposure task. BoxPlots show median, IQR, min and max values. Variables with normal distribution also show a marker indication the mean.

tential contexts for virtual navigation, the main advantages and disadvantages of VirtualLeap and VirtualWalk, potential improvements to such an application, and the originality or distinguishing features of this application.

Exploring a Known Area. All participants were very positive about being able to explore POIs in a popular route and wanted both to increase their knowledge about known POIs and to discover places they were unaware about. One participant stated: *"I live here for 19 years, and I've been to the Strip District, but I didn't know a lot of these places even existed. So you get all this good information"*.

Contexts for Virtual Navigation. Among scenarios where participants would use such an application, all but one referred that it would be useful both in known and unknown places, usually mentioning it in general terms. A more concrete example to explore known places was their own neighborhood, while unknown places can include, for instance shopping or touristic activities. One participant commented that he could not say *"how many people say, where would you like to eat? And you don't know anything! And it would be neat to pull out an application like this and find something close, and the ratings, all these things.. is really neat"*. Another participant referred that "having this knowledge could balance the power in the relationship", by being able to suggest places that are on a particular route.

Modalities Pros and Cons. Participants' comments regarding their favorite functions were scattered across the system functionality. For instance, 3 participants referred that they liked to have the ability to control the speed in VirtualWalk. Eight participants were able to see advantages in both modalities, supporting that both are useful, each in their own context. Ten participants referred to VirtualWalk as the way to convey a better spatial understanding of the route, while four participants pointed the slower exploration as its disadvantage. VirtualLeap on the other side, is able to provide a faster overview of a route and is more efficient when their goal is focused on browsing POIs. One participant stated: *"[VirtualWalk] (...) I think negative, it's gonna take you longer to get the overall information [but] you might have more intuition of how long it takes to get from one restaurant or POI to the next."*

Future Improvements. All but two participants referred to navigational transit information as the main kind of information to add to the system. This includes bus stops, more information about intersections and crossings and sidewalk information including temporary construction. Additionally, one participant referred that he would like to have *"an auditory recording without even opening the app (...) sometimes me and my wife go on cruises, (...) we may want to put together a couple of recordings of virtual streets (...) and just have a virtual with the streets and the POIs."*

Originality. All participants were enthusiastic about being able to explore a location before-hand, for instance by stating that it is the *"best virtual way to explore the route (..) you can actually navigate!"*. A distinguishing factor of our application was the ability of simulate the navigation and at the same time grasp the knowledge surrounding POIs and their exact location within the route. One participant stated: "not only do you get directions, but you get your surrounding businesses (...) and what they do and what they are and how they are rated... is really neat. You can get that stuff with Google if you look for the place itself, but this turn-by-turn addition is really nice."

6. DISCUSSION

Building on the results obtained, we discuss our main findings and contributions:

Virtual navigation enabled blind users to build accurate sequential representations of the environment. The route reconstruction task showed that most participants were able to build a mental representation of the sequence of steps in a route. Although we believe that the knowledge about the POIs can be leveraged when navigating the real world, we anticipated that the ability to discover POIs along a route, could also increase the cognitive load. Still, most participants were able to recognize the different street blocks and direction of turns, while placing at least three POIs in their respective street block. Five participants, in each of the conditions, were able to recall the whole route structure and at the same time all POIs, placed in the correct block and sequence. This ability to build a mental representation in a sequential structure [21, 32] was also evident when participants guided the researcher when exposed to the real-world environment. All participants were able to reach the destination, where seven out of thirteen were able to do that without making any error. In this task, the POIs were essential landmarks for providing accurate instructions, but also to recover from errors. Participants that were not sure about their location often chose a landmark they knew in order to restart the navigation and were then able to succeed and reach the destination.

VirtualLeap and VirtualWalk were equally able to support the creation of a mental representation of the environment, but users' preference depends

on their goal. All metrics related to the route and POI knowledge provided no significant difference between the two methods. However, participants took significantly more time to use VirtualLeap than VirtualWalk, suggesting that the first may require a greater memory effort to obtain a similar cognitive mapping accuracy. While most participants would like to have the ability to use both methods, their comments point towards using VirtualWalk when the goal is to have an accurate cognitive map of the route, while using VirtualLeap when the goal is to have a quicker overview or to focus on the discovery and exploration of POIs.

Accurate estimation of length is a challenge. The main challenge to build an accurate representation of the route was the street length estimations. This result is not unexpected, in particular for the *VirtualLeap* modality, as previous research based on verbal descriptions (or navigation instructions) reported the difficulty to estimate distances [35]. However, we were expecting that VirtualWalk would provide a better understanding of the relative lengths of each street block. Although some participants referred that it gave "*a better perspective of length and the time it takes*", overall that was not reflected in participants' performance. Although guiding the researcher in the real world did not require a fully accurate sense of the distances, participants where generally aware of long and short distances; and they were very accurate when basing their instructions on landmarks that preceded a turn. Two participants stood out as they were able to recall all POIs and made very accurate estimations in the real-world task, but were also able to reconstruct the LEGO route (with the two modalities) without making any error regarding the sequential ordering of the route. Although these were the two youngest participants (41 and 42 years old), we could not find any effect of age in route nor POI metrics.

Virtual navigation had high perceived usefulness and acceptance. The main advantage of our approach was the ability to simulate and control the navigation, while at the same time being guided and informed by relevant information in the route. This was perceived as beneficial both in terms of building a mental representation of a route and as a way to discover relevant POIs in a route, which was referred as a boost in independence and knowledge that can be leveraged in their interaction with sighted peers.

7. CONCLUSIONS

Prior exploration of an environment by VI people can increase their spatial knowledge without the risks and cognitive load of direct exploration [5]. In order to overcome users' absent/fragmented knowledge about the real-world, we hypothesized if sequential representations of the environment containing information about turn-by-turn instructions and POIs could be used to increase route knowledge. We built a smartphone app with two virtual navigation methods and conducted a user study to assess how could they support sequential representations of the real-world.

Results have shown no significant differences between VirtualLeap and VirtualWalk, but have shown VI people's ability to build an accurate sequential representation of the route structure, complemented with POIs along the route. Most participants were also able to locate the POIs in their respective street block (at an approximate location). Moreover, in a subsequent exposure to the real world, participants were able to use the POIs as landmarks as they guided the researcher to the destination. While providing accurate sequential information, most participants were not able to retain the relative lengths of the streets blocks, which suggests the need for complementary approaches that enable learning other specific aspects of a route independently.

Subjective feedback also placed the ability to simulate the navigation while being informed about the POIs along the street as the main distinguishing aspect of our approach. Participants highlighted its ability to provide a spatial understanding of the route not only to increase the person's confidence, but also for trip planning based on the POIs explored. The most important feature to increase the usefulness of virtual navigation is the inclusion of information related to transit or navigation, such as more detail about the shape of intersections and traffic signs (including audible pedestrian signals), information about sidewalks, crosswalks and bus stops. In order to integrate this information, future work should try to understand how to convey larger amounts of information without overwhelming users. Such knowledge and the interaction with the system in a simulation mode, may help understanding how to convey timely and adequate information in the real world as well.

8. ACKNOWLEDGMENTS

This work was sponsored in part by Shimizu Corp, JST CREST grant (JPMJCR14E1) and NSF NRI grant (1637927).

9. REFERENCES

[1] Blindsquare ios application. http://blindsquare.com/. Accessed: 2017-05-04.

[2] D. Ahmetovic, C. Gleason, C. Ruan, K. Kitani, H. Takagi, and C. Asakawa. Navcog: a navigational cognitive assistant for the blind. In *Proceedings of the 18th International Conference on Human-Computer Interaction with Mobile Devices and Services*, pages 90–99. ACM, 2016.

[3] N. Banovic, R. L. Franz, K. N. Truong, J. Mankoff, and A. K. Dey. Uncovering information needs for independent spatial learning for users who are visually impaired. In *Proceedings of the 15th International ACM SIGACCESS Conference on Computers and Accessibility*, page 24. ACM, 2013.

[4] J. R. Blum, M. Bouchard, and J. R. Cooperstock. What's around me? spatialized audio augmented reality for blind users with a smartphone. In *International Conference on Mobile and Ubiquitous Systems: Computing, Networking, and Services*, pages 49–62. Springer, 2011.

[5] A. M. Brock, P. Truillet, B. Oriola, D. Picard, and C. Jouffrais. Interactivity improves usability of geographic maps for visually impaired people. *Human–Computer Interaction*, 30(2):156–194, 2015.

[6] J. L. Campbell, C. Quincy, J. Osserman, and O. K. Pedersen. Coding in-depth semistructured interviews: Problems of unitization and intercoder reliability and agreement. *Sociological Methods & Research*, 42(3):294–320, 2013.

[7] E. C. Connors, E. R. Chrastil, J. Sánchez, and L. B. Merabet. Virtual environments for the transfer of navigation skills in the blind: a comparison of directed instruction vs. video game based learning approaches. *Frontiers in human neuroscience*, 8:223, 2014.

[8] R. G. Golledge. *Wayfinding behavior: Cognitive mapping and other spatial processes.* JHU press, 1999.

[9] W. H. Gomaa and A. A. Fahmy. A survey of text similarity approaches. *International Journal of Computer Applications*, 68(13), 2013.

[10] T. Guerreiro, K. Montague, J. Guerreiro, R. Nunes H. Nicolau, and D. J. Gonçalves. Blind people interacting with large touch surfaces: Strategies for one-handed and two-handed exploration. In *Proceedings of the 2015 International Conference on Interactive Tabletops & Surfaces*, pages 25–34. ACM, 2015.

[11] H. Kacorri, S. Mascetti, A. Gerino, D. Ahmetovic, H. Takagi, and C. Asakawa. Supporting orientation of people with visual impairment: Analysis of large scale usage data. In *Proceedings of the 18th International ACM SIGACCESS Conference on Computers and Accessibility*, pages 151–159. ACM, 2016.

[12] S. K. Kane, M. R. Morris, A. Z. Perkins, D. Wigdor, R. E. Ladner, and J. O. Wobbrock. Access overlays: improving non-visual access to large touch screens for blind users. In *Proceedings of the 24th annual ACM symposium on User interface software and technology*, pages 273–282. ACM, 2011.

[13] B. F. Katz, S. Kammoun, G. Parseihian, O. Gutierrez, A. Brilhault, M. Auvray, P. Truillet, M. Denis, S. Thorpe, and C. Jouffrais. Navig: augmented reality guidance system for the visually impaired. *Virtual Reality*, 16(4):253–269, 2012.

[14] R. Kitchin and R. Jacobson. Techniques to collect and analyze the cognitive map knowledge of persons with visual impairment or blindness: issues of validity. *Journal of Visual Impairment and Blindness*, 91(4):360–376, 1997.

[15] R. L. Klatzky, J. M. Loomis, A. C. Beall, S. S. Chance, and R. G. Golledge. Spatial updating of self-position and orientation during real, imagined, and virtual locomotion. *Psychological science*, 9(4):293–298, 1998.

[16] R. L. Klatzky, J. M. Loomis, R. G. Golledge, J. G. Cicinelli, S. Doherty, and J. W. Pellegrino. Acquisition of route and survey knowledge in the absence of vision. *Journal of motor behavior*, 22(1):19–43, 1990.

[17] V. I. Levenshtein. Binary codes capable of correcting deletions, insertions, and reversals. In *Soviet physics doklady*, volume 10, pages 707–710, 1966.

[18] J. M. Loomis, R. G. Golledge, and R. L. Klatzky. Navigation system for the blind: Auditory display modes and guidance. *Presence: Teleoperators and Virtual Environments*, 7(2):193–203, 1998.

[19] M. Lumbreras and J. Sánchez. Interactive 3d sound hyperstories for blind children. In *Proceedings of the SIGCHI conference on Human Factors in Computing Systems*, pages 318–325. ACM, 1999.

[20] S. Mascetti, D. Ahmetovic, A. Gerino, and C. Bernareggi. Zebrarecognizer: Pedestrian crossing recognition for people with visual impairment or blindness. *Pattern Recognition*, 2016.

[21] S. Millar. *Understanding and representing space: Theory and evidence from studies with blind and sighted children.* Clarendon Press/Oxford University Press, 1994.

[22] D. R. Montello. Spatial cognition. In N. J. Smelser and B. Baltes, editors, *International Encyclopedia of the Social and Behavioral Sciences*, pages 7–14771. 2001.

[23] C. Morency, M. Trépanier, and M. Demers. Walking to transit: an unexpected source of physical activity. *Transport Policy*, 18(6):800–806, 2011.

[24] H. Nicolau, J. Jorge, and T. Guerreiro. Blobby: how to guide a blind person. In *CHI'09 Extended Abstracts on Human Factors in Computing Systems*, pages 3601–3606. ACM, 2009.

[25] R. Nordahl, S. Serafin, N. C. Nilsson, and L. Turchet. Enhancing realism in virtual environments by simulating the audio-haptic sensation of walking on ground surfaces. In *Virtual Reality Short Papers and Posters (VRW), 2012 IEEE*, pages 73–74. IEEE, 2012.

[26] S. A. Panëels, A. Olmos, J. R. Blum, and J. R. Cooperstock. Listen to it yourself!: evaluating usability of what's around me? for the blind. In *Proceedings of the SIGCHI Conference on Human Factors in Computing Systems*, pages 2107–2116. ACM, 2013.

[27] R. Passini, G. Proulx, and C. Rainville. The spatio-cognitive abilities of the visually impaired population. *Environment and Behavior*, 22(1):91–118, 1990.

[28] L. Picinali, A. Afonso, M. Denis, and B. F. Katz. Exploration of architectural spaces by blind people using auditory virtual reality for the construction of spatial knowledge. *International Journal of Human-Computer Studies*, 72(4):393–407, 2014.

[29] J. J. Rieser. Access to knowledge of spatial structure at novel points of observation. *Journal of Experimental Psychology: Learning, Memory, and Cognition*, 15(6):1157, 1989.

[30] J. Rowell and S. Ungar. Feeling our way: tactile map user requirements-a survey. In *International Cartographic Conference, La Coruna*, 2005.

[31] J. Su, A. Rosenzweig, A. Goel, E. de Lara, and K. N. Truong. Timbremap: enabling the visually-impaired to use maps on touch-enabled devices. In *Proceedings of the 12th international conference on Human computer interaction with mobile devices and services*, pages 17–26. ACM, 2010.

[32] C. Thinus-Blanc and F. Gaunet. Representation of space in blind persons: vision as a spatial sense? *Psychological bulletin*, 121(1):20, 1997.

[33] W. R. Wiener, R. L. Welsh, and B. B. Blasch. *Foundations of orientation and mobility*, volume 1. American Foundation for the Blind, 2010.

[34] R. Yang, S. Park, S. R. Mishra, Z. Hong, C. Newsom, H. Joo, E. Hofer, and M. W. Newman. Supporting spatial awareness and independent wayfinding for pedestrians with visual impairments. In *The proceedings of the 13th international ACM SIGACCESS conference on Computers and accessibility*, pages 27–34. ACM, 2011.

[35] K. Yatani, N. Banovic, and K. Truong. Spacesense: representing geographical information to visually impaired people using spatial tactile feedback. In *Proceedings of the SIGCHI Conference on Human Factors in Computing Systems*, pages 415–424. ACM, 2012.

Opinions and Preferences of Blind and Low Vision Consumers Regarding Self-Driving Vehicles: Results of Focus Group Discussions

Julian Brinkley
University of Florida
432 Newell Drive
Gainesville, FL 32611
1 (352) 392 - 1200
julian.brinkley@ufl.edu

Brianna Posadas
University of Florida
432 Newell Drive
Gainesville, FL 32611
1 (352) 392 - 1200
bposadas@ufl.edu

Julia Woodward
University of Florida
432 Newell Drive
Gainesville, FL 32611
1 (352) 392 - 1200
julia.woodward@ufl.edu

Juan E. Gilbert
University of Florida
432 Newell Drive
Gainesville, FL 32611
1 (352) 392 - 1200
juan@ufl.edu

ABSTRACT
Fully autonomous vehicles, commonly referred to as self-driving vehicles, are an emerging technology that may hold tremendous mobility potential for individuals who are blind or visually impaired who have been previously disadvantaged by an inability to operate conventional motor vehicles. This study explores the opinions of 38 participants who are blind and low vision, through the use of focus group methodology, regarding this emerging self-driving vehicle technology. Participants were overwhelmingly optimistic about the potential for independence and mobility that self-driving vehicles may provide but were concerned that the needs of individuals with visual impairments were not being adequately considered in the development of the technology. Participants also raised questions about how the technology would satisfy their need for situational awareness, how the technology would enable blind or visually impaired operators to verify their arrival at their desired location and a host of issues related to parking, vehicle location and roadside assistance. Participants also expressed a preference for smartphone and speech input capabilities as a primary means of system interaction. These findings suggest that at a minimum more needs to be done to engage individuals with visual impairments in the development of self-driving vehicle technology and to increase awareness of manufacturer efforts.

CCS Concepts
• **Human-centered computing → User studies**

Keywords
Self-Driving Vehicles; Blindness, Low Vision, Accessibility; Advanced Driver Assistance Systems.

1. INTRODUCTION
As self-driving vehicle technology transitions from the realm of science fiction to scientific reality, the enormous benefits of this technology have become ever more broadly discussed. Removing error prone human beings from the driving process may potentially eliminate the types of traffic accidents that claim thousands of lives annually and results in costly property damage and loss [13]. Self-driving vehicle technology itself may render personal vehicle ownership obsolete as transportation is increasingly consumed as a service [3]. This, in turn, may change the financial models of a host of major industries and the physical design of cities themselves [5, 23]. To realize these benefits consumer adoption of such a paradigm shifting technology is critical given the potentially high costs of the technology and the potential safety concerns of automated driving [4]. While discussions of the impact of self-driving vehicle technology taking place in academia, regulatory bodies and in industry are being accompanied by wide ranging consumer and user research there are still large knowledge gaps as it relates to the needs and preferences of specific groups of users. It has been suggested for instance that most self-driving vehicle technology being developed is not in fact accessible to individuals with visual impairments [18]. This may be at least partially attributable to a knowledge gap as it relates to the needs and preferences of individuals with visual impairments regarding self-driving vehicle technology.

The present study was designed to contribute to the literature an exploration of the opinions and concerns of blind and low vision consumers regarding self-driving vehicle technology. Using focus group methodology, 38 people who are blind and low vision participated in eight focus groups over a two-day period. Participants were asked to provide their general opinions regarding self-driving vehicles, comment on their hopes for the technology, reflect on their concerns, and express their preferences regarding interaction mechanisms among other topics in a semi structured group discussion lasting approximately one hour. We believe that this work furthers our goal of contributing to the literature research that furthers the understanding of the needs and preferences of users with a range of visual impairments as it relates to emerging self-driving vehicle technology. Research of this type will become increasingly critical if universal access to this technology is to be realized.

2. Related Work
There have been a number of studies in recent years that have investigated public opinion regarding automated driving conceptually, have explored consumer preferences regarding specific self-driving vehicle technologies and have examined related user needs.

ASSETS '17, October 29-November 1, 2017, Baltimore, MD, USA

ACM ISBN 978-1-4503-4926-0/17/10…$15.00
https://doi.org/10.1145/3132525.3132532

In a 2013 survey conducted by Continental AG in Germany, China, Japan and the U.S., 59% of respondents considered automated driving to be a "useful advancement" but 31% of respondents in all three countries found the development of automated vehicles to be "unnerving" [24]. Sixty six percent of U.S. respondents for instance indicated that they were "scared" by the concept of automated driving. Respondents were also skeptical of the reliability of the technology with 74% of respondents in China and 50% of respondents in the U.S. indicating that they did not believe that it would function reliably.

In 2013 professional services company KPMG conducted a focus group study with a total of 32 participants across California, Chicago and New Jersey [8]. Their results showed that women (median = 8.5 on a scale from 1 to 10) were more willing to use self-driving vehicles than men (median 7.5). Safety was a dominant topic of discussion during the focus groups with many participants expressing skepticism that the technology would work properly. Participants were near unanimous in expressing a need to be able to take control of the vehicle at will for a variety of reasons. Some participants expressed a lack of trust in the automated systems and expressed comfort in having manual controls available. Participants also expressed joy in driving and appreciated having manual controls as an option.

Howard and Dai in a 2013 survey explored the opinions of 107 respondents in Berkley, CA regarding self-driving vehicles [6]. Respondents indicated that safety (75%) and convenience (61%) were the most attractive features of the technology. More than 40% of respondents expressed willingness to either purchase a fully self-driving vehicle as their next vehicle or to retrofit their existing vehicle with self-driving technology if such an option were made available. Respondents indicated that liability concerns and the potential cost were the least attractive features of the technology.

In a 2014 survey involving 1,533 respondents in the U.S, U.K. and Australia, Schoettle and Sivak found that more than 60% of respondents in all three countries were aware of the technology and more than 50% had positive expectations about its potential benefits (e.g. less traffic congestion, shorter travel time) [20]. Respondents in all three countries expressed concerns about self-driving vehicles however. Across all three countries the most significant concerns were expressed regarding system/equipment failure, followed by vehicle performance in unexpected situations. Additionally, more than 90% of respondents expressed some degree of concern regarding the legal liability of drivers/owners of self-driving vehicles. A majority of respondents in all three countries expressed some interest in having self-driving technology but were generally unwilling to pay extra for it.

Payre, Cestac and Delhomme conducted a public opinion survey in 2014 of French drivers to investigate opinions on fully automated driving [19]. The study examined attitudes and acceptability of fully automated driving technology among 421 drivers finding that men and those scoring highly on the driving-related sensation seeking scale were more willing to use a fully automated vehicle and were more inclined to purchase a self-driving vehicle. Older respondents were less likely to indicate that they would purchase such a vehicle but showed higher acceptance of the technology. Respondents expressed a preference for full automation on highways, in traffic congestion, for automatic parking and when impaired by drug use or alcohol.

Ipsos MORI conducted a public opinion survey in 2014 involving 1,001 British respondents to investigate attitudes related to cars and technological developments surrounding the automotive industry [16]. Only 18% of those surveyed felt that it was important for car manufacturers to focus on driverless technologies while 41% indicated that it was unimportant. Older people (55+) were less likely to embrace the technology than the youngest group (16 to 24) and 50% of those aged 55+ felt that the technology was unimportant compared to 30% of those in the 16 to 24 age group.

A similar study was conducted by Kyriakidis, Happee and de Winter who conducted an international public opinion survey in 2015 involving 5000 respondents from 109 countries to investigate user acceptance, concerns and willingness to buy partially, highly and fully automated vehicles [10]. A plurality of respondents (22%) indicated that they were unwilling to pay any money for a fully automated driving system, while 5% indicated a willingness to pay more than $30,000 for it. Respondents were most concerned about software hacking/misuse, legal issues and safety.

In a 2016 survey involving 618 respondents in the U.S, Schoettle and Sivak found that among those surveyed the most frequent preference for vehicle automation was, in fact, "no automation" followed by a preference for partially self-driving vehicles [21]. Approximately 16% of respondents indicated a preference for self-driving vehicles. Over 90% of respondents expressed some degree of concern regarding self-driving vehicles when presented with a scenario where a self-driving vehicle would be their only means of transportation. The vast majority of respondents also expressed a desire for manual vehicle controls (e.g. steering wheel, gas pedal and brake) with 94.5% of respondents indicating that they would like a self-driving car to have such controls to enable a human driver to take control in the event of an emergency. In terms of entering a route or destination in a self-driving vehicle, 38% of respondents preferred the use of a touchscreen compared to 34.5% who preferred the use of a voice commands, 7.9% preferred the use of a personal portable device.

Bansai, Kockelman and Sing in a 2016 study involving 347 respondents in Austin, Texas found that respondents on average were willing to pay $7,253 to add Level 4 automation or full self-driving capabilities to their vehicles [2]. This stands in contrast to the findings of much of the previously described research but is largely consistent with the findings of Daziano, Sarria and Leard [4] who found in a 2017 study involving 1,260 respondents that the average household was willing to pay $4,900 for self-driving capabilities.

Each of the previously described studies had specific foci but contributed generally to the understanding of public opinion and consumer preferences as it pertains to self-driving cars. We believe that the present study is somewhat unique in that it explores the preferences of blind and low vision consumers whose preferences and concerns, we argue, have not been adequately explored in the recent literature.

3. METHOD

The use of focus group methodology was chosen over other methods because it provided the research team with an opportunity to elicit subjective perspectives regarding the research topics. This approach also allowed for a significant amount of flexibility to pursue themes that emerged during the course of discussion.

3.1 Participant Recruitment

Interested individuals were invited to participate if they fulfilled the following criteria: age 18 or above and currently considered themselves to be a visually impaired person based on an accompanying definition that defined that as blindness or with limited vision not correctable by glasses or contact lenses. Advertisements indicated that interested individuals should also have transportation to one of two focus group locations in north central Florida. Participants were recruited by email, newsletter and social media announcements distributed by organizations serving individuals with visual impairments in north central Florida and by vocational rehabilitation organizations. Those interested in participating were asked to call or email for additional information and scheduling. The Institutional Review Board of the authors' university approved this study and each participant provided written informed consent the day of his or her focus group session. Participants were compensated with a $20 prepaid gift card for their participation.

3.2 Description of Participants

Eight focus groups were conducted over a two-day period in two separate locations in north central Florida. In total, 38 participants were involved in the study in groups of between 4 and 6 people. Participant demographics are provided in Table 1. Study participants had a mean age of 51.5 (range = 18 to 90 years old) and a household annual income that ranged from under $15,000 to over $99,000. Twenty-two participants self identified as blind and 16 self-identified as low vision. Krueger and Casey have argued that focus group participants should share similar characteristics (e.g. gender group, age-range, social class background) in order to encourage open dialogue within the group but with enough variation to allow for contrasting opinions [9]. An attempt was made to group participants near their preferred location in accordance with this principle with a primary factor of similarity being a participant's characterization of their vision loss and a secondary factor being their age. No other factors were considered for the purpose of constructing the focus groups (e.g. race, gender, education). During the screening and scheduling process participants were briefly presented with functional definitions of blindness and low vision [12]. They were then asked to choose the definition that *best* characterized their degree of vision loss. As a result of this approach, when feasible, participants were placed in a group with other individuals who similarly characterized their vision loss as either blind or low vision. Where placement in such a group was not possible, typically due to logistical or scheduling constraints, an attempt was made to place the participant in a group with at least one individual of similar age. This placement was irrespective of whether or not the majority of the group's participants had expressed a different degree of vision loss. The approach resulted in one group that was predominantly composed of blind persons, one group predominantly composed of low vision persons and one group evenly split by degree of vision loss. The remaining three groups were relatively homogeneous in terms of age and predominantly composed of blind persons with each consisting of older participants (55+). The remaining groups were each slightly weighted towards blind participants in terms of composition though each group contained at least two low vision participants.

Table 1. Focus Group Demographics.

Variable	Female (n = 20)	Male (n = 18)
Degree of Vision Loss		
Blind	45.0	72.2
Low Vision	55.0	27.7
Age Range		
18-24	10.0	22.2
25-34	0.0	16.6
35-44	5.0	11.1
45-54	15.0	11.1
55-64	30.0	27.7
65-74	30.0	5.5
75+	10.0	5.5
Ethnicity		
White / Caucasian	90.0	61.1
Black / African American	10.0	16.6
Hispanic	0.0	16.6
Mixed Race	0.0	5.5

3.3 Procedure

Each focus group lasted approximately one hour with a procedure that was identical for each session. After each participant was seated in the meeting space, the informed consent document, which had been emailed to each participant in an accessible format the day before each focus group, was read aloud by the study moderator. Participants were then provided with assistance, as needed, signing the informed consent document. After being provided light refreshments, a brief ice breaking exercise was led by the focus group moderator to introduce participants to one another and encourage interaction between participants. A semi structured interview followed. Between three and five days following the focus group session a telephone interview was conducted with each participant. This interview provided an opportunity to ask follow up questions of study participants after a period of reflection and to gather additional demographic information. This paper reports on the results of the semi structured interview as well as relevant demographic data.

3.4 Focus Group Guide

We created a semi-structured script to elicit information from participants regarding self-driving vehicles [22]. Questions focused on participant understanding and awareness of current developments regarding self-driving vehicles, hopes and aspirations for future self-driving vehicle technologies, concerns related to the accessibility of self-driving vehicles and opinions regarding the legal environment for the use of this technology by individuals with visual impairments. The focus group guide was pilot tested with three participants in a group setting prior to beginning data collection to ensure that it was comprehensible and comprehensive.

3.5 Data Capture and Transcription

Each focus group session was video recorded and transcribed verbatim by a professional transcriptionist prior to analysis. The completed transcript was then verified by a member of the research team against the original recordings.

3.6 Analysis

In preparation for analysis all transcripts were entered into MAXQDA [14], a computer program for qualitative data analysis. After initially familiarizing ourselves with the data two investigators independently coded all quotations from participants (JB and JW). For each researcher this hybrid process began with a small set of a priori codes agreed upon by the research team in advance then continued with codes inductively identified within the data. Each coding was then categorized and refined by each researcher independently. Both independent analyses were then merged into a single definitive version by a third researcher (BP) with any disagreements in coding and categorization settled by this third researcher and agreed upon by the research team collectively.

4. RESULTS

Results of the analyses of focus group data are organized around six major thematic findings: 1) self-driving vehicle concerns, 2) potential benefits of self-driving vehicles 3) licensing and training, 4) the human-machine interface of self-driving vehicles, 5) purchase considerations and 6) risk and trust. Across the eight focus groups self-driving vehicle concerns were raised 223 times followed by 151 comments related to the potential benefits of self-driving vehicles. Comments associated with licensing and training occurred 121 times and were followed by comments related to the human-machine interface of self-driving vehicles (88) and vehicle purchase considerations (74). Issues related to risk and trust were the least discussed, occurring 33 times. In many instances more than one theme was addressed in a single conversational turn.

4.1 Self-Driving Vehicle Concerns

4.1.1 Are the needs of individuals with visual impairments being adequately considered in the development of autonomous vehicle technologies?

While opinions varied, most participants expressed the view that the needs of individuals with visual impairments were not being adequately considered in the development of autonomous vehicle technologies (57%). Negative experiences with past technologies were frequently cited as examples of why they believed these needs were likely being ignored:

> No, I don't / I don't think they do. And they didn't when they invented the quiet car. And that's, you know, that was an invention that's plagued me. I mean, I love hybrid vehicles and what they do for the environment, but I hate hybrid vehicles and how dangerous they are. They're like sharks in the water now. You don't know when it's coming up behind you. It may strike. (P38)

> I know that in the past with all the new technology that's come out so far, blind people have been kind of an afterthought. (P37)

Many participants (37%) expressed a belief that the technology presently exists to solve most autonomous vehicle accessibility challenges but that manufacturers need to be made aware of the importance of the issue:

> Like, on the side like Tesla and Uber and whatnot, I'm sure there's someone somewhere thinking about that, but I don't think it's in, like, the forefront. (P34)

> If you KNOW of all these obstacles, they can be overcome. And the technology, it pretty much exists now. It's just a matter of marrying that technology, you know? (P17)

4.1.2 Parking, Orientation and Vehicle Location

A variety of issues were raised related to the parking of an autonomous vehicle, orientation to a destination upon parking and the location and identification of a visually impaired operator's vehicle at the conclusion of a trip.

Forty four percent of participants expressed concerns regarding their ability to provide parking guidance to an autonomous vehicle without the ability to see the surrounding area. Some of the concerns expressed related to safety:

> How do you try to set a car to park where you want it to park if you can't see where to show it to park or tell it to park or whatever? You might be parking in the / across a railroad track. (P12)

Some expressed concerns related to convenience and practicality, with travel to shopping malls being a frequently provided example of the need to tell a self-driving vehicle specifically where to park:

> When you pull into a shopping mall, you know, you got like this one out here is, you got Penney's on one end, Sears in the back and Belk's on the other end. Well, you know, you need to be able to tell it... (P11)

The ability to orient oneself to the desired destination (e.g. a building's front door) upon arrival to a location was a widely discussed topic. Thirty nine percent of participants felt that this was an unanswered question that would need to be addressed by the technology:

> Now, if I drive up in a car and get out of the car, how do I know where the door is? In other words, there's a...the car has to do a lot besides just drive. (P24)

One participant raised questions about how the technology would enable her to orient herself to her desired destination in the event that she were dropped off in a parking lot:

> And there's also, you know, if it takes you to a location and it like drops you off in the middle of like a parking lot, you know, which building or which direction that your actual destination is? You know, something that would also, like, help you figure that out and know where that is. (P23)

In response, another participant (P21) suggested dedicated autonomous vehicle parking to aide in general orientation.

Twenty eight percent of participants raised questions about the technology necessary to enable an autonomous vehicle operator with visual impairment's to locate his or her vehicle in a large crowded space like a shopping center parking lot. A number of solutions were expressed across focus groups to include programming the vehicle to return at a specified time and location (P30, P32), to key chains designed to vibrate based on proximity to the vehicle (P34).

4.1.3 Location Verification

The desire for a vehicle feature that would enable an operator with visual impairments to verify his or her arrival at a desired location was a topic of great interest. A majority of participants across focus groups (53%) commented that such a feature was important to some degree and that they would be concerned about inadvertently getting out of the vehicle in the wrong place. A commonly expressed view was that the technology should provide some type of back up system to prevent such an occurrence:

> I think my operating system should take care of it. You know? It's like she'd…she'd take care of everything. So, I think the operating system should say, "Don't get out of the car. You're in the wrong…you're in a field." (P32)

In many cases the expressed desire for this feature closely related to negative experiences with automotive navigation systems where the participant had observed these systems lead others in the wrong direction, make errors or otherwise fail to operate properly. One participant's comment was representative of many regarding this topic:

> …you know, I've experienced on MV, you know, our public transportation that, you know, the GPS saying "You have arrived at your destination" and, you know, and the driver says, "No, we haven't." So, you know, it's not all it seems. Like GPS is fallible, you know, at times. (P20)

4.1.4 Situational Awareness

Many participants expressed desire for a vehicle feature that would, at any given time, provide information on an operator vehicle's relationship to other vehicles, landmarks, pedestrians, obstacles and the final destination. Forty five percent of participants across focus groups expressed a view that the self-driving vehicle's technology should be able to provide such information in real time to mirror the type of information that a sighted operator would have available through the use of cameras, mirrors and sight:

> I think it would make the person sitting in the car feel a little bit more at ease. You know, that you know, since you can't see where you're going or where you're at, that it would tell you like, "Well, you know, we are like half a mile away from your destination." (P2)

> …you don't necessarily know, like, where you are in relationship to where you're actually going. Something that might help you, like place, like where you are. (P23)

4.1.5 Interaction with Non-Autonomous Vehicles

Participants generally expressed skepticism that autonomous vehicles would be able to successfully operate alongside non-autonomous vehicles due to the unpredictability of human drivers (63%):

> I think that the fact that they have to interact with people driving is a downfall too, because, you know, people are really bad drivers. I ride with my daughter all the time and the people constantly running red lights, cutting us off and doing things, you know. And I would…you know, you would wonder how the car would react to things like that. (P33)

> My downside is…To me, my – this is my opinion – I just don't see an autonomous car being able to react to human error that quickly. (P25)

Many participants (39%) commented that as autonomous vehicles became more common and displaced non-autonomous vehicles on the road they believed the interaction problem would lessen as captured in this exchange between three participants in group six:

> Well, I think the autonomous vehicles are like the flu shot. The more people that get the flu shot, (P25 laughs) the less chance of an epidemic. The more autonomous vehicles that are on the road… (P27)

> The more of them that are on the road, the safer the roads will be. (P26)

4.1.6 Help and Roadside Assistance

Thirty nine percent of study participants raised questions regarding how to and whom to ask for help in the event of a vehicle breakdown or unforeseen event. While the overwhelming majority of participants stated that they had never owned or operated a vehicle, the suggested approaches took the form of a type of monitoring and assistance service similar to General Motors' OnStar [11] which was specifically named several times:

> Yeah, that would be good, if they had some kind of like, like a home center (P2: Yeah. Yeah), you know, that paid attention. Like a security system for cars that keeps track of where your car is going. So, if you're lost or something, you're able to get help. (P4)

> Well, I…I think about something along the lines of – and I've never used it before, but, you know, something along the lines of OnStar. In other words, you know, if you get into some trouble, if there's vehicle trouble, you know, with the actual vehicle itself, being able to call, you know, somebody to come and help you. 'Cause, obviously, if I was riding it by myself and the car had a problem and was maybe automatically pulled over, I wouldn't know where I was. (P20)

4.1.7 Legal Liability

A small number of participants raised questions regarding legal liability in the event of an accident (13%). Some participants expressed concerns about the seemingly unsettled liability questions in the event of an autonomous vehicle accident while several blind participants expressed concerns that they would be automatically assumed to be liable as captured in this exchange between two participants in group two:

> You can't even be your own witness? (laughs) (P6)

> (laughs) Yeah, you're just getting blamed for it for sure. (P5)

4.2 Potential Benefits of Self-Driving Vehicles

The majority of participant comments in the study that focused on the potential benefits of self-driving vehicles centered on the potential for increased independence, personal mobility and the potential for time savings versus participants' existing means of transportation.

4.2.1 Independence and Mobility

Forty seven percent of participants specifically referenced "independence" when referring to the potential benefits of self-driving vehicles. Many of those commenting expressed a hope that self-driving vehicles would enable them to no longer rely on friends, relatives or public transportation for their transportation needs:

> I would definitely say the benefit would be to not have rely on people to take you (P6 nods) around. That you could just get up and go whenever you want to, whenever you want to. (P7)

> Independence and the ability to go from point A to point B without having to ask somebody to drop what they're doing to do that for you. (P16)

Within the context of the discussion regarding independence several participants specifically discussed a desire for basic transportation capabilities that would enable them to return to work as expressed by one blind participant:

> You know, I think one of the things that's important to understand is, you know, everybody is looking at these high-end abilities, you know, things like luxury, comfort, you know, safety about, you know, an ability to go anywhere. I don't think that we have to start there. You know, if I could purchase an AV that…I was in home healthcare sales rep, but, you know, two years ago. You know, I…Every week, I called on the same doctor's offices, the same hospitals, the same nursing homes. You know, I ran the same route every day, on time. You know. And if I could have a vehicle that I could program to do nothing but that route and now to get here and maybe the grocery store, I would be totally 100% happy. (P16: Definitely, yeah.) You know? And I think that's one of the things that these engineers are missing is: they're trying to make the all-inclusive, you know, panacea, you know. And that's not really what people with disabilities are concerned with. (P14: Right.) Yea it would be nice to have. But we're just looking for the basic mobility and independence that most people totally take for granted.

Participants in the study commented on the impact that the inability to operate a personal vehicle had on their daily lives. Participants indicated that it impacted where they lived, their diet, their shopping habits, their medical care, their employment and their ability to visit friends and relatives. Nearly all participants responded positively to the potential independence and mobility benefits of self-driving vehicles (97%):

> Well, the idea of being able to get in a car at the time you wanted to and go wherever you want it to and get in it and come back home when you wanted to, it would mean an awful lot, I think. (P12)

One blind participant indicated that she did not see any benefits however (P29).

4.2.2 Time Savings

Of participants commenting on the topic (18%), opinions were overwhelmingly positive about the potential time savings of the use of a self-driving vehicle over their current forms of transportation, which, in most cases was public transportation, friends or family. Many shared personal stories about their daily challenges or the challenges of friends with visual impairments and how these challenges could potentially be overcome with the use of a self-driving vehicle:

> I know a guy who goes to work and he spends three hours to get there and like two hours coming home. And that's for 25 years he's been doing that. (P25: Oh my God!) So, can you imagine how valuable that time is that he is losing? (P26)

> And…And what you…What people don't realize what you could in 30 to 45 minutes, it takes on a bus two hours to four hours. [P28: Or more.] Like getting here. (P25)

4.3 Licensing and Training

The discussion of legal and regulatory issues related to self-driving vehicles centered on laws that could potentially restrict access to individuals with visual impairments. Broadly within the study these discussions generally focused on the potential requirement that self-driving vehicle operators possess a valid driver's license or on potential training requirements.

More than half of participants (55%) expressed concerns about the prospects of laws being put in place that would effectively prevent individuals with visual impairments from operating self-driving vehicles. The most concerning prospect for many was the requirement that a valid driver's license be required to operate a self-driving vehicle. Several participants expressed the view that this amounted to a form of discrimination.

> So, I think they would have to make some laws, like he was saying, to…for people not to do that. 'Cause we have rights too. (P3)

> But regardless, I'd really…I personally hate…That's what ADA is all about. (P25: Yeah.) (P24)

The topic elicited a variety of comments however and some degree of disagreement with several participants suggesting that a driver's or operator's license of some kind should be required to, at a minimum, promote safe operation and prevent children or individuals with limited cognitive abilities from operating self-driving vehicles alone:

> I think, the first thing that comes (P19: Safety.) to my mind would be, you know: Would…I mean, it seems logical that if we're gonna operate something like that we'd have to get a driver's license. And I…I'm just not sure how that's gonna work. (laughs) (P20)

> I would say, you don't put a sixteen-year-old behind the wheel. (P38)

In many of these discussions within the study a compromise of sorts that seemed acceptable to the group that emerged was the concept of an "operator's license" that could be earned through a training program and testing:

> When you drive a normal car you gotta go and get your driver's license and take a class, so there should probably be a class to take for this, too. I think. I mean, that would make sense. Maybe not that extensive or whatever, but, you know, just like all the safety issues and stuff like that. It would make sense to have that. (P5)

> And I think to be on the safe side and keep you from having some issues, I think it's better that you have to take a test. (P31)

4.4 The Human Machine Interface of Self-Driving Vehicles

The discussion of the human machine interface (HMI) of self-driving vehicles focused on the manner in which participants anticipated that they would interact with a self-driving vehicle and their preferences in this regard.

The vast majority of participants (71%) anticipated that self-driving vehicles would implement some type of speech interaction capability. For example:

> I hope it's so that you can just get in the car and say, "I want to go to "such and such church" and it'll take you there. And I hope I can get in and say, "I want to go home", when it's over. (P11: Well) I hope they can simplify it somewhat. (P12)

Concerns were expressed about the accuracy of speech input however with personal experiences with voice recognition errors in Apple's Siri [7] being cited as examples by several participants.

Participants expressed a variety of opinions however regarding their preferred primary means of interacting with a self-driving vehicle. While some expressed a preference for speech input, several expressed a desire to interact with the vehicle primarily through the use of their smartphone as captured in this exchange in group five:

> Because like most visually impaired or blind individuals, like we have smart phones. So, is there a way to put it in through our phone that it will sync with the car? Well, I'm not saying "Is there a way?" but "Could there be a way?" I guess, that's what I'm asking. I guess, that would probably be the number one thing. (P21)

> I think that would probably be a good idea 'cause a phone is something I can, like, hold up closer to me so I can see it easier. And also, it will read it back to me, like, that's already accessible in that way versus like having to look at something else. And I'd also say to make like buttons or different things maybe more distinguishable so you know which one is which. (P23)

The use of a touchscreen to interact with an autonomous vehicle was described by many participants as a backup means of interaction. One participant with low vision who favored the use of a smart phone as a primary means of interaction preferred the use of a touchscreen as a backup form of interaction in the event that her smartphone failed albeit with an iPhone like "voiceover" feature that would indicate what icon was being touched. Several blind participants disagreed with this comment however citing past problems with voiceover and the inaccessibility of standard touch screen displays.

4.5 Purchase Considerations

Vehicle purchase considerations as it related to self-driving vehicles largely revolved around cost, vehicle maintenance and the presence of backup systems.

Most participants who commented on the topic (24%) expressed a view that while the costs are at present unknown, self-driving vehicles would likely be costly, if not prohibitively so. For example:

> ... let's face it, most of these vehicles to begin with, they're gonna be economically prohibitive for most of us to be able to purchase and maintain. (P36)

Eleven percent of participants also commented about the uncertainty of repair costs or even where or how to get the vehicle repaired or maintained. For example:

> And since it's run mainly by technology, you know, where do you take it for its 50,000 overhaul or whatever? (P19)

A small number of participants (8%) expressed concerns about the reliability of primary self-driving vehicle systems. These participants questioned what would happen if primary systems failed during vehicle operation and considered the presence of a backup system to be a key purchase consideration. For instance:

> It must have. What if the main system malfunctions, you know, and it can't literally drive you? Well, if you're on the interstate and it malfunctions, would they have like a backup system? (P29)

4.6 Risk and Trust

Participants expressed a broad range of views as it related to whether or not they would trust in the safety and reliability of self-driving vehicle technology.

Some participants (5%) rejected the idea outright as too risky as did one blind participant:

> ...I just would not feel full trust at turning myself totally loose with any type of a / Even if it's a computer. And I've worked with computers too long that I know they can make / get a glitch in them. And I think there is still a possibility of risk. (P1)

Sixteen percent of study participants raised concerns regarding the possibility of malfunctions due to computer viruses and hacking. One participant stated for example:

> Computers aren't infallible. You know, they get viruses, they get / other people get in and take control. You know? So, you have to think about all that stuff, too. And that would make me very nervous. (P10)

Of the 76% of participants who commented on the topic, many indicated that they viewed riding in a self-driving vehicle as being no more risky than riding with a human driver:

> The risk involved. For me, it's no, even more than getting in the car of my wife. (P11)

Some participants however indicated that they would actually feel safer in a self-driving vehicle:

> But we almost daily risk our lives by getting into a vehicle (P25: Oh yeah, I agree!) with a stranger who may be the worst driver. (P29: That's true, yes.) (P28: Yeah.) They may be drunk, they may be on drugs, they may have stayed up all night fighting with their girlfriend. Whereas the autonomous vehicle does not get distracted, does not get tired. I think it's just way, way, way safer. (P28: I agree.) (P27)

A blind participant who had recently lost his sight described to the group being driven by his wife who had never driven before and was in the process of learning to drive:

> She's got to learn it. So now I'm riding in a computer that's learning, you know, a self-taught computer. So instead of having, you know, the option of maybe a program glitch happening, I'm riding a computer that doesn't have a clue what it's doing yet. You know? So I'd feel safer in an AV. (P17)

For some participants the potential independence and mobility benefits simply outweighed any risks. One participant who was progressively losing her sight and no longer had the ability to drive stated:

> Pitfalls? None. I don't care if they crash me into a wall, I'll wear a helmet. I just want to get out of my house. I don't care. I'll be a test driver. I just want out. I just want my freedom. They outweigh any / any problems. I'll sign a liability waiver. (P32)

5. DISCUSSION

5.1 General Opinions Regarding Self-Driving Vehicles

The vast majority of participants expressed an awareness of self-driving vehicle technology. All but one participant within the study indicated a belief in their general understanding of the technology when asked at the outset of their respective focus group. Participants expressed views that, while somewhat skeptical, were generally more positive than the related literature [20, 21] however as it pertained to the benefits of self-driving vehicle technology. The overwhelming majority of participants were resolute regarding their belief that self-driving vehicles could potentially be life-changing technology for them personally. While the majority expressed a view that there are considerable unknowns regarding the technology that need to be addressed, they were generally optimistic about the potential personal benefits. Participants also expressed optimism for society at large believing that self-driving vehicles could potentially make driving generally safer, while reducing the impact on the environment.

Concerns regarding the potential legal liability of owners/drivers/operators of self-driving vehicles have been raised as a substantial concern in the related literature [6, 20]. Participants expressed similar concerns in the present study but generally related these concerns to their visual impairment and not the absence of an active driver, as is typically the case in the related literature. Several participants questioned whether there would be a presumption of their liability if a self-driving vehicle were to be operated by a person with visual impairments and how an individual would defend his or herself from spurious legal claims without the ability to provide visual testimony regarding an accident. These concerns, while similar, are somewhat different from the legal liability issues raised in the related literature that often explore whether legal liability should be assigned to the vehicle manufacturer or operator.

5.2 Human Machine Interface

Our findings suggest that the Human Machine Interface (HMI) of a self-driving vehicle for a person who his blind or low vision will likely need to do more than simply allow an operator to input a route or destination. The HMI for an operator who is blind or low vision will likely need to serve this purpose while also satisfying the need for situational awareness, location verification and other, as yet unspecified needs.

Study participants' desires for a self-driving vehicle HMI closely aligned with their degree of vision loss and their age. Blind participants generally expressed preferences for both speech input capabilities and the use of a smartphone application. Many participants anticipated that self-driving vehicles would utilize speech input as a default means of interaction but were wary of the system inaccurately interpreting their utterances or of generally poor performance based on past experiences with Apple's Siri [7], Microsoft Cortana [15] and Amazon Alexa [1]. Many participants indicated that they found their personal smartphone to be very accessible and would prefer to control a self-driving vehicle using a smartphone application if possible though they acknowledged that a backup system would be necessary in the event that they did not have a phone or their battery died. Blind participants were extremely resistant to a standard touchscreen, viewing them as being entirely inaccessible with several indicating some acceptance of a touchscreen with Apple "voiceover" [25] capabilities.

Participants with low vision also expressed preferences for both speech input capabilities and the use of a smartphone application but also expressed an interest in touchscreen interaction. Like blind participants, many participants with low vision expressed a belief that self-driving vehicles would utilize speech input as a default means of interaction but expressed somewhat less concern about the potential for voice recognition problems. Participants with low vision also found their personal smartphones to be very accessible and expressed a desire to control a self-driving vehicle using a smartphone application if possible. Participants with low vision expressed interest in the use of a touchscreen, largely as a backup to the use of a smartphone application, but suggested the incorporation of contrasting colors, enlarged buttons and Apple "voiceover" [25] capabilities. Our findings stand in contrast to those of Schoettle and Shivak [21] who, in a survey presumably of sighted respondents, found that a plurality of respondents preferred touchscreen interaction. It is important to note that relatively younger (under 30) blind and low vision participants in the present study were the most emphatic about the desire to use their personal smartphone or a smartphone application as a control device for a self-driving vehicle with older participants accepting of the concept but open to other approaches.

Studies by Schoettle and Shivak [21] and KPMG [8] have suggested that a majority of potential operators of self-driving vehicles have a preference for manual controls to allow the vehicle to be controlled by a human operator in an emergency situation or for enjoyment. A very small number of the participants of the present study expressed a similar desire. All but one of these participants were people with low vision who felt that they should have some ability to control the vehicle in an emergency situation if they observed a potential hazard.

The need for the self-driving vehicle's technology to provide some means to satisfy the need for situational awareness while in transit and to aide the operator in verifying their arrival at the correct location was expressed by the majority of participants in the study. Most participants expressed some concerns about traveling without having some awareness of the direction that they were traveling in and their immediate surroundings (e.g. current street, surrounding vehicles, buildings, pedestrians). Participants also expressed hesitance about getting out of the vehicle upon arrival, especially in the case of a self-driving taxi that would perhaps immediately leave, without assurances that they had arrived in the correct location. These concerns were closely related to skepticism regarding the reliability of GPS technologies and negative assumptions regarding the technologies that would be used to input desired destinations (e.g. unreliable speech systems). Older participants (55+) were especially concerned about the ability of the HMI to relay information regarding parking options and building locations. Many of these older participants expressed a belief that the challenge of getting from the vehicle to their desired building or final destination and back would be nearly as complicated a technical challenge as the development of the self-driving vehicle itself. While the majority of participants felt that these challenges could be solved with existing technology they were unsure how.

5.3 Self-Driving Vehicle Cost

Much of the self-driving vehicle literature of the past decade has suggested that in cases where people would consider owning self-driving vehicle technology these same individuals in most instances would not consider paying extra for it [10, 20]. Recent studies [2, 4] have suggested a break from this trend, finding that consumers may be increasingly willing to pay for self-driving vehicle technology depending upon the cost. In the present study only a few participants took the position that they were unwilling to pay anything extra for autonomous vehicle technology with very few being steadfast in this view. While not every participant verbalized a position on the issue, only one participant indicated during the discussion that they would not be willing to pay for a self-driving vehicle.

In the study the question for many participants was not whether they were willing to pay or pay a premium for this technology but rather whether they would be able to afford what many assumed would be very costly technology. This question was exacerbated by the fact that the overwhelming majority of participants had never owned or purchased a vehicle before and therefore many indicated that they had little direct frame of reference for vehicle costs, self-driving or otherwise. Several participants in the study expressed an interest in the Tesla brand and the "Autopilot" feature specifically [17]; indicating that they had conducted research on related features and pricing. These participants, coupled with those who had exposure to vehicle pricing from past experience, friends and relatives, ultimately helped to frame the discussion around vehicle costs in several of the groups. The majority of groups arrived at an estimate at or near $100,000 that seemed to make reference to the believed cost of a near-autonomous Tesla that was often discussed in the same context. This cost for most participants was viewed as unaffordable though quite a few participants indicated that they were willing to pay that or more if that was what it would cost for a self-driving vehicle. Many of the participants espousing this latter view were older participants (55+) who questioned whether the technology would become commercially available soon enough for them to benefit.

5.4 Legal and Regulatory Issues, Licensing and Training

Discussions related to the legal environment for self-driving vehicles, the licensing requirements for their operation and the need for training were cordial but generally contentious throughout the study. In some cases, participants indicated that their concerns were admittedly based on second hand information or rumors. The majority of the study's participants however indicated that they had been following national and local discussions around these issues with many participants indicating that they believed, based on these discussions, that it was possible that individuals with visual impairments would effectively be blocked from owning or operating self-driving vehicles. Of particular concern were two types of laws: 1) laws requiring that an individual operating a self-driving vehicle have the ability to take over control in the event of an emergency and 2) laws that would require a licensed driver to operate a self-driving vehicle.

Participants were split regarding laws that would require an individual operating a self-driving vehicle to have the ability to take over as necessary. While some participants found this premise to be unreasonable given that such a vehicle would be designed to be fully automated, others argued that present or near-future technology would exist that would enable a blind or low vision driver to safely bring a vehicle to a stop in the event of an emergency. These participants, while in a minority, did not believe that such a law would therefore prevent the operation of a self-driving vehicle by individuals with visual impairments.

While some participants were overtly against the idea of requiring a conventional driver's license, some participants felt that a license of some sort should be a requirement given the serious nature of vehicle operation, self-driving or otherwise. These participants repeatedly raised concerns about the prospect of children or people with cognitive disabilities operating self-driving vehicles. Those against licensing raised a number of arguments against it but the majority viewed it as an attack on their civil liberties and as overt discrimination against persons with disabilities. In all but two of the focus groups the discussion gradually trended towards the concept of an "operator's license" that would require a certain amount of training on the operation of self-driving vehicles generally but would not exclude individuals with physical disabilities from ownership or operation.

5.5 Risk, Trust and Safety

Much of the recent literature on self-driving vehicles and reliability, risk, trust and safety find that most people are concerned that self-driving vehicles will not function reliably [8, 20, 24]. While the present study included participants who held this view, the majority expressed the view that self-driving vehicles are at least as safe human drivers. Some participants expressed a view that self-driving vehicles would be safer than humans and for some the potential independence and mobility benefits simply outweighed what they viewed as minimal safety risks. Overall the attitude expressed towards the technology was generally more trusting than that expressed in much of the related literature. A small number of participants raised questions about the potential for software hacking, a topic found to be of importance to those surveyed by Kyriakidis et al. [10], but it was a topic of limited discussion within the study and the issue generally did not appear to undermine trust in the technology.

5.6 Consideration of User Needs

Many participants shared impassioned personal stories while discussing whether or not they felt the needs of people who are blind or low vision were being adequately considered in the development of self-driving vehicles. While opinions varied, most participants expressed the view that their needs were being largely ignored. In all cases, evidence for this was not any experience with an inaccessible self-driving vehicle, as none of the participants had first hand experience with the technology, but was instead negative experiences in other areas of their lives related to other technologies. Many participants expressed a view that technology was often designed and developed without adequate input from people with disabilities generally and was often forced upon them without adequate training or explanation. A number of participants commented that major companies routinely moved to new technologies without properly considering the needs of people with disabilities and potential concerns regarding inaccessibility. The movement towards touchscreen soda machines was cited several times by participants as a problematic technology that was being broadly introduced without proper consideration of accessibility concerns. Several participants described challenges that they had faced in having their accessibility concerns addressed on a local and state level and questioned their ability to have their concerns addressed by, arguably, much more difficult to reach international businesses. The majority of participants specifically cited awareness as a key issue. Many expressed a belief that the technology and technical capability currently exists to make self-driving vehicles universally accessible but questioned whether manufacturers and decision makers were generally aware of the importance of doing so. At a minimum these findings suggest that more needs to be done to reach out to organizations that serve people who are blind and low vision and to people directly to better inform them about what is being done to develop accessible self-driving technology. At the same time more, in fact, may need to be done to make self-driving vehicle technology more accessible while including more stakeholders with a range of visual impairments in the design and development process.

5.7 Limitations

While the use of focus group methodology has its merits, group composition is a recognized weakness. Despite our care in implementing Krueger and Casey's [9] guidelines our design choices regarding group composition may be called into question. Given the topic of study we argue that our chosen variables, degree of vision loss and age, were rather logical choices. Disagreement can be found however in our manner of implementation. While our goal in implementing the guidelines was to structure each group according to degree of vision loss and participant age range, due largely to recruitment, scheduling and logistical constraints several of the focus groups ended somewhat mixed in terms of degree of vision loss and participant age range. Generally low vision persons were underrepresented in most groups as most were slightly weighted towards blind persons. Our use of a functional definition as opposed to medical definition of vision loss may also have impacted our groupings. Given the active participation of nearly all participants in the focus groups it is our opinion that the aforementioned limitations had little impact on the discussions themselves however.

6. CONCLUSION AND FUTURE WORK

The present study was designed to contribute to the literature a study that explored the needs and preferences of blind and low vision consumers as it relates to self-driving vehicles. Using focus group methodology we asked participants to comment on their general opinions regarding self-driving vehicles conceptually, their hopes for the technology, their major concerns, and their preferences regarding modes of interaction among other topics. Our findings suggest that blind and low vision consumers may view fully self-driving vehicles more favorably than consumers generally and may have a greater degree of trust in the safety and reliability of the technology. At the same time, if the results of our focus groups are reflective of general attitudes of people with visual impairments, many believe that their specific needs are not being adequately considered in the development of the technology. We believe that this work furthers our goal of contributing to the literature research that furthers the understanding of the needs and preferences of users with a range of visual impairments as it relates to emerging fully autonomous vehicle technology.

7. ACKNOWLEDGMENTS

We thank the members of the community in north central Florida for spreading awareness about the research and the local organizations that provided facilities in support of the research effort.

8. REFERENCES

[1] Alexa: *https://developer.amazon.com/alexa*. Accessed: 2017-04-17.

[2] Bansal, P. et al. 2016. Assessing public opinions of and interest in new vehicle technologies: An Austin perspective. *Transportation Research Part C: Emerging Technologies*. 67, (Jun. 2016), 1–14. DOI:https://doi.org/10.1016/j.trc.2016.01.019.

[3] Cusumano, M.A. 2014. How traditional firms must compete in the sharing economy. *Communications of the ACM*. 58, 1 (Dec. 2014), 32–34. DOI:https://doi.org/10.1145/2688487.

[4] Daziano, R.A. et al. 2017. Are consumers willing to pay to let cars drive for them? Analyzing response to autonomous vehicles. *Transportation Research Part C: Emerging Technologies*. 78, (May 2017), 150–164. DOI:https://doi.org/10.1016/j.trc.2017.03.003.

[5] Greenblatt, J.B. and Saxena, S. 2015. Autonomous taxis could greatly reduce greenhouse-gas emissions of US light-duty vehicles. *Nature Climate Change*. 5, 9 (Jul. 2015), 860–863. DOI:https://doi.org/10.1038/nclimate2685.

[6] Howard, D. and Dai, D. 2014. Public perceptions of self-driving cars: The case of Berkeley, California. *Transportation Research Board 93rd Annual Meeting* (2014).

[7] iOS - Siri: *http://www.apple.com/ios/siri/*. Accessed: 2017-04-17.

[8] KPMG 2013. Self-Driving Cars: Are We Ready?

[9] Krueger, R.A. and Casey, M.C. 2009. *Focus Groups A Practical Guide for Applied Research*. Sage Publications.

[10] Kyriakidis, M. et al. 2015. Public opinion on automated driving: Results of an international questionnaire among 5000 respondents. *Transportation Research Part F: Traffic Psychology and Behaviour*. 32, (Jul. 2015), 127–140. DOI:https://doi.org/10.1016/j.trf.2015.04.014.

[11] Learn About OnStart: *https://www.onstar.com/us/en/home.html*. Accessed: 2017-04-17.

[12] Low Vision and Legal Blindness Terms and Descriptions - VisionAware: *http://www.visionaware.org/info/your-eye-condition/eye-health/low-vision/low-vision-terms-and-descriptions/1235*. Accessed: 2017-04-17.

[13] Marinik, A. et al. 2014. Human factors evaluation of level 2 and level 3 automated driving concepts: Concepts of operation. (2014).

[14] MAXQDA: Qualitative Data Analysis Software | Windows & Mac: *http://www.maxqda.com/*. Accessed: 2017-03-19.

[15] Microsoft Cortana Dev Center: *https://developer.microsoft.com/en-us/cortana*. Accessed: 2017-04-15.

[16] Missel, J. 2014. *Ipsos MORI Loyalty Automotive Survey*.

[17] Model S Autopilot Press Kit | Tesla Motors: *https://www.teslamotors.com/presskit/autopilot*. Accessed: 2016-07-07.

[18] National Federation of the Blind Resolutions for 2016 | National Federation of the Blind: *https://nfb.org/2016-resolutions*. Accessed: 2017-01-16.

[19] Payre, W. et al. 2014. Intention to use a fully automated car: Attitudes and a priori acceptability. *Transportation research part F: traffic psychology and behaviour*. 27, (2014), 252–263.

[20] Schoettle, B. and Sivak, M. 2014. A survey of public opinion about autonomous and self-driving vehicles in the US, the UK, and Australia. *Ann Arbor: The University of Michigan Transportation Research Institute: Transportation Research Institute*. (2014).

[21] Schoettle, B. and Sivak, M. 2016. Motorists' Preferences for Different Levels of Vehicle Automation: 2016. *University of Michigan Sustainable Worldwide Transportation*. (2016).

[22] Self-Driving Vehicle Focus Group Questions: *www.jbrinkley.com/projects/self-driving-vehicle-focus-groups/focus_group_script.pdf*. Accessed: 2017-06-15.

[23] Snyder, R. 2016. Implications of Autonomous Vehicles: A Planner's Perspective. *Institute of Transportation Engineers. ITE Journal*. 86, 12 (2016), 25.

[24] Sommer, K. 2013. *Continental Mobility Study 2013*.

[25] Vision Accessibility - Mac: *https://www.apple.com/accessibility/mac/vision/*. Accessed: 2017-04-17.

DroneNavigator: Using Leashed and Free-Floating Quadcopters to Navigate Visually Impaired Travelers

Mauro Avila Soto[1], Markus Funk[1], Matthias Hoppe[1],
Robin Boldt[1], Katrin Wolf[2], Niels Henze[1]
[1]University of Stuttgart (Pfaffenwaldring 5a, 70569 Stuttgart, Germany)
[2]HAW University of Applied Sciences Hamburg (Finkenau 35, 22081 Hamburg, Germany)
firstname.lastname@vis.uni-stuttgart.de[1] – firstname.lastname@haw-hamburg.de[2]

ABSTRACT

Although a large number of navigation support systems for visually impaired people have been proposed in the past, navigating through unknown environments is still a major challenge for visually impaired travelers. Existing systems provide navigation information through headphones, speakers or tactile actuators. In this paper, we propose to use small lightweight quadcopters instead to provide navigation information for people with visual impairments. Using a leashed or free-floating quadcopter, the user is navigated by the distinct sound that the quadcopter emits and a haptic stimulus provided by the leash. In a user with 14 visually impaired participants, we compared leashed quadcopter navigation, free-floating quadcopter navigation, and traditional audio navigation. The results show that compared to audio navigation, participants navigate significantly faster with a free-floating quadcopter and make fewer navigation errors using the quadcopter navigation methods.

CCS Concepts

•**Human-centered computing → Empirical studies in HCI; Accessibility systems and tools;**

Keywords

Navigation Aid; Visual Impairments; Quadcopter; Drones

1. INTRODUCTION AND BACKGROUND

In 2012, there were 285 million persons with visual impairments, including 39 million persons that were considered blind [17]. People with visual impairments face a number of challenges in daily life. Especially being able to navigate through known and unknown environments becomes challenging without vision. Today, the most common tools used by persons with visual impairments are the white cane and guide dogs. While both offer great support for fine navigation, they do not provide support for gross navigation - medium-term strategies including orientating, reaching waypoints, and following a path along a route.

ASSETS '17, October 29-November 1, 2017, Baltimore, MD, USA
© 2017 ACM. ISBN 978-1-4503-4926-0/17/10...$15.00
DOI: https://doi.org/10.1145/3132525.3132556

Figure 1: A user is using a leashed quadcopter to navigate in unknown indoor environments. The user can perceive the directions both by hearing the auditory feedback that the quadcopter naturally emits and by feeling the tactile feedback on the handle.

A number of electronic mobility aids for people with visual impairments are commercially available (see Roentgen et al. for an overview [19]). An even larger number of approaches and systems has been proposed by previous research. Previous research focused on providing navigation information through auditory (e.g. [10, 16, 24]) or tactile feedback (e.g. [2, 8, 9]). Auditory feedback is typically provided through headphones [10] or bone-conduction headphones [24]. Using 3D audio to display waypoints can further improve blind users' navigation performance [4, 13]. Tactile feedback is provided by diverse systems and through various body parts. Common approaches include smart-canes [5, 23], tactile belts [9, 22], wheeled robots on a leash [15], and tactile vests [12, 21].

A novel approach that has recently been proposed is providing navigation information using small lightweight quadcopters [3, 14]. The work is mainly inspired by work on the use of quadcopters as companions for outdoor activities [6, 18, 20] and combining tactile and auditory modalities for navigating visually impaired travelers [11]. Similar to more traditional auditory navigation systems that use 3D audio to provide navigation information, quadcopters can provide

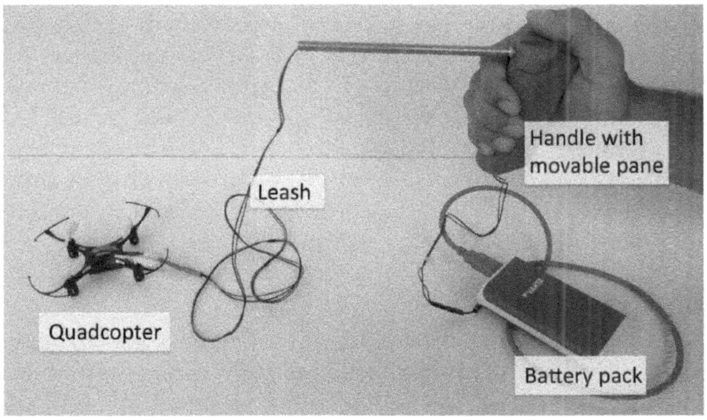

Figure 2: Our leashed quadcopter navigation prototype. The quadcopter is connected to a handle using an electric wire which acts as a leash. The handle has a movable pane with a 3D-printed arrow on top. This arrow can convey a direction as the leash lets the arrow always point into the direction of the quadcopter. Further, the handle is connected to an external USB battery pack, which can be carried by the user.

directional information through their position relative to the user and the sound they naturally emit. This was also used by previous work to guide two blind runners [1] in a Wizard of Oz study. Previous work, however, did not study if quadcopters can provide helpful information to blind users in everyday navigation tasks.

In this paper, we investigate the potential of quadcopters as navigation support for persons with visual impairments (see Figure 1). We extend previous work on quadcopters for visually impaired persons by providing tactile feedback in addition to the auditory feedback provided by the quadcopter's rotors. Through a leash that connects the user and the quadcopter the user can not only hear but also feel the direction of the quadcopter. In a study with 14 visually impaired participants, we compared leashed quadcopter navigation, free-floating quadcopter navigation, and traditional audio navigation. We show that the quadcopter-based approaches enable participants to significantly navigate faster and make fewer navigation errors.

2. DRONENAVIGATOR

We developed two prototypes of a multi-modal feedback system that provides navigation information for visually impaired users. The first prototype is a free-floating quadcopter which uses spatial audio to guide a visually impaired traveler. The second prototype uses a leashed quadcopter to combine advantages of auditory and tactile systems. Previous work typically provides spatial audio by positioning and rendering a virtual 3D sound relative to the user's position (e.g. [4, 13]). The resulting audio signal is conveyed through speakers, headphones, or bone conduction headphones. Instead, of using a virtual sound source for providing directional information, we provide directions through an actual sound source that can be moved in 3D. Therefore, our two prototypes use a quadcopter that can be freely moved in space (see Figure 1).

For both prototypes, we decided to use a small and lightweight quadcopter to ensure safe operation even in crowded environments. Therefore, we use an Eachine H8 Mini quadcopter, which is 13.5×13.5cm wide, 2.8cm high, and weighs 20 grams.

2.1 System: A Free-Floating Quadcopter

Similar to previous work [3], our free-floating prototype is an unmodified quadcopter, which provides auditory information through the sound the quadcopter naturally emits. We use a Wizard of Oz approach to fly the quadcopter at a distance of 1m in front of the participant. The quadcopter is flown at an altitude similar to the participants shoulders above the ground. If there are stairs up or down along the route, the quadcopter will change its height indicating that a change in altitude will follow soon.

2.2 System: A Quadcopter on a Leash

Our second system extends the prototype by Avila et al. [3] and makes it more durable by mounting a leash on the quadcopter. Using a leash has two main benefits. The first benefit is, that the leash is connecting the visually impaired traveler with the quadcopter, which creates a tactile feedback. Considering tactile feedback approaches, previous work relied on using multiple vibrotactors. Directional information can be provided by spatially arranging a discrete number of vibrotactile actuators (e.g. [9, 22, 23]. In contrast, we enable the user to also feel the position of the quadcopter to provide tactile feedback. To increase the tactile experience, we designed a handle that converts the pulling of the quadcopter into an appropriate tactile stimuli for the visually impaired traveler. To achieve that, we extended a handle with a pane, which is rotatable and has a 3D printed arrow on its tip (see Figure 2). Further, the tip of the handle is connected to a small pipe, which converts the direction in which the leash is pulled by the quadcopter into a rotation that is perceivable by the visually impaired traveler.

The second benefit of the leash is that it provides a connection to the quadcopter, which enables us to power it using an external battery. To extend the quadcopter's flight duration, we integrated an additional battery with $10,000mAh$ into the handle. The additional battery extends the flight time from 5-8 minutes to approximately 5 hours. Using an external battery further enables us to remove the original battery from the quadcopter, which compensates for the additional weight of the leash. For the leash, we use a standard insulated electric wire which is 1m long. Similar to the free-floating quadcopter navigation system, the leashed quadcopter also flies at an altitude similar to the participants shoulders and also indicates upcoming stairs using a change in altitude.

3. EVALUATION

For evaluating the two proposed quadcopter guidance approaches, we conducted a study with 14 visually impaired or blind participants. We compared the two approaches to state of the art audio navigation. In the following, we describe the method and the results of the study.

3.1 Design

The experiment follows a repeated measures design with the used guidance approach as the only independent variable with three levels (free-floating quadcopter, leashed quadcopter, and audio navigation). As dependent variables, we measure the Task Completion Time (TCT), the number of errors, and the Raw NASA Taskload Index (RTLX) [7]. To minimize learning effects we used 3 equally long and equally difficult routes as navigation task. We counterbalanced the order of the guidance approaches and counterbalanced the used routes according to the Balanced Latin Square.

3.2 Apparatus and Navigation Routes

The study compares the two quadcopter-based systems, to an audio navigation baseline. We designed the audio navigation according to state-of-the-art navigation systems and enhanced them with feedback about the current state. This results in three navigation instructions: *"continue straight"*, *"turn left"*, and *"turn right"*. The instructions to make a turn were presented 2 meters before the turn had to be made. Further, the *"continue straight"* instruction was presented every 5 meters. To ensure a perfect triggering of the auditory instructions according to the participants position, all instructions were triggered manually by a Wizard of Oz. Inspired by related work [25], we chose to present the auditory navigation instructions on bone conduction headphones in order to be able to additionally perceive the sound from the environment. For our study, we were using the Aftershokz Sportz M3[1] bone conduction headphones, which are connected via Bluetooth to a smartphone. The Wizard of Oz was carrying the smartphone and triggering the audio instructions using the Custom Soundboard[2] app.

We chose to conduct our experiment in an indoor navigation context. Therefore, we designed three routes that were equally long and equally difficult. The length was approximately 60m for each route. All routes contained a staircase with the same number of steps on the staircase and entering a door with the width of 95cm. Further, we made sure that all routes contained a reverberating and dull sounding environment. We made sure that there were no passersby when conducting the study. Therefore, the routes can be seen as a controlled study environment. Other type of routes might provide additional insights.

3.3 Procedure

After welcoming the participant and explaining the purpose of the study, we informed the participant about the data, which we collect during the study, and asked for a written consent. Then, we collected the demographics of the participants and gave a general introduction about the three navigation systems that we are using in the study. Due to counterbalancing, the order of the conditions was different across the participants. Before starting the first condition, we gave the participant some time to get familiar with the navigation system. Once the participant felt familiar, we started the experiment at a defined starting point of the current route. We instructed the participant to start following the instructions that are provided by the navigation system. However, we told them to additionally use their white cane. After the experimenter started the study, the TCT and the number of navigation errors were measured. The TCT is measured from the starting point to the end point of the route. As a navigation error, we counted when the participant was walking three or more steps with more than a 45° offset away from the target position. The errors were independently counted by two experimenters, who were walking behind the participant in a distance of 1m in all three conditions. For all conditions, the navigation instructions were triggered by one of the two experimenters, who was acting as a Wizard of Oz. After reaching the end position of the route, we asked the participant to fill an RTLX questionnaire. We repeated this procedure for the remaining two conditions. After all conditions, we were asking the participants for their opinion about the presented navigation systems through a semi structured interview.

3.4 Participants

We invited 14 visually impaired participants for our user study. Thirteen of the participants were completely blind and one participant had a remaining vision of 5%. All of the participants were white cane users. The participants were aged from 21 to 74 years (M = 51.69 years, SD = 15.09 years). None of the participants was familiar with the quadcopter guidance systems, nor were they familiar with the routes that we used in our study. We recruited the participants using the first author's personal contacts to a social group for visually impaired and blind persons. As participating in our user study was on a voluntary basis, we did not compensate the participants for taking part in our study. The runtime of the study was approximately 45 minutes.

3.5 Results

We statistically compared the TCT, number of navigation errors, and the RTLX score using a one-way repeated measures ANOVA. Mauchly's test showed that the sphericity assumption was violated for the number of navigation errors ($\chi^2(2)$=10.208, p=.006). Therefore, we used the Greenhouse-Geisser correction to adjust the degrees of freedom (ϵ=.636 for the number of navigation errors). Further, we were using a Bonferroni correction for all post-hoc tests.

First, we analyzed the TCT, i.e. the time that the visually impaired travelers took to complete the routes (see Figure 3a). The participants were fastest using the free-floating quadcopter navigation (M = 82.29 sec, SD = 18.97 sec), followed by the leashed quadcopter (M = 94.07 sec, SD = 20.58 sec), and the audio navigation (M = 98.57 sec, SD = 16.32 sec). A one-way repeated measures ANOVA revealed a significant difference between the approaches, $F(2, 26) = 4.41$, $p = .022$. The post-hoc tests revealed a significant difference between the free-floating quadcopter and the audio navigation ($p < 0.05$). The effect size estimate shows a large effect ($\eta^2 = .254$).

When analyzing the number of navigation errors that the participants made during the study (see Figure 3b), the audio navigation led to the highest number of navigation errors (M = .86 errors, SD = 1.03 errors), followed by the free-floating quadcopter and the leashed quadcopter, which both had exactly the same average number of navigation errors (M = .14 errors, SD = .36 errors). A one-way repeated measures ANOVA revealed a significant difference between the approaches, $F(1.272, 16.53) = 6.25$, $p = .021$. The post-hoc tests revealed a significant difference between the audio navigation vs. the free floating quadcopter and the audio navigation vs. the leashed quadcopter (all $p < 0.05$). The effect size estimate shows a large effect ($\eta^2 = .325$).

Finally, considering the perceived workload that the participants experienced using the different navigation systems measured using the RTLX score (see Figure 3c), the participants rated the audio navigation as inducing the least

[1] http://aftershokz.com/products/sportz-m3
[2] https://play.google.com/store/apps/details?id=ix.com.android.CustomSoundboard&hl=en

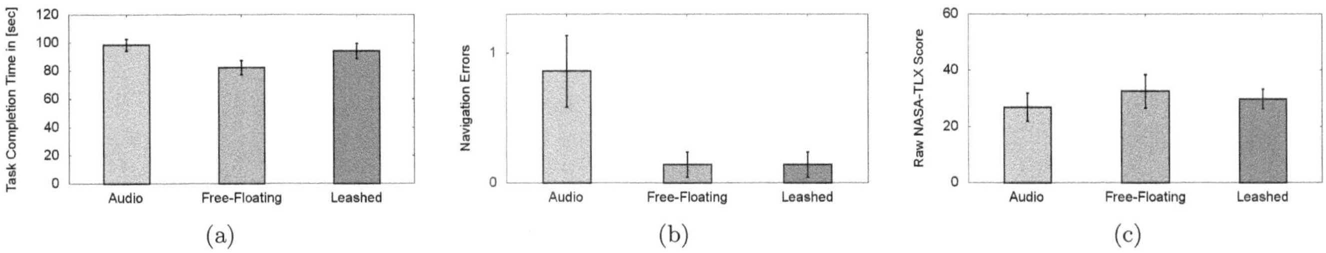

Figure 3: The results of the user study. (a) The Task Completion Time in seconds that was needed for each navigation method. (b) The average amount of navigation errors. (c) The perceived cognitive workload measured using the RTLX score. All error bars depict the standard error.

workload ($M = 26.93$, $SD = 18.83$), followed by the leashed quadcopter navigation ($M = 29.79$, $SD = 13.34$), and the free-floating quadcopter navigation ($M = 32.5$, $SD = 22.01$). A one-way repeated measures ANOVA could not reveal a significant difference between the conditions ($p > 0.05$).

In the semi-structured interview, we asked the participants which navigation system they considered being the best one in the study. 8 participants preferred the auditory navigation. This was followed by 4 participants who preferred the free-floating quadcopter navigation and 2 participants preferring the leashed quadcopter.

Participants' preferences for the auditory navigation was also visible in the answers to the questions of the semi-structured interview. However, the participants were suggesting to improve the auditory navigation as they found it was too *"coarse when giving the directions"* (P8) and therefore is *"inaccurate"* (P1, P3, P4, P8, P14). Also they would have liked to *"receive more accurate directions - e.g. in three meters turn to two o'clock"*. Compared to the two quadcopter conditions, participants mentioned that *"the auditory navigation condition is not continuous"* as feedback was not always present like in the quadcopter conditions.

Considering the free-floating quadcopter, the participants liked that they did not have to carry a device with them at all times. P11 stated that *"the free-floating quadcopter is great because I can focus completely on my white cane"*. However, other participants were skeptical because *"[they are] not sure if the free-floating quadcopter navigation will work in noisy environments"*. Two participants stated that on the one hand, they could *"precisely tell the position of the quadcopter but [are] having a hard time estimating the distance to the quadcopter"*. Some participants did not like the quadcopter because they found that *"the sound of the rotors is annoying after some time"* (P2, P5, P7, P12, P14) and would like to use a different frequency of sound when using a continuous auditory feedback.

When being asked about the leashed quadcopter, the participants were generally positive although only two participants considered it the best navigation system. Two participants liked that *"[they] can feel the distance to the quadcopter using the leash"* (P1, P11) and P4 especially liked the tactile component *"because this would also work in loud environments"*. Other participants liked how the handle was designed because they stated that *"it is nice to have an arrow in the hand that shows [them] the way every time"* (P1, P4, P6, P8). On the other hand, participants disliked that *"[they] had to carry an additional thing [referring to the handle] during the navigation while using the cane"* (P7, P12) as this occupies both of their hands.

4. DISCUSSION AND CONCLUSION

In this paper, we investigated using small light-weight quadcopters as a navigation device for visually impaired travelers. We extended previous work [3], which proposed using free-floating quadcopters as navigation systems, by presenting a quadcopter on a leash. Our leashed prototype extends the auditory navigation instructions that are emitted by the quadcopter with a tactile navigation through creating a tactile sensation on the quadcopter's handle. Through a user study with 14 visually impaired participants, we compared the free-floating quadcopter navigation system and our leashed quadcopter navigation system to a state-of-the-art audio navigation system.

The results reveal that participants using a free-floating quadcopter as a navigation system were significantly faster compared to the auditory baseline navigation system. Considering the number of navigation errors the participants made during the study, we found that the state-of-the-art audio navigation leads to significantly more navigation errors compared to both quadcopter navigation systems. The qualitative feedback revealed that the participants found the quadcopter navigation more accurate as it was giving a continuous feedback in the direction of travel. Main limitation of both quadcopter-based approaches is emitted sound which can be annoying and raises concerns considering the social acceptability of both quadcopter conditions.

One important direction for future work is the potentially annoying sound and the social acceptability when using a small quadcopter as a navigation device for visually impaired travelers. We envision a number of technical directions to potentially improve both aspects. Using quadcopters that produce less sound or integrating active noise control into the system could improve the social acceptability and the probability to be annoying. Unfortunately, a lower volume could make it harder to localize the quadcopter. Thus, there is a need to find a suitable sound design for quadcopter-based navigation systems. We are interested in exploring the use additional auditory feedback combined with active noise reduction. This would allow full control over the sound generated by the quadcopter that could be targeted only in the direction of the user.

Another direction we are interested in is how the acceptance of small quadcopters changes when the audience knows that it is an accessibility device. We expect similar effects as for guide dogs. While dogs are not necessarily socially acceptable in many situations, guide dogs are typically considered acceptable. Also, as safety of both visually impaired user and passersby are our priority, we want to work of a solution, where the quadcopter is protected with a cage.

5. ACKNOWLEDGEMENTS

This work is funded by the DAAD – SENACYT Cooperation program and the German Research Foundation within the SimTech Cluster of Excellence (EXC 310/2).

6. REFERENCES

[1] M. Al Zayer, S. Tregillus, J. Bhandari, D. Feil-Seifer, and E. Folmer. Exploring the use of a drone to guide blind runners. In *Proceedings of the 18th International ACM SIGACCESS Conference on Computers and Accessibility*, pages 263–264. ACM, 2016.

[2] T. Amemiya and H. Sugiyama. Haptic handheld wayfinder with pseudo-attraction force for pedestrians with visual impairments. In *Proceedings of the 11th International ACM SIGACCESS Conference on Computers and Accessibility*, Assets '09, pages 107–114, New York, NY, USA, 2009. ACM.

[3] M. Avila, M. Funk, and N. Henze. Dronenavigator: Using drones for navigating visually impaired persons. In *Proceedings of the 17th International ACM SIGACCESS Conference on Computers & Accessibility*, pages 327–328. ACM, 2015.

[4] J. R. Blum, M. Bouchard, and J. R. Cooperstock. What's around me? spatialized audio augmented reality for blind users with a smartphone. In *Mobile and Ubiquitous Systems: Computing, Networking, and Services*, pages 49–62. Springer, 2012.

[5] J. Borenstein and L. Ulrich. The guidecane-a computerized travel aid for the active guidance of blind pedestrians. In *Robotics and Automation, 1997. Proceedings., 1997 IEEE International Conference on*, volume 2, pages 1283–1288. IEEE, 1997.

[6] E. Graether and F. Mueller. Joggobot: a flying robot as jogging companion. In *CHI'12 Extended Abstracts on Human Factors in Computing Systems*, pages 1063–1066. ACM, 2012.

[7] S. G. Hart. Nasa-task load index (nasa-tlx); 20 years later. In *Proceedings of the human factors and ergonomics society annual meeting*, volume 50, pages 904–908. Sage Publications, 2006.

[8] N. Henze, W. Heuten, and S. Boll. Non-intrusive somatosensory navigation support for blind pedestrians. *Proc. Eurohaptics*, 2006.

[9] W. Heuten, N. Henze, S. Boll, and M. Pielot. Tactile wayfinder: A non-visual support system for wayfinding. In *Proceedings of the 5th Nordic Conference on Human-computer Interaction: Building Bridges*, NordiCHI '08, pages 172–181, New York, NY, USA, 2008. ACM.

[10] S. Holland, R. D. Morse, and H. Gedenryd. Audiogps: Spatial audio navigation with a minimal attention interface. *Personal and Ubiquitous Computing*, 6(4):253–259, 2002.

[11] R. D. Jacobson. Navigating maps with little or no sight: An audio-tactile approach. In *Proceedings of the workshop on Content Visualization and Intermedia Representations (CVIR)*, 1998.

[12] L. A. Jones, M. Nakamura, and B. Lockyer. Development of a tactile vest. In *Haptic Interfaces for Virtual Environment and Teleoperator Systems, 2004. HAPTICS '04. Proceedings. 12th International Symposium on*, pages 82–89, March 2004.

[13] B. F. Katz, S. Kammoun, G. Parseihian, O. Gutierrez, A. Brilhault, M. Auvray, P. Truillet, M. Denis, S. Thorpe, and C. Jouffrais. Navig: augmented reality guidance system for the visually impaired. *Virtual Reality*, 16(4):253–269, 2012.

[14] B. Kim, H. Y. Kim, and J. Kim. Getting home safely with drone. In *Proceedings of the 2016 ACM International Joint Conference on Pervasive and Ubiquitous Computing: Adjunct*, pages 117–120. ACM, 2016.

[15] V. Kulyukin, C. Gharpure, J. Nicholson, and G. Osborne. Robot-assisted wayfinding for the visually impaired in structured indoor environments. *Autonomous Robots*, 21(1):29–41, 2006.

[16] J. M. Loomis, R. G. Golledge, and R. L. Klatzky. Navigation system for the blind: Auditory display modes and guidance. *Presence: Teleoperators and Virtual Environments*, 7(2):193–203, 1998.

[17] S. P. Mariotti. Global data on visual impairments 2010. *World Health Organization*, 20, 2012.

[18] S. Mayer, P. Knierim, P. W. Wozniak, and M. Funk. How drones can support backcountry activities. In *Proceedings of the 2017 natureCHI workshop, in conjunction with ACM mobileHCI'17*, volume 2 of *natureCHI'17*, page 6, 2017.

[19] U. R. Roentgen, G. J. Gelderblom, M. Soede, and L. P. de Witte. Inventory of electronic mobility aids for persons with visual impairments: A literature review. *Journal of Visual Impairment & Blindness*, 102(11):702, 2008.

[20] A. Romanowski, S. Mayer, L. Lischke, K. Grudzień, T. Jaworski, I. Perenc, P. Kucharski, M. Obaid, T. Kosizski, and P. W. Wozniak. Towards supporting remote cheering during running races with drone technology. In *Proceedings of the 2017 CHI Conference Extended Abstracts on Human Factors in Computing Systems*, pages 2867–2874. ACM, 2017.

[21] H. Z. Tan, R. Gray, J. J. Young, and R. Traylor. A haptic back display for attentional and directional cueing. *The Electronic Journal of Haptics Research*, 3(1), 2003.

[22] K. Tsukada and M. Yasumura. *ActiveBelt: Belt-Type Wearable Tactile Display for Directional Navigation*, pages 384–399. Springer Berlin Heidelberg, Berlin, Heidelberg, 2004.

[23] Y. Wang and K. J. Kuchenbecker. Halo: Haptic alerts for low-hanging obstacles in white cane navigation. In *2012 IEEE Haptics Symposium (HAPTICS)*, pages 527–532, March 2012.

[24] J. Wilson, B. N. Walker, J. Lindsay, C. Cambias, and F. Dellaert. Swan: System for wearable audio navigation. In *2007 11th IEEE International Symposium on Wearable Computers*, pages 91–98, Oct 2007.

[25] J. Wilson, B. N. Walker, J. Lindsay, C. Cambias, and F. Dellaert. Swan: System for wearable audio navigation. In *Wearable Computers, 2007 11th IEEE International Symposium on*, pages 91–98. IEEE, 2007.

A Pilot Deployment of an Online Tool for Large-Scale Virtual Auditing of Urban Accessibility

Manaswi Saha[1,2], Kotaro Hara[1,3], Soheil Behnezhad[1], Anthony Li[1],
Michael Saugstad[1], Hanuma Maddali[1], Sage Chen[4], Jon E. Froehlich[1,2]
[1]University of Maryland; [2]University of Washington; [3]Carnegie Mellon University; [4]University of Michigan,
{manaswi, soheil, saugstad, hmaddali, antli, jonf}@umd.edu; kotaroh@cmu.edu; sagec@umich.edu

(a) Example mission screen (b) Virtually walk and explore city streets guided by mission map (c) Find and label accessibility features and problems

Figure 1. *Project Sidewalk* uses basic game design principles to engage online volunteers in virtually auditing urban accessibility in Google Street View.

ABSTRACT
We present *Project Sidewalk*, a new online tool that allows anyone—from motivated citizens to government workers—to remotely label accessibility problems by virtually walking through city streets. Basic game design principles such as interactive onboarding, mission-based tasks, and stats dashboards are used to train, engage, and sustain users. We describe the current Project Sidewalk system, present results of a pilot public deployment with 581 users, and discuss open questions and future work.

Keywords
Urban accessibility; crowdsourcing; mobility impaired users; GIS

1. INTRODUCTION
Geographic Information Systems (GIS) such as Google Maps, Waze, and Yelp have transformed the way people travel and access information about the physical world. While these systems contain terabytes of data about road networks and points of interest (POIs), their information about *physical accessibility* is commensurately poor. GIS websites such as Axsmap.com, Wheelmap.org, and AccessTogether.org aim to address this problem by collecting location-based accessibility information provided by volunteers (*i.e.*, crowdsourcing). While these efforts are important and commendable, their value propositions are intrinsically tied to the amount and quality of provided data. In a survey, Ding *et al.* [3] found that most accessibility-oriented GIS sites suffer from serious data sparseness issues (*e.g.*, only 1.6% of the POIs in Wheelmap had data entered on accessibility). One key problem is that these sites rely on local populations with physical experience of a place, which dramatically limits who can supply data.

In contrast, we are exploring a different approach embodied in a new interactive tool called *Project Sidewalk*, which enables volunteers to contribute physical-world accessibility information by *virtually* visiting a location in Google Street View (Figure 1). Rather than pulling solely from a local population, our potential pool of users scales to anyone with an Internet connection and a web browser. Project Sidewalk extends previous work in virtual auditing tools, including *CANVAS* [1], *Spotlight* [2], *Bus Stop CSI* [5], and *Tohme* [7], all which demonstrate that tool-mediated virtual audits of urban infrastructure have high concordance with traditional physical audits. However, these tools were not publicly deployed, were focused on small spatial regions, and relied on specialized user populations (*e.g.*, public health researchers [1, 2]) or paid crowdworkers [5, 7]. As Project Sidewalk is designed to engage and train non-expert volunteers in a complex task—that is, accessibility audits—our work is also strongly linked to and additionally informed by work in citizen science [4], which similarly seeks to engage non-experts in collecting and processing data through novel interactive tools (*e.g.*, Zooniverse.org).

As initial work, our research questions are exploratory: how can we engage, train, and sustain volunteer users in virtual accessibility audits? What types of users participate (*e.g.*, GIS enthusiasts, government workers, concerned citizens, or perhaps those directly impacted by accessibility problems)? How do volunteers differ in labeling behavior and quality compared to experts? Is it feasible to rely purely on volunteers or must data be supplemented by paid crowd workers? To begin addressing these questions, we report on an initial pilot deployment of Project Sidewalk in Washington DC. We first describe the Project Sidewalk system before providing a brief, high-level analysis of the data we have collected thus far. We close with a discussion of future work plans.

2. PROJECT SIDEWALK
Project Sidewalk culminates five years of research in virtual auditing interfaces for accessibility (see [6] for a history). We build on the labeling interfaces in [5, 7] but extend our system to: (i) interactively train volunteers about the tool and urban accessibility; (ii) incorporate basic game design principles such as missions and progress tracking to improve user engagement; and (iii) allow open-world exploring (similar to first-person video games) to increase street and sidewalk coverage. Such changes have required a substantial engineering effort: the Project Sidewalk open-source github repository has 2,155 commits from 20 team members and 118,207 lines of developed code in Scala, Javascript, and Python.

To use Project Sidewalk, visit http://projectsidewalk.io on a laptop or desktop (touchscreens are not currently supported). Upon clicking the '*Start Mapping*' button, new users are greeted by a multi-stage interactive tutorial to learn about the user interface and

ASSETS '17, October 29-November 1, 2017, Baltimore, MD, USA

ACM ISBN 978-1-4503-4926-0/17/10.
https://doi.org/10.1145/3132525.3134775

basic accessibility concepts. Once the tutorial is complete, users are auto-assigned a neighborhood in DC and are given their first mission (Figure 1a). Missions route users through specific streets in a neighborhood; as the user walks virtually along this path, they find and label street and sidewalk accessibility features (curb ramps) and problems (sidewalk obstacles, missing curb ramps, no sidewalks, *etc.*). After identifying a problem, the user is asked to provide a severity rating on a scale from '1' to '5' where '5' represents an impassable barrier for someone in a manual wheelchair. Once a mission is complete, users are greeted by a 'mission complete' screen along with a 'cheering' sound effect. Users are then assigned a new mission and the cycle continues. Users can choose to contribute anonymously or to register and login. Registered users can check their contribution activity on an analytics dashboard. Currently, however, there is no way to view or compare other users' contributions.

3. PILOT DEPLOYMENT

We launched a pilot deployment in September 2016, which was advertised through word-of-mouth and social media. Thus far, 581 users have contributed 71,873 accessibility labels across 504 miles of DC streets (nearly 50% of all streets in the city)—see Figure 2. On average, our users complete 3.6 missions (*SD*=13.8), which accounts for an average of 2.9 miles audited/user (*Med*=1.0; *SD*=8.8). As mission lengths vary, to examine auditing time, we calculated the average time to complete 1,000ft (~305 meters): 16.9 mins (*SD*=11.2). Of the 581 users, 315 (54.2%) chose to register and login. These registered users contribute a majority of labels: 58,887 *vs.* 12,986 for anonymous. In terms of the labels themselves, *curb ramps* comprise 64.3% of our data, followed by *no sidewalks* (17%), *missing curb ramps* (7.2%), *obstacles in path* (5.6%), and *surface problems* (4.9%)—see Table 1. These labeling statistics are raw counts and contain redundancies as users can label a problem multiple times from different viewpoints. Future post-processing is necessary to aggregate redundant labels into individual issues.

Labels	Total	Anon. Only	Avg. Severity (SD)	Labels/mile
Curb Ramp	46,213 (64.3%)	9,182	1.2 (0.5)	91.6
No Sidewalk	12,230 (17.0%)	1,293	N/A	24.3
Missing Curb Ramp	5,191 (7.2%)	1,285	3.8 (1.1)	10.3
Obstacle in Path	4,044 (5.6%)	673	3.1 (1.3)	8.0
Surface Problem	3,552 (4.9%)	465	2.3 (1.2)	7.0
Other	643 (0.9%)	16.1%	N/A	4.7
Total	71,873	12,986		1.3

Table 1. A breakdown of data collected in the pilot deployment. Label severity is a scale from '1' to '5' where '5' is worst.

We have also begun analyzing qualitative comments from email, social media, and our tool's 'feedback' form. Generally, responses have been positive: multiple city DOTs have inquired about deploying in their cities, and ADA specialists have provided helpful suggestions. Reported problems include not always understanding *where* to apply labels (*e.g., "should driveways be labeled as curb ramps?"*), ambiguity between label types (*e.g.,* some problems could legitimately be labeled both an 'obstacle in path' and a 'surface problem'), and technical issues (*e.g.,* 24% of our site visitors used unsupported browsers).

4. DISCUSSION AND CONCLUSION

While our pilot deployment demonstrates the potential of Project Sidewalk to train and use non-expert volunteers to virtually audit urban infrastructure for accessibility, there is much work to be done. We have three major goals: (i) to develop a robust, reusable platform for crowdsourcing urban accessibility data that can be deployed in any city in the world that has Google Street View; (ii)

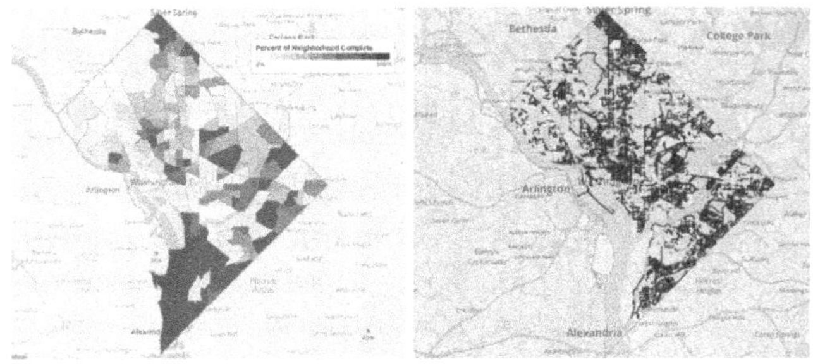

Figure 2. (a) A choropleth of Washington DC showing neighborhood completion rates (*Avg completion rate*=54.7%; *SD*=29.7%) and (b) a map showing the 504 miles of audited DC streets (in black).

to increase scalability using machine learning (extending [7]); (iii) to support the development of novel accessibility-aware GIS applications that leverage Project Sidewalk's unprecedented data (http://projectsidewalk.io/api).

Towards (i), Ding *et al.*'s [3] survey of GIS accessibility sites focused on data completeness rather than quality—both are important. While we have not yet analyzed the accuracy of our labels, our prior work [6, 7] suggests 80-90% correctness. We are currently designing verification interfaces to help analyze and improve labeling accuracy. Once complete, we plan to launch a full deployment in Washington DC followed by 3-5 more U.S. cities, which will allow us to compare accessibility characteristics across regions. Towards (iii), we have begun building a suite of accessibility-aware GIS tools that leverage Project Sidewalk data such as *AccessScore*, which provides an at-a-glance view of neighborhood accessibility, *AccessRoute* that personalizes route suggestions based on a user's mobility level, and *AccessModel* that explores accessibility correlates with socio-economic, census tract, and other location-specific data. Finally, we are exploring hybrid volunteer + paid worker approaches. We estimate that auditing a city as large as DC with Project Sidewalk on Mechanical Turk at $7.25/hr (US minimum wage) would cost around $14,000 (including the 20% Amazon commission). In comparison, a traditional audit costs orders of magnitude more.

5. REFERENCES

[1] Bader, M.D.M., Mooney, *et al.* 2015. Development and deployment of the Computer Assisted Neighborhood Visual Assessment System (CANVAS) to measure health-related neighborhood conditions. *Health & Place.* 31, (Jan. 2015), 163–172.

[2] Bethlehem, J.R., Mackenbach, J.D., *et al.* 2014. The SPOTLIGHT virtual audit tool: a valid and reliable tool to assess obesogenic characteristics of the built environment. *International Journal of Health Geographics.* 13, 1 (Dec. 2014), 52.

[3] Ding, C., Wald, M. and Wills, G. 2014. A Survey of Open Accessibility Data. *Proc. of W4A* (NY, USA, 2014), 37:1--37:4.

[4] Haklay, M. 2013. Citizen Science and Volunteered Geographic Information: Overview and Typology of Participation. *Crowdsourcing Geographic Knowledge: VGI in Theory & Practice.* D. Sui, S. Elwood, & M. Goodchild, eds. Springer. 105–122.

[5] Hara, K., Azenkot, S., Campbell, M., *et al.* 2015. Improving Public Transit Accessibility for Blind Riders by Crowdsourcing Bus Stop Landmark Locations with Google Street View: An Extended Analysis. *ACM Trans. Access. Comput.* 6, 2 (Mar. 2015), 5:1--5:23.

[6] Hara, K. & Froehlich, J. 2015. Characterizing & visualizing physical world accessibility at scale using crowdsourcing, computer vision, & machine learning. *ACM SIGACCESS Newsletter.* 113, 13–21.

[7] Hara, K., Sun, J., Jacobs, D. & Froehlich, J. 2014. Tohme: Detecting Curb Ramps in Google Street View Using Crowdsourcing, Computer Vision, and Machine Learning. *Proc of UIST'14,* 189-204.

ActVirtual: Making Public Activism Accessible

Disha Bora, Hanlin Li, Sagar Salvi, Erin Brady
Indiana University-Purdue University Indianapolis
Indianapolis, IN 46202
{dishbora, lihanl, salvis, brady}@iupui.edu

ABSTRACT
Technology-mediated public activism has grown popular in recent years with the high uptake of social media. Facebook and Twitter have become venues for activists to participate in online activism, or organize offline activism events. However, due to accessibility barriers in physical environments and accessibility issues in social media, people with disabilities continue to face challenges when they engage with such social movements. We interviewed 22 disabled activists about how they used technology to mediate civic engagement and barriers they faced. We present preliminary findings from these interviews and describe a potential solution named ActVirtual, a mobile platform for accessible activism. Our future work will include implementing and testing ActVirtual with users to make online and offline activism more accessible.

Keywords
Accessible activism, public protests, accessible technology.

1. INTRODUCTION
Accessibility is an imperative in social spaces (*e.g.*, public transport, malls, and civic engagement activities like elections) [2]. Technological advancements have helped to make these everyday spaces accessible for people with disabilities to some extent, but accessibility in civic activities like rallies and protests has mostly been overlooked because of their transient nature. In-person rallies can raise many environmental, physical, and social constraints for people with disabilities. Actions like protesting with a crowd, marching from one point to another, and handling noise can be challenging for people who need mobility assistance, have chronic illness or fatigue, or any other range of disabilities.

As an alternative, people with disabilities have started to use a variety of online platforms to educate and advocate about disability rights [2] and accessibility issues [3]. Existing forms of online activism include signing e-petitions, joining online advocacy groups, posting about social causes and even organizing entire movements [4]. Accessibility in public activism not only needs to consider the ongoing research on physical spaces [1] to address environmental and physical barriers [6], but also connect this to existing online forms of activism for accessibility.

In this poster, we identify and articulate design requirements from 22 interviews conducted with disabled activists. After identifying key findings, we present our ongoing design solution and development of ActVirtual, a mobile application that aims to make public activism more accessible.

2. ACCESSIBILITY IN ACTIVISM
Our research was inspired by a virtual 'march' carried out by an online group of disabled activists protesting for social rights in January 2017 [5]. The Disability March was an online contingent of the 2017 Women's March on Washington, DC. The Disability March included a website[1] created by some 20 volunteers inviting people with disabilities to post personal stories as a form of representation. The website further expanded to several social media channels including Facebook, Twitter, and Instagram.

2.1 Methods
We recruited 22 activists with disabilities for semi-structured phone interviews which lasted around average of 45 minutes. Sixteen of these 22 respondents had participated in the Disability March, and the majority (18) were female owing to the nature of this march. The participants had disabilities like visual and mobility impairments, chronic illnesses, and mental illnesses, including a wide range of both physical and invisible disabilities.

In our interviews, participants identified the barriers faced while taking part in offline and online forms of activism. We then asked them about the role technology had played in supporting their activism. Three researchers interviewed, transcribed, and analyzed the key findings in the initial phase of the study and then brainstormed design solutions. The identified design requirements were sketched as low-fidelity design solutions by another researcher and then iterated in brainstorming sessions.

2.2 Key Findings
Our findings identified respondents' roles as both participants and organizers of activism, roles which were not mutually exclusive. All our interviewees shared their experiences with participating in activism online (*e.g.*, social media) and in-person (*e.g.*, physically attending protests). Participants had advocated for many causes, and many felt that their disability, which had first led them to disability advocacy, was an impetus to become more involved in a wider range of political and activist causes.

The respondents appreciated the ways they could contribute to the protest by uploading pictures, sharing posts, and descriptions online. One respondent who couldn't attend the march in-person due to her mobility issues mentioned how her friend who went live streamed a video of the march to her in her home, which made her feel involved. Due to the availability of social media and their online presence, activists found ways to communicate and organize the alternative Disability March event.

Our interviews highlighted physical and technological accessibility issues. Respondents listed barriers like transportation to the venue, no mobility aids, dealing with crowded spaces, and finding information about events as major concerns.

> *"If it's snowing then I won't be able to go. So, transportation issues. I have only used motorized scooter in last few years, so I need accessible transportation, [I] just can't get in anybody's car" – P16*

Participants also reported experiencing exhaustion after marches.

ASSETS '17, October 29-November 1, 2017, Baltimore, MD, USA

ACM ISBN 978-1-4503-4926-0/17/10.
https://doi.org/10.1145/3132525.3134815

[1] www.disabilitymarch.com

For online technological barriers, the respondents encountered web accessibility problems including untagged images, dizziness from auto playing videos, and scrolling feeds.

> *"Facebook is not accessible….People take screenshot and post it. That is not working for a screen reader" – P11*

People who could not go to a march in-person mentioned using *proxies,* a physical representation of them at the offline marches. Our respondents who were unable to leave home (*e.g.*, due to mobility issues) appreciated the idea of a proxy person or an object taking part in the march with their name. This concept made them feel more involved in the march while they participated virtually through online activism.

> *"I have heard, my friend in Disability March carried a list of such people in her shoe, I thought that was cool" – P17*

Four of our respondents had experiences with organizing marches and making them accessible. From our interviews, we understood that online technologies like email, Facebook groups, and Google Docs played a major role in facilitating the organizer's efforts to plan and coordinate the march. However, organizers identified challenges like coordinating the online and offline events, assigning roles, and accommodating a variety of disabilities.

Some of the suggestions proposed by respondents included improving information access about events and transportation methods; finding people to accompany them to the events; and participating in both online and offline activism simultaneously.

3. DESIGN CONSIDERATIONS

Building upon our interview findings, we are designing a mobile application called ActVirtual. The target users for this mobile application are activists and organizers with disabilities.

3.1 For Activists

The design incorporates and provides accessible solutions to activists who want to participate in offline or online activism. For offline, ActVirtual facilitates collaboration between activists, including arranging transportation or carpooling, connecting with nearby activists for physically marching, or setting up emergency contacts, to support the activists on the day of in-person marches.

The online barriers involved dealing with web accessibility failures with help of assistive technologies (for example, alternate text description for images), and designing a focused solution without involving the complexity of social media platforms. We concluded from our interviews that some members of the disability community preferred an online or virtual component for every offline march. ActVirtual has options for the online participants to choose ways by which they can participate in the march, either by posting images and protest messages or choosing an in-person proxy marcher to represent them in the march.

3.2 For Organizers

In ActVirtual, users can register as an organizer, then collaborate, plan, and update the march details easily. The respondents had reported that many times, there is not enough information provided in the first place about accessibility of the event. Our design solution combines simple and effective presentation of information, includes online chat and one click help options for easy mediation of the protest between the volunteers and organizers. Organizers can directly manage the roles assigned and moderate the protest messages, even assign special disability assistance service to volunteers through general chat screens. Such use of assistive online technology will serve the disability community to be more inclusive in the society at large.

Figure 1. ActVirtual sample designs. Activist design page *(left)*, Organizer design page *(right)*.

4. FUTURE WORK

The interview findings and brainstorming sessions gave us a lot of insights on how technology mediated activism can help people with disabilities take part in future protests and rallies. Our findings show that there is a lot of scope to improve the online community of activists for people with disabilities. The ActVirtual mobile application will be designed and developed to help bring public activism closer to home for people with disabilities while giving them accessible options to participate in online, offline, or both forms of activism. Future work involves developing a fully functional accessible application and testing it with people with disabilities for improving further. We aim to fundamentally make social events more accessible in nature.

5. REFERENCES

[1] Hara, K. et al. 2015. Improving Public Transit Accessibility for Blind Riders by Crowdsourcing Bus Stop Landmark Locations with Google Street View: An Extended Analysis. *ACM Transactions on Accessible Computing (TACCESS)*. 6, 2 (2015), 5.

[2] Harris, S. et al. 2012. Civic Engagement and People with Disabilities: The Role of Advocacy and Technology. Journal of Community Engagement and Scholarship; Tuscaloosa 5, 1: 70–83.

[3] Li, H. and Brady, E. 2016. #accessibilityFail: Categorizing Shared Photographs of Physical Accessibility Problems. *Proceedings of the 18th International ACM SIGACCESS Conference on Computers and Accessibility* (New York, NY, USA, 2016), 277–278.

[4] Mercea, D. 2013. Probing the Implications of Facebook Use for the Organizational Form of Social Movement Organizations. *Information, Communication & Society*. 16, 8 (Oct. 2013), 1306–1327.

[5] Virtual march helps people with disabilities join the Women's March on Washington: *http://mashable.com/2017/01/18/disability-march-womens-march-on-washington/*. Accessed: 2017-04-25.

[6] Wang, Z. et al. 2009. Instant Tactile-audio Map: Enabling Access to Digital Maps for People with Visual Impairment. *Proceedings of the 11th International ACM SIGACCESS Conference on Computers and Accessibility* (New York, NY, USA, 2009), 43–50.

An Exploratory Case Study to Support Young Children with Spinal Muscular Atrophy (SMA)

Sheng Miao, Ziying Tang, Jinjuan Heidi Feng
Computer and Information Sciences Department
Towson University
Towson, MD21252, USA
{smiao1, ztang, jfeng@towson.edu}

Amanda Jozkowski, Molly Lichtenwalner
Department of Occupational Therapy
and Occupational Sciences
Towson University
Towson, MD21252, USA
{ajozkowski, mlicht4@towson.edu}

ABSTRACT
In this paper, we describe a preliminary case study that examines the challenges faced by very young children with Type I Spinal Muscular Atrophy (SMA) and how technology may help these children live a more independent life. Several input solutions were examined to support interaction between a young patient and computer-based systems. We started working with the patient when he was two and a half years old. The challenges observed and lessons learned regarding both working with very young children with severe disabilities and the use of specific technical solutions are discussed.

CCS Concepts
• Human-centered computing -> Accessibility ->Empirical studies in accessibility •Accessibility technology

Keywords
Young children, Spinal Muscular Atrophy (SMA); Sensor

1. INTRODUCTION
Spinal Muscular Atrophy (SMA) is an autosomal recessive neurodegenerative disease characterized by degeneration of spinal cord motor neurons, atrophy of skeletal muscles, and generalized weakness [1]. The incidence of SMA is about one in every 6,000 to 10,000 live births with a carrier frequency of one in 50 [2]. Nowadays, SMA affects more than 750,000 patients worldwide and is the number one genetic killer of infants and toddlers [3]. SMA affects an individual's motor neurons in a range of ways depending on the particular type; people with SMA are often unable to walk, many cannot sit up unassisted, and (in the most severe forms) are unable to eat and breathe. Although researchers have identified the gene that causes SMA, and potential parents can be screened to find out if they are a carrier, there is currently no known treatment or cure [1].

2. CHALLENGES AND OBJECTIVES
Our research team worked together with a very young patient Kevin[1] with Type I SMA and his family since Kevin was two and a half years old. While Kevin is fully intact cognitively, he is unable to function independently in many domains. He uses a tracheostomy tube and ventilator to breathe, and requires assistance to sit and to hold his head up. He wears an exoskeleton and other assistive/mobility devices to help him utilize his minimal movements (due to extreme muscle weakness), and must have 24-hour supervision to monitor his vital signs. Despite these challenges, he and his family, together with a large and dedicated team of physicians and therapists, have made incredible strides toward making his life as "typical" as possible. He enjoys looking at books, listening and dancing to music, watching his pet fish, playing with playdough and puzzles, and going outside to the park and the zoo.

[1] *The participant's name has been changed to protect anonymity*

ASSETS'17, Oct. 29–Nov. 1, 2017, Baltimore, MD, USA.
ACM ISBN 978-1-4503-4926-0/17/10.
DOI: http://dx.doi.org/10.1145/3132525.3134772

One area that Kevin's parents are struggling with is helping him communicate and control his environment as desired. His parents spoke about his intelligence and obvious desire to interact and engage with the world, but they felt that he was completely dependent on others for all aspects of his care and participation. They envision Kevin as being able to independently participate – for example he might wake up, call for his mother, turn on the lights in his bedroom, and then select and start playing a computer game while he was waiting to be fed. Currently, to perform these tasks, Kevin would need someone to notice he was up, turn on the lights for him, ask him what he wanted, set up a communication device or attempt to interpret his vocalizations (he is unable to form words due to low facial muscle tone), bring over a switch-adapted toy or computer tablet, hook up his hands and position everything correctly, and then stay with Kevin to make sure everything is in place and usable. Kevin is not capable of repositioning devices by himself if they are moved. In addition, many of the products currently available require too much force for Kevin and other children with Type I SMA to actuate, or they are not as sensitive and accurate as needed for the desired applications.

We believe that Kevin has the potential and the underlying capacities to be able to operate devices such as an eye-gaze communication system, a power wheelchair, a personal environmental control system, etc. if appropriate input devices are identified to fit his unique constellation of needs. The following section will discuss one specific aspect of our project: the design and preliminary evaluation of the input solutions.

3. TENTATIVE INPUT SOLUTIONS
While building the communication and environment control systems for Kevin, one of the main challenges is the channel of input due to his extremely limited physical and vocal capabilities. Eye-gaze based solution had been evaluated and yielded promising results. But the eye-gaze based solution can be intrusive in the context of communication. Regarding hand

controlled input solutions, the following characteristics were identified based on parents' input and observations:

- Customizable (i.e., can be modified/adapted for others with Type I SMA and similar disorders)
- Affordable/accessible to people in the SMA community
- Usable (does not take more than 5 minutes to set up and can be easily understood and modified by families who are not technically trained)
- Durable
- Responsive/sensitive
- Accurate
- Allows for maximal functional movement patterns (i.e., palms of hands are not obstructed so they can still be used for play)

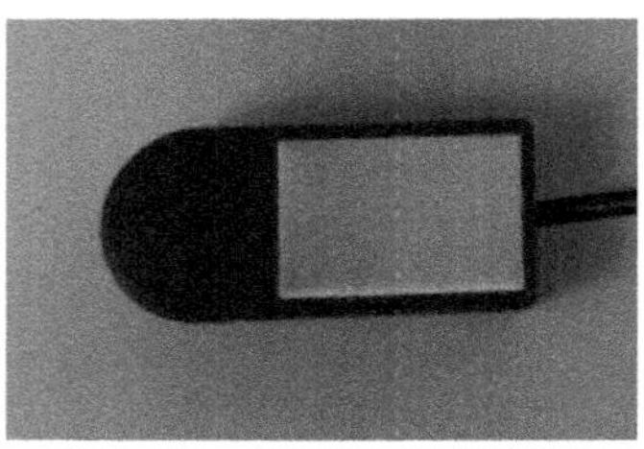

(1a)

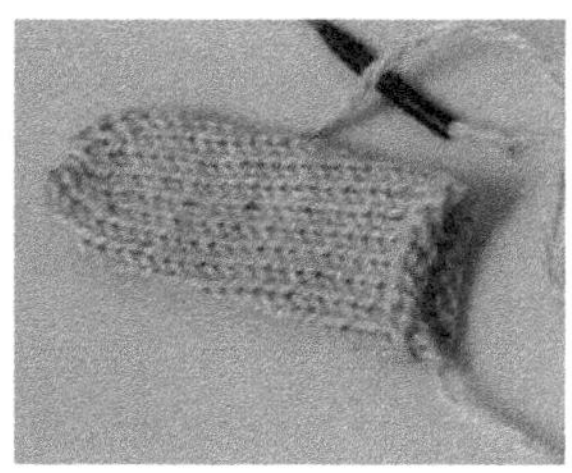

(1b)

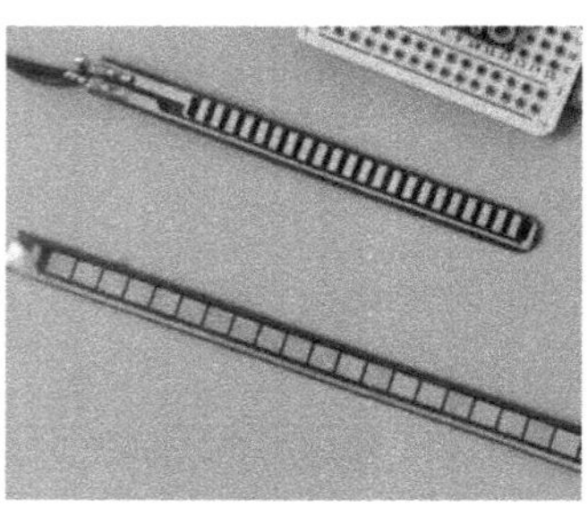

(1c)

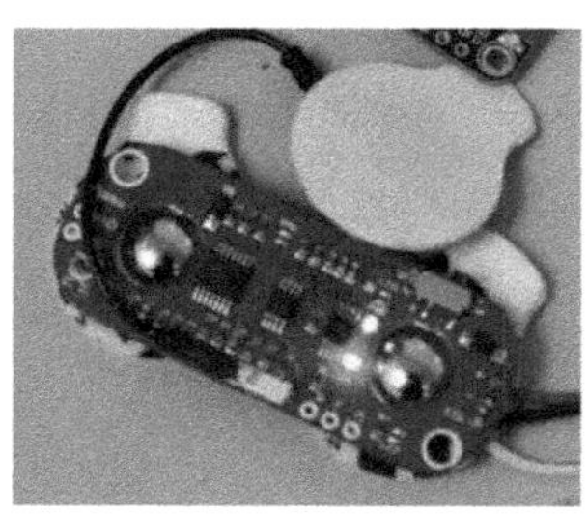

(1d)

Figure 1. Demonstration of four input solutions: (a) micro light switch; (b) conductive fabric thread; (c) flexible sensor; (d) EMG-based muscle sensor

Based on the above listed criteria, we chose and tested four types of input techniques as demonstrated in Figure 1. Figure 1a illustrates a micro light switch that we positioned under Kevin's index and middle fingers. Figure 1b illustrates a finger cot that we knitted for the size of Kevin's hands using conductive fabric thread. Figure 1c illustrates two flexible sensor with different lengths. Figure 1d illustrates an EMG-based muscle sensor.

Figure 2. Demonstration of the flexible sensor solution during testing

Figure 2 shows a customized approach to attach a flexible sensor on to a glove specifically made for Kevin's hands to better capture the intended movements.

4. RESULTS AND CONCLUSIONS

A preliminary evaluation of the solutions suggests that the micro light switch might be the solution that offers a reasonable balance between efficiency and accuracy. Several challenges and design considerations for the targeted population have also been observed. First, substantial amount of the hand movements are passive and it is very difficult to differentiate passive movements from intentional movements. Second, the threshold for movement detection needs to be set very carefully. High threshold may make it too hard for the patient to generate detectable movement, while low threshold may make the system too sensitive and incapable of filtering out noises in the movements. We also found that the thresholds can be quite different between the two hands if the muscle tone of one hand is stronger than the other. Third, collecting empirical data from very young children with severe disabilities takes much longer time and preparation compared to neurotypical adult users. The tasks must be age appropriate and highly engaging. In this study, we developed an interactive game based on Kevin's favorite character, the minions, to evaluate the input solutions. Even with this customized game, Kevin had often times lost interest in the middle of a task and refused to continue.

Currently, we are recruiting more young children with SMA to evaluate the input solutions. Like many health conditions, the capabilities of young children with SMA vary substantially. Data from more target users will help better understand how to identify and customize effective solution(s) for a particular user.

5. ACKNOWLEDGMENTS

We would like to thank Kevin, his family, and his support team for their enthusiastic participation and truly insightful feedback on various aspects of the project.

6. REFERENCES

[1] Lunn, M. R. and Wang, C. H. 2008. Spinal muscular atrophy, *The Lancet*, vol. 371, no. 9630, 2120–2133.

[2] Ogino, S., Leonard, D., Rennert, H., Ewens, W., and Wilson, R. 2002. Genetic risk assessment in carrier testing for spinal muscular atrophy, *American Journal of Medical Genetics*, vol. 110, no. 4, 301–307.

[3] American Occupational Therapy Association & American Occupational Therapy Foundation. 2011. Occupational therapy research agenda. *American Journal of Occupational Therapy*, 65(Suppl.), S4–S7.

Assessing Collaboration between Autistic Players — An Engagement Metric

Deborah Sturm
Dept. of Computer Science
College of Staten Island
Deborah.Sturm@csi.cuny.edu

Kristen Gillespie-Lynch
Dept. of Psychology
College of Staten Island
Kristen.Gillespie-Lynch@csi.cuny.edu

Michael Kholodovsky
Dept. of Computer Science
College of Staten Island
Michael.Kholodovsky@cix.csi.cuny.edu

ABSTRACT

We developed an engagement metric that is embedded in a two-player Kinect game. The game is designed to help autistic people interact and collaborate with each other and others. Each level has two phases - initially the players work on a task independently. In order to complete the task they must collaborate and agree. We added a component to assess the level of in-game cooperation. Using face tracking we developed a metric to automatically quantify collaboration based on the amount of time each player individually and together engage with one another. This can replace the time-consuming hand-coded evaluations. We also designed collaborative reward games including one that encourages players to interact with each other.

CCS Concepts

•**Human-centered computing** → *Collaborative and social computing;*

Keywords

Autism; Collaborative Games; Cooperation; Engagement

1. INTRODUCTION

Among the criteria for diagnosing Autism Syndrome Disorder are difficulties socializing and collaborating with others [1]. Autistic individuals often report that they communicate more effectively through computer-mediated communications than with in-person interactions and immersive computer-mediated interventions are more effective at promoting generalizable social skills than less dynamic interventions [3]. Many Autism studies examine attention patterns for diagnostic and predictive purposes [7].Several collaborative apps and games have been developed for players on the autism spectrum. Some use tabletops while others employ tablets ([2], [8],[5]). These games strengthen several social skills including turn taking compromise, empathy and joint attention. In order to help autistic people transfer skills to the real world, Whyte et al. suggest that computer- mediated games include multiple players along with blended computer and in-person interactions[9].

ASSETS '17 October 29-November 1, 2017, Baltimore, MD, USA

ACM ISBN 978-1-4503-4926-0/17/10.

DOI: https://doi.org/10.1145/3132525.3134795

Figure 1: Collaborative phase for anger level

2. CONNECTING THROUGH KINECT

Our collaborative game is immersive and dynamic [4]. The game is designed to support generalizable social skills by providing players with a hybrid intervention where they simultaneously engage with a peer or sibling digitally and in-person and by teaching participants how to interpret complex emotions using varied cues Standing next to each other, player complete collaborative emotion matching puzzles by moving images using Kinect technology with hand gestures. The game has two phases in each level; an independent phase where the players move their own pieces and a collaborative phase where they have to agree on the next move. Our storyline involves a boy who is initially bullied by a group of children but later stands up to the group and is ultimately included. In Figure 1 the scene shows the character confronting the bullies and the players need to agree on his emotion during the collaborative phase.

2.1 Engagement Metric

Khoshelham and Elberink [6] report on the accuracy of the Kinect sensor data and conclude that the sensor data is noisy especially when the players are far from the Kinect. We used more robust face point cloud values along with the skeleton values to compute player orientation. In order to quantify the level of engagement, we developed an engagement metric to measure player interaction. The player can look towards the other player by turning their head alone or their body with their head or both. To capture the body movement, we subtract the distance between the z component of the shoulder vertices. We then add this to the head distance (unless the head is facing forward while the body is rotated). Given

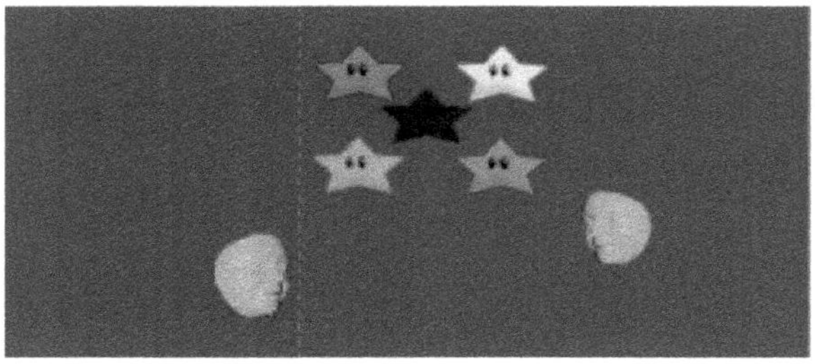

Figure 2: Engagement Reward Game

a player index, the Turn function, T, returns the distance from the sensor: $T(P) = (+/-)(dist(LM_{chin}, Sensor) + SO$, where LM_{chin} is the vertex for the chin landmark from the facial point cloud, and SO is the shoulder offset. The engagement metric for the player on the left is: $E_{PL} = \frac{\sum_{i=0}^{n} TR(PL)_i}{n}$ and on the right: $E_{PR} = \frac{\sum_{i=0}^{n} TL(PR)_i}{n}$ Finally the combined engagement metric is the average the players' metrics: $E = \frac{E_{PL}+E_{PR}}{2}$.

At the end of each level the players agree on a reward. In one reward game meant to encourage interaction between the players, we display the face mesh that we use for tracking the players faces. When the players move their heads the face mask changes to blue. If they look towards each other at the same time, the masks both turn green, a sound effect plays and an animations plays (see figure 2). Players, both typically developing and those on the spectrum have reacted very positively to this game and enjoy controlling the mask with their head movement.

3. PRELIMINARY OBSERVATIONS

In order to validate our metric, we first conducted controlled experiments with timed engagements and confirmed that these matched the generated metric. We then videoed and hand-coded 4 sessions with two players with each session coded by 3 raters. We found that the coders' scores were not consistent - showing that hand-coding can be subjective. Moreover it was difficult to measure short glances that are less than one second. In a longer study, we tested one level of the game with 14 players, recording their engagement levels for the first and second half of the level. Except for one pair, we verified that there was minimal interaction during the independent task, increased engagement during the collaborative portion and the highest level of engagement after the joint task was completed. This seemed to reflect their combined sense of accomplishment. Since each session is approximately one half hour long it can take three hand coders a total of 9 hours to process 6 sessions to record their evaluations of how engaged the players were during gameplay. Our current approach with the automatic engagement metric objectively quantifies this in real time.

4. DISCUSSION AND FUTURE WORK

The engagement metric quantifies aspects of player social interaction and can be used to verify or substitute for hand coding game-play. The engagement metric module is independent of our collaborative game and can therefore be added to any Unity-based Kinect game or project. The collaborative reward games are separate scenes and can also be used in other two-player Unity games. In order to encourage even more player interaction, we plan to add a pause moment before they choose the correct emotion for the scene. The players will hopefully interact and discuss what to do next and then proceed. Not all engagement uses eye contact; people also collaborate during a shared task by speaking. We observed that some players cooperated while talking without significant turning. We hope to extend the engagement metric to include player speech. We can do this using speaker diarisation to partition any speech into segments according to player identity. We also intend to improve the metric by weighting the contributions according to time so that short glances have lower weights in the metric.

5. ACKNOWLEDGMENTS

This project has been supported by an interdisciplinary research grant awarded to the first two authors.

6. REFERENCES

[1] A. P. Association et al. *Diagnostic and statistical manual of mental disorders (DSM-5®)*. American Psychiatric Pub, 2013.

[2] A. Battocchi, F. Pianesi, D. Tomasini, M. Zancanaro, G. Esposito, P. Venuti, B. Sasson, E. Gal, and P. Weiss. Collaborative puzzle game: a tabletop interactive game for fostering collaboration in children with asd. In *ACM International Conference on Interactive Tabletops and Surfaces*, pages 197–204, 2009.

[3] K. Gillespie, P. Brooks, C. Shane-Simpson, N. Gaggi, D. Sturm, and B. Ploog. Selecting computer-mediated interventions to support the social and emotional development of individuals with autism spectrum disorder. *Special and Gifted Education: Concepts, Methodologies, Tools, and Applications*, 2016.

[4] K. Gillespie, G. Goldstein, D. Smith, A. Riccio, M. Kholodovsky, C. Merendino, S. Leskov, R. Arab, H. Elsherbini, P. Asanov, and D. Sturm. Connecting through kinect: Designing and evaluating a collaborative game with and for autistic individuals. In *Conference on Human-Computer Interaction*, 2017.

[5] J. P. Hourcade, S. R. Williams, E. A. Miller, K. E. Huebner, and L. J. Liang. Evaluation of tablet apps to encourage social interaction in children with autism spectrum disorders. In *SIGCHI Conference on Human Factors in Computing Systems*, pages 3197–3206, 2013.

[6] K. Khoshelham and S. O. Elberink. Accuracy and resolution of kinect depth data for indoor mapping applications. *Sensors*, 12(2):1437–1454, 2012.

[7] P. Mundy, M. Sigman, and C. Kasari. A longitudinal study of joint attention and language development in autistic children. *Journal of autism and developmental disorders*, 20(1):115–128, 1990.

[8] S. Sharma, S. Srivastava, K. Achary, B. Varkey, T. Heimonen, J. S. Hakulinen, M. Turunen, and N. Rajput. Promoting joint attention with computer supported collaboration in children with autism. In *19th ACM Conference on Computer-Supported Cooperative Work*. ACM, 2016.

[9] E. M. Whyte, J. M. Smyth, and K. S. Scherf. Designing serious game interventions for individuals with autism. *Journal of autism and developmental disorders*, 45(12):3820–3831, 2015.

Blocks4All Demonstration: a Blocks-Based Programming Environment for Blind Children

Lauren R. Milne, Catherine M. Baker, Richard E. Ladner
Paul G. Allen School of Computer Science
University of Washington, Box 352350
Seattle, WA 98195-2350
milnel2@cs.washington.edu, cmbaker@cs.washington.edu, ladner@cs.washington.edu

ABSTRACT
Blocks-based programming environments, such as Scratch and Blockly, are designed to make learning programming easier for young children. They are increasingly being used for both formal and informal curriculum, such as many of Code.org's hour of code projects. However, these block-based environments rely heavily on visual metaphors and interactions, making them inaccessible for blind children. We describe our initial design of a touchscreen-based blocks environment that is accessible for blind children.

CCS Concepts
•Human-centered computing → Accessibility → Accessibility systems and tools • Applied computing → Education → Interactive learning environments

Keywords
Accessibility; blind, children; educational technology; touchscreen interactions.

1. INTRODUCTION
Computer science education for K-12 children is an important topic both in the United States and globally. The hour of code, first launched by Code.org in 2013, is a popular outreach effort that has encouraged millions of students to try programming projects [3]. To make programming more engaging for young children, much of the programming is taught using blocks-based programming environments: visual environments that rely on users dragging and dropping "blocks" of code consisting of statements that fit together like puzzle pieces. In fact, of the 162 hour of code projects on the Code.org website designed for pre-readers through age 8, 79 of them use blocks-based environments [3].

Unfortunately, because they rely so heavily on visual elements, current programming environments, like Scratch [8] and Blockly [2] do not work well with screen readers and are therefore not accessible for blind children. This renders much of the current K-12 computing curricula unusable for these children. To remedy this, we are exploring techniques to make these blocks-based environments accessible to children who are blind or who have low-vision.

ASSETS'17, October 29-Novermber 1, 2017, Baltimore, MD, USA

ACM ISBN 978-1-4503-4926-0/17/10.
https://doi.org/10.1145/3132525.3134774

In this demonstration, we show our initial prototype, a tablet-based iOS application that allows blind children to access to the same features that make blocks-based languages usable and engaging for sighted children: (1) a lack of syntax errors due to blocks that are units of code, as opposed to a text-based approach (2) code creation using a menu of blocks that relies on recognition instead of recall, and (3) strong spatial hints about scope to indicate if a block is inside a conditional or loop statement.

2. RELATED WORK
There are many blocks-based programming environments. They were initially made popular with the creation of Scratch, with the intention of making programming accessible to and fun for all children. Google has created the Blockly library [2], which allows anyone to embed a blocks-based code editor into their applications.

Although most of these applications are not accessible with a screen reader, there have been attempts to explore how to make them accessible, using hierarchical menus that can be navigated with a screen reader on a desktop computer [1, 5, 6], so that structural information such as nesting level is conveyed via the level of hierarchy in the menu. Ludi et al. [7] explored adding audio cues, such as spearcons (sped-up speech) and earcons (sounds such as musical notes) to a modified version of Blockly to help blind users navigate and understand the structure of code. We used many of the design elements from these studies, but adapted them to a touch-screen interface.

3. DESIGN PRINCIPLES
We followed three main guidelines to inform the initial design of our application:

1) *Design for sighted children, blind children and children with low vision.* To give access to much of the existing curriculum available with blocks-based languages, we chose to try to preserve features and explore touchscreen interactions that could be used non-visually and could be integrated into current visual environments.

2) *Design for mainstream technology, already in use.* Touchscreen devices, especially iOS devices are popular in the blind community [11]. We have found in a previous study that they are popular with young children who are blind and many of them were more familiar with the techniques to use touchscreen-based screen readers as opposed to those on desktop computers [9].

3) *Design for children.* Blind children may be less familiar with desktop screen readers and may benefit from the spatial exploration that a tablet-based interface provides. We plan to explore this when evaluating our tool.

4. BLOCKS4ALL DESIGN
In our initial prototype, we created a simplified block-environment, which supports the same features as ScratchJr [4], a tablet-based

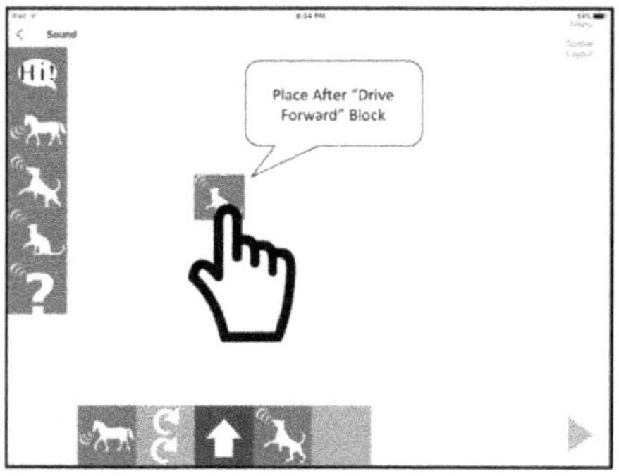

Figure 1. Audio-guided Drag and Drop interface with audio cues for understanding code structure.

environment designed for children aged 5-7. We are running user studies with four children to explore accessible methods to (1) move and connect blocks from the toolbox to the workspace, (2) modify blocks and (3) make the program structure, including hierarchical statements in the form of repeat loops, understandable.

We created an iOS application that works with VoiceOver using high contrast for children with low vision control. The current application can be used to control a Dash robot [12], focusing on non-visual controls such as movement and sounds.

4.1 Application Layout

The application is designed so that all the elements can easily be located. The toolbox is on the left side of the screen and the play button is on the right, which is similar to existing blocks-based environments. Based on early user studies, one major difference in our application is that blocks are all the same size and are placed in a single row on the bottom of the screen, and we do not currently support multiple "islands" of blocks. This is to make blocks easier to find and navigate.

4.2 Adding Blocks

We currently support three techniques to add and move blocks in the workspace: (1) an audio guided drag-and-drop, similar to the Tickle application [10], and two forms of select, select drop, (2) one in which the user selects a block and then a location in the workspace and (3) one in which they select a location in the workspace and then a block, similar to Accessible Blockly [1].

4.3 Exploring Program Structure

To facilitate exploring blocks in workspace, the blocks are all the same size and are evenly and horizontally spaced on the bottom of the screen. We are exploring two methods to indicate nested statements: (1) using a spatial relationship to bump blocks up if they are nested and (2) using begin and end repeat blocks and audio cues to indicate nesting.

4.4 Modifying Blocks

Currently, we support only statement-level blocks, and have not explored introducing variables and expressions at the block level. To support statements and expressions, they are built into the blocks as menus of options. We are exploring pop-up menus and scroll menus to allow children to modify blocks.

5. FUTURE WORK

We are running user studies with children who are blind or who have low-vision to test out and refine our prototypes. In the future, we would like to explore: (1) how to convey block type information (conveyed via shape in visual languages) by using sound cues or only making the correct type of blocks selectable, (2) using spatial

Figure 2. Select, Select Drop interface starting from workspace with spatial cues indicating code structure

layouts to convey complex hierarchical information such as conditionals, and (3) how to convey run time information with the code, perhaps allowing users to "walk through" the code using gestures and receiving audio feedback.

6. ACKNOWLEDGMENTS

This work supported by the National Science Foundation Graduate Research Fellowship under Grant No. DGE-1256082 and a SIGCSE special projects grant.

7. REFERENCES

[1] Accessible Blockly: *https://blockly-demo.appspot.com/static/demos/accessible/index.html.* Accessed: 2017-06-16.

[2] Blockly: *https://developers.google.com/blockly/.* Accessed: 2017-06-16.

[3] Code.org: Anybody can Learn: *https://code.org/.* Accessed: 2017-06-16.

[4] Flannery, L.P. et al. 2013. Designing ScratchJr: Support for Early Childhood Learning Through Computer Programming. *Proc. 12th International Conference on Interaction Design and Children* (New York, NY, USA, 2013), 1–10.

[5] Koushik, V. and Lewis, C. 2016. An Accessible Blocks Language: Work in Progress. *Proc. ASSETS '16* (New York, NY, USA, 2016), 317–318.

[6] Lewis, C. 2014. Work in Progress Report: Nonvisual Visual Programming. *Psychology of Programming Interest Group.* (2014).

[7] Ludi, S. et al. 2016. Exploration of the Use of Auditory Cues in Code Comprehension and Navigation for Individuals with Visual Impairments in a Visual Programming Environment. *Proc. ASSETS '16* (New York, NY, USA, 2016), 279–280.

[8] Maloney, J. et al. 2010. The Scratch Programming Language and Environment. *Trans. Comput. Educ.* 10, 4 (Nov. 2010), 16:1–16:15.

[9] Milne, L.R. et al. 2014. BraillePlay: Educational Smartphone Games for Blind Children. *Proc. of the 16th International ACM SIGACCESS Conference on Computers & Accessibility* (New York, NY, USA, 2014), 137–144.

[10] Tickle: Program on your iPhone and iPad: *https://www.tickleapp.com/.* Accessed: 2017-02-27.

[11] WebAIM: Screen Reader User Survey #6 Results: *http://webaim.org/projects/screenreadersurvey6/.* Accessed: 2017-06-19.

[12] Wonder Workshop *Blockly iOS Application for Dot and Dash Robots.*

CollabAll: Inclusive Discussion Support System For Deaf and Hearing Students

Anthony Peruma [1]
axp6201@rit.edu
[1] Department of Software Engineering
Rochester Institute of Technology
Rochester, NY, USA

Yasmine N. El-Glaly [1,2]
yasmine@se.rit.edu
[2] Department of Computer Science
Faculty of Science, Port Said University
Port Said, Egypt

ABSTRACT

Even with advances in technology, group meetings between hearing and deaf and hard-of-hearing (D/HH) students can be challenging for all participants. This paper introduces CollabAll, a system that aims to better facilitate productive meetings between D/HH and hearing students. CollabAll provides D/HH individuals with a mechanism to actively participate in making decisions and getting their point across in team meetings. CollabAll enables every team member to create discussion topics for their meeting, track the person currently communicating and the current topic being discussed along with providing a mechanism for 'polite' interruptions. Early feedback from participatory design and focus group studies indicated a positive user experience.

CCS Concepts

•**Human-centered computing → Accessibility systems and tools;** *Collaborative and social computing systems and tools; Participatory design;*

Keywords

Deaf; Meetings; Mixed Groups; Turn Taking; Discussions

1. INTRODUCTION

Modern educating practices promote the need of having inclusive classrooms over specialized classrooms for the education of Deaf or Hard of Hearing (D/HH) students [1]. As such, universities provide American Sign Language (ASL) Interpretation services for students in the classroom, with an interpreter facilitating communication between D/HH students and the educator. For most part of the lecture, communication is one-way (from educator to the classroom). However, as part of the course content educators incorporate group projects and activities into the syllabus; with groups usually comprising of a mix of D/HH and hearing students.

As claimed by Stinson et al. [10] in their study of interactions between D/HH and hearing students, D/HH students are disadvantaged by mixed group activities as it involves discussions and collaboration between multiple individuals, most of whom are not skilled in ASL interpretation. Some of the key issues that have been noticed during group activities include: (1) Multiple students speaking at the same time, (2) No set meeting agenda/structure, and (3) Deaf cultural insensitivity. D/HH students are disadvantaged at meetings with hearing students since a D/HH student would need to keep track of the person communicating, the interpreter, and interruptions. This leads to the D/HH student missing out on the discussion and also finding it difficult to interrupt the person currently speaking.

To provide a more inclusive environment for D/HH students in meetings, we propose our novel system, CollabAll, to break the barriers that prevent D/HH and hearing students from collaborating productively and equally.

2. RELATED WORK

Prior research has been primarily around textual representation of speech/sound in an educational context. More specifically, the works focus on auto generation of caption and transcripts [7, 6] as well as automatic speech to text translation [8]. However, the studies do not touch upon face-to-face group meetings, where there is a possibility of multiple people speaking at the same time. Additional research in this area includes the integration of multiple visual sources for seamless content delivery [2, 9, 4, 3]; some of which also includes the use of commercial products such as Adobe Connect[1] to aid in content delivery. These research works were mainly limited to improving the visual attention of the consumer, and as such did not investigate effective face-to-face group collaboration. Further, using such systems for small (ad-hoc) meetings is not cost-effective due to the required infrastructure and prior setup.

3. CollabAll SYSTEM AND INTERFACE

CollabAll is built as a responsive web based system[2], each participant in the meeting has the ability to access the web site using any Internet enabled device. Through the web site, a participant can be added to multiple 'Groups', setup the discussion points for the meeting using 'Cards', customize 'Interjections' for the group's meeting and run and participate in the meeting. A participant can politely interrupt a person communicating (e.g. 'Slow Down!', 'Don't Understand!', etc). As depicted in Figure 1, the 'Meet Now'

[1] http://www.adobe.com/products/adobeconnect.html
[2] https://collaball.github.io/

ASSETS '17, Oct. 29–Nov. 1, 2017, Baltimore, MD, USA.

ACM ISBN 978-1-4503-4926-0/17/10...$15.00.
DOI: https://doi.org/10.1145/3132525.3134800

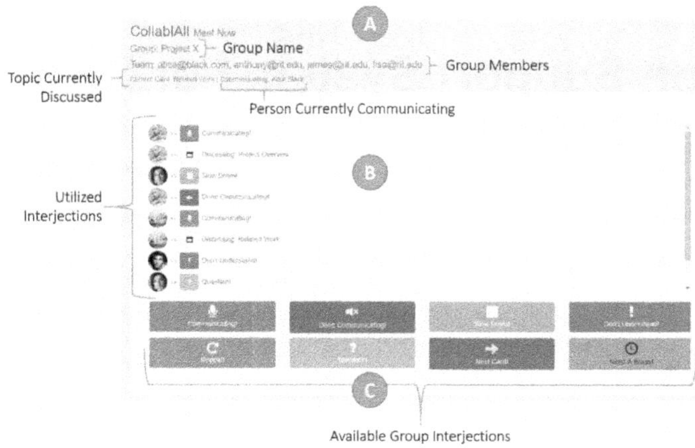

Figure 1: The CollabAll user interface.

screen is utilized when the group meets. Within this screen, the section marked 'A' contains information such as the group name, members, the person currently communicating and the current topic of discussion. The interjection feed section, marked 'B', contains a feed of 'Interjections' issued by meeting participants. The feed is sorted in chronological order. Next to each 'Interjection' the avatar (or name) of the user will be displayed. The list of available Group Interjections is shown in the section marked 'C'. The 'Interjections' are rendered as buttons, which when clicked, notifies all participants of the interjection. The notifications are instantaneous and appear in the feed. It should be noted that, given the importance of ASL [5], CollabAll does not aim to eliminate the need for ASL or even an ASL Interpreter; it merely supplements the services of an ASL Interpreter.

4. PRELIMINARY USER STUDY

We employed a participatory design approach involving a team of D/HH consultants and life experts to aid in the design of the system. Findings from the participatory design session led to enhancements in the initial prototype.

We evaluated the final design of the prototype in controlled Focus Group studies comprising of five hearing and two deaf students that ranged in age from 21 to 27. In-addition to surveys, the studies were monitored by two researchers that observed the group and took notes. Our studies involved having a group of students discuss predefined topics and perform tasks associated with these topics. An ASL interpreter was recruited to facilitate communication. Our observations from the study showed that participants: (1) took turns in communicating and (2) used interjections to convey the need for talking, agreeing, and disagreeing. We also observed that hearing students at times forgot to use interjections; however, the deaf students always used the interjections feature. Further, the deaf students usually took the lead in initiating and discussing activity tasks.

All individuals that we interacted with were asked to complete a survey[3]. Our analysis points to users being satisfied with the effectiveness, intuitiveness and ease of use of the system. We support these findings by qualitative user feedback such as: "Deaf people like me can easily follow along and see who is speaking without feeling lost/confused".

[3]https://github.com/CollabAll/survey

5. CONCLUSIONS AND FUTURE WORK

We used an iterative multi-phased approach in designing and building CollabAll. Preliminary studies via participatory design and focus group sessions along with open discussions at meetings and conferences, and researchers observations have demonstrated promising results of the system and also shows the need for such a system.

We plan on conducting a formal and in-depth study of CollabAll in both, controlled and in-the-wild settings, to further understand the effectiveness, shortcomings and improvements of the system.

6. REFERENCES

[1] A. S.-L.-H. Association et al. Inclusive practices for children and youths with communication disorders. 1996.

[2] A. Brando, H. Nicolau, S. Tadas, and V. L. Hanson. Slidepacer: A presentation delivery tool for instructors of deaf and hard of hearing students. In *Proceedings of the 18th International ACM SIGACCESS Conference on Computers and Accessibility*, ASSETS '16, pages 25–32, 2016.

[3] A. C. Cavender. Using networked multimedia to improve educational access for deaf and hard of hearing students. *SIGACCESS Access. Comput.*, (89):18–21, Sept. 2007.

[4] A. C. Cavender, J. P. Bigham, and R. E. Ladner. Classinfocus: Enabling improved visual attention strategies for deaf and hard of hearing students. In *Proceedings of the 11th International ACM SIGACCESS Conference on Computers and Accessibility*, Assets '09, 2009.

[5] L. Elliot, M. Stinson, J. Mallory, D. Easton, and M. Huenerfauth. Deaf and hard of hearing individuals' perceptions of communication with hearing colleagues in small groups. In *Proceedings of the 18th International ACM SIGACCESS Conference on Computers and Accessibility*, ASSETS '16, 2016.

[6] R. Kheir and T. Way. Inclusion of deaf students in computer science classes using real-time speech transcription. In *Proceedings of the 12th Annual SIGCSE Conference on Innovation and Technology in Computer Science Education*, ITiCSE '07, pages 261–265, 2007.

[7] W. S. Lasecki, R. Kushalnagar, and J. P. Bigham. Helping students keep up with real-time captions by pausing and highlighting. In *Proceedings of the 11th Web for All Conference*, W4A '14, pages 1–8, 2014.

[8] S. S. Prietch, E. J. dos Santos, and L. V. L. Filgueiras. A mean for communication between deaf and hearing pairs in inclusive educational settings: The sessai app. In *Proceedings of the 12th Web for All Conference*, W4A '15, pages 27:1–27:2, 2015.

[9] J. Reis, E. T. Solovey, J. Henner, K. Johnson, and R. Hoffmeister. Asl clear: Stem education tools for deaf students. In *Proceedings of the 17th International ACM SIGACCESS Conference on Computers and Accessibility*, pages 441–442. ACM, 2015.

[10] M. Stinson and Y. Liu. Participation of deaf and hard-of-hearing students in classes with hearing students. *Journal of Deaf Studies and Deaf Education*, 4(3):191–202, 1999.

Developing Interfaces for Rehabilitation: A Graduate Level Course for Students from Multiple Disciplines

Ravi Kuber
UMBC
rkuber@umbc.edu

ABSTRACT
This paper describes the design of a graduate level course focusing on developing interfaces for purposes of rehabilitation, catering to students from multiple disciplines. Students work on projects relating to the needs of individuals with disabilities, under the supervision of internal and external mentors. The course has been designed to help students develop both research and mobile interface technical design skills. Course structure and deliverables are described, along with the challenges faced and lessons learned from multiple offerings of the course.

CCS Concepts
CCS → Social and professional topics → Professional topics → Computing education → Computing education programs.

Keywords
Accessibility; Graduate Course; Inclusive Design; Rehabilitation;

1. INTRODUCTION
A graduate level course entitled 'Developing Interfaces for Rehabilitation', offered through the Department of Information Systems at UMBC, provides an opportunity for students to focus in depth on rehabilitative and assistive technologies to better support users with diverse abilities. The course appeals to students from a range of disciplines including Human-Centered Computing, Computer Science, Psychology and Education, attracting those with professional or personal interests in designing for rehabilitation. In this paper, we describe the format of the course, skills which are developed, along with the lessons learned through offering the course. The aim is to offer guidance to instructors interested in teaching rehabilitative interface design to students from an array of educational backgrounds.

2. RELATED WORK
Courses have been developed to introduce computing and non-computing students to topics relating to universal access, disability, technology and society [6] and assistive technologies [11]. Best practices have been developed to support instruction (e.g., [8, 10]), either for targeted courses or integrated into the curriculum as a whole. These include providing real-world learning environments to students, exposing them to accessibility topics in multiple ways, and the need for instructor initiative to support learning [8]. However, opportunities exist for providing courses with a greater emphasis on rehabilitation or remediated initiatives, which may provide users with the skills to utilize assistive technologies.

ASSETS '17, October 29-November 1, 2017, Baltimore, MD, USA

ACM ISBN 978-1-4503-4926-0/17/10.
https://doi.org/10.1145/3132525.3134784

3. COURSE DESIGN
3.1 Objectives, Topics and Course Structure
The objectives of the course developed at UMBC, are to (1) gain an understanding of the challenges faced by individuals with disabilities, and examine the ways that needs may change over time; (2) demonstrate an understanding of a functional approach to the assessment of rehabilitation and assistive technology needs; (3) apply design concepts to interfaces for rehabilitation. Topics covered include introductions to needs assessment, adaptive system and multimodal interface design, robotic, prosthetic and orthotic interventions, design for mobility, and ergonomic and workspace design. Weekly readings from texts such as Cook and Polgar [3], Cooper et al. [4] and other conference papers, are suggested to supplement each class.

Each class is divided into two sections, a lecture component, followed by an interface design practical. Lectures focus on the ways in which technologies can be designed to support users with disabilities. These are often interspersed with in-class activities to consolidate knowledge gained from the lecture. Students learn to use drag-and-drop style mobile prototyping tools (MIT AppInventor 2 [7]) by following a set of tutorials, with a view to applying skills developed to the design of a mobile rehabilitative game as part of a final project. Although programming experience is advantageous, students without experience are welcomed.

3.2 Guest Lectures
Similar to the best practices identified in [8], lectures from subject-matter experts complement the course by providing alternative perspectives on ways to support rehabilitation. Examples include (1) rehabilitation engineers from local organizations, such as V-Linc [9], who cater to the needs of users for whom off-the-shelf products may not support; (2) clinicians specializing in physical medicine and rehabilitation (physiatry) to provide an overview of the ways in which they work in concert with other professionals (e.g. speech therapists, occupational therapists) and rehabilitation designers to support individuals with disabilities; (3) educational technologists to discuss evidence-based instructional practices and technical solutions to support learning in K-12 environments for children with emotional and learning disabilities. Students are able to gain an insight into the strategies adopted by professionals and identify ways to position themselves, should they wish to pursue careers in these areas.

3.3 Mentorship for Projects
Prior to the beginning of the course, applications are solicited for external mentors to set and supervise group-based projects. External mentors include educational specialists, speech therapists, occupational therapists, and physiatrists from the local area. Students meet with external mentors three times either face-to-face or remotely per semester to discuss progress. Internal

mentors are also recruited who can offer day-to-day guidance relating to techniques for interface design or evaluation.

3.4 Course Deliverables

- **Individual reports**. Students address a research question through evidence from scholarly papers. Research questions relate to topics such as technologies to assist the rehabilitation of stroke survivors, supporting skill development among individuals with disabilities etc. The aim is to equip students with skills in critically analyzing papers relating to rehabilitative interventions.
- **Semester-long group projects** relate to designing rehabilitative solutions (e.g. games to support improvements in behavior, strengthen word building skills, prompting solutions for daily living tasks, apps to support/promote movement of joints and muscles). Deliverables include a **detailed report** describing the design and evaluation of a mobile game, and a **poster** summarizing the research conducted. This is presented at an event, to which mentors and members of the campus community are invited. Students are able to practice disseminating their research at the event.

4. OPPORTUNITIES

- The course attracts a small number of students with disabilities, in addition to students with experience of working in rehabilitation environments. **Leveraging student experience** to offer insights into rehabilitative practices has been found valuable to foster discussion within the class.
- Students have been able to **continue the relationship with their mentors**, extending their semester projects by conducting larger scale evaluations of interfaces. These have led to a range of publications [2,5], and helped to inspire the development of outreach activities [1]. The partnership with mentors allows students not only to **focus on a topic of interest which may not be covered in depth** due to issues of time, but also allows the university to maintain **links with organizations and community groups** in the local area.

5. LESSONS LEARNED

- **Managing mentor's expectations for the project.** It is made clear from the outset, that due to the relatively short duration of the course, students will likely be able to deliver a functional prototype of a system, not a final, polished version. Projects can be extended into independent studies/theses, where more time can be invested into design and evaluation.
- **Recruitment of subjects**. A class IRB protocol is submitted prior to the beginning of the semester. Students are able to familiarize themselves with the ethical considerations in order to conduct studies. Due to the restrictive nature of the protocol, coupled with logistical issues recruiting disabled users, testing is conducted with individuals without disabilities. To gain greater exposure to the needs of individuals with disabilities, approaches similar to those of [6] will be adopted, where the technical interactions of disabled users from videos sourced from video-sharing sites (e.g. YouTube) can be analyzed.

6. CHALLENGES FACED

- **Difficulties performing usability studies with children.** Projects suggested by educational specialists from K-12 environments have been difficult to evaluate with their own students aged below 18. Mentors are asked to have IRB protocols in place at their own institution to expedite the process of testing with target user groups.
- **Mobile prototyping alternatives.** While students with programming knowledge may favor developing gaming interfaces using different languages/tools, challenges can be faced by those with limited programming experience. Alternative tools are suggested to design interactive prototypes (e.g. Axure, Balsamiq, JustInMind).

7. ACKNOWLEDGMENTS

We thank Dr. Amy Hurst for her input to course development.

8. REFERENCES

[1] Anthony, L., Prasad, S., Hurst, A. and Kuber, R. 2012. A participatory design workshop on accessible apps and games with students with learning differences. In *Proceedings of the 14th International ACM SIGACCESS Conference on Computers and Accessibility.* ACM, New York, NY, 253-254, DOI=http://dx.doi.org/10.1145/2384916.2384979.

[2] Carrington, P., Kuber, R., Anthony, L., Hurst, A., and Prasad, S. 2010. Developing an interface to support procedural memory training using a participatory-based approach. In *Proceedings of the 26th Annual BCS Interaction Specialist Group Conference on People and Computers,* British Computer Society, 333-338.

[3] Cook, A.M., and Polgar, J.M., 2014. *Assistive technologies: Principles and Practice*. Elsevier Health Sciences.

[4] Cooper, R.A., Ohnabe, H., and Hobson, D.A. 2006. *An Introduction to Rehabilitation Engineering*. CRC Press.

[5] Krishnaswamy, K., and Kuber, R. 2012. Toward the development of a BCI and gestural interface to support individuals with physical disabilities. *In Proceedings of the 14th international ACM SIGACCESS Conference on Computers and Accessibility*, ACM, New York, NY, 229-230, DOI=http://dx.doi.org/10.1145/2384916.2384967.

[6] Kurniawan, S.H., Arteaga, S. and Manduchi, R. 2010. A general education course on universal access, disability, technology and society. In *Proceedings of the 12th international ACM SIGACCESS Conference on Computers and Accessibility,* ACM, New York, NY, 11-18, DOI=http://dx.doi.org/10.1145/1878803.1878808.

[7] MIT AppInventor2 - http://appinventor.mit.edu

[8] Putnam, C., Dahman, M., Rose, E., Cheng, J. and Bradford, G., 2016. Best practices for teaching accessibility in university classrooms: cultivating awareness, understanding, and appreciation for diverse users. *ACM Transactions on Accessible Computing (TACCESS)*, 8(4), Article No. 13, DOI=http://dx.doi.org/10.1145/2831424.

[9] V-Linc – http://www.v-linc.org

[10] Waller, A., Hanson, V.L. and Sloan, D. 2009. Including accessibility within and beyond undergraduate computing courses. In *Proceedings of the 11th International ACM SIGACCESS Conference on Computers and Accessibility,* ACM, New York, NY, 155-162, DOI=http://dx.doi.org/10.1145/1639642.1639670.

[11] UMBC Assistive Technologies Class (HCC741) - https://umbcassistivetech.wordpress.com

DytectiveU: A Game to Train the Difficulties and the Strengths of Children with Dyslexia

Luz Rello, Arturo Macías, María Herrera, Camila de Ros, Enrique Romero and Jeffrey P. Bigham
Change Dyslexia
{luz,camila,maria,arturo,enrique,jeff}@changedyslexia.org

ABSTRACT

In this demo we present *DytectiveU*, a game with 35,000 exercises to train the cognitive abilities related to dyslexia. To personalize the exercises, the game takes into consideration 25 indicators grouped in performance measures, language skills, working memory, executive functions and perceptual processes. The main contribution of this approach is to train dyslexia from a holistic point of view addressing not only the difficulties in reading and writing but also other cognitive abilities that are related to dyslexia and/or contribute to create coping skills to overcome dyslexia. The game is available for Android, iOS and Web (PC/Mac).

Keywords

Dyslexia, Training Exercises, Serious Games, Cognitive Skills

Categories and Subject Descriptors

K.4.2 [**Computers and Society**]: Social Issues—*Assistive technologies for people with disabilities*

1. INTRODUCTION

Approximately 1 in 10 people has dyslexia, a disorder that leads to children who, despite conventional classroom experience, fail to attain the language skills of reading, writing, and spelling commensurate with their intellectual abilities [4]. Computer interventions to support dyslexia in Spanish mainly focus on training reading fluency but do not specifically focus on other cognitive skills that are related to dyslexia, such as visual spatial attention, working memory or auditory perception.

In this demo we present *DytectiveU*,[1] the first application to support 25 cognitive abilities related to dyslexia in order to train the difficulties but also to empower the strengths of children with dyslexia which are crucial to develop coping skills to overcome dyslexia.

[1]Available for iOS, Android and Web at: https://dytectiveu.org/

ASSETS '17 October 29-November 1, 2017, Baltimore, MD, USA

ACM ISBN 978-1-4503-4926-0/17/10.
DOI: https://doi.org/10.1145/3132525.3134773

Figure 1: Characters of DytectiveU (up); and an example of an exercise targeting the executive function of activation and attention and the linguistic skills of phonological and lexical awareness (down).

2. RELATED WORK

In the mobile markets we found two scientifically validated apps. To support Spanish reading fluency we found *Galexia*,[2] with is composed of 24 sessions. It was evaluated with 46 participants (dyslexia and poor readers) showing significant improvements in reading skills between the pre-tests and post-tests [3].

To support the spelling there is *Piruletras (Dyseggxia)*,[3] with 5,000 exercises that integrate linguistic patterns found on errors written by people with dyslexia using a corpus of real errors [1]. The tool was evaluated with 48 children with diagnosed dyslexia showing significant improvements in their spelling performance after four weeks of use [2].

[2]Available for Android at: https://goo.gl/cfxiF8
[3]Available for iOS at: https://goo.gl/SPPNsQ

Language Skills	**Performance Measures**
Alphabetic Awareness	Reading Comprehension
Phonological Awareness	Reading Speed
Syllabic Awareness	Natural Spelling
Lexical Awareness	Arbitrary Spelling
Morphological Awareness	Writing Speed
Syntactic Awareness	Error Recognition
Semantic Awareness	Error Correction
Orthographic Awareness	
Prosodic Awareness	
Working Memory	**Executive Functions**
Visual (alphabetical)	Activation and attention
Auditory (phonology)	Sustained attention
Sequential (auditory)	Simultaneous attention
Sequential (visual)	
Perceptual Processes	
Visual discrimination and categorization	
Auditory discrimination and categorization	

Table 1: The 25 indicators used in DytectiveU for the personalizing of the exercises.

3. CONTENT DESIGN

Exercise Design. *DytectiveU* has 35,000 exercises that were manually created by linguists, psychologists and computer scientists using two language resources: (a) the linguistic pattern extracted from a corpus of errors made by people with dyslexia [1] using linguistic data mining; (b) language resources generated using natural language techniques. The exercises include all the linguistically motivated exercises validated in our previous work [2]. There are 54 types of exercises depending on the linguistic element and cognitive ability they target and 11 different interactions, *e.g.* find an element in whack a mole interaction, click over an element in a sentence, or delete a letter (see Figure 1, down).

Cognitive Abilities. Each of the exercises is tagged with three or more of the 18 cognitive abilities and 7 performance measures shown in Table 1.

Challenges. The tool is composed of 64 challenges (around 15-20 minutes long) that include a set of exercises. The set of exercises per challenge vary from child to child depending on their age and the personalization performed.

Personalization. For each exercise we gather a set of dependent variables (*number of clicks, hits, speed, accuracy* and *efficiency*) that are subsequently mapped with each of the cognitive abilities. Then, depending on the user performance per cognitive ability in comparison with the users of their age, we select subsequent challenge's exercises in order to strengthen the weakest cognitive skills and challenge the strongest cognitive skills with more difficult exercises.

Reports and Challenge Generation. The tool presents two type of reports: (i) and evaluation of the player compared to the percentile of the rest of players of the same age (see Figure 2), and (ii) the evolution of the player in time per cognitive skill. The measures used are *Accuracy* (percentage of correct exercises) and *Efficiency*, taking into account *Accuracy* and *Speed*.

There are two versions of *DytectiveU*, one for families

Figure 2: Example of an evaluation report of the language skills after playing a challenge. English translation in blue.

showing reports with performance measures only and *DytectiveU PRO* designed for professional therapists. *DytectiveU PRO* allows the therapist to access to more detailed reports (one per cognitive skill) and the manual personalization of the exercises.

4. PROOF OF CONCEPT AND FUTURE WORK

We accomplished a crowd-funding campaign to fund the development of *DytectiveU* and involved the contributors of the campaign in the creation process of the tool. We invited then to a Proof of Concept workshop in Madrid where 12 families with children with dyslexia -from 6 to 18 years old- and 6 professional therapists attended. The results of workshop were materialized in functionalities of the tool, such as the use of reports; some gamification strategies of the game; and the design of the characters (see Figure 1).

For future work we plan to carry out a longitudinal evaluation of *DytectiveU* in schools to measure the impact of the methodology on the performance of children with dyslexia.

5. REFERENCES

[1] L. Rello, R. Baeza-Yates, and J. Llisterri. A resource of errors written in spanish by people with dyslexia and its linguistic, phonetic and visual analysis. *Language Resources and Evaluation*, 2016.

[2] L. Rello, C. Bayarri, Y. Otal, and P. Pielot. A computer-based method to improve the spelling of children with dyslexia using errors. In *Proc. The 16th International ACM SIGACCESS Conference of Computers and Accessibility (ASSETS 2014)*, Rochester, USA, October 2014.

[3] F. Serrano, J. B. Sánchez, and M. G. Olmedo. Galexia: Evidence-based software for intervention in reading fluency and comprehension. In *INTED2016 Proceedings*, pages 2001–2007. IATED, 2016.

[4] World Federation of Neurology (WFN). Report of research group on dyslexia and world illiteracy. Dallas: WFN, 1968.

ICT to Aid Dental Care of Children with Autism

Mariasole Bondioli
Susanna Pelagatti
University of Pisa
Lungarno Pacinotti 43, 56124 Pisa
{mariasole.bondioli,
susanna.pelagatti}@di.unipi.it

Maria Claudia Buzzi
Marina Buzzi
IIT-CNR
via Moruzzi 1, 56124 Pisa
{claudia.buzzi, marina.buzzi}@iit.cnr.it

Caterina Senette
IIT-CNR
via Moruzzi 1, 56124 Pisa
caterina.senette@iit.cnr.it

ABSTRACT

Dental health in children with autism presents many challenges, due to their different perception of sensory experience and difficulty accepting unknown social contexts. The dental care setting presents strong sound-visual stimulations that can upset a patient with autism, often forcing dentists to administer chemical sedation in order to deliver dental care. In recent years, several technology-enhanced systems and apps have been proposed to help people with autism adapt to new contexts and cope with distressing social situations. Our study explores the potential of personalized digital tools for familiarizing these children with dental procedures and environments, and teaching them how to perform proper oral hygiene at home. A 3-month study to test ICT tools created to control children's anxiety and avoid sedation was carried out involving researchers, developers, dentists, psychologists, parents and ten children with autism observed under natural conditions during their first dental care cycle. The results appear to confirm the potential of personalized technology to reduce anxiety in professional settings, increasing children's wellbeing and safety and encouraging oral hygiene as part of their daily routine.

CCS Concepts

• **Human-centered computing~Participatory design** • *Human-centered computing~Accessibility systems and tools* • *Applied computing~Healthcare information systems*

Keywords

Autism; Dental health; Web application; Cognitive games

1. INTRODUCTION

The behavior of patients with autism spectrum disorder (ASD) makes the delivery of oral hygiene and dental treatment a big problem due to their different sensory perceptions. Recent studies acknowledge ASD children's difficulty approaching dental visits and performing daily oral care as the most significant factors in their poor oral health. Their higher rate of pathologies in fact can be related to a lack of prevention in oral care, which usually is not appropriately delivered to meet their special needs [5]. Children with autism need to be supported during dental visits by an interdisciplinary plan of action that takes into account the individual's specific needs and implements strategies to promote better dental health [5]. To increase the probability of successful dental treatment of ASD patients, the dentist should have an in-depth interdisciplinary understanding of the autism syndrome as well as of behavioral principles for therapeutic intervention. Barry [4] examined the problems encountered by children with autism when accessing dental care, using a questionnaire completed by 112 subjects (parents), suggesting some intervention guidelines involving photos and social stories (which are a subset of the ICT activities attempted in our study).

ASSETS '17, October 29-November 1, 2017, Baltimore, MD, USA

ACM ISBN 978-1-4503-4926-0/17/10.
https://doi.org/10.1145/3132525.3134799

The effectiveness of ICT in teaching various skills has been confirmed by several studies. Video modeling [10] and visual programs for the development of social skills [3] are increasingly used. The literature reports the use of video materials to obtain the cooperation of ASD children during a dental visit, for instance to visually teach the children how to brush their teeth [9]. Visual scheduling has also been very useful for helping the child understand and accept sequences of activities [6]. Isong et al. [5] tested two types of electronic screen media – a Google glass (sun-glass-style video eyewear) and a DVD reader – showing that their use was beneficial in reducing fear and uncooperative behaviors in ASD children undergoing dental visits. However, they used the child's favorite digital movies or videos performed by a normal-typical child in a general dental setting. Personalization may increase the intervention's usability and efficacy, so we use videos and pictures made during the child's own dental sessions, making the child an active participant in content creation. This exploratory study investigates the use of ICT to engage and simplify dental care for children with autism by actively involving the subject; the aim is to define a general methodology to enhance current practice.

2. THE STUDY

Ten children 6-12 years old (age range covering the permanent dentition process) were recruited from among young patients with autism seeking access to dental care at a public hospital in Pisa. The group, identified with the help of the no-profit association Autismo Pisa Onlus, included nine low-functioning children (three non-receptive and non-verbal, three receptive non-verbal, and three receptive verbal) and one high-functioning. Two different multidisciplinary teams were enrolled: clinical professionals (dentists and neuropsychiatrist) and ICT researchers. Two dental professionals and one neuro-psychiatric expert defined the clinical protocol. Parents had a crucial role, especially by assisting and supervising recommended activities at home. One dentist supervised the overall procedures and interacted with parents; the other delivered oral care to children, assisted by the hygienist when necessary. An ICT researcher, present at all children's visits, recorded observational data of children's behavior. The protocol includes: (i) identification of figures and roles to involve; (ii) the number and frequency of visits to plan with the children; (iii) the amount, type, and collection of data needed to characterize the children; (iv) activities to perform during visits; (v) definition of the materials to be used. The first meeting helped the dentist get to know each child (and his/her parents) and test the child's reactions to simple requests such as to sit in the dental chair or open their mouth. A questionnaire was administered to the caregivers to collect data related to the child's oral condition, dental hygiene habits, sensory disturbances, the child's autism condition, and the use of technological devices such as tablets and smartphones.

2.1 Activities

The children's training was structured to include three different types of activities: medical procedures, educational activities (during the visits) and homework using a kit of personalized digital resources (video and games) that the dentist provided to each child's family. Visits were scheduled as weekly appointments (45 min) for each child over a 3-month period. The venue was always the same clinical room, to avoid confusion and ease familiarization. The dentist (helped by the ICT researcher) collected resources (part of the kit) gradually, visit by visit, personalizing them in all the intervention phases. The kit was given to the child to be used at home in order to prepare the child for the next appointment. Children were actively involved in resource collection using a tablet (especially as a camera) in order to create a constantly updated personal multimedia archive. Moreover, the dentist provided each child with typical dental objects such as mirror, probe, toothbrush, gloves and protective glasses, inviting the child to simulate their use at home, assisted by caregivers.

2.2 Materials

Examples of materials used in this study to support the familiarization process are: 1) **Cognitive learning games**, to familiarize the patient with dental procedures in an amusing way. In ASD children, games are used to stimulate learning through imitation [1], [2], [10] and to capture user attention and collaboration in performing specific tasks. Four kinds of customizable digital games: memories, puzzles, sequences and matching exercises. Sequences proved to be particularly helpful in teaching "how things happen" and how to communicate with clinical staff. As Menzies et Al. [7] highlighted in their study "the most important aspects of communication from the patient were identified as being *yes*, *no* and *stop*". 2) **Audio, video and photos** indexed by visit date, to keep track of the important phases of the visit. The child can navigate his/her resources and show them to parents, relatives or friends. 3) **Interactive PDF files** equipped with sound effects: particularly useful for narrating stories that introduce the dental environment, procedures and/or objects. This allows associating positive elements with a stressful event and can help reduce resistance to change. 4) **Videos** reproducing all actions from the arrival at the clinic to the child sitting in the dentist's chair. The videos are essential for activating the imitation. Seeing familiar people performing target actions can help the child's imitation process [8]. Crucial attention is devoted to technical details such as freeze frame, zoom, audio-visual aids and graphics that transform the footage into a powerful educational tool.

3. RESULTS AND CONCLUSION

This study investigated whether technology can make dental care more efficient, effective and pleasant for ASD children. Starting from previous research, we investigated how to take advantage of every child's interest in gaming and multimedia content, to facilitate ASD children's dental care. Results of this study appear to confirm the feasibility of the proposed approach and the positive role of technology support: (i) Eight out of ten children responded to this approach positively, modeling their behavior and becoming increasingly collaborative, visit by visit; (ii) Nearly all caregivers manifested satisfaction with the approach due to their active involvement. (iii) Caregivers strongly committed to the protocol, who respected the weekly schedule, felt that the child-parent relationship was reinforced, and the corresponding five children successfully completed the dental protocol in the scheduled time. In contrast, three children who missed half or more of the scheduled sessions due to caregiver issues were also unable to complete the familiarization protocol and then their dental procedures in the time scheduled. Flexible and dynamically customizable technology could adapt to the specific needs and preferences of each child, aiding the familiarization process and reducing anxiety in professional settings, increasing children's wellbeing and safety.

Starting from these results, we extracted the requirements of a Web environment for easy creation, management and fruition of digital resources for ASD children and dentists, in an accessible structured framework. As future work, we will apply participative design and early prototyping to create the MyDentist platform.

4. REFERENCES

[1] Aresti-Bartolome, N., Garcia-Zapirain, B. (2014). Technologies as support tools for persons with autistic spectrum disorder: a systematic review. Int. journal of environmental research and public health, 11(8), 7767-7802.

[2] Artoni, S., Pelagatti, S., Buzzi, M. C., Buzzi, M., and Senette, C., Technology-enhanced discriminative programs for children with autism. Proc. of the 8th Int. Conf. on Pervasive Computing Technologies for Healthcare 331-334 (2014)

[3] Ayres, Ayres, K. M., Maguire, A., McClimon, D. Acquisition and generalization of chained tasks taught with computer based video instruction to children with autism. Education and Training in Developmental Disabilities, 493-508 (2009)

[4] Barry, S. M. (2012). Improving access and reducing barriers to dental care for children with autism spectrum disorder. University of Leeds.

[5] Isong, I. A., Rao, S. R., Holifield, C., Iannuzzi, D., Hanson, E., Ware, J., Nelson, L. P. Addressing dental fear in children with autism spectrum disorders: a randomized controlled pilot study using electronic screen media. Clinical pediatrics, 53(3), 230-237 (2014)

[6] Kientz, J. A., Hayes, G. R., Westeyn, T. L., Starner, T., Abowd, G. D. Pervasive computing and autism: Assisting caregivers of children with special needs. IEEE Pervasive Computing, 6 (1) (2007)

[7] Menzies, R., Herron, D., Scott, L., Freeman, R., Waller, A. (2013). Involving clinical staff in the design of a support tool improve dental communication for patients with intellectual disabilities. In Proceedings of the 15th International ACM SIGACCESS Conference on Computers and Accessibility (p. 55). ACM.

[8] Oberman, L. M., Ramachandran, V. S., Pineda, J. A. Modulation of mu suppression in children with autism spectrum disorders in response to familiar or unfamiliar stimuli: the mirror neuron hypothesis. Neuropsychologia, 46(5), 1558-1565 (2008)

[9] Pilebro, C., Bäckman, B.Teaching oral hygiene to children with autism. International Journal of Paediatric Dentistry, 15(1), 1-9 (2005)

[10] Tereshko, L., MacDonald, R., Ahearn, W. H. Strategies for teaching children with autism to imitate response chains using video modeling. Research in Autism Spectrum Disorders, 4(3), 479-489 (2010)

Identifying and Mitigating Technology-Related Anxiety

Kelly Steelman
Michigan Technological University
1400 Townsend Drive
Houghton MI 49931 USA
steelman@mtu.edu

Charles Wallace
Michigan Technological University
1400 Townsend Drive
Houghton MI 49931 USA
wallace@mtu.edu

ABSTRACT

Our experience with digital literacy tutoring for older adults confirms other research that identifies technology-related anxiety as a significant barrier for this constituency. Based on established theories of instructional design, we hypothesize that anxiety impairs the development of digital literacy skills by consuming critical cognitive resources. Our research with experienced tutors reveals numerous strategies for mitigating anxiety and motivates the development of anxiety-aware instructional and design frameworks, and new anxiety scales that better reflect current devices, services, and threats

CCS Concepts

•Social and professional topics → Seniors; •Applied computing → Collaborative learning; *Personal computers and PC applications;* **•Human-centered computing →** *Empirical studies in accessibility;*

Keywords

Digital literacy; Senior citizens; Accessibility; Anxiety

1. TECHNOLOGY-RELATED ANXIETY: A BARRIER TO DIGITAL ENTRY

Technology related anxiety (TRA) constitutes a formidable barrier to entry for many newcomers to the digital world [4]. It is associated with resistance to computer use [4, 12], poor task performance [2, 6] and impaired learning of computer skills [7]. Indeed, we conceive of this domain-specific anxiety as an accessibility issue that requires special care in both technology design and instruction.

Since 2011 our BASIC (Building Adult Skills in Computing) program has provided digital literacy tutoring to our local community [1, 10]. Many patrons report feeling anxious using technology and seek help because they have been forced to adopt a new technology as services and functions move exclusively online. Our experience suggests that anxiety not only hinders adoption but also stifles the skills needed for long-term digital independence.

Through a cognitive task analysis eliciting best practices from our tutors, we have identified a pattern of successful guided learning strategies [10], many explicitly directed at identifying and mitigating anxiety. Tutors emphasize *wayfinding* (deliberate, goal-directed search) combined with *exploration* (heuristic, breadth-first traversal). Our tutors report that anxiety coincides with an unwillingness to explore and an excessive reliance on rote memorization of sequences to accomplish specific tasks—a fragile knowledge that cannot support the rapid pace of technological change. Anxiety, it seems, is interfering with the learning process itself.

2. ANXIETY AS RESOURCE DRAIN

Through what mechanism(s) does anxiety impair performance and learning? Two prominent theories of instructional design [11, 8] posit that meaningful learning requires sufficient cognitive resources to process new information and connect it with prior knowledge in long-term memory. When processing demands exceed the learner's cognitive capacity, the learner experiences cognitive overload and learning will be impaired. These theories suggest that high levels of anxiety should impair the development of digital literacy skills.

Attentional Control Theory (ACT) [5] specifically identifies anxiety as a source of resource consumption. Executive memory resources are required for three primary functions: inhibition of disruptions from task-irrelevant stimuli, shifting attention between tasks, and adapting to changing task demands. Anxiety produces decrements in tasks that rely upon these functions. Notably, these functions are critical to wayfinding and exploration, as both tasks require users to maintain one or more goals while avoiding distractions. ACT, therefore, suggests that anxiety must be addressed to release the cognitive resources necessary for the development of higher-order digital literacy skills. These theories also suggest that the costs of anxiety may be exacerbated for individuals with lower levels of cognitive capacity, due to aging, cognitive impairments, or other factors.

3. IDENTIFYING TRA

In order to mitigate technology-related anxiety, we must first be able to identify anxious users. Although numerous scales are available to assess computer anxiety (e.g., [6, 9, 12]), many were developed well over a decade ago to assess anxiety and self-efficacy associated with desktop computer use. These scales include questions about outdated

ASSETS '17 October 29-November 1, 2017, Baltimore, MD, USA

ACM ISBN 978-1-4503-4926-0/17/10.

DOI: https://doi.org/10.1145/3132525.3134820

technology (e.g., floppy discs). Likewise, as many of these scales were developed before the advent of smartphones, tablets social media, cloud computing, and even Google, they lack questions about these popular modern technologies and functions.

To our knowledge, there is no anxiety scale that encompasses the full range of modern computing devices and their respective functions and applications. Our work with the BASIC program suggests several sources of anxiety that may not be well captured by older computer anxiety scales, including online phishing scams, identity theft, viruses and malware, cloud-based storage, online shopping, and social media privacy settings.

4. MITIGATING TRA

Our analysis reveals that tutors use numerous strategies to mitigate anxiety. For example, many tutors employ a *sandbox* technique, creating temporary accounts or documents allowing learners to play and practice without risking their personal data. Tutors also *commiserate* with learners, expressing their own frustration about poor design and assuring learners that many problems reflect more on the device than on the learner. Likewise, tutors admit when they do not immediately have a solution, giving patrons the thrill of *stumping the expert* and giving tutors the chance to model their problem solving process.

Inspired by such practices, we propose an anxiety-aware design toolkit. This toolkit will allow web developers to implement accessibility functions that extend the value of the interaction of a tutoring program, or substitute for it if no such program is available. We propose three scaffolded accessibility functions designed to mitigate anxiety:

- *Show My Options.* Design elements will provide the option of a simplified roadmap pointing out directions of importance for newcomers. With appropriately tagged web elements, users can consult the website for relevant options, highlighted with extraneous detail temporarily obscured. Web content will offer users a clearer picture of directions to go—including "escape routes" back to a known safe state.

- *Play It Forward.* With design elements from our toolkit, high-risk website options, or those that could be perceived so, can be appropriately tagged with links to appropriate play-it-forward material. A user who wishes to see the effects of the action without committing can request a sandboxed simulation of consequent actions.

- *Annotate.* Our toolkit will permit generation of "dynamic breadcrumbs" associated with function rather than place. Through appropriate tagging of elements in the website design, users can record key workflows and subscribe to changes. As web design modifications trigger changes to those workflows, users can be informed of them and alerted to new ways of achieving the same functionality.

5. TRA: A CROSS-CUTTING ISSUE

To date, technology-related anxiety appears to have not been widely considered as an accessibility issue in computing. A review of ACM's accessibility literature (the ASSETS conference proceedings and the TACCESS journal) yielded no articles, other than our own, with the keyword "anxiety." A search of the ACM Full-Text Collection yielded only 7 in the last 30 years that include the phrase "computer anxiety", with only a few including tech anxiety or tech acceptance as dependent measures in the assessment of various technologies (e.g., [3]).

We believe that this issue could well be a cross-cutting concern worthy of attention in a wide range of accessibility efforts. For instance, participants testing new assistive approaches may be experiencing unacknowledged technology-related anxiety, posing a significant confounding factor. In addition, if anxiety consumes cognitive resources, those with fewer resources to start may be most impaired.

6. REFERENCES

[1] K. Atkinson, J. Barnes, J. Albee, P. Anttila, J. Haataja, K. Nanavati, K. Steelman, and C. Wallace. Breaking barriers to digital literacy: An intergenerational social-cognitive approach. In *Proceedings of 18th International SIGACCESS Conference on Computers and Accessibility*, pages 239–244, 2016.

[2] M. Brosnan. The impact of computer anxiety and self-efficacy upon performance. *Journal of Computer Assisted Learning*, 14:223–234, 1998.

[3] M. Conci, F. Pianesi, and M. Zancanaro. Older adults' attitude towards a monitoring technology. In *Proceedings of the 28th Annual European Conference on Cognitive Ergonomics*, pages 143–146, 2010.

[4] S. Czaja, N. Charness, A. Fisk, C. Hertzog, S. Nair, W. Rogers, and J. Sharit. Factors predicting the use of technology: Findings from the center for research and education on aging and technology enhancement (create). *Psychology and Aging*, 21(2):333, 2006.

[5] M. W. Eysenck, N. Derakshan, R. Santos, and M. G. Calvo. Anxiety and cognitive performance: Attentional control theory. *Emotion*, 7(2):336–353, 2007.

[6] R. K. Heinssen, C. Glass, and L. Knight. Assessing computer anxiety: Development and validation of the computer anxiety rating scale. *Computers in Human Behavior*, 3:49–59, 1987.

[7] G. Marcoulides. The relationship between computer anxiety and computer achievement. *Journal of Educational Computing Research*, 4:151–158, 1988.

[8] R. Mayer and R. Moreno. Nine ways to reduce cognitive load in multimedia learning. *Educational Psychologist*, 38(1):43–52, 2003.

[9] C. Murphy, D. Coover, and S. Owen. Development and validation of the computer self-efficacy scale. *Educational and Psychological Measurement*, 49:893–899, 1989.

[10] K. S. Steelman, K. L. Tislar, L. C. Ureel, and C. Wallace. Eliciting best practices in digital literacy tutoring: A cognitive task analysis approach. In *Proceedings of HCI International*, 2017.

[11] J. Sweller. *Instructional Design in Technical Areas.* ACER Press, 1999.

[12] G. Torkzadeh and I. Angula. The concept and correlates of computer anxiety. *Behavior and Information Technology*, 11:99–108, 1994.

Independent Word Discovery for People with Aphasia

Mmachi G. Obiorah[1], Anne Marie Piper[2], Michael Horn[1]
[1]TIDAL Lab, [2]Inclusive Technology Lab
Northwestern University, Evanston, IL
obiorahm@u.northwestern.edu, {ampiper, michael-horn}@northwestern.edu

ABSTRACT

Augmentative and Alternative Communication (AAC) devices help people with speech-language impairments due to aphasia express themselves more independently and fluently. However, current AACs are still limited in that they must be pre-programmed with common words or phrases prior to use. When people with aphasia encounter unexpected and unplanned situations or contexts, they may have difficulty using their AAC device to generate the desired speech. We present the design of an AAC application that uses image recognition technology to give people with aphasia just in time access to words. Our design automatically carries out an extensive retrieval of words associated with a captured image. The relevance, accuracy and usefulness of each word can then be verified independently by the user through an intensive retrieval of images associated with each word.

Keywords

Aphasia; Augmentative and Alternative Communication Devices

1. INTRODUCTION

Word finding difficulty is a symptom of aphasia in which an individual is unable to generate spoken language associated with a an idea, object, or action. AAC devices (e.g., Lingraphica[1], Dynavox[2]) attempt to address word finding difficulties by providing a bank of words, often text coupled with images, and organizing those words in a recognizable order. The person with aphasia is then trained to use the device to retrieve words when he/she needs them. Many AAC devices allow the user to expand and customize the device's vocabulary, although this tailoring takes time and speech-language pathologists often perform device customization. AAC devices rely heavily on the presence of other people to explore new words and extend or reorganize the device's vocabulary. In addition, AACs are usually programmed prior to use and therefore may be less useful in novel situations.

Generally, people with aphasia are able to recognize symbols and images in spite of having either expressive or receptive speech-language impairments. This ability to recognize images and symbols is often applied in the design of AAC devices to support the user in sentence composition using captioned icons. Yet, a significant limitation is that both the text and the image sets are static and do not adapt to new stimuli in the user's environment. In our work, we explore a design that supports users of AACs in independently associating texts, images, and sounds in novel situations. We hypothesize that our design will empower users by reducing their reliance on external parties for novel word captioning and support users in exploring their environment.

2. RELATED WORK

While there are many different forms of aphasia and each individual presents slightly differently, word finding is a common challenge across this population. As a result, both commercial products and academic researchers have invested considerable effort in addressing word finding challenges through the use of AACs. Specifically, the ability for an individual to use an AAC effectively depends on their ability to search for, identify, and select the desired word or phrase in time for communication. To help achieve just-in-time speech through an AAC, many existing systems (e.g.Proloquo2go[3], Lingraphica[1]) organize words into hierarchical representations, and words are accessed by navigating through the hierarchy. Hierarchical representations, though useful, can become too deep, complex, and confusing for many users [2].

As an alternative approach, Nikolova et al [2] explored the use of semantic relatedness, or the frequency of occurrence of words together and how much one word brings another to mind. They found that structuring available word choices based on semantic relatedness out performed a hierarchical organization for sentence composition except when finding the initial word in the sentence. Similarly, Epps et al. [1] used location tracking and specialized algorithms to retrieve words from the Internet and supply them to the AAC. Their method complemented the base vocabulary of the AAC and was adaptive based on the location of the user.

Our work, like Epps et al [1], addresses just-in-time word retrieval. However, we do this through image recognition, which supports extensive retrieval of words and allows the user to independently determine the accuracy or relevance of the retrieved words by associating each word with descriptive images.

3. DESIGN OF PHOTOSEARCH

To better understand the process of speech-language therapy and word finding challenges, we have observed seven adults with aphasia during a total of 43 hours of therapy. Additionally, we collaborated with four clinicians. Our observations and discussions with clinical experts focused on becoming familiar with aphasia and the process of therapy; understanding how current AACs are used within therapy and how they can empower/disempower people with aphasia; and investigating how AAC's can be better designed to support people with aphasia. We

[1] https://www.aphasia.com/
[2] https://www.tobiidynavox.com/
[3] http://www.assistiveware.com/product/proloquo2go

ASSETS '17, October 29-November 1, 2017, Baltimore, MD, USA

ACM ISBN 978-1-4503-4926-0/17/10.
https://doi.org/10.1145/3132525.3134790

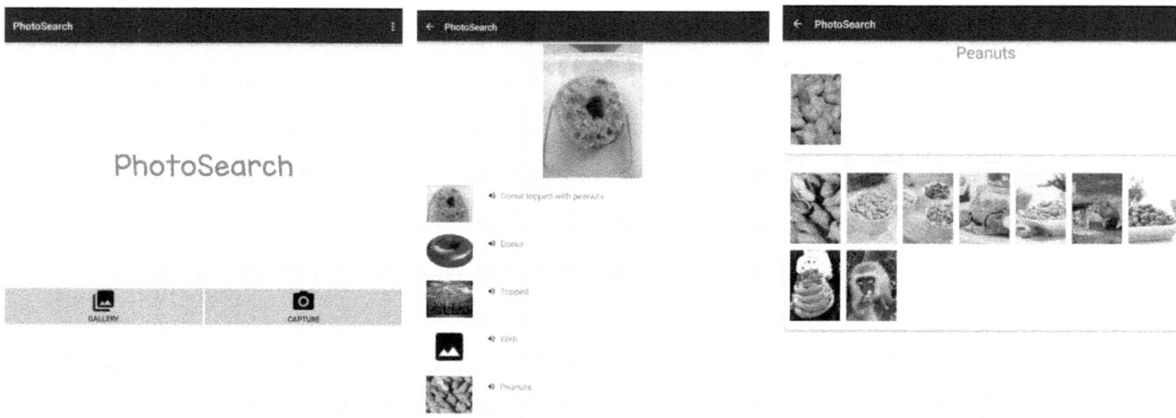

Figure 1: ***Left:*** **The user can either select an existing image from the gallery or take a new photo.** ***Center:*** **The captured photo is captioned. In this case, it is captioned as "Donut topped with peanuts". Each word is listed below and associated with a descriptive image.** ***Right:*** **When the word "Peanut" is clicked more images that describe the word "Peanut" are retrieved. The images are ordered according to a prediction confidence.**

took field notes from our observations and discussions with experts. Preliminary analysis of these data led to the design of a new approach to a word finding application.

4. SYSTEM DESIGN

We created an Android application called PhotoSearch, which captions images automatically. Image captioning for PhotoSearch is powered by the CloudSight[4] API. Users take a photo of their environment and the system returns text-based tags associated with that image. The tags include nouns associated with objects in the image as well as adjectives, such as the color of the object and type of material of the object (e.g., wood, paper). As a result, a single image capture serves as an access point to a variety of words (see Figure 1). Since people who have aphasia vary in their ability to access written and spoken language but may still have the ability to recognize images, the application presents each term to the user along with a separate image for each term (retrieved from the Openclipart[5] project and Pixabay[6]). The application then provides text-to-speech functionality for each word-image description. The descriptive image helps the user to distinguish and identify the meaning of each retrieved word while also serving as a link to more images associated with the word. If the user clicks the descriptive image, the application displays a page with even more descriptive images associated with this initial word (as in Figure 1 where 'Peanut' was clicked). This is intended to help the user to independently establish a level of confidence in the accuracy of the retrieved word as well as iteratively and independently find the desired word. Images are ordered on the display screen according to a prediction algorithm confidence that is based on content based image retrieval.

5. CONCLUSION AND FUTURE WORK

Our ongoing work involves working with speech-language pathologists to use this application within a clinical setting. We are first testing our application with several speech-language pathologists to further inform the design, understand potential usability problems, and identify use cases. In addition, feedback from initial tests will inform our design iterations and our final design, which we plan to test with people with aphasia.

Even though our application tries to help the user establish confidence in the association of a word with an image, word sense disambiguation is a difficult problem to solve. We intend to further explore establishing confidence in the accuracy of the retrieved word by including a social component to the application where a structured request for help from a caregiver or family members can be made by the user of the application.

The loss of independence in communication is one of the most difficult aspects of aphasia. PhotoSearch applies image recognition and captioning to better support people with aphasia in discovering new words independently in diverse contexts.

6. ACKNOWLEDGMENTS

We thank NUCASLL for their support with data collection and for their advice and feedback throughout this study.

7. REFERENCES

[1] C. Demmans Epps, J. Djordjevic, S. Wu, K. Moffat, and R. M. Baecker. Towards providing just-in-time vocabulary support for assistive and augmentative communication. *In Proceedings of the 2012 ACM International Conference on Intelligent User Interfaces,* IUI '12, pages 33-36. ACM, 2012.

[2] S.Nikolova, M. Tremaine, and P. R. Cook. Click on bake to get cookies: Guiding word-finding with semantic associations. *In Proceedings of the 12th International ACM SIGACCESS Conference on Computers and Accessibility*, ASSETS '10, pages 155-162. ACM, 2010.

[4] https://cloudsight.ai/
[5] https://openclipart.org/
[6] https://pixabay.com/

Interactive Urdu Braille Learning System for Parents of Visually Impaired Students

Muhammad Zahid Iqbal
Department of Computer Science
Information Technology University
Lahore, Punjab
Pakistan
MSCS14043@itu.edu.pk

Suleman Shahid
Department of Computer Science
Lahore University of Management Sciences, Lahore
Punjab, Pakistan
suleman.shahid@lums.edu.pk

Mustafa Naseem
ATLAS Institute
University of Colorado, Boulder
Colorado, USA
Mustafa.Naseem@colorado.edu

ABSTRACT

Braille literacy is one of the core pillars of education for visually impaired children. Previous studies have highlighted the importance of Braille for Visually impaired children by suggesting that students who read Braille outside of the classroom have higher reading speed and fluency. In resource –constrained countries, such as Pakistan, the visually impaired students may acquire the knowledge of Urdu Braille at special education schools. However, there is a dearth of resources for the parents of such children, when it comes to learning Urdu Braille. Therefore, we designed a web-based Urdu Braille Translator and interactive Braille learning tool to enhance the Urdu Braille learning experience for parents of visually impaired. The usability study of this tool was conducted with 15 parents of the visually impaired students.

KEYWORDS

ICT for Education; Special Education; Braille learning; Self-Learning

ACM CLASSIFICATION KEYWORDS

Human Factors, Performance, Languages, Evaluation

1. INTRODUCTION

Literacy of visually impaired people is a challenge all over the world. It is a mammoth task especially in developing countries. According to the WHO, 285 Million people are estimated to be visually impaired worldwide: 39 million are visually impaired and 246 have low vision [1]. According to a survey of National Federation for visually impaired, "less than 10 percent of the 1.3 million people, who are legally visually impaired in the United States are Braille readers" [2]. Xu, and Cheng developed applications based on TeslaTouch, a system that provides tactile sensation to moving fingers on touch screens [3]. Brailleplay has accessible games for Smartphone that teach Braille character encodings [4].

HoliBraille is a system to enables Braille input and output on mobile devices by using vibrotactile motors [5]. Furthermore, Braille Bug developed for learning English Braille through words games has been presented by *American Foundation for the Blinds* [6]. Besides the above mentioned systems, Araki developed self-learning system using speech technology for visually impaired to learn through audio dialogue [7]. *BrailleTouch* is an eye-free text entry in the Smartphone [8]. V-Braille is Braille touch on the standard phone using the touch screen [9].

The focus of this research is to develop an Urdu Braille Translator and an interactive application, which can assist parents to learn Urdu Braille.

Urdu Braille

Urdu Braille is six dotted (same as English Braille) Braille language used for teaching visually impaired teachers. It followed the UNESCO standard [2]. Urdu is written as Persian style from left to right but Urdu Braille written as Right to left.

2. URDU BRAILLE TRANSLATOR AND LEARNING APPLICATION

First, we developed a web-based Urdu Braille Font and an Urdu Braille Translator as per the standards proposed by the UNESCO [2]. Figure 1 is explaining our web based Urdu Braille translator.

The translated Urdu script can be imported to PDF or directly sent to embosser. Our custom Braille font for Urdu can be downloaded[1]to be used in the MS Word.

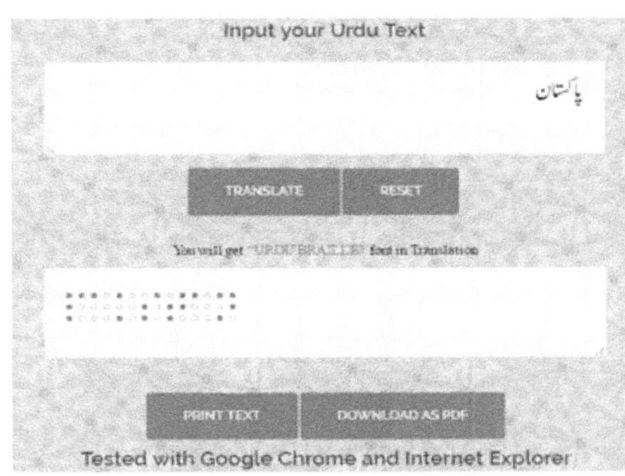

Figure 1: Web based Urdu Braille Translator

In the next step, we developed an Urdu Braille learning application for parents of visually impaired students. The Braille learning application has four main modules:

(1) A multiple-choice interface (figure 2) where against each picture learners see multiple Braille words and their task is to pick

ACM ISBN 978-1-4503-4926-0/17/10.
https://doi.org/10.1145/3132525.3134809

[1]http://urdubraille.com/Urdu-Braille.zip

the right word. If they pick a wrong word, an explanation is given and they are asked to go ahead with the learning exercise.

(2) An Urdu Braille reading module where participants are shown a Braille word and their task is to pick the right Urdu word.

(3) A fill in the blank module where learners are shown a Braille word and they are asked to type in the right Urdu word in the provide space.

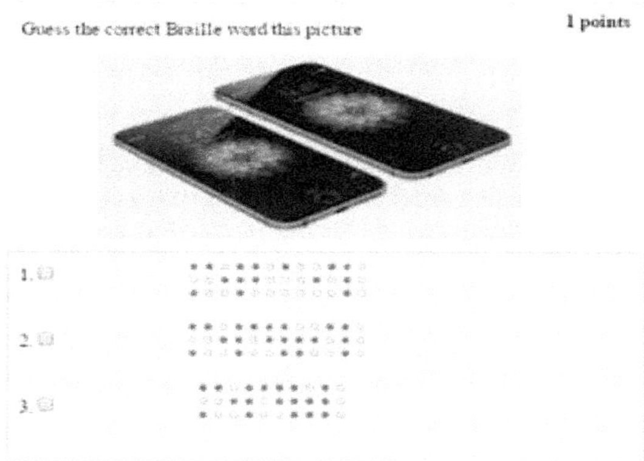

Figure 2: Braille learning application – MCQs interface.

3. USABILITY TESTING

For testing the usability of both the application, we tested the method of learning Braille through self-learning Application with 15 parents (aged 28-45) of visually impaired students who never used Braille before.

We conducted five (5) tests in a period of one month with 15 parents. For these tests, the participants used Urdu script from *BBC Urdu* and translated it by using Urdu Braille translator. On the basis of their learning from translated Urdu script, they used online Braille learning application. In the Figure 3, Results are presented for all five tests. Before using these tests, parents were briefed with the use of application each and every step.

Average Attempted questions: Average questions attempted by all fifteen (15) participants. (Questions attempted /15)

Average correct Questions: Average of correct questions from attempted questions. (Correct Questions /15).

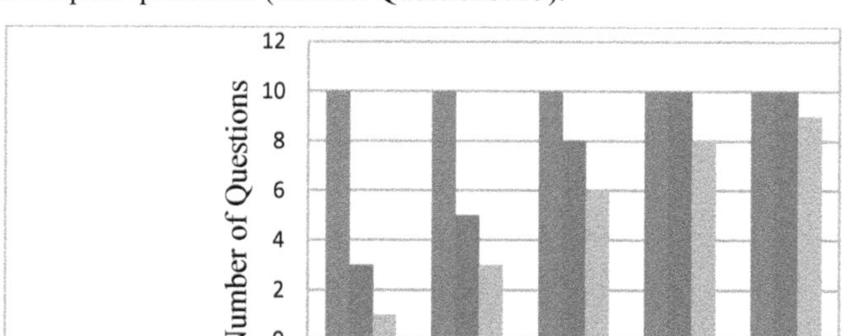

	Test 1	Test 2	Test 3	Test 4	Test 5
Total Questions Per Test	10	10	10	10	10
Average Attempted Question	3	5	8	10	10
Average Correct Questions	1	3	6	8	9

Figure 3: Five (5) Test bases comparison for 15 participants.

During the process of evaluation, the participants had different views to share about educating a special child. One of the Braille instructors suggested that *"Visually impaired students need individual attention from teachers and there is lot more effort required to start their early education". However, according to* one of the parents, *"start of early life education for my child was impossible due to mobility and accessibility issues".*

A female participant shared a view that, *"the idea of using the method of early classes textbooks (using the new system) is great to create interest and ease in learning".*

4. CONCLUSION & FUTURE WORK

A gradual increase in the participant learning by attempting questions correctly proved from the tests helped us to measure the effectiveness of the application. The printed Urdu text to Braille translation system has many interesting applications in schools, libraries and offices, where instructions and notices are to be read. Urdu Braille Translation system can be used for reproducing Urdu textbooks and publications for visually impaired people.

Training the parents in Braille language will enable them to help their children in studying efficiently while sitting in their homes. This study has opened interesting avenues for future. We aim to introduce this application in special educational schools which can guide parents and help them to learn the Braille.

5. REFERENCES

[1]. World Health Organization, "Fact Sheet: Visual impairment and visually impaired", October 2013, Web, July 01, 2014

http://www.who.int/mediacentre/factsheets/fs282/en/

[2]. Mackenzie, C. "World Braille usage." UNESCO,(1954).

[3]. Xu, Cheng, et al. "Tactile display for the visually impaired using TeslaTouch." CHI'11 Extended Abstracts on Human Factors in Computing Systems. ACM, 2011.

[4]. Milne, Lauren R., et al. "BraillePlay: educational smartphone games for blind children." *Proceedings of the 16th international ACM SIGACCESS conference on Computers & accessibility*. ACM, 2014.

[5]. Nicolau, Hugo, et al. "HoliBraille: multipoint vibrotactile feedback on mobile devices." *Proceedings of the 12th Web for All Conference*. ACM, 2015.

[6]. American Foundation for the Blinds *"Braille Bug"* http://braillebug.afb.org/

[7]. Araki, Masahiro, Kana Shibahara, and Yuko Mizukami. "Spoken dialogue system for learning Braille." *2011 IEEE 35th Annual Computer Software and Applications Conference*. IEEE, 2011.

[8]. Frey, Brian, et al. "From texting app to Braille literacy." CHI'12 Extended Abstracts on Human Factors in Computing Systems. ACM, 2012.

[9]. Jayant, Chandrika, et al. "V-braille: haptic Braille perception using a touch-screen and vibration on mobile phones." *Proceedings of the 12th international ACM SIGACCESS conference on Computers and accessibility*. ACM, 2010

JustPoint: Identifying Colors with a Natural User Interface

Sergio Mascetti
Università degli Studi di Milano
and EveryWare Technologies
sergio.mascetti@unimi.it

Andrea Gerino
Università degli Studi di Milano
and EveryWare Technologies
andrea.gerino@unimi.it

Cristian Bernareggi
Università degli Studi di Milano
and EveryWare Technologies
cristian.bernareggi@unimi.it

Silvia D'Acquisto
Università degli Studi di Milano
silvia.dacquisto
@studenti.unimi.it

Mattia Ducci
Università degli Studi di Milano
mattia.ducci
@studenti.unimi.it

James M. Coughlan
Smith-Kettlewell Eye
Research Institute
coughlan@ski.org

ABSTRACT

People with severe visual impairments usually have no way of identifying the colors of objects in their environment. While existing smartphone apps can recognize colors and speak them aloud, they require the user to center the object of interest in the camera's field of view, which is challenging for many users. We developed a smartphone app to address this problem that reads aloud the color of the object pointed to by the user's fingertip, without confusion from background colors. We evaluated the app with nine people who are blind, demonstrating the app's effectiveness and suggesting directions for improvements in the future.

CCS Concepts

•**Human-centered computing** → **Empirical studies in accessibility; Accessibility technologies; Accessibility systems and tools;** *Mobile computing;* •**Computing methodologies** → *Object recognition;*

Keywords

Assistive Technology, Hand Recognition, Color Detection

1. INTRODUCTION

People with severe visual impairments usually have no way of identifying the colors of objects in their environment, such as clothing, food or other items. While a number of useful mobile smartphone apps are available to recognize colors and speak them aloud, they require the user to center the object of interest in the smartphone camera's field of view, which often poses significant difficulties for the user.

We describe *JustPoint*, a smartphone app that reads aloud the color of the object that is pointed to by the user's fingertip. The users can explore the object surface by moving their finger across it, obtaining the desired color information without confusion from background colors.

ASSETS '17 October 29-November 1, 2017, Baltimore, MD, USA

ACM ISBN 978-1-4503-4926-0/17/10.
DOI: https://doi.org/10.1145/3132525.3134802

Our paper makes two main contributions: (i) an evaluation of a real-time fingertip detection technique, and (ii) the application of this technique to the task of color identification, which allows a blind user to point to a specific region to identify. We distinguish our contributions from the following past work. VizLens [1] performs real-time fingertip detection, but there is no explicit evaluation of fingertip detection, and it is not applied to the task of color identification. Access Lens [2] performs real-time fingertip detection and color identification, but it uses a laptop and a webcam rather than a smartphone, and there is only limited analysis of the system's ability to identify colors for visually impaired users. GIST [3] performs real-time fingertip detection and color identification, but it relies on a special depth camera rather than a standard smartphone camera. Finally, OrCam (http://www.orcam.com/) implements real-time fingertip detection using special-purpose hardware, but there are no publications describing the details of the algorithms used, and it does not perform color identification.

2. THE *JUSTPOINT* APP

JustPoint is an iOS prototype application whose primary purpose is to read aloud the color of the *target area*, i.e., a circular area located close to the fingertip in the direction it's pointing. This is obtained by acquiring frames from the device camera, detecting the target area with a computer vision technique, computing the name of the target area color and informing the user accordingly.

The computer vision technique processes video frames captured by the device's camera in five main steps (see Figure 1). First, the image is pre-processed with a blur filter. Then, skin detection is performed using the threshold-based technique proposed in [4]. The third step is to decide which skin-colored region(if any) is actually a hand. We start by considering each contiguous skin region as a candidate, then we prune this set according to two criteria: size and shape (i.e., template match). In the next step the coordinates of the pointing fingertip have to be found. This computation is based on the idea that the fingertip is generally the vertex of the hand's convex hull that has the largest distance from the center of mass. The center of the target area is determined in the last step by extending the line segment that begins at the hand's center of mass and passes through the fingertip.

While this recognition technique is generally stable, it sometimes reports false positives (i.e., shapes that are erroneously detected as a hand) or false negatives (i.e., the hand

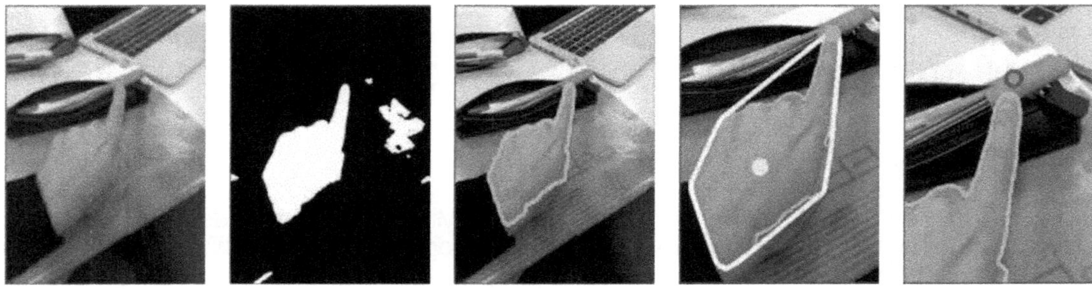

(a) Pre-processed (b) Skin detection (c) Hand detection (d) Fingertip detection (e) Target area

Figure 1: Five main steps of the single frame processing procedure.

is visible but is not detected). During app testing we observed that, in some cases, the app has a sequence of correct recognitions interwoven with incorrect ones. This results in a confusing sequence of readings for the user. In order to make the output more stable, *JustPoint* aggregates results among successive frames.

3. EVALUATION

We conducted both 'computational-based' experiments - aimed at assessing the effectiveness of the computer vision technique - and a 'human-based' evaluation - aimed at evaluating *JustPoint*'s effectiveness and ease of use.

Computational-based experiments use a test-set of 100 images collected from about 30 sighted users. Half of these images contain a hand in the "pointing position" (as in Figure 1(a)), while the others do not contain a hand. Each of these image was manually annotated indicating the target area. Overall, precision is 0.87 and recall is 0.89 (Table 1).

Image set	TP	TN	FP	FN
Images with hand	42	0	3	5
Images without hand	0	47	3	0
All images	42	47	6	5

Table 1: Computational-based evaluation results

'Human-based' evaluation was conducted with 9 blind participants who, after a short training, were asked to complete 3 tasks, each consisting of recognizing, by using *JustPoint*, an object in a set of 3, indistinguishable by touch. For example, in the first task participants had to identify a box of strawberry candies, which is mainly red, distinguishing it from other two boxes. Credit cards were used in the second task and bottles in the third.

All the participants were able to complete the first and the second task by providing the correct answer in less than 2 minutes for each task (on average 79 sec. for task 1 and 82 sec. for task 2). In the third task 3 participants gave the wrong answer. This task also turned out to be more time demanding than the others (123 sec. on average). Based on the comments and on the report by the observer, two reasons account for the difficulties encountered in the third task. First, it was challenging for the participants to point the finger on the bottle and hold it steadily in one location; second, the participants failed to hold the bottle with one hand, while maintaining, with that hand, the correct pointing configuration; consequently in some cases *JustPoint* failed to recognize the correct target area.

4. CONCLUSIONS AND FUTURE WORK

We have described *JustPoint*, which was designed to solve the problem of how people with severe visual impairments can identify the colors of objects, including objects that are small or contain multiple colors in a small area. The evaluation shows promising results in terms of both hand detection reliability and app effectiveness judged by end users.

While the hand-detection technique is generally effective, most errors are due to errors in skin identification. So, we intend to experiment with alternative techniques for skin detection. Alternatively, existing solutions based on machine learning can be adapted for skin detection or for the entire process of target area identification. From the point of view of human-computer interaction, we wish to explore the use of a wearable (e.g., eyeglass-mounted or head-mounted) camera. We will also investigate the possibility of augmenting the text-to-speech interface with sonification techniques.

ACKNOWLEDGMENTS

James M. Coughlan was supported by NIH grant 5R01EY025332 and NIDILRR grant 90RE5024-01-00. Sergio Mascetti was supported by grant "Fondo Supporto alla Ricerca" under the project "Assistive Technologies on Mobile Devices".

5. REFERENCES

[1] A. Guo, X. Chen, H. Qi, S. White, S. Ghosh, C. Asakawa, and J. P. Bigham. Vizlens: A robust and interactive screen reader for interfaces in the real world. In *Proc. of the 29th Annual Symp. on User Interface Software and Technology*. ACM, 2016.

[2] S. K. Kane, B. Frey, and J. O. Wobbrock. Access lens: a gesture-based screen reader for real-world documents. In *Proc. of the SIGCHI Conference on Human Factors in Computing Systems*. ACM, 2013.

[3] V. Khambadkar and E. Folmer. Gist: a gestural interface for remote nonvisual spatial perception. In *Proc. of the 26th annual ACM symposium on User interface software and technology*. ACM, 2013.

[4] N. A. A. Rahman, C. W. Kit, and J. See. Rgb-h-cbcr skin colour model for human face detection. In *MMU Int. Symp. on Inf. & Comm. Tech.*, 2006.

Making Facial Expressions of Emotions Accessible for Visually Impaired Persons

Hendrik Buimer
Radboud University
Nijmegen, The Netherlands
h.buimer@donders.ru.nl

Thea van der Geest
HAN University of Applied Sciences
Arnhem, The Netherlands

Abdellatif Nemri
University of Twente
Enschede, The Netherlands

Renske Schellens
Radboud University
Nijmegen, The Netherlands

Richard van Wezel
Radboud University
Nijmegen, The Netherlands

Yan Zhao
University of Twente
Enschede, The Netherlands

Keywords
Vision-impaired persons; facial expressions; emotion recognition; vibrotactile output; wearables

1. INTRODUCTION
Our R&D project is set up in a Human-Centered Design and Engineering process; the prospective user group is involved in various stages of the process. We are designing, developing, testing, and evaluating a wearable system that helps people with visual impairments to perceive facial expressions of emotions. In earlier studies concerning the needs and problems that visually impaired persons encounter in daily life, including interviews we have conducted amongst visually impaired persons, respondents identified their inability to perceive non-verbal cues of conversation partners as a critical issue in their daily life contacts. They ranked this issue as one of the most pressing problems that should be high on the R&D agenda. [1, 4, 6]. We took their expressed need as a starting point for a R&D project on facial expression recognition.

To convey the emotions expressed by the conversation partner, we used a vibrotactile belt, because the haptic modality does not interfere with the other modalities used in most social interactions, such as sound and vision.

The system (see Figure 1) consists of:

1. An eye-level camera which captures the face of the conversation partner in real time, which can be clipped on to any pair of spectacles;
2. The emotion recognition software FaceReader which detects facial expressions and classifies those into one of six basic emotions (i.e. anger, disgust, enjoyment, fear, sadness, surprise) [3, 7, 12];
3. A belt worn on the waist, connected through USB or Bluetooth, with six vibrotactile units each assigned to one of the emotions [11]. The principle is that when the system detects an emotion, the user feels a vibration on the location associated to the detected emotion.

ASSETS '17, October 29-November 1, 2017, Baltimore, MD, USA

ACM ISBN 978-1-4503-4926-0/17/10.
https://doi.org/10.1145/3132525.3134823

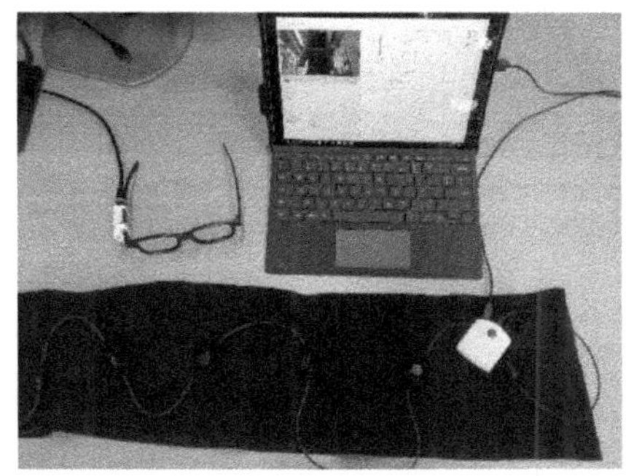

Figure 1 Picture of the current version of the system, existing of a camera clipped-on to spectacles, emotion recognition software running on a tablet, and a vibrotactile belt.

In an earlier study ([2], full paper currently under revision), we have presented the results of a controlled experimental study where people with visual impairments (VIPs) and sighted persons were asked to determine what emotions were presented to them. The images displayed were photos, videos, and additional auditory cues (affect bursts) which are used as validated stimuli in emotion research [5, 8–10]. In this controlled experimental setting, VIPs proved to be able to perceive and recognize emotions from facial expressions at almost the level of sighted persons, and significantly more than without the support of the system. For example, the correct identification of emotional facial expressions from photos without sound cues increased from 14.2% to 82.5%. More importantly, VIPs ventured to imagine how such a system could be applied in situations in daily life, such as work related meetings. To see whether this promise of usefulness for daily life situations like work place conversations could be fulfilled, we wanted to answer an important question: how well would the system perform in more realistic usage contexts, such as an actual one-on-one conversation? In such situations, new challenges arise, such as changing lightning conditions and moving conversations partners who are not always watching directly at the wearer of the system.

The goal of the study we are presenting was to determine whether the earlier developed wearable assistive technology would benefit visually impaired users in realistic usage contexts.

2. METHOD
2.1 Participants
Eight people with visual impairments were participating in the study. The participants, four women and four men, had an average age of 46(±15.8) years old. Five of whom were fully blind, the others were partially sighted. Four of the participants had congenital visual impairments, while the others became visually

impaired at a later stage in life and had been able to see facial expressions in the past.

2.2 Procedure

Participants were invited to participate in two sessions: a training session and an experimental session. The training session, which took place at a location preferred by the participants – most often at their home – lasted about two hours. The participants were presented with pictures and videos of facial expressions of emotions, with and without auditory cues [8, 9]. Over the course of the training, the number of complementary auditory cues decreased, meaning that ultimately the participants had to rely on the vibrotactile cues to determine the emotion expressed in the images.

Two weeks later, the participants were invited to the lab for the experimental session. First, the participants went through another (short) training session. Then the VIPs were asked to engage in a mock job interview with an actor, who played the role of the director of a fictive company. The actor was instructed to keep the conversation as realistic as possible, without the use of any exaggerated facial expressions. The mock job interview consisted of two 15-minute conversations, during one of these the system was worn by the participant.

After the job interview conversations, we conducted semi-structured exit interviews with the participants. We asked questions regarding the users' experiences, perceived usefulness, possible contradictions between their perceptions and the emotions signaled by the system, the economic and financial value of the system, possible improvements of the system, and social acceptance.

2.3 Data collection and preliminary results

During the earlier controlled experimental study, participants showed that the vibrotactile cues were easy to learn and to interpret. In the training sessions, these findings were confirmed, as participants achieved percentage-correct scores of over 95% in the stimuli without complementary auditory cues.

During the observations, various data collection methods were used. Firstly, video-captures were made of the facial expressions of both the actor and the participant of the study, which were combined with a graphical representation of the belt output. This gives us the opportunity to analyze the performance of the system, and checking whether the facial expressions of the actor are recognized by the system and mirrored by the visually impaired conversation partner. The actor annotated his performance in several captured sessions, so we can check whether the system does recognize the emotion expressions that the actor intended to show. The videotapes will be analyzed for emotion expressions by two independent coders.

Additionally, the emotion recognition software logged its performance frame by frame. This so-called emotion log will be used to determine at what times the software surpassed the threshold that was set for each emotion, enabling us to determine the exact times when the system conveyed emotions to the user. We can combine those timestamped data with the video recordings.

From the analysis of the video footage, combined with the emotion log, we expect to draw conclusions about the accuracy of emotion recognition software in realistic settings, as well as insights in the ability of system users to interpret and use cues conveyed by the system while being engaged in a conversation. Preliminary analysis showed that the wearable system is not always conveying correct information to its users, which is problematic and requires improvements before it can be applied as assistive technology. Possible explanations for this difference compared to the earlier controlled experimental setting, are changing lightning conditions and a moving conversation partner, resulting in different viewing distances and angles, making it more challenging to aim the camera at the target.

Finally, we interviewed the participants about their experiences with using the system in a realistic conversation. Besides the findings from the analysis of the video footage and the emotion log, participants also perceived a mismatch between the emotion conveyed by the system and the emotion they perceived from auditory cues. Nevertheless, during moments of silence, the system was perceived helpful to have some idea of what was going on. Even though the recognition of emotions was not always correct, participants were positive about location and the easiness of the vibrotactile cues conveyed by the system. While three participants found it difficult to interpret the cues during the conversation, the others stated they could stay engaged in the conversation while being able to interpret the vibrotactile cues at the same time.

3. ACKNOWLEDGMENTS

There are no conflicts of interest to declare. The research was funded by INTERREG and was approved by the Research Ethical Committee of the University of Twente.

4. REFERENCES

[1] Broerse, J. et al. 2015. *Een onderzoeksagenda vanuit cliëntenperspectief.*

[2] Buimer, H.P. et al. 2016. *Enhancing emotion recognition in VIPs with haptic feedback.*

[3] Ekman, P. 1992. An argument for basic emotions. *Cognition & Emotion.*

[4] Van der Geest, T.M. and Buimer, H.P. 2015. User-centered priority setting for accessible devices and applications. *Mensch und Computer 2015 – Workshopband* (Stuttgart, 2015), 383–389.

[5] Hawk, S.T. et al. 2009. "Worth a thousand words": absolute and relative decoding of nonlinguistic affect vocalizations. *Emotion.* 9, 3 (2009), 293–305. DOI:https://doi.org/10.1037/a0015178.

[6] Krishna, S. et al. 2008. A Systematic Requirements Analysis and Development of an Assistive Device to Enhance the Social Interaction of People Who are Blind or Visually Impaired. *Workshop on Computer Vision Applications for the Visually Impaired.* (2008).

[7] Kuilenburg, H. Van et al. 2008. Facereader 6.1 – How do they do it? (2008), 10000.

[8] Lima, C.F. et al. 2013. When voices get emotional: a corpus of nonverbal vocalizations for research on emotion processing. *Behavior research methods.* 45, 4 (2013), 1234–45. DOI:https://doi.org/10.3758/s13428-013-0324-3.

[9] Olszanowski, M. et al. 2015. Warsaw set of emotional facial expression pictures: A validation study of facial display photographs. *Frontiers in Psychology.* 6, JAN (2015), 1–8. DOI:https://doi.org/10.3389/fpsyg.2015.00516.

[10] Van der Schalk, J. et al. 2011. Moving faces, looking places: Validation of the Amsterdam Dynamic Facial Expression Set (ADFES). *Emotion (Washington, D.C.).* 11, 4 (2011), 907–920. DOI:https://doi.org/10.1037/a0023853.

[11] Science Suit: 2014. *http://www.elitac.nl/science-suit/.*

[12] Den Uyl, M. et al. 2005. FaceReader: an online facial expression recognition system. *Measuring Behavior 2005 5th International Conference on Methods and Techniques in Behavioral Research* (2005), 589–590.

Predictive Link Following Plug-In For Web Browsers

Lyle Pierson Stachecki, John Magee
Department of Mathematics and Computer Science
Clark University, Worcester, MA, USA
lyleps@gmail.com, jmagee@clarku.edu

ABSTRACT

We demonstrate a target-aware pointing assistance software plug-in for web browsers. Web browsing can be difficult for people with motor impairments because of small links and cluttered web pages. The lack of high-precision movements presents a challenge for such interfaces because clicks may miss a link, or links may be followed unintentionally. Our approach is based on Predictive Link Following which alleviates the difficulties with link selection when using mouse replacement interfaces by predicting which link should be clicked based on the proximity of the cursor to the link. We previously presented and evaluated this method as lab-based experiments that were restricted to our custom web pages. We here demonstrate a plug-in for web browsers that allows our method to work on any web page. This publication accompanies the public release of the software as a freely-available download.

CCS Concepts

•**Human-centered computing → Accessibility systems and tools;** *Accessibility technologies;*

Keywords

Accessibilty; web browsing; mouse replacement interfaces; target-aware pointing

1. INTRODUCTION

People with motor impairments may use adaptive mouse devices or mouse replacement interfaces to control the pointer in point-and-click computer interfaces. Example adaptive devices include modified mice, trackballs, mouth joysticks, and touchpads. Mouse-replacement interfaces can include Computer Vision based systems allowing control via head movements or other body parts, and eye-gaze systems that control a pointer based on where the user looks at the screen.

However, many point-and-click tasks can be difficult due to low dexterity, limited mobility, involuntary motions, or the nature of the interface. Particularly with dwell-time based selection interfaces, it can be difficult to stop the pointer motion over a link to activate a click in the precise spot. Small links are especially difficult to select, resulting in the user "missing" the link. Closely clustered links make the problem worse: users may unintentionally follow a nearby link. A low threshold for dwell-time selection can also cause unintended link selection, a phenomenon known as the "Midas Touch" problem.

The aforementioned difficulties have been observed by the second author and his collaborators in Camera Mouse[1] [1], users over a period of many years. The Camera Mouse is a computer vision mouse replacement system intended for people with severe motion impariments. It allows the control of a mouse pointer through head motion or other body motion. These observations have been the primary inspiration for the creation of the predictive link approach to assist users with web browsing.

Assistive pointing systems can be target-aware or target-agnostic. Click actuation can be physical, manual, or inferred. Target-aware pointing systems are difficult to generalize because the pointing interface needs to be informed of the locations of each of the targets. This is a problem because the pointing device is typically controlled by the operating system and sends mouse events to the software application to make interaction decisions.

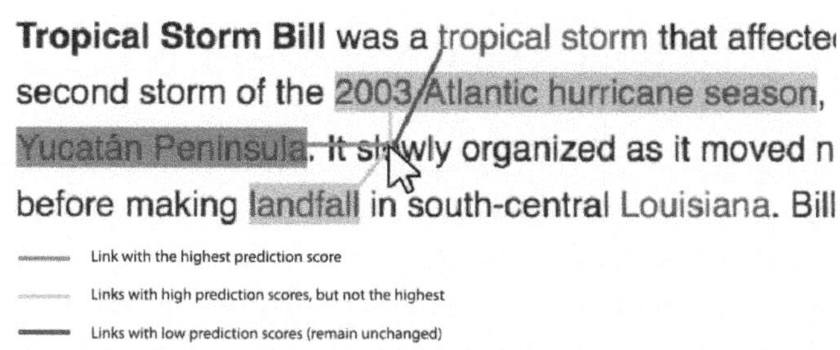

Figure 1: The distance from mouse pointer to bounding box of all links is calculated and contributes to the current link score. Selection normally requires clicking within the bounding box; our system can take into account near-misses. The link with the current highest score is highlighted red, while nearby links with high scores are highlighted orange.

[1] Available at: http://www.cameramouse.org

ASSETS '17 October 29-November 1, 2017, Baltimore, MD, USA

ACM ISBN 978-1-4503-4926-0/17/10.
DOI: https://doi.org/10.1145/3132525.3134776

Our approach is a plug-in for a web browser that intercepts mouse click signals and instead follows links based on analysis of the user's mouse movement behavior. The software accumulates a score based on pointing *near a target* to assist in selecting the target even when the user is unable to actually click on it.

Many applications such as email and social media are now "web based", meaning they run as web pages within a web browser. The way web browsers render web pages exposes the location of all links to scripts and plug-ins. Therefore, our application can retrieve the location of all links on a page and will work with most web pages and applications. This approach thus opens a wide range of applications to target-aware pointing techniques.

2. PREDICTIVE LINK FOLLOWING

Our algorithm analyzes mouse movement and clicks before instructing a web browser to follow a link. Our software is implemented as plug-in for web browsers. This allows it to work with most web pages and with hardware or software that controls the pointer. The system parameters allow it to be configured for different users' abilities and preferences. The proximity of mouse actions to every link on a web page contribute to its prediction score which is used to decide if the link should be followed (see Fig 1). In this way, clicks are no longer *commands* to follow a link, instead becoming an indicator of the user's intention. A click that barely misses a link can still cause the link to be followed.

Each link a at time t has a prediction score $P_t(a)$:

$$P_t(a) = \tau * P_{t-1}(a) + \texttt{pointer}(a)$$

Where τ is a time decay factor, and $\texttt{pointer}(a)$ is a function related to the action of the mouse pointer in the current time instant:

$$\text{pointer}(a) = \frac{1}{(\text{dist}(a, \textit{mousepoint}) + 1)^{\beta}} * \gamma$$

where β affects how much the distance from a link to the click increases the score, and γ weights the click score. These parameters are configurable by the user. The function is used to accumulate a score for how likely a user is trying to click on a particular link a based on the distance from the pointer to the link.

When a click is detected, if $P_t(a) > \texttt{threshold}$, the link a is followed and all scores reset to zero.

3. EXPERIMENTAL EVALUATION

The authors and their collaborators previously reported experimental evaluations of two iterations of the Predictve Link approach.

In the first study [2], seven participants used the Camera Mouse to control the mouse pointer with their heads. Four of the seven participants experienced better performance with the predictive algorithm, while one reported equal performance and two reported worse performance. Qualitatively, the participants noted that they were able to click links that they would have missed with traditional dwell-time. Many of the errors in the initial trial were caused by links being followed unintentionally as a new page loaded. The current software can prevent this by disabling clicking while the page is loading.

In the second study [3], an improved algorithm was tested using an eye-gaze system, the Tobii EyeX. Seven new participants conducted trials comparing predictive link clicking and blink clicking. All participants in this trial reported better performance with predictive link than with the blink-clicking condition. Qualitatively, it was observed that the additional jitter present in eye-gaze control seemed to favor the preditive-link approach since a score is accumulated over time rather than a link being selected by an instantaneous click.

4. DEMONSTRATION CONFIGURATION

The accompanying demonstration at ASSETS '17 consists of a laptop configured with several input devices: laptop touchpad, external mouse, the Camera Mouse, and Tobii EyeX devices. A web browser with the predictive-link plug-in will be running with several popular web pages for the participants to try.

A short interactive demonstration typically involves the Camera Mouse for pointer control. Attendees are invited to sit or stand at the laptop and control the pointer using their head motion as captured by the computer-vision based system. They may try traditional dwell-time clicking and our predictive-link clicking approaches on several web pages. If time allows, additional input devices and configurations may be tested by attendees.

A task to follow a series of links on Wikipedia will also be offered so that participants may time themselves and compare their performance using dwell-time versus predictive link.

We will solicit feedback from people at the demo, and invite them to leave their contact information. We will also provide cards with software download instructions.

5. CONCLUSION

This publication represents the first public release of our software as a freely available download. Development of our system is ongoing and feedback from those who try our system will be incorporated into future versions. Future plans include using machine learning to set the system parameters for a particular user's abilities. We also plan an opt-in to participate in research data collection based on crowd-sourced usage. We will continue to evaluate future iterations of the system with users with various motion abilities, involuntary motions, and alternative interfaces.

6. ACKNOWLEDGMENTS

The authors would like to thank Jiri Roznovjak and Jason Vazquez-Li for their asstance with the predictive link algorithm. The authors thank NSF (1551590) for partial support of this work.

7. REFERENCES

[1] M. Betke, J. Gips, and P. Fleming. The camera mouse: Visual tracking of body features to provide computer access for people with severe disabilities. IEEE Trans. Neural Systems and Rehabilitation Engineering, 10:1-10, 2002

[2] J. Roznovjak, and J. Magee. Predictive Link Following for Accessible Web Browsing. ASSETS'15, pp 403-404. Oct. 2015.

[3] J. Vazquez-Li, L. Pierson Stachecki, and J. Magee. Eye-Gaze With Predictive Link Following Improves Accessibility as a Mouse Pointing Interface. ASSETS'16, pp 297-298. Oct. 2016.

Prime III: Voting for a More Accessible Future

Simone A. Smarr, Imani N. Sherman, Brianna Posadas, Juan E. Gilbert
Computer & Information Science & Engineering Department
University of Florida
Gainesville, Florida
ssmarr, sherman , bposadas, juan @ufl.edu

ABSTRACT

In 2012, about one-third of voters with disabilities reported having issues when voting in a polling place [7]. Although the Help America Vote Act (HAVA) was passed in 2002, it is clear that there is room for improvement within the domain of accessible voting. Prime III is a voting technology that addresses many issues that plague other accessible voting systems. By addressing the needs of different communities, Prime III has become a ballot marking system that allows all voters to vote on one machine. This demonstration will showcase the accessibility features of Prime III and how it can be used in elections.

Keywords

accessible voting, universal design

1. INTRODUCTION

The 2000 United States Presidential Election exposed the voting infrastructure [10], as well as, voting issues [1], and inspired The Help America Vote Act (HAVA) to address the problems. In 2003, Prime III was developed to address the issues [2] [3], and many still remain[6]. As an open source, multimodal ballot marking system, it was the first of its kind. The system is purely software, thus allowing the election officials to purchase their choice of off the shelf hardware. The ballot and its options can be read by the user or read to the user. The user can make selections with their voice, the touchscreen, or button switches. During this demo, users will be able to utilize each of these options.

2. MOTIVATION

The US Election in 2000 brought attention to voting technology issues. For example, punch card ballots like the butterfly ballot caused confusion for voters and issues with determining voter intent. In 2002, HAVA was passed which created "new mandatory minimum standards for states to follow in several key areas of election administration" [9]. It pushed states to improve voting infrastructure and voting accessibility for people with disabilities.

While HAVA brought attention to the need for accessible voting systems, voters with accessibility needs still have less privacy and use a different voting system than other voters. A study conducted with 180 blind individuals showed that blind voters struggle with poll worker interactions and desire the ability to tailor the system based on their expertise levels[4]. In 2012 about one-third of disabled voters reported issues with voting in person[7]. Some common difficulties were reading the ballot, understanding how to use the equipment, waiting in line and writing on the ballot. Issues like these faced by those with differing abilities need to be addressed to create an accessible voting experience. Prime III is a secure, electronic ballot marking system that is creating an accessible voting experience for all users.

3. THE SYSTEM

Prime III is designed to create an equal voting experience independent of the voters' ability or disability. Typically the Prime III set-up includes a touch screen device, headset, printer, and a two-button textured switch, all of which are available off the shelf, Fig 1. Prime III provides multiple modes including in person voting, absentee voting and vote tabulation. Prime III utilizes a color-blind safe color scheme and includes options for visually impaired users. Since only 12% of blind individuals can read braille it was necessary to develop a more accessible input for voters of low or no vision. [8].

To vote with Prime III, users have the option to vote by voice, touch or both interchangeably. An audio voice feature can guide them through the voting process using the integrated text-to-speech engine. There is also the option to utilize the two button switch to navigate through the ballot if voters are unable to use the touch screen. Voters never need to verbally say who they are voting for when voting by voice, they simply say "vote" to select their choices, which ensures privacy.

The interface is meant to be easy to understand for all users. Voters are shown one contest per screen, and a side menu displays all the contests with the current contest highlighted. Voters can select their choices which are confirmed visually and audibly. A review of the voter's ballot is presented before submitting the ballot for print and is also accessible to the voter throughout the voting process. For security purposes, Prime III is capable of printing a paper ballot with the selections to ensure that there is a paper trail and determine if any software tampering has occurred. The

ASSETS '17 October 29-November 1, 2017, Baltimore, MD, USA

ACM ISBN 978-1-4503-4926-0/17/10.
DOI: https://doi.org/10.1145/3132525.3134771

Figure 1: Prime III set up with a large touch screen, wireless QR scanner, wireless headphones, wireless switch and a thermal printer.

ballot can be printed in different formats depending on the needs of the precinct.

4. FOCUS GROUPS

This past year focus groups were conducted with visually impaired voters to determine their thoughts on the issues with current voting systems and on ways they can be improved. Issues discussed included having to wait for the machine to be set up and the inability to ensure that their vote remained private [5]. These are problems that Prime III addresses. The system is purely software and would only require the poll worker to turn on the computer and open the software. Also, with Prime III, the majority of voters would not need assistance and therefore would have the ability to vote independently and privately. Participants also commented on the over simplicity of the switch button used in the current Prime III set up. The research team is now working on exploring different options to replace or improve the current switch button.

5. DEMONSTRATION DETAILS

In this demonstration we will present Prime III as it could be used within a voting precinct. Attendees will first be introduced to the Prime III software and the possibilities Prime III presents for the future of voting. Demonstrators will then walk attendees through the process of voting with Prime III. The demonstration set up will include multiple Prime III stations to allow attendees to also have a chance to interact with the system. The demonstration will show the different modes of Prime III (in person voting, absentee voting and vote tabulation) as well as the accessibility features that are built into it. Going through a sample ballot will show the audio capabilities of the system that can assist voters with any needs.

6. IMPACT/FUTURE WORK

Prime III is currently being used as the accessible voting machine in the state of New Hampshire. After its use in the 2016 primary and general election, voters were receptive of the software and election officials have opted to continue using it for the future. Prime III was created to be "The Voting Machine" and not just the accessibility machine. But its use in New Hampshire is the first step towards ensuring that everyone can vote on the same machine, independently and privately regardless of accessibility need, language spoken, or voting location.

7. ACKNOWLEDGMENTS

This material is based upon work supported by the U.S. Election Assistance Commission (EAC). Opinions or points of view expressed in this document are those of the authors and do not necessarily reflect the official position of, or a position that is endorsed by, EAC or the Federal government.

This material is based in part upon work supported by the National Science Foundation under Grant Numbers IIS-0738175. Any opinions, findings, and conclusions or recommendations expressed in this material are those of the author(s) and do not necessarily reflect the views of the National Science Foundation.

8. REFERENCES

[1] AGRESTI, A., AND PRESNELL, B. Misvotes, undervotes and overvotes: The 2000 presidential election in florida. *Statist. Sci. 17*, 4 (11 2002), 436–440.

[2] CROSS, II, E. V., MCMILLIAN, Y., GUPTA, P., WILLIAMS, P., NOBLES, K., AND GILBERT, J. E. Prime iii: A user centered voting system. In *CHI '07 Extended Abstracts on Human Factors in Computing Systems* (New York, NY, USA, 2007), CHI EA '07, ACM, pp. 2351–2356.

[3] DAWKINS, S., SULLIVAN, T., ROGERS, G., CROSS, II, E. V., HAMILTON, L., AND GILBERT, J. E. Prime iii: An innovative electronic voting interface. In *Proceedings of the 14th International Conference on Intelligent User Interfaces* (New York, NY, USA, 2009), IUI '09, ACM, pp. 485–486.

[4] PINER, G. E., AND BYRNE, M. D. The experience of accessible voting. *Proceedings of the Human Factors and Ergonomics Society Annual Meeting 55*, 1 (2011), 1686–1690.

[5] POSADAS, B., SHERMAN, I. N., MAHENDRAN, D., BURAGLIA, G., AND GILBERT, J. E. A focus group study of blind voters in alachua county. (in press).

[6] SCHUR, L., ADYA, M., AND KRUSE, D. Disability, voter turnout, and voting difficulties in the 2012 elections. *Report to US EAC and RAAV* (2013).

[7] SCHUR, L., AMERI, M., AND ADYA, M. Disability, voter turnout, and polling place accessibility*. *Social Science Quarterly* (2 2017).

[8] TOUSSAINT, K. A., AND TIGER, J. H. Teaching early braille literacy skills within a stimulus equivalence paradigm to children with degenerative visual impairments. *Journal of APplied Behavior Analysis 43*, 2 (Summer 2010), 181–194.

[9] US ELECTION ASSISTANCE COMMISSION. Help america vote act.

[10] WAYNE, L. The 2000 election: The voting system;close vote illuminates hodgepodge of ballots. *The New York Times* (November 2000).

Real-Time Depth-Camera Based Hand Tracking for ASL Recognition

Brandon Taylor
Carnegie Mellon University
5000 Forbes Ave
Pittsburgh, PA 15213
+1 412 268 2000
bttaylor@cs.cmu.edu

Anind Dey
Carnegie Mellon University
5000 Forbes Ave
Pittsburgh, PA 15213
+1 412 268 2000
anind@cs.cmu.edu

Dan Siewiorek
Carnegie Mellon University
5000 Forbes Ave
Pittsburgh, PA 15213
+1 412 268 2000
dps@cs.cmu.edu

Asim Smailagic
Carnegie Mellon University
5000 Forbes Ave
Pittsburgh, PA 15213
+1 412 268 2000
asim@cs.cmu.edu

ABSTRACT
Accurate real-time depth camera-based tracking of limbs, fingers and faces would be of great use to the field of Sign Language Recognition (SLR). While aspects of depth-based tracking have been applied to SLR, technological limitations have previously forced trade-offs between the resolution necessary to track finger positions and the field of view necessary to track the signer's body. Only recently, with improvements in cameras and computing power, have algorithms been developed which boast the capability of maintaining accurate finger tracking over an appropriately sized volume of space.

In this paper, we employ the publicly available Sphere-Mesh [1] hand tracking algorithm to collect and recognize ASL handshapes. In doing so, we demonstrate recognition rates comparable to other state of the art handshape classifiers using simple naïve Bayesian classifiers that can run in real-time.

CCS Concepts
• **Social and professional topics~Assistive technologies** • *Computing methodologies~Shape representations*

Keywords
Sign Recognition; ASL; Hand Tracking

1. INTRODUCTION
Sign Language Recognition (SLR) has long been a motivating goal for high-precision hand tracking systems. Over the past few years rapid improvements in available depth cameras has led to significant advances in 3D hand tracking and gesture recognition. We propose that recently released hand tracking algorithms offer many opportunities for further advancement of the recognition of American Sign Language (ASL).

The primary focus and contribution of this paper lies in validating the Sphere Mesh algorithm [1] as an reliable tool for collecting hand pose estimates. We did this by collecting data from ten participants and using the Sphere Mesh algorithm to estimate their hand position, orientation and pose. A simple Naïve Bayesian classifier then achieved 70% classification accuracy across the ASL alphabet for a typical, previously unseen signer.

ASSETS '17, October 29-November 1, 2017, Baltimore, MD, USA

ACM ISBN 978-1-4503-4926-0/17/10.
https://doi.org/10.1145/3132525.3134777

2. Background
2.1 Handshape Classification
While linguist differ in their counts of Handshapes, most place the number between 40 and 50 [2]. However, most research related to ASL Handshape detection does not extend beyond the 24 static alphabet signs (the signs for 'J' and 'Z' require motion and are often disregarded). Pugeault and Bowden were early adopters of the Microsoft Kinect for fingerspelling recognition [3]. The dataset, which consists of only the 24 static ASL alphabet handshapes, from their study was made available and has been used by a number of researches. Different classification techniques have been used to achieve recognition rates ranging from 47% to 84% [3, 4].

While these studies present a baseline for fingerspelling recognition using depth cameras, it's worth drawing attention to the work by Thangali and Dilsizian [5, 6]. To our knowledge, these efforts represent the only work on ASL handshape classification trained to recognize a comprehensive set of handshapes achieving 32% and 84% accuracy over sets of 82 and 77 handshapes, respectively. However, it is unclear whether these approaches are feasible for real-time handshape recognition. Thangali reported and average of 2.43s needed for their most effective approach, while Dilsizian made no direct mention of processing time.

2.2 Advantages of Real-time Hand tracking for ASL
The goal of the hand tracking algorithm we use is to provide complete hand pose, orientation and location information. The set of ASL Handshapes and Palm Orientations are a subset of the possible hand configurations reported by these algorithms. Observing Relative Hand Locations and Movements are both prerequisite to hand tracking. Focusing on algorithms that use full-body view depth cameras assures RGB video that can be used for facial and body-skeletal tracking to achieve means of capturing all five ASL parameters.

If we are able to correctly recognize the parameters contained within the hand tracking data, then we have the means to output transcribed representations of the signer's actions. Accomplishing that would allow a recognition system to provide useful data to an ASL corpus that could be used to advance research in the field of Sign Language Translation.

3. Study Design
The primary goal of this study was to measure the effectiveness of currently available, model-based tracking algorithms to capture the entire set of ASL handshape features. To answer this question,

we followed the common practice of focusing on only the 24 static ASL alphabet handshapes. We leave the expansion of our approach to a more complete set of handshapes to future work.

3.1 Data collection

We recruited 10 participants for our study. Participants were seated at a desk in front of a computer monitor with an Intel SR300 camera placed on top of it. We ran Tkach et al's open-source Sphere Mesh [1] algorithm to collect the data. Each participant was given a yellow wristband to place on their left wrist as required by the algorithm and a manual calibration of the handmodel's size parameters was performed.

Participants were presented with a series of 24 handshape prompts (the static ASL alphabet) on the monitor and instructed to begin each collection sequence by spreading their fingers and directing their palm toward the camera. When they were confident they understood the handshape presented in the prompt, users initiated recording by pressing the space bar. They were then asked to move their hand from the initialization pose to the prompted handshape and designated orientation. Participants pressed the space bar again to end the recording sequence at which point the next prompt was presented automatically. Data Analysis

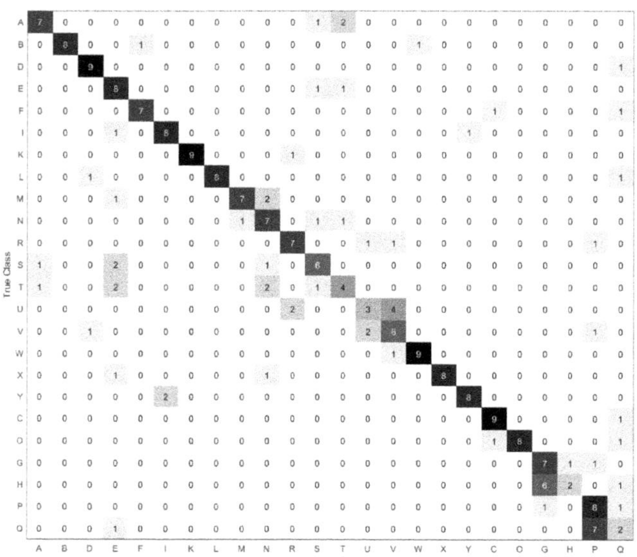

Figure 1. The Confusion Matrix for ASL Alphabet classification. The true class is shown on the y-axis, with the predicted class shown along the x-axis. Each participant recorded each letter once, so the rows will sum to 10. The 'G' and 'H' conditions are an exception due to a recording error.

During data collection, estimates of the hand poses were generated and rendered in real-time. The pose estimate generated by Tkach et al.'s algorithm is defined by Θ, a vector of 28 values representing the 28 degrees of freedom in the hand model presented by [7]. The first 6 values represent the global position and orientation of the hand. The rest of the values correspond to individual joints. For each frame of recorded depth data, Θ is optimized to fit the measured data providing a measure of the hand pose at that given time. Every recorded sequence began with the user's hand in the same pose and ended in the prompted handshape and palm orientation. Since we were not interested in the transition for most of our analysis, we simply select the final hand pose, Θ, as descriptive of the prompted pose.

For this work, we used only the joint data from Θ (ignoring global position and orientation) produced by the algorithm as the features to classify. We used naïve Bayesian classifiers throughout the study.

3.2 ASL Alphabet classification

To make as direct a comparison as possible to prior work examining ASL Handshape classification, we focused on the subset of Handshapes and Palm Orientations that make up the 24 static ASL alphabet signs. We followed two training procedures and built naïve Bayesian classifiers for ASL alphabet detection this analysis. For the sake of alphabet classification, we included the global orientation data provided by the hand tracking model in addition to the hand pose data.

The first procedure followed the leave-one-subject-out procedure that many studies employing the Pugeault data set used to examine signer independence [3]. In total we trained 10 classifiers so that each subject could be treated as a previously unseen signer. Across participants, this approach achieved an average classification accuracy of 69.9%. The confusion matrix is shown in Figure 1. Individual average classification accuracy ranged from 54.2% to 83.3% across users. This result indicates that the Sphere Mesh Algorithm provides comparable levels accuracy to prior work while running in real-time.

4. Conclusions

In this paper we demonstrated the feasibility of a publicly available real-time hand tracking algorithm to for recognizing ASL handshapes. We achieved nearly 70% classification accuracy on average across the ASL alphabet for an unseen signer using a simple classifier. We believe that this demonstrates significant promise for approaches to ASL recognition based on real-time hand tracking algorithms.

5. REFERENCES

[1] Tkach, A., M. Pauly, and A. Tagliasacchi. 2016. Sphere-Meshes for Real-Time Hand Modeling and Tracking. *Proceedings of SIGGRAPH Asia, ACM Transactions on Graphics* 35.

[2] Battison, R. 1978. Analyzing Signs. In *Lexical Borrowing in American Sign Language*, 19–58. Silver Spring, MD: Linstok Press.

[3] Pugeault, N., and R. Bowden. 2011. Spelling It Out : Real – Time ASL Fingerspelling Recognition University of Surrey. *The Hand: Computer Vision Workshops (ICCV Workshops), 2011 IEEE International Conference on*: 1114–1119.

[4] Keskin, C., F. Kiraç, Y. E. Kara, and L. Akarun. 2012. Hand pose estimation and hand shape classification using multi-layered randomized decision forests. *Lecture Notes in Computer Science (including subseries Lecture Notes in Artificial Intelligence and Lecture Notes in Bioinformatics)* 7577 LNCS: 852–863.

[5] Thangali, A., J. P. Nash, S. Sclaroff, and C. Neidle. Exploiting Phonological Constraints for Handshape Inference in ASL Video.

[6] Dilsizian, M., P. Yanovich, S. Wang, C. Neidle, and D. Metaxas. 2013. A New Framework for Sign Language Recognition based on 3D Handshape Identification and Linguistic Modeling: 1924–1929.

[7] Tagliasacchi, A., M. Schroder, A. Tkach, S. Bouaziz, M. Botsch, and M. Pauly. 2015. Robust Articulated-ICP for Real-Time Hand Tracking. *Computer Graphics Forum* 34: 101–114.

Sign Language Support System for Viewing Sports Programs

Tsubasa Uchida, Taro Miyazaki, Makiko Azuma, Shuichi Umeda, Naoto Kato, Hideki Sumiyoshi, and Yuko Yamanouchi
NHK (Japan Broadcasting Corporation)
Tokyo, Japan
+81-(0)3-5494-3438
{uchida.t-fi, miyazaki.t-jw, azuma.m-ia, umeda.s-hg, katou.n-ga, sumiyoshi.h-di, yamanouchi.y-fg}@nhk.or.jp

Nobuyuki Hiruma
NHK Engineering System, Inc.
Tokyo, Japan
+81-(0)3-5494-3386
hiruma.nobuyuki@nes.or.jp

ABSTRACT
To expand the services that are based on Japanese Sign Language (JSL) for deaf and hard of hearing people, we developed a support system for viewing sports program. The system provides sign language computer graphics (CG) animations and other auxiliary information such as text, image, and notifications automatically generated from game metadata. Results obtained from gathered opinions showed that the system is effective for understanding the situation when a game is interrupted.

CCS Concepts
• Human-centered computing → Accessibility → Accessibility systems and tools · Social and professional topics → User characteristics → People with disabilities

Keywords
Japanese Sign Language; JSL; Accessibility Technology; Avatar;

1. INTRODUCTION
Deaf communities in Japan are strongly demanding more sign language services. Although sign language interpretation should be provided by human beings, this is difficult due to the shortage of interpreters. To expand the services based on Japanese Sign Language (JSL), we have developed a system that generates computer graphics (CG) animation of JSL gestures. In this report, we describe our prototype support system that aims to enable deaf and hard of hearing viewers to enjoy viewing sports programs.

2. RELATED WORK
Weather information is a quite suitable first approach for sign language animation systems. Since the domain includes many fixed pattern expressions, various studies have been made about sign language weather forecasting [1][2]. We also selected weather information as the first research target, and developed a prototype system for automatically generating JSL CG animations using fixed-pattern weather forecast data [3].

We are now expanding our domain to sports, which requires more vocabulary and more real-time content generation than that needed for weather information. Several studies tried to generate sign language CG animations on the basis of sports game data [4][5]. However, in these previous studies, the sign language CG animation was completely independent from the game coverage. Of course, as game coverage is very important for people watching sports programs, appropriate support for sign language should reflect the content without disturbing one's viewing. To address these issues, we developed a prototype support system for viewing sports programs by substituting sign language CG and other auxiliary information such as text, images, or notifications using fixed-pattern data distributed during sports events.

ASSETS '17, October 29-November 1, 2017, Baltimore, MD, USA

ACM ISBN 978-1-4503-4926-0/17/10.
https://doi.org/10.1145/3132525.3134768

3. Support System Overview
3.1 Prototype system configuration
We developed a prototype support system for viewing sports programs. Figure 1 shows its configuration.

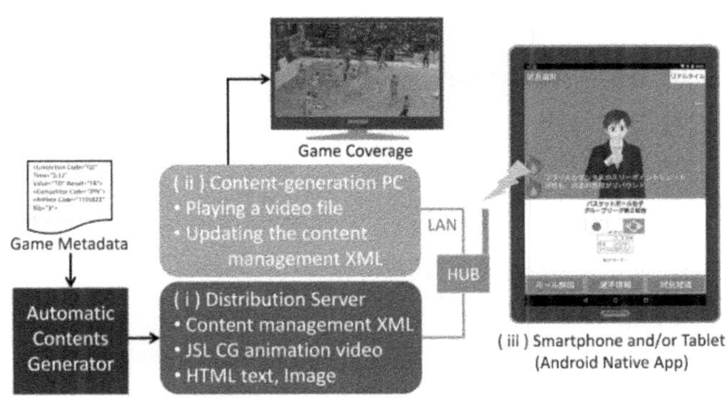

Figure 1: Configuration of the prototype support system.

(i) Distribution Server: The server holds distribution data for events such as JSL CG animation video files, HTML text, image data, and content management XML for managing them. Two types of content management XML are prepared. In the video XML, a JSL CG animation video related to the occurring event, a link to the latest HTML text, and an image are described. The real time XML includes five levels of sound to represent the excitement in the game coverage, and flag information for the timing of a whistle or buzzer in the case that game interruptions are described.

(ii) Content-generation PC: The PC plays a video of the game coverage and updates the content management XML in the delivery server. It synchronizes the timing of the coverage with various contents.

(iii) Smartphone and/or tablet: The application acquires various data on the distribution server, and sequentially displays the contents on the screen. We decided to use a smartphone and/or tablet to provide the support information as it would be desirable to avoid hindering the game coverage with sign language on the same screen.

3.2 Application details

The application provides JSL CG animation and other auxiliary information corresponding to the game situation. The application UI and function are shown in Figure 2.

JSL CG animation: The application displays three types of JSL CG animation: the game situation, the rule commentary, and the game digest. These animations were generated as MP4 videos automatically in advance on an event basis using game metadata sent in real time. The game situation video is automatically played to match the game coverage's timing, and the rule commentary and game digest videos are played at the timing specified by the user.

Other auxiliary information: The application complements audio information by using the vibration function of the smartphone or tablet with images and text information. The sounds of whistles and buzzers are important to understand what is happening in the game, so using the device's vibration function helps viewers understand the content of sports programs. As well as that, for interpolating realistic sensations such as the voices of an excited audience, the sound level of the game coverage in real time can be visualized by the number of icon images given. In addition, the latest score and player information can be also presented in text and images.

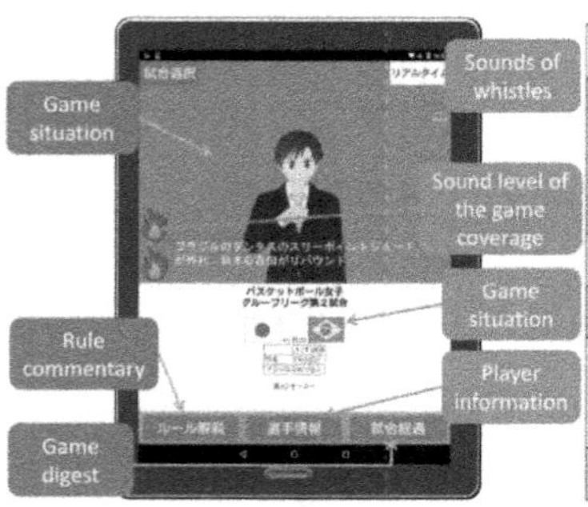

Function	Contents	File Format	Timing
Game situation	JSL CG	MP4	Automatic
	Text Image	HTML	Automatic
Rule commentary	JSL CG	MP4	Manual
Game digest	JSL CG	MP4	Manual
Sounds of whistles	Vibration	XML	Automatic
Sound level of the game coverage	Image	XML	Automatic
Player information	Text Image	HTML	Manual

Figure 2: Main screen and function of the support application.

4. Opinion Survey

On the basis of the prototype system, we built a demonstration environment for basketball games, and conducted a survey to gather the opinions of deaf and hard of hearing people on the system. The survey participants, whose age ranged from 20 to 40 years, were four deaf people (two females and two males) and one male (Coda) sign language interpreter who had been born to deaf parents. They were shown a video of a basketball game that was about three minutes long and included scenes in which the referee blew his whistle and interrupted the game. The application provides 13 game-situation videos, three rule-commentary videos, and three digest videos conveyed in JSL. The content on the demonstration system was generated manually from actual metadata. The questionnaire included queries about the need for JSL videos, the delay tolerance of displayed JSL content, and eye-movement workload. The various opinions gathered were basically classified into positive and negative comments as follows.

Positive opinions: The many positive comments gathered included opinions that JSL and other support information was helpful for understanding the situation when the game was interrupted. Some participants also commented that their enjoyment of the game was furthered by rule explanations in JSL, which helped them to understand unfamiliar terms, and by statistical information about the players.

Negative opinions: As we had anticipated, there were a number of comments stating that the JSL video was not necessary for the event to be understood when watching only the game video. Some participants also recommended that it would be better to overlay JSL video on the game video for reducing eye-movement workload.

Taking the opinion gathering results into consideration, we concluded that the ideal function of the support system would be for the user to be able to access the information subjectively at his/her convenience when needed. We are gathering opinions from various people of different ages, sexes and sports preferences; however, the support information required will depend on various factors, such as personal preference and affinity for sports. Although the system has only been tested for basketball games, we estimate that the necessary support information and presentation timing will change if the event type is changed. We will continue to verify the functionality of the system, and also carry out quantitative evaluation experiments of an improved system based on system requirements in the future.

5. CONCLUSION

We developed a support system for viewing sports programs using a sign language CG system. The results obtained from gathered opinions showed that several of the system functions are effective for enabling viewers to better enjoy sports programs. We are now gathering opinions on the system from deaf and hard of hearing people and incorporating those opinions into the system by adding necessary functions or deleting unnecessary functions. In the future, we will improve the system with the goal of producing services that can be provided when broadcasting sports events such as the Olympics, Paralympics and Deaflympics.

6. ACKNOWLEDGMENTS

The authors would like to express their deepest appreciation to the deaf people, hard of hearing people, and sign language interpreters who cooperated in our research.

7. REFERENCES

[1] I. Zwitserlood, M. Verlinden, J. Ros, and S. van der Schoot, "Synthetic Signing for the Deaf: eSIGN," Proceedings of the Conference and Workshop on Assistive Technologies for Vision and Hearing Impairment, CVHI 2004, 2004.

[2] J. Oh, S. Jeon, M. Kim, H. Kwon, and I. Kim, "An Avatar-Based Weather Forecast Sign Language System for the Hearing-Impaired," Proceedings of the 10th IFIP WG 12.5 International Conference on Artificial Intelligence Applications and Innovations, pp. 519–527, 2014.

[3] N. Hiruma, M. Azuma, T. Uchida, S. Umeda, T. Miyazaki, N. Kato, and S. Inoue, "Automatic generation system of Japanese sign language (JSL) with CG animation of fixed pattern weather information," ABU Technical Journal 264, pp. 2–5, 2015.

[4] M. Romeo, A. Evans, D. Pacheco, and J. Blat, "Domain specific sign language animation for virtual characters," International Conference on Computer Graphics Theory and Applications (GRAPP 2014), pp. 487–494, 2014.

[5] A. Othman, O. El Ghoul, and M. Jemni, " SportSign: A Service to Make Sports News Accessible to Deaf Persons in Sign Languages," Lecture Notes in Computer Science, Vol. 6180, pp.169–176, 2010.

Tangibles + Programming + Audio Stories = Fun

Varsha Koushik and Shaun K. Kane
Department of Computer Science
University of Colorado Boulder
Boulder, CO 80309 USA
{varsha.koushik, shaun.kane}@colorado.edu

ABSTRACT

Block-based programming languages enable novice programmers, including children, to learn the basics of programming. However, most block-based programming languages are not accessible to blind and visually impaired users because they rely upon visual drag-and-drop interaction, and because they typically create visual output. To improve access to block-based programming languages, we introduce Story Blocks, a programming toolkit that uses tangible blocks to represent story components, and which produces output in the form of accessible audio stories and games. Story Blocks provides an introductory programming environment that can be enjoyed by people of all abilities.

Keywords

Accessibility; Programming; Tangible Computing

1. INTRODUCTION

Block-based programming languages, such as Scratch and Blockly, provide novice programmers with support in learning programming languages. In particular, creating programs by combining blocks can show a novice how a program is structured, and can allow a novice to see whether a program is correctly assembled. Block-based programming languages often support the creation of simple animations and games so that young programmers can quickly create engaging content [2].

While block-based programming languages offer many benefits for novice programmers, most block-based languages are not accessible to blind and visually impaired users. This inaccessibility is caused primarily by two issues. First, block-based languages are programmed using drag-and-drop interactions on a graphical user interface, and these user interfaces are not easily translated for screen reader users. Second, the output of block-based languages often takes the form of graphic animation or games that are not accessible (and therefore not engaging) to blind learners.

To explore alternative input and output modes for block-based programming, we introduce the Story Blocks programming environment (Figure 1). In Story Blocks, users create programs by assembling physical blocks that represent characters and actions within an interactive story. The user can then scan this program using a mobile device camera. The program is executed as an audio story on the mobile device. Thus, Story Blocks provides both accessible tools for creating programs as well as universally accessible output. Creating more accessible programming tools may support children of all abilities in exploring computer science.

ASSETS '17, October 29-November 1, 2017, Baltimore, MD, USA

ACM ISBN 978-1-4503-4926-0/17/10.
https://doi.org/10.1145/3132525.3134769

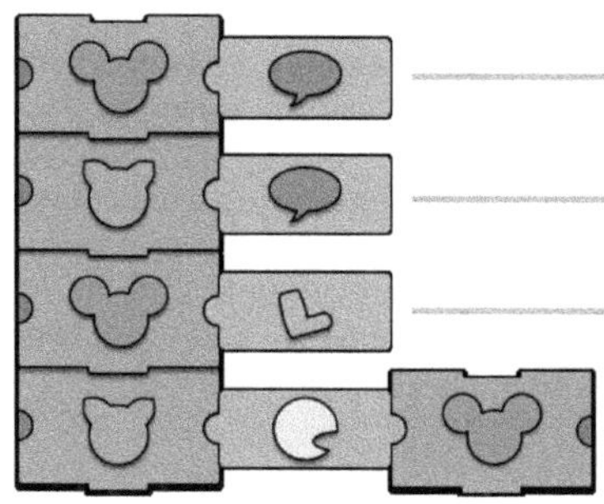

Figure 1. The Story Blocks programming language uses tangible blocks as the basis for programs. These blocks offer tactile features that allow them to be used by both blind and sighted users. The user assembles a program by connecting blocks, and captures an image of the program on a mobile device. The program is then executed on the phone in the form of an interactive audio story.

2. RELATED WORK

Several programming languages have been designed to support accessibility for blind and visually impaired users. Quorum [11] is a text-based programming language that provides explicit support for programming via a screen reader. Other researchers have explored ways to provide access to block-based languages by adding audio. Ludi [8] proposed extending the block-based language Blockly to provide access for screen readers. PseudoBlocks [7] is a nonvisual pseudo-spatial programming language that allows users to manipulate blocks using keyboard commands, and provides program output via speech. Blocks4All [9] allows users to explore a block-based program by touching a touch screen and receiving speech feedback. Story Blocks provides non-visual access to block-based code, but uses tangible input in addition to audio feedback.

Tangible programming tools also offer the potential to increase access to block-based programming. Strawbies [4] enables children to control an on-screen character by assembling a series of instruction blocks; blocks are scanned by a mobile device camera and are used to direct an on-screen character. Project Bloks [1] supports block-based programming by assembling a series of blocks with embedded sensors and actuators. However, these systems use blocks that are only identifiable visually. In this work, we are exploring how the tangible design of blocks can be used to create programs that are readable by a blind or visually impaired user. Project Torino [12] adopts a similar approach to Project Block, but is specifically designed to support both blind and sighted children. Users can assemble programs in Project Torino by connecting blocks with a cable, and can create programs that output music or spoken audio. However, Project Torino requires sophisticated hardware devices for each block, and thus may not scale well to large numbers of learners, such as in a large classroom. Story Blocks builds upon these tangible programming tools, but focuses on the design of low-cost tangible blocks that can be used to create expressive audio output.

Enabling novice programmers to create stories and games can be effective in encouraging programming practice, especially for younger learners. Alice [3] and Storytelling Alice [6] are block-based programming tools that enable novice programmers to write programs that control on-screen characters. Story Blocks explores programming of audio stories and simple games as a way to provide compelling non-visual output for novice programmers.

3. STORY BLOCKS

Our ongoing work in the Story Blocks project is motivated by the following goals. First, we wish to provide tangible access to block-based programming languages that can be used by both blind and sighted users. Second, we wish to enable the creation of compelling non-visual programs for novice programmers. Finally, we wish to support scalability of the system, enabling multiple students in a classroom to create programs simultaneously. These goals have been embodied in the current Story Blocks prototype.

3.1 System Design

The Story Block programming language consists of a series of physical blocks that can be joined together to create a program (Figure 1). In the current prototype, these blocks are made from low-cost materials and fabricated using a 3D printer or laser cutter. Each block is designed to be identifiable by its shape and color so that blocks can be identified by both blind and sighted users. As in other block-based programming languages, the shape of each block indicates how it may connect to other blocks. Blocks are marked with a distinctive dot pattern, such as a reacTivision tag [5], so that they may be tracked by the system.

The current prototype supports three types of blocks: character blocks, which represent characters in the story such as the Cat, Mouse, and Princess; action blocks, which represent actions taken by the characters, such as talking, eating, and running; and control blocks, which support conditional branching, looping, and other aspects of program flow. Figure 1 shows a simple Story Blocks program in which a cat encounters a mouse.

The blocks used in this system are constructed from passive materials such as cardboard, wood, or plastic. Execution of the program is controlled by a companion application running on a PC or mobile device. A user can compile their program by capturing a photo of the blocks. Once the program is loaded into the application, the user can execute the story using standard screen reader commands. For each line of code, the companion application will read the next part of the story. The companion application can embellish each line by adjusting the text-to-speech voice to represent different characters, and by adding atmospheric music and sound effects. While the current prototype only supports static stories, future versions of Story Blocks will support the creation of interactive stories and audio games.

4. CURRENT PROGRESS

Our current prototype supports the creation of simple stories with a limited number of characters. We intend to extend the current system by adding additional characters and actions, and by providing additional support for playing atmospheric sound and music. We are also investigating alternative designs for the blocks themselves, exploring tradeoffs between different block sizes, materials, and tracking methods.

We are also beginning a study of how K-12 students and teachers use Story Blocks. In particular, we hope to gather feedback about the current prototype and to explore how students and teachers may integrate Story Blocks into their current activities.

5. CONCLUSION

While block-based programming languages offer many opportunities for novice programmers, many of the features of these languages remain inaccessible. By combining tangible input with engaging audio output, Story Blocks may offer a compelling approach to introducing programming concepts to students with a variety of abilities.

6. ACKNOWLEDGMENTS

We thank Clayton Lewis, Mike Horn, Erin Buehler, Lauren Milne, and Richard Ladner for their feedback on this work.

7. REFERENCES

[1] Blikstein, P., Sipitakiat, A., Goldstein, J., Wilbert, J., Johnson, M., Vranakis, S., Pedersen, Z. and Carey, W. (2016). Project Bloks: designing a development platform for tangible programming for children.

[2] Brennan, K., and Resnick, M. (2012). New frameworks for studying and assessing the development of computational thinking. In *Proc. AERA '12,* 1-25.

[3] Cooper, S., Dann, W., and Pausch, R. (2000). Alice: a 3-D tool for introductory programming concepts. In *Journal of Computing Sciences in Colleges 15, 5,* pp. 107-116.

[4] Hu, F., Zekelman, A., Horn, M., and Judd, F. (2015). Strawbies: explorations in tangible programming. In *Proc. IDC '15,* 410-413.

[5] Jordà, S., Geiger, G., Alonso, M., and Kaltenbrunner, M. (2007). The reacTable: exploring the synergy between live music performance and tabletop tangible interfaces. In *Proc. TEI '07,* 139-146.

[6] Kelleher, C., Pausch, R., and Kiesler, S. (2007). Storytelling Alice motivates middle school girls to learn computer programming. In *Proc. CHI '07,* 1455-1464.

[7] Koushik, V., and Lewis, C. (2016). An accessible blocks language: work in progress. In *Proc. ASSETS '16,* 317-318.

[8] Ludi, S. (2015). Position paper: Towards making block-based programming accessible to blind users. *IEEE Blocks and Beyond Workshop*, 67-69.

[9] Milne, L. R. (2017). Blocks4All: making block programming languages accessible for blind children. *ACM SIGACCESS Accessibility and Computing* 117, pp. 26-29.

[10] Schanzer, E., Fisler, K., Krishnamurthi, S., and Felleisen, M. (2015). Transferring skills at solving word problems from computing to algebra through Bootstrap. In *Proc. SIGCSE '15*, 616-621.

[11] Stefik, A., and Siebert, S. (2013). An empirical investigation into programming language syntax. *ACM Transactions on Computing Education 13*(4), Article 19, 40 pages.

[12] Thieme, A., Morrison, C., Villar, N., Grayson, M., and Lindley, S. (2017). Enabling collaboration in learning computer programing inclusive of children with vision impairments. In *Proc. DIS '17,* 739-752.

The Participatory Design of an Adaptive Interface to Support Users with Changing Pointing Ability

Aqueasha Martin-Hammond[1], Foad Hamidi[2], Tejas Bhalerao[2], Abdullah Ali[3], Catherine Hornback[2], Casey Means[4], Amy Hurst[2]

[1]School of Informatics and Computing
Indiana University-Purdue University Indianapolis
Indianapolis, IN, USA
aqumarti@iupui.edu

[2]Information Systems Department
University of Maryland, Baltimore County
Baltimore, MD, USA
{foadhamidi, tejasb1, cat19, amyhurst} @umbc.edu

[3]DUB Group
Information School
University of Washington
Seattle, WA, USA
xyleques@uw.edu

[4]Department of Computer Science
Rhodes College
Memphis, TN, USA
meaac-16@rhodes.edu

ABSTRACT

Individuals who experience temporary, intermittent, or gradual changes in pointing ability may encounter frustrating experiences when using computer input devices. Personalized pointing systems that automatically assess changes in performance and provide individualized information and assistance may benefit these users. However, there has been little inquiry into this populations' expectations for interacting with these types of systems.

We describe a participatory design process in which we used a technology probe to assess the information needs and expectations of 27 individuals who experience occasional changes in pointing ability, through interactions with and discussion regarding a high-fidelity personalized pointing prototype. Participants preferred notification and adaptation interactions that provided them with control and explanation of system actions, instead of abstract notifications and automatic adaptations. We describe how we applied these finding in the design of the PINATA system.

CCS Concepts

Human-centered computing → Accessibility → Accessibility systems and tools

Keywords

Pointing problems; Web Navigation; Adaptive Systems

1. INTRODUCTION AND BACKGROUND

For individuals that experience temporary, intermittent, or gradual changes in pointing ability due to a physical impairment, environmental issue or age, using an input device to interact with user interface elements can be difficult. An individual with early stage Parkinson's disease may experience significant differences in his or her ability to control the mouse depending on medication regimen or time of day [4]. Alternatively, a younger adult's ability to control a mouse may change depending on his or her sleep schedule, excitement, or caffeine use [4]. An older adult user may experience changes in hand mobility due to the natural aging process [5]. These individuals may not have been diagnosed with motor impairment, and may not identify as assistive technology users. They may be unaware of changes, or if aware, may find it difficult to identify assistive technology solutions that can support their dynamically changing needs, leading to frustrating computer experiences and further impeding their computer use [1, 4, 6].

Systems that provide personalized (or adaptive) pointing support are a promising solution for individuals that experience changes in pointing ability because they can adapt to user behavior and provide real-time assistance tailored to immediate needs [6, 7]. However, researchers have yet to identify the information needs and expectations when interacting with these systems.

2. INCLUDING USERS IN DESIGN

To include participants in the design process of PINATA as early as possible, we developed and used a prototype of the system as a design probe [2]. We used the prototype to demonstrate different forms of *notifications*, mechanisms to inform the user about their pointing performance, and *assistance activation modes*, mechanisms to activate interface modification to assist with pointing tasks (e.g., zooming in the screen). Figure 1 shows the 3 notification designs that were shown to the participants.

We recruited 27 participants with diverse abilities: 12 younger adults (18 – 34 years), 10 older adults (ages 65 years or older), and 5 adults (ages 55 years or older) with early-stage Parkinson's. No participants reported impairments that would completely impede their use of a computer; 23 participants reported experiencing intermittent difficulty when using a pointing device.

We engaged participants in interview sessions where we demonstrated each of the notifications and had them interact with the prototype. We asked the participants about their preferences with respect to notification visibility, information delivery, information needs, and assistance information and activation preference. After collecting the data from our users, we conducted a thematic analysis and identified three themes to inform the system's design.

3. DESIGN RECOMMENDATIONS AND IMPLEMENTATIONS

After collecting the data from our users, we conducted a thematic analysis and identified three themes to inform the system's design. In the following subsections, we present the three main themes that emerged and how we incorporated them into the prototype.

3.1 Put the User in Control

Most participants (78%) preferred a system that combined automated assistance with explicit user input. The participants wanted to be able to control the type of errors that were detected and how the system would respond. One participant provided the example of "predictive text" when typing and mentioned that automatic assistance can be annoying when it suggests words other than what they were trying to type.

ASSETS '17, October 29-November 1, 2017, Baltimore, MD, USA

ACM ISBN 978-1-4503-4926-0/17/10.
https://doi.org/10.1145/3132525.3134810

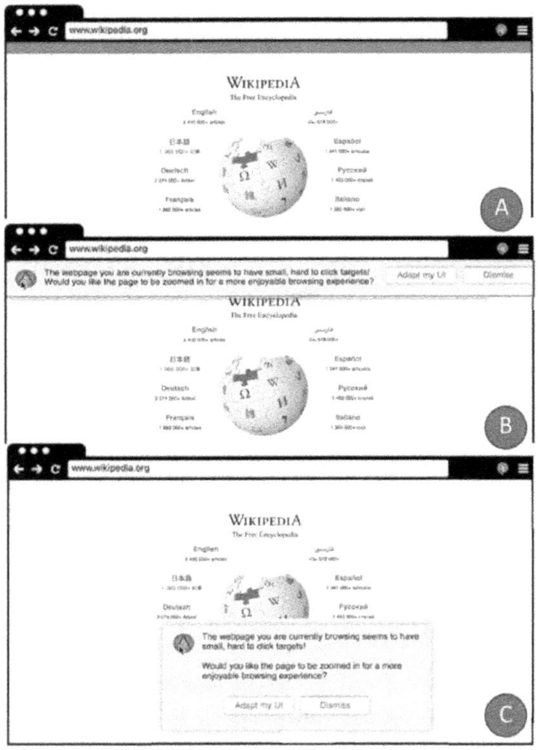

Figure 1. The Bar notification (A) consists of a horizontal bar. The Bar+ notification (B) includes text and interactive buttons. The Dialog box (C) is a popup alert with text and buttons.

To implement this preference, we provide users with a settings window (see Figure 2) that allows them (and their caregivers) to tweak different system settings, including the type of detected errors and the frequency of notifications provided. Additionally, the system allows the users to download and view all the data PINATA collects to automatically detect errors.

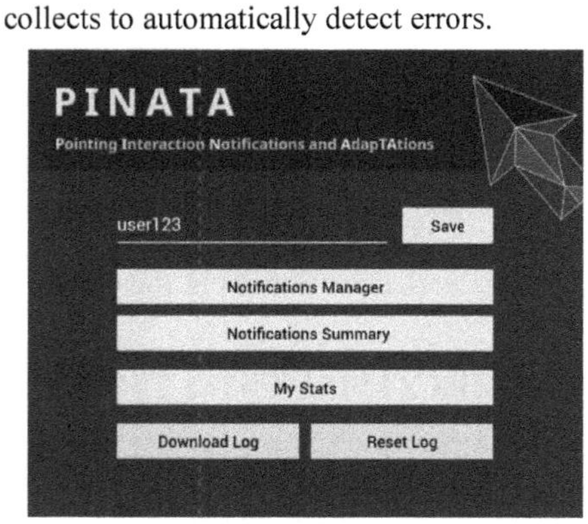

Figure 2. PINATA allows each user to review and specify their preferences.

3.2 Keep the User Informed

Participants did not like the Bar Notification because it did not explain why a notification was given. Instead, participants preferred the dialog box (63%) or Bar+ (30%) notifications because they provided this information and obvious support. This result is in accord with previous recommendations (e.g., [3]).

We incorporated this preference into PINATA's current design by providing textual information about why a notification is provided, with an option to see more information about it. For example, if a user had difficulty clicking on links, a message would state, "In the last 10 minutes, 75% of links have been too small to click. Would you like to zoom in on the page?". The user can then choose to deploy adaptation, get more information or ignore the message.

3.3 Help the User Trust the System

Most of our participants were confident that a computer could provide accurate automatic adaptations (85%) and provide them quickly (70%). However, many users (78%) were concerned about trusting that the system could act in accordance to their needs and preferred an activation mode that required their confirmation.

We implemented a *mixed-initiative* approach to activating assistance, where the user can confirm and activate the assistance when it is suggested by the system. Once the user is familiar with system, they have the choice to automate the assistance activation.

4. CONCLUSION

We investigated how individuals who experience intermittent or gradual declines in hand mobility want to be notified about pointing changes and their preference for assistance activation. We learned that users wanted systems that could 1) build trust by acting in a way that met individual user expectations, 2) keep them informed, and 3) put them in control of decision-making. We described how these preferences were incorporated into our PINATA system.

5. ACKNOWLEDGMENTS

This project was funded by a NIDILRR grant #-90DP0061-01-00.

6. REFERENCES

[1] Gregor, P., Newell, A. and Zajicek, M. 2002. Designing for dynamic diversity: interfaces for older people. In *Proc. ASSETS'02*, 151-156.

[2] Gaver, B., Dunne, T., and Pacenti, E. 1999. Design: cultural probes. *Interactions*, *6*(1), 21-29.

[3] Kulesza, T., Stumpf, S., Burnett, M. and Kwan, I. 2012. Tell me more?: the effects of mental model soundness on personalizing an intelligent agent. In *Proc. of CHI '12*, 1-10.

[4] Moffatt, K. and McGrenere, J. 2009. Exploring Methods to Improve Pen-Based Menu Selection for Younger and Older Adults. *Trans. Access. Comput.* 2, 1, Article 3, 34 pages.

[5] Pak, R., and McLaughlin, A. C. 2010. *Designing displays for older adults.* Boca Raton, FL: CRC Press.

[6] Peissner, M., Häbe, D., Janssen, D. and Sellner, T. 2012. MyUI: generating accessible user interfaces from multimodal design patterns. In *Proc. of EICS '12*, 81-90.

[7] Rothrock, L., Koubek, R., Fuchs, F., Haas, M., and Salvendy, G. 2010. Review and reappraisal of adaptive interfaces: Toward biologically inspired paradigms. *TIES*, *3(1)*, 47-84.

Towards a Sensor-based System for Assessing and Monitoring Powered Mobility Skills in Children

Roxana Ramirez Herrera[1], Catherine Holloway[1], Behzad Momahed Heravi[1], Tom Carlson[2]

[1]UCL Interaction Centre
University College London,
Gower Street, London, WC1E 6EA, United Kingdom
{roxana.herrera.15, c.holloway, b.heravi}@ucl.ac.uk

[2]Aspire CREATe Centre for Rehabilitation Engineering and Assistive Technology
University College London,
Stanmore, HA7 4LP, United Kingdom
t.carlson@ucl.ac.uk

ABSTRACT

Children with motor or cognitive impairments who require powered mobility at a very young age will face social and environmental barriers that make learning how to use the mobility device a challenging task. We present a first approach of a framework to help therapists and service providers to assess and monitor how children use their mobility device, which results from the combination of a plug and play inertial sensor, and the support of the Assessment Learning tool (ALP) from Nilsson and Durkin. We performed a formative study on four able-bodied children using an electric wheelchair. Results suggest it is possible to measure children's driving skills with this approach, and that results can be mapped to the validated ALP tool. We present the limitations of our study and the direction of future work.

Keywords

Powered mobility; assessment and monitoring; children; wheelchair skills; IMU.

1. INTRODUCTION

During infancy, independent movement enables children to interact with the world and this exploration contributes to their social, emotional, cognitive, visual and perceptual development [2][4]. In children with certain motor impairments, the lack of independent mobility within their first years of life can severely limit this interaction, compromising their development and contributing to passivity and dependence [4]. The provision of powered mobility devices (such as electric wheelchairs) has shown to compensate for the potential development issues posed by immobility [5]. These benefits however, are diminished without adequate training and practice, particularly for those children with cognitive or sensory limitations which are in greater need of guided personalized support [5]. An effective personalized training therapy depends not only on therapy sessions but also on the correct assessment and follow-up of the child's driving skills at each of its developmental stages[5]. Yet, public healthcare systems often find themselves unable to provide enough or even any type of qualified or personalized clinical support in the long term [2]. In consequence,some children's development will largely depend on when and how much they practice powered mobility at their everyday setting, such as home or school. Hence, we propose a sensor-based system for assessing and monitoring powered mobility skills in children in their everyday settings (see Figure 1).

ASSETS '17, October 29-November 1, 2017, Baltimore, MD, USA

ACM ISBN 978-1-4503-4926-0/17/10.
DOI:https://doi.org/10.1145/3132525.3134813

Figure 1. Diagram of proposed framework.

The system would need to objectively measure the level of driving skills of children and be validated against the current assessment method performed by healthcare practitioners. As a first step, we present our framework and a formative study in which we use an inertial measurement unit (IMU) to measure the child's driving learning stage.

2. RELATED WORK

The Assessment to Learn Powered mobility use (ALP) in early childhood is a fairly recent qualitative tool designed by Durkin and Nilsson that has been successfully used and appraised in the UK and Sweden [6]. It identifies eight ascending stages in the process of learning powered mobility use: novice, curious novice, beginner, advanced beginner, sophisticated beginner, competent, proficient and expert. Each stage description provides extensive cues for the therapist in five different observational categories: "level of attention," "activity and movement," "understanding of tool use," "expressions and emotions," and "interaction and communication" [6]. Like the ALP, existing assessment tools used for driving skills are typically subject to the therapist interpretation.

Wheelchair usage in particular has been characterized by a range of sensors to objectively measure driving behavior within both the users' daily environments and controlled settings for rehabilitation or evaluation [7]. Inertial sensors (IMUs) are the most recurrent sensor type, and their wide use can be attributed to the simplicity of installation and recently decreasing price in the market [3]. Most of these studies however, have been performed with adult users and some with able-bodied subjects, while only a few with children; the latter studies taking place mostly in controlled environments [4]. These studies have used existing assessment tools, or have proposed their own evaluation parameters, but have not used yet the ALP scale. To our knowledge, no studies have been performed on children under the age of 5, in their everyday settings. .

3. CONCEPT PROPOSAL

Our framework (see Figure 1) proposes the use of a plug and play sensor (an IMU) that will be distributed to the legal guardians of toddlers that use powered mobility. This plug and play device will be powered by the electric wheelchair, making it easy to use and reducing the barrier to taking part in the study.

The child will use the wheelchair within their everyday settings (for example, school, home or therapy center), and relevant parameters for their skills characterization will be recorded. This plug and play device will automatically transfer, via Bluetooth, pre-recorded data to a smart phone at regular intervals (for example, once every two days). Data will then be transferred via Wi-Fi to the Cloud, in which it will be processed, analyzed and distributed to researchers, therapists and electric wheelchair providers.

The first stage of the framework development will be to extract information from current users that have already been assessed using the ALP tool and classified to one of the 8 learning stages. Finding enough children at each stage of development would be challenging in a local area. However, using this platform could enable us to surpass geographical constrains and collect and record power assistive usage of children on a larger scale and simultaneously. During the processing stage, usage patterns can be extracted which can be used to create a database of average parameters for each of the stages. This can work as a guiding principle for classifying users at the second stage of the framework. Data analysis can also highlight the potential difficulties that the user might be experiencing while using the wheelchair when compared to a baseline.

The final system will include a database that allows remote assessment of powered mobility skills to help whenever needed. due to restrictions on time or location, access to therapist's live evaluation is difficult if not impossible. The system can assess the user and guide the parents, caregivers or therapist on strategies for intervention when appropriate. The baseline will be constantly updated as users join the network.

4. FORMATIVE STUDY

We performed a formative study to explore whether an IMU plug and play prototype could be used to describe the learning stage of the child from the ALP observational category "activity and movement". We recruited four able-bodied children between 4 and 5 years old, and asked them to perform a set of 12 tasks within a rectangular area, using the Bugzi[1] (Figure 1), an indoor powered wheelchair for toddlers, controlled with a joystick. The tasks involved moving with the chair in a straight line between two points, following rectangular or triangular trajectories, and a free trajectory period. Each session was video recorded, and triaxial acceleration and angular rate of the Bugzi were measured with the IMU sensor (accelerometer and gyroscope). These signals were filtered and plotted for each child in MATLAB. From these plots, we identified 4 types of movements: idle, rotation to the left, rotation to the right, and straight line. Each child's skill level was classified using the ALP through a mixture of researcher observations both in person and on re-watching the video. From these observations and IMU data, we figured that the time each child spent performing different types of movement could be indicative of their skills level. The time spent on each type of activity was calculated by an algorithm which classified the types of movements by comparing both acceleration and angular rate against thresholds which were empirically deduced form observing several plots. Data suggests (see Table 1) that a higher amount of rotations (either left or right on the chair) represents constant correction of the trajectory and maps to the child who scored the lowest on the ALP tool. On the other hand, the child who scored the highest, performed confidently on the use of the wheelchair and executed less rotations when performing tasks. The other participants did not differ significantly on straight movement performance. These findings are congruent with Nilsson's and Durkin's observational descriptions.

Table 1. ALP classification and percentage of time per activity

Child	ALP stage	%time rotating	%time straight line
1	expert	17.6	57.3
2	proficient	23.5	52.8
3	proficient	35.4	56.1
4	competent	40.7	30.3

5. CONCLUSION AND FUTURE WORK

As a first step to developing the sensing component of our framework, we propose the use of an IMU plug and play prototype. The data from our formative study suggests a relation between the level of competence of Bugzi driving, and the amount of time that the children spent rotating the chair, which is probably due to trajectory correction. Future work will improve the experimental design to better deal with the challenges of working with children, such as dealing with their playfulness with the mounted camera and sensor. Since the tool is created to look at functional output rather than disability, we believe these results are useful indicator of what would have been captured with disabled children. However, this needs to be validated. As our results are preliminary and our sample group is not representative, we will then proceed with the collection of more data from a larger number of participants both able-bodied and motor impaired in their everyday settings. Lastly, we will proceed to use a more efficient and automatic algorithm for movement type classification, by taking advantage of the many machine learning tools available.

6. ACKNOWLEDGEMENTS

This project was funded by the Queen Elizabeth's Foundation for disabled people, and by CONACyT.

7. REFERENCES

[1] Bugzi - MERU: *http://meru.org.uk/what-we-do/bugzi/.*

[2] Feldner, H.A. et al. 2015. Why the time is right for a radical paradigm shift in early powered mobility: the role of powered mobility technology devices , policy and stakeholders role of powered mobility technology devices , policy and stakeholders. *Disabil Rehabil Assist Technol.* early onli, April (2015).

[3] Fu, J. et al. 2016. A novel mobile-cloud system for capturing and analyzing wheelchair maneuvering data : A pilot study. *Assist Technol.* 28, 2 (2016), 105–114.

[4] Livingstone, R. and Field, D. 2014. Systematic review of power mobility outcomes for infants , children and adolescents with mobility limitations. *Clin Rehabil.* 28, 10 (2014), 954–964.

[5] Livingstone, R. and Paleg, G. 2014. Practice considerations for the introduction and use of power mobility for children. *Dev Med Child Neurol.* 56, 3 (2014), 210–221.

[6] Nilsson, L. and Durkin, J. 2014. Assessment of learning powered mobility use--applying grounded theory to occupational performance. *J Rehabil Res Dev.* 51, 6 (2014), 963–74.

[7] Routhier, F. et al. 2016. Data Logger Technologies for Manual Wheelchairs: A Scoping Review. *Assist Technol.* 00, 00 (2016), 1–8.

Towards Improving Predictive AAC using Crowdsourced Dialogues and Partner Context

Keith Vertanen
Michigan Technological University
Houghton, MI, USA
vertanen@mtu.edu

ABSTRACT

Augmentative and Alternative Communication (AAC) devices typically rely on a language model to help make predictions or disambiguate user input. We investigate how to improve predictions in two-sided conversational dialogues. We collect and share a new corpus of crowdsourced everyday dialogues. We show how language models based on recurrent neural networks outperform N-gram models on these dialogues. We demonstrate further gains are possible using text obtained from an AAC user's communication partner, even when that text is partial or contains errors.

1. INTRODUCTION

Communicating with an AAC device poses many challenges such as generating text sufficiently fast to take part in conversations, controlling the delivery of pre-entered text, conversation turn-taking, and expressing emotion [3]. Here we focus on the problem of generating text quickly by investigating ways to improve AAC device predictions during real-time conversations.

Predictive AAC devices typically use a language model. The language style and two-sided nature of everyday conversations is different from many of the common data sources used to train language models.We show how crowd workers can easily generate everyday conversational dialogues and how recurrent neural network language models (RNNLMs) [4] improve modeling of these crowdsourced dialogues.

AAC devices typically use only the AAC user's side of a conversation. We show gains are possible by modeling both sides of the dialogue. This might be possible by performing speech recognition on the person speaking with an AAC user. Speech context was used in the Converser AAC interface which recognized noun phrases from the speaking person and incorporated them into utterance templates [7].

Here we use the entire speech recognition result as context to a language model trained on dialogues. We show gains are robust even to substantial simulated recognition errors. Finally, we show how knowing even a single word of context from a partner's turn can improve predictions.

ASSETS '17 October 29-November 1, 2017, Baltimore, MD, USA

ACM ISBN 978-1-4503-4926-0/17/10.
DOI: https://doi.org/10.1145/3132525.3134814

A:	What's your favorite dessert?
B:	Molten Chocolate Lava cake with Raspberries
A:	Oh my God, that sounds grand!
B:	Yes, let's go get some!
A:	I've been dying to try that new cafe. Maybe it's on their menu?
B:	I'll pull it up online and find out.

Table 1: A dialogue created by Amazon workers.

2. EXPERIMENTS

To generate data for our experiments, we had Amazon Mechanical Turk workers think of a question they might ask someone. These questions were shown to other workers who decided if a question was plausible and, if so, to create a response. We continued this process until six turns were completed. Each turn extension took about two hours and cost $20. We collected 1,419 six-turn dialogues. We used 60% as a training set, 20% as a development set, and 20% as a test set. Overall workers invented plausible and creative dialogues (Table 1). We have made the dialogues available[1].

2.1 Predicting AAC user turns

First, we investigated predicting the AAC user turns in the test set without using the partner dialogue turns. We assumed the 2nd, 4th, and 6th turns were the AAC user. We report per-world *perplexity* on these turns (8K total words). Perplexity measures the possible options for the next token given the current context, e.g. a random digit sequence 0-9 has a perplexity of 10. Lower perplexity is better.

We used all dialogue turns, treating each turn as an independent training example (46K total words). We trained interpolated modified Kneser-Ney 4-gram models with no count cutoffs and a 35K vocabulary. We used Twitter as a large training set as it is a close match to AAC-like data [6].

The dialogue data was word-for-word better than Twitter, lowering perplexity from 285 to 160 (Table 2). However, using 50M words of Twitter data was much better, cutting perplexity to 81. Instead of random Twitter data, we selected 50M words using cross-entropy difference selection [5] with an in-domain model trained on 25% or 100% of the dialogues. This lowered perplexity to 76 and 73 respectively. This shows the value of having a large number of dialogues.

We trained RNNLMs on the cross-entropy selected Twitter data. An RNNLM with 250 sigmoid units had a perplexity of 89 (Table 3). Using 250 gated recurrent units and Noise Contrastive Estimation (NCE) lowered perplexity to

[1] http://keithv.com/data/turk-dialogues.txt

Training data	Words	PPL
Twitter, small amount of data	46K	285
Crowd dialogues	46K	160
Twitter, large amount of data	50M	81
Twitter, select w/ 25% crowd dialogues	50M	76
Twitter, select w/ 100% crowd dialogues	50M	73

Table 2: N-gram perplexity varying training data.

Model	PPL
Baseline Twitter RNNLM	89
+ gated recurrent units, NCE	78
+ maximum entropy	67
+ interpolate Twitter 4-gram LM	63
+ unigram cache	62
+ dialogue RNNLM	61

Table 3: RNNLM perplexities with added features.

78. Training a maximum entropy model in the network lowered perplexity to 67. Next we linearly interpolated the RNNLM and the N-gram model with a weight optimized on the development set. This resulted in a perplexity of 63, better than either model alone. Since words often reoccur in a dialogue, we added a unigram cache which reduced perplexity to 62. Finally, adding an RNNLM trained on just the crowdsourced dialogues lowered perplexity to 61.

2.2 Using partner turns

We tested using context from the partner turns to help predict the AAC user turns. Due to our relatively small crowdsourced corpus, we instead used dialogues from movies [1]. We trained an RNNLM treating each dialogue as a training example (3.8M words, 81K dialogues). For comparison, we tested the model on just the AAC user turns without partner turns (the test set used previously). Without partner turns, the RNNLM had a perplexity of 93. If instead the model made predictions based on both sides of the dialogues, perplexity dropped to 81. Thus, the RNNLM was able to use partner turns to improve predictions. A 6-gram N-gram language model was less capable and had a perplexity of 95.

The previous experiments assumed a perfect transcript of partner turns. We simulated speech recognition errors by injecting an error at a word in a partner's turn with some probability. 80% of errors were substitution errors, 10% insertion, and 10% deletion. Substitution and insertion errors used a random in-vocabulary word. Even at error probabilities up to 0.7, partner turns improved predictions (Figure 1). We then interpolated the two-sided dialogue model with the best model from the previous section. With perfect partner transcripts, this lowered perplexity from 61 to 54. Using turns with a 0.2 error probability only slightly

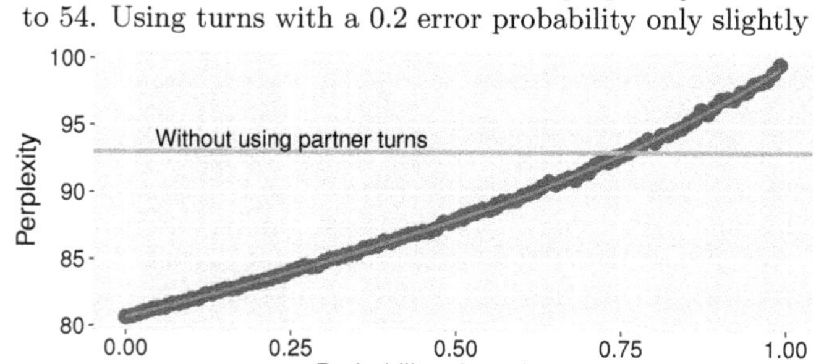

Figure 1: Perplexity with simulated rec. errors.

increased perplexity to 55. Thus it appears likely even with recognition errors, partner turns can inform predictions.

Instead of using the entire speech recognition transcript of a partner's turn, we could instead use just selected words, e.g. the non-stop words recognized with the highest confidence. Alternatively, a partner could explicitly suggest relevant words via a mobile app as in the AACrobat prototype [2]. We simulated this by using the word in the first turn with the lowest unigram probability. We trained an RNNLM on 1M words of Twitter data containing this word. As a baseline, we trained an RNNLM on 1M words of random Twitter data. The baseline RNNLM was interpolated with the two-sided RNNLM with partner turns having a 0.2 error probability. This reduced perplexity from 55 to 54. If instead we interpolated an RNNLM trained on data with the rarest word from the first turn, perplexity was 51.

3. CONCLUSIONS

Our experiments highlight some of the state-of-the-art language modeling methods available for improving predictive AAC. They also show how crowdsourcing dialogues can provide useful training data. We show how context obtained from speech recognition might be incorporated to improve AAC interface predictions. The speech-based improvements appear to be robust to recognition errors. This suggests speech context may be viable in real-world AAC interfaces.

We used only a small dialogue collection and a fraction of available Twitter data. Further work is needed to scale to larger amounts of data. We measured performance on dialogue turns contributed by crowd workers. Our improvements need to be validated in offline experiments with data from AAC users or in text entry studies with AAC users.

4. REFERENCES

[1] C. Danescu-Niculescu-Mizil and L. Lee. Chameleons in imagined conversations: A new approach to understanding coordination of linguistic style in dialogs. In *Proc. CMCL*, 2011.

[2] A. Fiannaca, A. Paradiso, M. Shah, and M. R. Morris. AACrobat: Using mobile devices to lower communication barriers and provide autonomy with gaze-based AAC. In *Proc. CSCW*, 2017.

[3] S. K. Kane, M. R. Morris, A. Paradiso, and J. Campbell. "At times avuncular and cantankerous, with the reflexes of a mongoose": Understanding self-expression through augmentative and alternative communication devices. In *Proc. CSCW*, 2017.

[4] T. Mikolov, M. Karafiát, L. Burget, J. Cernocký, and S. Khudanpur. Recurrent neural network based language model. In *Proc. Interspeech*, 2010.

[5] R. C. Moore and W. Lewis. Intelligent selection of language model training data. In *Proc. ACL*, 2010.

[6] K. Vertanen and P. O. Kristensson. The imagination of crowds: Conversational AAC language modeling using crowdsourcing and large data sources. In *Proc. EMNLP*, 2011.

[7] B. Wisenburn and D. J. Higginbotham. An AAC application using speaking partner speech recognition to automatically produce contextually relevant utterances: Objective results. *Augmentative and Alternative Communication*, 24(2).

Towards Supporting Individuals with Situational Impairments in Inhospitable Environments

Flynn Wolf, Ravi Kuber
Department of Information Systems
UMBC
Baltimore MD 21250
{flynn.wolf, rkuber} @umbc.edu

Dianne Pawluk
Department of Biomedical Engineering
UMBC
Baltimore MD 21250
dtpawluk@vcu.edu

Brian Turnage
City of Richmond Fire and Emergency Services
Richmond VA 23219
brian.turnage@richmondgov.com

ABSTRACT
In this paper, we describe an approach to develop alerts for individuals experiencing situationally-induced impairments and disabilities (SIIDs) in inhospitable environments, with a view to support situational awareness and decision making. Our research focuses on the needs of firefighters whose visual and auditory channels may be restricted while performing tasks, resulting in cues sometimes being missed. Through a series of contextual interviews, scenarios have been developed focusing on areas where alerts are required. A participatory-approach has been adopted with the aim of developing perceivable, meaningful and respected alerts, designed to better resist the impacts of SIIDs.

CCS Concepts
CCS → Human-centered computing → Accessibility → Empirical studies in accessibility.

Keywords
Situationally-induced impairments and disabilities;

1. INTRODUCTION
Situationally-induced impairments and disabilities (SIIDs) are faced by individuals regardless of ability when the situation itself places demands on the user's attention, sensory and motor ability [4,5]. Researchers have traditionally focused on identifying SIIDs faced by mobile device users while ambulatory (e.g. [1]). However, other groups also experience SIIDs in settings which are inhospitable. Examples include the issues faced by firefighters. Presence of thick smoke can restrict the ability to identify other firefighters and gestural cues, and even the reading of gauges located on their turnout gear. Orienting position and wayfinding within a burning structure can also pose challenges when vision is impaired, resorting to firefighters relying on the use of tactile cues (e.g. manually following a hose line to identify the exit to the structure). Noise from sirens, ventilation fans, pneumatic tools, and combustion of the structure may impact the ability to identify auditory alerts presented via communication devices or via voice. The cognitive and physical demands imposed by the inhospitable and rapidly-changing settings, can result in difficulties establishing situational awareness (SA).

ASSETS '17, October 29-November 1, 2017, Baltimore, MD, USA

ACM ISBN 978-1-4503-4926-0/17/10.
https://doi.org/10.1145/3132525.3134783

Our research aims to examine ways in which alerts to firefighters can be designed which better resist the impact of SIIDs. By presenting alerts which can be discerned when facing situational, contextual and environmental challenges, we aim to heighten levels of SA and to better inform decision making to remain safe in hazardous environments. In this paper, we describe an approach to identify and design alerts to better support firefighters when performing duties in the field.

2. RELATED WORK
Researchers have proposed a range of wearable solutions to support firefighters in action, where alerts are presented using one or multiple channels. Alerts vary from communicating the presence of dangerous gas concentrations and temperatures [6,7] to the relative distance of obstacles which may be encountered [2]. While care has been taken in the design of these alerts, the design process may have considered the impact of the SIIDs experienced by firefighters, which would affect perception. Further work is needed to develop cues which better support firefighters facing inhospitable conditions when performing duties.

3. CONTEXTUAL INTERVIEWS
Open-ended interviews were conducted with a total of six safety officers and senior fire service personnel from two districts (one urban, one suburban), and a range of firefighters from stations within these locales. Participants were asked to describe the ways in which SA can be gained in inhospitable and rapidly changing environments, the types of alerts currently present and their efficacy, along with the description of other situations where alerts would be beneficial.

Findings suggested that *temperature-related alerts were not specifically presented to firefighters when working at the scene of a fire*, meaning that they should rely on combination of their assessment of the environment, and communication with others (e.g. notifications from other firefighters, incident commanders based outside the structure) to identify whether temperatures have surpassed unsafe levels. Other areas included the need for *communicating the presence of hazards* to other firefighters (i.e. holes in the floor), alongside the *confusion caused by multiple alerts* presented via the same sensory domains (e.g. auditory alerts via radio and from body worn equipment (e.g. SCBA) within a short period of time, especially if these were impacted by situational, contextual or environmental factors.

The points raised were transformed into sets of scenarios relating to firefighters using location-independent wearable devices to receive alerts, similar to an approach adopted by [3]. These were then illustrated for successive participatory design workshops. In order to determine the validity of the resulting scenarios, checks were made by the original interviewees (domain experts).

Example of a scenario (abridged): A hazard has been detected by one firefighter in smoke-filled warehouse. The firefighter near the hazard (hole) attempts to communicate its position to other firefighters but cannot yell loudly enough above sounds of the burning structure. He is unsure if his radio message informing the Incident Commander about its presence has been received.

4. PARTICIPATORY-BASED APPROACH

A set of design workshops were conducted, where groups of 4-8 firefighters, staff with incident commanding experience, and interface designers could work as a team, to design alerts to better meet the needs of firefighters facing inhospitable environments. Participants' experience varied considerably (3-35 years service).

Scenarios developed (described in Section 3) were presented in sequence to the teams, along with illustrations of the steps taken by firefighters in each rich story. Participants were asked to consider the conditions faced by the *actors* in the scenarios, and describe whether alerts would be useful to support SA and decision making, and if so, how these could be designed using graphical, auditory and/or tactile feedback. Design suggestions could be made verbally or illustrated. These suggestions would be developed into cues by the researchers for presentation in successive design workshops, presented via a PC (e.g. visual and auditory cues) or tactile motors. Participants were asked to reflect upon each others' ideas. The same scenarios were presented to new groups of participants. Facilitation by the interface designers was aimed to strengthen alerts which had been designed or triggering new design ideas. It was envisaged that after a number of sessions, consensus on design would be reached.

5. PRELIMINARY RESULTS

Participants from all three workshops conducted, were generally able to provide detailed feedback on the scenarios presented, and relate these to their own personal experiences or times when alerts had been missed. All participants from the first workshop agreed that cues would need to be quick to interpret, as time could not be wasted attempting to discern different forms of feedback. Mappings would need to be simple and intuitive, due to the cognitive demands faced while firefighting. If many cues were presented at one time, it could lead to confusion resolving each of these cues, leading to discussion about either improving salience or if presented via multiple devices, temporarily halting cues from one device in order to attend to alerts from another device.

Tactile feedback was found to be of interest in all workshops, as vibrational output is rarely used to support firefighters, thereby gaining the user's attention. However, a wearable device would need to be positioned close to the skin, otherwise if affixed to the outside of turnout garments (which are thick in nature), signals would be attenuated. The hand was not thought to be a practical site for presentation, as it may be encumbered with equipment, or may be moving around which may make a sensation difficult to perceive. Suggestions were made to present tactile cues within the facemask itself, to provide users with the best chance of perceiving and responding to the alerts, without needing to spend time donning additional equipment.

In terms of auditory and tactile mappings, the second team suggested associating the pitch and amplitude respectively, to the severity of the situation (i.e. unsafe temperatures, presence of a hazard). This design suggestion was then strengthened by third group, that different levels of threat should be presented via these channels, rather than a continual increase in intensity which may be ignored after a period of time. While technologies worn by firefighters contain visual alerting devices (e.g. LEDs), these were thought to be difficult to identify when smoke is present, unless presented within the facemask heads-up display. Participants from the later workshops highlighted the need to convey information through multiple means using redundant information, to heighten the likelihood of noticing the cues. Suggestions were also made to customize mappings depending on the situation or context. A set of workshops have been planned to discuss these ideas in more detail. Resulting cues will then be evaluated in both simulated and real-world environments.

6. REVIEW OF APPROACH

The participatory-based approach has enabled participants from different levels of the fire service to come together to design cues to ensure that different perspectives are considered in the design process. While firefighting staff have been able to provide key domain knowledge within the workshops, interface designers were able to offer suggestions from their experiences developing salient cues. Observations revealed that both groups have been able to work together to formulate design suggestions, and to learn from one another to better support the design process.

7. ACKNOWLEDGMENTS

We thank Captain Douglas Clevert, and the staff at City of Richmond and Chesterfield County Fire and Emergency Services. This work is supported through the National Institute of Standards and Technology (Award: 60NANB16D281).

8. REFERENCES

[1] Abdolrahmani, A., Kuber, R., and Hurst A. 2016. An empirical investigation of the situationally-induced impairments experienced by blind mobile device users. In *Proceedings of W4A*, Article No: 21, DOI=http://dx.doi.org/10.1145/2899475.2899482.

[2] Carton, A., and Dunne, L.E., 2013. Tactile distance feedback for firefighters: design and preliminary evaluation of a sensory augmentation glove. In *Proceedings of the 4th Augmented Human International Conference,* 58-64, DOI= http://dx.doi.org/10.1145/2459236.2459247.

[3] Kuber, R., Yu, W. and McAllister, G., 2007. Towards developing assistive haptic feedback for visually impaired internet users. In *Proceedings of SIGCHI Conference on Human Factors in Computing Systems*, 1525-1534, DOI=http://dx.doi.org/10.1145/1240624.1240854.

[4] Pascoe, J., Ryan, N. and Morse, D., 2000. Using while moving: HCI issues in fieldwork environments. *ACM Transactions on Computer-Human Interaction*, 7, 3 (2000), 417–437, DOI=http://dx.doi.org/10.1145/355324.355329.

[5] Sears, A. Lin, M., Jacko, J. and Xiao, Y. 2003. When computers fade: Pervasive computing and situationally-induced impairments and disabilities. In *Proceedings of HCI International*, 1298–1302.

[6] Streefkerk, J.W., Vos, W., and Smets, M., 2012. Evaluating a multimodal interface for firefighting rescue tasks. In *Proceedings of the Human Factors and Ergonomics Society Annual Meeting*, 56, 1 (2012), 277-281. DOI=http://dx.doi.org/10.1177/1071181312561054.

[7] Walters, K., Lee, S., Starner, T., Leibrandt, R., and Lawo, M., 2010. Touchfire: towards a glove-mounted tactile display for rendering temperature readings for firefighters. In *Proceedings of International Symposium on Wearable Computers (ISWC)*,1-4, DOI=http://dx.doi.org/10.1109/ISWC.2010.5665862.

Unobtrusive Monitoring of Parkinson's Disease Based on Digital Biomarkers of Human Behaviour

Julio Vega, Caroline Jay, Markel Vigo, Simon Harper
School of Computer Science. University of Manchester, UK.
firstname.lastname@manchester.ac.uk

ABSTRACT

Parkinson's Disease impairs the motor, cognitive and emotional functioning of people. Clinicians do not get an accurate image of the disease because patients visit them every six months and their symptoms can change within hours. Technology has been used to tackle this problem, but most approaches disrupt people's routines or are uncomfortable to use. We aim to monitor Parkinson's in an unobtrusive, longitudinal and naturalistic way based on digital biomarkers inferred from smartphone-collected heterogeneous data. We use Parkinson's clinical scales and self-reporting of symptoms as ground truth to evaluate our methodology. Here, we present three insights we gained after tracking four people 24/7 for four months: a) the monitoring smartphone needs to be people's primary device, b) participants prefer a paper diary for symptom self-reporting, and c) social and phone interaction will be explored as digital biomarkers. We expect this approach to improve patient's quality of life and the efficiency of health services.

CCS Concepts

•**Human-centered computing → Empirical studies in ubiquitous and mobile computing;**

Keywords

Parkinson's Disease; Smartphone; Health monitoring

1. INTRODUCTION

Parkinson's Disease is a neurodegenerative disorder that affects around ten million people worldwide. Each person with this condition (PwP) develops a different subset of motor and non-motor symptoms that decrease their quality of life. Traditional health assessment can be inaccurate because clinicians examine PwP during short sessions every six months but symptoms vary within hours. Furthermore, the clinical scales used during these visits are expertise-dependant and prone to recall and cognitive biases.

ASSETS '17, Oct. 29–Nov. 1, 2017, Baltimore, MD, USA.

ACM ISBN 978-1-4503-4926-0/17/10.

DOI: 10.1145/3132525.3134782

In consequence, understanding Parkinson's progression is invaluable to support patients and medical personal. If clinicians had a detailed model of how symptoms change, they could tailor medication to each person's condition. This, in turn, would allow PwP to manage their symptoms better and enhance their quality of life by reducing the impact of Parkinson's in their routines, facilitating their access to daily activities, and stopping them from dwelling on the disease.

Researchers have used off-the-shelf wearables and smartphones equipped with movement, ambient and location sensors to try to tackle these issues [3]. In general, these devices are objective and more precise than traditional methods. Nevertheless, most previous approaches are tested under controlled conditions, are uncomfortable to use because they need to be attached to people's bodies, or are disruptive, asking people to perform assessments tasks periodically. These issues make Parkinson's monitoring unfeasible over an extended period. Although there is evidence that supports longitudinal and naturalistic monitoring of this disease [2] and other conditions [1] using smartphones, they rely on GPS only. Thus, we believe this idea can be improved by fusing multiple data sources including interaction, inertial, environmental and web data.

2. METHODOLOGY

We propose a novel longitudinal, naturalistic and unobtrusive methodology to monitor Parkinson's. It is known that symptoms affect different aspects of people's routines and activities; therefore, we hypothesise that if we identify and quantify the fluctuations of these behavioural phenotypes, then we can measure the severity of a subset of symptoms using digital biomarkers (DB) as a proxy. We define a DB as a set of metrics that quantify a human habit and we infer them based on smartphone-collected data. However, we want to highlight that this methodology is device agnostic and its main contribution lays in its analysis algorithms.

Our methodology has three stages. Data collection, where a smartphone carried by each participant collects social, environmental, location and interaction data 24/7 for 12 months. We do not require participants to perform any assessment tasks or carry the device in any particular way and only instruct them to use the phone as they would normally do. The smartphones run an in-house version of the Aware Framework in the background that logs, encrypts and sends data to our servers every hour.

The second stage, data analysis, has two tasks: inferring DBs and generating a Profile of Living (PL). In the first one, we clean and combine the collected data to infer a set of metrics that represent a DB. For example, if we were analysing human mobility we could compute metrics like the places a person visits the most, the time they spend on each of them, the distance they travel, etc. using location, spatial, inertial, WiFi and Bluetooth data. During the second task, we identify the trends of these metrics and measure their fluctuations to build the PL. A PL is a concept we propose where each of the DB's metrics are split in two, the portion at the beginning of the monitoring period represents a personal baseline while the rest are deviations from that initial segment. Going back to our previous example, we can analyse a metric in different time granularities (i.e., visited places per day), define that the baseline period is one month and then create a synthetic score that quantifies if a person visited fewer or more places in the following 11 months.

In the final stage, evaluation, the DB's metrics fluctuations are mapped to changes in the severity of Parkinson's symptoms to discover if they are correlated. The severity of symptoms is measured every six weeks using clinical scales that quantify the motor, cognitive, emotional and well-being state of a person. These scales include the full MDS-UPDRS (golden standard in clinical practice), ACE-III, PDQ-39, NMSQuest, Stroop test, verbal fluency test, reaction time test, and sustained attention test. Also, we collect the self-reported severity of our participants' three main symptoms at least once a day using a four-point interval scale that goes from "No severity" to "High severity".

3. INSIGHTS GAINED

In September 2015 we carried out a pilot study monitoring two PwP for twelve weeks collecting 29 different data sources [5]. Based on this data, monitoring approaches from the literature, and Parkinson's symptoms and clinical scales, we identified five DBs that could be explored: phone interaction, episodes of going up/down stairs, people's indoor routines, motor activities, and social interaction.

In March 2017 we started a one-year monitoring study with four PwP. Participants could use an Android phone running the data collection software either as their main or secondary device and use a set of four Bluetooth buttons to self-report their symptoms. After four months we got three insights that reshaped our study.

First, three participants used their monitoring phone as a secondary device. Therefore, it was not actively being used and could be forgotten during the day. Due to these usage patterns, and Android's battery saving strategies, we collected data only in 40% of the total monitored period compared to 80% for the participant using the phone as their primary device. This led us to install Aware in their main devices (iPhones) with the drawback of collecting ten fewer data sources than Android.

Second, the decision of using Aware for iOS alongside interviews with our participants, allowed us to decide what DBs will be analysed. All participants stated they do not keep their phones with themselves at home; thus, episodes of going up/down stairs and indoors routines are less likely to be recorded, so they were dropped. However, now that all participants are using an instrumented smartphone as their main device, we could capture location, accelerometer, screen events, ambient noise, Wifi and Bluetooth data. These sources are relevant for quantifying the social and phone interaction DBs which will be our primary focus. What is more, research suggests a correlation between interaction data and cognitive performance [4] and between mobility data and depression [1]; both symptoms of Parkinson's. Although motor activities might be amenable for computation, we discarded it because we want to work on a thin slice of this problem only. Accordingly, we will analyse the following metrics from the chosen DBs: phone usage sessions, typing speed, and typing errors for phone interaction; and visited places, time spent at home, distanced travelled, calls made and received, time surrounded by people (given by Bluetooth profiling), among others, for social interaction.

Third, the Bluetooth buttons for self-reporting stopped working with our Android phone due to technical problems. Thus, we iteratively co-designed with PwP a diary printed in a double-sided A5 booklet with one page per day, each page having three entries containing three symptoms to be ranked. Participants valued the flexibility and sense of presence the diary gave them compared to digital approaches. This was reflected by compliance of filling in the diary for 97% of the time over 196 days.

4. CONCLUSION

Due to the exploratory nature of this work and the idiosyncratic characteristics of Parkinson's we are interested in a personal and not a cross-sectional analysis of the social and phone interaction DBs. We consider each participant a case study and will present the results of our analysis in the context of their individual subset of symptoms. This means that a small cohort of participants is a desired feature in this project and that future work under the same line of research should explore the generalisation of our findings in a bigger sample of PwP. If successful, this approach could have a significant impact on the quality of life of PwP by saving them time, reducing the physical and psychological burden related to traditional clinical assessment methods, and improving the precision of treatments and interventions. In turn, this will lessen clinicians' workload and improve the efficiency of health services.

5. REFERENCES

[1] L. Canzian and M. Musolesi. Trajectories of depression. In *Proceedings of the 2015 ACM International Joint Conference on Pervasive and Ubiquitous Computing - UbiComp '15*, pages 1293–1304, New York, New York, USA, 2015. ACM Press.

[2] J. Liddle, D. Ireland, S. J. McBride, S. G. Brauer, L. M. Hall, H. Ding, M. Karunanithi, P. W. Hodges, D. Theodoros, P. A. Silburn, and H. J. Chenery. Measuring the lifespace of people with Parkinson's disease using smartphones: proof of principle. *JMIR mHealth and uHealth*, 2(1):e13, 1 2013.

[3] D. Pan, R. Dhall, A. Lieberman, and D. B. Petitti. A mobile cloud-based Parkinson's disease assessment system for home-based monitoring. *JMIR mHealth and uHealth*, 3(1):e29, 1 2015.

[4] M. Pavel, H. Jimison, T. Hayes, J. Kaye, E. Dishman, K. Wild, and D. Williams. Continuous, Unobtrusive Monitoring for the Assessment of Cognitive Function.

[5] J. Vega. Monitoring Parkinson's Disease Progression Using Behavioural Inferences, Mobile Devices and Web Technologies. *Proceedings of the 25th International Conference Companion on World Wide Web*, pages 323–327, 2016.

Value Sensitive Design for Neurodiverse Teams in Higher Education

Annuska Zolyomi[1], Anne Spencer Ross[2], Arpita Bhattacharya[3], Lauren Milne[2], Sean Munson[3]
[1]The Information School, [2]Computer Science & Engineering, [3]Human Centered Design and Engineering
University of Washington
{annuska, ansross, arpitab, milnel2, smunson}@u.washington.edu

ABSTRACT
In a neurodiverse team, such as one comprised of students with autism and neurotypical students, social interaction and cognitive styles differ. We used a Value-Sensitive Design (VSD) approach to explore the role of technology in supporting the diverse values of neurodiverse teams. We conducted interviews with higher education disability services staff, followed by interviews with students with autism. We analyzed the students' values using the Q-Methodology. We found that key values of students with autism are: *freedom from stigma, individual comfort, social comfort, social connection*, and *team cohesion*. Through a VSD technical investigation, we found that current collaboration and affective technologies focus on supporting *social connection* and *team cohesion*. However, these technologies tend to not enable tailoring the user experience for the *individual comfort* that can benefit autistic users.

CCS Concepts
Human-centered computing – Collaborative and social computing; Accessibility – Empirical studies in accessibility

Keywords:
Autism; neurodiversity; value-sensitive design; collaboration

1. INTRODUCTION
According to a study by the U.S. Department of Education [5], 47% of young adults with autism enrolled in a postsecondary institution within 6 years of graduating from high school. Among that group, only 35% of that group earned a degree, as opposed to a 51% completion rate for the general population. In higher education, class-based teams require students to work together in a high-pressure and unpredictable environment. For a team to function, the students need to use collaboration skills including communication, planning, and organization. Some class-based teams will be neurodiverse, such as those comprised of students with autism and neurotypical students. The team dynamics of neurodiverse teams will be constructed by the skills and working styles of all team members. Individuals with autism have diverse social, communication, and cognitive styles that influence their social dynamics and their approach to performing at school or work. In related research [4], adults with autism reported feeling pressure when communicating face-to-face: managing eye contact, interpreting the expressions of others, and responding at the right tempo. Interpersonal and workplace challenges can include "difficulty interpreting nuance in the meaning of coworkers' statements, difficulty interpreting coworkers' emotions, difficulty dealing with office politics, and difficulty handling conflicts" [3]. To explore the role of technology in supporting neurodiverse teams, we used a Value-Sensitive Design (VSD) approach [2]. VSD facilitates a close analysis of the ways that stakeholder values are supported or inhibited by technology. We conducted VSD conceptual, empirical, and technical investigations focusing on our research questions: (1) What are the values of autistic students in relation to class-based team-work? (2) How does team-focused technology support stakeholder values? We conducted semi-structured interviews with five higher education disability services staff, followed by semi-structured interviews with seven students with autism. This paper reports on our preliminary analysis of our interviews with the higher education staff, as well as the students' Q-Methodology ranking of value statements [4]. We found that, within the context of class-based teams, autistic students value *freedom from stigma, individual comfort, social comfort, social connection,* and *team cohesion.* Through our technical analysis, we found that collaboration and affective technologies support general notions of *social connection* and *team cohesion.* However, there is opportunity for technology to better support needs around *individual comfort.*

ASSETS '17, October 29-November 1, 2017, Baltimore, MD, USA.

ACM ISBN 978-1-4503-4926-0/17/10.
https://doi.org/10.1145/3132525.3134787

2. METHOD
For our VSD conceptual investigation, we drew from related work and autism-related online blogs and forums to determine the stakeholders who would be directly or indirectly affected by technologies. For the key stakeholders, we identified their core values (e.g. *individual comfort*) related to team work and identified trade-offs between values inherent in different technology concepts. For our first phase of empirical investigation, we conducted interviews with five employees of student disability services. Based on our conceptual analysis and staff interviews, we generated 15 value statements representing the emerging values. For instance, the values of *freedom from stigma* and *social connection* were reflected in statements such as "I want my teammates to know I have autism" and "I do not want to stand out as different than my teammates." The value of *individual comfort* mapped to statements such as "It is helpful for me to talk with someone about how my team is doing." and "I want things to be straight-forward." For our second phase of empirical investigation, we conducted in-person or online semi-structured interviews with seven adults with autism (4 female; 3 male) who were enrolled in college either currently or within the past two years. Interview questions and value statements are available upon request. Per the Q-Methodology, the participants ranked the value statements along a "strongly disagree" to "strongly agree" scale. In the five-column template, the participants were required to place two statements in the "strongly" disagree/agree columns, three in the "mostly" agree/disagree columns, and five in the middle "no opinion/mixed feelings" column. Finally, we conducted a VSD retroactive technology investigation of the team-based technologies we identified during our literature review and empirical investigations. Our team

analyzed how these technologies met or conflicted with the values of our participants.

3. FINDINGS

3.1 Values of Neurodiverse Teams

The stakeholders for technology designed to support neurodiverse teams include members of a class: student(s) with autism, neurotypical teammates, other classmates, the teaching assistant, and the professor. There are also stakeholders who are not directly involved in a class setting: peers and family of individuals with autism, and university employees who work in student disability services, information technology, and administration. An even broader set of stakeholders are the policy makers and funders of the university, including public and private funders. Our investigation focused on the perspectives of students with autism.

Students with autism value *freedom from stigma*, with four interview participants strongly agreeing (and three having mixed opinions) that there is a stigma associated with autism. Some participants cited perceived stigma as a reason for sometimes not disclosing their diagnosis to teammates or professors. Five participants expressed that although they feel there is a stigma associated with autism, this is stigma perceived by others, not self-stigma, so they prefer to be open about their autism. These students tended to be upfront about their preferred communication and work styles. Autistic students value *individual comfort*, which we define as being able to interact and work in ways that feel physically, emotionally, and intellectually natural to oneself. Autistic students value *team cohesion*, which is the degree to which members of a team contribute to a task at hand and foster productivity by setting and attaining meeting goals [6]. Team cohesion can benefit from enhanced interpersonal *social connection* (i.e.; connecting on a personal level in addition to a professional level). However, all our participants favored straight-forward, predictable team interactions. The majority of our participants preferred spending meeting time on project tasks, rather than discussing topics unrelated to the project. All the participants expressed underlying concerns about privacy and trust inherent in *social connection, individual comfort,* and *social comfort*. *Social comfort*, which we defined as following social norms and supporting each other's needs, can be difficult for all stakeholders depending on the team dynamics and the level of open, supportive communication.

3.2 Values of Technologies Supporting Teams

Adults with autism actively use Computer Mediated Communication (CMC), such as online communities, to foster relationships, although there are disadvantages [1]. Burke et al. speculate the social affordances of CMC can work well for these adults due to technology affordances of highly-structured environments without extraneous stimuli, asynchronous communication, visual anonymity, and privacy. Exploring technology-based social awareness, Williams et al. designed a smart scarf, SWARM [7], that used lights to convey the wearer's physiological state. Although designed for a range of users with disabilities, the scarf was inspired by weighted vests, which are used by some in the autism community for physical and sensory comfort. Our technical analysis found that primary technologies designed for teams can be placed in two categories: (1) tools that support collaborative work both for content sharing (Google Drive and Microsoft SharePoint) as well as project coordination and communication (Slack and email); and (2) affective computing prototypes designed for teamwork settings (SmartHeliosity [6] and SWARM). The content sharing and electronic communication tools allowed for asynchronous communication and fewer non-verbal social cues to interpret, therefore, generally supporting *social connection, freedom from stigma*, and *social comfort*. However, students with autism may feel constrained by the tools since they do not offer customizations or features to address issues around *individual comfort*. For instance, some individuals with autism are highly visual thinkers, while others may rely on text. Existing tools tend to require teams to use one mode, without the flexibility of different views for different users. The affective technologies are designed to communicate the emotional state of an individual or a team to promote *team cohesion* and *social connection*. However, students with autism may want more explicit support from affective technology, such as discrete naming of emotional states rather than communicating via ambiguous colors. They may prefer more personal and private expressions of emotions depending on their *individual comfort* needs, which can change over time.

4. CONCLUSION AND FUTURE WORK

Our VSD approach allowed us to begin developing a holistic understanding of the dynamics of neurodiverse teams. We identified primary value tensions within a team regarding *team cohesion* and the need for *freedom from stigma, individual comfort,* and *social comfort*. Another key tension was between *social connection* and *team cohesion*. In future work, we will complete our analysis of the interviews with higher education staff and autistic students. We will create a design framework to brainstorm technology-based tools to facilitate teamwork. Although technology cannot eliminate value tensions, we hope to identify opportunities for technology to mediate tensions leveraging strategies already used by stakeholders—such as fostering collaborative reflection and decision making by enabling communication with trusted peers and staff.

5. REFERENCES

[1] Moira Burke, Robert Kraut, and Diane Williams. 2010. Social Use of Computer-Mediated Communication by Adults on the Autism Spectrum. In *Proc. CSCW '10*, 425–434. DOI: https://doi.org/10.1145/1718918.1718991

[2] Batya Friedman, Peter H. Kahn Jr, and Alan Borning. 2006. Value Sensitive Design and information systems. In *Human-computer interaction in management information systems: Foundations*. M.E. Sharpe, 348–372.

[3] Meredith Ringel Morris, Andrew Begel, and Ben Wiedermann. 2015. Understanding the Challenges Faced by Neurodiverse Software Engineering Employees: Towards a More Inclusive and Productive Technical Workforce. In *Proc. SIGACCESS '15*, 173–184.

[4] Kathleen O'Leary, Jacob O. Wobbrock, and Eve A. Riskin. 2013. Q-Methodology as a Research and Design Tool for HCI. In *Proc .SIGCHI '13*, 1941–1950.

[5] C. Sanford, L. Newman, M. Wagner, R. Cameto, A.-M. Knokey, and D. Shaver. *The post-high school outcomes of young adults with disabilities up to 6 years after high school: Key findings from the National Longitudinal Transition Study-2 (NLTS2)*. SRI International, Menlo Park, CA.

[6] Oliver Stefani, Milind Mahale, Achim Pross, and Matthias Bues. 2011. SmartHeliosity: Emotional Ergonomics Through Coloured Light. In *Proc. Conference on Ergonomics and Health Aspects of Work with Computers*, 226–235.

[7] Michele A. Williams, Asta Roseway, Chris O'Dowd, Mary Czerwinski, and Meredith Ringel Morris. 2015. SWARM: An Actuated Wearable for Mediating Affect. In *Proc. International Conference on Tangible, Embedded, and Embodied Interaction (TEI '15)*, 293–300. DOI: https://doi.org/10.1145/2677199.2680565

WeLi: A Smartwatch Application to Assist Students with Intellectual and Developmental Disabilities

Hui Zheng, Vivian Genaro Motti
George Mason University
Fairfax, VA, US
hzheng5;vmotti@gmu.edu

ABSTRACT
To explore the potential of smartwatches in special education, we designed, developed and evaluated WeLi – a wearable application that assists students with intellectual and developmental disabilities (IDDs) in educational environments. By integrating a mobile application with a smartwatch solution, the WeLi application assists students with IDDs and their assistants, facilitating collaboration, communication and planning. WeLi provides features for intervention, self-regulation for mood and reminders. The findings from the user studies show that the students and their assistants are enthusiastic about adopting the novel technology in classroom settings.

CCS Concepts
• Human-centered computing • Ubiquitous and mobile computing • Social and professional topics • Assistive technologies.

Keywords
Intellectual and Developmental Disabilities (IDDs); Wearables; Special Education; Assistive Technologies; Smartwatches

1. INTRODUCTION
Despite having a large potential for diverse applications, wrist-worn devices are especially popular as fitness trackers and smartwatches. Little is known about the potential of wrist-worn technologies as assistive technologies, particularly to support students with IDDs in special education. To support students with IDDs and facilitate the communication and support between the students and their assistants, we developed WeLi – a wearable application implemented through user-centered design that assists students with IDDs in post-secondary education environments.

WeLi has been deployed in Mason Life (masonlife.gmu.edu), a post-secondary program for young adults with IDDs who desire a university experience in a supportive environment. To attend classes, each student receives continuous assistance from a staff member. The member sits near the student in class and intervenes when needed, for instance to inform the student of what to do next, to remind the student when to ask questions, and to keep the student focused, calm or silent. As the students follow regular courses, the assistance provided by the staff may disturb their colleagues.

ASSETS '17, October 29-November 1, 2017, Baltimore, MD, USA

ACM ISBN 978-1-4503-4926-0/17/10.
https://doi.org/10.1145/3132525.3134770

Having a staff member always around, may also cause discomfort or stigma to the student. By using WeLi, an M&W (mobile + wearable) application, the staff can sit in the rear of the classroom and send notifications to the student via a mobile phone. The student receives a personalized notification directly on his/her watch in a timely fashion.

2. ASSISTIVE SMARTWATCHES
Wrist-worn technologies have been explored as assistive technologies for users with disabilities in recent years. Still, little is known about the application in special education. Existing applications include: (1) a bracelet with LED lights that supports the communication of children with autism enhancing physical touch [1]; (2) a smartwatch app that alleviates the anxiety and stress of adults with ADHD and mild forms of attention deficit, providing tools for time management, guided meditation, and positive message priming [2]; (3) a wearable app designed to help children with neuro-developmental disorders, that detects behavioral problems and manage those through interventions [3]; and (4) a wrist- band developed to analyze anxiety levels of adults with autism by recording the user interaction with a digital stretch band [4]. Interviews with adults with mild cognitive impairments were conducted to understand better the potential of wearables in supporting them in their job, family and health settings [5].

3. WEARABLE LIFE (WELI)
The WeLi app was developed for Motorola G5 Plus smartphones with Android 7.0 Nougat, and Sony smartwatches 3 SWR50, enabling staff members to send interventions from their phones, which are paired with the student's watch. For real-time assistance in class, each notification sent to the student's watch is displayed on the screen after a quick vibration (800 milliseconds) to minimize the class disturbance and ensure it is still noticeable. The notifications can be sent manually or automatically (programmed) by the staff, and they are personalized and flexible, not always requiring immediate feedback from the student.

To elicit the requirements for WeLi, a user-centric design process was followed. After IRB-approval, two semi-structured interviews were conducted with three staff members and a demonstration app was implemented for pilot study. Then, five focus groups were conducted, being three with staff members and two with Mason Life students. Each session had five to eight participants and lasted around one hour. The results of the focus groups led to the development of five features in the app: prompting, self-regulation, checklist, countdown and alarm. To refine the requirements, terminology and features of the WeLi app, a survey with 32 staff members was conducted. As a result, three additional features were included in the app: survey, rewards and settings. All features are described in the next sections.

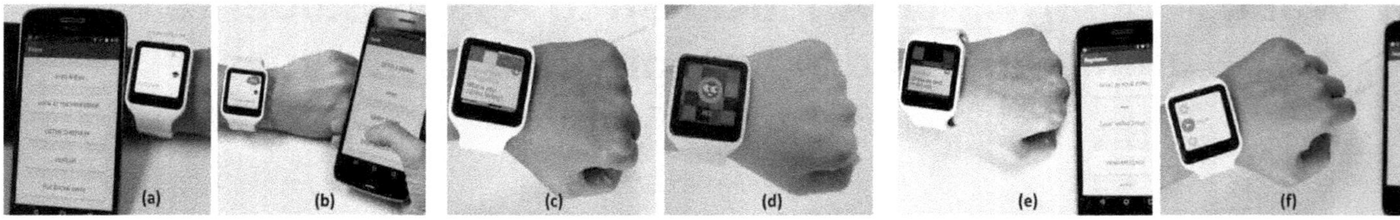

Figure 1. User interfaces illustrating the WeLi mobile and wearable application: (a) Focus, (b) Quiet, (c, d) Question and Answers for mood assessment, (e, f) Mood levels.

3.1 Prompting

Prompting provides four options for notifying the student: "Focus", "Quiet", "Participate", and "Rewards". For each option, specific messages can be chosen, e.g.: "Eyes ahead" (Figure. 1a) and "Listen carefully" under "Focus" in case the student is distracted in class. Similarly, there are several message choices for "Quiet" (Figure. 1b) and "Participate". For the "Rewards", when the student performs well in class, he/she receives a notification, such as: "Awesome", for encouragement. Every reward is counted as a star and the total is sent to the student at the end of class.

3.2 Self-Regulation

As the students have been trained with 'the zones of regulation' (www.zonesofregulation.com), this approach is employed for self-assessment of the student mood. The students select a 'zone' according to their current emotion in class by selecting among four color options: blue, green, yellow, and red (Figure 1c, Figure 1d). The feedback about the color-zone is shown on the staff's phone triggering another notification question that asks about their specific 'level' of the mood (Figure 1e). The possible answers are high, medium and low (Figure 1f) which are also sent to the staff's phone.

3.3 Checklist and Survey

Before each class, the readiness checklist is sent to the student to check whether he/she has for instance the necessary materials available and his/her phone is set to silent mode. The items checked by the student on the watch are informed on the staff's phone too. The survey has been implemented to ask students about their feedback in class.

3.4 Countdown, Alarm and Settings

The alarm enables the staff to set repeating notifications. The staff can set a certain time for the alarm to repeat every week and notify the student automatically, such as: "Be patient! Only 10 minutes left" to be sent 10 minutes before class ends. The countdown can be used for the class break or snack break, to send a reminder to the student asking him/her to come back to the classroom when the time is over. As the vibration precedes each notification, the staff can set it to be stronger or weaker using the settings feature.

4. FINDINGS

To evaluate WeLi, a usability study was conducted with seven students with IDDs. The study had two sessions with four and three students each. Each student was accompanied by a supporting staff and a note-taking observer.

The "prompting" and "self-regulation" features were evaluated. For the "prompting", five notifications were sent to the students' watches. For the "regulation", the student interacted with the watch to submit a reply. To choose the 'Zone', the student need to swipe the watch screen horizontally and choose one 'color'. To choose the 'level', the student needs to scroll vertically and choose one answer. To compare the two interaction styles, the horizontal scroll had only one mistake (out of 28 operations), in which the student confused the green icon with the blue one. Although there is text below each icon, we realized it is not enough, so we will make the icon more distinguishable by pattern and color. For the vertical style, six mistakes (out of 28 operations) were made by four students, among which one mistake was that a student selected two answers 'Medium' and 'High' rather than one because the items displayed on one screen are too small. The other five mistakes were that three students clicked the default 'Speak' Android Wear option for voice input. The study results indicate that the horizontal style is easier to interact with. Overall, the students were enthusiastic about the app and willing to use it in class. Besides, the staff learned how to use the app quickly and were delighted to adopt it in class.

5. ACKNOWLEDGMENTS

This material is based upon work supported by the National Science Foundation under Grant No.1314342. Any opinions, findings, conclusions or recommendations expressed in this material are those of the author(s) and don't necessarily reflect the views of the National Science Foundation.

6. REFERENCES

[1] K. Suzuki, T. Hachisu, and K. Iida. Enhancedtouch: A smart bracelet for enhancing human-human physical touch. In Proc. of CHI'16, pages 1282–1293, USA, 2016.

[2] V. Dibia. Foqus: A smartwatch application for individuals with adhd and mental health challenges. In Proc. of ASSETS'16, pages 311–312, USA, 2016.

[3] C. Zakaria and R. C. Davis. Demo: Wearable application to manage problem behavior in children with neurodevelopmental disorders. In Proc. of MobiSys'16, pages 127–127, Singapore, 2016.

[4] W. Simm, M. A. Ferrario, A. Gradinar, M. Tavares Smith, S. Forshaw, I. Smith, and J. Whittle. Anxiety and autism: Towards personalized digital health. In Proc. of CHI'16, pages 1270–1281, USA, 2016.

[5] V. Dibia, S. Trewin, M. Ashoori, and T. Erickson. Exploring the potential of wearables to support employment for people with mild cognitive impairment. In Proc. of ASSETS'15, pages 401–402, Portugal, 2015.

"I Always Have to Think About It First": Authentication Experiences of People with Cognitive Impairments

Jordan Hayes
Syracuse University
Syracuse, NY
jhayes05@syr.edu

Xiao Li
Syracuse University
Syracuse, NY
xli188@syr.edu

Yang Wang
Syracuse University
Syracuse, NY
ywang@syr.edu

ABSTRACT

Authentication is a mundane yet often integral part of people's experiences with computing devices and Internet services. Since most authentication mechanisms were designed without explicitly considering people with disabilities, these mechanisms may pose significant challenges for these users. In this paper, we report results from a contextual inquiry study on the authentication experiences and challenges of people with cognitive impairments. We identified a number of difficulties our participants experienced, such as remembering usernames and passwords, typing on the keyboard, logging out from their existing online accounts and being aware of errors. We hope the insights we found will indeed make future authentication systems more accessible and easier to use for users with cognitive impairments.

CCS Concepts

•**Security and privacy → Authentication; Usability in security and privacy;** *Social aspects of security and privacy;*

Keywords

authentication, security, cognitive impairments, HCI

1. INTRODUCTION

Authentication is one of key mechanisms to protect computer users' privacy and security. However, using these authentication systems can be significantly difficult for people with disabilities. In this paper, we focus on the authentication experiences of people with cognitive impairments, defined as those which "affect a person's ability to learn, process and/or remember information, communicate, or make decisions" [2]. In order to understand how our target population uses computers and Web services in a natural environment, we used a contextual inquiry research method where we conducted semi-structured qualitative interviews along with observations of how participants completed everyday authentication tasks they perform on a regular basis.

ASSETS '17 October 29-November 1, 2017, Baltimore, MD, USA

ACM ISBN 978-1-4503-4926-0/17/10.
DOI: https://doi.org/10.1145/3132525.3134788

2. RELATED WORK

Several research studies have examined the experiences users with and without cognitive impairments face in terms of general web accessibility, computer use and authentication. Rocha et al. surveyed and observed a group of users with intellectual disabilities and found that most participants had difficulty manipulating the keyboard [4]. Sevilla et al. analyzed current Web accessibility technologies regarding the needs of users with cognitive impairments and found some participants had less difficulties using an adaptive web interface. [5] Dosono et al. examined the difficulties and experiences of visually impaired users finding their participants encountered multiple accessibility and authentication obstacles [1]. Ma et. al (2013) involved users with Down syndrome who performed better remembering passwords than those without cognitive impairments but had difficulty remembering mnemonic passwords or passphrases.[3].

3. METHODS

To better understand the difficulties and challenges users with cognitive impairments may have, we conducted a contextual inquiry study in which we recruited seven participants from November 2015 to May 2016, at the location of their choice and conducted semi-structured interviews while observing them performing regular authentication tasks. We used a pre-screening survey to identify eligible participants, which consisted of three main parts: first we obtained participants' demographics, computer configurations and overall authentication experiences, as well as their opinions of online security and privacy. Then we guided the contextual inquiry and observed participants performing authentication tasks on a clearly defined set of concerns representing a set of common authentication scenarios we covered in our previous

Table 1: Demographic information of participants

ID	Age	Gender	Self-description
P1	30-40	Female	Learning Disabilities
P2	40-50	Male	Cerebral Palsy
P3	20-30	Male	Aspergers Syndrome
P4	30-40	Female	Anxiety
P5	61	Male	Dyslexia, Dyscalcula
P6	40-50	Male	Aspergers Syndrome
P7	19	Female	Vestibular Disorder

paper, such as computer system, email, banking/financial, shopping and social media websites [1]. We wrapped up the study by asking participants to reflect upon their experiences and provide suggestions to improve their authentication experiences. This semi-structured interview format allowed room for conversation and adjustment. Each participant gave informed consent via a form containing information about what was expected of them and that they could withdraw from the study at any time. Upon their permission, we took audio and video recordings of them doing the tasks. We turned the camera away from participants' screens when entering passwords in order to protect their privacy. This study was approved by the university's Institutional Review Board (IRB). The demographics of participants are listed in Table 1.

We analyzed data by reviewing the interview transcripts and audio/video recordings. We decomposed each transcript into various parts of the study components and then coded the data using a grounded theory approach [6]. We developed approximately 15 qualitative codes to summarize the most relevant findings we learned from each participant, which we clustered into sets of high level themes, including difficulty remembering passwords, error awareness, typing, CAPTCHAs and logging out of websites. Not all participants performed every task as some of them refused to log into their financial accounts or they did not have social media accounts.

4. RESULTS

Four participants (P1, P3, P5, P7) saved their credentials using browser-based password managers, while three manually entered their credentials. The four who saved their credentials claimed it was faster and easier to use, and this mechanism released them from the necessity of remembering their passwords. P2 recalls not resetting passwords for sites that he does not use regularly but makes an effort to do so for accessing sensitive information. P3 also experienced difficulties remembering his password while attempting to log into Facebook, failing three times and ultimately resetting his password. P4 struggled to remember the exact syntax of her username when attempting to log into Facebook, pondering over whether or not she used the correct one: *"and I always have to think about it first, because I have so many different ones."* P5 expressed difficulty remembering how to spell his passwords since he attributes his learning disability to frustration with his short-term memory. Therefore, he occasionally writes down his passwords and sometimes use the same password for multiple sites.

One participant had difficulty recognizing an important error regarding the syntax of one of his login credentials. Some websites, such as Google will remind users the validity of their credentials by showing a line of red text indicating an error under the incorrect credentials as well as a red frame to highlight the box containing incorrect information. Furthermore, some websites only say the username and password do not match rather than telling which specific credentials are incorrect. These visual indications did not successfully alert the attention of P6, who consequently had difficulties being aware of which credentials he incorrectly entered, failing to recognize the need to enter *".com"* into his email address in order to successfully log into Gmail.

Three participants chose to enter website names into the address bar and click the link from the Google search results than directly enter the actual URL. P5 referred to the fact that doing so was *"the only way [he] learned how to do it."*. P2 needed assistance from his aide to enter in his usernames and passwords for him because of challenges related to his hands' dexterity resulting from his cerebral palsy. He said he would rather use his voice to dictate information into his computer: *"Yeah. My voice is my strongest accent. As far as typing stuff, I'm not able to type very well...I could speak faster than I could type."*

5. DISCUSSION

Our results suggest that while some of the difficulties or challenges of users with or without cognitive impairments in authentication are similar at the surface, the root causes of their challenges tend to differ. Authentication designs intended to help users with cognitive impairments must consider both the challenges and their underlying causes to address the differences users with and without cognitive impairments may face when logging into and out of websites.

6. CONCLUSION

Current authentication interfaces are not accessible for users with cognitive impairments. Our study provides a nuanced account of various difficulties these users encounter with authentication. As the security community actively creates new authentication mechanisms, they should take into account the various characteristics of users and potential challenges they may face. We hope the authentication community can use our study insights to make their mechanisms more accessible.

7. ACKNOWLEDGMENTS

The contents of this paper were developed under a grant from the National Institute on Disability, Independent Living, and Rehabilitation Research (NIDILRR grant number 90DP0061- 01-00). We thank our participants for sharing their insights.

8. REFERENCES

[1] B. Dosono, J. Hayes, and Y. Wang. "i'm stuck!": A contextual inquiry of people with visual impairments in authentication. In *Eleventh Symposium On Usable Privacy and Security (SOUPS 2015)*, pages 151–168, Ottawa, 2015. USENIX Association.

[2] V. L. Hanson, A. Cavender, and S. Trewin. Writing about accessibility. *Interactions*, 22(6):62–65, 2015.

[3] Y. Ma, J. Feng, L. Kumin, and J. Lazar. Investigating User Behavior for Authentication Methods. *ACM Transactions on Accessible Computing*, 4(4):1–27, 2013.

[4] T. Rocha, M. Bessa, L. Magalhães, and L. Cabral. Performing universal tasks on the Web. *Proceedings of the XVI International Conference on Human Computer Interaction - Interacción '15*, pages 1–7, 2015.

[5] J. Sevilla, G. Herrera, B. Martínez, and F. Alcantud. Web accessibility for individuals with cognitive deficits. *ACM Transactions on Computer-Human Interaction*, 14(3):12–es, 2007.

[6] A. Strauss and J. Corbin. *Basics of Qualitative Research: Grounded Theory Procedures and Techniques.* Sage Publications, Inc., 1990.

Augmented Reality for the Literacy Development of Deaf Children: A Preliminary Investigation

[Extended Abstract]

Aziza Almutairi
King Saud University
Information Technology Department
Riyadh, Saudi Arabia
aziza.m.m@hotmail.com

Shiroq Al-Megren
King Saud University
Information Technology Department
Riyadh, Saudi Arabia
salmegren@ksu.edu.sa

ABSTRACT

This paper reports the on-going research on the development of an Augmented Reality (AR) application for the literacy development of hard of hearing children, particularly deaf children that rely on Arabic Sign Language (ArSL). Preliminary studies were conducted to determine the visual needs of deaf Arabic learners when reading using three different instruments and targets: interviews with teachers, observation of deaf children, and questionnaire from their parents. Results from teachers and parents indicate a preference for multiple resources, primarily ArSL, including photos and videos. Students, on the other hand, performed better with finger-spelling and poorly in ArSL. This disconnect between both achievements highlights the importance of considering various perspectives in the development of AR that targets literacy in younger children.

CCS Concepts

•Human-centered computing → Accessibility systems and tools;

Keywords

Augmented reality; deaf; hard of hearing; DHH; Arabic sign language; ArSL.

1. INTRODUCTION

Literacy is critical for children's growth as it significantly impacts educational, vocational, and social development. The reading process requires two related factors: language familiarity and decoding. Decoding is the process that leads to understanding the mapping between the language and the printed text [2]. Deaf children face a disadvantage on both factors: no early access to a familiar language and a lack of phonemic awareness via decoding [3]. Deafness is categorised by educators, in functional terms, as being hard of hearing or deaf, where the former is able to function auditorily with amplification, whereas the latter is not [6].

Recent reports from the General Authority for Statistics in Saudi Arabia declared 76,902 registered individuals that are deaf or hard of hearing where Arabic Sign Language (ArSL) is the native language [5]. Sign language (SL) is realised in the visual modality. A deaf person decodes the printed word into various forms: articulation, finger-spelling, or SL [7]. Decoding into SL was found to be the most effective and is often supported by various reading techniques, such as chaining or sandwiching [4]. The difficulty of ArSL lies in its neglect of diacritics that leads to difficulties understanding words out of context. For instance, the Arabic word for 'man', رجل, without diacritics can also mean 'leg'.

Visual literacy is the ability to understand ideas represented visually in static or dynamic forms [1]. Deaf children's visual literacy can be developed with the support of Augmented Reality (AR) [8]. There are several benefits of AR in education: seamless integration with reality, increased motivation and attention, information accessibility, and creativity. In this paper, we describe the preliminary investigations to identify the visual needs of deaf students to develop literacy competence. The objective of these studies is to identify the learning behaviours of deaf students and visual communications utilised for literacy. The study also aims to informatively identify media favouritism to be used in AR.

2. INTERVIEWING TEACHERS

Semi-structured interviews were conducted in Arabic with three female teachers with a mean age of 44 years and a standard deviation (SD) of 7.93 years. All interviewees are current teaching professionals from Al-Amal Deaf Institute in Riyadh, Saudi Arabia. Each session lasted approximately two and a half hours, was held at the teachers' place of work and audio recorded. First, general information was collected, followed by current teaching practices, typical printed text representations, and recommendations for the AR application after the teachers were shown AR applications.

2.1 Results

The interviews were transcribed and then translated into English. A thematic analysis was used to elicit meaning from the transcriptions. The following themes were identified:

- Vocabulary: All teachers stated that deaf students had problems identifying a word out of context or its con-

ASSETS '17 October 29-November 1, 2017, Baltimore, MD, USA

ACM ISBN 978-1-4503-4926-0/17/10.
DOI: https://doi.org/10.1145/3132525.3134789

notations. One teacher highlighted students' difficulties in understanding synonyms and antonyms.

- Sign Language: The interviewees agreed that SL is their primary means of communication with students.
- Teaching techniques: Surprisingly, the teachers agreed that no teaching methods were used for reading.
- Technical resources: Projectors were utilised to display videos and pictures to clarify taught words.
- AR Input: Two teachers advocated for printed books for elementary students.

3. OBSERVING STUDENTS

Six students were observed from Al-Amal Institute in two sessions: first graders (mean 9.6 years, SD 2.64) and fifth graders (mean 14 years, SD 3.46) groups. All were female students with moderate to severe hearing loss. Observations were recorded and sessions lasted two hours. Several linking tasks were presented to the students to gauge media favouritism and visual fluency. For each task, students were asked to associate a printed text with a media (either video, pictures, SL, or finger-spelling). The texts were chosen from the original courseware previously covered earlier in the semester with the aid of the teacher. For instance, students were presented with an image of a camel and asked to match the picture against its text. Another task required the students to associate a full-bodied or hands-only image of an SL interpreter with its text. For each task, the media was linked separately against text.

3.1 Results

As anticipated, fifth grade students generally performed better than first grade students in the linking task. All fifth graders were able to associate the right pictures with its corresponding printed text. However, this was not the case for first graders. Students had more difficulty with videos than they did with photos, where only one student from fifth grade was able to complete the association correctly. All the students struggled with ArSL, which was unexpected as ArSL was anticipated by the teachers' to be the most effective means when developing the tasks. Two first graders failed in completing any of the ArSL tasks, while the third student could only answer one correctly. Finger-spelling proved easy for fifth graders - all students completed the tasks successfully. First graders were observed signing the letters along with the photos to help associate them with the printed text and performed relatively well.

4. SURVEYING PARENTS

Parents of deaf children play a vital role in developing their reading ability. A questionnaire was used to collect information on deaf children's literacy from their parents. It utilised both open- and close-ended questions to gather information pertaining to a deaf child's literacy development. The questionnaire was distributed online to the teachers and various forums. Of the 37 responses received, only 14 were from parents of deaf children. The rest of the respondents were either deaf themselves or related to a deaf child.

4.1 Results

One section of the survey enquired about reading and SL proficiency. 65% of the children knew ArSL and 71% could read. Parents ranked family and schools for the deaf as having the strongest role in developing reading and SL. Some of the reading difficulties identified include the following: a weak linguistic crop, comprehending meaning of words, associating word with SL, and a child's inability to associate the alphabet to SL. All children were considered technologically competent and familiar with touch smartphones and/or tablets. The children mainly used these devices for entertainment, whereas only 43% used them for educational purposes. Parents stated that videos are a favourite among children, followed by pictures and finally animation. SL and finger-spelling had a weak preference at 29% and 15%.

5. DISCUSSION AND CONCLUSION

Interviews conducted with teachers of deaf elementary school children showed that they advocated for the use of ArSL to represent printed text. They suggested supplementing ArSL with pictures and/or videos. Observations of deaf students identified a weakness in ArSL, but the students fared better with finger-spelling. The observations also demonstrated the importance of showing the interpreter's face and body. Questionnaire results from parents of deaf children supported the suggestion of the teachers about the inclusion of photos and videos, but the parents gave these forms of media a higher priority over SL. Surprisingly finger-spelling was neither suggested by parents or teachers, but the observation found its utility in demonstrating the development of vocabulary and SL. While teachers pushed for SL as the best form of representation, the students struggled with mapping SL with its corresponding printed text. These findings highlight the importance of utilising a mixed media approach with AR to consider relevant perspectives to a child's reading progression. For future work, a participatory design approach will be adopted to develop an AR application that balances favoured media for mobile devices.

6. REFERENCES

[1] Elkins, J. The concept of visual literacy, and its limitations. *Visual Literacy* (2008).

[2] Goldin-Meadow, S., Mayberry, R. I., and Read, T. O. How Do Profoundly Deaf Children Learn to Read? *Learning Disabilities Research & Practice* (2001).

[3] Hanson, V. L. Phonology and Reading : Evidence from Profoundly Deaf Readers. *Haskins Laboratiories Status Report on Speech Research* (1989).

[4] Humphries, T., and MacDougall, F. Chaining and other links: Making connections between American Sign Language and English in Two Types of School Settings. *Visual Anthropology Review* (2000).

[5] Kingdom of Saudi Arabia General Authority of Statistic. Demographic survey, 2016.

[6] Musselman, C. How Do Children Who Can't Hear Learn to Read an Alphabetic Script? A Review of the Literature on Reading and Deafness. *Journal of deaf studies and deaf education* (2000).

[7] Treiman, R., and Hirsh-Pasek, K. Silent reading: Insights from second-generation deaf readers. *Cognitive Psychology* (1983).

[8] Uluyol, Ã., and Sahin, S. *Augmented reality: A new direction in education.* 2016.

Augmented Reality Magnification for Low Vision Users with the Microsoft Hololens and a Finger-Worn Camera

Lee Stearns[1], Victor DeSouza[1], Jessica Yin[3], Leah Findlater[2,5], Jon E. Froehlich[1,4]

[1]Department of Computer Science
[2]College of Information Studies
University of Maryland, College Park

[3]Poolesville High School
Poolesville, MD

[4]Computer Science and Engineering
[5]Human Centered Design and Engineering
University of Washington

lstearns@umd.edu, vdesouza@umd.edu, jessica.y.phs@gmail.com, leahkf@umd.edu, jonf@cs.umd.edu

ABSTRACT
Recent technical advances have enabled new wearable augmented reality (AR) solutions that can aid people with visual impairments (VI) in their everyday lives. Here, we investigate an AR-based magnification solution that combines a small finger-worn camera with a transparent augmented reality display (the Microsoft Hololens). The image from the camera is processed and projected on the Hololens to magnify visible content below the user's finger such as text and images. Our approach offers: (i) a close-up camera view (similar to a CCTV system) with the portability and processing power of a smartphone magnifier app, (ii) access to content through direct touch, and (iii) flexible placement of the magnified image within the wearer's field of view. We present three proof-of-concept interfaces and plans for a user evaluation.

CCS Concepts
• Human-centered computing → Accessibility technologies • Computing methodologies → Mixed / augmented reality

Keywords
Visually impaired; wearable computing; assistive technology; augmented reality; reading printed text; magnification

1. INTRODUCTION
Augmented reality (AR) has the potential to enhance the accessibility of the physical world for people with visual impairments (VI). One important emerging application area is the magnification and enhancement of visual information. Traditional methods such as closed-circuit television (CCTV) systems and other desktop video magnifiers [2] allow users with some residual vision to magnify and display content on a large screen. Many users also rely on magnifying glasses or smartphone-based magnifiers [1], which are more portable but offer a limited visual area and require the user to hold a device while reading. In contrast, a wearable AR system is portable and always available, provides a perceptually large display, and can allow for magnified output that is visually co-located with or even overlaid on top of the original content within the wearer's field of view.

In this poster paper, we introduce a novel AR magnification approach that combines a finger-worn camera to capture visual content with a transparent head-worn display for displaying a magnified and/or adjusted view of that content—in our case, using a *Microsoft Hololens* device [5]. Two previous approaches to magnifying information on a head-worn display have used video see-through displays where a video feed from a head-worn camera is displayed on screens in front of the user's eyes along with computer-generated content [3, 8]. In contrast, our approach does not restrict the user's field of view to only the camera view, allows for small finger movements to select the content to magnify (as opposed to head movements), and allows for 3D virtual content to be overlaid within the physical world. This lattermost characteristic is enabled by the Hololens API, which provides robust 3D mapping and motion tracking to make AR content appear as if it is fixed in place in the physical world.

ASSETS '17, October 29-November 1, 2017, Baltimore, MD, USA

ACM ISBN 978-1-4503-4926-0/17/10.
https://doi.org/10.1145/3132525.3134812

Figure 1. Prototype Hololens and finger-camera system: (a) reading a magazine article; (b) close-up view of the camera.

To date, we have implemented a proof-of-concept system with three interface variants for sensing, processing, and displaying magnified and/or adjusted images (*e.g.*, pictures, text). We describe these interfaces and associated design considerations, discuss plans for future user evaluations, and enumerate open questions for assistive AR applications. Our contributions include: (i) a preliminary investigation of a finger-mounted camera with an AR display for viewing printed or other non-tactile information and (ii) a proof-of-concept AR system with three distinct interface options for displaying magnified visual content.

2. PROTOTYPE HARDWARE
Our prototype system (Figure 1) includes a head-worn Microsoft Hololens unit and an Awaiba NanEye Idule camera worn on the index finger via a custom ring. Similar cameras have been applied for automated reading of printed text [6, 7] but here we use it solely as a digital magnifier. Currently, the camera connects to a laptop, which processes the video feed and communicates with the Hololens over Wi-Fi. While the Hololens is bulky and relatively heavy, its advanced capabilities and high-resolution display allowed us to quickly prototype and explore novel AR interfaces. In the future, we envision a fully wearable, lightweight system.

3. INTERFACE DESIGNS
To explore the magnification design space afforded by the combination of a head-worn display and finger-worn camera, we designed three interface options that vary in how the magnified AR view is displayed (Figure 2). Similar to *ForeSee* [8], we also implemented and explored real-time image processing techniques

(a) Fixed position on 2D AR display (*i.e.*, fixed within the wearer's field of view). (b) Fixed position on 3D surface or midair, in this case rendered flat on the magazine page. (c) Dynamic finger tracking, where magnified view follows and hovers above the finger.

Figure 2. The three viewport positions in our prototype system, which vary in how they present the magnified view to the user.

such as color and contrast changes to enhance legibility for low-vision users.

Design 1: Fixed Position on 2D AR Display. Our first design places the AR content at a fixed position within the user's field of vision, no matter how they move their head. We envision this design working similarly to other wearable heads-up displays such as Google Glass [4] but allowing for greater customization of the size and position of the magnified information. These parameters can be adjusted to account for user preference or vision level (*e.g.*, at the periphery for users with macular degeneration). This design is simple to implement and easy to understand but also partially obstructs a portion of the user's vision at all times.

Design 2: Fixed Position on 3D Surface. A second design places the display at a fixed position in 3D space, creating a virtual screen (the magnified image) on any surface the user chooses (*e.g.*, on a table or wall or on the document that the user is reading) or floating in midair. This design has the advantage of not occupying a part of the user's vision, instead staying at a fixed location in the world no matter how the user moves. This type of display may also more seamlessly integrate the virtual and physical worlds with content overlaid alongside or even in place of the original text in the physical world. However, this design requires more complex processing and user interactions, and since the virtual display is partially transparent, it may not work well for all locations.

Design 3: Dynamic Finger Tracking. In our third design, the display is positioned floating above the finger as it glides along the page. This design helps prevent disorientation by keeping the display as close as possible to the touched location so that the user can more easily view both. The interaction is similar to holding a physical magnifying glass or smartphone magnifier except that the user can do so at a greater distance and does not need to hold a physical device in hand, leaving the fingers free to touch the page. This design is the most complex, requiring reliable finger tracking and continual updating as the user moves, and it is possible that the motion of the display may distract from the content.

4. DISCUSSION AND OPEN QUESTIONS

Below we discuss open questions related to our system's design, plans for user evaluations, and our long-term vision for AR-based assistance for low-vision users.

The Hololens allowed us to easily prototype and experiment with novel AR designs; however, it has limitations that should be addressed for future versions of the system—specifically its size and relatively narrow display area centered in the user's field of view. Similarly, our finger-worn camera hardware is somewhat large fore regular use, and more importantly is not fully wearable—it currently relies on a separate computer for power and streaming images to the display.

While we have focused primarily on how and where to display the magnified content, designing appropriate user interactions is also important. For each of our interface designs, the user should be able to customize the magnification level, position, text processing, and other settings. Interacting with the system could be done via hand gestures or speech recognition (both are common with the Hololens). Future usability testing here is necessary to determine an appropriate interaction model.

To assess our three AR designs, we plan to conduct an evaluation with low-vision participants comparing the designs in terms of usability and comprehension. We will also compare finger-worn and head-worn cameras to explore the tradeoffs of each and compare our AR-based magnification approach against the current status quo—a handheld smartphone magnifier.

We also envision a future AR system that goes beyond simple magnification. For example, if combined with optical character recognition, the system could change fonts (*e.g.*, [8]) or read the text aloud as needed using text-to-speech. Content could be dynamically enhanced and placed over the original, although for legibility, the AR overlays would need to be opaque rather than the semi-transparent holograms that are currently possible with the Hololens. Future systems could also include touchscreen text and image manipulation features such as highlighting or copy and paste, potentially broadening the appeal to users with any level of vision.

5. ACKNOWLEDGMENTS

This work was supported by the Office of the Assistant Secretary of Defense for Health Affairs under Award W81XWH-14-1-0617.

6. REFERENCES

[1] Apple. iOS Accessibility Features: *https://www.apple.com/accessibility/iphone/vision/*.

[2] American Foundation for the Blind. CCTVs/Video Magnifiers: *http://www.afb.org/prodBrowseCatResults.aspx?CatID=53*.

[3] eSight Glasses: *https://www.esighteyewear.com/technology*.

[4] Google Glass: *https://www.google.com/glass/start/*.

[5] Microsoft Hololens: *https://www.microsoft.com/hololens*.

[6] Shilkrot, R., Huber, J., Wong, M.E., Maes, P. and Nanayakkara, S. 2015. FingerReader: a wearable device to explore printed text on the go. *Proc. CHI 2015*, 2363–2372.

[7] Stearns, L., Du, R., Oh, U., Jou, C., Findlater, L., Ross, D.A. and Froehlich, J.E. 2016. Evaluating Haptic and Auditory Directional Guidance to Assist Blind People in Reading Printed Text Using Finger-Mounted Cameras. *TACCESS*. 9, 1 (Oct. 2016), 1–38.

[8] Zhao, Y., Szpiro, S. and Azenkot, S. 2015. ForeSee: A Customizable Head-Mounted Vision Enhancement System for People with Low Vision. *Proc. ASSETS 2015*, 239–249.

Automatic Environment Adjustment for Emotional Disabilities

Shannon Duvall
Elon University
2320 Campus Box
Elon NC 27244
1-336-278-6232
sduvall2@elon.edu

Scott Spurlock
Elon University
2320 Campus Box
Elon NC 27244
1-336-278-6192
sspurlock@elon.edu

Robert Duvall
Duke University
Box 90129
Durham NC 27708
1-919-660-6567
rcd@cs.duke.edu

ABSTRACT
One often-overlooked area for assistive technology is help for those with emotional needs. Since these individuals may not emote in a typical way, most techniques for affective computing will not work for this population. Further, the applications that detect emotion are generally concerned with helping the user with some task, not simply helping them with their emotional difficulties. In this work, we present React 2 Me, a system that uses ambient technology to detect multimodal behavioral cues that may indicate emotional distress and adjust the environment to help the individual regulate their emotions.

CCS Concepts
• **Human-centered computing→Accessibility**

Keywords
Assistive technology; User experience; Affective computing; Ambient Intelligence

1. INTRODUCTION
While there are many efforts in assistive technology for those with physical disabilities, there are many fewer options for those with emotional disabilities. The field of affective computing is devoted to analyzing the emotion of a person based on everything from posture, gesture, facial expression, and physiological data. However, those with emotional disabilities do not necessarily show emotions in the same way that others do. Furthermore, for existing interactive systems, the reaction to the emotion once identified is generally application-specific, such as a game that adjusts difficulty based on the player's level of frustration. [3]

We present the creation of "React 2 Me", a software system that integrates easily obtained, relatively cheap, and portable hardware to make an interactive space for those with emotional disabilities. While the system can run interactive applications, its main function is to detect posture, sound, and movement, translate that into an action specific to the user, and adjust the ambient environment of the room, such as the lighting and music of the room. It can detect some self-injurious behaviors and alert caregivers if needed.

ASSETS'17, Oct. 29–Nov. 1, 2017, Batlimore, MD, USA.
ACM ISBN 978-1-4503-4926-0/17/10.
DOI: http://dx.doi.org/10.1145/3132525.3134816

2. RELATED WORK
There is a wide range of disabilities that include some form of emotional impairment: either sensing others' emotions, expressing their own emotions, or having appropriate emotional responses to stimuli. Garay et al classify six different types of disorders (visual, hearing, learning, mobility, developmental, and anxiety) that generally include some difficulty with affect processing. [4] For this population, traditional affect detection methods may not be effective. Santos et al further postulate that no one approach will be inclusive of all individuals with emotional difficulties. [7] Therefore, rather than trying to interpret the user's emotion, our system simply recognizes stereotypical behaviors of those with disabilities, as described by Berkson et al [2]. These behaviors can be cues to emotional state, although which state is indicated may well be specific to the user.

Equally as important as detecting emotion is what is done with the information. The field of ambient intelligence is concerned with helping users "behind the scenes" while running an application. For example, Hudlicka et al created a GUI for Air Force pilots that changes to adapt to the level of pilot stress. [5] Rather than helping the user accomplish some task, we would like to use the affect cues of the user to calm, soothe, or stimulate the user, or alert caretakers as needed. Previous findings show that color and music can affect mood [1,6]. Again, rather than assume positive or negative effects of stimuli, we allow the user to define the reaction of the system to the behavioral cues.

3. REACT 2 ME SYSTEM
Our overall goal is to create software that can be paired with various input and output devices to detect multimodal behavioral cues and adjust the environment accordingly. The result is an inexpensive, portable, and customizable way to understand and ease the discomfort of those with emotional disabilities.

3.1 System Components
The system uses mostly gaming devices meant for a single user for input. Because of this, it is best if one user at a time interacts with the system. Those with emotional disabilities often do not emote in a standard way, so having only one user also makes the system customizable and more effective for our target population.

Currently, the system integrates APIs for the Kinect, LeapMotion, and Philips Hue light system. The Kinect can localize the user within the space, recognize words, and detect gross motor movement. The LeapMotion device works in a smaller area and detects fine motor movements, gestures, and pointing. The Philips Hue lights enable us to programmatically change the lighting in the room, including making color schemes that are calming, adjusting dimness and brightness, and controlling specific bulbs separately.

This is not to say the user must purchase these devices, since the computer running the system also provides means of standard input and output, including mouse, keyboard, sound, and graphical display. To date, we have generally used this system with the computer running the application in hiding (under a table) and displaying any graphics with a projector. We encourage the participants to interact with the physical objects in the space rather than the technology.

3.2 Multimodal Behavior Cues

The user interface for the system presents a list of "triggers" which are the various states our system can detect. Triggers include physical phenomena like sitting, standing, lying, moving slowly, and moving quickly. Button or mouse movements, sounds at various levels, and even specific words can also be triggers. We have also included as triggers several forms of stemming, or self-stimulation, that are common among people with disabilities. These include rocking, biting oneself, head-banging, and "flapping", a characteristic movement of the arms and hands.

3.3 Behavior Interpretation

Behaviors can indicate different emotions for different people. For example, a child with emotional challenges may well cry when happy as well as when sad. Moving quickly may mean happiness for one individual and anxiety for another. Rather than trying to interpret the emotion behind the behavior, we instead ask the user (or care taker) to select the appropriate system responses to different behavioral cues, or combinations of cues.

3.4 Multimodal Reactions

When in this setup mode, the triggers are mapped to a series of reactions, such as sending text or email, turning lights on or off, changing light colors, changing music or sound effects, or starting various applications like games. Depending on the input and output devices the user decides to acquire, different triggers and reactions become available in the interface.

4. RESULTS

To date we have done informal runs with our system to test for functionality and usability. We have:

- Asked actor participants to perform some of the trigger gestures while another observer participant recognized when they did or did not occur. We used this information to test and refine our definitions of the triggers.
- Had school children (not necessarily disabled) use the interactive space as "stations". One station played music to match body motion and one station allowed users to say a color and then use their finger to "draw" virtually on a displayed screen.
- Used the system in a school specifically for kids with special needs, including participants with severe physical and severe emotional disabilities. The space included posters with animals and with colors on the wall. Our system would make sound effects when the children pointed at the various places on the posters (Figure 1). Informally we can say that every participant (~8) enjoyed the experience, several asked to have more than one turn, and even those with severe physical disabilities could interact with the posters. In one case, a teacher helped a student hand-over-hand to point, and the system was able to respond appropriately.

Figure 1. Responding to Pointing

5. FUTURE WORK

Our current work is to polish the interface for mapping triggers to reactions and do a usability study on the interface specifically and the system as a whole. We would also like to test how effective the system is at reducing emotional discomfort and engaging users.

Finally, we would like to use the system to study the mapping between triggers and emotional states. By applying machine learning techniques, we hope to discover individually personalized patterns in triggered emotional states, allowing for dynamic adjustments to the environment to help individuals preventatively rather than reactively.

6. REFERENCES

[1] Adams, F., Osgood, C. 1973. A cross-cultural study of the affective meanings of color. Journal of Cross-Cultural Psychology) 4,1 (June 1973), 135-156.

[2] Berkson, G., & Davenport, R. K. 1962. Stereotyped movements of mental defectives. American Journal of Mental Deficiency, 66, 849–852.

[3] Cearreta, I., López, J.M., López de Ipiña, K., Garay, N., Hernández, C., Graña, M. 2007. A study of the state of the art of affective computing in ambient intelligence environments. Interacción 2007 (VIII Congreso de Interacción Persona-Ordenador, II Congreso Espanol De Informatica - CEDI 2007), 333–342.

[4] Garay, N., Cearreta, I., Lopez, J.M., Fajardo, I. 2006. Assistive Technology and Affective Mediation. Human Technology: An Interdisciplinary Journal on Humans in ICT Environments 2,1 (2006), 55-83.

[5] Hudlicka, E., Mcneese, M.D. 2002. Assessment of User Affective and Belief States for Interface Adaptation: Application to an Air Force Pilot Task. User Modeling and User-Adapted Interaction 12, 1 (February 2002), 1-47. DOI=http://dx.doi.org/10.1023/A:1013337427135

[6] Juslin, P.N. & Sloboda, J.A. (ed.) (2001) Music and emotion: theory and research. Oxford ; New York : Oxford University Press.

[7] Santos, O. C., Rodriguez-Ascaso, A., Boticario, J.G., Salmeron-Majadas, S., QuirÃ³s, P., Cabestrero, R. Challenges for Inclusive Affective Detection in Educational Scenarios. Universal Access in Human-Computer Interaction. Design Methods, Tools, and Interaction Techniques for Inclusion Lecture Notes in Computer Science (2013), 566-575.

Caption Placement on an Augmented Reality Head Worn Device

Chris Schipper
Miami University
schippcj@miamioh.edu

Bo Brinkman
Miami University
bo.brinkman@miamioh.edu

ABSTRACT
Head worn augmented reality devices present new opportunities for creating assistive devices. This work investigates possible locations for captions for one-on-one conversations from a visibility and usability standpoint. Even in a one-on-one conversation there are interesting design challenges. We investigate 3 main factors: 1) Reference frame for captions (viewport or world coordinates); 2) Relation to the viewer (track the viewer's view, or track the speaker); and 3) Relation to speaker's face (most desirable vertical offset for captions). In this preliminary work, we argue that world coordinates are preferable (for reference frame), and then present our work in progress on the other factors.

CCS Concepts
• **Human-centered computing~Mixed / augmented reality**
• **Human-centered computing~Accessibility**

Keywords
Deaf; Hard-of-hearing; Captions; Augmented Reality; AR; HWD

1. INTRODUCTION
In this work, we explore the possibility of improving everyday communication for those who are D/HH (deaf or hard of hearing) by means of a head-worn video see-through augmented reality application. By performing speech-to-text operations in real time and displaying said text on the HWD (head worn device) for the user we hope to improve quality of conversations between those with and without hearing disabilities so that they are more enjoyable and communication for the deaf and hard of hearing users is easier. Speech to text functionality and AR view management are provided by the Microsoft HoloLens platform. Our contribution is to identify and investigate 3 factors that affect placement of live captions on a HWD.

The first of these is the reference frame for the captions. Specifically, we are looking at viewport versus real-world coordinates. Captions will always be rotated to face the viewer (the plane of the captions will be perpendicular to the view direction), and will be placed at an offset l, which is a 3D vector. In viewport mode, l is rotated based on the rotation of the main camera, and then added to the location of the main camera to produce the final location for the captions. In world coordinate mode l is simply used as the caption location with no modification. If, in viewport mode, we set the captions at the bottom of the viewport, and the user moves or rotates, the captions remain at the bottom of the viewport. In world coordinate mode the captions stay at a fixed place in the world. We will permit l to change, but only gradually, to provide the viewer some stability when trying to read the captions. If we did not make this restriction then the distinction between world and viewport reference frames would not be meaningful, because any l in one reference frame can easily be converted to an l' in the other reference frame.

The second factor we investigate is the placement of captions in relation to the speaker's face. There are advantages and disadvantages to placing the caption above, on, and below the face of the speaker. In essence, what is the most effective vertical offset for caption placement on a speaker?

The third factor, which only applies to world coordinate mode, is caption placement in relation to the viewer. Is it better to have captions follow the view of the user, or to track the speaker? (In viewport mode the captions will always follow the view of the user.)

We have not conducted formal experiments for this project; The project serves as a proof of concept for future works involving similar technologies with head worn devices.

2. RELATED WORK
There is a variety of work showing that DHH users find live captioning of speech useful. Mirazaei, Ghorshi, and Mortazavi [2] developed an augmented reality application that allowed deaf and hard of hearing users see speech-to-text in real time similar to the method described above; however, they did not perform their experiments with a HWD. Their work did investigate multiple methods of caption placement (speech bubbles and subtitles), but in a window-based app on the computer screen. Their experiments found that the majority of users would use this technology to assist in communications with ordinary people.

There have been other studies suggesting that real-time capture of audio and transcription to text in the classroom is helpful as well. In another study, conducted by Prietch et al. [3], it was found that deaf and hard of hearing users were willing to begin using a speech to text system in their everyday life because they "considered it important as an alternative of communication". Because of these works, we expect that our technology will be useful, and focus on determining how changing the caption placement can make it even more so.

There has not been as much work on optimal caption placement. Hu et al. determined that having captions follow the speakers on television shows reduces eyestrain when compared to traditional placement (at the bottom of the screen) [1]. It is important to note that this research was for videos on a screen, not for a head worn AR application. We wondered whether or not this idea would be useful in the type of application we are investigating.

ASSETS '17, October 29-November 1, 2017, Baltimore, MD, USA

ACM ISBN 978-1-4503-4926-0/17/10.
https://doi.org/10.1145/3132525.3134786

3. SYSTEM DESIGN

This research was carried out using a Microsoft HoloLens as the HWD, an array of microphones (from a Sony PS3 Eye camera), and a Raspberry Pi. The array of microphones is used to determine where sounds originate in the real world via differences in time delays. The Raspberry Pi powers the microphones, implements detection and tracking of sounds, and provides that information as a simple web service. The Microsoft HoloLens takes the data from the sound tracker and uses it to determine where a person is speaking from in the real world. For speech-to-text we used the microphones and libraries provided by the Microsoft HoloLens.

Figure 1. "Viewport locked" mode.

There are three different captioning modes that were tested using our system. The first is "viewport locked" mode. When using viewport locked mode, captions always stay within the field of view of the user, as seen in Figure 1; They will move with the user's field of view as their head rotates, always facing the user. This mode of captioning can take place with the captions at the top of the user's field of view, in the center, or at the bottom.

Figure 2. "Speech bubble" mode.

The second method of caption placement, "viewport delayed" mode, uses world coordinates, but still following the user's direction of view. Similar to the "viewport locked" method, the captions continuously face the user and follow their gaze; however, the captions move at a delay when the user rotates their head which we believe improves readability.

The third captioning method, "speech bubble" mode, involves dynamically placing captions on the speaker (see Figure 2). In this mode the captions are placed on the speaker as they speak.

4. EVALUATION AND DISCUSSION

This project is a work in progress, with our next step being to perform focus groups with the DHH community and other stakeholders, leading towards more rigorous evaluation. Our current goal was to build and test a proof of concept.

In our initial testing we have already discovered that the prior results mentioned above are unlikely to be directly applicable to head-worn devices. The cited works all used transcription systems where transcription results were displayed on a screen of some kind (on a TV screen, computer screen, or the screen of a phone or tablet) in a mode similar to our "viewport locked." Because the screen is either stationary or hand-held by the user the caption text is stable and easy to read in "viewport locked" mode. With the head-worn display we found this to no longer be the case. We found that when we read text we make many small head movements (some voluntary, some involuntary). In "viewport locked" mode this causes the captions to move, which tends to interrupt reading. We found both "viewport delayed" and "speech bubble" modes preferable to "viewport locked."

We also found vertically positioning subtitles in line with the speaker's face was preferable to positioning significantly above or below. In our experience these produced little to no strain on the eyes to read; however, the captions on the bottom and top were slightly straining to read over time. Our findings differ from [1–3] because they were not testing conversational applications. We found that during discussion the listener often makes eye contact with the speaker, and it is most comfortable to have the captions be in line, therefore, with the speaker's eyes. The downside is that the captions may sometimes hide the speaker's face.

Between "speech bubble" and "viewport delayed" it is not yet clear which is preferable for 2-person conversations. When using "speech bubble" mode the user loses the ability to read what the speaker is saying while looking away from them; however, it also clears up the viewport by only showing text when the user is looking at the speaker. We hypothesize that in a multi-speaker environment dynamic captions would be more useful. With multiple people speaking, it is difficult to determine who is saying what without attaching the words to the speaker.

5. CONCLUSIONS AND FUTURE WORK

Based on our work on this project so far, we conclude that the optimal caption placement for head-worn augmented reality applications is likely to be different from what is optimal for stationary screens or for hand-held applications. We found "viewport locked" mode to be very unusable with the HWD, while other researchers found it sufficient for their applications ([1–3]).

Our next step will be to convene a focus group of D/HH individuals, as well as D/HH educators and other stakeholders to gather formative qualitative feedback on our work. This will eventually lead to experimental evaluation and comparison of the different caption placement strategies we have identified.

6. REFERENCES

[1] Hu, Y. et al. 2015. Speaker-Following Video Subtitles. *ACM Trans. Multimedia Comput. Commun. Appl.* 11, 2 (Jan. 2015), 32:1–32:17.

[2] Mirzaei, M. et al. 2012. Helping Deaf and hard-of-hearing people by combining augmented reality and speech technologies. *Proc. 9th Intl Conf. Disability, Virtual Reality & Associated Technologies* (2012), 149–158.

[3] Prietch, S.S. et al. 2014. A Speech-To-Text System's Acceptance Evaluation: Would Deaf Individuals Adopt This Technology in Their Lives? *Universal Access in Human-Computer Interaction. Design and Development Methods for Universal Access* (Jun. 2014), 440–449.

Checklist for the Accessible Media Player Evaluation

Lourdes Moreno
LaBDA Group, Computer Science Department, Universidad Carlos III de Madrid, Spain
lmoreno@inf.uc3m.es

María González-García
LaBDA Group, Computer Science Department, Universidad Carlos III de Madrid, Spain
mgonza1@inf.uc3m.es

Paloma Martínez
LaBDA Group, Computer Science Department, Universidad Carlos III de Madrid, Spain
pmf@inf.uc3m.es

Yolanda González
Accessibility Consultant
ILUNION Tecnología y Accesibilidad
ygonzalez@consultoria.ilunion.com

ABSTRACT
Nowadays, consumption of video content is extremely high and the corresponding technology must be accessible in order for people with disabilities to be able to access it. For this reason, the user agents or media players used to access video content must be accessible. This poster presents a checklist that includes indicators which can assist in the design and evaluation of accessible media players.

Categories and Subject Descriptors
H.5.2 [Information Interfaces and Presentation]: User Interfaces – interaction style, theory and methods, graphical user interface.

Keywords
Accessibility, media player, evaluation

1. INTRODUCTION
Consumption of multimedia content on the Internet is constantly increasing and video streaming is changing people's viewing habits. Furthermore, because of the high growth in the use of mobile devices such as tablets and smartphones, not only has Internet use been generalised everywhere, but also the creation of video content that is shared and watched on social networks such as YouTube, Vimeo or Facebook is also commonplace. There are more and more users watching TV programs or series from their computers instead of their televisions. Although it is still far from the rates of traditional TV, Video on-Demand (VoD) or video multicasts (real time streaming) are growing very quickly, especially among younger consumers. Some examples are the BBC iPlayer in the UK or the Over The Top (OTT) broadcasting services that companies as Netflix or Hulu offer. Also, multimedia is frequently used for education, both face-to-face education and distance e-learning (formal education or the fashionable Massive Open Online Courses -MOOCs-), and it is also used in work environments for training.

One of the biggest issues for people with disabilities is the access to the video content. People who are hearing impaired need the availability of caption, screen reader users need the availability of audio description, and people with mobility impairments, the biggest issue is keyboard navigation to actually play and control the video. The media player should allow the users to access to multimedia content, regardless of whether or not they have a disability.

ASSETS'17, Oct. 29–Nov. 1, 2017, Baltimore, MD, USA.
ACM ISBN 978-1-4503-4926-0/17/10.
DOI: http://dx.doi.org/10.1145/3132525.3134791

2. CHECKLIST FOR ACCESSIBLE MEDIA PLAYER
There are a very extensive regulatory framework and standards with regards to accessibility such as the Web Content Accessibility Guidelines 2.0 (WCAG 2.0), User Agent Accessibility Guidelines 2.0 (UAAG 2.0) and Media Accessibility User Requirements. Even though these standards and guidelines are complete and exhaustive and were developed for all types of agents and users, those developers and evaluators who focus solely on media players may find them not very user friendly. After carrying out preliminary works [1] [2] and an exhaustive study of the standards, this work has identified what indicators should be taken into account to validate the accessibility of a media player. It presents a checklist that includes checkpoints grouped by type. The checklist helps to avoid passing over any of the checkpoints, depending on the level of compliance with the standards' success criteria. Table 1 shows the checklist with the mapping of each checkpoint with the UAAG 2.0 and WCAG 2.0 success criteria (with level conformance AA).

The WCAG transversal requirements have been integrated. For example, according to one of the UAAG guidelines, they must be in compliance with the WCAG. However, this is not an easy task nor is it quickly evaluated. For this reason, the WCAG 2.0 criteria are defined on the checklist in different groups. Also of the accessibility requirements of the multimedia content, the accessibility requirements of the media players must comply with the aim of achieving a complete accessibility [1]. Providing an audio description may not be useful if users cannot access it via their keyboards. Likewise, low-contrast subtitles may not be helpful a hearing-impaired individual.

This checklist has been used as a method of evaluating players such as YouTube and Vimeo; it was conducted by three experts where the Kappa index obtained was a substantial agreement among reviewers. The purpose is to provide a method which fills a gap concerning the evaluation of web accessibility based on conformance with standards.

ACKNOWLEDGMENTS
This work is supported by the eGovernAbility-Access project (TIN2014-52665-C2-2-R).

REFERENCES
[1] Lourdes Moreno, Paloma Martínez and Belén Ruíz-Mezcua. 2008. Disability Standards for Multimedia on the Web. IEEE MultiMedia 15(4): 52-54

[2] María González-García, Lourdes Moreno, and Paloma Martínez. 2015. A Model-Based Tool to develop an Accessible Media Player. ASSETS '15. ACM, New York, NY, USA, 415-416.

Table 1. Checklist for the accessible media player

CODE	ACCESSIBILITY CHECKPOINT	DESCRIPTION	UAAG 2.0	WCAG 2.0
1	**CONTENT**			
1.1	Alternative audio content	Check if the media player offers alternative content to the audio content		1.2.2, 1.2.4
1.2	Alternative visual content	Check if the media player offers alternative content to the video content		1.2.3, 1.2.5
1.3	Alternative content synchronisation	Check if audio and video tracks remain synchronised across the required range of playback rates	2.10.4	
1.4	Different file extensions	Check if the media player allows different files extensions for the alternative content		
2	**CONTROLS**			
2.1	Keyboard access	Check if all functions can be operated via the keyboard using sequential or direct keyboard commands	2.1.1	2.1.1
2.2	No keyboard traps	Check if the user can move focus away from an interactive element or control using the keyboard alone	2.1.3	2.1.2
2.3	Stop, pause, play, progress bar	Check if the media player provides mechanisms to stop, pause and play the playback and to show the state of the content	2.10.5, 3.1.3	
2.4	Volume	Check if the user can adjust the volume of each audio track independently from other tracks, relative to the global volume level set through operating environment mechanisms	G: 1.5 (1.5.1)	1.4.2
2.5	Highlighted items	Check if the elements can be visually distinguished when they are selected, focused or enabled	1.3.1	
3	**INTERFACE**			
3.1	Resize	Check if the user can resize the viewport of the media player	1.8.8	
3.1	Customize display of controls	Check if the user can customize the display of the media player controls	G 2.7 (2.7.1), 2.3.5	
3.2	Contrast	Check if the contrast of the different colours that appear in the interface satisfy level AA requirements		1.4.3
3.3	Easy to use	Check if the media player is easy to use	Principle 2 and 3	Principle 2 and 3
4	**SETTINGS**			
4.1	Alternative content preferences (colour, font, size)	Check if the user can change the preferences of the alternative content (captions)	1.4.2	
4.2	Allow persistent accessibility settings	Check if the accessibility features established by a user persist between sessions	2.6.1	
4.3	Menu position configuration	Check if the position of the menu can be configured	2.7.1	
4.4	Shortcuts/Access key	Check if the user can navigate via shortcuts	G 2.3	
4.5	Change menu's controls	Check if the user can modify (add, delete, etc.) the controls of the menu according to his/her preferences	2.7.1	
5	**UTILITIES**			
5.1	Search alternative content	Check if the media player allows user to search text within alternative content (captions)	2.4.1	
5.2	Automatic transcription	Check if the media player can provide automatic transcription of alternative content		
6	**HELP**			
6.1	Accessible documentation	Check if the media player offers documentation about the player itself in a format that meets the success criteria of WCAG 2.0 level "A" or higher	3.2.1	
6.2	Describe accessibility features	Check if the media player describes its accessibility features	3.2.2	
7	**ACCESSIBILITY POLICY**			
7.1	Provide policy of accessibility	Check if the media player provides a policy of accessibility		

Evaluating Author and User Experience for an Audio-Haptic System for Annotation of Physical Models

James M. Coughlan and Joshua Miele
The Smith-Kettlewell Eye Research Institute, San Francisco, CA 94115 USA
{coughlan, jam}@ski.org

ABSTRACT
We describe three usability studies involving a prototype system for creation and haptic exploration of labeled locations on 3D objects. The system uses a computer, webcam, and fiducial markers to associate a physical 3D object in the camera's view with a pre-defined digital map of labeled locations ("hotspots"), and to do real-time finger tracking, allowing a blind or visually impaired user to explore the object and hear individual labels spoken as each hotspot is touched. This paper describes: (a) a formative study with blind users exploring pre-annotated objects to assess system usability and accuracy; (b) a focus group of blind participants who used the system and, through structured and unstructured discussion, provided feedback on its practicality, possible applications, and real-world potential; and (c) a formative study in which a sighted adult used the system to add labels to on-screen images of objects, demonstrating the practicality of remote annotation of 3D models. These studies and related literature suggest potential for future iterations of the system to benefit blind and visually impaired users in educational, professional, and recreational contexts.

CCS Concepts
• **Human-centered computing→Accessibility**

Keywords
Blindness; low vision; 3D models; tactile graphics.

1. INTRODUCTION
Many people who are blind or visually impaired have insufficient access to a wide range of everyday objects needed for daily activities that require visual inspection on the part of the user. Such objects include printed documents, maps, infographics, appliances and 3D models (e.g., 3D-printed) used in STEM education, and are abundant in schools, the home and the workplace.

A common way of enhancing an object's accessibility is to affix braille labels to its surface. However, there is limited space available for braille labelling and it is inaccessible to those who don't read braille. A powerful alternative is the use of audio labels, which enable audio-haptic exploration of the object, whereby the user explores the surface naturally with the fingers and queries locations of interest. Audio labels can be associated with specific locations on tactile models and graphics in a variety of ways, including by placing touch-sensitive sensors at locations of interest, overlaying a tactile graphic on a touch-sensitive tablet, or using a camera-enabled "smart pen" that works with special materials [4]. While effective, these methods for producing audio labels require each object to be customized with special hardware and materials, which is costly and greatly limits their adoption.

By contrast, computer vision-based approaches, in which a camera tracks the user's hands as they explore an object, have the advantage of offering audio-haptic accessibility for *existing* objects with minimal or no customization. Several projects have employed this computer vision approach over the years, including Access Lens [3] for facilitating OCR, the Tactile Graphics Helper [1] to provide access to tactile graphics to students in an educational context, and VizLens [2] for making appliances accessible.

Our "CamIO" (short for "Camera Input-Output") project applies this computer vision approach to provide audio-haptic access to arbitrary 3D objects, including 3D models, tactile graphics, relief maps and appliances. It builds on our earlier work [5], but now uses a conventional camera (like Magic Touch [6]) instead of relying on a depth camera, and includes a new tool to create annotations for any rigid 3D object (not just 3D printed ones).

We describe recent developments, including improvements to the end-user software and a new tool to facilitate the creation of annotations specifying the information available for an object. Three user studies were performed, including a formative study to suggest possible UI improvements, a focus group study to assess the ways that people who are blind would want to use CamIO and another formative study to verify the usability and effectiveness of the annotation tool. The results of the user studies are discussed and highlight directions for future development of CamIO.

2. APPROACH
CamIO was conceived by one of the co-authors (who is blind) and has been iteratively improved based on ongoing user feedback with a user-centered research and development approach. Blindness rehabilitation professionals stressed the inconvenience of the Microsoft Kinect depth camera platform, so we modified our approach to accommodate a standard camera.

The new CamIO system consists of two main components: (a) the Explorer system (Fig. 1a) for end users who are blind or visually impaired, and (b) the Creator annotation tool that allows a sighted assistant to define the *hotspots* (locations of interest on the object) and the text labels associated with them. Both components are implemented on a standard laptop using its built-in camera; a preliminary version of Explorer also runs on Android.

Explorer uses computer vision to track the location of the user's *pointer finger* (usually the index finger), and whenever the fingertip nears a hotspot, the text label associated with the hotspot is announced using text-to-speech. Note that the user can explore the object naturally with one or both hands, but receives audio feedback on the location indicated by the pointing finger. Computer vision processing is simplified using a special black-and-white "fiducial" pattern board (Fig. 1a), which makes it easy to estimate the object's 3D pose (rotation and translation relative to the camera), and a multi-color fingertip marker (Fig. 1b).

ACM ISBN 978-1-4503-4926-0/17/10.
https://doi.org/10.1145/3132525.3134811

Creator allows a sighted assistant to define digital annotations, which specify the hotspot locations and associated text labels for an object of interest. The assistant indicates hotspot locations by clicking on the appropriate location in two different images of the object taken from different vantage points and typing in the corresponding text labels. This process allows the annotations to be authored remotely, even without physical access to the object.

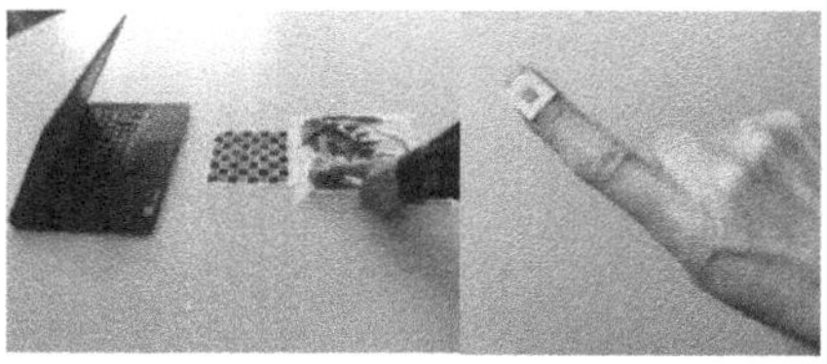

Figure 1. (a) CamIO system, showing laptop, object (relief map) and fiducial board. (b) Close-up of fingertip marker.

3. USER STUDIES

The first user study was a formative study we conducted with three completely blind volunteer participants (two male and one female, ages from 23-32). All three participants were able to use Explorer to independently read aloud the hotspots on a 3D-printed airplane model and a model of the Chrysler building, and expressed enthusiasm for the project. They suggested bug fixes and improvements, which were later implemented, including a new dwell gesture to trigger the announcement of additional hotspot information (when available).

Next, a focus group study was conducted to assess how blind adults are likely to use CamIO, which functions they want, and how they should be implemented. The study recruited five blind adults with ages ranging from 29-55 who had experience with braille reading, tactile graphics or haptic exploration and employment history as a blind adult. The participants were shown how to use Explorer, and used it for themselves to explore two objects: the 3D printed airplane and a Mackie 8-channel audio mixer.

Several dominant themes emerged from the study. (1) **Common use cases** include independent exploration of maps and models, access to appliances in the home or workplace, and educational applications including museum exhibits. (2) **New UI features**: better feedback was desired to help with proper positioning of the object relative to the camera, an audio signal indicating when the pointer finger exits a hotspot region, explicit feedback indicating when a secondary label is available, and the use of additional finger gestures. (3) **New authoring capabilities**: accessible authoring functions (including the ability to customize existing labels), the use of a stylus to define hotspot locations, and the use of crowdsourcing approaches to obtain annotations. (4) **Strengths**: the software-defined annotation approach that "[separates] accessibility from the original design of the object," a "natural" and "responsive" interface that permits "fluid exploration without interruption" and the presence of multiple layers of information. (5) **Weaknesses**: visibility problems (especially maintaining the visibility of the fingertip marker), the incidence of incorrect feedback, and the need for annotations for each object of interest.

A final formative study focusing on annotation was conducted with one volunteer participant, an adult female with normal vision. We trained her to use Creator and then had her annotate two objects by herself. For each object she was given a list of five hotspots to annotate, including the label name for each hotspot. (The Creator tool was pre-loaded with the two views of each object.) She took approximately 5-10 minutes to complete the annotations for each object, which we verified were correct. Note that she was able to complete the annotations independently without holding the objects or seeing them in person. She conveyed valuable feedback about Creator that we will address in the future, including her wish for a better understanding of how accurately she needed to click the mouse to specify the hotspot locations, and for a zoom feature to help her resolve fine spatial details.

4. CONCLUSIONS AND FUTURE WORK

We have described recent developments of the CamIO project, including improvements to Explorer, the new Creator tool, and user studies. The new CamIO approach has the advantage that it will be able to operate on any standard platform (both mobile and laptop) without the need for an external depth camera. The Creator tool allows a sighted person to perform remote annotation of an object without the need for physical access to it.

Overall, the user studies confirmed our belief that the CamIO project is likely to be of great interest to many people who are blind and that it has real-world potential. The studies suggest many avenues for future development, including UI improvements and new functionalities such as making authoring functions accessible.

Future work will include continuing to port the CamIO system to the smartphone/tablet platform. In particular, Creator will be ported to a browser platform, which will not only eliminate the inconvenience of downloading and installing the tool but also opens the possibility of crowdsourcing the annotation process, so that multiple people can contribute annotations for a single object.

We are also exploring possible applications of the CamIO approach for users who have low vision, who may prefer a visual interface that displays a close-up view of the current hotspot region (with the option of digitally rendering this view without the fingers obscuring it), instead of (or in addition to) an audio interface.

5. ACKNOWLEDGMENTS

This work was supported by NIH grants 5R01EY025332 and 2 R01 EY018890, and NIDILRR grant 90RE5024-01-00.

6. REFERENCES

[1] Fusco, G., & Morash, V. S. (2015). The tactile graphics helper: providing audio clarification for tactile graphics using machine vision. *Proc. 17th Int.'l ACM SIGACCESS Conf. on Computers & Accessibility* (pp. 97-106). ACM.

[2] Guo, A., Chen, X. A., Qi, H., White, S., Ghosh, S., Asakawa, C., & Bigham, J. P. (2016). VizLens: A Robust and Interactive Screen Reader for Interfaces in the Real World. *Proc. 29th Annual Symposium on UI Software & Tech.* ACM.

[3] Kane, S. K., Frey, B., & Wobbrock, J. O. (2013). Access lens: a gesture-based screen reader for real-world documents. *Proc. SIGCHI Conference on Human Factors in Computing Systems* (pp. 347-350). ACM.

[4] Miele, J. (2010). Talking Tactile Apps for the Pulse Pen: STEM Binder. *25th Annual Int.'l Tech. & Persons with Disabilities Conference (CSUN)*, March 2010.

[5] Shen, H., Edwards, O., Miele, J., & Coughlan, J. M. (2013). CamIO: A 3D computer vision system enabling audio/haptic interaction with physical objects by blind users. *Proc. 15th Int.'l ACM SIGACCESS Conf. on Computers and Accessibility* (p. 41). ACM.

[6] Shi, L., McLachlan, R., Zhao, Y., & Azenkot, S. (2016). Magic Touch: Interacting with 3D Printed Graphics. *Proc. 18th Int.'l ACM SIGACCESS Conf. on Computers and Accessibility* (pp. 329-330). ACM.

Exploring the Community of Blind or Visually Impaired People on YouTube

Woosuk Seo
University of Washington
Information School
Seattle, Washington 98195
seow@uw.edu

Hyunggu Jung
University of Washington
Department of Biomedical Informatics and Medical Education
Seattle, Washington 98195
hyunggu@uw.edu

ABSTRACT

We explore a community of blind or visually impaired (BVI) people through video blogs (vlogs) on YouTube. Many researchers have used vlogs as a means of identifying communities of video bloggers (vloggers). Nevertheless, little is still known about how BVI vloggers interact through vlogs in video-based social media. To fill the gap, we identified BVI vloggers and types of the vlogs they produced by analyzing videos on YouTube. Also, we found how BVI vloggers were connected with each other through vlogs. To our knowledge, this is the first attempt utilizing vlogs to understand the community of BVI people on YouTube.

Keywords

Blind; Visually Impaired; Vlogs; YouTube; Online Community; Accessibility

1. INTRODUCTION

The number of people sharing videos on social media (e.g., YouTube) is increasing. As of June 2017, it is reported that the total number of YouTube users is over 1,000,000,000 [8]. In addition, 44% of all internet users in the world watch a vlog each month [7]. As the demand of vlogs increases, it is important to understand benefits of vlogging. It is known that personal and contextual disclosure by a video medium build social support among vloggers with chronic illness and commenters on YouTube [2]. Vlogging also enables people to share knowledge with other people in the similar situations (e.g., medication treatment of cancer patients) [3].

Along with the growth of vlogs, researchers investigated the communities of vloggers with diverse background in video-based online communities. One study focused on the population of YouTube users with motor impairments [1]. This study revealed how they interacted with touchscreen devices by analyzing YouTube videos. Another study focused on the population of patients with Anorexia Nervosa [5]. This study showed how the patients expressed their symptoms and experiences to a public audience through vlogs by analyzing metadata, such as viewers' comments, text of script, number of views and subscribers on the vlogs produced by the patients. Nevertheless, to our knowledge, no prior studies investigated how BVI vloggers interact through vlogs. To fill the gap, we collected and analyzed vlogs produced by BVI vloggers on YouTube.

ASSETS '17 October 29-November 1, 2017, Baltimore, MD, USA

ACM ISBN 978-1-4503-4926-0/17/10.
DOI: https://doi.org/10.1145/3132525.3134801

2. METHOD

We gathered videos produced by BVI people on YouTube. To extract the videos, we queried them from YouTube using combinations of a conditional keyword ("visually impaired" or "blind") and a vlog keyword ("vlog", "vlogs", "vlogger", "vlogging" or "blog"). We focused on reviewing vlogs where BVI people talk to viewers in order to understand how BVI people share their thoughts and stories with others. The eligibility criteria for identifying videos were: 1) video must contain either "blind" or "visually impaired" in its title and/or description, 2) video features only one person. Instead, we excluded commercial, marketing, sponsored, or product review videos that focus more on advertising products or organizations, as well as game plays or animated videos that do not feature the vlogger. After eliminating duplicates, we identified a final set of vlogs produced by individual BVI vloggers.

Next, we watched the collected vlogs to identify the characteristics of each vlog and tagged them with codes based on the similarities between them using an open coding method [4]. We then used the codes to assign one of the following categories to each vlog: Tag, Q&A, How-To/Guide, Awareness, and Daily log. A Tag vlog is produced when a vlogger is mentioned by another vlogger to answer certain questionnaire and recommend other vloggers to produce similar videos. For instance, Visually Impaired People Tag vlogs consist of 10 questions (e.g., What is the best part about being blind or visually impaired?) that help BVI vloggers present their vision conditions and share their thoughts or stories about blindness with others. On the other hand, in Q&A vlogs, vloggers voluntarily answer a specific question or a set of questions from friends, family, comments, or other resources. How-To/Guide vlogs explain structured steps or processes that viewers can follow while Awareness vlogs provide information or advice about lifestyle, experiences, or community of BVI people. Daily logs are videos in which vloggers share their thoughts or stories about their daily life. Among the categorized vlogs, we watched Tag vlogs again

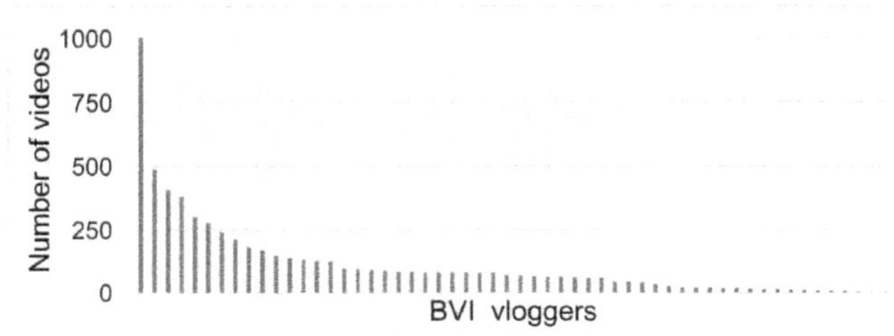

Figure 1: The distribution of the numbers of videos across 56 BVI vloggers.

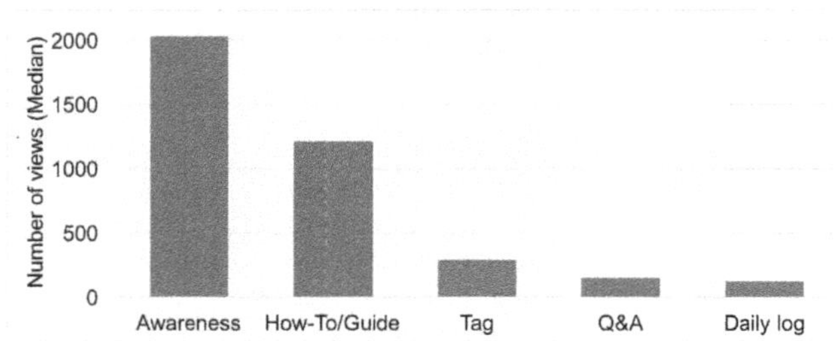

Figure 2: The popularity of the categorized vlogs is represented by the median of the numbers of views.

to identify BVI vloggers producing the vlogs. We traced the next tagged vloggers from the identified vloggers to investigate how they are connected each other through the vlogs.

3. FINDINGS

We found 56 individual BVI vloggers (37 females) after reviewing 115 filtered vlogs. The vloggers produced 6,178 videos in total (avg: 110.3, std: 160.4). This high standard deviation indicates that there is a large gap between those who produce many videos and those who do not (see Figure 1). Also, we identified five distinctive categories of vlogs produced by the vloggers that present the characteristics of the vlogs: 37 Daily logs, 35 Awareness, 20 How-To/Guide, 16 Tag vlogs, and 7 Q&A. In particular, the Awareness category was most popular to viewers, as the median of numbers of views for Awareness vlogs was the highest (see Figure 2). In addition, we identified how 29 BVI vloggers were connected with each other by Tag videos (see Figure 3). Each node represents an individual vlogger and is labelled with his/her initial. Each arrow indicates the direction of influence from one to the other by tagging. This connected network of vloggers shows that vlogging may facilitate social and peer supports between them.

4. CONCLUSION AND FUTURE WORK

The primary contribution of this study was to explore community of BVI people through vlogs on a video-based social media. In addition to common empirical investigation process, our study shows that the method analyzing the vlogs and vloggers could be alternative strategy to identify the needs of BVI people who use video-based social media, such as YouTube. Similar to having supports from public audience on other social media platforms [6], vlogs provide open communication channels for BVI people. This suggests potential opportunities for designing tools to facilitate communication among BVI people. As for the future work, we

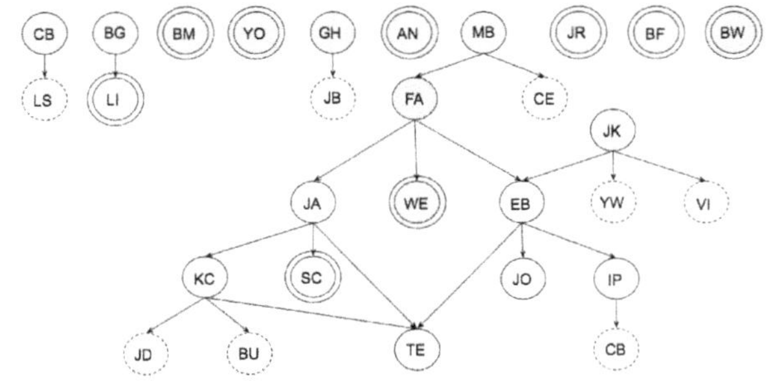

Figure 3: Yellow-colored nodes represent BVI vloggers who produced Tag vlogs we identified voluntarily, white-colored nodes the next tagged vloggers, concentric-circled nodes the vloggers who do not tag others, and dotted-line nodes the vloggers who were tagged by others but did not produce vlogs yet.

plan to conduct interviews with BVI vloggers on the connected network to identify their needs and barriers when interacting with other vloggers or viewers. In particular, the large variation of the numbers of videos produced by BVI people suggests the needs of conducting separated interviews for those who produced many videos and for those who did not based on the level of vlogging experience.

5. ACKNOWLEDGMENT

The authors would like to thank Dr. Richard E. Ladner for his support in reviewing the draft.

6. REFERENCES

[1] L. Anthony, Y. Kim, and L. Findlater. Analyzing user-generated youtube videos to understand touchscreen use by people with motor impairments. In *Proceedings of the SIGCHI Conference on Human Factors in Computing Systems*, CHI '13, pages 1223–1232, New York, NY, USA, 2013. ACM.

[2] J. Huh, L. S. Liu, T. Neogi, K. Inkpen, and W. Pratt. Health vlogs as social support for chronic illness management. *ACM Trans. Comput.-Hum. Interact.*, 21(4):23:1–23:31, Aug. 2014.

[3] L. S. Liu, J. Huh, T. Neogi, K. Inkpen, and W. Pratt. Health vlogger-viewer interaction in chronic illness management. In *Proceedings of the SIGCHI Conference on Human Factors in Computing Systems*, CHI '13, pages 49–58, New York, NY, USA, 2013. ACM.

[4] P. M. Quinn. Qualitative research and evaluation methods. *California EU: Sage Publications Inc*, 2002.

[5] E. Veer. Hiding in plain sight:'secret' anorexia nervosa communities on youtubetm. *NA-Advances in Consumer Research Volume 38*, 2011.

[6] S. Wu and L. A. Adamic. Visually impaired users on an online social network. In *Proceedings of the SIGCHI Conference on Human Factors in Computing Systems*, CHI '14, pages 3133–3142, New York, NY, USA, 2014. ACM.

[7] K. Young. *Over 4 in 10 watch vlogs*, 2016 (accessed June 30, 2017). http://blog.globalwebindex.net/chart-of-the-day/over-4-in-10-watch-vlogs/.

[8] YouTube. *YouTube for Press*, 2017 (accessed June 30, 2017). https://www.youtube.com/yt/about/press/.

Feasibility of Using Automatic Speech Recognition with Voices of Deaf and Hard-of-Hearing Individuals

Abraham Glasser, Kesavan Kushalnagar, and Raja Kushalnagar
Rochester Institute of Technology
Rochester, NY 14623
{atg2036, krk4565}@rit.edu, raja.kushalnagar@gallaudet.edu

ABSTRACT

Many personal devices have transitioned from visual-controlled interfaces to speech-controlled interfaces to reduce costs and interactive friction, supported by the rapid growth in capabilities of speech-controlled interfaces, e.g., Amazon Echo or Apple's Siri. A consequence is that people who are deaf or hard of hearing (DHH) may be unable to use these speech-controlled devices. We show that deaf speech has a high error rate compared to hearing speech, in commercial speech-controlled interfaces. Deaf speech had approximately a 78% word error rate (WER) compared to a hearing speech 18% WER. Our findings show that current speech-controlled interfaces are not usable by DHH people. Based on our findings, significant advances in speech recognition software or alternative approaches will be needed for deaf use of speech-controlled interfaces. We show that current speech-controlled interfaces are not usable by DHH people.

CCS Concepts

•Human-centered computing → Accessibility; Accessibility design and evaluation methods;

Keywords

Automatic Speech Recognition, Deaf Speech, Hearing Speech, Word Error Rate, Deaf, Hearing

1. RELATED WORK

Prior research has investigated how the lack of a feedback loop for deaf people who cannot hear their own speaking results in poor speech quality due vowel errors, intonation errors, and length errors [1, 2]. ASR software is generally trained with speech samples from hearing people, which results in very poor recognition of deaf speech. Even when used with limited possibilities, e.g., single digits, ASR for deaf speakers with poor speech intelligibility yielded a 13% Word Error Rate (WER) [3], compared to nearly no errors for hearing speech [4].

ASSETS '17 October 29-November 1, 2017, Baltimore, MD, USA

ACM ISBN 978-1-4503-4926-0/17/10.
DOI: https://doi.org/10.1145/3132525.3134819

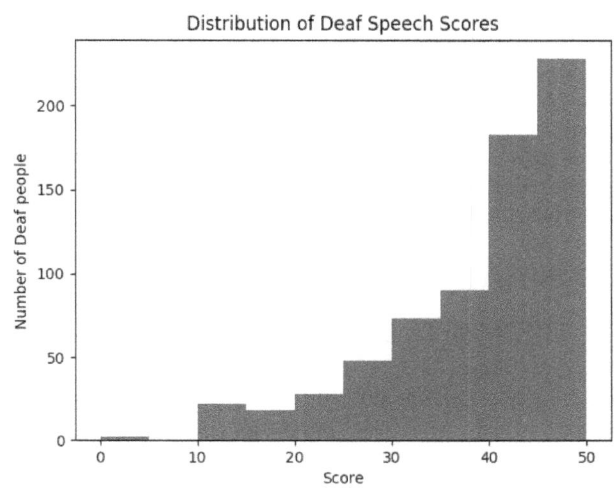

Figure 1: Distribution of Clarke Sentence Scores.

2. METHODOLOGY

2.1 Deaf Speech Dataset

We sampled from a subset of a large speech dataset of 650 deaf and hard of hearing (DHH) individuals at the National Technical Institute for the Deaf at Rochester Institute of Technology, which has an enrollment of around 1100 deaf and hard of hearing students. The dataset consisted of samples taken from DHH individuals who took the Clarke Sentences intelligibility test [5]. The test has 60 sentence lists, each with 10 sentences of 10 syllables. The number of words varies across the sentences and lists. Each audio file has one speaker speaking one list from the Clarke sentence list. In each audio file, the speaker says the sentence number and then proceeds to say that sentence, and repeats until all the ten sentences are spoken. The audio files were recorded by one individual, then the samples were sent to a speech pathologist. The speech pathologist assigned an intelligibility score from 0 to 50. The score is computed by looking for 50 target words within the sample for credit. A score of 50 would indicate that the deaf person is generally intelligible to the speech pathologist, while a score of 30 means difficult to understand, and a score of 0 means completely unintelligible. About half of all deaf individuals had scores of under 40, which is usually unintelligible to people not used to deaf speech, as shown in Figure 1.

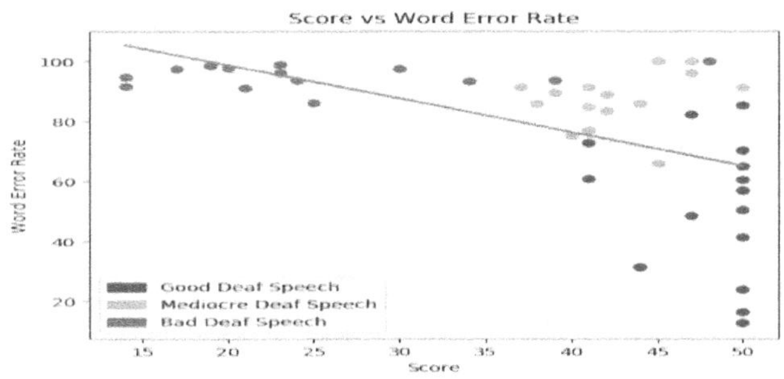

Figure 2: Intelligibility rating vs Word Error Rate

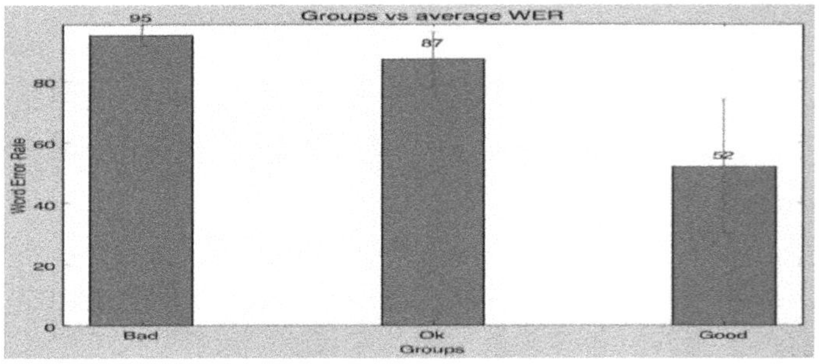

Figure 3: Group vs average WER

2.2 ASR and WER Analysis

We used the Microsoft Translator Speech API to create transcriptions for each audio file. This API is used by businesses for transcriptions. As a commercial level software, it matches other similar transcription software [6, 7, 8]. We also used the National Institute of Standards and Technology Speech Recognition Scoring Toolkit (SCTK) Version 2.4.0.4 for the Word Error Rate calculations [9].

3. ANALYSIS RESULTS

3.1 WER for Hearing Speakers

We calculated the ASR transcription and WER analysis results for five hearing subjects who read various lists from the same Clarke Sentences database, The speech samples were recorded with a cell phone in a noisy environment with background noise in a lab with many people speaking and computers, which is similar to common use-case scenarios in using phone ASR services. The average WER was 18%. While the speech recognition was not close to perfect for hearing people, it was still passable. These numbers are expected from the current state of the art technology. The majority of voice command interfaces are currently found in cell phones and home assistants, which are often used in noisy environments. If we had repeated these recordings in the same setting as the deaf speech samples, we would expect an even lower WER.

3.2 WER for Deaf Speakers

We ran a sample of the deaf speech database through the Microsoft Translator Speech API. We used 45 total samples that were chosen by a naive listener who determined 15 good samples (40+), 16 mediocre samples (30-40), and 14 poor files (10-30). The error rates were extremely high over all samples at 77%, including 53% WER for the good samples.

The average WER and standard deviation was calculated for each group, as shown in Figure 3.2. The average WER for the good speech group was significantly less than either the mediocre group or bad speech groups; a t-test comparison between the good and mediocre groups yielded $p < 0.01$.

4. CONCLUSIONS

The current WER of Microsoft Translator was too high for comfortable use. They were significantly poorer in performance compared to hearing people under similar conditions. There are a number of factors that have an impact on the accuracy of automatic speech recognition systems with deaf speech. The results also show much greater variance among deaf speakers, compared with hearing speakers. In order for ASR systems to recognize deaf speech as well as it does hearing speech requires a huge database of deaf speakers. While conceptually simple, it is still challenging. The deaf population is relatively small compared to the size of the hearing population, and have far more varied backgrounds.

ASR systems are trained using huge hearing speaker datasets. The results show that even deaf speakers with "good" speech have worse accuracy compared with the average hearing speaker. Although the Clarke Sentence test is useful for speech pathology evaluation, it is less useful for providing more feedback to DHH people about the usability of current ASR interfaces, since the top rating of 50 does not distinguish between DHH speakers with high ASR accuracy and those with less ASR accuracy. It would be helpful to develop an automated test that provides feedback to DHH people on their use of ASR services such as Siri or Alexa.

5. REFERENCES

[1] M. S. Thirumalai and S. G. Gayathri. *Speech of the hearing impaired.* Central Institute of Indian Languages, 2004.

[2] Mary J. Osberger and Nancy S. McGarr. Speech production characteristics of the hearing impaired. *Journal of Speech, Language and Hearing Research*, 8:221–283, 1982.

[3] C Jeyalakshmi, V Krishnamurthi, and A Revathy. Deaf speech assessment using digital processing techniques. *Signal & Image Processing: An International Journal (SIPIJ)*, 1(1):14–25, 2010.

[4] George R Doddington. Phonetically sensitive discriminants for improved speech recognition. In *Acoustics, Speech, and Signal Processing, 1989. ICASSP-89., 1989 International Conference on*, pages 556–559. IEEE, 1989.

[5] Vincent J. Samar and Dale Evan Metz. Criterion validity of speech intelligibility rating-scale procedures for the hearing-impaired population. *Journal of Speech, Language, and Hearing Research*, 31(3):307–316, 1988.

[6] Richard Eckel. Microsoft researchers achieve speech recognition milestone, Sep 2016.

[7] Google's speech recognition technology now has a 4.9% word error rate, May 2017.

[8] George Saon. Reaching new records in speech recognition, Mar 2017.

[9] National institute of standards and technology, June 2017.

FingerVoice: A Syllable Based Input System via Fingers Touching

Wenjie Chen[1], Yangyang Ma[1], Zhilei Chai[2, 3], Mingsong Chen[1]

[1]MoE Engineering Research Center for Software/Hardware Co-Design East China Normal University Shanghai, China wjchen@sei.ecnu.edu.cn

[2]State Key Laboratory of Mathematical Engineering and Advanced Computing Wuxi, China

[3]School of IoT Engineering Jiangnan University Wuxi, China

ABSTRACT

This paper proposes a novel input system via fingers touching, called *FingerVoice*. Instead of traditional letter based input system, it is based on syllables. Fingers on the left hand stand for consonants while fingers on the right hand for vowels. Fingers from both hands touch each other to form a syllable. We use a pair of gloves with conductive finger caps to detect the touch. As an example, the implementation of Chinese is presented in details. By connecting it to a smart phone via Bluetooth, a utility speaking system is implemented to help the speech-impaired to "speak" via smart phone. Our experimental result shows that this syllable based input device is faster than letter based input devices.

1. INTRODUCTION

Speech is a natural communication form among humans. Unfortunately, there are 1.5 percent of the world's population suffered from varied forms of speech impairments [1]. Voice can be played with any smart system, but how to input their thought is still a problem. In fact, input module plays an important role in any information system. The typical input device for traditional computer, such as a keyboard is inconvenient to be carried on the person, and it is difficult for the visually-impaired. Some glove-based input devices have been invented for compactness and flexibility [2-5]. Typically, buttons are used to detect finger touches against each other or against a desktop. A combination of chording finger touches represents for a letter. Text is typed letter by letter and the input speed is limited by the recognition of the simultaneous touches. Sidney proposed a neural network approach with complicated gloves to control speech synthesizer [6].

Instead of letter by letter, in this poster, we propose a system to input syllable by syllable, which is named as *FingerVoice*. Our major contributions are as follows. 1) We propose the novel idea of syllable based input method, which is more natural and faster than any letter based input method. The syllable is input by fingers touch. 2) We implement this idea by a pair of smart gloves, and we design the fingers expression codes for both the consonants and vowels of Chinese as an example. 3) We develop an Android App on smart phone to "speak" the syllable received from the gloves via Bluetooth .

ASSETS '17, October 29-November 1, 2017, Baltimore, MD, USA

ACM ISBN 978-1-4503-4926-0/17/10.
https://doi.org/10.1145/3132525.3134806

2. SYSTEM OVERVIEW

2.1 Syllables and fingers touching

In most languages, a word consists of one or more syllables, and a syllable consists of consonant and vowel phonemes. In our system, we use fingers touching to express syllables instead of letters. The left fingers express the consonant part, while the right express the vowel. For example, the touched thumb and index finger of left hand means a constant phoneme 'd', and the right thumb denotes 'a' . Then, when these three fingers touched together, a syllable 'da' is spelled. In order to operate freely in the air, we prefer touch among fingers only to touch between fingertips and desktop.

2.2 System prototype

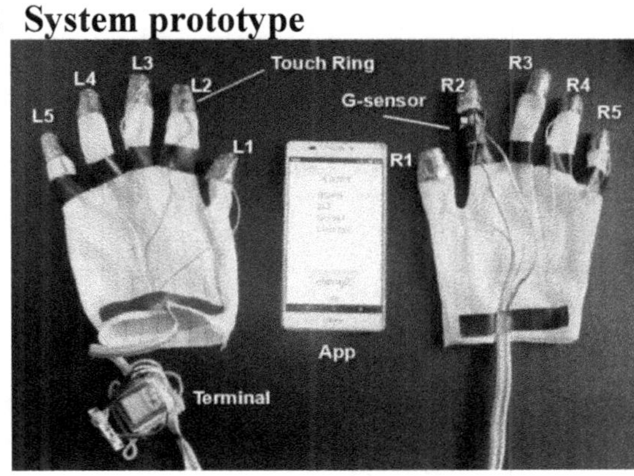

Figure 1. System prototype

The system is implemented as a pair of gloves as shown on Figure 1. Each finger (*labeled as L1... L5, R1... R5*) wears a conductive cap to probe whether it touches with others. The caps on both hands connect to a terminal on the left wrist. The terminal detects fingers touching state and sends it via wireless channel to the remote smart phone, where an App will interpret the syllable and pronounce it. In Chinese, a syllable may have 5 tones. To express them, we set a g-sensor on the right index finger. When the two hands touched, its posture will determine the tone of this syllable.

2.3 System work flow

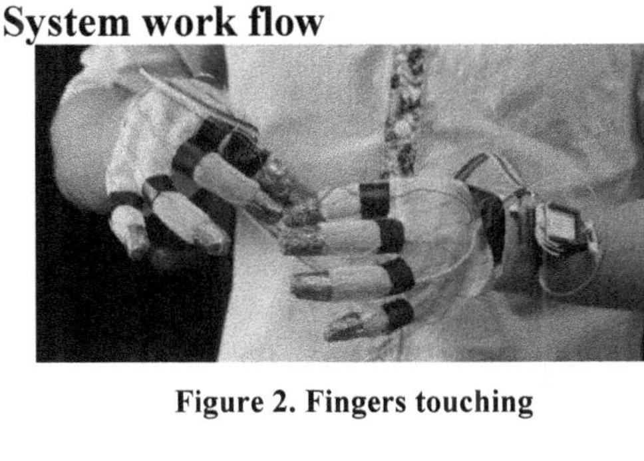

Figure 2. Fingers touching

i) As shown in Fig.2, the user touches several fingers on both hands and keep a finger gesture for tone information. ***ii)*** The terminal detects the fingers touching state and g-sensor state, and encodes them to a syllable code, such as "`L12+R123, \`", which means the left fingers L1, L2, and right fingers R1, R2 and R3 are touched together, and the fourth tone is used. The syllable code is sent to the remote smart phone. ***iii)*** In the smart phone, the language configuration have been already configured. Here we use Chinese. Then we get syllable index from the syllable code, "`diàn`". ***iv)*** Then, with the syllable index, we can pick up the sound of the syllable from the syllable voice library, and play it.

3. ENCODING FOR CHINESE

3.1 Consonants and vowels in Chinese

Table 1. Codes for consonants (left fingers combinations)

No.	consonant	fingers	bit code	No.	consonant	fingers	bit code
1	b	1	00001	13	q	34	01100
2	p	2	00010	14	x	45	11000
3	m	3	00100	15	zh	1245	11011
4	f	4	01000	16	ch	1345	11101
5	d	12	00011	17	sh	2345	11110
6	t	13	00101	18	r	5	10000
7	n	14	01001	19	z	1234	01111
8	l	15	10001	20	c	134	01101
9	g	123	00111	21	s	234	01110
10	k	124	01011	22	y	145	11001
11	h	125	10011	23	w	135	10101
12	j	23	00110	24	**(zero)**	12345	11111

Table 2. Codes for vowels (Right fingers combinations)

No.	vowel	fin-gers	same as	bit code	No.	vowel	fin-gers	same as	bit code
1	a	1		00001	19	un	234	ün	01110
2	o	2	uo	00010	20	ün	234	un	01110
3	e	3		00100	21	ang	2345		11110
4	i	4	er	01000	22	eng	1245		11011
5	u	5		10000	23	ing	1235		10111
6	ü	45	ui	11000	24	ong	1345	iong	11101
7	ai	14		01001	25	ia	145	ua	11001
8	ei	34		01100	26	iao	124		01011
9	ui	45	v	11000	27	ian	123		00111
10	ao	12		00011	28	iang	1234	uang	01111
11	ou	25		10010	29	iong	1345	ong	11101
12	iu	245		11010	30	ua	145	ia	11001
13	ie	134		01101	31	uai	345	üe	11100
14	üe	345		11100	32	uan	135	üan	10101
15	er	4	i	01000	33	üan	135	uan	10101
16	an	15		10001	34	uang	1234	iang	01111
17	en	35		10100	35	uo	2	o	00010
18	in	125		10011	36	**(zero)**	12345		11111

In Chinese, a character pronunciation is composed of an initial consonant part and a vowel part. There is no final consonant.

We use fingers of the left hand to express the **consonants**. There are 32 possibilities for 5 fingers. It is enough for the 23 initial consonants in Chinese. In addition, because some characters only have the vowel part, we set a "zero initial consonant". All the initial consonants and their respective codes are listed in Table 1. To make it easy to remember, the table is sorted complying with the China standard and grouped by the pronunciation regulation.

Right fingers are used to express the **vowels**. Chinese has 35 vowels, which is beyond what 5 fingers can express. Fortunately, not all combinations between the consonants and the vowels are valid. Therefore, some vowels may share the same code and it can still be distinguished by the initial consonants. Table 2 lists the vowels and their finger combinations. In addition, we also add a "zero" vowel to express the consonants themselves. Moreover, we define some special functions for "zero consonant" combining with "zero vowel", such as to cancel the last misspelled syllable.

3.2 Tones

The 5 tones are designed as Fig. 3, which could be probed by g-sensor on the index finger. The position of other fingers are not concerned, so they can move to any comfortable position.

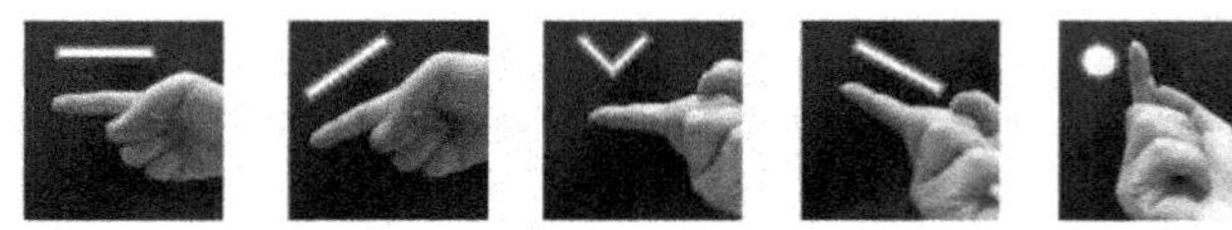

Figure 3. Fingers angles for tones of Chinese

4. CONCLUSION

We proposed a syllable based input device by fingers touching. It can be used to "speak" voice on a smart phone, or to type text on PC or consumer electronics. Our experiment shows that the input speed can reach 92.3 words/minute after 1 hour training. The finger code for Chinese has been illustrated. What's more, other languages can also be supported.

5. ACKNOWLEDGMENTS

This work is supported by China 863 Program (2015AA015304), Shanghai NSF (15ZR1410000) and MoE Industry/University Co-Education Program (Google, 201701003026).

6. REFERENCES

[1] Talkitt. http://nocamels.com/2014/08/amazing-app-talkitt-allows-people-with-speech-impairments-to-speak-clearly/

[2] Murao, Kazuya. "Wearable text input interface using touch typing skills." in Augmented Human International Conference, 2015, pp. 207-208.

[3] R. Wada, T. Nonaka and T. Hase, "Glove input interface with switches on fingertips," in 15th International Symposium on Consumer Electronics (ISCE), IEEE, Singapore, 2011, pp. 95-97.

[4] B. Bajer, I. S. MacKenzie and M. Baljko, "Huffman Base-4 Text Entry Glove (H4 TEG)," in 16th International Symposium on Wearable Computers (ISWC), Newcastle, 2012, pp. 41-47.

[5] keyglove. www.keyglove.net

[6] glovetalk. www.cs.toronto.edu/~fritz/absps/glovetalkii.htm

Goby: A Wearable Swimming Aid for Blind Athletes

Annika Muehlbradt, Varsha Koushik, and Shaun K. Kane
Department of Computer Science
University of Colorado Boulder
Boulder, CO 80309 USA
{annika.muehlbradt, varsha.koushik, shaun.kane}@colorado.edu

ABSTRACT

We introduce Goby, a swimming aid that provides audio feedback for blind and visually impaired athletes. Goby's activity tracker is worn on the thigh and uses a downward-facing camera to track the swimmer's position in the pool. Goby detects when the user is swimming outside the lane or approaching a wall, and warns the user via an audio notification. In this paper, we introduce the Goby prototype and share formative feedback about the prototype from blind and sighted swimmers.

Keywords

Accessibility; blindness; wearable computing; fitness

1. INTRODUCTION

Swimming is a whole-body, aerobic exercise with low impact on the body. Most people, regardless of their age or physical fitness, can include swimming as part of their exercise plan. However, swimming in a shared pool can be challenging for blind and visually impaired people, as it can be difficult to track one's position in the pool. Without the ability to accurately track their location, an untrained swimmer may veer outside their lane, bump into the pool wall, or even collide with another swimmer.

Currently, some blind swimmers address this challenge by swimming with a specially trained aide known as a "tapper," who can warn the swimmer about nearby swimmers or other obstacles [2]. The tapper observes the swimmer from outside the pool, and taps the swimmer with a long foam pole when it is time to change direction. While a human tapper may enable someone to swim effectively, the need for any sighted aide can place an undue burden on the athlete, who must recruit and coordinate with that aide whenever they wish to exercise [4].

In this work, we explore how a wearable device can be used to track a swimmer's location in the pool and provide feedback about the swimmer's position relative to the swim lane or other obstacles. We introduce Goby, a wearable device that tracks a swimmer using computer vision and provides feedback via audio cues. Goby's design is based on iterative prototyping with trained swimmers, and is intended to balance accurate tracking with comfortable use. In this paper, we document Goby's development, describe the current prototype, and present feedback from a preliminary evaluation of the prototype. Based on our preliminary research, we believe that a wearable swim tracker may be used to support blind and visually impaired athletes while swimming independently.

ASSETS'17, Oct. 29–Nov. 1, 2017, Batlimore, MD, USA.
ACM ISBN 978-1-4503-4926-0/17/10.
DOI: http://dx.doi.org/10.1145/ 3132525.3134822

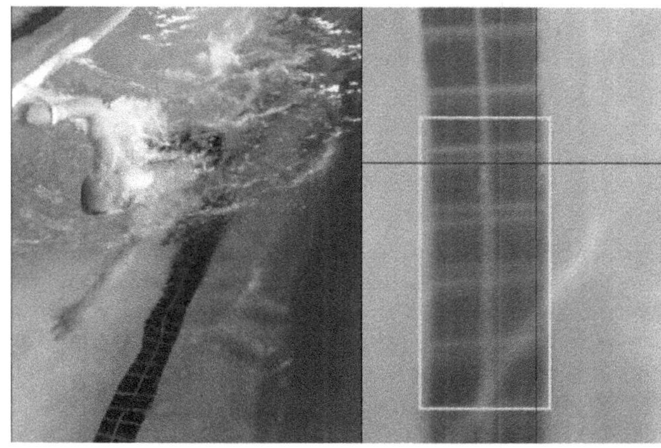

Figure 1: Goby is a wearable device that provides audio feedback for swimmers. Left: A swimmer wears the Goby prototype in the pool. Right: Goby's wearable camera identifies and tracks a lane marker at the bottom of the pool.

2. RELATED WORK

Assistive technologies can support blind and visually impaired athletes by providing information about their position or form. For example, Folmer [1] introduced an aerial-robot-based guide for runners, in which the runner could track the sound of the robot's rotors to follow a designated running path. Eyes-Free Yoga [3] used a depth-sensing camera to track a user's form, and provided audio prompts to correct the user's posture. As illustrated by these examples, a common challenge in providing access to fitness activities is balancing tracking accuracy with the obtrusiveness of the technology. For example, the eyes-free yoga system requires a depth-sensing camera, which limits its portability and prevents outdoor use. In this work, we explore the use of wearable activity trackers, which may be used in a wide variety of situations.

Relatively little research has addressed the accessibility of swimming for blind and visually impaired people. One prior attempt to support accessible swimming was Aqualert II, a device that was placed on a cable above a pool and projected a continuous spray of water down onto the swim lane [5]. While blind swimmers found Aqualert useful, it required significant effort to install. In contrast, our work leverages a wearable form factor to provide swimmers with feedback even in uninstrumented pools.

3. ITERATIVE DESIGN PROCESS

While developing our wearable swimming aid, we explored a variety of sensing methods and form factors. To sense the swimmer's position, we tested cameras, accelerometers, and ultrasonic sensors. Each sensing approach offered some trade-offs in comparison to other approaches. For example, we found that ultrasonic sensors were accurate even in turbulent water, but were less accurate than optical sensors at short ranges.

We also tested several different form factors and body locations, each of which also offered trade-offs. For example, a wrist-worn device may be more comfortable than a device worn on the thigh, but may be less accurate in tracking the user's position while swimming. Our current prototype, described here, attempts to balance tracking accuracy and comfort. We also discuss opportunities for improving this system in the future.

4. GOBY

Goby is a wearable swim tracker that is worn on the swimmer's thigh (Figure 1). Goby tracks the swimmer's position using computer vision, and provides audio feedback via a set of waterproof Bluetooth earphones.

The current Goby prototype is based on a Raspberry Pi 2 board, paired with a 1080p USB webcam and a 6000-mAh rechargeable battery pack. The components of the prototype are bound together using elastic bands, and the assembly is sealed in a waterproof plastic bag. In total, the prototype cost about $100 USD.

Goby is worn on the swimmer's thigh, and is attached to the body via a Velcro strap. During our preliminary testing, we found that placing Goby on the thigh provided the camera with a consistent view of the bottom of the pool while minimizing discomfort. The Goby prototype can easily be adapted to fit swimmers of different ages and sizes. The battery pack enables Goby to be used for several hours between charges.

A major goal of this project is to track a swimmer's location using a wearable device alone, without requiring the pool itself to be instrumented. Goby uses computer vision to track the lane markers painted on the bottom of the pool. Goby's software is implemented as a custom Python application and uses the OpenCV library. Goby tracks the lane marker at a rate of 30 frames per second. For each frame, Goby identifies the major contours in the frame, which should correspond to the lane marker at the bottom of the pool. By comparing the orientation of the lane marker to the swimmer's position, Goby can identify whether the swimmer is following a straight path or deviating from that path (Figure 1). Goby also identifies the wider T-shape that is present at the end of the lane marker, and can thus determine when the swimmer has reached the end of the lane. While this system has only been tested in a small number of pools, we are optimistic that this approach can be used across a variety of pool sizes and marker designs.

Goby notifies the user of their position via the paired Bluetooth earphones. Goby speaks the messages "swim left" and "swim right" if the swimmer veers off track, and says "wall" as the swimmer reaches the end of the lane. These messages are repeated every three seconds until the swimmer adjusts their trajectory. If the swimmer is on the correct path, Goby speaks the message "on track" every ten seconds.

5. PRELIMINARY DESIGN FEEDBACK

To gain feedback about Goby's premise, form factor, and feedback methods, we presented Goby at a design expo at our university. Because we could not easily demonstrate Goby in an actual swimming pool, we created an artificial pool marker on the floor using colored tape. Guests at the design expo were able to test the prototype by attaching the sensor to their leg, donning the headphones, and walking across the marker. We also showed a video of the Goby prototype being worn in a swimming pool. We asked each participant to provide feedback about their experience.

During this event, approximately thirty individuals tested the Goby prototype, including two blind individuals and one individual with low vision. Overall, our informants were enthusiastic about the prototype, and wished to try it out in an actual pool. Informants offered several suggestions for improving Goby's feedback: some found the repeated speech instructions to be distracting, and suggested replacing the speech feedback with non-speech tones. Others suggested changing the intensity of the sounds to indicate how far off-course the swimmer had drifted or how close they were to the wall.

6. LIMITATIONS AND FUTURE WORK

While our research team has tested Goby in several underwater settings, including a public pool, we have not yet tested the prototype with blind swimmers. Evaluating Goby with blind swimmers will provide us with valuable insights about the hardware form factor, tracking methods, and feedback modes.

A major limitation of the current prototype is that its tracking method relies upon the presence of easily legible lane markers. Thus, Goby currently cannot be used in open water, in situations in which the lane markers are not visible (e.g., in dim lighting or cloudy water), or with lane markers that look significantly different than the markers we have tested with. These issues may be addressed by improving Goby's visual sensing capabilities, such as by adding a light source to the camera, or by combining Goby's visual tracking with other sensing methods, such as an ultrasonic sensor. Alternately, users could carry a set of temporary markers that could be used in unmarked pools or even in open water.

A second limitation is that Goby must be worn on the thigh, which some swimmers might find uncomfortable, and which may be incompatible with some swimming styles, such as the backstroke. In the future, Goby could be extended to support different swimming styles and body placements.

Finally, we have identified several opportunities for improving Goby's tracking capabilities and feedback modes. In addition to identifying obstacles, future versions of Goby could also track a swimmer's speed, distance traveled, or calories burned. Goby could also be extended to provide haptic feedback, which might be preferable for some users, such as deaf-blind swimmers or those who listen to music while swimming.

7. ACKNOWLEDGMENTS

We thank Derek Reimer, Bill Casson, and Floyd Mueller for their helpful feedback. We also thank the Fort Collins Club for the use of their pool facilities.

8. REFERENCES

[1] Folmer, E. (2015). Exploring the use of an aerial robot to guide blind runners. *ACM SIGACCESS Accessibility and Computing*, (112), 3–7.

[2] Paciorek, M. J., and Jones, J. A. (1989). Sports and Recreation for the Disabled: A Resource Manual. Benchmark Press, Inc.

[3] Rector, K., Bennett, C. L., and Kientz, J. A. (2013). Eyes-free yoga: an exergame using depth cameras for blind & low vision exercise. In *Proceedings of ASSETS '13*, article 12, 8 pages.

[4] Rector, K., Milne, L., Ladner, R. E., Friedman, B., and Kientz, J. A. (2015). Exploring the opportunities and challenges with exercise technologies for people who are blind or low-vision. In *Proceedings of ASSETS '15*, 203–214.

[5] Scheib, K. M., and Ponchillia, P. E. (1999). The Aqualert II: An end-of-lane signaling device for swimmers who are visually impaired. *RE: view*, *31*(1), p. 32.

HOMER: An Interactive System for Home Based Stroke Rehabilitation

Aisling Kelliher, Jinwoo Choi, Jia-Bin Huang, Thanassis Rikakis
Virginia Tech
Blacksburg, Virginia, USA
{aislingk, jinchoi, jbhuang, rikakis}@vt.edu

Kris Kitani
Carnegie Mellon University
5000 Forbes Avenue
Pittsburgh, Pennsylvania, USA
kkitani@cs.cmu.edu

ABSTRACT
Delivering long term, unsupervised stroke rehabilitation in the home is a complex challenge that requires robust, low cost, scalable, and engaging solutions. We present HOMER, an interactive system that uses novel therapy artifacts, a computer vision approach, and a tablet interface to provide users with a flexible solution suitable for home based rehabilitation. HOMER builds on our prior work developing systems for lightly supervised rehabilitation use in the clinic, by identifying key features for functional movement analysis, adopting a simplified classification assessment approach, and supporting transferability of therapy outcomes to daily living experiences through the design of novel rehabilitation artifacts. A small pilot study with unimpaired subjects indicates the potential of the system in effectively assessing movement and establishing a creative environment for training.

CCS Concepts
Information interfaces and presentation (e.g., HCI)

Keywords
Stroke rehabilitation, interactive neurorehabilitation, home based care, assistive technology, health, aging

1. INTRODUCTION
Stroke is the leading cause of disability in the United States and the most common neurological disorder worldwide. Although large-scale studies point to the effectiveness of long-term therapy in facilitating recovery, the cost, availability of facilities and experts, and issues with reliable transportation, limits the amount of supervised therapy that stroke survivors can receive in the clinic [5]. In response, home-based unsupervised therapy has emerged as a possible viable alternative, which can be effective in conjunction with therapy in the clinic or even as the primary mode of therapy [1]. Pervasive health technologies present rich opportunities for leading and supporting efforts here, although considerable personal and technical challenges remain, including patient non-compliance and adherence, reproducing a supervised therapist experience without the therapist present, and technology or design related issues including system size, system complexity and robustness, and home privacy intrusion. Building on our prior interdisciplinary work in creating large-scale rehabilitation systems for hospitals and clinics [2], we present our approach in developing an interactive system for unsupervised upper extremity stroke rehabilitation in the home. The HOMER system is designed to occupy a small footprint in the home, capture and analyze the most significant movement features, and motivate use through a set of therapy objects that promote problem solving capabilities.

ASSETS '17, October 29–November 1, 2017, Baltimore, MD, USA

ACM ISBN 978-1-4503-4926-0/17/10.
https://doi.org/10.1145/3132525.3134807

2. RELATED WORK
Home based interactive rehabilitation therapy can be defined as computer-assisted therapy with limited engagement of the therapist (either through remote supervision or a limited number of visits to the home). Recent developments using low-cost interactive technologies such as tablet computers and the Kinect increase the possibility of long-term, affordable home managed care through tangible, augmented, virtual, and mixed reality applications [2, 3, 4]. In tandem with these technical developments, therapeutic approaches to stroke rehabilitation have also evolved considerably in the last decade, with an emerging focus on patient use of goal-driven, active problem solving strategies, and therapist experimentation with activities of everyday relevance [5]. Integrating these advancements, our goal is to produce a robust and affordable interactive system oriented towards creative problem-solving through the use of "enriched" therapy objects that align carefully with activities of everyday living [6].

3. HOMER SYSTEM
Our interactive rehabilitation system for the home consists of an inscribed mat (see Fig 1a), six custom designed therapy artifacts and their container (see Fig 1b and 1c), a table mounted Kinect camera, a mini-computer module clamped underneath and a tablet device with a custom web application (see Fig 1a). The system is designed to fit on typical tabletop surfaces found in the home, such as a kitchen, dining room, or computer/office table. The mat (laid out on a table) acts as a stage on which the user performs each rehabilitation activity using the objects individually or in combination. The Kinect is integrated into a modifiable table–mounted stand which allows for maximal visibility of the upper body of the user. The tablet device hosts the interactive web application presenting the training protocol, including the activity instructions.

The set of objects in our system are designed to support cross-mapping and generalizable activity strategies through their open-ended affordances, combinatorial possibilities, and perceived correlation with diverse artifacts of daily living (e.g. drinking from a glass, turning a key, unscrewing a jar etc.). The current system set consists of three base objects (tapered can, hourglass, covered tripod), and three tops (teardrop, checker, round ball) that can be used individually or variously combined by stacking, or in the case of the can and teardrop top, screwing together. The objects can be grasped and manipulated in a wide variety of ways

Figure 1. a) The HOMER system including mat, objects, tablet and Kinect; b) set of 6 objects; c) combining two objects

corresponding to the primary identified hand grasps, (see Fig 1c) thus lending themselves to rich cross-mapping opportunities.

We use the Kinect 2 camera to passively measure hand movements and train grasp classifiers for the three primary hand grasps (medium wrap, power sphere and precision pinch). We also use the Kinect 2 SDK body tracking algorithm to track the positions of both shoulders as a proxy for torso movement. This combined approach provides coverage for the key movement features as defined by our prior work [2], namely: 1) end effector activity over time and space (reach time, trajectory, velocity profile); 2) hand shape (grasp analysis); 3) torso compensation; and 4) object behavior. Our movement assessment module aims to judge the quality of the activity by identifying six key types of performance errors typically observed by the therapists on our team during therapy including low speed; indirect movement path; dropped object; misplaced object; incomplete task; and torso compensation.

4. PILOT STUDY

We tested the feasibility of the current version of the system through a small pilot study with 15 healthy subjects engaged in completing tasks developed by the team therapists, using unimpaired and simulated impaired movements. Our goal with this study was to safely identify and eradicate any system errors that could potentially confuse, frustrate, or possibly injure vulnerable users in a forthcoming clinical trial.

Participants were instructed to use the web application on the tablet device to access and move through the activity protocol by themselves, and at their own pace. Participants were instructed to complete 12 distinct reach/grasp/transport activities using the set of 6 objects, with each activity repeated 4 times. For the first two repetitions for each activity, the participants were instructed to complete the activity as accurately as they could and at normal speed. For the third and fourth repetitions, the participants were instructed to complete the activity, but each time with one of the 6 performance errors noted above.

5. FINDINGS AND DISCUSSION

The system functioned smoothly throughout the study, with no technical hardware failures and correct communication maintained between the various system devices. All 15 participants completed the study within the assumed 1-hour timeframe and all demonstrated observable growth in fluency and confidence with the system as they progressed through the activities. Overall our system was able to detect 5 of the 6 performance errors (>0.7 recall), which suggests that our current movement assessment implementation is able to identify a particular simulated performance error with decent accuracy. In debrief interviews after the study, participants also noted how the objects and protocol tasks reminded them of various everyday activities, with one stating that they liked how the objects didn't obviously "give away" what they could be, or what they could be used for, indicating that the setup succeeded in prompting them to think creatively during the exercise. Building on these insights, we are currently extending our approach beyond functional error detection to support a broader capture and analysis of the participant's action goals. This revised system will be used in an upcoming trial with 10 stroke patients, which will help us further assess the potential of our approach.

6. REFERENCES

[1] Anderson, C. et al. Stroke rehabilitation services to accelerate hospital discharge and provide home-based care. *Pharmacoeconomics,* 20(8): 537–552, 2002.

[2] Baran, M. et al. Interdisciplinary concepts for design and implementation of mixed reality interactive neurorehabilitation systems for stroke. *Physical therapy,* 2015;95:449-460

[3] Kirk, P. et al. Motivating Stroke Rehabilitation Through Music: A Feasibility Study Using Digital Musical Instruments in the Home. In *Proc* CHI '16, 1781-1785.

[4] Webster, C and Celik, O. Systematic review of Kinect applications in elderly care and stroke rehabilitation, *J. of Neuroengineering and Rehab.,* vol. 11, pp. 1–24, 2014.

[5] Wolf, S. et al. Assessing wolf motor function test as outcome measure for research in patients after stroke. *Stroke,* 32(7):1635–1639, 2001

[6] Wu, C. et al. Effects of object affordances on reaching performance in persons with and without cerebrovascular accident. *Am J Occup Ther.* 1998 Jun;52(6):447-56.

Needs and Challenges of Post-Acute Brain Injury Patients in Understanding Personal Recovery

Yamini Karanam, Andrew Miller, and Erin Brady
School of Informatics and Computing, Indiana University, Indianapolis
535 W. Michigan St, Indianapolis IN, 46201
{ykaranam,andrewm,brady}@iupui.edu

ABSTRACT
Recovery from brain injury is a complex and longitudinal process consisting of clinical recovery, illness management, and personal recovery. Lack of initiatives to create awareness about expected recovery and tools for helping patients understand their progress make the personal recovery journey challenging and frustrating. In this paper, we discuss results from interviews with five post-acute brain injury patients about their needs and challenges in understanding their personal recovery.

Keywords
Brain injury; personal recovery; patient awareness; rehabilitation.

1. INTRODUCTION
Brain injury is a structural damage or physiological disruption of brain function and is a leading cause of death and disability around the world. This condition could be a result of external force, illness, stroke, substance abuse, or tumors acquired after birth. It may cause temporary or permanent impairment in areas such as cognitive, emotional, metabolic, motor, perceptual and sensory brain function. In addition, brain injury patients are more susceptible to long-term emotional problems, such as anxiety and depression.

Recovery from brain injury is a complex construct that depends on severity of brain injury, time since injury, and other psychological and social factors. Recovery may not mean that the "suffering has disappeared, all the symptoms removed, and the functioning completely restored" [1]. It is not a linear process, involving more than relief from acute clinical symptoms and occuring even if symptoms reoccur. It changes the frequency and duration of symptoms and is characterized by growth, setbacks and periods of little and rapid change [2]. Side effects from medication, accidents, or other complications arising from brain injury can worsen the frequency and duration of symptoms, hamper recovery and make understanding the course of recovery unintuitive for patients.

Recovery is also complicated by the diverse communities of practice involved. Different stakeholders and practitioners understand recovery differently, causing a disparity in the understanding of personal recovery among brain injury patients, caregivers, and clinicians which can severely impact rehabilitation [6, 10]. The medical system currently focuses on and supports clinical recovery (remission as measured by neuroimaging tests and neuropsychological assessments) and symptom-based illness management (including symptom control and long-term symptom monitoring. Less attention is paid to *personal recovery*, or the holistic process of working toward feeling 'normal again' [2] A lack of standardized practices for rehabilitation and education leaves patients without awareness of the condition, understanding of expected recovery, and options for rehabilitation [4].

Patients are often unaware of the expected course of personal recovery and its impact on functional domains [8]. Patient self-awareness through an understanding of personal recovery predicts quality of life and impacts rehabilitation outcomes more than the severity of brain injury over time [9]. Thus, there is an urgent need to improve understanding of personal recovery and operationalize recovery for various stakeholders through patient understanding. Patient understanding of personal recovery includes *intellectual awareness* (knowledge of a particular problem), *emergent awareness* (recognizing a problem when it occurs), and *anticipatory awareness* (ability to predict that a problem is likely to occur) [5]. Intellectual awareness provides the foundation for emergent and anticipatory awareness. Factors that lead to impaired intellectual awareness are a lack of adequate information for analyzing past knowledge, impaired abstract reasoning, denial, and self-deception [5, 6]. The goal of this study is to understand patients' needs and challenges in acquiring adequate information to develop intellectual awareness and enable emergent and anticipatory awareness.

2. METHODS
We conducted semi-structured interviews with five post-acute brain injury patients, recruited from an online support group for post-surgery pineal tumor patients. We asked about self-awareness of impairments, similar to the protocol proposed by Fleming et al., and about course of recovery, rehabilitation, tracking and managing symptoms, and participation in clinical decision-making [7].

3. PRELIMINARY FINDINGS
All interviews were audio-recorded. We transcribed and analyzed interviews using six-phase essentialist/realist thematic analysis [3]. The age of the participants ranged from 22 - 54 years and the duration after surgery ranged from 2 months to 3 years. However, they experienced symptoms few years before diagnosis or surgery.

RQ1: How do patients recovering from brain injury currently track and understand their personal recovery? Lack of clinical or healthcare practices to measure personal recovery leaves the burden of tracking and understanding personal recovery entirely to patients. Our goal is to understand their current practices - data collection instruments, analysis, and insights obtained.

Most participants reported recording pain levels or sleep patterns manually (excel sheet, iPhone app for migraine, paper and pencil) or using a wearable device (Fitbit). The participants explained that logging this information helped them with externalizing the list of symptoms they experience each day and confirm the correlation between symptoms and triggers. P5 spoke about the impact of journaling on reflection and self-awareness. They expressed the need for tangible sources of data that could be used to see trends and communicate their experiences with their healthcare providers.

P5: *"I would write in my journal and that has helped me too because when I would go back I would be able to see oh look at*

ASSETS '17, October 29-November 1, 2017, Baltimore, MD, USA

ACM ISBN 978-1-4503-4926-0/17/10.
https://doi.org/10.1145/3132525.3134794

this, my health was really getting bad here back in August and ... here's the comparison to June you know it was very helpful"

Participants understood their recovery by self-experimentation and trial and error. They gained an intuitive understanding of their abilities and impairments through observation of daily living.

P2: *"I guess just figure then like it was my new normal and avoid anything I could, find my triggers, see any doctor that I could."*

RQ2: What are their needs and challenges in this process? Analyzing and reflecting on large amounts of diverse data is challenging without the help of external tools. Our goal is to understand the metaphysical process through which patients gain insights. Through this, we aim to understand what needs and challenges they face in acting on their insights.

Participants stated that the online support group was their main source of information and emotional support. They acquired information about complications of brain injury anecdotally through the stories of other people on the group. They were introduced to the support group either while browsing for information or through another brain tumor survivor. Participants reiterated that the consequences of brain injury and the course of recovery are unique for everyone. Although some of their symptoms were similar to other patients on the support group, the experience of the symptoms and the effect of impairment depends on functional domains such as work, interpersonal relationships etc.

Participants tracked symptoms manually only to discontinue later due to the effort it required.

P1: "Current challenge [is to] chart exactly when it starts. Because there are some days when I wake up with a migraine and obviously I don't know what time it exactly started or what could have caused it".

They believed that data alone did not convey their experience of symptoms without interpretation of how they affected well-being and quality of life.

P3: *"The MRI shows that everything is fine I would say I have recovered except for the fatigue issues and double vision."*

RQ3: How is this information used in collaborative care among various stakeholders? We aim to investigate the challenges patients face in the process of communicating an insight to his/her clinician as an input to clinical decision making.

Healthcare providers did not set expectations for setbacks or assess overall well-being. On inquiring, participants were informed by their healthcare providers that they were not informed of the continued complications in order not to cause anxiety about recovery. Patients reported that their healthcare providers' perspective of recovery was very different from their actual recovery. Although they did not conclusively state reasons for this, they speculated that this could be a limitation in the knowledge in the field of neurology. P4 reported that she consulted a neurologist who is a doctor of osteopathy. She reported that his evaluation of her health included well-being while her other doctors who hold M.D.s did not account for it in their assessments. They reported reduced quality of life due to this disparity.

P3: "*...unless you had your brain messed with I don't think you know how it feels... I don't think doctors really get it.*"

Healthcare providers accounted for recovery from only acute clinical symptoms and set expectations accordingly. Often, they could not anticipate or explain the cause of other complications arising from brain injury. They expected patients to rehabilitate within a few weeks to months. However, participants reported recurring symptoms and new complications preventing them from returning to their pre-injury lives. This simplified perspective of recovery from clinicians may inhibit communication with patients.

Healthcare providers may also be reluctant to use patient generated health data (PGHD) in clinical decision making. P1 was dissuaded from collecting his sleep data first using an excel sheet later with a Fitbit because his healthcare provider refused to use it in validating his concerns. Participants reported that their healthcare providers did not consider this data credible.

P1: "*When I logged my sleep patterns in excel for 6-7 months, my doctors refused to even look at it.*"

4. CONCLUSIONS AND FUTURE WORK

Our results show that most participants tracked their symptoms using personal memoirs, paper or mobile based trackers, or wearable devices. However, they understand their overall recovery intuitively. Healthcare providers are reluctant to use the insights obtained through this process due to issues with validity and reliability. Given its individualistic and complicated nature, we believe that personal health informatics has the potential for leveraging the use of patient generated health data in patients' everyday lives and clinician encounters. In future work, we will conduct longitudinal studies collecting data about health-related quality of life to capture a patient's *perception* of symptoms and functional status. This data is useful to quantify the degree to which a disease or treatment impacts a patient's life in a valid and reliable way. We will use it to co-design and evaluate *exploratory visualizations* iteratively to enable reflection and self-awareness in patients and evaluate how visualization tools facilitate self-advocacy and participation in clinical decision making for patients.

5. REFERENCES

[1] Anthony, W.A. 1993. Recovery from mental illness: The guiding vision of the mental health service system in the 1990s. *Psychosocial Rehabilitation Journal*. 16, 4 (1993), 11–23.

[2] Barber, M.E. 2012. Recovery as the new medical model for psychiatry. *Psychiatric Services (Washington, D.C.)*. 63, 3 (Mar. 2012), 277–279.

[3] Braun, V. and Clarke, V. 2006. Using thematic analysis in psychology. *Qualitative Research in Psychology*. 3, 2 (Jan. 2006), 77–101.

[4] Cioe, N. 2012. Factors influencing post-acute brain injury rehabilitation treatment outcome. *Dissertations*. (May 2012).

[5] Crosson, B. et al. 1989. Awareness and compensation in postacute head injury rehabilitation. *Journal of Head Trauma Rehabilitation*. 4, 3 (Sep. 1989), 46–54.

[6] Flashman, L.A. and McAllister, T.W. 2002. Lack of awareness and its impact in traumatic brain injury. *Neurorehabilitation*. 17, 4 (2002), 285–296.

[7] Fleming, J.M. et al. 1996. Self-awareness of deficits in adults with traumatic brain injury: how best to measure? *Brain Injury*. 10, 1 (Jan. 1996), 1–16.

[8] Pagulayan, K.F. et al. 2006. A Longitudinal Study of Health-Related Quality of Life After Traumatic Brain Injury. *Archives of Physical Medicine and Rehabilitation*. 87, 5 (May 2006), 611–618.

[9] Soberg, H.L. et al. 2013. Health-related Quality of Life 12 months after severe traumatic brain injury: A prospective nationwide cohort study. *Journal of Rehabilitation Medicine*. 45, 8 (Sep. 2013), 785–791.

[10] Stotland, N.L. et al. 2008. The recovery concept: clinician and consumer perspectives. *Journal of Psychiatric Practice*. 14 Suppl 2, (May 2008), 45–54.

On How Deaf People Might Use Speech to Control Devices

Jeffrey P. Bigham[1], Raja Kushalnagar[2], Ting-Hao Kenneth Huang[1], Juan Pablo Flores[3,4], Saiph Savage[4]

[1] Carnegie Mellon University, <jbigham,tinghaoh>@cs.cmu.edu
[2] Gallaudet University, raja.kushalnagar@gallaudet.edu
[3] Universidad Nacional Autonoma de Mexico, jp@juanpabloflores.com
[4] West Virginia University, saiph.savage@mail.wvu.edu

ABSTRACT

Smart devices connected to the Internet are proliferating. To reduce costs of devices that have traditionally been inexpensive (toasters, microwaves, printers, etc), many of these devices have chosen to use a speech interface rather than a visual one. This transition has been hastened by the increasing capabilities of speech interfaces, exemplified by products like Amazon Echo and Apple's Siri. A consequence of these products moving to voice control is that people who are deaf and hard of hearing (DHH) may be unable to use them. In this paper, we briefly introduce two technical approaches we are pursuing for enabling DHH people to provide input to these devices: *(i)* human computation workflows for understanding "deaf speech," and *(ii)* mobile interfaces that can be instructed to speak on the user's behalf.

CCS Concepts

•Human-centered computing → *Accessibility theory, concepts and paradigms; Empirical studies in accessibility;*

1. INTRODUCTION

More and more devices are becoming speech-controlled, now that speech recognition is becoming better, and more devices are becoming "smarter" and thus need an interface for users (Figure 1). Speech is often preferred because devices using speech can avoid display screens that are expensive and bulky, and difficult to operate in a hands-free way. There are speech-controlled devices that are quite general (*e.g.*, Amazon's Alexa, Google Home, and Apple's HomePod), and those that are quite specific (*e.g.*, microwaves. Unfortunately, speech input/output is inaccessible for people who are deaf, and that is the only way to access much of the functionality of today's smart devices.

In this poster, we present initial work on enabling deaf people to access speech-controlled devices. We first overview the problem, and demonstrate that deaf speech is not recognized by current speech recognition technology. We then present initial work exploring whether human computation might be a more effective way to recognize deaf speech, and finally present evidence that using an accompanying mobile application that produces speech on behalf of the user may be a more fruitful path forward. We conclude with challenges for future work in this area.

ASSETS '17 October 29-November 1, 2017, Baltimore, MD, USA

ACM ISBN 978-1-4503-4926-0/17/10.

DOI: https://doi.org/10.1145/3132525.3134821

Figure 1: Voice-activated devices have become common-place. Users can use voice to control their smart watches, mobile phones, personal assistant devices such as Amazon's Echo or Apple's HomePod, voice-activated vacuum robots, even smart cars. However, most voice-activated devices are not accessible to deaf people.

2. RECOGNIZING DEAF SPEECH

Deaf speech is the speech produced by deaf individuals. Because the individual cannot hear their own speech, deaf speech generally sounds different from the speech of hearing people (the so-called deaf accent). Unlike a true accent, deaf speech is characterized by large variation in pronunciation both between individuals and within a single individual. This variation can lead to difficulty in understanding, even among people familiar with deaf speech or even those familiar with the specific speech of an individual [5]. As a result, speech recognition, including that on today's proliferating smart devices, does not work for most deaf people [2].

To begin exploring the problem of recognizing deaf speech, we collected a corpus from five deaf individuals, each of whom contributed 10 common commands [4] used to control the Amazon Echo device. Example commands included: "Alexa, what is the weather today?", "Alexa, stop.", "Alexa, tell me about the movie Ghost in the Shell." We chose to use Echo as a platform of inquiry because of its popularity, because of its state-of-the-art speech recognition capabilities, and because, despite its popularity, much of its functionality, cannot be accessed without speech (even though there is an accompanying mobile application).

We first explored how well state-of-the-art general speech recognition works in understanding the commands that deaf people produce for controlling an Amazon Echo device. For this purpose, we took all of the commands that deaf individuals produced, inserted them into Google's Speech Recognition system, and calculated the word error rate (WER). The word error rate helps us asses the performance of a speech recognition system as it measures the number of words that the system correctly identifies. We found that Google's Speech Recognition system had an average word error rate of over 40 % and a standard deviation of .4. In other words, over 40 % of the words that a deaf person pronounced were on average incorrectly classified. Notice that this error is much larger than Google's standard word error rate, which is less than 5 % [6]. Given that state of the art speech recognition did not work especially well on deaf speech, we next explored how human computation might work for understanding this speech. We posted to Amazon Mechanical Turk our 50 clips of deaf people stating different commands. Workers were pretty good at understanding the speech of one of our participants (who became deaf later in life, and whose speech was most understandable). However, this method overall worked much poorer than via automated speech recognition systems. With human computation we had an average word error rate of over 90 %, and a standard deviation of .62.

As a modification of this, we posted the speech samples again, along with the 10 phrases, and asked workers to simply choose which of the 10 phrases was most likely to be the one said. Workers were much better at this. Workers were incorrect in only 33 % of cases, *i.e.*, 67 % of the commands were correctly classified through this approach. Overall, we expect recognizing deaf speech to remain challenging with both automatic and human-powered approaches, although for some individuals it may be possible to develop hybrid recognition approaches that work.

3. INTERFACES TO PRODUCE SPEECH

In addition to improving the accuracy of automatic recognition of deaf speech, one potential direction is to empower deaf people to generate natural speech easily. If smartphones can convert text (or deaf speech) to speech that the devices such as Amazon's Echo can understand, smartphones can act as convenient and powerful tools to intermediate deaf users and voice-controlled devices. While the technology of speech synthesis (also known as Text-To-Speech, TTS) have been developed for decades~[1], literatures had little to say about its capability of generating speech commands for personal assistant devices. To understand the feasibility of using smartphones as a TTS device for communicating with voice-controlled devices, we manually typed the text of ten Alexa commands that were used in our previous speech recognition study into a TTS application[1] powered by Google Speech Recognition via an LG's Nexus 5X Android phone, and then had the phone display the synthesized speech to an Amazon's Echo device. We found that Echo was able to understand speech produced from text-to-speech and respond with valid answers in all ten trials. However, we found that some parameter tuning allowed for the best recognition. In particular, we found that the phone volume needed to be set fairly loud for it to work, and the phone needed to still be fairly close to the device. It may be difficult for a person who is unable to hear their device to do this efficiently, and so likely one challenge going forward will be to give users feedback about good placement of the phone and the audio it is outputting.

4. FUTURE WORK

Our on-going work focuses on two main activities, as represented by the preliminary work discussed here. First, we are attempting to create speech recognition that is likely to work for deaf speech. We are working with speech recognition researchers to build models that adapt to deaf speech. This is difficult because deaf speech is variable from person to person, and even within the same person across different times.

We are also pursuing more complex human computation workflows that may allows crowd workers to better recognize deaf speech. We are borrowing the iterative model from Turkit that may allow a sequence of workers to do better than a single worker [3]. We are also implementing human interface equivalents to the language models used by speech recognition systems. For example, if a particular device can only recognize certain templated commands, we are exploring ways to have workers interact within those constraints. This may make them more efficient and accurate.

Finally, we are building a mobile application that can produce speech on behalf of the deaf user. The design of this application will necessarily go beyond simply producing speech, by also providing feedback to the user about how well the produced speech was understood and recognizing speech and other audio output from the device as well.

[1] `https://codepen.io/SteveJRobertson/pen/emGWaR`

5. CONCLUSION

In this paper, we have presented an initial investigation of the accessibility challenges presented by speech-controlled devices for deaf users. Using a sample of inputs to these devices using deaf speech, we first demonstrated that off-the-shelf speech recognition does not work well for this user group. We then presented two alternative approaches for enabling deaf people to interact with these devices: *(i)* using human computation to recognize the speech, and *(ii)* using text-to-speech functionality on a mobile application to produce the speech.

6. REFERENCES

[1] Sadaoki Furui. 2000. *Digital speech processing: synthesis, and recognition.* CRC Press.

[2] Linda~G Gottermeier, Carol~L De~Filippo, R~Aja Kushalnagar, and Bonnie~L Bastian. 2016. User Evaluation Of Automatic Speech Recognition Systems For Deaf-hearing Interactions At School And Work. *Audiology Today* 28, 2 (2016), 20–34.

[3] Greg Little, Lydia~B Chilton, Max Goldman, and Robert~C Miller. 2009. Turkit: tools for iterative tasks on mechanical turk. In *Proceedings of the ACM SIGKDD workshop on human computation.* ACM, 29–30.

[4] Taylor Martin and David Priest. 2017. The complete list of Alexa commands so far. (April 2017). `https://www.cnet.com/how-to/amazon-echo-the-complete-list-of-alexa-commands/`

[5] Nancy~S. McGarr. 1983. The Intelligibility of Deaf Speech to Experienced and Inexperienced Listeners. *Journal of Speech, Language, and Hearing Research* 26, 3 (1983), 451–458. DOI: `http://dx.doi.org/10.1044/jshr.2603.451`

[6] John Shinal. 2017. Making sense of Google CEO Sundar Pichai's plan to move every direction at once. (May 2017). `http://www.cnbc.com/2017/05/18/google-ceo-sundar-pichai-machine-learning-big-data.html`

Perceptions of Mobile Device Authentication Mechanisms by Individuals who are Blind

Flynn Wolf
Department of Information Systems
UMBC
Baltimore, MD 21250
flynn.wolf@umbc.edu

Ravi Kuber
Department of Information Systems
UMBC
Baltimore, MD 21250
rkuber@umbc.edu

Adam J. Aviv
Department of Computer Science
USNA
Annapolis, MD 21402
aviv@usna.edu

ABSTRACT
This paper describes an exploratory study focusing on the methods of mobile authentication currently utilized by individuals who are blind. Perceptions of security are discussed, along with the trade-offs with usability and accessibility. A tactile aid for a mobile authentication interface was introduced to participants to obtain preliminary feedback on its design. The aid was found to offer promise for supporting orientation, which could be used support novice users, and provide assistance when the mobile device must be used privately in public spaces.

CCS Concepts
Human-centered computing → Accessibility → Empirical studies in accessibility.

Keywords
Authentication; Blind; Mobile Devices; Security; Tactile

1. INTRODUCTION
Authentication mechanisms are often used to secure access to mobile devices, where personal and sensitive data may be viewed or stored. While PINs and graphical patterns (prescribed sequence of on-screen strokes) can be entered quickly into mobile authentication interfaces, the predominantly graphical nature of these interfaces can pose challenges for individuals who are blind. Difficulties can in part be attributed to the limited nature of assistive technologies. Furthermore, challenges can be faced identifying the threat of observation attacks when interacting with authentication mechanisms.

In this paper, we describe an exploratory study examining the perceptions of current authentication mechanisms, focusing solely on mobile authentication interfaces. A mobile tactile aid, originally proposed for eyes-free interactions [6], was also evaluated with individuals who are blind to determine its potential for supporting orientation when authenticating entry.

2. RELATED WORK
Researchers have begun to explore issues of privacy and security among individuals who are blind, which may impact their interactions with technologies [2,4]. While users are able to log-in using PINs in conjunction with assistive technologies such as Voiceover, and are able to mask content from the screen using built-in functionality, studies have suggested that users are unaware or not concerned about potential security threats, limiting their use of password-protected screen locks [2]. Limitations of assistive technologies have been found to impact non-visual authentication [4], as time can be spent attempting to input data and verify system status. Furthermore, interfaces which are largely graphical in nature (i.e. pattern unlock screen) are difficult to use with screen readers, as positional information can be challenging to convey through audio.

Technologies have been proposed to support individuals who are blind with the process of authentication. Examples include the use of on-screen taps which can be entered with one or more fingers [2]. The solution limits the risks of visual or aural eavesdropping. Accessible password managers have also been designed to limit help users deal with complex password policies and a large number of online accounts [3]. However, further work is needed to improve access to existing authentication mechanisms. In this paper, we describe a study focusing on the perceptions of mobile authentication interfaces by individuals who are blind, and introduce an assistive tool, designed to support users when entering PINs and graphical patterns.

3. SEMI-STRUCTURED INTERVIEWS
Semi-structured interviews were conducted with three legally-blind users, all of whom relied on the use of assistive technologies for interaction with their mobile devices (Table 1). The participants, all of whom described themselves as intermediate to advanced mobile device users, were asked about their experiences with authenticating entry to mobile devices, and questions related to privacy and security during this process.

Table 1: Participant demographics

	Sight status	Sex	Age range	Preferred assistive technology
P1	Legally-blind (No vision)	F	21-30	TalkBack (Android)
P2	Legally-blind (Light perception)	M	31-40	Voiceover (iOS)
P3	Legally-blind (Some vision)	M	21-30	Magnification with some use of TalkBack (Android)

P1, a fully blind user, preferred not to lock her Android device. She took this approach because unlocking methods were "too difficult to manage routinely". While she had experience entering PINs, time would be spent listening for auditory feedback from the screen reader during this process. Errors could be made on occasion (if the finger slips), which could be both frustrating and time-consuming if re-entry was needed. In contrast, the other participants were very enthusiastic about using fingerprint authentication, as this was faster and more reliable than making PIN entry attempts. Fingerprint authentication, however, still required occasional PIN entry as a backup. Both P2 and P3 highlighted that they had spent time and effort learning the spatial

ASSETS '17, October 29-November 1, 2017, Baltimore, MD, USA

ACM ISBN 978-1-4503-4926-0/17/10.
https://doi.org/10.1145/3132525.3134793

position of digits on the PIN entry screen, to help them more accurately locate digits for entry.

P3 had also linked his device-based biometric reader to a password manager, allowing the fingerprint to quickly unlock both the device and authorized applications. Entering alphanumeric passwords was "otherwise always a hassle." P2 who had greater levels of vision available in the past, had interacted with the pattern unlock screen, but had not felt secure when using simple patterns in public places or in unfamiliar surroundings. P3 was aware of the benefits of using stroke-based patterns, but felt that these would be challenging to perform consistently with assistive technologies.

All participants were aware of potential threats around them. For example, P1 was concerned about her passwords or other secure details being overheard by others, especially in a closed vehicle. While the volume of her screen reader could be reduced or headphones could be used to minimize the likelihood of a threat, these actions impeded her hearing for other purposes. However, because she felt that she "could not defeat these risks" she was content to leave her phone unlocked, and instead limit sensitive information stored or accessed via her phone.

4. TACTILE AID STUDY

Tactile aids have shown promise helping visually impaired users explore mobile and touchscreen interfaces [5]. We examined whether an assistive tactile aid could support spatialization of two common mobile authentication types, PIN and 3x3 graphical grid patterns. Two web-based mockups of these interfaces, with a tactile aid feature, were presented to participants. When using the aid, tactile cues indicated when the pointing finger touched grid or PIN buttons, prior to starting to enter the passcode. To further help spatialization, the vibration pattern differed at the location of the first digit of the passcode to be entered. This aid intended to help a visually impaired user find interface landmarks, prior to entering a passcode. Standard tactile cues for button selection were also presented during authentication. Participants were asked to explore the interfaces and offer feedback, and to determine if it could realistically support blind users. They were also asked to enter in sample PINs and patterns of four and six-digit lengths.

5. PRELIMINARY FINDINGS

Responses from participants indicated that the tactile cues clearly informed them of the starting point of a PIN entry attempt, and the vertical and horizontal edges of the interfaces. Cues were presented passively and offered the benefits of discretion, without the user drawing unwanted attention from others, or needing to cede their broader situational awareness by needing to wear an audio headset. Presenting information relating to the starting point was thought to offer promise to novice users, who were not used to identifying targets on the numberpad interface, or who may easily lose position and find it difficult to reorient on the interface. However, further cues may be needed to continuously support the user while entering the remainder of the PIN. P3 also demonstrated that using his current mobile device with assistive technology, unique audio cues are presented when the finger leaves the numberpad area while entering a PIN, which can assist a distracted mobile user. A tactile version of this feature was suggested for the app.

Participants felt that for users who had been utilizing smartphones for a while, the screen was so well mentally-mapped out that tactile feedback may only be beneficial under certain circumstances. For example, in scenarios where headphones had been forgotten and discretion was needed, or in situations when the device was in a non-intuitive position (e.g. the phone at an angle in a pocket or bag, as the user may want to maintain privacy of the interaction, as described by [1]).

Mixed responses were received regarding the aid when interacting with the pattern unlock interface. While tactile feedback was found to be helpful, P3 was able to enter grid-based patterns with a 52.3% rate of accuracy (SD=0.31) in ten grid entry attempts using the aid. Further work will be conducted to investigate ways to support user awareness of where strokes have been made on the interface, to better support users when entering/ checking patterns.

6. CONCLUSION AND FUTURE WORK

This paper has described a preliminary study examining perceptions of mobile authentication mechanisms, and the use of a tactile aid to support spatialization and orientation when using PIN and graphical patterns. A study is currently in progress examining use of the applications in situations where the screen cannot be observed, to better understand means of supporting accessible authentication under these conditions. The results of this should inform more secure and usable authentication designs for blind users. As the next step in the research, we aim to modify instances when tactile feedback is presented when performing authentication interactions to determine whether greater assistance can be provided to the user.

7. ACKNOWLEDGMENTS

This work is supported through the Office of Naval Research (Award: N00014-15-1-2776).

8. REFERENCES

[1] Abdolrahmani, A., Kuber, R., and Hurst A. 2016. An empirical investigation of the situationally-induced impairments experienced by blind mobile device users. In *Proceedings of W4A*, Article No: 21, DOI=http://dx.doi.org/10.1145/2899475.2899482.

[2] Azenkot, S., Rector, K., Ladner, R., and Wobbrock, J. 2012. October. PassChords: secure multi-touch authentication for blind people. In *Proceedings of the SIGACCESS Conference on Computers and Accessibility (ASSETS)*, 159-166, DOI=http://dx.doi.org/10.1145/2384916.2384945.

[3] Barbosa, N.M., Hayes, J., and Wang, Y. 2016. UniPass: design and evaluation of a smart device-based password manager for visually impaired users. In *Proceedings of the Conference on Pervasive and Ubiquitous Computing,* 49-60, DOI=http://dx.doi.org/10.1145/2971648.2971722.

[4] Dosono, B., Hayes, J., and Wang, Y. 2015. "I'm stuck!": a contextual inquiry of people with visual impairments in authentication. . In *Symposium on Usable Privacy and Security (SOUPS),* 151-168.

[5] McGookin, D., Brewster, S., and Jiang, W.W. 2008. Investigating touchscreen accessibility for people with visual impairments. In *Proceedings of the 5th Nordic Conference on Human-Computer Interaction: Building Bridges*, 298-307, DOI=http://dx.doi.org/10.1145/1463160.1463193.

[6] Wolf, F., Kuber, R., and Aviv, A.J. 2016. Towards non-observable authentication for mobile devices. In *Symposium on Usable Privacy and Security (SOUPS) – Posters Section.*

Rapid Prototyping of Accessible Interfaces With Gaze-Contingent Tunnel Vision Simulation

Rie Kamikubo
The University of Tokyo
Tokyo, Japan
rkamikub@iis.u-tokyo.ac.jp

Keita Higuchi
The University of Tokyo
Tokyo, Japan
khiguchi@iis.u-tokyo.ac.jp

Ryo Yonetani
The University of Tokyo
Tokyo, Japan
yonetani@iis.u-tokyo.ac.jp

Hideki Koike
Tokyo Institute of Technology
Tokyo, Japan
koike@cs.titech.ac.jp

Yoichi Sato
The University of Tokyo
Tokyo, Japan
ysato@iis.u-tokyo.ac.jp

ABSTRACT

Active involvement of users with disabilities is difficult to employ during the iterative stages of the design process due to high costs and effort associated with user studies. This research proposes a user centered design (UCD) strategy to incorporate the use of gaze-contingent tunnel vision simulation with sighted individuals to facilitate rapid prototyping of accessible interfaces. Through three types of validation studies, we examined how our simulation techniques can provide the opportunity for continued evaluation and refinement of the design. Our simulation approach was effective in emulating scanning behaviors caused by tunnel vision along with grasping user feedback to recognize user interface and usability criteria early in the design cycle.

Keywords

Accessibility design; Rapid Prototyping; Simulation; Gaze Tracking.

1. BACKGROUND

UCD assumes an iterative design process, and by rapidly generating prototypes, technology designers have the increasing opportunity to test and refine their design with users. In theory, the inclusion of users should also encourage the development towards accessible solutions [7]. Some variations of UCD specifically advocate constant communication between designers and users with disabilities [3, 8].

Despite the emphasis on inclusion in UCD, active involvement of users with disabilities is difficult to practice. According to [1], user studies are time consuming and costly, and the diverse range of abilities of users complicates the designing of inclusive interfaces. For instance, people with low vision suffer from varying levels of visual impairment [5]. Even from the same eye disease such as Retinitis Pigmentosa (RP), the progression of constricted visual fields, as well as poor visual acuity or light sensitivity, varies among individuals. There are practical challenges for designers in conducting representative user trials or quickly getting a sense of how a person with a visual disability would experience the interface. Moreover, repeated tasks and sessions involved in user studies require great physical effort especially from the users with disabilities.

Due to a number of challenges in incorporating the perspective of users with disabilities, simulating possible interaction patterns has been introduced for evaluation. For example, low vision simulation programs including predicted models [1] are available. Low-tech simulation glasses are also well known to cheaply support the designers [2]. However, they lack the immediacy and the ease of transition between observing interaction patterns via wearable simulators and directly refining the development. While employing self-observation techniques is necessary, we need to encourage the use of simulation as part of the design cycle to grasp subjective and objective evaluation measures.

2. GAZE-CONTINGENT SIMULATION IN DESIGN PROCESS

Our research proposes a design process that utilizes a gaze-contingent interface to simulate a visual impairment and assist in the simulation of the impairment in accessible interface design and evaluation. In this work, it emulates "tunnel vision" by estimating the real-time gaze position of a person to represent limited peripheral vision (Shown in Figure 1) such as that found in RP. Our simulation technique responds to the following objectives: developers can 1) quickly observe the effects of prototypes under a simulated visual condition and 2) recruit sighted participants for representative user trials to gain simulated user feedback. As illustrated in Figure 2, paths labeled as (1) and (2) respectively correspond to meet the two aforementioned purposes in the design process.

Even though our current version of the simulator focuses on

ASSETS '17 October 29-November 1, 2017, Baltimore, MD, USA

ACM ISBN 978-1-4503-4926-0/17/10.
DOI: https://doi.org/10.1145/3132525.3134803

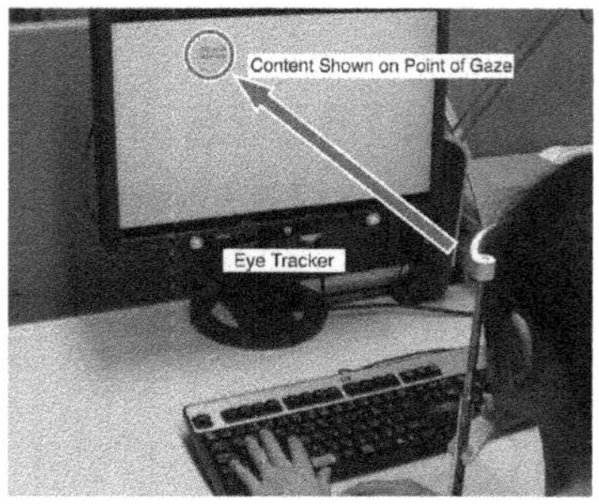

Figure 1: Sighted participant seeing a web page under a five degree field of the content at the real-time gaze position. This size of the area technically corresponds to how the field of view is restricted to central vision [9]

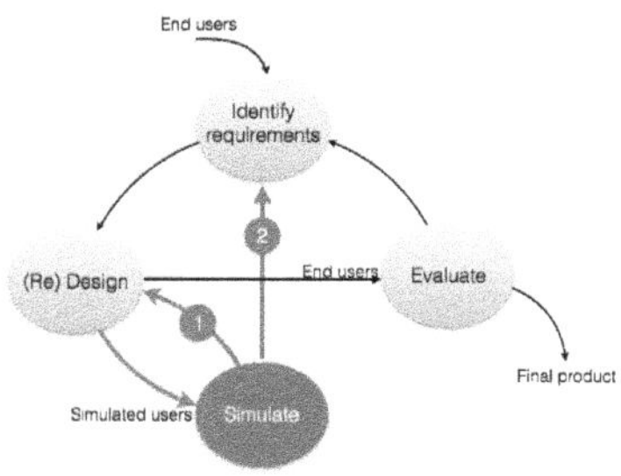

Figure 2: Simulation incorporated in the UCD process composed of 3 stages [6]. The path labeled as (1) serves for inspecting prototypes for redesign, whereas the path labeled as (2) goes through evaluation studies of the prototypes, both under simulated conditions of users with disabilities.

a certain visual impairment, we aim to pave the way for our simulation technique to offer the immediacy and flexibility to directly refine the design while examining simulation effects. It is then important for simulated evaluation studies to allow for collecting both subjective and objective data on the designed interface. To validate our design approach, we designed visual navigation aids and investigated how our tunnel vision simulation can be used to reveal similar design and evaluation input on our prototypes as those captured by RP users with limited peripheral vision.

3. FINDINGS

Through three types of validation studies conducted, we found that the gaze-contingent tunnel vision simulator can be used to identify basic interface problems and obtain user feedback from simulated tunnel vision participants. From the eye movement study, we examined that the simulator affected sighted individuals on their scanning behaviors regarding a number of saccadic movements that exceeded the simulated visual angle. These scanning pattern characteristics were similarly found for increased saccade frequency under tunnel vision [4]. Moreover, the simulated user interface (UI) and usability evaluation studies against our prototypes addressed necessary quantitative and qualitative results that corresponded with the RP participants.

From UI testing, we were able to explore design alternatives and verify which one to carry forward to the next usability testing stage. Out of five prototypes tested, both simulated tunnel vision and RP groups showed similar visual preference over one navigation cue with a radial design. It was found to be simple for the users with tunnel vision to visually reach the target by tracking the static lines for navigation instructions. It received highest ratings for the ease of completing visual-search tasks for web content. In usability testing, our navigation aid was analyzed to limit cognitive load of both groups for layout understanding. While statistical evaluation was also feasible due to controlled test conditions offered by the simulation approach, we saw the importance of enabling developers to consider human factors from simulated subjective perspectives.

It is important to note that we do not advocate completely excluding the actual end users in the design cycle. Especially at the initial user research and near the end of the higher-fidelity prototyping cycle, understanding consequences or coping strategies involved in an impairment day-to-day experiences will give the designers insights in forming new accessible requirements. Simulated evaluation is beneficial to easily check and modify their low- to mid-fidelity prototypes. We aim to lessen a certain amount of cost regarding time and effort in constantly inspecting basic interface changes.

4. CONCLUSION & FUTURE WORK

This paper presents a starting point for utilizing the gaze-contingent tunnel vision simulator in a continual design-evaluation cycle. Our future work primarily involves investigating the effects of different simulation-based techniques from the viewpoints of the developers. We also need to support configuration for multiple visual conditions. We hope to provide a new paradigm to facilitate rapid prototyping developments of accessible interfaces.

5. REFERENCES

[1] P. Biswas, P. Robinson, and P. Langdon. Designing inclusive interfaces through user modeling and simulation. *International Journal of Human-Computer Interaction*, 28(1):1–33, 2012.

[2] J. Goodman-Deane, S. Waller, A.-C. Collins, and P. J. Clarkson. Simulating vision loss: what levels of impairment are actually represented? 2013.

[3] R. E. Ladner. Design for user empowerment. *interactions*, 22(2):24–29, 2015.

[4] G. Luo and E. Peli. Patients with tunnel vision frequently saccade to outside their visual fields in visual search. *Journal of Vision*, 6(6):505–505, 2006.

[5] A. Openshaw, K. Branham, and J. Heckenlively. Understanding cone dystrophy. *Michigan: University of Michigan: Kellogg Eye Center*, pages 11–16, 2007.

[6] J. Preece, H. Sharp, and Y. Rogers. *Interaction Design-beyond human-computer interaction*. John Wiley & Sons, 2015.

[7] K. Shinohara, C. L. Bennett, and J. O. Wobbrock. How designing for people with and without disabilities shapes student design thinking. In *Proceedings of the 18th International ACM SIGACCESS Conference on Computers and Accessibility*, pages 229–237. ACM, 2016.

[8] J. O. Wobbrock, S. K. Kane, K. Z. Gajos, S. Harada, and J. Froehlich. Ability-based design: Concept, principles and examples. *ACM Transactions on Accessible Computing (TACCESS)*, 3(3):9, 2011.

[9] B. H. Zeavin and G. Wald. Rod and cone vision in retinitis pigmentosa. *American journal of ophthalmology*, 42(4):253–269, 1956.

Reaching Out: Investigating Different Modalities to Help People with Visual Impairments Acquire Items

Sooyeon Lee, Chien Wen Yuan, Benjamin V. Hanrahan, Mary Beth Rosson, John M. Carroll
Center for Human Computer Interaction, College of Information Sciences and Technology
Pennsylvania State University
University Park, PA 16801
{sul131, tuy11, bvh10, mrosson, jcarroll}@ ist.psu.edu

ABSTRACT
We present a lab study of multiple feedback designs for guiding small-scale arm-and-hand movement for people with visual impairments (PVI), so that they can reach out to and grasp an item on a shelf. Little attention has been paid to the guidance of small-scale arm-and-hand movements by PVI, yet this is an essential element of product acquisition in a grocery shopping task and other similar daily activities. We developed a feedback interface that allowed us to explore two types of auditory feedback (speech and tones), haptic vibration feedback, and a combination of both. The result of the study demonstrated that the multi-modal navigational feedback, specifically speech and haptic, was the most effective and preferred mode for small-scale navigation.

CCS Concepts
• **Human-centered computing~Empirical studies in accessibility** • **Human-centered computing~Accessibility technologies**

Keywords
Auditory feedback; haptic feedback; multimodal feedback; people with visual impairment

1. INTRODUCTION
Finding a wanted object and obtaining it with small-scale arm-and-hand motion is a frequently occurring activity in our daily lives; most of us would not think twice about grabbing a bottle from the pantry. Sighted people understand their relative locations to the surroundings and easily adjust their positions to accomplish various tasks. However, for people with visual impairments (PVI), reaching out and grabbing an object is quite challenging, and is even more so when the environment is unfamiliar (e.g., a store rather than a home). Activities like locating a glass of water, reaching out, and grabbing it from the dinner table, or retrieving a product from a grocery shelf requires careful and accurate arm-and-hand navigation guidance. Unless PVI are in a familiar space, they must either depend on assistance for moving their body or parts of their body to carry out such tasks, or use other sensory input (e.g., auditory or haptic) to understand what to do.

ASSETS '17, October 29-November 1, 2017, Baltimore, MD, USA

ACM ISBN 978-1-4503-4926-0/17/10.
https://doi.org/10.1145/3132525.3134817

Most existing research on PVI assistance has studied large-scale whole-body movement; little investigation has focused on small-scale movements of the arm and hand. Because such movements are both small in scale and brief in time, it is critical that PVI receive timely delivery of helpful information. We have been studying the nature and modality of such feedback as part of a larger project aiming to leverage state-of-the-art computer vision technologies in assisting PVI in daily tasks such as shopping. In this brief paper we report a study of five different directional feedback signals using a combination of sensory modes; we assessed the effectiveness of each signal type in guiding small-scale, arm-and-hand movements to reach to and grasp an object.

2. RELATED WORK
Previous research has investigated the presentation of directional information via the auditory channel (e.g., speech or non-speech like sonification), the haptic modality, or a combination of both [4][6][7]. In general, multi-modal feedback was found to be more effective, as predicted by multi-resource theory [8]. These existing studies examined support of large-scale body navigation, such as information needed in way-finding guidance. We contribute by exploring similar issues for small-scale, arm-and-hand movement navigation needed in object acquisition, such as in VizLens [2], GIST [5], ABBI [9], Kim et al., [3], Hong et al. [1], and Zhao et al. [10].

We extend previous research in three ways: 1) we focus on small-scale arm-and-hand movement; 2) we contrast multiple feedback options; and 3) we study grocery shopping as a context, identified by PVI as one of their most challenging daily tasks.

3. EXPERIMENT

3.1 Prototype and Feedback Design
To study the effectiveness of different modalities in small-scale arm-and-hand guidance, we used a prototype composed of a haptic glove and a bone conduction headset. The former was used for delivering haptic stimulation and the latter for conveying auditory feedback. The bone conduction headset enables PVI to receive not only the directional information but also ambient sounds with which they need to understand the surroundings.

We experimented with five different types of feedback: speech, non-speech, haptic vibration, a combination of speech and haptic, and a combination of non-speech and haptic. Synthesized voice was used for the speech feedback; tones (beeping sounds at different frequencies) were generated as non-speech feedback. Haptic feedback consisted of vibration signals delivered to different locations on the hand (left, right, top, bottom). Each type of feedback was mapped to six arm+hand adjustments (left, right, up, down, stop, reach forward) and two larger-scale movements (step forward, step backward). To make the feedback as intuitive and distinguishable as possible, we used spatial mapping (e.g., signal display on the left location for presenting a direction left) and various patterning with using different parameters such as duration and frequency. All feedback types were delivered in a continuous rhythm (e.g., sending continuous beeps to indicate moving left or right until the participant reaches the correct angle/position).

3.2 User Study

We used a Wizard of Oz (WOz) protocol to simulate computer vision and corresponding feedback; the human agent was required due to the instability of the current computer vision algorithm. We created a grocery shelf mockup in the lab and evaluated the five feedback conditions using eleven PVI (M:5; F:6) recruited from the local chapter of National Federation of the Blind (NFB). A research team member performed as the WOz operator using a pre-defined script.

For each trial, we positioned the participants in front of the product within a reachable distance. We provided training for each type of feedback at the beginning of each trial; we allowed participants to repeat the training as many times as needed. All participants performed 15 trials (3 trials X 5 feedback conditions). We used a Latin-square design to counterbalance the order of feedback conditions experienced by each participant.

We recorded the completion time for each trial along with number of errors made before object acquisition (errors included both incorrect product retrievals and an incomplete task). We also recorded the number of training requests. After the 15 trials, the participants rated each feedback condition on a 7-point Likert scale (1 = Not at all helpful and 7 = Extremely helpful); a semi-structured interview was conducted to gather qualitative data about experiences using each type of feedback.

4. RESULTS

4.1 Performance

A one-way ANOVA on completion times revealed significant differences among feedback conditions: $F(4, 160) = 4.84$, $p < .001$. A post-hoc analysis with Bonferroni confirmed significant differences ($p < .05$) between the vibration-only and the speech + vibration feedback; between tones + vibration and speech + vibration feedback. Another one-way ANOVA test with trial orders showed that no evidence of a learning effect across the three repetitions of each feedback condition.

4.2 Perceived Preference and Helpfulness

The analysis of preference ratings led to the following rank order: 1) speech-only ($M = 6.8$, $SD = 0.4$); 2) speech/haptic combination ($M = 6.4$, $SD = 1.5$); 3) haptic-only ($M = 5.7$, $SD = 1.3$); 4) tones-only ($M = 4.9$, $SD = 1.6$); and 5) tones/haptic combination mode ($M = 4.8$, $SD = 1.7$). Consistent with the performance result, the interviews revealed that a speech/haptic combination was most preferred; speech-only was second; and tones/haptic and haptic-only mode were least preferred.

Note that speech-only was rated most positively, but the interview responses placed it in second place. This may have been due to expectations for lowered effectiveness in noisy settings such as a grocery store. Participants told us they liked the combination of speech and haptic because the haptic feedback reinforced the speech and these two channels complement each other. The participants found the tones and haptic-only harder to discriminate and confusing at times.

5. CONCLUSION

We designed five feedback signals using speech, haptic, and non-speech information. We ran a study to examine effectiveness of each feedback mode for guiding arm-and-hand movement for reaching out and picking up items on grocery shelves. Our mixed method research showed that PVI performed best with a combination of speech and haptic feedback and it was also reported as most preferred in participants' comments. Our work extends the body of work on multi-modal feedback for PVI.

6. ACKNOWLEDGMENTS

This material is based on work supported by the National Science Foundation under Grants No. 1317560.

7. REFERENCES

[1] Hong, Jonggi, Lee Stearns, Tony Cheng, Jon E Froehlich, David Ross, and Leah Findlater. "Evaluating Angular Accuracy of Wrist - Based Haptic Directional Guidance for Hand Movement," n.d., 195–200.

[2] Guo, A., Chen, X. A., Qi, H., White, S., Ghosh, S., Asakawa, C., & Bigham, J. P. (2016, October). VizLens: A robust and interactive screen reader for interfaces in the real world. In *Proceedings of the 29th Annual Symposium on User Interface Software and Technology* (pp. 651-664). ACM.

[3] Kim, K., Ren, X., Choi, S., & Tan, H. Z. (2016). Assisting people with visual impairments in aiming at a target on a large wall-mounted display. *International Journal of Human-Computer Studies*, *86*, 109-120.

[4] Fiannaca, A., Apostolopoulous, I., & Folmer, E. (2014, October). Headlock: a wearable navigation aid that helps blind cane users traverse large open spaces. In *Proceedings of the 16th international ACM SIGACCESS conference on Computers & accessibility* (pp. 19-26). ACM

[5] Khambadkar, Vinitha. "GIST : A Gestural Interface for Remote Nonvisual Spatial Perception," 2013, 301–10.

[6] Merabet, L., & Sánchez, J. (2009). Audio-based navigation using virtual environments: combining technology and neuroscience. *AER Journal: Research and Practice in Visual Impairment and Blindness*, *2*(3), 128-137.

[7] Paneels, S., Anastassova, M., Strachan, S., Van, S. P., Sivacoumarane, S., & Bolzmacher, C. (2013, April). What's around me? Multi-actuator haptic feedback on the wrist. In World Haptics Conference (WHC), 2013 (pp. 407-412). IEEE.

[8] Wickens, C. D. (1991). Processing resources and attention. *Multiple-task performance*, *1991*, 3-34.

[9] Wilson, G., & Brewster, S. A. (2016, October). Using Dynamic Audio Feedback to Support Peripersonal Reaching in Young Visually Impaired People. In *Proceedings of the 18th International ACM SIGACCESS Conference on Computers and Accessibility* (pp. 209-218). ACM.

[10] Zhao, Y., Szpiro, S., Knighten, J., & Azenkot, S. (2016, September). CueSee: exploring visual cues for people with low vision to facilitate a visual search task. In *Proceedings of the 2016 ACM International Joint Conference on Pervasive and Ubiquitous Computing* (pp. 73-84). ACM.

Real-time Activity-sensitive Wearable Ankle Edema Monitoring System For Elderly and Visually Impaired Heart Failure Patients

Ahmad S Manshad, MD
Rush University Medical Center
Department of Internal Medicine
Chicago, Illinois, USA
ahmad_s_manshad@rush.edu

Muhanad S Manshad
New Mexico State University
Department of Computer Science
Las Cruces, New Mexico, USA
mmanshad@nmsu.edu

Sara S Manshad
New Mexico State University
Department of Biology
Las Cruces, New Mexico, USA
msara@nmsu.edu

ABSTRACT
Heart failure (HF) is a leading cause of hospital admissions and readmissions, and carries significant morbidity and mortality in the elderly patient population. Worsening ankle edema is an early sign of an acute HF exacerbation and needs to be carefully monitored. We present the AnkleBracelet, a prototype of a real-time, activity-sensitive, wearable assistive device for monitoring ankle edema specifically designed for elderly, blind, and visually impaired patients. This device provides unobtrusive data regarding changes in ankle edema to encourage behavioral change through multimodal feedback and interaction. Data can be transmitted remotely to maintain a constant connection between physicians and their patients. This device has a patient-centered design that is evidence-based and was derived from a series of collaborations with cardiologists at Rush University Medical Center.

CCS Concepts
*H.5.2 [**User Interfaces**]: User-centered design, Haptic I/O, Input devices and strategies; K.4.2 [**Social Issues**]: Assistive Technologies for Persons with Disabilities.*

Keywords
Heart failure; Haptic Feedback; Accessibility; Elderly; Blind and Visually Impaired; Multimodal; Assistive Technology; Wearables.

1. INTRODUCTION
Heart failure (HF) is a chronic and disabling condition characterized by reduced blood flow out of the heart. It is predominantly a condition of the elderly with patients over the age of 65 constituting the majority of HF cases in the United States [1]. Elderly patients presenting with HF have the highest readmission rates and ultimately the poorest outcomes [9]. Therefore, early detection of HF symptoms through patient awareness and self-care is of utmost importance.

Self-care for HF encompasses a spectrum of behaviors including recognition of early warning signs and medication adherence and self-adjustment. Self-care is particularly difficult for elderly patients with HF as they commonly have a complex profile characterized by multiple co-morbidities and age-related changes such as the loss of hearing, visual acuity, and impaired functional status [3].

ASSETS '17, October 29-November 1, 2017, Baltimore, MD, USA © 2017 Copyright is held by the owner/author(s).
ACM ISBN 978-1-4503-4926-0/17/10.
https://doi.org/10.1145/3132525.3134792

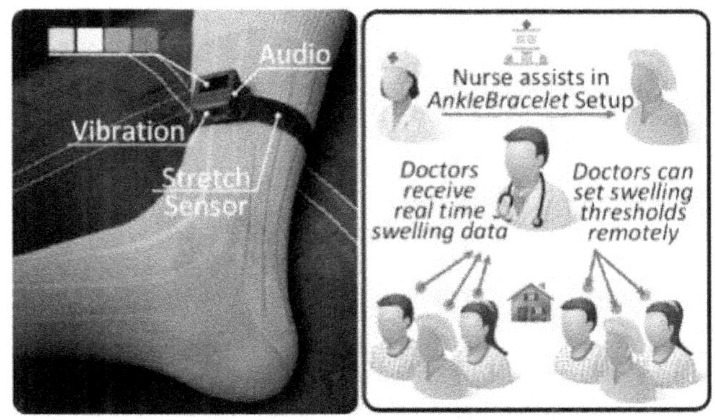

Figure 1. AnkleBracelet prototype (Left); device set up and remote monitoring (Right).

When these factors are combined with low income, lack of education, and unavailability of support, the ability to master the complex treatment regimen required for successful self-care of HF is compromised.

Among all HF self-care activities, symptom monitoring is the least well-performed [8]. Ankle edema is one particularly important early warning symptom, and if left unmanaged, may result in significant cardiac overload. Although many physicians are aware of the importance of monitoring edema, accuracy and consistency in assessing edema has been a challenge. The most widely-used technique is a subjective assessment where the patient applies pressure with his/her index finger to a single location on the ankle. This technique captures pit depth and the time needed for the skin to return to its original appearance (recovery time) as a single edema score ranging from 0 to 4. While this classic method is commonly used, it has not been proven to be sufficiently objective, reliable, or sensitive in assessing edema even by clinicians [2]. This can be especially daunting when performed by elderly patients with underlying impairments in cognitive, visual, mobility, and/or tactile function.

Few studies describe the use of non-invasive, wearable devices that use sensors to monitor ankle edema [4]. These devices are in early developmental phases and do not provide a sensible feedback system based on baseline ankle edema levels. Furthermore, they fail to relay information in an accessible format (audio, visual, or tactile feedback) to accommodate patients with functional impairments. Without an appropriate, patient-centered reminder system, these devices are unlikely to reinforce patients to self-initiate an appropriate response plan. This can undermine patient autonomy and prevent development of behaviors that improve self-care.

In this paper, we describe a real-time, activity-sensitive, wearable device designed to detect ankle edema in HF patients who are elderly, blind, or visually impaired. The AnkleBracelet uses a set of sensors to allow for accurate and reliable assessment of ankle edema and identification of body posture and activity. The AnkleBracelet measures changes in ankle edema and informs patients when certain thresholds in change have occurred to guide in initiating a response plan. Using a wireless module, this device sends user data directly to the physician for closer surveillance of swelling measurements to allow for timely intervention.

2. ANKLE-BRACELET: AN EVIDENCE-BASED, PATIENT-CENTERED DESIGN

The design of AnkleBracelet originates from a series of focus groups with three active, full-time cardiologists at Rush University Medical Center in Chicago.

- *Accurate Ankle Edema Measurements:* Among the various modalities used to assess ankle edema, circumference measurements are among the most reliable and accurate [2]. The AnkleBracelet was affixed with a flexible stretch sensor to assess ankle edema in a manner similar to ankle circumference measurements.
- *Posture Detection*: Ankle edema varies with changes in posture (e.g. supine, sitting, standing) [6]. To account for this variability, the AnkleBracelet uses an accelerometer to detect patient posture and interpret ankle edema while in a standing position.
- *Collaborative Monitoring*: Based on the 2010 Heart Failure Society of America guidelines, patients and physicians are encouraged to collaborate on a HF action plan [5]. HF action plans are divided into green, yellow, orange, and red zones corresponding to a stable, worsening, acute, and emergent states; with each state corresponding to a customized response plan. The AnkleBracelet is incorporated into the HF action plan to alert patients of changes in ankle swelling using the same colored graded zones (Figure 1).
- *Data Accessibility to Physicians*: Home-monitoring systems in HF patients have demonstrated the value of providing physicians with remotely-accessible data [7]. The AnkleBracelet uses a wireless module to transmit ankle swelling data to physicians.
- *Multimodal Feedback*: Functional and cognitive impairments are strong independent predictors of mortality in elderly patients with HF [3]. The AnkleBracelet accommodates patients with underlying impairments by providing multimodal (audio, visual, and haptic) feedback.

3. HARDWARE AND SOFTWARE

AnkleBracelet has been developed from scratch, using affordable off the-shelf hardware components. The device provides multimodal feedback via sound/speech, vibration and visuals via screen color changes depicting appropriate swelling stages. Software implementation is a custom application using a special set of algorithms to detect baseline ankle edema values, incremental changes in swelling when correct body posture is detected, and controlled vibration feedback via unique frequencies according to current swelling stage. All swelling data is transmitted in real-time through wifi, and is accessible by healthcare providers via a web application.

4. CURRENT STATUS

A prototype (Figure 1) has been developed to prove our concept. A number of formal evaluation activities are currently underway, including: NASA TLX (Task Load Index) workload assessment and SUS (system usability scale). Current participants will include a set of elderly patients with known HF, and a set of Blind and Visually impaired individuals. Participants will be tasked to utilize AnkleBracelet for a short period of time. During this time we will measure ankle swelling reliability, data transfer, and healthcare provider control.

5. REFERENCES

[1] Ammar KA, Jacobsen SJ, Mahoney DW, Kors JA, Redfield MM, Burnett JC Jr, Rodeheffer RJ. Prevalence and prognostic significance of heart failure stages: application of the American College of Cardiology/American Heart Association heart failure staging criteria in the community. Circulation. 2007 Mar 27;115(12):1563-70.

[2] Brodovicz KG, McNaughton K, Uemura N, Meininger G, Girman CJ, Yale SH. Reliability and feasibility of methods to quantitatively assess peripheral edema. Clin Med Res. 2009 Jun;7(1-2):21-31.

[3] Cacciatore F, Abete P, Mazzella F, Viati L, Della Morte D, D'Ambrosio D, Gargiulo G, Testa G, Santis D, Galizia G, Ferrara N, Rengo F. Frailty predicts long-term mortality in elderly subjects with chronic heart failure. Eur J Clin Invest. 2005 Dec;35(12):723-30.

[4] Fallahzadeh R, Pedram M, Ghasemzadeh H. SmartSock: a wearable platform for context-aware assessment of ankle edema. Conf Proc IEEE Eng Med Biol Soc. 2016. Aug;2016:6302-6306.

[5] Heart Failure Society Of America. Nonpharmacologic management and health care maintenance in patients with chronic heart failure. J Card Fail. 2006. Feb;12(1):e29-37.

[6] Man IO, Glover K, Nixon P, Poyton R, Terre R, Morrissey MC. Effect of body position on foot and ankle volume in healthy subjects. Clin Physiol Funct Imaging. 2004 Nov;24(6):323-6.

[7] Maric B, Kaan A, Ignaszewski A, Lear SA. A systematic review of telemonitoring technologies in heart failure. Eur J Heart Fail. 2009 May;11(5):506–17.

[8] Moser DK, Doering LV, Chung ML. Vulnerabilities of patients recovering from an exacerbation of chronic heart failure. Am Heart J 2005; 150:984.

[9] Vinson JM, Rich MW, Sperry JC, Shah AS, McNamara T. Early readmission of elderly patients with congestive heart failure. J Am Geriatr Soc. 1990 Dec;38(12):1290-5.

Recognizing Clothing Colors and Visual Textures Using a Finger-Mounted Camera: An Initial Investigation

Alexander J. Medeiros[1], Lee Stearns[1], Leah Findlater[2,5], Chuan Chen[3], Jon E. Froehlich[1,4]

[1]Department of Computer Science
[2]College of Information Studies
University of Maryland, College Park

[3]Poolesville High School
Poolesville, MD

[4]Computer Science and Engineering
[5]Human Centered Design and Engineering
University of Washington

ajmed@umd.edu, lstearns@umd.edu, leahkf@umd.edu, riverchen@gmail.com, jonf@cs.umd.edu

ABSTRACT

We investigate clothing color and visual texture recognition using images from a finger-mounted camera to support people with visual impairments. Our approach mitigates issues with distance and lighting that can impact the accuracy of existing color and texture recognizers and allows for easy touch-based interrogation to better understand clothing appearance. We classify image textures by combining two off-the-shelf techniques commonly used for object recognition achieving 99.4% accuracy on a dataset of 520 clothing images across 9 texture categories. We close with a discussion of potential applications, user evaluation plans, and open questions.

CCS Concepts

• **Human-centered computing → Accessibility technologies**

Keywords

Blind; visually impaired; wearables; texture recognition

1. INTRODUCTION

For people with visual impairments, color and texture information are frequently inaccessible. Standalone commercial devices such as *Color Teller* [2] or smartphone apps such as *Color Identifier* [5] allow users to identify colors and hear them read aloud. However, accuracy varies depending on ambient lighting and distance from the target surface. Also, these systems do not support recognition of visual textures or allow users to quickly query multiple locations—both of which are important to recognizing clothing [3]. Outside of commercial products, Yuan *et al.* [11, 13] investigated simple color and texture classification algorithms to identify clothing from static images. However, their approaches are again affected by distance and ambient lighting and do not allow for efficient interaction to identify more complex patterns.

In contrast, we introduce a wearable system using a small camera and co-located illumination source (an LED) worn on the finger. This system should enable access to color and texture information through touch, allowing users to move their finger across an article of clothing and combine knowledge of physical materials gained from their own sense of touch with automated audio feedback about visual appearance. This approach builds on a small but growing body of work, including our own [6, 10], that uses finger-mounted wearable cameras to support visually impaired users in a variety of activities. Our approach is most closely related to *Magic Finger* [12], which was not intended specifically for visually impaired

ASSETS '17, October 29-November 1, 2017, Baltimore, MD, USA

ACM ISBN 978-1-4503-4926-0/17/10.
https://doi.org/10.1145/3132525.3134805

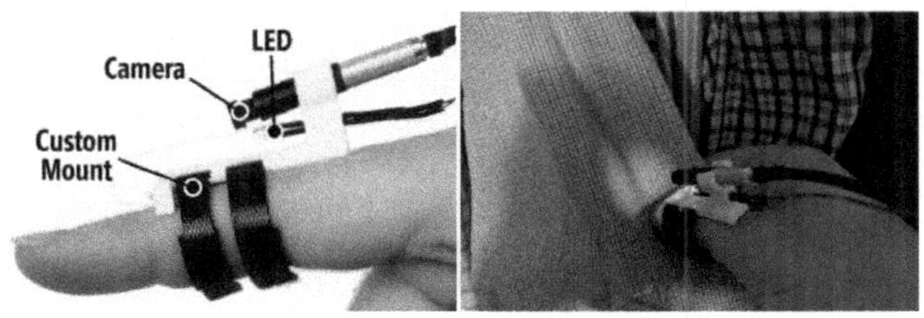

Figure 1. Prototype wearable camera and LED system: (a) Close-up view of system, (b) Identifying an article of clothing.

users but which similarly uses a finger-mounted camera to classify touched surfaces including seven clothing textures. However, Magic Finger's classification approach was simplistic and would not scale well to a large database of textures. In contrast, our algorithmic approach is based on that by Cimpoi *et al.* [4], which combines two complementary features commonly used for object recognition to achieve state-of-the-art texture classification performance. To examine this approach with a finger-wearable camera, we conducted a classification experiment on a small custom dataset of 520 images across 9 visual texture categories and 29 articles of clothing, achieving 99.4% accuracy.

Our contributions include: (i) extending our finger mounted camera system [6, 10] to support robust color and visual texture recognition accessed through touch, (ii) a small but novel dataset of close-up clothing images captured using this system, and (iii) results of applying a state-of-the-art texture classification approach to our dataset. Because this work is at an early stage, we also cover open questions and challenges that will need to be addressed as we implement an interactive system for visually impaired users.

2. CAMERA AND ALGORITHMS

Our prototype system uses a small, endoscopic camera (*Awaiba NanEye GS Idule*) mounted on top of the finger to capture images of the touched surface (Figure 1). The camera provides 640×640px images with a 30° field of view and can focus from 15mm.

To identify textures, we use the classification approach described in [4], which combines two complementary features to improve classification performance. First, we detect deep convolutional activation features (DeCAF) using a pre-trained deep convolutional network. As in [4], we repurpose the *AlexNet* [7] image classifier for identifying textures by removing the last two softmax and fully connected layers. Second, we use scale-invariant feature transform (SIFT [8]) descriptors extracted densely at multiple scales. The SIFT features are combined into a single descriptor using the Improved Fisher Vector (IFV [9]) formulation. The result is two feature vectors of length 4,096 and 40,960 for DeCAF and IFV respectively, which are used as inputs (separately or concatenated together) to a support vector machine for classification.

We focus primarily on visual *texture* classification since few researchers have attempted to make this information accessible for visually impaired users. However, our *color* recognition approach

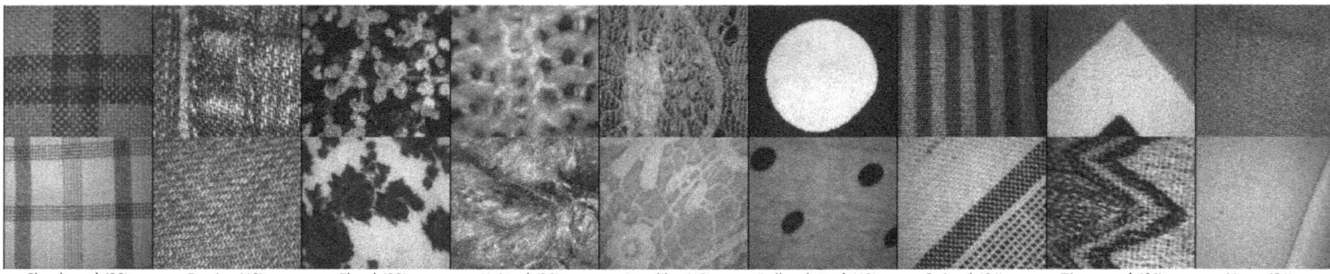

Figure 2. Examples of the 9 clothing textures included in our dataset. The numbers in parentheses indicate the quantity captured for each class.

also has some advantages over existing solutions. Our wearable system uses touch-based interactions to constrain the camera's distance from the target surface and includes a bright LED to overpower the effects of ambient light (allowing for more consistent color recognition). Furthermore, we use a color detection approach based on superpixel segmentation [1] that allows multiple colors to be detected simultaneously (one per superpixel) helping users to better understand how an article of clothing appears.

3. DATASET AND EXPERIMENTS

The results reported in [4] were promising but did not focus on clothing textures and used images from online sources that differed greatly from our target domain. It was unclear how well the approach would extend to close-up images captured by a finger-mounted camera. To answer this question, we collected a dataset of 520 images across 29 articles of clothing, which spanned 9 clothing texture categories (Figure 2). These categories are a subset of the 47 included in [4]; we eliminated categories that rarely describe clothing (*e.g.*, "bubbly"), combined those that are visually similar (*e.g.*, "striped", "banded), and added two new categories: "denim" and "none". We controlled for and varied the distance (5cm *vs.* 12cm), rotation (0° *vs.* 45°), and perspective of the camera (90° *vs.* 45°), as well as the tension of the fabric (taut *vs.* hanging naturally). The dataset was collected by one person over three months.

To assess performance, we conducted a classification experiment computing accuracy as the number of test samples classified correctly. We also explored the effect of training set size to determine whether a small user-gathered training set would be sufficient. Figure 3 shows classification accuracy using DeCAF and IFV features separately and together as the training set size increases averaged across 40 random samples.

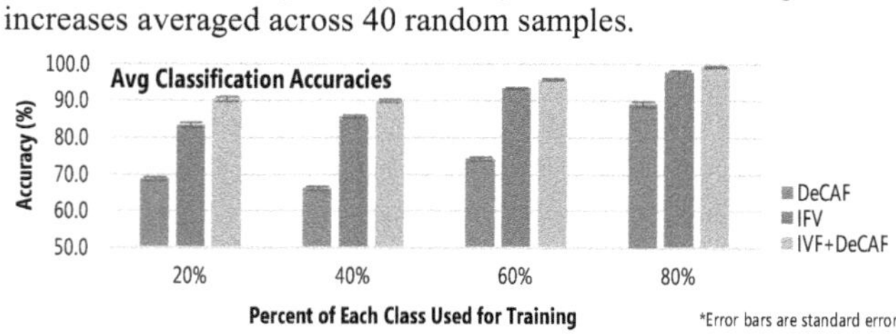

Figure 3. Accuracies using individual and combined features.

As with [4], in each case the combined result is best, demonstrating the advantage of using complementary texture features. However, unlike [4], our DeCAF results are significantly lower than IFV. This is likely because DeCAF requires a large amount of training data to perform well while IFV does well even with the small amount that we provided.

4. DISCUSSION AND OPEN QUESTIONS

Our results demonstrate the feasibility of recognizing clothing textures using close-up images from a finger-mounted camera. Even with a small amount of training data across a variety of variables, we achieve high classification accuracy. However, our dataset was captured under controlled conditions, so future work will need to investigate performance with a much larger, more varied dataset and conduct a user study with a real-time system.

We envision a few different scenarios in which visually impaired users could benefit from our proposed system. First, users could train the system to recognize customized articles of clothing in their own closet gathering training examples like those included in our dataset. Our results suggest reliable performance even with a small number of training examples. Second, we could draw upon larger texture datasets such as [4] to train a general-purpose classifier, which would allow users to access information about unfamiliar articles of clothing (*e.g.*, while shopping). Our approach should allow users to quickly explore a surface and combine their sense of touch with visual texture and color information to make informed decisions about what to wear or buy. How best to convey this information to visually impaired users is an open question.

5. ACKNOWLEDGMENTS

This work was supported by the Office of the Assistant Secretary of Defense for Health Affairs under Award W81XWH-14-1-0617.

6. REFERENCES

[1] Achanta, R., *et al.*. 2012. SLIC Superpixels Compared to State-of-the-Art Superpixel Methods. *TPAMI*. 34, 11: 2274–2282.

[2] Brytech Color Teller: *http://www.brytech.com/colorteller/*.

[3] Burton, M.A., *et al.*. 2012. Crowdsourcing Subjective Fashion Advice Using VizWiz: Challenges and Opportunities. *Proc. ASSETS 2012*, 135–142.

[4] Cimpoi, M., *et al.*. 2014. Describing Textures in the Wild. *Proc. CVPR 2014*, 3606–3613.

[5] GreenGar Studios. Color Identifier: *https://itunes.apple.com/us/app/color-identifier/id363346987?mt=8*.

[6] Findlater, L., *et al.*. 2015. Supporting Everyday Activities for Persons with Visual Impairments Through Computer Vision-Augmented Touch. *Proc. ASSETS* 2015, 383–384.

[7] Krizhevsky, A., *et al.*. 2012. ImageNet classification with deep convolutional neural networks. *Proc. NIPS 2012,* 1097–1105.

[8] Lowe, D.G. 2004. Distinctive image features from scale-invariant keypoints. *IJCV*. 60, 2 (2004), 91–110.

[9] Perronnin, F., Sánchez, J. and Mensink, T. 2010. Improving the Fisher Kernel for Large-Scale Image Classification. Springer, Berlin, Heidelberg. 143–156.

[10] Stearns, L., *et al.* 2016. Evaluating Haptic and Auditory Directional Guidance to Assist Blind People in Reading Printed Text Using Finger-Mounted Cameras. *TACCESS*. 9, 1: 1–38.

[11] Tian, Y. and Yuan, S. 2010. Clothes Matching for Blind and Color Blind People. *Computers Helping People with Special Needs SE - 48*. Springer Berlin Heidelberg. 324–331.

[12] Yang, X.-D., *et al.*. 2012. Magic finger: always-available input through finger instrumentation. *Proc. UIST 2012*, 147–156.

[13] Yuan, S., *et al.*. 2011. Clothing matching for visually impaired persons. *Technology and Disability*. 23, 2 (Jan. 2011), 75–85.

Sign'Maths: An Interactive Dictionary in French Sign Language

Camille Nadal
IRIT
Université Toulouse 3 – Paul Sabatier
118 route de Narbonne
31062 Toulouse, France
Camille.Nadal@irit.fr

Christophe Collet
IRIT
Université Toulouse 3 – Paul Sabatier
118 route de Narbonne
31062 Toulouse, France
collet@irit.fr

ABSTRACT

Sign'Maths is an online dictionary that gives deaf students access to mathematical definitions in Sign Language. In this study, we investigate a new approach that uses Sign Language as a means to navigate and access online content.

CCS Concepts

•Human-centered computing → Accessibility technologies; •Applied computing → *Interactive learning environments;*

Keywords

Deaf Education, Sign Language, ICT in Education

1. INTRODUCTION

Sign Language (SL) has been legally recognized in France by the Handicap law in 2005 which underlines its educative, pedagogical and cultural legitimacy [2]. Since then, Deaf youths have access to education in French SL. However, though teaching is provided in their mother tongue – i.e. French SL -, the majority of the pedagogical resources uses written French. Thus, an important part of the learning process relies on the students' ability to read and understand French as their second language. Moreover, when learning new concepts, Deaf students have to learn related French vocabulary in order to understand the given examples and exercises' instructions. Consequently, their knowledge of French will likely impact their learning in all disciplines. This is particularly true in science education where Deaf students have a problem in visualizing abstract concepts [7]. We aim at lowering the importance of French language skills in Deaf education by providing educational contents in SL. In this paper, we introduce Sign'Maths, a web-based dictionary that gives access to learning contents in French SL.

ASSETS'17, Oct. 29–Nov. 1, 2017, *Baltimore, MD, USA*

ACM ISBN 978-1-4503-4926-0/17/10.

DOI: http://dx.doi.org/10.1145/3132525.3134804

2. RELATED WORK

In the 21st century, we have observed numerous attempts to give Deaf Community access to ICT (Information and Communication Technologies) and e-learning. In 2004, Straetz *et al.* [8] created a bilingual web-based learning system for Deaf adults which allowed to retrieve a German SL video translation for each text block of the page. The same year, Debvc and Peljhan [3] provided a web-based tool that allowed the students to watch video clips of lectures along with slides and subtitles. In 2007 in Jordan, Khwaldeh *et al.* [5] developed interactive content and interactive tools to enable "interactivity between instructor/teacher and Deaf pupils". This included online conferences and chatting rooms where pupils can communicate with teachers or with one another. Augmented Reality was first investigated by Zainuddin *et al.* as a means to support Deaf Education. They created in 2010 an AR Science book [9] to help Deaf students in visualizing abstracts concepts. In 2014, Jones *et al.* [4] studied how a head-mounted display could help pupils in learning to read by visualizing both signs and words. Another study conducted by Adamo-Villani and Anasingaraju [1] based on the use of Augmented Reality was carried out in 2017. It focused on mathematics learning for the Deafs and used 3D holograms to translate lessons in real time. In the light of that, a website offering education support for abstract concepts learning and that would make possible to access lessons using SL only would be an interesting approach to explore.

3. CONTRIBUTION

Sign'Maths consists of an online interactive dictionary for mathematics addressed to Deaf students. We investigate if an interface entirely in SL would be meaningful for users. Sign'Maths offers definitions of concepts introduced in high school and college. Indeed, the lack of standardization of signs related to these concepts impedes the understanding and the exchange of information among students and teachers. To address the lack of signs to express mathematics concepts, a group of teachers expert in SL and mathematics is working on the creation new signs. They are also producing videos in SL of mathematics definitions that are progressively added to Sign'Maths.

Figure 1 presents a first version of Sign'Maths where navigation and access to definitions are made through SL videos. We chose to make videos play in a loop, an approach supported by Jean-Louis Brugeille [6], a Deaf expert in SL and academic inspector for teaching in SL.

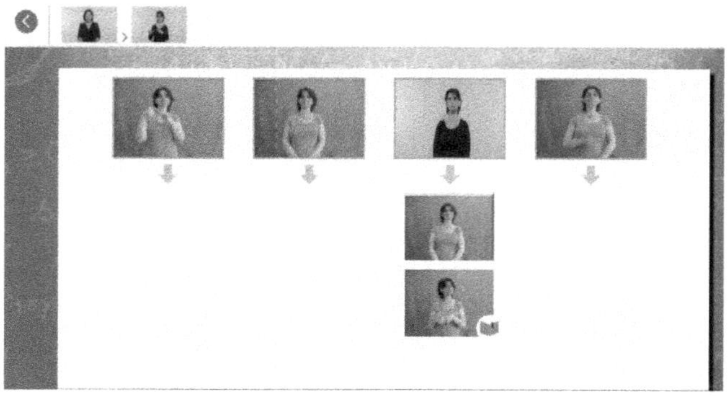

Figure 1: Sign'Maths with access by Sign Language

A framed tile represents a chapter and an arrow points at the notions it covers. A notion that could be expanded into sub-notions is represented by a stack. Clicking on the book icon open the notion's definition. Ariane's thread and back button allow easy return to previous chapters.

Another version, where SL videos are replaced by graphics illustrating underlying concepts and subtitled in French, can be seen in Figure 2.

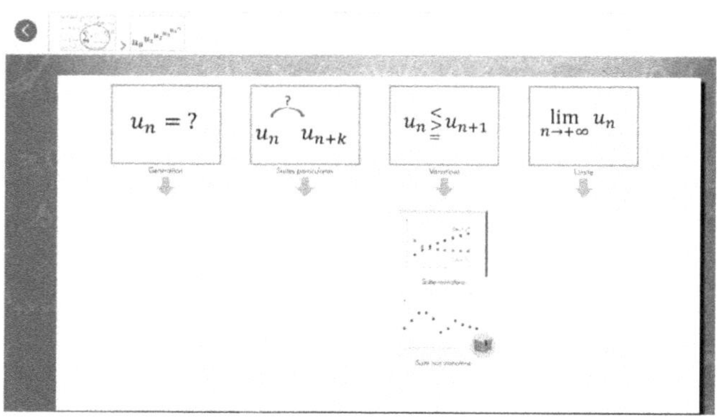

Figure 2: Sign'Maths with access by French and graphics

In this version, SL translation is available on tiles mouse-over. Thus, the user can get the same information in three different forms.

Finally, the definition page is shown in Figure 3. The definition video may include hypermedia links redirecting to prerequisites' definitions when needed. A User-Centered Design approach has been followed to design and test the interfaces. Tests are currently in progress to evaluate the performance and satisfaction of participants when using Sign'Maths SL interface and determine how French indications impacts the usability and User Experience.

4. CONCLUSIONS AND PROSPECTS

Sign'Maths stands out by putting SL at the core of a pedagogical tool. Tests primary results show that participants appreciate the extensive use of SL in the interface. However, due to the ubiquity of written text in their Education, they agree that French indications are needed to support navigation and would be helpful for a search-by-word tool. Finally, participants appreciate the use of graphics to complement SL and written information. Because mathematics cover abstract concepts, the use of visual information such as diagrams and signs can have a positive impact on Deaf students' learning. The search of unknown mathematical words will be addressed by adding a text search function. Future work will investigate how an entry in SL can be used to search for signs in video definitions.

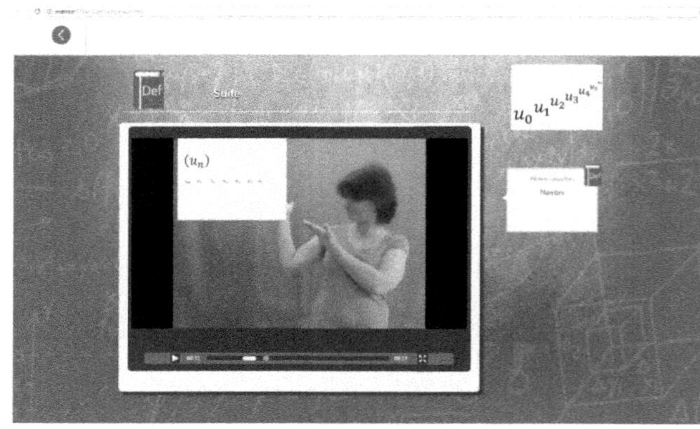

Figure 3: Definition page of "convergent sequence"

5. REFERENCES

[1] N. Adamo-Villani and S. Anasingaraju. *Holographic Signing Avatars for Deaf Education*, pages 54–61. Springer International Publishing, 2017.

[2] P. Dalle. La place de la langue des signes dans le milieu institutionnel de l'éducation : enjeux, blocages et évolution. *Langue française*, 137(1):32–59, 2003.

[3] M. Debevc and Ž. Peljhan. The role of video technology in on-line lectures for the deaf. *Disability and Rehabilitation*, 26(17):1048–1059, Sept. 2004.

[4] M. Jones, N. Bench, and S. Ferons. Vocabulary acquisition for deaf readers using augmented technology. In *VAAT, 2014 2nd Workshop on Virtual and Augmented Assistive Technology*, pages 13–15. IEEE, 2014.

[5] S. Khwaldeh, N. Matar, and Z. Hunaiti. Interactivity in deaf classroom using centralised e-learning system in jordan. In *The 8th Annual Postgraduate Symposium on the Convergence of Telecommunications, Networking and Broadcasting*, Liverpool, 2007.

[6] E. Leroy and J.-L. Brugeille. Ressource en auto-formation : Langue des signes française : quelle évaluation pour une langue sans écriture ? https://goo.gl/C7fBbM. Video in French SL, 2015-02.

[7] N. Megat Mohd. Zainuddin, H. Badioze Zaman, and A. Ahmad. *Learning Science Using AR Book: A Preliminary Study on Visual Needs of Deaf Learners*, pages 844–855. Springer Berlin Heidelberg, Berlin, Heidelberg, 2009.

[8] K. Straetz, A. Kaibel, V. Raithel, M. Specht, K. Grote, and F. Kramer. An e-learning environment for deaf adults. In *Conference proceedings 8th ERCIM workshop "user interfaces for all"*, 2004.

[9] N. M. M. Zainuddin, H. B. Zaman, and A. Ahmad. Developing augmented reality book for deaf in science: the determining factors. In *ITSim, 2010 International Symposium in Information Technology*, volume 1, pages 1–4. IEEE, 2010.

TacTILE: A Preliminary Toolchain for Creating Accessible Graphics with 3D-Printed Overlays and Auditory Annotations

Liang He[1,3] Zijian Wan[2] Leah Findlater[2,4] Jon E. Froehlich[1,3]

[1] Computer Science, [2] Information Studies, University of Maryland
{lianghe, ziwan, leahkf, jonf}@umd.edu

[3] Computer Science & Engineering University of Washington
{lianghe, jonf}@cs.uw.edu

[4] Human Centered Design & Engineering, University of Washington
leahkf@uw.edu

ABSTRACT

Tactile overlays with audio annotations can increase the accessibility of touchscreens for blind users; however, preparing these overlays is complex and labor intensive. We introduce *TacTILE*, a novel toolchain to more easily create tactile overlays with audio annotations for arbitrary touchscreen graphics (*e.g.*, graphs, pictures, maps). The workflow includes: (i) an annotation tool to add audio to graphical elements, (ii) a fabrication process that generates 3D-printed tactile overlays, and (iii) a custom app for the user to explore graphics with these overlays. We close with a pilot study with one blind participant who explores three examples (*floor plan*, *photo*, and *chart*), and a discussion of future work.

CCS Concepts

• **Human-centered computing ~ Accessibility technologies**

Keywords

Blind users; visual impairments; tactile overlays; 3D printing; accessible graphics; speech; touchscreens.

1. INTRODUCTION

While mobile screen readers have improved access to touchscreen devices for people with visual impairments, graphical information such as maps, charts, and images are still difficult to convey and understand. One solution is to employ physical overlays that are placed on top of the screen, providing tactile information and constraining input to only specific locations [1,4,6,7]. The *Talking Tactile Tablet* [5], for example, allows users to place tactile sheets (*e.g.*, made from swell paper) on top of a tablet that can then sense a user's touches. *LucentMaps* [2] uses 3D-printed tactile maps with embedded capacitive material that, when overlaid on a touchscreen device, can generate audio in response to touch. Finally, *Touchplates* [4] employs physical overlays with cutouts that can be recognized by a touchscreen device and may be extended to domain-specific tactile graphics (though the focus was on input such as keyboard guides).

An important limitation with these tactile overlay approaches, however, is scalability: each graphic (map, chart, image) requires its own custom overlay and complementary audio annotations. These are typically not easy to create. A related solution to this scalability problem—though not focused on touchscreen overlays—is Façade [3], which allows blind users to take a picture of a smooth appliance interface (*e.g.*, microwave keypad) and semi-

ASSETS '17, October 29-November 1, 2017, Baltimore, MD, USA
© 2017 Copyright is held by the owner/author(s).
ACM ISBN 978-1-4503-4926-0/17/10. https://doi.org/10.1145/3132525.3134818

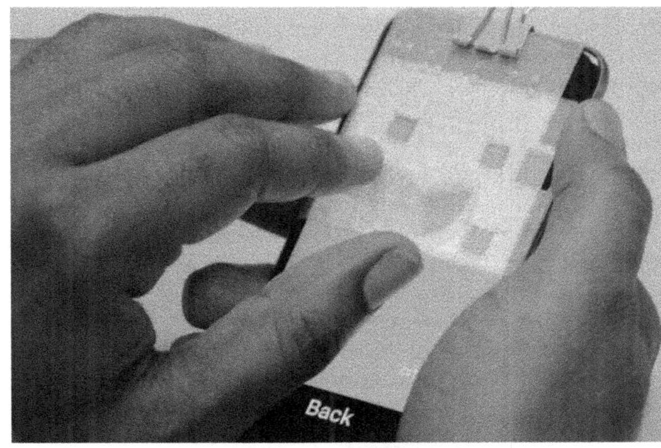

Figure 1. A blind user using an overlay to explore a pie chart on a phone. The cutouts (in green) allows the user to interact with the touchscreen and hear relevant audio descriptions at those locations.

automatically generates a 3D-printed guide to place on the interface, including braille in place of the original printed text. However, Façade is limited to relatively simple appliance interfaces and does not include audio annotations.

In this poster paper, we introduce *TacTILE*, a novel toolchain to support the creation of audio-annotated 3D-printed tactile overlays for touchscreens. TacTILE includes (i) an annotation tool to add audio to graphical elements, (ii) a fabrication process that generates the 3D-printed overlays, and (iii) a custom app for the user to explore graphics with these overlays. As initial work, each pipeline stage is preliminary—*e.g.*, the tactile overlays are generated manually rather than automatically—but our ultimate vision is to dramatically lower the barrier to generating tactile overlays with audio annotations for touchscreen applications. We close with brief results from a pilot study with one blind participant and discuss future work.

2. PROTOTYPE TacTILE PIPELINE

We have focused on three areas thus far: (i) building a GUI-based annotation tool that allows adding audio to the touchscreen element(s) exposed by the tactile overlay; (ii) creating a fabrication process to generate 3D-printed textural overlays with cutouts from 2D graphics; and (iii) implementing an iOS app that allows users to interact with the audio-annotated tactile overlays (Figure 1). The first two stages currently require a sighted user, after which a blind user can download the design to print and load into our custom app. We envision that, ultimately, the second stage will be automatically executed and also be accessible to blind users.

2.1 Annotation Tool

To support the ability to add audio recordings to graphics, we implemented a GUI-based annotation tool using *Processing*, *Minim*[1], and *ControlP5*[2]. In this tool, a sighted user can load an

[1] http://code.compartmental.net/tools/minim/

[2] http://www.sojamo.de/libraries/controlP5/

image by clicking the 'LOAD' button. Annotations are added by clicking the 'TAG' button, placing a rectangle (which represents the interactive cutout), and linking to a pre-recorded audio clip button (Figure 2a; the active annotation is shown in green). While we envision directly embedding the audio into the graphic file as metadata for flexible reuse, we currently link to the external file which is used in our custom app later.

2.2 3D-printed Tactile Overlay

The second step in the process is to design the tactile overlay both to convey graphical information through the 3D print (*e.g.,* via textures, raised lines, *etc.*), as well as to allow access to the audio annotations via cutouts in the print (Figure 2). Overlays are composed of three parts: the name of the overlay in braille, the 3D-printed tactile elements representing the underlying graphic, and the audio-encoded cutouts (Figure 2b). As a proof-of-concept, we created the tactile overlays manually: we first generated a 3D model from the 2D graphic using *Image to Lithophane*, an online sketch-to-3D model tool (http://3dp.rocks/lithophane). We then used *Rhino* (rhino3d.com) to create the braille name and cutout regions for the audio tags. Multiple 3D-printed layers are used to distinguish foreground and background, especially for photos, in the overlay. Ultimately, we envision that our toolchain will do this automatically and allow the user to better customize the tactile elements.

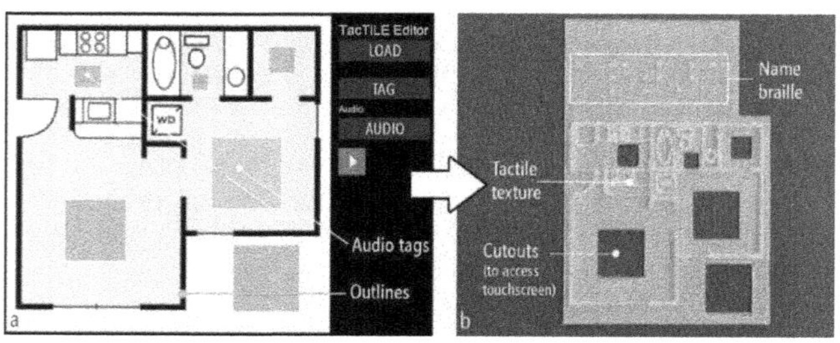

Figure 2. Converting a floor plan from 2D graphic to 3D-printed tile: (a) the annotation tool; (b) 3D-printed tactile overlay.

2.3 Interactive App

The third step employs our custom iOS app. Within the app, the blind user can use the tactile overlay with the app at any time by placing and aligning it at the top of the touchscreen and dictating the name (based on the braille). Interaction involves exploring the tactile overlay by touch and activating the pre-encoded audio annotations by tapping touchscreen areas exposed by the cutouts.

3. PILOT USER STUDY

As an initial pilot study to assess the usability of the interactive overlays created by our workflow, we designed six overlays in three graphical categories for an iPhone 6S sized device: two floor plans, two charts (pie and bar), and two photos (people and scenery). We recruited one male volunteer (39 years old; born with glaucoma and cataracts) who is proficient with screen readers and braille. The study session took ~1.5 hours. The participant was asked to explore the six graphics using the tactile overlays and our iOS app and to describe the details of each graphic. We then solicited open-ended concerns, suggestions, and comments on the overall experience.

Overall, the participant held a positive attitude toward the overlays and our app. First, he could correctly orient the tactile on the touchscreen. Then, he could identify major embedded information, such as graphical objects' spatial details in the floor plans and charts, but missed some details such as people's facial expressions in the photos. Except for the distracting guide lines in the bar chart, charts were reported as easiest to understand. Similar to [4], the participant suggested that cutout shapes other than rectangles might indicate different types of content or audio annotations. Also, the participant felt that some cutouts were too small, so future tools should limit sizes. Extending from prior work [5], standardized symbols or commonly used graphics were preferred rather than complex embossing on the overlay. For example, a simplified tree symbol can be used in photos instead of the current engraved replication of a real tree. Additionally, he suggested that it could be useful to receive feedback not only on the location being touched, but also about the surroundings. For example, touching a bedroom on the floor plan could also describe that the bedroom is to the left of the living room, providing more context.

4. CONCLUSION AND FUTURE WORK

Building on [2] and [4], we combine auditory feedback and 3D-printed tactile overlays to enhance the accessibility of touchscreens, particularly for graphical data. While each of these two components has been explored in prior work, our primary contribution is in designing a reusable workflow, called TacTILE, that enables the creation of audio-annotated 3D-printed tactile overlays for accessible graphics. In future work, we plan to (i) support different types of auditory feedback (*e.g.,* data sonification) using the cutout shapes; (ii) improve the algorithm for tactile overlay generation with standardized graphics; (iii) automate the generation of the physical overlay with braille and cutouts in a standalone program; and (iv) provide feedback on what parts of the graphic have already been explored so that the user can ensure they have covered all areas.

5. ACKNOWLEDGEMENTS

We thank the Columbia Lighthouse for the Blind for their support and participation in our pilot study.

6. REFERENCES

[1] El-Glaly,Y.N., Quek, F., Smith-Jackson, T. and Dhillon, G. 2013. Touch-screens are not tangible: fusing tangible interaction with touch glass in readers for the blind. In *Proc. of TEI '13*, 245-253.

[2] Götzelmann., T. 2016. LucentMaps: 3D Printed Audiovisual Tactile Maps for Blind and Visually Impaired People. In *Proc. of ASSETS '16*, 81-90.

[3] Guo, A., Kim, J., Chen, X., Yeh, T., Hudson, S.E., Mankoff, J. and Bigham, J.P. 2017. Facade : Auto-generating Tactile Interfaces to Appliances. In *Proc. of CHI '17*, 5826-5838.

[4] Kane, S.K., Morris, M.R. and Wobbrock, J.O. 2013. Touchplates: Low-cost Tactile Overlays for Visually Impaired Touch Screen Users. In *Proc. of ASSETS '15*, 22.

[5] Landua, S. and Wells, L. 2003. Merging Tactile Sensory Input and Audio Data by Means of The Talking Tactile Tablet. In *Proc. of Eurohaptics* (vol.3).

[6] McGookin, D., Brewster, S. and Jiang, W. 2008. Investigating touchscreen accessibility for people with visual impairments. In *Proc. of NordiCHI '08*, 298.

[7] Pawluk, D.T., Adams, R.J. and Kitada, R. 2015. Designing haptic assistive technology for individuals who are blind or visually impaired. *IEEE Transactions on Haptics* 8(3), 258–278.

Teaching Inclusive Thinking in Undergraduate Computing

Nidhi Palan
Golisano College of Computing and Information Sciences
Rochester Institute of Technology
Rochester, NY 14623 USA
nxp4195@rit.edu

Vicki Hanson, Matt Huenerfauth
Golisano College of Computing and Information Sciences
Rochester Institute of Technology
Rochester, NY 14623 USA
{vlh, matt.huenerfauth}@rit.edu

Stephanie Ludi
Department of Computer Science and Engineering
University of North Texas
Denton, TX USA
stephanie.ludi@unt.edu

ABSTRACT
With the increasing importance of accessibility awareness and knowledge as both a moral imperative and an employment differentiator, it is incumbent on educational programs to have demonstrated ability to teach these skills. We report on our year-long evaluation of university students' accessibility awareness and knowledge following a week of accessibility lectures as part of courses on Human-Computer Interaction (HCI). We report gains in awareness and knowledge when accessibility lectures were part of the course. We describe the test battery developed to measure these skills, and describe our ongoing longitudinal research to measure the effectiveness of several interventions for teaching inclusive thinking in undergraduate computing courses.

CCS Concepts
• Social and professional topics ~ Professional topics ~ Computing education • Human-centered computing ~ Accessibility

Keywords
Computer science education, accessibility, ethics

1. INTRODUCTION
We report on a study that investigates the efficacy of lectures about accessibility as a means of teaching inclusive thinking. There is a growing awareness among employers of the need to hire developers knowledgeable about accessibility and inclusion [2][6]. Despite calls for more accessibility-aware developers, even recent publications have noted the lack of principled methods for teaching accessibility [3][5]. Several approaches have been reported anecdotally, but there have been few attempts to measure outcomes. Most commonly, degree programs include accessibility content in upper-level undergraduate courses on accessibility, or in courses on related topics, e.g. human-computer interaction (HCI) [1][4][5][7].

2. METHOD
We used pre- and post-tests to measure changes in student attitudes and awareness about disability and creating accessible technology. The study was conducted as part of required courses in Information Technology (IT) and Software Engineering (SE). At Rochester Institute of Technology, students majoring in IT or SE are required to take a course in HCI (a separate course for each major). The HCI courses for both majors contain a semester-long project, in which teams of 4-5 students design a mobile app, website, or desktop application while following a design process and submitting progress reports. Both classes currently provide a week of lectures on: (1) diversity of human sensory abilities, including experiences of people with common visual impairments and who are Deaf/deaf or hard of hearing; (2) human motor system and various movement impairments; (3) diversity in human cognitive or learning abilities; (4) common assistive technologies for accessing computers (e.g. screen readers, magnification, alternative input tools); (5) U.S. legal requirements for technology accessibility; (6) key aspects of website design for accessibility (e.g. alt text, captioned media). In general, our survey questions (described below) are related to this lecture content. The survey began with an IRB approved informed consent statement, indicating that the questionnaire was voluntary and it would not affect the outcome of their course grades.

ASSETS'17, October 29-November 1, 2017, Baltimore, MD, USA

ACM ISBN 978-1-4503-4926-0/17/10...$15.00
DOI: https://doi.org/10.1145/3132525.3134808

2.1 Measurement Instruments
Participants in the pre- and post-tests (beginning and end of semester) completed the following battery of tests:

(1) Scenario: Participants were presented with the voting machine problem scenario from Ludi [4]. The scenario included requirements to design a voting kiosk for state elections. Participants were asked two open-ended questions about the scenario. **Design Question:** The first question asked them to discuss key points that they would keep in mind in the design of the voting system. **Evaluation Question:** The second question asked what potential addressed voters they would test the kiosk prototype with in order to gain feedback on the new design. The scenario did not mention disabilities. The two questions were designed to be unbiased/neutral, so any mentions of accessibility by the students were based on their awareness of accessibility importance in the design and evaluation of software.

(2) Accessibility Survey: This survey first asked about ***accessibility awareness***. Students were asked to indicate whether they either had *knowledge of* or *personal experience with* people with specific disabilities (low vision, blindness, hearing loss, autism, learning disabilities, intellectual disabilities, motor disabilities, or older people). For each, radio button options were used to indicate either a) *knowledge of* or b) *personal experience with* each case.

Second, there were questions about ***accessibility knowledge*** in design and development. Participants were asked to indicate whether they had *read about* (scored as 1 point) or *had done* (scored as 2 points) website development for people with disabilities (8 items with radio button choices).

Next, they were asked if they were *familiar with* (scored as 1 point) or had *taken into account* (scored as 2 points) each of several accessibility issues in web design (e.g., CSS, alternative text, colors, etc.) and if they had accounted for each when designing websites (10 items with radio button choices).

There was a further set of questions in which they were asked whether they were *familiar with* or had *taken into account* each of several accessibility issues in accessible software design (e.g., screen-reader interfaces, avoiding responses that require a fixed time limit, etc.) (6 items with radio button choices).

The final two items were Yes / No questions asking whether they had previously been involved in the design / development of websites or software and, if yes, whether accessibility issues had been taken into account (1 point for each "yes" response).

A SurveyMonkey survey was created with the above instruments, in the order above. Students in participating classes were asked to complete the pre-test during the first 2 weeks of the semester and the post-test during the last two weeks of the 16-week semester.

3. RESULTS

In our two semesters of testing, 49 students completed both the pre- and post-test. Our reported analyses were only on this sample who had completed scores for both.

3.1 Scenario

To evaluate whether students considered accessibility in the voting scenario, we assigned a binary score to participants' responses to each of the two open-ended questions: whether or not their response mentioned accessibility. Thus, for both pre- and post-testing, each student could have a score of 0, 1, or 2 – if they had mentioned accessibility in response to neither, one, or both of the questions.

There were more accessibility mentions at the end of the semester than at the beginning (for both, $Mdn = 1$, $Range = 0$ to 2). This repeated-measures ordinal data was analyzed using the Wilcoxon Signed-Rank test, with the pre- and post-test scores found to be statistically different ($W = -134$, $Z = -2.69$, $p<.01$, two-tailed).

Combining the pre- and post-test scores, accessibility was mentioned in 34% of the participants' responses to the **design question** and in 59% of their responses to the **evaluation question**. This difference in accessibility mentions for the two questions was significant, $X^2(1) = 12.46$, $p<.001$.

3.2 Accessibility Survey

For ***accessibility knowledge***, each student could receive a total score from 0 – 50. A Wilcoxon Signed Rank test ($W = 997$, $Z = 5.44$, $p<.001$, two-tailed) determined that the median accessibility knowledge scores were significantly higher in the post-test ($Mdn = 32$, $Range = 0$ to 35) than the pre-test ($Mdn = 18$, $Range = 0$ to 50).

4. DISCUSSION

Results reported here show gains in undergraduate students' ***accessibility awareness*** and ***accessibility knowledge*** following one week of lectures on people with disabilities and on accessibility in HCI courses. To our knowledge, this is the first such quantitative evidence. Important for future work is the demonstrated effectiveness of our battery in measuring such changes.

The voting scenario test in our battery found clear gains in students' considering users with disabilities in a design task. Using this scenario, Ludi [4] originally examined potential differences in inclusive thinking about software design and evaluation. We found the instrument also sensitive to detecting increased awareness following courses that contained accessibility lectures.

The accessibility survey developed for our research was a sensitive measure of changes in ***accessibility knowledge***. In contrast to no significant changes in ***accessibility awareness***, there were significant self-reported gains in ***accessibility knowledge*** following the week of lectures in HCI courses.

The measures of ***accessibility awareness*** and ***accessibility knowledge*** are broad categories, each with multiple aspects. We believe these categories are useful in considering whether varied teaching interventions promote an understanding of the technical aspects of accessibility and / or whether they promote an awareness of the need to consider accessibility requirements during development.

5. FUTURE WORK

The current work reports on one teaching intervention during the first year of a four-year longitudinal study. Our long-term project goal is to gather information about comparative longitudinal gains regarding of multiple teaching interventions. The full longitudinal study, in progress, examines the effectiveness of interventions involving a team project related to accessibility, a classroom interaction with someone having a disability, and a team project in which a team member has a disability.

6. ACKNOWLEDGMENTS

This material is based upon work supported by the National Science Foundation under award number 1540396. We thank Ashley Miller for her contributions to early phases of this research project.

7. REFERENCES

[1] *Computer Science Curriculum 2013: Curriculum Guidelines for Undergraduate Degree Programs in Computer Science*. 2013. Retrieved 20 April, 2017 from https://www.acm.org/education/CS2013-final-report.pdf.

[2] Ladner, R.E., May, M. 2017. Teaching Accessibility. In *Proceedings of the 2017 ACM SIGCSE Technical Symposium on Computer Science Education* (SIGCSE '17). ACM, New York, NY, USA, 691-692.

[3] Lewthwaite, S., Sloan, D. 2016. Exploring pedagogical culture for accessibility education in computing science. In *Proceedings of the 13th Web for All Conference* (W4A '16). ACM, New York, NY, USA, Article 3, 4 pages.

[4] Ludi, S. 2007. Introducing accessibility requirements through external stakeholder utilization in an undergraduate requirements engineering course. In *Proceedings of the 29th international conference on Software Engineering (ICSE '07).* IEEE Computer Society, Washington, DC, USA, 736-743. DOI=10.1109/ICSE.2007.46

[5] Putnam, C., Dahman, M., Rose, E., Cheng, J., Bradford, G. 2016. Best Practices for Teaching Accessibility in University Classrooms: Cultivating Awareness, Understanding, and Appreciation for Diverse Users. *ACM Trans. Access. Comput.* 8, 4, Article 13 (March 2016), 26 pages. DOI=http://dx.doi.org/10.1145/2831424

[6] Teach Access. 2017. Retrieved April 28, 2017 from http://teachaccess.org

[7] Shinohara, K., Bennett, C. L., Wobbrock. J. O. 2016. How designing for people with and without disabilities shapes student design thinking. In *Proc. 9th international ACM SIGACCESS conference on Computers and accessibility (Assets'16).* ACM, New York, NY, USA, 123-130.

The Accessibility of MOOCs for Blind Learners

Aleksandra Królak
Lodz University of Technology
Wólczańska 211/215
90-924 Łódź, Poland
+48 426312715
akrolak@p.lodz.pl

Weiqin Chen
HiOA
PO box 4 St. Olavs plass
0130 Oslo, Norway
+47 67238671
weiqin.chen@hioa.no

Norun C. Sanderson
HiOA
PO box 4 St. Olavs plass
0130 Oslo, Norway
+47 67238673
nsand@hioa.no

Siri Kessel
HiOA
PO box 4 St. Olavs plass
0130 Oslo, Norway
+47 67238672
siri.kessel@hioa.no

ABSTRACT

The development of Massive Open Online Courses (MOOCs) has provided unique learning opportunities for many people. In the meantime, the lack of accessibility in some MOOCs has also created barriers for diverse learners. In this paper, we present the preliminary results from a study on the accessibility a selected set of MOOCs on the Coursera platform for blind learners who use screen readers and Braille to interact with computers and mobile devices.

CCS Concepts

• **Human-centered computing→ Accessibility →Empirical Studies in accessibility**

Keywords

Massive Open Online Course (MOOC); Accessibility; Blind; Screen reader; Braille

1. INTRODUCTION

According to the World Health Organization (WHO), an estimated 285 million people worldwide are visually impaired, of which 39 million are blind and 246 have low vision [5]. Massive Open Online Courses (MOOCs), as a type of e-learning and distance education, provide unique learning opportunities for underprivileged people, people with disabilities, elderly, and people who live in countries with poor infrastructure. However, the lack of accessibility in MOOCs has also created barriers for diverse learners. Blind learners often face challenges such as lack of support for keyboard navigation and poor compatibility with screen readers. According to [3], there has been limited research focused on accessibility within MOOCs and particularly in user-based empirical studies.

The goal of this research is to identify accessibility issues in diverse MOOCs for blind learners by conducting user-based studies and provide recommendations for improving the accessibility.

2. METHOD

This exploratory study took a qualitative approach towards identifying barriers and issues encountered by blind users of screen readers and Braille devices partaking in MOOC courses. Barriers and issues encountered by users are often found in the user interface of a MOOC platform. Consequently, to ensure all participants were exposed to the same user interface, the researchers chose one MOOC provider, Coursera, as the case for this study. Typically, MOOC courses continue over several weeks, with weekly modules and exercises for students. Although observation sessions can disclose many barriers and issues encountered by users, it is not feasible to observe users over a longer period such as the length of a full MOOC course. Therefore, this study based its data collection on weekly self-reporting from participants completing the MOOC course in their own home. Thus, the methods chosen for data collection approach contain elements of case studies and diary studies.

Seven participants, of which 3 female and 4 male, were recruited through the Polish Association of the Blind in cooperation with the Institute of Electronics at the Lodz University of Technology. The participants were between 38 and 52 years of age with a good level of English proficiency. All of them use computers daily both at work and at home, including office tools, email clients, and browsers. All participants use screen readers for both PC and mobile devices, and two of the participants also use Braille technologies such as Electronic Braille Notetaker and Braille Display. Three of them had some experience with online learning. The participants were given information both orally and via email about what was expected of participants, their rights to withdraw from the study, and the agreed disbursement, before agreeing to partake in the study. All participants also signed a consent form.

Each participant was asked to complete a 4-week MOOC course offered by Coursera. They could choose a course topic within the area of their own interest. The only limitations given by the researchers were the length of the course (4 weeks) and the course provider (Coursera). Participants were asked to take notes on any barriers and issues encountered during the course, and report these to the researchers after each completed course week. The reporting was done through answering predefined open-ended questions in a document and sending the document via email. Before the start of the MOOC courses, each participant answered a semi-structured questionnaire to collect demographical information about participants, including assistive technology and previous experience with online learning.

3. PRELIMINARY RESULTS

The preliminary results of the study are presented in this section according to the four principles in the Web Content Accessibility Guidelines (WCAG 2.0) [4].

3.1 Perceivable

This principle requires that users must be able to perceive all the information and user interface components presented. The accessibility issues reported by the participants testing Coursera courses include lack of labels for buttons, especially the search form button and buttons in forms for entering text answers for test questions, lack of alternative text for graphical elements, and auto-start of time-based media that disturbs the screen readers.

ASSETS '17, October 29-November 1, 2017, Baltimore, MD, USA.

ACM ISBN 978-1-4503-4926-0/17/10.
https://doi.org/10.1145/3132525.3134796

3.2 Operable

This principle requires that the user must be able to operate and navigate with any type of input device, at his or her own pace, and receive feedback in case of errors. The main issue reported was related to poor header structure that caused problems with navigation. Examples of this problem are at the Home Page, where the first level header is followed by a third level header immediately, or at the My Account Settings page, which starts with a third level header instead of a first level one. Another issue was the lack of keyboard access to radio buttons for self-assessment. The buttons were clickable, but contained no text description. The participants were provided with enough time to complete the tasks and reported good error management.

3.3 Understandable

This principle requires that the content must be understandable for users. The participants reported that the courses have a clear, logical structure, there are no unexpected elements used, and all instructions are simple and easy to understand. The only issue was the lack of confirmation before submitting some information.

3.4 Robust

This principle requires that the content must be created in such a way that it can be interpreted reliably by as many user agents and assistive technologies as possible. The participants used a large number of tools for accessing the courses, including Windows, macOS, iOS, Apple TV and Android operating systems and web browsers such as Internet Explorer, Google Chrome, Mozilla Firefox, and Safari, as well as assistive technologies such as NVDA and Voice Over screen readers. The participants were able to complete the chosen courses with any of the third party technologies. However, some compatibility issues were reported by the participants, including incorrect reading of the button labels with links when using Google Chrome and very slow operation of Internet Explorer when used with the NVDA screen reader.

4. DISCUSSION

Studies conducted by Al-Mouh et al. [1] involved two blind or partially sighted learners and Coursera courses in selected disciplines including technology, design, humanities and physics. Bohnsack & Puh [2] conducted accessibility evaluation of five MOOC platforms (Udacity, Coursera, edX, OpenCourseWorld and Iversity) with blind users. The main issue identified for all MOOCs was the lack of correct language markers for screen readers. This issue was also reported by the participants in our research.

The above-mentioned user evaluations, both performed in 2013, show that the participants faced problems such as lack of notification for modal window opening, no alternative text for graphical elements, inappropriate heading structure disturbing the operation of screen readers, lack of labels for buttons, and no keyboard access to some form functions. All these were confirmed by the participants in our study. Since the two previous studies in 2013 some improvements have been made by Coursera, including better error handling, logical structure of the courses, and compatibility with mobile browsers.

Our study revealed additional problems with the accessibility of the selected. By default the auto-play option is enabled. It is difficult for blind learners to quickly locate Pause and Play buttons in order to stop the playback since there are no ARIA tags for these buttons. We have also found that different subpages in a course have the same title or invalid titles and include unnamed links which cause difficulties in navigation, e.g. on the welcome page of "Gender and Sexuality: Diversity and Inclusion in the Workplace" course link is read in the form "b14a700a78d0a0d225271160521e2a6c". There are also different accessibility issues in different web browsers, for example, Internet Explorer slows down the work of screen reader when playing multimedia content, in Chrome the links are read as webpage addresses in some courses (e.g."Dog Emotion and Cognition"), when trying to sign in to courses using mobile Firefox browser, the screen displays information that this browser does not support Coursera courses. Another identified problem is the lack of descriptions of radio buttons in the self-assessment form and course assessment form. Blind learners are not able to complete them because it is not possible for them to know which box to click. There is also lack of keyboard access to these items.

In our study, the iOS mobile app for Coursera was also tested. The main issues identified were the lack of access to the transcription of subtitles for some videos, lack of assigned roles to several elements (e.g. Course Info, Notes, Resources), no reaction to some gestures controlling Voice Over screen readers and limited amount of information presented in comparison to the full web version.

5. CONCLUSION AND ONGOING WORK

In this paper we have presented the preliminary results from a qualitative study aiming at identifying the accessibility issues in MOOCs for blind learners who use screen readers and Braille to interact with computers and mobile devices. Despite of the accessibility policy and continuous efforts by Coursera in making the platform and courses accessible, our participants still encountered barriers and issues when taking the MOOCs. The data analysis used for attaining the preliminary results presented in this paper was an informal analysis where the researchers read the delivered reports and summarized the feedback from the participants. Currently we are planning a more systematic analysis, e.g., Deductive Thematic Analysis, on the qualitative data collected in the study. Furthermore, we plan to recruit more participants with diverse visual impairments, extend the scope of the study to more MOOCs and platforms, and conduct in-depth interview and user testing to gain a better understanding of the accessibility of MOOCs for learners with visual impairments.

6. ACKNOWLEDGMENTS

The authors would like to thank all the participants in the study for their invaluable feedback and the anonymous reviewers for their constructive comments.

7. REFERENCES

[1] Al-Mouh, N. A., Al-Khalifa, A. S. and Al-Khalifa, H. S. 2014. A first look into MOOCs accessibility: The case of Coursera. *Computers Helping People with Special Needs. Springer International Publishing. Lecture Notes in Com- puter Science*, 8547 LNCS (PART 1), 145–152.

[2] Bohnsack, M. and Puhl, S. 2014. Accessibility of MOOCs. *International Conference on Computers for Handicapped Persons. Springer International Publishing*. 141–144.

[3] Iniesto, F., McAndrew, P., Minocha, S. and Coughlan, T. 2016. The current *state of accessibility of MOOCs: What are the next* steps? *Proc. of Open Education Global Conference 2016*, (April 12-14, 2016), Krakow, Poland.

[4] WCAG 2.0 http://www.w3.org/TR/WCAG20/

[5] WHO | Visual impairment and blindness www.who.int/mediacentre/factsheets/fs282/en

Towards Brain-Computer Interface (BCI) and Gestural-Based Authentication for Individuals who are Blind

Sidas Saulynas and Ravi Kuber
UMBC
Baltimore MD 21250
{saulyn1, rkuber} @umbc.edu

ABSTRACT

This paper describes an exploratory study examining the feasibility of using Brain-Computer Interface (BCI) and gestural technologies to support individuals who are blind during the authentication process. Four legally-blind participants were asked to don the Emotiv Epoc headset, and authenticate entry using gestural cues, emotional cues and mental commands. Findings highlighted that while BCI and gestural technologies may be slower and less accurate to use compared to four digit PINs, levels of perceived security were higher, as some of these cues were thought to be more difficult for third parties to replicate. A trade-off between perceived security and usability was evident.

CCS Concepts

Human-centered computing → Accessibility → Empirical studies in accessibility.

Keywords

Authentication; Blind; Brain-Computer Interface technologies; Gestural technologies;

1. INTRODUCTION

Maintaining privacy and control of one's data has become more of a challenge due to the number of threats present. Tokens which are inputted for device authentication are vulnerable to various eavesdropping or observation attacks [6]. Protecting one's data from being compromised requires users to be vigilant of their surroundings. However, for individuals who are blind, difficulties are faced during this process. In addition to the threat of observation attacks which may go undetected, any negative interaction experience when accessing authentication mechanisms can be exacerbated for blind users due to such factors as restrictions imposed by assistive technologies and inappropriate design of authentication interfaces [4].

If tokens could be entered inconspicuously, input would be less vulnerable to observation attacks. Brain-Computer Interface (BCI) technologies offer potential to support the authentication process. Thoughts cannot be viewed by observers. No other current input modality possesses this true inconspicuous input quality [5], which offers promise to users whose visual channel is blocked or restricted. In this paper, we describe a study examining the feasibility of BCI and gestural technologies, as an alternative input modality for inputting a 4-token authentication code.

ASSETS '17, October 29-November 1, 2017, Baltimore, MD, USA

ACM ISBN 978-1-4503-4926-0/17/10.
https://doi.org/10.1145/3132525.3134785

2. RELATED WORK

Through a series of semi-structured interviews, Ahmed et al. [1] revealed that when considering physical privacy, blind users' concerns include lack of independence (reliance on others) and worries regarding eavesdropping from others. To provide more accessible alternatives for authentication, technologies have been developed to support individuals with visual impairments. Examples include the PassChords solution [2] where authentication tokens are entered by tapping several times on a touch surface with one or more fingers. Other solutions include sequences of pin-based patterns, which were shown to be memorable over a period of time [4]. While studies have considered the potential of BCI to support authentication (e.g. Thorpe et al. [7]), these have yet to exploit the range of cues which can be obtained using off-the-shelf technologies or consider the needs of users with diverse abilities. Our study described in this paper, has aimed to examine the feasibility of using the Emotiv Epoc headset [3] for this purpose.

3. METHODOLOGY

Four legally-blind participants were recruited for purposes of the study (3 males, 1 female, mean age: 32.25). They were introduced to the Emotiv Epoc headset and accompanying software. Mental commands, emotional states and facial expressions (termed "gestural cues") can be obtained from the user using the headset.

Table 1. Input tokens used for each authentication task

Type	Token 1	Token 2	Token 3	Token 4
4-digit PIN	2	4	8	9
Facial Exp.	Blink	Smile	Clinch Teeth	Left Wink
Emotion State	Excite	Excite	Frustr.	Engage
Mental Cmd.	Push	Pull	Lift	Drop
Mixed Methods	Lift	Engage	Blink	Push

Participants were then asked to use an adapted version of an authentication interface described in an earlier study [5], where additional auditory cues were presented to provide greater awareness of content on the graphical interface. To simulate as closely as possible, the familiar task of 4-digit authentication, participants were asked to input four prescribed sets of mental commands, emotional states and gestural cues (termed "tokens"). These needed to be entered in a prescribed order to authenticate entry (see Table 1). The process would terminate after all four tokens were detected or would automatically time out if any token took longer than two minutes to detect. Each cue type was tested separately as well as one authentication task that was a mixture of all three. As a control, 4 digit PINs were also entered by participants. Prior to the authentication tasks, approximately 20-

25 minutes was spent practicing the input tokens to be used. Also, there were six training sessions for each mental command token as these needed to be specifically trained and the signature EEG patterns for each participant stored in a profile log [5]. The speed and accuracy of input were recorded. After completion of the task, participants were presented with a 5-point Likert-scale (5=highest) questionnaire relating to levels of perceived security when accessing the solution and the quality of the user experience. Interviews were also performed to solicit suggestions on strengthening the interface.

4. RESULTS & DISCUSSION

The rate of accuracy and task time taken are shown in Table 2. Findings suggest that in comparison to entering a four digit PIN, lower levels of accuracy were experienced and more time was spent when authenticating using BCI and gestural conditions. Entering a sequence of emotional states was found to be faster and entered more accurately compared with the other BCI and gestural conditions. In terms of subjective user experience (Table 3), emotional states and facial expressions were selected as representing the most superior experience, while mental commands were almost unanimously thought to offer a poorer user experience. Detection rates for facial expressions (62.5%) did not vary considerably from emotional states (68.75%). However, they on average took 21 seconds longer to enter, which could be frustrating for users. In terms of perceived security, participants rated the 4-digit PIN condition lowest (1.75 out 5).

Table 2. Performance by condition

Type	Rate of Accuracy	Avg Speed (sec.)	Avg Perceived Security (Likert Scale 1-5 *5=highest*)
4-digit PIN	100.00%	1.455	1.75
Facial Exp.	62.50%	31.01	2.75
Emotion State	68.75%	10.05	4.25
Mental Cmd.	12.50%	54.03	4.50
Mixed Methods	50.00%	26.39	5.00

Table 3: Quality of subjective user experience

Type	Highest Quality Subjective Experience	Lowest Quality Subjective Experience
Facial Exp.	2	1
Emotion States	2	0
Mental Cmd.	0	3
Mixed Methods	0	0

Although the rate of accuracy entering PIN-based authentication stimuli was 100%, worries about third parties viewing or eavesdropping were evident. As one participant noted, "[4-digit PINs are not secure]…because if there is anyone else around…unless you've taken steps…it's not going to be very secure." The mixed condition was found to offer greater levels of perceived security, as there were multiple choices of token which could be selected for an authentication sequence, some which were not visible to third parties (e.g. mental commands, emotional states). One participant commented, "…whatever mental image you've created…even if you have the same mental images as somebody else, the way it's going to be done is not going to be duplicated, as no-one can see it". Responses highlighted that participants were willing to trade-off usability (in terms of task time) for conditions which offer higher levels of perceived security. However, it was thought that BCI and gestural technologies would need to be enhanced considerably, prior to their deployment for purposes of mainstream authentication.

5. CONCLUSION AND FUTURE WORK

This paper described an exploratory study examining the use of a commercially available BCI and gestural headset as a potential means of supporting authentication by individuals who are blind. While the findings suggest BCI and gestural technologies may offer promise, the scale of the study was small. The next logical step in the research would be to widen the sample of participants, and to evaluate over a period of time to assess the memorability of self-selected vs researcher-selected tokens.

6. ACKNOWLEDGEMENTS

This work was partly supported through the Office of Naval Research (N00014-15-1-2776). We thank Charles Lechner (UMBC) for his assistance with the development of the system.

7. REFERENCES

[1] Ahmed T., Hoyle R., Connelly K., Crandall D., and Kapadia A. 2015. Privacy concerns and behaviors of people with visual impairments. In *Proceedings of the 33rd Annual ACM Conference on Human Factors in Computing Systems*, 3523-3532, DOI=http://dx.doi.org/10.1145/2702123.2702334.

[2] Azenkot S., Rector K., Ladner R., and Wobbrock J. 2012. PassChords: Secure multi-touch authentication for blind people. In *Proceedings of the 14th International ACM SIGACCESS Conference on Computers and Accessibility*, 159-166, DOI=http://dx.doi.org/10.1145/2384916.2384945.

[3] Emotiv Epoc. Available: http://www.emotiv.com/

[4] Kuber R. and Sharma S. 2012. Developing an extension to an existing tactile authentication mechanism to support non-visual interaction. In *Proceedings of the IASTED Conference on Human-Computer Interaction*, 190-198, DOI=http://dx.doi.org/10.2316/P.2012.772-009.

[5] Saulynas S. and Kuber R. 2017. Towards the use of brain-computer interface technologies as a potential alternative to pin authentication. *International Journal of Human-Computer Interaction*, DOI=http://dx.doi.org/10.1080/10447318.2017.1357905.

[6] Saxena N. and Watt J. H. 2009. Authentication technologies for the blind or visually impaired. In *Proceedings of the USENIX Workshop on Hot Topics in Security*.

[7] Thorpe J., van Oorschot P. C., and Somayaji A. 2005. Pass-thoughts: authenticating with our minds. In *Proceedings of the 2005 Workshop on New Security Paradigms*, 45-56. DOI=http://dx.doi.org/10.1145/1146269.1146282.

User Experiences When Testing a Messaging App for Communication Between Individuals who are Hearing and Deaf or Hard of Hearing

Lisa Elliot, Michael Stinson, Syed Ahmed, and Donna Easton
National Technical Institute for the Deaf
Rochester Institute of Technology
Rochester, NY 14623
{lbenrd, msserd, sxy1056, dlencr}@rit.edu

ABSTRACT

This study investigated user experiences of participants testing a prototype messaging app with automatic speech recognition (ASR). Twelve pairs of participants, where one individual was deaf or hard-of-hearing (DHH), and the other one was hearing used the app, with the hearing individual using speech and ASR and the DHH one using typing. Participants completed a standardized decision making task to test the app. Regardless of hearing status of the participants or the type of device used, participants were generally satisfied with the app. These findings indicate that ASR has potential to facilitate communication between DHH and hearing individuals in small groups and that the technology merits further investigation.

CCS Concepts

• Human-centered computing → Accessibility → Empirical studies in accessibility • Human-centered computing → Collaborative and social computing → Empirical studies in collaborative and social computing • Human-centered computing → User studies • Human-centered computing →Ubiquitous and mobile devices

Keywords

Deaf; hard-of-hearing; small groups; communication; automatic speech recognition; mobile devices

1. INTRODUCTION

Individuals who are deaf or hard of hearing (DHH) must sometimes participate in small groups with individuals who are hearing. Unfortunately, DHH individuals often face barriers to full functioning in these groups, resulting in limited contributions to the group. For example, DHH employees must meet with hearing employees who do not know sign language, and sign language interpreters or real-time captioning is often not available for these meetings; consequently, the hearing and DHH employees often have difficulty communicating with each other [1, 2, 3]. Automatic speech recognition (ASR) holds exciting promise for making spoken content accessible for DHH individuals in situations where interpreters or providers of captioning often are not available. If ASR can facilitate communication between DHH and hearing individuals, it could become a popular application in these settings. Current ASR, however, is imperfect, especially in the noisy and complex environment of multi-party meetings.

Although ASR has potential to facilitate communication in small groups, there has been little use of ASR in this capacity. A survey of 108 D/HH students who participated in internships in settings where they had to regularly interact with non-signing hearing employees revealed that ASR was the least used method for communicating with hearing employees among 8 technologies (e.g. others were computer word document, etc.) [4].

The purpose of this study was to examine user experiences of a prototype messaging app for mobile devices with an ASR feature for a conversation between two people, where one individual was DHH, and the other was hearing. The hearing individual used speech and ASR to produce text and the DHH individual typed. The user experiences provide critical feedback for future app refinement and use in a variety of settings.

ASSETS'17, October 29-November 1, 2017, Baltimore, MD, USA.
ACM ISBN 978-1-4503-4926-0/17/10.
DOI: http://dx.doi.org/10.1145/3132525.3134798

2. METHOD

2.1. Design

Twelve pairs of students, each with one hearing and one DHH participant, used prototype messaging software for mobile devices to communicate while completing a standardized decision making task: (a) In one set of four pairs, the hearing participant used ASR and the DHH participant used typing on the smartphone keyboard; (b) in a second set of four pairs, the hearing participant used ASR on a phone, and the DHH one used typing on a full sized keyboard connected to a tablet computer; and (c) in the third set, the hearing participant used ASR and the DHH one used typing, with both having tablet computers with keyboards.

2.2 Participants

A total of 24 students participated in the study. The subjects were comprised of DHH (n=12) and Hearing students (n=12). Participants were recruited by posters, personal contacts and social media on the campus of a northeastern university.

2.3 Materials and Procedures

Materials consisted of a prototype messaging app with ASR and typing features to generate texts, Android smartphones, Android tablet computers, full-size Bluetooth keyboards and a collaborative task. In the conversation thread, the app underlined and italicized words produced with ASR that were below a 75% confidence level. Prior to the collaborative activity, participants received 15 minutes of training with the app, including a brief video and practice opportunities. The activity used to elicit conversation from the students while using the app was a collaborative task that presented students with a survival situation, "Lost at Sea." Participants needed to decide the survival value of 10 items that they could bring with them on a raft when escaping their sinking ship. Hearing participants used ASR to produce their messages and typed when correcting errors produced with ASR. DHH participants typed all their messages. After the collaborative task, participants completed an online survey about their satisfaction and experiences with the app. The survey included 19 closed- and open-ended questions about ease of use, message comprehension, collaboration, and errors.

3. RESULTS

3.1 Closed-Ended Responses

Participants rated their agreement with 13 statements on a 5-point Likert-type scale (1=strongly disagree; 5=strongly agree). Items included statements on the following topics: (a) Ease of use (5 items); (b) Comprehension (3 items); (c) Collaboration (3 items); and, (d) Errors (2 items). ANOVA tests reveal few significant differences based on hearing status or type of mobile device used, and no significant interactions between the hearing status x device use.

Hearing Status. ANOVA tests showed only one statistically significant result with regard to participant hearing status. Hearing participants found that it was easier to send a message with the app than did the DHH participants (p=.046, F =.4.477).

Mobile Device Type. With regard to type of mobile device used during the trial (phone vs. tablet), individuals using tablets were more likely to report that their partners understood them enough to do the experiment task (p=.000, F = 20.087). In addition, tablet users also agreed more often with the statement that errors produced with ASR made it difficult to understand the information exchanged during the experiment task (p =.043, F=4.632).

3.2 Open-Ended Responses

Respondents were also presented with up to five open-ended questions pertaining to their experiences (10 participants were only presented with the first four questions). The questions included: (a) How helpful was the ASR when reading or producing messages? (b) What did you like best about the app? (c) What did you like least about the app? (d) What was your experience using the messaging app to communicate with your partner in the experiment? and, (e) Please comment on your experience using the phone, tablet or keyboard for this experiment. The responses were coded using content analysis, resulting in three consistent themes: accuracy, features, and speed. In addition, several questions included responses corresponding to the themes of ease of use, and communication. Type of device did not seem to influence responses to the questions.

Accuracy. Respondents most often commented on accuracy. Users did notice errors on occasion, however most respondents were satisfied that the system had "pretty good accuracy." Hearing users remarked that being able to correct errors by typing was appreciated, although DHH users noted that error correction slowed communication.

Features. Users were generally positive about features, including text and font colors and voice recognition.

Speed. DHH and hearing users both commented on the speed of the app. Comments from users suggested that the app enabled fast communication, and one DHH user commented that the app was "smoother and faster" than another app that is currently used by the general public.

Ease of use. Comments by all users were favorable, for example the comment by a hearing user: "it was intuitive, anyone who has used a messaging app before will easily understand how to use this one." Another user who is DHH commented, "It's easy to use and I think it'd be helpful to use in meeting and such between hearing and hard-of-hearing people."

Communication. As the latter comment relating to ease of use suggested, respondents felt that the app helped to facilitate and normalize communication. One DHH user commented that: "It was basically like having a normal conversation and we were both kind of laughing a little bit." A hearing user recognized that the app made communication easier: "I find it easier to share my ideas in speech rather than typing. It allowed me to communicate with a hard of hearing student while still speaking."

4. CONCLUSION

This study investigated perceptions of use of a prototype messaging app with ASR and typing features. Regardless of hearing status of the participants or the type of device used, participants were generally satisfied with the app. These findings indicate that ASR has potential to facilitate communication between DHH and hearing individuals in small groups and that the technology merits further investigation.

5. ACKNOWLEDGMENTS

This material is based on work supported by the National Technical Institute for the Deaf.

6. REFERENCES

[1] Foster, S. and MacLeod, J. 2003. Deaf People at Work: Assessment of Communication Among Deaf and Hearing Persons in Work Settings. International journal of audiology, 42 (2003), 128-139.

[2] Punch, R., Hyde, M., and Power, D. 2007. Career and Workplace Experiences of Australian University Graduates who are Deaf or Hard of Hearing. Journal of deaf studies and deaf education 12, 4 (2007), 504-517 doi:10.1093/deafed/enm011

[3] Stinson, M., and Buckley, G. (Eds.) 2013. Taking the risk: Acquiring and living with a cochlear implant. Rochester, NY. RIT Press.

[4] Elliot, L., Stinson, M., Mallory, J., and Huenerfauth, M. 2016. Deaf and Hard of Hearing Individuals' Perceptions of Communication with Hearing Colleagues in Small Groups. In: Proceedings of the 18th Annual International Conference on Computers and Accessibility (ASSETS16), ACM, New York, NY, USA, 271-272. http://dx.doi.org/10.1145/2982142.2982198

Using Automatic Speech Recognition to Facilitate Communication Between an Individual who is Hearing and One who is Deaf or Hard of Hearing

Michael Stinson, Syed Ahmed,
Lisa Elliot, Donna Easton
National Technical Institute for the Deaf
Rochester Institute of Technology
Rochester, NY 14623
{ msserd, sxy1056, lbenrd, dlencr}@rit.edu

ABSTRACT
This study investigated use of automatic speech recognition (ASR) in 12 pairs where one individual was deaf or hard-of-hearing (DHH), and the other one was hearing, with the hearing individual using speech and ASR and the DHH one using typing. Each of the pairs used prototype software for messaging to communicate while completing a standardized decision making task. Results suggested that ASR produced text at a faster rate than a keyboard. When both participants used keyboards, they exchanged more messages than when one or both of them used a smartphone with a miniature keyboard.

CCS Concepts
• Human-centered computing → Accessibility → Empirical studies in accessibility • Human-centered computing → Collaborative and social computing → Empirical studies in collaborative and social computing

Keywords
Deaf; hard-of-hearing; small groups; communication; automatic speech recognition

1. INTRODUCTION
Individuals who are deaf or hard of hearing (DHH) must sometimes participate in small groups with individuals who are hearing. Unfortunately, DHH individuals often face communication barriers in these groups [1,2]. Automatic speech recognition (ASR) holds exciting promise for making spoken content accessible for DHH individuals in situations where interpreters or providers of captioning often are not available. ASR may facilitate communication between DHH and hearing individuals by producing text faster [3].

The purpose of this study was to examine:

1. Speed of exchange of information as a function of whether the individual used ASR or typing, and of the type of keyboard that the individual used to produce text. Full size keyboards may produce text more rapidly than phone ones.
2. Incorrect productions of words that the ASR produced (i.e. errors) and the correction of these errors. If ASR marks a word as likely to be a production error, users may be more likely to correct it.

ACM ISBN 978-1-4503-4926-0/17/10.
https://doi.org/10.1145/3132525.3134797

2. METHOD
In this experiment, 12 pairs of students, each with one hearing and one DHH student, used prototype software for messaging to communicate while completing a standardized decision making task: (a) In one set of four pairs, the hearing student used ASR and the DHH student used typing on the miniature keyboard on smartphones; (b) in a second set of four pairs, the hearing student used ASR on a phone, and the DHH one used typing on a full sized keyboard connected to a tablet computer; and (c) in the third set, the hearing student used ASR and the DHH one used typing, with both having tablet computers with keyboards.

2.1 Participants
A total of 24 students participated in the study. The subjects were comprised of DHH (n=12) and Hearing students (n=12). Participants were recruited by posters, personal contacts and social media on the campus of a northeastern university.

2.2 Materials and Procedures
Materials consisted of a prototype for messaging with ASR and typing for participants to communicate with each other, Android smartphones, Android tablet computers, full size keyboards and a collaborative task. The software prototype marked words produced with ASR that were below a 75% confidence level with underlining and italicization. The prototype automatically recorded and time stamped each spoken or typed word and displayed the confidence level for that word. The activity used to elicit conversation from the students while using the messaging prototype was a collaborative task that presented students a survival situation, "Lost at Sea." Participants needed to decide the survival value of 10 items that they could bring with them on a raft when escaping their sinking ship. Hearing students used typing to correct errors produced with ASR.

3. RESULTS
3.1 Exchange of Information
The first set of analyses examined the data produced by the messaging prototype on exchange of information between the DHH and hearing participants. Table 1 shows the mean number of words produced/per minute in messages, number of messages for

the collaborative task, and number of words for the task for each of the three combinations of keyboards for DHH and hearing participants. Users of ASR (hearing) produced words at a faster rate during messaging than did the typing (DHH) ones, $F(2,24) = 24.02$ $p < .0001$. Furthermore, when both participants had full keyboards and tablets they produced more messages than the other two groups did; when the ASR user had a phone and the typing user had a full keyboard, they produced the second most messages; and when both individuals had smartphones, they produced the fewest messages, $F(2, 24) = 4.74, p < .05$.

3.2 Word Errors and Corrections

The next set of analyses also used data produced with the messaging prototype, but focused on words produced by the ASR user, who was hearing. A coder identified errors and corrected words from the downloaded word information. These analyses compared the words, words identified as errors, corrected words, and uncorrected words for marked and unmarked words. Table 2 shows these data. More words were unmarked than were marked, $t(1, 11) = 7.68, p < .001$. In addition, ASR users corrected all of their errors for marked words but sometimes did not correct errors for unmarked words, $t(1, 11) = 2.05, p < .10$

3. CONCLUSION

This study investigated speed of exchange of messages, and production and correction of error words generated with ASR.

Table 1

Mean Number of Words per Minute, Messages, and Words for Hearing and DHH Participants for Three Keyboard Combinations

	Measure		
Keyboard combination and hearing status	**Words per minute**	**Messages**	**Words**
	M (SD)	**M (SD)**	**M (SD)**
Both have smartphone			
Hearing (ASR)	80.99 (6.26)	33.75 (16.80)	238.50 123.38
DHH (typing)	54.27 (32.99)	26.25 (12.37)	159.50 86.65
DHH has keyboard/tablet; hearing has smartphone			
Hearing (ASR)	96.53 (4.37)	41.75 (8.06)	244.00 (122.42)
DHH (typing)	39.86 (13.16)	34.75 (16.15)	203.25 (77.34)
Both have keyboard/tablet			
Hearing (ASR)	84.16 (13.81)	52.75 (6.19)	306.50 (56.67)
DHH (typing)	47.28 (22.21)	46.25 (13.07)	255.75 (66.35)

Table 2

Words, Error Words, Corrected Words, and Uncorrected Words for Those that were Marked or Unmarked

	Word Type			
Measure	**Marked (below 75% confidence)**		**Unmarked (above 75% confidence)**	
	Mean	SD	Mean	SD
Words	49.17	23.81	213.83	85.25
Error Words	3.50	4.92	4.50	4.37
Corrected Words	3.50	4.92	2.58	2.84
Uncorrected Words	0	0	1.92	3.23

Results suggested that ASR produced text at a faster rate than a keyboard. Furthermore, when both participants used full sized keyboards, they exchanged more messages than when one or both of them used phones with a miniature keyboard.

In regard to error words, ASR generated few errors relative to the number of words produced. When the error words were marked, users of ASR always corrected them; however, when the error words were unmarked, the users sometimes did not correct them. It appears that the mark up may help users of ASR recognize and correct that error.

These findings indicate that ASR has potential to facilitate communication between DHH and hearing individuals in small groups and that the technology merits further investigation.

4. ACKNOWLEDGMENTS

This material is based on work supported by the National Technical Institute for the Deaf.

5. REFERENCES

[1] Foster, S. and MacLeod, J. 2003. Deaf people at work: Assessment of communication among deaf and hearing persons in work settings. *International Journal of Audiology*, 42 (2003), 128-139.

[2] Punch, R., Hyde, M., and Power, D. 2007. Career and workplace experiences of Australian university graduates who are deaf or hard of hearing. *Journal of Deaf Studies and Deaf Education* 12, 4 (2007), 504-517 doi:10.1093/deafed/enm011

[3] Ruan, S., Wobbrock, J., Liou, K., Ng, A., and Landay, J. 2016. Speech is 3x faster than typing for English and Mandarin text entry on mobile devices. *arXiv Preprint*. arXiv: 1608.07323.

COSMA: Cooperative Self-Management Tool for Adolescents with Autism

Myeonghan Ryu, Eunkyung Jo, Sung-In Kim
Seoul National University
{rmh0313, mrke07, adult11}@snu.ac.kr

ABSTRACT
Adolescence is a challenging period for individuals with autism because they undergo radical physical, emotional, and social transitions. We describe our setup to support the self-management of adolescents with autism for assisting adaptive transitions. We propose COSMA, an interactive mobile application that allows both individuals with autism and their caregivers to cooperatively manage, plan, reflect on, and improve behavior. COSMA is a self-management tool for adolescents with autism, including behavioral goal setting by means of the co-contract process, self-reporting while performing everyday tasks, and cooperative reflection to support their smooth transition to adulthood.

CCS Concepts
• Human-Centered Computing→Interaction Design • Social and professional topics→User characteristics.

Keywords
Autism; adolescents; puberty; self-management; behavior change

1. INTRODUCTION
Individuals with autism present a variety of behavioral challenges derived from deficits in social interactions and restricted, repetitive patterns of behavior, interests, or activities [1]. While adolescence is a difficult time for most individuals, it is especially difficult for adolescents with autism. Such individuals struggle to understand rapid and often drastic physical and emotional changes as well as ever-changing social expectation [3]. Of the many strategies used to mitigate difficulties for individuals with autism and their caregivers, self-management is a popular approach to helping adolescents with autism learn skills for independence through the modification of problematic behaviors [2]. In recent years, there have been various assistive technologies using smart devices such as smartphones to help with the self-management of individuals with autism [4]. Our aim is to develop a prototype of an assistive mobile application that can support a smooth transition to adulthood for adolescents with autism. To do this, we conducted a semi-structured interview with five parents of Korean autistic youths and five autism specialists in Korea. We were able to identify day-to-day difficulties and challenging behaviors displayed by adolescents with autism that are described below. Drawing on the formative user research findings, we propose a prototype of COSMA, which is a cooperative self-management tool for adolescents with autism.

ASSETS '17, October 29-November 1, 2017, Baltimore, MD, USA

ACM ISBN 978-1-4503-4926-0/17/10.
https://doi.org/10.1145/3132525.3134825

2. FORMATIVE USER RESEARCH

2.1 Participants and Method
Our caregiver participants had children diagnosed with autism spectrum disorder whose ages ranged from 10 to 16. All clinician participants were individuals who had regularly consulted with adolescents with autism and their parents as certified autism specialists. The interview questions for participants included the topics, challenges, and characteristic of adolescents with autism and their use of digital devices.

2.2 Findings
We gained a detailed understanding of the day-to-day difficulties of adolescents with autism and their challenging behaviors such as sexual inappropriateness, aggression, and noncompliance increased during puberty. We also identified the current practices and strategies that adolescents with autism and their caregivers use to collaboratively manage, plan, reflect upon, and improve the adolescents' behavior. To develop an intervening medium for successful transitions, we focused on identifying ways to support the self-management of behaviors.

2.2.1 Negotiating Behavioral Goals with Parents
The participating parents invested a great deal of effort in setting goals to change their children's behaviors. However, goals generated solely by parents were not persuasive, as parents' constant prompting to follow behavioral plans did not affect children's behavior. Parent–adolescent conflicts also take place when adolescents are given the initiative for determining their tasks or behaviors. However, our participants had attempted to resolve conflicts by encouraging both parents and children to add a negotiation process to their scheduling. Thus, we take the negotiation process into account when designing the self-management system.

2.2.2 Encouraging Self-Reflection in a Daily Context
According to the participants, adolescents with autism are expected to improve their behavior and, eventually, to better understand themselves. Reflecting upon past events helped a child understand the contexts and triggers of his problematic behavior. Therefore, to ensure successful behavior modification, it is imperative to collect the information about the targeted behavior. The parents and therapists, however, had limited access to the information. For instance, some of our adolescents with autism did not want to share their secrets or their innermost feelings with their parents. Thus, the adult caregivers (mostly parents) collected the information about their children through various channels, such as their children's school teachers, therapists, and peers, as well as those peers' mothers.

3. THE DESIGN OF COSMA
To support cooperative goal setting and self-reflection in a daily context, we have developed a system called COSMA. It is a mobile-based cooperative self-management application for

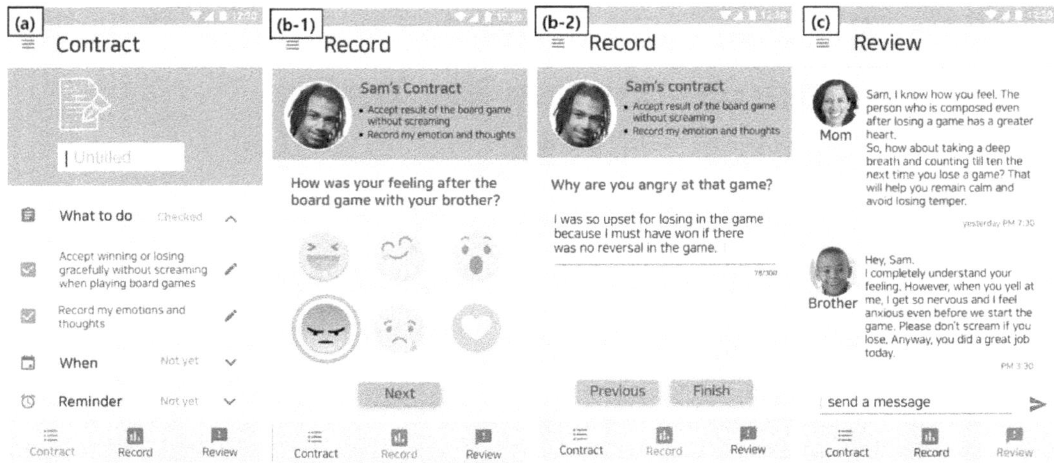

Figure 1. Three stages of COSMA : (a) Contract: Create a new contract, (b-1) Record: Rate mood, (b-2) Record: Describe a reason for the mood rated, (c) Review: Check reviews of behaviors over the contract period.

adolescents with autism, including behavioral goal setting by means of making co-contract between adolescents and their caregivers, self-reporting while performing everyday tasks, and cooperative reflection.

3.1 COSMA Feature Description

In general, COSMA functions under three stages of self-management activities. We will explain each stage using a concrete scenario about Sam, a teenager who enjoys playing board games with his younger brother, as an example.

3.1.1 Co-Contract for Plausible Goal Setting

This stage seeks to build consensus for plausible behavioral goal setting between adolescents with autism and caregivers. This contract includes target behaviors, rewards, the duration of the contract, and the detailed condition of reminder. In the case of Sam, he has the problem of screaming in anger every time he is defeated in a game. To correct this behavior, Sam's mother would like to propose a contract for two things: 1) accept winning or losing gracefully without screaming when playing board games; and 2) record emotions and thoughts through COSMA immediately after playing the game. After writing a contract with target behaviors, the duration of the contract, and the reward for the target behavior, she sends the contract to her son. Sam reads the contract sent by his mother through COSMA, writes the feedback on the contract and sends it back to his mother (Figure 1.a).

3.1.2 Self-Monitoring of Everyday Tasks

As expressed in the findings above, adolescents are expected to improve their behaviors by reflecting upon past activities; therefore, the self-monitoring of activities throughout the day is critical. For instance, whenever Sam loses in a board game while playing with his brother on the weekend, he first comes out of the room yelling at his brother. However, as soon as Sam comes up with the contract, he takes out his cell phone and starts to record his feelings through COSMA. On COSMA, Sam checks the "angry" icon to answer the question asking his emotion status(Figure 1.b-1). Additionally, he answers the question "Why are you angry?" with "I was so upset for losing in the game because I must have won if there was no reversal in the game." (Figure 1.b-2). After writing his feelings on COSMA, he feels more relaxed and begins to reflect his behaviors.

3.1.3 Cooperative Reflection

The last stage we designed is the cooperative reflection, in which adolescents with autism reflect their behavior by receiving feedback from their caregivers and therapists based on the collected data. For example, Sam's mother and younger brother check the data that Sam has recorded and write a review for him. In the review, Sam's mother expresses sympathy for his feelings first and then suggests an alternative method, such as taking a deep breath and counting to ten instead of screaming in a similar situation. In his brother's review, he asks Sam not to yell at him even if he loses in a game because he becomes nervous when Sam screams and gets anxious even before starting a game with him in the next time. After checking the reviews, Sam begins to think about his brother's feelings and decides to follow his mother's advice instead of screaming next time (Figure 1.c).

4. CONCLUSION AND FUTURE WORK

Much like other adolescents, adolescents with autism experience problems caused from their puberty, and because of their autistic characteristics, they experience much more difficulties. The key to decrease their difficulties is to help them reflect themselves and smoothly communicate with their caregivers. Based on formative findings, we suggest COSMA, which is a mobile-based application for self-behavioral management. In the near future, we will evaluate the working prototype with adolescents with autism, their caregivers, and therapists in a field setting.

5. REFERENCE

[1] American Psychiatric Association. 2013. DSM-5 Autism spectrum disorder fact sheet. *Arlington, VA: American Psychiatric.*

[2] Liu, Y., Moore, D. W., and Anderson, A. 2015. Improving Social Skills in a Child With Autism Spectrum Disorder Through Self-Management Training. *Behaviour Change* 32, 4: 273–284. https://doi.org/10.1017/bec.2015.14

[3] Tantam, D. 2003. The challenge of adolescents and adults with Asperger syndrome. *Child and adolescent psychiatric clinics of North America* 12, 1: 143–163.

[4] Ulgado, R. R., Nguyen, k., Custodio, V. E., Waterhouse, A., Weiner, R., and Hayes, G. 2013. VidCoach: A Mobile Video Modeling System for Youth with Special Needs. *Proceedings of the 12th International Conference on Interaction Design and Children - IDC '13*: 581–584. https://doi.org/10.1145/2485760.248587

Crowdsourcing the Installation and Maintenance of Indoor Navigation Infrastructure

Cole Gleason
Human-Computer Interaction Institute
Carnegie Mellon University
5000 Forbes Ave
Pittsburgh, PA 15213
cgleason@cs.cmu.edu

ABSTRACT

Indoor navigation systems, especially for people with visual impairments, often require intensive data collection and instrumentation to install and maintain over time. The most accurate navigation systems require experts to install many Bluetooth beacons or similar technologies throughout the environment. After hardware installation, data samples must be collected to construct a signal model of the environment to be navigated. The demands of this intense upfront workload and ongoing updates pose barriers for widespread adoption of navigation systems.

This document describes LuzDeploy, a system to break these installation and maintenance workflows into small, simple tasks that be completed by volunteers with little to no training. A Facebook Messenger bot coordinates the overall deployment by assigning volunteers to beacon placement, data collection, or quality assurance tasks that take only a few minutes to complete. These tasks may be batched to do more or less work, depending on the amount of time the volunteer is able to contribute. LuzDeploy allows building owners and managers to distribute the difficult task of installation and maintenance. By making these workloads easier for non-experts, LuzDeploy aims to increase adoption of indoor navigation systems and make unfamiliar spaces more accessible to people who wish to navigate independently.

CCS Concepts

• **Human-centered computing → Accessibility technologies** • *Social and professional topics → People with disabilities.*

Keywords

Individuals with visual impairments; Physical crowdsourcing; Indoor navigation assistance.

1. INTRODUCTION

Navigating unfamiliar environments is a challenge for people with visual impairments, as most of the wayfinding aids available are signs or other visual features. GPS systems have made this easier outdoors where the user can almost always be located and routed, but GPS signals are not reliable enough for accurate and robust indoor navigation systems. Researchers have proposed approaches using other technologies such as RFID tags or Bluetooth beacons [3]. However, instrumenting indoor environments with these after-market sensors and maintaining them over time is costly, as usually only experts are able to maintain this infrastructure.

For example, the NavCog system [1] uses Bluetooth Low-Energy beacons to locate the user to within a meter of their actual location. To install the system, a beacon must be placed about every 5 meters in a building's hallways. Then, a system administrator samples the Bluetooth signals using a mobile phone every meter. These samples are used to generate a map of the indoor space for localization. As the beacon go missing, their batteries lose power, or the environment changes, the map needs to be updated with fresh samples. If the administrator does not constantly monitor the health of the navigation system, both hardware and data, the navigation application will not be reliable when a person with a visual impairment arrives at the building.

These installation and maintenance workflows make navigation systems costly to adopt, as experts must be brought on-site or new employees must be trained to properly maintain these systems. Instead, LuzDeploy breaks these workflows into small tasks that can completed by non-experts in minutes. Volunteers simply need to message a Facebook Messenger chatbot, which assigns tasks to install beacons, sample data, or check on the health of the infrastructure.

2. LUZDEPLOY

There are 3 main components to LuzDeploy: 1) a Facebook Messenger chat bot that communicates with volunteers, 2) an online map interface for the building, and 3) a companion iOS application used in some tasks to collect Bluetooth data.

2.1 LuzDeploy Bot

The LuzDeploy Bot is a server that coordinates the volunteers, assigned tasks, and remaining work. Using Facebook Messenger to communicate with the physical crowd of volunteers eases onboarding, as users likely already have the appropriate app and do not need to create a new account. The bot walks new users through the consent process, suggests a new random task to volunteers every day, and reminds them of unfinished tasks.

For the NavCog example, it keeps a record of which beacon is placed in which location in the building and gathers Bluetooth samples collected from volunteers. When volunteers start these two tasks, they can specify how many beacons they want to place or samples they would like to collect. The bot will find a cluster of needed work in the building for them, reducing travel overhead. It also asks volunteers to check on the health of the beacons in a segment of hallway every week.

ASSETS '17, October 29-November 1, 2017, Baltimore, MD, USA

ACM ISBN 978-1-4503-4926-0/17/10.
https://doi.org/10.1145/3132525.3134827

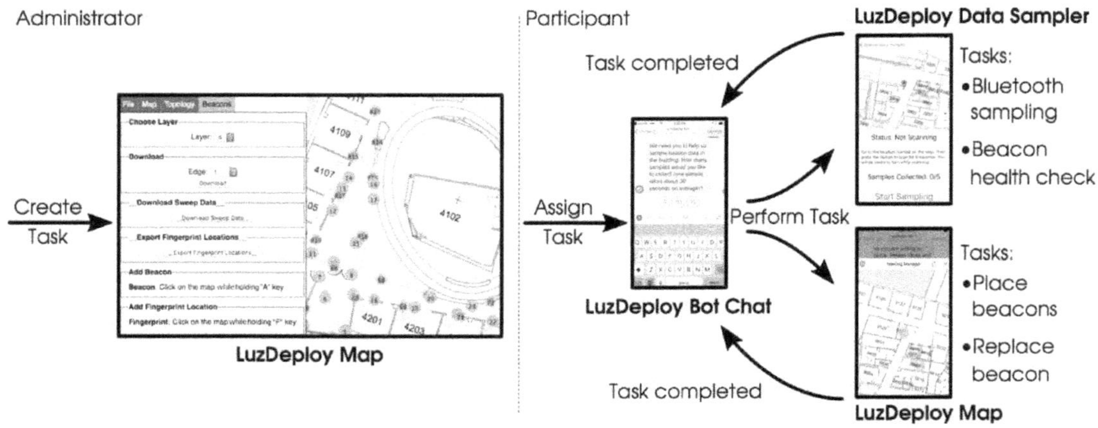

Figure 1: LuzDeploy components: The administrator uses the online Map interface to create the data for beacon placement, sampling, and health check tasks, which are dispatched by the LuzDeploy Bot to participants through Facebook Messenger. Then, the Bot uses either the Map or Data Sampler application to guide the participants to complete the assigned task.

2.2 LuzDeploy Map

The LuzDeploy Map is a modified version of the online map interface used by administrators in the NavCog system. Similarly, administrators using LuzDeploy to install NavCog can specify beacon and data sample locations on the map, which are turned into tasks for volunteers.

2.3 LuzDeploy Data Sampler

Some tasks require sampling Bluetooth signals at a specific point or checking on the health of the Bluetooth beacons in the building. A companion iOS application, the LuzDeploy Data Sampler, is available for these tasks. After volunteers install this on their phones, links in the conversation with the LuzDeploy Bot open the data sampler with pre-loaded task parameters. This data sampler includes a map view of the task, along with instructions on sampling the data. When finished, the user is redirected back into the Messenger conversation where they can get a new task.

When volunteers work on tasks, one step is usually to travel to a physical location in the building. In these cases, the map is shown to the user in a read-only mode with a specified point or hallway segment highlighted.

3. STUDY

We used LuzDeploy to install and begin maintenance of NavCog on the Carnegie Mellon University campus in two sessions.

3.1 Session 1

The first session took place on a single day from 4PM to 10PM in the computer science building of the university. Multiple members of the research team recruited students walking through a heavily trafficked hallway near a building entrance. Overall, 89 participants participated in placing 99 beacons. Most only placed a single beacon, as LuzDeploy did not have beacon batching enabled in this session. This lead to significant walking overhead between tasks, so many participants decided to leave the deployment effort after completing the first task.

One week after the deployment, a visual inspection of each installed beacon was performed by two members of the research team. NavCog does not need the beacons to be placed exactly at a fixed point [2], so the beacons were inspected to see if they were within 1 meter of the location marked on the building floor plan. Of the 99 beacons deployed in the building, 73 were on the designated map marker or close enough and 6 beacons were missing entirely.

3.2 Session 2

Rather than a single-day event, the second session took place over four months, and without a constant presence from the research team. In this session, beacon batching was enabled, so 25 participants placed a total of 97 beacons in the second session, resulting in an average of 3.9 beacons per person (2.7 per task over 36 tasks).

After the second session, we again visually inspected the placed beacons to measure the placement accuracy. We found that 83 beacons had been placed correctly, and only 12 were too far from the intended location or not found. Two beacons placed in this session were found broken during the inspection.

4. FUTURE WORK

Our initial studies show that physical crowdsourcing is a feasible approach to instrumenting buildings for blind navigation systems. We intend to complete further study sessions to evaluate the effectiveness of this approach with different crowd populations, locations, and incentive mechanisms. These studies will help us improve and generalize LuzDeploy so that any building can be quickly instrumented and maintained over time, supporting widespread adoption of blind navigation infrastructure.

5. REFERENCES

[1] Ahmetovic, D., Gleason, C., Ruan, C., Kitani, K., Takagi, H., and Asakawa, C. 2016. NavCog: a navigational cognitive assistant for the blind. In *Proceedings of the 18th International Conference on Human-Computer Interaction with Mobile Devices and Services* (MobileHCI '16). ACM, New York, NY, USA, 90-99. DOI: http://dx.doi.org/10.1145/2935334.2935361

[2] Ahmetovic, D., Murata, M., Gleason, C., Brady, E., Takagi, H., Kitani, K., and Asakawa, C. 2017. Achieving Practical and Accurate Indoor Navigation for People with Visual Impairments. In *Proceedings of the 14th Web for All Conference on The Future of Accessible Work* (W4A '17). ACM, New York, NY, USA, Article 31, 10 pages. DOI: https://doi.org/10.1145/3058555.3058560

[3] Fallah, N., Apostolopoulos, I., Bekris, K., and Folmer, E. 2013. Indoor Human Navigation Systems: A Survey. *Interacting with Computers.* 25, 1 (Jan. 2013), 21–33. DOI: http://doi.org/10.1093/iwc/iws010

Identifying Visual Cues to Improve Independent Indoor Navigation for Blind Individuals

Cameron Cassidy
Texas A&M University
400 Bizzell St,
College Station, TX 77413
ccassidy4138@tamu.edu

ABSTRACT
The idea of using technology to help those with visual impairments navigate has been studied extensively. However, most of these systems focus on getting the user from place to place, rather than helping the person get a better sense and intuition of their environment. Providing blind people with the same intuitive clues that sighted persons have may allow them to better navigate physical spaces, and also feel more empowered to freely explore the physical location. For this purpose, we have begun to study the process that sighted individuals use for familiarizing and getting a sense of their environment. We believe our results will show it is possible to enhance the navigational capabilities of blind people by providing access to the same clues used by sighted people to get a sense of their environment.

1. INTRODUCTION
We live in an inherently visual world. As such, most indoor spaces are planned for easy visual navigation. However, this leads to problems for those with visual disabilities. For blind individuals, navigation can be a barrier to independence, education, and employment [1]. For sighted individuals, traversing an unfamiliar indoor location is done through a combination of conscious observation and much more subtle visual cues [3]. We believe that if these subtle cues can be identified and presented to another sense, it may help those with visual disabilities find their way around indoors. Our primary goal is to provide blind people with the same visual cues used by sighted individuals. Most navigation systems for the blind focus on informing blind people of where they should go to reach their desired destination [2,4,5].

However, these approaches do not worry with informing blind people of key aspects of the physical space in which they are in. This can lead blind people to have limited understanding of their surroundings which can limit their explorations. Another major difference is the goal of our system versus that of the more traditional approaches. While most systems attempt to guide a user to a predetermined destination, we aim to give the user a sense of place and a mental image of their surroundings. Hopefully, this will empower blind people to better navigate and explore indoor spaces.

Most research approaches also require installation of systems, complex mapping schemes [5], or expensive hardware [2]. We believe that a more elegant solution can be achieved through a single device, with hardware found in most smart phones. The benefit of this over the aforementioned systems is universality. It would be usable in most indoor spaces, while its competitors are limited to locations with the appropriate mapping and hardware. Our research will consist of two parts. The first part involves using a combination of an eye tracking device and interviews to understand the type of visual clues that sighted people use to navigate and get a sense of their environment. In the second, we will develop a system that recognizes these visual clues, and give blind people access to them. We will then conduct a user study to understand the strengths and limitations of this approach.

ASSETS'17, Oct. 29–Nov. 1, 2017, Baltimore, MD, USA.
ACM ISBN 978-1-4503-4926-0/17/10.
DOI: http://dx.doi.org/10.1145/ 3132525.3134828

2. A SENSE OF SPACE
In this research we focus on providing blind people with clues that will empower them to get a better sense of the spaces in which they are navigating. What it means to have sense of the environment can mean many things. Thus, we break unknowns faced by a blind person into two categories - things which they know exist in the space, but they don't know the location of; and others that they don't know exist in a space, and they also don't know the location of. An example of the first would be restrooms; it is quite obvious that a blind person would have difficulty finding a restroom. However, many businesses do not have one – and a blind person may simply assume that one is far away or not available, when one is actually fairly close.

A vending machine would be an example of the second type. Someone may enjoy a soda, but may not even think to ask where to get one. Why would they? It is uncommon to have a vending machine in a building and asking strangers to help locate something can be daunting. In this case, the individual does not know if it exists and they also do not even think to ask, though it would be nice to know. Thus in order to help blind people get a better sense of the space, we need to allow them to specify what they're looking for and help them find it. We also need to find a way to give users knowledge of things which are potentially unknown to them, without overloading them with information. We believe this can be accomplished by understanding the information that sighted people use to comprehend a space.

3. UNDERSTANDING VISUAL CUES
So far, we have recruited sighted individuals to understand the type of visual clues they use to navigate and make sense of their environment. For this purpose, the sighted participants were brought to different indoor locations, and outfitted with an eye tracking device. Participants were then asked to use an eye-tracker and talk out loud, while they conduct different tasks with different levels of difficulties in the indoor location (e.g., "find a location for studying"). So far, 6 participants have found 3 locations each, for a total of 18 locations being found.

4. STUDY GOALS

After finishing all the studies, we will analyze the eye tracking data and interview responses to identify the key clues that sighted people use to navigate. This will accomplish 2 things. The first, it will provide insight into the needed specifications of the system. It will also identify what visual cues sighted people rely the most heavily on, and thus, may be of greater use to blind people.

5. THOUGHTS ON THE SYSTEM

In this section, we will discuss some early ideas on the system's design. After a bit of brainstorming, we have narrowed prospective hardware down to two platforms, Google Glass and a smart phone with a rear facing camera. Both of these devices have their own pros and cons from a technical standpoint, which we have tried to identify and listed below. Of course, an individual user's preference of interaction would have a drastic impact on which device is chosen.

5.1 The Passive Smart Phone Interface

This interface assumes that the blind user would show their phone's camera the area immediately around them. The phone would then relay information to the user editorially. This system would be easy to implement. However, because the user needs to know when to pull out their phone and scan, a lot of information could be missed! This is one major drawback of this approach.

5.2 The Vigilant Smart Phone Interface

This interface assumes that the smart Phone is strapped to the front of the user, and would always be active. This would mean the user does not have to hold the phone or know when the app is needed. There are a few downsides to this approach however. When lots of information is relayed to the user notification fatigue, where users experience stress and tone out information can occur. Another major downside is the area seen by the camera; smart phone cameras are only able to analyze a rather small arc of what is around the user.

5.3 A Google Glass Interface

This last interface utilizes a Google Glass. This device has a fish eye camera with a larger diameter. Thus, it is active at all times and is able to see more than the previous systems. However, Google Glass carries a high price tag and would not be available for most users, as it is still in beta testing. We also have concerns about the battery life of the device.

5.4 What's Next? A User Study

Our goal with our evaluation is to understand the degree to which our system helps unsighted people to have a better sense of their space. For this purpose, we will recruit participants with severe visual impairments. We will conduct a between subjects study, where one group will be exposed to our system and the other will use their traditional indoor navigation tools. We will ask participants in each group to conduct navigation tasks in different buildings. We will study how successful people are completing these different navigation tasks, as well as how much they feel they can do activities in the space, and general knowledge they have of the environment.

6. CONCLUSION

In conclusion, we expect our research to discover and quantify visual cues used by sighted people for indoor navigation. We aim to show that giving blind people access to these cues will help with navigation and familiarity in a new space. Hopefully, this will inspire a new type of navigation systems, which focus less on point A to B navigation, and more on giving blind people a sense of the space where they are in.

7. REFERENCES

[1] Brady, E. L., Sato, D., Ruan, C., Takagi, H., and Asakawa, C. 2015. Exploring interface design for independent navigation by people with visual impairments. In Proceedings of the 17th International ACM SIGACCESS Conference on Computers & Accessibility. ACM, 387–388.

[2] Ganz, A., Gandhi, S. R., Schafer, J., Singh, T., Puleo, E., Mullett, G., and Wilson, C. 2011. PERCEPT: Indoor navigation for the blind and visually impaired. In Engineering in Medicine and Biology Society, EMBC, 2011 Annual International Conference of the IEEE. IEEE, 856–859.

[3] Gärling, T., Lindberg, E., and Mäntylä, T. 1983. Orientation in buildings: Effects of familiarity, visual access, and orientation aids. *Journal of Applied Psychology* 68, 1 (1983), 177.

[4] Guerrero, V., and Ochoa, L. 2012. An Indoor Navigation System for the Visually Impaired. In sensors. *IEEE*, 8236–8258..

[5] Willis, S., and Helal, S. 2005. RFID information grid for blind navigation and wayfinding. In Wearable Computers, 2005. Proceedings. Ninth IEEE International Symposium on. IEEE, 34–37.

Participatory Design Using Sensory Substitution Devices with Tactile and Audio Feedback

Ella Tuson, Samantha Hughson, Christina Zymaris, Ryan King
Department of Mathematics and Computer Science
Clark University, Worcester, MA, USA
{btuson, shughson, czymaris, ryaking}@clarku.edu

ABSTRACT

Blind or visually impaired persons may experience challenges forming a mental map of the world around them. Our goal, in this participatory study, was to bridge the gap found in current technologies for a blind woman by creating a model utilizing tactile feedback. To achieve this goal, we designed three prototype sensory substitution systems. These prototypes attempted to aid our participant in crafting a world around her by providing auditory or tactile feedback in accordance to her proximity to an object. Each used a different form of output for the user: audio, vibration, or pressure. All of the stimuli produced by the models was managed by a researcher in place of a computer-vision algorithm. From our participant's feedback, we hope to develop a device that will provide the user a physical sensory substitution experience of sight.

CCS Concepts

•**Human-centered computing → Accessibility systems and tools;** *Accessibility design and evaluation methods;*

Keywords

Accessibilty; participatory design; blind individuals; sensory substitution; tactile feedback

1. INTRODUCTION

With the rate of advancements in computer vision and haptic feedback technologies, a great number of sensory substitution devices using both tactile and auditory feedback have been developed to aid individuals who are blind or visually impaired [3]. However, no available technologies exist that the subject of this study, denoted as TC, has found to fulfill her needs. Blind from birth, TC has occasionally experienced some physical sensations that she associates with sight, such as feeling her eyes "pulled" towards a bright area like a window. Visual depth perception exploits parallax due to different location of eyes to estimate distances to objects; eye muscles assist in moving and focusing the eyes to objects at various distances. While TC has tested various technologies, she has found that many tactile sensory substitution technologies, such as the tongue based electrotactile vision substitution system [2], are difficult for her to use and do not provide the physical experience of sight that she described to the research team. Likewise, TC has had little success with auditory simulation systems, ruling out the use of a system similar to EyeMusic [1].

Our intent is to work with TC over a period of time to develop assistive technologies which are unobtrusive and which suit her expressed needs, rather than what a sighted researcher believes her needs to be. The sighted researchers' misunderstanding of the descriptions of a physical sensation by the participant has been a significant challenge of the research team, similar to challenges in navigation assistance noted by Williams et al. [5].

ASSETS '17 October 29-November 1, 2017, Baltimore, MD, USA

ACM ISBN 978-1-4503-4926-0/17/10.
DOI: https://doi.org/10.1145/3132525.3134826

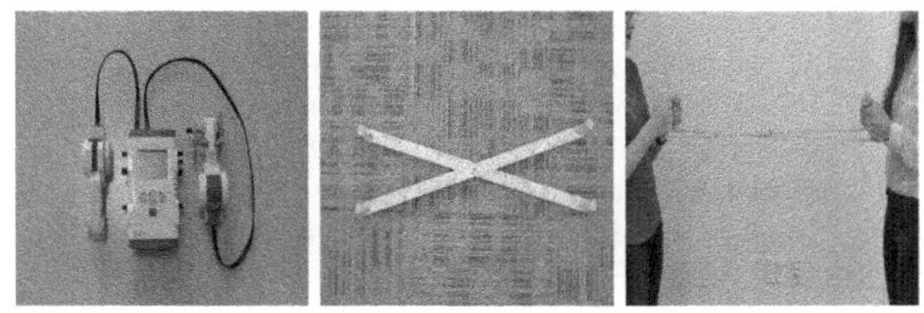

Figure 1: From left to right: LEGO Mindstorms motor; Third prototype apparatus; Third prototype evaluation setup.

2. EXPERIMENTAL EVALUATION

Our research is a preliminary step in the participatory design process through which a system will be created which uses computer vision to analyze images from a video camera and translate the results of the analysis into some form of haptic output. Due to the nature of this project, we chose to begin by developing the output system. The design of the output is key because it delivers the physical experience of sight to the user. In order to focus on the design of the output, we decided to substitute possible computer vision processes with a human researcher (i.e. a "Wizard of Oz" experiment).

2.1 Apparatus

We developed three prototype devices to perform a preliminary evaluation case study with TC. The first device used sound as the stimuli. This device was chosen due to the existence of many other assistive technologies which incorporate sound [2]. A researcher manually played a beeping noise from a laptop to indicate the distance between TC and another researcher. The second device was similarly constructed to test a stimuli common in assistive technologies. It used a small LEGO Mindstorms motor run at different speeds to generate vibrations that indicated distance. The third prototype incorporated a device made up of two yardsticks connected by a bolt in the middle in such a way that the device could be opened and closed like scissors. The device exerted pressure on TC's hands depending on how far different objects were from her, simulating parallax. TC held onto one side of the device, and the other was manned by a researcher. Though the pressure device was tested using distance, the original design was inspired by TC's desire to understand the shape of different objects using pressure, like one would when making pottery.

For the first two tests, TC wore a Samsung Gear VR headset that recorded first-person video. A Samsung phone was connected to this headset that streamed the current video feed to the laptop of a researcher. That researcher could then identify what TC was looking at and the distance to said item using the Distance Meter application. The researcher then administered the stimuli depending on which prototype was being implemented.

2.2 Procedure

While all three prototypes varied in the nature of stimuli, each was tested in a similar manner. TC was first introduced to each prototype and gained confidence through a few trial sessions. The test was then performed and TC gave feedback about the usefulness of each prototype. This feedback was recorded by a researcher.

The first test used sound as a cue for distance. While TC sat and looked directly ahead, one of the researchers would move toward and away from her. Depending on the distance between TC and the researcher, a corresponding number of beeping sounds were played in succession.

Following our evaluation using auditory feedback, we implemented a similar system using tactile feedback with the LEGO Mindstorms motor. Once again, TC was seated with a researcher a few feet away. The motor, controlled by another researcher, vibrated at an increased rate the closer the first researcher was to TC, and likewise decreased in intensity the further the researcher was from TC.

The final test used pressure as the outputted stimuli. Using the aforementioned device with yardsticks, a researcher moved TC's hands closer or further apart depending on the distance between TC and the researcher. Though the VR headset could have been used in this test, we decided against it since its video output would have been obstructed by a researcher controlling the handheld device.

2.3 Results

With our first prototype that utilized auditory feedback, TC felt that she "could gauge pretty accurately how far [away] someone was", which met our goal of providing a basic measure of distance. However, TC noted that incorporating auditory complexity into a more developed system would likely provide challenges and speculated, "I might not be able to make sense of it".

The LEGO Mindstorms prototype, presented a method of conceptualizing space through tactile feedback (vibrations) using the motor's technology. Our one-dimensional system of decreasing rumble intensity when moving further away from TC proved effective in allowing her to measure distance. However, its simplicity and limitations were noted. In a debriefing meeting, TC stated "speed is a key facet of my visual experiences" and proposed that using vibration intensity as an indicator of object density may be a possible modification to the prototype.

The final test using the pressure prototype garnered the most positive feedback in our trials. TC was excited to see progress on a model that attempted to simulate eye movement and found the prototype "easy to understand." She suggested that for a more complete model "incorporating rotation would be important." Following this suggestion, we disassembled part of the third prototype to allow for rotation of TC's hands and evaluated this new system of conveying parallax. TC gave a positive response to the rotational system and noted that it may lead to the inception of a useful product in the future.

3. CONCLUSION

After completing our evaluation, we have concluded that our future focal point will be to enhance the pressure prototype, which was the device built to exert pressure on TC's hands in order to better fulfill her desire for a physical experience of sight that she described. We intend to simulate eye movement by incorporating rotation in order to express distance. We plan to introduce TC to a vibrotactile device inspired by the VibroGlove [4]. Our next device would provide the sensation of a user's hands being pushed and rotated in different directions, mimicking the ways in which eyes move. This would enable the user to identify the distance to an object in front of him or her. TC's wish of visualizing an environment through utilizing tactile feedback can be approached through this model, and we believe the model we have presented typifies TC's aspirations.

4. ACKNOWLEDGEMENTS

The authors would like to thank Tasha Chemel, Bezawit Ayalew, Tiffany Kayo, John Magee, and Diane Theriault.

5. REFERENCES

[1] S. Abboud, S. Hanassy, S. Levy-Tzedek, S. Maidenbaum, and A. Amedi. EyeMusic: Introducing a "visual" colorful experience for the blind using auditory sensory substitution. *Restorative Neurology and Neuroscience*, 32(2):247–257, 2014.

[2] P. Bach-y Rita and S. Kercel. Sensory substitution and the human-machine interface. *TRENDS in Cognitive Sciences*, 7(12):541–546, 2003.

[3] A. Cassinellia, E. Sampaio, S. Joffily, H. Lima, and B. Gusmão. Do blind people move more confidently with the tactile radar? *Technology and Disability*, 26(2):161–170, 2014.

[4] S. Krishna, S. Bala, T. McDaniel, S. McGuire, and S. Panchanathan. VibroGlove: an assistive technology aid for conveying facial expressions. In *CHI EA 2010*, pages 3637–3642, 2010.

[5] M. Williams, C. Galbraith, S. Kane, and A. Hurst. "Just let the cane hit it": how the blind and sighted see navigation differently. In *ASSETS '14*, pages 217–224, 2014.

VocalIDE: An IDE for Programming via Speech Recognition

Lucas Rosenblatt
Brown University, CMU HCI
6324 Douglas St.
Pittsburgh, PA 15217
lucas_rosenblatt@brown.edu

ABSTRACT

We believe that developing tools using a publicly available speech recognition API can provide a basis for keyboard free programming. We set out to develop a specialized voice-based IDE for this purpose. Early research revealed the strengths and limitations of current vocal text editors and environments. We report on a Wizard of Oz (WOz) experiment we conducted asking participants to edit code using vocal instructions given to a "human computer." Following the study, we developed a prototype, VocalIDE, which implements specialized editing mechanisms to better facilitate vocal programming.

CCS Concepts

• **HCI ⇒ Interaction devices ⇒ Sound-based input / output •HCI ⇒ Interactive systems and tools ⇒ User interface toolkits • HCI ⇒ Accessibility ⇒ Accessibility technologies**

Keywords

speech recognition; IDE; upper-limb impairment;

1. INTRODUCTION

While 6.7% of Americans have upper limb physical impairments [1], less than 4% of developers report having any physical disability whatsoever [2]. This suggests that those with upper body disabilities are under-represented in the developer community. One potential reason for this disparity is that coding remains inaccessible to those who struggle with or cannot use standard keyboards. Current coding practice implicitly requires the use of a keyboard. This requirement prevents a person who cannot type on a keyboard from coding. While soft keyboards or specialized trackballs might allow a user to code, these systems can be inefficient, difficult to learn, or expensive [5]. They are also primarily for general computer use rather than specialized to the domain of computer programming

IDEs have yet to be fully supported by easy-to-use speech-to-text software. Most programming languages contain varied commands that must be associated with speech patterns. Systems have been built by individuals for personal use, and for those willing to dedicate a significant amount of time to learning a new "language" (see Tavis Rudd's system [7] and Ben Meyer's VoiceCode [6]).

A system of voice programming is an expert task; it will always require some user education/instruction in order for interactions to produce results (sample commands, understanding of editing mechanisms, etc.). In both Rudd and Meyer's solutions, a new user must learn a whole host of non-natural vocal commands to be able to effectively use the software. Yet asking a user to memorize a new language discourages adoption, and this instructional period should be minimized. Conventional user experience wisdom suggests that by reducing use "friction" (in this case educational overhead), users will have a higher system adoption rate.

ASSETS'17, Oct. 29–Nov. 1, 2017, Batlimore, MD, USA.

 ISBN 978-1-4503-4926-0/17/10…$15.00.

DOI: http://dx.doi.org/10.1145/3132525.3134824

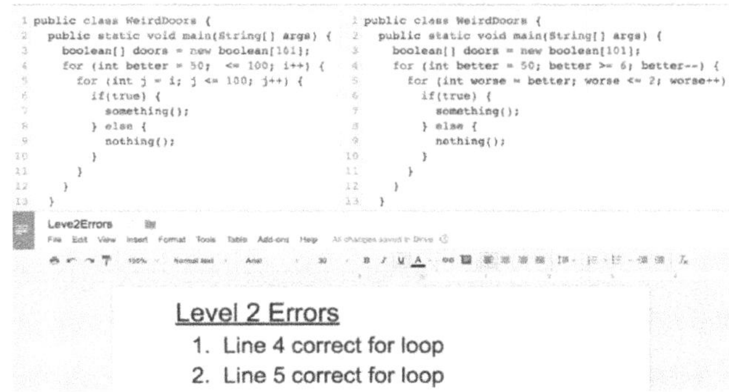

Figure 1. Participants were asked to correct the code on the left until it matched the code on the right using vocal instructions.

2. PRELIMINARY STUDY

An initial Wizard of Oz study (WOz) was conducted, seeking to gain an understanding of user instincts when giving vocal commands to a computer. What commands are programmers inclined to give a computer (using their voices) in order to write and edit code? What are the largest points of friction, and the most difficult tasks to complete? The study was conducted with 10 participants, none of whom had motor impairments, but who each had some coding experience. Future studies will be conducted on those who have upper limb impairments. The average participant age was 20 years ± 1.15, the study was conducted on 5 men and 5 women, and the average years of programming experience was 2.7 ± .95. All had taken a college programming course, and more than half had taken a high school programming course.

2.1 Method

Participants were asked to direct a "human computer" (a researcher) to correct code that was provided to them. The participant's screen mirrored the display of the "human computer's" screen, who operated the text editor according to a

P	LD	Common words w/ %	Time
1	16.33	"right" 39 %, "backspace" 9.4 %	7:26
2	26.13	"jump-to" 10.0 %, "space" 6.7 %	9:54
3	24.20	"the" 10.1 %, "after" 5.9 %	10:46
4	20.30	"and" 9.5 %, "then" 9.3 %	10:55
5	21.91	"the" 9.1 %, "after" 6.6 %	10:36
6	35.81	"to" 6.4 %, "line" 6.4 %	9:00
7	25.36	"to" 7.4 %, "backspace" 7.0 %	10:26
8	28.47	"type" 6.6 %, "to" 6.1 %	13:57
9	33.90	"the" 13.2 %, "line" 7.1 %	10:42
10	26.17	"type" 13.4 %, "to" 6.9 %	10:02

Table 1. Notice that participants shared a common vocabulary, but that all of the Lexical Densities (LD) suggest inefficiency, falling below 45+ (normal speech).

very literal interpretation of participant's speech. During each of six levels, the participant was presented two blocks of code. The right of their screen displayed the correct and complete code, and the left displayed a similar code snippet that contained some errors (Figure 2). Participants were instructed to speak to the "human computer" to transform the incorrect code into the correct code. Errors in the code were listed to control for variation in debugging time and strategy.

2.2 Level Generation

Levels were created following an analysis of common Java code and errors. The 50 most in-linked algorithm pages from rosettacode.org formed a common Java corpus. We ran further text analysis to create a standard of common Java syntax. Thanks to Jackson, Carver et al. [3] we had an approximation of the 20 most common Java errors. We used this knowledge to create realistic, common errors on each level of the study. This rigorous process ensured that levels were representative of important/common challenges a programmer faces when writing/editing Java code.

2.3 Results

The study showed that participants used different commands when vocal programming, although they shared approaches. The most common word was "the", and the most common significant words, barring articles ("the", "to", etc.), were "right," "line," "space," and "after." Significant words were navigational in nature, suggesting that a majority of participants spent their words on referencing locations in the code. For closer text analysis, we use lexical density (LD) (a measure of significant words in a text, or how many words contribute to the overall meaning of a text) [4]. The overall lexical density of the participant corpus was 6.9%, which is far less than average speech (one study suggests that speech interviews tend to have a lexical density of ~45%) [4]. This suggests that users are inefficient with natural speech vocal commands. A number of individuals typed letter by letter, while some participants provided new feature insight that we had not yet conceptualized (for example: combine "search" and "type" into one command "change").

3. WORKING PROTOTYPE: VOCALIDE

Drawing from research and the results of our WOz study, we developed VocalIDE using websafe javascript. VocalIDE is a fully capable voice-to-code editor. VocalIDE allows users to program using a myriad of vocal commands. Users can enter new text by word or by letter, enter syntax (+,.,\},) etc.) by common name, navigate using line numbers or minute cursor commands, and select instances of words or phrases anywhere in the document. This constitutes what we deem the "basic" usable functionality of vocal text editor. The results of the WOz study indicate that a user expects for each of these inputs or editing mechanisms to be available.

VocalIDE ignores most articles and filler words, attempting to search a command string for pertinent or significant command information. The WOz study suggested that users will include these words that do not contribute to meaningful commands. Ignoring them provides a smoother transition as the user becomes accustomed to the platform.

The WOz study suggested that users are ineffecient when navigating text using vocal commands. Furthermore, close context editing (i.e. single word level) and wide context changes (i.e. file navigation) are difficult to do with ease and accuracy using vocal commands. To address this, we proposed and implemented Context Color Editing, or CCE. CCE follows the cursor position, and highlights individual syntax and words on the cursor's line, as well as the lines above and below it. The user need only say a color for that color's highlighted text to become the active selection. CCE also highlights file tabs for quickly changing between the current open file. The goal of CCE is to allow users to be more efficient with their commands, replacing cumbersome sentence structures with short, quickly spoken colors. The entire document can be navigated using CCE alone, and we found that the introduction of CCE greatly improved close context editing ability of users by allowing them to be less accurate with their selection commands (as they could quickly reselect with color commands) and faster with their general navigation.

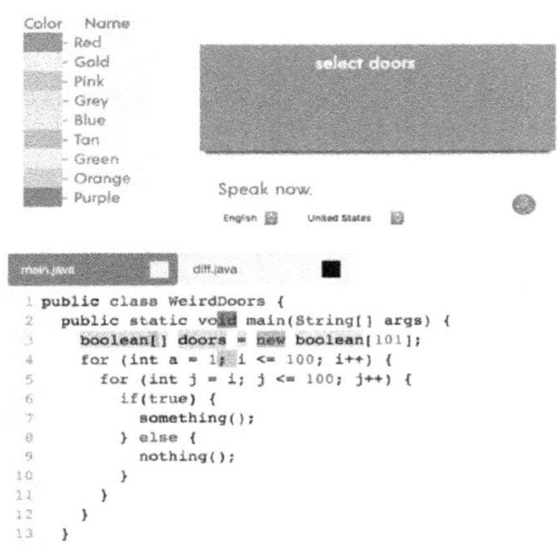

Figure 2. Active prototype with CCE (a "select doors" command has just been recorded). The main.java and diff.java tabs can be swapped using vocal CCE shortcuts.

4. FUTURE WORK

Another study will soon be conducted with participants who have limited upper body, arm or hand dexterity; following the study, the participants will be interviewed and the system adjusted according to their specific needs. CCE will be expanded into more visual feedback vocal navigation selection tools (for file navigation and running code).

5. REFERENCES

[1] Brault, M.W. July 2012. *Americans With Disabilities: 2010.* U.S. Department of Commerce.

[2] IGDA. October 2005. *Game Developer Demographics: Exploration of Diversity.* U.S. Department of Commerce.

[3] Jackson, J, Cobb, M, and Carver, C. 2005. Identifying top Java errors for novice programmers. In *FIE'05. Proceedings 35th Annual Conference.* T4C-T4C.

[4] Johansson, V. 2008. *Lexical diversity and lexical density in speech and writing.* Working Papers 53. 61-79 pages.

[5] Mackenzie, I. S, Zhang, S. X, and Soukoreff, R. W. 1999. Text entry using soft keyboards. *Behaviour & Information Technology.* 18, 4 (1999).

[6] Meyer, B. Accessed May 23, 2017. *Advanced voice-control Platform.* https://voicecode.io/.

[7] Rudd, T. http://pyvideo.org/pycon-us-2013/using-python-to-code-by-voice.html. Using Python to Code by Voice. PyVideo.org, Accessed May 23, 2017

Personal Perspectives on Using Automatic Speech Recognition to Facilitate Communication between Deaf Students and Hearing Customers

James Mallory
NTID/RIT
52 Lomb Memorial Drive
Rochester, NY 14623
585-475-2865
jrmnet@rit.edu

Michael Stinson
NTID/RIT
52 Lomb Memorial Drive
Rochester, NY 14623
585-475-6596
msserd@rit.edu

Lisa Elliot
NTID/RIT
52 Lomb Memorial Drive
Rochester, NY 14623
585-475-6596
lisa.elliot@rit.edu

Donna Easton
NTID/RIT
52 Lomb Memorial Drive
Rochester, NY 14623
585-475-6596
dlencr@rit.edu

ABSTRACT
Automatic Speech Recognition (ASR) and the wide use of smart phones and their apps have allowed huge inroads when preparing deaf and hard-of-hearing (D/HH) students to be effective and productive in the hearing workplace. This paper presents both a hearing instructor's experiences and a deaf researcher's observations when preparing deaf and hard of hearing students as computer technicians for the hearing work place.

CCS Concepts
Human Centered Computing →Automatic Speech Recognition
This paper includes the use of technology by and in support of Individuals who are deaf or hard-of-hearing (D/HH). The authors present innovative contributions to smart phone technology and apps that improve the accessibility of everyday life of D/HH individuals.

Keywords
Smart phones; deaf and hard of hearing; phone apps; WhatsApp; research; deaf in workplace. automatic speech recognition; deaf education; small group interaction; technology

1. INTRODUCTION
One author teaches a technical capstone course each semester where groups of five to twenty D/HH students finishing their AAS Applied Computer Technology (ACT) degrees are required to implement projects in Rochester and surrounding area businesses. Communication between D/HH students and hearing business owners and managers can be quite cumbersome when there are no interpreters around so the instructor had students and the business owners use a smart phone app named WhatsApp for communication purposes. Researchers monitored these interactions and their observations are detailed in this paper.

The second author is one of the researchers on the team and is deaf. He has repeatedly experienced frustration in following group conversations with non-signing hearing persons. Although he benefits from a cochlear implant, conversations in groups, especially when there is background noise, are challenging for him. In particular, it can be difficult to remember specific points discussed in a conversation and use the information in follow up work after the group conversation. In part, these experiences provided inspiration for this research project to explore use of automatic speech recognition to facilitate communication between D/HH and hearing persons in meetings when an interpreter is not available.

In contrast to educational settings, where legislation and practice promote accommodations such as sign language interpreting, cost-effective methods to facilitate D/HH individual's communication in the *workplace* are not available. Automatic Speech Recognition (ASR), software that converts audio input of human speech into text displayed on the screen, holds exciting promise for making spoken content accessible for people who are D/HH

This paper will report on an in-progress study that has completed 10 field trials, 5 with ASR technology, including display of speaker's comments, with students in the Applied Computer Technology (ACT) major within the NTID Information and Computing Studies (ICS) program. The study has been examining the extent that ASR has potential, whether participants can adapt to the use of ASR, and whether they modify their speech or behavior to enable communication. These D/HH students, as part of their project or work experience, have regularly interacted with hearing customers without interpreting support.

2. METHODOLOGY
During three semesters, ASR implementation using WhatsApp was used with 28 students at four different locations. Twenty-one of these 28 students were observed by the one of the other authors, including Michael Stinson who himself is deaf. Five field trials occurred with ASR and five occurred without ASR. The ASR that was used was a feature in the WhatsApp application on both Android and iPhone smart phones. The study was conducted on-site at three different businesses in the Rochester area. Customers included hearing business owners of a swimming pool and patio supply story, a paddling center, and a manager and a senior technician at Fix-in-a-Zip Mobil device repair business.

Participants were 21 signing deaf students and 6 hearing customers who did not know sign language. The study used observational checklists, field notes, and participant ratings to identify ways that D/HH and hearing workers may use an ASR

ASSETS'17, October 29-November 1, 2017, Baltimore, MD, USA.

ACM ISBN 978-1-4503-4926-0/17/10.
https://doi.org/10.1145/3132525.3134779

tool. For the trials with ASR, the transcripts that were produced with ASR and with students using texting were examined.

The technology used was an app called WhatsApp. It sets up a conversational stream. Students or customers were free to add to it at any point during the life of the project. The hearing business owner would speak into their phones and use the ASR aspect of WhatsApp and the D/HH students would text back as seen in Figure 1 below.

The following pictures illustrate how communication occurred between hearing customers and D/HH students. Figures 2 and 3 show use of sign language interpreters at the site to facilitate communication. Figures 4-7 show these same hearing customers and D/HH students communicating with each other using ASR and texting using the WhatsApp smart phone application.

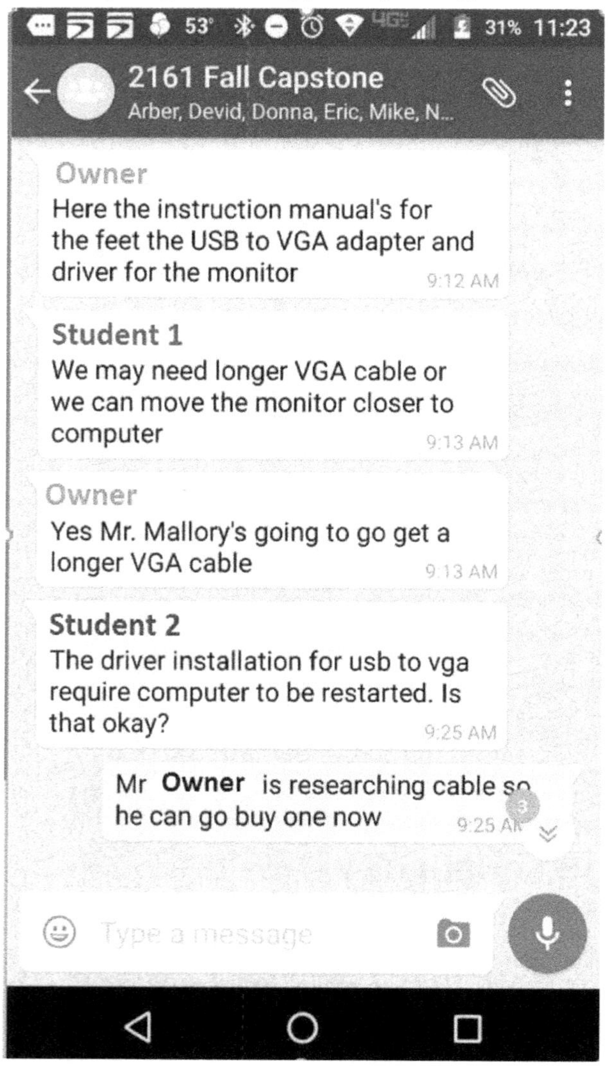

Fig. 1: Phone screen capture of WhatApp and ASR use.

Fig. 2: Author Mallory (right) interpreting for manager at a company prior to ASR Implementation.

Fig. 3: Using interpreter (4th from left) with hearing business owner (5th from left) on site at a business prior to implementing ASR.

Fig. 4: Owner (far left) Using ASR with D/HH students at place of business.

Fig. 5: Manager (foreground, back turned) Using ASR with D/HH students and with Deaf Author Stinson (far right) who is observing the interaction.

Fig. 6: Owner Using ASR with D/HH students at place of business.

Fig. 7: Sr. Technician training D/HH students at place of business using ASR.

3. RESULTS

Results indicated that ASR in conjunction with smart phone apps might benefit communication between hearing and deaf individuals in small group communication where an NTID instructor oversees the project but is occasionally not at customer-student meetings. Observations of the five field trials without ASR indicated that deaf students typically used writing or text messaging to communicate with hearing customers. Hearing customers tended to write out basic information in response to questions or comments of deaf students. When they needed to initiate conversations with deaf students, customers wrote basic information. Observations of trials with ASR indicated that customers needed to become familiar with using ASR, as using ASR to communicate with deaf students was new. Once they began to use ASR, customers appeared to use it with relative ease, and the ASR seemed to ease communication with deaf students. Based on visual inspection of transcripts and observations of students and owners, ASR was generally accurate enough for participants to rely on the text display. In the surveys of deaf students' perceptions of ASR, all twelve students rated ASR as either somewhat or very helpful for communicating with hearing customers. A few more students stated that they received more information from hearing customers with ASR than stated that they received about the same amount of information without ASR. Whether a student was deaf or hard of hearing made a difference in responses, with hard of hearing students being less reliant on ASR.

Some challenges occurred with the mobile device repair business. The senior technician working with the students (Figure 7) had to pick up and put the phone down frequently when he was showing what to do with smart phone repairs. The authors and this technician experimented with behind the ear Bluetooth devices which helped, but WhatsApp still requires that the user hit the "send" button to deliver the message. In future studies the authors would like to implement a watch instead of a traditional smart phone and an ASR app that does not require the use of a send button.

3.1 Title and Authors TBA

4. ACKNOWLEDGMENTS

Our thanks to Rochester area business owners and managers for collaborating with us for this study. With their permission, we acknowledge them by name here. Specifically we would like to thank John and Gene Easton, owners of Ace Swim and Leisure, Ken Altfather, owner of Baycreek Paddle Center, and Mr. Chris Camelio, owner Fix-In-A-Zip Device Repair and Home Solutions. We would also like to thank and acknowledge manager Kristin DiQuattor and senior technician Tim Odonell at Fix-In-A-Zip who spent considerable time working with our students and our researchers.

5. REFERENCES

[1] Acero, A., Deng, L., Kristjansson, T.T., Zhang, J.: HMM adaptation using vector taylor series for noisy speech recognition. In: Proceedings of Annual Conference of International Speech Communication Association (INTERSPEECH), pp. 869–872 (2000)

[2] Bahl, L., Brown, P., de Souza, P., Mercer, R.: Maximum mutual information estimation of HMM parameters for speech recognition. In: Proceedings of International Conference on Acoustics, Speech and Signal Processing (ICASSP), pp. 49–52 (1986)

[3] Baker, J., Deng, L., Glass, J., Khudanpur, S., Lee, C.H., Morgan, N., O'Shgughnessy, D.: Research developments and directions in speech recognition and understanding, part i. IEEE Signal Process. Mag. **26**(3), 75–80 (2009)

[4] Baker, J., Deng, L., Glass, J., Khudanpur, S., Lee, C.H., Morgan, N., O'Shgughnessy, D.: Updated minds report on speech recognition and understanding (research developments and directions in speech recognition and understanding, part ii). IEEE Signal Process. Mag. **26**(4), 78–85 (2009)

[5] Biem, A., Katagiri, S., McDermott, E., Juang, B.H.: An application of discriminative feature extraction to filter-bank-based speech recognition. IEEE Trans. Speech Audio Process. **9**, 96–110 (2001)

[6] Bilmes, J.: Buried Markov models: a graphical modeling approach to automatic speech recognition. Comput. Speech Lang. **17**, 213–231 (2003)

Cyborg Pride: Self-Design in e-NABLE

Peregrine Hawthorn
Monroe Community College
Rochester, NY
peregrinetodd@gmail.com

Daniel Ashbrook
Rochester Institute of Technology
Rochester, NY
daniel.ashbrook@rit.edu

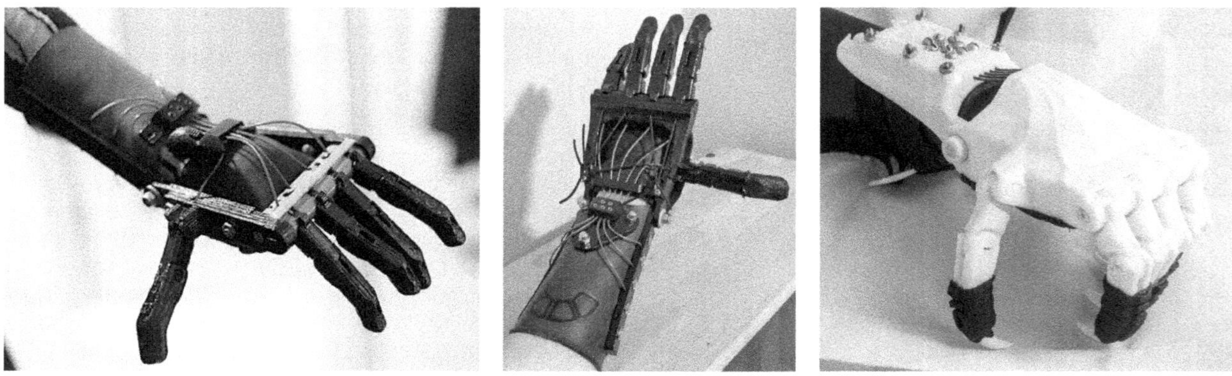

(a) (b) (c)

Figure 1: A partial progression of the first author's hands. (a) Snap-together RoboHand[1] (image courtesy of Jen Owen); (b) Talon hand 3.0[2] (image courtesy Peter Binkley); (c) The hand currently in use, a very highly customized Osprey[3] design.

ABSTRACT

The e-NABLE community is a global, distributed, loosely coordinated effort to design, produce, and deliver upper-limb assistive technology to those in need. e-NABLE's volunteers are often 3D-printing enthusiasts who are driven to use their skills to improve the lives of others. Volunteers provide the devices they produce to recipients around the world; these recipients are mainly children, but some are adults as well. While e-NABLE and its participants have received much attention from the media, little has been written about the experiences of the e-NABLE device users themselves. In this paper, we document the experiences of one user of an e-NABLE hand, detailing in a first-person account the journey from a recipient to an active participant and advocate for self-efficacy.

1. INTRODUCTION

Physical prostheses have been used for thousands of years to replace the function or appearance of a missing body part. Prostheses can be purely—or mainly—cosmetic, aiming to look as much like the original as possible, and can also to varying degrees recreate functionality. Prosthetic technology has always been customized to the end user: while human anatomy naturally varies from person to person, the morphology of missing body parts can vary much more, resulting from congenital factors or injury. While both professionals and amateurs have always created customized assistive technology (AT) [4], in recent years the rise in availability of consumer-level fabrication equipment—especially 3D printers—has allowed for the emergence of a new sharing culture of designs, strategies, and sometimes even physical assistive technology devices themselves.

The e-NABLE community—a globally distributed, loosely organized group of volunteers who design, customize, fabricate, and deliver 3D-printed upper-limb assistive technology to those in need—is a prominent example of this new paradigm of AT production [6]. The devices produced by e-NABLE volunteers combine body-powered functionality with a customizable, but usually non-realistic aesthetic, enabling recipients to grasp and—to a certain extent—manipulate objects while avoiding the traditional "hook" prosthetic.

As yet, there is little published data following up with recipients of these devices to assess the long-term impact of the prosthesis on their lives. It is known from the literature that as many as one in three users of assistive technology may stop using, or abandon, the devices [7], but data specific to e-NABLE is not available. In this report, we add one data point: the first author of this paper is both a recipient of an e-NABLE hand and an active participant in the community. We discuss the experiences of Peregrine with his e-NABLE hands and the community, describing how the device has interacted with and changed his body, life, and sense of self.

1.1 e-NABLE

In earlier work, we described e-NABLE as a community in detail and related some of the challenges that volunteers and clinicians

[1] `https://www.thingiverse.com/thing:92937`
[2] `https://www.thingiverse.com/thing:229620`
[3] `https://www.thingiverse.com/thing:910465`

ASSETS '17, Oct. 29–Nov. 1, 2017, Baltimore, MD, USA.

ISBN 978-1-4503-4926-0/17/10...$15.00.
DOI: `http://dx.doi.org/10.1145/3132525.3134780`

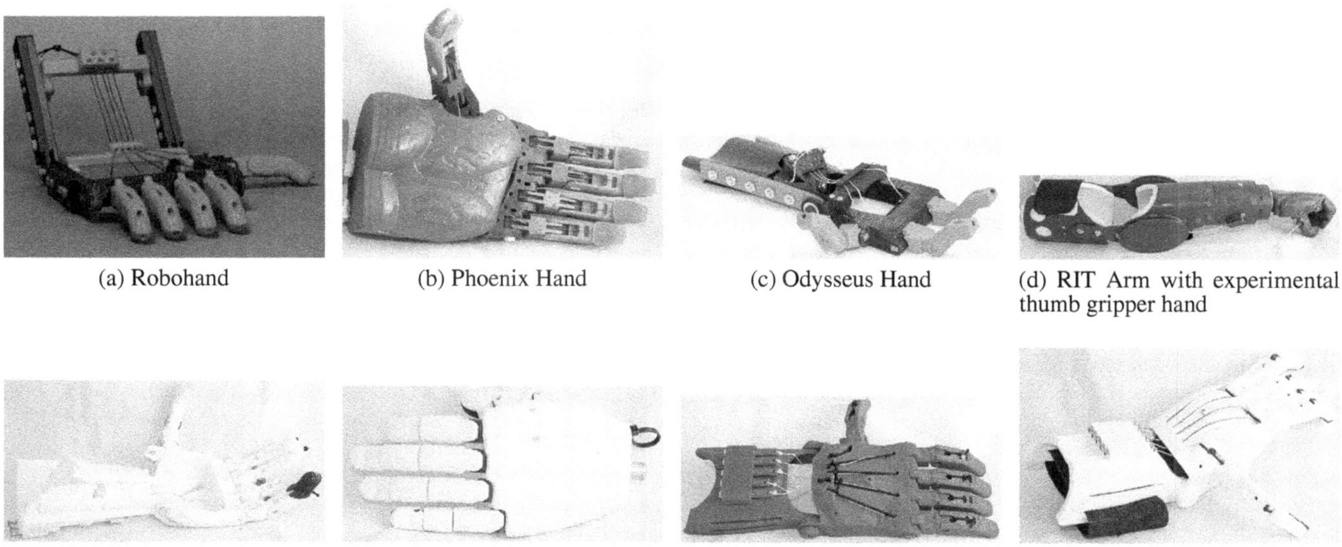

(a) Robohand (b) Phoenix Hand (c) Odysseus Hand (d) RIT Arm with experimental thumb gripper hand

(e) Cyborg Beast (f) Flexy-Hand (g) Raptor Hand (h) Raptor Reloaded

Figure 2: A variety of hands and arms developed in connection with the e-NABLE community. (a) is ⓒⓒ by MakerBot; the other images were taken by the last author at RIT's e-NABLE lab.

encounter when trying to work together [6]. For context, here we will briefly summarize some of those findings, as well as add more detail about the e-NABLE devices themselves.

e-NABLE is primarily represented by a private Google+ online forum (members must request to be admitted, but the acceptance criteria is very liberal). This Google+ community includes over 9,800 members, and continues to grow. Community members can take on any of several roles within e-NABLE, and frequently have more than one role. Potential recipients and parents of recipients participate in the community discussions, as well as general 3D printing hobbyists who are interested in volunteering. Medical professionals, clinicians, and orthotists/prosthetists occasionally lend their expertise to community discussions. Device designers share announcements of new designs with the wider community, and seek volunteers to print new designs on a wide variety of printers for beta testing. A matching team pairs fabricators with recipients. Community organizers announce opportunities to take part in conventions, Maker Faires, and other face-to-face events.

There is no single "e-NABLE device;" rather, the e-NABLE community uses a constantly-evolving array of upper-limb assistive devices. All of these devices share the mechanical property of providing basic grasp assistance and the aesthetic property of appearing—at least to a certain extent—somewhat like a human hand. Although 3D printing is the primary method of producing devices, many designs include a significant portion of non-printed parts. These can include elastic bands, specialized screws, hook-and-loop fasteners, leather, foam padding, and micro gel fingertips. Not all of these components are widely available, leading to design principles around using easy-to-source hardware.

e-NABLE's fabricators provide a number of types of devices that effect a gross grasping motion, using a cable-pull mechanism to cause the fingers to close. Devices are available both for recipients with a transradial or higher amputation ("arms") or wrist or lower ("hands"). For hands—the focus of this experience report—the devices are actuated by wrist flexion.

e-NABLE has a beta testing process for validating candidate device designs, which is documented in the online community. This device validation process includes selecting an appropriate open license, documenting assembly instructions, drafting a bill of materials with sources for all non-printed parts, documenting the results of print tests and user tests, and determining a support plan for questions that may be generated by users. All of this documentation is then submitted to e-NABLE's Strategic Planning Committee for approval.

When a device design is approved for wide release, source files are posted to a publicly-accessible repository, such as Thingiverse[4] or Youmagine[5]. A link to the design is added to the list of devices on the e-NABLE website[6], and announcements of the new design are posted to the Google+ e-NABLE community.

Figure 2 shows a number of the hands and arms that have been developed in connection with the e-NABLE community.

2. RELATED WORK

Beyond our own work [6], discussed above, the e-NABLE community, its members, and the technology it produces have been a topic of some academic interest. With reference to the e-NABLE community itself, Homan et al. used textual and network analysis techqniues to comment on the origins and evolution of the Google+ online forum [3].

From a clinical perspective, some effort has been focused on the "development of the 3D-printed devices as well as considerations around actual production. Zuniga et al. have published several papers on construction and fitting of e-NABLE devices [10, 11, 9], including a brief report on one to three months of usage by eleven children. The authors found that using the device correlated to some improvement in life quality, and that the amount of use varied considerably. Researchers have also taken advantage of the customizability of 3D-printed technology to rapidly prototype task-specific prosthetic devices, such as a violin bow holder [2].

[4] `http://www.thingiverse.com`
[5] `https://www.youmagine.com/`
[6] `http://enablingthefuture.org/upper-limb-prosthetics`

Hofmann et al. reported on the perspectives of e-NABLE-involved clinicians and makers who attended an e-NABLE summit. They noted the tensions between the clinicians' "do no harm" professional ethical stance and the makers' desire for rapid iteration and unbridled creativity [1].

Some researchers have investigated the experiences of end users of personalized assistive technology. Profita et al. investigated the customization activities of hearing aid and cochlear implant users, finding that device wearers saw decorating their devices as a medium for self-expression [8]. Similarly, Bennett et al.'s study of 14 individuals with upper-limb difference showed that those who chose to use prostheses integrated them as part of their self-identity, often enhancing this effect by aesthetic customization. In an interesting contrast to the first author of this paper, Bennet et al.'s study included five e-NABLE recipients, none of whom used their 3D-printed—or any—prosthesis with regularity.

Finally, Meissner et al. described a series of workshops intended to give people with disabilities an opportunity to learn and use making skills by themselves [5]. They found that participants were interested in learning and exercising skills and in building technology to help themselves and others—interests that mirror our own findings of motivations of volunteers in e-NABLE [6].

3. THE EXPERIENCE OF AN E-NABLE DEVICE USER

In this section, the first author provides a first-person account of his experiences as an e-NABLE user, community participant, and advocate for self-efficacy for people with disabilities.

3.1 Early Experience

My name is Peregrine Hawthorn, and I was born without fingers on my left hand. Growing up, I was often ridiculed for my difference, and made to feel physically inferior to all my peers. My family was poor, so we never considered any sort of assistive technology.

It wasn't until I was 18 years old, after I had graduated from high school, that I discovered 3D printing, and the ability to create my own set of fingers. My father was the first to get a 3D printer—the Solidoodle 2—and it was an ordeal to get successful prints out of it, but after about 3 months of modifying and fiddling with the printer, we managed to print and assemble a Snap-Together Robohand (Figure 2a). I very quickly got used to having an extra five fingers, and I often found myself trying to, and sometimes failing to, resist the urge to grab something simply because I now could. Since I put on my first hand, it's been an integral part of who I am and what I do. Today, I design and build hands, in addition to wearing and using them.

The first hand I made (Figure 1a) provided a fantastic experience, but was sub-par on almost every level. Before we could even make a hand, we had to change designs from the "official" Robohand to the Snap Together Robohand released my Makerbot, due to the fabrication instructions being incomplete and referencing parts not included in the design files. Once we assembled a functional hand, it was bulky and didn't fit me very well. The forearm was small and inflexible, and the plastic wrist joints didn't line up well with my wrist. I couldn't use it to do more than to gesture or to drag a small amount of weight, as too much pressure would start to warp the palm. It hurt to wear for more than a few hours at a time because the cable guides in the forearm and back of the hand weren't fixed in place, causing them to turn and dig into my arm under physical stress.

One of the earliest modifications to the hand involved using a hacksaw. The original RoboHand's attachment to the wrist involved two parallel bars, which doesn't fit well on adults. We cut off parts of the knuckle block to make the sides slope in towards my wrist. We also dipped the ends of the palm and the arm bars in boiling water to soften them and bent them with pliers to give me a better fit. However, where the physical function was lacking, we were able to customize my new hand to my liking, with stamped leather and glossy black fingers to give a "Darth Vader" feel to my new fingers. Despite having no prior experience 3D printing, we were able to construct a rudimentary hand from my fathers experience with other materials like leather and thermoplastics: skills I quickly picked up as I did further post-print modifications and repairs on subsequent hands.

Once my hand became comfortable enough that I could use it to lift more than a couple of pounds, with the addition of padding and slightly more rounded corners, I began losing fingers about as fast as we could print replacements. A combination of poor print quality and thin, delicate parts meant that the finger joints would break frequently, sometimes without me even noticing until hours later. This would be fixed, mostly by identifying weak points by fractures and bulking them up until they stopped breaking. This was a clumsy method, but effective within the confines of what I was capable of. The more elegant changes came later when I started fusing parts that didn't need to be printed separately anymore because of desktop 3D printing advancements allowing for greater overhangs and sturdier layer adhesion.

Most of the early modifications happened on the design file end, and the bulk of those were done by my father, the far more experienced 3D modeler among us. However, most of those early changes were informed by my use and suggestion. Until I learned to use modeling programs like Blender, TinkerCAD, Solidworks, and Fusion 360, I mostly made post-printing modifications like finding better materials for finger pads, or using different metal hardware that allowed me to more easily make adjustments on the fly. All the modifications we made for durability, we devised ourselves, as no one else in e-NABLE had much experience with parts breaking. However, we did pull some structural inspiration from models like the Cyborg Beast for my eventual plastic upper, as well as 3D printed washers for large snap pins in the wrist to replace steel bolts with nylock nuts I continually lost.

Shortly after I got my first hand, I began working. I worked backstage at a local theater, building sets, assisting quick changes, and fixing broken microphones during the show. After that, I worked for Fed-Ex sorting packages. After that, I joined Americorps NCCC, FEMACorps, and traveled around the country aiding disaster recovery efforts in Oklahoma, Northern Texas, and Southern California. Upon graduation out of the AmeriCorps program, I worked in event setup, creating and setting up decor for weddings and events, doing everything from moving very large base plates to building centerpieces.

Each and every one of these jobs was a testing ground for the latest iteration of my limbs. Each step of the way I improved the base features of my hand like bulking up fragile parts or using better grip material as I found it, or making the fit more dynamic and adaptable to different amounts of clothing or fitting around uniforms. Most of these modifications were made to the original design files in Blender, which I learned from my father and online tutorials. I also would make regional or task-specific changes to match different jobs, like attaching a flashlight to my wrist when working backstage, making my hand able to convert into a hip water bottle holder in AmeriCorps, or insulating my fingers with rubber to allow me to unravel yard upon yard of cord, and change light-bulbs on live wire without the risk of electrocution. Later I would also thicken portions of my hand that I intended to use as a hammer, and add claws that allowed me to manipulate very small objects when building prototype electronics. These modifications were usually made post-print, or made quickly in easier to use, but less powerful, modeling software like TinkerCAD.

Relatively early on in this adventure, I was contacted by Ivan Owen, the maker who designed the original Snap-Together Robohand. We were both in the Seattle area at the time, and after meeting up and sharing our stories, he directed me to a group on Google+ called e-NABLE. e-NABLE is an online group of people from around the world who had taken an interest in developing and distributing 3D printed upper limb prostheses. Many of the designs were highly temperamental, but some of the early ideas in that community became instrumental in the later development of upper limb prostheses today. I quickly found a place in this community as one of the most vocal and articulate users of the devices developed there.

3.2 About My Hand

In my experience designing and using upper limb assistive technology, the most important thing is that it be comfortable. This means that it is not only easy on the user when they are at rest or preforming light actions, but when they are under the greatest stress that they can expect to endure. It is not enough to be comfortable in the lab, when it's first put on. It must continue to be comfortable in heat and cold, while carrying significant weight, and under sustained use.

To fulfill these requirements when designing and building a hand, I prefer to use leather as a base, and either foam or silicone for padding. Despite the trademark aspect of my assistive devices being that they are 3D printed, to avoid abrasion issues I don't let any of that printed plastic touch my skin. I remain separated from the plastic by a thick layer of leather, secured in place with machine screws into the plastic and with nylon straps and tri-glide adjusters (Figure 3).

The general construction of my prosthetic devices has changed only slightly in the years that I've been wearing them. All custom parts are 3D printed in ABS plastic in a fused deposition printer. I then sand those parts to remove any stray bits of plastic, hold them at approximately 110°C to improve layer adhesion and overall strength, and then expose them to a cloud of acetone vapor to vitrify and smooth over the rough print lines. This makes the otherwise porous and rough surface strong, smooth, and easy to keep clean. I then mount these parts to leather with either machine screws (newer hands) or rivets (older hands). Leather is a fantastic material here, because it's very easy to use, and is significantly more comfortable than any printed plastic structure. Braided actuator cables are sometimes tied to screws or printed bars, but I prefer to use nylon monofilament cables that I affix with set screws in the forearm and fingers. Originally this preference was purely aesthetic, but this later became the foundation of how I removed elastics from the actuation system, relying on stiffer cabling that both close and open my fingers.

Form and function play an integral role in my relationship with my prosthetic hands. This is also true for e-NABLE recipients: among child users, I observe them often preferring a particular look over usefulness or durability. This makes sense, as they often use 3D printed limbs on a social level, rather than a physical one. It is far more important that their limb be a "character-themed hand" than that it be able to carry lots of weight for long hours. In the future, it would be nice if hand designs allowed for more customization, beyond the colors parts are printed in. I could see space for designs or a signature being useful in helping a device feel more like a part of the user. Other small customizations like a slot for frequently used items, or decorative attachments have had some success, but they've been few and far in-between, and none have been seen as more than just a novelty one-off device.

Despite its importance, this kind of personalization can often be hindered by a social barrier. If a volunteer is making a hand, free of charge, it's not uncommon for a recipient to feel like any requests are imposing and taking advantage of the kindness of others. It can be considered charity work, not a business, and as such the recipient may not feel entitled to ask for much customization. This issue can be exacerbated by the fact that most users are young enough that most communication passes through their parents on its way to an e-NABLE volunteer, and thus most possibility for creative expression is dulled across communication channels.

When I create my own limbs, there is no such barrier: I can spend as much time and effort on them as I like (Figure 3). I have rubber work glove parts on my fingers and large claws simply because I wanted to try it out and thought it might look nice; they turn out to be useful for holding different kinds of objects and for pulling sleeves and gloves onto my unaffected hand. I put protruding bolts on my bracer because I felt the extra strength they might provide would be worth the sharp edges. I used three different methods to affix my actuator cables into my fingertips because I was tired of them popping out under excessive strain. I worked for a few hours just to create the aesthetic design on the back of the piece that I felt I should have there. I experimented with steel brushes to give the white plastic the look of bone. I even printed finger connector pins in three different colors so I could coordinate them with my clothing. In my customization, I went far beyond what I would ever consider asking anyone else to do for me, particularly if I felt somehow indebted to them for this service.

It has been my observation that, as all e-NABLE hands are made for printing and assembly by inexperienced DIY "makers" or others of similar skill level, any hand that can be successfully distributed must be made of easily acquirable parts, such as those that can be purchased at a hardware store. Generally, a low-end 3D printer is the only piece of specialized equipment we can expect anyone to have access to. This dramatically reduces the variety of solutions available for designing DIY assistive technology. This means that, as a designer, I need to make everything easy to source, fit, and make, as well as make every design robust against failure from many angles. My personal hand uses metal hardware, leather, nylon straps, heavy gauge fishing line, and rubber work gloves. I deliberately chose all of these as easy to find and easy to work with. The digital files for my hand also contain many variations of the same part with different levels of joint tolerance, to accommodate for scale and to correct for low quality printers' tendency to over-extrude.

For me, and for many others, the hand and all of the modifications are not just about function, but about the social aspect, especially for kids. In school, most children haven't yet learned yet how to be decent human beings, and they will pick on any differences they can find. If you can go from being the kid with the weird hand to the kid with the cool robot hand, you can go from being an outcast to the kid everyone wants to be friends with. In that way, the social aspect can be even more important than the functionality of the hand.

3.3 Cyborg Identity

My own social experience as a congenital amputee has been a generally troubled one. Mostly through between the grades of one and four, I was consistently made fun of and considered "other" by my peers. However, beyond that, most people either made a point of ignoring or simply didn't notice my limb difference. I also got very good at hiding it, always covering my affected hand in photos and wearing baggy long sleeve shirts that covered my affected limb. It wasn't until I was 18 and made my first assistive hand that I began

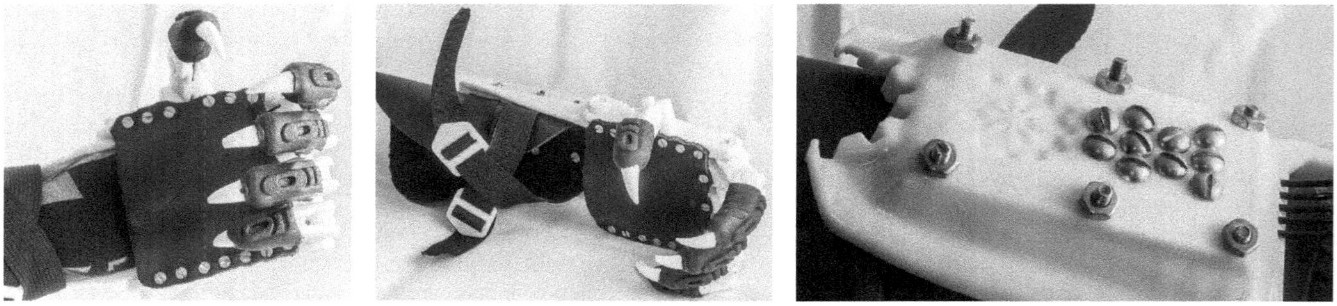

Figure 3: Images of Peregrine's current hand with its modifications. Left: claws allow fine manipulation and the ability to pull on sleeves and gloves on the right hand. Center: crossed straps provide a more comfortable fit than a single one. Right: a close-up image of the aesthetic customizations, including brass hardware, protruding bolts, and gear-shaped finishes.

to display my hand again. Now I don't hide my hand partly because, physically, I can't. The device I wear is too big to fit in any pocket, and eclipses my unaffected hand. However, the more prominent reason I display my prosthetic hand is because of the role I had in making and designing it, and how happy I am with the results. Every assistive device I've worn highlights my limb difference. Because of this, every hand I wear is designed to celebrate that difference. My first hand was a glossy black with bright blue actuation cables. Today my hand is bright white to contrast with the black I usually wear, further putting my hand in the spotlight, and has symbols of personal significance embossed into the forearm that mirror a necklace given to me.

As someone who grew up with depression, it had always been difficult to associate with myself. I rarely had any strong feelings about things happening to me, and never had much interest in self-improvement. The only things I ever got excited about were things I had made. I would go far out of my way to find and hoard scrap and raw material to make things with. When I began to make my own limbs, I became my own project. I became a prototype to be refined as I use, break, repair, and redesign my body—my self.

Today, I feel a responsibility for my own body parts. I am able to be independent and to maintain myself. If part of my hand breaks, I don't have to ask someone else to fix it. I have an understanding of how it works and what its limitations are. I can upgrade myself as needed, and I can see the same thing happening for other people: in the future, they might design their own hands to specialize them to what they want to do, whether it is fine-grained manipulation, holding a glass of wine, or moving heavy boxes around.

I see myself as a work in progress, and as something worthy of of improving and upkeeping. I think this is one of the greatest things that someone could get out of this experience: not just the hand, but the idea that you are worth improving, and that you have the ability to improve yourself.

Acknowledgements

This material is based upon work supported by the National Science Foundation under Grant No. IIS-1464377.

4. REFERENCES

[1] Megan Hofmann, Julie Burke, Jon Pearlman, Goeran Fiedler, Andrea Hess, Jon Schull, Scott E Hudson, and Jennifer Mankoff. 2016a. Clinical and Maker Perspectives on the Design of Assistive Technology with Rapid Prototyping Technologies. In *ASSETS '16: Proceedings of the 18th international ACM SIGACCESS conference on Computers & accessibility*. 1–6.

[2] Megan Hofmann, Jeffrey Harris, Scott E Hudson, and Jennifer Mankoff. 2016b. Helping Hands: Requirements for a Prototyping Methodology for Upper-limb Prosthetics Users. In *CHI '16: Proceedings of the 2016 CHI Conference on Human Factors in Computing Systems*. New York, New York, USA, 1769–1780.

[3] Christopher Michael Homan, Jon I Schull, and Akshai Prabhu. 2017. On the Genesis of an Assistive Technology Crowdsourcing Community. In *Proceedings of the 2017 CHI Conference Extended Abstracts on Human Factors in Computing Systems*. ACM Press, New York, New York, USA, 1003–1011.

[4] A Hurst and J Tobias. 2011. Empowering individuals with do-it-yourself assistive technology. In *The proceedings of the 13th international ACM SIGACCESS conference on Computers and accessibility*. 11–18.

[5] Janis Lena Meissner, John Vines, Janice McLaughlin, Thomas Nappey, Jekaterina Maksimova, and Peter Wright. 2017. Do-It-Yourself Empowerment as Experienced by Novice Makers with Disabilities. In *Proceedings of the 2017 Conference on Designing Interactive Systems*. ACM, New York, New York, USA, 1053–1065.

[6] Jeremiah Parry-Hill, Patrick C Shih, Jennifer Mankoff, and Daniel Ashbrook. 2017. Understanding Volunteer AT Fabricators: Opportunities and Challenges in DIY-AT for Others in e-NABLE. In *CHI '17: Proceedings of the 2017 CHI Conference on Human Factors in Computing Systems*. ACM, New York, New York, USA, 6184–6194.

[7] Betsy Phillips and Hongxin Zhao. 2010. Predictors of Assistive Technology Abandonment. *Assistive Technology* 5, 1 (Oct. 2010), 36–45.

[8] Halley P Profita, Abigale Stangl, Laura Matuszewska, Sigrunn Sky, and Shaun K. Kane. 2016. Nothing to Hide: Aesthetic Customization of Hearing Aids and Cochlear Implants in an Online Community. In *Proceedings of the 18th International ACM SIGACCESS Conference on Computers and Accessibility*. ACM, New York, New York, USA, 219–227.

[9] Jorge M Zuniga, Adam M Carson, Jean M Peck, Thomas Kalina, Rakesh M Srivastava, and Kirk Peck. 2016. The development of a low-cost three-dimensional printed shoulder, arm, and hand prostheses for children. *Prosthetics and Orthotics International* 41, 2 (April 2016), 205–209.

[10] Jorge M Zuniga, Dimitrios Katsavelis, Jean Peck, John Stollberg, Marc Petrykowski, Adam Carson, and Cristina Fernandez. 2015. Cyborg beast: a low-cost 3d-printed prosthetic hand for children with upper-limb differences. *BMC Research Notes* 8, 1 (Jan. 2015), 10.

[11] Jorge M Zuniga, Jean Peck, Rakesh Srivastava, Dimitrios Katsavelis, and Adam Carson. 2016. An Open Source 3D-Printed Transitional Hand Prosthesis for Children. *JPO: Journal of Prosthetics and Orthotics* 28, 3 (July 2016), 103–108.

Deaf, Hard of Hearing, and Hearing Perspectives on using Automatic Speech Recognition in Conversation

Abraham Glasser, Kesavan Kushalnagar, and Raja Kushalnagar
Rochester Institute of Technology
Rochester, NY 14623
{atg2036, krk4565}@rit.edu, raja.kushalnagar@gallaudet.edu

ABSTRACT

Many personal devices have transitioned from visual-controlled interfaces to speech-controlled interfaces to reduce costs and interactive friction, supported by the rapid growth in capabilities of speech-controlled interfaces, e.g., Amazon Echo or Apple's Siri. A consequence is that people who are deaf or hard of hearing (DHH) may be unable to use these speech-controlled devices. We show that deaf speech has a high error rate compared to hearing speech, in commercial speech-controlled interfaces. Deaf speech had approximately a 78% word error rate (WER) compared to a hearing speech 18% WER. Our findings show that current speech-controlled interfaces are not usable by DHH people. Based on our findings, significant advances in speech recognition software or alternative approaches will be needed for deaf use of speech-controlled interfaces. We show that current speech-controlled interfaces are not usable by DHH people.

CCS Concepts

•**Human-centered computing** → **Accessibility; Accessibility design and evaluation methods;**

Keywords

Automatic Speech Recognition, Deaf Speech, Deaf, Hearing

1. INTRODUCTION

About 30 million people in the United States have bilateral hearing loss [1], and about 1 million are functionally deaf [2]. Speech production quality is correlated with hearing loss [3], which can lead to both speaking and listening difficulties. Around half a million people in United States communicate visually through American Sign Language (ASL), and use it as their primary means of communication [4]. Deaf or hard of hearing (DHH) people usually cannot understand speech unaided, and usually depend on additional support such as hearing aids or speech-to-text technology, compared with their hearing (H) peers. Simple low-technology aids such as using paper and pen to write back and forth or to text back and forth can work, but are about 3-4 times slower than spoken or signed communication, and is not effective for sustained communication.

ASSETS '17, Oct. 29–Nov. 1, 2017, Baltimore, MD, USA.

ISBN 978-1-4503-4926-0/17/10. . . $15.00.
DOI: https://doi.org/10.1145/3132525.3134781

1.1 Automatic Speech Recognition

Many personal devices offer aural interfaces (e.g., phones) that use Automatic Speech Recognition (ASR) and Text-To-Speech (TTS). Aural interfaces are being rapidly adopted as they have become reasonably accurate and easy-to-use, through significant advancements in speech recognition, machine learning and context sensing services. With increasing interest in IoT (Internet of Things) devices, voice-controlled personal assistants have also become popular as standalone computing devices in home and office environment, as they are cheap, convenient and reasonably accurate.

1.2 ASR Barriers

DHH users cannot easily use these aural interfaces because the ASR services used in these interfaces are inaccurate at recognizing deaf people's speech, which have wide variation and disfluencies, even for short commands and requests [5]. The acoustic and linguistic characteristics of speech associated with DHH people is different from non-DHH people, and usually varies dramatically as a function of hearing loss and onset [3, 6]. As a consequence, Automatic Speech Recognition (ASR) systems trained on speech from non-DHH people perform poorly for recognizing deaf speech [7]. In particular, even if the deaf person had highly intelligible speech, commercial ASR services could not recognize many spoken words, and participants were dissatisfied with the service [8].

1.3 Conversational Barriers

DHH and H people face diverse challenges in spoken language communication with each other in conversational settings, especially in multiple-talker settings such as in classrooms and workplaces. In contrast with H listeners, DHH listeners have manage competing tasks such as shifting attention between multiple visuals. They have to connect incomplete segments together, while searching for cues to know where to pay attention. As a result, even when provided with accurate real-time text through captioners, they receive only 50%-80% of the information, compared to 84%-95% for H peers [9]. Similarly, HH participants have to make sense of reduced speech information through their hearing aids. Both groups need flexible accessible technology solutions for upward mobility [10].

2. PERSPECTIVES

This experience report describes the accessibility challenges by two deaf, one hard of hearing and two hearing participants, including the authors, in using Automatic Speech Recognition (ASR) applications on personal devices for commands and group conversation. Deaf, hard of hearing and hearing speakers and listeners have different challenges and accessibility needs in mixed group conversation in most settings, including academic and workplace settings. We discuss how current ASR applications enhance access by deaf and hard-of-hearing individuals. We also examine how ASR applications enhance communication exchanges between deaf or hard-of-hearing persons and hearing persons in the classroom or workplace.

2.1 Deaf Participants

The deaf participants reported that their challenge was in accessing and following spoken information and in conveying information efficiently and quickly to others in group settings. They preferred to use ASR for one-to-one conversation in quiet settings, so that ASR could accurately display and read the words of their communication partners. Sometimes they also use ASR to speak and convey information quickly to their communication partners especially if their speech clarity is sufficiently close enough to that of their hearing peers.

2.2 Hard of Hearing Participants

The hard of hearing participant usually did not have conversational challenges in quiet or one-to-one settings. Instead, the participant often had difficulties in multi-speaker or noisy settings, because the audio signal was degraded, or with multiple information sources, and/or talkers with dialects or accents [11].

Even with the latest hearing aids that incorporate noise reduction algorithms that are capable of improving listening-alone performance, the participant was not able to make up for the adverse effects of having to concentrate on following speech, and or dealing with competing tasks such as taking notes or shifting attention between multiple speakers or visuals, which is common for hard of hearing listeners [12].

2.3 Hearing Participants

The hearing participants did not have difficulty in speaking or listening to other hearing peers in most settings, but had difficulties in conversing with deaf or hard of hearing speakers, especially if they did not have prior experience with the deaf or hard of hearing person. Hearing listeners use similar cognitive-perceptual processing adaptations to better understand speech under adverse listening conditions, either noise (environmental degradation) or dysarthric speech (source degradation) [13].

2.4 Deaf-Hearing Communication

Deaf or hard of hearing speakers usually have wide variance in speech production. Figure 1 shows the distribution of speech samples from about 650 deaf people as rated by speech pathologists [14]. Each of these samples and ratings were based on an assessment of intelligibility and comprehensibility, using a set of sentences called "Clarke Sentences"[1] with ratings from 0 to 50.

[1]https://www.ntid.rit.edu/slpros/assessment/intel/sentence

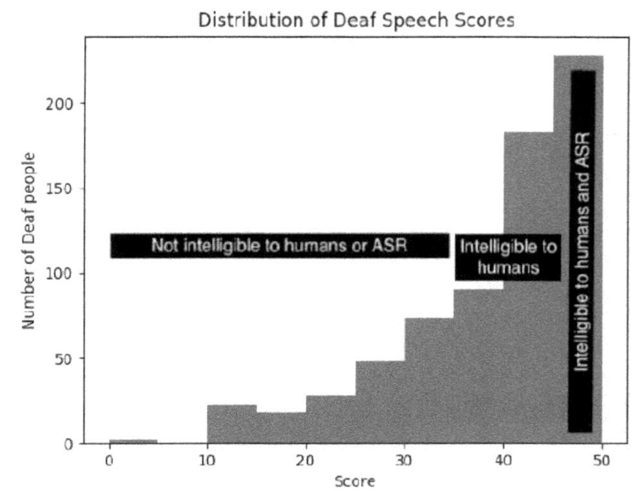

Figure 1: Distribution of Deaf Speech scores.

Hearing listeners usually cannot adapt and understand DHH speakers with ratings of between 0 to 30. If they have a lot of experience listening to deaf speech, they can adapt their cognitive processing strategies to follow DHH speakers with ratings between 30 to 45. If they do not have prior experience, they can follow DHH speakers with ratings from 45 to 50 with some effort. So, hearing speakers with little prior experience are able to understand fewer than half of DHH speakers on average.

2.5 ASR Services

ASR services are rapidly improving due to large investments in aural interfaces for use in wearables, cars, robotics, and machines. The incorporation of large datasets with millions of speakers has led to higher accuracy with a wider range of speech patterns, such as Microsoft at 6% in late 2016 [15] and Google at 5% in early 2017[16].

However, ASR services are trained with large speech sets under good audio conditions and adapt poorly to adverse audio conditions, either noise or speech [17]. While new algorithms have shown promise in handling the dysarthric speech variation [18], they need large datasets, which can be difficult to get. An ASR evaluation with the Clarke Sentence samples drawn from DHH speakers rated 5.0, yielded a Word Error Rate (WER) of about 53% [14], which is generally too high. Other ASR problems include lag, jitter, and acquisition factors such as fidelity, ambient noise and microphone quality. ASR services still had word error rates of 20-25% for lectures [11].

2.6 Accuracy

The text accuracy for real-time speech-to-text needs to be sufficiently high to be useful. Studies have shown that DHH people will use real-time speech-to-text, such as ASR, if its accuracy is least 85% [19] to 90% [20] or higher.

2.7 Lag and Jitter

The lag time for ASR needs to be short enough to be usable. Lag time for ASR becomes worse as the amount of data to be analyzed increases and causes processing delays. Similarly variance in processing time significantly bothers

Figure 2: Logos of various ASR platforms used

users. They cannot effectively participate in discussions or dialogues if lag time is more than 5 seconds [19], or if variance is more than 2-3 seconds [11].

3. METHODS

To investigate the capabilities of current ASR applications, from Fall 2016 through Summer 2017, five participants used one or more of seven ASR applications on their personal devices in everyday, real-world settings for conversations.

3.1 Users

One of the deaf participants did not use spoken conversation with hearing peers and typed on the phone and used ASR for conversing with non-signing peers. The other deaf participant used spoken conversation with hearing peers in face-to-face conversations, and used ASR in group conversations.

The hard of hearing participant used spoken conversation with hearing peers in face-to-face conversation, and used ASR in group conversations.

The hearing participant used spoken conversation with hearing peers in both face-to-face and group conversations, and used either ASL or ASR with the hard of hearing and deaf peers.

3.2 Contexts

The purpose of using the ASR applications was to assess the usability of the applications in face-to-face spoken language interactions by providing a visible text representation of speech in the following contexts:

- Classroom communication
- Job Interviews
- Conversation
- Speech production practice

3.3 Applications

The participants used and evaluated the following ASR apps: DEAFCOM, Dragon Dictation, Siri, Virtual Voice, Ava, Google Assistant, and Amazon Alexa, as shown in Figure 2. These apps were chosen because they were available for free and had been rated at least 3.5 out of 5 for user satisfaction in the store.

1. DEAFCOM by askjerry Communications is aimed at DHH to use for conversation, with a simple interface that is quick to start. Its description is: ".... For a non-hearing or hard-of-hearing person, the application will allow faster communication with deaf persons. For deaf users, the software can assist in faster communication and may also be used as a useful tool when practicing your speech".[2]
2. Dragon Dictation by Nuance Communications is for all users as a voice recognition system: " ... an easy-to-use voice recognition application powered by Dragon ...."[3]
3. Siri by Apple, is for all users as an aural interface assistant: "Talk to Siri as you would to a friend and it can help you get things done, like sending messages, placing calls, or making dinner reservations ...."[4]
4. Virtual Voice by Gareth Hannaway Communications is aimed at DHH to use for conversation, with a simple interface that is easy to read: "It is designed to use the text to speech (TTS) and the speech recognition features of your Android device. It was created with deaf and/or mute people in mind, so they can communicate with others without the need for sign language or lip reading".[5]
5. Ava by Ava, is aimed at DHH to use for conversation in pairs or groups: "Ava shows you who says what. Ava shows you what people say, in less than a second. Easy communication is only a tap away."[6]
6. The Google Assistant by Google, is for all users as an aural interface assistant: "Meet your Google Assistant. Ask it questions. Tell it to do things. It's your own personal Google, always ready to help."[7]
7. Alexa by Amazon, is for all users as an aural interface assistant: "Using Alexa is as simple as asking a question.The more you talk to Alexa, the more it adapts to your speech patterns, vocabulary, and personal preferences."[8]

3.4 Evaluation

The participants downloaded the apps to their personal iPhone or Android device (or directly used the device), and evaluated their use in the contexts listed above.

[2] play.google.com/store/apps/details?id=defcom.v1
[3] www.dragonmobileapps.com/android/
[4] www.apple.com/ios/siri/
[5] play.google.com/store/apps/details?id=appinventor.ai_Gareth_Hannaway_420.VirtualVoice
[6] https://www.ava.me/
[7] https://assistant.google.com/
[8] https://www.amazon.com/Amazon-Echo-And-Alexa-Devices/b?ie=UTF8&node=9818047011

All participants reported that when they used the apps under ideal circumstances, the captions spoken by their hearing peers were accurate, with minimal lag and jitter. The ideal circumstance was to use the app with excellent WiFi coverage, in quiet one-to-one settings with hearing peers with American accents when discussing general topics. The apps did well in all contexts, when used for five minutes or less, regardless of whether it was used in a classroom, informal conversation, job interviews or speech production practice in which the text displayed by an app was used as an indicator of the intelligibility.

3.5 Duration

After continuous conversation for more than five minutes, five of the seven apps (interactive assistants and apps for the deaf, but not ASR service apps) showed significant time lag in quiet settings, especially in classroom settings, which tend to have multiple speakers who speak fast. The hearing and hard of hearing participants reported that on some occasions the time lag resulted in dropped words, while the deaf participants did not report this phenomenon.

3.6 Noise

All apps exhibited significant lag more quickly (within a minute) and jitter (variance) when there was background noise, which happened often in all contexts. They all inserted random text as well. The lag occurred even when the background noise was not noticeable to hearing peers in the room.

Accuracy was also disappointing when there was any level of noise in the environment. The combination of inaccurate transcription and time lag was very frustrating for the deaf and hard of hearing participants, and they reported that there was much work yet to be done to make these apps useful enough to put away pencil and paper.

3.7 Multiple speakers

All apps had significant lag more quickly (within a minute) and jitter (variance) when there were multiple speakers, in all contexts. The lag occurred even when the background noise was not noticeable to hearing peers in the room.

For most applications, the deaf users could not tell who was speaking and often became confused and frustrated. On the other hand, hearing peers who had concerns about communicating with deaf or hard of hearing individuals felt more at ease when they were able to use the apps, even in noisy or multi-speaker settings.

3.8 Hearing Accents

All apps also had more lag, jitter and were less accurate when the speech had variance from standard American speech patterns when the speaker had an accent from another country. In addition to being less accurate, the apps often inserted random text.

3.9 Deaf Speech/Accent

Most apps did not recognize the different prosody, pitch, and articulations of deaf speakers, even for the apps that were aimed at use by deaf or hard of hearing users. These DHH specific apps had less lag time, but still had high error rates. For purposes of facilitating speech intelligibility, most of the DHH evaluators, regardless of their mode of communication, did not find the speech recognition apps to be usable. The DHH evaluators were quite disappointed to find that they uniformly failed to recognize their speech and they tended to attribute this failure to differences in their own articulation, pitch, and prosody. The alternative of switching to a text-to-speech or text-to-text function resulted in significant slowing in conversational interactions.

4. LESSONS LEARNED

When using ASR technology, deaf, hard of hearing and hearing people report different ways of interacting with the technology. The following lessons were learned from daily experience with the technology. In most situations, the settings were not ideal, and the level of accuracy and degree of latency characteristic of the apps were not adequate to enhance speech reception in face-to-face interaction. We experienced a disruptive display of text that did not match in time what the others were saying. More needs to be done so that the text is synchronous with the speech. When the authors ignored the speech or did not speechread, it was useful to have access merely to the overall context of the message via keywords that the apps could display.

In summary, regardless of context, the main factors for app usability were:

- Noise (e.g., music)
- Speech produced with an accent
- Multi-talker speech or side conversation
- Disfluent speech or speakers with emotion.

The shared use of ASR apps by both deaf and hearing people drew them into a collective learning experience:

4.1 Deaf users

> We are not the only ones with problems understanding .... That we're not the only ones. There's non-disabled people out there who are having the same problems ... you feel equal.

> The idea today is that everyone should make a small effort to make the conversation work. Of course a minimal effort, but the burden should not be on the deaf person alone. Everyone works together.

> The app is difficult to use. I prefer to use paper and pen as it is more reliable and easier to use.

4.2 Hard of hearing users

> It's telling me that at least I'm not the only person that might have a problem understanding. Like, I know that sometimes when you've got a disability you feel like you're the only one ... I just don't want it to benefit us. I'd like to see it work for everybody

> I cannot use Alexa at my parents' house, as I cannot understand its responses after I give it a command.

4.3 Hearing users

> I am very satisfied with using ASR apps for looking up simple queries on the web. I did not realize that the apps are not accurate or easy to use for conversational use with deaf friends.

5. CONCLUSIONS

ASR has been constantly updated and improved for over 50 years. However, ASR has been and continues to be focused on hearing speakers who have low variance and in their speech. It is difficult for deaf and hard of hearing individuals, even those who use voice on a regular basis, to be fully comfortable with ASR. They cannot dictate to ASR services reliably, because there is a big variance their speech, even if their speech is understandable by their hearing peers. Hearing peers use additional information such as experience with common deaf speech patterns, visual cues to accurately understand the DHH speaker. So, even if the deaf person can be understood by hearing peers, all ASR services currently tested do not reliably provide accurate or usable transcripts.

5.1 User Interface

DHH individuals report that the hearing peer's patience and attitude matters, especially when the hearing peer has never used ASR before. The DHH individuals note that hearing peers often get frustrated with the user interface design of the ASR app itself, since these interfaces are not intuitive to use for conversational use. The DHH users said that it would be ideal if ASR systems could tell the user if repetition of a specific word was needed rather than the whole word. Using a system like this might increase the interaction of users with the device.

5.2 Visual Interface Feedback

A big barrier to interaction with ASR devices is that DHH individuals do not have access to the verbal output from these devices after speaking commands to it, i.e., verbal inputs. Many interfaces are voice only, and are inaccessible to many DHH individuals. Some ASR devices are able are able to display verbal responses as text on the screens of paired personal phones. However, many new devices on the market do not have any visual interface and and do not connect with personal phones.

A couple of personal phones with ASR services have recently added text input capability in addition to voice input capability, which makes these services more accessible for DHH individuals. But because text interfaces are slower than speech interfaces, these text interfaces are not as appealing as voice interfaces for using these devices as a personal assistant. DHH individuals typically cannot monitor their own speech inflections and volume, and it is important to provide users good feedback about good placement of the phone and associated speech volume.

Although some DHH individuals are able to use ASR systems such for transactional use, almost all DHH individuals are uncomfortable using these systems for sustained conversational use, as the systems have higher than tolerable error rates, especially in less than perfect settings. Whenever there are errors, the errors are time consuming to fix and the presented text cannot be edited for accuracy or clarification.

Putting aside the problems facing deaf people using their own voices with ASR, there are still user interface accessibility issues. For example, if it was practical for ASR technology to be used in conversations between multiple deaf and hearing individuals, the ASR interface should be quick to open, and display contextual cues, such as speaker identification.

5.3 Algorithms

Although ASR services show significant improvement in laboratory settings [16, 17, 21], DHH and hearing users experience significant performance issues, especially in the critical settings of the classroom and workplace. New technological advances and enhanced engineering are needed to bring the errors down much further in order to make speech recognition useful under difficult yet practical and realistic conditions [22], particularly to control noise and side-talk interference, perhaps with better noise canceling algorithms, more advanced microphone array techniques, and through use of a lapel mic, Bluetooth streaming, and/or Wi-Fi Direct, and to ultimately convince deaf and hard-of-hearing persons that speech recognition technologies are better than pencil and paper when trying to communicate to a person with typical hearing when it counts in the classroom or on the job.

5.4 Speech Quality

In addition to noisy backgrounds, many speakers, especially those who are deaf, have low volume, and directional microphones can make a significant difference. It would be helpful to include external microphone support for microphones that can be either plugged in or connected with Bluetooth. This could be a lapel type of mic that is clipped on the person, or a more central hardware piece with multiple microphones. These could indeed do both directional beam forming or omni directional capturing. Most applications need fairly loud speech samples for optimal accuracy, that is, the speech signal has to be much larger than the background noise.

5.5 App Support

People have frustrations with lack of Internet connections and battery and space usage, so it should be an objective to make ASR apps efficient. People who have little or no experience using ASR technology may not know how to interact with the app. Thus, clear, intuitive user interfaces need to be added to the ASR apps so that the conversation will have better flow and comfort. Apps are typically limited and have a certain amount they will transcribe in a time period. It has been observed that some apps require purchases for more usage. This is disadvantageous because Deaf people should not have to work harder and give up more to have equal access to information.

6. RECOMMENDATIONS

In order to improve ASR service support for conversational use between deaf, hard of hearing and hearing users, it is critical to include their perspectives and experiences in their ASR app use. Evaluations and surveys need to recruit people with different backgrounds and use. This way, the developers and researchers will be able to work with accessibility in mind and have their products benefit a wide spectrum of people.

6.1 Aural Interface Access

The increased popularity of wearables and personal devices with aural interfaces is likely to pose an significant barrier for use of aural interfaces. Most aural interfaces' ASR services are inaccurate at recognizing deaf people's speech, because their speech has wide variation and disfluencies, even for short commands and requests, let alone long speeches. They cannot easily use or interact with the aural interfaces in today's wearables or devices. Deaf users prefer to use interfaces through which they can interact with high accuracy, low variance and low lag time. Although communicating through typing and writing has high accuracy and low variance, they are slow and introduce a lot of lag time. For deaf individuals with low intelligibility ratings, it is unlikely ASR services will be able to recognize their speech, due to the high variance in their speech.

6.2 Visual Interface Access

Deaf signers, like hearing speakers, have high accuracy, low variance and low lag time in communication through sign language. Deaf signers would prefer and benefit from a visual interface that can recognize and produce sign language, and has high accuracy, low variance and low lag time. Similarly, hard of hearing people regardless of whether they pick a aural, visual, aural-visual or aural-visual-tactile interface, would prefer that it have high accuracy, low variance and low lag time.

Writing or typing is used as a last resort by both hearing and deaf or hard of hearing individuals in conversational use. Although it is understood by both parties, and is accurate, it is far slower than speaking or signing. The text representation carries less emotion and inflections, when compared to speech or sign, even the text representation is supplemented with emojis.

7. REFERENCES

[1] Frank R. Lin, John K. Niparko, and Luigi Ferrucci. Hearing Loss Prevalence in the United States. *Archives of Internal Medicine*, 171(20):1851, nov 2011.

[2] B B Blanchfield, J J Feldman, J L Dunbar, and E N Gardner. The severely to profoundly hearing-impaired population in the United States: prevalence estimates and demographics. *Journal of the American Academy of Audiology*, 12(4):183–9, apr 2001.

[3] Sven L. Mattys, Matthew H. Davis, Ann R. Bradlow, and Sophie K. Scott. Speech recognition in adverse conditions: A review. *Language and Cognitive Processes*, 27(7-8):953–978, sep 2012.

[4] Ross E. Mitchell, Travas A. Young, Bellamie Bachleda, and Michael A. Karchmer. How Many People Use ASL in the United States? Why Estimates Need Updating. *Sign Language Studies*, 6(3):306–335, 2006.

[5] C Jeyalakshmi, V Krishnamurthi, and A Revathy. Deaf speech assessment using digital processing techniques. *Signal & Image Processing: An International Journal (SIPIJ)*, 1(1):14–25, 2010.

[6] Leo De Raeve. A Longitudinal Study on Auditory Perception and Speech Intelligibility in Deaf Children Implanted Younger Than 18 Months in Comparison to Those Implanted at Later Ages. *Otology & Neurotology*, 31(8):1261–1267, oct 2010.

[7] Kinfe Tadesse Mengistu and Frank Rudzicz. Comparing Humans and Automatic Speech Recognition Systems in Recognizing Dysarthric Speech. pages 291–300. 2011.

[8] Linda G. Gottermeier and Raja S. Kushalnagar. User Evaluation of Automatic Speech Recognition Systems for Deaf-Hearing Interactions at School and Work. *Audiology Today*, 28(2):20–34, 2016.

[9] Marc Marschark, Patricia Sapere, Carol Convertino, and Jeff Pelz. Learning via direct and mediated instruction by deaf students. *Journal of deaf studies and deaf education*, 13(4):546–561, 2008.

[10] Marc Marschark, Venetta Lampropoulou, and Emmanouil K Skordilis. *Diversity in Deaf Education.* Oxford University Press, 2016.

[11] Raja. S. Kushalnagar, Walter S. Lasecki, and Jeffrey P. Bigham. Accessibility Evaluation of Classroom Captions. *ACM Transactions on Accessible Computing*, 5(3):1–24, 2014.

[12] Karen L. Anderson. Access is the issue, not hearing loss: New policy clarification requires schools to ensure effective communication access. *SIG 9 Perspectives on Hearing and Hearing Disorders in Childhood*, 25(1):24–36, 2015.

[13] Stephanie A. Borrie, Melissa Baese-Berk, Kristin Van Engen, and Tessa Bent. A relationship between processing speech in noise and dysarthric speech. *The Journal of the Acoustical Society of America*, 141(6):4660–4667, jun 2017.

[14] Abraham Glasser, Kesavan Kushalnagar, and Raja Kushalnagar. Feasibility of Using Automatic Speech Recognition with Voices of Deaf and Hard-of-Hearing Individuals. In *The 19th International ACM SIGACCESS Conference on Computers and Accessibility*, pages 334–336, 2017.

[15] W Xiong, J Droppo, X Huang, F Seide, M. Seltzer, Andreas Stolcke, D Yu, and G Zweig. The Microsoft 2016 conversational speech recognition system. In *2017 IEEE International Conference on Acoustics, Speech and Signal Processing (ICASSP)*, pages 5255–5259. IEEE, mar 2017.

[16] John Shinal. Making sense of Google CEO Sundar Pichai's plan to move every direction at once. *CNBC*, May 2017.

[17] Ming Tu, Alan Wisler, Visar Berisha, and Julie M. Liss. The relationship between perceptual disturbances in dysarthric speech and automatic speech recognition performance. *The Journal of the Acoustical Society of America*, 140(5):EL416–EL422, Nov 2016.

[18] Myungjong Kim, Younggwan Kim, Joohong Yoo, Jun Wang, and Hoirin Kim. Regularized Speaker Adaptation of KL-HMM for Dysarthric Speech Recognition. *IEEE Transactions on Neural Systems and Rehabilitation Engineering*, pages 1–1, 2017.

[19] Mike Wald. Using automatic speech recognition to enhance education for all students: Turning a vision into reality. In *Frontiers in Education, 2005. FIE'05. Proceedings 35th Annual Conference*, pages S3G–S3G. IEEE, 2005.

[20] Richard Kheir and Thomas Way. Inclusion of deaf students in computer science classes using real-time speech transcription. *ACM Sigcse Bulletin*, 39(3):261–265, 2007.

[21] Wayne Xiong, Lingfeng Wu, Fil Alleva, Jasha Droppo, Xuedong Huang, and Andreas Stolcke. The microsoft 2017 conversational speech recognition system. Technical report, August 2017.

[22] Dong Yu and Li Deng. *Automatic speech recognition: A deep learning approach.* Springer, 2014.

Author Index

www.ingramcontent.com/pod-product-compliance
Ingram Content Group UK Ltd.
Pitfield, Milton Keynes, MK11 3LW, UK
UKHW051412290926
15471UKWH00009B/1568

9 781450 356817